THE WAR
ILLUSTRATED

LIEUT.-GENERAL SIR BERNARD LAW MONTGOMERY, K.C.B., D.S.O.

*From the portrait by Capt. Neville Lewis, official South African war artist, exhibited at the National
Portrait Gallery, London, May 1943. Reproduced by permission of the Government of South Africa*

THE WAR
Illustrated

Complete Record of the Conflict
by Land and Sea and in the Air

Edited by
SIR JOHN HAMMERTON

Volume Six

The SIXTH VOLUME OF THE WAR ILLUSTRATED
contains the issues numbered 131 to 155, covering the period from
the summer of 1942 to the late spring of 1943. In dramatic
intensity, in the importance of the events that have fallen to be
recorded within its pages, this volume may well challenge comparison with its predecessors. As it opened, the 8th Army in
Libya was suffering a severe reversal of fortune. The loss of
Tobruk was felt as keenly as that of Singapore earlier in the year,
and the retreat into Egypt was watched with gloom, even apprehension. It was a dark hour, yet (as our pages record) a glorious
dawn was about to break. By the time this volume had half
run its course the 8th Army, re-equipped and re-armed and led
by a general whose name was soon to ring round the world,
swept over Rommel's lines at El Alamein and drove him and his
vaunted Afrika Korps (not to mention his Italian allies) out of
Egypt, out of Cyrenaica, out of Tripolitania, out of the Mareth
Line into the furthermost tip of Tunisia. It is a great story, and
makes grand reading. For years and generations to come men
will draw inspiration from the tale of the heroic deeds of the
Desert Army, captained by the intrepid Montgomery and the
wise and skilful Alexander—and from those not less heroic performed
by Anderson's 1st Army, with whose amazingly complete triumph
in Tunisia the volume closes.

But if the war in Africa has filled many of our pages with a
topic of absorbing interest, we have not forgotten that this war is
indeed world-wide to an extent not approached by the war of a
generation ago. Asia and Australia, the Americas and all the
world's seas and oceans have been involved to a greater or lesser
extent in the bloody struggle, and so have come within the
all-including sphere of our pictorial record. Then there is
Russia . . . In the history of the War the defence of Stalingrad
will occupy a place of highest honour, of supreme importance ;
and we have striven to pay a not unworthy tribute to the deathless
valour of the soldiers of the Soviet.

As we close the volume a new chapter seems about to open. In
Europe millions of unhappy serfs are waiting the hour of their
deliverance from Hitler's yoke. In all the countries of the United
Nations the tempo of production, the degree of martial readiness,
mounts and mounts. To what end ? To what fresh fields of
conquest ? Not this volume but the next will show.

Published 2000
Cover Design © 2000
TRIDENT PRESS INTERNATIONAL
ISBN 1-58279-105-8 Single Edition
Printed in Croatia

General Index to Volume Six

*T*HIS *Index is designed to give ready reference to the whole of the literary and pictorial contents of* THE WAR ILLUSTRATED. *Individual subjects and persons of importance are indexed under their own headings, while references are included to general subjects such as Tunisia, War in; Pacific; U.S.A., etc. Page Numbers in italics indicate illustrations.*

List of Maps and Plans

Index of Special Drawings and Diagrams

Vol 6 # The War Illustrated Nº 131

Edited by Sir John Hammerton

6d FORTNIGHTLY

JUNE 26, 1942

INTO BATTLE, or as near the actual thing as the rigorous training under modern conditions can make it. An infantryman, yelling a weird war cry, leaps through a wall of flame. The strenuous conditions of fighting today demand a far more realistic course of battle drill than formerly : the baptism of fire is not delayed until the soldier reaches the front line. See the article in page 14, and further Illustrations in pages 15 to 18.

Photo, The Daily Mirror

NO. 132 WILL BE PUBLISHED FRIDAY, JULY 10

ALONG THE BATTLE FRONTS

by Our Military Critic, Maj.-Gen. Sir Charles Gwynn, K.C.B., D.S.O.

THE period here under review was marked by events of far-reaching importance, although neither side could claim clear cut victory on land.

GERMANY

Terrific as their effects were, the four-figure raids of May 30 on Cologne and June 1 on Essen are even more important as indications of what is to come when American aircraft add their weight to that of the R.A.F. Under such attacks not only will the war industries of Germany be affected to a degree that must eventually cripple her powers of offensive action, but obviously the whole economic organization of the country will be disturbed by the necessity of clearing wreckage, carrying out essential repairs, evacuating large sections of the population and redistributing food supplies. The effect of these and subsequent raids may not be immediately felt on the fighting fronts, for it must be assumed that great reserves of munitions have already been collected there, though in view of the demands made to meet the Russian winter offensive they are unlikely to be sufficient for prolonged intensive operations failing a constant and immense flow of replacement from home resources.

Sir Charles GWYNN
Photo, Bassano

The preceding raids on Rostock and Lübeck aimed at more immediate results on troop movement to Finland, and on output of U-boats and aircraft. What the effect on German morale may be is unsafe to forecast, for a spirit of desperation may be engendered.

RUSSIA

Timoshenko's offensive in the Kharkov region ended on May 31, although before that date Von Bock's counter-attack, which from Izyum dangerously threatened his left flank and communications, had been defeated after heavy fighting.

By disrupting German plans for an early offensive towards the Caucasian oil fields, of which the capture of Kerch was evidently the opening move, Timoshenko achieved his main object. There can be no doubt that the troops Von Bock used for his counter-

RUSSIAN FRONT: The Kharkov area, showing the pocket caused by the Soviet advance south of the city. The arrow indicates the direction of Von Bock's flank attack.
By courtesy of The Times

attack were those designed to strike into the Donetz basin in cooperation with a direct attack on Rostov, and probably with an attempt to cross the straits at Kerch. Kharkov itself would also probably have been the base of an attack to cover the left of the southern thrust, and to turn the Russian defences on the Donetz. Timoshenko therefore not only compelled the Germans to expend men and great quantities of accumulated material, but forced them to take action in directions which upset their arrangements.

The drive towards Caucasia will probably be re-staged, for it is even more important for the Germans to deprive Russia of oil than it is to obtain new sources of oil supply for themselves. But Timoshenko has secured a position from which he can threaten the flank of a southern offensive and check a cooperative attempt from Kharkov. He may have hoped to force the Germans to withdraw from Kharkov by outflanking it, but he does not appear to have made a determined effort to capture the city which, strongly defended, might have been desperately costly. He may be well satisfied with the results achieved, for, as in the case of Stalin's winter offensive, the effects produced on the German army were of more importance than the recapture of territory. The winter offensive was primarily intended to compel the Germans

to fight under conditions of terrible hardships and to prevent recuperation. The effect aimed at was long term and moral. Timoshenko's object, on the other hand, was to remove an immediate danger. In neither case was it intended to initiate a decisive counter-offensive for which, as Stalin has said, the time has not yet arrived.

The fact that so many "hedgehog" key points are still held by the Germans may have disappointed onlookers, but it must be realized that under winter thaw conditions it was impracticable to employ heavy weapons against them, and that in the neighbourhood of railways German defences could be strongly held. It was at a distance from railways, where supply conditions limited the size of detachments, that Russian lightly-armed troops achieved successes.

A feature of the recent fighting has been the increased power of Russian armaments. Tanks, both of Russian and Allied construction, are fully a match for those of the Germans, and aircraft are definitely superior. In meeting counter-attacks the new Russian anti-tank rifle proved its value. It enables the infantry to protect themselves against tank attack, a long-felt want, although artillery support and heavy anti-tank weapons are still essential. These, however, are easier for the enemy's artillery to knock out of action than the less conspicuous weapons of well-entrenched infantry.

What will be the developments of the immediate future is uncertain. Although the southern German offensive has been postponed, there are indications that an offensive is in preparation having the primary object of relieving pressure on the "hedgehog" key points of the German salient west of Moscow. This may indicate an intention to revive the threat to the capital.

AN offensive in the Leningrad region seems also probable, though possibly only with the object of strengthening the investing force east of the city which has with difficulty retained its position during the winter. Leningrad itself is still strongly defended, and an attempt to take it by assault seems improbable so long as it can be closely invested. An attempt to by-pass the city, such as was defeated at Tikhvin last year, may be made; for Vologda, on the Moscow-Archangel railway, is a tempting objective, since its capture would interrupt the inflow of Allied munitions. A renewal of attempts to capture Murmansk is also threatened.

There is, of course, a possibility that German plans may again be forestalled by Russian offensives, and the Russian salient formed during the winter south of Lake Ilmen, is a potential danger to the communications of the northern German armies.

At the moment, although strong local attacks and counter-attacks are reported at a number of places, the intentions of the opponents are obscure and, in a major sense, there is a lull on the whole front.

LIBYA

Rommel on May 27 ended the stalemate which since the beginning of the year had existed in Libya. Intensified bombing of Malta has made it impossible to use the island as an offensive base and this had enabled strong reinforcements to reach Libya in comparative safety. They probably were not sufficient to justify a far-reaching attempt to invade Egypt, but they must at least have convinced Rommel that he was strong enough to defeat General Ritchie's 8th Army. Desert conditions and indifferent communications set

SOVIET ANTI-TANK GUNNERS have done excellent work in the Kharkov battles, using a specially long-barrelled weapon which takes two men to handle. The one in the photograph had just put two enemy tanks out of action.
Photo, Planet News

a limit to the size at which Ritchie's army could be maintained, and the desert afforded unique opportunities for a Panzer attack on his vulnerable communications.

Difficulties of supply and great distances made invasion of Egypt a much more ambitious project unless a cooperative attack from the east, or possibly a strong air-borne attack from Crete, could be relied on. It is therefore unnecessary to assume that Rommel aimed at more than the defeat of the 8th Army, the recapture of Tobruk and Bardia, and the re-establishment of his position at Halfaya. The moral effect of such a success would have been great, although it would have had no material effect on the situation in Russia.

It is possible that Rommel may have underestimated Ritchie's strength, knowing the demands that had been made for reinforcement of the Far Eastern theatre. It was no secret that Australian and other troops that had fought in Libya had gone east. It is probable too that he counted on finding Ritchie's tanks still under-gunned and his anti-tank weapons too light, for the "General Grant" tanks and 6-pdr. anti-tank guns had been well-kept secrets.

Ritchie's strongly entrenched position with its belt of minefields at Gazala was clearly too strong to be overrun by a direct attack, but south of Bir Hacheim his flank was open, though to turn it meant a long detour involving a vulnerable supply line. The situation closely resembled in reverse direction that which faced Auchinleck last November with the exception that in each

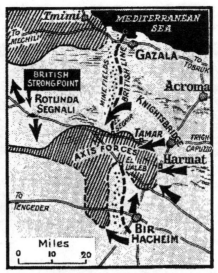

LIBYAN FRONT, showing the scene of the fierce fighting early in June. Black arrows indicate British counter-thrusts.
By courtesy of The Daily Telegraph

coast road between Tobruk and Gazala, and a great tank battle went on for three days in the Knightsbridge area where Ritchie had only just established a strong position which now, with its anti-tank guns, formed a valuable pivot, resisting all attacks. The failure of two other features of his plan added to Rommel's difficulties; he had

On June 5 Ritchie's troops which had been closing in on Rommel's bridge-head launched a determined attack against it. Fierce fighting ensued with attack and counter-attack during which Rommel again attempted to break out eastwards using all available armoured reserves which had by now joined him from the west. This attempt was again repulsed and Rommel again fell back into the gap.

He then concentrated on an attempt to capture Bir Hacheim, using heavy guns, tanks and dive-bombers. With the pressure on the position reaching such intensity, and with supplies running short, General Ritchie decided to withdraw the garrison, and this was successfully accomplished on the night of June 10. Rommel might claim a success of considerable moral importance and some improvement of his position, but he had paid a heavy price; and Ritchie, relieved of a responsibility, was at greater liberty to concentrate his armoured troops.

Whether Rommel will now abandon his offensive and withdraw to his original position or fight it out remains to be seen. It is evident however that he can now have little hope of victory and risks decisive defeat. If he withdraws he may be able to re-establish stalemate conditions, but with Malta recovering its potentialities as an offensive base since the withdrawal of the Luftwaffe from Sicily his prospects of receiving reinforcements on a large scale must be small. Should he fight it out to a clear cut decision and be heavily defeated, the whole situation in Libya and in the Mediterranean may be changed.

A feature in the battle has been the greatly increased part the R.A.F. has taken in the ground fighting which indicates a definite change of tactical policy.

FAR EAST
Of the Far Eastern situation I have little to say. Control of sea communications, by air or naval action, is still the dominating issue.

In Burma the Japanese are in possession, undisputed except by air counter-attacks; but General Alexander's fighting withdrawal gained valuable time. The monsoon season and lack of roads make a serious attack on India from Burma by land for the moment out of the question; while at the same time the reinforcement of both the land and air forces in India and Ceylon would seem to make an amphibious attempt prohibitively dangerous. Fighting on the Burma Road continues and the Chinese have had considerable success. Their object may be to retain their hold on the western end of the road in order eventually to be in a position to cooperate in any attempt to reopen communications. It seems improbable that the Japanese aim at invading China seriously by such a roundabout route.

Their major operation against China is in Chekiang with the defensive purpose of denying it as a base for American air forces. The Chinese are resisting stubbornly, and the Japanese operations in the Canton region are probably intended to prevent the reinforcement of the Chinese in Chekiang and to exhaust China's munition reserves.

CHINA FRONT, where in the Chekiang area the Japanese are on the offensive.
By courtesy of The Times

Page 3

GEN. RITCHIE, directing the Libyan battle from his advanced headquarters. With him on either side are two corps commanders, Lt.-Gen. Willoughby Norrie (left) and Lt.-Gen. Gott. On right, Knightsbridge, no more than a name in the desert, but the scene of a great tank battle: below the name is the map reference.
Photos, British Official: Crown Copyright

case Tobruk was in British hands. Wavell's bold decision to hold on to Tobruk had far-reaching effects. Now Tobruk and probably Bardia were the advanced supply bases for the 8th Army, and Rommel's primary intention was to interrupt communication between them and Gazala even if he failed to capture them at once.

With about half his Panzer troops Rommel swept round Ritchie's open flank, and his advanced detachments succeeded in reaching the coastal road both east and west of Tobruk though they could not maintain their hold on it when counter-attacked, and in danger of failure of supplies, fell back on the main body which was itself faced with supply difficulties.

Bir Hacheim, which Rommel had hoped to carry by a *coup de main*, and thus shorten the detour of his supply services, had resisted all attack; and it was not till two gaps had been cut in the minefields north of Bir Hacheim that the danger of running short of petrol and ammunition was reduced.

Rommel in spite of his difficulties made desperate efforts to establish himself on the

hoped to break through the Gazala defences near the coast road while at the same time a force was to land close behind them. The South Africans repelled the former attack and the Navy broke up the latter.

But Rommel had strong forces to the west, and in order to get in direct touch with them and to ease his supply problems he drew back into the gaps in the minefield establishing strong defences at their eastern exits. Under cover of this protection he succeeded in capturing the locality held by a Brigade of the 50th Division which separated the two gaps; and thus improved his position by throwing them into one. There followed a comparative lull partly due to heavy dust storms and partly to exhaustion and the necessity of regrouping forces. Rommel's intentions were not clear, but he was still strong and certainly not prepared to admit failure. He made several attacks on Bir Hacheim which the Free French, though now isolated and running short of supplies and ammunition, magnificently defeated with the aid of British mobile troops operating against the rear of the attackers.

Hard Knocks for Hitler's Afrika Korps

IN LIBYA British troops standing by a German medium tank destroyed by our gunfire. A weapon that has played a considerable part in the recent battles in the Western Desert is the new six-pounder anti-tank gun produced entirely in British factories.

GEN. LUDWIG CRUE-WELL (below), Rommel's Chief of Staff and commander of the German Afrika Korps, was captured on May 29 when, inspecting the battle from a Fieseler-Storch plane, he was shot down. The bullet-ridden plane made a forced landing inside the British lines. The photograph shows General Cruewell climbing out of a British armoured car after being brought back to headquarters.

FREE FRENCH troops, left centre, going into action with anti-tank guns. At Bir Hacheim, vital point S.W. of Tobruk, the Free French forces put up a magnificent stand. " All France looks to you with pride," ran a message from Gen. de Gaulle to their Commander, Gen. Koenig. But on June 10, after a 16-day siege, the survivors of the garrison were withdrawn at Gen. Ritchie's Order.

GENERAL GRANT TANKS at a British forward Tank H.Q. in Libya before going into action. This new American-built 28-ton tank is the heaviest so far used in the Middle East. Its fire power is tremendous. The tank is so strongly armoured that though one General Grant was hit at 100 yards the crew were saved.

Photos, British Official: Crown Copyright

The 'Kamerad' Cry in the Western Desert

DESERT SURRENDER, as the lone survivor of the blazing German tank in the background walks with his arms up across the sand to the victorious British Bren-gun carrier. Here is a dramatic war photograph, radioed from the new transmission station at Cairo, which gives a vivid idea of the kind of individual tank duel which is part of the Western Desert struggle. Rommel's objective was presumably to capture Tobruk by a concerted sea and land action, but according to General Auchinleck his initial offensive went completely awry.   *Photo. British Official: Crown Copyright*   **Page 5**

Well Done, Horses (and Dogs) of the Red Army!

When we pay tribute to the magnificent valour of Soviet Russia's fighting men, let us not forget the horses—yes, and the dogs, too—without whom the battle could not have been sustained, and who, like their masters, have had to pay a heavy price in death, mutilation and just plain suffering.

RUSSIA has millions of horses in service with the Red Army; without them, in spite of the railways and the immense number of motor vehicles, it would be impossible to maintain the constant stream of supplies to the millions of men holding the thousand-mile-long front. Hundreds of thousands are actually in the firing line, hauling guns and ammunition wagons; great numbers more are harnessed to ambulances and supply vehicles. Then, of course, there is the Russian cavalry—in particular the famous Cossacks, who in this war, as in all the wars for centuries past, have had a notable part to play.

The Russians are using dogs, too, on a larger scale it would seem, than is the case in the British Army or with the Nazis. They have many jobs, but a new task which has been demanded of them is the dragging back from the battlefield of wounded Soviet soldiers after these have been placed on little sledges by the first-aid men. Alsatians are chiefly used for this job, but Airedales have been found capable, and many of the larger mongrels are also employed because of their usual intelligence. For this work the dogs have to be not only strong, but swift moving, since with temperatures far below freezing-point the wounded man's life may well depend on the speed with which he is dragged back on his little sledge to the dressing-station. It is interesting to learn that few of these Red Cross dogs have been wounded, probably because they move so close to the ground.

Casualties among the horses, however, have been (as might be expected) very large. Not only have numbers of them been killed on the field of battle, but many more have been wounded, while all must have suffered terribly during the winter. Day after day they have had to labour deep in snow or mud, dragging heavy loads across country which has been reduced by shell-fire to a quagmire; some may have been acclimatised to the bitter cold, but those who have been drawn from the warmer districts of the Soviet Union must have suffered indescribably. Yet it is good to know that the Red Army men have done all in their power to alleviate the lot of their horses; and from all reports the Russian Army Veterinary Service is highly efficient.

Recently Reuter's Special Correspondent in Moscow made a trip to the frontal zone with a view to investigating the Russian treatment of their horses, both cavalry and transport animals; and on the whole his report will be read with pleasure by animal-lovers—even though these can never be properly reconciled to animals becoming involved in all the devilries of man-made war. The Russian cavalry units, we learn, have their own veterinary surgeons, and every effort is made to save the wounded horses, if at all possible. Most of the veterinary treatment is given with the units themselves or in the immediate neighbourhood of the front; but the Red Army has also a service

SOVIET RED CROSS NURSE on horseback on the way to the front. Formerly in a factory in Gorky, she has been doing valuable work tending the wounded.   *Photo, British Official*

of lorries specially constructed to take three horses at a time, so that the more severely wounded can be conveyed to hospitals in the rear.

"The veterinary centre which I visited," writes Reuter's Correspondent, "is one of nine such in Moscow itself, and I was told by Mr. Alfiorov, Regional Inspector of Veterinary Services, who with the veterinary surgeon in charge showed me the various sections, that it was representative, though not the best. It was devoted to surgical treatment, infectious cases being taken to special hospitals. The centre has an electrically-controlled operating table for horses, invented by a Russian professor, which stands vertical while the horse is strapped on, and slowly moves down, pulling the horse with it. It has also an X-ray department, and an artificial sunlight section in which I saw

a horse receiving rays to speed up what had been a septic shoulder sore. There are also physico-therapy and clinical laboratories, and a permanent hospital department for nursing civilian horses and pets.

"When the Germans approached Moscow, the veterinary centres in the city were able to receive cases direct from the front, from such regions as Krasnaya Polyana, and a number of stables are still permanently kept open to receive cases of wounds needing surgical treatment. One horse brought in during the Moscow battle, after having been wounded in the field, belonged to a high officer who several times visited his mount. During the period of the bombings a number of horses were treated who were suffering from shell splinters and like injuries. No horses were lost.

"I spoke also with the official responsible for re-establishing veterinary services in the areas of Moscow province regained from the Germans. I learned from him some of the difficulties of work in the regions burned out by the enemy. In some towns and villages, however, the enemy did not have the time to do all the damage they wished, and to such places the veterinary services had been transferred. From another veterinary surgeon I learned that about sixty per cent of the cases of injury to horses are to the legs, fairly frequently various types of inflammation being diagnosed. When I asked whether lameness in horses at the front was treated locally I was told that this was impossible, as lameness was regarded by the Soviet veterinary services as a serious matter, and such cases were usually sent to the rear for diagnosis. I carried away from my visit an impression, gathered from these experts, that the services they represented were fully aware of the value of the work which the horse is doing for the Soviet Union, and that their work was to some extent linked up with the normal services of inspection of State-owned animals."

But although the Russian veterinary services are large and admirably equipped, the prolonged and terrible battles of the last year have made grave inroads on their strength. Veterinary supplies are by no means inexhaustible and, indeed, in some departments they are running short. When this was realized the Royal Society for the Prevention of Cruelty to Animals resolved to do what it could, and through its War Animals (Allies) Fund it has supplied the Russian Veterinary Corps with considerable quantities of equipment. Most of the veterinary supplies sent consist of drugs and dressings, but the consignments have also included veterinary surgeons' wallets; veterinary officers' field chests, complete with instruments and drugs; syringes, X-ray outfits, anaesthetics, breathing tubes for horses, etc. The wallets and field chests are particularly welcome, since they are used by the mobile veterinary workers on the actual battlefield; but the R.S.P.C.A. is hoping to raise sufficient funds to permit the establishment of permanent veterinary hospitals in the interior, where the more seriously wounded animals can be given attention and rest.

These hospitals must be fitted with sling harnesses for wounded horses and up-to-date X-ray apparatus, and although many such hospitals are already in existence, many more are needed. To help provide them is a form of war effort which should be sure of a ready response from Britain's animal-lovers.

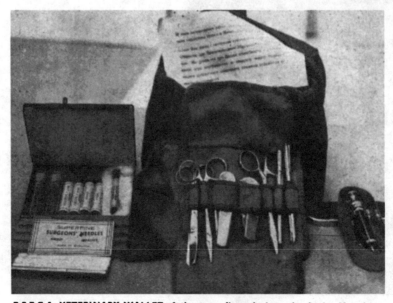

R.S.P.C.A. VETERINARY WALLET of the type dispatched to the Soviet Veterinary Corps. The wallets cost £5 each, and the Society aims to send 2,000 of them. Many thousands of horses, used for cavalry and transport, have been helping the cause of freedom on the East Front. Here is an opportunity of alleviating the sufferings of this noble animal involved in " man's inhumanity to man."   *Photo, Topical Press*

Russian Fighters and Their Animal Comrades

Lack of roads and economy of mechanical power have brought the horse to the fore on the Russian fronts. Here are some mounted scouts reconnoitring in the bright winter sunshine.

A Red Army cavalryman using his horse's back as a gun rest. Right, Soviet horseman testing the edge of his blade before going into action.

Remounts for the Soviet Army being examined and classified at a cavalry centre. The winter campaign in Russia would have been impossible without equine aid. Right, Service dogs transporting a machine-gun across the snowbound countryside.

Photos, Ministry of Information, Planet News

THE WAR IN THE AIR

Specially Contributed by Capt. NORMAN MACMILLAN, M.C., A.F.C.

A NEW phase in the air war over Europe began on the night of Friday, May 29, the thousandth day of the war. Seven days earlier Bomber Command raided St. Nazaire, German U-boat base in Occupied France. Then a week of bad weather deferred large-scale operations. On the night following the thousandth day the R.A.F. struck at German "auxiliary" war industry.

For three hours onwards from midnight, the Gnome-Rhone aero-engine factory (1,000 workers) at Gennevilliers, the Goodrich rubber factory at Colombes, and other targets near Paris were bombed. Gennevilliers power station, supplying the whole industrial area of north-west Paris, was razed.

Capt. N. MACMILLAN
Photo, Raphael

On the following night, with the moon rising almost to the full, the greatest bombing force the world has ever seen rose from the aerodromes of the United Kingdom and flew to raid Cologne, the third greatest city of Germany; 1,130 four-engined Stirling, Halifax, Lancaster, and twin-engined Manchester Whitley, Wellington and Hampden bombers—a force twice as numerous as the largest sent by Germany over any British city, and transporting a quadrupled bomb load—were concentrated over the target, and in 90 minutes dropped 3,000 tons of bombs. (Compare this with the total of 6,402 tons dropped by the British air forces on the Western Front from July 1916, to November 1918.)

Air Vice-Marshal J. E. A. Baldwin and other senior officers flew with the crews under their command.

Fighter, Coastal, and Army Cooperation Commands made diversionary attacks against aerodromes and other targets.

The German anti-aircraft defences, nowhere greater than around Cologne and its approaches, were saturated by the weight and plus ten-aircraft-a-minute speed of attack. Soon they were unable to maintain efficient defence. The fires of Cologne were visible from aircraft flying over the Dutch coast 140 miles distant. For several days after the attack reconnaissance aircraft were unable to photograph Cologne owing to the pall of smoke rising from the burning city to 15,000 feet.

Two nights later a force of 1,036 bombers attacked the Ruhr. Essen was the main target, but in the factory-smoke-filled air of the moonlit sky, it is not always easy to pick out a given factory. Captains of aircraft were given freedom to select alternative targets in Duisburg, Oberhausen and elsewhere ; the size of the target area, measuring about 40 miles by 15, enabled this large force to operate despite somewhat unfavourable cloud conditions.

All aircraft in both raids were British in design and manufacture. Their all-British crews came from the Commonwealth. Forty-four aircraft were lost in the first four-figure raid ; 35 in the second ; a percentage of 3·66. The rate of aircraft loss, which is held to be too costly to replace, was fixed by Air Chief Marshal Sir Hugh Dowding, who won the first Battle of Britain against the Luftwaffe, at 10 per cent.

Air Marshal A. T. Harris, C.-in-C. Bomber Command, who organized the great-scale air raids, is one of the world's outstanding air commanders. I remember him as a fighter pilot in 45 Squadron in 1917, when, flying Camels in France, he scored successes against the Albatrosses of the German air force. He invented an ingenious device for counting the number of rounds fired from the twin Vickers machine-guns. His ante-Cologne order to his bomber crews was typical : " Let them have it on the chin."

Lt.-General H. H. Arnold, Chief of the U.S. Army Air Forces, and Rear-Admiral John H. Towers (who commanded the four U.S. Navy Curtiss flying-boats that set out to fly the Atlantic in 1919, and who taxied his boat to Horta, Azores, after forced-landing on the ocean), now Chief of the U.S. Navy Bureau of Aeronautics, came to England during the last week in May (see illus. p. 28). Soon U.S. crews and bombers will join the British crews in the raids against Germany.

During the day preceding the Ruhr raid, about 1,000 fighters of Fighter Command made sweeps over occupied territory. Frequently escorting Boston and Hurribombers, these fighters have kept up their constant pressure on the west central coastline of Europe and its hinterland.

Germany's threatened reprisal raids on two successive nights were made against Canterbury. Damage was done. The attacks were on a relatively small scale. German aircraft losses were from 10 to 12 per cent, including those shot down over bases in Europe.

Medium-scale British raids were directed against Essen and Bremen on June 2 and 3.

For two nights before Thursday, May 28, when Rommel launched his latest attack in Libya, Axis aircraft raided Allied rear areas, keeping troops alert, but doing little damage. Allied aircraft raided enemy bases, camps, aerodromes, and motor transport in Africa and Sicily. With the outbreak of battle, every unit of the R.A.F. roared into action against troops, supply columns, fuel tankers, and aerodromes ; aircraft included Hurricanes, Tomahawks, Kittyhawks, Bostons, Beaufighters, and, for the first time in Africa, Spitfires.

Three U-boats were reported sunk by Brazilian coast patrol aircraft off Pernambuco between May 23 and 28. In the Pacific, Allied air raids were made against Amboina, Lae, Rabaul. Five Japanese Zero fighters were shot down.

Statements by General Alexander after the retreat of the British army from Burma to India, and by Admiral Sir Andrew Cunningham on relinquishing the Mediterranean Command, which he had held since January 1939, show that it is now generally recognized that air cover is an essential pre-requisite to success in all operations by land or sea. In the oceans aircraft carriers must provide the facilities to achieve that end.

U.S. Army and R.A.F. aircraft attacked Japanese forces in Burma, raiding aerodrome, river craft, and power station at Rangoon, the aerodrome at Akyab, steamers on the Mayu and Chindwin rivers, barracks and stores at Kyaukpyu. The American Volunteer Group from China, bombed Japanese fortified positions west of the Salween river.

British, American, and Chinese pilots flew 8,616 refugees—women and children first—from Burma to India. U.S. Army Air corps carried 4,228. One plane brought out 72 refugees in one trip. R.A.F. planes dropped 100,000 lb. of food to evacuating parties on the ground, and food, boots, and shoes to British troops retreating over the hills.

The Commonwealth—Australia, Canada, New Zealand, United Kingdom—Air Training Plan has been extended to March 31, 1945, by conference in Ottawa. It assures the training of air crews in adequate numbers for the huge air programme that lies ahead. Britain will contribute half the cost.

Russo-German air operations have remained tactically directed towards targets in the field and forward supply routes on land and at sea. The Russian Air Force uses rocket propulsion to discharge anti-tank bombs from Stormovik low-level bombers, and have applied the same gear to their Hurricane (British-built) bombers.

The U.S. Curtiss-Wright C43 " Commando " army transport aeroplane can carry field guns and reconnaissance cars.

IN CANTERBURY, the Dean, Rev. Hewlett Johnson, inspecting the damage which resulted from the raid on the night of May 31. Two churches, a newspaper office and two schools were among the buildings destroyed. The victims included the town clerk and his wife. *Photo, Associated Press*

What the 1,000 Bombers Did to Cologne

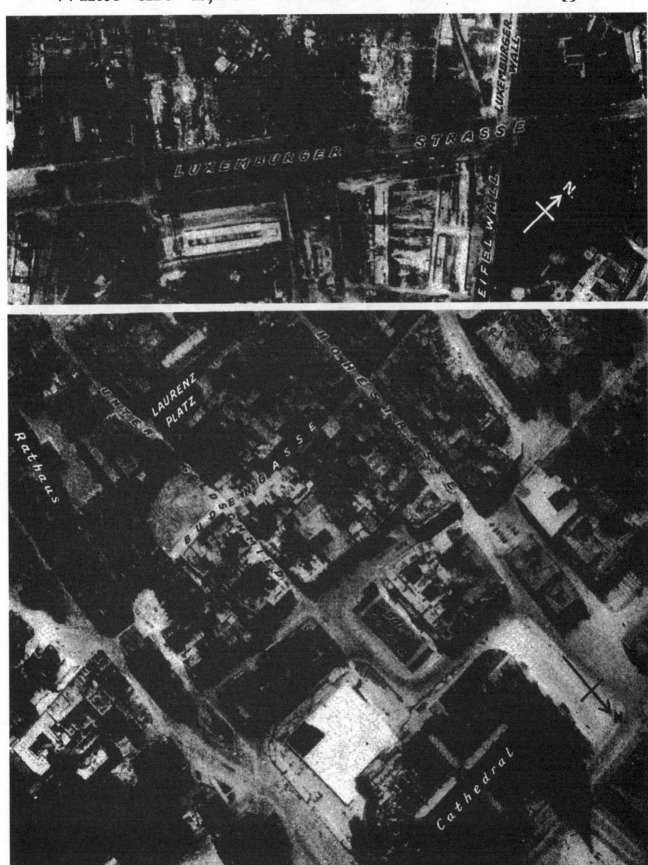

DEVASTATION IN COLOGNE after the 1,000-bomber raid on May 30 revealed in R.A.F. photos taken several days later, when at last the pall of smoke had been dissipated. The cathedral, seen in the bottom right-hand corner, was spared, receiving only superficial damage from blast. Heavily blitzed areas totalled 5,000 acres of industrial property, including gasworks, tire factories, the Deutsche Wagen Fabrik A.G., the Humboldt Deutsche Motoren A.G., and the Humboldt Deutsche works at Koeln-Kalk. The photograph at the top shows the destruction in the neighbourhood of the Luxemburger Strasse and Eifel Wall.

Photos, British Official : Crown Copyright

Back from Cologne, Greatest Raid in History

Back from their great raid over Cologne, some members of the crews are celebrating with smiles and the familiar "thumbs up" signal the doom of many a Nazi munition works.

R.A.F. navigator, back from Cologne, handing over his maps to a member of the W.A.A.F.

Air Vice-Marshal J. E. A. Baldwin, who flew with the bombers to Cologne so that he could "see things for himself."

ON May 30, 1942, the 1,001st day of the war, 1,130 British-manned aircraft took part in the greatest aerial offensive in history to date. The target for that night was Cologne. 13,000 men, roughly divided between the ground and the air, were organized to the minute. Machines were tuned up, bombs were put in the racks and crews were briefed. While the bombers winged their way to the main objective, machines of the Army Cooperation Command were engaged in diversionary attacks on enemy aerodromes . . .

The raid was brilliantly described by a Flying Officer who was a bomb-aimer in a Lancaster. Puzzled by the unusual light over enemy territory, the navigator consulted his chart. The city, he thought, was much too far away to be seen. So great, however, were the fires caused by early arrivals over the target that it was actually Cologne. "The glare was still there like a huge cigarette-end in the German black-out. On and on the plane went until it 'flew into the smoke.' Down in my bomb-aimer's hatch I looked at the burning town below me. I let the bombs go. As we crossed the town there were burning blocks to the right of us, while to the left the fires were immense. Buildings were skeletons in the midst of the fires ; sometimes you could see what appeared to be frame-works of white-hot joists. The blast of the bombs was hurling walls themselves across the flames."

At first the Germans strove to discount the size and effect of the raid. But the massiveness of the onslaught could not be hid. "Gone for ever is the Cologne that we knew," said the Koelnische Zeitung ; and neutrals spoke of 20,000 killed and of a vast army of refugees.

General view of Cologne showing the cathedral and main railway station. In the background, stretching for miles, is the vast industrial area. Right, three Canadian members of the crew of a Halifax bomber enjoying a cup of tea at a U.S. mobile canteen, after being briefed.

Photos, British Official ; P.N.A., Sport & General, Associated Press

In America Ships Are Being Mass-Produced

SUBMARINE CHASER, nearing completion in the Defoe shipbuilding yards at Bay City, Michigan. By the upside method of construction—that is, hull uppermost—it is possible to turn out such a ship in a week, whereas in the orthodox manner it would take six weeks.

Entire forepeak section of a Liberty ship's bow of prefabricated material being hoisted into place at the California Shipbuilding Corporation's yard at Wilmington (below). Mass-produced ships of this kind are welded together and not riveted, thereby saving time, manpower and deadweight. All ships being built in America for Britain will be welded.

Two more Liberty ships, as the U.S.A.'s new merchantmen are popularly styled, nearly ready for Freedom's war. In deference to a very old custom, eyes have been painted on their prows as a charm against the perils of the sea.

New U.S. submarine being launched at a Wisconsin shipyard on Lake Michigan (above). After being fitted and passing her naval tests she will be christened the U.S.S. Peto.

Nine new ships at a fitting-out dock are part of the vast new U.S. armada (right). The striped drums on their sterns are gun-emplacements. These ships will soon be playing their part in keeping the Allied lifelines open.

Photos, Associated Press, Wide World, Keystone

House-to-House Fighting in a Soviet Town

Specially drawn by Haworth for THE WAR ILLUSTRATED

"THE BATTLE FOR 'X' (said a recent dispatch from the Russian front) is not yet over, but day by day the Germans are being driven back towards the centre of the town." This drawing illustrates some of the tactics and weapons employed in street fighting of this type.

The Germans are here depicted in possession of a block of buildings, from which they can direct withering fire along several important roads. This house, typical of Russian domestic architecture, is heavily fortified, being defended by an anti-tank gun (A) and anti-tank rifle (B) on the ground floor, a heavy machine-gun (C) on the first floor and numerous riflemen stationed at the windows.

A frontal attack being virtually impossible, the Russians have worked their way round side streets, clearing houses and overcoming resistance as they go. Protected by covering machine-gun fire from (D) and from windows behind this machine-gun, the attackers have reached the roof at (E) and are breaking in. All windows on that side of the Nazi stronghold are under fire; e.g. the German soldier (F) is driven back from his window. It must be imagined that a similar attack has been launched

on the opposite flank not only from the roof (G) but also at street level (H). The party carrying out this latter move are seen crouched under cover, their objective being the heavy door (J) leading to the rear of the German anti-tank gun and anti-tank rifle positions which are holding up the main Russian advance. One man (K) has darted forward and flung a grenade at the heavy door, taking cover himself immediately. Another (L) of the party prepares to throw should it be necessary.

Party (G) have made the best progress of all and are seen in the act of attacking the defenders from the rear. They have "mouseholed" their way along the eaves and attics of adjoining houses and are now seen entering the strongpoint by the roof. German snipers (M) are held up by a Russian (N) with a sub machine-gun whilst another (O) prepares to demoralize defenders below by firing a shattering volley through the floor. Meanwhile, others of the same patrol have torn a hole in the roof; one man (P) is seen dropping through to assist his comrades (Q) who are breaking down the door preparatory to hurling a grenade into the machine-gun nest established in the room within.

With Timoshenko's Army Outside Kharkov

CAPTURED NEAR KHARKOV, a group of German prisoners taken by Red Army men during fierce fighting for a village. Right, camouflaged in white overalls Soviet soldiers advance on Yuknev.

UNITS OF THE RED ARMY under Marshal Timoshenko storming German defences on the Kharkov front. The position, originally forest land, was cleared by the retreating Nazis, but trees and their stumps were left about to impede the Russian advance.

IN THE UKRAINE lumber and brushwood make hard going for Soviet infantrymen. Left, a rubber dinghy comes in handy for German soldiers crossing a flooded street in a town on the East Front.

Photos, British Official: Crown Copyright; Planet News, Keystone

Battle School: The 'Real Thing' in Training

Much has been heard recently of the new battle drill which is now an established part of the training of the British Army. Below we give some account of its origin, of what it attempts to do, and of how it does it ; and more may be learnt from the series of photographs which are given in the pages immediately following.

UP a slope towards us twenty men are running slowly and heavily. They wear a kind of combination overall and battle-dress, black and shiny with water, streaked with dull red, daubed with mud. Some of their faces are purple with extreme exertion, others are white or yellow. Round them three or four instructors prance and skip, gesticulating with short sticks, and shouting hoarsely : " Hurry, hurry, hurry ! On, on ! There are Huns at the top of the hill ! Get at them ! Kill them—hurry ! They'll get you if you don't get them : On, on ! " The men stumble to the top of the hill and stand swaying wearily and begin to take their muddy rifles to pieces and clean them. When they've done that a whistle blows and they close together automatically, and stumble away at the double.

So Richard Sharp of the B.B.C. describes the conclusion of the " assault course " at one of Britain's new battle schools. There are a number of these schools now, one in every Command, and all are under the direct control of General Sir Bernard Paget, Commander-in-Chief of the Home Forces. For the most part they were started by individual commanders, and they still retain a distinct individuality in the methods adopted to turn out officers and men capable of standing up to the test of modern war. In them battle drill is carried to a high pitch of realistic perfection, although it is now being extended to all the infantry.

What is battle drill ? In brief, it is the training of men in the circumstances as near as may be of actual battle, so that when they are confronted with the " real thing " they will know instinctively what to do and how to do it. It dates from about the time of Dunkirk, when there were many officers who realized from their experience of the fighting in France that the British soldier, although as brave as the bravest, a good shot with the rifle, and a handy fellow enough with the bayonet, was hardly to be compared with the Germans in the tactics of modern warfare. He knew little of infiltration, and as often as not his handling of his weapons—other than the rifle—left something to be desired. (This was hardly to be wondered at, since the number of Bren guns, anti-tank rifles, etc., issued before the war was very limited.) Chief of those who urged the modernization of training was General Sir H. Alexander, upon whose tactical notes drawn up after Dunkirk the new methods are largely based.

How to enter a house suspected of being occupied by the enemy. The door is kicked open, the soldier holding his Tommy gun at the ready.
Photo, The Daily Mirror

The old formal drill of the barrack square was, in fact, the battle drill of Waterloo. A new age has brought with it a new kind of war, and a new kind of war demands new methods. So new battle drills have been, and are being, devised. Details vary, but in general the section adopts arrow-head formation, in which each man has a designated task, whether it be as leader, Bren gun 1 and 2, grenadier, sniper, and so on. Special drills have been worked out for clearing forests and crossing rivers ; and so complex and various are they that the full course at a battle school may take the whole of a very full and arduous sixteen days.

There are both offensive and defensive drills for sections and platoons, companies and battalions, and all through the aim is to ensure that each man, from the private to the colonel, shall know automatically what part he has to play in battle. Not the least of the difficulties which distinguish the new drill from the old, is that it involves the use of live ammunition from all infantry weapons, while the men engaged are also exposed to very realistic dive-bombing by aircraft.

To return to Richard Sharp's description, the particular battle school he visited has for its commander a lieutenant-colonel of twenty-one, and in the class were majors, captains,

lieutenants and sergeant-majors. All were dressed alike in impersonal denim, with no marks of rank, and all were treated alike. The day which ended with that charge up the slope had begun with a lecture on hate, delivered in the " hate room," which is hung with photographs from Nazi-occupied Europe, of people starving and sick, of the dead lying in heaps. The commandant explained that if you hate your enemy you are likely to kill him more quickly and efficiently. After the lecture the men, with rifles, bayonets fixed, and packs on their backs, had run a sort of race. First they had lain on their backs and clawed their way with bleeding hands under a nest of barbed wire ten yards wide. They had gone under and over the low hurdles, throwing themselves at them ; then through burning paraffin, wincing and screwing up their eyes, but hurrying on ; then through deep water, and under more barbed wire with Bren-gun bullets cutting a crease in the grass just in front of them (*see* photos, pp. 16, 17).

Another " hazard " is what is called the " haunted house " (*see* photo on the left). It is a cottage filled with booby-traps and supposed Germans—cardboard figures which pop up from behind shelves and peer round chimneys, lie in wait behind closed doors and in cupboards or lurk on the dilapidated stairs. As you push open the front door a mine goes off, filling the little room with smoke. A soldier with a tommy-gun lets fly—with live ammo.—and with grim determination makes his way from room to room, upstairs under a hail of tins and buckets of dirty water, whirling round and tut-tutting with his gun as enemy figures appear with disconcerting suddenness, in front and behind, at this side and on that. Altogether, then, an immense amount of ingenuity has gone to the planning of the battle drills and the assault courses in particular, and it is not unnatural that the men who take part in them, however sceptical and " browned off " they may feel at the beginning, soon show the most eager interest. But the course at the battle schools is a gruelling one ; not all the students can manage to make the circuit, and those who fail—usually for physical reasons—are at once returned to their units.

General Paget recently wrote to all the Army Commanders strongly condemning the use of strong and offensive language to urge students to greater efforts during training. " While troops will respond to a lead," he said in a letter to the Army Commanders, read at the Assembly of the Church of Scotland in Edinburgh, " they will not be driven on by abusive language. When such language is used by N.C.O.s to officer-students, I consider it is most harmful to discipline." A second point he criticized was " the attempt to produce a blood lust, or hate, during training. Such an attitude is foreign to our British temperament and any attempt to produce it, by artificial stimulus, is bound to fail. Officers and N.C.O.s must be made to realize the difference between this artificial hate and the building up of a true offensive spirit, combined with the will-power which will not recognize defeat."

After packing their rifles, equipment and clothing in their groundsheets and gas capes, soldiers in training at one of the Battle Schools set up in the Commands cross a river. In this way clothes and equipment are kept more or less waterproof, and the bundles themselves, being buoyant, act as a support for the swimmers.

Photos, British Official : Crown Copyright

Britain's Soldiers at Battle Drill

Battle Drill is now a recognized feature of the British Army's training, and at Battle Schools
in various parts of the country—this photograph was taken at one in Northern Ireland—
men are trained to fight under conditions approaching as near as possible the "real thing."
A descriptive account of the new methods is given in the opposite page.

15

'Over the Top' in the Assault Course

Photos, British Off
& General, The

1. The Assault Course begins : advancing through explosions and barbed wire. 2. " Flattening out " before a hail of live ammunition from Bren-guns. Tracer bullets are furrowing the sand in the immediate foreground. 3. All in the day's march—or swim—an infantry officer reaches the top of a 30 ft. wall. 4. Infantry crawling through a muddy "hazard."

16

Attack! Attack! Always Attack!

5. Through fire and water they go under conditions similar to real warfare. 6. With full
equipment, steel helmets and rifles, troops swimming a reservoir. 7. Soldiers advancing
through a barbed-wire obstacle under instructors' fire. 8. A wire-cutting party clearing the
way for an advance by Bren-gun carriers, charges exploding to represent mortar fire.

17

In Scotland Today: Germany Tomorrow!

Photos, British Official · Crown Copyright

Preparing for the " second front," these troops of the Scottish Command are carrying out
landing exercises at night with gun-cotton charges exploding in the lake and tracer ammunition being fired within a few feet of them.   Live ammunition is the order of modern training.
In the upper photograph is another landing-party coming ashore under a smoke screen.

Here and There in the India That Isn't British

In all the prolonged and widespread discussions concerning what is called the Indian problem, little has been heard of those territories in India which are neither British nor ruled by Indian princes, i.e. Portuguese India and French India. These are the subjects of the article that follows.

As everyone knows, India—the vast peninsula or sub-continent which has its crown in the towering peaks of the Himalayas and its. foot in the warm waters of the Indian Ocean—is divided between British India and the India of the Princes. i.e. those Indian states which have treaties of alliance with the British Crown. But there are also two other Indias, so far as political allegiance is concerned ; there is a Portuguese India and a French.

Of these the more important, both in area, and population, is Portuguese India, which consists of Goa, with the islands of Angediva, São Jorge and Morcegos on the Malabar coast ; Daman (Damão) on the Gulf of Cambay, north of Bombay; and Diu, on the other side of the Gulf, on the coast of Gujerat. All in all, these have an area of 1,537 square miles, with a population of some 600,000.

All are relics of the days when Portugal was the world's greatest commercial and colonizing power. Goa was captured in 1510 by the famous Portuguese captain, Affonso d'Albuquerque. An attempt by the local king to eject the Portuguese was defeated, and Goa became the capital of the whole Portuguese Empire in the Orient.

The customs and constitutions of the native village communities were left practically untouched, save that the rite of suttee (widow-burning) was abolished, but on the native framework was erected an imposing edifice of military, commercial, and ecclesiastical power, so that " Golden Goa " rivalled in splendour the empire of the Moguls. Its great days were at the close of the sixteenth century and the opening of the seventeenth ; then the appearance of the Dutch in the Indies led to Goa's gradual decline. When a hundred years later Clive set about establishing British power in India, Goa was well nigh deserted by all save priests and monks ; its arsenal, its quays, its palaces and even many of its churches were in ruins, while its streets were overgrown with grass. And such it has remained for the most part, a city of ruins and ancient memories. In the most notable of its surviving churches, that of Bom Jesus, are enshrined the mortal remains —still in a fair state of preservation—of St. Francis Xavier, the Apostle of the Indies, who died in 1552 in China, and was reburied in Goa two years later. The present-day capital of the colony is Panjim, or New Goa, which possesses a modern port as well as the usual complement of Government buildings. On the other side of the Mandavi estuary is Mormugão, which is linked by railway with the British Indian system.

Daman has been Portuguese since 1558—the year in which our Queen Elizabeth came to the throne ; attached to it are the territories of Dadará and Nagar Havili, which were occupied considerably later. The soil is fertile, and there are some fine teak forests ; there are also some salt works and shipyards.

Diu comprises the island of that name and a small district (Gocola and Simbor) on the mainland. Once it was an important port, but the water is not deep enough for large ships and its trade is now decayed.

Now let us turn to French India. This consists of five separate colonies or provinces —Pondicherry, Chandernagore, Karikal, Mahé and Yanaon—which together cover an area of 196 square miles with a population of some 300,000 ; each province is divided into communes, with their own municipal institutions. Most important is Pondicherry, whose Governor is Governor-General of the French possessions in India ; there is also an elected General Council, and the colony used to have its representatives in the French Senate and Chamber in Paris.

Those who remember their reading of Macaulay's vivid pages will not need to be reminded of the rivalry between the French under Dupleix and the English under Clive ; and Pondicherry (which was originally founded by French settlers in 1683) was Dupleix' base in his bid for a French empire in India. In 1748 Admiral Boscawen laid siege to it unsuccessfully, but Coote took it from Lally in 1761. Restored to France some years later, the British captured it again in 1778 and its fortifications were destroyed. Twice more it was restored to the French and captured by the British, but since 1816 it has remained in French possession, although

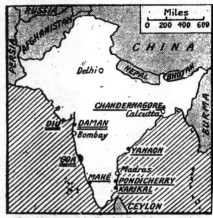

it is entirely surrounded by British territory. The town of Pondicherry has some fine public buildings, cotton and bone mills, and in the adjoining countryside rice and grains are the chief crops.

Chandernagore is a pocket-handkerchief of a territory—it contains only three square miles with a population of under 40,000—on the Hooghly, some twenty miles above Calcutta. It became a French settlement in 1688, and in the Dupleix period enjoyed considerable importance. Like Pondicherry it has changed hands time and again, until in 1816 it became French for good. Today it is described as a quiet riverside town.

Karikal was captured by the French from the Rajah of Tangore in 1739, and after the usual vicissitudes, was restored to them by the British in 1817. It has an area of fifty-three square miles, and a population of about sixty thousand, who engage in commerce with Ceylon and (in normal times) with the Straits Settlements. Mahé (area 26 square miles, population 13,000) is the only French possession on the west coast of India. Like Pondicherry, it used to have its representative in the French Parliament; but economically it is in decay. As for Yanaon, there is little that can be said about it, save that it is five square miles in extent, and that it has some 5,000 people.

Governor of French India is M. Louis Bonvin. On September 9, 1940 he announced his adhesion to General de Gaulle, who nominated him to the Council of Defence of the Free French Empire.

IN OLD GOA, the church of Bom (the good) Jesus, where the body of St. Francis Xavier, the Apostle of the Indies, was laid to rest in 1554. Except for a few churches Old Goa is now in ruins. Pangim, or New Goa, has been the capital of the Colony since 1843.   *Photo, E.N.A.*

PONDICHERRY. (left), capital of French India, lies about 100 miles south of Madras. Right, the statue in the town of J. Francois Dupleix, who founded the French colony, and became governor of the province in 1741.   *Photo, E.N.A.*

Nearing the End of a Weary Road in Burma

BRITISH SOLDIERS—they are men of the King's Own Yorkshire Light Infantry—on patrol in the Tharrawaddy sector, Burma. The "Koylies" were the first British troops to go into action against the Japanese in Burma, and they were continuously engaged on the Sittang River front.

INDIAN TROOPS (below) who assisted the Chinese forces at Toungoo, and who had fought their way gallantly through the encircling Japanese, passing along a road north of Toungoo. Though we were compelled to evacuate Burma our efforts there, said General Wavell, "saved India from what might have been a serious situation."

"KOYLIES" on the Burmese front. In a statement to the Press at New Delhi on May 29 General Wavell said, "The Burma campaign is over for the time being, but some day I hope we will fight it again the other way round." Of the troops who went from India to Burma more than four-fifths got back.

On the road to Moulmein, third largest town in Burma, this important bridge was destroyed by our retreating forces. Japanese engineers erected an emergency gangway, and in this photograph some Jap units are seen crossing the river.

Photos, British Official: Crown Copyright British Newsreels; Wide World

x

x

In Madagascar the British Assume Control

Rear-Adm. E. N. SYFRET and Maj.-Gen. STURGES inspecting British troops in Diego Suarez, after the surrender of the fort and port to combined British naval and military forces on May 7.

One of the British landing-craft used in the taking of Diego Suarez, carrying a motor ambulance. Although there was some severe fighting with the Vichy forces, our total casualties in the engagement, according to Mr. Eden, amounted to less than 500.

Photos, British Newsreels

Imitation is the sincerest form of flattery. A small Madagascan looks up to the tall British soldier on sentry in Diego Suarez harbour. One of the clauses in the terms for the surrender of Madagascar was that the territory would remain French and would be restored to French sovereignty after the war.

AT ANTSIRANE, the scene at the British headquarters, after the surrender of Diego Suarez. The French naval, military and air respresentatives (backs to camera) are facing the British combined services delegation, including Rear-Admiral E. N. Syfret, Commander of the British Naval forces.

Photos, British Official: Crown Copyright

H.M.S. PENELOPE, 5,270-ton cruiser, at Malta. Behind this laconic statement is a story of pluck and resource that must take its place among the proudest annals of the British Navy. Penelope (Captain A. D. Nicholl, D.S.O., R.N.) was singled out for attack by Axis aircraft, and for two weeks was subjected to some of the heaviest raids in Malta's experience. For the greater part of every day the **Penelope's guns were in continuous action, and it**

was a case of all hands, including stewards and cooks, to the guns which were kept going in spite of a veritable hail of bomb and flying splinters. The ship was repeatedly hit, but repairs were carried out under fire while the Penelope's guns hit back at the raiders. Almost to schedule the ship was got ready for sea. Capt. Nicholl was wounded, but continued to direct operations without rest or respite. H.M.S.

Penelope, notwithstanding her damage and her exhausted crew, put to sea. On the following day she was shadowed by two float planes, and during the morning a Ju. 88 and four Italian torpedo-bombers attacked, but the cruiser retaliated with such fury that the enemy planes were beaten off. Then followed other raids in swift succession. These, too, were frustrated. A critical moment arrived when a

force of six torpedo bombers delivered a torpedo attack, but, superbly handled, the cruiser was not hit. Fourteen Ju. 88s came over, and one bomb fell near the Penelope. A single Ju. 88 made a final effort, but failed, and Penelope reached Gibraltar. Now H.M.S. "Pepper-Pot," as she is nicknamed because of her 1,000 bomb-holes, is under repair in a U.S. port, while her Captain, and several of her complement have been decorated.

Photo, British Official: Crown Copyright. Badge by Permission of the Controller, H.M. Stationery Office

THE WAR AT SEA

by Our Naval Correspondent
FRANCIS E. McMURTRIE

A FTER a period of comparative quiescence, following their repulse in the Coral Sea action, the Japanese resumed activity in the Indian Ocean and Pacific at the end of May.

Their most important move was made against Sydney, headquarters of the Allied naval forces in the South-West Pacific.

F. E. McMURTRIE
Photo, Fox

Here, at-least four submarines of "special" type managed to enter the harbour on the night of May 31, but accomplished nothing beyond torpedoing an ex-ferry vessel used as a naval depôt ship. All four submarines were destroyed by gunfire or depth charges. One of them has already been salved from the shoal water in which she sank, and is reported to be somewhat bigger than the midget type used in the attack on Pearl Harbour on December 7, 1941. The latter were stated by the U.S. Navy Department to be 41 feet in length, but according to messages from Sydney, the vessel recovered there is at least 60 and possibly nearly 75 feet long.

It would appear, therefore, that the Japanese, finding the tiny craft used in their Hawaiian attack to be a failure, have now built somewhat bigger vessels in the hope of overcoming the defects of the original design. To judge from the fate of the four submarines at Sydney, this hope does not seem to have been realized.

In all probability these small submarines were launched from a depôt ship of some description, which must have approached within 100 miles of the Australian coast to give her brood a chance of success. Naturally every effort will have been made to run down and sink this parent vessel, but she is probably a fairly fast ship and has therefore been able to make her escape. Australian and Dutch aircraft engaged in hunting for her were fortunate enough to locate four enemy submarines at sea, off the New South Wales and Queensland coasts. Three of these are considered to have been destroyed beyond doubt, having been bombed as they were about to submerge. They were larger vessels than those which entered Sydney Harbour, and were evidently cruising independently against commerce. One of them had torpedoed a ship just before she was intercepted. A bomb which hit the submarine amidships caused her to break in two and sink, with the loss of all but five of

her complement of 42. It is possible that she was either Ro. 33 or Ro. 34, submarines of 700 tons, launched in 1933-34, and armed with four torpedo tubes and a 3-inch gun.

At Diego Suarez, the naval base in the north of Madagascar occupied by British forces as a precautionary measure, a Japanese submarine attack was defeated on May 30. In order that the enemy might gain no useful guidance for the future, the Admiralty refrained from publishing details of this affair, beyond stating that no casualties were sustained in any of H.M. ships. A claim made in Tokyo to have damaged a battleship of the Queen Elizabeth type and a cruiser of the Arethusa class on this occasion, has been definitely denied. Probably it was made in the hope of eliciting some sort of information.

O N June 3 an air raid was delivered on Dutch Harbour, the U.S. naval station in the island of Unalaska, on the south-eastern edge of the Bering Sea. As headquarters of the U.S. Navy in Alaskan waters, this harbour is of some importance, though it is by no means a first-class naval base. Nor is it well adapted as a starting-point for attack upon Japan, 2,000 miles distant, weather conditions in the intervening seas being bad for most of the year. Four bombers and 15 fighters carried out this raid, which lasted 15 minutes. High-explosive and incendiary bombs were used, but no damage of note was done. Two further visits from enemy aircraft followed, but no more bombs were dropped. It seems fairly certain that the planes came from an aircraft-carrier. In this way the Japanese may have hoped to excite popular apprehensions on the Pacific coasts of the United States and Canada to such an extent as to divert forces which could be more usefully employed elsewhere.

A much more serious affair was the attack on Midway Island, an American naval air station, 1,125 miles to the N.W. of Hawaii. According to official communiqués issued by Admiral Chester W. Nimitz, Commander-in-Chief of the U.S. Pacific Fleet, the attack was opened on June 4 by a strong force of bombers from enemy aircraft-carriers. After American fighter aircraft had repulsed these with heavy loss, Japanese naval forces approached the island. Up to the time of writing, these had been decisively defeated with the loss of two if not three aircraft-carriers, with all their planes. This is of the first importance, since it is upon the possession of an adequate force of aircraft-carriers that supremacy in the Pacific largely depends. One or two more aircraft-carriers have been more or less badly damaged, as have three battleships, four cruisers, and three naval auxiliaries or transports.

This is the heaviest blow that has so far been inflicted on the Japanese at sea, and

JAPANESE SUBMARINE being raised from Sydney Harbour. It is one of those sunk in the abortive Japanese raid on the night of May 31. *Photo, Australian Official*

may well prove to be a turning-point of the war. That it should have occurred over the possession of a minor position such as Midway may seem strange; but probably the enemy considered it a thorn in their side, from which U.S. reconnaissance aircraft could keep watch over their dispositions in the Marshall Islands and neighbouring groups, 1,000 miles and more to the south-westward.

If the enemy idea was to catch the defenders of Midway napping, after an interval of nearly three months since the island was last attacked, they certainly miscalculated badly.

In the Atlantic, U-boat attacks on shipping off the American Atlantic coasts continue to cause serious concern. On June 5 it was announced in New York that the Royal Navy was assisting U.S. naval forces with corvettes and trawlers to combat this menace, in view of the limited experience which our Allies have had in anti-submarine warfare. So long as the enemy are able to sink merchant vessels faster than they can be replaced, the war is by no means won.

A NOTHER phase of the German war against shipping can be seen in the constant air attacks upon convoys proceeding to North Russia. Owing to the proximity of enemy air bases in Norway and Finland, the Germans are invariably able to attack in force, while our defending fighters, fewer in number and often obliged to descend into the sea when their fuel is exhausted, are faced with an unequal contest. Though the recent German claim to have destroyed 18 ships in a single convoy has been described by the Admiralty as exaggerated by 175 per cent, these losses cannot be regarded with equanimity.

In the Mediterranean the Italian fleet shows no sign of enterprise. On the few occasions on which it has ventured to sea it has been so severely mauled that it now prefers to remain in port, except when obliged to provide escorts for supplies and reinforcements despatched to Libya. If it had not been for the tremendous force which the Luftwaffe concentrated on Malta in recent months, it is doubtful whether Rommel would have been able to renew his strength sufficiently for his recent advance in the Western Desert to have been undertaken.

AMERICAN TANKER sunk off the Georgia coast on April 8. Shell holes can be seen, and the smoke coming from the fo'c'sle is proof that the tanker was shelled after being torpedoed. Flying above is a U.S. Naval patrol plane. *Photo, Keystone*

Now Mexico Is Added to Our Company

Following the sinking by German U-boats of several Mexican tankers and merchantships, President Camacho asked the Mexican Congress for a declaration of war against the Axis Powers. This was granted, and from noon on May 28 Mexico was joined with the United Nations as their ally in the world-wide struggle.

ACCOMPANIED by soldiers, bands, and waving flags, officials of the Republic of Mexico on June 1 paraded the streets of the capital and the principal cities and towns to read a proclamation of war against Germany, Italy, and Japan. This was in accordance with old-time custom, dating back to the days when Mexico was a colonial province of Spain, but in fact the Republic was at war already.

Four days before, on May 28, President Avila Camacho addressed a special session of Congress assembled in Mexico City. Mexico, he said, was a peaceful nation and the last war in which she had been engaged was that against the invading French in 1862 ; but the recent sinking by German submarines of two Mexican tankers "in a cowardly ambush" made it necessary for Mexico to defend her honour and the principles of all liberty-loving people. "The dictators have

that the first of the great modern revolutions broke out—in 1911, when President Diaz, who had been virtual dictator of the republic for more than thirty years, was overthrown by Francisco Madero, whose slogan was "land and liberty." The story of the years that followed is as confused as it is blood-stained, but while presidents have come and presidents have gone, the revolution has gone on. Expropriation of the great landowners and the dividing up of the feudal estates into holdings for the peons, or Indian peasants ; the disestablishment of the Catholic Church because of its political activities, and the nationalization of its large properties (other than the churches themselves) ; and the attempt to bring the great foreign oil interests, in particular the Mexican Eagle and the Royal Dutch-Shell groups, under full Government control—these are persistent features of the Mexican revolution. In 1938 the foreign

many. At that time, too, the country was torn by civil war as rival gangster politicians struggled for office and its spoils. It is fortunate, indeed, that for some years past the republic has been governed on strong but constitutional lines by two men who are likely to live long in their country's history. The one is General Lázaro Cárdenas, who succeeded Calles as President in 1934 and forthwith embarked on a programme of far-reaching social reforms, constituting a "new deal" not unlike, and possibly inspired by, Roosevelt's in the great republic to the north. Cárdenas it was who fought and defeated the "oil imperialism" of the British and American trusts, nationalized the railways and big industries, and distributed millions of acres among the landless peasants. The other is General Camacho, who succeeded Cárdenas as President in November 1940 ; under him the trend to State Socialism has gone on, though it has not been—at least some say—quite so pronounced.

So today, Mexico—third in size and second in population of the Latin-American republics ; she is as big as Germany, Spain, France and Italy combined, and there are nearly twice as many Mexicans as there are Canadians—is our ally. From the purely military point of view her adhesion is not perhaps of any great significance, since her regular army numbers only some 40,000 men; her air force is tiny, and her navy consists of a handful of patrol vessels used in coastguard and police work. Her mercantile marine comprised, in 1939, fifty-six vessels of a gross tonnage of 38,373. But her strategic and economic importance is hardly to be exaggerated. For some months past Mexico has joined with the U.S.A. in measures for coastal defence, and the latter has had the

MEXICO, as this map indicates, is of vast importance, economically and politically. Much of the world's oil is produced in the republic, and the country is infinitely rich in other resources. Moreover, Mexico's entry into the war brings the United States 2,450 coast miles nearer the Panama Canal, the defence of which is vital to the United Nations.

By courtesy of News Chronicle

attacked us" (he went on). "The nation understands that we have done all that was possible to avoid entering the war—all but passive acceptance of dishonour. Mexico expects each one of her sons to do his duty."

While promising that Mexican troops would not be sent to serve out of the continent, the President asked—indeed gave a pledge—that Mexico would collaborate to the full in continental defence and would co-ordinate its activities with those of the other American nations defending themselves and the hemisphere. The assembly cheered and cheered again as the President sat down, and hastened to give him the powers he required, viz. to declare a state of war with the Axis Powers and govern by decree for the duration of the war, the usual parliamentary guarantees being suspended during the emergency.

In Mexico the declaration of war against the Axis was received with general satisfaction, since of all the American republics Mexico has claim to be considered as the most firmly anti-totalitarian. Moreover—though this will seem hard to believe by those who think of Mexico as a land of dictators and bandits—she is genuinely democratic and to a very large extent socialist. It was in Mexico

oil companies were expropriated, and this led to the severance of diplomatic relations with Britain. Mexicans, however, regarded the act as a symbol of national sovereignty and independence, and it is satisfactory to recall that last October terms were agreed for the purchase of the oil properties.

Then in foreign affairs Mexico's record of opposition to the aggressor powers is hard to beat. In 1935 she condemned German rearmament ; she never recognized the Italian seizure of Abyssinia ; she protested against Hitler's invasion of Austria, and was the only country in the world to give asylum to those who had fought against Fascism in Spain. It was in Mexico, too, that Trotsky found a refuge. Mexican public opinion was bitterly contemptuous of the Munich settlement, and for years it gave the principle of collective security ardent support. Then, although the country is not Communist—there are still no diplomatic relations between Mexico and Moscow—the entry of Soviet Russia into the war greatly strengthened her already strong sympathies with the democratic countries.

In the last war Mexico was neutral, showing at times a pronounced bias against the U.S.A. and Britain and in favour of Ger-

right to land its aeroplanes on Mexican aerodromes for a 24-hour stay ; but now the U.S. Navy will be able to use twenty-two Mexican ports on the Pacific and the Gulf of Mexico, Mexican aerodromes will be generally available, and the defence of the Panama Canal will be made vastly more effective. Moreover, Mexico's enormous mineral wealth will be flung into the scale on the side of the United Nations. The mass of the Mexican people are shockingly poor, in spite of all the well-intentioned reforms of recent decades ; but the country in which they live, and whose surface has as yet hardly been scratched, is immensely rich. Most important of all, of course, are the oil deposits : in 1939 Mexico produced over six million tons of crude petroleum—more than Rumania and almost as much as the Netherlands East Indies, although small enough compared with the 168 million tons produced in the U.S.A. Then, finally, now that Mexico has entered the war on our side, our enemies are deprived of a possible jumping-off ground for the invasion of America, north or south. All in all, then, we have good reason to be pleased and proud that Mexico is now to be numbered in the great and growing company of the United Nations. E. ROYSTON PIKE

In the Land of the Aztecs and Oil Kings

MEXICO CITY, the main square, with the cathedral and Government Palace. The cathedral was begun as far back as 1572, and occupies the site of the Aztec temple of Huitzilpochtli. Mexico is the oldest city in North America, and was rebuilt by Cortes following his overthrow of the Aztec power in 1521.

MT. POPOCATEPETL, which means "smoking mountain," with her sister volcano, Ixtaccihuatl, meaning the "white woman," in Aztec. Situated about forty miles south-east of Mexico City, Popocatepetl, second highest peak (17,876 ft.) in the country, has an eliptical crater of over two thousand feet at its widest part and 673 ft. deep below the lowest part of the rim.

Scene of enthusiasm outside the National Palace in Mexico City following President Camacho's declaration of war against the Axis on June 2. The posters call the Mexicans to resist Nazi aggression.

NEAR TAMPICO, oil refineries on the north bank of the Panuco River, in the state of Tamaulipas. Tampico is the centre of export for the oil trade, and as a result of the temporary loss of the Allies' wells in Malaya and Dutch East Indies, is likely to play a great part in the United Nations' plans for victory.

Photos, Paul Popper. Planet News

THE HOME FRONT

by Our Special Correspondent
AUGUSTUS MUIR

As I survey the Home Front during these midsummer weeks of 1942 I see a Britain that is braced for action. There have been times when the nation's muscles have relaxed for a space: it was as if the tension had been too high, the pace too hot to maintain. A graph of this mental and muscular tension would be informative. It touched a high spot in the days of Dunkirk. Fluctuating for a time, it seemed to move downward at the end of last year. Recent events have called forth a new spate of national energy. I see a Britain that has transformed itself not only into a fortress, but into a vast arsenal that resounds with the clamour of productive machinery. War-material rolls from our factories like a dark tidal-wave. On the Home Front, too, the pruning-hook is busy: everything in our daily lives that fails to help in the war effort is being cut away. A pruning-hook is a handy implement; but a sharp axe cuts deeper. There are those who cry for the axe.

Burning Problem of Coal

The problem of coal has been agitating the minds of many. Both the Lords and the Commons have had their say; the big tub has been thumped in some sections of the Press. The tussle about the Beveridge rationing scheme for fuel went on for weeks. The problem of the mines and miners is like a running sore. Many people want immediate out-and-out nationalization, and the man-power question in the mines is critical. Part of the labour at the coal-pits is unskilled; the miners' leaders declare that the wages paid for such work are far below the average the men could get in other industries. Faced with a demand for a minimum wage of £4 5s. for the hewer at the coal face, the coal owners have retorted that the hewer has been earning more than this figure in the better pits, in some cases reaching £6 per week, and even in the poorer coal fields averaging £4. A few weeks ago it was stated that 80,000 tons had been lost by recent strikes in the north of England, the chief cause being the resentment of the lower-scale miners at the fat pay envelopes of their own wives and sisters in other industries. If the whole problem is not settled with good-will on both sides, the outlook may be grim before we get through next winter. We cannot afford to let one single machine producing war material stand idle for one hour through lack of fuel.

The Minister of Agriculture has made a new call on farmers. More land must be ploughed up, since with a battle-line that girdles the globe, with munitions pouring out from our seaports and raw materials flooding in, it is inevitable that cargo space for food must shrink as the months go by. The old cry of "Speed the Plough" has a new potency at this stage of the war. The Wiltshire agricultural committees have declared their ability to plough up another 20,000 acres. "Good," replied Mr. Hudson, the Minister of Agriculture; "I expect you to do another 30,000." The farmers will respond, we may be sure, in an eager fighting spirit.

Some heartening details have been released by the Ministry of Home Security about the raids on certain of our towns. After the dire experiences in the early part of last year, when some of the Civil Defence Services were stretched to the uttermost in repeated blitzes, a lot of re-organization has been carried out. The National Fire Service has been welded into a great unit that is now fighting fit; and the "good neighbour" policy among towns has been working on full throttle in what the Press called the Baedeker raids. Mutual aid has, in fact, been organized all over the country; and we have examples in the prompt help Bristol gave to Bath and Plymouth to Exeter in the brutal Hitlerian orgy of destruction when historic buildings were ground into dust.

Carry Your Gas Mask!

The Civil Defence authorities have been releasing tear gas on the public at unexpected times and places. These tests cause inconvenience, but surely only a fool would grumble. Not so long ago the Prime Minister made a solemn announcement that if Germany used poison gas against any of the Allies, Britain would at once reply with poison gas. This threat was not made without grave thought. With a people as well protected as we are in Britain, gas is a weapon that can succeed only if we are taken by surprise. In Bristol last month, hundreds of aircraft workers were caught in an invasion exercise and blinded with tear gas: they had "forgotten" their gas-masks.

In a few days' time the number of private motor-cars on British roads will be still further reduced. Gone is the basic petrol ration, by which a motorist of the good old

days of a year ago could travel his forty or fifty miles per week. If he wished, he could go to dog-races, to the cinema, or for a sniff of country air. Austerity has clamped down on this with a sharp metallic click: from July 1 onward pleasure motoring is dead. The insurance companies have agreed to a considerable discount in premiums, in some cases about 20 per cent, because presumably there will be fewer accidents. Yet the prices of secondhand cars show a firm market.

CONCRETE SLEEPERS are now being used by the Southern Railway to replace the standard wooden pattern when repairs are necessary. This is one of many Home Front devices to conserve the use of timber. *Photo, Fox*

Clothing control, extended this month, has Austerity as its keynote. After consulting with the Board of Trade, the publishers of Paper Patterns have been carrying out experiments that will interest every woman. Styles are to be restricted, but the publishers are anxious to include pleats, frills, and other trimmings in their patterns. There is a reason for this. Home-made frocks do not come under the Government ban: they may be made as frilly as the heart desires. Officials of the Board of Trade were staggered when certain statistics were put before them no less than one-fifth of women and children's clothes in this country are made at home. With no Austerity curb on home-made frocks, the number is likely to increase.

Meantime, the weather has helped housewives. Green vegetables, an essential part of diet, have been fetching astronomical prices. Drought caused a green vegetable scarcity, but rain came in the second week of May. A cabbage of average size had been costing eighteen pence; a few drenches brought them down to fourpence—the pre-war figure, which I put on record with satisfaction, at a time when "the war" is too often used as an excuse for petty profiteering of the most flagrant kind.

Food and Drink in the News

Towards the end of this month housewives have been hoping to purchase the dried eggs sent across in a huge consignment of 144 million from the United States. A new process has made it possible for eggs to be sent in this dried form, a 5 oz. tin equalling 12 eggs, thus saving cargo space. Since the manufacturing capacity for milk products had reached its maximum in the middle of May, milk was taken off the rationing scheme; and there was heated controversy in certain newspapers about the Food Ministry's action in their slow-down in the canning of fruit and vegetables. To those with a sweet tooth and the means to pander to it, the rationing of sweets will sound the knell to one form of indulgence. No doubt the Black Racketeers will ply their shifty trade, and most people would like to see penalties increased, even to the inclusion of flogging; for Black Market operations in Germany the penalty is death. To strike a more genial note, soft drinks are to be controlled. The universal scowl on the faces of schoolboys changed to a smile when it was learned that control would not mean restriction in quantity; for the Government is merely anxious to "pool" the production of mineral waters and fix prices, the result being considerable factory space available for the storage of other goods.

Even banking facilities are to be pooled. Plans are afoot to release for the Services many young men and women in the Big Five and other banks. Not that bankers have been reluctant to get into uniform; of the 60,000 employed before the war more than half are now in the forces, and over one-tenth of the 9,000 branches in this country have already been closed. But still greater concentration is being demanded, and Sir Kingsley Wood has set up a committee that will consider the release for other duties of those who work behind the familiar but formidable brass rails. Both the Stock Exchange and Lloyds have also contributed a notable portion of their personnel. For the first time in history there was talk the other day of women working "on the floor" of the Stock Exchange. However deep the horror of some old members at this innovation, it is only another example of the passing of the old ways. A new order—very different from Hitler's—is being born before our eyes.

The Changing Face of Wartime London

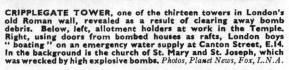

CRIPPLEGATE TOWER, one of the thirteen towers in London's old Roman wall, revealed as a result of clearing away bomb debris. Below, left, allotment holders at work in the Temple. Right, using doors from bombed houses as rafts, London boys " boating " on an emergency water supply at Canton Street, E.14. In the background is the church of St. Mary and St. Joseph, which was wrecked by high explosive bombs. *Photos, Planet News, Fox, L.N.A.*

Here and There With the Roving Cameraman

AMERICAN LEADERS IN BRITAIN. They are, left to right, Major-Gen. D. D. Eisenhower, Chief of the Operations Section of the United States, Major-Gen. B. B. Somervell, Chief of the U.S. Army Services of Supply, a great organizer who gained experience during the U.S. economic depression ; Admiral J. H. Towers, Chief of the U.S. Navy Bureau of Aeronautics ; and Lieut.-Gen. H. H. Arnold, United States Air Force Chief. "It is obvious," remarked Gen. Arnold, recently, "that no offensive against Nazi-occupied Europe can succeed without air superiority, and we mean to have it."

H.M. THE QUEEN chatting with an old pensioner in the grounds of the Royal Hospital, Chelsea, on the occasion of Oak Apple Day anniversary, May 29, the birthday of Charles II, founder of the Royal Hospital. During the intensive night raids on London in the autumn of 1940, the Hospital was hit by Nazi bombs.

TO SAVE PETROL, the Ministry of Transport are asking road transport operators to convert part of their fleets to the producer gas system. Photograph shows gas units behind commercial lorries at a London garage.

COASTGUARDS have now a khaki battle-dress in place of the navy blue uniform. In this photograph the old and new uniforms are seen being worn side by side somewhere on the coast.

THREE NEW NAVAL V.C.s. For their gallantry in the Commando raid on St. Nazaire on March 27-28, Commander R. E. D. Ryder, who commanded the Naval forces, Lt.-Commander S. H. Beattie, R.N., of H.M.S. Campbeltown, and Able-Seaman W. H. Savage, were given the V.C. Seaman Savage was a pom-pom gunlayer in a motor gunboat. Though completely exposed under heavy fire, he fired continuously into enemy positions ashore and the attacking ships until he was killed at his gun.

Photos. British Official : Crown Copyright ; Associated Press. Central Press, G.P.U., The Daily Mirror, P.N.A., L.N.A., Planet News, Topical Press

Our Tokyo Raid Gave the Japs a Shock

With the decorating of the man who led the American bombing raid on Tokyo on April 18 (*see* p, 681, Vol. 4), he was revealed as Brigadier-General James Doolittle, who gave the following brief account of his exploit.

EVERY plane of our attacking force was specially equipped, and every man volunteered for the raid. They practised the plan of attack for weeks.

Extreme care was taken not to bomb non-military targets. We did not bomb the Imperial Palace. I gave special instructions not to bomb the palace, although there would have been no difficulty in doing so, had we desired.

The success of the raid exceeded our most optimistic expectations. Each plane was assigned specific targets, and the bombardiers carried out their expert duties with remarkable precision. Since the raid was made in fair weather in the middle of the day and from a very low altitude no trouble whatever was experienced in finding the exact target.

Apparently there was no advance warning of the raid, as we experienced little hostile reaction. Not more than thirty Japanese pursuit planes were observed during the flight, and these were completely ineffective. Several we know were shot down. The pilots seemed somewhat inexperienced and were evidently not up to the standard of those encountered in active theatres.

We approached our objectives just over the housetops, but bombed at 1,500 feet. The target for one plane was the navy yard in South Tokio, in reaching which it had passed over what apparently was a flying-school, as there were a number of planes in the air.

One salvo made a direct hit on a new cruiser or battleship under construction. It was left in flames. Another illuminated a tank factory.

After releasing our bombs we dived again to the tree tops and went to the coast at that altitude to avoid A.A. fire. Along the coastline we observed several squadrons of destroyers and some cruisers and battleships.

About 25 or 30 miles to sea our rear gunners reported seeing columns of smoke rising thousands of feet in the air. One of our bombardiers strewed incendiary bombs along a quarter of a mile of an aircraft factory near Nagoya.

Flying at such low altitudes made it very difficult to observe results. We could see them strike, but our own field of vision was greatly restricted by our speed. Even so, one of our party observed a ball game in progress. The players and spectators had not started to run for cover until just as the field passed out of sight.

We would like to have tarried and watched later developments from fire and explosion, and even so we were fortunate to receive a fairly detailed report from the excited Japanese radio broadcasts. It took them several hours to calm down to deception and accusation.

In general, the objectives of the raid began north of Tokyo and extended south in an area about 40 miles long and 5 to 20 miles wide.

We Drew V's at Night in Oslo's Streets

Norwegians have suffered drastic penalties for their opposition to German rule, but, as described in the following story received from Oslo by the Norwegian Ministry of Information, they keep their spirit of defiance.

THE first time the V campaign appeal was broadcast from London there was very little reaction in Oslo. Certainly a few people began to use the V sign as a greeting, but that was all.

After the second appeal was broadcast my friend and I started drawing V's at night, and for four consecutive nights we two were almost the only V campaigners in the centre of Oslo. The first night we were in action we went round with chalk drawing huge V's in all the most conspicuous places. Among other places we drew one in the Karl Johansgate, the main Oslo street, and I sat in a window opposite during the whole of the next afternoon watching the passers-by. This V of ours aroused real enthusiasm ; I saw many delighted faces. Most people saw the significance and enjoyed the joke, but others could not see anything particularly Norwegian about the sign, and in some cases they stopped and asked one another what it meant.

I had tasted blood, however, and was determined to make a serious offensive next night. As soon as it grew dark my V's began to appear—chalk-white V's on dark walls and pitch-black V's on light walls. But the anticlimax came the next morning. The Germans had launched a gigantic counter V campaign. Our V's were completely dwarfed by the fine huge stencilled V's of the Germans. Only then did the people begin to take the matter seriously, for they were not only following the appeal from London but defying the Germans at the same time. Nearly everybody used the V sign and tapped out V's in Morse code. I decided not to give up in the first round ; I had seen the effect of our V's, and I knew that one Norwegian V —for Victory—had a very much greater effect than a hundred German V's.

They Had to Repaint the Wall !

That night we two went the rounds again with two buckets, one of pitch and one of whitewash. We drew enormous V's and decorated them with H7 for King Haakon VII, thus : one which we drew on the quisling Ministry of Supply remained there for three whole days, and even when it was painted over it still showed through as plainly as before. It caused such a sensation that a fortnight later the whole wall was repainted.

During the same night we had our first contact with our German rivals. We were drawing on one wall of a corner house when my friend noticed that there was someone round the corner. We finished our V and then investigated. There stood two quislings, one stencilling a fine V on the other wall of the house, and one sticking up posters. Three German policemen, including an officer, were superintending. We went quietly past them, and continued our work in another street. In the centre of Oslo alone that night we met three similar Nazi parties busy at work, and in the course of the night we clashed many times with these—our technically superior—rivals. They pasted over our V's, while we tore down their posters, painted over their V's and drew new ones. The Germans then started painting V's on the pavements ; we followed at fifty yards distance, crossing

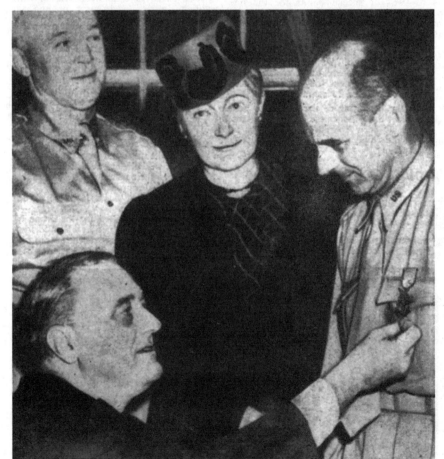

HE BOMBED TOKYO, and received the Congressional Medal of Honour which was personally pinned on his tunic by President Roosevelt ; Brig.-Gen. J. H. Doolittle at the White House, with the President, Lt.-Gen. H. H. Arnold, Air Forces Commander, and Mrs. Doolittle on the occasion of the ceremony. The Tokyo raid is described by General Doolittle in this page. *Photo, Wide World*

THE V SIGN has become the great passive offensive in Norway. It has, of course, two meanings, Verloren, which means lost in German, and Victory for the United Nations. In an article in this page a Norwegian describes how the V campaign was spread in Oslo, his country's capital.
Photos by courtesy of the Royal Norwegian Government

them out or painting them over with an improvised stencil. With the latter the German signs were altered from

GERMANY WINS to GERMANY WINS VERLOREN
on all V fronts on all V fronts

" Verloren " is German for lost.

At one moment, when we were painting on the pavement, a Norwegian policeman came running towards us. We took the offensive and walked quickly towards him. He was obviously disconcerted, for he ran right past us and up to the place where we had been painting. There he turned and set off in pursuit of us, but after we had dodged once round a church and up a few more streets we were able to continue our work undisturbed. We had to stop work at 3.30 a.m. when it grew too light, but the Germans continued until 5 a.m.

After that night the V campaign spread all over the town. People tore down German posters and outlined V's in stairways, lifts, etc. Some people were caught in the act and imprisoned for three or four months.

On the following night we continued our work. We altered a German V opposite the guard-room at the Palace so effectively that even after it had been painted over by the Germans next morning it still showed and aroused great enthusiasm. Even today the words can still be read—" Germany Verloren." We spent one night drawing V's on the doors and windows of all well-known Nazis—we got special paints for the fine window-panes of a particular Nazi glazier, and to remove that V it would be necessary to scratch it off. Shops in the centre of the town which were unlucky enough to get German V's on their windows were forbidden to remove the sign. We therefore helped these people by decorating the German V's as described, and next day the shopkeeper would be ordered to remove them.

At the beginning of the campaign people smiled at the childishness of the Germans in setting up their counter-offensive, but later they quite simply ignored the Germans' prolific sign-writing.

follow, but after four days of uneventful travel we lost our way. That is to say, I and an advance guard of four others did.

At length we came to a tiny Chinese village and persuaded the headman to lend us a guide. Off we went with bamboo torches flaring. The track was still bad and presently we found it blocked by a huge dim shape, a wild bison.

" Don't look at him," said the guide as we skirted the snorting beast. " It makes them charge. Pretend he's not there." It was difficult, particularly when he began to follow us and I was the last in the line. Almost as soon as he gave up we heard something padding on dry leaves near us and saw, reflecting in the torchlight, the baleful eyes of a tiger. It too kept up with our party for some time, but eventually padded away.

When we finally reached our destination we found the main party already there. Now the hill trek began, and we discarded all possible kit for it. For two days we clambered along hillsides with precipitous drops below us. Only the Sealyham dog with us was happy about this mountaineering. After the hills there were three days of river wading. That is where our feet got soft and were cut with stones.

One night we found we were camping near a herd of wild elephants. Just as we began to get used to their trumpetings we were startled again by the approach of a single low-flying plane. In case it was a Japanese we doused our fires.

But while we waited for the drone of the engine to die away, panthers moved into our camp and we had to relight the fires to frighten them away. All the while a tiger was snarling

We Trekked to India Through a Burmese 'Zoo'

Among the civilian refugees who made the 250-mile journey to India on foot through the Burmese jungle was Mr. Leonard Pinchbeck, of Lincolnshire, who told the following story of his adventures to the Daily Herald correspondent, Victor Thompson.

ON April 22 I was told in Mandalay—or what was left of Mandalay after the Japanese bombs—that the enemy was near, and that I was to join a party of civilians and frontier force men making for India. They were leaving from the railway station a few miles away.

When the train started somebody produced three bottles of beer to celebrate our escape from the bombs. Beer! We hadn't seen it for months.

Eventually we crawled into Shwebo—to find it bombed and burning. By quieter stages we finally came to a point where we had to leave the train and go by road.

Sixty-seven of us set out next day under the guidance of a forestry official. One other white man and I were his two lieutenants. The rest of the party were Indians, Burmans and people of mixed race. After one day's trek with bullock carts, which we pushed along at a dizzy speed of three miles an hour, our leader was recalled and we had to go on

without him. He left with me detailed instructions concerning the route we must

Camouflaged with foliage pulled from surrounding bushes, a Chinese sniper crouches in a Burmese jungle. In this page is a vivid description of a trek through a forest teeming with wild beasts.
Photo, British Newsreel

on the other side of the river. I began to feel I was camping in the Zoo. I certainly wasn't sorry when the misty morning came.

That day we came to a place where we could hire canoes. For the next three days we travelled in two large dug-outs, poling, rowing and pushing them over shallows. Leaving the river our caravan trailed 22 hot miles up into the hills. It was the most gruelling stretch of all, but nobody fell out.

When we reached camp that night it was alive with rumours spread by other refugees that the Japanese were already ahead of us. As we lay in the open wondering what to do, heavy rains broke and put out our fires. Wet and miserable, we decided next morning that the Japanese could go to blazes. and pushed on. Our clothes were rags, our feet were blistered and bleeding. Mosquitoes and sandflies were getting busy on some of us. But we were nearing the frontier. Still climbing, we did a two-days march at heights up to 6,500 feet above sea level, sleeping wet amid the clouds. Then on the Indian border we struck a real path. We slept that night on the outskirts of a refugee camp. In the middle of dreaming about that bad night, I was awakened by an alarming din outside. Dacoits were attacking some of our party and were trying to rob them of their poor bundles. My shot-gun scared them off—and that was our last excitement except a hair-raising lorry ride around precipices.

Before long we were smoking real cigarettes instead of dried coconut fronds, and drinking great draughts of water which at least didn't turn brown—the danger signal—when we put permanganate crystals in it. I met my wife and baby in India 23 days after leaving Mandalay. On foot we had covered 250 miles. My weight is nearly two stone less than it was. In fact, I totted up the lost weight of the whole party, and it came to half a ton. Still, we all got through.

IN BURMA, buildings at Maymyo—twenty-five miles north-east of Mandalay—in flames as a result of Japanese bombing. This photograph was taken when General Joseph Stilwell, American Commander of the Chinese forces, had his headquarters in the town.
Photo, Associated Press

OUR DIARY OF THE WAR

MAY 28, 1942, Thursday   *999th day*
Russian Front.—Fierce German attack repelled in Izyum-Barvenkovo sector.
Mediterranean.—Aerodrome at Catania, Sicily, raided by R.A.F.
Africa.—Heavy fighting between armoured forces round Knightsbridge.
China.—Kinhwa besieged from all sides by Japs.
Australasia.—U.S. submarines sank or damaged four enemy ships.

MAY 29, Friday   *1,000th day*
Air.—R.A.F. made heavy attack on Gnome-Rhone aero-engine works and Goodrich rubber works near Paris.
Russian Front.—German attacks still held in Izyum-Barvenkovo sector.
Mediterranean.—Catania again raided by R.A.F.
Africa.—Fierce fighting E. of our main positions ; British counter-attacks at Knightsbridge.
Burma.—U.S. heavy bombers raided Myitkyina aerodrome.
China.—Japs occupy Kinhwa after bitter street fighting.
Australasia.—Allied airmen raided Dilli, Rabaul and seaplane base at Tulagi.
Home.—Seven enemy aircraft destroyed off S.E. and N.E. coast.
General.—Prague announced execution of two Czech families following attack on Heydrich.

MAY 30, Saturday   *1,001st day*
Air.—R.A.F. in biggest attack of war raided Cologne and the Ruhr with more than 1,000 bombers.
Russian Front.—Soviet High Command announced success of Russian attack at Kharkov in forestalling German attack.
Africa.—Germans made two gaps in minefield W. of Knightsbridge.
Burma.—U.S. heavy bombers again raided Myitkyina aerodrome.
Indian Ocean.—Jap submarines attacked harbour of Diego Suarez, Madagascar.
Australasia.—Allied bombers made night attack on Lae, Kupang and Dilli.
General.—Forty-four Czechs, including ten women, executed in Prague.
Lieut.-Gen. F. N. Mason MacFarlane apptd. Governor and C.-in-C., Gibraltar.

MAY 31, Sunday   *1,002nd day*
Mediterranean.—R.A.F. raided Messina.

Africa.—German armoured forces concentrating in gaps of minefield on Trigh Capuzzo.
Home.—German " reprisal " raid on Canterbury.
General.—Twenty Czechs executed.

JUNE 1, Monday   *1,003rd day*
Sea.—Admiralty announced loss of H.M. cruiser Trinidad.
Air.—R.A.F. raided Essen and the Rhur with 1,036 bombers.
Mediterranean.—Submarine base at Augusta, Sicily, raided by R.A.F.
Africa.—German attacks on Bir Hacheim repulsed. Gen. Cruewell, Commander of Afrika Korps, captured.
Burma.—Rangoon attacked by heavy bombers of U.S. Army Air Force.
Australasia.—Jap submarines raided Sydney Harbour. Jap bombers made daylight raid on Pt. Moresby ; Allied bombers raided Rabaul, Lae and Salamana.
General.—Mexican declaration of war signed by President Camacho.
Execution of 27 more Czechs.

JUNE 2, Tuesday   *1,004th day*
Air.—Essen and the Ruhr again raided by strong force.
Mediterranean.—Pantellaria and Cagliari raided by R.A.F.
Africa.—British armoured forces occupied Tamar, W. of Knightsbridge.
Burma.—R.A.F. bombers attacked Oyster Island, off Akyab.
Australasia.—Allied airmen raided Rabaul, Tulagi and Atamboea in Timor.
Home.—Five enemy aircraft shot down over S.E. England.

JUNE 3, Wednesday   *1,005th day*
Air.—Bremen attacked by strong force of bombers.
Africa.—Further attacks on Bir Hacheim driven off by Free French.
China.—On Chekiang front Japs launched attack on Chuhsien.
Indian Ocean.—British occupied Ambilobe, Madagascar.
U.S.A.—Dutch Harbour, Alaska, attacked by Jap aircraft.
General.—Lord Louis Mountbatten, Chief of Combined Operations, in America. Twenty-one Czechs executed.

JUNE 4, Thursday   *1,006th day*
Mediterranean.—Syracuse bombed by R.A.F.
Africa.—Attacks at Bir Hacheim again repulsed.
Burma.—U.S. bombers raided Rangoon.
Indian Ocean.—British occupied ports of Vohemar and Antalaha, Madagascar.
China.—Gens. Stilwell, Brereton and Chennault arrived in Chungking.
Australasia.—Allied submarine sank enemy transport and two supply ships.
Pacific.—Jap aircraft attacked Midway Island.
General.—Special Service troops made reconnaissance raid in Boulogne-Le Touquet area.
Heydrich died from wounds received on May 27. Twenty-four Czechs executed. Hitler and Keitel visited Field-Marshal Mannerheim in Finland.

JUNE 5, Friday   *1,007th day*
Air.—Strong force of bombers raided the Ruhr.
Russian Front.—Germans launched attack on Sevastopol.
Mediterranean.—Night raid by R.A.F. on harbour of Naples.
China.—Japs captured Foochow.
Australasia.—Announced that six Jap submarines had been sunk in five days.
Pacific.—Sea and air battle continuing off Midway Island.
General.—Thirty Czechs executed.

JUNE 6, Saturday   *1,008th day*
Air.—R.A.F. made heavy attacks on port of Emden.
Russian Front.—German attacks on Sevastopol repelled.
Mediterranean.—Nine enemy aircraft shot down over Malta. Messina raided.
Africa.—British armoured units reached Harmat. Two attacks on Bir Hacheim repelled by Free French.
China.—In Chekiang Japs occupied airfield outside Chuhsien.
Pacific.—Adm. Nimitz announced that Jap losses off Midway Island were two or three aircraft carriers lost with all aircraft, three battleships damaged, four cruisers and three transports damaged.
General.—Execution of 13 more Czechs announced.

JUNE 7, Sunday   *1,009th day*
Russian Front.—Stubborn fighting continued round Sevastopol.
Africa.—British artillery stopped enemy armoured forces at Knightsbridge. French repulsed another attack at Bir Hacheim.
Pacific.—Adm. Nimitz reported withdrawal of Jap fleet from Midway Island.

JUNE 8, Monday   *1,010th day*
Sea.—Admiralty announced loss of H.M. trawler Bedfordshire.
Air.—Strong force of bombers raided the Ruhr by night.
Russian Front.—Enemy attacks on Sevastopol repelled with heavy loss.
Mediterranean.—R.A.F. bombed aerodrome at Heraklion, Crete, and naval base at Taranto.
Africa.—Heavy attack on Bir Hacheim repulsed after fierce fighting.
Burma.—U.S. bombers made their first daylight raid on Rangoon.
Australasia.—Sydney and Newcastle, N.S.W., shelled by Jap submarine.
General.—Fourteen Czechs executed.

JUNE 9, Tuesday   *1,011th day*
Sea.—Admiralty announced that H.M. submarine Turbulent sank Italian destroyer and three supply ships in Mediterranean.
Africa.—British armoured forces and Free French drove off large-scale attack at Bir Hacheim.
China.—British and American air force units arrived in China.
General.—Execution of 41 Czechs.

ANGLO-RUSSIAN TREATY

May 20.—Mr. Molotov, Russian Foreign Minister, arrived in Britain for discussions with the British Government concerning the military and political situation.
May 25.—Agreement on all points secured.
May 26.—Treaty of Alliance and Mutual Assistance between Britain and Russia signed at the Foreign Office.
May 29.—Mr. Molotov arrived in Washington. In the course of ensuing conversations " full understanding " reached.
June 4.—Mr. Molotov left Washington on his return journey to Moscow via London.
June 11.—The Alliance announced by Mr. Eden in the House of Commons.

AT the beginning of yet another volume of THE WAR ILLUSTRATED one is tempted to speculate on what will be its contents. But, remembering the many unexpected events that it has been our lot to record and illustrate in the preceding five volumes, the temptation is easily overcome. When I planned and launched the publication in September 1939 little did I guess that well nigh three years later I should be looking back on Russia's mighty stand against Germany, with whom she had signed a pact in August 1939 ; on the unveiled hostility of Nazi-led France to her ally of 1939 ; on the temporary passing of so much of the British colonial empire in the East into enemy hands !

IT would be no exaggeration to say that hardly anything has happened in this amazing war "according to plan." And that goes for the Nazis as well as for the British ; for in some ways the very speed with which most of Hitler's opening blows succeeded had a dislocating effect upon his follow-up ; just as his astounding and entirely unforeseen hold-up in Russia resulted from the rapidity of his invasion, which Stalin helped to achieve by a strategic retreat to positions that bogged the invaders in a winter of frustration.

So you will understand why I am making no vain prophecies about the probable contents of our Sixth Volume. I can say with some confidence, however, that it will be the most vitally interesting of the whole series, no matter how long THE WAR ILLUSTRATED may continue or how soon it may end. For before next winter arrives, even if we have not reached decisions, we shall be able to discern the shape of things to come with more certitude than at this moment. What chiefly harasses one is the question of ways and means. Thus far, we have every reason to be satisfied with the way we have surmounted difficulties that beset our progress since that dreadful day when France collapsed, as all the major evils we have since suffered can be dated from that day. To the shameful defection of Vichy France, far more than to any lack of British foresight or preparation, we owe the disasters that have fallen upon us in every area of the War, by land, by sea and air.

INDO-CHINA was the real crux of the situation in the Far East, and when the Vichy traitors meanly surrendered it to the Japs while they valiantly fought Britain for Syria an entirely new Japanese approach to Malaya and India became possible, and years of preparations, made when the Anglo-French Alliance had every prospect of enduring reality, became worse than useless. To the end of the chapter the course of the War will be affected by that great catastrophe of June 1940. Looking back on the two years that have since been lived through, the British people have abundant cause for pride and none at all for shame. And this I assert with the gravity of our losses clearly in mind ; and despite the lugubrious moanings of our native-born Cassandras.

ONE might add that the French betrayal was also the root cause of most that we have had to suffer in the Battle of Britain and the Battle of the Atlantic. World history can yield no such heroic chapters as the recovery of British power and the creation of such striking force as our mass bombing of Cologne on May 30/31 disclosed, in face of any country's former ally and nearest neighbour's complete subjection to a ruthless enemy. Every port of France and all her industrial resources have been turned by enemy action against her former ally, who still strives to prove her friend. If it should happen—and signs are not awanting that it may—that the French navy

---

---

should be surrendered to Germany and the whole of French Africa in the North and West pass into German control these, indeed, would be the bottommost dregs of the bitter cup which France has asked Britain to drain. One might add and stress all that, but it is better to express the hope that such ignominy may not come to pass, that such waters of Marah may yet be sweetened by another Mosaic miracle.

WELL, it is my hope that by the time this Sixth Volume of ours has been completed (say in eleven months from now) it will embody the record of the great decisive events that are now being prepared by the United Nations : the Robber Nations will have been made to disgorge most, if not all of their plunder, and if the conflict is still going on the aggressors will be on the defensive, manoeuvring for peace and the cheapest way of escape from a punishment that must be made to fit their crimes. Then another year should see the stage set for Democracy's day of judgement. All this I

imagine cannot be dated much earlier than two summers hence. Which means that if we are able to secure the materials of production THE WAR ILLUSTRATED will run to a total of at least seven, and possibly eight volumes. I certainly hope and believe that the final event will not throw this estimate far out. And there, after all, I have let myself in for something very like a forecast, which I had intended to avoid. But I'll let it stand at that !

MY readers will notice certain changes in our contents which I have introduced as more suitable to its fortnightly issue. In the earlier phases of the War, and so long as we were able to maintain weekly publication, I felt that our available space was best utilized by going to press as late as possible and recording all outstanding events of the preceding week as effectively as we could with the information at our command. But a new method of treatment is now desirable ; hence the three main chronicles of the War's progress which begin in this number. Each of these will provide a continuous survey of the things that happen within its writer's particular field of interest every fortnight. There will be no effort to supply " hot " news, but rather expert appreciation of the news which you have been reading in the daily papers. Special contributions on topics of immediate interest will also appear in every number, sometimes supplementing those discussed in the regular chronicles, but more often dealing with isolated subjects. In this way readers of THE WAR ILLUSTRATED will acquire an orderly and authoritative understanding of the events that are happening in every theatre of the War.

THE collaboration of so eminent a military expert as Maj.-Gen. Sir Charles Gwynn, K.C.B., D.S.O., who has been my valued colleague as Military Editor of that highly successful Standard History, The Second Great War, since its start in October 1939, is something on which I can congratulate my readers and myself ; for there is no more engaging writer on military affairs and none better informed than Sir Charles. His contribution Along the Battle-Fronts will keep my readers in touch with the implications of things recorded and will build up a rational conception of the War from which all hasty judgements have been excluded.

I AM happy also in my other collaborators. Capt. Norman Macmillan, M.C., A.F.C., is in the front rank of writers on aeronautics, two of his books, The Art of Flying and Air Strategy, being standard works ; while Mr. Francis McMurtrie, A.I.N.A., has specialised for many years on naval affairs, and as editor of Jane's Fighting Ships he holds a unique position of technical authority. You will thus be assured in each number of THE WAR ILLUSTRATED of maintaining contact with the best sources of expert opinion on all that concerns the land, air, and sea developments of the War. If space can be found for a regular chronicle of the Home Front on similar lines I may also make that provision, but that will depend to some extent on the varying urgency of providing for adequate treatment of the large topics of general interest that will surely claim our attention from time to time.

Printed in England and published every alternate Friday by the Proprietors, The Amalgamated Press, Ltd., The Fleetway House, Farringdon Street, London, E.C.4. Registered for transmission by Canadian Magazine Post. Sole Agents for Australia and New Zealand : Messrs. Gordon & Gotch, Ltd. ; and for South Africa : Central News Agency, Ltd. June 26, 1942. S.S. *Editorial Address :* JOHN CARPENTER HOUSE WHITEFRIARS, LONDON, E.C.4.

HEROES OF BIR HACHEIM. Of a surety the true France is expressed in the smiling and confident bearing of these two Free French warriors who fought most valiantly in the defence of Bir Hacheim. The Free French brigade under General Koenig held out for sixteen days. They destroyed about 70 Axis tanks, inflicted severe losses in men and material on the German and Italian forces, and in night raids liberated a number of our own men who had been taken prisoner. The garrison of Bir Hacheim was withdrawn on June 10.

Photo, British Official: Crown-Copyright

ALONG THE BATTLE FRONTS

by Our Military Critic, Maj.-Gen. Sir Charles Gwynn, K.C.B., D.S.O.

THE fortnight ending June 22 was full of tense situations—for our Army perhaps the most tense since the days of Dunkirk —although, of course, less crucial. There is no denying that in Libya we suffered a severe and disconcerting reverse, and did not escape serious disaster.

On the whole, however, the tide of war continued to flow in favour of the Allies. In Russia, Sebastopol maintained its magnificent resistance to desperate attempts to storm the fortress ; and a renewed effort by Von Bock to eliminate Timoshenko's menacing salient south of Kharkov failed after incurring heavy losses.

In the Pacific, although the Japanese secured a foothold in the Aleutian Islands, they paid a heavy price, having admittedly suffered naval losses comparable to those incurred at Midway Island. These, added to those of the Coral Sea and Midway Island, have completely changed the balance of sea power in the Pacific. Japan's losses of aircraft-carriers, her most formidable weapon, have been particularly severe ; while American losses in all classes of ships have been comparatively light. Even in Libya, where we have to admit a disaster, Rommel had only partly achieved his main object—the destruction of Ritchie's Army—and had not yet become a serious menace to Egypt.

LIBYA With his usual promptitude
.... Rommel, after our withdrawal from Bir Hacheim, made use of his recovered liberty of manoeuvre to revert to his original plan, which aimed at cutting off Ritchie's troops at Gazala and blocking their line of retreat to Tobruk.

Striking east with a strong Panzer force and motorized infantry, he attempted to rush Ritchie's El Adem post, but was driven off by the garrison and our armoured forces. Wheeling north, he attempted to reach the coast road west of Tobruk, using the whole of his armoured strength. Heavy fighting occurred round the defensive " boxes " of Knightsbridge and Acroma, and for a time it seemed that the situation would turn decisively in our favour. For it was a risky move ; Ritchie's army was well under his hand, and his armoured troops and air force made it difficult for Rommel to maintain his ammunition and petrol supplies.

Then on Saturday, June 13, occurred one of those incidents which in a battle of manoeuvre may in a few minutes change the whole aspect. Whether as a protective measure or as an intentional trap Rommel, or one of his subordinate commanders, had concentrated a number of heavy anti-tank guns in a well-concealed position at Bir Behaffar, south of Acroma. A trap in the event it proved to be, for a concentration of our armoured troops, evidently moving in close formation to attack, were suddenly met with overwhelming fire at close range and suffered disastrous casualties, leaving Rommel with decisive predominance in armoured strength.

The situation of the S. African and 50th British Divisions in the Gazala position and of the garrison of the Knightsbridge post at once became precarious in the extreme. Ritchie promptly ordered their withdrawal— a very difficult and dangerous operation, carried out successfully next day.

The South Africans, with all their equipment, fought their way back by the coastal road with insignificant losses, their first withdrawal being covered by the 50th Division, which remained in position—and, later, by the Acroma post and a vigorous counter-attack delivered by a much-depleted armoured division. The 50th Division also got away successfully by most brilliant tactics. Instead of retiring in the obvious direction covered by a rearguard, they struck westward into the Italian position, taking two divisions by surprise and throwing them into confusion. Doing all the damage they could in their passage, they wheeled south ; and eventually by a long detour through an area where the enemy was in possession, they reached safety. Whether the plan was conceived by General Ritchie or by the G.O.C. of the Division, it was an amazing example of what may sometimes be achieved by taking the unexpected course

Rommel was in no condition to make a serious attack on our new positions before they were organized. His men admittedly were too exhausted, what with fighting and the heat. A small force, attempting to strike eastwards towards Halfaya, was sharply repulsed by the Sidi Rezegh post, and Ritchie had time to complete his dispositions ; occupying the old Tobruk perimeter and also a strong position on the top, and not as formerly at the bottom, of the Halfaya escarpment above Sollum. The situation was therefore much the same as it was before Auchinleck's offensive last November.

Then came serious disaster. Rommel at first moved east with his armoured divisions towards Halfaya, while his main infantry and artillery body closed in round Tobruk. Then suddenly, when within 25 miles of the new position at Halfaya, he turned his armour about and, acting with the speed for which he is famous, on June 20 launched an attack on Tobruk with his whole strength preceded by heavy bombing by his Stukas. Attacking from the east, his armour forced its way through the perimeter defences, still incompletely protected by minefields ; and his infantry followed through the gap. Then his tanks went on, and the end came on Sunday morning. Our troops fought gallantly, but probably they had not had time to organize their defences thoroughly, and there may have been a shortage of anti-tank guns. No doubt Rommel had received stronger reinforcements than was expected, but one must conclude that the reviving power of defence has not yet proved invulnerable to determined and skilful attack.

Rommel's success was no doubt due largely to his resource, vigour and daring. He probably had advantage in the heavy tanks, of which he seems to have plenty in reserve, for though our " General Grant " tanks were good there were not enough of them. The same applies to our new anti-tank gun ; and no doubt Rommel made very skilful use of his numerical strength in this class of weapon.

Air power seems to have had surprisingly little influence on the course of the battle. The R.A.F. attacks on Rommel's supply service, persistent and gallant as they were, never apparently caused serious interruption :

LIBYAN COLUMN of British motorized infantry, widely spread out so as to avoid casualties, in case of an attack by dive-bombers, moving into action. All around stretches the vast expanse of the desert, barren and grim.
Photo, British Official : Crown Copyright

THE WESTERN DESERT, showing places involved in the fighting for Tobruk, which fell into enemy hands on June 21. After the evacuation of Bir Hacheim Rommel virtually surrounded the port and attacked it with overwhelming strength and drive.
Courtesy of The Observer

and Rommel, except at Bir Hacheim, and at Tobruk, owed little to his Stukas. The air attacks made on our communications with Egypt did little damage, and may have had a reconnaissance purpose, to test defences, if an attempt to establish a block with airborne troops, reported to be assembled in Crete, is contemplated.

The question is certain to be asked, how did it happen that our armoured divisions fell into the trap, which so materially altered the whole situation? Normally it might be expected that it would have been discovered by advanced patrols or cooperating aircraft; but it would be grossly unjust to assume neglect of precautions. Probably dust had something to do with it, necessitating close dispositions in order to maintain contact; and if aircraft were working with the column it is easy to miss well-posted troops using the concealment immobility gives. Very low flying would not help, for if visibility is too low to give a view of an object as it is approached the difficulty of distinguishing it in the flash of passing over is very great. Consider how little can be seen of near-by objects from a railway carriage, and multiply the speed of the train by four.

All the strategical text books warn retreating armies not to take refuge in fortresses, but to retain their mobility at all costs. The

KHARKOV FRONT, where throughout June the Red Army under Marshal Timoshenko attacked, and was attacked by, von Bock's Nazis. *By courtesy of The Times*

GEN. VON MANNSTEIN (left) with one of his divisional commanders discussing plans for an all-out attack on Sebastopol. *Photo, Keystone*

advisability of holding Tobruk has consequently been questioned in some quarters. But wars cannot be fought on a literal interpretation of theoretical doctrines, and every situation requires analysis. In the first instance, it is still uncertain whether Ritchie's decision was imposed on him by the difficulty of withdrawing his whole force to the frontier, or whether it was deliberately taken. Assuming the latter, there were arguments in favour of the decision. It would prevent large accumulations of stores falling into the enemy's hands and deny him the use of the best port in Cyrenaica, and if Rommel intended to attack the Halfaya position he would have to leave a strong investing force at Tobruk to safeguard his communications. He would, therefore, be more vulnerable to counter-attack.

On the other hand, there was the risk that he might concentrate his whole force to attack the isolated position at Tobruk. But the defensive possibilities of the place had been proved, and it may have been thought that they had been increased by the power

IN THE CRIMEA von Mannstein made desperate efforts to take Sebastopol. German and Rumanian divisions were sacrificed altogether regardless of loss. *By courtesy of The Daily Mail*

of new anti-tank weapons to repel armoured attack. Possibly Rommel's residual strength and power to launch an attack before the defences were fully organized were underestimated. The conditions in this respect were less favourable than when Wavell made his decision, for Rommel was stronger and his communications shorter. Against this, Ritchie had at Halfaya a stronger force than Wavell possessed, and it might shortly recover its offensive potentialities. Failing such recovery, a prolonged occupation of Tobruk would have imposed a heavy strain on the Navy; for the enemy air force in Crete exposed sea communications to constant air attack, and the port itself would be under persistent attack from near-by airfields.

Perhaps the worst feature of Rommel's success is that it adds to the difficulty of the naval situation in the Mediterranean. His own sea communications have become more secure and ours less so. Possibly the appearance of the really long-range Liberator bombers in the Middle East, which must be most unwelcome to Italy, will partly compensate for the loss of our advanced airfields in Libya. They may also have a marked effect on the situation in Russia.

RUSSIA
During the period under review, the situation was as tense at Sebastopol as in Libya. All through the fortnight desperate German attacks succeeded each other with hardly an interval, but the garrison, though hard pressed, fought magnificently and made frequent counter-attacks. Owing to the nature of the ground the Germans admitted that in most sectors tanks could not operate, and that they had to rely on infantry, supported by intense bombing attacks and artillery bombardment.

What that meant in casualties when attacks were repulsed we learnt in the last war; and one must conclude that the Germans considered the capture of the fortress to be of vital importance. Why would not investment of the place have sufficed? Is it because troops could not for long

be spared for the purpose, or aircraft to prevent the use of the port by the Black Sea Fleet? It seems more probable that the Germans require the port themselves in order to ease the supply problems of a major offensive in the south; especially that part of it which might operate from Kerch. Railway communications running east and west in South Russia are few and follow circuitous routes. Those served by the port of Sebastopol would gain immensely in value by its capture and are perhaps essential to the maintenance of a major offensive.

Von Bock's renewal of the attack on the Kharkov front was also evidently a preliminary operation. It met with little success and was immensely costly.

If and when a major offensive does come the preliminary operations may have robbed it of much of its sting; and if it has to be postponed till preliminary operations reach a successful conclusion, the time lost will be hard to recover. Already we have reached the anniversary of the opening of last year's campaign in which lack of time was so much in evidence.

Moscow radio has commented on the failure of tanks against the new power of anti-tank weapons, and draws the conclusion that deep penetration by Panzer thrusts are unlikely to be attempted in future. That, of course, would mean slower operations than those of last year.

FAR EAST
The situation in the Aleutian Islands is obscure, and it remains to be seen whether Japan will retain her footing in the islands. If she does it is unlikely to prove of much value to her unless she becomes engaged in a war with Russia. Possibly the enterprise had that possibility in view, but under existing conditions it involves the maintenance of still another line of sea communication, and it has meant immediate and heavy naval losses.

Reduction in number of her aircraft-carriers must practically prohibit any further amphibious adventure which cannot be closely supported by shore-based aircraft. That, of course, reduces the danger of invasion of Australia and India.

SOVIET TANKS coming into action in the Kharkov sector. Above, Red Army gunners with an anti-tank gun on a tractor on the lookout for Nazi movements. *Photos, U.S.S.R. Official* **Page 33**

At Close Quarters with the General Grants

MAN THE TANKS! The order has been given, and British crews are doubling towards the fleet of American General Grants lined up on the Libyan sands. This new tank, mass-produced in the U.S.A. during last winter, and since shipped to the Middle East, played an important part in the fierce battles of the Cauldron and Knightsbridge.

Preparing for further encounters with the Panzers, a General Grant being loaded with ammunition somewhere in the desert.

A line of General Grants moving up for battle. Heavily armour-plated, some of these new tanks have survived direct hits.

MAINTENANCE MEN of the Royal Tank Regiment removing one of the tracks of a General Grant. Oval, ramming home a shell inside a tank. Right, cleaning the 75-mm. gun. The General Grant weighs about 28 tons and mounts two guns—a 37-mm. and a 75-mm. Though much " boosted " before the battle, after the fall of Tobruk it was stated that the General Grants were already obsolescent in America, had vulnerable spots, and were too slow. Certain it was that there were not enough of them.

Photos, British Official: Crown Copyright

In the Libyan Inferno Round About Acroma

South African Mortar Section in action in the Western Desert. The South Africans, under Major-General Pienaar, were ordered by General Ritchie to withdraw from Gazala on June 13. Under cover of the 50th Division the daring manoeuvre was carried out, and the South Africans suffered only six casualties.

Beneath, R.A.M.C. stretcher-bearers and medical officer on their errand of succour.

Photos, British Official

British supply column being bombed near Acroma. Here a single British tank division gallantly resisted two German armoured divisions, supported by a motorized division, for a whole day before they were compelled to retire. Right, running into an ambush this enemy vehicle was caught by our gunners. The crew leapt out and put up their hands. I Beneath, British soldier displays the Swastika flag behind a captured Nazi.

The 'Fighting French' at Bay at Bir Hacheim

" Now we shall be able to show you that true Frenchmen still fight—and fight better than Germans."
So ran a message to the British Commander from the Free French troops who, after cooling their
heels in Syria for months of unwelcome inactivity, were sent to join our Eighth Army in Libya.
Below we tell how they more than made good their promise.

BIR HACHEIM ! Just a spot on the map of the Western Desert, and in the desert itself a four-mile-long plateau of sand and stone, with in the middle a well, now as dry as the barren waste round about. But there came a day when it was turned into a formidable fortress, planted thickly with guns, sown with minefields, bordered with belts of wire. And to garrison it there came a little army—perhaps 4,000 men in all—who fought under the flag of Free France. They were a mixed crowd : Bretons fought shoulder to shoulder with Parisians, Senegalese sharp-shooters lay in the trenches beside native warriors from New Caledonia in the far-distant Pacific ; the Foreign Legion was there, too, with Spanish Republicans, veterans of the war against Franco, some Germans who were still prepared to fight and if need be die for freedom, an American, and a handful (four officers and a dozen men) of British liaison troops. There were also two British women—an Australian girl and a doctor married to a French doctor ; throughout the battle they peeled potatoes, helped in the field kitchens and gave a hand to the ambulance and hospital workers.

Set at the southern extremity of General Ritchie's line, Bir Hacheim was a vital spot ; and from its slight rise the French were able to command the desert for far afield, so that Rommel's communications were constantly threatened To attack Ritchie's army in the rear, as was apparently Rommel's plan, the Germans and their Italian allies had to run the gauntlet of the Bir Hacheim guns. So the order went out from Rommel : " Bir Hacheim must be taken," and again, " The French at Bir Hacheim must be wiped out to the last man."

But Rommel had not allowed for General Joseph Koenig—that valiant 42-year-old soldier who after fighting the Germans in the snows of Narvik and over the fields of Normandy was now to his great joy face to face with them again. According to report he had sworn never to sheathe his sword until his native Alsace was liberated from the Nazi yoke. He approached his present task in a mood of sublime simplicity. " My orders are to hold Bir Hacheim. I hold Bir Hacheim."

So the attack began. At 7 a.m. on May 27 seventy Italian tanks tried to penetrate the minefields surrounding the plateau.

" We opened fire at two thousand yards with our 75s, which we got from the Vichy French after the Syrian campaign," said a sergeant of the French Foreign Legion. " They are wonderful guns. I watched tank after tank explode. At about a thousand yards we had destroyed fifteen tanks, but others still came on and we kept knocking them out. Two actually got into the minefields ; by extraordinary luck they did not strike a single mine and were within 200 yards of my gun before they were hit. At that range, they went up in little bits."

The attack was completely shattered and the survivors lumbered hastily away across the desert. But on the field of the encounter thirty-five Italian tanks flamed and smouldered.

Cheered by their success, the garrison in daring mood sent out patrol after patrol, who played havoc with the enemy's supply columns and shot up many an infantry post. On June 1 British armoured cars which had assembled at Bir Hacheim swept out and occupied Rotunda Segnali, a point well behind the Axis lines, whence they harassed Rommel's columns.   This exploit and others like it made it all the more necessary for the enemy to subdue Bir Hacheim. So further assaults were planned, and delivered, with tanks, artillery and Stuka

dive-bombers. On June 2 an infantry attack in force with strong artillery support was withered by the French machine-gunners. The next day fierce shelling began, and this continued almost uninterruptedly by day and by night until the end. Bombing raids, too, were frequent. In almost contemptuous disregard of their losses in men and machines the enemy still came on, but it was not until June 8 that they succeeded in effecting their first penetration of the minefield.

Well did Bir Hacheim earn its nickname of the " lost inferno." Koenig's men were described as " ghosts " by an Italian prisoner. " We are beginning to believe that Bir Hacheim is held by phantom Frenchmen," he said ;. " we cannot believe that they are still alive after the terrific pounding we have been giving them for the last ten days." He added, " Perhaps the Legion

GENERAL KOENIG, Commander of the Free French Forces, whose valiant stand at Bir Hacheim against the Axis is among the great episodes of the war. . Though the little garrison was compelled to retreat, their resistance was of vital importance. " Yours is an example for all of us," said General Ritchie in a message to this Alsatian hero.
Photo, British Official

has been up to its tricks again "—a reference to the old ruse of the French Foreign Legion in the fighting in the Moroccan desert of propping dummies against the parapets and putting rifles into their hands, so as to draw the enemy fire. A French War Correspondent gave a vivid description of yet another tank attack.

" Spitting sand from their teeth and shaking it from their hair," he wrote, " General Koenig's lean, grim, unshaven ghosts rose to the occasion once again. As soon as the Axis armoured forces were sighted the alarm was flashed to every man. The French held their fire, and then at a given signal they let them have it. The desert seemed to shudder at the concerted bark of their 75s mingled with the staccato rattle of machine-guns. German tanks stopped in their tracks, or slowed round in circles, churning up the sand like great jungle beasts in their death-throes."

Still tattered and begrimed the French Tricolour with the Lorraine Cross hung proudly over the desolate little plateau. The air was heavy with fumes from the smoking guns. All around were the shattered remains of many a score of derelict tanks, amongst which moved parties of grave-diggers, burying the heaps of enemy dead.

Though sorely reduced in numbers, Koenig's men were fighting like maniacs.

Five times at least Italian officers advanced with a white flag, and called upon General Koenig to surrender. Each time they were received with a blunt refusal, even jeers, and the French in their refusals got ruder and ruder. At last their stock of epithets had practically given out, and they had come to the exceedingly rude and quite unprintable word which General Cambronne is reported to have used at Waterloo when the English summoned the remnants of Napoleon's Old Guard to surrender.

Attack followed attack, and still the Free French kept up their magnificent defence. Still, too, the R.A.F. continued to give the greatest support and encouragement to the beleaguered garrison. " When we get out of this," said one soldier from Paris, " I will kiss the first R.A.F. officer I see, whether he likes it or not. And after that I will have a hot bath." And a Breton remarked as a British plane swooped from the clouds and drove off a Stuka about to dive on to the French positions, " that is the only collaboration we want.' One day the defenders of Bir Hacheim sent a message to the R.A.F. : " Bravo, merci pour le R.A.F." ; to which the R.A.F. answered, " Bravo, merci pour le sport."

For more than a fortnight the bitter conflict went on. " We don't feel that we are defending some insignificant oasis in the Libyan desert," said one man, " we feel we are defending our own homes in Nantes and Versailles." All were greatly cheered to hear of a message from General de Gaulle. " All France looks to you in her pride. Please convey this message to your men." So ran the message, and General Koenig was quick to pass it on as he strode about the plateau, tireless, joking and whistling in tuneless fashion.

By June 7 the enemy had assembled ten thousand men around Bir Hacheim—Italians for the most part, but including a large number of picked Nazis, with plentiful tanks and artillery. Gradually the weight of numbers began to tell, and they were able to get up their guns within a short distance of the French entrenchments. But always a small gap was kept open, and through this the defenders were able to receive a trickle of supplies. At length on June 10 General Ritchie decided that Bir Hacheim had done its job, and he gave orders that Koenig and his men should be withdrawn.

The operation was entrusted to a column of the British Seventh Motorized Brigade, and at the appointed hour, 11 p.m. on June 10, the garrison began to file on foot through the narrow gap in the southern sector of the minefield to where the Brigadier had lorries in waiting. Swiftly they were embussed and driven off some miles to the west, where R.A.S.C. parties were ready to receive them with hot tea and other drinks, food and cigarettes. At the same time another and smaller party made their withdrawal in lorries, taking with them some of their guns ; these were not so fortunate, since they were attacked by the enemy and suffered some casualties. Forty ambulances accompanied the British rescue column, and in these were loaded all the wounded that were capable of being moved.

But some of the garrison had to be left behind to cover the retreat of their comrades. To the last they kept up their fire, until on the morning of June 11 the Germans and their Italian jackals swept over the plateau in triumph. More than 2,000 prisoners were claimed, with many guns and vehicles, and 1,000 dead were said to have been found on the devastated slopes. But the honours of war rested surely with the Fighting French.

'All France Looked to Them in Pride'

Free French anti-aircraft gunners on the Libyan front. Left, photograph radioed from Cairo shows some of the heroes of Bir Hacheim who for more than a fortnight kept at bay the 90th Light German Division and the Italian motorized Trieste Division.

French 75-mm. gun in action. The Free French Brigade in the Middle East comprises the Foreign Legion, French colonial troops and other units under command of General de Larminat and General Koenig.

Left, War Sister Kelsey, a Londoner, who served on the Libyan front as theatre sister for the Free French mobile hospital at Bir Hacheim. Above, Free French Marines at a 25-mm. anti-tank and A.A. gun in Libya.

Photos, British Official: Crown Copyright

THE WAR IN THE AIR

by Capt. Norman Macmillan, M.C., A.F.C.

In the fast-moving panorama of the air war, some events appear to invest themselves with the significance of isolation. Dramatic as these happenings often are, it is a mistake to regard them as things apart. Strategically, they are a part of the World War. The prudent observer must endeavour to fit them into their proper places, just as the pieces of a jigsaw puzzle must be so fitted to get the balance of the picture right. Such an event was the Battle of the Mediterranean Convoys which preceded the fall of Tobruk.

While the Libyan tank-air battle raged fiercely after the German break-through at Bir Hacheim, two great sea-air battles developed over and around the passage of two British convoys in the Mediterranean Sea. The land and sea battles were generally reported as separate events. They cannot be so regarded. They were closely linked. An examination of both together gives an important clue to Axis air strategy.

Malta must be regarded as Britain's Middle East advanced air base. The use of Malta enables the R.A.F. to bomb southern Italy, Sicily, and Sardinia. It enables Britain to bring air pressure to bear upon the shipping supply lines of the Axis across the Mediterranean between Italy and Tripoli. It therefore exercises a restraining influence upon Axis supply bases of departure and arrival on the north and south Mediterranean shores and upon the inter-connecting routes. That is why Malta was the subject of intense air attack prior to the opening of Rommel's spring 1942 offensive.

Malta is like an ocean aerodrome anchored 1,100 miles from Gibraltar and 650 miles from the nearest point of the Egyptian frontier. One of the most densely-populated areas of the world, it is not self-supporting. Supplies for its population and for its garrison must be taken there to enable it to function as an air base. The aircraft can be flown there, but bombs, torpedoes, petrol, oil, and spares must be transported by ship, or Malta will lose her offensive power.

From Alexandria to the battlefields of Libya stretches the desert. The straight line distance to Tobruk is 350 miles. Overland transport can be used, but larger quantities of vital war supplies can be carried in ships. The R.A.F. and S.A.A.F. were pounding away at Rommel's tank and motorized

Army and R.A.F. personnel refuelling and reloading a Spitfire on a Malta aerodrome. A brief lull followed the concentrated Axis air raids on the island prior to Rommel's Libyan offensive, but when enemy forces reached the Egyptian frontier the bombing attacks on Malta were renewed.
Photo, British Official

columns thrusting eastwards in Cyrenaica; under the command of Air Vice-Marshal "Mary" Coningham (the nickname is a corruption of Maori, Coningham being a New Zealander) Boston and Kitty-Bombers struck many times a day at enemy columns and tanks, and definitely halted by air power alone several German armoured attacks on some of our defended positions. Fighter screens prevented enemy fighters from getting through to attack our bombers, and for days on end not a single Boston was lost. For three weeks this operation continued non-stop from dawn to dusk, sixteen hours a day. But Rommel's forces still came on.

Huge supplies must have got through to the German Afrika Korps while Malta was under its spring travail from the air.

But Rommel's supplies were clearly being used up faster than he could continue indefinitely to replace them, during this, the fifth Libyan battle. The storm of war lashed fiercer than ever before. At the moment when the British Eighth Army was in strategic retreat to defensive positions in its rear, two convoys set out for Malta, one from Gibraltar, the other from Alexandria via Tobruk—timed to split up Axis opposition by their synchronization.

The Axis armies were left, with a minimum of air support, to fend for themselves, while almost the full brunt of Axis air power in the Mediterranean was diverted to the task of preventing the convoys from reaching Malta, which, to Rommel, mattered more than Tobruk.

The greatest sea-air battle ever fought raged for four days from June 13. The convoys were escorted by warships. The one from Alexandria was escorted by shore-based fighters. Beaufighters, each armed with three cannon-guns and four machine-guns, flew 300 miles westwards from Malta to meet the oncoming convoy somewhere between Cagliari and Bizerta.

An Italian fleet steamed southwards from Taranto naval base. Another Italian fleet thrust northward between Tunisia and

Significant event in the Mediterranean war zone in June was the appearance in action of 4-engined Liberator bombers flown by American crews. Fifteen of these huge planes made a raid on the oilfields at Ploesti in Rumania; while others helped to bomb Italian warships during the attack on the Malta convoys.
Photo, British Official

Pantelleria, presumably to try to force the eastward-bound convoy close to the coast of Sicily where it would be within easy reach of shore-based dive-bombers. The Italian warships found they were not fighting warships, but aeroplanes. The fleet from Taranto was met 220 miles north-west of Tobruk by four-engined Liberator bombers flown by American crews and carrying heavy bombs, followed by torpedo-carrying aircraft. That fleet of two battleships, three cruisers, and ten destroyers turned and fled northwards with 23 hits on one battleship and 15 on another and both on fire. A cruiser was sunk, and other ships damaged. That fleet never got within five hours' steaming range of the British convoy. This convoy, attacked by aircraft, failed to reach Malta, but got some supply ships into Tobruk.

The threatened sea action in the Sicilian narrows developed into another major battle.

Aircraft fought aircraft to get at the ships and to protect them. Warships of both sides were attacked with bombs and air-borne torpedoes; the merchant-ships were similarly attacked. Losses were suffered by both sides. The surviving ships of this convoy reached Malta. In both battles the enemy lost at least 65 aircraft, the United Nations, for their part, lost 30—dual evidence of the severity of the air action.

Axis air power was here used strategically to weaken our future position in preference to concentrating all their air power upon the battlefield. The flexibility of Axis air power is one of its features. The United Nations' air action was purely tactical.

Our supply lines are our greatest weakness. The Axis know that. They know, too, that air power can dominate supply lines when they pass within its reach. For that reason, air supremacy is for us a condition imperative for victory. But, while we are toiling towards the goal of air supremacy, we can answer the Axis air attacks upon our supply lines if we choose to do so strategically.

Thus: We can blot out Axis supply ports on the northern shore of the Mediterranean by mass bomb raids on one port after another. Rome is a vital Italian railway communication centre—that makes it a military objective; others are Bologna and Pisa. These three cut all railway routes running south through Italy. And we might destroy the entrances to the trans-Alpine tunnels; or failing that, destroy Genoa. Such are our answers to Axis air interference with our convoys. By such means as these we can surely do something to deplete Rommel upon the battlefield.

Meanwhile, by mining the Baltic from the air we are impeding Axis supplies to their front in North Russia. Large numbers of Axis ships have been sunk. The air-mine is a weapon that Germany must regret she began to use. In the shallow waters of the Baltic it is particularly effective. It has recoiled upon her with a vengeance there.

Kittyhawks Seeking Their Prey in Libya

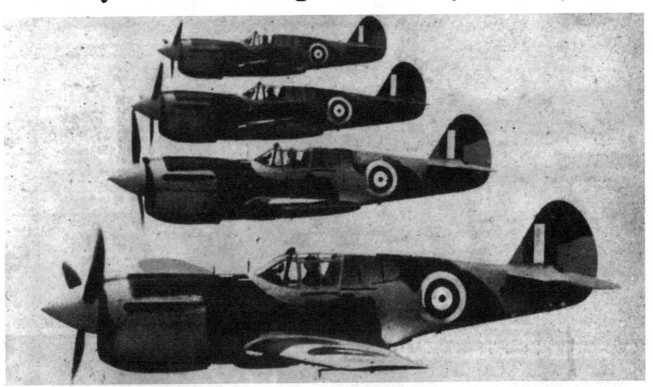

U.S.-made Kittyhawks in flight over Libya. Left, R.A.F. armourers bombing up a Kittyhawk on an advanced aerodrome in Libya preparatory to a raid on Rommel's positions.

CURTISS HAWK P. 40E—the Kittyhawk is P. 40D—with all guns ablaze during gunnery practice on the new Curtiss Wright firing range in Buffalo. Oval, a Kittyhawk fighter belonging to the famous R.A.F. "Sharknose" Squadron landed during a sandstorm in the Western Desert, a mechanic on top of one of the wings guiding her. Though no details of the Curtiss Hawk P. 40E's firepower have been released, this American machine is among the most heavily armoured in existence.

Photos, British Official; Crown Copyright; Keystone

'Down Under' They Mean To Be On Top

American and Australian soldiers refuelling a U.S. Army Flying Fortress at the Alice Springs aerodrome. "In all areas you will find Americans commanding Australians and vice versa," said Gen. Brett, Cdr. of the Allied air forces.

Japanese pilot, captured after his Zero plane crashed on the beach at Port Moresby, Papua, on his way to the prison camp. Centre left, General MacArthur (in profile), hero of Corregidor and Allied Supreme Commander in the South-West Pacific, conferring with Lt.-General V. A. K. Sturdee, Chief of the General Staff, and Mr. F. M. Forde, Australia's Army Minister.

Members of an Australian Coast Artillery Unit firing their heavy gun. The war in Australia has, so far, been confined to air duels and raids between Japanese forces based in the Dutch East Indies and Australian and American aircraft operating from Australian aerodromes.

Photos, Keystone, Sport & General, Planet News

At Canterbury the Nazis Bombed the Library

IN REVENGE FOR COLOGNE the Nazis raided Canterbury on the night of Sunday, May 31. The Cathedral Library was hit, and in the foreground of this photo some soldiers are seen clearing up the debris. Though it housed one of the oldest collections of books in England, the Library was a modern structure and its greater treasures had been removed to a place of safety. The Cathedral itself was not hit, although, said Dean Hewlett Johnson, it was singled out and dive-bombed.

Photo, Keystone

We Dropped a Tricolour by the Arc de Triomphe

Fl.-Lt. A. K. GATWARD of the Coastal Command who dropped the Tricolour by the Arc de Triomphe in Paris and cannon-shelled the German-occupied Ministry of Marine building.

I'D never been to Paris before, but it looked exactly as I imagined it would : we studied a lot of guide books and photographs before we set out. We took a bearing from the Eiffel Tower and came in smack over the Defence Monument, and then headed straight for the Arc de Triomphe. I said to Sergeant Fern, my observer, "Are you ready with the first flag ?" And he said, "Yes, I'm ready all right, but the slip-stream is nearly breaking my arm." He was pushing this weighted and furled flag down a flare shoot into the slip-stream from the propellers, and at the right moment he let her go. Vichy says it fell right on the tomb of the unknown warrior.

One of the things we wanted to look at particularly was the Ministry of Marine, because it was crammed with Huns, and we had something for them. We turned south a bit towards the river so we could come square up to the Ministry, and we were in line at a range of about five hundred yards before we let fly with our four cannons, and I saw the sparks flying off the building. We hadn't any time to see whether the shells burst inside, but a good deal went through the window. We sprayed the place from base to apex and we only cleared the roof by about five feet. While I was doing this Fern was shouting encouragement and pushing out the second flag, which we hoped would fall slap across the front door.

From Fl.-Lt. Gatward's broadcast, June 17

SCRAPING PARIS ROOFS Fl.-Lt. Gatward took his bearings by the Eiffel Tower, seen in the distance beyond the wing of his plane. Sometimes his machine was even below the level of the roofs. A second Tricolour was dropped near the Ministry of Marine in the Place de la Concorde. The whole flight from the time the aircraft was airborne until it returned to its base occupied 150 minutes, and was carried out without any serious interference by the enemy. The upper photo, also taken during the flight, shows a corner of the Jardin des Tuileries, running behind which is the Rue de Rivoli, where the Gestapo H.Q. are situated.

Photos, British Official ; G.P.U.

Molotov Makes History in Britain and U.S.

Three of the photographs in this page illustrate Mr. Molotov's visit to this country to sign the Twenty Years' Treaty of Alliance between Great Britain and Northern Ireland on the one hand and Soviet Russia on the other. They are (1) Mr. Molotov greeted on his arrival in England by a senior Air Force Officer ; (2) Mr. Molotov arriving by an L.N.E.R. special train at a London suburban station with (right) Mr. Maisky and Mr. Anthony Eden ; (3) Mr. Molotov signs the Treaty on May 26 at the Foreign Office. On his left are Mr. Eden, Mr. Churchill and Mr Attlee, while Mr. Maisky is on his right. (4) President Roosevelt and Mr. Molotov in Washington, where the latter arrived on May 29. (5) Reading to the workers in a Moscow factory the text of the Anglo-Soviet Treaty.

Photos, British Official ; Russian Official ; Fox, Keystone

Britain and Russia Allies For Twenty Years

In London on May 26 there was signed the Anglo-Soviet Treaty of Alliance—an event which history will probably rank as among the greatest and most portentous happenings of the war. The story of the Treaty's framing and signature is given below, while in the preceding page are reproduced a number of relevant photographs.

"I AM glad to be able to inform the House that his Majesty's Government have concluded a treaty with the Union of Soviet Socialist Republics which confirms our alliance with that country during the war against Germany and her associates in Europe."

Tremendous cheers greeted this declaration made by Mr. Anthony Eden, Britain's Foreign Secretary, in the House of Commons on the afternoon of June 11. There were more cheers when Mr. Eden stated that the Treaty provides that " after the war our two countries will render each other mutual assistance against any further attack by Germany or her associates," and still more cheers for the further provision that Britain and Russia and the other United Nations are to cooperate in the peace settlement and during the ensuing period of reconstruction on the basis of the principles set out in the Atlantic Charter.

Briefly, Mr. Eden reviewed the course of events which had led up to this dramatic stroke of high policy. He recalled the evening of June 22 last year when, only a few hours after Hitler began his invasion of Russia, Mr. Churchill affirmed that the Russian danger was our danger and that we would give to Russia whatever help we could and make common cause with the Russian people. He recalled the Anglo-Soviet agreement of July 12, Lord Beaverbrook's visit to Moscow in September, and his own visit in December. Since then conversations had been continuing, and when the discussions had made sufficient progress the British Government had suggested that Mr. Molotov should come to London to embody the agreement in a formal treaty. Meanwhile, Mr. Molotov had been invited by President Roosevelt to visit him in Washington. Arrangements were made accordingly for the Russian Commissar of Foreign Affairs to come to London, and then go on to the United States. He arrived in London on May 21.

Few secrets—and never, perhaps, one of such momentous import—have been better kept. It was on the morning of May 20 that Mr. Molotov descended from a giant Russian aircraft which came to land at an aerodrome somewhere in Northern Britain ; accompanying him were Mr. Sobolov, Secretary-General of the Peoples' Commissariat of Foreign Affairs, Lt.-Gen. Shelovski, Maj.-Gen. Issayev, and a large team of military and diplomatic advisers. Having divested himself of his heavy flying gear, Mr. Molotov chatted with Mr. Maisky, Soviet Ambassador in London, who was there to greet him, and inspected the guard of honour formed by the R.A.F. and a famous regiment drawn up on the aerodrome. Shortly afterwards he and his party entered a special train and sped on their way south. The train stopped at a London suburban station, where Mr. Molotov was greeted on the platform by Mr. Eden, Sir Alexander Cadogan, Permanent Under-Secretary at the Home Office, and General Nye, Vice-Chief of the Imperial General Staff. Then he was whirled away by car to Chequers, the Premier's official residence in the country, which Mr. Churchill had placed at his disposal.

Negotiations began next morning in the Cabinet Room at 10, Downing Street, with Mr. Churchill in the chair. After an exchange of compliments the conference got straight down to business.

During the following days six other meetings were held, most of them in Mr. Eden's room at the Foreign Office, with Mr. Pavlov and Brigadier Firebrace acting as interpreters. Each day Mr. Molotov came up from Chequers ; each night he returned to the Buckinghamshire seat. Little progress was made, until there came an evening when Mr. Molotov had a long talk " somewhere in the country " (presumably at Chequers) with Mr. Eden and Mr. Churchill. Mr. Maisky acted as interpreter, and the discussion continued into the small hours. At this meeting Churchill and Molotov really got together, and learnt to appreciate and understand one another. They covered the whole field of the war—in particular the

TREATY OF ALLIANCE

Part I. Art. I. In virtue of the alliance established between the United Kingdom and the Union of Soviet Socialist Republics, the High Contracting Parties mutually undertake to afford one another military and other assistance and support of all kinds in the war against Germany and all those States which are associated with her in acts of aggression in Europe.

Art. II. . . . undertake not to enter into any negotiations with the Hitlerite Government or any other Government in Germany that does not clearly renounce all aggressive intentions, and not to negotiate or conclude except by mutual consent any armistice or peace treaty with Germany or any other State associated with her in acts of aggression in Europe.

Part II. Art. III. . . . declare their desire to unite with other like-minded States in adopting proposals for common action to preserve peace and resist aggression in the post-war period. Pending the adoption of such proposals, they will after the termination of hostilities take all the measures in their power to render impossible a repetition of aggression and violation of the peace by Germany or any of the States associated with her in acts of aggression in Europe.

Art. IV. Should one of the High Contracting Parties during the post-war period become involved in hostilities with Germany . . . the other High Contracting Party will at once give to the Contracting Party so involved in hostilities all the military and other support and assistance in his power . . .

Art. V. The High Contracting Parties . . . agree to work together in close and friendly collaboration after the re-establishment of peace for the organization of security and economic prosperity in Europe . . . and they will act in accordance with the two principles of not seeking territorial aggrandizement for themselves and of non-interference in the internal affairs of other States.

Art. VI. . . . agree to render one another all possible economic assistance after the war.

Art. VII. Each High Contracting Party undertakes not to conclude any alliance and not to take part in any coalition directed against the other High Contracting Party.

Art. VIII. The present treaty . . . comes into force immediately on the exchange of the instruments of ratification . . . Part I shall remain in force until the re-establishment of peace between the High Contracting Parties and Germany and the Powers associated with her in acts of aggression in Europe. Part II shall remain in force for a period of 20 years . . .

questions of opening a second front on the Continent this year, and of supplies to the Soviet Union ; and when they broke up the main lines of the treaty had been settled. The next day the British and Soviet delegations settled down to consideration of the terms in detail, and by the evening of Whit Monday (May 25) the final draft of the treaty had been drawn up and approved. The following day Moscow signified its approval, and at 5.30 on the afternoon of Whit Tuesday the treaty lay ready for signature on the table in Mr. Eden's room at the Foreign Office. On the British side sat Mr. Churchill and Mr. Eden, Mr. Attlee and Sir Archibald Sinclair, while Mr. Molotov was accompanied by his own delegation and Mr. Maisky.

The only speeches were delivered by Mr. Eden and Mr. Molotov. " We are met in a world at war," said Britain's Foreign Secretary, " when our two countries are together at grips with the common enemy. Under the impact of war we have found that understanding which escaped us in the uneasy years of peace. The treaty which we have just signed engages us to continue the struggle together until the victory be won." But, went on Mr. Eden, " One day the war will end. One day the common enemy will be defeated, and there will be peace again. We must see to it that this time peace endures. In the treaty which we have signed we pledge ourselves to work together for this purpose." Then Mr. Molotov. He described the treaty between the U.S.S.R. and Great Britain of alliance in the war against Hitlerite Germany and her accomplices in Europe, and of cooperation and mutual assistance after the war, as an important political landmark in the relations between Britain and the Soviet Union. The treaty was essential, not only to the peoples of the U.S.S.R. and Britain, but to those of other countries. " All peoples who have experienced the aggression of the German-Fascist Imperialists, or whose freedom and honour have been threatened, and may still be threatened, by the Hitlerite band of robbers, oppressors and ravishers—all these will express their satisfaction at the conclusion of this historic treaty."

Shortly after signing the treaty Mr. Molotov (who in the intervals of the discussions had been received in audience by the King) visited a fighter station in company with Mr. Churchill, and with Mr. Maisky as his guide inspected war damage in London set off to Washington, where he arrived on May 29 and remained as the President's guest until June 4.

Conversations were carried out at the White House which resulted in the conclusion of the Lend-Lease Agreement between Russia and the U.S.A. ; and " a full understanding was reached with regard to the urgent tasks of creating a second front in Europe in 1942." Returning from Washington Mr. Molotov stayed for another brief space in London, and then proceeded to Moscow.

Only when he had arrived back there, and only then, did security reasons permit the disclosure of his visits and their fruit. Mr. Eden's statement in the House of Commons was made, as we have seen, on June 11 ; and immediately afterwards an announcement was issued by the Foreign Office. This was interesting chiefly because of the statement, in almost the same words as that of the Washington announcement, that " full understanding was reached between the two parties with regard to the urgent tasks of creating a second front in Europe in 1942 " ; it also stated that discussions had taken place on the question of improving the supplies of aeroplanes, tanks, and other war material sent to Russia.

Throughout the world of the United Nations the conclusion of the Alliance was hailed with the greatest satisfaction. Mr. Stalin and Mr. Churchill exchanged congratulatory telegrams, and the King and President Kalinin most cordial greetings.

Speaking in the House of Commons after Mr. Eden, Mr. Lloyd George said that " had the treaty been a fact some years ago, many grave blunders in foreign policy would have been avoided. Not only that, this war could never have occurred."

A Big Raid on Germany Is Planned

Here are the men entrusted with the greatest aerial offensive in history. They are Air Marshal A. Travers Harris, Chief of Bomber Command (seated) with his Chiefs of Staff, Air Vice-Marshal R. H. M. S. Saundby and (left) Air Vice-Marshal R. Graham. Top, the Station Commander with a Boston III crew discusses in the operations room the "target for tonight."

The Heavy Bombers Take-Off

R.A.F. personnel having received their orders, big raid operations begin. (1) Armourers checking over the bombs before loading them into a Stirling. (2) Crew of one of the Wellingtons going aboard in the dusk. (3) A twin-engined Manchester setting forth for enemy territory. Many types of machines took part in the huge raid on Cologne on May 30.

Over the Target and Back Again

Nearing their objective, flak becomes increasingly furious, as may be seen in photograph (4).
Nothing daunted, however, the Stirling has dropped its bombs and is returning to base (5).
In photograph (6) are two of our many pilots who were once "so few." Their attitude has
been summed up in the words " Brave yet cautious, cool yet daring."

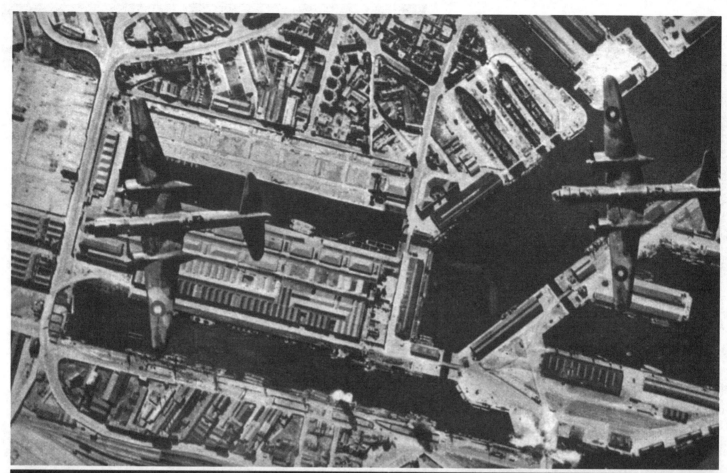

The Raiders Report Success

In the upper photograph Boston bombers are seen over Le Havre docks during a daylight attack. Bombs are exploding across the dock gates while others have burst among the barges. Beneath, the Intelligence Officer is interrogating members of R.A.F. crews who have just returned from the raid. All facts are carefully recorded.

Tobruk Was Taken By Storm at Last

For 517 days—from January 21, 1941 to June 21, 1942—we held Tobruk. Then, what had been for so long " a thorn in the flesh of the German troops on the road to Egypt " was stormed by Rommel's army of Germans and Italians. Here then is the story, so far as it can be told at the moment, of yet another enemy triumph, as disastrous in its way and even more unexpected than the fall of Singapore earlier in the year.

" WELL, boys, it was not quite so bad this time. We've caught the Tommies at last." So Rommel was heard to remark to some of his men in a pause in the fighting within the perimeter of the fortress of Tobruk.

It was Saturday afternoon, June 20, and although the battle was to rage for hours more, Tobruk's fate was already sealed. Very likely its fate was sealed days before— on the previous Saturday when General Ritchie's tanks were caught in Rommel's ambush south of the Trigh Capuzzo between Knightsbridge and El Adem ; that was indeed —so it would seem—a stricken field, one on which our armour was shattered beyond immediate repair. Following this defeat Gazala had to be evacuated ; and soon afterwards Acroma and El Adem were also abandoned, since Rommel was now pushing on in overwhelming strength. Possibly on Thursday (June 18) and certainly by Friday night, Tobruk was isolated once more, and every hour that passed added to the force with which it was encompassed. Thousands of lorries were observed making their way up the coast road from Derna ; arrived at the Axis by-pass, south of Tobruk, they unloaded at every key point more guns, more troops, more supplies. Late on the Friday night two German columns which Rommel had sent on reconnaissance towards the Egyptian frontier re- turned from the Bardia district to Sidi Rezegh, where their tanks were added to the great number already assembled. Mean- while in Tobruk a mixed force of British, Indians, South Africans and their allies, supported by all too few tanks and guns, were striving to put the place into a fresh state of defence. They strove manfully, and soon the trenches and defence works, largely silted up with sand since Tobruk was left in a backwater last December, were manned by the men in khaki.

During twilight on the Friday evening Rommel brought up his troops to within easy striking distance. This, according to an account issued by the German News Agency, was his decisive masterstroke : " to install them in their new positions without giving them an hour's rest and send them in to attack Tobruk early next morning."

At 5.20 a.m. on June 20 the assault was launched. First there was a furious attack by fifty German and Italian dive-bombers on the first line of field fortifications ; the air- cover of the defence was nil. While the bombs were still thundering down, shaking the earth for hundreds of yards, batteries con- centrated on a gap only three miles wide in front of Ed Duda, facing the south-east corner of the Tobruk defences, put up a " veritable drum-roll of shelling against the front lines."

" As the range was lengthened," to continue our quotation from the German account, " our sappers rose from their quickly-dug ditches to clear up mines and cut wires in the forefield. Despite violent artillery and machine-gun fire,

they advanced rapidly. Our tanks were faced with deep, cunningly excavated tank traps running the length of the defence line, presenting an obstacle difficult to overcome. Here the pioneers had to create a bridge for the tanks, and they went to work at three points at the same time. They pushed tank bridges, previously carefully assembled on wheels, into the ditches, and mounted them under the cover of the ditches themselves. The tanks could then go on and occupy the fortifica- tions with their fire, while the columns were able to flow on undisturbed through the gap and deep into the inner fortification works."

While the tanks spread out in fanwise fashion, lorry-borne infantry from the Ger- man 15th Armoured Division and the 90th Light Division, supported by the Italian Trieste and Ariete Divisions, followed close behind or were hurled in wave upon wave, completely regardless of casualties, on the defences to left and right of the gap.

Rommel did not trouble himself with what was happening away from the gap. The batteries followed close on the guns and tanks ; every ten minutes they changed their positions to shell the targets with unparalleled effectiveness. More and more of the enemy came towards us with their hands up. Tanks sent to attack us were shot up by our tanks and pressed back. Enemy batteries were quickly found and ground to dust. The number of blazing vehicles rose from minute to minute."

Riding at the head of the tempestuous advance in his light armoured car, Rommel reached the crossing of the El Adem-Tobruk road with the Via Balbia at 11.30 a.m. He was then already eight miles inside the perimeter. By 4.45 p.m. the main positions were completely in German hands, although some of the coastal guns were still firing, and heavy fighting was still going on near the town. During the night fuel dumps,

TOBRUK, looking across the harbour from the coastal road which runs to Gambut and Bardia. In the background are the white-walled houses of the town, and not far from the shore lies a half-submerged merchantman. As told in this page, the place was overrun by Rommel's forces in 26 hours.
Photo, British Official

One force of tanks, estimated to number between 30 and 40 (reported Richard Mac- Millan of the British United Press), was widening the gap in the south-east of the defences ; another strong armoured force, strongly supported by infantry, dashed down the main El Adem-Tobruk road. The British Commander sent out two strong tank forces to meet them, but they encountered an uninterrupted hail of shells from every piece of artillery the Germans could drag on to the escarpment. One by one our tanks went up, and after five hours of bloody struggle the Axis tanks were in control of the highway. Then wheeling to the east, the Germans took in the rear those who were still resisting the thrust from the south-east ; still bigger tank forces dashed against the British artillery and overran the divisional H.Q. ; yet another group forced its way towards Tobruk.

It was at 9 a.m., according to the German account, that Rommel's infantry, tanks and artillery broke through the minefields into the inner ring.

" The British thundered at the narrow gap with numerous batteries without causing anything more than a temporary nuisance to the ever- rising tide of attack. Soldiers who had not slept for days drove the defenders of Tobruk before them. Whatever fortifications lay to the left and right of the gap were taken or forced to surrender.

fired by the defenders, went up in flames, and when Sunday dawned a thick pall of black smoke covered the harbour.

In the early morning of Sunday the garrison of Fort Pilastrino surrendered, but small fortifications in the outer ring continued fighting until the afternoon. In Tobruk itself the struggle continued, and up to late in the evening R.A.F. reconnaissance planes reported that fighting was still going on.

All through Saturday the General Officer Commanding the garrison had been in com- munication with Eighth Army H.Q., al- though he had to move his headquarters hourly from one place to another inside the perimeter. But after 7 o'clock on Sunday morning there were no more messages.

" At seven a.m. this morning," said a special announcement issued in Rome at 1.43 on Sunday afternoon, " a British officer presented himself at the command of our 21st Army Corps to offer in the name of the Commander the surrender of Tobruk fortress. Axis troops have occupied fortress, town, and harbour. 25,000 prisoners, including several Generals, have surrendered." The booty was stated to be considerable, and the capture of Bardia was also reported.

Not until 12.7 a.m. on June 22 was it officially confirmed in London that " Tobruk has fallen." A few hours later Hitler pro- moted Rommel to the rank of Field-Marshal.

United Nations Day in London and New York

THE KING AND QUEEN taking the salute on the occasion of the United Nations Day celebration on June 14. They are seen (close to the bottom edge of the photograph) on the platform facing the Victoria Memorial in front of Buckingham Palace. In the photograph (radioed from America—hence the slightly fuzzy appearance) at the top of the page a detachment of the Royal Navy is marching through Fifth Avenue in New York, as part of the programme of United Nations Day in the great American city.

Photos, Planet News, G.P.U.

The Beat of Liberty in the Heart of England

FLAGS OF FREEDOM, representing twenty-five Allied Powers, in the Market Place, Aylesbury, during the celebration of United Nations Day on June 14. It was from Aylesbury, a typical English country town with associations with John Hampden, that the ceremony was broadcast. The American-born mayor, Mrs. Olive Paterson, read a Government message, while United States troops (on left) and units from other Allied forces paraded.

Photo, Wide World

THE WAR AT SEA

by Francis E. McMurtrie

ONCE more the importance of ample air support for naval forces operating in narrow waters has been emphasized. So far as can be gathered from the various accounts that have been published of last month's convoy action in the Mediterranean, surface forces did not come into contact except for a brief period. Most of the damage inflicted on the enemy was by air attack. For the first time in the Mediterranean American aircraft took part in the operations.

On this occasion, to give supplies a better chance of getting through, two strongly escorted convoys sailed simultaneously, one from Gibraltar under Vice-Admiral A. T. B. Curteis, the other from Alexandria under Rear-Admiral Sir Philip Vian. The latter force, having passed supplies into Tobruk, was steering a course towards Malta when air reconnaissance reported an Italian force, including two battleships of the Littorio class, four cruisers and eight destroyers, at sea south of Taranto. During the night of June 14 and next morning attacks were made by Allied aircraft, including bombers manned by American Army personnel and British torpedo planes. Several bomb hits were made on the two battleships, causing fires. A torpedo hit may also have been scored on one of them. A heavy cruiser of 10,000

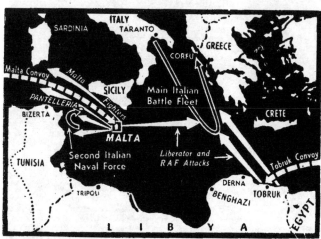

CENTRAL MEDITERRANEAN, showing the scene of convoy actions just before the fall of Tobruk. Two convoys, one from Gibraltar and the other from Alexandria, reached Malta and Tobruk respectively. The battles, in which a 10,000-ton Italian cruiser and at least two destroyers were sunk, are indicated by arrows.

Courtesy of The Daily Mail

tons, belonging to the Trento class, was set on fire by bombs and ultimately sunk by torpedo from one of our submarines. At least one smaller cruiser and a destroyer were also damaged. As a result the enemy altered course to the northward and retreated to the Taranto naval base.

On the same morning another Italian force was driven off by British torpedo aircraft off the island of Pantelleria, between Sicily and Tunisia. It was composed, according to an Italian official statement, of the cruisers Eugenio di Savoia and Raimondo Montecuccoli, and the destroyers Ugolino Vivaldi, Lanzerotto Malocello, Ascari, Orione and Premuda, under the command of Rear-Admiral Alberto da Zara, aged 53. One of Admiral da Zara's cruisers was set on fire during the engagement, and a destroyer was almost certainly sunk.

Throughout the week-end, on June 13, 14 and 15, many bombing attacks were intercepted, heavy fighting taking place. On one occasion a raiding force of 40 Junkers 87s

and Ju.88s, escorted by more than 20 Messerschmitt 109s, was intercepted. Undoubtedly considerable losses were inflicted on the Axis air forces in this action, 43 planes being certainly destroyed, and probably 50 per cent more. In attacks made on the eastern convoy the enemy lost at least 22 aircraft. (For a description of the air aspect of the battle *see* page 40).

It has been emphasized by the Admiralty that Axis claims to have sunk four British cruisers and to have damaged a battleship and an aircraft carrier are fantastic and without foundation.

Though the difficult operation of escorting convoys through the danger zone between Italy and Tunisia and Libya was not accomplished without loss, the object of delivering supplies to the garrisons of Malta and Tobruk was effected in spite of the enemy's efforts to intercept the convoys. Thus as much success as could be expected in such circumstances was gained by the Allied forces. Had the Italian squadrons stayed to fight it out, there is no doubt that the success would have been far more decisive; but for good reasons, based on sad experience in the past, the Italian Navy never risks encountering our fleet at sea if it can avoid it.

In all, the British losses amounted to one cruiser, four destroyers and two smaller vessels, besides 30 aircraft. At the lowest estimate, the enemy lost a heavy cruiser, two destroyers, a submarine and 65 aircraft, besides having one of their best battleships torpedoed and put out of action.

There are five Italian battleships in service. Two are modern ships of 35,000 tons, the Littorio and Vittorio Veneto; and the other three are rebuilt ships of 23,622 tons, the Giulio Cesare, Andrea Doria, and Caio Duilio. A sixth ship, belonging to the latter type, was the Conte di Cavour, reduced to a wreck by the British torpedo attack from the air at Taranto in November 1940; she is not believed to be fit for further service.

ON June 12 the United States Navy Department revealed details of the operations in the Coral Sea during the first week in May, which for reasons of security could not be published earlier.

Though surface forces were never in contact, it is considered that the Japanese lost 15 warships, all from air attack. The United States force, which was under the command of Rear-Admiral Frank J. Fletcher, lost only three. The action began with an air attack on Japanese ships in the vicinity of Tulagi, in the Solomon Islands. In this affair 12 Japanese ships were sunk or badly damaged, and six aircraft destroyed. The Americans lost three planes. On May 7 an attack was made on the main enemy force in the Louisiade Islands, resulting in the sinking of the new 20,000-ton Japanese aircraft-carrier Ryukaku, which received ten torpedo and 15 bomb hits. Caught just as she was turning into the wind to launch her aircraft, she took most of them

Admiral C. W. NIMITZ, C.-in-C. of the U.S. Pacific Fleet, right, on the occasion of a visit to Midway Island. With him is Commander C. T. Simard, commanding the Naval Air Station on the island. *Photo, Associated Press*

to the bottom with her. A heavy cruiser was also sunk.

Counter-attacks by enemy aircraft were beaten off, more than 25 Japanese aircraft being brought down as compared with six American. In the afternoon, however, the enemy located the U.S. naval oiler Neosho and an escorting destroyer, the Sims, of 1,570 tons, sinking the latter and so badly damaging the former that she foundered some days later.

On May 8 a further attack was made on the Japanese force, a second 20,000-ton aircraft-carrier, the Syokaku, being bombed and torpedoed. When last seen she was badly on fire. A counter-attack was concentrated on the U.S. aircraft-carrier Lexington, of 33,000 tons, which was hit by two torpedoes and two bombs, this being the last incident of the action. Though the fires raging in the Lexington were extinguished, and she was able to proceed at a speed of 20 knots, a tremendous internal explosion occurred several hours later, due to ignition of petrol vapour from leaks caused by the torpedo damage. After five hours of vain endeavour she had to be abandoned, blew up and sank.

IN the action off Midway Island between June 4 and 7 aircraft-carriers again played the principal part, though the surface ships do not appear to have come within 100 miles of each other. Full details have yet to be published, but Admiral Chester W. Nimitz, Commander-in-Chief of the United States Pacific Fleet, considers that two Japanese aircraft-carriers, identified unofficially as the Akagi and Kaga, each of 26,900 tons, were sunk, as well as a destroyer. One or two more aircraft-carriers, three battleships and four cruisers received damage of a more or less extensive nature. (*See* page 61).

On this occasion the only American warship lost was a destroyer, torpedoed by a Japanese submarine. Some damage was sustained by a U.S. aircraft-carrier. Apparently the enemy casualties were mainly due to air attack, though the destruction of one of the aircraft-carriers was caused by three torpedoes from an American submarine.

Following on the Coral Sea losses, this Japanese defeat off Midway seems likely to be the turning-point of the naval war in the Pacific. In tonnage the Japanese fleet has lost about 45 per cent of its aircraft-carriers, a type of war vessel of which the importance can hardly be exaggerated.

'Abandon Ship!' Last Minutes of the Lexington

U.S. AIRCRAFT - CARRIER LEXINGTON, 33,000 tons, just before she blew up on May 8 in the course of the battle of the Coral Sea. Her crew, being unable to put out the fires, are leaping into the sea to be rescued by destroyers. On the right is another photograph of the Lexington, her entire length ablaze, and in the smaller illustration is a view of the carrier with aircraft aboard during pre-war manoeuvres off the Virginia Cape. The Lexington was hit by two Japanese torpedoes and at least two bombs. She caught fire, and although the crew worked heroically for more than five hours to put out the flames it was impossible to save her. Captain F. C. Sherman gave orders to abandon ship, and 92 per cent of the Lexington's company were rescued before she sank.

Photos, Planet News, Wide World

Midway Was a Victory for the United States

Most important of the three Midway Islands, situated in the Pacific Ocean about 2,800 miles from Tokyo, is Sand Island above; on the right is a close-up of the island showing rows of tough grass planted as a barricade against the ceaseless drift of sand. Beneath, the landing stage at Midway, with a pan-American clipper in the lagoon. The battle of the Midway Islands, on June 7 proved a heavy defeat for the Japanese navy. The United States Navy spokesman revealed at Honolulu on June 12 that probably four Japanese aircraft-carriers, including two of the heaviest type, were destroyed in this action, and that many other vessels, including three battleships, were damaged.

SAND ISLAND: a caterpillar-tractor preparing land for the building of a seaplane base (left). Right, baby albatrosses, or goonies, on a Midway Island beach. The map indicates the position of Midway, relatively to Tokyo, San Francisco and Dutch Harbour in the Aleutians. Japanese forces operating in the last-named area were also heavily hit by American torpedo bombers, a cruiser being reported to have been sunk and an aircraft-carrier damaged.

Photos, E.N.A.; Map by courtesy of The Daily Mail

Dutch Harbour: War at the 'Top of the World'

While the tempo of the war in the more southern regions of the Pacific seemed to slacken somewhat, there were reports of Japanese activity in the far north, in the Aleutian Islands, which might presage a move either against Alaska and the North American mainland, or against Siberia in Soviet Asia. Some account of this new " top of the world " war area follows.

DUTCH HARBOUR bombed by the Japanese! How many people when they read the American Navy Department's announcement on June 4 were able to put their finger on the spot which marks Dutch Harbour on the map? At once, or at last, they found it—in the Aleutian Islands, that long chain of dots that joins America and Asia not so very far south of the Arctic Circle (*see* map opposite). If the atlas were an old one they would probably not find it at all, and only those with a globe could appreciate the full significance of the news. For a globe makes it plain that the shortest distance from North America to Eastern Asia—Japan in particular—runs through or near those same islands. That is the " top of the world " route, where the trail was first blazed by Soviet flyers in 1937.

Strung out like a chain between the two great land masses, the Aleutians cover a distance of some 1,200 miles from end to end. There are 150 of them, but most are small and very few are inhabited—which is not surprising since they are hardly pleasant places in which to live. Fogs are almost perpetual, for it is here that the comparatively warm ocean breezes make contact with the bitter blasts from the Arctic. The rainfall is very heavy; the winters are long and often severe, while the summers are short and never more than cool. Hardly a tree is to be seen on any of the islands, although between May and September the ground is covered with rich grass, thickly sown with flowers. A continuation of the mountains in Alaska, the islands are themselves the summits of a chain of volcanoes; and there are numerous cones which are still active. The coasts are rocky and dangerous to approach, and from the shore the land rises immediately to steep and rugged mountains.

In this inhospitable region the human family is represented by the Aleuts, a branch of the Eskimo stock, and as such resembling the Eskimos in features, in language, and in culture. Years ago, before the Aleutians became part of the Russian Empire, there were said to be 25,000 Aleuts on the archipelago, but ere long they were almost wiped out by the barbarities of the white traders, who went to the islands to secure the furs of the seal and sea otter and the blue and Arctic fox. Twenty years ago the population was given as 1,080, and the natives are probably not much more numerous today. But in addition to the natives the Aleutians possess a large population drawn from the armed forces of the U.S.A. For the islands are now American, and though their economic importance is of small account, in the strategy of the Pacific they have a great and growing place.

Politically, the Aleutians form part of the Territory of Alaska, one of the components of the U.S.A. Until 1867 Alaska belonged to Russia, but in that year all the Tsar's possessions in America were sold to the United States. The price paid was $7,200,000, and Mr. Secretary Seward, who negotiated the purchase, was scoffed at by his countrymen for having made what they regarded as a very poor bargain. For years Alaska was called " Seward's folly " and a " giant ice-box "; and it was not until the eighteen-nineties, when Seward had been dead for twenty years, that his foresight was vindicated. Then the discovery of gold put Alaska on the map, and to gold there were soon added copper and silver, coal and timber and enormously rich fisheries. Alaska, which in size is equal to one-fifth of the continental U.S.A., is indeed one great treasure-house of economic resources which still await full exploitation.

But the Aleutians are not among Nature's favourites; climate and soil and configuration all conspire against any agricultural, industrial or commercial development on a large scale. The natives have always lived by fishing and hunting, supplemented by basket-making on the part of the women; their agriculture is represented by little more than some not very productive vegetable plots. The Americans are there for other purposes; it is war, and the preparations for war, that have led to their immigration.

Most important of their settlements is Dutch Harbour on the island of Unalaska, one of the largest in the chain. Here there is a first-class harbour, two miles long and half a mile wide, which, moreover, has the great advantage of being ice-free all the year round. At Dutch Harbour the Americans have constructed a base for their naval, army and air forces; fringing the shore are great oil tanks, huge depots of military stores, a radio station and a shipyard, where (so it is rumoured) submarines are being constructed. There are aerodromes, too, and aircraft factories and repair shops.

It was only about a year ago, soon after the Germans had invaded Russia, that Col. Knox, U.S. Navy Secretary, announced that Dutch Harbour was to be developed as an American base. The decision was soon acted upon.

" Into Dutch Harbour and Unalaska," Alec Hunter wrote recently in the News Chronicle, " roared construction crews—about 2,000 husky, hard-bitten, hard-living engineers, industry's soldiers of fortune. Already there was an unspecified number of Army and Navy men to man the base. These descended on what was originally a quiet herring-fishing village with a native population of 300 Aleut Indians. Saturday nights in Unalaska were tough. There are six liquor stores, one saloon—Black Floyd's Unalaska Cocktail Bar. It is, in spite of everything, orderly. The military police and the U.S. deputy marshal see to that."

From Dutch Harbour to Tokyo is 2,850 miles, and to the Japanese naval base of Paramushiro some 1,600 miles (Paramushiro is in the Japanese Kurile Islands, just south of the Russian peninsula of Kamchatka). Aircraft-carriers based on Dutch Harbour might well then threaten Tokyo. No wonder the Japanese Admiral Matsuaga declared a few months ago " that as soon as the Arctic fog had lifted " the Japanese air force would make Dutch Harbour one of its objectives.

That promise was carried out (as we have seen) on June 3, when Dutch Harbour was twice attacked by Japanese planes. A week later Imperial Japanese Headquarters in Tokyo issued a communiqué stating that " Japanese naval units operating in the Eastern Pacific carried out a surprise attack on Dutch Harbour, Alaska, as well as on the entire Aleutian Island group, and continued raids on enemy positions there on June 4 and 5." After a reference to fierce attacks made on Midway Island, the communiqué went on to claim that on June 7 Japanese naval units in close cooperation with the military " reduced a number of enemy positions in the Aleutian Islands, and are now continuing operations there."

To some extent these claims were confirmed by the U.S. Navy Department: there had been landings by the enemy at Attu, most westerly of the islands, it was announced, and at Kiska in the Rat group. Attu—800 miles from the northern islands of Japan and a little more from Dutch Harbour—is a desolate spot of very doubtful military value; as often as not it is buried in fog or swept by storms, and its only inhabitants are reported to be about a hundred primitive Aleuts, a half-breed trader, and an employee of the Weather Bureau and his school-teacher wife.

Much more important is Kiska, which is stated to have one of the best harbours in the Aleutian group. Though it is still undeveloped, this harbour might be of considerable use to the Japanese fleet and air force. From its aerodrome, which is stated to have run-ways long enough to allow four-engine bombers to take off, Japanese aircraft could operate against Dutch Harbour, which, as stated above, is only some 800 miles to the east. Kiska is also 800 miles from the Russian base of Petropavlovsk in Kamchatka—a fact which might well be of considerable importance in the event of Soviet Russia coming into the war.

Following the announcement of the Japanese landings there was little fresh news from the Aleutian front. The U.S. Navy Department revealed that air attacks against the Japanese forces were continuing. " The foul weather and fog characteristic of this locality at all seasons are hampering our reconnaissance and attack operations, but reports to date indicate that at least three cruisers, one destroyer, one gunboat and one transport have been damaged, some severely." Then the operations were blanketed again in fog as thick as that which for six days out of seven shrouds the Aleutians.   E. ROYSTON PIKE

THE JAPANESE OCTOPUS. In this ingenious conception of the war in the Far East Japan is represented as an octopus, with far-reaching tentacles stretched out towards Australia, New Zealand, Midway, Alaska, China and India. Had the United Nations the appropriate strategy, and the weapons essential to that strategy, the direct way of destroying Japan's power would be to strike at Japan herself and thereby stop the heart of this " sprawling beast." In that event the tentacles would fall limp and release their grip from territories now in Japanese possession. Though a super-plane attack in force is impracticable at present, we may well see in time a fleet of giant bombers of the Douglas B-19 and Glenn Martin flying-boat size which might attack Japan direct across the 3,100 miles from Alaska to Tokyo.
Illustration from Victory Through Air Power, by Major de Seversky. By permission of Hutchinson & Co.; Copyright, Pinker, Ltd.

Men of the Sea, They're Planning the Next Convoy

TYPICAL CONVOY CAPTAINS, Messrs. Brown of Glasgow, F. W. Faviant of Gravesend and L. A. Shuttleworth of Sunderland, exchanging experiences before attending a conference to settle the procedure to be adopted on the next voyage.

Captain McInnes (above) hails from Glasgow, and that rugged Scots face, inscribed with a grim humour, is known in many a port. To bring home the goods he is obviously ready to defy all the U-boats in the world. Left, the Convoy "Brains Trust," who are in charge of the Trade Division at the Admiralty. Here are some of the men who plan the struggle upon which all battles depend—the fight to keep the seas open. They are, left to right, Captain Bittleston, Commander Morey, Vice-Admiral King, Commander Leggatt and Captain Schofield.

Beneath, an outgoing convoy assembled at a selected rendezvous. Anchors have been dropped, and barrage balloons raised, while the masters of the vessels have gone ashore to receive final instructions.

Photos, G.P.U.

Our Submarines and Theirs: a 'Bag' of Exploits

A U-boat has been sighted by a Whitley aircraft of the R.A.F. Coastal Command in the Bay of Biscay. In a few seconds the bomber is over the enemy and bombs have been accurately placed. As they explode a huge column of water ascends into the air, as seen in photograph No. 1. Two minutes later the conning-tower of the U-boat, forced to the surface by the explosion, appears, No. 2. In the third photograph a large patch of oil, nearly 200 yards in diameter, and air bubbles denote the complete destruction of the enemy submarine. So the ceaseless war against Hitler's sea-wolves continues.

Photos, British Official ; G.P.U., Lafayette

Emanating from Rome, these photographs (above) show an American merchantship going to her doom soon after she had been struck by an enemy torpedo.
Photos, Keystone

One of the bravest deeds of the war was revealed when Lt. P. S. W. Roberts, R.N., and P.O. Thomas Gould (right and left, above) of H.M. submarine Thrasher, were awarded V.C.s. The Thrasher had sunk a supply ship on February 16. She survived a depth charge, but when she surfaced after dark two unexploded enemy bombs were discovered in her gun-casing. Lt. Roberts and P.O. Gould volunteered to remove them. They had to lie full-length to carry out their dangerous task. Having dealt with one bomb, they pushed the second for about twenty feet until it could be lowered over the side. The photograph shows A, where the first bomb penetrated, and, A1, where it was discovered (left). B indicates where second bomb was found, and C shows P. O. Gould in casing hatch through which the bomb was dragged.

Cheers and Smiles Caught By Our Camera

WORKERS OF THE WEEK, three women specially chosen and honourably mentioned by the Ministry of Supply. The first is Mrs. Edith Foster, "blue girl," or supervisor, in a Welsh royal ordnance factory. Mrs. Foster is in charge, under a foreman, of 14 machines.

Mrs. Alice Watts, mother of six children, who has registered 100 per cent attendance in a north-west ordnance factory. Also a blue girl, she is in charge of a number of girls filling shells, bombs and anti-tank mines. She has never missed a day's work. Two of her daughters are in the same factory.

Mrs. Rose Jackman (right) bends copper pipes for Spitfires, doing it with her bare hands. "It's the knack of suddenly putting all your strength into your wrists that does it," says Rose.

H.M.S. PENELOPE, familiarly known as H.M.S. "Pepperpot," showing part of her splinter-riddled sides caulked with wooden pegs. The cruiser was continuously attacked for two weeks by Axis bombers while she was in Malta Harbour, but fought off the planes, put to sea and was brought safely to port.
(See also page 22)

Beneath : the ship's company of the U.S. flagship cheering King George on the occasion of his visit to the U.S. Navy with the Home Fleet. His Majesty is aboard the small auxiliary vessel, Morialta, thereby conferring a unique honour on the Merchant Navy by reviewing the Fleet from the bridge of a merchantman. The Morialta is flying the signal "Splice the Main brace," which means a double portion of rum for all wherewith to drink the King's health.

MINISTER OF FUEL, Major G. Lloyd George, appointed head of the new Government department to deal with the coal and fuel problem. The second portrait is of Group Capt. G. N. Ambler, who has been appointed Commandant of the Royal Observer Corps in succession to Air Commodore A. D. Warrington-Morris. Commodore Ambler joined the Auxiliary Air Force in 1931 and commanded Nos. 608 (North Riding) and 609 (West Riding) Squadrons. On right, Lord Swinton, who has been appointed Minister Resident with Cabinet rank in West Africa. Lord Swinton was Secretary of State for Air from 1935 to 1938.

Photos, British Official: Crown Copyright ; B.B.C., Central Press, G.P.U., Topical Press

I WAS THERE!

'Give Me a Moonlight Night and My Hurricane!'

Destroying enemy bombers over the home bases is known as "intruding"
to the night-fighters of the R.A.F. One of the most successful intruders,
Squadron-Leader MacLachlan, gave some account of his nocturnal operations
in a broadcast on May 18.

MOST of us night fighters are too fond of our mornings in bed to go flying around in the daytime. Give me a moonlight night and my old Hurricane and you can have your Spitfires and dawn readiness. We've no formation flying to worry about, and no bombers to escort. In fact, nothing to do but amuse ourselves once we've crossed the French coast.

I must admit that those miles of Channel with only one engine bring mixed thoughts, and one can't help listening to every little beat of the old " Merlin " as the English coast disappears in the darkness. I always get a feeling of relief and excitement as I cross the French coast and turn on the reflector sight, knowing that anything I see then I can have a crack at. We have to keep our eyes skinned the whole time, and occasionally glance at the compass and clock.

As the minutes go by and we approach the Hun aerodrome we look eagerly for the flare paths. More often than not we are disappointed. The flare path is switched off as soon as we arrive and up come the searchlights and flak. But if you're lucky it's a piece of cake. The other night I saw the Jerries when I was still some distance away. They were flying round at about 2,000 feet. I chose the nearest and followed him round. He was battling along at about 200 miles an hour, but I soon caught him and got him beautifully lined up in my sights before letting him have it.

The effect of our four cannon is incredible after the eight machine-guns I had previously been used to. Scarcely had I pressed the button when a cluster of flashes appeared on the bomber and a spurt of dark red flame came from its starboard engine. The whole thing seemed to fold up then and fall out of the sky. I turned steeply to watch it crash, and as I did so I saw another Hun about a mile away, coming straight for me. In half a minute he was in my sights, and a second later his port petrol tank was blazing. I gave him another short burst for luck and then flew beside him. It was just like watching a film. A moment before he hit the ground I could see trees and houses lit up by the dark red glow from the burning machine. Suddenly there was a terrific sheet of flame, and little bits of burning Heinkel flew in all directions.

I flew straight back to the aerodrome to find another. Unfortunately, all the lights had been switched off, and though I circled for some time I found nothing. So I cracked off for home. I looked back once and could still see the two bombers burning in the distance, and a few searchlights trying vainly to find me.

Well, when your petrol and ammunition are nearly gone you are faced with the old Channel again. If you've got something, as I had that night, you leave enemy territory with a sort of guilty conscience—somehow you feel they've got it in for you and that everyone's going to shoot at you. It's a sort of nervous reaction, I suppose. The whole thing seems too easy to be true. Ten to one there's no Hun within shooting distance and the ground defences are quiet. That makes it all the worse, and I generally weave about till I'm half-way back across the Channel. Out over the Channel you can hear your ground station calling the other aircraft of the squadron and you count the minutes and look eagerly for the coast.

At last, in the distance, you see the flashing beacon and soon you are taxi-ing in to your dispersal point. I dread the look of disappointment on my mechanic's face if my guns are unfired. But if the rubber covers have been shot off I've scarcely time to stop my engine before I am surrounded by the boys asking what luck I've had. My whole squadron—both ground crews and pilots—are as keen as mustard, and I must say they've put up a terrific show. Since April 1 the squadron has destroyed eleven aircraft for certain and probably three more.

The lion's share of this total goes to my Czech Flight-Commander Kuttelwascher (*see* page 746, Vol. 5). He's a first-class pilot and has the most uncanny gift of knowing just

Sqdn.-Ldr. J. A. F. MacLACHLAN, D.F.C. and Bar, who describes a moonlight raid in this page, has an artificial arm, having lost the original limb in a fight over Malta.
Photo, British Official

which aerodrome the Huns are going back to. He'll look at the map and say, " I'll go there tonight ! " possibly to some unobtrusive aerodrome. Sure enough, even if the others see no activity, he certainly will. One night we agreed to visit a certain aerodrome, but five minutes before we took off old Kuttel changed his mind and went to another. I got to my aerodrome to find it covered with fog, while he calmly knocked down three !

Now, finally, a word of tribute to our aircraft and those who make them. I fought with Hurricanes in the Battle of Britain, in Malta and in Libya, and they're still as good as ever. For the kind of night work on which we're engaged we couldn't wish for a more reliable and effective aircraft.

What the Americans Told Me About Midway

These first eye witness stories of the Japanese defeat in the sea and air
battles off Midway Island on June 3 and 4 were told to Reuter's correspondent by American participants in the action.

IT was on June 3 (said General Willis Hale, Commander of the U.S. Bombardment Command) that two Japanese fleets were first reported to be approaching Midway Island. One of the fleets, composed mainly of transports, was coming from the west. The other—the battle fleet—was coming from another direction. Orders were flashed to U.S. Army bombers lined up and waiting for just such an opportunity.

That afternoon the Army bombers made their first contact with the enemy far west of Midway. They sent their bomb loads screaming down from a medium altitude, damaging a cruiser or a battleship, one transport and a destroyer.

The Japanese air attack on Midway on the following day was anticipated. U.S. Army and Navy planes were in the air when the enemy arrived. Flying Fortresses were attacking the Japanese battle fleet from a high altitude. Colonel Walter Sweeney, who led the Fortresses, said :

" We first made contact with the enemy far out in the Pacific on the afternoon of June 3. There were over twenty ships in columns with the big ships in the centre. We circled westward and came in with the sun at our backs. When the Japs sighted us they immediately deployed, each ship turning individually and trying frantically to avoid attack. We were at medium altitude owing to the clouds, and we found the antiaircraft fire more accurate than we had anticipated. We picked out the biggest ships as targets and laid our bombs in a pattern.

" At dawn the next day we hopped off for another attack on the same force, but soon got orders to attack another and larger force. We found them.

" There was a big battle line with destroyers outside them, cruisers, then battleships, and away at the back, carriers. The ships

KAGA CLASS Japanese aircraft-carrier, similar to those described in the eye witness story of the battle of Midway appearing in this page. Of the two ships of this class engaged in this naval action one is said to be a total loss.
Photo, Associated Press

Shouting orders to the twenty-five-pounder guns from one of the fire-posts in the Western Desert.   *Photos, British Official*

smashed carrier. They would pass over the carrier, soar out of sight, and then come back again in a sort of hopeless desperation. Night fell, and the stranded planes were swallowed up in darkness.

Crouched in his rubber boat, Gay saw great glowing patches in the sky which he guessed to be searchlights of Japanese rescue ships looking for survivors from the wrecked carriers. Three times he heard violent explosions which he believed may have been demolition charges.

Then, several hours after the sun rose, a U.S. navy patrol plane rescued him. As he flew back to the base, Gay told me, the sea could be seen covered with patches of oil and littered with empty Japanese rafts.

The whole story is one of the cool courage and firm determination of young Americans who fought until dizzy from lack of sleep and did things with their planes that the machines had never been built to do.

started frantic manoeuvres, but our pattern of bombs blanketed a carrier. A few Zeros who came up showed faint-heartedness.

" We returned to Midway, reloaded, and were over the enemy again at 4 p.m., when we found a carrier and a capital ship lying dead without headway and burning. We then got a heavy cruiser. High-level bombing is effective in attacks like these. Nothing can escape us since we can lay bombs in patterns which no ship can avoid."

Another vivid eye witness story of the sea and air battle was told me by Ensign Gay, 25-year-old torpedo-plane pilot. On June 4 he came upon three Japanese carriers with less than ten miles between the first and last, protected by a great screen of destroyers and cruisers. Two of the carriers were of the Kaga class—the only two known to exist of these massive 26,900-ton giants which carry 50 to 60 planes. One of the carriers was blazing fiercely as Gay arrived, and the other two were taking on their planes.

Gay launched a torpedo at a Kaga carrier before being shot down at 11 a.m. ; his machine-gunner and wireless operator were killed, but he managed to " pancake " his plane on the sea and to extricate himself from the wreckage. He recovered a rubber life-raft, and from this he saw something of the terrific battle.

U.S. bombers screamed into action, hurling bomb after bomb at the vulnerable Japanese ships. Gay saw the other two carriers squarely hit. Tremendous fires burst from the vessels, and great billows of smoke churned up, with great flames shooting out from the tips of the black columns. Every few minutes explosions inside the burning carriers sent new gushes of smoke belching upwards. One of the Kaga class ships was certainly a total loss, while the last he saw of the other carriers was as they were being pursued by U.S. forces.

As the afternoon drew to a close the Japanese made frantic efforts to help the remaining giant carrier. A cruiser tried to come alongside, but seemed unable to get close enough, so she opened up with her big guns, presumably to scuttle her. Some time later a destroyer managed to get close enough to take off survivors still on board.

All this time Japanese planes were hovering in the air above, with nowhere to land but in the sea or on the blazing decks of their

Twenty-five-pounder guns light up desert darkness at the moment of firing. A fine action photograph from the Libyan front. A Scots photographer, who was captured but escaped in the hurly-burly which has characterized so much of the fighting in the Western Desert, describes his adventure below.

The Germans Caught Me As I 'Snapped' Them

A Scots photographer who was captured by the Germans in Libya and escaped after a short stay in the enemy lines, told the following story—so typical of the confused desert war—of his adventures.

I WAS captured when the lorry in which I was riding found itself among a German armoured column. At first I thought the Germans were prisoners, and I began to take photographs of them—until firing began. One of the men in the back of the lorry shouted that there was a German armoured car firing on us. We soon found that a tank was also firing at us, and machine-guns appeared to be spitting fire everywhere. We jumped out and took cover, but we were too late and were captured.

We were taken to the headquarters of this German column, which numbered about 200 vehicles, consisting of armoured cars, a few tanks, lorries full of infantry and scores of scout cars. One of the German N.C.O.s gave me an Italian cigarette and, when the tobacco began to fall out, remarked : " It's just like the Italians—no good." Others told me they would be in Tobruk on May 27, and said " We have Churchill by the throat this time."

A German lieutenant ordered me to accompany him into the desert—a 40-mile trip which I didn't appreciate, as we were in the van of advancing artillery and armoured cars. We were met by a heavy hail of artillery fire when going down an escarpment,

and I noticed that two of the enemy vehicles were destroyed. When we arrived at the bottom of the next escarpment we were numbered and told to keep away from the unit. The lieutenant said that anyone attempting to escape, or having a weapon or live rounds of ammunition in his pocket would be shot.

Later, the artillery fire from the British troops became extremely accurate, and all the vehicles which had been captured with us were rushed forward. An officer armed with a tommy-gun was left to look after the prisoners.

Then the shooting became dead accurate, and the prisoners were left to themselves. Several, including myself, landed in the welcome safety of a slit trench, where we lay doggo for three hours. Some Germans stopped and looked at us, but, thinking we were dead, passed on.

When it was dark enough I managed to collect about 50 other ranks and found a pocket compass. This, however, was not very accurate, and we had to depend on the moon for our direction. With a halt of ten minutes in every hour, we walked 25 miles and eventually struck the main Tobruk-Bardia road—and safety.—*Reuter.*

I Went to France With the Commando Men

For nearly an hour in the early morning of June 4, 1942, German defences on
the French coast between Boulogne and Le Touquet were put into confusion
by the "smash and grab" Commando raid described here by the Exchange
Telegraph Co.'s war correspondent, Edward Gilling.

OUR voyage to the French coast was
uneventful. Weather conditions were
absolutely perfect, with the red glow
from the setting sun flooding a calm sea. The
Commandos, wearing shorts and stockings,
and with their toggle ropes round their waists
and soft woollen hats, sat quietly in the
assault boats talking in whispers. As we
neared the French coast searchlights were
switched on and swung low over the sea.
We held our breath many a time when it
seemed certain that we must be picked up,
but after a few anxious seconds the lights
were switched off.

The Commandos, many of whom had to
wade waist deep from their assault craft,
advanced over the dunes, some of them
reaching some distance inland after cutting
their way through the barbed wire defences.
It was not until the Commandos had actually
established themselves on the foreshore that
the German defences opened fire, following
upon the firing of a white Very light which
illumined the beach and threw a spotlight on
the Commandos racing towards the dunes.
The defences tried to set up a cross-fire, but,
in the end, tracer bullets from one German
machine-gun post could be seen streaking
across the sands point-blank at a fellow
gunpost. The Commandos were able to
get through the wire defences and carry out
their reconnaissance and gather the information which they were there to seek. Two
searchlights were switched on by the defenders, and the German machine-gun posts
directed their fire against the assault craft
lying off, obviously with the object of preventing the re-embarkation of the troops
that had landed.

The Army commander who led the assault
up the beach ordered the withdrawal after
the Commandos had completed their task, a
single bugle note ringing out above the rattle
of machine-gun and rifle-fire. Immediately
the Commandos began to make their way
back to the boats, the last party to leave
consisting of a lieutenant and half-a-dozen
men. Under cover of a smokescreen the
troops were re-embarked and made their
way out to sea with the German defences
still firing wild and sporadic bursts at the
diminishing targets.

After putting out a mile off-shore, it was
decided that, in order to ensure that no one
had been left behind, one of the craft should
put back to the beach for a final look round.
Finding no one waiting on the beaches, the
commander of this craft decided to enjoy a
Parthian shot with long bursts of fire from
Bren guns and every other type of armament
aboard.

This craft had only just left the beach
when in the brilliant moonlight we suddenly
spotted R.A.F. machines overhead diving
low to the shore, and a series of heavy explosions followed as they dropped their
bombs all along the foreshore in and about
the defences. Shortly after dawn, as we
were making our way from the French coast,
we saw a squadron of Spitfires flying low over
the water towards us, and for the remainder
of the voyage home the R.A.F. fighters
continually circled the convoy. One or two
straggling craft, however, fell astern of us
and these were made the object of a sudden
swoop by four Messerschmitts which attempted to dive-bomb and machine-gun
them. The enemy aircraft were met with a

BACK FROM BOULOGNE! Some of the
men who took part in the Commando raid in
the Boulogne-Le Touquet area on June 3. A
description of this exploit appears in this page.
Photo, British Official

fusillade of fire from the boats and after a
few minutes were driven off. Apart from this,
the return voyage to a South Coast port was
without incident. Small crowds gathered at
the port and watched the Commandos come
ashore and drive to their billets.

OUR DIARY OF THE WAR

JUNE 10, 1942, Wednesday   1,012th day
  Russian Front.—In Kharkov sector
Germans passed to offensive.
  Mediterranean.—R.A.F. raided Taranto and Crete by night.
  Africa.—Garrison of Bir Hacheim
withdrawn on Gen. Ritchie's order.
  Australasia.—Rabaul raided by Allied
bombers.
  Home.—King's visit to Home Fleet
revealed that units of U.S. Navy were
operating in British waters.
  General.—Prague radio announced
that all men of Czech village of Lidice
had been shot, women sent to concentration camp, children to "educational
centres," and village razed to the ground.

JUNE 11, Thursday   1,013th day
  Russian Front.—Heavy attacks on
Sebastopol; Germans also attacking at
Kharkov.
  Mediterranean.—Harbours of Tar-
anto and Piraeus raided by R.A.F.
  Africa.—Our armoured forces engaged
enemy E. of Harmat.
  General.—Mr. Eden announced sign-
ing of Anglo-Soviet Pact on May 26.
Execution of 34 Czechs announced.

JUNE 12, Friday   1,014th day
  Russian Front.—Stubborn fighting for
Sebastopol. Germans still attacking at
Kharkov.
  China.—Chuhsien occupied by Japs.
A.V.G. shot down 9 out of 18 Jap planes
raiding Kweilin.
  Australasia.—Allied planes raided
Rabaul and Gasmata in New Britain.
  U.S.A.—Navy Dept. confirmed Jap
landing at Attu, in Aleutians.
  Home.—Further reinforcements of
Canadian troops arrived in Britain.
  General.—Execution of 18 Czechs.

JUNE 13, Saturday   1,015th day
  Russian Front.—Heavy fighting in
Kharkov sector; Sebastopol beat off
attacks.
  Mediterranean.—Heraklion and Tar-
anto raided by R.A.F.
  Africa.—Severe fighting between ar-
moured forces S. of Acroma.
  China.—Japs entered Nancheng, S. of
Nanchang.
  Australasia.—Twenty-seven Jap
bombers raided Darwin. Allied bombers
raided shipping at Simberi, New Ireland.

Home.—More U.S. troops arrived in
N. Ireland, escorted by U.S. naval forces.

JUNE 14, Sunday   1,016th day
  Sea.—Admiralty announced loss of
H.M. submarine Olympus.
  Russian Front.—Fighting continued in
Kharkov and Sebastopol sectors.
  Mediterranean.—Convoy from Alex-
andria bound for Malta encountered 2
Italian battleships, 4 cruisers and 8
destroyers.
  Africa.—Troops round Acroma and
1st Armoured Division covered with-
drawal from Gazala of 1st S. African
Division and 50th Division.
  China.—Japs from Chekiang occupied
Yushan in Kiangsi.
  Australasia.—Jap bombers and fighters
intercepted off Darwin. Allied bombers
raided Sohana in Solomons.
  General.—Four American bombers
made forced landing in Turkey.

JUNE 15, Monday   1,017th day
  Russian Front.—Fierce fighting round
Kharkov and Sebastopol.
  Mediterranean.—In air attacks on
Italian fleet attacking westbound convoy,
cruiser sunk, battleship torpedoed, and
22 enemy aircraft shot down.
  Australasia.—Extensive raid on Dar-
win by 27 Jap bombers. Allied bombers
attacked Kupang, Lae and Salamaua.
  General.—Argentina and Chile warned
by Germany that vessels entering N.
American "blockade zone" after June 26
do so at their own risk.

JUNE 16, Tuesday   1,018th day
  Air.—Targets in Ruhr and Rhineland
bombed by night.
  Russian Front.—German attacks
beaten off at Sebastopol and Kharkov.
  Mediterranean.—Convoy from Gib-
raltar reached Malta with serious losses
after violent air attacks.
  Africa.—Enemy attacks repelled at
Sidi Rezegh and Acroma.
  China.—Kwangfeng, Kiangsi, evacuated
by Chinese.
  Australasia.—Town and harbour of
Darwin raided by 27 heavy Jap bombers.

JUNE 17, Wednesday   1,019th day
  Air.—Submarine base at St. Nazaire
bombed by night.
  Russian Front.—Fierce attacks on
Sebastopol repelled.
  Mediterranean.—R.A.F. bombed
Heraklion and Kasteli, Crete.
  Africa.—Our forces withdrew from El
Adem and Sidi Rezegh.
  Australasia.—Port Moresby attacked
by 18 Jap bombers.

JUNE 18, Thursday   1,020th day
  Sea.—Admiralty announced loss of
H.M. minesweeper Fitzroy.
  Russian Front.—Germans claimed to
have stormed main fortifications in N.
of Sebastopol defences.
  Africa.—Eighth Army holding strong
fortified positions on Libyan frontier and
in Tobruk area.
  Australasia.—Port Moresby raided
by 18 Jap bombers.
  General.—Mr. Churchill arrived in
U.S.A. for discussions with President
Roosevelt.
  Germans announced that two men who
shot Heydrich had been captured and
executed.

JUNE 19, Friday   1,021st day
  Sea.—Admiralty announced loss of
H.M destroyer Wild Swan after fight
in Atlantic against 12 German bombers,
of which six were brought down.
  Russian Front.—Fierce fighting for
Sebastopol.
  Air.—Emden and Osnabruck raided by
R.A.F.
  Africa.—Two enemy columns advanc-
ing eastward turned back towards
Tobruk.
  Australasia.—Allied bombers made
heavy attack on aerodromes and shipping
at Rabaul.
  General.—Germans executed General
Alois Elias, former prime minister of
Czech puppet government.

JUNE 20, Saturday   1,022nd day
  Air.—Docks at Le Havre bombed by
day. Strong force of bombers raided
Emden by night.

  Mediterranean.—Targets in Crete
attacked by R.A.F. Seven enemy aircraft
destroyed over Malta.
  Africa.—Enemy attacked Tobruk perimeter in great strength and penetrated
the defences. Enemy bombers attacked
Egyptian coast between Sidi Barrani
and Fuka.
  Burma.—R.A.F. bombed Akyab and
Magwe.
  Australasia.—Admiralty announced
that H.M. submarines had sunk three Jap
supply ships in Strait of Malacca. Allied
bombers again raided Rabaul and Lae.
  General.—Telegraph Station at Este-
van Point, Vancouver Island, shelled by
submarine.

JUNE 21, Sunday   1,023rd day
  Air.—R.A.F. bombed Dunkirk docks.
  Russian Front.—Enemy succeeded in
driving wedge into Sebastopol defences.
  Mediterranean.—R.A.F. attacked tar-
gets in Greece and Crete.
  Africa.—Tobruk captured by Rommel.
  U.S.A.—Coast of Oregon shelled by
unidentified craft. Navy Dept. confirmed
Jap landing in Kiska, Aleutians.
  Home.—Four German bombers des-
troyed in night raid on Southampton.

JUNE 22, Monday   1,024th day
  Air.—R.A.F. bombed Dunkirk docks.
  Russian Front.—Fierce fighting con-
tinued at Sebastopol and Kharkov.
  Africa.—Slight enemy activity in
Egyptian frontier region.
  Burma.—R.A.F. bombers raided Akyab
and Magwe.
  General. — Argentine merchant
steamer Rio Tercero sunk by U-boat off
New Jersey.

JUNE 23, Tuesday   1,025th day
  Air.—R.A.F. again bombed Dunkirk.
  Russian Front.—Slight withdrawal by
Russians in Kharkov sector.
  Africa.—Enemy moving south from
Gambut.
  Burma.—Akyab harbour and aero-
drome bombed by R.A.F.
  China.—Kweiki, Kiangsi, recaptured
by Chinese.
  Home.—Small-scale raid on E. Anglia;
three enemy aircraft destroyed.
  General.—Announced that 73 Czechs
executed in last three days

Editor's Postscript

No matter how much one may agree with the published opinions of any writer, if, on occasion, one finds him writing nonsense it is one's duty to say so. And I venture to discharge this duty by drawing the attention of my readers to these ill-considered words of Sir Ernest Benn in a recent issue of "Truth":

"Why is it that no member of the Government, so far as I know, and no speaker on the B.B.C., so far as I have heard, has yet told us that we are living on the charity of Canada and the United States; that without the free gift of sustenance from these sons and brothers and cousins we should today be in a condition not perhaps as bad as Greece, but getting very near to it? Can it be that we have sunk so low in the spirit of dependence, that we are so saturated with the mentality of doles and subsidies, that Britons who were once the antithesis of slavery have become such pulp-like paupers as to eat from the hand of charity without a thank you or without a thought as to how they might escape from that position? I decline altogether to believe it."

I AM glad Sir Ernest declines to accept the preposterous proposition which he presents to us (like the ghost in Hamlet) in "such a questionable shape." For it is quite at variance with the spirit that is claimed to inform the journal which gave it print. God help the world if there were any measure of truth in it! Britain is no beggar, sponging on her children nations or on her kith and kin beyond the seas. Canada is doing superbly in this hour of peril, America magnificently; but neither is showering largesse upon an indigent relative. And it is an insult to Britain even to frame so foolish a question. Britain has (so far) saved "the two Americas," Australia, and every country where men are now standing up for freedom, by her own stupendous efforts since the fall of France, and every ounce of energy, every penny of financial help that America and the British Dominions can contribute to this tremendous task of resisting the organized might of the dictator powers is no more than the charity that begins at home: it is needed no less for their own protection and survival than for Britain's. Had Britain (as the military leaders of France anticipated, save those few who followed De Gaulle) surrendered to Germany on a day in June 1940 all would soon have been over for the freedom-loving nations of all the Five Continents and that madman's dream of Germanic world-conquest might well have come to pass, or the Hundred Years' War that Japan is prepared for (says Tojo!) would now be dragging on with little hope of the eventual triumph of the democratic peoples.

AT the outset of the praiseworthy campaign of paper-saving and the surrender of old printed matter for re-pulping, a worthy magistrate somewhere in Scotland told his townsfolk that only two books were needed in any home—"Your Bible and your bank book." Why he didn't go the whole hog and say that any book other than a bank book was sheer luxury I can attribute only to the old Scottish superstition that the very paper on which a Bible is printed acquires a measure of holiness, yet the Scots have risen to greatness largely because of their readiness to follow a logical argument no matter where it leads them. I thought of that Scottish magistrate ("I'm no' a man, I'm a magistrate" is a historic Scots rebuke) when quite recently the English town of Stockton had the brilliant idea of dedicating a mile of old books to the Salvage drive, and the ceremony began with the Mayor's placing an old family Bible on the ground as the first item in the mile-long offering of his fellow-citizens. "Ma conscience!" must have exclaimed that Scottish magistrate if he ever heard of such sacrilege. Personally, I rejoiced at the liberal-mindedness that prompted this action. And I remembered with admiration an eminent Sunday-school worker of my acquaintance forty years ago who threatened to throw in the fire his housemaid's Bible because that lazy lassie spent too much of her time reading it instead of getting on with her housework. In an age when all sorts of stupid superstitions are again raising their once diminished heads it is worth emphasizing that no greater sacredness inheres in the actual printed paper of a Bible than in the printed pages of any other sort of book, so that when the family Bible is used to prop up a window-sash no irreverence should be attributed to the act. "For the letter killeth, but the spirit giveth life." If many old copies of the Bible found their way to the Salvage dumps it is more than probable that they were among the least soiled of those literary offerings, and the more welcome on that account.

A LITTLE lunch in wartime. Noted at a restaurant just a week before rationing. Lunchers: two very ordinary-looking persons, a young woman of no particular allure in an indeterminate dark blue uniform, youngish man, rather foreign ("if you know what I mean") in appearance. Began with cocktails or sherries (say 3s. each), melon 6s. each, half cold lobster, 7s. 6d. each, fresh peaches, 5s. 6d. each, coffee, and quite possibly brandies to follow, but I had to leave before they had attained to that joyous conclusion, though not without having seen them empty a large bottle of white burgundy (20s.). Total of lunch, including table money and ten per cent tip, minimum £3 14s.; if brandies followed, say £4 5s. 6d. A bit thick? Hence need for rationing.

THESE sour-stomached and self-appointed mentors of our statesmen, soldiers, sailors, airmen—these valiants of the pen who know everything, but, being internationally minded, suppress any impulse to encourage a belief in the modest merits of their more numerous but less intelligent fellow countrymen—have been doing their best in their gloomy little circles to belittle Britain's new effort in the air. To raid Cologne with a thousand planes in 90 minutes doesn't please them at all, at all, as they sip their weak tea and munch their buns in Bloomsbury byways. "With this technique, accuracy of aim must have been sacrificed to indiscriminate bombing," so moans a melancholic commentator in The New Statesman. The photographs taken by the R.A.F. to illustrate the results of their historic Cologne raid do not confirm this criticism of our bomber squadrons. From the same journalistic source Mr. Churchill can always get some sage advice on how to do his job.

DEAR MR. NEWSAGENT—I am afraid that you do not always read this postscript, and I am not altogether surprised, as I know how little time you have in these days of reduced staffs and increased pressure to get through with the trying task of distribution. But I should be glad if this brief note catches your attention, although it is no more than a repetition of one that appeared some months ago.

Our Publishing Department inform me that although I drew attention to the necessity for newsagents to avoid writing names and addresses of customers on the front page of THE WAR ILLUSTRATED, this habit is still too common. It makes no difference, of course, to subscribers who do not intend to have their fortnightly Parts bound into volume form, but it is a very undesirable practice from the point of view of the subscriber who collects the loose Parts for binding purposes, as the outer pages are now designed for binding in the volume and ought to be preserved as clean and spotless as possible. Indeed, it seems to me that a subscriber has the right to insist that his newsagent will in no case write his name and address in pencil on any part of the publication merely to suit his own convenience in distributing. A number of cases in which the address has actually been written in ink have also been reported and that seems to me quite inexcusable. Do please oblige our publishers by bearing this in mind.

Printed in England and published every alternate Friday by the Proprietors, The Amalgamated Press, Ltd., The Fleetway House, Farringdon Street, London, E.C.4. Registered for transmission by Canadian Magazine Post. Sole Agents for Australia and New Zealand: Messrs. Gordon & Gotch, Ltd.; and for South Africa: Central News Agency, Ltd. July 10, 1942. S.S. Editorial Address: JOHN CARPENTER HOUSE, WHITEFRIARS, LONDON, E.C.4.

AMERICA IN N. IRELAND : a sentry on board a U.S. destroyer which has put in at the great American naval base that has been constructed at Londonderry, second city of Northern Ireland. A year ago Magee's Fields, as the site was named locally, was a stretch of tufted and boggy pastureland; now, where only sheep used to roam, American ships engaged in the Battle of the Atlantic are repaired and refitted. Even before the base was officially finished ships put in for overhaul, the first arrival being the U.S. converted fishing schooner Albatross, on January 17. The Commandant, Capt. Larson, says: "Give us any ship that's in trouble, and we'll see it home." *Photo, Planet News*

ALONG THE BATTLE FRONTS

by Our Military Critic, Maj.-Gen. Sir Charles Gwynn, K.C.B., D.S.O.

THE defeat of the Eighth Army in Libya and its retreat far into Egypt was serious and alarming—all the more so because danger was unexpected. The Allied main bases in the Middle East, and in particular the chief base of our fleet in the Mediterranean at Alexandria were suddenly threatened. Not until Rommel, by July 5, was brought to a standstill at El Alamein, and Auchinleck had gained time for reinforcements to arrive, did the situation begin to clear. At the same time, the fall of Sevastopol in spite of its magnificent resistance, which had cost the enemy such heavy losses, represented Axis progress, liberating the troops employed in the siege.

The long-expected German offensive in Russia has opened, and after a slow start, in which it suffered heavy losses, it has had an alarming measure of success. When the Don was crossed and Voronezh reached in the first week of July, Timoshenko's southern armies, which bar the way to Caucasia, were in obvious danger.

In the Far East I am inclined to think that a Russo-Japanese War may be the next development, but the situation still remains somewhat obscure.

EGYPT After the fall of Tobruk it would have been courting further disaster for Auchinleck, with the depleted Eighth Army, to attempt to stand on the frontier against Rommel's greatly superior forces. There was no alternative but to withdraw with all speed to a position where reinforcements could most quickly reach him, and where Rommel's opportunities for enveloping manoeuvre would be reduced. Attempts to delay pursuit by taking up rearguard positions would have been highly dangerous against an enemy possessing speed of movement and the wide spaces of the desert in which to manoeuvre.

It was hoped that a stand to gain time might be made in Wavell's old defences at Mersa Matruh, a position which, on account of its good water supplies, it was important to deny to the enemy. But the speed and

'AUK' AT THE FRONT. On June 25 Gen. Auchinleck decided to assume command personally of the 8th Army in succession to Gen. Ritchie. His Battle H.Q. is, it will be seen, a covered lorry.
Photo, British Official: Crown Copyright

strength of Rommel's pursuit gave no time for the reorganization of the position or for the arrival of adequate reinforcements. The attempted stand might easily have led to catastrophe but for the magnificent fight of the battle-experienced and fresh New Zealand division.

Further retreat was necessary to El Alamein, where the coastal plain is at its narrowest and where outflanking movements are confined by the marshy Qattara depression. To El Alamein reinforcements and supplies had shorter distances to travel, and another joint was added to Rommel's immensely long line of communications.

Auchinleck had not left the pursuer entirely unopposed, but the opposition offered was mobile, not static. Small fast-moving "Jock" columns harassed the enemy, striking, as opportunity offered, at his supply services and flanking detachments. The R.A.F., too, redoubled their attacks to cause the maximum amount of damage and delay. Delay probably was slight, but damage inflicted was bound to reduce the enemy's residual strength and power of manoeuvre which called for great expenditure of petrol.

The retreat was evidently a difficult and critical operation, and quite apart from any question of General Ritchie's competence, Auchinleck was no doubt right to assume direct command himself. It was a situation in which the Commander had to be solely responsible for every decision and the one who could give orders for movements of reinforcements. It was not a situation which admitted consultation, explanations, or calls for help.

Mr. Churchill has told us that Rommel's offensive was primarily a forestalling operation, and although I did not know we were preparing for a summer offensive, I had from the first believed that was its intention.

The intensified attacks on Malta had indicated, of course, that Rommel was being heavily reinforced, but their slackening off before he struck suggested that he had no far-reaching object in view. It seemed more probable that he aimed only at defeating Ritchie's army and driving it back across the frontier, thereby making his own position secure during the period in which all available Axis resources would be needed in Russia. That Rommel was prepared to exploit success to the utmost is characteristic of the man, but he certainly carried exploitation to the point of risk. The doubtful factor was whether he was relying on the cooperation of a Crete-based, airborne force to which, when he closed on Egypt, he would be able to give fighter protection that could not be provided from Crete. I confess I felt anxiety on this point, especially when it appeared that Rommel was husbanding his Luftwaffe reserves and not disputing to the utmost the air superiority of the R.A.F. This certainly suggested that he might be keeping them for cooperation with an airborne attack. Reports that the Cretan force had been transferred to Russia could not be relied on, and no doubt the threat it implied must have affected Auchinleck's dispositions.

That Rommel arrived at El Alamein with troops nearing exhaustion and having

LOADING A TANK with refilled machine-gun belts—a frequent scene in the battle in the Western Desert. On June 15 the 8th Army lost 230 tanks out of the 300 engaged.
Photo, British Official: Crown Copyright

suffered from air attacks is evident. Auchinleck's seizure of opportunities for counter-attack immediately was therefore obviously right.

Rommel naturally attacked without hesitation what he believed to be a badly-shaken army, but he was in a better condition to deal with hastily-organized static defences than to conduct the battle of rapid manoeuvre which Auchinleck imposed on him. To take advantage of the enemy's exhaustion and limited immediately-available supplies, and not merely to stop him, was clearly Auchinleck's policy.

The R.A.F. and S.A.A.F. cooperation was altogether admirable, and evidently their direct intervention in the battle had a most heartening effect on our tired troops as well as achieving concrete results.

RUSSIA With the evacuation of Sevastopol on July 3 ended one of the most glorious sieges in history. Seldom or never has a fortress been subjected to such prolonged and intensive assaults or to assaults backed with such a weight of armament.

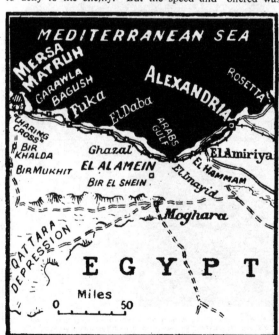

BATTLE OF ALEXANDRIA. Here is the battleground where the fate of Egypt may well be decided. Particularly fierce was the fighting near El Alamein, where there is a gap of only 45 miles between the Mediterranean and the Qattara depression. *Courtesy of The Daily Telegraph*

Seldom, too, has the resistance of the besieged served so valuable a strategic purpose, contributing as it did to delay, weaken, and disarrange the German plans for a great offensive.

That offensive has now been launched on the central and southern sectors, but the maintenance of its energy and ultimate scope may be affected by the costly preliminary operations necessitated by the Russian resistance at Kerch and Sevastopol and by Timoshenko's forestalling Kharkov offensive. Kerch and Sevastopol caused delays and cost the Germans a heavy price, and it took three major counter-attacks to drive Timoshenko from the threatening position he had won. The third did succeed, by crossing the Upper Donetz, in establishing a starting line for a major offensive on this part of the front, but Timoshenko has regrouped his troops behind the Oskol river and is ready to meet attack. It seems almost certain, however, that the main German thrust will be delivered farther south, with the Donetz basin and Rostov as immediate objectives, but with the ultimate aim of cutting off the Red Army from its vital oil sources in the Caucasus.

The offensives which have opened in the Kursk and Bielgorod regions north of Kharkov have succeeded in attaining their object of establishing a footing across the Don and of interrupting Russian lateral railway communications between Moscow and Rostov in order to protect the main thrust, when it is delivered, from counter-attack on its left flank. The attack delivered at Gzhatsk at the head of the salient pointing towards Moscow appears to have been on a smaller scale, and may have been intended mainly to imply a threat to the capital which would compel the retention of large Russian reserves to ensure its security. None of these last three offensives has met with the immediate initial success which almost always was achieved by German thrusts last year. Only after heavy fighting and by reckless expenditure of Panzer troops did the Kursk offensive result in a breakthrough.

The opening phases of the German offensive have certainly been of a very different order from those of last year which were marked by deep Panzer penetrations and Russian retreats. A period of hard slogging, close-range fighting appears to be probable in which the Russians are in no way inferior to their opponents. The Germans, however, still retain the initiative, and though their strength has undoubtedly diminished they can, with the advantages of the initiative, mass for attack at selected points. Their main offensive may not yet even have started, and when it does one must

RUSSIAN FRONT, illustrating in particular the direction of Von Bock's drive between Kursk and Kharkov against Voronezh and the Don. *By courtesy of The Times*

expect that it will be made with maximum violence and with great reserves to maintain its impetus. The liberation of considerable forces from the Crimean theatre may have been awaited in order to strengthen the reserves of the main blow.

On the whole, the situation is not too discouraging. Last year the Germans were strong enough to carry out offensives with three different geographical objectives—Leningrad, Moscow, and the Ukraine industrial areas, with Moscow as the chief. This year it seems probable that, initially at least, the main offensive will be in the south, combined with a holding offensive on the Moscow front ; and that on the Leningrad front the Germans will remain strategically on the defensive, content merely to hold their positions investing the city.

That Russia will prove even stronger and more determined than last year is evident,

and she may be expected to retain general air superiority—though not to an extent that would prevent the Germans achieving temporary local superiority at their selected places.

FAR EAST There was a marked lull in Far East operations during the fortnight ending July 8.

In Burma, owing to supply difficulties during the wet season, the Japanese have been compelled to withdraw their advanced troops to areas with railways and good roads. The threat of invasion of India by land is in consequence temporarily removed.

The whole situation is one for speculation rather than for comment on events, and speculation must be confined to courses open to the enemy. My own opinion is that, in view of her naval losses, Japan cannot risk further ambitious amphibious enterprises under existing circumstances ; and that if she had contemplated major amphibious attacks on India or Australia they must be abandoned or postponed, especially as both countries have been heavily reinforced. This would leave the bulk of the Japanese Army uncommitted. How could she use it ?

Part of it she is using to secure control of the airfields in China from which her home bases might be attacked, but is she likely to use her whole surplus strength in an attempt to crush Chiang Kai-shek while his supply lines are cut ? In spite of what some Japanese spokesmen are reported to have said, I think it improbable. Japan has already learnt that even when Chiang was weakest his complete destruction evaded her. China under present circumstances, except in the matter of airfields, is no immediate threat to Japan ; and her future depends on the progress of the Allied cause as a whole.

On the other hand, Japan has shown how sensitive she is for the security of her home bases against air attack, and Vladivostok remains a potential danger. While Russia is engaged in her struggle with Germany and the Japanese Army is not largely committed, there is surely an apparent opportunity for eliminating the danger, while at the same time assisting her confederate in the World War. There are reports that Japan is reinforcing her Manchurian army, and I confess the main factors in the strategical situation make me credit them. Japan's Aleutian enterprise would seem to be directed against Russia as much as against the U.S.A. The positions Japan has won in the south have gone far to prevent direct assistance being given to Russia by her allies should she be attacked. Japan must husband her naval and air resources for the defence of her gains, but it is on them rather than her army that she relies for retaining the positions won.

IN THE KHARKOV SECTOR fierce fighting continues between Timoshenko's Red Army and Von Bock's Hitlerites, as the Russians style their enemy. Here are two photographs radioed from the battle-front. That on the left shows two Red Army men waiting with deadly concentration the approach of the enemy ; powerful "tank-bursting" machine-gun, grenades and Molotov cocktails are all ready to give the foe appropriate greeting. Then the second photograph is of a number of German soldiers holding their helmets and arms high in the air in token of surrender to the Red Army tank detachment occupying the foreground. *Photo, British Official: Crown Copyright*

Rommel's Tanks Speed Across the Desert

IN LIBYA, some of the Axis "armour" comes under heavy fire. Right, below, Field-Marshal Rommel—the General received his promotion on the morrow of his storming of the British stronghold of Tobruk—and the Italian General Bastico conferring before the battle.

AXIS TANKS, spread out in battle formation over the undulating sand, give the appearance of battleships as they go into action. Above, German anti-tank gun waiting for the arrival of British tanks. The Afrika Korps is well equipped with anti-tank guns—5 and 4 centimetres and 88 mm. (3·46 in.). The last, originally an anti-aircraft weapon, fires a 20 lb. shell at the rate of 15 to 20 rounds a minute.

Photos. Keystone, Associated Press

Britons in Action in the Battle of Egypt

GEN. SIR C. AUCHINLECK, C.-in-C. in the Middle East, takes the salute from some of the 750,000 men under his command.

OUTSIDE MERSA MATRUH, British gunners, stripped to the waist, are seen in action under fire. Mersa Matruh was evacuated on June 29. The photo was radioed from the battle zone.

IN EGYPT, British infantry patrols on reconnaissance in the shade of a group of palm trees. Right, linesman of the Royal Corps of Signals repairing telephone and telegraph lines, broken by enemy fire or the stress of weather, in the Western Desert.

Help for India!   The Convoy Makes Port

The biggest convoy ever to leave Britain, consisting of some of the most famous liners belonging to the United Nations, arrives off India, laden with troops and equipment for the defence of the Empire—a wonderful effort in organization and courage.

Coming down to solid earth after weeks on the rolling wave, a group of British soldiers avail themselves of a dockside crane.

INDIA AT LAST, after the long and perilous voyage. Troops lining the decks of one of the largest ships. Right, Indians taking an interest in one of the tanks which, with a great number of planes and guns, were disembarked at various ports.

Photos. G.P.U.

How the 'Herrenvolk' Treat the Poles

THE NEW ORDER OF DAMNATION, such is the literal truth of the Herrenvolk idea, now applied to German-occupied territory in Europe. You either become slaves to the execrable German race, are treated like cattle and lose your identity as human beings, or you protest and suffer torture or death or both. In the photograph above a crowd of men and women from Poland and Russia are about to be transported to Germany as forced labourers. At the top of the page, left, two Poles suspected of sabotage (one has obviously been struck in the face) are under escort ; and right, a suspect is undergoing a brutal third degree.

PAGE 71   *Photos, Polish Ministry of Information, Associated Press*

THE WAR IN THE AIR

by Capt. Norman Macmillan, M.C., A.F.C.

DURING the period Saturday, June 20, to Friday, July 3, 1942, air power played an important part in the operations in Libya and the Crimea.

The trend of contemporary British thought was dominated by the defeat of the British Eighth Army in Libya, the fall of Tobruk on June 21 after a 26-hours' assault, and the subsequent retreat of the British Imperial Forces eastward from the Libya-Egypt frontier, past Mersa Matruh, to its stand 65 miles west of Alexandria for the beginning of the second great battle with Marshal Rommel's forces at El Alamein on July 2.

The importance of the outcome of this battle for Alexandria was enhanced by the evacuation of Sevastopol by the Russians on July 3 after a siege lasting nearly 8 months.

It is impossible at such close historical range to disentangle all the components which go to the making of victory or defeat in a particular battle, but just as the development of modern weapons has placed in the hands of generals the power of swift concentration of instruments of war with great destructive properties, so a general, to achieve success. must not only employ his own weapons with superlative precision of timing, but must deny the use of a proportion of equivalent weapons to the enemy.

These principles were applied by the Germans in the fifth battle of Libya and in the siege and capture of Sevastopol. In each case air power was used to obtain the desired object, but its application was in the one case indirect, and, in the other, direct.

The strategic setting of the two battles was similar. The contesting armies fought close to the seaboard. It was thus possible for all three arms of war to be engaged in active operations. The conditions were ideal for the employment of the speed, hitting power, and mobility of the air weapon.

The Russians and the United Nations each possessed surface sea superiority in the Black Sea and the Eastern Mediterranean respectively. At sea the smaller surface forces which opposed them were supported by submarines and air forces. In each case the superiority in surface sea power was unavailing against the combined pressure of all arms of the enemy. Both actions show that surface sea power does not possess the quality it formerly had of applying tremendous pressure upon an enemy and his lines of supply. As the range of guns has not altered appreciably during the past 25 years, the cause of the altered position of sea power must be ascribed to the development of air power.

This new situation in war was recognized by the United States within six months of her entry into the war, and the decision was taken during the period under review to build no more U.S. battleships at present, but to concentrate instead upon aircraft-carriers, aircraft, cruisers and smaller vessels (*See* p. 86).

Brigadier-General William Mitchell, Assistant Chief of the Army Air Service of the United States, was regraded to the substantive rank of Colonel in consequence of his too open advocacy of air power in the summer of 1925. Six months later he was out of the army for good, deprived of rank, after a court-martial which tried him following his issue of a public statement which upheld his views in strong terms. This year the United States Government restored his rank, and posthumously (he died in 1936) promoted him to the rank of General. The type of bomber which first bombed Tokyo is called the " Mitchell."

The United States had to learn the lessons of Pearl Harbour, Wake Island, the battles of the Coral Sea and Midway Island, the fall of Malaya and Burma to re-cast their decision on the battleship-building programme. Now they are determined to possess " a terrific concentration of air striking power over the oceans."

Air striking power over the water played a considerable part in the German successes in Libya and the Crimea.

IN my previous commentary (*see* p. 40) I described the battle of the British convoys in the Mediterranean and pointed out how, even in the middle of a major land battle, Rommel had no hesitation in disengaging air power from immediate tactical employment in the field to prevent our convoys from running their full supplies to Malta.

If our convoys got to Malta, Rommel's own convoys would be imperilled in their trans-Mediterranean journeys to his bases.

We had air superiority over the battlefield. But Rommel had air superiority over the Central Mediterranean zone—in Libya, Tripoli, Sicily, Italy, Greece and Crete. The result of the action showed that Rommel had air superiority in the strategic sense, while our superiority was tactical. The lesson for

BOSTON BOMBER being bombed up by its South African ground crew prior to taking off for another raid. S.A.A.F. planes have valiantly supported the R.A.F. in Libya.

the future is that air supremacy—not simply local superiority—is the prime air power consideration in this war.

AIR supremacy includes the enjoyment of air bases. Rommel's victory at Gazala caused our Army to retreat, and with its retreat the R.A.F. lost its airfields. Tobruk was left without air cover. The German Stuka dive-bombers could operate unmolested. They drove the first breach in the defences of Tobruk.

Air power and secure air bases are synonymous terms. Air power is at its best in offensive action. It is less effective during retreat. This has been proved time and again during the past 25 years. The one shining exception was the Battle of Britain, wherein the conditions were exceptional.

During the siege of Sevastopol the Russian sea communications were constantly imperilled by German air power. The Germans possessed better air bases for action against the fortress city than the defenders, who were, in the later stages; beleaguered. The Germans used their air power to pound the Russian communications and positions ; in these circumstances the Russians put up a stout defence. Here the tale is the same story of the enemy's possession of superior strategic air bases.

There is a twofold lesson to be learned from these tragic defeats. It is that the strategic disposition of air power is even more important than its tactical employment. The second follows from the first, but the first does not follow from the second. Dispositions of all forces must therefore take into primary consideration the disposition of air forces. Norway, Greece, Crete, and now Libya all fell because tactical air defence was attempted without strategic air strength.

IN the air war against Germany, Emden and Bremen were the principal targets : Emden, a port for the intake of iron ore from the Baltic en route to the Ruhr ; Bremen, producer-city of submarines and trans-ocean aircraft. Bremen was the target for our third 1,000-bomber raid, concentrated into one hour and a quarter on the night of June 25, followed by additional raids on the nights of June 27 and 29 and July 2.

If we take the war out of the realm of the localized battlefields, and regard it as a world war, it will be seen that these raids on German industry are in a still greater sense just what Rommel did in the Mediterranean. Indeed, it can be said (although we have not yet got all our strength together by any means) that our strategy is even more widely placed than Germany's. The official announcement that United States bomber squadrons will soon operate with ours from the United Kingdom in the war against Germany is further evidence of a world strategy which should mean that this is Hitler's last year of opportunity for victory.

SHOT DOWN IN THE DESERT, this German Messerschmitt Me 110 long-range two-seater fighter is one of the Nazis' many casualties in their conflict with the air forces of Britain and South Africa. " Here at home," said Mr. Churchill in a telegram to Air Chief Marshal Tedder, " we are all watching with enthusiasm the brilliant, supreme exertions of the Royal Air Force in the battle now proceeding in Egypt."

Photos, British Official: Crown Copyright

Today Britain Too Has Glider Troops

Oval, an R.A.F. instructor with an Army pupil in the cockpit of a glider. Top left, glider about to land gliding over another on the ground.

A FLIGHT OF GLIDERS flying in formation towed by training aircraft. Right, above, a glider seen from the towing aeroplane. The Glider Training School is now an essential part of army mechanization. Airborne troops take a course in glider flying under the supervision of R.A.F. pilots. It was in the Battle of Crete that gliders were first used on any large scale. For invasion tactics the glider has advantages in that troops can be dropped near their objective.

Photos, P.N.A., G.P.U.

Now the W.A.A.F. Is Three Years Old

Prior to large-scale bombing operations, the W.A.A.F.s are more than usually busy folding parachutes.

W.A.A.F. driver wishes "Good luck" to the bomber crew whom she has driven to the dispersal point.

CUTTING THE CAKE on the occasion of the recent W.A.A.F. birthday celebrations is Air Commandant K. J. Trefusis Forbes, while the cooks look on. Right, members of the W.A.A.F. filling vacuum flasks and packing rations for bomber crews in readiness for night operations. In the circle, a W.A.A.F. radio-operator contacting R.A.F. crews during the third four-figure raid over enemy territory—to Bremen on June 25, 1942. These photographs were taken on the W.A.A.F.'s third birthday.

Photos, British Official; L.N.A., G.P.U.

In West Africa the R.A.F. Build an Aerodrome

Hurricane fighter being wheeled on to an aerodrome somewhere in West Africa. Only a short time ago this site was indistinguishable from the tropical jungle which still encompasses it on every side.

Beneath, West African head-quarters of a Royal Air Force flying boat squadron, and flying boat and marine craft base. The hut has been called Piccadilly as a reminder of London town. Under the mosquito net, which has been tied up, an officer is enjoying a book and a pipe of tobacco in between spells of duty.

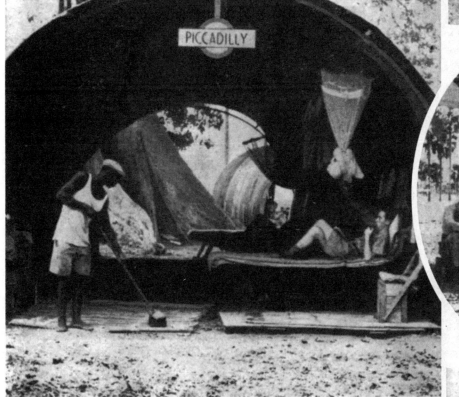

WEST AFRICANS clearing the bush to extend the aerodrome, under supervision of the adjutant (right). Oval, a ground crew sheltering from the tropical heat under the wing of a bomber.

Here, at this West African outpost, men of the R.A.F., working with reconnaissance bombers, flying boats and fighter squadrons, are doing an important job. The heat is terrific and comforts are few, but these remote defenders of freedom manage to keep cheerful and healthy.

Photos, British Official: Crown Copyright

America's Naval Base in Northern Ireland

U.S. NAVY police squad leaving their ship at the great new American Naval base at Londonderry, in Northern Ireland. Below, U.S. Marines changing guard.

The Londonderry base was built by 800 American technicians, members of the Naval Civil Engineering Corps mostly, assisted by about 2,000 local workers. The contract was signed on June 12, 1941 ; the first shipload of material arrived from across the Atlantic on July 8, work began on August 1, and on February 5 this year the base was officially declared in commission.

Capt. W. J. LARSON, Commandant of the base ; he is a veteran of the U.S. Queenstown base in the last war. Beneath, U.S. sailors scrubbing hammock covers on the quay.

Back to their ship after shore leave. American bluejackets stationed at Londonderry have won widespread popularity in Ulster.

Photos, Fox, Planet News

Here's Luck to the U.S. Forces in England

THE FOX

OVER HERE, a quartette of the advanced units of the vast force which the United States is sending to Britain in readiness to take part in the European theatre of war, enjoy a glass of English ale at the sign of the Fox, a typical English inn somewhere in the country. Mine host and hostess are glad to welcome, as we all are, these men from the great American Republic.   *Photo, P.N.A.*

Egypt: Between the Desert and the 'Ditch'

Only a day or two after the storming of Tobruk, Rommel swept across the frontier into Egypt with a view to securing those supreme prizes, Alexandria on the Nile delta, and the Suez Canal. In this article we present some facts necessary for an understanding of the new battle-zone.

THE land of Egypt! For thousands of years it has been the battleground of empires, the scene of conflicts which have decided the fate of the world for many a hundred years. Conqueror after conqueror has stood on the banks of the Nile and in the shadow of the pyramids—colossal erections, yet not so colossal as the pride of the Pharaohs which caused them to be built out of the rock, cemented by human sweat and tears and blood. Alexander and Caesar, Saladin and Napoleon—they have come, had their little day, and have gone. Time after time, through age after age,

> While the dark shades of forty ages stood
> Like startled giants by Nile's famous flood;
> Or from the pyramid's tall pinnacle
> Beheld the desert peopled, as from hell,
> With clashing hosts, who strew'd the barren sand.

Now once again Egypt is the cockpit of warring armies. Once more, as Rommel's armoured columns forge ahead through the green ribbon. Of those 16 millions Cairo, the capital, claims nearly a million and a half; the great port of Alexandria has a population of about 700,000, and Port Said about 125,000. Another three-quarters of a million or so have their homes in more or less urban areas, but for the rest the people are country-dwellers or *fellahin*, who are engaged as their fathers have been engaged since before history began in cultivating the intricate patchwork of fields carved out of the mud deposited by the Nile. As often as not, their agricultural methods are so primitive as to recall those pictured on the walls of the ancient tombs, but the fellah of today enjoys one advantage denied his ancestors in the shape of the magnificent system of artificial irrigation which British administrators and engineers have given to Egypt. British Imperialism could wish for no better monument than the great dam at Aswan, which bottles up and conserves the flow of water

signed in 1936, provides for the use of Egyptian communications by Britain in time of war, and also recognizes her special interests in the defence of the Suez Canal zone. This zone runs from Port Said to Suez, a distance of about a hundred miles. It is only two hundred yards wide, yet within it contains a full-gauge railway, a first-class high road, one of the most important and most used of the world's electric cables, sweet water conduits—and the Canal.

OPENED in 1869, the Suez Canal is the property of a French company, the *Compagnie Universelle du Canal Maritime de Suez*, which has its head office in Paris at 1, Rue d'Astorg. In normal times it is controlled by a board of management consisting of thirty-two administrators—nineteen French, ten British (three appointed by the Government and seven by the shipowning interests), two Egyptian, and one Dutch. The majority of the shares are in French hands, but the British Government owns the largest single block of shares—295,000 out of 652,000. Its holding was originally acquired in 1875, when Disraeli made a spectacular deal with a spendthrift Khedive; the purchase price was £4 million, and it has been stated that more than £40 millions has been received in interest, while just before the war the shares were included in our national balance-sheet at £32 millions.

Britain is not only the largest individual shareholder in the Canal, but British vessels are the most numerous of those making use of it. Thus of the 5,277 ships which went through the Canal in 1929, 2,627 were British; next in order came Italy, the Netherlands, Germany, France, Norway and Greece, and so on down to China's one.

But though the Company is an international concern, though its management is predominantly French, in this present time of war the Canal is under the complete control of the British Empire. The zone from end to end is one great military camp, just as it was in the last war, when it was threatened from the east front—not as today from the west; there was one day in February 1915 when the Turks actually reached the further bank of the Canal. Theoretically the Canal, in accordance with the terms of its charter, is open to the ships of all nations in wartime as in time of peace; theoretically there is nothing to prevent German ships, Italian and Japanese ships from making the passage—nothing save the existence at either end of British naval forces. The banks are controlled by the Egyptian Camel Corps; anti-aircraft guns are spaced throughout the Canal's length, and at entrance and exit a great boom is let down each night to prevent the passage of submarines. A close watch is kept for mines, and every ship making the passage is rigorously searched. From the air the Canal is not particularly vulnerable since it has no locks to be put out of action; the chief dangers to be guarded against are sabotage, air-sown mines, and a vessel sunk by design or accident across the fairway.

Port Said, at the northern end of the Canal, has (as was said above) a population of 125,000; facing it across the Canal is Port Fuad, where are the headquarters of the Canal administration. Near the middle of the Canal is Ismailia, standing on the fine road which runs beside the "ditch" from end to end; here are situated the headquarters of the Canal Brigade of the British Army, the Naval authorities, and the Egyptian Military Governor. Then at the southern end is Suez, a dirty and dilapidated Arab town of some 50,000 population, connected by a causeway with the Egyptian garden city of Port Tewfik. **E. ROYSTON PIKE**

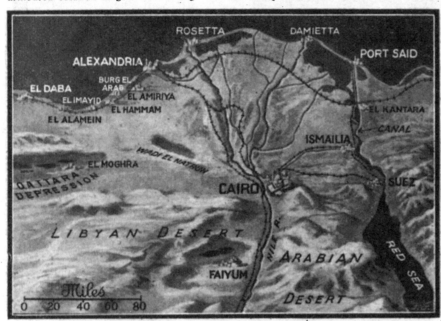

ALEXANDRIA—CAIRO—SUEZ. Although Egypt is some six hundred miles long, measuring from the Mediterranean to the Sudan border, and covers an area of 383,000 square miles—more than six times the size of England and Wales—all that matters is the Nile Valley, the Delta and the adjacent Suez Canal zone. This map, indeed, covers the most thickly populated and politically and commercially important regions. *Specially drawn for* THE WAR ILLUSTRATED *by Félix Gardon*

billowing clouds of dust to meet Auchinleck's "battle groups," the desert is peopled with "clashing hosts as from hell." But the conflict of today is of a size and character that would have staggered even Byron's genius to describe. He wrote of an Age of Bronze: we live in an age of steel and oil.

What sort of a place is this land of Egypt? It is a country born of a river and sustained by a river; and without that river it would soon fail to be distinguished from the sterile desert which bounds it on east and west.

BUT that region—the Nile valley, that is, with the Delta behind Alexandria where the great river broadens out and forms many a branch to meet the Mediterranean—is but a fraction of what the geographers call Egypt, is only some 13,000 square miles out of a total area of 383,000 square miles. Yet it comprises practically all the settled area. For the rest Egypt is a collection of deserts—the Libyan (dotted here and there at vast intervals with oases), the Arabian, and Sinai.

As might be expected, most of Egypt's 16 million people live in the Nile valley; only a few thousand Arabs make their homes in the oases and in the dreary and desolate region which lies on either side of the Nile's

born of the snows in the Abyssinian highlands, so that the superabundance of one season may compensate for the lack of the next. Wheat, barley and maize, rice and sugar cane, beans and onions are among the principal crops; and the production of cotton has assumed increasing importance.

Old as Egypt is, it is one of the most juvenile of modern states. From the day when Cleopatra killed herself to avoid shameful exposure in Caesar's triumph to only recently, Egypt formed part of the succession of empires which have ruled along the Mediterranean fringe. The British went there in 1882, although Egypt was nominally included in the realms of the Sultan of Turkey until 1914, when, following Turkey's entry into the war against us, a British protectorate over the country was proclaimed, and the pro-Turk khedive was deposed, and an Egyptian prince given the title of Sultan of Egypt. The protectorate came to an end in 1922, whereupon the Sultan was proclaimed king; the present sovereign is his son, King Faruk I, a young man of twenty-two. But although Egypt has her independence, Britain occupies a privileged position in the country, since the Anglo-Egyptian Treaty of Alliance,

War Comes to the Land of Egypt

With the fall of Tobruk and Mersa Matruh, Rommel's way lay open for the battle of Egypt. So once again the Pyramids, ancient when Europe was peopled by barbaric tribes, look out on mortal strife as R.A.F. bombers pass to and fro with their loads of death. In the larger photograph Egyptian sentries are patrolling the frontier between Egypt and Libya.

Britain's Life-Line of Empire

1. From Port Said to Suez runs for a hundred miles the Suez Canal ; this is a typical stretch.
2. Egyptian gunners, part of the Canal's defences. 3. An aerial view of the Canal, which runs dead straight from Port Said as far as Ismailia at the entrance to the Bitter Lakes. The minimum width is 196 ft. 10 in. and the maximum draught allowed for ships is 34 ft.

Photos, Mrs
Pop

Wartime Glimpses of the Suez Canal

The Anglo-Egyptian Treaty of Alliance of 1936 provided for the defence of the Canal by joint British and Egyptian forces; in (4) is seen an Egyptian anti-tank gun in the desert beside the " ditch."   5. At Port Said is this statue of Ferdinand de Lesseps, the French diplomatist and engineer who built the Canal. 6. Another view of the Canal.

These Names Spell the Egypt of Today

With the invasion of Egypt, Cairo (seat of British G.H.Q.) assumed an ever more martial aspect; this photo shows an Egyptian Bren-gun post at a bridge approach. Alexandria, Britain's great naval base in the Eastern Mediterranean, is the subject of the upper photograph. "Alex" is also Egypt's chief commercial port.

Do We Yet Know Why We Lost Tobruk?

While the news of the Tobruk disaster was still fresh in men's minds the House of Commons debated a motion of censure on Mr. Churchill's Government. On the second day the motion was rejected by 475 votes to 25; but the result did not dispel the disquiet with which the course of the campaign in the Western Desert was watched.

WHY did Tobruk fall? Why, seven months after Mr. Churchill declared that in Libya "this is the first time we have met the Germans at least equally well armed and equipped," and six months after he told the House of Commons that General Auchinleck had set out to destroy the entire armed forces of the Germans and Italians in Cyrenaica, " and I am bound to say that it seems probable that he will do so," —why after these hopeful expressions should there so soon come a time when the Imperial Forces in the Western Desert were in full retreat and Egypt and the Suez Canal were definitely threatened by Rommel's swift-moving panzers? These were some of the questions put by M.P.s in the debate which took place in the first two days of July. They were answered, but only in part.

None seems to have been more surprised than Mr. Churchill at the swift reversal of fortune in the Libyan battle. The fall of Tobruk, with its garrison of about 25,000 men, in a single day, was utterly unexpected—unexpected not only by the House and the public at large but by the War Cabinet, the Chiefs of the Staff, by General Auchinleck and the High Command in the Middle East.

"On the night before its capture we received a telegram from General Auchinleck that he had allotted what he believed to be an adequate garrison, that the defences were in good order, and that 90 days' supplies were available for the troops."

Mr. Churchill heard the news in Washington, where he had arrived on June 18 to consult with President Roosevelt on the prosecution of the war.

"When on the morning of Sunday the 21st I went into the President's room, I was greatly shocked to be confronted with a report that Tobruk had fallen. I found it difficult to believe, but a few minutes later my own telegram, forwarded from London, arrived. I hope the House will realize what a bitter pang this was to me. . . ."

A few moments later Mr. Churchill revealed that the opposing armies drawn up in the desert in the middle of May numbered about 100,000 a side: more exactly, Ritchie had 100,000 men and Rommel 90,000, of whom 50,000 were Germans. We had a superiority in the numbers of tanks (though not, it transpired, in quality) of perhaps 7 to 5. We had a superiority in artillery of nearly 8 to 5. Throughout the battle our army enjoyed superiority in the air. Lastly, we had better and shorter lines of communication than the enemy.

Even after the fall of Bir Hacheim on June 10 the battle was equal, but on June 13 there came a change.

"On that morning we had about 300 tanks in action, and by nightfall no more than 70 remained, excluding the light Stuart tanks ; and all this happened without any corresponding loss having been inflicted on the enemy . . . with this disproportionate destruction of our armour Rommel became decisively the stronger."

After a reference to the " many evil consequences that] followed inevitably on this one day's fighting," Mr. Churchill made it clear that the army in Libya had been overpowered and driven back not because of any conscious or wilful grudging of reinforcements in men or material. During the last two years, he announced, more than 950,000 men had been sent to the Middle East theatre of war, together with 4,500 tanks, 6,000 aircraft, nearly 5,000 pieces of artillery, 50,000 machine-guns and over 100,000 mechanical vehicles. And this at a time when we were not only threatened with invasion at home but, during the latter part, were sending large supplies to Russia.

Mr. Churchill spoke at the end of the debate. The other Government spokesman, Mr. Lyttelton, spoke almost at the beginning, in reply to the proposers of the censure motion, Sir John Wardlaw-Milne and Sir Roger Keyes. The critics alleged that so far from answering the indictment he made a speech for the prosecution.

Dismal indeed was the picture drawn by the Minister of Production. A tank engaged in the Libyan fighting was the Crusader. " And what a tank ! " some of his hearers must have murmured as Mr. Lyttelton went on to say that it was unreliable and unsuitable for desert conditions. There was something incorrigibly wrong with the fan-driving assembly, so that the cooling system broke down. The traverse of the gun was interfered with if the lid of the secondary turret was up, and the driver's vision was

GUEST OF HONOUR. *From a cartoon by ZEC ; Courtesy of The Daily Mirror*

too limited. Moreover—well-nigh incredible this—" the turret was too small for the man of ordinary physique." For the rest, Mr. Lyttelton could promise that new and better tanks and guns were under production and would be delivered in due course ; while, as for dive-bombers, the orders were placed by Lord Beaverbrook in June 1940 and deliveries were now being received. " Some dive-bombers have already reached one theatre of war and others are on their way."

Almost without exception every speaker in the debate was critical to a greater or lesser degree. The newspapers throughout the country were even more condemnatory, whether in their " leaders " or in the reports they published from their correspondents at the front. The Daily Telegraph published a striking article, " By a Correspondent recently returned from Libya." According to this writer, there was no disposition to take the initiative. The whole idea was to wait for Rommel and see what he did. " Let Rommel and his Afrika Korps do all the hard work in the summer months under the

blazing sun, in blinding dust storms "—this, he said, reflected the attitude of those Staff Officers with whom he conversed when he suggested that Rommel might not wait until the cool of the autumn. There were almost two armies in the Middle East, he went on, the Army of the Desert and the army in Cairo ; and he quoted the favourite wisecrack : " If Rommel gets to the Pyramids and G.H.Q. turns out in its own defence, for the first time in his career Rommel will be outnumbered." Rommel was able to act more swiftly because he was unorthodox : he even sent out his orders " in clear," thus avoiding waste of time in de-coding.

Writing in the same issue, Christopher Buckley, The Daily Telegraph's Special Correspondent with the 8th Army, roundly declared that " some part of our defeat must be attributed to the tendency still existing to place officers in important commands over armoured units, whose chief qualification has been cavalry experience."

This point was elaborated by Major Oliver Stewart in The Evening Standard. " This is," he said, " a war of motoring ; motoring by land and sea and air. It is not blood and tears we want, but grease and oil. Field-Marshal Rommel is a great motorist. Opposing him are great fox-hunters, or great traditional soldiers—men of sterling courage, ready at a moment's notice to have their heads blown off, longing for the tremendous clash of battle between equally matched forces, but not ingenious, not mechanics. not engineers. . . ."

And here, to conclude, is a passage from the speech made on the second day of the debate by Mr. Aneurin Bevan. " This is a proud and brave race," he said, " and it is feeling humiliated. It cannot stand the holding out of Sevastopol for months and the collapse of Tobruk in 26 hours . . . It wants leadership. It is getting words . . . This nation can win, but it must be properly led, it must be properly inspired, and it must have confidence in its military leadership. Give us that and we can win the War . . .'

Sevastopol's Epic of Imperishable Glory

During the Crimean War, not quite ninety years ago, Sevastopol made history when for a year it withstood the assault of the combined armies of Britain, France and Turkey. Now a second siege of Sevastopol has ended. But Sevastopol's name and fame will live as an inspiration for generations to come.

"SEVASTOPOL has fallen." From Hitler's headquarters came the news in a special announcement on the evening of July 1.

"The German and Rumanian war flags have been hoisted on the fortress, town and harbour," went on the announcement. "German and Rumanian troops, commanded by Col.-Gen. von Mannstein, effectively supported by the air corps commanded by Col.-Gen. von Richthofen, mastered at noon today the strongest land and sea fortress in the world after 25 days' bitter fighting. Strong forts, fortifications built into rock and underground positions, concrete and earth bunkers, and innumerable field entrenchments were taken in exemplary collaboration between the two armies. The number of prisoners and amount of booty cannot yet be estimated. The remnants of the beaten Sevastopol army fled to the Khersonese Peninsula. They are being pressed together into a small area, and face destruction."

More details of the Russians' "last desperate defence" were contained in a statement issued by the German High Command.

"Dive-bombers opened the way for infantry through the positions in and around Nikolayevska. Heavy bombs, dropped from a low altitude, tore terrific blocks from the rock walls, which buried large parts of the Russian trenches. A similar effect was obtained by bombing the entrances to rock tunnels, thus silencing enemy batteries which were too well concealed for the German artillery. The destruction caused in the inner town of Sevastopol by previous German attacks was increased during yesterday. Barracks, railway depots and electricity and gas works went up in flames. Ships at anchor in the harbour were hit during the raid and several of them were sunk."

Sevastopol's siege began in November 1941, when von Mannstein's troops overran the Crimean peninsula, as far as the outer defences of the great Russian fortress-port. An attempt at that time to carry the place by storm cost the Germans sixteen thousand dead. During December a second attack was launched, and in the course of the seventeen days it lasted the German killed were reported to number 45,000. Followed a five months' lull—or rather near lull, since air raids were frequent. Then on June 5 the third attack was launched, and it was soon apparent that this time it was to be pressed to the bitter end. When it began, the Soviet C.-in-C., Admiral Umashev, told his troops : "If Sevastopol must fall it must cost the Germans 100,000 men. If you make the enemy pay this price, your sacrifice will not have been in vain." The defenders saw that the Germans did indeed pay the price, since even before the final assault the third attack had cost the lives of 50,000 German and Rumanian soldiers.

When the attack was in its second week Lt.-Gen. Dietmar, the Nazi military commentator, admitted, in a broadcast from Berlin, that the attempt to reduce Sevastopol was certainly no easy one. The approaches to the fortress, he pointed out, were ideal for the defence in every particular, since they consisted of many deep ravines and steep-sided gorges, which made direct shelling practically impossible. Everywhere there was excellent cover for the defenders, who

had constructed positions deep in the rock, immune to even the most powerful guns or mines. Numerous natural caves provided roomy shelter for men and materials. Then coastal batteries and armoured and concrete defence positions made the Soviet defence particularly strong. Nor did the guns point only out to sea, as at Singapore . . . In the fighting, tanks were condemned to play a minor part or no part at all. Thus it was that even more than usual the brunt of the fighting fell upon the infantry.

Long before the end the inevitability of Sevastopol's fall was realized by soldiers and citizens alike. Yet there was no sign of weakening. Air raids were so frequent that the warning was no longer given, but the 60,000 people who remained in the city out of the original 130,000 or so still "carried on." In large measure they lived their lives underground, where in caves and in artificial galleries they had established factories and canteens, newspaper offices,

RUSSIA'S CRIMEAN STRONGHOLD : A plan of Sevastopol's fortifications, given in the Nazi paper, Voelkischer Beobachter. Individual forts, 1 to 5, were named by the Russians : Maxim Gorki, Molotov, Siberia, Stalin and Lenin. Sevastopol fell to the enemy on July 1.
Courtesy of the Daily Herald

dormitories and first-aid posts—even schools, until 15,000 children were evacuated with their mothers by warships of the Black Sea Fleet. Even the theatre continued in operation, and Moscow's Grand Guignol company played to crowded houses.

Ere long most of the city had been converted into rubble by shelling and bombing.

"Sevastopol does not stand any more," said the Soviet writer, Petrov, in a telephone message to Moscow. "There is no town left, no more acacia trees or chestnuts ; no more clean, shady streets and little parks. Now each day is like a year. The fire upon us is heavier than ever before in the history of the war. Every yard of the yellow, rocky ground of the city is pocked with shell and bomb. Every day the enemy infantry attacks, believing nothing can be left after such a hell ; and every day the yellow rocks of Sevastopol come to life again—come to life again with a deadly fire from her defenders."

Another description of life in the doomed city came from the Russian playwright Boris Voytechov, who reached Sevastopol after the third offensive had begun. The Germans, he reported, were trying to break the people's nerve with terror-bombing. Apart

from screaming bombs they had rained down on the city pieces of railway lines, wheels, and ploughs. But the nerves of Sevastopol were different from those of Cologne or the Ruhr. The ordeal was being borne with stoical courage; the anonymous heroes of Sevastopol carried on. The electric power plant and telephones were still working. Unexploded land-mines were promptly cleared from the streets. Everybody was carrying a rifle or hand-grenades, and every enterprise had organized its defence groups so that the city bristled like a hedgehog. At one point on the front fighting was in progress in vineyards and orchards less than six miles from the city. Yet the nerves of those fighting on its shores were as calm as the Black Sea. "The scent from acacia drowns the stench of charred timbers, and by the light of star-shells and rockets the familiar façade of the city looks unchanged."

Fort after fort in the defence range was carried by assault—Fort Stalin, Fort Molotov, Fort Lenin, Fort Maxim Gorki. The last, said a German correspondent in a broadcast from Berlin, was a formidable fortress.

"Fort Maxim Gorki (he said) went on fighting even after it had been captured. It sounds unbelievable, but it is true. Although the upper storeys of this fort are in our hands and the battle line has moved some 1,400 yards forward, Soviet soldiers are beneath us, deep underground in the lower storeys of the fort, and continue to put up resistance. We have sent negotiators to explain to them that further resistance is useless, but they refuse to listen ; they will not come out. While we succeeded in forcing several hundred Soviet soldiers out of the upper storeys, blasting them out with hand-grenades and explosives hurled through the apertures, we cannot reach these last men.

"Never before," he continued, "have we seen such armour-plate, such concrete walls, and, above all, such a kind of concrete, which is quite new to us. Fort Maxim Gorki had 13-in. guns, which continued to blast away even after our shock units and storming guns had been brought up to close range. They went on firing at a range of less than 800 yards, and even 500 yards. We have still to deal with other forts. One, a very large artillery bastion, has been by-passed by our troops, but continues to hold out in our rear. We still have to silence heavy Soviet coastal batteries, the huge guns of which have been turned inland and shell us incessantly."

As the end drew near Russian commandos made a daring landing at Yalta on the Crimean coast well behind the enemy lines, and Sevastopol's defenders themselves delivered an almost incessant series of counter-attacks. But the enemy came on in inexhaustible strength. Fort Malakhov was stormed on June 30, and on the same day it was claimed that Rumanian troops in a rapid advance had taken the harbour and town of Balaclava. The next day the Germans were in Sevastopol itself. But there were no negotiations for surrender, no appeal even for an armistice. Days later von Mannstein was reported to be capturing the city street by street, even house by house, since the Russians, both garrison and civilian population, refused to lay down their arms.

"The Germans have gained nothing but a heap of ruins," said Moscow radio; and "Let us fight like the men of Sevastopol" became the Russian people's slogan.

Last Days in the Verdun of the Soviets

It was announced from Hitler's headquarters on July 1 that Sevastopol had fallen to German and Rumanian troops under the command of Colonel-General Mannstein, supported by Col.-Gen. Richthofen's air forces, after 25 days of the fiercest fighting. The photograph on the right shows Nazi infantry attacking Soviet defences.

The greatest heroism was shown by Russian nurses in tending the wounded under fire. Below is Medical Nurse Antipova rendering first aid to a wounded Russian commander during the defence of Sevastopol. For eight months the Russians held out against the enemy, and it is computed that its capture cost Hitler 100,000 dead.
Photos, Keystone, Planet News

Much of the life of beleaguered Sevastopol was carried on in caves and artificially-constructed shelters carved out of the rock on which the city is built. Centre right, Russian women are sewing underwear and other warm garments for the defenders of Sevastopol in one of these underground places of refuge.

Anti-aircraft gunners on a Soviet armoured train beating off an enemy raid in the Sevastopol sector. Dive-bombing played an important part in the Nazi plan for reducing the fortress. Bombers screamed down in power dives incessantly, dropping their loads, returning to their bases 25 miles away, and attacking again within half-an-hour.
Photos, British Official: Crown Copyright.

THE WAR AT SEA

by Francis E. McMurtrie

WITH the rapid advance of General Rommel's forces over the Egyptian frontier and past Mersa Matruh, the idea seems to have arisen in many minds that our fleet in the Eastern Mediterranean would have no alternative but to retreat at once through the Suez Canal into the Red Sea.

In fact, this by no means follows in such event. Should the invaders reach Alexandria it would deprive the fleet of its principal base, with most of the extensive resources that have been concentrated, there. Nor is there another port available which can compare with Alexandria so far as strategic position and harbour facilities are concerned. Port Said might be a useful substitute, were it not for the obvious fact that, with Alexandria in enemy hands, a position only 145 miles away would soon become untenable. It may be assumed, therefore, that the bases from which our warships would continue to operate would be Haifa and Beirut, the principal ports of Palestine and Syria.

Haifa is quite a modern city, with a harbour on which large sums have been spent in recent years. Beirut, though much older, has been improved considerably under the French regime in Syria. Cruisers and destroyers could make good use of both ports.

ANOTHER problem which has aroused public anxiety is the fate of the French squadron laid up at Alexandria. This comprises the old battleship Lorraine, of 22,189 tons displacement, armed with eight 13·4-inch guns; the heavy cruisers Suffren (9,938 tons), Duquesne and Tourville (both 10,000 tons), all three armed with eight 8-inch guns; the cruiser Duguay-Trouin, 7,249 tons and eight 6·1-inch guns; the destroyers Basque, Forbin and Le Fortuné, each 1,378 tons, four 5·1-inch guns and six torpedo tubes; and the submarine Protée, 1,379 tons, one 3·9-inch gun and eleven torpedo tubes.

It was in the first week of July 1940 that an agreement was reached between Admiral Sir Andrew Cunningham, Commander-in-Chief of the Mediterranean Fleet, and Admiral Godfroy, commanding the French squadron at Alexandria, by which the latter force was immobilized. All ammunition, torpedo warheads, breech-blocks of guns, and oil fuel were landed, and the crews repatriated to France, with the exception of small parties of shipkeepers.

In the event of Alexandria being endangered there is no doubt good care would be taken to ensure that these French ships should not fall into enemy hands. Presumably they would be taken through the Suez Canal to some safe port a considerable distance away; indeed, the naval base at Diego Suarez, Madagascar, occupied by British forces last May, has been mentioned in this connexion. Failing their removal, it may be regarded as certain that steps would be taken to render the ships useless to the Germans or Italians, i.e. they would be blown up or sunk if that became necessary.

CASUALTIES suffered in the convoy actions in the Central Mediterranean in the middle of June comprised a cruiser and six destroyers, the names of which have now been released. They were H.M.S. Hermione, a cruiser of 5,450 tons launched in 1939, and armed with ten 5·25-inch "dual-purpose" guns; and the destroyers Bedouin, 1,870 tons; Nestor, 1,690 tons; Hasty, 1,350 tons; Airedale, Grove, and Kujawiak, each of 904 tons. The Nestor belonged to the Royal Australian Navy and the Kujawiak to the Polish Navy.

It is understood that the Hermione was torpedoed by an enemy submarine while returning to her base, and that the Nestor was sunk by our own forces after she had been disabled in action with hostile aircraft.

Enemy losses on this occasion, it should be noted, included one Italian cruiser of 10,000 tons, two destroyers and a submarine sunk, a battleship seriously damaged, and at least 65 and probably 87 aircraft destroyed. We lost 30 aircraft.

In the United States the decision has been taken to suspend for the time being the construction of five huge battleships of 65,000 tons that were ordered last year, and concentrate upon building more aircraft-carriers. Six battle cruisers of about 27,000 tons, the Alaska, Guam, Hawaii, Philippines, Puerto Rico and Samoa, will be re-designed and completed as aircraft-carriers, as will a number of the 10,000-ton cruisers of the Cleveland class, 32 of which are being built.

In view of the important part which naval aircraft have played in the Pacific, there can be no doubt that this decision is a wise one.

ATLANTIC ESCORT. Even before America's entry into the war U.S. warships played a great part in convoying ships to Britain, but of late months their work has been greatly intensified. This photo was taken on a U.S. escort vessel engaged on convoy work in the North Atlantic; beyond is one of the ships of the convoy. *Photo, New York Times Photos*

Not only are the Axis Powers inferior to the Allies in the number of their capital ships, but the United States Navy already has ten new battleships approaching completion or well advanced in construction. These are the 45,000-ton Iowa, New Jersey, Missouri, Wisconsin, Illinois and Kentucky, and the 35,000-ton South Dakota, Massachusetts, Indiana and Alabama. With this margin of superiority in capital ships, it is far more urgent to complete additional aircraft-carriers with which to follow up the heavy blow dealt to the Japanese Navy off Midway Island early in June. It is now known that the enemy losses in that action included the four aircraft-carriers Akagi and Kaga, both of 26,000 tons, Soryu and Hiryu, both of 10,050 tons. Adding these to the destruction of the Ryukaku, of 20,000 tons, in the Coral Sea fighting, it is clear that Japan has been deprived of 60 per cent of her aircraft-carrier tonnage, without taking into consideration the heavy damage believed to have been inflicted on the Syokaku of 20,000 tons.

IN these circumstances it may be expected that arrangements will be made to build as rapidly as possible a considerable number of medium-sized aircraft-carriers, which could not only be completed in less time than bigger ships, but would involve a smaller loss of material and personnel if sunk.

At the same time, no doubt, every endeavour will be made to deliver at an early date those aircraft-carriers of larger size already in hand, such as H.M.S. Implacable and Indefatigable, of 23,000 tons, due for completion this year; and the 11 American ships of the Essex class, ordered in 1941, which are reported to be of about 25,000 tons. Quite a number of new merchantship hulls are known to have been converted into escort aircraft-carriers, for duty in convoy protection.

It is possible that in the not far distant future a new design of capital ship will be evolved, in which the strong protection of the present-day type of battleship will be combined with flight deck accommodation for a considerable number of aircraft, including torpedo-bombers and fighters.

U.S. AIRCRAFT-CARRIER WASP which, it was revealed on July 1, recently accomplished ferry trips to the Mediterranean carrying aeroplane reinforcements for beleaguered Malta. On one occasion R.A.F. fighters, after taking off from the Wasp, went straight into action with the enemy over Malta. This photograph was taken in December 1939, as the new 21-million-dollar ship left a yard of the Bethlehem Steel Corporation. *Photo, New York Times Photos*

Another Torpedo for the Battle of the Seas

SUPERCHARGED WITH DEATH, a torpedo, fresh from the factory, is being manoeuvred into position for loading into one of our submarines. The torpedo has proved to be one of the deadliest weapons ever invented. During 1914-18 no fewer than 4,000 merchant ships of all nationalities were destroyed by torpedoes, and in this war the tonnage of naval and other craft lost has reached astronomical figures. All modern torpedoes are driven by compressed air.

Photo, Associated Press

Welcome Home to the Victors of Midway

HEROES OF MIDWAY ISLAND BATTLE, (4) in this page of Midway photos, being greeted by their comrades at Oahu Field, Hawaii. 1, U.S. destroyer and army bomber circling a column of smoke marking a crashed Japanese plane ; 2, an air sergeant at Oahu Field examining the damaged windflap of a Flying Fortress ; 3, Maj.-Gen. W. H. Hale and Lt.-Col. W. C. Sweeney, Jr., being interviewed on their return ; 5, name-plate of a B-26 Medium Bomber, all that was worth salvaging after the plane returned to its base.

Photos, Keystone

Bombed Into Ruin by America's Flyers

JAPANESE CRUISER, of the Mogami class, after she had been bombed by American naval planes in the Battle of Midway Island during the first week in June. (See pages 54 and 61.) Superstructures have been reduced to scrap-iron and the whole deck is a mass of flame and smoke. Top, a terrifying impression of the shattered monster, her guns knocked out, with one dipping towards the sea, a cauldron of fire amidships, and sailors huddled at stern and bows.

Photos, Keystone

THE HOME FRONT

by Augustus Muir

LABOUR disputes have always been among the primary symptoms of a social structure in the act of readjustment. However deeply strikes are to be deplored in the present critical days, the actual working time lost by them is much smaller than one might conclude after reading headlines in certain sections of the Press. An Industrial Commissioner, quoting the statistics for April and May of this year, showed that in the Scottish coal-mining industry the time lost by strikes was a quarter of one per cent, and the shipbuilding loss was actually less than one-sixth of this figure. Absenteeism is largely attributed to young people who have become "stale" after intensive spells of overtime. Meanwhile two million more men and women are to register for war work: men up to 50, women up to 45. Young men transplanted from industry to the fighting forces will thus be replaced by older operatives; and rapidly-expanding war factories will have fresh personnel. The problem of the key-worker must be tackled with constructive imagination.

The President of the Amalgamated Engineering Union has warned engineers that the "fluidity of labour" is of signal importance; it might be necessary, for instance, to move arms workers to shipbuilding. As one industry reaches saturation point, a switch-over of personnel will be vital in the achieving and maintaining of 100 per cent production. To this end the Ministry of Supply has been cooperating with the Ministry of Labour to complete schemes for a nation-wide "labour pool." Of the thirty-three million men and women between the ages of 14 and 65, twenty-two million have been mobilized for the armed forces, Civil Defence, and war production; and the Labour Minister, Mr. Bevin, has made the resounding claim that no other country in the world's history has ever so fully mobilized its man-power. And to provide the sinews of war the House of Commons the other day voted another thousand million sterling. This makes a total of ten thousand million pounds—already more than the *total* cost of the War of 1914-1918.

Farmers in Scotland have touched a new peak in potato planting, and look for a production of over a million tons this autumn. There is word of this year's harvest being a bumper one generally in the north; and Scottish farmers, smallholders, and crofters have succeeded in bringing another 200,000 acres under the plough since last autumn, thus adding a total of 600,000 acres since the first winter of the war. The figures for England are no less encouraging; and the latest demand of Mr. Hudson, Minister of Agriculture, is for another half-million acres to be brought under the plough this autumn. City volunteers are now being mobilized all over England to help in the harvest; land clubs are being formed, and school children

TOPICS

Time Lost by Strikes · New Call-Up for War Industry · A "Labour Pool" · Cost of the War · A Bumper Harvest · The Woolton Food Zones · Control of Milk Distribution · Coal and the Miner · Cut in Motor Coach Services · Help for Small Traders · Government Control Tightening.

will spend holidays in harvest camps. It is estimated that 20,000 boys and girls will have enrolled with farmers by August.

With a sharp pencil and large-scale map, Lord Woolton has divided the United Kingdom into sectors, each being a new food zone. This will mean a big drop in the cost of distribution, for retailers will be obliged to draw their supplies only from wholesalers within their zone boundary; and the edict will affect 15s. of every 20s. spent by the average housewife. Similar plans have already been in operation for certain commodities. One has heard too much about goods being carried long distances, only to be hauled back to retailers in the locality whence they came.

THE Food Minister startled the House of Lords the other day by holding up a small green disk about the size of a 5s. piece. He assured his astounded peers that it contained enough concentrated vegetables to feed a family of twelve: "Fresh vegetables," he declared, "for our troops in the desert!" One wonders what our troops will think of the green agglomerate! But there is news of a new dried meat process that will mean a saving in cargo space: indeed, caterers have

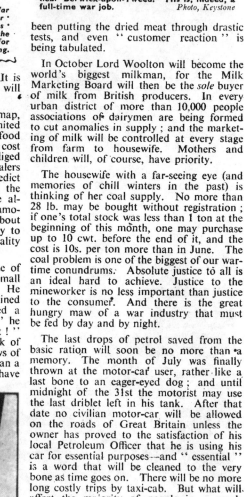

FISHERMAN HOME GUARD on Holy Island, near Berwick-upon-Tweed. His is, indeed, a full-time war job.   *Photo, Keystone*

been putting the dried meat through drastic tests, and even "customer reaction" is being tabulated.

In October Lord Woolton will become the world's biggest milkman, for the Milk Marketing Board will then be the *sole* buyer of milk from British producers. In every urban district of more than 10,000 people associations of dairymen are being formed to cut anomalies in supply; and the marketing of milk will be controlled at every stage from farm to housewife. Mothers and children will, of course, have priority.

The housewife with a far-seeing eye (and memories of chill winters in the past) is thinking of her coal supply. No more than 28 lb. may be bought without registration; if one's total stock was less than 1 ton at the beginning of this month, one may purchase up to 10 cwt. before the end of it, and the cost is 10s. per ton more than in June. The coal problem is one of the biggest of our wartime conundrums. Absolute justice to all is an ideal hard to achieve. Justice to the mineworker is no less important than justice to the consumer. And there is the great hungry maw of a war industry that must be fed by day and by night.

The last drops of petrol saved from the basic ration will soon be no more than a memory. The month of July was finally thrown at the motor-car user, rather like a last bone to an eager-eyed dog; and until midnight of the 31st the motorist may use the last driblet left in his tank. After that date no civilian motor-car will be allowed on the roads of Great Britain unless the owner has proved to the satisfaction of his local Petroleum Officer that he is using his car for essential purposes—and "essential" is a word that will be cleaned to the very bone as time goes on. There will be no more long costly trips by taxi-cab. But what will affect the majority of people in a much more drastic way is the cut in public coach services. We may as well face the fact: all travelling is discouraged except for journeys that are necessary.

OF vital interest to small traders whose profits have vanished with the scarcity of goods is the Government proposal of assisted liquidation. This should ameliorate many a difficult case where the shopkeeper has been grimly hanging on with bankruptcy as the only certain thing in an uncertain future. On the other hand, some traders are flourishing. In secondhand furniture, for example, scarcity has been the fluent excuse for prices having doubled and trebled. But the Board of Trade is taking control; no longer will prices continue to mount skyward. The entire basis of commodity trading is being radically revised, and Government control is tightening upon every branch of our lives.

'MATILDAS' FOR RUSSIA being shipped at a British port. Such is a daily scene at certain docks where convoys for munitions assemble to collect the "tools" which British workmen are making to help their Soviet comrades.   *Photo, Central Press*   PAGE 90

Pleasure Motoring Stops 'for the Duration'

IN LONDON, one solitary car in Lincoln's Inn Fields, on the morning of July 1, 1942, when the "no pleasure motoring" order came into force. The parking sign remains as a relic of the car age. Left, the effect of the new law in the Strand.

IN NEW YORK, West Side Highway before and (right) after petrol restriction. Whereas cars used to be numbered in hundreds a minute, now with the rationing of "gas" they are few and far between.   *Photos, Topical Press*   PAGE 91

King and People in the Eye of the Camera

WORKERS OF THE WEEK above, Mr. Richard Harris, army aircraft employee, who helps to make our great bomber raids possible. Mr. Harris has worked for the aircraft industry for ten years and, in his spare time, he is an Air Training Corps instructor. Right, Mr. Fred Shapley, 44-year-old foreman of the tool room in a Midlands Royal Ordnance factory, which he improvised from some old machinery and a shed. The whole works is now dependent on his shop.

KING GEORGE on the occasion of the royal visit to American troops in Northern Ireland. His Majesty spent eight hours with the troops, carried out an inspection and assisted at manoeuvres. In this photograph King George is seen riding in an American "Jeep" army car driven by Lieut. Russell F. Mann, of Oxford, Iowa.

SURBITON'S ANSWER to the loss of the Borough's adopted warship, the Wild Swan, which cost over £500,000, was to begin saving another half million to replace the vessel. At a presentation ceremony on June 25 the Mayor handed Vice-Admiral Sir Robert Hornell a replica of the Borough coat of arms, and received from Sir Robert a replica of the ship's badge. Above right, H.M.S. Wild Swan, which was attacked by 12 enemy bombers off the west coast of France on June 17. Badly damaged, she also collided with a Spanish trawler and sank, but six German aircraft were destroyed.

THE NEW STEN GUN (right) is being mass-produced at Royal Ordnance factories at a cost of less than £2 each. It can be fired as an automatic, or used for single shot firing, either from the shoulder or from the hip.

Photos, B.B.C., Associated Press, New York Times Photos, Wright & Logan, Sport & General

I WAS THERE! Eye Witness Stories of the War

They Quite Like Us A.R.P. Wardens Now!

Reprinted from the Manchester Guardian, this article by Bernard Lennon affords an interesting and amusing sidelight on the changing attitude towards the "P.B.I." of Civil Defence brought about by the experience of "blitz" conditions.

"THE P.B.I. of Civil Defence—that's us," said old Mattinson when the wardens brought up the rear of the parade held in connexion with Warship Week. "Mugs all along the line," he said afterwards. "Remember before the war started?"

Most of us did remember. About the time of Munich there had been the distribution of respirators, to use the official phrase, though by the time the work was accomplished neither the recipients nor the distributors indulged in such high-flown language. The wardens were blamed for all the discomforts of the long queue. They were told repeatedly why other centres and different hours would have been more convenient.

It is doubtful whether even that ordeal was as bad as the calls we made on householders a month or two before the war began. Had everybody in the house a gas mask? Had a gas chamber been prepared? Had everyone received a carton for his or her gas mask? What were the dimensions of the garden or the backyard? The responses could hardly be called warm. There was little open opposition, to be sure, but there was no lack of looks to express the thoughts which were not put into words. We were told there was not going to be a war and were left to imagine what kind of lunatics we were to be wasting our own and other people's time on fools' errands. Many people seemed to take delight in letting us stand on the doorstep in pouring rain or a cutting wind. Even the friends on whom we called seemed to consider us fanatics who had to be humoured.

We remembered all this and we remembered old Mattinson's comment on the wardens when it was announced not so long ago that we had to undertake a house-to-house examination of gas masks, and we showed little enthusiasm. The work was to be done in pairs, and partners made their arrangements in an atmosphere of mutual commiseration.

On the night that Conway and I began our rounds there was a biting wind with occasional squalls of rain. We had visions of ourselves standing on doorsteps while mocking eyes watched our numbed fingers fumbling with head-harness, stretching the face-piece, testing the elasticity of the rubber band, removing and replacing the inlet valve. We discussed whether a truculent or an apologetic tone would be the more suitable and compromised on politeness. We knocked at our first door. It opened.

"We have called on behalf of the Wardens' Service. Could we see the gas masks, please?" "Yes, certainly. Come in. Come in. It's cold out there."

Conway and I looked at one another, and I saw his eyebrows lift as we followed the young woman into the house. "It's the wardens, mother," she called out as she went to gather the family respirators together. When we had passed them both mother and daughter became talkative, treating us as if we were the confidants of the C.I.G.S. Would Hitler use gas next time? When would the war be over? We extricated ourselves with soothing words and wondered whether this treatment was a flash in the pan.

At the next house we were also asked in. The gas masks were again brought forth promptly and readily. The examiners were again treated as a cross between Delphic oracles and experts in the higher strategy.

It was the same all that evening and the next evening and every evening till our area was completed. We were received with smiles and allowed with reluctance to depart. We were offered cups of tea, biscuits, even cigarettes. We were overwhelmed with sympathy at having to spend our valuable time like this. "You shouldn't be coming here," said one man. "You ought to make us come to you." Then he proudly showed us the piece of railway line which had embedded itself in his asphalt garden path.

Apologies were showered on us if anyone had mislaid a mask and had kept us waiting, or if we had had to call a second or third time at a house before finding anyone at home.

Our experience was not exceptional. Every warden reported the same welcome,

'HOW'S YOUR RESPIRATOR?' A familiar scene during the recent overhaul of gas masks, as the Civil Defence warden goes from house to house about his duty.

the same readiness to comply, the same desire for advice, the same belief in the wardens' omniscience.

"Perhaps," suggested someone, "it was the uniform that did the trick." "Don't you believe it," said old Mattinson. "Remember that we had a blitz last year."

"And what about the wardens now? Do you still think they're the Poor Blooming Infantry of Civil Defence?" "Maybe I wasn't so far wrong as you seem to think," retorted Mattinson, who was a corporal in the K.O.R.L. a quarter of a century ago. "The P.B.I. won the last war, didn't they?"

Daily I Thanked My Lucky Star—and the French

An Englishman who lived in Occupied France from June 1940 to October 1941, expecting daily to be caught by the Germans, gave this account of the friendly help he received from the French until he reached safety at Lisbon.

BEFORE the war I was working in Nantes and when war broke out I sent my wife and boy to England and carried on with my job. When the Germans arrived I was unable to get away and had to remain in Nantes, where I was helped by French friends. After some six weeks there was a general tightening-up by the German authorities, and I had to move. I thought that Paris was the best place in which to hide until I could get out of Occupied France.

In Paris, thanks to many French friends, I lived for fifteen months, until October 1941. I had no money and no papers except my British passport. What was perhaps worse was that I was unable to get ration cards. However, all the French people I met were pleased and anxious to help me. They kept me supplied with food, sharing their own scanty rations, and supplied me with lodgings. I had to change my address several times, although I was always careful to see that I was not being followed on my way home. Every day I thanked my lucky star—and the French—for every day I expected to be caught by the Germans.

At night if by accident I was unable to get back home before the curfew I went with friends to a cabaret or to a café, which remained open all night, and there I had to remain until five o'clock in the morning, rubbing shoulders with drunken Germans. Sometimes a German would speak to me and I would reply in my best French, but the French and the Germans kept very much apart in such places. Often in the Underground French people would look at the

SEARCHING THE RUINS, an A.R.P. squad among the debris of a house at Bath. Civil Defence, which was once regarded by the public as a kind of joke, if not a nuisance, is now recognized as an essential and honoured part of the great war for freedom. A warden recounts some recent experiences in this page. *Photo, Sport & General*

BOUND FOR TOBRUK was this naval stores ship before the fall of the Libyan stronghold. A writer in this page describes how certain British ships got away from Tobruk under enemy fire.
Photo, British Official: Crown Copyright

At about five o'clock all naval personnel having any kind of arms were ordered to fall in. Only a few naval units and one small schooner were in the harbour at this time. From the time the road was cut four days previously most of Tobruk's supplies had been brought by sea—as during the last siege. I was told to bring my craft alongside and did so. We stood by there awaiting orders for about two hours, while the demolition parties carried out their duties.

The next thing I saw was five or six German tanks on the other side of the escarpment. We saw four or five of our soldiers shoot up one of the tanks and then plunge into the water and swim to a small boat in which they pulled over to us.

In the evening we learned officially that there had been a general break-through. I rang up headquarters from a gun position and was told this. About this time the German tanks were coming over the hill from the east down the road into the town, backed by armoured cars. Then the order came—be ready to move.

Then the enemy put over the biggest bombardment I have ever seen. Tanks were firing at the ships while the harbour and town were being shelled and bombed. All kinds of ammunition were used. Shells and bombs were exploding all around, but we suffered no casualties.

The armoured forces were now so close that we were ordered to sail. All ships had been made ready with steam up since the siege began. I could not get my ship—a small craft—away because she had been hit by a shell. We hopped ashore and saw all the ships leaving. I got aboard another vessel just as she was letting go and we all moved out. There were shells falling all around now and we had one hit. At this time we were in a rather isolated corner of the harbour and could not see if any ships took on troops before leaving. The ships were firing pom-poms and other light weapons at the enemy and the din was terrific.

As we moved out the enemy put down a curtain of shells from guns of every kind over the boom entrance, so that all ships would have to pass through it. We went through at full speed and were not hit.

Then Stukas arrived and bombed the town. Up to the last half-hour no damage had been done to any of the few important or inhabited buildings in the town, and when we left four buildings which were not hit in the previous bombardments were still standing.

Naval demolition squads blew up everything essential before we left. Certain craft had been detailed to stay behind for demolition parties, practically all of whom were taken off. They continued working until the last moment, even when enemy armoured forces were in the town.

There were only naval personnel in the town—the Army were all around it. Practically everyone in the town or on the shore managed to get away in craft, but the bulk of the army was left behind. By the time the last ship left the enemy armoured forces were all around the harbour.—*Reuter*

Germans sitting around and then look at me and solemnly wink. They could see that I was English.

At one of my lodgings I used to go down to the "loge" of the concierge to play "belote" with him and to listen to the B.B.C. One night I asked the concierge what he would reply if he were asked by the authorities to identify me. "My dear sir," he replied, "you are not one of my tenants, I have never seen you before, and I have never seen you visiting one of my tenants. 'Belote, et rebelote.'"

Finally I got down near to the "line." How I crossed the line I cannot explain, but I succeeded in getting out of France and into Portugal.

I believe that practically all the French people will welcome the English with open arms when they land in France—ask them what happened at St. Nazaire. This did not surprise me, for in all the fifteen months I was in Paris I met many people in the streets who had known me before the war, but not once was I in danger of being denounced. I hope there will be a special decoration after the war for those people who, at the risk of their lives, helped me and others, without hope of reward, to hide from the Germans.—*The Manchester Guardian*

Our Ship Was Shelled by Tanks at Tobruk

How British warships, with naval demolition parties, escaped at the last minute from Tobruk harbour under the guns of German batteries and tanks is told here by a young naval officer who was among the last to leave.

THOUGH there was no organized evacuation of Tobruk, the defenders were determined to reorganize and fight their way out. Tobruk town and harbour had been shelled for some days fairly heavily, but not until Saturday, June 20, did the bombardment become really vicious. The Germans used everything they had from two-inch shells upwards, even anti-tank guns.

Bombing was going on on the other side of the escarpment with Junkers 88s and Stukas coming over all the time, blasting the gun positions and concentrating on one gun at a time to knock them out in preparation for the tank charge. No bombing was directed at us. In fact, as far as the Navy was concerned, the bombing and shelling were more of nuisance value than anything else, and we continued with our work as if nothing was happening. But on Saturday afternoon the big stuff started to come over. I had been on coastal patrol the night before, so had turned in and slept despite the bombardment. When I got up at 3.30 p.m. it was not very bad, although things were popping off all over the place. I left the building in which I had been sleeping at four o'clock and met some troops who had just come down the escarpment. They told us that they had been cut off by the enemy. This was the first we knew of the break-through.

We Laid Mines in Enemy Waters

A recurring and often little-noted item of news is that "mines were laid in enemy waters." Here, broadcast by a Flight Lieutenant on minelaying duty, is an account of what that operation entails.

THE other night we set off in one of our bombers for those enemy waters in which our mine was to be laid. A mine is really a sort of delay-action bomb dropped into the water. You see it flop out of the aircraft and go sailing down on its parachute. It sinks into the water very quietly ; no flame, no flash, no leaping debris such as a big bomb may make. The mine just sits there waiting. Just think what it means to the enemy, that night after night British aircraft buzz round that long coastline from Narvik to Bordeaux, along which its convoys must go carrying the products of occupied Europe. The convoys must hug the shore, or else our bombers, motor torpedo boats or submarines will get them. But along those shores, in the shallow waters, our minelaying aircraft have been at work the night before.

It was a dirty night on which we went out, with cloud down to within a few hundred feet above the sea. We flew above it. The trouble with flying above cloud like that is that you may not be able to tell where you are, and your mine must be dropped just where you want it. However, for us that night the question largely solved itself.

As soon as we reckoned we were off the enemy coast we began to see searchlights and flak. Those of our crew who had been in these parts a good many times before had little difficulty in fixing our position. Soon we found a flak barrage going up to port as well as to starboard. That told us definitely where we were. Down through the cloud we went, lower and lower. At last we came out of the greyness, and then just a few feet below was the sea, rough and brown and cold, and too near for comfort. Back we went into the cloud.

Immediately I heard the bomb-aimer's voice over the inter-com.: "Bomb doors open." Then I heard a clonk as the mine was released. Then the bomb-aimer's voice: "Bomb gone," the pilot's voice: "Bomb doors shut." On the way home I thought, "Well, it's there."

Probably, of course, the enemy knows that these channels are now dangerous, but, if so, it means that all his convoys will have to put in to port. For days, probably, a fleet of his minesweepers will have to come out seeking for what we've dropped. Maybe they won't find it, or maybe our mine will be detected and swept up. But then, just as the channels are clear again, the next dark night they will hear the drone of our bombers. They will wonder if all those channels aren't dangerous again. And maybe they will be, or maybe somewhere else will be.

GERMAN MINESWEEPERS operating in the North Sea. How mines are laid by British in enemy waters from an aeroplane forms the subject of an article in this and the preceding pages.
Photo, Planet News

Then they'll have to decide whether to send the convoys through and risk half-a-dozen laden ships going to the bottom, or start their sweeping all over again. For this is one of the great advantages of dropping mines from aircraft. A minelayer or a sub- marine can't revisit a minefield once it's been laid ; if it did, it would probably be blown up on its own mines. But an aircraft can come back and back, keeping up the supply, laying more mines just after the enemy has swept up the old ones.—*The Listener.*

OUR DIARY OF THE WAR

JUNE 24, 1942, Wednesday *1,026th day*
Russian Front.—Heavy fighting continued on Kharkov front.
Africa.—British withdrew from Sollum and Sidi Omar.
China.—A.V.G. raided Hankow and other Jap bases.
Australasia.—Allied reconnaissance 'planes over Kendari, Celebes.
Home.—Five enemy raiders shot down in attacks on Midlands and E. Anglia.

JUNE 25, Thursday *1,027th day*
Air.—More than 1,000 R.A.F. bombers raided Bremen.
Russian Front.—Russians evacuated Kupiansk, S.E. of Kharkov.
Mediterranean.—Our submarines torpedoed three supply ships.
Africa.—Rommel's main forces advanced on Matruh.
Burma.—R.A.F. bombers raided Akyab.
Australasia.—Allied air raids on Dilli, Salamaua and Rabaul. Jap fighters intercepted over Port Moresby.
Home.—Major-Gen. Eisenhower, commander of U.S. Forces in European Theatre, in London.

JUNE 26, Friday *1,028th day*
Russian Front.—Heavy fighting in Kharkov and Sevastopol sectors.
Africa.—Rommel's forces 15 miles from Matruh.
U.S.A.—Jap shore installations at Kiska, Aleutians, raided by U.S. bombers.

JUNE 27, Saturday *1,029th day*
Air.—Another heavy raid by R.A.F. bombers on Bremen.
Russian Front.—Several attacks on Sevastopol repelled.
Africa.—Our forces closed with the enemy round Mersa Matruh.
Pacific.—U.S. bombers flew 2,000 miles from Hawaii to bomb Wake Island.
Australasia.—Night raids by Allied bombers on Tulagi, Lae and Salamaua.

JUNE 28, Sunday *1,030th day*
Air.—Submarine base at St. Nazaire bombed by night.
Russian Front.—Germans started offensive in Kursk area, 100 miles N. of Kharkov.
Africa.—Heavy fighting continued round Mersa Matruh.
Australasia.—Allied land forces made a raid on Jap garrison at Salamaua, New Guinea.

U.S.A.—U.S. army bombers again attacked Kiska, Aleutians.

JUNE 29, Monday *1,031st day*
Air.—Strong force of R.A.F. bombers raided Bremen.
Russian Front.—Heavy German tank attacks repelled at Kursk ; German advance at Sevastopol.
Africa.—Mersa Matruh evacuated by our troops.

JUNE 30, Tuesday *1,032nd day*
Russian Front.—Attacks at Kursk and Sevastopol still being held by Russians.
Africa. — No large-scale fighting ; Germans reported to have passed El Daba.
Indian Ocean.—S. African land and air forces officially stated to be in Madagascar.
Australasia.—Allied bombers raided Lae and Rabaul.

JULY 1, Wednesday *1,033rd day*
Russian Front.—Germans claimed capture of Sevastopol.

Africa.—German tanks and infantry attacked our positions at El Alamein.
China.—American Army Air Force raided Hankow aerodrome.
Australasia.—Allied bombers attacked airfield at Kendari, Celebes, making 1,700-mile flight.

JULY 2, Thursday *1,034th day*
Air.—Powerful force of bombers again raided Bremen.
Russian Front.—Fighting developed in Bielgorod and Volchansk direction.
Africa.—German attack on El Alamein continued. Allied bombers made heavy raid on Tobruk.
Indian Ocean.—British forces occupied island of Mayotte, between Madagascar and Africa.
Australasia.—Allied bombers twice raided Dilli, Portuguese Timor.
U.S.A.—U.S. bombers damaged three Jap transports off Agattu Island, W. Aleutians.

JULY 3, Friday *1,035th day*
Sea.—Admiralty announced that ships lost in Malta convoy attacks in June were cruiser Hermione, destroyers Bedouin, Hasty, Grove and Airedale and Polish destroyer Kujawiak. Australian destroyer Nestor also lost.
Russian Front.—Evacuation of Sevastopol announced by Russians. Large-scale German attacks at Kursk, Bielgorod and Volchansk.
Africa.—Our forces counter-attacked in El Alamein area.
U.S.A.—Kiska, Aleutians, again attacked by U.S. bombers.

JULY 4, Saturday *1,036th day*
Air.—Six planes manned by U.S. airmen took part in joint attack with R.A.F. on aerodromes in Holland.
Russian Front.—Heavy fighting continued at Kursk, Bielgorod and Volchansk.
China.—U.S. bombers raided aerodrome at Canton.
Australasia.—Allied aircraft made heavy raids on Lae and Salamaua.
U.S.A.—U.S. submarines torpedoed three Jap destroyers at Kiska and one at Agattu, Aleutians.

JULY 5, Sunday *1,037th day*
Africa.—Our land and air forces continued to attack in the area of El Alamein.
U.S.A.—U.S. submarine torpedoed Jap destroyer near Kiska, Aleutian.

JULY 6, Monday *1,038th day*
Russian Front.—Russians retired at some points W. of Voronezh. North of Orel Russians launched attack.
Burma.—Enemy troop concentrations on Chindwin River bombed by R.A.F.
Australasia.—Allied bombers raided Lae and Salamaua and made night raids on Solomons and Dutch Timor.

JULY 7, Tuesday *1,039th day*
Russian Front.—Fierce fighting round Voronezh and Stary Oskol ; Germans claimed capture of Voronezh.
Mediterranean.—Twenty-five Axis aircraft shot down over Malta in 24 hours ; R.A.F. bombed Messina by night.
Africa.—Mobile columns engaged enemy at El Alamein ; intensive bombing by our air forces.
Australasia.—Jap bombers raided aerodrome on Horn Island, Torres Straits.
Home.—Maj.-Gen. C. Spaatz appointed to command U.S. air forces in Europe.

MR. CHURCHILL'S THIRD VISIT TO AMERICA

Arriving in America on June 18, Mr. Churchill held in Washington a number of conferences with President Roosevelt and the American and British advisers. On his return to London on June 27 a joint statement was made public, of which the following are the main points.

In the matter of production of munitions of all kinds, the survey gives on the whole an optimistic picture. The previously planned monthly output has not reached the maximum, but is fast approaching it on schedule.

Transportation of the fighting forces, together with the transportation of munitions of war and supplies, still constitutes the major problem of the United Nations.

While submarine warfare on the part of the Axis continues to take a heavy toll of cargo ships, the actual production of new tonnage is greatly increasing month by month.

The United Nations have never been in such hearty and detailed agreement on plans for winning the war as they are today.

Detailed discussions were held with our military advisers on methods to be adopted against Japan and for the relief of China.

While our plans, for obvious reasons, cannot be disclosed, it can be said that the coming operations which were discussed in detail at our Washington conferences, between ourselves and our respective military advisers, will divert German strength from the attack on Russia.

The Prime Minister and the President have met twice before, first in August 1941 and again in December 1941. There is no doubt in their minds that the over-all picture is more favourable to victory than it was either in August or December of last year.

Editor's Postscript

FOR some months now the swiftly moving events of the War have made it impossible to keep pace with their speedy recording in the more carefully compiled pages of our fortnightly issue, especially since wartime exigencies have imposed certain working conditions upon us which could never obtain in peacetime. That is why our text pages have recently undergone a change which is designed to keep our readers fully acquainted with the progress of the War in all essential details as seen through the eyes of our expert contributors at the time of writing. But readers should remember that at least a fortnight must elapse between our going to press and their reading our pages. The B.B.C. bulletins and the daily papers keep everyone supplied with the "hot" news, while THE WAR ILLUSTRATED comes along each alternate Friday with its balanced contents of picture, chronicle and comment, building up steadily into a unique pictorial record of the War. That has been its function since its first number, but during its weekly issue and while almost normal conditions of production continued, our pages trod more closely on the heels of the news, a fact which had the defects of its merits whenever the battle fronts became "fluid," as in some sections of the Russian front and later in Libya.

OUR changed treatment has met with general approval, judging from the many complimentary notes I have received from readers, though I deliberately discourage correspondence now on account of the paper situation—and postage costs. And the fact remains that whoever finds himself, when the War is over, in possession of a complete set of THE WAR ILLUSTRATED, will have a unique collection of contemporary chronicle enriched with an immense and well ordered photographic record which is not only beyond all rivalry at present, but is secure from any future competition. In the War of 1914-18 much the same thing happened, in even more remarkable circumstances, for out of a dozen weekly competitors of THE WAR ILLUSTRATED of that historic time I had the editorial satisfaction of seeing only one surviving at the date of the Armistice ! Today THE WAR ILLUSTRATED stands alone in its field, and, despite difficulties unimagined in 1939, enjoys a circulation substantially greater than its precursor of 1914.

HOW's this for a bit of bright bureaucracy ? A commercial printer known to me has a large and weighty piece of machinery which has seen forty years' service and is now little better than junk. It can no longer be used with economy. In a London showroom stands a similar machine of more modern design, unused, and for sale. This the printer found after much searching. He agreed to buy it and turn in his old machine as metal replacement for salvage. The dealer has been flatly refused permission to sell, though the Government department concerned has been provided with all details of the proposed transaction. Thus the printer cannot continue economically to use his worn-out machine for essential commercial stationery, the owners of the new machine have to let it stand idle in their showroom, and the Iron Salvage is deprived of a valuable free contribution. The Salvage sleuths would probably prefer to snaffle some antique iron gate or railing ; indeed, two or three gates would be needed to provide an equal weight of metal which this printer is anxious to part with. What fun we are going to have after the War eliminating this sort of bureaucratic nonsense !

ON the principle of trying anything once, I occasionally buy some publication whose contents I feel will offend my intelligence, just to see "what fools these mortals be." I shall not particularize my latest purchase beyond remarking upon its strident advocacy of superstitions, which flourish whenever trouble breeds credulity. A study of its pages provided me with a good half-hour's diversion, and especially with this gem of wisdom introducing an elaborate astrological study by that noted seer Mr. R. H. Naylor :

"Nobody drives a car with his eyes shut ; none is so foolish as to ride a bicycle blindfold. Fighting a war is infinitely more dangerous than driving a car or riding a bicycle. All the more imperative, therefore, to look where we are going. And, believe me, mankind faces that which cannot be estimated or understood from past mass-experience."

How perspicacious ! Believe me, tomorrow will be Friday, for I'm writing on a Thursday.

ALTHOUGH much that the periodical in question contains is offered under the pretence of "Science" I would suggest that "Superstition" would be a more fitting general title for it than the one it bears. Indeed, I have been shocked at the evidence which it provides for the growing mental confusion of the age. As significant as any of its literary contents is an advertisement offering any reader for 2s. 9d. a gold-plated amulet which contains "nine drops from a famous Wishing Well" (unnamed) and has the peculiar merit of enabling its possessor to secure the fulfilment of nine wishes. One of its purchasers has already won £30, another picked up the "Unity Pool" (whatever that may be), and yet another has wished for a thing which she didn't expect to get and yet she got it ! This strikes me as pretty good value for 2s. 9d., especially the gold-plating, as last week I noticed a jeweller in Victoria Street was offering 39s. 6d. in exchange for one sovereign ! But I had always thought that the traditional number of wishes was three, as in "The Monkey's Paw" and a multitude of other cautionary tales. Possibly the nine drops from that Wishing Well represent a generous reserve in case of some failures. The best of well-wishers, or wishing-wellers, could hardly expect to find in every wish a good egg.

NOT long ago I had evidence of how very near one can be to the scene of a lively air raid without knowing anything about it. Visiting friends in a certain village which lies something less than ten miles from a much bombed seacoast on a day of real June sunshine, we were enjoying the quietude and beauty of the scene so keenly that the common feeling of the company in that walled garden of old-world fragrance was : How distant seemed the horrors of war from such a haunt of peace ! But a visitor arriving shortly after tea brought the news that there had been a sharp raid on the nearest coast town, with some casualties and a fair amount of material damage— and this was going on while we sat there rejoicing in our peaceful environment. Yet in five or six minutes the attacking bombers could have been over our tea-party, once again demonstrating the advantage of living in the country, where houses are few and scattered and objects worthy of bombing fewer still.

IN my own rural retreat, during recent months, there was much to tempt my pen to lyrical comment upon many unsuspected charms of country life and the manifestations of Nature. Though lack of space restricts such observations as I would like to set down, I must allow myself a passing remark on the perversity of Mother Nature. While hedges of recently planted cypresses, reared with tender care and transplanted at the right time, were roughly handled by the unexpected cold winds that came out of season and destroyed many of the young bushes, turning their vivid green of life into the rusty red of death, I had to arrange for the felling of several rows of beautiful willow trees whose luxuriant growth had seriously overshadowed our kitchen garden last year. Each one of these numerous willow trees had been originally a rough, rootless post, from which only the bark had not been stripped, used for the support of garden fencing, and yet without exception they had all struck roots and developed into graceful trees whose branches reached 20 feet high !

Lt.-Gen. R. G. W. H. STONE, D.S.O., M.C., who has been appointed G.O.C. of the British troops in Egypt. He was formerly Assistant Commandant, Sudan Defence Force. *Photo, British Official: Crown Copyright*

Printed in England and published every alternate Friday by the Proprietors, The Amalgamated Press, Ltd., The Fleetway House, Farringdon Street, London, E.C.4. Registered for transmission by Canadian Magazine Post. Sole Agents for Australia and New Zealand : Messrs. Gordon & Gotch, Ltd. ; and for South Africa : Central News Agency, Ltd.—July 24, 1942. S.S. *Editorial Address :* JOHN CARPENTER HOUSE, WHITEFRIARS, LONDON E.C.4

Vol 6 # The War Illustrated N° 134

Edited by Sir John Hammerton

6d FORTNIGHTLY   AUGUST 7, 1942

RED ARMY MACHINE GUNNERS engaging the enemy at close quarters in a German-occupied village at the southern end of the vast Eastern Front. Towards the end of July the situation in this sector became increasingly grave for our most gallant allies. "There the question is being decided," said the Soviet newspaper Red Star; "will the enemy succeed in his aims or shall we stop him, delivering such a blow as will clear the road for victory ? Can we stop the enemy ? The answer is undoubtedly, Yes !"   Photo, Planet News

NO. 135 WILL BE PUBLISHED FRIDAY, AUGUST 21

ALONG THE BATTLE FRONTS

by Our Military Critic, Maj.-Gen. Sir Charles Gwynn, K.C.B., D.S.O.

IN the third week of July the general situation had become grave and alarming. Germany's 1942 offensive had developed in even greater strength than was expected. Although it had been evident that during the winter and spring her air power and armour had been husbanded with extreme economy, it was uncertain how far they would be concentrated for the attainment of a single object.

It is now practically certain that she is staking her whole available offensive strength to secure control of the Caucasian oil supplies both for her own use and to deny them to the Red Army.

The crucial question is whether she will be able to maintain the great effort she is making. She has already spent much on preliminary operations, and the tenacity of the Russians at Voronezh has disturbed the even development of her plans.

Communication between the Russian central armies and the lower Volga has been kept open, and consequently the northern flank of the German drive is not secure. On the other hand, the southern wing of the offensive has made rapid progress in the area between the Donetz and the great loop of the Don. Timoshenko's armies here have been forced to retreat southwards, and his troops west of the Donetz in particular may be cut off.

Much must depend on whether Russian forces which have retreated south retain sufficient fighting capacity to exhaust the impetus of the German advance.

It is conceivable that Timoshenko will not attempt to withdraw his troops west of the Donetz, but leave them to fight it out, accepting the risk of encirclement. If the Germans were held up west of the Donetz for a considerable time, their drive east of the river, with lengthened lines of communication, might lose its momentum. The progress of its main bodies shows signs of becoming slower. Critical as the situation is for our ally, the enemy must have his anxieties. Having played for high stakes, he cannot afford to lose, and the Russians have given evidence of their toughness.

EGYPT In Egypt about the same time the situation was still critical, for although Auchinleck had made a great recovery, there remained an element of uncertainty while Rommel's armour strength remained formidable. Neither side was in a

position to take risks : Auchinleck especially so, and his policy of compelling his opponent to expend his resources piecemeal was evidently sound.

During the first week of July the crisis in Egypt reached its peak. It was an anxious question whether Auchinleck would be able to muster sufficient strength to prevent a renewal of Rommel's advance.

By the end of the week it became clear that, temporarily at least, Rommel had shot his bolt. His attempt to rush the defences at El Alamein had been repulsed by the South Africans, and attempts to turn them in the south had been frustrated by mobile columns. But probably the work of the Empire air forces—R.A.F., South African and Australian—was the decisive factor. By maintaining continuous intensive attacks on the enemy's supply columns, airfields and concentrations of troops, and by intervening in actual ground engagements,

his supply organization, repaired damaged armour and given his troops rest. His main infantry formations, chiefly Italian, held the coastal road sector ; his armour was concentrated behind the centre of his front, while his right, turned sharply back for some 20 miles to protect his communications, was held by mobile detachments and small posts.

If at this time Auchinleck had received sufficient fresh reinforcements, a n d had had armour in adequate quantity, there would have been an obvious opportunity for a counter-offensive on a major scale against Rommel's tired force. But the Eighth Army was still very exhausted, and reinforcements, especially of armour, were not yet sufficient to justify an attempt which if it failed would have disastrous consequences, and which if it succeeded could not be relentlessly exploited.

WESTERN DESERT battlefront on July 19, showing how the 8th Army gained ground in all three sectors. In the battle for the Ruweisat ridge the enemy lost about 25 tanks, chiefly at the hands of our anti-tank gunners on the 6-pounder batteries.
Courtesy of News Chronicle

they accomplished three objects : they left the enemy short of supplies, especially of water ; they gave him no opportunity to rest ; and they contributed to his discomfiture when he advanced to attack.

During the second week of the month Rommel was therefore compelled to adopt a defensive attitude, though no doubt with the intention of renewing his offensive as soon as he had received reinforcements, developed

Auchinleck did not leave his opponent undisturbed to recover his offensive power. Mobile detachments raided and harried the enemy, and air activity was constantly increased.

On July 10 he made his first move to recover ground by advancing his right about five miles to Tel el Eisa. It is not yet clear whether this was in order to add depth to his position or to forestall an attack. The operation, which had a definitely limited

TANKS ON THE MOVE in the forward areas of the North African battlefield. While the British armoured units manoeuvre across the desert under a sun so intense that the outside steel becomes too hot to touch and the inside is a suffocating inferno, the R.A.F. supports the advance with a terrific and relentless barrage on aerodromes and landing-grounds nearest the battlefield. By the middle of July the main British armour was in place along the central positions facing the bulk of Rommel's Panzers.

Photo, British Official : Crown Copyright

objective, was very successful, 2,000 prisoners, mainly Italian, and some guns being captured, and commanding ground occupied.

In the following days the enemy made a number of counter-attacks, both by day and night, using tanks to support his infantry, but without committing his main armoured force. It was a period of confused fighting in which ground was lost and recovered in a series of attacks and counter-attacks, but in the end our troops remained in possession of the essential features they had captured.

WHILE this fighting about Tel el Eisa was still in progress, on July 14 Auchinleck struck again 10 miles farther south, penetrating the Axis positions on the low Ruweisat ridge, which runs for some eight miles parallel to the coast.

Although not a strongly marked feature, the ridge commands a wide view, and Rommel evidently attached importance to it, for he counter-attacked violently. This time he called on his carefully husbanded Panzer divisions, and our own armour intervened to support the infantry in the positions they had captured. A tank battle, which at one time seemed likely to develop into a decisive test of armoured strength, ensued, and went on throughout the 15th and 16th, to be followed by a lull. Both sides had suffered casualties, but neither had a preponderance of strength sufficient to justify taking risks in forcing an issue ; and neither had made mistakes in manoeuvre which could not be rectified by evasion.

Rommel had nevertheless been forced to expend much of the reserve supplies he had been attempting to accumulate, and to bring into action reserves of his air force and armour which he had evidently been husbanding for a major operation.

IT is clear that the tank battle developed from a comparatively minor operation, and that neither commander had deliberately planned a far - reaching operation. With Alexandria so close behind him, Auchinleck obviously must act cautiously. Rommel, on the other hand, may risk an early decision, for with his long line of communications exposed to air attack he can hardly hope to receive reinforcement on a scale which would compensate for the deterioration of his army due to wastage from attrition and summer conditions in the desert.

If he does not feel strong enough to renew his offensive within a short period it seems probable that he may be compelled to withdraw, possibly to Mersa Matruh, where conditions would be more favourable for building up his strength and where he would be less vulnerable to harassing attacks. The superiority which our air forces have established and their increased range of action, due to the appearance of American heavy bombers, are becoming a vital factor in the situation : for it must affect the rate at which Rommel can receive accessions to his strength and the conditions under which his troops have to live.

RUSSIA

The first three weeks of July saw a grave deterioration of the situation in Russia. The German claim to have captured Voronezh was soon proved to be premature, but by reckless expenditure of life Von Bock by the middle of the month had succeeded in crossing the Don in strength and in forming a strong bridgehead that included a footing in the town. And from the neighbourhood of Orel to this point he had established a defensive front which protected his left flank from counter-attack by Zhukov's armies.

The intensity of the fighting testified to the importance both sides attached to Voronezh. If the Germans captured it they would secure one of the few places where a railway crosses the Don and can be used for the maintenance of an army operating east of the river.. From Voronezh an army could either strike south, turning the Don defences, or strike east, interrupting the railways which run from the Volga river ports to the Moscow region, while at the same time prolonging the northern defensive flank of the offensive. The Russian counter-attacks, which not only denied Voronezh to the enemy but endangered the German troops that had crossed the river, represented therefore a most encouraging success.

RUSSIAN FRONT. The enemy armies were heroically held by Timoshenko at Voronezh, but farther south they gained ground in their drive towards Stalingrad, and the Russians announced on July 19 that Voroshilovgrad had been abandoned.
Courtesy of Daily Sketch

Unfortunately, the German drive from the Kharkov region achieved much more than that from the Kursk front. Having crossed the Oskol at Kupiansk it advanced rapidly eastwards to the Don and south-eastwards through the great tract of corn-growing country between the Don and Donetz, which at this season offered a perfect surface for Panzer tactics.

ONCE the line of the Oskol was lost, there was no other obstacle which could be held till the Don was reached. The Russians therefore retreated, rearguards fighting tenaciously and leaving small centres of resistance which, holding out to the last, delayed the German main bodies. In their advance the Germans overran the very important Moscow-Rostov railway, which had provided the main lateral communication between the northern and southern Russian armies. They made no attempt, however, to cross the Don, but swung southwards, aiming at isolating the whole of Timoshenko's left wing in the Donetz basin and cutting its vital railway communication with Stalingrad. Up to July 22 no attack was made from the west towards Rostov, but the Russians in the Donetz basin were under heavy pressure from the north. Clearly there was a danger that the whole of the rich territory west of the Don would fall into German hands, and Russian troops there, even if they made good their retreat, would lose their main sources of supply. Would they in such circumstances be able to check a German advance into Caucasia or across the Don towards Stalingrad ?

The successful resistance at Voronezh should enable reinforcements to reach Stalingrad and the line of the Don in that neighbourhood, but the importance of protecting traffic on the great Volga waterway which carries oil to the north cannot be overestimated. The stand at Voronezh may, therefore, prove a decisive factor in the further development of the situation.

MARSHAL VON BOCK, commander of the German armies assailing Voronezh and Rostov, listens to a description of the fighting given by Gen. Lindemann, in command of an infantry division (top). The railway lines between Taganrog and Orel are the object of the most bitter contest ; the lower photo shows Red Army men defending a vital sector.
Photos, Ministry of Information, Sport & General

The Eighth Army Goes Into Action in Egypt

WITH AUCHINLECK'S INTREPID ARMY. 1. British troops cautiously approach a burning enemy supply truck. 2. Men of the Rifle Brigade in an advance Motor Brigade column sent to locate and harass enemy supply lines ; a raiding party such as this may be away for days at a time. 3. Digging a pit for a 3·7 A.A. gun. 4. Radioed picture showing an infantryman creeping forward to the attack under heavy shelling. 5. Scots Guards advancing under cover of tanks at El Alamein.

Photos, British Official: Crown Copyright

At Alamein Rommel's Drive Was Halted

ON THE DESERT BATTLEFIELD. Top, El Alamein, which, although it consists only of a railway station and a few poor dwellings, has given its name to one of the great battles of the War. Centre, tanks being moved up to the front on special transport lorries. Bottom, enemy prisoners seen as they marched into our lines; one British soldier sufficed as an escort to the long column of battle-weary and discouraged men.

Photos, British Official: Crown Copyright

Five Years: China's Great Fight For Freedom

On July 7 China entered upon the sixth year of her heroic resistance to the Japanese invader.
The struggle which the Japanese referred to at first half-contemptuously as an "incident" has
developed into one of the longest and most bitterly contested wars of modern times.

NOT many of us worried very much about China in those summer months of 1937 when the Japanese, having spent half-a-dozen years in digesting Manchuria marched into the northern provinces of China proper. Reading of the skirmish between little parties of Japanese and Chinese troops at Marco Polo bridge, a few miles from Peiping, we thought that it was just a skirmish, one more inconsiderable clash in a long period of Sino-Japanese friction. Yet those few shots fired in the half-light five years ago have led to the death and mutilation of millions, the devastation of provinces as big as some European countries, the burning of great cities and of an uncountable multitude of villages, death and rape and arson on a scale hardly approached in all the many bloodstained and fire scorched pages of history.

That was on July 7, 1937. Five years have passed, and the sound of those few shots is still reverberating through the hills and across the seemingly boundless plains of China. At the outset it looked as if the Japanese would have it all their own way; vastly superior in equipment and training, if not in numbers, they drove the undisciplined hordes of the Chinese levies before them, and by the end of the war's first month claimed to be in full possession of both Tientsin and Peiping. But as the months passed Chinese resistance stiffened. For five tremendous weeks they strove desperately to hold Shanghai, losing 150,000 men in the process: Blasted out of the great port by Japanese bombers, guns, and tanks, they made a fresh stand at Nanking; and when that, too, fell they continued the fight as they withdrew up the Yangtze valley to Hankow. In October 1938, when we were still feeling relieved, if more than a little disgusted, at the results of the Munich Conference, Hankow was captured by the Japanese, and a few days later fell Canton, the great commercial metropolis of the south. But after these speedy and spectacular triumphs Japan found increasing difficulty in overcoming the opposition of Chiang Kai-shek's regulars and of the great host of irregulars who kept up the struggle within territory which, on the map, was included within the sphere of Japanese occupation.

FOR it must be emphasized that much of Japan's conquests are "paper": she has neither the men nor the material to hold down and exploit the huge areas invaded by her armies, and perforce has to content herself with maintaining control of the seaports, industrial centres, principal railway junctions, and the vital strategic points born of China's geography. Thus it is that Chinese courts still hold sway far within territories that are nominally Japanese, and Chinese guerilla bands keep up the war in regions which have been "conquered" long ago. So vast is China, indeed, that there are some districts even near the main war zone where Japanese soldiers are still an unfamiliar sight.

But there is not a town, not a village or hamlet in the country, wrote The Times correspondent in Chungking recently, which has not learnt in the past five years to dread the drone of enemy bombers. The aeroplane has brought the war home to the dwellings of the remotest glens of the far interior. "I have heard a Chinese woman silence a crying child with the admonition, 'Fei chi, Fei chi' (planes, planes), much as English mothers in Border castles were wont to chide errant children by reminding them of Black Douglas."

And there, it is suggested, we have one of the chief causes of Japan's undoing. China has seen many invasions during the last four thousand years or so; many conquerors have come, and some of them have

CHINA, showing (shaded) the areas occupied by the Japanese in the course of five years of war. In recent weeks the invaders have launched a new offensive designed to secure the vertical railways from Manchukuo to Canton and the bulge in Chekiang to Japan, whence planes might set out to bomb the Japanese cities.

stayed long enough to be absorbed in the vast Chinese mass. But for the most part the conquerors have taken care to respect the lives and ways of the great bulk of the population; seldom if ever have they resorted to mass terrorism. But the Japanese have brought a new sort of war to China, one far more terrible, far more universal. The story of the bombing of defenceless cities has horrified the peace-loving and eminently civilized Chinese; and even worse in Chinese eyes is the tale of horror of occupied areas, carried far and wide throughout the country by the millions of refugees. To quote another sentence from The Times correspondent, "Nothing can diminish the loathing with which the Chinese view the bestial attacks on their women, especially in a country where not long ago adultery was punished by burial alive amidst the execrations of the villagers."

Huns and Tartars, Mongols and Manchus: worse, far worse, than the worst of these invaders of the past are the Japanese of today. Slaughters and burnings may be forgotten, if not forgiven; but the humiliations and obscenities, the horrible happenings that accompanied—to take but one instance—the sack of Nanking, can never be wiped from the memory of a great and proud, albeit peaceful, people. Small wonder, then,

that again this year the Double Seventh—the seventh day of the seventh month, the anniversary of the incident of July 7, 1937—was made the occasion for great demonstrations of national unity and resolve to continue the struggle until China's soil is purged of the invader's hateful presence.

BUT can China continue the war, if not indefinitely, at least for years? In the past five years she has paid a terrible price. Up to the end of 1941—up to the end of the period, that is, when China was grappling single-handed with the arch-aggressor of the Orient—the Chinese Army had suffered the loss of six millions killed and wounded; as for the losses inflicted upon the civilian population and the extent of the material damage, no estimates can be forthcoming: they cannot be computed in figures or expressed in words. Yet still China has continued the fight; nor in drawing up the balance sheet of the five years of war do we find nothing to be placed on the credit side.

Only since 1937 has China risen to the full heights of her nationhood; the Revolution that began in 1911 gave her strength, the war with Japan has given her unity—unity such as has not been hers for many a hundred years. Again, though the war has ravaged more than a quarter of her territory, though much that the Japanese have not destroyed the Chinese themselves have "scorched," in spite of all these things China today is, in some ways, economically stronger and more sound. No longer is industry concentrated along the eastern seaboard and in the Treaty Ports which were under foreign dominance: the stern necessities of war have led to vast migrations of industry as of people, so that today provinces which five years ago were the most backward and benighted now lead the way in industrial development, in education, and in all the arts of cultured existence.

THESE things are to the good, and they are full of encouragement—but not for the immediate future. China is weary and hard pressed: she must have help, and that help her allies of the United Nations are ready to give. But how? All the Chinese coast-line is in Japanese hands, not one of her many ports is functioning save for the enemy's ships. On land, too, the situation is black. Indo-China was a door, but that was closed last year. Then there was the Burma Road, well described as China's lifeline; but it is a lifeline no longer, since the Japanese have overrun Burma.

True, other routes are being developed—from U.S.S.R. through Sinkiang to Lanchow; from Sadiya in Assam (British India) to Chungking across the mountains; and from Lhasa in Tibet to Chengtu. But of these only the first is stated to be in actual use, and that involves a haul of thousands of miles across largely unpeopled desert, so that camels and donkeys have to be relied upon rather than motor lorries. Then there is the air; it has been estimated that a fleet of 150 large transport planes, operating from bases in India, each carrying 75 tons per month, could make good the loss to China of the Burma Road.

The Chinese, it has been stated, are holding down 31 Japanese divisions, more than 600,000 men; and only from China can the Japanese islands and cities be bombed. But there is here more than a selfish interest. Out of the darkness and loss and bitter disappointments of these weary years of war China shines like a beacon of hope, holding out the promise of a better and fuller life for all the many millions of common humanity.   E. ROYSTON PIKE

Since 1937 They Have Kept the Japs at Bay

CHINESE GIRLS—like this nurse, a member of the American Baptist Surgical Unit, tending an injured soldier behind the lines—have been at the front for five years.

Air-raid cave shelter at Chungking, capital of Free China, into which the young population cheerfully stream when an alert warns them of the approach of Japanese bombers.

Smiling girl students of Lingkiang College who, when they were evacuated from Shanghai, set up new quarters with their own hands at Chungking, built a road, and levelled athletic grounds.

Below, Gen. Hsiung Shih-Fei, head of the Chinese Military Mission in Washington, and Lt.-Gen. Hugh Drum, commanding the U.S. First Army, salute the American flag in New York.

DISABLED CHINESE SOLDIERS work at cooperative wool-spinning (above). Centre oval, Adm. Chen Shao-Kwan is seen standing between Lt.-Col. McHugh, U.S. Naval Attaché, and Brig. Grimsdale, British Military Attaché, just after he had accepted the gift of three gunboats at Chungking. One, U.S.S. Tutuila, was the last remaining American warship in Free China waters ; the others were H.M.S. Falcon and H.M.S. Gannet. These vessels once patrolled the Yangtse with their guns pointed against the Chinese, protecting their own nationals ; now they point at the invaders of China and are manned by Chinese sailors.

Photos, British Official ; The Daily Mirror, L.N.A., Keystone

THE WAR IN THE AIR

by Capt. Norman Macmillan, M.C., A.F.C.

THE air war has raged without interruption over the Far East, in the Australasian zone, on the Russian front (where our allies estimate that more than 3,000 enemy craft were destroyed during the two months' fighting for Sevastopol and Voronezh), in North Africa, Malta, Western Europe, and the Arctic, where German bombers attacked an Archangel-bound convoy for several days.

The seriousness of shipping losses to the United Nations' supply lines was stressed by the holding of a secret session of Parliament, and during the period under review—from Saturday July 4 to Friday 17—Bomber Command continued its counter-offensive against the German submarine campaign and Axis shipping supply lines.

Details became known about the attack on Bremen on the night of July 2/3 by a force which included Halifax, Stirling, and Lancaster bombers. In the space of half-an-hour the bombers shot down two enemy fighters, and left widespread fires behind them, especially in the dock area. One Halifax, thrown on to its back by a shellburst while making a steeply banked turn, went into a spin, but its pilot righted his heavy craft (a tribute to British design) and went on to drop his load.

Wilhelmshaven was raided on July 8/9 ; 4,000-lb. bombs were dropped. This was the first official intimation of the use of bombs of this size by the R.A.F. Large four-engined bombers have made it possible to use these bombs, whose destructive effect causes havoc over a wide area. The Ruhr, including Duisburg, a large port on the Rhine, was pounded on the night of July 13/14. These were the three main night attacks during a period when weather interfered with operations.

ON July 11 Lancasters attacked Danzig in daylight. The Lancaster is fast ; she sounds like a train roaring through a tunnel. The Germans must loathe the sound of these aircraft passing over their heads. Flying through thunderclouds rising from 800 feet to 15,000 feet, the aircraft were iced-up and charged with static electricity. Some had to turn back, but a strong force reached Danzig before twilight, and dived low over the submarine yards (where as many as fifteen submarines can be fitted out simultaneously) and left fires after the bomb-bursts. Theirs was a flight of 1,700 miles.

A simultaneous attack was made on Flensburg, the Baltic submarine port, close to the Danish frontier. This daylight attack was repeated on the 16th, and Stirlings bombed submarine yards near Lübeck. On the same day the Ruhr was also attacked in daylight by single aircraft. During four nights of this period mines were laid in enemy waters.

Twenty-nine bombers were lost in all operations.

ON July 4 (American Independence Day) United States' crews cooperated for the first time with Bomber Command. Twelve Bostons, six manned by U.S. crews, set out, and attacked the Dutch airfields of Hamstede, Alkmaar, and Valkenburg, concentrating their bombs and bullets on hangars, administrative buildings, and dispersal points. Two of the American-manned aircraft and one of the British were lost.

Two remarkable sea rescues are worthy of record. Pilot Officer Holbrooke Mahn was piloting his R.C.A.F. Hampden bomber off the Frisian Islands at about 200-300 feet when one engine failed. There was no time to jettison the bombs before the Hampden hit the water with a crash. The rubber dinghy opened. But there was no food and only two quarts of water. On the eighth day the navigator died, on the ninth the gunner. On the thirteenth day the pilot caught and killed a seagull, sucked its blood and ate the fish in its gut. That bird saved his life. He was picked up next day, weak, but still alive.

On July 8 an anti-submarine patrol Whitley bomber of Coastal Command came down in the Bay of Biscay 100 miles from the Spanish coast. A second Whitley sighted smoke from a Very cartridge fired from the dinghy. Other Whitleys kept watch, lost the dinghy in the night, picked it up again in the morning. A Sunderland went out. It spotted the smoke of the last Very cartridge possessed by the dinghy's crew. The flying boat made a tricky landing on a nasty swell, and the crew of six from the Whitley were taken aboard and flown home after a 24-hours' drift.

A Catalina flying-boat had a duel with a U-boat in the Mediterranean. The Catalina's bombs beat the U-boat's guns, and the submarine sank stern first. The Catalina attempted to alight to pick up about 30 survivors, hit a tremendous swell, broke her hull, but got into the air again and limped home—without the survivors.

Heavy air fighting in the El Alamein area of the Western Desert brought cooperation between air and ground forces to a new peak of efficiency. Bombers raided Benghazi,

Wing-Cdr. 'PADDY' FINUCANE, D.S.O., D.F.C., whose death was announced on July 17. The radiator of his Spitfire was hit by a machine-gun on the French dunes when returning from the biggest fighter sweep ever made, and crashed into the sea. Finucane, Britain's fighter ace and victor of 32 air combats, was only 21. *Photo, Sport & General*

Tobruk, and many other places. Ground-fighting forces saw the enemy being pounded from the air just ahead of their positions by our bombers and fighter-bombers. During one period of 24 hours 130 bombers, escorted by 127 fighters, attacked enemy concentrations south-west of El Alamein ; 75 Kittyhawk bombers attacked transport on El Daba aerodrome ; 166 Spitfires and Hurricanes carried out sweeps at hourly intervals over the battle area ; at night 84 Wellingtons, eight Liberators, and six Blenheims bombed motor transport concentrated in the El Daba area and shipping off Benghazi. On July 10 Allied fighters went over wave after wave for hours on end. Beaufighters attacked troop transport aircraft and enemy shipping creeping along the coast. The battle continues . . .

A South African Air Force fighter squadron encountered 14 Stukas about to peel off into a dive on one of our positions. The Stukas were escorted by fighter aircraft. The S.A. Hurricanes waded in, led by 28-year-old Cape Town Major Le Mesurier, crashed 13 Stukas and one Messerschmitt 109 in a few seconds—a record !

DURING the first eleven days of July 83 enemy aircraft were destroyed over Malta, where the battle of attrition from the air continues ; 78 aircraft (of which 29 were bombers) were shot down by our fighters. We lost 21 fighters, but saved nine of their pilots.

The first Czech fighter squadron with the R.A.F. is now two years old ; it flies cannon-gun and machine-gun Spitfires, and has destroyed 43 enemy aircraft. Altogether Czech pilots have destroyed 118 enemy aeroplanes.

The second anniversary of Polish Air Force day was July 16. On July 3, when German aircraft attempted a raid on the Midlands, No. 303 Polish Squadron shot down two Junkers 88s. This squadron has the second highest score in Fighter Command. Up to July 15, 1942, its bag was 175 enemy aircraft ; more than 100 were destroyed in the Battle of Britain with Hurricanes ; it now has Spitfires. Polish 302 Squadron, formed in August 1940, shot down 35 enemy aircraft up to July 15. Polish fighter pilots have destroyed 464 enemy aircraft altogether.

During June Fighter Command and anti-aircraft guns accounted for 83 enemy aircraft ; intruder patrols destroyed 12 enemy bombers over bases in Europe, bringing the score to 31 for the first six months of 1942. During June 69 fighters were lost by Fighter Command ; five pilots were saved.

THIS FIESELER STORCH German aircraft, captured on the field of battle, is now used by the R.A.F. for reconnaissance purposes and air-to-ground cooperation in the Egyptian battle zone. The Fieseler Storch is a high-winged monoplane, so built that the pilot can take off or land within a distance of little more than 50 yards. Rommel uses one at the front in Egypt. *Photo, British Official*

War's Whirlwind Sweeps the Summer Sky

IN ENGLAND NOW it is the time of harvest. A farmer pulls up his team as a formation of Coastal Command aircraft roar above the field on their way to make a sweep over Northern France. From the peace of the sun-bathed countryside, where the grain is being garnered, in what it is hoped, and believed, will be the most bountiful harvest within the memory of living men, to the clatter of enemy ack-ack above the damaged French ports, is a matter of minutes only.

Photo, The Daily Mirror

Lancasters Flew 1,750 Miles to Danzig and Back

AVRO LANCASTER is Britain's latest heavy bomber. Its dimensions are: span, 102 ft. ; length, 69 ft. ; height on ground, 19 ft. 7 in. Maximum speed, about 300 m.p.h. The engines are four Rolls-Royce Merlins ; three-bladed constant speed airscrews are fitted. Like the Stirling and Halifax the Lancaster has power-operated nose, tail, and dorsal gun turrets.

Lancasters were used for the famous daylight raid on the submarine diesel-engine plant at Augsburg in April, and on July 11 several squadrons made daylight flights to Danzig and Flensburg on the Baltic. These photographs show (1) an Avro Lancaster in flight ; (2) the pilot's cockpit and the front gun turret above the bomb aimer's position ; (3) the dorsal gun turret ; and (4) rear view.

Photos, British Official ; G.P.U.

Yet More Airfields in Britain's Countryside

WORKS SERVICE SQUADRONS have been established in the R.A.F., their job being the repair, maintenance, and extension of aerodromes. Above, filling in a bomb crater ; right, laying a metal track runway.

R.A.F. men making a concrete perimeter road round an airfield in the West of England. This work was formerly carried out by Army units or by firms of civilian contractors.

CANADIAN ARMY ENGINEERS constructing an airport in Great Britain. Above, travelling concrete machine making a runway ; right, sand and cement are brought in trucks to feed the giant machine.

Eyes of the Army ～ And Much More Besides

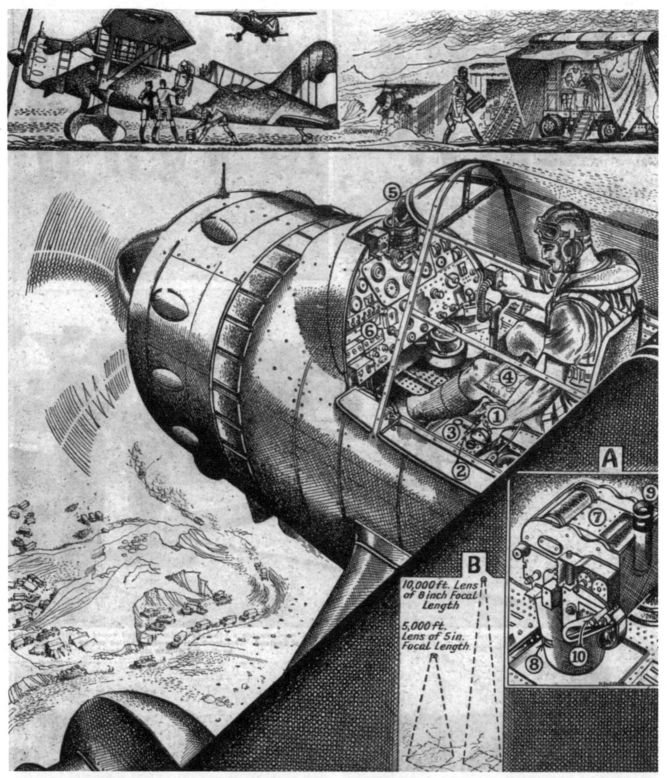

Specially drawn by Haworth for THE WAR ILLUSTRATED

ARMY-R.A.F. COOPERATION was in its infancy during the Battle of France in the summer of 1940, and after Dunkirk many hard words were said by Tommies who failed to understand why they had seen so few aircraft supporting them in action. But some time after the fall of France the Army Cooperation Command of the R.A.F. was formed, and as a result liaison between the two Services has been greatly improved. Many of the Army Coopera aircraft are piloted by officers who have been seconded from the Army to the R.A.F.

Every Army Commander must know what the enemy is doing, where his strength is being massed, and where his strongest fortifications are in defence. This information, and much more besides, is provided by the Army Cooperation squadrons, and the large drawing above shows the pilot of a Westland Lysander Army Cooperation plane—one of the several types used for this work—observing and photographing an enemy position. His left hand is grasping the control knob (1), which operates the electrically-driven camera placed farther back in the plane. As he does this he is looking down through the camera sighting device (2), which is trained through a lens in the floor (3). The pilot has his map handy (4), and the compass is just in front of him. The small button on top of the control stick fires the forward machine-guns, and the gun sight is at (5). The row of switches (6) are for bomb selection. Besides the pilot there is an air gunner in the rear, but the main protection is provided by an escort of fighter planes.

DIAGRAM (A) shows details of the camera, which weighs about 35 lb., and takes photographs automatically, varying the shutter interval according to the height of the plane and its ground speed, so that each exposure overlaps slightly the preceding one. The magazine carrying 125 exposures is seen at (7), the lens position and control at (8). As shown in this diagram, the camera is fixed pointing vertically downwards, to take photographs for map-making purposes; but it may also be hand-operated for taking views at oblique angles. In this case the sighting apparatus (9) is used; the hand-operating handle is at (10).

DIAGRAM (B) shows the differing areas photographed by the camera at varying heights. Lenses with focal lengths up to 20 in. are used for great heights.

The topmost drawing shows the scene when the pilot has returned to his base. The rear gunner is handing over the camera to the ground staff, who will develop the contents in quick time in their mobile developing van. The pilot is seen carrying his maps to the H.Q. of the Air Intelligence liaison officer.

Russia Burnt and Blasted by the Fire of War

IN THE CRIMEA, three of the last inhabitants leaving the battered city of Kerch after the Russian High Command ordered its evacuation (top). Centre, bowed with fatigue and melancholy, a Russian family in the Ukraine drags the harrow over a field which has now to be tilled for the benefit of the conquerors. Bottom, a single German soldier flees to shelter in a wrecked Russian town from which the Nazis are being driven by artillery counter-attack.

Photos, Planet News, Keystone, New York Times Photos

UNDER THE SWASTIKA

Sidelights on Life and Things in France Today

A celebrated Frenchman of letters, who has written widely in the critical journals of Paris and London and did work of the greatest value to Anglo-French relationships during the War of 1914-18, sends us these interesting notes on values as they obtain today in the France of Hitler and Laval. We give the article here as the first of a new feature dealing with life in the occupied and Nazi-dominated countries.

MISINFORMATION may have many sources other than those fed so bounteously by Dr. Goebbels, and some of them perfectly guileless. Things are said in good faith which by repetition start rumours completely opposed to the facts. I read lately in a popular London daily that many fine villas on the French Riviera are being sold " dirt cheap." It was in a reported conversation with a tennis champion just returned from Unoccupied France. This lady added that English people were extremely well treated there, a point on which all travellers concur.

But I was the more surprised at what she said concerning these dirt-cheap villas, as a few days before I had met a Frenchman recently escaped from Occupied France. He is a businessman, little prone to flights of imagination, and a stickler for realities. We had been talking about trade and finance under the German invader, and he gave me some reliable facts. According to the examples he quoted, there has been an amazing increase in the value of landed property. He told me of various properties which we both knew ; one near Issoudun, in the centre of France, fat land, fertile in wheat, which had been sold for ten thousand francs an acre, and another in Normandy, pasture and apple orchards, which had reached twenty thousand francs, these figures being respectively five and ten times their pre-war values. A whole estate near Lyons, with a big house and extensive farm buildings, which had been bought for 380,000 francs in 1936, changed hands a few months ago for two million francs !

WHY, then, should villas on the Riviera go for " dirt prices " ? It was hard to believe, with all respect to the alleged statements of the tennis star, so I resolved to verify my doubts. As in the case of all wishful thinking, that was easier said than done. For a time I had no notion where to find credible information. I came across that by chance.

There is a place in London where privileged professional people can see quite a number of the current French daily papers. There I go regularly to peruse them, not that I would say I read them, from the " Premier

' THE LAUGHING BUCCANEER': Laval as a French cartoonist sees him, with swastikas decorating his collar, tie and cuffs, and the Nazi emblem superimposed on the miniature French flag over which he gloats. The original drawing was received by the B.B.C. from Montpellier on April 25.

Paris," or rather " Premier Vichy "—i.e. the editorial leader, as they say in England—to the classified advertisements, or " smalls." The news is usually out of date and the comments more or less insidious, in the Paris papers especially, and no wonder their French readers hardly believe a word of what they print. Their advertisement columns, however, are revealing and instructive. Indeed, it is there that the future historian may find an exhaustive documentation on many subjects essential to the writing of a complete history of the present economic and political vicissitudes of my unhappy country.

French dailies have never carried a display of advertisements comparable with the English press, although provincial papers devote a much larger proportion of their space than those of Paris to advertisements. Advertising experts agree that the contrast is explained by the fact that the French public is restive to any sort of propaganda ; they smell a rat at any " réclame," any puff or boost.

At the present time there is such a shortage of every kind of goods that most traders have nothing to boost and do not advertise. It is the other way about : the customer asks for second-hand articles. In the provincial papers, which are published in a single sheet, the classified advertisements—and these are very few—concern chiefly agricultural equipment, factory machinery, millwright work, tools and plant that are no more to be found in the shops. Farmers advertise also for farmhands, who are very scarce since most of them are war-prisoners.

IN the Paris newspapers employment bureaux insert alluring offers for skilled labour ; and the more alluring they sound the more likely are they to be inserted for the benefit of German manufacturers. Sometimes you come upon some queer item when people in want of cash offer such articles as furs, clocks, watches, furniture, " a pair of shoes nearly new, size 9," and " nearly new " also, " a lounge suit for a young man." Hotels also advertise unobtrusively for holidays, but none on the Channel and Atlantic coasts, and very few on the Mediterranean coast. All mention " cuisine soignée " and " normal provisioning," whatever it may mean in this time of restrictions and rationing. No doubt the black market comes into play here.

Then, opening the Figaro, I discovered unexpectedly the customary column of special advertisements under the heading " Immeubles à vendre." I turned to the Temps : there it was, too, just as before the war. Remembering the assertions of the tennis champion, I went eagerly through the lists of those " real estates for sale," and found that a good many were situated on the Riviera. As the properties were to be auctioned through a law official, an " avoué " or a " notaire," an upset price was mentioned, and it was easy to calculate that it was not " dirt cheap " ! Compared with pre-war prices, the proportion was five and six times as much, and no final at that.

What is the explanation ? Owing chiefly to the crushing indemnity that France has to fork out daily to the invader, currency is increasing in huge proportions, and the value of money deteriorating accordingly. People who are making profits are chary of keeping their paper money, which when peace comes will not even be worth the paper it is printed on, nor are they trusting transferable securities. So they turn to " real estate," whose value can but increase, especially if it is producing crops, ploughed land, grazing land, woodland and vineyards. That, with manual labour, will remain the real capital, the unchangeable assets, " real estate," as the English term so aptly describes it ; that is the kind of investment that appeals to the Frenchman.

A SMALL advertisement which I found by itself among the lot bears out that these cautious people, well advised about realities, have also less material preoccupations. Their intellectual needs are not disregarded, and a well-known circulating library offers " an interesting profit " to " persons " able to canvass for subscribers, promising the prompt supply of all new books. It will be easy work, it says, " as the taste for reading is so readily developing in all social classes." The French may go short of food and fuel, but it would appear from this modest notice that they are whetting their appetite for spiritual provender.

IN PARIS gloom reigns instead of gaiety. Here is the Place de la Concorde in May 1942. Apart from the German transport lorries, the only vehicles to be seen are bicycles and an occasional brougham belonging probably to French aristocrats of the old regime. On the right is the Ministry of Marine, which in June was sprayed with shells from the aircraft flown by Fl.-Lt. Gatward (see page 44) in his daring roof-top raid. *Photo, Keystone*

At Sunset the Convoy Sets Sail

Seen from beside the guns in the stern of a British destroyer, a convoy of Allied merchantmen stream away to the horizon and beyond. Perchance the ships are carrying men and
tanks and guns to one of our armies overseas. Or they may be bound for the Arctic, and
their safe arrival will mean yet another link in the chain of Anglo-Russian comradeship.

Dawn~The Convoy Well On Its Way

As the sun comes up on a new day the ships are revealed in line ahead (1), flags flying from the masthead and smoke pouring from the regiment of funnels. The convoy presses on (3). The "umbrella" of kite balloons is raised into the sky (2) as a precaution against enemy aircraft which may be tempted into making a mast-high bomb-dive.

Balloons that Beat the Dive-Bomber

The kite-balloons—little sisters of the barrage-balloons which float above Britain's cities and vital dockyards and munition centres—are taken out to sea in a depot-barge (4), where they are transferred to a naval drifter which hauls them to the ships of the convoy (5). Hundreds of dive-bombing attacks have been frustrated by these balloons.

Sunrise~In Sight of Port

Photos, British Official : Crown Copyright : Central Press

The voyage is over.   The convoy has completed its passage, the task of the guardian warships and ever-watchful planes has been safely completed.   But in a few hours, or days at most, the ships will be heading for the open sea again.   And Illustrious—the aircraft-carrier whose impressive shape we see below—will be writing fresh pages in an already glorious history.

114

So This Is How the Americans See Us!

Before they cross the Atlantic, American soldiers are given an official War Department publication called "A Short Guide to Great Britain." As will be seen from the extracts given below, it is written in racy language, and its 32 pages provide a delightfully fresh and not too unflattering —we are relieved to note•!—representation of our national home and character.

IN their major way of life British and American people are much alike. They speak the same language, they both believe in representative government, in freedom of worship, in freedom of speech. But each country has minor national characteristics which differ. It is by causing misunderstanding over these minor differences that Hitler hopes to make his propaganda effective.

The British are reserved, not unfriendly. You defeat enemy propaganda not by denying these differences exist, but by admitting them openly and then trying to understand them.

A 'REGULAR GUY' of the U.S. Overseas Forces now in this country. P.N.A.

For instance, the British are often more reserved in conduct than we are. On a small, crowded island, where 45,000,000 people live, each man learns to guard his privacy carefully, and is equally careful not to invade another man's privacy. So if Britons sit in trains or buses without starting up a conversation with you it doesn't mean they are being haughty and unfriendly. Probably they are paying more attention to you than you think, but they don't speak to you because they don't want to appear intrusive or rude.

Another difference. The British have phrases and colloquialisms of their own that may sound funny to you. You can make just as many " boners " in their eyes.

IT isn't a good idea, for instance, to say " bloody " in mixed company in Britain. It is one of their worst swear words. To say " I look like a bum " is offensive to their ears, for to the British this means that you look like your own backside. It isn't important, but just a tip if you are trying to shine in polite society.

American wages and American soldiers' pay are the highest in the world. When payday comes it would be a sound practice to learn to spend your money according to British standards.

They consider you highly paid. They won't think any better of you for throwing money around. They are more likely to feel that you haven't learned the common-sense virtue of thrift.

The British Tommy is apt to be specially touchy about the difference between his wages and yours. Keep this in mind, use common sense, and don't rub him the wrong way.

The British are tough. Don't be misled by the British tendency to be soft-spoken and polite. If they need to be they can be plenty tough.

THE English language did not spread across oceans and over the mountains and jungles and swamps of the world because these people were pantywaists. Sixty thousand British civilians—men, women and children —have died under bombs, and yet the morale of the British is unbreakable and high. A nation does not come through that if it does not have plain, common guts.

At first you will probably not like the almost continual rains and mists and absence of snow and crisp cold. Actually the City of London has less rain for the whole year than many places in the United States. Most people get used to English climate eventually.

Although you will read in papers about " Lords " and " Sirs," England is still one of the great Democracies and cradle of many American liberties. Personal rule by king has been dead in England for nearly 1,000 years. Today the King reigns but does not govern. British people have a great affection for their monarch, but they have stripped him of practically all political power. It is well to remember this in your comings and goings about England.

Be careful not to criticize the King. The British feel about that the way you would feel if anybody spoke against our country or our flag. Their King and Queen stuck with the people through blitzes, and had their home bombed just like anyone else. So their people are proud of them.

In general, more people play games in Britain than in America, and they play the game even if they are not good at it.

The British have theatres and movies (which they call cinemas) as we have, but the great place of recreation is the " pub."

A "PUB" (or public-house) is what we would call a bar or tavern. The usual drink is beer, which is not an imitation of German beer, as our beer is, but ale (but they usually call it beer or bitter). The British are beer drinkers and can " hold it." Beer is now below peacetime strength, but can still make a man's tongue wag at both ends. You will be welcome in British pubs as long as you remember one thing—the " pub " is the poor man's club or gathering-place where men have come to see their friends, not strangers.

You will naturally be interested in getting to know your opposite number—the British soldier (Tommy) you have heard and read about. You can understand that two actions on your part will slow up friendship—swiping his girl and not appreciating what his Army has been up against. Yes, and rubbing it in that you are better paid than he is.

Keep out of arguments. You can rub the Briton the wrong way by telling him " We came over and won the last one." Each nation did its share, but Britain remembers that nearly 1,000,000 of her best manhood died in the last war. America lost 60,000 in action. Such arguments, and the War Debts along with them, are dead issues.

The British don't know how to make a good cup of coffee. You don't know how to make a good cup of tea. It is an even swap.

The British are leisurely, but not really slow. Their crack trains held world speed records, a British ship held the Transatlantic record, a British car and British driver set up world speed records in America.

You will find the British money system easier than you think.

DON'T show off or brag or bluster— " swank," as the British say. If somebody looks in your direction and says, " He's chucking his weight about," you can be pretty sure you are off base. That is the time to pull in your ears.

The British will welcome you as friends and allies, but remember that crossing an ocean does not automatically make you a hero. There are housewives in aprons and youngsters in knee pants in Britain who have lived through more high-explosives in air raids than many soldiers saw in first-class barrages in the last war.

If you are invited to eat with a family, do not eat too much, otherwise you may eat up their weekly rations. Don't criticize food, beer, or cigarettes to the British. Remember they've been at war since 1939.

Don't make fun of the British speech or accents. You sound just as funny to them, but they will be too polite to show it.

You will soon find yourself among kindly, quiet, hardworking people who have been living under a strain such as few people in the world have ever known. In your dealings with them let this be your slogan: " It is always impolite to criticize your hosts ; it is militarily stupid to criticize your Allies."

And This Is Our Men's Guide To America

By way of companion to the above, here are some of the most interesting paragraphs from a small blue-covered pamphlet, "Notes For Your Guidance," which is handed to every young Briton who goes to the U.S.A. for flight training.

YOU will not be expected to tell your hosts and hostesses what is wrong, in your opinion, with them and their country. During this war, and probably after, our fate is closely bound up with that of the United States, and we shall need in this country people who understand the American viewpoint and interpret to us their reactions.

You are going to America as guests. Therefore, you will receive almost unbounded hospitality, the American standard of hospitality being as high as any in the world. Remember, that there is just as high a standard expected of the guest as of the host. You will be expected to feel and show appreciation. Do so.

The Americans are a tremendous nation who have built up standards different from our own in many ways. Expect Americans to be different from us. After all, their forefathers and predecessors in the continent fought to be independent of us. Grant them to be so in your mind as they are in fact.

You are going to the United States to learn. To learn your job, and, in doing so, to learn to like and understand Americans. This is almost as important as your technical training.

For Englishmen, ways of speech are often bound up with ideas of class distinction. Of course, there are differences in any country between the speech of the so-called well-educated and that of the ill-educated, and America is no exception, but you must beware of transferring unconscious assumptions drawn from your English experience to totally different conditions. The United States were a revolutionary, equalitarian country all the time the frontier was moving west, and, in spite of changes, remain so in sentiment to this day. Speech is not an index of class position, either way.

Just as we have a kind of stage Irishman and stage American in the national gallery of literary mythology, so the Americans have a stage Englishman. Don't be offended if you are measured up against certain characters in Dickens, or more likely against Bertie Wooster and Jeeves. It is poetic justice—and you will live down the comparison, and be taken as a regular guy when your hosts get to know you.

You will find plenty of sportsmanship and a code of what is and what is not done. But it is not always our code, and you may be surprised at some of the things that are done.

Don't expect the stately minuet of cricket, with its elaborate etiquette, on the baseball field, and remember that barracking is part of the art of the game. The idea is to win, not just to have a game. That idea is not altogether unknown in some games in other parts of the English-speaking world—and it is not a bad idea for a fighting man.

Under the Stars and Stripes They Go to War

AMERICA AT WAR. On Independence Day—July 4, the anniversary of the Declaration of Independence in 1776—200 recruits (above) were sworn into the armed forces of the U.S.A. in front of the Liberty Bell at Philadelphia. - Left, American Red Cross army nurses, heroines of Bataan, being decorated for bravery by Surg.-Gen. James C. Magee. Below, three U.S. Consolidated Patrol bombers on duty off the grim coast of Alaska.

Photos, Keystone, New York Times Photos

Australia and America : Comrades in Arms

IN NEW GUINEA, at a new American air base, Gen. M. Scanlan (centre) greets Gen. Ralph Royce, head of the Pacific Air Forces (left), and Lt.-Cmdr. Lyndon Johnson.

Near an Australian airfield American ground staff have stored numbers of 500-lb. bombs, aided by the camouflage of giant ant-hills.

Target practice by a U.S. anti-aircraft battery on the Australian coast. Left, two P-39 fighter planes take off for combat from New Guinea.

Photos, Keystone

THE WAR AT SEA

by Francis E. McMurtrie

SINCE my last article was written, the outstanding event at sea has been the brief and abortive excursion into the Barents Sea of the German squadron from Trondheim, comprising the 40,000-ton battleship Tirpitz, the pocket battleships Admiral Scheer and Lützow, the heavy cruiser Admiral Hipper, and seven destroyers.

On July 6 this squadron was sighted emerging from the shelter of the Norwegian fjords by a Soviet submarine. Fortunately this submarine was commanded by an exceptionally daring and experienced officer, Commander Lunin, whose exploits had already gained him the distinction of " Hero of the Soviet Union," rather more than equivalent to our D.S.O. He succeeded in torpedoing the Tirpitz before the accompanying destroyers could intervene ; though for a short time these hunted energetically for the submarine, they soon abandoned the chase in order to close round the stricken ship. Next morning the entire squadron was sighted by Soviet reconnaissance aircraft steaming southward along the Norwegian coast, evidently returning to Trondheim.

Commander Lunin's prompt and skilful action is considered to have averted an attack by the enemy squadron on an Allied convoy which was then on its way to Murmansk, where it duly arrived in safety.

Whatever the extent of the damage inflicted upon the Tirpitz, it is likely to necessitate her proceeding to Kiel or some other German port for dry-docking and repair. Thus the threat to Atlantic communications which her presence at Trondheim has exercised may be temporarily lifted, since she is much the most formidable unit of the squadron.

It has been pointed out that, since the Russian submarine would naturally have submerged immediately she had fired her torpedoes, the only indication of their having found a target would have been the sound of the explosion. It is suggested, therefore, that the ship struck may not have been the Tirpitz, but one of the destroyers.

While it is true that there must always be an element of uncertainty in an attack carried out in these conditions, the time which elapsed between the discharge of the torpedo and the sound of its detonation should give an approximate idea of the distance it has run. Presumably this would have been taken as a guide by Commander Lunin when he reported that in ·his opinion the Tirpitz was the ship hit. It seems only fair, therefore, to accept this conclusion in the absence of positive evidence to the contrary. A hasty German denial that the Tirpitz suffered any damage need not, of course, be taken seriously.

IN the Baltic the Soviet submarine service has also been very active. Twice within recent weeks the regular ferry service between Sassnitz in Germany and Trelleborg in Sweden has had to be suspended on account of the presence of Russian submarines ; and now the number of ships sunk or attacked has become so considerable that a state of emergency has been declared along the whole of the German and German-occupied Baltic coasts. No ships are allowed to put to sea without official permission, and arrangements are being hastily improvised to provide escorts wherever possible. This means that the busy iron-ore trade will be slowed up to

allow vessels to proceed in convoy, with a detrimental effect on the supplies of ore upon which the enemy munitions industry depends.

A somewhat similar situation developed during the last war, when in 1915 British submarines under Commander (now Admiral Sir Noel) Laurence held up this same trade for weeks. In those days the Russian submarine service was far less efficient than today, and could afford the British flotilla little aid ; but it has evidently digested the lesson and is putting it into practice.

Until recently far too little was heard of the constant patrols which are being carried out in the Channel and North Sea by

what are officially referred to as our light coastal forces, an expression covering motor torpedo-boats, motor gunboats and motor launches. These never hesitate to take on superior forces of German craft of the same kind, which, for no particular reason, are referred to in Admiralty communiqués as " E-boats." It would have been less confusing to have employed the German term " S-boat," an abbreviation of *Schnellboot*, meaning " high speed boat."

On the night of July 9 two of our light coastal craft were on patrol off the French coast when they encountered six German minesweepers. Acting on Nelson's favourite signal, " Engage the enemy more closely," they pressed home their attack to point-blank range, sinking two of the minesweepers and damaging three others. Neither of our vessels suffered any casualties.

Less than a week later— in the early hours of July 15 —a patrol flotilla under the command of Lt.-Cdr. R. P. Hichens, R.N.V.R., intercepted a small enemy convoy off Cherbourg. This comprised a laden oil tanker, escorted by two heavily-armed trawlers and at least three of the S-boats already mentioned. An attack on the escort was pressed home to within 100 yards, both German trawlers being severely damaged. Our forces thus burst through the enemy screen and attacked the tanker, which was set on fire from stem to stern and was later seen to be sinking. All our craft returned safely to port without any fatal casualties.

It is reported that fire from our 20-milli-

metre Oerlikon guns was particularly effective, one of the enemy craft being seen to burst into flames after being hit by Oerlikon shells at close range. She is believed to have become a total loss, but our two boats were too busy inflicting damage on the enemy to be able to stop and investigate the results of their devastating fire. Low visibility alone enabled the enemy force to scatter and make good their escape after suffering severe damage and many casualties.

In the official report it is stated that the calmness and undisturbed efficiency of our crews in the face of intense fire enabled them to deal effectively with the superior enemy force. Casualties on our side were slight.

Lt.-Cdr. R. P. HICHENS, D.S.C., R.N.V.R., awarded the D.S.O. for determination and coolness in the protection of a convoy. The day this was announced, the light forces he was leading sank a well-protected tanker off Cherbourg. *Photo, News Chronicle*

RUSSIAN SUBMARINES, one of which is seen here, have been very active lately in the Baltic, with the result that the flow of Swedish iron ore to Germany has been seriously disrupted. In 1940 the Soviet Navy was reported to include 170 submarines, and no doubt the number has since been increased. *Photo, British Official: Crown Copyright*

Remains of a U-boat which was rammed by a tanker off the U.S. coast. The bows were badly damaged, the armour plates of the conning tower dented, and the periscope bent.
Photo, Associated Press

Ships and Planes on the Northern Patrol

British shipping routes in northern waters are guarded not only by H.M. destroyers and other naval craft, but by units of the Fleet Air Arm. Here a destroyer is seen from a patrolling naval aircraft.

In his endeavours to stop the shipments of Allied tanks and aeroplanes to Russia, Hitler has based some of his large warships, such as the Tirpitz, Scheer and Hipper, and a fleet of Stukas and long-range bombers on Tromsö and other northern Norwegian ports. Admiral Sir John Tovey, C.-in-C. Home Fleet, one of whose jobs it is to keep open these British supply routes, is thus faced by the perpetual danger of attack from the air and also the possibility of these powerful ships emerging from their lairs to attack Allied convoys.

H.M.S. Northern Sky, once a member of the Grimsby fishing fleet and now a naval trawler on Northern Patrol, forgathers with a former colleague in the North Atlantic. A boat has been lowered and is pulling towards the fishing trawler, the crew of which have offered the gift of a supply of freshly caught fish to their friends, whose job now consists in seeking a more deadly and even more elusive prey.

Photos, British Official

Testing the guns of a Fulmar fighter on the deck of an aircraft-carrier engaged in patrolling the Northern trade routes. The Fairey Fulmar is a two-seater monoplane carrying eight machine-guns, four in each wing. Other machines used by the Fleet Air Arm are the Walrus, the American Grumman Martlet, and the Albacore. In northern waters the Germans have the advantage of land-based aircraft, for they have made use of the 24 hours of summer daylight to construct speedily numerous air fields in northern Norway, from which their aircraft can locate and attack Allied convoys destined for Russia.

Our Daily Round in War-torn Malta

Written by George Fabri, a correspondent of The War Illustrated in Malta, this article tells of the ordeal to which the gallant Maltese nation has been, and is still being, subjected at the hands of the enemy air forces.

THE Nazi " good morning " to the little island of Malta is in the form of a reconnaissance plane, crossing the island at a " safe " height, out of range of the A.A. deadly fire. (Not very long ago both German and Italian radio stations credited Malta with being provided with a system of " new, heavy and secret anti-aircraft defences.") A few minutes later a raiding force of Junkers 88 dive-bombers, heavily escorted by Me. 109s, approach the Fortress Island, to be followed later through the day by as many as seventeen raids.

Target No. 1 is, undoubtedly, the big air-field in the heart of the island. In the course of a single day as many as ten or more raids are directed against it. Target No. 2 is another aerodrome, not so large or important as No. 1. Target No. 3 is the harbour area. This last target receives extra attention from the Nazi Air Force when a movement of shipping is apparent.

By day the Luftwaffe attacks in raiding force, varying from three to five planes. The average is 5 Ju. 88s with, say, twice that number of yellow-nosed Me. 109 fighter escort. If the sky is cloudy the Luftwaffe has a good shield to cover its movement. Flying at a great height, they keep crossing the island at half-hourly intervals, searching for gaps in the clouds through which to jettison their bombs. These tip and run raids, aimed with little precision and frustrated by the intense A.A. barrage, cause negligible damage, because a very high percentage of the bombs fall harmlessly in the sea or in the soil. Occasionally bomb-carrying Me. 109s swoop from a great height and let go their bombs. The general rule, though, is for these bomb-carrying fighters to stay in the region of 15,000 ft. and carry out high-level bombing.

On cloudless days the Luftwaffe's activity against Malta relatively diminishes, because of an insufficiency of cloud cover and the fear of the rough manhandling they will receive from the hands of the Hurricane patrolling squadrons.

The early morning reconnaissance plane sees to it that he does not go too deeply into the island. He entertains a healthy respect for our Hurricanes and A.A. fire. Dive-bombing is generally carried out on these fine, cloudless days. The Luftwaffe contents itself with a few determined dive-bombings directed mainly against the harbours and Target No. 1. One thing, however, is worth noting in regard to these raids : dive-bombing as it is carried out today by Nazi pilots falls very short and does not stand comparison with what the Luftwaffe used to do a year ago.

At night the Nazi planes cross the island singly or in very small groups. Search-lights probe the sky for them, and very often succeed in illuminating the night raiders. When conditions permit, Hurricanes, night fighters, generally piloted by D.F.C.s, patrol the skies over Malta. A problem which is not always realized is the difficulty the night-fighter pilot encounters in intercepting the incoming enemy raider. The smallness of the island, 17 miles by 9, favours the raider who, on seeing that things are getting pretty hot, can easily evade the night fighter and make out to sea without fear of any possible interception. The Nazi pilot knows that the British night fighters' fire is accurate and deadly, and he therefore refrains from crossing the island too many times, contenting himself with going round and round the island out of range of the searchlights. When the Nazi night blitzer finds out that he has to deal only with the A.A.s he becomes bolder. He stays for stretches of time, until he is relieved by another plane, generally a Ju. 88 or a Heinkel 111.

Considering the weight of bombs daily dropped on Malta military damage is very small, though civilian damage is very great.

ONE day last spring a crime equal to the destruction of Rotterdam, Belgrade and Warsaw was entered in the " Crimes Book " of the Axis—when 300 of Kesselring's bombers strove to destroy the old and beautiful city of Valetta, the city built by Grand Master Jean de La Valette, the city built " by gentlemen for gentlemen," a veritable treasure-house of history and antiquity. In the sunny, cloudless afternoon the bombers made a deliberate, devastating, devilish attack. All those monuments, which took tens and even hundreds

L.A.C. ALBERT OSBORNE, who was a taxi-driver before enlisting in the R.A.F. and becoming a torpedo-man, was posthumously awarded the George Cross for " unsurpassed courage and devotion to duty " during fierce air attacks on Malta.

of years to build, were destroyed by the Luftwaffe in a few minutes. As the pall of smoke and dust slowly lifted, Valetta, the proud and fair city, showed to all its children the gaping wounds inflicted upon her by a merciless enemy. Among the irreplaceable losses are many a stately " Auberge " of the Knights, the Banqueting Hall and the Staircase of the Palace, and the Opera House. The people were stunned to witness such destruction ; but they were still Maltese, who had inherited from their fathers that iron will to carry on, with bulldog tenacity, and never to stop fighting until victory was assured. Feeling the greatest sorrow for their devastated city, they filled every wall with the exhortation to " Bomb Rome." Valetta is as dear to us as Rome is to the Italians. A consoling element amid this destruction was that casualties numbered less than ten.

His Majesty the King, conscious of the island's full contribution towards the war effort, and informed of the terrible ordeal Malta was passing through, graciously awarded the George Cross to Malta—a singular honour, never given before to any community in the British Empire. The following is the text of the telegram received by his Excellency, General Sir William Dobbie, Governor and C.-in-C., Malta, from the Secretary of State for the Colonies,

" I have it in command from the King to convey to you the following Message :—

" ' To honour her brave people I award the George Cross to the island fortress of Malta to bear witness to a heroism and devotion that will long be famous in history.—GEORGE R.I.' "

WORDS cannot express the satisfaction and pride felt by every Maltese and Service-man as he heard of the King's most gracious award to the island. Faces brightened as the news was read over the B.B.C. The daily Times of Malta, which displayed the welcome announcement, together with a photograph of his Majesty, was eagerly bought. Raids, bombs and barrages were all forgotten. Malta was feeling very happy.

Far from damping their spirits, the 24-hour offensive against the British fortress in the Central Mediterranean has aroused in the Maltese nation a determination to carry on, unflinchingly and undaunted, with their usual jobs, and has kindled in their hearts an " offensive " spirit to carry the war to the enemy's door.

AT MALTA two Bofors guns figured in a ceremony when they were handed over by the Royal Marines to the Royal Artillery. Vice-Adm. Sir Ralph Leatham, K.C.B., is seen inspecting the guns and their teams before handing over to the Commander of the Royal Artillery (second from right).
Photo, British Official: Crown Copyright

The Fighting French Celebrate the Bastille's Fall

Before the parade Gen. de Gaulle laid a tricolour wreath at the foot of the equestrian statue of Marshal Foch in Grosvenor Gardens, London.

BASTILLE DAY—July 14, the anniversary of the French Revolution in 1789—was observed by the Fighting French everywhere. Above, men of the first Fighting French Commando unit parading at Wellington Barracks on July 14; they are drawn from the Fusiliers Marins, and wear khaki battledress and the French naval cap with red pompon. Below, Gen. de Gaulle presenting decorations.

VOLONTAIRES FRAN-ÇAISES, the equivalent of our A.T.S., drawn up on the parade-ground for inspection by the leader of Fighting France, as the de Gaulle movement is now styled.
Photos, Associated Press, Topical, Keystone, Sport & General, Planet News

Mme. Jeannette, Army telephonist, received a Croix de Guerre for devotion to duty during the Dunkirk evacua-

Here the Army's Pigeons Go to School

ONLY A BABY, but in the course of a few months this young pigeon, now being cared for by a Corporal of the Army Pigeon Service, will have learnt its job.

AT THE BILLET the birds of the Army Pigeon Service have their individual, well-appointed quarters. Here they are rested after a "lesson" and their flights; here, too, the young are reared.

OFF THEY GO! Taken some distance from their billets, the pigeons are released from the basket; and at once they set out on the homeward journey. A good homer can cover 40 miles in an hour.

Photos, Planet News, L.N.A.

Messages are carried in little metal cylinders which (as seen in this photograph) are attached to the pigeon's leg.

AS in the last war so in this, the Army Pigeon Service is proving its usefulness. The Royal Corps of Signals has its own pigeon units, each under the control of a Pigeon Officer—usually one accustomed to handling pigeons in civilian life. Most of the birds have been loaned by pigeon fanciers for the duration of the War.

Carrier pigeons are used by Signals units in cases where the utmost degree of secrecy must be observed, and also in emergencies when radio communication is impossible and other means of signalling have broken down. They will fly round storms or over heavy concentrations of gas; they never stop for a "meal," though if very thirsty they will come down to take a drink of water they have spotted from the air. A good homer flies at the speed of 40 m.p.h., though exceptionally a bird may cover 60 miles in an hour's flight.

Pigeons were used during the siege of Paris in 1870, and during the Great War both French and British maintained an excellent pigeon service on the Western Front; the first birds were sent across the Channel from England in March 1916. Similar services were established at Salonica and in Egypt and Mesopotamia.

Berlin Camouflaged Against Our Bombers

FEAR OF THE R.A.F. has led to an extensive system of camouflage in the capital of the German Reich. Below, the Lietzen Lake, in the crowded industrial suburb of Charlottenburg, transformed so as to give the effect of a suburban landscape: coloured nets and "roof tops" have been supported on poles driven into the lake's floor. Top, a large building in the Kaiser Damm shrouded in coloured netting so as to deceive the R.A.F. into thinking they are flying over meadows.

Photos. Associated Press

Wartime Subjects for the Roving Cameraman

WASTE PAPER being unloaded from barges near a paper mill, where it will be converted into essentials of war. The need for paper salvage is as urgent as ever, and in every house, shop, and office facilities should be provided for its collection.

AWARDED THE V.C. : Cdr. Anthony Cecil Capel Miers, D.S.O., R.N.," for valour in command of H.M. submarine Torbay in a daring and successful raid on shipping in a defended enemy harbour, planned with full knowledge of the great hazards to be expected during 17 hours in waters closely patrolled by the enemy. He attacked in full daylight in a glassy calm. When he had fired his torpedoes he was heavily counter-attacked, and had to withdraw through a long channel with anti-submarine craft all around and continuous air patrols overhead."

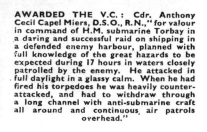

These four American airmen (below) were decorated by Maj.-Gen. Carl Spaatz, commanding the U.S. Air Force in Europe, for their part in the daylight raid on German aerodromes in Holland on July 4. They are (left to right) Sgt. Bennie Cunningham, Sgt. Robert Golay, Lt. Randall Dorton, and Maj. Charles C. Kegelman. The last-named flew home on one engine, the other being on fire, after his aircraft had been so damaged by A.A. fire that it struck the ground.

Fuel shortage has now become a serious war problem. Left, one of the many ex-miners released from the Army and sent back to the mines to help build up coal stocks. Below, fuel briquettes being used on a Southern Railway goods traffic engine in order to save coal.

Photos, British Official: Crown Copyright ; Planet News, L.N.A., Topical Press, Keystone

I WAS THERE!
Eye Witness Stories of the War

When I Left Germany Last May . . .

Released with other American journalists in May, 1942, after five months' internment in Germany, Joseph W. Grigg, Jr., describes in the following article, reprinted from The Spectator, the differences he found in life on the home front in Germany and England.

THE contrast between living conditions in Germany and Great Britain which I found when I arrived in London a few weeks ago was overwhelming. Germany has just passed through its grimmest winter since 1918. The food situation deteriorated markedly during the first four months of this year. The Germans froze in their homes because the catastrophic state of their transport system made it impossible to bring coal to the big cities. Nerves became frayed. Grumbling, despondency and war-weariness increased on the home front.

Superficially, there is much that Berlin and London have in common. People stumble around in the same black-out. There is no great difference in the basic rations. There are queues, propaganda posters, thin newspapers and uniforms everywhere. You meet some of the same wartime shortages, and hear people grumbling about much the same sort of annoyances. But in everything of real importance there is no comparison between the two countries. Food, drink, general living conditions, morale and, above all, confidence in the outcome of the war—in all these Great Britain is so far ahead of Germany that there are times when someone coming direct from Germany finds it hard to remember that this is a country at war at all.

There is absolutely no question that Britain is eating better than Germany. In Germany today practically every article of food is rationed, and ration coupons have to be given up in restaurants as well. That means in practice that the average German gets considerably smaller rations than the Briton who eats at least one meal a day in restaurants or canteens. The potato crop froze in Germany last winter, and potatoes were rationed for the first time. Green vegetables of any sort were practically unobtainable,

and the average German family was living to a large extent on turnips, red cabbage and sauerkraut. Bread in Germany is rationed, and the ration was cut during the winter—a particular hardship to working-class Germans owing to the potato shortage. The standard of the bread also deteriorated very noticeably. Today there is no white bread of any sort available, and the standard bread is heavy, soggy and sour-tasting. Full milk is available only to expectant and nursing mothers and small children. Even skimmed milk is severely rationed, and in winter is sometimes unobtainable altogether. The cheese ration is much smaller than in Britain. Since the beginning of the war the Germans have had no real coffee, tea or cocoa and practically no chocolate. They have to drink ersatz coffee made of roasted barley or rye, and various types of herbal tea or peppermint tea. An indication of how badly the Germans miss real coffee and tea is seen in that fact that the black market price of coffee now stands around £4 a pound, and of tea around £6 10s.

Ration Cards for Cigarettes

Drink of all kinds has become even scarcer than in this country. German beer now has practically no alcoholic content. Spirits have almost disappeared from sale altogether. Even Hock and Moselle wines have become scarce and fantastically expensive. As far back as a year ago good Berlin restaurants were charging £10 a bottle for 1937 vintages. The tobacco situation is much worse than in this country. After months during which cigarettes were almost unobtainable a tobacco ration-card was introduced last December. The ration for men is three to four cigarettes a day, and for women three every other day. Women under 25 or over 55 are not entitled to a ration card at all.

The problem of footwear for German children is met by the establishment of secondhand depots where outgrown but not yet outworn shoes can be exchanged. *Photo, E.N.A.*

The shortage of all kinds of consumer's goods has become so severe during the past eighteen months that shop counters are almost bare. There is a clothes-rationing card in Germany as in Great Britain, but the ration is frequently only theoretical, as it is practically impossible to buy clothes. Women, for instance, are entitled to six pairs of stockings a year, but often spend months searching the shops before they can find a pair. Mending wool, which also comes on the clothing card, is another thing that is almost unobtainable. The clothes that can be bought are of bad ersatz material that wears out quickly, particularly if it has to be laundered with wartime soap-substitute. Shoes can only be bought with a special permit. Most German women now wear wooden shoes with straw or canvas tops. Shop-windows well stocked with good leather shoes which you see in England are a thing of the past in Germany. Leather shoes are only obtainable after an official has visited your house and searched the cupboards to confirm that the shoes really are urgently needed. In summertime no permits for leather shoes are given at all. Queues are generally much longer than in London. Among the articles I notice one can buy here which have disappeared almost altogether in Germany are shoe-laces, darning wool, leather soles, shaving cream and string.

Little Bomb Damage—As Yet

In Germany practically all building has been stopped, except for the most urgent work approved by the State. The clothing industry has almost ceased production for civilian purposes. Owing to shortage of labour it takes at least six months to get a suit cleaned —if the cleaners accept it at all—and about a year and a half to get one made. Owing to shortage of labour, as well as to save petrol, about 75 per cent of the omnibuses in Berlin have been taken off the streets. Taxis also have almost disappeared, and only persons on urgent official business or sick people on the way to hospital are allowed to take one at all. Infringements of these restrictions are severely punishable. The result is that the streets of Berlin are almost denuded of traffic today. There is no such thing as a traffic jam any more.

On the debit side of the balance there is London's bomb damage. Berlin has experienced about one hundred air-raid alarms since the beginning of the war. But with three or four exceptions none of the raids has been heavy, and the German capital still has to experience its first genuine blitz.

CAFÉ LIFE IN BERLIN still goes on, but it is ersatz coffee, made from grain, that is drunk, and there are no rich cakes to be eaten with it, and no cigar to follow. The open-air café shown here is in the Kurfürstendamm. A surprising feature is the number of young men not in uniform. *Photo, E.N.A.*

BIR HACHEIM (see page 38) was memorable for the great stand of the Free French who, under Gen. Koenig, held out for so long against tremendous odds. In this striking photograph an attack is being made on Bir Hacheim by dive-bombers. *Photo, Forces Françaises Libres.*

'Now It's Hell in Bir Hacheim'

A few hours before General Ritchie gave the order to evacuate Bir Hacheim on June 10, a French correspondent sent this last message from the beleaguered garrison. We reprint it by courtesy of La France Libre.

Now it is hell. A short time ago a strange, unreal silence hung over this grim, battle-scarred little plateau—a silence broken only by the groans of the enemy wounded who, under the protection of the white flag, the Germans are removing from the outskirts of the positions held by Koenig's "ghosts" for fifteen days and nights of mounting fury.

But for the last half-hour artillery and bomber aircraft have been relentlessly, nerve-rackingly pounding our defences. The last attack, which was flung back with severe loss to the enemy—and with some loss to ourselves—surpassed all others in ferocity.

Artillery, dive-bombers, infantry and tanks —the enemy gave us everything he had. The first wave of tanks blew up on the minefields laid by our engineers at great danger to themselves. The next wave was nailed to the ground by our 75s, which for days on end have been barking death and destruction and which are largely responsible for transforming Bir Hacheim into a cemetery of tanks.

I should say some 50 to 100 enemy tanks litter the battlefield—grim hulks which resemble the skeletons of prehistoric monsters.

Rommel—who has latterly been signing the notes calling on Gen. Koenig to surrender —flung more and more metal into the attack, and though his losses grew proportionately greater, some of the tanks broke through our defences and rolled right up to our guns.

When our guns were overrun, it was man against tank. At one post held by the Foreign Legion a German tank scored a direct hit at 20 yards. The officer commanding the post —a calm young man from Saint Cyr—burnt his regiment's standard so that it should not be captured, and then called on his men to attack. With incendiary grenades in their hands, they flung themselves on the tanks like infuriated hornets.

There are some things I can never forget :

The légionnaire who, with blood streaming from his face, climbed on to a German tank and emptied his revolver through an aperture, killing all the occupants.

The sergeant-major who destroyed seven tanks.

The gun crew who, when a shell stuck in the breach of their cannon at the height of the battle, gambled their lives by knocking the shell out with a hammer.

In less than two hours Koenig's men destroyed 37 tanks. Somehow, incredibly, the attack was repelled. The Germans and Italians retreated, seemingly appalled by the blind fury of the defenders.

That moment will always live in my mind. The tanks withdrawing, screening the fleeing infantry. On the ground a ghastly chaos—a mingling of shell craters, dead and wounded Frenchmen, Germans and Italians.

In that moment of victory no cries of triumph, only the indescribable expression of defiance of the blackened, exhausted French.

Since then, and up to 30 minutes ago, there was that uncanny silence.

Now they are pounding us again, and hard. The shelling and bombing are rising to a crescendo. We are straining our eyes to see what they are preparing in the darkness beyond our lines . . .

At this point the message broke off.

'The Hermione Reared Up Like a Huge Whale'

How men sang and joked in the oily sea while awaiting rescue after the torpedoing of the cruiser Hermione in the Mediterranean convoy battles in June was described by survivors who reached Alexandria.

Lieut. Sidney Beadell, of West Dulwich, London, a former Fleet Street cameraman and now a Naval photographer, said : I was having a cup of cocoa in the charthouse of the Hermione when there was a terrific crash. The ship gave a violent shudder and heeled over sharply.

All the lights went out except the emergency lamps. I was flung across the charthouse, but managed to wrench open the door and got up the narrow ladder to the bridge, where I saw the captain directing a signalman who was flashing a red lamp asking for assistance. I grabbed a camera which I had left on the bridge and went down to the ship's waist.

It was impossible to get the whalers out owing to the heavy list. When the order was given to abandon ship some men jumped into the water, while others slid down the hull. The man standing next to me said he couldn't swim, but he jumped and found a piece of wood to hold on to. There was absolutely no panic, and the men were very cheerful, although the water was thick with oil. There was no moon, but the stars were bright.

I swam away from the ship and when I looked round her bows were rearing up like a huge whale. Then she went down stern first. Some of her depth charges exploded on immersion, making us feel as if we were

H.M.S. ARGUS, a former liner converted into an aircraft-carrier, figured in the Malta convoy action of June 14-16. The smoke seen in the background is from one of the 43 enemy planes that were shot down either by naval aircraft or by A.A. fire from the convoy and escort warships.

Photo, Fox

BOMBS IN THE MEDITERRANEAN. As told in this page, the convoy of which the Hermione was part of the escort was attacked violently from the air and suffered serious losses. The photograph shows bombs exploding near an escorting battleship. *Photo, British Official: Crown Copyright*

being ripped open. After swimming for nearly an hour I found a float with an officer on it. He dragged me on to it and then we dragged on two other fellows. One was the sick bay officer, who had medical supplies slung round his neck and a torch which he kept flashing.

We were unable to use the paddles as these were lashed to the float and we had no knife, so we used our hands instead. But the strong current carried us farther and farther from the destroyers which were picking up survivors. Finally we managed to free the paddles, reached a destroyer and were hauled aboard.

Another officer said: I was in the director tower of the cruiser when there was a colossal explosion on the starboard side. The order to abandon ship was given

within five minutes. Timber was cut away and thrown over the side and men clung to the pieces of wood and to floats. Except at the point where she was hit almost everyone below managed to get up before the ship sank. I jumped over and swam away to avoid being sucked down; then I found a float.

While in the water the men sang songs such as It's a Bit Wet, and We're All Together Now, and although the water was thick with oil nobody lost his cheerfulness for a moment.

Here is the story of the battle as told by another of Hermione's crew:

We started westwards with a strong force. On Sunday evening, June 14, there was a

dive-bombing attack. Then planes started dropping flares.

The next day we were bombed all day by Stukas. I have never seen such a terrific barrage as every ship put up. It was like a Christmas snowstorm. The whole sky was a great mass of white bursts of A.A. shells.

The destroyer Airedale was struck by three bombs during the attacks, and sank almost immediately. She just blew up in a great cloud of smoke. I thought it impossible that there could be any survivors, but nearly all were saved.

The Australian destroyer Nestor had to be taken in tow after being hit by a bomb, and subsequently had to be sunk.—*Reuter*

OUR DIARY OF THE WAR

JULY 8, 1942, Wednesday   *1,040th day*
   Sea.—Moscow announced that German battleship Tirpitz had been torpedoed and damaged by Soviet submarine in Barents Sea.
   Air.—Strong force of R.A.F. bombers raided Wilhelmshaven at night.
   Russian Front.—Russians evacuated Stary Oskol; fighting still going on west of Voronezh.
   Mediterranean.—Day and night raids on Malta.
   Africa.—In El Alamein sector our fighting patrols took some prisoners.
   Burma.—R.A.F. bombers made intensive attacks on Jap-occupied territory.

JULY 9, Thursday   *1,041st day*
   Sea.—Russians sank two transports and tanker in Baltic.
   Russian Front.—Stubborn fighting west of Voronezh and round Rossosh.
   Mediterranean.—Thirteen enemy aircraft shot down over Malta.
   Africa.—Our mobile columns engaged enemy units and forced them to move northwards.
   China.—Chinese recaptured Nancheng, Ihuang, Tsungjen and Changsuchen.
   Australia.—Allied aircraft raided Dilli in Portuguese Timor.

JULY 10, Friday   *1,042nd day*
   Sea.—British submarine sank two enemy supply ships in Mediterranean.
   Russian Front.—Rossosh evacuated by Russians; fighting round Kazemirovsk, to the south.
   Africa.—At El Alamein our troops attacked in northern sector and made five-mile advance; in southern sector enemy advancing eastwards was engaged.
   China.—Japs made new landing in Chekiang at Juian, near Wenchow.
   Australasia.—Jap bombers made heavy attack on barracks and shipping at Port Moresby.

JULY 11, Saturday   *1,043rd day*
   Air.—Several squadrons of Lancaster bombers attacked submarine building yards at Danzig and Flensburg by day.
   Russian Front.—Fierce fighting on outskirts of Voronezh; battles also raging at Kantemirovka and Lisichansk.
   Africa.—Our troops in northern sector consolidated positions in captured territory; 2,000 prisoners taken. Light naval units and naval aircraft attacked Mersa Matruh.

China.—Japs occupied Wenchow on Chekiang coast; Chinese recaptured Futou Island near Foochow.
   U.S.A.—Jap cruiser bombed at Kiska, Aleutians.
   Australasia.—Jap bombers attacked shipping at Port Moresby, where, it was announced, American troops are stationed.

JULY 12, Sunday   *1,044th day*
   Russian Front.—Russians evacuated Kantemirovka and Lisichansk; fighting at approaches to Voronezh and in neighbourhood of Boguchar.
   Africa.—Enemy attack driven off in northern sector. Heavy raid by R.A.F. on Tobruk.
   Burma.—R.A.F. bombers attacked Jap concentrations in Kalewa area.

JULY 13, Monday   *1,045th day*
   Sea.—Announced in Canada that three Allied ships had been torpedoed and sunk in Gulf of St. Lawrence.
   Air.—Strong force of bombers attacked Ruhr by night.
   Russian Front.—Fierce fighting round Voronezh and Boguchar; further Russian withdrawal east of Lisichansk.
   Africa.—Enemy tank and infantry attacks beaten off in northern sector.

JULY 14, Tuesday   *1,046th day*
   Russian Front.—Fierce fighting round Voronezh and Boguchar.
   Africa.—Enemy tanks and infantry attacked at Tel el Eisa.
   Australasia.—Allied air units raided Alor Island, off Timor, and aerodrome at Salamaua, New Guinea.
   General.—Vichy rejected proposals by President Roosevelt for removal of immobilized French warships at Alexandria to a safe port.
   General de Gaulle's movement changed its name to "Fighting France" (La France Combattante).

JULY 15, Wednesday   *1,047th day*
   Sea.—Our light coastal forces destroyed a heavily-escorted enemy tanker off French coast.
   Air.—Nearly 200 Spitfires took part in intensive fighter sweeps over N. France.
   Russian Front.—Russians announced

evacuation of Boguchar and Millerovsk; heavy fighting round Voronezh.
   Africa.—In central sector our forces captured ridge to S. of El Alamein. In north enemy were partially successful at Tel el Eisa.
   Burma.—R.A.F. bombers renewed attacks at Kalewa.

JULY 16, Thursday   *1,048th day*
   Air.—Stirling bombers made daylight attack on submarine building yards at Lübeck and Flensburg. The Ruhr was also raided by day.
   Russian Front.—Fighting continued in area of Voronezh.
   Africa.—Tank battle developed in central sector for possession of Ruweisat ridge.
   Burma.—R.A.F. made low-level attacks on Akyab.
   China.—Chinese recaptured Tsingtien in Chekiang. Allied bombers raided Hankow.

JULY 17, Friday   *1,049th day*
   Air.—Single aircraft of Bomber Command raided the Ruhr in daylight.
   Russian Front.—Fighting round Voronezh and S.E. of Millerovsk.
   Africa.—Efforts to dislodge our troops in northern sector failed. Tobruk raided in force by heavy bombers, while our naval aircraft and light naval forces attacked Mersa Matruh.
   China.—Chinese recaptured Wenchow and Juian.
   U.S.A.—Washington announces that Japs have occupied undefended islands of Kiska, Attu and Agattu in the Aleutians.

JULY 18, Saturday   *1,050th day*
   Air.—Lancaster bombers raided the Ruhr in daylight. Russian bombers attacked Königsberg.
   Russian Front.—Fighting continued round Voronezh and S. of Millerovsk.
   Africa.—In central sector our troops advanced along Ruweisat ridge. Tobruk raided by our heavy bombers and Mersa Matruh bombarded by our naval forces.
   Burma.—R.A.F. bombers made attacks in Kalemyo area.
   China.—Chinese recaptured Hengfeng and Iyang in eastern Kiangsi. Allied

bombers made surprise attack on aerodrome at Canton.

JULY 19, Sunday   *1,051st day*
   Air.—Large-scale attacks by our bombers and fighters in N. France. By night four-engined bombers raided submarine building yards at Vegesack, near Bremen.
   Russian Front.—Evacuation of Voroshilovgrad announced by Russians; fighting continued in Voronezh area and S. of Millerovsk.
   Africa.—Our troops maintained their positions in all sectors. Since July 14 4,000 prisoners taken.
   China.—Allied air force bombed Jap headquarters at Linchuan. Chinese recaptured Chienteh in western Chekiang.

JULY 20, Monday   *1,052nd day*
   Sea.—Admiralty announced loss of H.M. whaler Cocker and H.M. trawler Kingston Ceylonite.
   Air.—Russian bombers again raided Königsberg.
   Russian Front.—In region of Voronezh the Russians captured a bridgehead.
   Africa.—Patrol activity on land; large-scale air attack on enemy aerodrome near Fuka. Navy again bombarded Mersa Matruh.
   China.—Japs recaptured Wenchow.
   Burma.—R.A.F. renewed their attacks on Akyab.
   Australasia.—Jap bombers damaged aerodrome in raid on Port Moresby.

JULY 21, Tuesday   *1,053rd day*
   Air.—R.A.F. fighters made low-level attacks in occupied France and Belgium. Single aircraft raided N.W. Germany by day; strong force of bombers raided Duisburg and the Ruhr by night.
   Russian Front.—Fighting continued in area of Voronezh and S.E. of Voroshilovgrad.
   Mediterranean.—Allied bombers made daylight raid on shipping in Suda Bay, Crete.
   Africa.—N.Z., Indian and S. African infantry launched attack on enemy positions during the night.
   Burma.—R.A.F. attacked coastal craft in Akyab area and Jap base at Kalewa.
   Australasia.—Allied bombers attacked Jap convoy off New Guinea.
   U.S.A.—Navy Dept. announced that American submarines had sunk three more Jap destroyers near Kiska.

Editor's Postscript

No matter how long the War goes on (and that's a subject on which now that I am far more optimistic I find some of the early optimists taking longer views!) the story of Malta will retain its epic quality. One's admiration goes out to these splendid islanders for their endurance in the greatest test to which any community has ever been subjected in the whole course of history, not excepting their remote ancestors of Carthage in their three years' resistance to the Romans. Watching a newsreel last night which had been "shot" on board a ship of that great convoy which fought its way through the savage air, sea, and undersea attack launched against it by the Axis, as the ship approached Valetta the picture of destruction that unfolded was terrific. Every one of the lovely old buildings that were steeped in history had been battered into shapeless ruin. It seemed hardly possible that human life could endure in such a shambles But the inhabitants of the star city of the Crusaders—"a city built by gentlemen for gentlemen"—were proving worthy of the knights of old.

From no single spot of British overseas resistance have I had so many letters. The most of my correspondents have been youths in their teens, who all write excellent idiomatic English, and display an enthusiasm for the British cause that is not outdone even in Britain itself. Although the Italian language and Italian names are common in Malta the local hatred of Italy is so intense that I have even had protests from my young readers there, whose own names are still Italian, because Italian names had been given to some places on the Island in a map I published, whereas these names had recently been discarded and others more English in form adopted! Although I have printed a number of extracts from my Malta correspondence, I have not been able to give more than a tiny part of the whole. One of Mr. Fabri's letters to me, recently to hand, resembled one of these lace-like patterns made by tearing newspaper, after it had passed the ordeal of the censor's scissors! But I am having some of Mr. Fabri's letters edited for a page in THE WAR ILLUSTRATED by piecing together the bits which the censor has left.

Meanwhile, that brilliant Maltese youth John Mizzi, from whose pen I've already given a number of interesting notes, has sent me many pages of manuscript about life in the Island, his latest letter coming to my desk only a few days ago after it had been just about three weeks on the way—pretty good postal work when it sometimes takes three days to get a letter from one part of rural England to another. Sometimes, note, but not often, though these delays do happen to me somehow. John Mizzi at sixteen has the makings of a very fine journalist. I know that at sixteen I could not have written so well; but in that far and tranquil past I didn't have matters of such moment to write about. The views of my young correspondent are no less interesting than his news, for they give a clue to what Maltese youth is thinking—and remember the total population of Malta is just about the same as that of Portsmouth: few but tough, obviously. In this last letter John Mizzi writes:

I have now received the parts of THE WAR ILLUSTRATED I asked for, and quite agree with what you say about the Navy. What a grand job they are doing! Had it not been for them I think the Empire would have been knocked out of the fight. The latest example of their work is arrival, through a blizzard of shells, bombs, and torpedoes, of a convoy to Malta. You should have seen our planes, scores of fighters of every type, taking off to protect the convoy. Unfortunately the range at which fighters can operate is not enough to ensure protection through the whole passage. But when the ships were near Pantellaria, our fighters met them and were in time to pounce on a formation of forty bombers and force them to jettison their bombs before reaching the target. After that the enemy left the convoy alone.

A sailor to whom I spoke told me that it was "quite all right" while it lasted. When our fighters began to shoot down the enemy bombers, he said, with a grin, that they wanted to cheer but couldn't; the guns had to continue firing. He had been on a gun for four days, and he pulled up his sleeve to show me his arm. The sun had turned it red hot and dotted it with blisters.

We here knew before any other place of the mauling the Italian fleet had got in "its lake." We were elated. When the Germans get it in the neck we are relieved, but when the Italians get it we go crazy. And we are nearly always going crazy, too! We like to see them have it, to see their planes come down as balls of fire. Their navy is made up of men without guts, men who only go out to sea when the ship's engines are tested to see whether they are still good after so much staying in port, and then they go and anchor again. The air force is made up of fighters not even able to match a Camel or an S.E.7. The pilots try to imitate the Germans with no slight trace of

MAJ.-GEN. CARL SPAATZ, appointed to command the U.S. Air Force in the European Theatre, was one of the first U.S. airmen to go overseas in the war of 1914-18. *Photo, Planet News*

success. Then think of their soldiers, so many of them now in India behind barbed wire! It's a good job Italy did not join us. We would then have had to defend Italy as well as ourselves. I hope we in Malta will have a large share in knocking Italy out of the fight.

So that's the spirit that wins in the long run and can suffer until victory. I think that Malta has already done an incalculable service to Britain and the world in standing up to the most vicious attacks which the Hun and his henchmen could devise and after the victory its reward will come. I ought to mention that whenever the youngsters of Valetta go parading through the ruins left by the latest air raid they carry banners on which the favourite slogan is "Bomb Rome!" Many of us would like to know that the modern monstrosities of Italian architecture with which Mussolini has plastered Rome were reduced to equal ruin with its ancient remains; but that is a task hardly possible of achievement without still further ruining those most precious of ancient survivals. It would suit equally to smother towns like Milan and Turin or Genoa and Naples where the enemy has many of his War factories and little that matters of beauty or antiquity that need be spared. Anyway, I'd rather reserve for Musso and his fellow gangsters—all creatures of a meaner mould than their German masters—a stickier fate than going out under British bomb and blast. "Bomb Munich" is my own slogan and it is beyond my comprehension why we have kept our aerial blows away from the holy city of Nazidom. Some day it must be blasted and I wish we had a modern Cato to keep on calling for that job to be well and quickly done.

I was interested to receive some time ago a letter from Mr. C. J. Hindle of Oxford with regard to the use of the word Hun as applied to Germans. My readers may remember that I made no attempt to trace it farther back than the notorious order of the late unlamented Kaiser to the German troops who were being sent to China at the time of the Boxer troubles; but it would appear from my correspondent that it has an earlier origin and the Kaiser was only using a suitable name for his soldiers, which will be found in Francisque Sarcey's Le Siège de Paris, where he writes: "nous les (les Prussiens) appelions des Pandours, des Huns, des Vandales."

So it would seem that even the comparatively decent Germans (as we had supposed them to be) of seventy years ago had earned the description of Huns from the literary Frenchmen of that date, who were never at a loss for the right and pungent word.

Since paper economy became imperative I have personally made great use of old envelopes which have brought me bills and company reports. Indeed, many of my investments are yielding me no other dividend these days. Its astonishing how a bit of gummed paper folded over the slit edge of an envelope enables you to re-use it. Post Office returns show that only one in ten of the envelopes is an old one re-used. The percentage could be raised to at least two out of three and this is what it must come to, as only 15 per cent of the pre-War Supply is now permitted by the Paper Controller.

Printed in England and published every alternate Friday by the Proprietors, THE AMALGAMATED PRESS, LTD., The Fleetway House, Farringdon Street, London, E.C.4. Registered for transmission by Canadian Magazine Post. Sole Agents for Australia and New Zealand: Messrs. Gordon & Gotch, Ltd.; and for South Africa: Central News Agency, Ltd.—August 7, 1942. S.S. Editorial Address: JOHN CARPENTER HOUSE, WHITEFRIARS, LONDON, E.C.4.

Vol 6

The War Illustrated

Nº 135

Edited by Sir John Hammerton

6d FORTNIGHTLY

AUGUST 21, 1942

U.S. AIRCRAFT-CARRIER YORKTOWN and other fighting ships of the American Navy throw up a heavy screen of A.A. fire to beat off a squadron of Japanese torpedo-carrying planes during the Battle of Midway Island in the Pacific last June. The aircraft-carrier and her escort were unsuccessfully attacked during a crucial phase of the battle by thirty-six enemy aircraft launched from the Japanese carrier Hiryu—subsequently destroyed; but in a further attack by torpedo aircraft the Yorktown (left) was hit.
Photo, Sport & General

NO. 136 WILL BE PUBLISHED FRIDAY, SEPTEMBER 4

ALONG THE BATTLE FRONTS

by Our Military Critic, Maj.-Gen. Sir Charles Gwynn, K.C.B., D.S.O.

DURING the second half of July the situation continued to deteriorate at a disturbing pace. It is true that the lull in the Far East might be considered advantageous to the Allies, as it gave time for expansion and organization of their forces. The limited success of Japanese operations in China and spirited resistance of the Chinese armies were also encouraging. But the losses inflicted on Japan's shipping and navy in the period were probably more than balanced by the quantities of raw material for war purposes she was now drawing from captured territories.

In Egypt, Gen. Auchinleck had ensured, temporarily at least, the security of Alexandria and the Canal, and had achieved some minor tactical successes ; but he had been unable to muster an adequate force in time to attempt a decisive blow against Rommel's army while it was still exhausted, and without reinforcements or an organized line of communications. The situation became one of temporary stalemate, neither side being strong enough to attempt a major offensive on a restricted front which denies possibilities of large-scale manoeuvre and involves frontal attacks on strongly defended positions. By pursuing an active policy, General Auchinleck may be able to slow down the rate at which Rommel can gather strength for a renewed attempt to reach Alexandria, while at the same time gaining time for accessions to his own strength to arrive from distant sources.

While conducting that policy he would have the advantage of better and shorter communications to his immediate base, and

his troops should consequently suffer less than the enemy from exposure to summer conditions. On the whole, the situation in Egypt has deteriorated only so far as hopes of an early and effective counter-offensive have had to be abandoned, leaving the threat to Alexandria in abeyance.

In Russia the deterioration of the situation was, of course, so far as ascertainable facts go, much more serious. Russia by the end of the month had lost the industrial area of the Donetz, the great food-producing areas in the bend of the Don, and her oil supplies were threatened.

The left wing of Timoshenko's armies on the Lower Don had been defeated after hard fighting ; its losses must have been heavy, and there was little hope of it being strongly reinforced. Its residual power of resistance depended on the degree of success achieved in carrying out a difficult withdrawal and on the strength of reserves in the Lower Don region still unused. The threat to Stalingrad and to the Volga waterway had also become very serious, but the possibility of reinforcing the defences there made the situation a degree less critical than on the left of Timoshenko's front.

The successful counter-attacks at Voronezh alone of the ascertainable facts are encouraging. There are, however, factors in the situation about which definite information cannot be obtained, but which may yet vitally affect the development of the situation favourably.

The Germans have achieved success by a maximum concentration of their offensive strength. The question is, how long can

IN EGYPT Rommel was checked by the Eighth Army at El Alamein. The map shows the battle front at the end of July.
By Courtesy of News Chronicle

READERS are asked to remember that the articles on the War by Land, Sea, and Air, specially written for THE WAR ILLUSTRATED by our expert contributors, should be read with at least a fortnight's perspective in mind. Of necessity these articles are written between two and three weeks in advance of publishing day and no attempt can be made in a fortnightly publication to be abreast of the latest news. The aim of our contributors is to present a well-considered review of the progress of the War from all points of view at the time of writing.

the momentum of their offensive be maintained, and to what extent has the resistance it has encountered exhausted its strength ? We do not know and can speculate only.

Russia, on the other hand, though she has lost so heavily in territory and in sources of war production, has still a great part of her army uncommitted. She has no occupied territories to garrison, and, except for the army she maintains in the Far East, she is free to use all of her reserve power. What its strength may be we have no exact knowledge, but it probably exceeds the reserve strength of Germany. If the part of her army which has had to meet the German blow retains sufficient strength to continue its resistance, an opportunity may arise for the employment of this reserve strength in counter-offensive action. Even if a counter-offensive were unable to make headway against stubborn German defence it might at least prolong the struggle into winter.

EGYPT In Egypt after the indecisive tank battle of July 15 and 16 there was a lull broken only by intensive air attacks on Rommel's troops and communications.

The lull continued until the night of the 21st, when Auchinleck launched an attack on his whole front. His chief objectives were to extend his hold on the ridges about Tel el

BRITAIN'S EIGHTH ARMY brought Rommel's forces to a pause in Egypt in the middle of July, and then made a series of counter-attacks. Left, officers of a mobile column hold a conference for a plan of attack ; these " Jock " columns have done extremely valuable work in harassing Axis forces. The nights are bitterly cold in the Western Desert, and the men (right) wearing greatcoats are warming themselves over an improvised brazier.

Photos, British Official: Crown Copyright

CROSSING THE DON by pontoon bridges the German thrust into the Caucasus was speeded up after the fall of Rostov at the end of July, when the enemy established four bridgeheads. Some of Von Bock's men are here seen making the crossing of the river. *Photo, G.P.U.*

Eisa in the north, the capture of the Ruweisat ridge in the centre, and to improve his position on the plateau bounding the Qattara depression in the south. Progress was made at all points, and in particular the whole of the Ruweisat ridge was captured. Throughout the 22nd Rommel counter-attacked strongly, but without again committing any large force of tanks. He recovered the western extremity of the Ruweisat ridge, where counter-attacks had been most violent, and the Tel el Eisa ridges changed hands several times. Thus our final gain of ground was inconsiderable.

On the whole, the results of the attack were somewhat disappointing, but it did, to some extent, improve the position, and inflicted losses on the enemy which effectively slowed down the recovery of his offensive strength.

There followed a lull of four days, during which the enemy worked at consolidating his position, now well protected by minefields. On July 28 Auchinleck attacked again in the northern sector to secure a further footing on the Tel el Eisa ridges. Several points were taken, but could not be held, as the rocky ground prevented rapid consolidation and troops were exposed to great concentrations of artillery fire. Isolated high points, though valuable for observation purposes, can seldom be held unless defences can be consolidated well beyond them, for they are inviting targets. In this instance minefields prevented tanks from gaining ground which the infantry might have consolidated. As a raid the operation had some success, but on the whole it was disappointing. The lull which followed it proved that nothing of importance had been achieved.

RUSSIA
In the latter half of July the great German drive southwards progressed alarmingly. West of the Donetz it was stubbornly resisted, but it was pressed there with special fury and was supported by an immense concentration of aircraft, tanks, and guns.

The first sign that Timoshenko had little hope of checking the drive short of Rostov was when the great industrial town of Voroshilovgrad was evacuated on July 19. Rearguard fighting continued, but by the 24th fighting was going on in the outskirts of Rostov and tanks had penetrated the outer defences. It was then only a question whether Timoshenko would sacrifice troops to fight for every house, or whether he would try to get as many away as possible to the other side of the Don. Wisely he took the latter course, and though his troops from the right bank were probably much disorganized in crossing the river under constant air attack, a substantial proportion must have got away safely since the Germans claimed no large number of prisoners.

Although the capture of Rostov was a sensational event it had probably no special strategic importance, for the city had lost much of its value to the Russians and its fall did not greatly facilitate further German operations. Like the Donetz Basin it was a loss that had to be written off. The main problem was how to check the impetus of the German drive on the line of the Don.

The Germans had reached the river on a broad front, and their attempt to cross it at Tsimlyanskaya, half-way between Rostov and its great bend, was particularly dangerous, for the Stalingrad-Novorossisk railway passes within forty miles of the river at this point — and this line was the only remaining railway communication with Timoshenko's left flank. Tsimlyanskaya, however, probably marked the centre of the army which had retreated in good order southwards between the Don and the Donetz, and the German attempts to cross the river failed a number of times in face of strong opposition before a bridgehead was established.

Even when a firm foothold had been gained, its reinforcement was difficult, and counter-attacks had, up to the end of the month, checked its extension, compelling the Germans to attempt crossing at other points.

As had been illustrated at Voronezh it is often easier to effect the crossing of a river than to deploy a force of offensive capacity across it. Vigorous and quick counter-attacks are therefore the main method of holding a river line, although air attacks may greatly add to the difficulty of reinforcing bridgeheads. Although by the end of July the Don had been crossed at several points, the problem of deploying the German Army on its left bank had not yet been solved except in the Rostov region.

Meanwhile, the left wing of the German drive had neared the elbow of the Don, close to the Volga and Stalingrad. It was meeting strong opposition on the right bank of the river, and had as yet made no attempt to force a crossing. Probably from lack of good communications the German force here was not at first of great strength, but the advance in the Donetz, by securing control of the railway to Stalingrad, may have enabled it to be reinforced. The attack therefore promised to grow in violence.

What the crossing of the Don would eventually cost the Germans, and what its effect in checking the momentum of their advance would be, were at the end of the month uncertain. It was also becoming doubtful whether they would be able to retain their footing across the river at Voronezh. They had not unlimited reserves to draw on in this region, for Russian attacks at Bryansk were threatening the northern defensive flank of their great offensive. The subsidiary offensive which they had opened in the Rzhev region had died down, possibly because reserves were needed at Bryansk, and there was an obvious danger that this would leave Zhukov with a freer hand to use his reserves offensively.

Serious as the Russian situation was, it certainly still had encouraging possibilities.

RUSSIAN FRONT. Here in this map is shown the North Caucasian area which by early August was largely overrun by the Nazi armies. Maikop and Grozny are rich oil-fields, and the strategical importance of the railway between Stalingrad and Novorossisk will be obvious.
By Courtesy of The Daily Telegraph

They Fought and Died to the Last Man

NEW ZEALAND TROOPS are serving on the El Alamein front in Egypt, where the menace from the air includes the deadly dive-bomber. Top, taking cover behind a supply truck, two New Zealanders aim at an approaching Stuka. Below, a radioed photograph showing the burial of the New Zealand crew of an A.A. gun. Firing was continued until the last man had fallen as the result of a ferocious dive-bombing attack. The pile of shell-cases is a mute witness to their devotion to duty.

Photos, British Official : Crown Copyright

New Zealand Will Remember El Alamein

IN THE WESTERN DESERT the New Zealanders fought most valiantly against Rommel's forces in conditions that called for superhuman endurance and courage. In the top photograph, supplies are being unloaded from Army lorries. Centre, Lt.-Gen. Sir B. Freyberg, V.C., G.O.C. New Zealand Forces in the Middle East, lies wounded (for the ninth time in his career) at a field-dressing station near Mersa Matruh. Below, exhausted Axis prisoners put into " the bag " by the New Zealanders.

Photos, New Zealand Official ; Sport & General

NAZI WAR METHODS on Two Fronts

Specially drawn for
THE WAR ILLUSTRATED
By Haworth

IN RUSSIA   **IN EGYPT**

EGYPT AND RUSSIA constitute two very different battlefields, yet in the one and the other the Germans, in their war-making technique, display an identical aim—that of increasing and concentrating artillery fire-power to its fullest and most deadly extent.

IN RUSSIA the Germans employ two types of "Assault Wagons." These are designed to give intense close support fire to the infantry in reducing strong points and in close street fighting. In the foreground (A) is seen a 105-mm. gun mounted on the Mark I P Z K (light) tank chassis. Normally a revolving turret with two machine-guns is mounted. Several types of gun have been experimented with, but the 105-mm. seems to be the largest yet mounted on this chassis. The armoured shield (1) provides shelter for the crew, who are here seen observing the result of previous fire and are preparing to reload (2). The driver of the vehicle is situated low and just in front of the gun layer turning the small wheel (3).

(B). This 75mm. gun (4) is mounted on the Mark III chassis (5)—normally mounting a 50-mm. gun on revolving turret. There is a crew of four including the driver. The commander is seen observing the shot (6) from the entrance to the very squat armoured cupola of the vehicle. In both these types of assault wagon the whole vehicle is aimed at the target, but on the vertical plane the action is normal. These guns are fed by small ammunition trailers, which draw up alongside to replenish them. Inset small circle shows one of the many heavy Russian tanks which have been used with such effective results on the Voronezh front. This one mounts a four-inch gun on a revolving turret.

IN EGYPT the Germans employ the 88-mm. anti-aircraft and anti-tank gun, the chief feature of these being mobility. In the background (C) the gun is on a travelling train pulled along by a powerful half-tracked lorry which carries the crew. At (D) the crew are preparing the gun for A.A. work. The front and rear sets of wheels are detached by lowering the gun to the ground and extending the side arms (7). In anti-tank work the wheels are usually kept in position (E) and the side arms only extended. The gun is here seen recoiling and ejecting the spent shell-case. The gun loader, wearing a heavy elbow-length glove, is at (8), the gun layer (9). Others of the crew are preparing to reload, whilst the Officer-in-Charge observes the fire (10). The shells fired weigh about 20 lb. each. Seen inset small circle our own 25-pounder gun, which many experts consider to be the most useful all-round gun.

When It Was 'Sitzkrieg' for the Nazis in Libya

During the summer and autumn of 1941 the German sergeant-mechanic who kept the diary from which the following extracts are taken was a member of Rommel's Afrika Korps on the Sollum front. It was a period of "sitz" rather than "blitz," and it is interesting to note his reactions to the trials and tribulations of that kind of desert war.

JULY. As I have no other book, this English one [it was a S.O. 135] from the aerodrome at El Adem must do. I've torn out some used pages, so it's quite serviceable. The latest news is not the war in Russia, but that two men from the battalion can go on leave every fortnight. I've worked it out that under this scheme we shall need five-and-a-half years. Marvellous, isn't it ? But I don't want leave that lasts only 21 days starting from Naples.

Then food here is now perfectly bloody. Today I had a little bit of cheese that provided just three thinly spread slices. I'd like to see the blurbs they're shoving in all the newspapers about our " splendid " grub out here. Here we sit like birds in the wilderness, so they give us food fit for owls. It's right enough to say that the German soldier adapts himself to his environment. Like a fool, I'd always wondered what the scorpions lived on. What do *we* live on, anyway ? Let's hope that at home they don't forget us altogether on account of the Eastern campaign. I do not want to start a mutiny here, but there is no doubt that they could do better for us.

No break again for Sunday. I've got to work so that the paper-war may flourish. Three loud cheers for the paper-war ! We started off the day again with an inoculation in the left breast, this time against cholera. If it goes on like this we shall shortly be walking medicine-chests.

It's dark already. Over there on the slope an Arab is piping away on his nerve-shattering instrument like a child of four. Today I lay the whole day in bed, feverish and trembling in every limb. I ate nothing all day but two bits of bread and marmalade. Has the tropical sickness got me as well ? The chief thing for me is to keep well. I don't want to see any medical orderlies ; they don't know themselves what they're doing. I've reached the stage that almost the whole company reached months ago. All pride in my health has gone. If this lasts another three weeks I'll be a useless wreck. But in spite of everything I'll grit my teeth and go through with it and not leave Africa before my unit leaves it.

I ate no more today than I did yesterday. Even my favourite dish, haricot beans well-cooked, couldn't tempt my appetite. My gorge rises at everything.

August. We get it pretty bad with British planes here. The beggars are here the whole time. Over Bardia one flare after the other is dropped. Now four of them are hanging there—and now the Tommies have laid their eggs. Of our Luftwaffe there's nothing to be seen. I think there must be away in Russia. Well, boys, just wait a moment ; when they're here again and a big air attack begins, then the old desert will heave with a vengeance.

'God Knows What the Italians Are At !'

Italians are here laying mines in front of ours. In the short time that we've been here three Italians have already gone up in the air while doing their job. God knows what they think they're at. We've laid some thousands without that happening. The Italians are gradually getting on my nerves.' The whole livelong day these friends of ours sound the air-raid alert—whether for a German or an Italian or a Britisher, they don't care a damn. Then they take to their heels and dive down their holes. When the All Clear sounds they first of all poke their heads out cautiously, and then creep forth. We don't let this comedy disturb us.

September. All day long we had our hands full with T-mines, H.E.s, shells, detonators, time fuses, and such like. In the evening I bathed both my feet in soapy water, for four scratches had festered and they've been open for fourteen days. At least twenty men are running around in this condition ; everything festers and refuses to heal. After I had bathed them the medical corporal came and removed the septic matter with his surgical pincers. Today a man is off to Catania in Sicily ; he has jaundice. What a life ! Another man has diphtheria. One has this and the other has that. Fifteen of us have stomach trouble. The health situation is ghastly. It's so sad I feel like biting my big toe for laughter.

The new Commander has forbidden the wearing of short trousers. So now you run about the whole day in longs and sweat like a pig. I don't know which is worse, the Commander, the flies, or the rats. To hell with it ! Are we in Africa or the Arctic

SITZKRIEG!—but not the version described in this article. A German officer sits alone in a prisoner-of-war camp in the Western Desert.   *Photo, British Official*

or a madhouse ? Everyone wants to go home. They say, quite rightly, " What are we doing here still ? We're not fighting." Only with a sense of humour is this bearable.

I spoke this morning with an Italian, one-third by speech, two-thirds by gestures. He told me the English would never attack Rome. It was too ancient, the Holy Father lived there, and Rome had on that account no A.A. I made it plausible to him that we might shortly be getting a move on, in order to reach Cairo. He showed precious little elation at the prospect. That these fellows have no longer any stomach for the fight is absolutely clear to me. Some of them have been here for twenty months, and have had no leave. Perhaps these figures will apply to us some day. God forbid !

Today that mad Italian bugler sounded the air-raid alert no less than eighteen times.

That makes thirty-six calls altogether. The Italians are by this time getting to be a real joke. They shoot at anything in the air providing it is far enough away.

At lunchtime eight British bombers flew over in close formation as calmly as you like. I'll have to get hold of a British A.A. gun. It's getting a bit thick that our friends are invariably permitted to go on their way undisturbed. Of course, the Italian flak hasn't fired a shot, for the bomber is the sort of thing that might, just conceivably, drop a bomb. They must see it's useless to try to placate the things by not shooting, for you can get a bomb in your eye ever so easily and then you've got to wear a glass eye or a black patch for the rest of your life. Is it tragedy or a comedy that's being played here ?

October. [For the first part of the month the writer is seriously ill. He has pains in the left thigh that cripple him. But throughout, as he records, he works indefatigably—and grouses half hysterically, as usual.]

Today, once again, we got rations for three days. I had such a pitiable hunger that I've already eaten my rations for tomorrow and the day after. What I'll eat then God alone knows. Perhaps I'll get another parcel. Isn't it perfect mockery what they offer us here for food ? Here, of all places, where you need more to keep your health than elsewhere. It doesn't matter a damn if we go to the dogs ; what matters is that Germany saves foreign exchange and will win the war.

'Best to Keep My Mouth Shut'

November. Shall I curse or shall I laugh ? Shall I kick things around ? I'll keep my mouth shut ; that's the best thing. On a Sunday they actually give us a quarter of a plate of food. But be content, you've got all you need ! What ? Not the case ? It's there in the papers ; you'll find it in the weekly illustrated. Then it *must* be true. Now I have really got fed up with the whole show. Nothing doing in front of us or behind ; in addition to which you've got to starve and every night we have a visit from the Royal Air Force. I'm going to apply for leave. They can stew in their own juice.

I want to go home. When I get back let's hope we shall get a move on. We can live on dry bread for all I care, so long as we get a move on. When we were shifting about all over the desert like Arabs we were always told, " Of course, supplies can't follow you ; you move so quickly. But it'll soon be better; we've everything stored in Tripoli." Now, we've been stationary for weeks and suddenly they have the cheek to tell us, " Yes, the English are sinking too much of our stuff." Nothing's simpler than that—you just work out the average quota of losses, send over enough extra to right the balance, and there you are. The thanks of the Fatherland go out to you, boys, sure enough. You see it more clearly every day. Divisional Orders say that numerous bags of parcels have been lost through enemy action. This should be made known to our parents ; it would save unnecessary questions afterwards. About ten parcels of mine must have gone to the devil. How do you like that ? They're not even in a position to safeguard the little needs and luxuries that we get from home. Everything sums up to this : " We're holding out in a lost post."

Yesterday we are again given three days' rations. It's simply incredible what we've got to put up with. Poor homeland, can you offer nothing better to your sons who are roasting in Africa's heat ?

THE WAR IN THE AIR

by Capt. Norman Macmillan, M.C., A.F.C.

ALLIED air activity everywhere continues on a growing scale. American squadrons now operate in the United Kingdom, in the Middle East, in China, and the Far East ; in Russia American-built Fortress bombers have been used to bomb strategic lines of communication. North American Mustang single-seat fighters have been shooting-up ground targets in France ; these aircraft are used by the R.A.F. Army Cooperation Command, and pending the opening-up of active ground warfare in Western Europe they are working in collaboration with the squadrons of Fighter Command.

Fierce and bitter air actions have continued along the active zones of fighting in Russia, each side striving to attain a measure of local domination in the air, and neither appearing to achieve their objective, so evenly do the air arms match one another. Yet the Red Air Force have bombed Königsberg, the important port and communication centre and capital of East Prussia, which has not been bombed by the R.A.F. This city of about 320,000 inhabitants is strategically well-placed as a feeder for the German forces facing the Leningrad, Moscow, and Bryansk zones. Its straight-line distance from British bases is 800 miles—too far for a summer night's raid. For the Red Air Force it must have meant an operational round flight of about 1,100 to 1,200 miles. All the Russian aircraft returned safely. The type of aircraft used was not disclosed. Evidently the Russian airmen met small opposition—further evidence of Germany's need to concentrate her air defences against the R.A.F. Apart from the material damage caused by this raid on Königsberg, the raid will have the useful strategic effect of causing the Luftwaffe still further to spread the ground-air defences against air raids.

While the extended German invasion of south Russia is a serious factor in the war situation, it must be borne in mind that for Germany, bent on conquest, this is the critical

year in which Hitler must stake everything he has got. It is now universally conceded that air superiority, employed tactically, has created the conditions necessary for every material conquest of this war. It follows that this condition is also necessary to enable the Allies to reverse the sequences of military exploitation which we have witnessed at our expense during the past three years. In the field the Allied air forces are apparently approximately equal to those of the enemy in Russia, Egypt, India, and the Far East ; while in Britain they are superior to those in Western Europe. We have reached this position after two years of great effort, for at the time of the Battle of Britain we were greatly outnumbered, as, later, we were

A STUKA CRASHES on the Egyptian battlefront. This radioed photograph was taken at the actual moment that the machine hit the ground. It was shot down on July 23 by British A.A. gunfire. The pilot had baled out, and became a prisoner of war. *Photo, British Official: Crown Copyright*

outnumbered in the Far East. In 1943 we shall have world air superiority, and with satisfactory organization should be able to concentrate excess air strength wherever required, and at the same time increase still further the air bombardment of Germany.

THE four-engined bombers — Stirling, Halifax, Lancaster—that are causing heavy damage in Germany by their capacity to carry large-size bombs and heavy bombloads had their origin as R.A.F. types in the findings of an Air Staff conference held at the Air Ministry in May 1936 to consider a heavy-bomber specification drawn up under the guidance of Air Vice-Marshal (as he now is) R. D. Oxland. Thus we see how slowly, even under the urgent stress of rearmament and the pressure of war, new types of aircraft come into service ; even then minor faults may be found under active service conditions, and have to be put right before the full flow of production can go smoothly. In this type of aircraft we are ahead of Germany. We now need them in ever greater numbers, for they are playing an important part in the campaign against the enemy submarine war.

From July 18 to 30 the principal targets for our home-based bombers were the Ruhr

and Rhineland, Hamburg, and Saarbrücken. In the Ruhr-Rhine area the main objective was Duisburg (raided July 21, 23, and 25), the largest inland port in the world, and a vital centre for the inflow and outflow of raw and finished materials from that great war-producing belt. Although they may not appear to be interconnected, the attacks made during the same period by Fighter Command and Army Cooperation Command upon railway engines in the occupied zone within their reach are in alignment with the bomber attack upon Duisburg, for both were directed against enemy communications. Interference with waterborne communications adds to the strain upon landborne communications, and vice versa ; when both are attacked the strain is greater.

The attack upon Hamburg on the night of July 26-7 must have had a shattering effect upon that city. Within 35 minutes more than 175,000 incendiary bombs fell upon the place, dropped by two waves of heavy and medium bombers, setting much of the old town on fire, causing fires all round the Aussen Alster lake, and many in the dock area. Anyone who knows Hamburg will realize that this is a blow heavier than any which the Luftwaffe has struck at Britain. The incendiaries were followed by high-explosives, including many 4,000-lb. bombs. The great German port and submarine-building base was raided again two nights later. These raids strike at the submarine menace direct, and are an important contribution to the Battle of the Atlantic. Saarbrücken was raided on July 29-30.

A FEW landmarks in the war have occurred in this period. Air Vice-Marshal K. R. Park, who commanded the No. 11 Fighter Group that played such a prominent part in the Battle of Britain, has taken over command in Malta from Air Vice-Marshal H. P. Lloyd as officer commanding the R.A.F. Mediterranean. In a special Order of the Day issued to all ranks A.V.-M. Lloyd, since knighted, disclosed that the enemy had to provide battleship escort for their convoys owing to action from Malta base. Last December the Germans transferred 400 aircraft in Sicily, mostly from units then in Russia and France, and the succeeding attack upon Malta was the most concentrated and sustained in the history of air warfare. But, he continued, " We destroyed and damaged so many aircraft that it weakened the German effort in Africa and also helped out the Russians . . . They are suffering from their great losses in this small island, whereas we are stronger than ever."

One of the County of London Auxiliary squadrons which fought in Britain and in Malta is now fighting in Egypt.

On July 21 R.A.F. Ferry Command celebrated its first birthday. During the year many American-built heavy and medium bombers and flying-boats have been flown across the Atlantic to Britain under the able direction of Air Chief Marshal Sir Frederick Bowhill, who handled the Coastal Command until he took over Ferry Command.

On July 26 a force of Spitfires in combat with Focke-Wulf 190s, Germany's crack fighters, shot down nine F.W.s, losing three Spitfires. One F.W. 190 was recently forced down and captured on the English south coast.

The Japanese landing at Buna in New Guinea has concentrated air action in that area. The landing was accompanied by new Japanese air attacks against Australian territory, notably Darwin and Townsville, but little damage was done. Meanwhile the monsoon in the Bay of Bengal has held up activity in the Burma-India zone ; but in spite of the terrible monsoon weather (which I know from experience) the R.A.F. have raided points in Japanese occupation, among them Akyab, Burmese port across the Bay.

New American Planes Already in Action

Here are some of the new American aircraft which are now in operation against the enemy. 1. The Grumman Avenger, the U.S. Navy's most recent type of torpedo bomber, used with deadly effect against the Japanese in the Battle of Midway Island. 2. Vultee Vengeance dive-bomber. 3. Britain's latest fighter from America, the Mustang, mainly used by the R.A.F. Army Cooperation Command in low-flying attacks on ground targets in German-occupied territory. 4. Boeing Flying Fortress, the formidable B-17E, in flight. *Photos, Keystone, Sport & General, P.N.A.*

Down to the Sea They Swoop to Save

A special smoke bomb (right) being fixed to a Walrus seaplane, employed by the R.A.F. Air-Sea Rescue Service.

AIR-SEA RESCUE SERVICE PILOTS of the R.A.F. are saving the lives of pilots forced down off our shores. Rescue work consists of a spotting plane dropping a rubber dinghy, marking the spot with a smoke bomb. A seaplane is then dispatched to pick up the stranded airmen. A Sunderland flying-boat (top) rescues airmen coming alongside in a dinghy. Attaching a container complete with dinghy before setting off (below left). Packing blankets into a Walrus seaplane (below right).

Photos, British Official; New York Times Photos, Planet News, Associated Press

Though Silent Now Bow Bells Will Ring Again

IN ST. MARY-LE-BOW, Cheapside, now open to the sky, the Ward of Cordwainer Club held a service on July 30, the first to take place there since the church was wrecked by enemy action. Through the ruined west window can be seen the dome of St. Paul's Cathedral, also a sufferer—though fortunately to a much slighter extent—during the raids of 1940-41. The Cordwainers' own hall in Cannon Street was destroyed in a German bomb attack a year or so ago.

Photo, Topical Press

U.S. Commanders on the World's War Fronts

Since the treacherous blow dealt by the Japanese at Pearl Harbour last December, the U.S.A.'s contribution to the armed forces of the United Nations distributed across the world has been growing fast. Some indication of the extent and far-flung quality of the American armies is afforded by this page of portrait-biographies of the most prominent generals in the field.

BRETT of AUSTRALIA

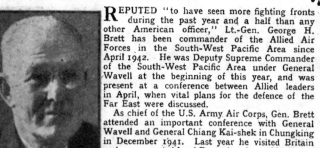

REPUTED "to have seen more fighting fronts during the past year and a half than any other American officer," Lt.-Gen. George H. Brett has been commander of the Allied Air Forces in the South-West Pacific Area since April 1942. He was Deputy Supreme Commander of the South-West Pacific Area under General Wavell at the beginning of this year, and was present at a conference between Allied leaders in April, when vital plans for the defence of the Far East were discussed.

As chief of the U.S. Army Air Corps, Gen. Brett attended an important conference with General Wavell and General Chiang Kai-shek in Chungking in December 1941. Last year he visited Britain and accompanied Lord Beaverbrook and Mr. Harriman on their lease-lend mission to the U.S.S.R. He later studied air force organization in Russia. Brett has the reputation of being blunt and outspoken. In the last war he specialized in aviation.

ANDREWS of the CARIBBEAN

COMMANDER of the Caribbean area, including the highly important Panama Canal zone, Lt.-Gen. Frank M. Andrews began his career at America's famous military academy, West Point, subsequently becoming a cavalry officer. During the last war he transferred to aviation, and after the Armistice was put in charge of the airservice of American forces on the Rhine.

Known as an "airmen's airman," General Andrews has held important air command posts for the past fifteen years, and was a firm believer in fighter planes being equipped with cannon before the war made them a necessity.

In 1933 he became the first head of the G.H.Q. Air Force, at that time intended to be a concentrated striking force of all types of military aircraft. The majority of these planes were dispersed throughout America and a system of centrilization had to be devised. Andrews co-ordinated this into the first assembled air power America possessed.

MAXWELL of MIDDLE EAST

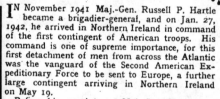

IN command of American operations in the Middle East, Maj.-General Russell Maxwell occupies one of the most vital positions of any American officer. He commands an army of American technicians whose purpose it is to supply and equip the forces of the United Nations in Egypt and the Middle East. Enormous assembly plants and repair shops designed for this end are now nearing completion in Eritrea. At Basra, at the head of the Persian Gulf, the work of engineers has brought into being highways and a railway to carry supplies to the Soviet armies in South Russia battling against powerful German forces in the fight for the Caucasus.

General Maxwell has outstanding organizing abilities and is responsible for the speed and efficiency with which these valuable supplies reach their destination. Originally an ordnance expert, he specialized in supply and economic warfare.

NIMITZ of the PACIFIC

SUCCEEDING Admiral Husband Kimmel in December 1941 as C.-in-C. of the U.S. Pacific Fleet, Admiral Chester W. Nimitz possesses splendid qualifications as an expert in submarine warfare. Before his promotion to the Hawaiian Command, he was Chief of the Navigation Bureau, a position which involved the assignment of Naval personnel. His present responsibilities are extremely vital, second only to those of Admiral King, C.-in-C. of the U.S. Navy.

The Japanese have found in Admiral Nimitz a shrewd and resourceful opponent—one who forestalls the enemy by the skilful dispositions of his forces operating over an extremely wide area. Large-scale reverses suffered by the Japanese—notably those of Midway Island and in the Battle of the Coral Sea—which involved considerable losses in men, ships, and aircraft, were largely the result of brilliant planning and co-ordination on the part of Admiral Nimitz.

HARTLE of NORTH IRELAND

IN November 1941 Maj.-Gen. Russell P. Hartle became a brigadier-general, and on Jan. 27, 1942, he arrived in Northern Ireland in command of the first contingent of American troops. His command is one of supreme importance, for this first detachment of men from across the Atlantic was the vanguard of the Second American Expeditionary Force to be sent to Europe, a further large contingent arriving in Northern Ireland on May 19.

Before his appointment Maj.-Gen. Hartle was commander of the 34th Infantry Division Camp at Claiborne, Louisiana, and he is among the youngest United States officers to hold the rank of major-general. He entered the Army before the last war as a second lieutenant of infantry, and subsequently spent some years as an instructor in military schools. He also attended the advanced course at America's Naval War College.

BONESTEEL of ICELAND

APPOINTED in September 1941 to command the garrison of American troops in Iceland, Maj.-Gen. Charles H. Bonesteel is a typical representative of U.S. Army tradition. From September 1941 to April 1942 he shared authority in Iceland with the British, and in April it was announced that he had been appointed to command the forces of the United Nations on the island. His job calls for an unusual degree of adaptability, for he maintains harmonious relations with the British Army and Navy, the R.A.F., Free Norwegian and Icelandic authorities.

The first contingent of American forces landed in Iceland in July 1941 to reinforce the British garrison, and one of the chief aims of Maj.-Gen. Bonesteel is to guard against attack from the Germans. The enemy covets Iceland not only as a base from which to attack Britain, but also as a menace to the North Atlantic.

BUCKNER of ALASKA

COMMANDING this vital area belonging to the U.S.A., Maj.-Gen. Simon Bolivar Buckner has mainly specialized in tanks. He is considered to be one of America's leading army lecturers. In 1933 he was Commandant of the Cadet Corps at the American Military Academy of West Point, being in charge of the cadets' discipline and drill.

Alaska has become a highly important strategical territory—its area is one-fifth of that of the United States and it has an extremely long coastline, coveted by the Japanese in their designs for the mastery of the Pacific. Under Maj.-Gen. Buckner's efficient command the Alaskan defence force has developed into a fine organization, one that can be relied upon to deal with an unscrupulous enemy.

Buckner began his career at Virginia Military Institute. During the Wilson administration (1921–1921) he was military aide at the White House. His father, who bore the same names, was a famous soldier and political leader, and was Governor of Kentucky from 1887 to 1891.

STILWELL of CHINA

G.-O.-C. the Chinese forces in Burma, Lt.-Gen. Joseph W. Stilwell arrived in Delhi on May 24, 1942, after an adventurous trek through Central Burma to the borders of Assam. Cut off from the outside world and travelling the greater part of the way on foot, General Stilwell and his staff had many adventures in forest and jungle.

During the Japanese invasion of Burma he made it clear that the enemy had superiority in numbers and that these great forces had been stretched out over a wide area. It was largely owing to Stilwell's brilliant leadership that the Chinese armies were kept intact after the Japanese broke through into Upper Burma.

Before he assumed command of the Chinese in Burma he was Chief of Staff to Gen. Chiang Kai-shek, an appointment announced in Chungking on March 10, 1942. After the Japanese occupation of Burma he consulted with Gen. Wavell in India. At the conclusion of these consultations Gen. Stilwell returned to China.

Americans in the Australasian War Zone

NEW GUINEA natives have made friends with these U.S. soldiers at Port Moresby (above). Supervised by an American negro soldier, native Kanaka workers (right) load a U.S. Army truck " somewhere in New Caledonia."

Returning to their Australian airfield after having carried out an effective bombing raid against the Japanese in the islands to the north, the crew of this American B.17 bomber is seen leaving its plane.

SYMBOLS OF VICTORY : Each of the torpedoes beside the skull and crossbones on the " Jolly Roger " flown by this U.S. submarine (above, left) represents a Japanese ship sunk in the south-west Pacific. The crew of this submarine has been decorated for bravery. American fighter pilots in Northern Australia (right) intently study a map. They are familiarizing themselves with important details of the territory which they must cover in their flights.

 Photos, Keystone, Planet News, Associated Press, Sport & General

THE HOME FRONT

by E. Royston Pike

"Is that a utility suit?" demanded an Hon. Member of the President of the Board of Trade the other day when the Commons were discussing the annual "Vote." "No, sir," replied Mr. Dalton, "because I am saving my coupons to the utmost I can. It is the better plan to expend coupons as slowly as possible having regard to the stock of clothes we possess. This suit" (he went. on to the accompaniment of cheers and laughter) "was made in 1930 and really it is too thin for the British climate."

Utility clothing, Mr. Dalton averred, had been very well received, especially by women. "One lady friend of mine told me yesterday that she was wearing a utility frock and that she liked it very much." Between 70 and 80 per cent of the total civilian production is now utility clothing. Among the utility goods now in course of production are pottery, hollow ware, such as kettles, pots and pans, and umbrellas—which are standardized in two sizes and will have only eight ribs instead of sixteen as now. Utility pencils, mechanical lighters, household textiles, cutlery and suit-cases are on the way, and in the case of jewelry it is proposed to limit production to clocks and watches, identification bracelets, cuff links, studs, and plain wedding-rings. Notwithstanding the war's impetus to betrothals there are sufficient engagement-rings in stock to last for several years, so no more are to be made for the present. Leather suit-cases are not being produced : perhaps they are not necessary since a haversack can contain all that is needful for a week-end's honeymoon. Lemon-squeezers, hair curlers, and electric dry-shavers are among the miscellanea whose production is banned ; and if you haven't already got a fountain-pen—well, you must write to *him* in Egypt or on the High Seas in pencil. Now it's Utility, Utility, all the time ; and the Utility Home will be practically complete in the autumn when utility furniture is expected to be in the shops in substantial quantities.

From furniture to food is not too sudden a step. As the war's third year draws to its close we are naturally concerned with the maintenance of the food front. Fortunately Mr. R. S. Hudson, Minister of Agriculture, was able in his Commons review on July 28 to give a fairly favourable account of our countryside as a food factory. Farmers are playing up well to the calls made upon them. It is yet too early to forecast a result

of this year's harvest, since in this matter we are always at the mercy of the weather, but we are assured that everything that man can do is being done to make it the biggest harvest ever. There has been a certain amount of waste in potatoes, and there is not much satisfaction to be derived from Mr. Hudson's statement that the Hamburgers were potatoless for ten days in early July. If the weather is reasonable, it is hoped to increase our wheat acreage by 600,000 acres ; and much more land is being put down to potatoes and sugar beet. In spite of the very unfavourable spring we actually produced ten million more gallons of milk than in the best pre-war years and thirteen million gallons more than last year. Not everybody was pleased, however, at the Minister's review, and Mr. Driberg, newly-elected member for Maldon, scored a point by a parody of Goldsmith's famous lines :

> Ill fares the land, to hastening ills a prey,
> Where *forms* accumulate, and *crops* decay.

Meanwhile we are being urged to save bread by eating more potatoes, for the very good reason that they are grown at home while the bulk of our wheat comes from abroad and takes much-needed shipping space. Lord Woolton has provided housewives with fifty recipes for using potatoes "round the clock." He has even presided at a Ministry of Food buffet luncheon at which all of the many different dishes were composed for the most part of potatoes ; he himself dined off Irish potato cakes and egg champ (made with dried egg), but some of the more stalwart guests tackled soup, cheese cookies, fish pie, scones and tarts, in all of which potatoes were a chief ingredient.

Rationing of chocolate and sweets began on Sunday, July 26, with a weekly allowance of 2 oz. per head. Some people had thought that children would receive a larger ration, but the Ministry of Food has taken the view that even for children sweets are not a necessity but a luxury. Furthermore, it is always open to parents to forgo their own ration in favour of their offspring . . . In spite of the usual eve-of-rationing rush, the country's 300,000 retail confectioners were well stocked for the beginning of this new venture in commodity control. No registration is needed, and people may buy sweets where they will on delivery of the necessary "points" cut from the personal rationing book—which made its début in this connexion.

To save fuel, oil and rubber, several hundred omnibuses are now parked during slack hours at certain points in Central London, one being along the carriage ways in Hyde Park.
Photo, Sport & General

Still the great Salvage Drive gathers impetus. Round London the racecourses are losing their iron railings, and even the graves in our country churchyards are being stripped of their iron surrounds. For my part, I can watch them go with the completest equanimity, for I have long been of the opinion that the last resting-places of the dead should not be cluttered up with Italian marble and the products of the metal foundry, but should be places "where the wild flowers wave In the free air."

Nor (devoted booklover though I am) do I see cause for much regret in the "miles of books" which are being launched in many parts of the country under the direction of the Wardens or the ever-useful W.V.S. Agreed, it costs a pang to separate from a volume that was purchased out of the slender purse of boyhood days or was "picked up" in some distant place in the long ago ; but there's consolation in the reflection that those vacant spaces on the library shelves may now be filled with an easy conscience—for books are still amongst the cheapest of life's goods, they are still unrationed or even taxed. So steel your hearts, out with the old books and add them to the literary snake crawling along the pavement—but *don't* throw away the string with which you tied the bundle. Since July 20 it has been a wartime crime to throw away string, rope and rags.

To conclude on a *colourful* note. In the House of Commons on July 23 Mr. G. Tomlinson, Parliamentary Secretary to the Ministry of Labour, referred to the "strange thing" that "though many of our girls don't object in the slightest to the risk of being blown to blazes, they *do* object to being turned yellow," and so scientists have been put to work on methods of preventing or minimizing this "facial decoration." In the next Sunday Express Mary Ferguson made it clear that the "yellow girls" are very few as compared with the last war. "In 999 cases out of a thousand," she wrote, "the girls on the 'yellow job' who put explosives into big and small bombs and into detonator caps have beautifully made-up faces. The Government has the cosmetics specially made for them, and supplies them free to every girl. The explosives workshops have beauty parlours and luxury ablution rooms." The one girl in a thousand who gets a yellow face is usually one who doesn't wash and make-up properly. "These girls, most of them young," concluded Miss Ferguson, "are heroines. They play with death all the time they work. Sometimes they lose their nerve. But for the most part they worry more about their complexions than the danger . . ." And that's not a bad facet of life in wartime Britain to finish up with.

REAPING FLAX is one of the tasks undertaken by the Women's Land Army. At this farm in Sussex a mechanical flax-puller is shown in use, while the girls accompany it up and down the field, rapidly stooking the stems. The revival of this industry is due to war conditions. *Photo, Topical*

Marshal Timoshenko • Hero of the Soviet Union

Well does the C.-in-C. of Russia's Southern Army Group merit his membership of the Order of his country's supreme heroes. At twenty his was the lot of a wretched peasant on a Bessarabian estate; today, twenty-seven years later, it is his brilliant generalship which time and again has brought to naught the stratagems of Hitler's ablest generals.

143

After a Year of Constant Battle

With desperate bravery the Russian rearguards fight to hold up the German advance. 1. Red Army infantry crossing a pontoon-bridge. 2. Radioed photograph showing Soviet soldiers advancing to dislodge the enemy from a village in the Crimea. 3. Red Army scouts engaged on a river reconnaissance. 4. Some of Timoshenko's reserves passing through Moscow.

Pho

On the Red Army's 1,000-Mile Front

Across the Russian countryside roars a German tank : a few seconds more and it will be halted by the Russian marksman aiming his anti-tank rifle from behind a wall (5). Soon the crew will be prisoners, marched (like those in 6 above) to the rear of the Russian lines. 7. A Red Army dispatch-rider hands over his dispatch near Voronezh.

Photos, U.S.S.R. Official; Planet News

Once Again the Cossacks Ride to War

For hundreds of years the fame of Russia's Cossacks has gone out to all the world. Today the Cossacks ride again, to victory or death ; but those shown here (top) wear steel helmets instead of their traditional round caps, and are armed not with silver-handled sabres but with sub-machine-guns. Below, a glimpse of Russian cavalry of another kind.

Rommel: The Man and the Myth

"If Rommel had been in the British Army," runs an oft-repeated quip, "he would still be a sergeant." But, as this article tells, it is quite wrong to suppose that Rommel is a "ranker" in the ordinary sense of the word. In fact, he is—well, here the "authorities" differ.

WHO is Rommel? Today he has his feet on the shifting sands of Egypt; he has booked for himself a place in history as the general who defeated Wavell, who stormed Tobruk, who smashed Auchinleck's armour and drove the remnants of the Eighth Army out of Libya. But when the historians come to write up his career they are going to have a hard job determining and disentangling the events of his earlier years. So much of Rommel's past is the subject of dispute—but the deficiencies and discrepancies are no brake upon the exuberant fancy of Dr. Goebbels' professional liars, busily constructing their pretty little myth about the "unbeatable general."

Up to now no one has produced Erwin Rommel's birth certificate, but he is presumed to have been born fifty years ago, in 1892. He seems to have sprung from lower middle-class stock, but what his father was —well, you can take your choice between a Bavarian workman, a butcher, a bricklayer, a professor of mathematics at Munich University, and a schoolmaster at Heidesheim in Württemberg. After education at a technical college (so it is said) young Rommel entered the Kaiser's army in 1910; this seems to be more or less agreed, but whereas according to one account he served in the ranks, according to another, and perhaps more probable, he was gazetted as a second lieutenant in the 124th Regiment of Infantry. At the outbreak of war in 1914 he was, or became, adjutant in an artillery regiment, and he was still only a lieutenant when in 1917 at Caporetto he bluffed a considerable Italian force into surrender. It was a bloodless victory, but the young subaltern's daring and resource were brought to the notice of the German High Command, and he was awarded the *Pour le Mérite*, the V.C. of Imperial Germany (as indeed it is of Hitler's Germany, too).

AFTER the collapse of 1918 Rommel left the Army and for a time was a student at Tübingen University. Two or three years later he contacted in some way or another Hitler's organization of Brownshirts, and in 1921, as an S.A. leader in Thuringia, he led a march on the Bavarian town of Koburg. The raid was the first of its kind, but it was marked by many of the features which soon became all too familiar: people were beaten up in the streets, the local police were temporarily overwhelmed, and for a few hours the Brownshirts were in control of the town—long enough for Adolf Hitler, then hardly notorious as a demagogue of the Munich beer-cellars, to take the salute as they marched past and to deliver one of his half-mystical, half-maniacal harangues. Then, the police having been reinforced, the Brownshirts dissolved into the crowd. But they had made history, and their leader was the young ex-officer with the black and silver ribbon on his breast.

After this brief emergence Rommel retired again into obscurity. Presumably he retained his membership of the Nazi party, but he was certainly not one of their recognized leaders; if he had been, he might have been shot with Roehm and his comrades in the bloody purge of June 1934. Not long after Hitler's rise to power Rommel returned to the Army, but another four or five years had to pass before his star was in the ascendant. Then, when Hitler was making his triumphal entry into the Sudetenland after Munich, something reminded him of the man who had captained that first of so many marches. Col. Rommel was put in charge of the Fuehrer's personal headquarters, and as such accompanied him to Poland.

FIELD-MARSHAL ROMMEL directing operations in the Western Desert, where his brilliant tactics, combined with superior forces, constituted a serious menace to the British positions in Egypt.
Photo, Sport & General

Shortly before Hitler's onslaught on the countries of the West, Rommel was given command of a Panzer division in France with the rank of lieutenant-general. It was an opportunity that he was quick to seize. His tanks—so it is said—were those which made the first dent in the French line at Sedan, and when the dent became a bulge and then a gap, they swept through and ranged far and wide behind the Maginot Line: they were reported in action on the Somme, at Cherbourg, and finally not far from Bordeaux. Knowing what we now know of Rommel, we can imagine the happy zest with which he harried the fleeing remnants of a broken and largely demoralized foe.

Even before Rommel left France for Africa, the Nazi propagandists were doing their best to boost his reputation. It was claimed that he displayed a "veritable genius for leadership." His success at Sedan,

creditable as it may well have been, was magnified out of all proportion: after all, the Germans had the advantage of long and careful preparation and of highly-trained and superbly-equipped divisions, while they were pitted against opponents whose arms were insufficient, whose leadership was contemptible, and whose movements were fatally hampered by a vast, uncontrollable flood of refugees. Even less evidence of military genius is afforded by that summer-time excursion across the smiling plains of central France. It was spectacular, yes; it was victory, victory all the way—but a conqueror's prowess is not to be dissociated from the quality of his foe.

WHY then does Dr. Joseph boost Rommel to the skies, while "soft-pedalling" von Bock and von Leeb, Weichs, Kleist, and the rest of the topmost flight of Germany's warrior chiefs, whose military achievements have been far more impressive, far more momentous, than any which even the most extravagant propaganda can ascribe to Rommel? Surely the answer is not far to seek. Bock, Leeb and Company belong to the professionals, they are "old school tie" men. They are Nazis, it is true, but they are Nazis from a sense of opportunism rather than persuasion; they support Hitler, they flatter him, they bow to his wishes (sometimes)—but the good Nazis may well suspect that if fortune should change the generals would put a bullet in the Fuehrer with never a moment's hesitation.

Unlike Hindenburg-Ludendorff in the last war, Rommel is not a typical product of the German general staff tradition. He is a typical S.A. tough; he is almost the only Army leader of high rank who has graduated from the ranks of the Party. As the Münchener Neusten-Nachrichten put it in an article not long ago, "General Rommel, who, as an old S.A. leader in Thuringia, derived his National Socialist ideology from direct personal relationship with the Fuehrer, is essentially the warrior type of the New Germany; in him are embodied its core of dogma, the untiring drive of the New Reich."

That is one reason for Doctor Goebbels' boostings. There is also a second. To quote from Die Zeitung, the German newspaper published in London, "The propaganda on behalf of the alleged genius is well calculated. It is intended to create the impression inside and outside Germany that nothing and nobody can withstand the new Marshal. It is a kind of Hindenburg-Ludendorff fabricated myth (*ersatz-mythos*)."

For our part we must, and do, admit that the Marshal and his Afrika Korps have done great things; we are not inclined to belittle in the least their successes on the African battlefield. But we must not "fall for" this latest of the Nazi myths. That myth of the last war, the Hindenburg-Ludendorff combination, seemed for months and years to bear all the marks of invincibility. Then came August 8, 1918. Rommel's myth, too, is *ersatz*.

What the Germans Found in Sevastopol

SEVASTOPOL IS IN GERMAN HANDS after an heroic defence of eight months. These photographs afford some indication of the bitter character of the struggle. Top left, German labourers start clearing up the debris ; right, part of the ruined city, with smoke rising from scores of smouldering buildings in the distance. Below, aerial view showing how the overwhelming superiority of the Luftwaffe laid waste the fortress-city.

Photos, Associated Press, Keystone

'Kamerad!' A Pocket of Nazis Surrenders

ON THE RUSSIAN FRONT. 1. German soldiers in a south-western battle area surrender to a Russian tank. 2. Two fighter pilots attached to the Soviet Northern Fleet, the naval force guarding the Barents Sea communications, enjoy a game of draughts between operations. The aircraft in the background is a U.S. Curtiss Kittyhawk fighter. 3. German soldiers, apprehensive of snipers, skirt a building fired by the Russians in the Donetz sector. 4. Artillery observers of the Red Army correcting the fire of their batteries.

Photos, U.S.S.R. Official; Planet News. Keystone

THE RED ARMY'S NEW ANTI-TANK GUN is here being demonstrated to a large class of officers and men at a reserve training camp behind the Russian battle front. In use this gun is supported on a low stand, the two legs of which fold back when the weapon is being carried, as will be seen in the illustration at the bottom of page 164, where also the muzzle is shown protected by a small piece of sacking. The long barrel increases the velocity of the hard-cored armour-piercing bullet. Each gun is manned by a crew of two.

Photo, Planet News

THE WAR AT SEA

by Francis E. McMurtrie

ACTIVITY in the English Channel and North Sea, commented on in page 118, has by no means abated. In the early hours of July 21 a small patrol of our light coastal craft under Lieut. H. P. Cobb, R.N.V.R. (aged 29), was in action with a superior enemy force engaged in escorting a supply ship up Channel. Despite the odds, our boats at once attacked, setting on fire an armed trawler and hitting various other vessels heavily, including the supply ship. Though one of our units, a motor gunboat, was set on fire and became a total loss, the enemy turned back to the westward and sought shelter in harbour.

To make the utmost out of the fact that for once we had lost a vessel, the Germans issued a distorted account of the action in which it was alleged that four British motor torpedo-boats were sunk as well as the motor gunboat. Incidentally, it was mentioned that the enemy force was commanded by Lieut.-Cdr. Wunderlich—which in German means " strange." He is certainly responsible for a strange story !

Five nights later another patrol, under Lieut. R. G. L. Pennell, R.N., intercepted two enemy trawlers, armed with high-angle guns, off the French coast. One of the trawlers was left sinking and the other was severely damaged. We sustained two minor casualties and some slight superficial damage.

Early on July 28 two more trawlers were caught by one of our patrols off Cherbourg, one being sunk and the other heavily damaged. Again there was no serious damage and only two casualties on our side.

NEXT, on the night of July 30-31, there were no fewer than three brushes in the Channel and North Sea, evidence of the keen eye kept on enemy movements by our patrols. Off Ymuiden, Holland, five armed trawlers were encountered by light coastal craft under Lieut. E. M. Thorpe, R.N., and engaged for ten minutes. In this time one of the enemy vessels was set on fire, but the action had then to be broken off, as one of our craft was disabled and had to be taken in tow and brought back to the base.

Less than an hour later the same enemy force was attacked by another of our patrols, under Lieut.-Cdr. N. H. Hughes, R.N.V.R., with the result that further damage and casualties were inflicted. The trawler previously set on fire was again hit, and the blaze increased to such proportions that there is little doubt she became a total loss. Only daylight obliged us to discontinue the fight. Though attacked repeatedly by enemy aircraft and shore batteries, our patrol suffered neither damage nor casualties.

Meanwhile, in the Channel, three enemy ships believed to be either seagoing torpedo-boats of 600 tons or minesweepers of similar size and appearance, accompanied by smaller craft of the motor gunboat type, were attacked by a patrol of our light coastal craft under Lieut. G. D. K. Richards, R.N. Unfortunately the action was too brief for much to be accomplished, but the enemy certainly received a number of hits, while we suffered neither casualties nor damage.

A FULL account has now been released of the Arctic convoy action, lasting for over four days at the end of April and beginning of May, in which four commanding officers won the D.S.O. These were Commander M. Richmond, H.M.S. Bulldog; Commander R. C. Medley, H.M.S. Beagle; Lieut.-Commander N. E. G. Roper, H.M.S. Amazon ; and Lieut.-Commander John Grant, H.M.S. Beverley. All these ships are destroyers, the last-named being one of those transferred from the United States Navy in September 1940.

As one of the two convoys involved was skirting a large patch of drift ice, three enemy destroyers of over 1,800 tons were sighted, all faster and more powerfully armed than the British vessels. The Bulldog at once led her consorts to the attack, fire being opened at 10,000 yards range in poor visibility conditions owing to snow squalls. Though the Amazon was hit, suffering casualties and damage, she remained in the line and continued to fire, and the enemy were forced to retire.

Half an hour later the German destroyers were sighted again, but retired as before on being attacked. Meanwhile the convoy had entered the ice pack, and in order to maintain touch the escort had to follow suit. A third attempt to break through was made by the enemy an hour afterwards, but was not persisted in after the British escort vessels had opened fire. Another attack came in another

hour, but this time the German fire was neither so accurate nor so intense, evidence of the damage sustained from our shells. Only one of the enemy destroyers seemed able to fire full salvos at the finish. Therefore when the fifth and final engagement began within half an hour, it lasted only ten minutes before the enemy retreated.

During these same operations we lost a 10,000-ton cruiser, H.M.S. Edinburgh. She was completed shortly before the outbreak of war, and was armed with twelve 6-in. and twelve 4-in. guns, and had a speed of over 32 knots. Her steering gear having been disabled by a torpedo attack from a U-boat on April 30, the destroyers Foresight and Forester and two Soviet destroyers came to her aid. An effort by the Forester to tow the cruiser proved abortive owing to the heavy sea running, so for about 16 hours the Foresight was taken in tow by the Edinburgh.

H.M.S. FORESTER, a destroyer which did heroic work in the action described in this page. Forced to stop by a hit in the boiler-room, which also killed her commanding officer, she continued to engage the enemy and finally got under way again. *Photo, Wright & Logan*

For 23 hours every effort was made by the engine-room staff to keep a correct course by the use of the engines, the number of different engine orders which had to be given in a single watch being as many as 64. Various attacks were made by U-boats, but all were frustrated by the Forester and Foresight, the two Soviet destroyers having returned to port. On the afternoon of May 1 another Soviet destroyer arrived with a tug, and the minesweepers Harrier, Niger, Gossamer and Hussar joined company. So heavy were the seas that the tug could not keep the Edinburgh on her course unaided, so the Gossamer was taken in tow by the cruiser to assist in steering.

Early next morning three large enemy destroyers appeared about four miles off, and were engaged by Harrier and Hussar. The Foresight and Forester did their best to close the range, and there was an intermittent running fight.

H.M.S. Forester was stopped by a shell in her boiler room. H.M.S. Foresight did her best to draw the enemy's fire upon herself, and hit one of the enemy ships so severely that she stopped.

Finally the enemy destroyers fired a salvo of torpedoes, one of which unfortunately struck the Edinburgh, rendering her completely unmanageable. The Hussar promptly laid a smoke screen to cover her, while the Harrier and Gossamer ran alongside, and, in spite of heavy seas, took on board all the cruiser's personnel except the guns' crews.

Both the Forester and Foresight continued in action, and although the latter was also hit and disabled for a time, the enemy had had enough and retired. When they reappeared, the Foresight scored a hit on the enemy destroyer which had stopped, causing a terrific explosion. When the smoke cleared she could no longer be seen. Soon afterwards there was a heavy explosion in another of the German ships, which then abandoned the fight.

Unfortunately the Edinburgh was so badly damaged that we had to sink her ourselves.

H.M.S. EDINBURGH, a cruiser of 10,000 tons, was torpedoed by a U-boat on April 30, 1942, while acting as part of the escort of a North Russian convoy, and her steering gear was disabled. Two days later, after a second torpedo attack, she had to be sunk by our own forces.
Photo, British Official; Crown Copyright

Women's War Work and How It's Paid

In this war to an even greater extent than in the last, women are playing a great and increasing part : indeed, they are almost everywhere save in the actual fighting line. This is the first of three articles on the subject by IRENE CLEPHANE ; it is concerned with women in the Services.

WOMEN began to train for service with the forces of the Crown before war began. The formation of the Auxiliary Territorial Service for women, on a basis similar to that of the Territorial Army, was announced in September 1938, shortly after Munich ; and in July 1939 the King approved the formation of a separate women's service under a woman to be called the Women's Auxiliary Air Force, which would take over certain duties with the Royal Air Force in time of war, duties that had previously been allocated to the A.T.S. ; at the same time the War Office appointed a woman Director of the A.T.S., whose strength was then 912 officers and 16,547 members. The Women's Royal Naval Service, known as the Wrens, was founded during the war of 1914-18 and re-formed on the outbreak of the present war.

Wrens are employed on shore service only, on work that will release men for duty afloat. Their duties range from cooking to driving lorries at night, and include ciphering, de-coding, and other confidential work. They do just enough drill to enable them to make a smart appearance on parade—not difficult to achieve in their neat navy blue uniform with the attractive little cap for rank and file, the three-cornered hat of old style naval pattern for officers.

Wrens may be either "mobile" or "immobile," the first being willing to move to any point where their services are required and receiving 4d. to 1s. a day more than the second, who are stationed at the point of enlistment—usually their home town, for many of the women in the Wrens are born on the coast, and often have long-standing family associations with the Navy.

BY August 1940 some 7,000 Wrens were serving, and a call for a further 600-700 recruits a month went out, wanted mainly as cooks, but also as wireless operators, clerks, and stewards. For the first time the Admiralty allowed women to be admitted to the Royal Naval Cookery Schools at Portsmouth, Devonport, Rosyth, and

W.R.N.S. DISPATCH RIDER hands a message to the Officer of the Day of a destroyer returned from patrol duty. Girls who enter this branch of the Service must have experience of motor-cycling and running repairs.
Photo, British Official

Chatham ; and candidates were accepted up to the age of 49 if they had had previous experience. Though Wrens work ashore only, a wide field of experience is open to them : by December 1941 (when their numbers had risen to 20,000) they were serving not only in the big home ports, where one of their duties was to plot the Battle of the Atlantic, but also in the Orkneys and the Outer Hebrides, Gibraltar and Singapore.

Rank in the Wrens runs on parallel lines with that of men of the Royal Navy, from Superintendent, which equals Commander, to Wren, which equals A.B. Pay in the ranks ranges from 1s. 4d. to 3s. 8d. a day, plus board, lodging and clothing.

Helping the Men Who Fly

IMMEDIATELY war started the W.A.A.F. sent out a call which met with a ready response for cooks, mess orderlies, equipment assistants, motor-transport drivers, clerks, telephone and teleprinter operators, and fabric workers—either trained or willing to train. Pay for an airwoman begins at 1s. 4d. a day (plus a wartime allowance of 4d. a day), with increases for proficiency in a trade and for length of service. Junior officers receive 7s. 4d. a day, senior officers £1 2s. 4d. In all cases board and lodging are found, and the airwomen receive clothing as well.

The first 8,000 members of the W.A.A.F. had nearly completed their training by the end of 1939, but recruits continued to be called for, and to come in. In May 1940 a special call was made for cooks, kitchen hands, seamstresses and upholsterers (as balloon fabric workers), and for candidates for special confidential duties. The need for cooks was so great that the minimum height was reduced in July 1940 from 5 ft. 2 in. to 4 ft. 10 in.

The duties undertaken by airwomen were constantly extended. In September 1940 a new school was opened to train them as code and cipher officers ; in April 1941 they began to train to take the places of men on barrage balloon stations ; and in October 1941, owing to a shortage of suitable men, W.A.A.F. officers began to be appointed to act as assistant adjutants in mixed units : they were empowered to give orders and make decisions affecting men as well as women, but were not allowed to administer disciplinary action over airmen, or to command units composed entirely of men.

The Government decision in December 1941 to introduce conscription of young unmarried women brought a rush of candidates to the W.A.A.F. By the end of January 1942 it was the largest women's service in the world embodied in a single organization : it had a strength exceeding that of the whole R.A.F. at home and abroad before the war. It included 51 trades.

The Women in Khaki

UNDOUBTEDLY the attractiveness of the Air Force blue uniform and the feats of the R.A.F. had much to do with the partiality shown by recruits for the W.A.A.F. as against the A.T.S., the conditions in which came in for a good deal of criticism. But in the early days of the war service in the A.T.S. was popular enough. By October 14, 1939, 20,000 women were already serving in it, and recruiting went on with the object of doubling that number. Clerks, draughtswomen, drivers for light vans and cars, cooks, storewomen, switchboard operators, teleprinter operators, and orderlies were all

A.T.S. POLICEWOMEN serving in the South-Eastern Command, examine the papers of a woman driver of a military car.
Photo, Fox

wanted. Married as well as single women were asked to enrol, and if their husbands were serving they were allowed to continue to receive their marriage allowances.

A.T.S. recruits were paid 1s. 4d. a day (later increased by 4d. a day wartime pay), rising as they passed their tests. There was no allowance for dependants, however ; indeed, it was specifically stated at that time that "those who have to provide for dependants should seek other means of service" ! This attitude of the authorities changed as the need for women grew more pressing : in January 1940 allowances for dependants of women in all the forces were introduced, based on the contribution the serving women had been in the habit of making in civil life. They range from 7s. 6d. to 25s. a week, of which amount members have to contribute from 8d. to 1s. 9d. a day according to their rate of pay.

BY April 1940 A.T.S. units were established in France at the base ports and in the lines of communication areas. They were lodged in hostels or billets and lived under a semi-military code under which they were not allowed to leave their quarters except in pairs. With the withdrawal of the British army from France, the A.T.S. returned home too. But recruiting went on. On June 4, 5,000 drivers with at least one year's experience were urgently needed for immediate duty, and 1,000 cooks and 1,000 orderlies to cook for and wait on the returning B.E.F. In March 1941 A.T.S. began to train for work on anti-aircraft stations ; six months later the first mixed anti-aircraft battery was in action near London. A.T.S., it was found, proved the equals of men in operating all the intricate apparatus of an anti-aircraft post, but they do not handle the guns. The average age of the men and women in these mixed posts is about 20, and both men and women wear ordinary battledress. The women do shorter periods of duty than the men. A mixed battery got its first German aeroplane early in November 1941. An A.T.S. military police unit was formed in January 1942, and went on duty in the streets of London for the first time on February 10. Their work is intended to be advisory rather than disciplinary.

Here Are the ATS, the WAAF and the WRNS

A.T.S. GIRLS who "man" the predictors and range-finders are seen receiving instruction during a practice gas smoke attack at one of London's gun emplacements. The instructor is Sergeant Minnie Cropley.

FLEET AIR ARM WRENS at work on an aircraft. This section of the Service has become very skilled at performing intricate maintenance jobs such as acetylene welding, dope spraying, and so on.

VARIED WORK OF THE W.A.A.F. Left, loading a stretcher case into a hospital plane. Above, young amazons of the Balloon Barrage steady their charge while it is being made fast.

Photos, Daily Mirror, New York Times Photos, Associated Press, Sport & General

The Germans Fortify the Channel Islands

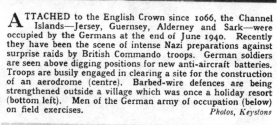

ATTACHED to the English Crown since 1066, the Channel Islands—Jersey, Guernsey, Alderney and Sark—were occupied by the Germans at the end of June 1940. Recently they have been the scene of intense Nazi preparations against surprise raids by British Commando troops. German soldiers are seen above digging positions for new anti-aircraft batteries. Troops are busily engaged in clearing a site for the construction of an aerodrome (centre). Barbed-wire defences are being strengthened outside a village which was once a holiday resort (bottom left). Men of the German army of occupation (below) on field exercises.

Photos, Keystone

From the Battlefield to the Hospital Ward

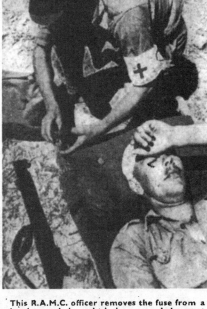

RED CROSS ambulances are regarded as legitimate targets by the enemy. An R.A.M.C. convoy was attacked by the Nazis in the Western Desert, and one of the ambulances was set on fire. The driver, though wounded, escaped, and is seen above being helped by his comrades. Stretcher bearers, below, carry the wounded through the dust and smoke of the Libyan battlefield.

This R.A.M.C. officer removes the fuse from a hand grenade brought in by a wounded man at a field dressing station in the Western Desert.

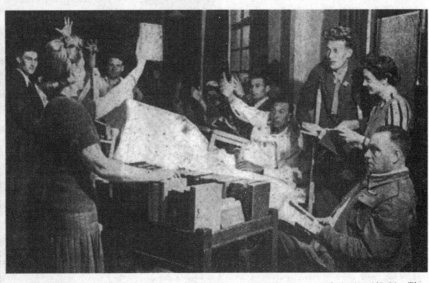

NURSED BACK TO HEALTH, these men learn to forget the horrors of the battlefield. The wounded soldier (left) walks on a pair of crutches which were made by the two boys at a country school to which they had been evacuated. Visiting the wounded every week, this Red Cross librarian (above) holds out a thriller. *Photos, British Official; Daily Mirror*

'On the Record' By Our Roving Camera

PRE-FABRICATED HUTS (right), comprising three dormitories, canteen, store, and two offices, were erected in sixteen days by a flying squad of 35 men. The purpose of these mobile builders is to reduce the delay between the date on which tenders are invited for constructional work and the actual start of operations by the contractor. In the foreground are three of the mobile vans, lettered "Ministry of Works Flying Squad," in which the men sleep.

Belgian Independence Day, celebrated on July 21, was memorable for a parade of Belgian Forces in Britain at Chelsea Barracks, London. M. Gutt, Belgian Defence Minister (below), is seen inspecting Belgian parachute troops during the ceremony.

H.M.S. SKATE (below), Britain's oldest destroyer, recently celebrated her silver jubilee in active service. Built in 1917, she is the last surviving ship of the "Admiralty R" class, and is the only three-funnelled destroyer in the Royal Navy. The Skate is one of the guardians of the convoys which run from a northern port, and her 25th birthday was spent at sea. During the past year she missed only one convoy, and she has travelled many thousands of miles during her gallant vigil of the seas.

Photos, Topical Press, Associated Press, Wright & Logan, Planet News

THE MITCHELL FAMILY were decorated by the King for having courageously carried on their work during bombardment and air attacks on their farm at Dover. Undeterred by repeated enemy raids, they went about their work of farming close to what has been nicknamed Hellfire Corner. Mr. Gilbert Mitchell (centre) received the George Medal. His wife, Mrs. Kathleen Mitchell (left), and her sister, Miss Grace Harrison, who is in the Women's Land Army, were each awarded the British Empire Medal.

ADMIRAL LEAHY (left), appointed by President Roosevelt on June 21 Chief of Staff of all the U.S. Armed Forces, succeeded Mr. W. Bullitt as American Ambassador to the Vichy Government in Jan. 1941, but was recalled after Laval's reinstatement.

President Roosevelt's Lease-Lend Administrator, Mr. Edward R. Stettinius, above, arrived in London in July. During his visit he conferred with the Prime Minister, Lord Woolton, and other Ministers, and made a tour of the country.

I WAS THERE! Eye Witness Stories of the War

I Saw the Indians Go into Action in Libya

This thrilling eye witness account of two days' fighting in the Libyan desert was given to a special correspondent of The Daily Telegraph by Capt. M. L. Katju, an observer in the Indian Army.

ON the night of June 4 the Indian Infantry Brigade formed up for an attack on the Germans east of Bir el Tamar. The moon was late ; the night chill. A great quiet hung over the desert. A few tanks took their station ahead followed by Bren gun carriers. Farther behind were the lorry-borne infantry. The men wore their great-coats and slept under the trucks while they waited.

At 2.50 the night exploded with the shock of many guns. The earth rocked. Men shed their greatcoats and sprang into the trucks. Their hour for action had come.

Without much opposition we reached our objective. Our success flare went up. Four minutes later the Scottish battalion, which had shared in the van of our attack, put up the same signal. The position was won.

As the opal light in the east thickened, the enemy ranged on us with black smoke and shrapnel. In front our tanks moved in and out, sparring and probing the enemy's strength. Behind our guns came up, lunging into close support. At the first clear light they opened fire. Our tanks, their job done, lurched back through our lines. On the out-skirts of our position figures scurried from black masses which exploded with shattering roars. Our sappers were blowing up the enemy tanks. They destroyed six.

The morning sun saw the hot dust masses cut by flashes. Before noon tanks began to press on the Scottish battalion. Our 25-pounders had no time to dig in, and the gunners began to suffer. An R.A.S.C. driver awaiting orders told me of his wife and daughters. "It's a fair twist, sir, having a home and kids and having to come to fight in this God-forsaken place. It's hardly worth having them," he said.

A heavy shell crumped overhead. A faint streak of blood showed on the driver's lip and chin. I saw him grow pale. "It's the end for me, sir," he said. Slowly he sank down, dying before the doctor could reach him.

Throughout that burning, breathless day the guns fought the tanks that milled restlessly around the horizon, awaiting a chance to close in to their butcher's work. Towards evening there was a lull.

'Proud Men, and Unafraid'

In the darkness I walked amidst the Indian infantry. They sat over their tea, chatting quietly. At any small jest, a dozen sets of white teeth gleamed. They were proud men, and unafraid.

Then in an instant the earth rocked and split. Shells screamed, to burst behind ; the blast of other shells too close to be heard struck our faces. Our 25-pounders instantly roared their reply with sharp crashes. The enemy pounded our guns. The gun teams, the men stripped to their waists, disappeared in mountains of sand.

In front, dust clouds that sheltered the enemy tanks crept closer. Restlessly moving in and out they awaited the death of our guns before they dared to close in on our infantry. One by one salvos of shells fell on our 25-pounders, leaving them askew, with figures strewn about. Officers ran up and crouched, solitary figures, loading and firing. Then the one undamaged gun was driven off. Our infantry were alone. Dust clouds edged up. Machine-gun bullets began to kick around, puffing up spurts of sand.

The doctor and I found a serviceable vehicle, loaded it with a small party of wounded and drove off to battalion H.Q.

Sighting a tank surrounded by British soldiers, we shouted with joy and drove furiously. Drawing near we noticed the men around the tank waving us away. We were within 20 yards before realizing that the men were prisoners and the tank a German one. We swerved and drove off.

We were within a hundred yards of the tank when its cannon and machine-guns opened fire on us. A cannon shell hit the rear of the truck—sparks flew out. Then the sergeant beside me slumped to the floor. He had been killed instantly.

The driver shouted, "The doctor's hit." That fine, brave man had been shot through the chest. In the next instant he was hit again. "Don't mind me, I'm finished. You must get out," he said. Tracer shells were coming from both sides. A tire blew off. We swerved and raced on.

Suddenly the shooting stopped. We drew into an open space, with no dust clouds. Lifting out several of the dead, we tied up the wounded, and a truck bore down on us. The doctor of another Indian regiment climbed out. He adjusted the bandages and told us to drive on.

A truck arrived filled with Indian soldiers under the command of a jemadar. He asked for the battalion. We told him his battalion

Carrying rifle with fixed bayonet in the left hand and kukri (curved knife) in the right, these Gurkhas typify the fighting quality (as described in this page) of the Indian troops in the Western Desert. *Photo, British Official*

had been engaged, and we feared overrun, and that they need not go forward. The jemadar shook his head. He had his orders to come and fight. He drove off to battle. British vehicles began to turn up. Soon we saw tanks lunging forward.

It's So Nice to See the Nazis Gorge in Oslo!

Judging from these extracts from a Norwegian housewife's letters which have reached the Royal Norwegian Government in London, there is no lack of food in Norway's capital—for the Germans ! The Norwegians have the unpleasant experience of watching their "protectors" gorge, while they themselves go on short—and ever shorter—rations.

THE last frozen potatoes have been cooked and eaten. Every day now, week in and week out, lunch consists of fish, without potatoes, and bad fish at that. For supper there are not more than one or two slices of bread, without butter or cheese. The authorities tell the people to make up with turnips, but these also are difficult to get and usually frozen.

In the last few months Norwegian families living in towns or industrial areas have had no butter or margarine at all ; but there is plenty of butter in the German restaurants and in the many thousand German house-holds. Norwegians spread their bread with a thin layer of jam—if they were lucky enough to get any fruit after the Germans had helped themselves to the harvest last year. The jam contains no sugar, only artificial sweetening : but it tastes all right. With this meal the Norwegian drinks half a glass of skimmed milk, which leaves not one white fleck on the glass. The Germans are so thoughtful : it is not necessary to wash the glass afterwards. But they are not so thoughtful for themselves, for their glass contains a thick white layer after they have drunk their creamy milk ; and they are not restricted to one glass, they have two or three —more than a quart a day if they like it. And while the Norwegian and his family have had to do without eggs for months, the German has an egg for breakfast every day.

No Norwegian family gets more than 200 grams (about 6 oz.) of poor quality sausage meat per person per month. But at the same time every German can have 500 grams (over 1 lb.) of pure meat every week. If he is the only German living in a

Norwegian house, he will have his meat dinner brought to his own room ; but if there are several Germans there they take infinite pleasure in sitting down to table and devouring their meat course right in front of the Norwegians, who get only their inevitable bad fish without butter. The Germans are, of course, also free to get a meat meal five days out of seven in their own restaurants. Imagine the pleasure for a really hungry Norwegian to follow a German in thought—into his restaurant on a meatless day. There will be served a meal consisting of rich meat soup, fresh meat with new green vegetables and potatoes, puff pastries with cream (it is forbidden to serve cream), rounded off with cigarettes and real coffee (which is unobtainable in the shops), and choice wines.

In one of the big Oslo stores recently many people were misled in a most distressing manner. On entering the shop they saw before them a counter loaded with the most delicious cheeses, butter, coffee, eggs and choice delicacies ; but when the Norwegian citizen ventured to approach this counter, he was bustled over to the opposite counter which, except for a few tins of spinach, stood bleak and bare. The first counter was reserved for his Germanic brothers.

Every German comes before a Norwegian citizen also where lodging is concerned. Should a German take a fancy to the apartments of a Norwegian citizen, an order makes it possible for the police to turn him and his family out, on the grounds either that the man is abroad or that he is an "enemy of the State." Every day sick and old people, mothers and children, are forced to leave their homes because a German wishes to live

RESTAURANT IN OSLO, once the famous Humia, now renamed Loewenbrau. It is reserved for the exclusive use of Germans, who have confiscated for its storerooms and cellars large supplies of food and drink. This photograph shows crates and barrels waiting to be taken in. *Photo, Keystone*

there. Of course, nothing is done to find new lodgings for the homeless.

But don't the Germans pay compensation for all they take? Naturally; they are no thieves, they are cultured people! The

German official often earns ten times the salary of a Norwegian, but as the money is drawn from the Bank of Norway, it is in fact the Norwegians who pay for their oppressors' extravagances.

Our Convoy Went Through 6 Days of Bombing

A six-day battle against attacking planes recently fought by one of the largest convoys to reach Russia with war supplies, was described by British seamen on their return to this country.

FOR nearly a week our convoy was shadowed by a German plane (said a Merchant Navy officer). Then the "fun" started.

Heavy bombers came through the clouds, and the most terrific barrage I have ever seen opened up. The sky was black with the smoke of bursting shells. The Germans scattered and were clearly put off their course by the fire. They reformed and swooped in again. As the planes passed over little more than mast-high we opened up with everything we had. Hits were scored.

But out of the clouds came more German planes. The roar of gunfire and the noise of crashing bombs went on almost non-stop for days. We got no sleep—no one appeared to want sleep. The German planes kept up the attack. There was barely a break of

half an hour between the raids. I saw more than a dozen of Jerry's planes crash in flames.

Then we got the signal to scatter. German naval forces had been sighted. Hardly had the convoy scattered than shells came crashing into the sea. Escorting warships sailed to meet the enemy, while we moved on, keeping our guns going at the midgets in the sky, who now did not appear to relish low-level bombing. In the distance we could hear the noise of heavy gunfire. That went on for hours.

Soon after we were again in action with the Jerry planes—this time torpedo bombers. Those pilots seemed to have charmed lives, until the Russian fighters came on the scene, charging head on, their guns blazing at the Huns. Most gallant of all was a Russian pilot in a single-seater fighter. He had been

making circles round a bunch of Huns, blazing away all the time. I saw pieces of the German planes falling. Then his guns were silent. He started to climb rapidly, swung round and dived at three torpedo-planes in a bunch 1,000 feet above the sea. The Russian plane crashed right in among them and all three Germans hit the sea together with the Russian plane on top of them. That Russian pilot sacrificed his life to save our ships.

One Russian ship, hit at 5 o'clock in the morning of the third day, was set ablaze. For more than twelve hours the crew, including six girls, fought the fire. They put it out. All day long the ship never swerved from its course, maintained its speed and its correct place in the convoy. When the Russian skipper signalled "Fire under control," he received an immediate reply from the commodore: "Well done!"

WE had six days of almost constant bombing raids (said Seaman Williams, of Anglesey). Our escort ship put up a magnificent barrage, but the Nazi pilots came right through it and gave us all they had.

We had a catapult plane on our ship and it was shot off to meet the attackers. The pilot was a young South African, and he went right up to break up the Nazi formations. We saw him bring down a large bomber and set off to chase another. I believe he got it, too, but a signal reached the bridge of our ship stating that the pilot was wounded and had had to bale out. He jumped clear of the machine and made a perfect parachute drop into the sea. A destroyer went to his rescue and took him safely aboard.

On the following day a direct hit was scored on our ship, and she began to sink immediately. Two boats were launched and one of them was only an oar's length from the ship's side when a bomb fell and the lifeboat was blown to pieces. Five of the men in it were killed.

In the other boat, where I was, we had to lie down on our faces to dodge bullets during machine-gun attacks by a Nazi plane. Luckily, none of us was injured, but our boat was shattered, and we found ourselves in the water clinging to driftwood. Because of the grand work of our naval escort none of us was in the water for long. The rescue ships ignored all risks in order that lives should not be lost.

There was never any darkness to give us protection from attack, and every man in that convoy was on duty throughout six days and nights without thought of rest or sleep. The convoy contained a number of American ships, and it was a miracle that, in spite of incessant bombing, so few ships were lost.

The Russians gave us a grand reception on our arrival, and when we saw how eagerly they tackled the job of discharging our cargoes we felt that our job in transporting them was well worth doing.

HEROES OF THE MERCHANT NAVY. The ships in their convoy were bombed and machine-gunned for six days and nights, but these five imperturbable men just went on with their job of helping to get supplies through to Russia. Their names (left to right) are: Frank Robinson and F. Gibson, from Liverpool; W. Williams, Anglesey; J. Rogan, Birkenhead; and F. Briggs, from Darwen, Lancs. Seaman Williams, whose ship was sunk by a direct hit, contributes above to the description of this hazardous voyage. PAGE 158 *Photo, Keystone*

THE ITALIAN SUBMARINE FERRARIS, having ventured for the first time away from the coasts of Italy, was damaged by a Catalina flying boat and finally sunk by H.M. destroyer Lamerton, a convoy escort ship, which chased her for 31 miles. These photographs, taken by the eye-witness whose story is given below, show (left) members of the submarine's crew struggling in the water while waiting to be picked up, and (right) some of the survivors, stripped save for their life-saving belts, arriving aboard the British warship.
Photos, N. Symmons

We Picked Up Forty-Four Unhappy Italians

Here in a few words Petty Officer Nicholas Symmons tells of an incident that came to break the monotony of a spell of convoy duty. At a time when the menace of the U-boats is being stressed in Press and Parliament, it is well to be reminded that the enemy is not having it all his own way.

DURING an attack on the convoy the night before, my ship, H.M.S. Lamerton, one of the convoy's escort, used up so much fuel owing to her high speed that she was ordered to leave the convoy, proceed to a port for oil fuel, and return to the convoy as soon as possible.

Three hours after we had left the convoy, one of the look-outs sighted a Catalina aircraft 17 miles away. A signalman successfully established communication with it by flashing.

The Catalina tersely replied : " Full speed ahead." She had sighted and damaged with depth charges the long-range Italian submarine Ferraris. The submarine must have sighted us then, as she decided to make off on the surface at 22 knots.

We gradually overhauled her, and opened fire with the forward guns when the range had been reduced to 9,600 yards. We were zig-zagging in case she loosed off any torpedoes and to fluster their range as they were firing

back with their after gun. Their firing was spasmodic and erratic, and the shells dropped some way off from Lamerton. We hit her four or five times, and brought her to a stand-still in a sinking condition. Her firing ceased, and she sank before we arrived on the spot. Nevertheless, we dropped a pattern of depth charges over the spot to make sure of it.

There were 44 very unhappy Italians bobbing about in the water waiting to be picked up. As they climbed aboard Lamerton, our captain sounded a series of . . . — (V) on the siren. The Catalina swooped low over our masts and did the victory roll. So ended the thirty-one-mile chase with the destruction of the Ferraris while on her first cruise away from Italy.

OUR DIARY OF THE WAR

JULY 22, 1942, Wednesday   *1,054th day*
Russian Front.—Fighting spread to area of Tsimlyanskaya and Novocherkassk, and continued round Voronezh.
Africa.—Heavy fighting developed on all sectors of the front ; our troops made some progress.
Burma.—R.A.F. raided river craft in coastal areas.
Australasia.—Japs made new landing in New Guinea at Gona, 120 m. north of Port Moresby. Allied bombers sank three transports.

JULY 23, Thursday   *1,055th day*
Sea.—Announced that British submarines in Mediterranean had sunk three enemy supply ships.
Air.—R.A.F. bombers raided Duisburg and other places in Ruhr and Rhineland. Russian Air Force bombed East Prussia.
Russian Front.—Fighting continued round Voronezh, Tsimlyanskaya and Novocherkassk, and spread to Rostov area.
Australasia.—Allied bombers raided Japs in Buna area of New Guinea ; dive-bombers attacked Gona.
Home.—Seven enemy aircraft destroyed in scattered night raids.

JULY 24, Friday   *1,056th day*
Russian Front.—Fighting continued in neighbourhood of Voronezh, Tsimlyanskaya, Novocherkassk and Rostov. Germans claimed to have taken Rostov.
Africa.—Patrol and artillery activity in northern and central sectors.
Australasia.—Jap bombers raided aerodrome at Port Moresby. Allied bombers attacked Jap installations at Gona.

JULY 25, Saturday   *1,057th day*
Sea.—Russian warships sank two transports in Gulf of Finland.
Air.—Strong force of R.A.F. bombers again raided Duisburg by night and many Russian bombers attacked Königsberg.
Russian Front.—Announced that Germans broke through in one Rostov sector ; fighting at Voronezh, Novocherkassk and Rostov.
Mediterranean.—Allied heavy bombers raided Crete.
Africa.—Land operations again confined to patrol and artillery engagements. Enemy reconnaissance planes over Nile Delta were destroyed or damaged.

Australasia.—Jap flying-boats made first raid on Townsville, Queensland. Allied bombers attacked Gona. U.S. Navy Dept. announced sinking of five more Jap ships by U.S. submarines.

JULY 26, Sunday   *1,058th day*
Air.—American Air Force pilots took part for first time in fighter sweeps over N. France. Very strong force of R.A.F. bombers raided Hamburg at night.
Russian Front.—Fighting continued in area of Voronezh, Tsimlyanskaya, Novocherkassk and Rostov.
Africa.—Land operations again limited. Allied bombers made heavy raid on Tobruk.
Australasia.—Patrols engaged Japs at Awala, inland from Gona. Jap aircraft raided Darwin.

JULY 27, Monday   *1,059th day*
Sea.—Russian warships in Barents Sea sank enemy submarine and transport.
Russian Front.—Evacuation of Rostov and Novocherkassk announced by Russians. Fighting continued round Voronezh and Tsimlyanskaya.
Mediterranean.—Thirteen enemy aircraft shot down over Malta.
Africa.—Severe fighting developed with heavy artillery duels.
Australasia.—Allied aircraft, including American dive-bombers, attacked Jap positions at Gona.
Home.—Number of scattered daylight raids over England.

JULY 28, Tuesday   *1,060th day*
Sea.—Russian warships sank three transports in Bay of Finland.
Air.—Hamburg again raided by strong force of R.A.F. bombers.
Russian Front.—Fierce fighting in areas of Voronezh, Tsimlyanskaya and Bataisk.
Africa.—Reduced activity on land.
Mediterranean.—Heavy bombers of Allied air forces raided Suda Bay, Crete.
Burma.—R.A.F. bombers attacked Akyab docks and Mandalay-Rangoon Rly.
Home.—Nine raiders destroyed in raids on Birmingham and elsewhere.

JULY 29, Wednesday   *1,061st day*
Air.—Fighters made many daylight raids over N. France. Strong force of bombers attacked Saarbrücken at night.
Russian Front.—Fierce fighting round Voronezh and at Tsimlyanskaya, Bataisk and S.W. of Kletskaya.
Australasia.—Allied ground patrols repulsed Japs from positions near Kokoda.
Home.—Birmingham was enemy's main night target ; 8 raiders destroyed.

JULY 30, Thursday   *1,062nd day*
Sea.—Light coastal forces were active during night in North Sea and Channel, and had three brushes with enemy.
Air.—Day raids over N. France, including St. Omer.
Russian Front.—German threat to Stalingrad railway becoming more acute. Russian resistance stiffening along R. Don.
Africa.—Bombs on outskirts of Cairo. Lull in desert fighting continued.
Australasia.—Japanese bombers attacked Port Hedland (W. Australia). Large formations of aircraft attempting to raid Darwin were completely broken up.
Home.—Nine enemy bombers destroyed during widespread night raids.

JULY 31, Friday   *1,063rd day*
Air.—Boston bombers raided St. Malo docks and aerodrome at Abbeville ; 11 enemy fighters destroyed for 8 British escort fighters missing. Heavy night raid on Düsseldorf, causing great destruction. 31 of our aircraft missing.
Russian Front.—German attacks S.W. of Kletskaya repulsed with great loss. South of Rostov enemy made further progress.
Australasia.—Heavy Allied raids on targets in New Guinea, New Britain, Solomons and elsewhere.
China.—During night operations on July 30 and 31 U.S. fighters destroyed 17 Jap aircraft in battles round Hengyang.

AUGUST 1, Saturday   *1,064th day*
Sea.—Night action in English Channel resulting in destruction of two E-boats and damage to other enemy units. In

darkness German ships fired on each other, and German shore batteries on their own forces.
Air.—Daylight raids on railway and other targets in N. France and on Flushing.
Russian Front.—Fierce engagements in areas of Kletskaya, Tsimlyanskaya, Kushchevsk and Salsk, rail junction 100 miles S.E. of Rostov.
Home.—Short night raid on Norwich

AUGUST 2, Sunday   *1,065th day*
Air.—Spitfires attacked railway targets and barges in Low Countries.
Russian Front.—German forces south of lower Don making rapid 3-prong advance. Two thrusts reached junction on Caucasus-Stalingrad railway ; third aimed at Yeisk, on Sea of Azov.
Africa.—Air warfare continued unabated, especially heavy attacks on Tobruk and other enemy ports.
Australasia.—Allied bombers continued attacks on Japanese in Papua and on naval units in Banda Sea.
Home.—East and south coastal raids by single enemy aircraft. Three raiders destroyed at night.

AUGUST 3, Monday   *1,066th day*
Air.—German floatplane destroyed during Coastal Command combats in Bay of Biscay.
Russian Front.—Red armies still holding enemy attacks in Don loop. South of Rostov Germans claimed to be near upper reaches of Kuban river.
Africa.—Egyptian front still quiet.
Home.—Single enemy bombers dropped bombs at places in E. and N.E. England and Midlands, and on seaside resort in S.W. area.

AUGUST 4, Tuesday   *1,067th day*
Air.—Night bombers attacked targets in the Ruhr.
Russian Front.—Retreat south of River Don continued. Germans claimed capture of Voroshilovsk. In Don loop Russians still resisting effectively.
Australasia.—Enemy shipping activity reported off Gona (Papua) area, suggesting arrival of reinforcements.
Home.—Daylight raids on two south-coast towns. Night attacks on S. and S.W. England and S. Wales. Six out of 30 raiders destroyed.

Editor's Postscript

ALL too soon September will be upon us, and Autumn days will be here again. Last night it happened that I was glancing through my copy of Old Moore's Almanack, amusing myself by checking off his prophecies against their fulfilment. I was surprised to find him remarkably accurate in his forecast for August so far as weather conditions were concerned, as witness: "The best harvest this country has probably ever known is likely to be gathered this month under ideal conditions, with every advantage which public interest will bring. More than ever is it recognized that, however important industrial life is, agriculture is in its ascendancy and a country like our own must find the foundation for its health and prosperity. Too long have fertile acres been suffered to remain idle, although idle hands have been waiting to turn them into producers of economic wealth for us all. But never again will such things be, and a cry for increased production and yet more production is the order of the day."

BEARING in mind that it is more than a year since these words were printed, that is certainly one up for the prophet. But, curious to know what he has in store for us in September, I read with some surprise that: "Under its new regime Japan shows an inclination to join up with the democratic Powers, realizing that its tremendous industrial output can be used to greatest advantage by the closest possible association with those nations who are fashioning the new world." Quite obviously this Old Moore (there are several, by the way) is on safer grounds when prophesying about seed-time and harvest than in projecting his prophetic vision a few months ahead into international relationships. The words I have quoted were published only six months before the resounding disaster at Pearl Harbour, but any prophet worth tuppence ought to have known that Pearl Harbour was just round the corner when he was writing. This particular "bloomer" probably registers a new high mark of guesswork in divination.

I SHALL, however, look out in September for "a new author with a book on revolutionary lines" who "arouses great interest." Does any month ever pass without bringing someone that answers that description? It sounds a safe enough shot at an inner on the prophetic dartboard, but I have just heard that Old Moore for 1943, conveniently forgetful of all the nonsense he wrote in 1941 concerning 1942, is already circulating his prophecies for 1944, and I must get my annual copy, for I look upon him as a source of innocent merriment. And I know there is a large element of truth in his Almanack, which reminds me that Lord Tennyson was born on August 6, a hundred and thirty-three years ago; that it was just twenty years (to my amazement) since Lord Northcliffe died on the 14th of the month, and August 22 is Sir Walter Citrine's fifty-fifth birthday. These are things that any person can find out without having recourse to the stars, and are worthier of acceptance. I also noticed that

two years ago, on the publishing day of this number of THE WAR ILLUSTRATED, Trotsky was murdered in Mexico; a significant fact to remember. For it was the "liquidation" of the Trotsky conspiracy that placed the Soviet Government in the position of unassailable strength that has enabled it to make so marvellous a stand against the German invaders. This and much more of great usefulness in forming a proper appreciation of the power, purpose, and capabilities of Stalin and the men around him, is clearly illustrated in the pages of that invaluable book, Mission to Moscow, by Joseph E. Davies, U.S. Ambassador to the Soviet Union from 1936 to 1938, a review of which, embodying some instructive extracts, I hope to include in an early issue.

KING HAAKON of Norway celebrated his 70th birthday on August 3, 1942, when all Norwegians, whether bond or free, paid tribute to their leader, who stands as the symbol of that liberty for which they are struggling.
Photo by Courtesy of the Royal Norwegian Government

THE long tongue of that lying jade, Dame Rumour, has been wagging briskly of late. And the more I hear of her waggings the more I am inclined to credit her with Teutonic parentage. But what surprises me is the credulity of quite intelligent persons. Here is one instance revealed to me in whisperings at a club table with much cautioning not to let it be known. But I'm going to shout it! It wasn't Essen that suffered the second of our thousand-bomber raids— it was a dummy town featuring all the landmarks of Essen, with dummy Krupp's works, great dummy breweries, dummy railway stations, a dummy monastery, dummy Minster and numerous dummy churches, and a dummy exchange! My informant couldn't tell me just where this dummy Essen had been built, but that's the place our thousand bombers smothered with their high explosives! Well, I haven't visited Essen, but its population is now (or was recently) nearly 700,000, and I know what

that implies: a town covering an area greater than Sheffield and not much less than Manchester. And I shall assert that any man, woman, or child who believes the Germans could have built up a dummy Essen, bigger than Sheffield, to delude our R.A.F. boys and make them waste their beautiful bombs on it (protecting the dummy, remember, with the heaviest type of anti-aircraft guns) is first cousin to the loons who saw the Russians coming through Scotland in 1915 and knew they were Russians by the snow on their boots. Yet it was a very able journalist who whispered this wonder tale in my ear and gave every sign of believing it. It didn't take me a split second to denounce it for sheer idiocy.

LET's examine the yarn. (1) Our R.A.F. pilot officers don't sail the skies looking for places like Essen anywhere but at Essen, especially when one thousand of them are all on the same target. The navigation officer can direct his plane over any town of that size by dead reckoning. His instruments do 90 per cent of the job for him. (2) A thousand pilots can't all go wrong; at least a few hundreds of them would get to the proper target! (3) "Great Fires" could not start up from papier mâché buildings and send their smoke thousands of feet into the air, while vast explosions in dummy buildings were being registered by all the observers. (4) And finally, if the idiocy were a truth, the energy that went to the making of the dummy town and its ack-ack defence was far greater than that involved in the dispatching of those thousand aeroplanes. Don't you think so?

THESE are the sort of lies that Goebbels would like us to believe, and I am convinced that only fifth columnists in England could invent them, or at least circulate them. My friend is no fifth columnist; he is a very patriotic and clever newspaper columnist, but more credulous by nature than I am, for he looks upon me as a very obstinate sceptic in all things. I shall say nothing about his other hush-hush news, none of which I credited, but will give only one other instance of Dame Rumour's wagging tongue. "Do you know that the inhabitants of X—— are to be evacuated at two hours' notice and the aged and infirm have all been advised to leave the town at once?" asked a lady friend of mine just returned from a visit to X——. "I don't, and I do not believe it's true," said I. "Have you seen the official notice?" I asked. "Oh, no," said the lady, "but my sister was told by her next neighbour that she had seen one." Consider the matter, please. A great seaside town is booked for evacuation at two hours' notice, yet some of its residents have to rely on their neighbours for this information. These neighbours haven't been officially warned, but they've "seen" a notice received by another householder. No notices were displayed on the hoardings. Believe that and you'll believe anything. Not that I think very highly of our local authorities anywhere. I urge all my readers to turn a deaf ear to any talk of this kind and to believe not one word of it until they have seen it in official print for themselves.

Printed in England and published every alternate Friday by the Proprietors, THE AMALGAMATED PRESS, LTD., The Fleetway House, Farringdon Street, London, E.C.4. Registered for transmission by Canadian Magazine Post. Sole Agents for Australia and New Zealand : Messrs. Gordon & Gotch, Ltd. ; and for South Africa : Central News Agency, Ltd.—August 21, 1942.   S.S.   Editorial Address : JOHN CARPENTER HOUSE, WHITEFRIARS, LONDON, E.C.4

Vol 6 # The War Illustrated Nº 136

Edited by Sir John Hammerton

6d FORTNIGHTLY   SEPTEMBER 4, 1942

CURTISS COMMANDO, already in mass production in America, is a 25-ton transport 'plane. This aircraft carries infantry, light artillery and one or more Jeeps, its purpose being to speed up reinforcements. The Curtiss Commando is the largest twin-engined military 'plane in the world, and has a wing span of 108 feet. In the foreground are seen three Jeep cars lined up behind a column of U.S. infantry-men. waiting to file into the aircraft. The cars are driven into the cabin by means of special ramps.   Photo, Associated Press

NO. 137 WILL BE PUBLISHED FRIDAY. SEPTEMBER 18

ALONG THE BATTLE FRONTS

by Our Military Critic, Maj.-Gen. Sir Charles Gwynn, K.C.B., D.S.O.

In the first half of August the deterioration in the general situation, so alarming at the end of July, continued, but at a slackening pace and less widespread. In Russia, though the Germans made deep thrusts in certain directions these did not immediately threaten vital points, and where the danger was greatest Russian resistance showed distinct signs of stiffening. It was, in fact, so firm that the Germans were compelled to seek new methods of overcoming it, widening their front of attack. That may make heavy demands on their resources and communications, but it had, combined with unsparing use of reserves, a measure of success which, by the middle of the month, again made the situation, especially on the Stalingrad front, critical in the extreme. Although the Russians made successful counter-attacks at various points there was little indication that they intended to attempt a counter-offensive on a scale which might materially affect the issue.

In Egypt the lull in the land battle was maintained—each side strengthening its defensive position while accumulating resources for offensive action. Little change in the situation therefore occurred.

It was in the Far East that the situation developed in a definitely encouraging manner with the Allied attack on the Japanese base in the Solomons. The operation strategically was defensive in nature, but it provided proof of the growing offensive power of the Allies and of the inherent weakness of the widely-dispersed Japanese positions with their vulnerable lines of communication.

Reduction in Allied shipping losses, which had for months reached alarming figures, is also encouraging, although as yet it is somewhat uncertain whether the reduction is due to redispositions of the enemy's attack or to undoubtedly improved results obtained from the Allied defensive and offensive measures. Reduction in losses must be maintained over a longer period before it is safe to draw definite conclusions.

RUSSIA

During the period under review undoubtedly the most encouraging feature in the Russian situation was the magnificent defence made by the Army protecting the approaches to Stalingrad against an ever-increasing weight of German attacks. In the elbow of the Don between Kletskaya and Kalach, where the German attempt to reach Stalingrad first opened, fighting was continuous and of ever-increasing intensity with heavy losses in men and material on both sides. The Germans, since they overran the Donetz basin, have had the use of the railway connecting it with Stalingrad, and such damage as it sustained has no doubt been made good and its gauge altered by now. It must contribute largely towards maintaining the vigour of the German offensive. In spite of this advantage the Germans made little progress within the Don elbow until the middle of the month, when they gained a footing on the west bank of the river south of Kletskaya from which counter-attacks failed to dislodge them.

Early in August another serious threat to Stalingrad developed. The Germans, having at last succeeded in extending their bridgehead at Tsimlyanskaya to the south-east, secured possession of Kotelnikovo on the Rostov-Stalingrad railway. From there they attempted to advance north-eastwards, directly threatening Stalingrad and the communications of the Russians fighting west of the Don at Kalach. The threat was all the more serious because the Rostov railway west of Kotelnikovo was by now in German hands and available as a new line of communication. Russian defence was, however, again stubborn and the advance was soon brought to a standstill. Fierce battles in which armour was extensively used followed, again with heavy losses on both sides; but the defence held firm, counter-attacking vigorously.

Checked in this north-easterly drive, the Germans, about the middle of August, started a new thrust eastwards up the valley of the Sal river; though whether this was intended to swing north towards Stalingrad, to continue eastwards towards Astrakhan at the mouth of the Volga, or to make for a point farther south on the Caspian coast was not apparent. Whichever line was taken the thrust was a new danger. On the Volga front there was therefore, about the middle of August, an alarming deterioration of the situation, although the Germans had been compelled to throw in many reserves and to extend their front into an area where railway communications were lacking.

On the Caucasus front the Germans had not been definitely checked, though their claims to have taken Maikop and Krasnodar were made prematurely. Fighting continued in both places long after the claims were made, and when Maikop was finally evacuated on August 16 the scorched earth policy was carried out effectively. The German drive in the Caucasus, by the middle of August appeared to pursue two distinct objects after it had reached the oil centres of Maikop and Krasnodar. In the west the capture of the naval bases at Novorossisk and Tuapse appeared to be the immediate object. This entailed an attempt to cut off the extreme left wing of Timoshenko's army, which had clung to its position in the Azov coast region south-west of Rostov. Threatened with encirclement this force appears to have made good its retreat, partly by sea, to the mouth of the Kuban river, where it could reinforce the troops defending the lower reaches of the river to cover Novorossisk. The Germans also made desperate attempts to cross the Kuban in the Krasnodar region from which the railway runs to Novorossisk; but they met stubborn resistance. From Maikop their advance along the railway to Tuapse was also checked.

It is evident that the Germans attach special importance to the elimination of the Black Sea fleet, presumably because they need sea communications to ease their transport difficulties. Till sea transport can be used heavy plant to repair damage to the oil-fields is not likely to be available, and such oil as may be obtained from the Maikop and Grozny oil-fields can hardly reach Germany over railways congested with military traffic. Germany may have sufficient oil for her military needs, but it is badly needed to maintain the economic life of Germany and occupied countries. The Black Sea fleet, while it can remain in action, also, of course, prohibits any amphibious attempt against Trans-Caucasia, and it is interesting to note that no attempt has been made even to cross the Straits of Kerch.

The other half of the Caucasian drive is mainly directed south-eastwards. From Armavir a panzer thrust penetrated far up the valley of the Upper Kuban, from which a road crosses the mountains to the Black Sea at Sukhum. This thrust reached Cherkessk, where it was checked, but whether it was an attempt to cross the Caucasus seems doubtful, because the Rostov-Baku railway is clearly the line by which a major attempt to invade Trans-Caucasia or to reach the shores of the Caspian must be made. On this line panzer troops reached Mineralniye Vody in the Caspian watershed. From there they threatened the Grozny oil-fields, and the northern end, at Ordzhonikidze, of the military road which crosses the mountains. This road, which rises to 8,000 feet and might easily be demolished, is not of importance as an avenue of invasion, but it would provide communication for a Russian force on the flank of an advance to Baku. In the Terek Valley, up which the road starts, is one of the richest deposits of manganese ore in the world, which, since Germany is in desperate need of the mineral, may be an incidental objective.

On the whole, it would seem, the main German objects are: to secure control of the Volga in order to interrupt Russian oil supplies, and to eliminate the obstacle the Black Sea fleet presents to the development of sea communications. I do not believe the Germans will dissipate their strength in attempting a major invasion of Trans-caucasia till these objects are attained.

MAIN GERMAN THRUSTS are here shown directed against Stalingrad and south into the Caucasus. On August 17 it was announced that the Russians had abandoned Maikop after destroying the oil wells. *By courtesy of The Daily Telegraph*

IN THE DON RIVER AREA lies some of the richest agricultural land of the U.S.S.R. The Kursk and Voronezh provinces had nearly 30,000,000 acres under cultivation, and although much of the gigantic harvest may have been gathered and removed eastwards before the enemy reached it, this photograph of von Bock's troops moving through a wheat-field proves that this was not achieved everywhere.
Photo, Keystone

They may push on towards the Caspian coast, from which air attacks might seriously interfere with Russian sea communications carrying oil and Allied munitions from Iran.

Except on the Volga and Caucasian fronts, the Germans are definitely on the defensive, and are hard pressed at Voronezh, Briansk and in the Rzhev region. The Russian attacks, though · vigorous, are not in the nature of a major offensive. They are presumably designed to exhaust German resources, prevent the transference of formations to the main theatre, and possibly to ·prepare the way for offensive action on a major scale.

EGYPT
On land up to the middle of August no event of importance occurred in Egypt, but signs were not lacking that both sides were preparing intensively for operations.

Allied air forces, including American squadrons, maintained constant attacks on the enemy's land and sea· communications. In particular, by sinking barges conveying material to Mersa Matruh they must have

inflicted much damage and delayed Rommel's preparations.

During the lull our troops have had much better opportunities for rest and recuperation than those of the enemy, which may prove an important factor.

The event of most strategic importance at that time in the Mediterranean theatre was the arrival of yet another convoy at

TULAGI, vital objective in the Solomon Islands from which U.S. forces seek to expel the Japanese, provided a strategic starting-point for enemy raids upon New Guinea and Australia. See also map p. 165.
By courtesy of The Daily Mail

Malta. The price paid was heavy, but the scale of the enemy's attempts to destroy the convoy, and the continued costly attacks on the island, are clear indications of the important offensive role Malta is playing.

FAR EAST
The successful landing of American Marines on the Solomon Islands, and the capture of the enemy's air base there, is of first importance. It may be assumed that the operation had primarily a defensive strategic purpose, and aimed at depriving the Japanese of a springboard from which further enterprises against New Caledonia, or even Australia, might start, and from which communications between the U.S.A. and Australia could be attacked. The primary object has already been attained, but it may be some time

before a secondary, though no less important, object is achieved—the establishment of an Allied base for offensive purposes. That object cannot be achieved till Japanese resistance is overcome, and it is likely to continue to be stubborn. The deployment of an adequate offensive force in, and its advance from, the bridge heads secured are certain to be slow, difficult and expensive operations, especially until shore air bases can be used.

What price has had to be paid by the Allied navies will probably not be revealed for some time. It may be heavy, though Japanese claims are evidently fantastic. Japan has also had naval losses, and any attempts she may make to assist her garrison are likely to be increasingly costly. She has here, in New Guinea and in the Aleutians begun to pay the penalty for the dispersion of her forces—dispersion. that, now that she is forced to adopt a defensive attitude, cannot be reduced. The Allies, on the other hand, are now able to concentrate for .offensive blows ; and each new air base secured will immensely facilitate and render less expensive the next step.

LIEUT.-GEN. W. H. E. GOTT, C.B.E., D.S.O., M.C., whose death was announced on August 11. General Gott was shot down while flying to Cairo on leave from the front.
Photo, British Official: Crown Copyright

VICE-ADMIRAL R. GHORMLEY, C.-in-C. of the U.S.-New Zealand naval command, directs operations, under Admiral Nimitz, in the Solomon Islands.   *New York Times Photos*

America's Famous 'Leathernecks' Go into Action

Photos, Keystone, New York Times Photos

U.S. MARINES were stated on August 12 to have made successful landings on three islands in the Solomons Group, and by August 21 had occupied an important airfield and were consolidating and improving their positions. These photographs show men of this famous corps in training. Above, leaving the parent-ship in a, rubber boat en route for the shore. Top, a landing effected, the assault troops advance to establish a beach-head.

United Nations Attack in the South-West Pacific

SOLOMON ISLANDS are now a crucial theatre of operations since Allied forces established bases there in August. 1. Tulagi, the scene of a landing by American forces. 2. Solomon Islands in relation to New Guinea and Australia. 3. View from Tulagi towards Makambo Island. 4. United Nations aircraft guards an Allied convoy near Port Moresby, New Guinea, and 5. Troops line up for inspection on arrival. Fighting continues in the Kokoda area of the island.

Photos, Black Star, E.N.A., Planet News. Map by courtesy of The Daily Mirror

Sweeney Todd of Tobruk Has No Customers Today

RAIDS ON TOBRUK have been made by R.A.F. bombers since its fall on June 21, and on the left three direct hits are being scored on two of the jetties during the night of July 9-10. Above, German ambulance car in front of a grimly humorous reminder of the British occupation.

HEROIC DEFENDERS OF TOBRUK who are now captives of the Axis. Among the units involved were elements of the 201st Guards (Motor) Brigade and the 32nd Army Tank Brigade; H.Q. 2nd South African Division, with the 4th and 6th South African Infantry Brigades; and the 11th Indian Infantry Brigade. There were also in the garrison units of medium A.A. and coastal defence, survey and searchlight artillery, and Royal Engineers, together with signal, service corps, and medical, ordnance, pay, pioneer and postal units, most of which were United Kingdom troops. Berlin claimed a total of 28,000 prisoners.

Photos, British Official: Crown Copyright; Associated Press

Hearty Welcome Back to the Aussies in Egypt

Australians recovering equipment from an Italian M 13 tank, one of many which were wrecked or abandoned in the fierce fighting west of El Alamein. It was in the Tel el Eisa area that Australian reinforcements were officially stated on July 12 to be in action, and to have advanced the British line by 5 miles. This infusion of fresh blood into the weary desert army proved an important factor in Gen. Auchinleck's stand at El Alamein.

Above and right, men of the Eighth Army in the El Alamein battle zone find among the Australian troops newly arrived in Egypt many old comrades with whom they had fought side by side in the earlier campaigns. The "Diggers" received an enthusiastic welcome, and many friendships were renewed.

In mid-August important changes were announced in the Middle East Command. Gen. Alexander succeeded Gen. Auchinleck as C.-in-C. Middle East; Lt.-Gen. Montgomery was appointed Commander of the 8th Army in succession to Gen. Ritchie, and Maj.-Gen. Lumsden became Commander of the 30th Corps in place of Lt.-Gen. Gott.

Photos, British Official: Crown Copyright

THE WAR IN THE AIR

by Capt. Norman Macmillan, M.C., A.F.C.

IT can be truly said that the air war is world-wide. Great and important air actions have taken place over the Bay of Biscay, Western Europe, the Mediterranean, the Caucasus, among the tropic islands north of Australia, and in the Aleutian Islands of the North Pacific. In the spreading character of the air war there is evidence of the increasing air power of the United Nations : no other explanation is possible. To those who believe —as I believe—that overwhelming air power is the key to ultimate victory, and that the door to peace is uncompromisingly barred until that key is forged, the events of the period here under review are of heartening trend, despite reverses in certain theatres of operations.

British reports on the air-sea battle which began in the Mediterranean on August 11 and ended with the arrival of the convoy at Malta three days later, make it clear that no greater battle between sea and air has been fought on the lines of communication during the three years of war.

H.M.S. Eagle, one of several aircraft-carriers included in the escort, was sunk by a U-boat the first day, and some of her fighters went down with her. About five hours later came the first enemy air attack. Bombers, torpedo-bombers and Stukas swarmed out from their bases in Sardinia and Sicily, but one attack after another was smashed either by our carrier fighters, which intercepted them out of sight, or by the tremendous barrage of shells from the naval and merchant ships. Losses were suffered in the convoy (*see* page 182), but it was known by the evening of Aug. 12 that 39 enemy aircraft had been destroyed that day. In the final stage of the

operation, that of protecting the convoy in the Sicilian Channel, R.A.F. long-range fighters from Malta also took part and destroyed at least ten machines. The total number of enemy aircraft certainly destroyed during the whole operation by our fighters and A.A. gunfire was at least 66, while we lost eight, four of the pilots being safe.

WHILE our supply lines are almost entirely dependent upon surface ships there is no other way to munition Malta (which also requires to import a large proportion of its food). Malta is important as a fixed, forward air base. Its importance has increased since the withdrawal of the Eighth Army from Cyrenaica to El Alamein. From Maltese aerodromes we have bombed Southern Italy, Sicily, and Sardinia. Our attacks on Naples were made from Malta. And because Malta lies astride Axis lines of communication across the Mediterranean, it must play an important part in future Allied operations in North Africa ; and would be almost indispensable to any attempt to invade Southern Europe. It is an unsinkable aircraft carrier. It has defied air bombardment. It would be a costly operation to attempt to take it by storm. The Axis could make such an attempt only by air, as in Crete. But there can be no comparison between defence organization in Malta and the improvised defences in Crete. The Axis, mindful of the wastage they have suffered in aircraft, and by contrast, of growing Allied strength in the air, would like to reduce Malta by siege.

SEVEN thousand miles from Malta, on the Californian coast, Mr. Henry Kaiser is to begin the construction of 70-ton Martin Mars flying-boats for air transport use. Twenty per cent of American multi-motor aircraft to be built for the U.S. Army are to be air transports. The United Nations cannot expect to begin to enjoy the benefits of air transport in safety and speed until 1943 is well advanced. Until then the air-sea battles of the high seas and the narrow waters must continue unabated. The critical character of the current year was created, and is still maintained, as much by the initial lead in air strength possessed by the Axis as by any other factor. But in 1943 the pendulum will have begun to swing the other way.

In the meantime, I sympathise with Captain L. D. Macintosh, D.S.C., who commanded H.M.S. Eagle for a bare six weeks. Captain Macintosh (*see* portrait, p. 182) has been with the air arm of the Navy for many years. I remember him when he was an observer in the Fleet Air Arm, in the days when the operational methods of present-day carriers were being slowly evolved, with experimental flying and tactical exercises proceeding side by side, as an officer keenly conscious of the importance of the air side of the Navy's work.

Fierce air combats began over the waters of the Bay of Biscay on July 28. Over the wide bay, from off Brest south towards the north coast of Spain, landplanes and flying boats of the Coastal Command have patrolled with ceaseless care to spot and attack U-boats on passage in and out of the French western

ports. Duels between the underwater craft and the aircraft have made it more difficult for German submarines to carry on their attacks against the Allied shipping lanes. The Marine section of the Luftwaffe was dispatched to the French zone to counter the activities of Coastal Command, in addition to the landplanes already there. First blood was drawn by an Australian squadron of Coastal Command, whose Sunderland flying boat shot a Messerschmitt 109 into the sea. A Wellington landplane shortly afterwards shot an Arado floatplane down and damaged another. Three Whitleys were attacked separately by Arados, but

WING-CMDR. J. M. FULTON, D.F.C., A.F.C., reported missing after the R.A.F. raid on Hamburg on July 28. He is credited with some sixty important operations.
Photo, British Official

fought them off. More combats occurred on July 30 when a Sunderland shot down one of three float-planes. A naval officer on board the Sunderland commented on the similarity between air and naval fighting tactics. On August 3 a Whitley was forced down on the sea by two Arados. Within five minutes another Whitley engaged the Arados and shot one down and drove the other off. Yet a third Whitley fought another Arado. On August 5 Coastal Command Beaufighters entered the Bay, shot down one Arado and damaged another. Since then the Bay has been quieter.

On August 8 United States naval forces assisted by U.S. and Australian aircraft, attacked the Japanese holding the Tulagi area in the Solomon Islands. Tulagi is the best naval anchorage in that area of the South Pacific. Contingent air attacks were made against the Japanese aircraft based in New Guinea, and at all aerodromes whence aid might be sent to the Japanese forces in the Solomon group. The air fighting continues. Simultaneously United States air forces attacked the Japanese base at Kiska in the Aleutian Islands of the North Pacific. Enemy transports were sunk in harbour, but fog made observations difficult. The operations are doubtless designed to prevent the Japanese movement towards Alaska via the Aleutian stepping stones across the ocean.

Air fighting was severe in Transcaucasia while the Germans advanced south-east and south from Rostov. Heavy losses in aircraft were claimed by both sides. Air fighting there was purely tactical.

The R.A.F. lost Wing-Commander John " Moose " Fulton, D.F.C., A.F.C., of Kamloops, British Columbia, when raiding Hamburg on July 28. He had flown on 60 operations, and was a brilliant leader.

ON July 30 Luftwaffe Ace Major Rudolph Pflanz scored his 51st claimed victory. Next day, when Bostons and Spitfires of Fighter Command raided the German fighter base at Abbeville they destroyed five F.W.190s and six Messerschmitt 109s ; in one of those German fighters Rudolph Pflanz was killed.

Bomber Command's main objectives during the first half of August were Düsseldorf, Duisburg-Ruhrort-Meiderich-Hamborn (three nights), Osnabrück, Mainz (two nights). These are all large industrial towns. A Czecho-slovak squadron of Bomber Command celebrated its second anniversary on August 6.

One Fighter Command station has reached a total of 900 enemy aircraft destroyed. At the end of July Fighter Command had destroyed a total of 4,452 enemy aircraft in daylight actions. During July the Axis lost 424 aircraft over Britain, Western Europe, the Middle East, and to the Royal Navy ; the R.A.F. lost 432.

AMERICAN BOMBER scores a direct hit on a Japanese transport off the Aleutian Islands. On August 12 it was reported that the enemy had lost 21 ships following heavy U.S. attacks.
Photo, Pictorial Press

Captured Fighter Gives Away Luftwaffe's Secrets

Half-inch compressed steel protects the pilot's head from both rear and frontal attack, while the cockpit cover can be jettisoned in an emergency.

GERMANY'S latest single-seater fighter aircraft, the Focke-Wulf 190, whose secret was closely guarded by the enemy, has now yielded up any mysterious quality it may have once possessed. Flight tests have been carried out by R.A.F. pilots on one of these machines which was recently forced down on the South Coast of England. The 'plane was so little damaged that British experts were able to dismantle and examine it minutely.

The F.W. 190 has appeared as a fighter bomber in daylight raids over this country, and carried a bomb load similar to that of our Hurricane fighter bomber, though it is able to pack its load into one 550 lb. bomb as compared with the Hurricane's two of 250 lb. Its maximum speed, attained at 18,060 ft., is 375 m.p.h. and it possesses greater manoeuvrability than other German fighters. Armament consists of four 20 mm. cannon installed in the wings and two 7.92 mm. machine-guns mounted on top of the engine cowling (see illus. bottom, right), and firing through the air-screw arc with an interrupter gear. The cannon fire 60 rounds each.

An outstanding feature is the master control ("Kommandeur") unit, relieving the pilot of many duties in the control of the engine, and providing against any mishandling on his part.

Possessing an extremely wide wing span and a finely tapered tail, the F.W.190 is seen in flight during one of its important R.A.F. tests.

When the machine is in flight the wheels retract inwards into the wings. Here the 'plane is taxi-ing across the landing field after one of its trials.

Achtung!
Haubenabwurf
durch Sprengladung
Abwurfhebel nicht berühren. Im Probefall
vorherige Sicherung des Schlagbolzens

DEMOLITION OF THE AIRCRAFT in the event of a forced landing can be effected by detonating an explosive charge inside the fuselage. On the left is a warning to the pilot against touching the operating lever. The efficiency of the F.W. 190 largely depends on its compact and powerful engine (right). This is a B.M.W. 14-cylinder air-cooled radial of 1,530 h.p., fitted with a two-stage supercharger—a development of the American Pratt and Whitney engine. The two machine guns, each designed to fire 1,000 rounds, are seen on the top.

Photos, E.N.A., G.P.U., Keystone

Malta is 'A Very Great Nuisance to the Axis'

BOMB-SCARRED AERODROME of Ta Venezia, one of the R.A.F. bases in Malta. I, aircraft sheds; 2, subterranean hangars; 3, stick of bursting bombs. Despite the recurring damage done to their base, it is from Ta Venezia that so many dauntless fighter pilots take off to do battle with the enemy. This and the photograph below are from Goebbels' paper, Signal.

On the eastern side of Malta (left) there are five airfields: I, Halfar; 2, Guidia; 3, Luca; 4, Krendi; and 5, Ta Venezia. Three of these are linked by a broad runway, 6. Aircraft parking grounds are shown at 7. Valletta harbour, 8, and Marsa Scirocco, 9, are the two chief bays in a much indented coast. During the month of July 147 enemy aircraft were brought down over and around Malta, of which 133 were destroyed by our fighters.

Air Vice-Marshal K. R. Park, C.B., D.F.C. (above), recently appointed Air Officer Commanding the R.A.F. Mediterranean in place of Air Vice-Marshal H. P. Lloyd. During the Battle of Britain he commanded No. II Fighter Group. It was his predecessor who gave the George Cross island the apt description quoted in our headline.

Photos, British Official & G.P.U.

Ferry Pilots Marooned in Greenland for 45 Days

HUSKIES TO THE RESCUE. One of the most dramatic air adventures of the war reached a happy ending when recently three men of the R.A.F. Ferry Command, who were missing for forty-five days, were brought back from Greenland in a U.S. flying-boat. They had flown a Hudson bomber to Newfoundland, and were waiting to cross the Atlantic when they were ordered to make a survey sortie over N.W. Greenland and then repair to Reykjavik, Iceland. But the flight to Iceland was rendered impossible by nightmare weather —dense sleet, icing and an electric storm which threw both compass and radio out of gear. Then one of the two engines failed. Petrol was nearly exhausted and a crash-landing had to be made on a sheet of water covered with ice, which immediately broke.

"We were getting ready to swim for it," related the pilot, "when we heard and saw something of a kind which only happens in story books. Dashing towards us across the wilderness of mountains, ice and water was a team of huskies, and behind them a line of men." These belonged to an American detachment who had come to establish a post. Near by was an Eskimo hamlet; otherwise there were no human beings for five hundred miles. The huskies were harnessed to the task of salvaging everything that could be quickly removed from the sinking plane. A wireless transmitter was improvised and faint signals sent out. Rescue was, however, impossible until, after forty-five days, a Catalina flying-boat was able to land and embark the Hudson crew.

Photo, British Official: Crown Copyright

We Trained For the R.A.F. in America

Just over a year ago there was a great need of increased training capacity for aircrews, and the U.S. Government offered to place training facilities in the United States at the disposal of the R.A.F.—an offer that was gratefully accepted. The article that follows is from the pen of one of the young men who were trained under the scheme. Now, however, the training capacity in the British Commonwealth has been so extended that it has been possible to relinquish the U.S. facilities in favour of U.S. Air Force cadets.

A FEW weeks ago I arrived back in England from the United States as a trained observer of the Royal Air Force—one of the many thousands who are completing their flying instruction undisturbed within the borders of that vast domain. It was my good fortune to be detailed along with many of my fellows for instruction in South Florida, where the subtropical climate, which had made the district famous as the World's Playground in happier times, was also found to be ideal for flying.

First, however, we were to spend a short term of preparation in Canada at a large depot camp where, for the first time in our two years, we could walk along brightly illuminated streets and gaze into shop windows gay with neon lighting.

When we arrived we found Canada at its loveliest. The snow was packed hard underfoot, and every tree, every roof-top, was hidden beneath a deep layer of white, which moulded sharp outlines into things of beauty.

Our new-found friends made us very welcome, inviting us at once to their own homes and firesides to ask us details of England as it is today: the England that is still the "Old Country" to them. Many of the people we met during our short sojourn there were folk who left England but a decade or so ago, and many were the yarns that went back and forth before the crackling fires. We found them quietly confident in the progress of the conflict, and justifiably proud of the contribution which Canada is making in men, money and munitions of war. They are lusty sons of Empire, these men from the teeming cities and vast forest solitudes of our great Dominion, and we felt privileged to be amongst them.

In a few days, though, we had to climb aboard our train for the long journey south. We pulled out of the station waving a cheery goodbye to our Canadian friends. Three days and nights went by while we thundered across a continent. Canada's snowlands disappeared before the industrial regions around Portland and Boston. These in turn were swallowed in the mightier masses of New York and Philadelphia. The white dome of the Capitol in Washington slid into view and as quickly vanished. Before us now lay the broad lands which somehow still hold the mystic spell and grandeur of the old South. Virginia, Carolina, and Georgia—in which last Margaret Mitchell found the fount and inspiration of her masterpiece "Gone with the Wind." Into the distance, on either side, the cotton and tobacco fields stretched away, brown as yet with the stubble of last year's crop. Little groups of dwellings flashed by with their Shanty Town appearance enchanting the eye. There we saw the inevitable veranda with its inevitable rocking-chair, and crowds of happy little coloured children waving joyously as we rumbled on.

We were glad to stow greatcoats about this time, for it was noticeably warmer. Then, on our last night aboard, we roared over the Florida State line and awoke to find ourselves in Miami with a hot sun shining overhead.

Miami is a very lovely city. The prevailing colour of its well-proportioned modern buildings is white, thus enhancing its fresh and clean appearance. Wide boulevards are carefully laid out and are set about with graceful palms which sway gently in the soft Atlantic breezes.

On arrival we were issued with our khaki uniforms of slacks and shirts, as regulation Royal Air Force blue is not the ultimate in comfort when the temperature is around eighty degrees in the shade and the air almost saturated. Our quarters and food were excellent, although some palates found the rather highly spiced dishes a little strange at first. Fruit there was in abundance, along with plenty of eggs and milk. I enjoyed every item of diet except one—the American hot-dog ; and that, I firmly believe, is manufactured from that precious commodity—rubber !

Since we arrived during a week-end there were no lectures for us until the following week, and we made the most of this first opportunity to look round the subtropical paradise in which we now found ourselves. The winter season was at its height, for although America had been engulfed in the War but a few weeks earlier, its grim effects had not yet reached out to mar the gaiety of Miami and its environs. Visitors from all over the United States still thronged the boulevards and gardens. In the happy crowds one could distinguish the easy drawl of the Southerner in contrast to the quick-clipped accent of the New Yorker. Again an olive skin would show the presence of the Latin, for Miami is one of the most cosmopolitan cities of the New World ; a fact which pleased us, for we wanted to get the unbiased general opinion of the Americans in their outlook on the War ; and here, if anywhere, it was to be found.

There are very few barriers of reserve to the American, and we rapidly made true-hearted friends. To many it came as a surprise and a profound revelation of Anglo-American unity to know that men from Great Britain had come so far for training, and we were hard put to answer their many

R.A.F. NAVIGATOR receiving instruction from a U.S. Naval Reserve pilot. Coastal Command navigator cadets are trained in the Breezy Point area of the Naval Air Station at Norfolk, Virginia, and are given actual experience as crew members of the U.S. Catalina flying-boats.

Photo, British Official: Crown Copyright

questions about conditions here. They follow our fortunes in England with close and sincere interest, but we found one of their impressions of England's size rather amusing : " It's so darned small," they would say, " don't all you folks get in each other's way ? " I have a sneaking suspicion that one or two of our friends believe one could stand on top of St. Paul's and see France on one hand and Ireland on the other !

The comfort of the fighting man is a very real thing to them and they show a great generosity in their efforts to this end. In our locality huge open-air shows were staged regularly for Army and Navy benefit, patrons often buying tickets at two or three times their face value and then turning them in for re-issue free of charge to men of the Services. All sorts of concerts and parties were arranged to make the men feel at home in new surroundings.

Our schedule of training was timed to such minute-by-minute detail that our spare time was very limited. From the first we were plunged into real hard work, spending hours every day in the lecture-halls under the eyes of men with long experience in navigating heavy aircraft. Much time was spent in practical work on instruments with which we were to be concerned in our flying. Weeks passed and we realized that terms such as " celestial azimuth," " reciprocal bearing," and " running fix " were no longer things of mystery to us. Eagerly we awaited the day when our first flight was to be made.

I remember now that cheerful bunch of fellows on the transport which took us to the flying base, the roominess of the aircraft, and the sudden drowning of speech as the huge engines coughed into life. A perfect day for flying, and very soon we were swinging in slow circles over the base, which looked like a toy model thousands of feet below. However, we were soon too busy to gaze idly at the panorama of houses, glades and sea. We quickly got down to a routine and, as our instructors put it, " ironed out the kinks in our navigation." We found the work to be of absorbing interest, particularly the night flying, where conditions as nearly as possible resembled those to be encountered in actual operations.

Days flew by, and before we knew it final examinations were looming up. A little extra ounce to reach the peak of perfection, the excitement and anxiety of the examinations themselves—and then the great day when, midst speeches and cheering, we graduated as the proud possessors of our own flying log-books. At last we had earned the right to call ourselves navigators. A few days of freedom with all the hard work behind us came and went, and there was genuine regret in all our hearts when we at last had to bid farewell to the many sincere friends we had made in that land of sunshine. Soon we were heading north again with visions of home and precious leave in our minds. We spent another day or two in the Canadian camp depot, where the snow had now fled before the gay flowers of summer, and then, under the watchful eyes of the British Navy, we ploughed our way towards Old England.

Britons Learn to Fly in Florida's Sunny Clime

AMERICA TAUGHT R.A.F. AIRCREWS at a time when the speeding-up of training was a matter of urgency. These are scenes at U.S. flying schools while this invaluable help was being given to Britain. Top, embryo pilots return from an instruction flight at Lakeland School of Aeronautics, Florida. Below, a class at the Riddle-Mackay Aero College, Florida, lined up to receive their wings from Air-Marshal D. S. C. Evill, then Chief of R.A.F. Training Units in the U.S.A. In front are British officers and personnel of the flying school.

Photos, Keystone, Planet News

THOSE THREE FATEFUL YEARS!

by Paul Tabori
Author of *Epitaph for Europe*

THREE years of war have changed Europe from a continent of uneasy peace, fitful prosperity and hectic brilliance into a vast expanse of misery, suspicion and slavery. Three years under Hitler or in his shadow have done more harm than the Thirty Years' War or the two centuries of Turkish rule. Mechanized war, total war, has wrought havoc at a speed that was still unknown in 1914-1918. In September 1939 there were four belligerents in Europe : today there are five neutrals left, and even Spain, Sweden, Turkey, Portugal and Switzerland belong to the class of non-belligerents and not to that of absolute neutrals, having chosen their ideological allegiance in some way or the other. It becomes more and more clear at the end of the third year that what we are experiencing is not a war but a vast series of revolutions of world-wide effect.

THERE were two great dividing lines, immense watersheds in the tragic landscape of these three years for Europe. The first was the fall of France ; the second the Nazi attack on Russia.

The fall of France destroyed the final vestiges of the great system of alliances which Clemenceau, Barthou and others had laboured so hard to build. This system had been weakened by the *Anschluss* and severely shaken by Munich. But when France fell and the greatest military power on the Continent lay prostrate, the remaining unconquered neutrals were either driven into Hitler's arms or reduced to helpless panic. Some of them roused themselves from this extreme terror and wrote deathless pages of courage and defiance in the history of Europe. Others sank into the morass of "collaboration" and became vassals. The fall of France was the deepest point of Europe's disgrace, the nadir of her humiliation. It created the myth of German invincibility ; it cut off Britain from the Continent.

The attack on Russia had the opposite effect. It was what many of the European nations had been praying for. They knew that Russia could not be defeated, or at least only at a cost which would destroy Germany in the end. For the Slav countries, Russia was still the big brother ; now that she was fighting, they had an ally, near enough to support and succour them. Even if they had no way of linking up with her armies, the underground army of saboteurs, guerillas, partisans was given everywhere a new lease of life, new hope, new opportunities. Hitler tried to turn the Russian campaign into a sham crusade of Europe against Asia (for some time the German communiqués spoke not of the Axis or German forces but of "European" troops), but this propaganda trick had a short-lived success. Today the majority of "volunteers" from Spain, Norway, Belgium and other "protected" countries have returned, sadder and wiser men.

THE three years of war have proved the idiocy of neutrality in peacetime ; the truth that no nation could stand aloof from others in distress. War has become indivisible, as M. Litvinov had maintained peace was ; and the exiled governments have already begun to create regional unions and look forward to a Europe not forced into the strait jacket of "blocs" but organized in natural groups, interlocking and interdependent.

The three years have produced heroes and villains in plenty. A half-baked Norwegian visionary has given his name to a whole brood of traitors. But there were traitors before Vidkun Quisling : smooth-tongued betrayers like Seyss Inquart and Guido Schmidt in Austria ; weak-kneed puppets like Hacha in Czechoslovakia, Horthy in Hungary and Antonescu in Rumania ; ambitious fanatics and schemers like Mussert in Holland, Degrelle in Belgium, Scavenius in Denmark ; odious mercenary scoundrels like Laval and Darlan in France, Neditch in Yugoslavia and King Boris in Bulgaria. Hitler's New Order proved to be broadminded about its local agents—a downright gangster like Ante Pavelitch, over-lord of unhappy Croatia, or an ex-gaolbird like Sano Mach in Slovakia were given more or less free hand to murder and plunder their compatriots. It is significant that almost everywhere the popular support of these quislings represents a small fraction of the nation. And it is to the eternal glory of both Poland and Russia that no man was found willing to serve the usurper. That is one of the main reasons why the Gestapo rages with special violence in these territories.

IF the three years in Europe have given us an especially repulsive set of villains, they have certainly brought forth a group of heroes, worthy of these tremendous times. Men like De Gaulle who proved to the world that France had not forgotten her noble traditions ; General Michailovitch whose epic struggle in the mountains of Bosnia and Montenegro must form one of the greatest chapters in human courage against desperate odds ; the millions of nameless Poles, Serbs, Greeks, Russians—all these represent a more than adequate balance on the credit side of Europe. The hostages dying daily by the score ; the Jews, walled up alive in the ghettos of Poland ; the intellectuals pressed into slavery in the labour camps— the silent heroism and endurance have proved once more that the spirit can be stronger and more tenacious than the most cold-blooded and systematic oppression the world has ever known.

POLITICALLY Europe has experienced another phenomenon, unparalleled in history. I am referring to the immense mass-migrations compared to which the movements of tribes and nations in the first ten centuries of the Christian era were mere "conducted tours." The Reich has catapulted its citizens to a dozen different countries as colonists, policemen, officials. In small Slovenia alone fifty thousand people have been dispossessed and herded into desolate districts. The peregrinations of the Jews alone surpass the Forty Years which Israel spent in the desert. All over Europe millions of people have been forcibly ejected from their homes and sent to unaccustomed, inhospitable places. And a smaller yet no less important trickle of migration is taking place constantly—thousands of men and women who can no longer stand German tyranny try to escape to freedom. Only a small percentage succeed, but the tales of these escapes alone show that Europe has not given in to the tyrant. Apart from millions of prisoners-of-war Germany has also drawn to its huge unhappy penitentiary large numbers of foreign workers.

THE political and social hierarchy of Europe has changed and stiffened. On top there is the *Herrenvolk* with the top-heavy ruling caste of Nazis and military leaders. Next come the "allies" who are in reality satellites. One of the most tragi-comic sights in Europe is Italy—having been a "partner" in the Axis, she has now become a third-rate power, her gimcrack Caesar fading into obscurity, her rich beauty easy German plunder, every phase of her national life controlled by the Nazis. Hungary and

PAUL TABORI has written in Epitaph for Europe one of the few war books that will outlive the War. In the current number of World Digest I wrote of him :

"Not many English writers can rival this fortunate Hungarian in command of our idiom, and none, it is safe to say, has had so complete a training in European affairs. To read his book is more fully to appreciate what is meant by a good European. The truth about every people in Europe, stated with the restraint which comes from knowledge and understanding, is told superbly well in Epitaph for-Europe."

My readers will, therefore, welcome the contribution which Mr. Tabori has expressly written for this issue and will be glad to know that he is to be a regular contributor to the pages of THE WAR ILLUSTRATED.—Ed.

Photo, Kelenyi

Rumania, the two jackals, are ready to fly at each other's throat if Germany should remove the leash. Bulgaria and Slovakia have also sunk to vassaldom. Finland's tragic case shows that you cannot sup with the devil however long your spoon's handle.

The satellites are followed in the hierarchy by the occupied and oppressed countries ; and in this category there is strict distinction between the "collaborationist" states who give comparatively little trouble and those more or less openly mutinous. On the whole it can be said that the daily sabotage acts, assassinations, passive and active demonstrations show that Hitler is actually farther today from subduing the continent than he had been these three years.

IN the spiritual field there are two main facts about Europe. One is the revival of religion and the defiance of the servants of God—Bishop Berggrav in Norway, the Orthodox Patriarch in Yugoslavia are only two examples of this proud, loyal courage —the other is the complete barrenness in creative arts. Hitler's Europe hasn't produced a single outstanding work in literature, the drama, the cinema or the fine arts during these years. You cannot create beauty under a whip.

Today Europe's heart is in London, the centre and magnet of the free. But millions of individual hearts are beating all over the unhappy continent, ready to combine and defy openly the monstrous plague of a diseased political creed. Europe is waiting, no longer hopeless as after the collapse of France or too exuberant as after June 22, 1941—waiting with sober confidence, patient grit, for the day when she will recover her soul and forget the long nightmare of these three years.

Photo, Keystone

What's the Riddle of these Photos?

In this and succeeding pages we print a series of striking photographs issued by German propaganda. Above is one that purports to show submarine shelters in course of construction on the French coast. "Very like a whale" as Polonius said. It looks a formidable rampart against British invasion. Its use for U-boats is less apparent.

On Channel Coast and Atlantic Shore:

Stretching for 130 miles along the north coast of France, the Germans claim that their Channel defences constitute a coastal Siegfried Line. (1) Long-range gun recently installed. (2) Blockhouse apparently devoid of guns or gun casemates; the portholes and chimneys are for ventilation. (3) Enemy artillerymen with so-called "champagne cocktail" shells.

Photos,

Hitler's Bastions Against Invasion

(4) German machine-gun post on a cliff-top acts as a defence against low-flying R.A.F.
bombers. (5) A gun crew makes ready. The Germans employ their heaviest guns to attack
British shipping in the Channel ; these guns are placed on rails and frequently moved,
since they present an obvious target (6) Guns firing from the railway siding of a factory

Photos, Sport & General, Keystone

Giant Fortress of Steel and Concrete

"Batterie Todt" (top), named after Fritz Todt, builder of the Siegfried Line, serves as an important link in the German system of Channel fortifications. This enemy stronghold on the French coast is camouflaged from the air and sea. The Battery is manned night and day. Men of the garrison (below) are seen rushing to the gun posts as the alarm signal sounds.

THE WAR'S MOST VITAL CONFERENCE
Churchill, Stalin and Harriman at the Kremlin

At four o'clock on Wednesday afternoon, August 12, three great American Liberator bombers, escorted by Russian fighters, approached the red roofs of Moscow, circled over the airport and quietly came to earth. That people of importance were arriving was apparent from the presence on the tarmac of M. Molotov, the Foreign Minister, Marshal Shaposhnikov, the Russian Chief of Staff, and other Soviet representatives, as well as the British and American Ambassadors, Sir Archibald Clark-Kerr and Admiral Standley, and Gen. Follet Bradley, of the U.S. Army.

As the first aircraft came to rest the guard of honour presented arms, and massed military bands struck up the British national anthem, followed by that of America and the Internationale. Out from the bomber stepped Mr. Churchill, a broad smile on his face, his fingers held aloft in the V sign. At the invitation of M. Stalin he had flown from Britain at the head of British and American delegations, in which was included Mr. Averell Harriman, for important conferences.

After greetings and introductions and an inspection of the tall, steel-helmeted guard of honour, two short statements by Mr. Churchill and Mr. Harriman were recorded on the airfield (*see* panel above). The delegates then faced a battery of Soviet photographers, and at last entered the fleet of waiting cars and were driven to the Kremlin. The citizens of Moscow had noticed in Gorky Street a number of exceptionally smart infantrymen and some Cossacks in parade uniform, but as yet they were unaware of the identity of the visitors whom they could just discern in the limousines as they sped past.

In addition to the Prime Minister, the British delegation included Sir Alexander Cadogan, Permanent Under-Secretary at the Foreign Office ; Gen. Sir Alan Brooke, Chief of the Imperial General Staff ; Gen. Sir Archibald Wavell ; Air Chief Marshal Sir Arthur Tedder, Chief of the Air Command, Middle East ; Sir Charles Wilson, the Prime Minister's personal physician ; Col. E. I. C. Jacob ; Commander C. R. Thompson, R.N., personal assistant to Mr. Churchill as Minister of Defence ; Lt.-Col. Dunphil ; and Mr. T. R. Rowan, the Premier's private secretary. Gen. Wavell did not arrive until Thursday, his plane having had to return to Teheran after taking off from there, owing to a slight mishap.

'UNTIL THE HITLER REGIME HAS TURNED TO DUST'

We are fully determined, whatever sufferings and difficulties lie ahead of us, to continue the struggle hand in hand with our comrades and brothers until the last remnants of the Hitler regime have turned to dust and remain in our memories as a warning and example for the future.
Winston Churchill

The President of the United States asked me to accompany the British Prime Minister on his most important journey to Moscow during this decisive moment of the war.
The President of the United States will agree to all decisions taken by Mr. Churchill. America will stand hand in hand together with the Russians.
Averell Harriman

The United States delegation, in addition to Mr. Harriman, included Maj.-Gen. Maxwell, Commander-in-Chief American Forces in Egypt, and Brigadier S. P. Sparlding. In all, the delegates totalled twenty.

On his way from Britain Mr. Churchill had met. Gen. Smuts at Cairo, and the talks between them lasted for more than a day. This was the first meeting of the British and South African Premiers in the present war.

The evening of their arrival in Moscow Mr. Churchill and Mr. Harriman had their first talk with M. Stalin, when M. Molotov and Marshal Voroshilov were also present. It lasted nearly four hours, for business had to be conducted through interpreters, and throughout the proceedings the Prime Minister, in the words of an observer, " worked like a beaver." It was suggested that after his journey he might have preferred rest and relaxation. Mr. Churchill poohpoohed the idea : " I never let pleasure clog the works of business." With him at this meeting were Sir Alan Brooke, Sir Alexander Cadogan and Sir Archibald Clark-Kerr. Mr. Harriman attended as the representative of President Roosevelt. The discussions, it was announced, were carried on " in an atmosphere of cordiality and complete sincerity."

The next day (Thursday) Mr. Churchill had a long talk with M. Molotov, and later a second meeting with M. Stalin. The Soviet leader smoked his famous pipe, Mr. Churchill his equally famous cigars.

On Friday there were further consultations and discussions, by the end of which the essential business had been transacted, so that evening the delegates relaxed at a great banquet given by their hosts at the Kremlin, in the room Catherine the Great used as a ballroom. The entire Soviet Politburo, which virtually decides Russian policy, had been invited to meet them, but there was nothing stiff or formal about the festivity. The speeches, of which there were 25, were light and witty, and the whole atmosphere one of complete friendliness. M. Stalin was in great spirits, cracking many jokes, and himself proposing several of the innumerable toasts. Mr. Churchill's sonorous voice was heard booming " To the President " as he rose, glass in hand, to the toast of President Roosevelt. M. Stalin wore his customary semi-uniform of light brown summer blouse, brown trousers and regulation black boots. Mr. Churchill had donned the " siren suit " which was so often noticed during his visit to America.

On Saturday Mr. Churchill and Mr. Harriman spent the day in the country near Moscow. Late in the afternoon a final meeting with M. Stalin took place, but this was more in the nature of a farewell, for complete and full agreement on the momentous subjects under discussion had been reached the previous day. Owing to these constant preoccupations the Prime Minister was able to see nothing of the life and activities of the great Soviet capital on this, his first visit. In the early dawn of Sunday morning he and his party left by air on their homeward journey.

On Monday evening, August 17, Moscow radio officially informed the Russian people of Mr. Churchill's mission, at the same time that the B.B.C. gave the news to British listeners. In the words of the London communiqué : " A number of decisions were reached covering the field of the war against Hitlerite Germany and her associates in Europe. This just war of liberation both Governments are determined to carry on with all their power and energy until the complete destruction of Hitlerism and any similar tyranny has been achieved."

In a last message to M. Stalin the Prime Minister said : " I am very pleased to have visited Moscow : firstly, because it was my duty to express myself ; and, secondly, because I am certain that our contact will contribute usefully to our cause."

THE HISTORIC MOSCOW CONFERENCE began one hour and a half after the Liberators had landed. The next day Mr. Churchill, who spent each night in the quiet countryside outside Moscow, drove back to the Kremlin with Sir Alexander Cadogan and had long discussions with M. Stalin and M. Molotov. This specially posed photograph shows, seated, left to right, Sir Alexander Cadogan, the Prime Minister, Mr. Harriman, M. Stalin and M. Molotov. The Conference Room was furnished chiefly with a 20-ft.-long table ; across its width the two leaders faced each other.

This was the Cost of the Passage of the Don

FIGHTING ON THE DON FRONT was unparalleled in its intensity as the Germans, disregarding their enormous losses, threw in fresh reserves. The top photograph shows an appalling scene of desolation in what was once the busy centre of a town on the Don after the Germans had captured the place. Russian bombers and heavy artillery ceaselessly pounded enemy tanks and lorries during the Germans' crossing of the great river. Below, a bridge and its approaches choked with the wreckage of enemy vehicles.

Photos, Sport & General, Keystone

Behind the Front with the Red Army

IN RUSSIA the importance of mechanized warfare is fully recognized. 1. Moscow railwaymen have built an armoured train and presented it to the Red Army. Members of the train's crew are seen lined up in front of it before leaving for a battle zone. 2. Radioed picture showing Soviet anti-tank units passing through a village on their way to the front. 3. Jumbled mass of captured enemy tanks brought to a special factory for repair, after which they will be used by the Red Army.

Photos, U.S.S.R. Official and Planet News

THE WAR AT SEA

by Francis E. McMurtrie

An important Allied offensive was opened in the South-West Pacific on August 7. In the course of this operation strong forces of the United States Marine Corps were landed on certain of the islands of the Solomon group, including Guadalcanar and Tulagi, and according to the latest news available at the time of writing are now " well established " there. In support of these landings repeated air raids have been made on Japanese bases at Rabaul, Lae, Salamaua and Buna, as well as on more remote spots such as Timor and the Kei Islands, an enemy-occupied group in the Banda Sea.

Units of the main United States Pacific Fleet have recently been added to the naval

H.M.S. EAGLE, one of the oldest British aircraft carriers, was sunk in the Mediterranean on August 11 while defending a vital convoy bound for Malta. She displaced 22,600 tons, accommodated 21 aircraft and was completed in 1924. Inset, Capt. L. D. Mackintosh, D.S.C., R.N., her commander, who was among the 930 officers and ratings saved. *Photos, Daily Mirror, Lafayette*

forces already assigned to the South-West Pacific sector, which include both American and Australian warships. Substantial damage has been inflicted on the enemy naval and air forces, though details are not likely to be published until the operation has been concluded.

With the object of calming anxiety in Japan, the Tokyo authorities have issued the wildest claims of devastation inflicted on the Allied forces, culminating in a broadcast on August 15 asserting that 11 cruisers, six destroyers and ten transports had been sunk. Most of this destruction is alleged to have been accomplished by torpedo aircraft, 21 of which it is admitted were lost " by hurling themselves with headlong crashes on to the decks of warships." This is not the first time this particular story has been put forward. It originated with the Italians, who before the war began were fond of boasting that their airmen were prepared to sacrifice their lives in this spectacular fashion to make certain of achieving hits. Actually the only Allied losses so far reported from official

sources comprise one cruiser sunk, and two cruisers, two destroyers and one transport damaged—a modest total compared with enemy claims. The enemy lost 36 aircraft in the initial landing operations.

Washington stated on August 17 that the only engagement between surface forces was fought on the night of August 8-9, when an enemy force of cruisers and destroyers attempted to attack our transports, but was heavily repulsed. It had previously been explained that the immediate objective was to expel the Japanese from the Tulagi area and to make use of that region for Allied purposes. Evidently it had been the enemy's purpose to use it as a base for offensive

operations against Allied positions covering the line of communications to Australia and New Zealand.

An initial surprise was effected, and though the enemy counter-attacked rapidly and with vigour, he failed to expel the landing parties. The great significance of the whole operation is that it marks the Allied assumption of the initiative against Japan. Previously it has always been the enemy who has done the attacking. Operations are under the immediate direction of Vice-Admiral Robert L. Ghormley (*see* portrait p. 163), who until April was United States Naval Observer in London, and under the general control of Admiral Chester W. Nimitz, Commander-in-Chief of the U.S. Pacific Fleet.

The garrison of Malta, whose dauntless defence has excited such admiration throughout the Allied countries, has again been reinforced and supplied by an important convoy under the protection of the Royal Navy. In the escort were included battleships, aircraft carriers, cruisers, destroyers and minesweepers, which were called upon to beat

off constant attacks by aircraft and U-boats. Italian cruisers and destroyers also approached from the Tyrrhenian Sea, but as soon as a striking force of aircraft assailed them they retreated without coming within range of our gunfire. One of our submarines, commanded by Lieut. A. C. G. Mars, R.N., succeeded in hitting two of the enemy cruisers (which included ships mounting both 8-inch and 6-inch guns) with torpedoes. Though there is no evidence that either was sunk, air reconnaissance showed that one had 60 ft. of her bows blown away.

Before this encounter developed, H.M.S. Eagle, an aircraft carrier of 22,600 tons, was torpedoed by a U-boat and became a total loss, though luckily 930 of her officers and men were saved. The Eagle had an unusual history. Laid down on the Tyne in 1913 as the Chilean battleship Almirante Cochrane, she was acquired by the Admiralty during the last war and completed as an aircraft carrier. Her design was therefore somewhat obsolete, but in spite of the fact that her maximum speed was 24 knots and her complement of aircraft only 21, she has done good work in the present conflict. Some of her planes took part, with those of H.M.S. Illustrious, in the famous torpedo attack on the Italian fleet at Taranto on November 11, 1940 ; and on various occasions her aircraft have disposed of Italian destroyers and submarines with which they have been in action.

Regardless of the Eagle's loss, the convoy continued on its way and after hard fighting reached its destination. In addition to the Eagle our losses include H.M.S. Manchester, a cruiser of 9,400 tons, completed in 1938, H.M.S. Cairo, an old cruiser of 4,200 tons, re-armed for anti-aircraft escort duties, and H.M.S. Foresight, a destroyer of 1,350 tons. Two enemy submarines were destroyed and at least 66 aircraft (possibly 93), while we lost only eight.

Vice-Admiral E. N. Syfret, who was in command of the whole operation, has worthily maintained the high tradition established during the first twelve months of the war with Italy by Admiral Sir James Somerville, who will always be remembered for his famous order : " The convoy must go through." Rear-Adm. A. L. St. G. Lyster was in command of the aircraft carriers, and Rear-Adm. H. M. Burrough of the light forces.

In case it may be questioned whether the retention of Malta is worth the naval, mercantile and air losses which have had to be sustained to keep the island supplied, it may be pointed out that it is the only bastion on the northern flank of our Mediterranean front which the enemy has been unable to overcome.

Malta has served the threefold purpose of affording a base for the interception of enemy supplies to Libya by submarines and light craft ; of providing an important intermediate stage for aircraft, and for air attacks on Axis sea communications and bases ; and of constituting a miniature but most effective " second front," which has been the means of keeping large numbers of enemy aircraft away from other theatres of war. Altogether not less than 800 enemy planes have been destroyed in abortive assaults on the Maltese stronghold.

An American merchant vessel has been sunk by a surface raider in the South Atlantic. The raider is described as a heavily armed vessel of mercantile design and appearance, with an extensive fuel supply, resembling in her main features the notorious Altmark. Germany possesses several such ships, which were undoubtedly designed for this purpose.

It is clear that no raider can afford to make more than fleeting appearances upon the trade routes, the bulk of her time being perforce spent in unfrequented areas lest she be sighted and run to earth. This necessarily sets a limit on the amount of destruction that she can accomplish in a given time.

Escorts Take Deadly Toll of Convoy Raiders

ITALIAN BOMBER (above), swooping to attack a British destroyer, has been hit by the ship's deadly pom-pom fire, and makes a determined bid to escape. A few minutes later the plane crashes in flames into the sea (left). These photographs were taken during an actual Axis attack on a Mediterranean convoy.

DAMAGED U-BOAT rises to the surface after having been successfully attacked by a British warship in a fierce encounter. Members of the crew who are seen standing in the stern of the submarine were rescued and taken aboard the warship as prisoners.

LEADING A CONVOY ESCORT into Malta harbour, this British destroyer reaches port after warding off enemy submarines and aircraft in the hazardous waters of the Mediterranean.

Photos British Official, Daily Mirror, Associated Press

Special Service Troops Prepare for 'The Day'

COMMANDOS IN ACTION have proved formidable fighters in raids on enemy-occupied territory such as the reconnaissance in force at Dieppe on Aug. 19. The photographs show the rigorous training which these men undergo in preparation for such combined operations. 1. Disembarking from landing-craft. 2. Preparing to jump ashore. 3. Advancing under cover of a smoke-screen across a beach. 4. Thrusting an explosive charge into a pill-box opening by means of a pole charge. 5. Part of the equipment carried by these troops is the dirk—a useful weapon which is worn inside the stocking.

Photos British Official: Crown Copyright

Indians Trek By Scottish Lochs and Hills

ROYAL INDIAN ARMY SERVICE CORPS units are here seen against an unfamiliar background. Stationed in Scotland, a team of pack-horses, top, begins the mountain climb as it carries stores and equipment beyond the reach of mechanized transport. Below, the pack-train has mounted to a higher altitude, while far below it stretches the lovely panorama of the Scottish countryside.

Photos, British Official

Women in Uniform: Civilian Work and Pay

Following her description of conditions of service in the three Women's Services (see page 152) IRENE CLEPHANE in this second article treats of those whom she describes as "civilians in uniform"—the women who serve in the N.A.A.F.I. canteens, the nurses in hospitals and first-aid posts, the cheery conductors on the bus and tram platforms, the green-and-khaki girls of the Women's Land Army, and the stalwart and ever-helpful women in the blue of the Police.

CIVILIAN women doing war work exceed in number those in the forces, and many of them also wear uniform. Take, for instance, the women in N.A.A.F.I. (Navy, Army, and Air Force Institutes), the official canteen organization whose object is to provide serving men with a homelike atmosphere in their hours of recreation. Women joining N.A.A.F.I. do not have to sign on for the duration—though they may be retained after the War if they wish to remain in its service. Uniform is worn, but there is no military discipline, for though so closely associated with the Forces, N.A.A.F.I. is not part of them. Rates of pay range from 20s. for counter, general, and kitchen assistants, to 45s. for fully qualified cooks, plus board, lodging, and uniform.

Then there is nursing, the service which calls more urgently than any other for recruits. Girls of conscription age can always volunteer for nursing, even if they wait until they are about to be "directed" to essential work of some kind. Nursing is of equal value to civilians and to the armed forces, especially in the present war when air raids mean thousands of civilian casualties. Many young women between 18 and 30 who feel a call to nursing as a career have already become student nurses, at a starting wage of £40 a year, plus board, lodging, laundry, medical attendance and uniform. Many nurses who had retired have returned to their profession. But the need still continues: a call for 5,000 more went out in the spring of 1942.

Women drawn to nursing who yet do not want to make it a career are doing splendid work in the Civil Nursing Reserve as Nursing Auxiliaries. The age limits are 18 to 55, and candidates need have had no previous nursing experience. Over 25,000 have taken up full-time service in hospitals and first-aid posts all over the country. In hospitals they are paid £55 a year and receive free board, lodging and laundry, or a cash allowance in place of them; in first-aid posts or medical-aid posts in shelters, they are paid £2 7s. a week and keep themselves.

During the period of heavy air raids the hospitals suffered many direct hits. A number of nurses were killed at their posts, and hundreds showed the most conspicuous heroism, attending to their patients under conditions of appalling horror, moving them when necessary from wrecked or burning wards without a thought for their own safety.

Forty Thousand Land Girls

The Minister of Agriculture recently announced that Great Britain is now producing two-thirds of its own food supply. The attainment of this fine result is due in no small measure to the skill and devotion of the Women's Land Army. This organization, though called an "army," is purely civilian. It resembles the Forces only in that its members have to promise to serve for the duration of the war, and to go where directed. First launched in 1916, during the war of 1914-1918, it was revived in June 1939. By the end of August 1939, some 9,000 volunteers had offered themselves, and 5,000 more were awaiting interviews. In those last momentous days before war started, members assisted for the first time in getting in the harvest. By the end of October over 1,000 were in full-time jobs; by the end of February 1940 nearly 4,000 had been placed, and the demand for their services was growing. The uniform of khaki corduroy breeches, green pullover, and jaunty little khaki felt hat (provided free at

yearly intervals) was becoming familiar in town and country.

Land Army girls receive 10s. a week, plus free board and lodging, during their training, which lasts four weeks. When they are trained the farmer for whom they have been working is expected to employ them. At the beginning of the war the minimum wage for a volunteer was 28s. for a 48-hour week. Following the granting last December of a national minimum wage of 60s. a week to male agricultural workers, women's wages, too, were raised, and members of the Women's Land Army now (August 1942) receive a minimum of 18s. for a 48-hour week after they have paid for their board and lodging. Though overtime is paid for extra, the rate of pay is not high for work that is hard in itself, requires considerable skill, involves long hours of outdoor work in all weathers, and

HARVESTING WHEAT in Hertfordshire, these girls belonging to the Women's Land Army are hard at work. Throughout the country thousands of women are ensuring that Britain's harvest of 1942 will be a record one.
Photo, E. W. Tattersall

frequently means complete isolation in unfamiliar surroundings, where even a bath may be an impossible luxury. One Cornish farmer remarked, "After the land girl is trained she is certainly worth more than we pay for her."

By the end of 1940, 9,000 Land Army members had been placed in jobs. By July 1941, 16,000 were at work in England and Wales, 1,300 in Scotland; and in that month the Queen became the patron of the W.L.A. In the summer of 1942 the number employed had risen to 40,000. Members of the Land Army are exempt from direction by the Ministry of Labour. Their work includes milking and dairy work, general farm work, fruit and vegetable cultivation, the care of livestock, tractor driving, and the hewing and measuring of timber.

The girl transport conductor is a commonplace today. In the London area alone, out of some 19,000 conductors of buses, trams and trolley-buses, 8,000 are now women. They work under the same conditions and for the same hours as the men. Blitz or no blitz, they all carry on. And though after

2 to 3 weeks training they start at 83s. 8d. a week, after 6 months on the road they are paid the men's minimum of 93s. a week, and thereafter work up to the same maximum, 99s. a week. The women conductors employed by the London Passenger Transport Board wear an attractive and comfortable uniform of jacket and slacks in pale grey piped with blue. More than one romance has developed during the two years women have been working as conductors, and the Board finds that a wife conductor behind a husband driver in no way impedes work. But besides the girls who punch the tickets, there is an army of women behind the scenes who keep the vehicles serviceable. All these "back room" duties, from cleaning the vehicles to overhauling their works, are now shared by women. Including those who work on the L.P.T.B. railways as porters, booking clerks, power house and boiler attendants, lamp changers, etc., the Board now employs some 13,000 women.

During the bad blitz period 1,000 women were employed to see to the feeding of the 100,000 people who nightly sought shelter in the London tubes. They worked in two shifts—an evening and a morning one—and were paid 6s. to 8s. a shift, working 6 shifts a week. This part of the Board's organization could be revived instantly at need.

The majority of the women in the service of the Board come from better-class factory jobs, but you may find a court dressmaker acting as a pipe-fitter's mate, a school teacher or a crooner as a conductor, a manageress of a teashop as a labourer, and so on.

Women on the Railways

Transport companies and local authorities all over the country are employing more and more women in jobs usually carried out by men. Forty-four Brighton trolley-bus women conductors recently set up a national record of regular attendance at work; absenteeism among them was less than one per cent. The main line railways too are employing women as porters, booking clerks, ticket collectors, cleaners, etc., in ever-increasing numbers. On the Southern Railway alone over 5,000 women were already engaged at the end of 1941 in place of men serving with the Forces.

The Home Office has more than once urged the appointment of more women police throughout the country, particularly in the neighbourhood of military establishments and munition works, where the presence of a helpful and sympathetic policewoman can often prevent disaster in the lives of thoughtless young women (and men). Some local authorities have listened to the Home Office's urgings—those usually which were enlightened enough to have women police before the war—but not nearly enough have responded. Candidates for work in the Metropolitan Police, which has always led the way in the employment of women, must be 24 to 35 years old, not less than 5 ft. 4 in. in their stockinged feet, and of sound sight out of doors without glasses. Pay during preliminary training (normally 11 weeks, reduced during the war to 4 weeks) is 40s. a week. Constables receive 56s. to 80s. a week, plus a war duty allowance of 2s. 6d. and a supplementary allowance of 7s. 6d.; sergeants receive up to 100s. a week, inspectors up to 145s. a week. The work of women police is advisory rather than repressive, and knowledge and understanding of human beings is an essential part of their equipment. Like the men of the police force, they are out in the blitz and in all conditions of weather.

Many and Varied Tasks of the Women's Services

TRACKING DOWN PARASITES liable to destroy prized tomato plants, these experts in research are engaged in highly important work for the Women's Land Army. They are here seen, hard at work at their horticultural research station in Hertfordshire.

N.A.A.F.I. GIRLS, above, are packing cakes into boxes at the central bakery of the command. These are to be dispatched to the many N.A.A.F.I. depots throughout the country. Over fifteen million cakes and pastries are made each year for the consumption of the forces.

VARIED DUTIES undertaken by women include the familiar ones of nursing and public transport work. Above, a nurse assists convalescent soldiers to enjoy the sunshine in the grounds of a Military Hospital. Two types of uniform worn by London bus conductresses are seen below. The three-quarter coat and grey slacks worn by the girl on the right have now become the official costume as opposed to the more restricted coat and skirt.

WOMEN'S AUXILIARY POLICE CORPS in the City of London was started in 1941, and has proved to be outstandingly successful. Duties include the driving of ambulances and clerical and canteen work. Here is a telephone operator. *Photos, Daily Mirror, Topical Press, Fox*

Our Roving Camera Ranges the Home Front

RECENT APPOINTMENTS. Admiral Sir Charles Kennedy Purvis, left, took up his duties as Lord Commissioner of the Admiralty and Deputy First Sea Lord early in August. He was recently C.-in-C. on the America and West Indies Station. Right, Brig.-Gen. Ira C. Eaker, Commander of the U.S. Bomber Force in Great Britain, who personally led its first raid on August 17, when Rouen was attacked by day.

NEW A.A. ROCKET defends merchant ships against enemy dive bombers. The rocket apparatus shoots parachutes with long wires attached to them into the sky and unless the enemy pilot swerves instantly off his course his plane becomes entangled in the "wire barrage." Above, rocket is seen carrying the wire aloft. Inset, parachute trailing the wire.

Soldiers of the Norwegian Army (right) march past King Haakon at the military parade which formed part of the celebrations in London of His Majesty's seventieth birthday on August 3. The King stands between Crown Prince Olaf and Crown Princess Märtha of Norway. The parade took place in Hyde Park.

GATHERING IN THE HARVEST, these soldiers at first glance appear to be camouflaged. They are lending valuable assistance to a Berkshire farmer during one of the busiest periods of the year

Photos, Central Press, Topical, Sport & General, Keystone

I WAS THERE!

Eye Witness
Stories of the War

With the R.A.F. I Dropped Food Over Burma

Refugees from Burma were helped on their way by food supplies dropped by R.A.F. and U.S. airmen who flew through the monsoon on their errands of mercy. Here is the story told by The Daily Telegraph special correspondent, L. Marsland Gander, who accompanied them on one trip.

STARTING from Calcutta in a big transport plane we flew through cloud and sunshine. Everything was dripping, including our sweating faces. Just before the take-off an air-raid alert caused droves of fighters to take the air, while our crew was on the ground eating ice-cream.

Nothing developed from the alarm. We took off and followed the red-brown snake of the Hooghly River, dotted with boats with square green sails. In a short time we were flying over immense tracts of flooded countryside. Villages and clumps of trees were made forlorn little islands, and great rivers spread formlessly over forest and rice-fields.

From time to time we plunged into clouds, hail lashed us like bullets, and our great wings quivered. Several hours later we were over the trim tea gardens of Assam. We came down from the cool heights to the steaming heat of this aerodrome.

Early next morning I boarded another transport from which the door had been removed, for the first food-dropping trip of the day. While I sat on a pile of sacks containing a ton of food and clothing, our pilot, a flight-lieutenant from Wicklow, Eire, pointed out our destination on a map. The weather having temporarily improved, we were headed for one of the most difficult places, where low cloud would make navigation impossible.

Down the centre of the plane ran a steel wire to which the crew attached themselves with safety lines. An aircraftman, formerly a London lorry driver, stood with his hand jocularly on the wire like a bus conductor about to ring the bell.

We took off towards the distant hills, keeping a sharp look-out for Japanese fighters, which have, however, been very quiet lately. A flight sergeant, an ex-manager of a Manchester store, who has been on 45 bombing raids in Europe and the Middle East, described to me the contents of the bundles. There were

rice meal, tinned meat, towels, soap, stockings, sandals, tea, sugar and a big parcel of books.

He told me that the party we were seeking had on the previous day spelt out with bully beef tins the message : "Thousand starving." He recalled that the piece de résistance of their food-dropping was a barrel of rum, sent down on two parachutes.

Now we were 8,000 ft. up over rugged hills covered to the summits with dark-green jungle. In all directions they extended endlessly, ridge on ridge, while here and there mysterious peaks poked through billowing cotton-wool.

In the dust-filled cabin the crew put on goggles and handkerchiefs over their heads and mouths as we neared our destination. Diving through a cloud ceiling, we began to spiral down in a bowl of mountains till, less than 600 ft. below, I saw a camp of bamboo huts in a clearing on a hilltop.

I caught a glimpse of a message in bully beef tins : " Drop food and drugs."

Then began a series of tricky " bombing runs " over the target. We had no parachutes. The method adopted was simply to stack up half a dozen sacks in the open doorway. An aircraftman, a former Cambridge farm labourer, braced his back against the cabin wall, and, on a light signal from the pilot, pushed the sacks out with his feet. With others I heaved and sweated at the sacks in a choking cloud of dust, and saw them whizzing down through space mostly well within the target area.

I saw several Indians staring upwards, oblivious of the danger from these 30-lb. sacks that went smashing down, sometimes crashing through the roof of huts. To them it was manna from Heaven. Nine times we flew over the camp and pushed out sacks. The figures below rushing to recover them seemed so close that I fancied a lasso could have hoisted them on board to safety, yet they were marooned by a flooded river.

The South African group captain who made the flight with us pointed out landmarks in this wild country. Finding and feeding these lost parties is temporarily his biggest task. He is fighting the monsoon more than the Japanese. There are rescue parties with elephants threading through the jungles who also have to be located and fed. Dumps are being formed. When there is a break in the monsoon the food planes fly from dawn till dusk. On one camp we visited seven tons of food were dropped in a few days.

At Night With My Tank in the Western Desert

The following description of a tanks' battlefield by night, when the supply lorries bring up petrol, water and food, and the tanks are serviced ready for the next day's fighting, was given in a letter from a British tank officer serving in Libya, which appeared in The Daily Telegraph.

WE had been fighting hard all the afternoon, and the going had been particularly stiff. In the lulls we watched the sun—as one always does, trying to will the thing down towards the horizon. How slowly it moves ! But at last it touches the horizon and twilight falls.

With darkness we can no longer clearly distinguish our target ; further firing is just a waste of ammunition. Suddenly we feel utterly weary as tensed nerves relax ; also we feel a great relief that makes many pray, for we have been reprieved for another day.

Over the air comes the voice of the colonel, telling us to rally to a given light signal. Up soars a light, and we take a bearing on it and

move towards it. All around us sound the throb of engines and creak of tracks. Other troops loom up in the gloom, recognize us and fall into their allotted places until the regiment is moving through the darkness in two long lines.

The gunner and the loader doze, exhausted, their faces coppery black with fumes. The driver strains to see the tank ahead, for there are no lights. He is the hero of every tank ; on his mechanical skill our lives depend. He alone can do nothing to hit back, can make no decisions. He can only watch and wait for orders.

Out of the gloom looms another column, silent compared with the boom of our huge engines ; our transport has arrived. It bears petrol, oil, water and food ; perhaps rum tonight. With it come the fitters and medical stores. Often there are wounded men lying on the backs of tanks, where they can be stretched out and kept warm over the engine.

Here and there fires blaze from burning tanks and lorries—relics of the day's struggle —and sometimes we have to make a small detour to avoid being illuminated by them.

Clusters of white illuminating lights rise at different points around us ; these are the Germans. It is no use going after them, as they are probably on the move, too. We should never find them, we might give away our position, and one can see little through the sights at night. There is no " gentleman's agreement " ; we should attack them if we could.

At last we halt and move into our protective formation around the " soft " vehicles— the lorries. The gunner and loader have to be shaken.

Discipline tells, and we move briskly. The driver tells his commander his petrol and oil requirements ; the gunner tells how much two-pounder and Besa ammunition he needs. The commander tells his squadron leader. Guns are cleaned and the tank is maintained. No matter how weary we may be, there is one tradition which will not be broken : the tank will be made mechanically perfect before

THROUGH THE BURMESE JUNGLE plodded refugees during the great retreat of May, 1942. This photograph, taken by a Daily Express correspondent who escaped safely to Assam, shows a line of Naga bearers who carried the party's baggage. The journey of 130 miles took seven days and led them over mountain ranges up to heights of 4,000 feet. *Photo exclusive to* THE WAR ILLUSTRATED

TANK MAINTENANCE is of the utmost importance in desert warfare and, as described in the text, it is the nightly duty of the crew, however weary, to see to their charge and make it ready for the morning before themselves seeking rest. But sometimes more than routine servicing is necessary, and this work is carried out by the Light Recovery Section of the Ordnance Corps. Above are seen two transporters, each with its Cruiser tank, which are being returned to the forward areas after re-conditioning. Inset, a mechanic overhauls a tank engine. *Photos, British Official*

dawn, the tank will be full of petrol and ammunition, and the tank will be spotlessly clean inside ; then some of us may rest.

The supply lorries move along the line, dumping our exact requirements. They have been following behind us as we fought throughout the day. They have been dive-bombed, they have been machine-gunned, they have been shelled—they have no armour. They will finish after midnight, and will rise long before dawn. Then they will go to their rendezvous with the R.A.S.C. and do the whole thing again. Those are the men who form our lifeline, the men of our regiment, our "echelon."

We heave up the heavy petrol tins, the five-gallon drums of oil, and the boxes of ammunition. We draw our rations and pack everything away ; and all the time the bitter wind is blowing. We cannot make tea, we cannot cook or even smoke, for we must not show a light.

The squadron sergeant-major comes along. He plods up the line, not very straight, for he is deadly tired. He has done his full share of work in his tank, he has reported to his squadron leader, and now he brings the orders round. One man per tank for guard. An hour and a quarter per weary man, and we have only five hours for sleep tonight. All members of the crew do guard in turn. To-night it is the loader, and he will be called at half-past two by the man from the next tank. He will listen for the slightest sound that might mean the approach of an enemy laager-raiding party. It is anxious work.

We train the guns outwards, and they are left loaded and cocked. Then we haul the tarpaulins off the backs of the tanks. On those we spread our blankets and roll our greatcoats for pillows. We fold the other half of the tarpaulin back over the beds to keep off frost and dew, place loaded revolvers handy and crawl under the blankets.

It seems but a moment before we hear our unhappy loader called to do his guard, and but another moment before the hum of engines tell us that the echelons are moving out to refill. It is still dark when a sentry shakes us. We roll our blankets and pack them and

stow the tarpaulins. We are quivering with cold and filled with dread anticipation. We wait for orders.

A voice yells "Start up," and almost immediately engines roar. It is a relief to have something to do. In a few minutes engines are warm. A pale streak on the horizon shows the dawn and tanks cautiously move out, just a little way. As the light increases they will move farther and farther until they command a view of the surrounding desert, and there they will await operational orders. If we are lucky they will wait long enough to prepare a hot breakfast.

We Were the R.A.F.'s Rearguard in Libya

The story of the rearguard action fought in the Western Desert by the Allied Air Forces, and of their final retirement from their landing ground almost under the noses of German tanks is told here by an R.A.F. officer.

WE were standing on the landing ground when the bombers returned from their last raid. It was nothing but an arid stretch of desert—a few tents and a thick cloud of dust kicked up by the constant take-off. All around were grouped the air crews, grimy and dust-covered from days of continuous fighting, but still cheerful.

Then the Bostons came back. They had been gone only a few minutes but their bomb racks were empty. The nearest column of tanks, they reported, was only about five minutes' flying time away. It might be on the landing ground within an hour or so. Everybody knew that the withdrawal could

not be longer postponed. Lorries took on board tents and the ground crews. The convoys of trucks formed up and moved quietly on across the desert. The air crews climbed into their Bostons and took off.

At the nearest fighter landing ground the squadrons were still up patrolling over the enemy columns only a few miles from their base. They flew and fought till nightfall.

Then the drama transferred itself to the dug-out which served as the fighter operations room on the landing ground. From time to time news of the enemy tank movements came in on the telephone. Outside in the cool quietness of the desert evening the fighters and bombers alike were dispersed around the aerodrome. All tents had been struck and piled on lorries ready to move off at short notice. Everybody slept out in the slit trenches or on the open ground.

The news that came in over the telephone was not reassuring. The nearest enemy tanks were only 15 miles away. At midnight they were being engaged by the Free French. An hour later the German tanks had been driven a little north on to Gambut aerodrome. At 2 a.m. they had been driven from there and nobody knew where they had gone in the darkness. The moon had set. It was said they had turned to the north-east towards us.

Messengers were sent round the camp shaking sleeping men by the shoulder and telling them to be ready to move off at first light. The hour before dawn was the most anxious, for the fighters and bombers still stood on the aerodrome and the German tank column still hovered somewhere near. We were gathered in the last tent left standing, drinking hot tea from a dixie and chewing bacon and sausage sandwiches to the light of a single hurricane lamp. The field telephone was still ringing with orders to get rid of any surplus aviation petrol, to demolish aircraft that were useless and could no longer fly.

Then it was light, and the shapes of the waiting aircraft gradually formed from the dimness of the landing ground. It was a magnificent sunrise. The trucks formed up into convoy. Two columns of black smoke rose into the air from where two useless aircraft had been fired. Then the squadrons began to take off.

It had been worth it. They had risked staying almost in the front line, so as to be able to strike at the enemy until the last moment. They had been within easy striking distance of the tanks. But now it was light the aircraft were away. The whole force had fought until the last moment and been withdrawn in safety. That was something of a triumph.

S.A.A.F. SQUADRON, serving with the R.A.F. in the Middle East, all packed up and ready to move to another desert landing-ground. Sudden removals such as this are frequently necessary in Western Desert warfare and the efficiency with which they are effected is well described in this page.
Photo, British Official

They circled the landing ground and headed towards the desert tracks to cover the withdrawal of the ground forces. We climbed into our trucks and rumbled slowly after them. All day it was just a steady trek across the desert, lines of trucks, everywhere choking dust, maps and compasses to study, cans of bully-beef for lunch, and a brew of hot coffee that the padre made on a fire of camel-thorn twigs. Overhead swept the

fighters on patrol and never a German aircraft came near us.

By evening we were at the new landing grounds and the whole force was re-formed. The withdrawal was done without fuss, hurry or concern. We came back steadily and brought all our gear with us. Within twelve hours the fighters were fully equipped to fight again and the bombers to recommence their raids.

OUR DIARY OF THE WAR

AUGUST 5, 1942, Wednesday 1,068th day
Air.—R.A.F. bombers raided targets in the Ruhr by night.
Russian Front.—Further German gains at Kotelnikovo, on Stalingrad-Krasnodar railway, and east of Tsimlyanskaya; fighting continued south of Byelaya Glina and Kushchevsk.
Mediterranean.—British submarine sank Italian supply ship and damaged another.
China.—American bombers attacked Jap installations near Hankow.

AUGUST 6, Thursday 1,069th day
Air.—Strong force of R.A.F. bombers raided Duisburg.
Russian Front.—Russians made further withdrawals at Kotelnikovo and Byelaya Glina. At Rzhev Russians gained ground.
Africa.—Land activity confined to artillery exchanges. U.S. Army Air Force bombers raided Tobruk.
China.—American bombers attacked Jap aerodrome at Tienho, near Canton.
Australasia.—Japs announced that their units had occupied the Kei, Aru and Tenimber islands between Timor and New Guinea. Allied bombers started day and night raids on Jap bases in New Guinea and the Solomons.

AUGUST 7, Friday 1,070th day
Russian Front.—German drive to Caucasus continued; Russians withdrew in direction of Armavir. In Stalingrad region fighting continued at Kletskaya and Kotelnikovo.
Australasia.—American and Australian forces started offensive operations against the Tulagi region of the Solomon Islands.
Home.—Sharp attack on East Anglian town in the early hours.

AUGUST 8, Saturday 1,071st day
Russian Front.—Fierce fighting in area of Armavir in Caucasus, and Kotelnikovo and Kletskaya in Stalingrad region.
China.—U.S. bombers raided aerodrome and docks at Canton.
Australasia.—In Solomon Islands operations, a Jap force of cruisers and destroyers was driven off by U.S. naval units during the night of August 8-9.
U.S.A.—A Task Force of the U.S. Pacific Fleet heavily bombarded Jap ships and shore installations at Kiska, Aleutians.

General.—Indian Congress Party resolution demanded British withdrawal from India and threatened campaign of civil disobedience.

AUGUST 9, Sunday 1,072nd day
Air.—Strong force of R.A.F. bombers raided Osnabrück.
Russian Front.—Germans claimed capture of Maikop and Krasnodar. Round Stalingrad Russians continued to put up strong resistance.
Africa.—U.S. Army Air Force heavy bombers made daylight raid on Benghazi.
Burma.—R.A.F. attacked Jap bases in N.W. Burma.
China.—U.S. bombers and fighters raided Haiphong in Indo-China.
Australasia.—Allied bombers made day and night raids on Rabaul, Gasmata, Salamaua and Kokoda.
U.S.A.—American navy patrol planes attacked Jap ships in Kiska harbour.
General.—Mr. Gandhi and leaders of Congress Party arrested.

AUGUST 10, Monday 1,073rd day
Russian Front.—Fighting continued round Armavir, Krasnodar and Maikop; Germans claimed capture of Piatigorsk. In the Don bend Russians countered many attacks.
China.—American Army Air Force bombers made low-level attack on Hankow.
Australasia.—Allied bombers continued raids on New Guinea and attacked Jap shipping off Timor.
General.—German authorities announced that 93 persons had been executed in different parts of France as reprisals for attacks on Germans.

AUGUST 11, Tuesday 1,074th day
Air.—Strong force of R.A.F. bombers attacked Mainz; Coblenz and Le Havre also raided. 16 bombers missing.
Russian Front.—German advance in Caucasus continued, with fighting at Cherkessk, Krasnodar and Maikop.
Mediterranean.—H.M.S. Eagle (aircraft carrier) lost as result of U-boat attack while escorting convoy to Malta

American heavy bombers attacked enemy cruisers in Navarino Bay, Greece.
China.—American fighter aircraft bombed Jap aerodrome at Nanchang.
Home.—Sharp raid on S.E. coast town.

AUGUST 12, Wednesday 1,075th day
Sea.—Free French H.Q. announced loss of submarine-chaser Reine.
Air.—Mainz again bombed by strong force. U.S. Army Air Force fighters took part in sorties over English Channel.
Russian Front.—Caucasus fighting continued round Maikop and Krasnodar; Russians withdrew in Cherkessk region. German attacks held round Stalingrad.
Mediterranean.—During passage of convoy to Malta H.M.S. Manchester (cruiser) was damaged by torpedo or mine, and subsequently sank. R.A.F. attacked aerodrome at Calato, Rhodes.
Africa.—Allied bombers attacked Tobruk and Sollum.
Australasia.—U.S. Marines consolidating their positions in three islands in vicinity of Tulagi. Flying Fortresses made daylight raid on Rabaul harbour.
General.—Mr. Churchill and Mr. Averell Harriman arrived in Moscow for discussions with Mr. Stalin.

AUGUST 13, Thursday 1,076th day
Sea.—Russian warships sank enemy submarine in Gulf of Finland and three transports in the Barents Sea.
Air.—U.S. Army Air Force fighter squadrons again took part in operations over the Channel and Northern France.
Russian Front.—Fighting in Caucasus spread to Mineralniye Vody, E. of Armavir. At Kotelnikovo the Russians counter-attacked.
Mediterranean.—British naval squadron under Admiral Vian shelled Rhodes.
Australasia.—Allied bombers made daylight attacks on Jap convoy off New Guinea.

AUGUST 14, Friday 1,077th day
Sea.—Admiralty announced that convoy had reached Malta despite attacks by U-boats, E-boats, and aircraft.
Russian Front.—Fighting continued round Mineralniye Vody, Maikop, and Krasnodar, where the defences were

penetrated. On Stalingrad front Russians counter-attacked.

AUGUST 15, Saturday 1,078th day
Air.—R.A.F. bombers raided western Germany in bad weather conditions.
Russian Front.—Fighting in Caucasus round Cherkessk, Mineralniye Vody, Krasnodar and Maikop.
Africa.—Our bombers raided Mersa Matruh, Tobruk, and Sollum.
Australasia.—Allied bombers attacked Jap installations on Timor. Enemy pressure increased in Papua.
General.—Five Dutchmen held as hostages for attack on German military train were executed.

AUGUST 16, Sunday 1,079th day
Air.—U.S. Army Air Force fighters again took part in sweeps.
Russian Front.—Evacuation of Maikop announced by Russians. On Stalingrad front Germans made some progress.
Australasia.—Allied bombers attacked Jap base at Timor. In New Guinea Japs occupied Kokoda airfield.
General.—Mr. Churchill left Moscow

AUGUST 17, Monday 1,080th day
Air.—U.S. Army Air Force Flying Fortresses raided railway marshalling-yards at Rouen by daylight. R.A.F. bombed Osnabrück by night.
Russian Front.—Heavy enemy attacks at Mineralniye Vody; in area of Krasnodar the Germans forced crossing of Kuban R.
Australasia.—Jap bombers caused damage and casualties in heavy raid on aerodrome near Port Moresby.
General.—Brazilian Government announced sinking of five ships, including army transport, by Axis submarines.

AUGUST 18, Tuesday 1,081st day
Air.—R.A.F. bombers raided submarine yards at Flensburg. Soviet bombers raided Danzig, Königsberg and Tilsit.
Russian Front.—Fierce German attacks in area of Krasnodar and Piatigorsk; slight Russian withdrawal near Stalingrad.
Mediterranean.—Admiralty announced that other ships lost in convoy action were anti-aircraft cruiser Cairo and destroyer Foresight.
General.—Announced that on his way to Moscow Mr. Churchill visited Cairo and the front at El Alamein.
Brazilian ships on high seas ordered back to port and coastal sailings cancelled.

Editor's Postscript

ONE of the most pleasantly profitable hours that I spend every week is devoted to the News Theatre, and many times I feel that the entertainment and instruction to be had in one of these is vastly better value for money than some of the over-praised full-length films I have recently seen. But as the lion's share in the programmes at the News Theatres is nearly always supplied from America, there is, I think, some danger of our English speech and native idiom being overlaid by Americanisms, not all which are worthy of acceptance. Some of the commentaries spoken by Americans strike so dreadfully on the English ear that one's sense of hearing rejoices in passing from one of these too American sound tracks to the purer and more agreeable speech from the lips of Leslie Mitchell, Stuart Hibbert, or other of the B.B.C. announcers whose voices are occasionally used by British film makers.

MY spirits always fall when I see a travel piece from America announced, for while I know that its photography will be impeccable, I also know that I am going to listen to the most banal comments in the least attractive phraseology, with one dreadful word recurring like the leitmotif in a more tuneful sort of composition. That word is pronounced and repeated four or five times in a five-minute film as "cullaful." The word in itself is not offensive if its use is occasional, but in America it almost rivals "wonnerful" as a sound expressing an idea for which the speaker has not a sufficient vocabulary. I could write at length on this important topic if paper were more plentiful, as I heard an American commentator in presenting a quite admirable film the other night twice use the unknown word "momento," which I took as a mispronunciation of "memento," and I just can't let that go without mention.

I THINK it is incumbent on all English school teachers to warn their children against having their speech corrupted by many of the sounds that accompany American films, and it might be a good exercise to get young people to note down any of the peculiar expressions they hear and report them at school for the teacher's opinion of their use. Incidentally, I have just had a letter from a reader suggesting that it would be worth while issuing a booklet of American phrases on the lines on which I dealt with French and Norwegian in the earlier numbers of THE WAR ILLUSTRATED. Sincerely as I admire the Americans and American institutions (always excepting gangsterism) I do not favour the interlarding of our English speech with Americanisms; but the student who is curious about these matters is already well supplied in American Usage, edited by Mr. H. W. Horwill and issued in similar form to Fowler's English Usage, by the Oxford University Press.

ABOUT forty years ago, when the War Gods were asleep and the London evening papers had to resort to stunts to hoist their circulations, a singularly stupid device was to employ some celebrity to "edit" the paper for one day—or it may have been one week—and the inimitable Dan Leno was chosen to displace the editor of The Sun. I recalled this today in having had rather an overdose of querulous criticism in our evening sheets, which are now reduced to the dimensions of the ha'penny press of forty years ago. For Dan put up an excellent show with the first (it may have been the only) number of the luminary he edited. His leading article was entitled "Whither are we Withering?" It was a joyous farrago of nonsense and was so characteristic that I think he actually composed it himself. As a constructive criticism of our war effort I have

MAJ.-GEN. MARK WAYNE CLARK, Commander of the U.S. Ground Forces in the European theatre of operations, has his headquarters in England. He is 46 years of age and was formerly Chief of Staff of Army Ground Forces at Washington.
Photo, Associated Press

little doubt it would bear reprinting today alongside much of the stuff which amateur strategists and excitable Second Fronters are getting into type.

THE scene, as described to me, a roof refreshment place in the West End whence an impressive view of the multitudinous barrage balloons can be obtained. An American military officer having a drink with an English friend. American: "Is this the sort of weather you usually have in August?" His English friend: "Oh dear, no. It's sometimes worse, but not often, and you must remember you're from California." American ("looking lazy" at the balloons): "Well, I can't help saying it's a helluva climate and you might do worse than cut down these balloons and let the whole darn place sink." The spirit of Mark Twain still inspires the humour of his countrymen.

MORE than two years ago I wrote a paragraph or two about the dishonesty which persists in the human race despite all the moralists and teachers and policemen throughout the Christian era. The occasion was my being informed by a railway director that the average number of hand towels stolen from Pullman car lavatories on his own line every year was fifty thousand. I have just read in my evening paper that the total number of such towels stolen from all the lavatories on the railways of the United Kingdom during the last twelve months was one million! My friend the director was evidently not overstating the pilferings on his own line, as a total on the same ratio for the whole railway system of the country would work out at only three hundred thousand! So it may be that in wartime thieving is done in triplicate like the forms of the bureaucrats. The stealing of a million hand towels involves a considerable proportion of one's fellow countrymen, unless it be that we owe it to a few only who, having started it as a hobby, may have made it a profession. Result: no more towels will be provided in train lavatories, excepting a few only in "sleepers."

WASPS have never been favourites of mine, or yours, I'll warrant. We're having a plague of them this autumn down in Sussex. But we are also having another plague: the Large White butterfly. And the wasps held my attention for a good half-hour after lunch yesterday while I watched them chasing and killing Large Whites! Seven or eight of these butterfly pests were accounted for in that time. The butterfly, like an insect bomber compared to a wasp, was pounced upon in flight by his fighter foe and brought crashing to the ground, where the victor made fairly short work of his prey by eating its head off! The game also gave me excellent opportunities for killing the wasps, which I did not neglect; but I felt some slight compunction when I realized for the first time that these unpleasant insects were doing a good job in thinning out the Large Whites, for they are the butterflies who devastate our cabbage patches.

"PERSONALLY I would rather miss a meal than miss my WAR ILLUSTRATED, and consequently I dare not say too much to my newsagent about the reprehensible practice of writing customers' names and addresses on the front page, concerning which I have complained many times, but so far to no purpose." This is a quotation from a letter received by me the other day from a Leeds subscriber, and while I do not wish to keep recurring to this topic, in quoting the foregoing I would repeat that with very little extra trouble in making their deliveries the newsagents could avoid this disfigurement of copies which are intended to be handled with unusual care and in many thousands of cases to be preserved for binding purposes. A list of the names and addresses of his regular subscribers to THE WAR ILLUSTRATED could be given to the messengers who distribute them. And with this aid to memory it should be possible to put each number into the hands of its purchaser without making the publication itself the guide to his address. As a class the agents are usually anxious and willing to cooperate, and any who take advantage of short supplies to adopt a "take it or leave it" attitude, are only the exceptions that prove the rule.

Printed in England and published every alternate Friday by the Proprietors, THE AMALGAMATED PRESS, LTD., The Fleetway House, Farringdon Street, London, E.C.4. Registered for transmission by Canadian Magazine Post. Sole Agents for Australia and New Zealand: Messrs. Gordon & Gotch, Ltd.; and for South Africa: Central News Agency, Ltd. September 4, 1942. S.S. *Editorial Address:* JOHN CARPENTER HOUSE, WHITEFRIARS, LONDON, E.C.4.

Vol 6   *The War Illustrated*   Nº 137

Edited by Sir John Hammerton

6d. FORTNIGHTLY   SEPTEMBER 18. 1942

HOME FROM DIEPPE after the fierce nine-hour raid by British, U.S. and Fighting French troops on August 19, these two Commandos—tired, battle-stained, but happy—have just stepped ashore at a British port. They triumphantly display the Union Jack which was planted by one of the first parties of British troops to land in the Dieppe area. The flag acted as a beacon to guide incoming raiders to the landing-stage, and assisted our men to find their way back to the waiting ships.   *Photo, Exclusive to* THE WAR ILLUSTRATED

NO. 138 WILL BE PUBLISHED FRIDAY, OCTOBER 2

ALONG THE BATTLE FRONTS

by Our Military Critic, Maj.-Gen. Sir Charles Gwynn, K.C.B., D.S.O.

NEITHER the Russian offensive west of Moscow, nor the Dieppe raid, nor the R.A.F. bombing attacks on Germany can effect an immediate amelioration of the situation. They are encouraging signs of the potential offensive power of the Allies, but till the main German offensive is brought to a standstill their effects will not be fully felt. They should, however, affect Germany's reserve of power to an extent that if her original offensive plan fails to produce decisive results it would be impossible for her to make a major attempt in a new direction this year.

At the end of August the situation in Russia remained as critical as ever, for although the German drive had received checks and been slowed down it was far from exhausted. In Egypt the situation remained in suspense, possibly because the Axis Powers were unwilling while the Russian struggle was at its height to engage in operations which, if prolonged, would make serious demands on their reserves, rather than because Rommel was not sufficiently strong to strike an initial blow.

IN THE FAR EAST the outlook had become definitely more favourable with the consolidation of the recapture of the Solomons and the remarkable successes achieved by the Chinese.

The possibility that the Japanese were concentrating their forces for an attack on Russia could not be ignored. Owing to the growing strength of the Allies and Japan's naval losses the probability of major attacks on India or Australia had receded, but an attack on Russia would—like the offensive in Chekiang—serve a defensive purpose, for, if successful, it would close the door to eventual counter-offensive by the Allies in a vital region.

Although Japan may undertake this or other offensive operations I consider that in the broadest sense she is now strategically on the defensive, and will remain so unless she can gain some tactical success which would retrieve the naval predominance in the Pacific lost in the Coral Sea and Midway Island encounters.

WESTERN FRONT

The story of the Dieppe raid is told fully elsewhere (*see* pages 196 to 201). The value of the raid cannot, of course, be tested by the amount of damage

DON BRIDGES destroyed by the Russians, are seen at a bend of the river in this photograph, taken from a German aircraft. The enemy's powerful bid to cross the Don imposed enormous losses upon the Germans, wave after wave of reserves being thrown in to force a decision.
Photo, New York Times Photos

sustained by the enemy, though the damage inflicted incidentally on the Luftwaffe was sufficient to have real importance.

As a rehearsal the raid showed only how the first scene of an opposed landing would go. Later scenes, such as the extension of the bridgehead, the deployment of a large army, and the landing of immense quantities of reserves of stores and equipment, are problems on which no light was thrown. Nor, in view of the short time covered by the raid, were any attempts made to interfere with the movements of the enemy's main reserves, which might have introduced features notable by their absence, but which discretion forbids mention.

In counting the cost of the raid it should be realized that it involved two major operations—disembarkation and, probably the more costly, re-embarkation.

The information obtained in the raid and the training and experience gained obviously are of great value, but can only be fully assessed by those in possession of complete reports.

The progressive increase in bombing Germany has been evidenced by its extension to new and more distant targets. With longer nights the extension will presumably become even more marked.

RUSSIA

When the Germans succeeded in crossing the Don at its elbow and in establishing a bridgehead from which panzer troops could operate, the fate of Stalingrad seemed to be sealed. Almost at once a serious panzer breakthrough and the development of a terrific air attack strengthened forebodings.

But once again the Russians, as last year at Moscow in its most threatened hours, reacted with amazing gallantry and displayed determined and efficient leadership. Stubborn defence and

prompt and well-directed counter-attacks inflicted heavy losses on the panzer spearhead and placed it in a precarious position.

The first German thrust was thus parried, but Von Bock, though checked, maintained pressure, and while bringing up reinforcements, savagely bombed Stalingrad ; partly no doubt in hopes of damaging morale, but presumably also to interrupt Russian regrouping movements and to destroy establishments producing munitions. Meanwhile the Russian force still retaining their hold on part of the area on the west bank of the Don within the elbow continued to make gallant counter-attacks, though they can hardly have been in sufficient strength to have had much more than a nuisance effect.

MORE important was the stubborn and active resistance offered to the German force directed north-east on Stalingrad from the Kotelnikovo direction. I had expected that this force would constitute the greatest danger to Stalingrad and that the direct attack across the Don might be postponed till the two attacks could cooperate closely. Possibly Von Bock considered this southern attack would suffice to draw off a substantial part of Timoshenko's available forces and that he could not afford to lose time. It would seem in any case that the operations on the

MOSCOW FRONT. At the end of August the Russians crossed the Upper Volga, west of Rzhev. The line in this map depicts approximate Soviet positions on August 30.
By courtesy of The Times

Caucasus front conducted with such a wide dispersion of force may have prevented the reinforcement of the Kotelnikovo army to a strength adequate for its role. There is a limit to which even the Germans can safely afford to disperse their immense strength.

On the Caucasus front itself, although the Germans continued in the last half of August to make progress, their advance was slowed down and the Russian resistance in the hills stiffened—though it hardly appears to have been quite as determined as at Stalingrad. On the whole, it seems possible that the Germans, intent on securing the maximum results in the short time remaining of the campaigning season, may have undertaken more than they can carry through. I can hardly believe, however, that they intend to attempt to overrun Transcaucasia this year ; and their attacks on the Caucasus passes may mainly be to secure an easily-held line with good lateral communications, pending further operations next year.

The attacks directed on Novorossisk and Tuapse, aimed at reducing the power of the Black Sea fleet, are of a different order and attempts to press them home must be expected.

It is difficult to estimate what prospects of success Zhukov's counter-offensive has. Rzhev, Briansk, and other key-points in the

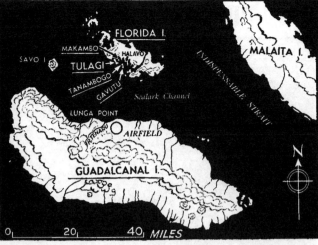

FIGHTING IN THE SOLOMONS resulted in the defeat of the Japanese, six important islands being firmly held by the Americans. U.S. forces in the Guadalcanal and Tulagi area established their positions despite frantic enemy attempts to dislodge them, and Japanese losses were accordingly heavy. A U.S. tank (above, left) makes its way to a forward position on Guadalcanal. American Marines in the background are seen resting during a lull in the fighting. The six islands occupied by the U.S. forces are underlined in the map, above right. *Photo, Keystone. Map, The Daily Mail*

German defensive front must by now be fortresses of great strength and well stocked with munitions and supplies of all kinds. Their capture, if they are held by adequate garrisons of good troops, which must be assumed, would be a great feat. The interruption of the railways by which communication with them still exists, would not produce immediate results, more especially as air transport could probably make good deficiencies in essential supplies.

Zhukov may capture the outer defences of the places, but the hard core of resistance will be immensely difficult to penetrate. It seems probable, however, that he will be able to destroy the value of the centres as springboards for a renewed offensive against Moscow, which presumably the Germans still contemplate or wish to maintain as a threat.

How far it may be possible for Zhukov to by-pass and invest the German strong points depends partly on the strength of Germany's defensive reserve, but an even greater obstacle to such a policy would be the lack of railways, especially when rain and snow limit motor transport. Few lines could be used, for practically all are blocked by German keypoints. The importance of Rzhev, Vyasma and Briansk lies, obviously, in the fact that they are great railway centres.

The apparent inability of the Russians to exploit success to the depth or with the rapidity achieved by the Germans is no doubt in part due to the difficulty of re-establishing railway communications where gauge has been changed from broad to normal. In the last war the Germans took the precaution of cutting down sleepers to a length that made them useless for broad-gauge reconstruction, and they have probably done this again.

Zhukov's offensive may make a valuable contribution towards exhausting German strength and in compelling them to undertake operations that formed no part of their preconceived plans, but I do not think it can be expected to achieve sensational, immediate changes in the situation.

EGYPT

Though Rommel had received strong reinforcements and was expected to take advantage of the August full moon, he made no move; and at the end of August the situation was still in suspense, with General Alexander's troops the more active. [General Sir H. R. L. G. Alexander's appointment as C.-in-C. Middle East in succession to General Auchinleck was announced on August 18, while at the same time Lt.-Gen. B. L. Montgomery became G.O.C. Eighth Army in Egypt].

The successful reinforcement of Malta and the activities of Allied submarines and aircraft on his sea communications may have made Rommel hesitate. The calls made on the Luftwaffe in Russia and for defence in Germany may also have left him with little hope of establishing air superiority.

It is more than ever evident that his invasion of Egypt was a remarkable exploitation of an opportunity, and not the development of a preconceived plan. It very nearly earned its reward, but it entailed the formation of a new plan which probably requires the assurance of continuous support in what might be prolonged operations.

FAR EAST

By the end of August consolidation of the recapture of Tulagi and adjacent islands in the Solomons was completed. The Japanese abortive attempts to retrieve the situation give proof of their discomfiture and it is surprising that they were not made in greater strength.

Their landing at Milne Bay in south east New Guinea shows an immediate intention to make a serious attack on Port Moresby, but the strategic intention may be mainly defensive to gain such control over the Torres Straits as would interfere with future offensive movements by the Allies.

MILNE BAY, New Guinea, was the centre of violent fighting when the Japanese attempted a landing on August 26. Australian troops repulsed enemy patrols. Map shows position of Milne Bay in relation to Port Moresby. *The Daily Mail*

The decisive defeat, under unfavourable conditions, of the Japanese landing is fresh proof of the quality of the Australian troops. General Clowes, whose conduct in the action has been commended, has earned the distinction of being the first general to fight in a landing battle on Australian territory. He must have just turned fifty, for he was in the first batch of cadets to join the Australian Royal Military College at Duntroon when it was founded in 1911. He was then an outstanding figure, good all round and a remarkable athlete. Though of a quiet personality, his strength of character and capacity for leadership were evident. Meeting him in England not many years ago I was delighted to find that he had lost none of his early aptitude. He is a Queenslander, but unlike most Queenslanders, is on the short side.

Chiang Kai-shek's armies have had remarkable successes and have already recovered some of the air bases, the denial of which to the Allies seemed to be the main object of the Japanese Chekiang offensive. It is difficult to believe that the Chinese could have made such progress if the Japanese had not decided to carry out at least a partial withdrawal of their armies, in order to concentrate their strength for a new enterprise.

If so, what will that enterprise be? To me it seems improbable, now that their Navy has been weakened, that they will attack India or Australia. Either would require larger forces than anything they have as yet used, and involve longer and more exposed lines of sea communications. An attack on Russia seems more probable, for although it would also entail large forces a considerable part of the army required is already on its starting line, and its sea communications would be immensely shorter and less vulnerable.

The bombing of Tokio, which probably provoked the Chekiang offensive, has shown how sensitive Japan is to a threat of attack on her home bases, and the elimination of the threat from Vladivostok may well appear to her a necessary defensive measure.

It is true that an air offensive might also be developed against Japan from China, but so long as Japan has control of her home waters she can reinforce her armies in China; and while she retains her hold on the Chinese coastal territory she is provided with a protective shield. The chance of securing a similar shield in Siberia may seem too good to be missed

---

Gen. the Hon. Sir H. ALEXANDER (left), it was announced on August 18, has succeeded Gen. Sir C. Auchinleck as C.-in-C., Middle East, while Lt.-Gen. B. L. MONTGOMERY (right) now commands the 8th Army in Egypt.

Photo, British Official

Speeding to Battle Across the Channel

THE LANDING AT DIEPPE by Allied troops in the great Combined Operations raid on August 19 was due in no small measure to the magnificent work of the Royal Navy. Invasion craft approach the French coast at dawn under cover of a smoke-screen (top). A view of Dieppe during the raid (centre). German coastal batteries and dive-bombing attacks failed to prevent the landing force from carrying out most of its objectives. Some idea of the fierceness of the enemy barrage can be judged from the bottom photograph.

Photos, Canadian and British Official

How Britain's Commandos Attacked Dieppe

Officially described as "a reconnaissance in force," the attack on Dieppe that was carried out on August 19, 1942, was the biggest and most successful "commando raid" to date. The following account is based on the communiqués issued by Combined Operations H.Q., made more vivid by passages from the stories of eye witnesses of the action.

FOR hours they had steamed across the star-spangled Channel towards the coast of France. Now shortly before dawn they arrived off Dieppe at the exact moment stated in the operation schedule. As Lt.-Cmdr. T. Woodroofe put it in a broadcast, "The Royal Navy had carried a large military force right through an enemy minefield in the middle of the night without loss —without, in fact, disturbing the sleep of any one of the soldiers it was carrying. . . . The passage across the Channel was a triumph for the professional sailor."

For their objectives the raiders had the testing by an offensive, on a larger scale than previously, of the defences of what is known to be a heavily-defended section of the coast; the destruction of German batteries, a radio-location station which has played a most important part in the German attacks

Maj. J. BEGG (left) led the Canadian tank crews into the attack. Maj.-Gen. J. H. ROBERTS, M.C. (right), commanded the military force.
Photos, Canadian Official

on our Channel convoys, German military personnel and equipment; and the taking of prisoners for interrogation. Heavy opposition was anticipated, since it was known that, as a consequence of our avowed aggressive policy, the Germans had recently been heavily reinforcing the coastal defences of the whole of the occupied territory. Before the day was out it was to be made clear that the enemy had brought additional troops and guns to the Dieppe area quite recently.

AT 4.50 a.m. or thereabouts the troops were put ashore on the beaches to the east and west of Dieppe, and in the front of the town itself, the landings being covered by a heavy bombardment by the naval guns and the R.A.F.'s aerial umbrella. First to achieve their objective were the men of Lord Lovat's No. 4 Commando, who sprang ashore west of Dieppe at Varengeville.

THE BATTLE OF DIEPPE. Two landings were made by tanks, Canadian infantry and engineers at Dieppe itself, when forces penetrated the town's defences. At Pourville and Puits the Canadians made pincer thrusts against Dieppe. A battery of 6-inch guns was destroyed at Varengeville and many Germans killed or taken prisoner. Canadian landing forces were sighted on their way to the shore and attacked by E-boats at Berneval. These men valiantly carried on, though they were unable to reach their objective—another battery. *Map, Daily Express*

They were entrusted with the destruction of a German battery, and only a few hours before they had been told by Admiral Lord Louis Mountbatten, Chief of Combined Operations, "Your task is most vital. If you don't knock out that German battery the whole operation will go wrong. You have got to do it even at the greatest possible risk." While half of the Commando, covered by mortar fire, made a frontal attack up the white cliffs, another half, led by Lord Lovat himself, landed a little farther west with the intention of taking the battery in the rear.

UP the cliffs went the Commando men, through narrow cracks and gullies which might have been death-traps had the Germans been more prepared. As it was, most of the remarkably few casualties were the work of snipers. Soon the mortars were in action against the German guns. Then, says A. B. Austin, representative of ten national newspapers, who had accompanied the Commando men to the beach, there came an explosion that seemed to be " the father and mother of all explosions," and presently there came back through the trees Major Mills Roberts, the leader of their part of the Commando force, and he was grinning with pleasure. " We've got their ammunition dump," he said; "mortar shell bang on top of it. Bloody fools—they'd got their ammunition all in one lot." A minute later came the message from Lord Lovat: " Flak gun demolished 06.50," and hard on its heels another: " Assault has gone in."

To get at the German gunners the attackers had to cross open ground under fire from carefully-concealed snipers. Two Commando officers fell and several men, but once across the battery wire, says Mr. Austin, it was man-to-man in as fierce an all-in struggle as anywhere that day.

Sniping from his office window was "Hauptmann und batterie Fuehrer" Schoeler, the battery C.O. A trooper kicked in the door, sprayed him with tommy-gun bullets. "Couldn't take him prisoner." he said; " it was him or me." Another trooper killed four Germans and got his section out of a nasty corner after his section and troop leaders had been killed. Working with him was an Army boxing champion fighting in his black and white laced boxing pumps. It was as much a fight of bayonet as of bullet. Troopers barged in and out of battery huts and the houses near, thrusting, stabbing, firing. On the battery commander's wall, along with the battery's list of

Lt.-Col. LORD LOVAT, whose No. 4 Commandos were the first men of the Dieppe raiding force to jump ashore, is seen above, left, comparing notes with an officer on returning to a home port. *Photo, British Official*

names, was an order of the day: " Dienstplan für mittwoch den 19 August, 1942," it was headed, and the first item after rising was: " 6.45–7.00 Frühsport " (" physical jerks "). The battery had its " frühsport " all right, and at the right time, but not quite of the planned type. Farther down the order of the day read : " 10.45–11.45 : Geschütz-exerzieren " (firing practice). Wednesday's firing practice was gravely upset.

When Lord Lovat and his men left the battery there was not a gunner alive except for some prisoners. The ammunition had been blown up, and the six great guns had been shattered by explosive charges detonated inside them.

MEANWHILE the attack on a second German battery to the east of Dieppe, near Berneval, was going not at all well. By a thousand-to-one chance it happened that an enemy convoy was passing along the coast just as the landing was about to begin, so

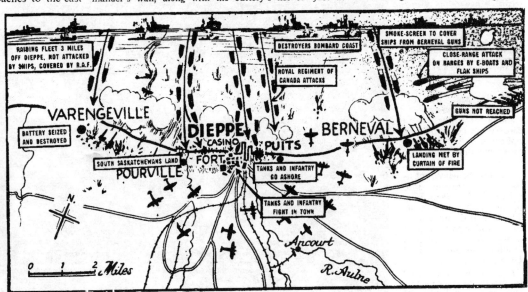

COMMANDO ATTACK ON DIEPPE
(Cont.)

that not only were the Commando craft severely damaged by German flak ships and E-boats, who held their fire until they were only about 200 yards away, but—much more important—warning was given to the Germans defending the coastal batteries.

So it was that (to quote from Reuter's correspondent, Alan Humphreys, who was in one of the tank-landing craft moving off shore) when the Commandos succeeded in landing on the assignment beach they simply walked into a curtain of fire. It came from every small arm the enemy could muster. The defenders even trained their anti-aircraft guns on the beach. Against this rain of death the Commandos, who had needed some measure of surprise to succeed, spent themselves in vain. The guns, first vital objective of the raid, were never silenced, despite the greatest efforts and sacrifices of the Commandos.

But though the attack in this sector was defeated, a small band of Commandos, too small to take the big guns by assault, sniped at them for four hours with exasperating diligence, so preventing them from bringing the full weight of their guns to bear on the crowded British anchorage at Dieppe.

While these two main parties of Commandos were going into action, "sneak" landings were made on the beaches of Dieppe by the South Saskatchewan Regiment at

craft dropped and tanks crunched their way across one of Europe's most popular peacetime playgrounds. With the tanks went the men of the Royal Canadian Engineers to clear the way for tanks to enter the town. There was also an infantry assault on the beach by the Royal Hamilton Light Infantry (of Hamilton, Ontario) and the Essex Scottish (of Windsor, Ontario). The battle was joined.

The thunder of battle rolled over the town of Dieppe ; the sky was filled with aircraft—British aircraft, bombers and fighters. At all levels and in all directions they flew, in twos, in fours, in twelves, in eighteens ; flying in line, in formation, in loose bunches ; flying straight, in great circles, in wide sweeps, in tortuous convolutions uncountable in their great number. " Just like bees round a beehive," said a Canadian corporal.

Equally amazing was the scene on the sea. From close inshore to three miles out lay an armada of all types of craft as thick as the fighters above them, most of them stopped, but with an occasional light craft cutting swiftly among them.

The hours passed. The time came for the withdrawal. A smokescreen along Pourville beach covered the return of the South Saskatchewans ; heading northward, the warships, bombed now and again, laid a really terrific smokescreen, while squadron after squadron of British bombers made a bomb line behind which the tanks and Canadian infantry who had managed to fight their way towards the centre of Dieppe were withdrawn. " As we came home," writes Reuter's correspondent, " the battered remnants of the tank force fought a rearguard action which Canada can well write into her military history."

Naval craft did not leave the French coast until it was known that every possible man had been taken off.

" We had left many brave men behind, and no one will know how or when they died, but we carried out our object," reports Lt.-Cmdr. Woodroofe. " We had safely transported a

large force of the Army across the Channel. We had landed them, including tanks, on the enemy coast ; we had lain off that coast for nine long hours, and brought the soldiers off again. Our losses in ships, comparatively speaking, were small ; but if it had not been for those Spitfires and the pilots who flew them, a good many of us would not have been in that flotilla steaming so bravely towards England.

" We had proved what we set out to prove— that we could transport a large force across the Channel, and land it on an enemy coast."

DIEPPE UNDER FIRE (right), a panoramic photograph taken during the raid. The photograph above of the Dieppe waterfront was taken by Army Cooperation aircraft several days before the raid on the French port. Workmen are seen running for shelter as the plane dives low. *Photos, British Official*

Pourville and by the Royal Regiment of Canada at Puits. Both encountered heavy opposition, which they overcame only with serious loss.

By now the whole coastline had sprung into activity as the Nazis flung up an immense barrage. The British destroyers replied, and a crescendo of heavy firing preluded landings on the beach at Dieppe itself.

As the bombardment ceased (reports Reuter's correspondent), the ramps of the landing

'Thumbs Up' at the End of a Memorable Day

RAIDERS RETURNING FROM DIEPPE are seen (1) embussing at their base port, watched by a group of interested spectators; exhausted and begrimed though they are, the men give the "thumbs-up" signal (2). Two more of the storming party (3), one slightly wounded. 4. These small boys get the thrill of their lives as they chat with one of the Commandos. 5. Blindfolded German prisoners, seen with their captors, receive their first impressions of England.

Photos, Exclusive to THE WAR ILLUSTRATED

THE WAR IN THE AIR

by Capt. Norman Macmillan, M.C., A.F.C.

IN MALTA the Army is helping the R.A.F. by doing building and repair work on the aerodromes, and servicing Spitfires and Wellingtons. Here two soldiers are loading a bomb train for a waiting aircraft. *Photo, British Official*

AT no period of the war has the vital importance of adequate air cover for surface operations been so strongly emphasized. Two operations of different kind have demonstrated this recently in unmistakable fashion.

The last Malta convoy, steaming from Gibraltar to the island fortress, had to run the gauntlet of enemy air attack coupled with the attacks of submarines and torpedo-motor-boats. As will be remembered (*see* page 168) the operation was not completed without loss—the Admiralty described it as a limited success ; but essential supplies did reach Malta. How important is its reinforcement with munitions and other articles can be understood when it is realized that in only one month of the German air attacks did more bombs fall on the whole of Britain than fell on Malta during last April. Sir Archibald Sinclair has said that 20,000 Maltese houses have been destroyed, including three-quarters of Valetta city, and from 30 per cent to 85 per cent of other towns.

In Malta the Army had to help the Air Force in ground maintenance. Air Vice-Marshal Sir Hugh Lloyd reported to the Air Minister : " But for the Army we should have been out of business. The aerodromes were in such a frightful state (from the bombing) that the rollers had to be used continuously for 24 hours on end. We were dependent on the Army. The Army was magnificent." All machinery and technical equipment had to be put underground. Rollers had to be protected by blast-proof pens.

THE most intense air battle ever fought, its fury transcending even the air battles of Britain, was fought over Dieppe from dawn to dusk on August 19. It was directed from the Fighter Command Group H.Q. commanded by Air Marshal T. L. Leigh-Mallory, C.B., D.S.O. (*see* portrait opposite), who

HURRICANE FIGHTERS, manned by the R.A.F. and specially adapted for operating from aircraft-carriers, were used for the first time in escorting the recent convoy to Malta. Up to that time all aeroplanes seen on the decks of aircraft-carriers were special naval types. *Photo, British Newsreel*

had operational control over units of Bomber and Army Cooperation Commands together with units of the United States Army Air Force and Allied Air Forces, for the occasion. This force provided the air cooperation for the Combined Services raid on Dieppe. The twin air objectives were : (1) to hold the air over Dieppe and the Channel so that our ground forces could land, carry out their task ashore, and re-embark, continuously protected from enemy air interference ; and (2) to force the Luftwaffe to fight.

Just as dawn broke and the barges, boats, and warships approached the French coast, Spitfires, Hurricanes, and Bostons attacked the beaches and batteries. Machine-gun bullets, cannon-shells, and bombs cracked and fell among the German troops. Cannon-

shells were fired into the anti-aircraft batteries in the Casino, gun emplacements on the beach, gun posts and defence positions on the headland of Dieppe.

Spitfires formed an air umbrella during the disembarkation, while Bostons attacked a heavy gun position east of the town. Hurri-bombers flew through a hail of flak from the centre of the town, ships in harbour, and the east and west cliffs to attack another heavy 4-gun battery a mile and a half south of Dieppe. Bostons and Blenheims laid smoke screens by dropping smoke bombs as our troops went ashore. Fighters were stepped up in layers from 100 feet to the sub-stratosphere at 30,000 feet, where vapour trails from two Spitfires formed a great V overhead.

Throughout the forenoon fighter squadrons kept up a relay of protective patrol over the area, while bomber squadrons with strong fighter escort dealt effective blows at troublesome enemy gun positions. After dropping its bombs, one bomber squadron fought its way out from the gun target allotted to it, through 25 enemy fighters. A patrolling Spitfire pilot said: " A battery west of the town was firing continuously and bashing at one little ship. Suddenly the whole battery went up in a huge orange flame which burned for half a minute. These guns fired no more."

ONE Hurri-bomber squadron finally silenced the coastal gun battery which held out longest on the cliffs east of Dieppe by attacks made at ground level.

Meanwhile, two squadrons of Flying Fortress bombers of the U.S. Army Air Force escorted by fighters of the R.A.F. and R.C.A.F. made a high level attack on the German fighter base at Abbeville, an aerodrome about 40 miles E.N.E. of Dieppe, causing bursts on buildings, runways, and dispersal areas, and starting fires. All Fortresses returned safely. The Luftwaffe was forced to call on fighters and bombers from the western zones in Belgium and Holland and elsewhere in France.

Army Cooperation Mustangs flew at ground level on reconnaissance, and, returning, reported the state of the battle to British and Canadian Army Air Liaison Officers.

MORE than 3,000 sorties were flown during the day. The air cover was complete. The very few German bombers who succeeded in breaking through the fighter shield were shot down. Every German who dropped a bomb near the Allied force was killed. The accuracy of their bombing was ruined as they were harried about the sky.

Ninety-three enemy aircraft were definitely destroyed, nearly half of them bombers ; more than 100 others were probably destroyed or damaged, but haze and smoke made it difficult for our pilots to see the end of their victims. We lost 98 aircraft of all types. Contrast these figures with those in the Battle of Britain when the Luftwaffe made the attack and lost aircraft in a ratio of five to one. Yet over Dieppe our pilots fought the flower of the Luftwaffe, in pilots and machines, for many of the best German fighter pilots were kept in France to guard against the R.A.F. Of the German aircraft destroyed, 48 were FW 190 and 29 were Dornier 217—Germany's latest fighters and bombers respectively.

The Allied force dropped more than 261,000 lb. of high explosive and anti-personnel bombs ; they fired tens of thousands of rounds of machine-gun and cannon-gun ammunition.

In addition to the R.A.F., the Allied forces included United States, Belgian, Czech, Polish, French, Norwegian, Canadian, and New Zealand air units—truly an international air force. Ground crews worked from 3 a.m. with a will. Their keenness made the thousands of sorties possible.

Next afternoon nearly 500 R.A.F., U.S.A.A.F., Dominion and Allied fighters swept over Northern France in a four-pronged sweep, while Fortresses bombed Amiens railway yards. The skies of France were quiet. The Luftwaffe was licking its wounds. Only the bombers were interfered with. All our aircraft returned.

On August 22 Spitfire pilots flew lower than 1,000 feet over Dieppe. Light flak alone greeted them. The heavy Dieppe batteries were unmanned and silent.

Bomber Command's main targets from August 15 to 29 were Osnabrück (50,000 incendiaries dropped), Flensburg, Frankfort, Wiesbaden, Kassel (locomotive and aircraft factories), Gdynia (Polish port used by the German Navy), Nuremberg (submarine Diesel-engine works), and Saarbrucken. We lost 85 bombers in these raids, and 8 more in lesser raids. In the same period Russian bombers attacked Berlin, Danzig, Stettin, and Koenigsberg, without loss.

THE Air Ministry is to investigate the circumstances of the Sunderland crash in Scotland in which H.R.H. the Duke of Kent was killed while flying to Iceland. I remember Squadron Leader Don, of No. 24 (Communication) Squadron, coaching Prince George, the Prince of Wales, and Prince Henry in flying at Northolt aerodrome in 1930. All three Royal brothers were keen pilots, but only the youngest became afterwards a serving officer in the R.A.F. All pilots who met the Duke will mourn him.

The R.A.F.'s Umbrella over Dieppe

Air Marshal T. L. LEIGH MALLORY, C.B., D.S.O., who directed the operations of the R.A.F. "umbrella" in the Combined Operations raid on Dieppe on August 19. He is the Air Officer Commanding the Group which, by reason of its location, was most concerned in the raid. Air Marshal Mallory has been responsible for the organization of Britain's Fighter offensive since 1940.

BOSTON BOMBER swoops in from the sea to silence a gun post at Dieppe; two bombs are dropping towards the target. The smoke screen is being laid by naval craft.

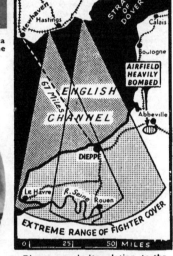

Dieppe area in its relation to the English coast, and the extent of the air cover provided by the R.A.F.

FIGHTERS IN THE RAID. Above, a Fighter formation which was one rib of the "umbrella." Right, U.S. mechanics servicing a Spitfire which, piloted by an American, took part in the operations. Circle, a Belgian ace who, in his Hurricane, led the Close Support Squadrons, the first to go over Dieppe. *Photos, British Official; Topical Press, Planet News, G.P.U. Map, The Daily Mail*

First All-American Raid on Nazi Europe

THE U.S. ARMY AIR FORCE on August 17, 1942, delivered a high-level attack on marshalling yards at Rouen. The giant formation of Flying Fortresses (1), protected by R.A.F. Spitfires, was led by Brig.-Gen. Ira C. Eaker (4), Commanding General U.S. Army Air Force Bomber Command, in the Yankee Doodle (2). Some of this aircraft's crew are seen in one of her gun turrets (3). The attack was completely successful, and every bomber returned safely to its base. For his part in this raid Brig.-Gen. Eaker was awarded the U.S. Army Silver Star (5). Two days later, as part of the Allied operations against Dieppe, two squadrons of Flying Fortresses attacked the German fighter base at Abbeville, and in the photograph below (6) bombs are seen bursting on specific targets : A, north dispersal area ; B, northern end of the N.E.-S.W. runway ; C and D, flak positions. In the right foreground are seven bombs released by a preceding aircraft.

Photos, British Official ; P.N.A., Barratt's

'Abandon Ship!'   Yet Another Atlantic Drama

ATTACKED BY A U-BOAT in the dawnlit waters of the Atlantic this tramp steamer is sinking rapidly.   But the crew is safe and has taken off from the doomed ship in lifeboats, one of which is seen as a small dark object in the centre of the photograph.   The men are cheered and comforted by the reassuring presence of a U.S. Army coastal patrol bomber as it circles overhead, watching over them until the arrival of the rescue ship which it has summoned.   On the extreme right is the wing-tip of the machine.   PAGE 203   *Photo, New York Times Photos*

Brazil's Vast Bulk to Weight the Scales of War

"In the face of acts of war against our sovereignty," ran an official statement issued by the Brazilian Government on August 22, 1942—the most important of the acts referred to being the sinking of 19 Brazilian merchantmen by Axis U-boats since January 19, "we recognize that a state of war exists between Brazil and the aggressor nations, Germany and Italy."

IN America are two United States, and the larger is not the one almost universally referred to in that expression. The United States of Brazil with its three-and-a-quarter million square miles exceeds by nearly 300,000 square miles the territory contained within the continental area of the United States of America.

Brazil is indeed one of the world's monster states, only surpassed in size by the Soviet Union and China. It is bigger than the whole of Europe without Russia, and takes up nearly half of South America. Its chief river, the Amazon, is the largest in the world, unless we count the Mississippi and the Missouri as one; some geographers put its length at 4,000 miles, but no one knows for certain, since some of its upper regions have never been trodden by a white man's foot. To a very large extent, indeed, Brazil is an unexplored jungle, yet on the jungle's fringe and along the seaboard are towns and cities as go-ahead, as rapidly growing, as prosperous and generally comfortable as any in the Old World or the New

AND its resources are a match for its bulk. The world's greatest iron reserves are hidden beneath its soil. Not so many years ago Brazil was the world's greatest, indeed the only, rubber-producing country, and in its jungles millions of rubber trees grow wild. Very considerable proportions of the world's supply of cocoa, sugar, tobacco, and cotton are produced in Brazil; while as for coffee —in Brazil millions of sacks are destroyed in time of glut, such is this mad world of poverty in the midst of plenty in which we live.

Politically, Brazil is a republic like all the other states of South America, but its traditions are Portuguese and not Spanish. From 1500, when it was discovered by a Portuguese admiral, until 1822 it was part of the dominions of Portugal; from then until 1889 it was an Empire ruled by a scion of the royal house of Braganza. Then as a result of a revolution—the first of many—it became a republic with a federal constitution modelled on that of the U.S.A. Such it still was in 1930, when the present President, Getulio Vargas, acquired or seized power. After suppressing one of two attempts at revolution by rival factions, Vargas decreed a new

constitution in 1934, and three years later carried out yet another coup d'état, which confirmed him in the position of dictator, which in fact he had been since his first election.

But, it has been urged, Vargas' dictatorship has little in common with that of Hitler or Mussolini. Under his rule Brazil is authoritarian but not totalitarian. Political parties have been suppressed; there is not even a government party as in Russia and Germany. Coloured shirts, badges, salutes and all the rest of the paraphernalia of present-day political partisanship are definitely banned. Brazilians seem for the most part to accept the dictatorship with a reasonably good grace, although there have been several abortive insurrections and the more incorrigible opponents of the Vargas regime have been given prison sentences of a savage length.

As for Dr. Vargas himself, it is difficult for most people, says John Gunther, to dislike him as he is always so friendly. He is one of the few smiling dictators, and his smile is not put on just to synchronize with the clicking of the camera's shutter. Although he is the most important political figure in South America, he has few enemies and is not given to vengefulness. He talks little: it is said of him that he can be silent in ten languages. His people make jokes about him—and he does not mind. When a newsreel in Rio shows pictures of the President playing golf his performance is such that the audience rocks with laughter.

ALL but his most bitter opponents agree that he has done great things for Brazil. Although his Government has abolished Trade Unions, its record for social legislation is claimed to be the most advanced in Latin America, except for Mexico and Uruguay. He has fostered agriculture and industry,

PRESIDENT VARGAS has been in power since 1930. Formerly a friend of Italy and Germany, he turned against them and their ideologies in 1938.
Photo, British Official

built railways and airports, and doubled the road mileage; done something for public health, and more perhaps for education. But, says Gunther, the regime like to think that their greatest achievement is in the realm of political unification and stability, and perhaps they are right. Before Vargas' time Brazil was more a collection of states—there are twenty-three of them, including the Federal District of Rio de Janeiro, the capital—than a state; since he achieved power he has struck deliberately at the privileges and powers of the individual states, even going to the length of burning their flags at a public ceremony. He has done his utmost to abolish separatism, and his avowed aim is to give his country a true national sense, to give it progress, unity and order.

No one can doubt that this sense of unity has been lacking in the past, largely because of the vast size of the country and the tremendous distances which separate the chief centres of population, but also because of the very mixed character of the some 40 million Brazilians themselves. In the south the population is dominantly white, but in the north negro blood predominates, while the Amazon basin is almost entirely peopled by Indian tribes. So far as the whites are concerned they are for the most part of Portuguese descent, but at various times there have been very considerable waves of immigration, particularly from Germany and Italy. The number of Germans in Brazil is stated to lie between 800,000 and 1,000,000, and there are perhaps twice as many more of German descent, mostly concentrated in the three southern states. The Italians probably number about 300,000, and the flourishing city of São Paulo has been described as being almost as Italian as Turin.

In the war with the Axis powers there is here obviously a fertile field for fifth-column plotters, and for years past Hitler has done all in his power to stimulate Nazism among the German elements in Brazil. But there is yet a third dangerously alien element—the Japanese, who are said to number some 200,000. The yellow invasion of Brazil began in 1912, and Japanese plantation companies, no doubt encouraged and subsidized by the Japanese Government, have succeeded in establishing in many parts of the country large and apparently prosperous colonies. As yet Brazil is not at war with Japan, but there is menace all the same in the presence of this host of yellow colonists.

WHAT in conclusion does Brazil bring to the aid of the Allied cause? She has an army of 100,000 regulars and 300,000 trained reserves; she has a navy including two battleships, two cruisers, and a number of smaller vessels; she has a small but expanding air force. She has a number of harbours, some of them excellent: Rio de Janeiro and Santos are the chief. Then there are her vast stocks and vaster resources of raw materials. But more important than these even is the strategical consideration that the western side of the vital Straits of Dakar—that 1,500-mile-wide stretch of the South Atlantic Ocean between the Brazilian and the African "bulges"—is now brought under United Nations' control.

AT RIO DE JANEIRO the anti-aircraft defences ringing the city have been considerably strengthened since Brazil severed diplomatic relations with the Axis Powers last January. In this photograph the crew of an A.A. battery directional range-finder are demonstrating its efficiency.
Photo, Planet News

South America's Largest Republic Our New Ally

FINE CITIES OF BRAZIL. 1. Bahia, a great seaport, is built on a cliff and along the shore, the two parts being connected by elevators and winding roads. 2. Waterfront of Pernambuco (Recife), capital of the state of the same name. 3. Rio de Janeiro, the superbly situated capital of Brazil, seen from the peak of Corcovado, one of the forest-clad mountains that rise almost from its streets. 4. Tropical trees and modern skyscraper in São Paulo. Map shows how Brazil can help the Allied cause. PAGE 205   *Map, The Daily Mail; photos, Dorien Leigh, Paul Popper*

So These 'Blond Beasts' Plan to Rule the World!

In the course of the fighting in Libya last March there was captured a secret German document concerning the function of the Armed S.S. in the Greater German Reich of the future. A brief account of its contents was cabled from Cairo at the time, but only since the document has been carefully studied in London has its full significance become apparent. A translation is included in the article that follows.

How will Hitler die ? Will it be peacefully in his bed like the Kaiser, whom the politicians vowed to hang at the end of the last war ? Will he fall in battle, or blindfolded before a firing-squad ? Will he be " bumped off " by his generals when his usefulness to them and their class has come to an end, or will he be torn to pieces by an infuriated mob ? There is room here for speculation of the most fascinating, if rather futile, kind. What is more to the point in the circumstances that now prevail is the discovery that Hitler himself has detected a threat to his place and power, and has taken steps to ensure, as far as may be, his hold on the one and the other.

At least, this would seem to be the most reasonable explanation of the Order which we now learn was issued by the Fuehrer two years ago—on August 6, 1940—on the occasion of the reorganization of his S.S. bodyguard. At first it was released only to generals down to and including corps commanders, but in March 1941 Keitel, Chief of

thought of Mr. Churchill's " Some chicken ! Some neck ! " For the first time since Napoleon's day there was one empire from Brest to Warsaw, from the North Cape to the Mediterranean ; some two hundred millions of the human race were included within the ranks of Hitler's subjects, serfs or slaves. Many of them, it might well be believed, were not in the nature of things " well-disposed to the Reich " : hence the necessity to establish a force of " State police troops " to maintain order, to suppress insurrections, even more to nip them in the bud by the relentless employment of headsman, hangman, and firing-party. To continue with the document :

This task can only be fulfilled by a State Police with men in its ranks of the best German blood, who unconditionally identify themselves with the philosophy of life which is fundamental to the Greater German Reich. Only a contingent composed of such men will resist in critical times disruptive influences. Such a contingent will feel a pride in its integrity, and will therefore never fraternize with the proletariat and with that

in such " unsavoury internal affairs." So Hitler had to fall back on his personal guards to do his murdering, and soon special formations of the S.S. were formed, comprising heavily-armed infantry, strong artillery formations, flame-throwing platoons, commando-troops, cavalry, and aircraft.

Always the S.S. has been a body of picked men : the Armed S.S. is, as The Times has put it, " the cream of the scum . . . a class of fanatical, utterly amoral, and ruthless robots." These Black Guards—blackguards in very truth—join the force for long periods of service ; and before they can join they must pass a very stiff racial test. By no means every German, not even the most pureblooded, fair-haired Aryan, can claim the right to enlist in their ranks. Nor may one of the S.S. marry the most Nordic-seeming fräulein. The common German people, the proletariat, are denied the *connubium* with men of the S.S.—with the object, as our document makes clear, of preventing " fraternization " with elements of the populace which might be lukewarm in their adherence to the Nazi scheme of things. Altogether, the Waffen S.S. is designed to supplant the aristocracy of birth, wealth and military rank, to constitute a Herren-caste over and above the Herrenvolk. They are the " blond beasts " of Nietzsche's famous phrase.

As we have learnt, the document was given a wider circulation in the spring of 1941. At that time, a few months before the invasion of Russia, the S.S. was not in good odour with the fighting-men of the regular army, who were jealous of the privileges and the safe existence of the men who might well have been styled Hitler's play-boys. So it was decreed that the Armed S.S., too, should go into action.

Returning home in the ranks of the Army after proving themselves in the field, the contingents of the Armed S.S. will possess the authority to carry out their tasks as " State Police."

And they did go into action, as the communiqués from Hitler's H.Q. in Russia soon made clear. They were most thoroughly " blooded."

But let us read on. Not only is the Waffen S.S. to ensure the good behaviour of the lesser breeds without the (Nazi) law ; it is to be held in readiness to combat disaffection within Germany itself, whether that disaffection springs from the masses of the people or from the ranks of the Army.

The use of the Armed S.S. at home is likewise to the interest of the Armed Forces themselves. It must never again be tolerated in the future that the German Armed Forces, conscripted from the whole people, should be sent into action in times of interior crisis against their own fellow-citizens (Volksgenossen). Such a step is the beginning of the end. A State which is compelled to resort to these measures thus renders itself incapable of sending its Armed Forces into action against the exterior foe, and thereby abdicates. Our history provides sad examples of this truth. From now on the task assigned to the Armed Forces will be solely and exclusively action against enemies of the Reich.

For tasks so great, so important, no mere police force would be sufficient. And the Waffen S.S. *is* no mere police force ; it is an army complete in itself. To an even greater degree than the S.S. and the S.A. of earlier years it is Hitler's private army, and its ten divisions constitute it a rival of the Army proper. It is the Fuehrer's insurance against the day when the Generals may judge that the time has come for the semi-divine Fuehrer to be translated to the Nazi Valhalla.

WAFFEN S.S. IN PARIS. Fresh from campaigning on the Eastern Front, they drive in army lorries along the Champs Elysées towards the Arc de Triomphe at a recent German military parade in the French capital. One of the primary functions of these Black Guards is to keep the people of the occupied countries in a state of terrorized quiet. *Photo. G.P.U.*

the Supreme Command of the German Armed Forces, ruled that it was highly desirable that the Fuehrer's views should be disseminated as widely as possible. Hence the document, a copy of which, marked " secret," was captured in Libya when the H.Q. of No. 2 Troop of the 75th Artillery Regiment was overrun last March. Here is the full text :

Re Armed S.S. On the occasion of the order for the reorganization of the Leibstandarte Adolf Hitler [this probably refers to the conversion of Hitler's S.S. Body Guard from a brigade to a division] on August 6, 1940, the Fuehrer laid down the principles on which the necessity for the Armed S.S. is based. These principles are summarized in the following text.

The Greater German Reich in its final form will not exclusively embrace within its frontiers national units *per se* well-disposed to the Reich. It is therefore necessary to maintain State police troops outside as well as inside the present core of the Reich, capable on any and every occasion of representing and asserting the internal authority of the Reich.

Here it is well to note the date when the Order was issued : the late summer of 1940, when a few weeks after France's collapse practically the whole of the Continent had echoed to the tread of Hitler's legions and it seemed that Britain too must very shortly fall. Already the Fuehrer was wringing our neck in gleeful anticipation, with never a

underworld which undermines the fundamental idea.

Moreover, in our future Greater German Reich only a police force trained to a soldierly mentality will possess the necessary authority in its relations with the other citizens (Volksgenossen).

Through the glorious events in the military sphere and through its education by the National Socialist Party our people has acquired such a soldierly mentality that a " sock-knitting police " (1848) or a " bureaucratized police " (1918) can no longer assert its authority. For this reason it is necessary that this " State Police " should prove itself in S.S. units at the front and should shed its blood like every other contingent of the Armed Forces.

Who are these State Police ? They are the Armed (Waffen) S.S., a most carefully selected and numerous division of the S.S. (*Schutz-staffeln*, protective squads) established by Hitler in 1928 as a sort of élite by the side of the S.A. (*Sturm-abteilungen*, Storm-troopers). The Waffen S.S. would seem to date from after June 1934, when the Roehm executions brought home to Hitler the necessity of having at his instant disposal a band of men who with never a question asked nor a sign of compunction were prepared to do anything and everything at his behest. Seemingly neither Goering nor Himmler were willing to employ the regular State police as executioners, while von Fritsch was equally firm against the use of the Army

Mr. Churchill Spies the Enemy

On his way to Moscow, and also on his return, Mr. Churchill called at Cairo, and in consultation with the political and military leaders reviewed the whole Middle East situation. The Premier also visited the front in Egypt, and here we see him surveying the desert across which, only a short distance away, lies Rommel's army.

At the Front in Egypt

(1) Mr. Churchill in Cairo with members of the Middle East War Council.   Back row : Air Chief-Marshal Tedder, Sir A. Brooke, Adm. Sir H. Harwood, Mr. R. G. Casey.   Front row : Field-Marshal Smuts, the Premier, Gen. Auchinleck and Gen. Wavell.   (2) Mr. Churchill with Sir S. H. Khan, and Gen. Wavell; and (3) with Sir A. Tedder and Gen. Auchinleck.

'Blimey, it's Winston!'

During his visit to the Alamein area, recently the scene of bitter desert fighting, the Premier received an overwhelming ovation from thousands of troops. (4) Inspecting a desert gun site. (5) Accompanied by Gen. Auchinleck, Mr. Churchill drives off from an aerodrome in the Western Desert. (6) Australian troops greet the Premier with a rousing cheer.

Running the Mediterranean Gauntlet

A fierce air and sea attack was launched by the enemy on August 11-14 upon a British Mediterranean convoy. These photographs were taken aboard H.M.S. Manchester, subsequently sunk by an E-boat. (1) A merchantman rides the storm. (2) Escorting warships, including H.M. aircraft-carrier Eagle (in foreground) which was sunk on August 11.

Women's Work and Wages: A Wartime Tribute

In this, the last of three articles in which IRENE CLEPHANE describes the work and wages of women in wartime, we are told of postwomen and the Post Office's women engineers, of the women of Civil Defence and the Fire Service, and of the great host of female workers in the engineering shops and munition works. Finally, there is a tribute to the housewives' who have done such grand and not always properly recognized work in caring for the evacuees.

THAT familiar peacetime figure, the postman, has now in many places become the postwoman. Uniformed postwomen were first seen during the present war in January 1941. They wore navy blue skirt and jacket piped with red, and a navy blue felt hat turned up at the side. Two months later trousers were issued as part of the official uniform to those women who preferred them; and a felt cap with a peak, reminiscent of the caps worn by Victorian postmen, was issued to postwomen and women mail van drivers after August 1941. By the end of 1941 the Post Office was employing 13,000 postwomen. Now (August 1942) there are nearly 15,000.

Soon after war began the Post Office began to take women into the telephone engineering service also. By June 1941 over 1,000 were working as repairers and fitters. Four months later it was announced that 2,000 skilled men had been released for more important work by the substitution of women, who were being trained at the rate of 500 a month to assist Post Office engineers. Today 4,500 women are working in the telephone engineering department, and by the end of this year there will be 5,000. Women Post Office engineers have, since the beginning of this year, received a working uniform of serge trousers and dungaree coats.

Wages vary with the age of the worker and her district: in London, postwomen earn from 36s. to 55s. for a 48-hour week (including mealtimes), compared with 36s. to 65s. for men; in the London suburbs, from 32s. to 52s.; in big provincial towns, from 33s. to 51s.; in the country, from 30s. to 45s. 6d. Women in the telephone engineering service earn from 32s. to 62s. a week. There is in addition a war bonus of 4s. to 10s. a week, according to the rate of pay.

IN Civil Defence women have done trojan service; they fill posts as air-raid wardens, ambulance drivers and attendants, canteen workers, cooks, clerks, cyclists and messengers, telephonists, drivers, etc. In October 1939, 4,396 women were in wholetime paid employment in the Auxiliary Fire Service; in September 1940 there were 5,000, and about half the personnel of the ambulance service were women drivers. At present there are some 25,000 wholetime paid fire-women.

During the worst bombing raids on London women everywhere—paid and voluntary—carried on with cool competence, without paying any attention to personal risks. During one night of raids—Monday, September 16, 1940—one mobile canteen staffed by Women's Voluntary Services served 3,000 cups of tea. Auxiliary Tanner, of the Women's A.F.S., was awarded the George Medal for a typical piece of cool courage: six serious fires were raging in her area, and for 3 hours, in spite of intense bombing, she drove a 30-cwt. lorry loaded with 150 gallons of petrol in cans from fire to fire, replenishing petrol supplies.

In April 1941 a call went out for 1,300 additional paid women as telephonists, watchroom workers, and canteen van workers for the A.F.S.; in July paid women dispatch riders were called for; in September 1941 more women recruits were wanted as motor-cycle dispatch riders, cyclist messengers, and drivers of heavy lorries, hose-laying lorries, motor-cars, canteen vans, store vans, and light vans; while Fire Force commanders were recommended to get indoor

work carried out as far as possible by women—a recommendation repeated in the strongest terms by a recent report of the Select Committee on National Expenditure.

At the beginning of the War women Civil Defence workers received a weekly wage of £2, since raised by gradual increases to £2 12s. A few better-paid posts, ranging up to £400 a year for senior area officers, are open to women in the now unified National Fire Service.

THE largest body of women war workers is in the engineering industry. Before women went into engineering in any large numbers, negotiations between employers and the Trade Unions resulted, in May 1940, in an agreement that, after six months at special rates, women who require no special supervision shall receive the basic rate and the

SCOTS POSTWOMAN, Miss Jean Cameron, setting out on her 14-mile daily round. As recounted in this page, there are now thousands of postwomen throughout the country. *Photo, Daily Mirror*

bonus applicable to men doing the same job. After the fall of France the demand for women in munition factories grew month by month, and it was mainly to fill these vacant jobs that the Government decided in March 1941 on the registration of women. Six months later the Government announced that women between 20 and 30 were liable to compulsory transference to essential work unless they were (1) already in full-time paid employment devoted as to 75 per cent to Government or export work; (2) in full-time paid employment in an undertaking scheduled under an Essential Work Order (under which employees cannot be dismissed or leave without the consent of the local National Service Officer); (3) in a reserved occupation; (4) married and responsible for a household; (5) had a child or children of their own under 14 living with them; (6) were expectant mothers. Wives of men serving with the Forces were not to be called upon to leave home.

DURING the first five months of 1942 the Ministry of Labour placed 757,845 women in all forms of industrial employment—370,000 in munitions. At the present moment there are 1,750,000 more women in

essential industries than there were before the war. This immense increase in the number of employed women has not been achieved without considerable dislocation of women's lives. For instance, London is sending 670 women a month to other parts of the country, Scotland 500 a month to England. Of the 300,000 people employed in the Government's ordnance factories, 60 per cent are women; and these factories are responsible for two-thirds of the gun output of the country. Output per worker has increased during the past year by 40 per cent. In 30 out of these 42 factories, women's hours are 55 or less, and reduction to this standard in the remaining 12 should be achieved by the end of October.

Except for a few very highly-skilled men working extremely long hours, spectacular wages are not being earned on munition work during this war. A recent article in the Manchester Guardian gave the following examples of women's wages. In one factory carrying on mixed heavy and light engineering, the top wage for women was 43s. for 47 hours' work, £2 11s. for 55 hours; extremely quick piece-rate workers could earn up to 25 per cent more. At another factory, girls doing semi-skilled work drew about £2 12s. a week after payment of income tax; during a short rush period exceptionally quick women working a 12-hour day 7 days a week earned up to £10. At a third factory, the average women's earnings were £2 10s. a week. At a fourth, the basic rate was 1s. an hour, working out at about 48s. a week, plus a bonus of 15s.

TWO special difficulties women have had in meeting the demands of industry: shopping, and the care of their young children. By finishing work early on one day a week, issuing cards to women workers enabling them to shop during hours specially allocated to them by the shops, and similar measures, the shopping difficulty has, with the cooperation of retailers, been mitigated. To take care of young children the Ministry of Health has encouraged local authorities to set up day nurseries in charge of a fully-trained matron with trained or partly trained assistants. The Ministry will make a grant up to 100 per cent of the initial cost, and will contribute 1s. a day to the cost of each child, the parents contributing 1s. and the local authority another 1s. to the estimated cost of 3s. per child per day. Some 1,000 wartime nurseries, able to take care of 52,000 children, are now open; another 500 are in preparation. But far more are needed, and suitable women are allowed to take up posts in these nurseries as their war work. Girls in training are paid £52 a year with meals while on duty. Posts at from £150 a year for nursery assistants to £180-220 a year for matrons are available for trained women.

Women have become cashiers in banks, assistants in provision shops, milk roundsmen, packers, even butchers' assistants. Stewardesses on board ship have continued their work, despite the dangers of life at sea in wartime. And in every corner of the countryside are devoted housewives caring for evacuees from our crowded cities—school children, mothers with babies, expectant mothers. The rewards in cash for this hospitality have been nil—the Government allowances have not always covered expenses; but these country and small-town women have rendered a service of inestimable value that has saved thousands of young lives from destruction or damage by bombs.

American Aid for the Hard-pressed Soviets

AT MURMANSK U.S. tanks (1) have been unloaded on to the quay after being safely convoyed through the Arctic. (2) American lorries lined up at a Persian port ready to be driven to Tabriz, 750 miles away, where they will be examined by U.S. specialists before being handed over. (3) An American pilot, who has ferried a bomber to a Russian-controlled airport, discusses the aircraft with the Soviet crew. (4) American-built tractor lorries hauling Russian guns through difficult country.

Photos, British Official; Associated Press, New York Times Photos, Planet News

In Stalingrad, Aim of Von Bock's Savage Struggle

KEY-CITY OF S.E. RUSSIA, against which Von Bock was reported to be hurling a million men at the end of August, Stalingrad is one of the U.S.S.R.'s largest industrial towns. 1, Central Square, showing the Obelisk of Freedom. 2, Soviet horse artillery enter a village, N.W. of the city, to aid counter-attacks against the enemy. 3, Citizens of Stalingrad watch tank-crews leave for the front. 4, Operatives pour out of the great tractor works of Stalingrad at the changing-over of shifts.

Photos, U.S.S.R. Official; Planet News, E.N.A.

SURVIVORS OF H.M.S. EAGLE swimming amidst floating wreckage before being hauled aboard another escort ship protecting a large convoy bound for Malta. She was sunk by a U-boat on August 11, but 930 of the ship's company were saved: an eye-witness account by a survivor appears in p. 221. Originally designed as a battleship for the Chilean Navy, H.M.S. Eagle was completed as an aircraft carrier in '924. Early in this war she hunted raiders in the Indian Ocean. She then joined the Mediterranean Fleet, and her aircraft engaged in operations off Tobruk and Fort Capuzzo, took part in the battle of Calabria, and conducted raids against Italian aerodromes. In 1941 the Eagle was harrying German supply ships in the South Atlantic, but in 1942 she returned to the Mediterranean.   *Photo, Exclusive to* THE WAR ILLUSTRATED

THE WAR AT SEA

by Francis E. McMurtrie

CHIEF place in the naval news continues to be occupied by the Allied offensive in the Solomon Islands area.

If there is one thing that is certain, it is that Japan cannot afford to allow this offensive to proceed unchecked. By following the Japanese method and using each island as a stepping-stone to the next, the reconquest of the whole of the Solomons and of the Bismarck group, farther to the north-westward, may be effected. This would inevitably extinguish the enemy invasion of New Guinea. Not only is it essential on purely military grounds that Japan should arrest Allied progress, but it is also fast becoming imperative from the point of view of prestige—or " saving face " as it is termed in the Far East.

No surprise was felt, therefore, when the United States Navy Department announced that a violent counter-attack had developed. On August 23 a strong Japanese naval force, which included at least one battleship, approached the south-eastern Solomons, occupied by American Marines, from the north-eastward. This squadron may have come from the enemy base at Truk, in the Caroline Islands, some hundreds of miles to the northward. Fortunately, the probability of some such counter-attack had been foreseen by Vice-Admiral Ghormley, whose forces were therefore disposed to meet it.

As in the majority of naval actions in the Pacific, there was no contact between surface ships. Instead, American naval aircraft and Army bombers of the Flying Fortress type attacked the enemy force while it was still at a considerable distance. Several enemy cruisers and a battleship were hit ; the aircraft-carrier Ryuzyo, of 7,100 tons, was severely damaged, and four hits were secured on a larger carrier, believed to be either the Syokaku or Zuikaku, of 20,000 tons. It will be recalled that the former was disabled in the Coral Sea action last May.

As a result of their mauling the Japanese withdrew. Undoubtedly the enemy must be feeling the handicap of losing so many aircraft-carriers, the Akagi, Kaga, Soryu and Hiryu having been sunk in the Midway Island action, and the Ryukaku in the Coral Sea. This leaves only two large and three smaller aircraft-carriers in service, though it is possible that others are completing.

Concurrently with this operation, strong air attacks were made on the aerodrome on Guadalcanal Island originally established by the enemy, but which had since been captured intact by U.S. Marines. At least 21 of the enemy, aircraft were shot down for the loss of only three American planes ; and in a further attack two days later 12 enemy machines were lost as against only one of the defenders. There is no doubt that the air defence was far stronger than the Japanese had expected.

Japanese Defeat at Milne Bay

Under cover of these attacks, and taking advantage of misty weather, three enemy transports, escorted by cruisers and destroyers, landed troops in Milne Bay, at the eastern extremity of New Guinea. In the course of their approach they had been sighted once, off the Trobriand Islands, where a warship described as a gunboat of about 1,000 tons was sunk by Allied aircraft. While the landing was in progress further air attacks were delivered, a transport and six landing barges being destroyed, and a cruiser and a destroyer receiving damage.

An attempt to reinforce Japanese patrols in Santa Isabel, an island to the north-west of Guadalcanal, was intercepted on August 28. Three Japanese destroyers and a seagoing torpedo-boat, loaded with supplies and equipment and possibly carrying some troops, were spotted by reconnaissance aircraft, who attacked the smallest vessel and set it on fire. Before dusk began a force of Douglas dive-bombers arrived and renewed the attack. One of the destroyers blew up and sank, and a second was heavily damaged and may not have survived. The third appears to have escaped under the shadow of the land.

Further particulars of the original landing in the Solomons (see p. 182) reveal that the Marines engaged were specially trained "raider battalions." Men composing these formations are taught to shoot from the hip with whatever weapon is at hand, to fight with knives, throw daggers, and employ any kind of violence necessary to put an enemy out of action in hand-to-hand fighting. They have to be strong swimmers, and able to march

seven miles an hour carrying full equipment. They must be able to direct their course by observing the stars, and to live in the open for long periods if required.

According to the Japanese the strength of the force was about 10,000 ; but this may be a statement made with the object of eliciting the true figure. It is known that all objectives were successfully occupied within less than 48 hours from the initial attack. Two large islands, Guadalcanal and Florida, and several small ones are now securely held as a result of this bold and skilfully conducted enterprise. In a small island off Florida is the harbour of Tulagi, where the enemy had established their headquarters, and adjoining it is Gavutu harbour, formed by the islets of Gavutu and Tanambogo, joined by a stone causeway. Not one of the Japanese garrison of these places surrendered, resistance continuing till all were killed, to the number of 600 or more.

BY the announcement of the loss of H.M. submarine Upholder, with her captain, Lieut.-Com. M. D. Wanklyn, V.C., D.S.O., R.N., and his officers and men, one is sharply reminded of the wonderful work which our submarines are accomplishing. In the Mediterranean, off the Norwegian coast, and in the Far East, they are ceaselessly on patrol in hostile waters, where the least failure to observe strict precautions is likely to result in destruction by depth-charge attack. Yet, in spite of this, the brave men who man our submarines are as cheerful and keen as any in the Royal Navy ; and the amount of damage done to enemy communications, especially those with North Africa, is remarkable. Scarcely a week passes without some achievement of our submarines being reported. Thus on August 29 it was announced by the Admiralty that the submarine commanded by Com. B. Bryant had sunk a large tanker, while others, commanded respectively by Com. J. W. Linton, Lieut. J. D. Martin and Lieut. A. C. Halliday, had damaged various supply ships and sunk one.

AN important part was played by the Royal Navy in the big raid on Dieppe (see p. 197). Not only were the invasion craft provided with strong escort on their passage across the Channel and back, but the enemy were effectually restrained from interfering by sea with the progress of the operation. Though the Luftwaffe did its utmost, it failed to stop either the landing or re-embarkation. Its sole achievement was to bomb the small destroyer Berkeley, which was so severely damaged that she had subsequently to be sunk by our own forces.

LANDING IN THE SOLOMONS, U.S. Marines are seen jumping ashore through the surf on the key island of Guadalcanal, their craft drawn in as close as possible to the beach. It was here on August 6 that the Japanese were taken by surprise at the beginning of the first phase of the Battle of the Solomon Islands. Once they had landed the Americans rounded up enemy groups in the jungle. All attempts on the part of the Japanese to dislodge the invaders from Guadalcanal were a dismal failure. PAGE 215

Photo, Planet News

When the Avila Star Was Sunk Off the Azores

S.S. AVILA STAR, a 14,443-ton Blue Star liner, sunk on July 5 by U-boat 300 miles off the Azores while homeward bound from Argentina.

STUMBLING ABOARD the Pedro Nunes is one of the 27 survivors who were landed at Lisbon on July 26 ; the 28th died an hour after rescue. During their long ordeal at sea rations had been reduced to two biscuits and ¼ pint of water per day.

IN THIS OPEN LIFEBOAT, one of seven launched, 39 persons, including two girls—Patricia Traunton and Mary Ferguson—set out to reach the African coast. Eleven died from injuries and exposure during the terrible twenty days that passed before the survivors were picked up by the Portuguese sloop, Pedro Nunes. *Photos, Associated Press, Fox*

PATRICIA TRAUNTON, still cheerful despite illness and injury, is shown (above) being carried ashore at Lisbon, and, below, wrapped in a Portuguese officer's cloak.

Britain's 6-Pounder on the Bench and in Action

IN THE MIDDLE EAST one of Britain's six-pounders is in action. This desert battery has changed over from the two-pounder to the six-pounder anti-tank gun, with most satisfactory results. The new weapon outranges the German 3-in. gun, and has remarkable armour penetration.

Completed six-pounder gun (left centre), one of large numbers now being turned out at a Royal Ordnance factory built since the war. More than half the operatives are women, and above is Miss Brenda Harris, once a thermometer-maker, who now works a drilling machine. Mr. Lyttelton, Minister of Production, paying a tribute to women in ordnance factories, said that they were doing skilled men's jobs really well, working 56 hours a week.

Barrels ready for sending to the finishing workshops (left). The six-pounder, named after the weight of the projectile, has a 2-in. calibre. It possesses a high rate of fire, and in this respect beats the slow-firing six-pounder which the Germans have mounted in their Mark III and IV tanks. The new British gun is very mobile, can be got into action in a minute, and requires a crew of five.

Photos, British Official: Sport & General, Keystone

HISTORIC SCENES IN MOSCOW were enacted on August 12, 1942, when Mr. Churchill arrived for his momentous talks with Stalin. The Prime Minister is seen with Mr. Molotov and Mr. Averell Harriman (top) at a march past of the Red Guards, the famous Moscow regiment. These men took the oath, "Stop Hitler—or die!" when the city was besieged last autumn. Mr. Harriman and the Russian Foreign Commissar stand on the Premier's right as the National Anthems of the three allies are played at Moscow airport, left. Marshal Shaposhnikov, Chief of the Soviet General Staff, is seen immediately behind Mr. Molotov. Maj.-Gen. Sinilov, commandant of the Moscow garrison, greets the Prime Minister (right).

VIEWS & REVIEWS Of Vital War Books

Stalin's Russia Seen by an American Ambassador

In this, the first of what is hoped will be a series of informative rather than critical reviews of books which have a definite bearing on the origins, course and future development of the war, we are enabled to report something of the Russian scene as it was viewed by an acute-minded and keenly observant American—Mr. Joseph E. Davies, U.S. Ambassador to the Soviet Union from 1936 to 1938. His book, Mission to Moscow, is published by Messrs. Victor Gollancz, Ltd., at 15s.

JOSEPH E. DAVIES, an American lawyer, who was U.S. Ambassador to the U.S.S.R., 1936-1938, Ambassador to Belgium and Minister to Luxembourg, 1938 to January, 1940, and then became Special Assistant to the Secretary of State in charge of War Emergency Problems and Policies at Washington.   *Photo, Topical*

WHEN Mr. Davies presented his credentials to Mr. Kalinin—it was on January 25, 1937—the President of the Soviet Union expressed his satisfaction that America should be represented in Moscow by an Ambassador who " by his training would take an objective view of conditions and would reserve his judgement until all the facts had been fairly seen in perspective." Superficial snap judgements, said Mr. Kalinin, were unfair ; and by way of illustration he pointed out that even though a visitor might see some drunkenness on the streets of Moscow, it would not be right for him to draw the conclusion that all Russians were drunkards. " See as much as possible of what we are doing and trying to do for the people, and assess it judicially and objectively "—that in effect was his counsel to the new Ambassador.

But Mr. Davies was in little need of the advice. He went to Russia with his eyes open, and from the outset he explained his own way of approach with the utmost frankness, even to Stalin himself. " Yes," the great man told him laughingly, " we know you are a capitalist, there can be no doubt about that." During the eighteen months Mr. Davies was in Russia he saw everything and everybody, listened a lot and said, it would seem, not very much. His book is evidence enough of his intense curiosity, of his determination to get behind the facade of propaganda, to pierce the screen of native exaggeration and foreign lies so as to see Russia and the Russians as they really were in those critical months when the cauldron of war was already being stirred.

AT the time of his arrival in Moscow the second Five Years' Plan had almost run its course, and many pages of his book are devoted to a description of what had been actually achieved. On the whole, our wealthy, deeply cultured and essentially liberal American was surprised by what he saw ; and the facts that he reported to Washington were received, it would seem, with considerable surprise. Yet in his view that achievement does not necessarily constitute an advertisement of the virtues of the Communist way of things. After a few months' stay he gave it as his considered opinion that " it is the enormous wealth of the Soviet Union and, particularly, the agricultural wealth of the country which enables this communistic and socialistic experiment to project and sustain itself with the apparent success which it has "; and one of his earliest conclusions was that Russia is not really a communistic state—at least, not in the usually accepted sense.

Russian workers, he was surprised to find, get what they earn. The communistic principle, " from everyone according to his abilities and to each according to his needs," has gone by the board. Production is stimulated by premiums and extra wages for service above the " norm." The profit motive and self-interest are the mainspring. Industrial plants are required to, and do, make a profit ranging from 5 to 30 per cent, which goes to the Central Government.

Somewhat later Mr. Davies accepted the view held by many Marxists that Russia is a Socialist State on the road to Communism, but he moved beyond John Strachey and his fellow Communist theoreticians in recognizing that patriotism would be the guiding

impulse of the future. " The idea of the world proletariat and revolution," he wrote, " has been set aside and replaced with the idea of a nationalistic Russia." Certainly in this respect the course of events during this last year of war has justified Mr. Davies' opinion ; many times it has been remarked that Stalin in his appeals to the Russian people to resist the invader has based the call upon love of the native soil rather than upon defence of the Bolshevik Revolution.

FOR much of the time that Mr. Davies was in Moscow society was convulsed by a succession of " treason trials "—of Radek, the well-known publicist, Sokolnikov, former ambassador to London, Marshal Tukhatchevsky and a group of his generals, ex-Commissar Rykov, Bukharin the Bolshevik theorist, and the rest. At the time it was almost universally believed outside Russia that these were a " frame-up " on the part of the Stalinists who hoped thereby to extirpate the remnants of the rival Trotsky faction. But Mr. Davies, who attended many of the sessions, saw the accused men in the dock, and heard them make their extraordinary confessions, concluded that there was plenty of substance in the charges and that the accused were fairly tried and justly condemned according to Soviet law.

'Fifth Columnists ? They Shot Them '

That was his opinion at the time, but he did not realize the full implications of the affair till some years later. In 1941, three days after Hitler had launched his invasion of the Soviet Union, Mr. Davies happened to be delivering a lecture at his old university in Chicago. " Someone in the audience asked : ' What about Fifth Columnists in Russia ? ' Off the anvil, I said : ' There aren't any—they shot them.' " He gave the reply on the spur of the moment, but on re-examining the evidence and his own notes he was more than confirmed in his conclusion.

WHAT actually had the conspirators planned ? Mr. Davies declares categorically that the principal defendants had entered into an agreement with Germany and Japan to aid them in a military attack upon the Soviet Union. They had agreed to, and actually cooperated in, plans to assassinate Stalin and Molotov, and to project a military uprising against the Kremlin which was to be led by General Tukhatchevsky. In anticipation of war they had agreed to, and had actually planned and directed, the sabotaging of industries, the blowing up of chemical plants, the destruction of coal mines and the wrecking of transport facilities. They agreed to perform and did these things pursuant to instructions received from the German General Staff, and they disclosed to Germany and Japan information vital to the defence of the Soviet Union. Apparently what they had in mind was the formation of an independent but considerably smaller state which would yield up large sections of the Soviet Union—the Ukraine and White Russia to Germany and the Maritime Provinces on the Pacific to Japan. Fortunate, indeed, was it for Russia—and in the event for us—that the conspiracy was nipped in the bud. " There were no Fifth Columnists in Russia in 1941," repeats Mr. Davies, " they had shot them. The purge had cleansed the country and rid it of treason."

Mr. Davies left Moscow in the summer of 1938, but from the embassy in Brussels he was able to watch at close quarters the rapid deterioration of European affairs. Deeply interesting are his pages concerning the happenings of 1939 : he reports a complete lack of realism in assessing Germany's military strength, although the Russians recognized as early as 1936 the menace of Hitlerism and the necessity for some system of collective security. They were ready to fight for Czechoslovakia, and expressed their willingness to cancel their non-aggression treaty with Poland so that their troops would be able to move through Poland to aid the Czechs in accordance with their treaty obligations. He speaks of the Moscow-Berlin pact as a " catastrophic calamity . . . probably one of the greatest diplomatic defeats the British Empire ever sustained "; and makes use of the striking phrase, " the Russian bear has taken a handsome revenge for being thrown out of Munich."

PERHAPS the most interesting and valuable of Mr. Davies' pages are those which constitute what he calls his " brief on the facts " —really a political, economic and social survey of the U.S.S.R. as he saw it. He notes the elements of weakness—such things as Russian native inertia and fatalistic quality, bureaucratic inefficiency, the tyranny over life and liberty exercised by the secret police, the substitution of worship of a man or men for the worship of God, the dangers of one-man rule and the hostility of the adjacent states. But there is much to be stated on the other side. He describes the resolute character of the Communist Party leadership and the impressive strength of the Red Army ; above all, he emphasizes the universal belief in " Father Stalin." " The strength of the present regime," he told Mr. Cordell Hull, " is found in the resolute, bold, and able leadership of Stalin. He has complete control of the army, the secret police, the newspapers, the radios, and the schools. Stalin is fast becoming, along with Lenin, the ' superman ' ideal of the masses. For the present this regime is firmly entrenched. There is always, however, the threat that hangs over dictatorships. Barring accident or assassination, coupled with a *coup d'état*, the present regime will persist for some time."

That was written in June 1938. What the future holds for Russia only a fool would venture to prophesy ; but at least Joseph E. Davies may claim that up to now events have not made mincemeat of his judgement of Russian men and things. E. ROYSTON PIKE

The Duke of Kent Killed on Active Service

THE KING'S YOUNGEST BROTHER, H.R.H. the Duke of Kent, killed in a flying accident in Scotland on August 25, latterly held the rank of Air Commodore, and was Chief Welfare Officer of the R.A.F. Home Command. While proceeding to Iceland on duty he met his death. He had flown thousands of miles since the outbreak of war, including a long air tour in the summer of 1941 in Canada and the U.S.A. to inspect the Empire Air Training schools. Later in the year he toured service establishments in Northern Ireland, and since 1939 he had inspected very many factories and Civil Defence centres, as well as Naval and R.A.F. establishments. In the photograph above he is seen at Queen Mary's Hospital at Roehampton.

MAJ.-GEN. R. L. McCREERY, D.S.O., new Chief of the General Staff, Middle East. As a cavalryman he captained the 12th Lancers polo team.

CORNISH TIN MINES have been re-opened and are being prospected and worked by sappers of the No. I Tunnelling Company of the Canadian Army in Britain. The loss of Malaya has made the home production of tin a matter of urgent importance to the Minister of Supply.

GEN. SIR H. M. WILSON, G.B.E., K.C.B., D.S.O., Chief of the newly-created Persia-Iraq army command. He has seen much service in the Middle East.

IN THE ENGLISH COUNTRYSIDE scenes of war and peace alternate. Left, a special mobile military policeman attached to a tank unit guides a Covenanter to a "harbour" in the woods. These highly-trained men have to acquire a detailed knowledge of roads suitable for rapid tank traffic and for swift mobilization and concealment. Right, boys from Aldenham School, Herts, help with the potato harvest.

I WAS THERE! Eye Witness Stories of the War

The Sea Poured Relentlessly Into the Eagle

The following description of the sinking of the aircraft-carrier Eagle in the Mediterranean on August 11 was written by Arthur Thorpe, Reuter's special correspondent, who was also rescued from the Ark Royal.

I WAS in an ante-room with three officers soon after 1 p.m. when two tremendous crashes shook me out of my chair. It seemed as though the walls of the room were tumbling in. We knew what they meant and leaped to the door. As we opened it two more violent explosions rocked the aircraft carrier. I heard steam hissing viciously and saw clouds pouring up from below into the broad aft deck across which we were running. As we dashed through the bulkhead to gain the upper deck the ship was heeling over crazily and water was washing about our feet.

We scrambled up the ladder to the upper deck with the ship listing over terrifyingly to the port side on which we were. The sea, normally ten feet below the rails, was surging ominously a bare two feet below them. We reached the quarter deck and grabbed anything we could to haul ourselves up the steeply sloping deck to the starboard side. Clutching the bullet-proof casing enclosing the quarter deck, I found myself next to a first lieutenant who was blowing up a lifebelt. I followed suit.

Looking round I saw the deck slanting more sharply than a gabled roof. Six-inch shells weighing over 100 lb. tore loose from their brackets and bumped down the cliff-like deck. Ratings on the port side saw them coming and flung themselves into the water to escape injury. Foolishly I asked No. 1 lieutenant, " Is she going ? " He nodded.

SEVERAL ratings, grasping the casing, clambered towards us. They fastened a stout rope to the deck, they slithered down into the thick oil welling out under the ship and coating the sea and drifted away. With perfect confidence in my lifebelt I slid down and let go.

I went under the waves, and when I rose to the surface I realized with horror that I had not put enough air into the lifebelt.

My head was barely above water. With all the poor swimmer's dread of deep water, I splashed and kicked clear of the ship. As I got out of the oil patch the sea became choppy and every wave washed clean over my head till I was dizzy. I gave myself up for lost.

No wreckage was near me which I could grasp. Then as a wave lifted me I saw a glorious sight—a cork float twenty yards off with sailors clinging round it. I fought madly to reach it. Three times my head went under and then I saw the float a few feet away. I snatched despairingly, but missed. Making another wild clutch, I felt my fingers grip.

HALF-A-DOZEN ratings holding on tried to loosen ropes to open the cork raft out. It was tied up like a round bundle. Their oily fingers made the task impossible. The water was quite warm, but I had difficulty in holding on firmly owing to my oil-smothered hands. Another rating swam up and caught hold, too. He told us his leg was broken. We helped him to crawl on to the centre of the bundle. As the waves broke over us I pulled myself up and saw the Eagle two hundred yards away. She was lying on her side. Down the great red expanse of the ship's bottom men like ants were sliding down into the sea.

Suddenly I felt a shock at the base of my spine. I knew it was a depth charge from a destroyer hunting the U-boat which had caused it. " She is going ! " gasped one of the men. Then came a mighty rumbling as the sea poured relentlessly into the Eagle, forcing out the air. The water threshed above her in a fury of white foam and then subsided. She had gone.

We looked hopefully around and cheered when we saw a destroyer a hundred yards away making for us. We were soon alongside. Ropes and cork lifebelts snaked down the side. Smiling faces encouraged us. My

H.M.S. EAGLE seen from one of her own fighters. Of the 21 aircraft which she was able to accommodate, some were in the air when the disaster happened, but others went down with her.   *Photo, P.N.A.*

sailor colleagues grasped the ropes and hauled themselves aboard. I clutched at a trailing rope, but could not hold on till a rating halfway up slid down and propped my body with his legs. I was feeling as weak as a kitten, but I managed to slip the looped rope under my shoulders. Just then a wooden ladder clattered down the side of the destroyer. I succeeded in climbing aboard with a helping pull under my shoulders, feeling half dead and as brown as a nigger from head to foot in the fuel oil.

The decks of the destroyer were crowded with survivors and scores more were being pulled aboard. We raided a bathroom and rid ourselves of most of the oil. The destroyer's officers and crew were wonderful. They opened up their kits and stores and soon we were all equipped with dry clothing. Many of us were sick through swallowing fuel oil, but tots of rum put our greasy stomachs right. We laughed at one another's quaint costumes. Some of the officers were dressed in long pants and vests ; others in football jerseys, grey flannels and coloured shirts. Some found shirts, but draped towels formed their clothing from the waist down.

OUR late ship's war-cry, " Up the Eagles ! " rang out earlier as Capt. Mackintosh came alongside on a float. He had held his command a bare six weeks. Then I saw an unforgettable scene. Another ship drew alongside, her decks packed with survivors.

As officers and men on the destroyer recognized those aboard her there was a glad bedlam of cries of recognition and bantering cheers.

I heard of many tales of heroism, of narrow escapes and humour. I met the commander first. He was wearing his gold-braided cap. He swam to the destroyer, but, knowing that gold-braided caps are irreplaceable now, he determined to stick to his and came aboard with his cap jammed on firmly.

A young Fleet Air Arm sub. swam to the ship with a rating minus a lifebelt on his back. " I heard him crying ' No Lifebelt,' he said. He climbed on to my shoulders. I told him to kick his feet. I swam with

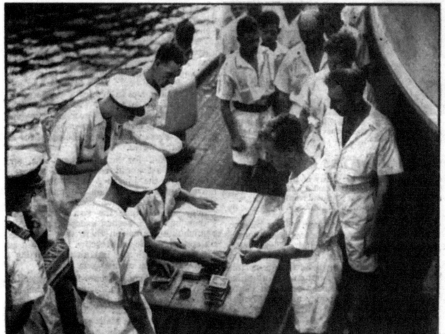

SURVIVORS OF H.M.S. EAGLE drawing their pay on arrival at Gibraltar. They had been provided with fresh kit by the crew of the destroyer which rescued them from the oily sea; a dramatic picture of the rescuers at work is shown in the exclusive photograph in page 214.

Photo, British Official: Crown Copyright

my hands and reached the destroyer after an exhausting fight.''

Another man on the port side of the flight deck had a leg broken by the blast of the explosion. Trailing his injured limb behind, he performed the astonishing feat of climbing up the flight deck and sliding down a rope into the water. He swam to a destroyer and was picked up.

In sharp contrast to these experiences was that of the first lieutenant, who left the ship after me.

All the men in " C " boiler room escaped. They swam in the fuel oil to the hatches,

scaled half a dozen ladders, and still had time to get away and be picked up.

Later in the afternoon the survivors were transferred to another destroyer. On her, too, we found the officers and men eager to do anything for us.

We heard the glad news that 929 officers and men had been saved from the Eagle. The ward-room of the destroyer that night looked like a common lodging house. Twenty-odd officers slept on chairs, on the floor, and in hammocks, dirty and unshaven and arrayed in a weird assortment of garments.

Lt. Sidebottom's megaphone, referred to in this page, which he used throughout the exciting action against the German R-boat ; as will be seen, it is pierced by bullets and shell splinters. *Photo, News Chronicle*

I Turned the Wheel Hard Over and Rammed

On August 16 our M.T.B.s engaged German R-boats in the Straits of Dover and sank or damaged four of them without loss to themselves. Lieut. D. C. Sidebottom, R.N.V.R., who commanded one of our patrols, told the following story of his part in the action to a News Chronicle reporter.

WE found the enemy much nearer the coast than usual. That stimulated every man aboard to extra effort. We made for the rearmost ship of the enemy formation and a violent action began.

We came to close quarters and ran into a hail of fire. I realized that my best chance was to ram, and I gave the order accordingly.

As we swept in a burst of pom-pom fire knocked out all four of the men on the bridge with me, including the coxswain at the wheel and my second-in-command. As the wheel swung over when the coxswain fell, the boat's head swung off and we passed under the stern of the German ship.

At the moment I was single-handed on the bridge, so I grabbed the wheel, turned it

hard over and rammed. The bow of my boat was forced right into the starboard quarter of the R-boat and we continued to drift on in company.

I tried to signal ''stop,'' but the telegraph was shot away and I had to get a rating to deliver the order. As we stopped the German ship tore herself free and made off. Later reconnaissance showed the vessel was sunk.

The second-in-command of Lieut. Sidebottom's boat said : " Though wounded in the leg by a shell splinter, Lieut. Sidebottom stood at the wheel as coolly as though on manoeuvres. A megaphone he held in his hand throughout the action was riddled by bullets and shell splinters.

spades. I did what the others did : that is to say, I unwillingly dug trenches and willingly buried dead Germans. But even the best of occupations grows tiresome after a time ; and so, after ten days, I said to myself, Why bury Germans who have been shot by someone else ? Why not shoot Germans for someone else to bury ?

I calculated about where the Polish lines could be, and during the night I disappeared. I reached Lwow. How I did it I cannot tell now. In Lwow I was caught by the German military police, and was thrown into a prison which had not been demolished, and in which I was given nothing to eat or drink. Time passed slowly, until one morning through the strange quiet came a rumbling noise. I jumped to the window and saw a Russian tank thundering by. World events had taken pity on my plight and changed my German prison into a Russian one—not, of course, for long. As soon as I had shown the Russians that I was a Czechoslovak who wanted to join in the fighting, I was given, in the proper order, something to eat, to drink, to smoke, clothes to wear, and the means of getting to Moscow. The Russians treated me and all the Czechoslovaks of whom I know extremely well.

IN Moscow I reconsidered the situation and said to myself : I can only reach France (where everything was still in order) by travelling around the globe. For this I need a great deal of money and a number of visas. I have a sister somewhere in the Antipodes, and so the Russians advised me to say that I wished to join her. They promised to give me an exit visa and thought that the Japanese would give me a transit visa. They said, further, that as soon as I reached Shanghai I should have less to worry about. Every half-hour boats were leaving Shanghai for all ports of the world.

So I asked for the necessary visa, and meanwhile set about earning the money I needed for the journey. As it happens, I am an optician in civilian life, and I found work immediately and made considerable money by the time the visa was granted. I then had all I needed except the visa for Manchukuo, of which there was, naturally, no representative in Moscow. I set out on my journey with the intention of getting a Manchukuo visa on the spot.

At one time I spent twenty-four days and as many nights in a train. Then I alighted and started working again for a time. As far as I can remember from what I read in some book or other, men made war in this way in ancient times. The soldiers sowed in spring, waited for the harvest, gathered the crops, ground the corn for flour, and then pushed on again.

RAMMING THE ENEMY SHIP provides a dramatic point to Lt. Sidebottom's description of his encounter with the R-boat, the story of which is given in this page. His brother officers are evidently amused at the gusto with which he demonstrates how it was done. *Photo, News Chronicle*

I Went Round the World to Join the Czechs

Recently there arrived in Britain to join his regiment in the Army of the Czechoslovak Republic a young Czech soldier who had spent two and a half years in making the journey. This story of his experiences is reprinted from the Czech newspaper Denni Hlasatel (Daily News), published in Chicago.

THE last legal act I performed in Europe was to purchase a ticket for the last performance in a cinema in the Ostrava district of Czechoslovakia, close to the frontier with Poland. I sat and watched the performance, within the bounds of the law, and then I stepped into the law of the prairie, but of a fiercer nature. As I came out of the theatre, in fact, I walked right into the arms of some Gestapo men who were rounding up recruits for war work in Poland. The war between Germany and Poland was already raging. I was only seventeen years old, but perhaps I looked older, although I doubt that

this really made a difference. They put me, together with others, into a lorry, and started us on our way to Poland. There were several stops en route, generally made to enable new Gestapo agents to make certain that the last group had not missed anything when searching us. During one such search I was relieved of my money and my watch ; during another I yielded up my leather coat.

We were at length deposited somewhere in Poland near a river, along the banks of which there had been some rather stubborn fighting done. We were given shovels and

I earned the means to continue my journey ; and, when I had collected enough money, I went on to Manchukuo. At the frontier station, as I descended from the train, I caught sight of the honourable guard. As the soldiers saw me they raised their guns, not to present arms but rather to stand ready for action. I was hurried off to police headquarters. There I was cross-examined. Japanese officers, who spoke Russian, examined me. They asked me all sorts of things about what I had seen on my journey, You can guess the kind of things they wanted to know. I answered plainly that I did not know anything. The examination lasted a long time ; and although I do not know a word of Japanese, I guessed that one Japanese officer said to another, " I have never seen such a blockhead before, let him go." They did, in fact, let me go ; but I had to wait seven days in that miserable hole, with the result that the first place I stayed at in Japan, when I reached there, was the hospital. It was a very modern American hospital. It was a pleasure to be ill there. The Americans, the doctors, and sisters gave me, a Czechoslovak in Japan, the means wherewith to continue my journey to France.

THEN I went on to Shanghai. There I reported for enlistment in the army and waited for a ship. Again I sowed and reaped. I was, among other things, a waiter and also a bodyguard. That is quite a common occupation in Shanghai, in which one can easily engage. I was a bodyguard to a certain important tobacco trader. His name was Wong. I received good pay—but not for long. Through the tender care of some gangsters in the pay of a rival trader, Mr. Wong was gathered to his forefathers.

Finally I had orders to sail. We stopped at Singapore and some African ports. The journey was safe and quiet.

Now here I am in England, in the Czechoslovak army. How many miles did I travel from Ostrava to England ? About 30,000.

CZECH TROOPS recently took part in a three days' invasion rehearsal in this country. Here is seen a member of a mortar crew sighting his weapon. Such men as these typify the fighting spirit of the Czechoslovak Army. The adventures of a Czech now serving with this army are recounted in the preceding page.
Photo, British Official

OUR DIARY OF THE WAR

AUGUST 19, 1942, Wednesday 1,082nd
Air.—Flying Fortresses attacked enemy fighter base at Abbeville.
Russian Front.—Evacuation of Krasnodar announced by Russians.
Africa.—Large contingent of U.S. Army Air Force arrived in Middle East.
Australasia.—Fortress bombers attacked Jap warships in the Solomons.
General.—Nine-hour Combined Operations raid in Dieppe area.

AUGUST 20, Thursday 1,083rd day
Air.—Nearly 500 fighters engaged in sweep over N. France while U.S. Fortresses bombed railway yards at Amiens.
Russian Front.—Fighting continued S.E. of Piatigorsk and S. of Krasnodar in Caucasus, and on Stalingrad front round Kotelnikovo and Kletskaya.
Africa.—S. African Air Force bombers raided Tobruk.
Australasia.—Loss announced of cruiser Canberra in Solomon Is. action. Jap unit of 700 men which landed in the Solomons was wiped out by U.S. Marines.

AUGUST 21, Friday 1,084th day
Sea.—Russian warships sank 3 enemy ships in Barents Sea and tanker in Baltic.
Air.—In air battle over North Sea, 11 Flying Fortresses destroyed or damaged 6 F.W. 190s.
Russian Front.—Fierce fighting continued in Don bend near Stalingrad.
Australasia.—Admiral Nimitz announced that on Aug. 17 U.S. Marines raided Makin, in Gilbert Is., and wrecked enemy seaplane base.

AUGUST 22, Saturday 1,085th day
Sea.—Admiralty announced loss of H.M. submarine Upholder.
Australasia.—U.S. Marines engaged in mopping up Jap forces on captured islands of Solomons.
General.—Brazil declared war against Germany and Italy.

AUGUST 23, Sunday 1,086th day
Sea.—Fourteen Danish fishing-vessels seized in prohibited waters and brought to British ports.
Air.—Emden bombed by two Wellingtons at midday.
Russian Front.—Fierce fighting continued for the Don crossings near Stalingrad.

Africa.—Tobruk harbour raided by our heavy bombers.
China.—Recapture of three important cities in Kiangsi announced by Chinese.
Australasia.—In raid on Darwin area 4 Jap bombers and 9 fighters were shot down.

AUGUST 24, Monday 1,087th day
Air.—U.S. Flying Fortresses bombed shipyards at Le Trait, near Rouen. R.A.F. made night raid on Frankfurt and Wiesbaden.
Russian Front.—Germans drove wedge into defences at Kotelnikovo.
General.—Mr. Churchill arrived in London from his visit to Moscow.

AUGUST 25, Tuesday 1,088th day
Russian Front.—Germans made further progress towards Stalingrad.
Africa.—New Zealand troops made successful raid on centre sector of El Alamein front.
Australasia.—U. S. Navy Dept, announced sea battle in Solomon Is., in which 2 Jap aircraft-carriers were damaged
Home.—Duke of Kent killed in aircraft accident while flying to Iceland.

AUGUST 26, Wednesday 1,089th day
Air.—Russian aircraft raided Berlin, Danzig, Königsberg, Stettin and Tilsit.
Russian Front.—Russians announced advance in regions of Rzhev and Kalinin.

Australasia.—Japs made fresh landing at Milne Bay, on S.E. tip of New Guinea, in face of heavy air opposition.

AUGUST 27, Thursday. 1,090th day
Air.—Bostons, with strong fighter escort, bombed Abbeville. Hurricane bombers hit four ships off Dieppe. U.S. Fortresses bombed shipyards at Rotterdam. R.A.F. made night attacks on Cassel and Gdynia ; 30 bombers missing.
Russian Front.—Bitter fighting in outskirts of Rzhev. German thrusts in area of southern Volga slowed down.
Australasia.—Japanese fleet, attempting to retake Solomons, withdrew. U.S. naval planes sank one Jap destroyer, probably sank another, left third burning.
General.—Lord Moyne appointed Deputy Minister of State at Cairo.

AUGUST 28, Friday 1,091st day
Air.—U.S. bombers attacked air-frame factory at Méulte, near Albert, and fighters swept St. Omer and Etretat regions. At night R.A.F. bombers raided Nuremberg and Saarbrücken ; 30 missing. Soviet bombers destroyed Finnish Army supply H.Q. at Helsinki.
China.—Chinese re-took Chuhsien.
Home.—Bombs fell on three omnibuses at Bristol, causing many casualties.

AUGUST 29, Saturday 1,092nd day
Sea.—Admiralty announced sinking by

submarine of three Axis supply ships and a tanker in Mediterranean.
Air.—Boston bombers attacked docks at Ostend and power stations in Lille-Lens area. U.S. Fortresses bombed aerodrome near Courtrai. Russian bombers attacked Berlin, Königsberg, Danzig, Stettin and other German towns.
Russian Front.—Further Russian counter-attacks north-west of Stalingrad and in Kletskaya area.
Africa.—British warships and aircraft bombarded Rommel's tank repair shops and store dumps at El Daba.
Australasia.—Allies now hold six main islands of Solomons. Jap planes raided American positions on Guadalcanal but were repulsed with loss of seven. Flying Fortresses made heavy night attack on aerodrome at Buka.
China.—Recapture by Chinese of air base at Lishui, in Chekiang announced.

AUGUST 31, Monday 1,094th day
Russian Front.—Germans claimed southern advance to within 15 miles of Stalingrad. Russians gained more ground in Kletskaya area.
Africa.—Rommel's forces launched attack on 8th Army's southern flank in El Hemeimat area.
Australasia.—Allied H.Q. announced withdrawal of Japs from Milne Bay, Papua, with heavy losses. Severe fighting in Kokoda area.

SEPT. 1, Tuesday 1,095th day
Air.—Strong force of R.A.F. bombers made night attacked on Saarbrücken. Soviet aircraft raided Warsaw.
Russian Front.—Defenders of Stalingrad made further withdrawal south of city. German forces to north-west, east of R. Don, almost encircled. Axis claimed capture of Anapa ; on Black Sea.
Africa.—Infantry attack in central sector repulsed. Rommel's tanks made headway in south.
Australasia.—Fierce jungle fighting at Kokoda, Papua.
Home.—Day attack on S.E. coast town Night raiders bombed towns in N.E. England.
General.—Maj.-Gen. G. R. Pearke.. V.C., commanding 1st Canadian Division appointed G.O.C.-in-C. Pacific Command. Togo, Jap Foreign Minister, resigned. Post taken over by Premier Tojo.

★════════ *Flash-backs* ════════★

1939
August 23. German-Soviet Pact of Non-Aggression signed
Sept. 1. Invasion of Poland.

1940
August 19. British evacuate Somaliland.
August 24. First bombs fall in central London ; 52 raiders destroyed.

August 25. First British bombs on Berlin.
August 26. Chad Territory declares for Free France, first French possession to do so.
August 31. Eighty-nine raiders destroyed over England.

1941
August 25. British and Russian forces enter Persia.

OUR admiration for the marvellous achievements and superb spirit of the Red Army need not involve equal admiration for all the national institutions of the Soviet Republics. But there are those in England who show a tendency in that direction. Our own vast Bureaucracy with which the War has saddled us and which will probably cling to its well-paid jobs for a generation after the War, is heading, here and there, along the Soviet paths of progress. It will be an evil day for Britain if it is allowed to proceed too far on one particular path : the monopoly of publishing and the press. It may be that the Soviet method of controlling all publishing enterprise is good for the Russian people in its present stage of national development, but no sensible person would advocate its substitution for our own free press and independent publishing. Yet we have already travelled a little way in that direction. H.M. Stationery Office appears inclined to enlarge its monopoly of official publications by entering the lists as a people's publishing house in subsidized competition with publishers whose energy and enterprise in open competition have rendered invaluable service to the nation for centuries.

A BEAUTIFULLY produced booklet telling the thrilling story of Ark Royal from her building to her sinking has just been issued by H.M. Stationery Office at ninepence : a quite uneconomic price if all costs of composition and production are reckoned. But that is not my complaint : the booklet contains a good deal of matter, both textual and pictorial, which would seem to have been withheld from the press for many months so that an " exclusive " value is given to this official story, which has slowly been compiled by some gentlemen at the Admiralty. The Battle of Britain was the first of these lavishly produced and admirably compiled official booklets which have taken the bookstalls by storm, and I have just received the latest ninepennyworth by Mr. Eric Linklater, The Highland Division, in an attractive series that already includes half-a-dozen titles. No independent publisher could provide such books, requiring heavy tonnage of the best printing paper, at the price charged. The purchaser, in buying his copies of these brightly written, instructive publications, does not pause to ask himself how much he should add to the nimble ninepence out of his taxes for the maintenance of the public departments concerned in their production. One detects, moreover, a growing jealousy on the part of H.M.S.O. towards independent publishers issuing books of national importance. In my opinion, any bureaucratic ambition to snaffle the popular publishing market ought to be firmly resisted, and at present I can perceive no such effort on the part of those makers of books who are so competent to supply the public with all the literature it requires and who represent a noble craft that has given hostages to English culture for full four hundred years. One further point : these beautiful booklets actually lose in value by bearing the imprint of H.M. Stationery Office : " propaganda," sneers the hostile critic abroad (or even at home). Is he altogether wrong ?

IN our valiant efforts to perform all that is required from each one of us by way of observing the numerous orders in which the liberty of the subject (laughingly so-called) has now been completely swamped, there is one direction in which punctilio is leading, I think, to a measure of waste. That is starting your black-out needlessly soon. Scores of thousands of conscientious householders begin about seven o'clock to get their houses properly blacked-out when the official hour is 7.45, let's say. Result, all is set for official darkness anything between fifteen minutes and half-an-hour in advance, and interior illumination starting so much earlier than need be involves the consumption of a good deal of electric current, gas, or paraffin that might otherwise have been avoided. At least that is what I have noticed in my own home and in the houses of others, and while one had better err on the right side, so far as the black-out is concerned, I think the possibility of waste lighting should be considered and the horrid, boring, nightly fag of blacking-out effected with neatness and dispatch to coincide with the advertised time. The only exception to this, I think, should be on unusually dark evenings, when (as happens occasionally) darkness has come upon us even sooner than the official time had allowed for. A million houses (not an improbable figure) each with even five minutes of extra black-out implies a mighty lot of ampere hours.

I WAS interested to read in a dispatch from one of the correspondents in Egypt that motor drivers and troops wearing sun helmets mean only one thing—new troops. " After a few days the men lose them, throw them away or hide them, because nobody wears them in the desert." I have often wondered why the pith helmet should be thought a necessary issue in tropical and sub-tropical campaigns. I have wandered all over Europe, Tunisia, Algeria, and Morocco, though not always in the height of summer, with nothing heavier than a panama and more often than not carrying that in my hand. In South and Central America I found that by going bareheaded I was more comfortable than wearing even the lightest of hats (a cap was worst of all), and during a motor tour through Spain in the heat of July I never once wore a head covering of any kind, nor did I notice many of the natives wearing any sort of hats, while on three Riviera holidays in blazing summers I entirely renounced headwear. My own theory is that if you perspire freely in strong sunshine you run no risk of sunstroke, while with a sun helmet or a panama you can sweat too much to be comfortable. Which may be all wrong from a doctor's point of view, but this paragraph I've just read about Tommy in the desert seems to give my opinion some support.

AT the beginning of the War I wrote, more than once, that the progress of hostilities would inevitably involve the need for surrendering a large measure (how large I did not then foresee !) of our long-boasted liberties. Hitler is primarily to blame that Democracy in the full and proper sense of the word must go into cold storage while we improvise methods of near-despotism to fight autocracies. We can still rejoice in our Parliament even though its wings may temporarily be clipped : we know its full feathers will sprout again. But there is a detestable feature of the French Revolution, the Russian Revolution, the Nazi Revolution—of all revolutions indeed—that has sprung up with our multitudinous wartime regulations which have created innumerable new legal offences : the anonymous letter. Petty jealousies, envy, personal dislikes, breed sneaks, spies and informers. I'm told that a large proportion of the prosecutions for alleged offences in petrol supply originate in anonymous complaints from disgruntled motorists, and I have had evidence that the anonymous letter-writer is busy in other directions trying " to get one back " on this person or that to whom he may have some ill will. Even if the accused has an excellent case and is exonerated by the court the informer has the vile satisfaction of having put him to wasteful trouble. Society is right in its contemptuous attitude to the malicious informer.

FOLLOWING upon my recent remarks on Dame Rumour, Paul Tabori, author of Epitaph for Europe, told me this delightful story which should find a place in any collection of wartime wit. It was current in Holland soon after the valiant and much-enduring Dutch had recovered sufficiently from the initial blitz to muster a smile again. The Nazis had built a dummy aerodrome somewhere in Holland to mislead the R.A.F. But to no purpose, for those eagle-eyed avengers twigged the trick and destroyed the dummy aerodrome a few days later by attacking it with dummy bombs.

ALLIED LEADERS at the Kremlin. This photograph, taken at one of the meetings of the Moscow Conference last month, is historic in that it was signed by both Mr. Churchill and Mr. Stalin. It shows the two Prime Ministers in genial mood. *Photo, British Official : Crown Copyright*

Printed in England and published every alternate Friday by the Proprietors, THE AMALGAMATED PRESS, LTD., The Fleetway House, Farringdon Street, London, E.C.4. Registered for transmission by Canadian Magazine Post. Sole Agents for Australia and New Zealand : Messrs. Gordon & Gotch, Ltd. ; and for South Africa : Central News Agency, Ltd.—September 18, 1942. S.S. *Editorial Address :* JOHN CARPENTER HOUSE, WHITEFRIARS, LONDON, E.C.4.

Vol 6 *The War Illustrated* N° 138

Edited by Sir John Hammerton

SIXPENCE

OCTOBER 2, 1942

BATTLE IN BRITAIN! Under conditions resembling as nearly as possible "the real thing," men undergoing a course at the Royal Marines Battle Training School in the West Country advance to storm a heavily-constructed and well-defended strong point. The Marines are trained to carry out landings, attack prepared positions, and face fire from live ammunition, and in a special assault course they are initiated in the highly-developed technique of unarmed combat and the overcoming of formidable obstacles, ranging from barbed wire to the scaling of high cliffs.

Photo, Central Press

NO. 139 WILL BE PUBLISHED FRIDAY, OCTOBER 16

ALONG THE BATTLE FRONTS

by Our Military Critic, Maj.-Gen. Sir Charles Gwynn, K.C.B., D.S.O.

WHEN Parliament met on Sept. 9 Mr. Churchill gave an encouraging review of the general situation. We have reason to think that it was not over-optimistic in spite of the increasingly serious situation in Russia.

In Egypt our position had been greatly improved by the defeat of Rommel's attack. In the Far East the Allies were steadily consolidating their defences and had made the first counter-offensive moves. In China Chiang Kai-shek's armies had struck back

ADMIRAL OKTYABRSKY (in oilskins), commander of the Russian Black Sea Fleet, is seen aboard the cruiser Krasny Krym. He was in charge of the naval base of Novorossisk, which the Russians evacuated on Sept. 11. Situated on the N. Caucasian coast, Novorossisk became the main Black Sea base for Russian warships after the fall of Sevastopol last July. *Photo, Keystone*

with much greater success than could have been expected in their isolated position. Mr. Churchill's report on the achievements of the Allied navies and on the progress made in the anti-U-boat campaign was particularly heartening; and his explanation of the purpose of the Dieppe raid confirmed the generally accepted view that it was a necessary and largely successful reconnaissance in force.

EGYPT On Monday, August 31, Rommel's expected attack on the 8th Army, under its new commander, Gen. Montgomery, was launched. The main position of the 8th Army did not extend from the sea to the Qattara Depression, but was L-shaped, running southwards from the coast to include the Ruweisat Ridge and then with its flank thrown far back eastwards. The gap between the angle thus formed and the Qattara depression was closed by minefields and guarded by mobile troops.

As was anticipated, Rommel's main attack with his armoured and motorized divisions struck at this gap; while his less mobile divisions, mainly Italian, delivered an attack, probably intended only to hold our troops to their ground, against the west-facing front of the position. The latter attack was easily repelled, sustaining heavy losses, but the main attack made progress through the minefields. Rommel was evidently repeating the tactics he employed in his original attack at Gazala, intending to bring our armoured troops to decisive action and then roll up the flank and cut off the retreat of the main body of our army. This time, however, he had not the open spaces of the desert available for rapid manoeuvre, and his advance through the minefields was perforce slow and deliberate. Furthermore, General Montgomery had no intention of

seeking a decisive armoured encounter against an opponent who still possessed some superiority in weight of armament, though not in numerical strength, and who was highly skilled in the employment of anti-tank artillery. Any serious reverse our armour suffered might have had disastrous results; it therefore fell back, harassing the enemy's force and inflicting casualties on it as opportunity offered—exploiting the advantage of its superior speed.

When he had got clear of the minefields Rommel turned sharp north, striking towards Montgomery's main line of communication; but here he found our turned back flank fully prepared to meet him with masses of 6-pdr anti-tank guns and 25-pounders. On Wednesday (Sept. 2) the crisis of the battle came; for Rommel, constantly losing supply vehicles from Allied air attacks and the harassing tactics of our armour, had no option but to attack our strong flank which, owing to his supply difficulties, he could not by-pass or turn. He launched his armour against it, but, failing to make an impression and suffering heavy casualties, retreat became the only course he could take. Slowly and deliberately he fell back in good order, retrieving many of his damaged vehicles, but leaving many on the battlefield which was in our possession.

Rommel had sustained a heavy reverse, but not a crushing disaster; for Montgomery, although he launched counter-attacks to recover lost ground and inflict punishment, was not in a position to deliver a counter-blow on a scale which alone could have gained a decisive victory. His enemy was still formidable and he himself was still awaiting the reinforcements dispatched at the time of the disaster in Libya. He had fought a highly successful defensive battle and, as he expressed it, " had given his enemy a bloody nose."

By the end of the week Rommel was back practically in his original position, but much

AXIS FORCES were pushed back westward of the Hemeimat minefields following Rommel's attempt to pierce our lines in the Egyptian desert at the beginning of September.
PAGE 226 *By courtesy of The Times*

RUSSIAN FRONT, showing the approximate battle-line in the early days of September. At Leningrad and Rzhev the Russians returned to the attack, but in the Stalingrad area Von Bock's Nazis were making tremendous efforts to reach the Volga. *By courtesy of The Times*

weakened and retaining only bridgeheads in our minefields. These might eventually facilitate renewal of attack, but it was evident that, with his land and sea communications constantly under attack by our Air Force and Navy, it would be some time before he could gather strength for a new attempt. A lull has again set in, and it may not be Rommel who will break it.

What was the scope of Rommel's intentions when he delivered his attack? Did he consider that he was strong enough to carry through a far-reaching invasion of the Nile Delta, or had he a more limited object? I suggest that his main object was to inflict another heavy defeat on the 8th Army and to drive it out of the El Alamein bottle-neck before it received further reinforcements. His hand was to some degree forced, and he was compelled to act before he had gathered strength sufficient for a more ambitious campaign.

THERE is, of course, no saying where he might have stopped if he had won a really crushing victory; but even if he had only forced the 8th Army to retire with heavy losses the situation for us would have been very serious. He would have gained a sally-port from which a more ambitious campaign could be launched when his strength had grown. Furthermore, if our Navy were forced to use a base farther east than Alexandria, Rommel's sea communications would be less precarious, and reinforcements released from Russia during the winter would no doubt have reached him. As a result of the battle he has not even achieved this limited object, but now finds himself in a weakened condition faced by Montgomery's growing strength. Moreover, the 8th Army has gained complete confidence in its new commander and suffered no serious loss.

The Allied Air Force played a great part in the victory and a new high standard of co-operation with the Army has been attained. Rommel's air force had been reinforced, though perhaps not to the extent that might have been expected, but it never was able seriously to challenge our air superiority or to achieve important results, even when used for concentrated attacks.

RUSSIA

With Von Bock concentrating the bulk of his forces on the Volga front and pressing his attack on Stalingrad regardless of cost, the situation by the middle of September had become more serious than ever. The Russian resistance continued to be magnificent, and the removal of shipping up the river was a sign that the battle would be fought out without thought of retreat.

Von Bock's first drive against the city from the north-west looked at one time likely to succeed, but it was met by strong counter-attacks and defeated. Then the attack from the Kotelnikov direction seemed to be most dangerous, but it was checked by stubborn Russian defence. In desperation, Von Bock, bringing up fresh reserves, then hurled them at the city from the west in the centre of his line. Maintaining his attack relentlessly with his armour, supported by immense concentrations of aircraft, he drove a wedge into the Russian defences, and slowly closed on the outskirts of the city—using his infantry prodigally to expand the opening made. The losses on both sides mounted at an appalling rate.

Russian reinforcements from the north, though in the later stage unable to reach the city, meanwhile strengthened the force which had retained its hold west of the Don in the Kletskaya area. Gallant attempts were made by these troops to bring relief to the city by counter-attacks on Von Bock's left flank; but though they had some success, these counter-strokes did not succeed in reducing the violence of the German main attack. Nor could the Russian Air Force seriously dispute the air superiority which the concentration of the Luftwaffe had locally established. Yet till the middle of the month Russian tenacity had checked all Von Bock's attempts to achieve decisive results.

In the Caucasus the weight of the German attack had obviously been reduced by the necessity of using all reserves on the Volga

MADAGASCAR, the Vichy French island controlling the southern gateway to the Indian Ocean. Here, on Sept. 10, Britain was again forced to take military action, and successful landings were made at various points on the west coast. *By courtesy of News Chronicle*

front. The drive eastwards along the Baku railway towards the Grozny oil-fields and the Caspian coast was maintained; but after a precarious foothold had been secured across the Terek river it was brought to a standstill sixty miles short of Grozny.

There had been no slackening, however, in the attack on Novorossisk and, five days after a premature claim by the Germans to have effected its capture, the Russians were forced to evacuate the port. It remains to be seen whether this loss will fatally affect the activities of the Black Sea fleet. If it is unable to prevent the Germans making use of the port for the supply of their southern armies the consequences will be serious. For sea communications would be of first importance to the enemy when autumn and winter weather reduces the relief that can be afforded by motor transport to railways. The Black Sea fleet can still use Tuapse and Batum, but Tuapse is threatened and Batum is not a good harbour or well-equipped port.

The Russian counter-offensive in the north maintains pressure, but has not yet achieved notable success. It is, however, a source of anxiety to the Germans, and its intensification east of Leningrad may develop into a major attempt to break the encirclement of the city.

WESTERN FRONT

There have been interesting and, possibly, important developments in the bombing attack on Germany. Bomber Command, without neglecting industrial establishments, has turned its attention especially to German railway communications. The remarkable bombing exploits of the Russians appear to have similar objectives.

It seems probable that attacks on communications, if carried out on an extensive scale, are more likely to have greater immediate effects on operations in progress than attacks on war

industries. An army engaged in active operations requires to be fed by an uninterrupted stream of supplies of all sorts. Interruption of the stream is at once felt, whereas the reserves, which industry is constantly building up, are certain to be adequate to maintain the stream over a considerable period.

The very successful daylight raids by Flying Fortress bombers at heights which make them immune to fire from the ground is also a promising development. The speed and powerful armament of these machines have, so far, also proved capable of protecting them against fighter attacks. With improved sights, daylight attacks even from the highest altitudes are more effective against small targets than those made by night, and few bombs are wasted.

MADAGASCAR

On Sept. 10 it was announced that our forces in Madagascar had landed at several ports on the western coast of the island and had met in some cases with sharp resistance. From these ports and from Diego Suarez, previously occupied, our troops advanced to occupy Antananarivo, the capital, and other important centres inland. These measures had clearly become necessary owing to the hostile attitude of the Vichy Government, and its refusal to allow the local authorities to establish relations with our occupying administration. There was reason to suspect facilities might be given to the Japanese to use unoccupied ports in the island as bases for U-boats or aircraft operating against

MAJ.-GEN. G. A. CLOWES, D.S.O., commanding the Australian forces who repelled with great loss the Japanese attack on Milne Bay, Papua, towards the end of August (see page 195). *Photo, Keystone*

our vital lines of sea communications to the the Middle East, which pass through the Mozambique Channel.

FAR EAST

In New Guinea the defeat of their landing at Milne Bay did not deter the Japanese from developing their main attack across the Owen Stanley Mountains towards Port Moresby.

As I was afraid, the physical obstacle of the mountains did not prove as insurmountable as many believed it would.

The defence is handicapped by the difficulty of learning quickly the enemy's movements, and by the absence of lateral communications by which reserves could be moved to danger points. Moreover, as the attack gains ground it can make use of the improvements the defenders have carried out on their rearward communications. The Japanese attack made somewhat alarming progress and crossed the crest of the range before it was checked some 40 miles from its objective. But the Australians, though forced to give ground, had not been defeated.

IN PAPUA, New Guinea, the Japanese drive southwards to Port Moresby, through the wild jungle tracks of the Owen Stanley Range, was halted by Allied troops, and bitter fighting ensued in the Kokoda-Efogi area. *By courtesy of The Evening Standard*

During the Lull in the Fighting in Egypt

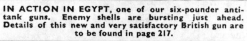

IN ACTION IN EGYPT, one of our six-pounder anti-tank guns. Enemy shells are bursting just ahead. Details of this new and very satisfactory British gun are to be found in page 217.

GENERAL STEWART TANK (nicknamed "Honey")—one of the many American tanks with British crews that are confronting Rommel's Panzers in the desert to the west of Egypt.

EN ROUTE TO CAIRO: wounded men being placed aboard a Red Cross aeroplane for quick transport from the fighting zone to the hospitals at the base.

EL HEMEIMAT, on the edge of the salt marshes that constitute the Qattara Depression, is only about 200 ft. high, but in that region it is conspicuous enough. It lies about 25 miles south of El Alamein, and here an Axis offensive was launched on August 31. Previous to the attack the enemy's renewed activity had been reported by our patrols, two of whom are seen left, making observations in this grim and desolate area.

Photos, British Official: Crown Copyright; Associated Press

Free China Launches a New Offensive

U.S. airmen, whose base is in India and whose job is to fly war supplies to China, are here seen receiving last-minute instructions before taking-off.

Supplies being loaded into one of the giant American transport planes which reach China from India along what has been termed the Burma Road of the Air.

In Sept. 1942 Chinese troops were attacking Nanchang and pressing eastwards beyond Chuhsien (whence Tokyo might be bombed), and had retaken Pakonghow and Yuan Tan on the Canton-Hankow railway.

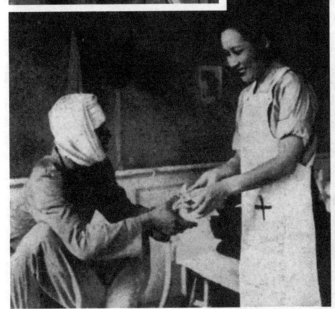

CHINA FIGHTS ON UNDAUNTED. Centre left, a young recruit to a Chinese military academy ; right, Maj. John Pun-Yung Hwang, a fighter ace who, after five years of very active service against the Japanese, has come to London as Air Attaché at the Chinese Embassy. Bottom left, Mme. Chiang Kai-shek, indefatigable in her work for the wounded, visits a military hospital ; right, a senior officer of the Chinese Army salutes men wounded in the North Hunan battle.

Photos, British Official ; Sport & General, Topical

After the Raid: German Photos of Dieppe

Photos, Keystone

" A HARD, SAVAGE CLASH, a reconnaissance in force, an indispensable preliminary to full-scale operations "—these were the phrases used by Mr. Churchill in his war survey of Sept. 8 to describe the attack on Dieppe. These photographs from an enemy source show : 1, Abandoned Canadian tank. 2, British prisoners assisting wounded men to stretchers under German escort. 3, British "tin hats" collected on Dieppe beach after the raid. 4, Burning landing-craft and damaged tanks on the shore.

America's Storming Parties in the Solomons

THE ATTACK ON THE SOLOMONS in mid-August was planned by Rear-Adm. R. K. Turner and Maj.-Gen. A. A. Vandergrift (I), the latter commanding the landing forces. 2, Black smoke rising from Tanambogo Island after Japanese defences had been bombed by American planes; top left is seen Gavutu Island. 3, U.S. Marines search for snipers in a palm grove on Guadalcanal Island. 4, Japanese machine-gun emplacement on Guadalcanal. 5, One of the amphibian tanks which landed the Marines on the island. *Photos, Keystone, Planet News, Central Press, Associated Press*

THE WAR IN THE AIR

by Capt. Norman Macmillan, M.C., A.F.C.

STRATEGICALLY, the air war has reached its most interesting stage. The moves of the opposing forces to their present geographical combatant positions have produced what President Roosevelt called, in a recent speech, " this global war "—an apt, if somewhat ugly, term.

The special significance of the strategic air situation is now the almost equidistant grouping of the vital zones. Note these ten examples : (1) Brest to Stalingrad ; (2) England to New York ; (3) New York to San Francisco ; (4) San Francisco to the narrows of the Bering Strait ; (5) the narrows of the Bering Strait to the main island of Japan ; (6) Japan to Port Moresby ; (7) Port Moresby to New Zealand ; (8) New Guinea to Singapore ; (9) Japan to the Bay of Bengal ; (10) the Bay of Bengal to the Caspian Sea—all represent a distance of between 2,500 and 3,000 miles. Some are separated by land masses, others by oceans, some by alternating land and sea.

Because British flying-boats have from the beginning had to face long Atlantic patrols, because American aircraft have always had to traverse great continental spaces, because Britain adopted the policy of the large bomber before the war began— the strategic situation in the air is swinging steadily in our favour. Britain and America have far surpassed Germany and Japan in the production of long-range aircraft of both land and sea-going types. Thus, almost for the first time in this war, the United Nations are approaching a strategically favourable air situation. The full benefit of this advantage will be reaped when the crops of the Northern Hemisphere are ready to be cut next year, but already we are gleaning something from the less bountiful harvest of the current air season. The dropping of 4,000-lb. bombs on the rear areas of Rommel's armies is known to have created great havoc, and caused much damage by blast. If Rommel has hitherto had the advantage

Alamein-Qattara Depression line, which began at 12.50 a.m. on Monday, August 31. Throughout the whole operation British, Dominion, and American air superiority was never in doubt, and it is noteworthy that the heavy bombers were the first to discover that Rommel's men were on the move.

On Sept. 2 and 3 all Allied records for the number of bomber sorties over the desert were broken, and in six nights over 1,000,000 lb. of bombs were dropped on Rommel's troops.

During the third year of the war ending on Sept. 2, the Middle East Command destroyed 1,417 enemy aircraft (not including those destroyed on the ground) for a loss of 1,114 aircraft.

IN the Far East the main centres of air activity have been in the New Guinea area and the Solomon Islands zone. Air action helped to repel the Japanese attempt to seize Milne Bay as a part of the offensive against Port Moresby. Australian resistance to the later infiltration advance of the Japanese forces across the Owen Stanley mountain range was assisted by Allied pilots who made low-flying bombing and machine-gun attacks against the Japanese forces. The Japanese base at Buna has been heavily bombed. In the Solomons, Japanese assaults against the islands retaken by the Americans met strong air defensive opposition. Fifteen Japanese bombers and five fighters were shot down in three days.

In Europe the Red Air Force has continued its attacks against Axis targets. During the fortnight from August 29 to Sept. 12 raids were effected against Budapest, Vienna, Jena, Berlin, Breslau, Warsaw, and Königsberg—a line within enemy territory roughly parallel to the Russian front and along which lie important Axis centres of communication and important war-industry targets.

Main targets of Bomber Command during this period were Saarbrücken, Karlsruhe, Bremen, Duisburg/Ruhrort, Frankfurt/ Rhineland, and Düsseldorf—all important manufacturing centres ; 70 bombers were lost in these raids. Air crews reported meeting heavier enemy anti-aircraft defences in guns and searchlights.

Latest figures show that during June and July 1942, some 13,000 tons of bombs fell on Germany compared with 8,500 in the same period of 1941, and 3,500 in 1940. During the three years of war ending Sept. 2, 1942, the Axis lost 8,985 aircraft in Britain, British waters, Europe and the Middle East against a British loss of 6,231 aircraft.

DUISBURG, the great German inland port situated between the rivers Rhine and Ruhr (see page 236), with both of which it is connected by canals, was heavily attacked by the R.A.F. on Sept. 6.   It is a highly important centre of communications, and its railway junctions, marshalling yards, and quays have been the target of many British bombing raids.

The importance to the air of the grouping of the combatant forces is most easily observed on a globe. A Mercator chart of the world is useless, because distances cannot be compared on it ; failing a globe, choose a map on which it is possible to measure distances in any direction from a standard scale. Then you will realize that lines of communication have become a problem of equal importance to both sides.

The advantage of shorter internal lines of communication which the Axis formerly possessed has disappeared so far as the air is concerned. The flying distances for both sides are now approximately equal along the communication lines. That, as much as the growing output of the United Nations' aircraft factories, contributes to the increased air strength of the Allies. German aircraft built in Rostock, Bremen, or in the factories in France which make German aircraft, must now fly as far as to reach the Trans-Caucasian front as if they had to cross the North Atlantic ocean.

in size of guns (both in and out of tanks) we are now able to beat him in the size of bombs.

The large bomb has a far greater radius of effect than a large shell of equal size, because the percentage of weight carried in the form of explosive is greater in the case of the bomb. Add to that the fact that a 4,000-lb. bomb is approximately twice as heavy as the largest shell, and it becomes possible to assess its worth in a place like the desert, where devastation over an area may be more valuable than extreme accuracy of aim with a limited area of effect. These are the pros and cons of the value of our large bombers versus Rommel's Stukas, which, because they are dive-bombers, are limited in the size of bomb they can carry.

THE pre-attack heavy bombing of Rommel's rear areas is held to have had an important bearing on his unsuccessful assault on the British positions along the El

DURING the period under review American Flying Fortresses bombed by day Rouen rail-yards, an aircraft factory near Albert, St. Omer aerodrome, Rotterdam shipyards and Utrecht rail-yards, and lost only two aircraft. On the last-mentioned raid, their fourteenth, they shot down 12 enemy fighters when flying without escort. The secret of their remarkable achievements lies in their turbo-superchargers, which give them exceptional engine-power at great heights. From this characteristic they are said to be 60 to 70 miles an hour faster than equivalent British bombers (although they carry a smaller bomb load), and they can operate at a greater height. They are thus about as fast as the FW 190 fighter—Germany's best—and are probably superior above 22,000 feet, at which height the performance of the FW begins to fall off. Their armament is the hard-hitting American half-inch machine-gun, mounted in blisters. Their performance with American crews has confounded the British technicians who some time ago criticized the Fortress.

During August 1942, the R.A.F. destroyed 247 enemy aircraft and lost 378 in Europe and Middle East zones.

How to Recognize American Bombers in Britain

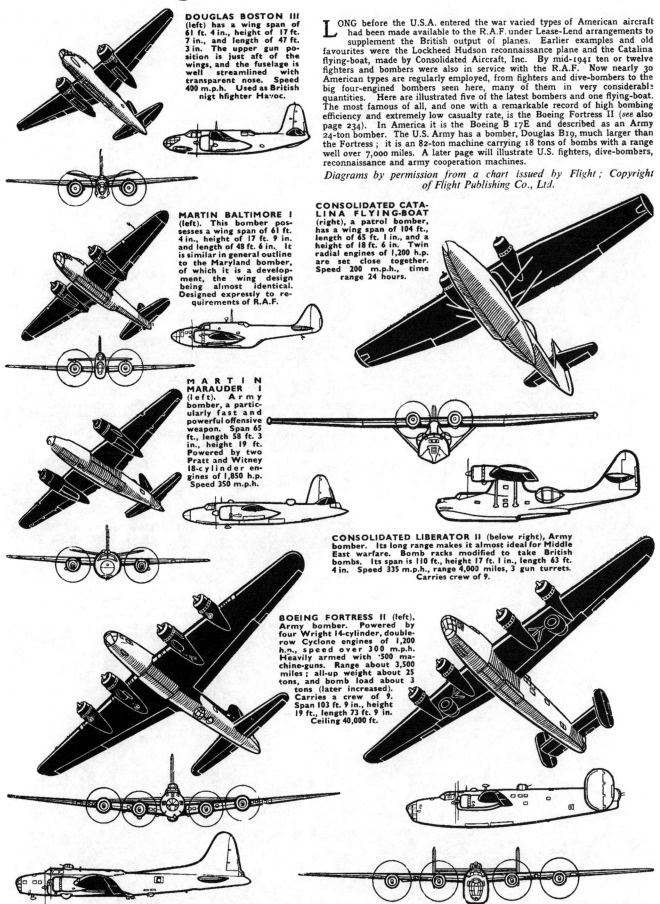

DOUGLAS BOSTON III (left) has a wing span of 61 ft. 4 in., height of 17 ft. 7 in., and length of 47 ft. 3 in. The upper gun position is just aft of the wings, and the fuselage is well streamlined with transparent nose. Speed 400 m.p.h. Used as British nigt hfighter Havoc.

LONG before the U.S.A. entered the war varied types of American aircraft had been made available to the R.A.F. under Lease-Lend arrangements to supplement the British output of planes. Earlier examples and old favourites were the Lockheed Hudson reconnaissance plane and the Catalina flying-boat, made by Consolidated Aircraft, Inc. By mid-1941 ten or twelve fighters and bombers were also in service with the R.A.F. Now nearly 30 American types are regularly employed, from fighters and dive-bombers to the big four-engined bombers seen here, many of them in very considerable quantities. Here are illustrated five of the latest bombers and one flying-boat. The most famous of all, and one with a remarkable record of high bombing efficiency and extremely low casualty rate, is the Boeing Fortress II (*see also* page 234). In America it is the Boeing B 17E and described as an Army 24-ton bomber. The U.S. Army has a bomber, Douglas B19, much larger than the Fortress; it is an 82-ton machine carrying 18 tons of bombs with a range well over 7,000 miles. A later page will illustrate U.S. fighters, dive-bombers, reconnaissance and army cooperation machines.

Diagrams by permission from a chart issued by Flight; Copyright of Flight Publishing Co., Ltd.

MARTIN BALTIMORE I (left). This bomber possesses a wing span of 61 ft. 4 in., height of 17 ft. 9 in. and length of 48 ft. 6 in. It is similar in general outline to the Maryland bomber, of which it is a development, the wing design being almost identical. Designed expressly to requirements of R.A.F.

CONSOLIDATED CATALINA FLYING-BOAT (right), a patrol bomber, has a wing span of 104 ft., length of 65 ft. 1 in., and a height of 18 ft. 6 in. Twin radial engines of 1,200 h.p. are set close together. Speed 200 m.p.h., time range 24 hours.

MARTIN MARAUDER I (left). Army bomber, a particularly fast and powerful offensive weapon. Span 65 ft., length 58 ft. 3 in., height 19 ft. Powered by two Pratt and Witney 18-cylinder engines of 1,850 h.p. Speed 350 m.p.h.

CONSOLIDATED LIBERATOR II (below right), Army bomber. Its long range makes it almost ideal for Middle East warfare. Bomb racks modified to take British bombs. Its span is 110 ft., height 17 ft. 1 in., length 63 ft. 4 in. Speed 335 m.p.h., range 4,000 miles, 3 gun turrets. Carries crew of 9.

BOEING FORTRESS II (left), Army bomber. Powered by four Wright 14-cylinder, double-row Cyclone engines of 1,200 h.n., speed over 300 m.p.h. Heavily armed with ·500 machine-guns. Range about 3,500 miles; all-up weight about 25 tons, and bomb load about 3 tons (later increased). Carries a crew of 9. Span 103 ft. 9 in., height 19 ft., length 73 ft. 9 in. Ceiling 40,000 ft.

IDENTIFICATION DRAWINGS of U.S.A. aircraft now in regular service with the R.A.F. and frequently to be seen in British skies. The characteristics of the machines are given in underside, broadside and head-on views to assist quick recognition. The drawings show the machines in relative sizes. The largest is the Liberator with a span of 110 ft., the Boston and Baltimore bombers being 61 ft. 4 in. These may be considered the principal American types of their classes operating with the R.A.F.

Flying Fortresses on an English Airfield

Two armament experts, one R.A.F. and the other American, overhauling the heavy calibre machine-guns in the base turret of a Flying Fortress. Below, a Fortress's tail, and (bottom right) air gunners engaged in a practice shoot.

American ground staff servicing a Flying Fortress. The U.S. Army Air Force in Britain is now so large that a special Service Command has been created to ensure a continuous flow of equipment to the aerodromes.

USED BY THE U.S. ARMY AIR FORCE on operations from R.A.F. bases, the Flying Fortresses are manned by American crews and serviced by American ground staff. These photographs were taken at a bomber station in England where hundreds of pilots, air-gunners, navigators and bomb-aimers receive their final training. Speed, high-flying, and their armament—they carry 12 machine-guns whose 5-inch ammo. has a longer range and greater hitting power than our 303-inch—make these giant planes most formidable opponents.

Photos, Photopress, Planet News

Fierce Battle in the City of the Cossacks

FIGHTING IN THE STREETS OF ROSTOV-ON-DON developed on an extremely fierce scale as the Germans forced their way through the suburbs of the city. The Russians evacuated Rostov on July 27, and with its fall the Germans were enabled to advance towards Stalingrad and the Caucasus, establishing a series of bridgeheads across the Don. Here are seen German infantrymen crawling forward, aided by field guns on the opposite side of the street.

Photo, Keystone

This Is the Ruhr We Bomb So Often

"Objectives in the Ruhr." How many times have we encountered that phrase in the Air Ministry's bulletins!— and we may expect it to be repeated time and again until the war is won. For the Ruhr, as this article makes clear, is one of the most important, perhaps the most vital, of the centres of Hitler's war machine.

I<small>N</small> geography the Ruhr is a little river which, rising in the hills of Westphalia, runs for some 140 miles to join the Lower Rhine at Ruhrort, between Düsseldorf and the Dutch frontier. But the term is commonly given a much wider, though rather indefinite, implication. The Ruhrgebiet, as the Germans call it—the Ruhr area or district—is not co-extensive with the

GOEBBELS IN COLOGNE observes for himself the result of an R.A.F. 1,000-bomber raid. Cologne, situated on the edge of the Ruhr, has been subjected to some of our most violent attacks.   *Photo, Keystone*

basin of the Ruhr, but stretches beyond it on all sides, even to the left bank of the Rhine. Roughly speaking, it includes the area between Duisburg and Düsseldorf and Dortmund and the much-bombed Hamm, but sometimes it is considered to reach as far south as Cologne. Furthermore, the Ruhr is not even an administrative area.

B<small>UT</small> if only a small portion of the Ruhr is taken up by the Ruhr basin, how has its naming come about? The answer lies beneath the soil through which the little river makes its way. Not far down—indeed, in the early days of the industry outcropping was the vogue—lie vast coal measures, some of the best coal in Europe, coal which can be converted most economically into excellent coke, and which is so gas-free that the miners can carry open-flame candles.

Most of the coal mines now being worked lie to the north of the river, between it and the Rhine-Herne Canal, but the name which first came into prominence a hundred years ago still sticks. "The Ruhr" is sure of its place in history.

In the Ruhr there are coal deposits estimated at 55,000,000 tons, representing considerably more than half of the entire coal resources of Germany. To these is to be added the best system of internal communications—the thickest network of railways, rivers and canals—in Europe; Duisburg is the continent's largest and most

important inland harbour, the world's largest river port; it is the chief link between northern Germany and the Baltic on the one side and southern Germany and the Danube valley on the other. To its docks come barges of a thousand tons and ocean-going vessels of 1,500 tons. Here, then, we have two of the prime essentials of modern heavy industry, coal and transport; the third, iron ore, has to be brought from a distance, though, thanks to the communications just mentioned, this is no expensive or difficult matter. Much of the ore comes from Sweden, while the balance is brought from French Lorraine.

H<small>ERE</small> we touch on a most interesting chapter in the history of capitalistic development. For a hundred years and more the iron ore of Lorraine and the coke of the Ruhr have been joined in the most fertile union; the only drawback is that between the two areas is drawn a frontier.

Economics has a way of getting round political barriers, however, and up to the war of 1914 most of the iron ore derived from the French mines in Lorraine was sent to the Ruhr. After 1918 that part of Lorraine which had been annexed by Bismarck in 1871 was returned to France, with the result that her resources of iron ore were vastly increased. But she was still as dependent as ever on the Ruhr's fuel, and special clauses were inserted in the Treaty of Versailles guaranteeing to France a regular supply at fixed prices of Ruhr coal and coke. The German iron and steel masters in Lorraine were expropriated, but with the compensation which they received from the German Government they erected new iron and steel works on the Ruhr, which they endeavoured so far as possible to keep supplied with ore from Sweden and Spain. The Lorraine steel barons were in no too happy a position, and their position became worse still when the Germans fell into arrears with the deliveries of Ruhr coke and coal.

At length, after many protests from France and Britain, French and Belgians marched into the Ruhr in 1923, and the district was not evacuated until the middle of 1925, when the mark had collapsed into utter nothingness, and Germany's economic and social system had been so disrupted that men listened with increasing eagerness to the wild denunciations and wilder promises of Hitler and his Nazis. Following the virtual collapse of Germany, the French, Belgian and German steel industries were joined in an international syndicate—a syndicate which, so far as is known, has continued to this day. Hitler's panzers, indeed, very effectively rubbed out the frontier lines in the summer of 1940.

To return to the Ruhr. Coal, transport and iron ore together have given birth to a vast concentration of coal mines, metal foundries, coke ovens, rolling mills, machine shops, railway engineering works, chemical and textile factories— altogether one of the world's greatest con

glomerations of economic power. In this, Germany's black country, even the black-out imposed by war is pierced by the fires flaming through the night. For miles the cities and towns are continuous. From Duisburg to Dortmund, a distance of some 35 miles, one town merges into the next: it is one long street all the way.

Situated a little to the north of the Ruhr, about half-way between the river and the Rhine-Herne Canal, Essen (as the whole world knows) is the chief seat of the Krupps armament firm—that great concern devoted to the making of death-dealing instruments which was founded in 1810 or thereabouts by Friedrich Krupp, was guided to greatness by Alfred, the "Cannon King," and whose destinies are now guided by Bertha Krupp's husband, Dr. Gustav Krupp von Bohlen und Halbach. In 1918 the Krupp works were employing 167,000 workers; ten years later the number had dropped to a mere 65,000, but by the summer of 1939 there were over 100,000 employees of the giant firm.

A glance at a plan of Essen shows that the Krupp "colonies" occupy most of the town; they are described as separate villages with schools and libraries, recreation grounds, clubs, stores and shops—altogether a modern settlement built on much the same lines as Andrew Undershaft's, described so brilliantly by G.B.S. in Major Barbara.

D<small>ÜSSELDORF</small>, with a population of over half a million, is the commercial and manufacturing centre of the Ruhr region; it is chock-a-block with metallurgical, engineering, machine-tool, glass and chemical works, paper, furniture, and enamel factories, textile mills, and breweries. Duisburg we have already mentioned; it includes Ruhrort, where the Ruhr runs into the Rhine, and Hamborn (pop. 530,000). Dortmund (pop. about the same as Düsseldorf) stands in the middle of the Westphalian coalfield; there are beds of iron ore in the neighbourhood, too, so that to some extent the town rivals Essen in the production of iron goods. Mülheim (pop. 136,000) is another manufacturing centre. Other Ruhr towns include Gelsenkirchen, Bochum, Oberhausen, Krefeld and Hagen. Then the interstices of this network of cities are filled with smaller towns and villages, where the serfs of Hitler's Reich sleep off the fatigue engendered by their long hours of toil.

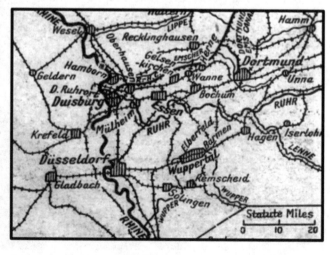

GERMANY'S VITAL TARGET, the highly industrialized Ruhr, has had to undergo innumerable R.A.F. raids, aimed at slowing up the enemy war machine. As will be seen, the area is a vast network of towns and communications.   PAGE 236

Vital Targets in Germany's Black Country

DÜSSELDORF, one of the greatest towns in the Ruhr concentration, was raided again by Bomber Command on the night of Sept. 10, and a mighty weight of H.E. and 100,000 incendiaries converted the city into a furnace. "The enemy's attack was fierce, and the test which the people had to suffer was hard," said a German war reporter in a broadcast; "stout hearts and determined courage were needed." Top left, Düsseldorf the morning after the previous raid of July 31 : top right, Dortmund Union Steelworks ; bottom, Krupp works at Essen. *British Official ; Dorien Leigh. E.N.A.*

To Battle in the Morning in Egypt

Very difficult it is for those who have no personal acquaintance with the Western Desert to visualize that grim waste where Montgomery's men and Rommel's strive so desperately for the mastery. Here, however, is a pen-picture which may serve to bring home, at least in some measure, the actual conditions of the desert war. It comes from Sergeant J. Lomas.

COULD anybody describe it? The din, rattle, clang, and crash of it. I've often thought they must be hearing us over in Manchester. The heat of the engine bakes your head and arms, and the rest of you goes blue with cold. Of course, you mustn't use lights, so you're in the pitch dark all the time, and it's very hard to see

LATEST TYPE OF GERMAN TANK put out of action during the fierce fighting in the Western Desert. Rommel was reported to have lost 100 tanks in his attempts to break through our positions in Egypt, and his losses in men were correspondingly heavy.
Photo, British Official: Crown Copyright

what's going on. Ahead of you is the back of the leading tank, behind is the nose of another, and that's all you can see in the darkness except dust, and there's always bags of that.

You halt dozens of times, perhaps a hundred of you altogether in a long line, then you carry on very slowly, in the same positions you'll be in when you go into battle in the morning. Of course, we like a smoke now and again to keep us awake, so we light a fag and keep it burning so as to save matches. Like a little red lamp in the dark, that is. Keeping the engines revving very slowly, so as not to make too much noise and give the show away, we get off the road, on the tricky little path through the minefields.

EACH tank commander climbs out on the front, keeping in close touch with the tank ahead because it's so easy to lose him. A man can walk over a mine easily enough, but a tank or lorry'll send them up in a proper earthquake. When we get through, then we switch off engines and fill up; but in the pitch dark. When all tanks switch off, it's quieter than a churchyard. Nothing moves in the desert, specially at night.

Then our troop officer comes over, running through the final details, and the word comes to mount and start up. So we whip off the gun coverings, check the breech actions, load both guns, and off we go. As soon as the tanks cross a narrow bridge over a trench we know we're headed straight for Jerry, and the sentry gives us a thumbs up for luck. Generally, we haven't got very far before shells start bursting all around us. We're inside our own barrage, that's why, so we turn round and circle about, till we're

behind it. Then we look through the periscope to try to see a bit of Jerry, or spot the flash of his guns. The barrage lifts, and we might see streams of tracer bullets ahead.

" Driver, swing left. Gunner, traverse right. Fire when on," yells our commander.

According to plan we swing left, into line ahead, and smash the enemy posts with all we've got. Heavy machine-guns and 2-pounders criss-cross with enemy fire, and all of a sudden there's a terrific shock, and sparks shower across my periscope. We've been hit, but there's no damage. Twenty yards away, our sister tank disappears with a bang which even shakes us. She's struck a mine, and when the dust settles, you can see she's heeled over, minus yards of track, with her gun pointing at the sky, out of it.

Slap in the middle of us is an armoured car of the King's Dragoon Guards, swapping machine-gun fire for everything Jerry's got. At such close range they must have had all the luck in the world. One hit even from light anti-tank stuff would smash right through it. There are carriers of the King's Own, too, small and nippy, right in the thick of it. The infantry, the long-suffering P.B.I., are there—as usual —and doing a marvellous job, and all.

The enemy's fire packs up, so you know job number one's been done. The enemy artillery barrage starts next, and you wonder who's going to cop it. You soon find out. You're outside your tank doing repairs, so you fall flat, and then start playing kids' games again, like " Last across the road," running like hell to get inside when you've got the chance, judging between the scream

and a short howl from a shell whether you've got it in your lap or not.

Shell fire is a terror in the open. Protected by armour, you're all right except from a direct hit; and even that doesn't always mean a great deal. But when it comes to lying on the floor under a continuous barrage of big stuff, it's not so funny. The shells seem to be barely missing you. Inside the tank you feel all right, even though the light from the periscope gets blotted out now and again by heaps of earth, till you might as well be in darkness. Then your spine starts curling up at every whine coming nearer and nearer, till you're all goose-flesh. I've actually seen a shadow of a falling shell in the sand before it hit, about the last six feet of its journey before it exploded.

YOU can't do much in a barrage except sit tight where you are. And that's not much use, because it might last three or four hours. If nothing's happened, you sigh with relief, and hope it broke Jerry's bloody heart to see you still there in spite of all his back-ache. When we start attacking, our 25-pdrs. open on a line in front of us. We form up watching the accurate shooting of the good old gunners, and cheering them on. They do a grand job, those gunners. Then it's our turn, and we advance toward our biggest headache of the day. We go on to the limit laid down, and once we get there, we just bang away as hard as we can go.

" Gun stopped ! " yells our gunner ; ' the damn thing's jammed."

I'd give anything for another pair of hands. The driver keeps on the move; I squirt a jet from a Pyrene extinguisher over the breech; and our 2-pounder bangs away, so nobody's wasting any time. The infantry's almost on top of us. There's no time for repairs on our sort of job.

Then, just to crown the lot, we see the maddest of all sights : A bayonet charge by a crack lot of County lads coming up behind us. Nothing can help them as they go into the smoke over the enemy posts flat out, like hundred-yard sprinters, looking like murder. And so they are.

Jerry hasn't got time to do anything between the end of the shelling and the lads coming at him, so he uses a bit of sense and puts his hands up. The sun shines down as though we were at Old Trafford.

That's Job number 2 done, and that's more or less what it's like in action. More or less . . .

Mr. Churchill on the ' Desert Army '

BEFORE I left [London] I had some reason to believe that the condition of the Desert Army and of the troops in Egypt was not entirely satisfactory.

✱ The Eighth Army, or the Desert Army, as I like to call it, had lost over 80,000 men. It had been driven back about 400 miles since May with immense losses in munitions, supplies, and transport. General Rommel's surprisingly rapid advance was only rendered possible because he used our captured stores and vehicles. In the battles around Gazala and in the stress of the retreat, and in the fighting at El Alamein, where General Auchinleck succeeded in stabilizing the front, the structure of the Army had become much deranged. Divisional formations had been largely broken up, and a number of battle groups or other improvized formations had sprung into being piecemeal in the course of the hard fighting.

✱ Nevertheless, as I can myself testify, there was a universal conviction in officers and men of every rank that they could beat the Germans man to man and face to face. But this was coupled with a sense of being baffled and of not understanding why so many misfortunes had fallen upon the Army. The spirit of the troops was admirable, but it was clear to me that drastic changes were required in the

High Command and that the Army must have a new start and a new leader.

✱ I therefore, after many heart searchings, submitted proposals to the War Cabinet for changing and remodelling the High Command . . . . I am satisfied that the combination of Gen. Alexander and Gen. Montgomery, with Gen. McCreery, a tank expert, is a team well adapted to our needs and the finest at our disposal at the present time.

✱ As far back as March last I asked President Roosevelt to lend me the shipping to transport an additional 40,000 or 50,000 men to the Middle East . . . The President placed at our disposal a number of American ships and at the critical moment we had rounding the Cape very large and well-equipped forces that could be directed to Egypt. It is to this that the improvement in our affairs or the maintenance of our affairs in that region can largely be attributed. . . .

✱ In spite of the heavy losses, the Army of the Western Desert is now stronger, actually and relatively, than it has ever been. So large have been the reinforcements which have reached this Army that what is to a large extent a new Army has been created while the fighting has been in progress.—*House of Commons, Sept. 8, 1942*

They Guard the Gate to Egypt

Between Marshal Rommel and the rich prize of Alexandria stands the 8th Army, commanded by Lt.-Gen. B. L. Montgomery—seen above (2) with Lt.-Gen. Horrocks on his right; while in supreme command of the Middle Eastern theatre of war is Gen. Sir H. Alexander (1). Our third photograph shows the crew of a Bofors gun in action at El Hemeimat.

239

In the Front Line of Africa's Defence

On the Egyptian battlefront in early September, Rommel's columns moved out to attack the 8th Army, only to be repulsed with considerable loss. These photographs show (1) U.S. tank commander observing from his turret; (2) South African with an armful of portable land-mines; (3) bomb about to be loaded into a Boston; (4) mobile telephone exchange.

Guns that Bark for Britain

When the Afrika Korps advanced it was severely handled by the British artillery. Here are three types of guns being used to good effect against the enemy : (5) a 4·5 long-range gun of a R.A. Medium Regiment ; (6) six-pounder anti-tank gun, used not only as a field-gun but also in increasing numbers on our heavy tanks ; (7) a 25-pounder goes into action.

Photos, British Official ; Fox

Quenching Their Desert Thirst

Fighting is dusty work in the Middle East, and the thirty N.A.A.F.I. canteens which patrol
the forward areas in Egypt are very welcome to our forces. As well as tea they bring
chocolate, cigarettes, newspapers and radio bulletins. Here also is a bar, " Ye Olde M.E.110 "
—made from its bullet-riddled tail—used by men of a Kittyhawk Squadron.

VIEWS & REVIEWS Of Vital War Books

Retreat in the East: A Correspondent's Picture

Eight months have passed since the news arrived of Singapore's fall—news that came with stunning force, so unexpected was the tragic blow and so terrific in its implications. The full story cannot yet be told, but Mr. O'Dowd Gallagher's Retreat in the East (Harrap, 8s. 6d.), reviewed here by Hamilton Fyfe, the veteran war correspondent, contains much that is of intensely vital interest.

MR. O'DOWD GALLAGHER, famous war correspondent, whose exciting adventures in the Far East are referred to in this page. He is at present serving with the Royal Armoured Corps.

Photo by courtesy of The Daily Express

NEVER in any war before this have newspaper men taken exactly the same risks as the fighting men. In some wars they have taken greater risks. When I was free-lancing in France during the early autumn of 1914, both Kitchener and the Germans said I should be shot if caught! One of the first and most famous of war correspondents, Archibald Forbes, went into action unarmed and liable to be treated as a spy if he were captured. But in this war reporters have been taken up in bombing planes, have gone with mechanized units into battle, have been in the thick of naval engagements. When Prince of Wales and Repulse went down, a Daily Express man, O. D. Gallagher, was in the latter. He just managed to escape with his life, after swimming for what seemed an eternity in the black-oil-covered sea.

His account of the fight in which battleship and cruiser were bombed and torpedoed for lack of aeroplane protection fills some of the most vivid pages in his exciting and grimly instructive book, Retreat in the East. The tense atmosphere on board before attack began, with loudspeakers sounding through the ship at frequent intervals to give news of enemy movements; the crash and roar of the bombs and bombers for just over an hour; then the order "Abandon ship!" and the plunge into warm, filthy water—the whole picture is clear and colourful. It thrills and saddens; it makes one alternately furious and proud.

Furious that these gallant ships should have been thrown away—for that is what it amounts to. Without aircraft protection they were helpless against the perfectly planned Japanese onslaught. To underrate this enemy's flying, or talk loosely about "suicide squads," is, Mr. Gallagher makes clear, foolish. They are not even reckless. They are like machinery. They know exactly what to do and they do it. They are more formidable than the Luftwaffe. Neither we nor the Americans knew how dangerous they were.

FOR some reason the hurling of Japan into the war found us unprepared in almost every way. Was this the fault of our diplomacy in Tokyo, or of Military Intelligence, or of the Government in London? Mr. Gallagher knows nothing about that, does not discuss it. But it will have to be discussed, and the blame apportioned, and punishment meted out. In Burma the local authorities "collapsed, could not stand the strain." The Governor loudly proclaimed Rangoon a second Tobruk (that was before its fall, of course) or Moscow. But nothing was done to stiffen the population, or get the ships with war material unloaded quickly, or cut through the ropes of officialism. The morale of civilians was "as flat as a punctured tire." They went on as usual, having parties, chattering secrets, voicing their lack of faith in the possibility of keeping the Japanese out. They knew Burma's weakness.

But if Burma was bad, Singapore was worse. The businessmen slacked and drank and lunched and dined out and slept after their heavy meals, according to custom. While they over-ate, airmen at the outpost of Khota Baru (much in the news at one period) were making meals off a couple of boiled potatoes with a thin layer of watery stew, bread and jam, and tea. Food could have been sent to them by the businessmen—but it wasn't. They howled when they were asked to raise more than a paltry sum by income tax, but they didn't worry about hardships suffered by the young men they relied on to save them from losing their incomes altogether.

Perhaps they might have behaved a little less stupidly and callously if the officials had not handed them out such reassuring dope. The Governor allowed the city to be caught with all its lights on for the first Japanese raid. Air-Marshal Brooke-Popham cheerily told newspaper men five days before the Japs started that "there were no signs that Japan was going to attack anyone," and that the aircraft he had "were quite good enough"—whereas in fact they were inferior machines, and shortly afterwards "many fine courageous pilots were lost in them."

AT that time there was not a tank in Malaya. According to the official view the enemy would not be able to use theirs, so what did we want any for? Mr. Gallagher quotes Anthony Eden's comforting words: "Singapore has not been neglected," and adds the scorching comment: "I am bound to suggest that Mr. Eden was misinformed."

Take one illustration of neglect. Everyone must remember the Causeway connecting Singapore with the mainland, and how it was "destroyed" to delay the Japanese advance. The island's chief water supply was piped across it. So, when it was cut, the water was stopped. But the Causeway was not effectively blown up. Only one end, the farther end, was damaged, and the Jap engineers repaired it in three hours. So the "impregnable fortress" of Parliamentary fairy-tales was lost, and with it a larger number of

British troops than ever surrendered in our history before, including a fresh division that arrived just before the end.

Wavell, says Mr. Gallagher, did all he could to get the transports carrying that division diverted to Burma, where they might have turned the scale. But no, they were landed at Singapore, sent straight into battle, and either killed or taken prisoner.

The whole story told in the book is one of blundering by the high-ups and magnificent courage in the rank-and-file. "Wherever I have seen fighting soldiers," the author testified, "heard their tales, known their losses, seen the results of their victories, I have found few that can stand up to the small-built fighting men from the British Isles. They are seldom commended, frequently disparaged, but they fight and suffer and die as few other men do."

That is considered praise from one who is well qualified to speak. Of the last five Christmas days he has spent four on active service—in Addis Ababa, Shanghai, Madrid, and on the French front at Arras (1939). He puts the Indians and Gurkhas also high on the roll of honour. A London-born soldier said to him: "Give me an Indian on my left and a Gurkha on my right and the three of us will fight our way to hell and back—if we've got enough ammunition." In those last half-dozen words lay tragic memories.

ANOTHER lot to win Mr. Gallagher's warm admiration were the airmen of the American Voluntary Group recruited for service with the Chinese and then transferred to Burma. A major-general on the spot "gave Burma three weeks" when the battle for the country began. "That it took six weeks for the Japanese to get to Rangoon was in part due to the magnificent fighting of the A.V.G." They "ran themselves in an honestly democratic way." This, Mr. Gallagher thinks, had a lot to do with their dash and competence.

It is a sorry tale, this of our Retreat in the East, a tale of muddle and miscalculation, silly optimism, lack of foresight. It could have been avoided, Mr. Gallagher suggests, though he does not actually say so—being a reporter, not a historian. It ought to have been avoided. We ought to know who were to blame, and they should be made to expiate their faults.

HAMILTON FYFE

SURRENDER OF SINGAPORE. This photograph from a Japanese source purports to show British officers on their way to negotiate with Lt.-Gen. Yamashita the terms of the city's surrender on Feb. 15, 1942. Lt.-Gen. A. E. Percival, G.O.C. Malaya, is on the extreme right of the picture. A Japanese officer walks in the centre of the group. (See Vol. 5, page 514).

Photo, Associated Press

PAGE 243

HOW THE RUSSIANS ATTACK: a Soviet photograph showing Red Army tanks and infantry going into action in the central sector of the Eastern Front. All through the summer fighting of the fiercest description has continued on the Russian plains. The losses have been terrific on both sides. Thus, between May 15 and August 15, says the Soviet Information Bureau, the Germans lost 1,250,000 officers and men, of whom 480,000 were killed. During the me period the Russians lost 606,000 men in killed, wounded and missing. The German loss s in tanks were 3,390, in guns 4,000, and aircraft 4,000. Corresponding Russian figures are given as 2,240 tanks, 3,162 guns, and 2,198 aircraft.

Photo, British Official: Crown Copyright

UNDER THE SWASTIKA

Europe's Youth Refuses to Be Hitler's Slaves

As PAUL TABORI writes in the article that follows, the young men and women of European countries overrun and held in subjection by the Nazi hordes are having a very raw deal. Yet, in spite of all, they hope and fight for the coming of a better day.

EVER since the First World War youth had had a very raw deal of life in Europe. Unemployment, the overcrowding of the professional classes, the springing up of totalitarian regimes, hit young people the hardest, turned them into rebels, or drew them into the regimented ranks of Fascist organizations. But these sufferings and vicissitudes were nothing compared with the abject slavery, the cruel decimation, which youth is enduring today under the swastika. News from all over Europe shows how young men and women, even the very children, are defying the Nazi blight or writhing under it. And it is perhaps this European youth which will form the vanguard of the great, super-national revolution against Hitler and his creed.

Youth is increasingly becoming cannon-fodder in Germany's Eastern campaign. When the Völkischer Beobachter printed the obituary notice of Otto von Keudell, *Fahnen-junker-Gefreiter*, who died for the Vaterland "shortly after his 17th birthday," it was only one of hundreds of similar cases. Germany has called up her sixteen-year-old boys and trained them hastily, and thousands of them have already suffered death or serious wounds in Russia. Mortgaging heavily her future, the Third Reich is killing off her young people faster than her declining birthrate can replace them.

You may remember the tragic fate of the Prague students who were rounded up a few months ago, taken to the big Stadium of the city, kept standing at attention for sixteen hours, and then some of them killed by machine-gun bullets and the rest sent to concentration camps and forced labour.

Czech youth continues the resistance, and is often driven to desperate measures to obtain the bare necessities of life. The Svenska Dagbladet reports that a few days ago four young Czechs—three boys and a girl—were sentenced to death by the Special Court in the Protectorate as *Volksschädlinge* (*i.e.* persons harmful to the community), guilty of " black slaughtering " and concealment of large quantities of crops. The truth behind this accusation was that the four young members of the same family killed a small pig because their mother was very ill and had to have fresh meat ; they also " concealed " seventy pounds of potatoes to have some provisions for the winter. This is justice as it is meted out in the former hunting-ground of the late unlamented Reinhard Heydrich.

IN the puppet state of Hungary youth has been completely transformed to serve the totalitarian purposes of besotted Horthy and double-crossing Premier Kallay. Some 125,000 girls have been organized in the female branch of the " Levente " movement, a counterpart of the Hitler Youth. The Minister of Education had to resign because he resisted the introduction of textbooks in the Nazi spirit—though the Minister, V. Homan, was of German origin. Even the Hungarian Scouts, who have taken third place after Britain and America at the world jamboree competitions in Copenhagen, have been changed into a semi-military organization, and Count Khuen Héderváry, the former Chief Scout, has had to make way for Major Farkas, a pro-Nazi army officer.

Education is almost at a complete standstill in Norway, where the clergy and the teachers have made such a courageous stand against the obnoxious Quisling. The Rudkan Dagblad reports that a schoolboy has been refused admittance to a secondary school because while at his elementary school he " behaved rudely to children of N.S. members "—the N.S. being Quisling's most unpopular party, Nasjonal Samling. Apparently children of elementary school age can also commit " political crimes " in Nazi-ridden Norway. At the same time it is still undecided whether schools in most parts of the country will restart after the summer holidays, and though Oslo University opened

for a new session on September 1, no new students were enrolled.

IN Denmark, according to the Fyns Tidende, the students held a great summer meeting at which the speakers emphasized that their present aim is " to preserve to the utmost possible extent Denmark's liberty and independence and to strive to regain absolute freedom. It is therefore occasionally necessary to make concessions which perhaps become humiliating to a free people ; but, honestly, we are not at present a free and independent people." Germany, being in desperate need of Denmark's agricultural products, permits a little more latitude and freedom of expression to the Danes than to her other vassals ; but two of the students taking part in this meeting have already been arrested and the others placed under police surveillance. Young Danish cyclists have refused to take part in a "non-political" sports rally at Milan. But twenty Danish " Labour Service " girls have been forced to go to Germany and attend a "leader course."

In Holland the latest, rather comic, effort of the local Nazis to entice youth into their ranks is taking the form of a " poetry competition " in which youths and girls between 14 and 25 have been invited to take part ; elocution competitions are also announced. But, according to the National Dagblad, which interviewed Adriaan van Hees, organizer of the contest, the response has been " most disappointing." Either young Dutchmen

are not of a poetical turn, or they refuse to turn out poetry at Nazi bidding.

The clandestine Belgian paper Le Peuple carries in its latest issue a tragic appeal to Belgian farmers to help save the country's youth. " Children," the paper writes, " cannot be saved by a few francs ; it must be done by bread, milk, meat and eggs. The children of respectable workers are fading away under the eyes of their parents . . . For two years now our young people who have left school cannot find a place in industry, in handicrafts, or in commerce. This must mean a very fair number of young unemployed, an easy prey for recruiters of labour for German industry or the notorious ' Walloon Guard.' Is anything whatsoever being done for these young people ? " Le Nouveau Journal has published an appeal to farmers, asking them to put up during the holidays students whose health is poor. " Our precious youth is wasting away, we must share all we have got to save it." But Belgian farmers, constantly plundered by the

EUROPEAN YOUTH in the Nazi-occupied countries is being inoculated with the pernicious doctrines of the enemy. On a visit to Graz, in the formerly Austrian province of Styria, Hitler reviews boys who have been enlisted in a Nazi-controlled youth formation. *Photo, Keystone*

Germans, have little left to help the young people of the cities.

From France comes the tragic tale of little Marcel K., son of a *rentier*, whose father had never meddled in politics and continued to live in his pleasant villa even after the German occupation. Marcel was the apple of his eye, a sturdy boy of ten. One day (so the story runs) Marcel was playing with two little girls at a level-crossing near his home. The crossing was guarded by German soldiers ; one of them chased the children away and hit one of the little girls a brutal blow. Little Marcel chivalrously stood up for her and shouted some insulting words which he hardly understood himself. The Germans stood him up against a tree and shot him—then carried his little body to his father's villa and dumped it at the gate. Monsieur K. almost lost his mind in his grief ; he tried everything to get " justice " from the local German authorities. Yet the same German soldiers guard the crossing.

IN Yugoslavia youth is taking an especially active part in resisting the invader and the various quisling bodies. Pavelitch, the *Poglavnik* (Fuehrer) of Croatia, was forced, according to the Nova Hrvatska, to draft all students enrolled at Zagreb University and at the economic and commercial high schools, into compulsory labour service, because " this appears to be the most suitable method of constant supervision." Even so, hundreds of students are escaping from the comparatively small area ruled by Pavelitch's *Ustacha* thugs and are joining the Slovenian guerillas.

THE WAR AT SEA

by Francis E. McMurtrie

As I write these lines news comes of a fresh piece of audacity by a U-boat in the Caribbean Sea. For 25 minutes a German submarine lay in Carlisle Bay, Barbados, and discharged at least five torpedoes into the port of Bridgetown, the island's capital. So far as can be gathered no damage of importance was inflicted. Shore batteries opened on the intruder.

It is not many months since a U-boat—possibly the same one—torpedoed a merchant vessel lying in the port of Limon, Costa Rica. The present attack may have been inspired by the recollection that during the last war the captain of the German cruiser Karlsruhe planned to raid Barbados. It was on Nov. 4, 1914 that the Karlsruhe, when within 300 miles of the island, was destroyed by the sudden explosion of her forward magazine. This catastrophe not only saved Barbados from being shelled, but ended the career of a surface raider which, in the space of three months, sank a greater quantity of Allied tonnage than any other vessel except the notorious Emden. Whether the idea came from that source or not, it seems probable that in the present instance the U-boat captain was also influenced by the smaller number of targets available owing to the extension of the convoy system to the Caribbean.

This attack on Barbados is likely to raise afresh the question of exercising stricter control over the French West Indies. It was on Feb. 21 that a German submarine put into Fort de France, Martinique, landed a wounded officer, and after obtaining supplies proceeded to sea again to resume her attacks on commerce. As a result the United States informed the Vichy Government that the use of French ports in the western hemisphere as bases for Axis ships or aircraft could not be permitted, and after some demur extracted an undertaking that there should be no repetition of this incident. In view of recent experience in Madagascar, it seems possible that U-boats may still be receiving information of ships' movements, etc., from French sources in the West Indies.

Clashes between light craft in the English Channel and the North Sea continue to be frequent. One such occurred in the early hours of Sept. 8, when two patrols of our coastal craft under Lieut. J. A. Eardley-Wilmot, R.N., and Lieut. A. R. H. Nye, R.N.V.R., intercepted an enemy supply ship bound for Cherbourg, under escort of armed trawlers and R-boats (motor minesweepers). A brisk action ensued at close range, and in spite of fire being opened on our forces by shore batteries, many hits were made on the enemy vessels. At least one torpedo struck the supply ship, the fate of which appears to be uncertain. Only one of our motor gunboats suffered slight damage, and there were no casualties.

In the Straits of Dover patrols under Lieut. M. Arnold-Forster, R.N.V.R., and Lieut. C. H. W. Andrew, R.N.V.R., intercepted another escorted supply ship. In the action which followed frequent hits were scored on two of the enemy escort craft, the guns of one being silenced. Two slight casualties and some minor superficial damage to one of our boats were all we suffered.

Clashes in the North Sea

Three days later there was a further series of actions off the Dutch coast. To start with, one of our offensive patrols under Lieut. P. G. C. Dickens, R.N. (son of Admiral Sir Gerald Dickens, a grandson of the novelist), intercepted and attacked a German convoy off the Texel. An enemy tanker, of medium size, was seen to disintegrate after being hit by a torpedo. A large "flak" (anti-aircraft) ship, forming part of the escort, is also believed to have been struck by a torpedo. A brisk action continued for some time after this, in the course of which an armed trawler and an R-boat were hit and very severely damaged.

Shortly afterwards a patrol of our light coastal craft, commanded by Lieut. J. B. R. Horne, R.N., intercepted a force of four enemy motor torpedo boats and severely handled one of them before they were able to escape. Later this patrol met two more German m.t.bs., and again one of the enemy vessels was severely damaged.

It would appear that these two enemy groups combined and were reinforced, for a group of about eight German coastal craft was intercepted and engaged a little later by a patrol under Lieut. E. M. Thorpe, R.N. At least three more of the enemy vessels received serious damage in the subsequent action. During this conflict one of our motor gunboats was set on fire badly. As there was no hope of being able to save her, Lieut. Thorpe ran his own motor gunboat alongside the burning vessel, took off survivors, and made certain that she would become a total loss and could not fall into the hands of the enemy. This last action, it should be noted, took place well after daybreak, within 25 miles of the Dutch coast.

I have been asked to explain the differences between the various types of coastal craft which are used in these encounters. The biggest of the British vessels are the motor gunboats, fast craft with a strong armament of pom-poms and heavy machine-guns. Of similar type, though slightly smaller and faster, are the motor torpedo boats, in which torpedo tubes are the predominant item in the armament. Motor launches, though no smaller, are the slowest and least heavily-armed of the three types, being used chiefly for escorting coastal convoys.

Of enemy vessels of corresponding categories, the so-called E-boats are actually known to the Germans as S-boats (*Schnellboote*), and are mostly armed as motor torpedo boats. R-boats (*Räumboote*) are motor minesweepers, resembling our motor launches in their general characteristics. "Flak" ships—a word compounded of the German initials *F.L.A.K.*, equivalent to A.A.—are craft of the coaster or trawler type, mounting high-angle guns.

In the region of the Solomon Islands, for the past fortnight, enemy opposition has been carried on chiefly by aircraft and submarines, which have resisted the landing of supplies and reinforcements for the U.S. Marine forces in Guadalcanal and adjacent islands. In the course of these operations the U.S. destroyer Blue, of 1,500 tons, and a small and old transport, the Colhoun, were lost. A heavy toll of enemy planes was exacted, and loaded landing-barges attempting to disembark enemy troops on Guadalcanal were sunk with heavy loss of life.

On Sept. 12 it was announced from Allied Headquarters in S.W. Pacific that a Japanese destroyer had been sunk off Normanby Island, in the Coral Sea, by Allied bombers.

On Sept. 2 the U.S. Navy Department, Washington, announced that American submarines in Far Eastern waters had sunk a Japanese light cruiser, two small cargo vessels, one medium-sized tanker, and a small steamer. Two large tankers were damaged and a medium-sized cargo ship probably sunk

H.M.S. SHROPSHIRE, British cruiser of the London class, has been given to the Royal Australian Navy to make up for the loss of H.M.A.S. Canberra, sunk off the Solomon Islands by a Japanese attack on August 9. Most of the latter's complement of 816 were rescued, but many of these were wounded, and the commanding officer, Capt. F. E. Getting, was killed. The new H.M.A.S. Canberra, as the Shropshire has been rechristened, was completed in 1929, displaces 9,830 tons, and carries eight 8-in. and eight 4-in. guns.

Photo, Charles E. Brown

Ships that Brazil Brings to the Allied Cause

THE BRAZILIAN NAVY includes two battleships and two cruisers (all built before the last war but recently modernized), three new destroyers, one older one and six more building, and many smaller vessels. I, Torpedo boat Piauhy, built in 1908 ; in the background is the training ship Almirante Saldanha. 2, One of the three modern submarines built in Italy for Brazil. 3, Cruiser Rio Grande do Sul ; she displaces 3,150 tons and carries ten 4·7-in. guns. 4, Minas Gerais, a 19,200-ton battleship, carrying twelve 12-in. and fourteen 4·7-in. guns. *Photos, Pictorial Press, New York Times Photos*

Merchantmen Have Their Own Fighters Now

CATAFIGHTERS—that is, aircraft launched from merchant ships to combat enemy bombers attacking convoys—have been particularly successful on the Murmansk route. They belong to the Merchant Ship Fighter Unit, and the merchantmen from which they are catapulted are known as Cam ships. Above are Flt.-Lt. D. R. Turley-George (left) and his spare pilot F/O. C. Fenwick, with their Hurricane on S.S. Empire Tide, also shown below left. Below right, the Hurricane is about to be catapulted from its runway. After dealing with the raider the pilot bales out and trusts to being picked up by one of the escort ships. His machine is almost always lost ; occasionally it may be near enough to land to get back.

Photos, British Official ; Associated Press

The Admiral Signalled: 'Proud to Have Met You'

THOSE merchantmen going stolidly on and on —never faltering, never wavering when one of their comrades was lost—stolidly on and on ; and although it seems invidious to draw attention to any one of so gallant a party, I simply must do so.

She had been uppermost in our thoughts from the moment we sailed, for she was a tanker carrying the most important and most dangerous cargo of all, and so very conspicuous from the air with her funnel right aft. Her name was Ohio, an American-built ship manned by a British crew, skippered by a very great man called Captain Mason. It was obvious that she would be a special target for the enemy, and sure enough she was hit by a torpedo at the same time as we were.

SHE was forced to stop, and later, as we went up alongside in the Ashanti, another merchantman was blazing not far off. It was that night when things weren't looking too good. Admiral Burrough hailed her from the bridge, "I've got to go on with the rest of the convoy. Make the shore route if you can and slip across to Malta. They need you badly." The reply was instantaneous. "Don't worry, sir ; we'll do our best. Good luck."

By next morning, by some superhuman effort, they had got the engines going and had caught us up in spite of having lost their compass and having to steer from aft. She then took

station on our quarter, and Ohio's next bit of trouble was when a Stuka attacking us was hit fair and square and crashed right into her.

For the rest of the forenoon she was always picked out for special attention, and time and time again she completely disappeared amongst the clouds of water from bursting bombs. But again and again she came through. Then at last one hit her. She was set on fire, but after a terrific fight they managed to get the flames under control. Her engines had been partly wrecked, but she just managed to make two knots and plodded on. Destroyers were left to look after her, but later she was hit again and her engines finally put out of action. Then they took her in tow, but the tow darted. During the night, with the help of a mine-sweeper from Malta, they got her a further twenty miles. All next day she was again bombed continuously, and towing became impossible. But that night she reached Malta.

IF ever there was an example of dogged perseverance against all odds, this was it. Admiral Burrough's last signal to Ohio was short and to the point : "I'm proud to have met you."

All that mattered was that supplies had to be got through to Malta—and they were.

—*Commander Anthony Kimmins, R.N., broadcasting as an eye witness an account of how the convoy got through to Malta during the fierce air and sea battle of August 12–14 (see page 182).*

Despite the enemy's long-sustained onslaught, the valiant oil-tanker Ohio got her valuable cargo of oil through to Malta. This photograph, taken from the deck of one of the escorting warships, shows the Ohio at the moment when she was torpedoed by a lurking U-boat—the first of a long series of mishaps most bravely overcome.

Photo,. Associated Press

GALLANT MASTER, GALLANT SHIP. Captain D. W. Mason (upper photo), Master of the S.S. Ohio, was awarded the George Cross on Sept. 4, 1942, for his part in the epic story of the Malta convoy. "Throughout he showed skill and courage of the highest order," ran the official announcement, "and it was due to his determination that, in spite of the most persistent enemy opposition, the vessel, with her valuable cargo, eventually reached Malta and was safely berthed." In the bottom photograph a huge smoke-column goes up from the 10,000-ton tanker as bombs from one of the attacking Stukas set her alight.

Photos, News Chronicle, British Newsreels

THE HOME FRONT

by E. Royston Pike

WHEN will women cease to be "news"? In the days when reading the newspapers was almost exclusively a masculine occupation it was understandable enough that columns should be filled with discussions and descriptions of the opposite and allegedly mysterious sex, while photographs of bathing belles, Gaiety girls, and Hollywood lovelies were always sure of selection by picture-editors with a keen eye for circulation. But even now, when lots of women read the papers, women are still news, just as they were in the days when for a woman to mount to the top of a bus was—well, something that was just "not done." And it must be admitted that women in wartime provide many an attractive and deeply interesting subject for a vivid pen. Here, for instance, is a White Paper, the Report of the Committee appointed by the Government six months ago to inquire into the amenities and welfare of the three Women's Services, which is both intensely readable and vastly informative—a social document, indeed, of the first importance.

VIRTUE has no gossip value. That pithy if not very profound remark may be taken as the Report's keynote. It will be recalled that at the time of the Committee's appointment there were many and widespread rumours of "immorality" and "drunkenness" on the part of the women and girls in the auxiliary services, the A.T.S. in particular; and those who retailed them with half-disguised gusto may, or may not, be relieved to know that the indictment has been completely disproved. The Committee of five women and three men, under the chairmanship of Miss Violet Markham (Mrs. Carruthers)—who was sent to France in 1918 to investigate very similar charges brought against the W.A.A.C. on similarly slender grounds—have visited camps and billets and training-schools in all parts of the country, carefully considered hundreds of letters, and made personal contacts innumerable. And what is their conclusion? That "we can find no justification for the vague but sweeping charges of immorality which have disturbed public opinion," and that "the nation has every reason to be proud of the women who are sharing the work of the soldiers, sailors and airmen."

But it is noteworthy that with a commendable broadmindedness they recognize the vast changes that time and circumstance have brought about in social conduct.

Thus of recent years "alcohol has become a symbol of conviviality for women no less than men, and has set a standard of social intercourse among people of all ages. Repeated rounds of cocktails involve a substantial consumption of spirits, and they are drunk by many girls who at heart would prefer a soft drink but fear to be dubbed 'not a sport' if they ask for lemonade or ginger beer." All the same, "the British have such a deep-rooted prejudice against uniforms" that the woman in uniform who is seen drinking a glass of beer in a public-house "becomes an easy target for careless talk about the low standards of the Services."

THEN in the matter of sexual behaviour standards have changed greatly in the last generation.

"The use of contraceptives has spread through all classes of society . . . The reticences and inhibitions of the Victorian period have been swept away to be replaced by frank and open discussion," although "there is a certain bravado in much talk that takes place between young people about sex questions, and theories are often paraded in conversation which are never put into practice. Shock tactics used against the shibboleths and conventions of their elders may prove good fun for the younger generation, but it is not surprising if the latter sometimes find themselves taken at their word." Statistics in so intimate a matter cannot prove very much either way, but the Committee puts on record the fact that whereas the illegitimate birth-rate among civilians in the age groups from which A.T.S. are recruited is approximately 21·8 per thousand per annum, the pregnancy rate for single A.T.S. women is 15·4. It should be borne in mind, of course, that a number of women are already pregnant before they are recruited for the Services. "We can say with certainty that the illegitimate birth-rate in the Services is lower than that among the comparable civilian population."

IN uniforms of khaki, Air Force blue, and navy, women have given bountiful proof of their courage and capacity during three years and more of war. Now the women in the home, office, and factory—there's not much doubt about *their* courage and capacity, either!—are (subject to a number of exemptions) about to be enlisted in Mr. Herbert

WOMAN IN THE NEWS. In peacetime glamorous film stars are among Fleet Street's favourite features, but now the spotlight is centred on women in the uniform of the Services or the garb of industry and transport—such as Jean Dale here, one of the 55,000 women employed on Britain's railways. *Photo, Keystone*

Morrison's army of fire watchers. But some women, and quite a lot of men, are up in arms against the decision.

Strong opposition has been voiced in Liverpool City Council on the grounds that women are exempted from fire-watching in the City of London, and that, from the point of view of morality, women should not be required to be about the streets of Liverpool at night. Moreover, it is said that there are plenty of men, and young men at that, who are dodging the fireguard roster. The London Chamber of Commerce, too, has joined in the protests; women, it feels, should not be employed on fire-watch in warehouses and old properties, where it is not possible to provide amenities. At the Trade Union Congress at Blackpool on Sept. 9, Mr. Hallsworth declared that the proposal ought to be resisted since "if there was any loss of life among women with husbands or sweethearts in the Services, there would be a strong revulsion of feeling against putting women to fight fire bombs"; and, besides, if women are to be enlisted, then they ought to receive the same rates of compensation for injuries as men—surely a most reasonable demand." And here is a typically feminine reaction: "We have all had to fight the fire bombs voluntarily in the past," a young woman working in Liverpool is reported as saying, "and women have done their share. But I couldn't stand a night in this office with all the rats and mice running about . . ."

And while on the subject of fires, in this war women are being conjured *not* to "keep the home fires burning." The fuel question has become increasingly serious—through dilly-dallying, assert the Government's critics—and Major Lloyd George and his experts at the new Ministry of Fuel have embarked on a great fuel-saving campaign.

"The Battle for Fuel is on" shriek advertisements in every newspaper; and householders are exhorted to study little diagrams from which their Fuel Targets may be deduced. Every individual is entitled to a personal allowance of 15 Fuel Units—a unit hitherto unknown to science, and one for whose birth no good reason seems to have been advanced; and for the rest, there are allowances graded according to the number of inhabited rooms and the situation of the house—in the North, Midlands, or the South. Criticism of the scheme has been loud and long. The Ministry has been charged with ignorance of the fact that in Britain the isotherms tend to range from west to east, and not from north to south: Essex is much colder than Cornwall, and the Western Isles of Scotland have milder winters very often than are experienced in London. Some unkind critics of our bureaucrats have suggested that the reason why the dwellers in the northern parts of the country are to get more fuel is because the many Civil Servants exiled there have cold feet! Then those who are dependent on paraffin urge that they are unfairly treated as compared with those who use coal, gas, and electricity. But, as the writer of a letter to the Daily Telegraph puts it very sensibly: "No doubt there are many flaws in the scheme, but it gives us housewives something definite to bite on, instead of just vaguely turning down the gas when the pot is boiling, hoping that this will help the war effort somehow."

SHORT socks and no hats! Here is Mr. Dalton at it again, compelling us to take yet another step—or rather two steps—along the road to wartime austerity. "I think we shall all more and more have to go without hats," he said the other day; "anybody who retains his natural hair ought to go without a hat." A few days later came the news that the Board of Trade has given instructions to manufacturers of "Utility" wear that no more normal-length socks are to be made during the war; henceforth men's socks are to be 9 in. in length as against 14½ in. as now worn.

Another item of interest on the clothing front is that the next instalment of coupons must go a bit farther, to March 31, 1943; in other words, the brown coupons are to be available for 5½ months as compared with 4½ months of the previous green coupons. As at present arranged the red coupons the last of the three blocks of twenty in the current book—are to last until July 31 next; but, warns Mr. Dalton, shipping losses have been heavy, and, although recently there has been some improvement, there is likely to be a severe strain on imports for some time ahead. So we are not to make plans on the assumption that we are going to get a new supply of coupons on August 1 of next year.

JUST a few figures to wind up with. "Out of every hundred occupied men and women in this country," Mr. Oliver Lyttelton, Minister of Production, told the Americans in a broadcast on August 27, "about 55 are working for the Government, either in the forces or in the factories, or in other branches of Government service; almost all the rest are doing work which, even if it serves the civilian population, is necessary to the conduct of the war. To reach our present level *you* would need to have very nearly 40,000,000 working for the Government."

That is the human aspect; now for the financial. "We have just completed three years of war," said Sir Kingsley Wood, Chancellor of the Exchequer, when asking the Commons to find a further £1,000,000,000 for the prosecution of the war. "In those three years the war has cost us £10,000,000,000 and, including the cost of the debt and our normal peacetime services, our total expenditure has been £12,100,000,000. Of this huge total we have met 40 per cent out of taxation."

And before the war Fascists told us—and there were some in this country who believed them—that we were a decadent people!

Tanks or Watches, R.E.M.E. Mends Them All

BRITAIN'S LATEST ARMY 'CORPS'—the Royal Electrical and Mechanical Engineers—came into being on Oct. 1, 1942. It is responsible for Army mechanical maintenance. Hauling an armoured vehicle from a ditch (left). Above, Polish fitters working on a tank.

'R.E.M.E.' will be primarily and chiefly responsible for maintaining the Army's machines in proper working order. Above, an A.T.S. engraver, attached to the Corps, works on repairing a gun sight. Below, Army mincing-machines are being put in order.

ASSEMBLING A 25-POUNDER GUN (above) is a job that demands strength and technical proficiency. Most of the men in the new Corps have been transferred from the Royal Army Ordnance Corps and the R.A. Service Corps. *Fox, Daily Mirror*

Brave Deeds Recalled by Our Roving Camera

HERO OF TOBRUK. Mr. H. A. Barker, to whom an M.B.E. was awarded on August 14, 1942, is a Y.M.C.A. official who, after the taking of Tobruk in January 1941 opened a centre in the town and, in spite of hardships and bombing, remained manfully at his post throughout the siege.

LONDON'S NEW DEEP SHELTERS (above), formed in sections of a new underground railway to be opened after the War, show many improvements over some of the older types. When completed they will sleep some 64,000 people—representing about half the present tube shelter accommodation.

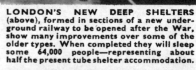

MALTA CONVOY AWARDS. Among the first D.S.O.s of the Merchant Navy are Captain David R. MacFarlane and Captain Richard Wren, who are thus honoured for "the great fortitude, seamanship and endurance they displayed in taking merchantmen through to Malta in the face of relentless enemy attacks." Above, Capt. Wren (in civilian clothes) talking to Rear-Admiral R. E. Burrough, C.B. ; below, Capt. MacFarlane.

U.S. PARADE IN LONDON, on Sept. 2, 1942, was a great success, when 300 American airmen, soldiers, and sailors marched through the City to lunch with Sir John Laurie, the Lord Mayor, in the Guildhall—that historic building has survived five centuries and two Fires of London. Here is the procession in Cannon Street with a freshly-visible St. Paul's in the background.

Photos, British Official: The Daily Express, Planet News, Sport & General, Daily Mirror

I WAS THERE! Eye Witness Stories of the War

'We Will Stick it in Malta. We Will Win'

"It means a lot to us to know that you in England are not forgetting us. It helps us to take it when we know we are not fighting unnoticed." So writes our young Maltese correspondent, John Mizzi, in another letter to the Editor, some of the most interesting passages of which are printed below.

ONE day in April last a Maltese L.A.C., training in Canada, stepped out of a train and went to the restaurant of the railway station. It happened that the Governor-General of Canada, the Earl of Athlone, came to the same restaurant just as the L.A.C. was sitting down. The earl stopped in the doorway and scanned the room. His eyes alighted on the word "Malta" on the aircraftman's tunic. He went up to him at a brisk pace with a smile on his face, gave him a friendly pat on the back, and sat down at the same table as the Maltese lad. He praised Malta, and before leaving—would you believe it ?—he invited the Maltese L.A.C. to pay him a visit at his home in Ottawa, if he ever happened to be there.

All this tribute to my little island, when you outside Malta don't even know three-fourths of what we have been enduring . . . We will stick it, though. Better this than hear the tramp of German jackboots and the unending bragging of the Italians. I *know* we will win. I feel it in my bones. I see Britain's air might growing here. I see Germany's biting the dust. The R.A.F. is grand. Had it not been for the Spitfires and the men who fly them Malta would have been in a far worse fix. I won't say Malta would have been crushed. Malta never will be crushed—never. God knows whom to protect, as much as we know Whom to ask for help. It is not very hard to see that Almighty God has his arms round little Malta.

If I look from my back window I see a house razed to the ground ; if I look from the balcony I see the spot where a boy was killed by a dirty Italian tip-and-run

raider. If I go into the garden I might tumble in a crater from an exploded D.A. bomb ; if I go on the roof I see the planes, the Spitfires confident and eager, the four-engined planes, and the sleek fast-moving Beauforts protected by the odd-shaped Beau-fighters ; and underneath this canopy of air might I see, through the tears in my eyes, I see destruction. My poor island blown to pieces, fields uplifted, and every corner the scene of some tragedy. But I see something else. I see the people weaving in and out of the rubble, laughing, confident in God, sure of victory ; and the spirit of the men of 1565, and of the murdered of 1940, 1941, 1942, looking on with sympathy and pride.

THERE is at a certain spot in Valetta a statue of Christ the King with Malta kneeling in fervent prayer at His feet (*see* photo right). This statue is on the outskirts of the city, and was surrounded by trees, situated in an airy place overlooking the two harbours. I wish you could see it now. More bombs have fallen round that spot than any other place in the whole world. The trees there now are leaning sideways, black and withering. The small garden around the monument is one huge crater, and all around there is devastation and desolation. But there God still reigns supreme, with Malta never losing faith at His feet. The statue is not even bruised. That is a sign from God. A man can be killed, but not his faith. Man may have his way, but God sees all and pays back in due time and in due proportions.

Not long ago bombs fell in our garden. The bomb-disposal squad men came, three in all, an officer and two N.C.O.s, to explode them. The lieutenant was a strapping lad of

CHRIST THE KING, the statue at Valetta, Malta, referred to in this page. This photo, taken before the war, comes from John Mizzi, the author of the accompanying text. Malta is depicted by the kneeling figure praying at the feet of the Saviour.

twenty-one, with red face and unruly hair. He and the other two were the coolest men on earth. They picked up the bombs as if they were loaves of bread, took them to a field and exploded them there. Father called them in and gave them drinks, and our neighbours gave them fruit, grapes or figs. They had been exploding bombs all day.

Well, the couple of N.C.O.s went to where my brother was looking at some "comics" and picked up one each. "Better than bombs," grinned one. "Haven't seen any of these for ages." They were human, after all, these men who were playing with death themselves to save others from death . . .

Surrounded by bomb craters and distorted trees, this is how the statue appeared last May before the concentrated bombing attacks by the Axis pounded Malta by day and by night. The scene has been transformed from one of peaceful beauty to a grimly realistic setting. The figure of Christ is poised against a background of war-scarred houses. The fury of enemy raids on Malta cannot defeat the heroic spirit of the island's inhabitants. In the words of a captured enemy pilot, "the only way to take Malta is to sink it."

Photo, Sport & General

BRITISH SAILORS ON A FREE FRENCH WARSHIP. Here are the three men whose experiences on La Moqueuse are given below. Left, William Beck, a signalman, who is 20 and lives at Preston, Lancs. Centre, R. T. Fryer, 21-year-old coder, who comes from Birkenhead ; this photograph confirms his own claim (see below) to have mastered the phrase " Donnez-moi du feu, s'il vous plaît." Right, J. A. T. Woods, also 21, whose home is in Surrey ; like William Beck, he is a signalman, and, like all the Englishmen aboard La Moqueuse, he is obviously on excellent terms with his French shipmates.
Photos, Forces Françaises Libres

We're English Sailors in Free France's Navy

Serving on board the Free French sloop La Moqueuse is a little group of English seamen, and here some of them describe how well they have settled down to work with their French shipmates.

Iᴛ was in Pompey Barracks about a year ago (it is William Beck speaking) I first heard of La Moqueuse. The Master-at-Arms said, " You're to go to the Moqueuse." " What's that ? " I asked. " French ship," he said. Well, I can tell you it was a bit of a poser, me not knowing a word of their lingo.

However, I arrived and found I wasn't the only Englishman on board, so that made it a bit less strange-like. Then I found that there wasn't much difference between the way the French matelots did things and the way we do 'em. Of course, all the names are different, but when you get to know them it isn't so bad, and it's wonderful what you can do with sign language if you try.

We find it pretty comfortable on board, and I took to their red wine—" Pinard," they call it—like a duck to water. The victuals are good, too. The only thing we English fellows don't like is all the garlic they put in the food, but we went and saw the cook about it and now he cooks a lot without any.

I'm a signalman ; by the way, all the British ratings on board are in the communications side of it. Our job is to help with all signals and things like that. You see, it's a bit hard for the Frenchies when they're out with British ships to take down signals and translate them quickly in English—so we're there to make it a bit easier.

I've seen quite a few places since I've been with the Moqueuse—French colonies for instance, which British people don't see so often ; and I've seen them go for the Jerries a few times, U-boats and aeroplanes mostly. And let me tell you this : The Free Frenchies are O.K.

To R. T. Fryer, a twenty-one-year-old coder on board the Moqueuse, the strangest thing on a French warship is the language difficulty.

Aˢ one becomes accustomed to it, however, one quickly begins to pick up small French phrases such as " Donnez-moi du feu, s'il vous plaît." Usually, however, we speak English, as most of the French boys have managed to pick up our language quite well and they prefer us to speak in English as they are all very keen to improve. However, of course, we like to show off our French, and so they do not have it all their own way, and often it happens that we speak in French and they answer in English. We can all tell the time like Frenchmen now

and are quite proud of ourselves. Naturally there are some phrases which we picked up quickly. If at any time we get into really deep water, there is always a dictionary at hand. My fellow watch-keeper could not speak any English when he first joined this ship, but through great use of the dictionary he is becoming very efficient, and similarly my French is improving by leaps and bounds.

The Free French are very keen about the part they are playing in this struggle, and they are never happier than when at sea chasing U-boats or shooting down enemy aircraft. If anyone ever had any doubts about the Free French Navy all they need do is to see these boys in action.

Then, to conclude, here is what another signalman, J. A. T. Woods, says about La Moqueuse.

Life on board the F.S. La Moqueuse comes very strange to English sailors at first. The routine and food, etc., are much different from an English ship, but of course you get used to things in time. It can be very monotonous, with a few high spots, such as French bugle calls and the English newspaper, Moqueuse Mercury (one copy daily), which is edited and published by our " Sparker."

Fun can be had in our efforts to speak French and trying to teach the Frenchmen English. One can very easily guess the type of words which are learnt first. Having been on the ship for over ten months, I have made good friends on board, and am able to get on very well with them. It's grand to be shipmates with men so eager to fight the common enemy, and wipe them from the earth to make it a better place to live in.

'Shake Hands! I'm From Tobruk'

A month after the fall of Tobruk Lieut. T. A. Nicol, of the Cameron Highlanders, walked into the British lines 300 miles away. Here is the story which he told to Norman Clark, News Chronicle War Correspondent.

Oᵁᴿ battalion position was on the outskirts of Tobruk perimeter. The enemy gave us time enough only to dig slit trenches a few inches deep, then unleashed bombs and shells upon us. Machine-guns and anti-tank 2-pounders, that's all we had. Every time we lifted our heads 25-pounders, captured by the enemy some time during the Eighth Army's withdrawal from Gazala, opened up point-blank at us. So we kept our heads down.

That went on all of Saturday (June 20)! Next morning we noticed big bodies of our troops marching down the road in fours. We couldn't make it out at all. To start with, we thought it a little too foolhardy ; and files of four of marching columns puzzled us. The enemy's guns, too, were not firing —except at us.

We could see groups of Italians walking about in front of us, smoking. Then seven Italian tanks began to move down the road firing straight ahead.

We were at the side of the road less than 100 yards away. We let the tanks come on, then with our single two-pounder picked them off, one by one, starting with the one bringing up the rear and working up to the front. That brought fire upon us, but our casualties were light.

For the rest of the day we lay low. At dusk we could see Italians walking about, still smoking glowing cigarettes. That wasn't like them, we thought, but communications

with the division had broken down, and until a runner returned we could but fight on.

After midnight a party came towards me with a white flag. We could see by the moon it was a German officer and three South African officers. He came up to me first and said the garrison had surrendered, that it was no use resisting, and that they didn't want to kill any more. " War is over for all of you," he kept on saying.

I passed him on to the colonel, to whom he announced that, unless the battalion surrendered and word was taken back to headquarters within an hour, the three South African officers, who were hostages for our good conduct, would be shot.

The colonel had no alternative. He called officers before him, told them the position, and said : " The battalion will fall in on the road at 5 a.m. with rations and kit necessary as prisoners of war." But apart from wounded I don't think a single officer obeyed the colonel's last order. We were so bitter about it all, we one and all decided to get away if we could.

Before the battalion fell in on the road— there must have been fewer than a platoon that were marched away—parties set out independently, carrying what water rations they could. Before it was light we made our way to a hole in the ground, and lay under a sheet of corrugated iron throughout the day.

At dusk I had a look out with my field-glasses. I could see little parties getting up out of holes all around us to make what distance they could during darkness. It did one's heart good to see so many taking the chance. They were everywhere one looked, climbing out of their hide-outs and stepping out for the frontier.

It took us a fortnight to get to the wire. We had no water left. We drank what rusty water we could drain out of the radiators of derelict trucks. A wounded corporal whose back was beginning to fester had to be left, as comfortable as possible, beside the road along which every now and again a lorry passed.

Another mile or two and we had to rest every 50 yards or less. Then I saw a barrel. "Petrol, I'll bet," somebody said. I said—something seemed to tell me it would turn out to be water—I said, " No, it's water this time, boys." They all laughed at me. But I crawled over, cupped my hand into it, tasted it. It was water. The others didn't believe me, but saw me gulping it down and stumbled up to the barrel—a 44-gallon barrel it was.

We gorged ourselves with it. Our tongues were black and swollen through drinking rusty radiator water. The skin on our faces was black, too. We just drank and drank. It made us sick. But we'd go away to vomit, then come back again.

After a night's sleep we made for the next well I could find on the map. When we got there we found near it a ration dump—tinned meat and vegetable stew, bully, dried fruits, cigarettes. We stayed there eight days recovering our strength. We couldn't believe any of our luck was true. But all the time we had before us the determination to get through after enduring so much.

We could see German trucks on the skyline and kept away from them. Then, one day, we held up a German lorry that came towards us and bowled along for miles—until we found ourselves inside an Italian wired position which was being shelled by our guns.

GERMAN TANK AT TOBRUK—a photo taken since Rommel's capture of the port on June 21, 1942. Tobruk was the scene of a combined operations raid on September 13, when our bombers and naval units bombarded the port and landing parties went ashore. After inflicting damage our forces withdrew. Two British destroyers, Sikh and Zulu, were reported sunk.
Photo, Associated Press

We abandoned the lorry and hid in a hole. An Italian came into it and said something. We mumbled back. Then he sat on the edge dangling his feet. We thought we were finished, and began hiding revolvers and our compass in the sand. We ate our last food before his eyes. Then he went away—to bring back more guards, we thought. Ten minutes passed. He didn't come back. We could see Italians everywhere, even Italian officers eating outside a mess truck. But nobody took any notice of us. When that Italian didn't come back and dusk fell I got down on my knees and said a prayer.

Then we walked through a hole made in the wire by a shell.

One morning I saw what I took to be bushes, and heard someone say, " Come on, it's five o'clock." Without thinking I looked at my watch. It was five o'clock.

Then I jumped—that was somebody speaking English. I had been almost too unconscious to realize it. Going up to the bush—it was a lorry—in the half light I pushed a revolver into a man's ribs. " Are you English ? " I demanded. " Yes, why ? " came the reply. " Thank God," I said. " Shake hands ! I'm from Tobruk."

OUR DIARY OF THE WAR

SEPT. 2, 1942, Wednesday   *1,096th day*
Air.—Strong force of R.A.F. bombers made heavy night attack on Karlsruhe.
Russian Front.—After stubborn fighting the Russians withdrew in one sector of the Stalingrad front.
Australasia.—Japs increased their attacks in Kokoda area of New Guinea.

SEPT. 3, Thursday   *1,097th day*
Russian Front.—Further slight withdrawal by Russians S.W. of Stalingrad.
Australasia.—Japanese made fresh landings in the south-eastern Solomons.
General.—Señor Suñer displaced from his position as Foreign Minister and President of the Political Junta of the Falange.

SEPT. 4, Friday   *1,098th day*
Air.—U.S. Fortresses made heavy daylight raid on Rouen. R.A.F. attacked Bremen by night, while Soviet bombers raided Budapest, Vienna, Breslau and Königsberg.
Russian Front.—German progress S.W. of Stalingrad halted by Russian defence.
Africa.—Rommel's armoured divisions withdrew to the west under pressure from our forces.
Home.—Attacks by bomb and rifle fire on several police stations in Northern Ireland.

SEPT. 5, Saturday   *1,099th day*
Russian Front.—Russians continued to hold up German progress towards Stalingrad and the Grozny oilfields.
Africa.—Enemy main concentrations continued to withdraw westward.
Australasia.—Attacks by Allied fighters and bombers on New Guinea aerodromes.

SEPT. 6, Sunday   *1,100th day*
Air.—American Flying Fortresses and Boston bombers made daylight attacks on airfields at Abbeville and St. Omer and air-frame factory at Méaulte. A strong force of bombers attacked Duisburg by night.
Russian Front.—Defenders of Stalingrad continued to hold their ground. Germans claimed capture of Novorossisk.
Africa.—Our forces harassed the enemy, who continued to move westwards.

Home.—Sharp air attack on north-east town.

SEPT. 7, Monday   *1,101st day*
Air.—U.S. Fortresses in daylight raids on Rotterdam and Utrecht shot down 12 enemy fighters without loss.
Russian Front.—Russians withdrew to new positions W. of Stalingrad ; fighting for Novorossisk continued.

SEPT. 8, Tuesday   *1,102nd day*
Air.—Daylight raids on docks at Cherbourg and Le Havre. Heavy night attack on Frankfurt.
Russian Front.—Further withdrawal by Russians west of Stalingrad. Germans reported that fighting was still going on in Novorossisk.
Africa.—R.A.F. bombers made heavy raid on Tobruk.
Australasia.—In New Guinea Japs advancing from Kokoda reached a point 10 m. N. of gap in the Owen Stanley Range.

SEPT. 9, Wednesday   *1,103rd day*
Air.—Whirlwind fighter-bombers in action for first time against shipping off French coast. Soviet bombers raided Budapest, Berlin and Königsberg.
Russian Front.—On South Volga front Russians again withdraw W. of Stalingrad. Germans broke into the suburbs at Novorossisk.

SEPT. 10, Thursday   *1,104th day*
Air.—A powerful force of R.A.F. bombers raiding Düsseldorf made the heaviest attack yet made on a moonless night.
Russian Front.—Three more places W. of Stalingrad evacuated by Russians. Street battles took place in Novorossisk.
Africa.—Our mobile columns and artillery engaged enemy tanks W. of Hemeimat.
Indian Ocean.—British troops began further military operations in Madagascar, making widespread landings on the west coast.
Australasia.—Fighting in New Guinea took a graver turn as the Japanese outflanked our positions in the gap in the Owen Stanley Range.

SEPT. 11, Friday   *1,105th day*
Russian Front.—Evacuation of Novorossisk announced by Russians. Round Stalingrad the Russians held their ground, and on the central and northern fronts continued to make progress.
Indian Ocean.—Our columns made progress inland from west coast of Madagascar.

SEPT. 12, Saturday   *1,106th day*
Russian Front.—Russians withdrew in sector S.W. of Stalingrad.
Africa.—Large force of bombers of

S.A.A.F. attacked landing-grounds E. of Mersa Matruh.
Burma.—R.A.F. heavy bombers raided Mandalay and Rangoon.
Australasia.—Japs launched large-scale air and sea attacks on American positions at Guadalcanal in the Solomons.

SEPT. 13, Sunday   *1,107th day*
Air.—Strong force of R.A.F. bombers made heavy raid on Bremen, while Soviet bombers attacked Bucharest and Ploesti.
Russian Front.—Russians held all their positions W. and S.W. of Stalingrad. On Barents Sea coast Soviet Marines made a " Commando " landing.
China.—Chinese forces recaptured Kufang on the Chekiang-Kiangsi railway.
Australasia.—Jap bombers made heavy attacks on airfield at Guadalcanal. During the night of Sept. 13-14 American positions were shelled by Jap surface craft.

SEPT. 14, Monday   *1,108th day*
Sea.—Canadian Navy Ministry announced loss of patrol vessel Raccoon and four merchant ships.
Air.—R.A.F. bombers attacked Wilhelmshaven in force.
Russian Front.—Germans made no advance in the battle for Stalingrad. On the Caucasus front the Russians withdrew at Mozdok.
Mediterranean.—U.S. bombers raided docks at Suda Bay, Crete.
Africa.—On the night of Sept. 13-14 our forces made seaborne raid on Tobruk in conjunction with heavy air attack.
Indian Ocean.—Our troops in Madagascar continued to make progress into the interior, meeting little opposition.
Australasia.—Jap bombers again raided airfield at Guadalcanal.
U.S.A.—Liberator bombers attacked Jap installations in the Aleutians, sinking or damaging several ships and aircraft.

Sept. 15, Tuesday   *1,109th day*
Russian Front.—German assault on Stalingrad reaching its height, with mass air attacks.
Mediterranean.—Our bombers attacked docks at Heraklion, Crete.
General.—Announced that Canadian casualties in Dieppe raid of August 19 totalled 3,350 killed, wounded and missing.

★————————— *Flash-backs* —————————★

1939
September 3. *Britain and France declared war on Germany.*
September 11. *B.E.F.'s presence in France announced.*

1940
September 3. *U.S.A. agreed to transfer 50 destroyers to Royal Navy.*
September 7. *In heaviest air*

attacks yet made on London, 103 German aircraft were destroyed.
September 15. *Battle of Britain reached its climax; 185 German aircraft shot down.*

1941
September 8. *Announcement of Allied raid on Spitzbergen.*
September 15. *Germans claimed to have reached suburbs of Leningrad.*

Editor's Postscript

THE fourth winter of black-out will presently be upon us. Few will regard it with indifference. One really does not get used to black-out; only those whose deeds are dark can welcome it. The sense of frustration which it spreads over so large an area of our social life is very wearing. Everywhere, but in London especially, the transport problem makes us acutely aware of petrol restrictions. Frantic cries of "taxi! taxi!" in shrill, stentorian, and cheery or beery voices that echo through the night make us more than ever conscious of the great service which the taximen, who brave the black-out dangers, render the community. With few exceptions they have done, and are doing, their job efficiently and in good temper. As one who uses taxis more than most, I consider they ought all to get double fare in black-out runs, especially at a late hour when their limited supply of petrol is nearing exhaustion. It is no uncommon thing for a driver to get stranded by endeavouring to carry an exigent fare beyond the distance he reckoned his juice would serve. Past eleven last night I heard a swaggering officer at the door of a Mayfair hotel command a driver to take him to Liverpool Street—no small stretch—and when the taximan quite reasonably pointed out that his petrol was insufficient to bring him back to his West-End garage, the officer blustered and insisted on getting into the cab, telling the driver he had better get a move on or he'd make trouble.

IT looks as though some adaptation of the "jitney" system, which allows taxis to carry several individual fares on the same route, may yet have to be permitted in London. Why shouldn't drivers follow certain routes, like the buses, and pick up or let down passengers by the way? The obvious answer is that the taximeter is set for one hire, and hopeless confusion would arise in respect to apportioning the fares, while trouble might inevitably result if drivers were allowed to exact what they wanted from each passenger; the old "pirate" days might be back again! Another and even greater objection would be that you might find yourself at too close quarters with tipplers, trulls, and thieves ... which settles it! Human ingenuity might be equal to inventing a night service that came between the taxi and the bus, but human character and common dishonesty stand in the way of its working.

TALKING of dishonesty, there was a case in the papers this morning of "the perfect clerk" who robbed his employers of more than £3,000 in eighteen months. He got four years and the police have recovered more than half of his swag. Perhaps he would have been glad of the four years had he got away with all his peculations. "Opportunity makes a thief," said Francis Bacon, and he spoke from experience, as he had done a bit "in a big way" himself when opportunity offered, though he got out of the £40,000 fine imposed upon him. Having no very high estimate of human honesty, I am certain that the present confusion will lead to an enormous increase in roguery. The monstrous growth of bureaucracy, enabling multitudes of men and women to handle sums of so-called public money which is passing from private possession into their clutches and being squandered in ways that are nominally "official" but criminally wasteful, can have no result other than a general debasing of the standard of honest dealings. Some day a painstaking statistician may be able to tell us how much of the £14,000,000 being daily "spent on the War" has honestly been applied in war effort. The wastage will call for astronomical figures to express it. And all that wastage is encouraging dishonesty and strengthening the natural bent of ordinary mortals towards carelessness in money matters and the property of others —a tendency that, even before the War, stood in little need of strengthening.

QUEEN WILHELMINA of [the Netherlands celebrated her 62nd birthday on August 31, 1942, amid the rejoicing of [thousands of her loyal subjects. She attended an important Dutch festival held in London. The Queen recently visited Canada and the U.S.
Photo, New York Times Photos

WHAT a chancy affair is death! As a Glasgow comedian, long before Harry Lauder made their school famous, used to put it: "We're here th' day an' awa' th' morn," like the Belfast boat." Through my own long day I have never been able quite to throw off my feeling of the impermanence of living things, have never needed a skeleton at my feast of life. A light heart has been an enduring help, but the sudden and unexpected withdrawals of familiar friends and acquaintances bring sorrowful thoughts that will not be denied. As today, when I read in my morning paper that William Murdoch, with whom I was talking a few weeks ago as full of life and kindliness as I have known him over many years, had died at the early age of 54. Since modern science has added some fifteen years to the Psalmist's allowance, so that 85 is now as common a "span" as three score and ten used to be, most men are still on the crest of life in their fifties. Murdoch was one of the finest pianists of his age, and as unlike the showman type of musician as could be imagined. A scholar, a profound student of his art, a master executant, and withal a modest and a charming companion. I have always thought that his acceptance in Norway as the ideal interpreter of Grieg's music was a singular honour, but perhaps it was not so strange that an Australian should be the favourite player of Norway's favourite composer, for both of them were of Scottish origin. If Murdoch's span has proved short it must have been gloriously worth while to him, and come the day when it may that's a great matter. His death might have had wider notice had he called himself Murdokovsky.

LOOKING across a far-stretching Sussex common this morning for the many thousandth time, I found myself still marvelling at the strangeness of the scene that first engaged me about midsummer, by which I mean the middle of June, for this year the summer has had neither a beginning, a middle, nor an end. Behold a journey back in time! A motor car in this rural landscape has become almost a rare sight, quite as unusual as when I first started driving one nearly forty years ago. But the bicycle has come into its own again. Numerous cyclists go skimming by on their silent wheels and only the laughter from little groups (for they are mostly young folk and have not yet learned to be unhappy) draws the eye to what the ear has first detected. My own cycling years in the green Midlands instantly flash back, though the astounding changes of nearly fifty years have passed between. Old motorist though I am, I sometimes wish this present vogue of the bicycle might long continue. But that is a vain thought, which reminds me of the hard-working Lancashire woman I knew in Bolton with her family of three delightful young children. As I complimented her on them she sighed and said: "Oh, if they could only stay like that and not grow up!" A whole world of vain thoughts is contained in that wish.

BUT I am apprehensive of what this new state of our highways and byways portends. Already in London I have noticed that the dithering jay walkers are increasing alarmingly and the motor drivers that remain have to face anew the trials that beset us in those early days when men, women and children, horses and dogs had not yet grown used to mechanical traffic. Children are playing again in the middle of the roads, and less often now do you notice pedestrians taking precautionary glances right or left; they just step off the kerb as though all wheeled traffic had ceased. In country lanes the only things to keep the wits of wanderers sharpened are Bren carriers and military wagons which make so much noise that they are really less dangerous to walkers than groups of cyclists or the infrequent car. Even the dogs, who have shown more adaptability than the humans in acquiring road sense, may now be in danger of losing it in such peaceful highway conditions as I have been looking at this morning, where, before the War, constant streams of motorists were passing in four directions all through the hours of the day and far into the night.

Printed in England and published every alternate Friday by the Proprietors, THE AMALGAMATED PRESS, LTD., The Fleetway House, Farringdon Street, London, E.C.4. Registered for transmission by Canadian Magazine Post. Sole Agents for Australia and New Zealand: Messrs. Gordon & Gotch, Ltd.; and for South Africa: Central News Agency, Ltd.—October 2, 1942. S.S. *Editorial Address:* JOHN CARPENTER HOUSE, WHITEFRIARS, LONDON, E.C.4.

Vol 6 — The War Illustrated — N° 139

Edited by Sir John Hammerton

SIXPENCE   OCTOBER 16, 1942

BRITAIN'S NEW TANK—the "Churchill"—possesses an astonishing speed and manoeuvrability, and, owing to its powerful armament, can be used as a pill-box. Early models were equipped with the two-pounder gun, but in the light of Libyan experience six-pounders are now fitted, giving this heavy infantry tank formidable fire-power. This photograph shows a "Churchill" moving off at speed after being landed from a tank landing craft during combined operational exercises.   *Photo, British Official: Crown Copyright*

NO. 140 WILL BE PUBLISHED FRIDAY, OCTOBER 30

ALONG THE BATTLE FRONTS

by Our Military Critic, Maj.-Gen. Sir Charles Gwynn, K.C.B., D.S.O.

Far from worsening, the situation during the second half of September steadily improved, although there was no outstanding event to mark progress.

The most satisfactory feature was the obvious German discomfiture at the failure to achieve decisive results anywhere on the Russian front, in spite of intensified exertions and reckless expenditure of lives. German spokesmen, unable to hide their disappointment, began to make excuses, and there were rumours of friction between Von Bock and Hitler. Again Russia in her hour of greatest peril has shown signs, not of collapse, but of renewed vitality.

Elsewhere, although the occupation of Madagascar was the only clear-cut success achieved by the Allies, they have held their ground in practically all theatres and have inflicted considerable losses on the enemy. Bombing attacks on Germany are steadily increasing in weight, and covering a wider area. If they have not yet perceptibly affected Germany's immediate war potentiality they must have compelled her to draw heavily on reserves, increased labour difficulties, and made the problem of finding adequate accommodation for large sections of the population during the winter very serious.

If there are as yet no indications where or when the Allies can achieve decisive victory over either the Axis or Japan, the prospects of the enemy gaining further substantial successes have definitely diminished.

RUSSIA

Throughout the whole of our period German attacks on Stalingrad increased in intensity. Every expedient was tried : concentration of bombing on small areas to obliterate the defences, bombardment by heavy siege guns, attacks by tanks in mass or infiltrating. All failed to crush the defence, and more and more infantry had to be used in street fighting, where the opponents were so closely locked that bombs and heavy shells could not support the attack for fear of destroying their own troops.

In this class of fighting the Germans met their match ; their advance became slower and slower ; extravagant, almost desperate, use of reserves failed to increase the rate of progress. Contrary to expectations, the Russians have been able to reinforce the garrison, though I doubt whether the report that they used submerged bridges to cross the Volga can be accepted.

Meanwhile, Timoshenko's counter-attacks from the north against Von Bock's left flank, which at first seemed merely gallant attempts to relieve pressure on the city, and too weak to produce much effect, grew in importance when they also were reinforced. Von Bock could no longer treat them lightly or rely on his despised Italian allies to protect his flank. German troops, including Panzer divisions, had to be employed to meet what had become a dangerous threat.

IN A RUSSIAN VILLAGE these Red Army men are charging through a farmyard, while some of their fellows put up covering fire from behind agricultural implements and military debris left behind by the Nazis in their flight. Scores of "inhabited places" have been retaken recently by the Russians after extremely bitter fighting. *Photo, British Official : Crown Copyright*

From a purely military standpoint, Von Bock must have begun to doubt whether it was really worth expending men and material in the attempt to complete the capture of the city by assault. He had already achieved a great part of his object, for he had practically destroyed Stalingrad as a centre of war industries, and had gained a position which enabled him to interrupt through traffic on the Volga. The attainment of his full object was evidently going to be no easy matter ; it would mean further loss of time and might necessitate damaging his own army more than that of his enemy.

If he left an investing force at Stalingrad to maintain the advantage he had already secured, might he not divert the bulk of his striking force to a more worthwhile object ? His army pressing in the direction of the Grozny oilfield and the Caspian was held up on the Terek river. By strongly reinforcing it, could he not set it again in motion ? During the winter it might well be more important to hold air bases on the Caspian from which shipping, carrying Baku

oil and Allied war material from Iran, could be attacked, than to be established on the banks of a frozen Volga. Since his capture of Novorossisk his troops there also had failed to make further progress. Did not they require reinforcements in order to capture Tuapse and thereby further restrict the activities of the Black Sea fleet ? Though he had captured Novorossisk the Russians were still in a position to prevent him making use of the port for the relief of the strain on his railways.

Cessation of attacks on Stalingrad would in any case relieve the strain on his communications, and allow him to give more weight to the Caucasus operations.

If Von Bock contemplated any such switch of his main effort, would Hitler consent ? The prestige of the Reichswehr was deeply committed, and failure to take Stalingrad, coming after failure to capture Leningrad and Moscow, would provide fresh proof that it was not invincible.

The situation was one that seemed likely to provoke a clash between military and political considerations. The growing strength and success of Timoshenko's counter-attack introduced a new complication. If it developed the weight of a major offensive it might not only relieve pressure on the city, but also make it impossible for Von Bock to reinforce the Caucasus front.

Berlin had also begun to show increased anxiety about Zhukov's offensive, which had so far only succeeded in maintaining sufficient pressure on the northern sectors of the front to prevent German troops being transferred to the southern theatre. Now Berlin suspected that the offensive had not developed its full strength, and spoke of large Russian forces assembling in the Moscow region.

Despite their great successes, the Germans evidently now realize that they have not broken Russia's offensive power. Committed to holding a front immensely longer than that of last winter, they obviously fear that the initiative which the Russians hold

STALINGRAD, the great Russian city for which Hitler's legions under Von Bock have been battling by day and by night for weeks, stands on the Volga, Europe's greatest river and here about a mile wide. German attacks are indicated by black arrows, and Russian counter-attacks by white ones. *By courtesy of The Daily Telegraph*

east of Leningrad, at Rzhev and to some extent at Voronezh, may be greatly extended.

EGYPT

The lull on the El Alamein front, after the defeat of Rommel's offensive, continued until another full moon excited expectations of operations on a larger scale than patrol activities and artillery exchanges.

The lull was, however, to some extent broken by the combined raid on Tobruk on Sept. 13-14 which, though expensive, must have seriously damaged Rommel's supply organization, for Tobruk had become his main base. The raid simultaneously carried out on Benghazi and Barce by a force that had started from Kufra oasis must, if not equally damaging, have been even more disconcerting.

A RAID by a land force 500 miles behind his front is a trouble no general is likely to consider a serious possibility. Now that it has occurred it will probably lead to further dispersion of Rommel's forces, both land and air. The great length of his communications must in any case have necessitated considerable dispersion of his fighting aircraft on protective duties, but now as well he will probably have to employ greater numbers of machines on somewhat wasteful reconnaissance patrols. The raid on the

mainly defensive, aiming at maintaining possession of territory she has secured. For that object her fleet must be kept in being, but ready to accept action only under conditions when she possesses a superior shore-based umbrella. Such offensive operations as she may now under-take will have mainly a defensive purpose and will be carried out by her army and air force without involving risks to her navy. Her operations in Chekiang had that character, and if, despite renewed assurances of neutrality, she attacked Russia, it would be so as to gain greater security against air attack.

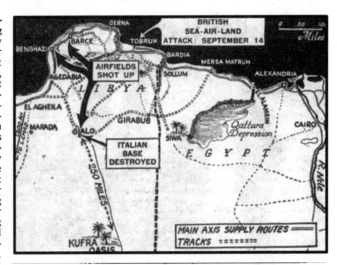

ROMMEL'S BACK-DOOR—Axis bases and ports in Libya—have been vigorously attacked by the R.A.F. of late weeks. Our bombers brilliantly backed up the daring attack on the Italian outpost of Gialo made by raiding columns of the 8th Army. *By courtesy of The Daily Express*

Attacks on Australia or India, on the other hand, could not be undertaken without exposing her navy to great risks. Her attempt to take Port Moresby is, I believe, with a view to closing the Torres Straits to

their exits has been proved still valid. At the exits the defence has better communications and greater freedom of manoeuvre, while the attacker is still cramped by the mountains. The New Guinea jungle may prevent the advantages thus possessed by the defence being fully exploited, and it would be unsafe to assume that air action will prevent, though it may slow down, the deployment of Japanese forces strong enough to test the defence seriously. There does not, however, seem to be much cause for anxiety.

MADAGASCAR

There is little to be said about the Madagascar operations beyond that they were admirably planned and executed.

Antananarivo, the capital, was entered by British troops on Sept 23, and the situation was reported to be quiet. M. Annet, the Vichy France governor-general, fled into the interior with a view to maintaining resistance, but it is to be hoped that the French will now accept the terms offered.

WAR AT SEA

The successful passage of the Northern convoys was a wonderful feat, and furnishes fresh proof that even the most vulnerable targets under the most unfavourable circumstances can be given a large measure of protection by the Navy and the Fleet Air Arm. The latter has now evidently aircraft of a quality up to requirements.

The menace of the U-boat still remains, and however much it may be reduced it will remain so long as the Germans can find crews to face the desperate risks entailed.

ADVANCING INTO ACTION for the first time, these men of a famous English County regiment are moving past the wrecked and burning hulks of enemy tanks during a fierce engagement in the Western Desert. Fighting in the barren wastes of Egypt, our troops have adapted themselves magnificently to the difficult conditions prevailing. *Photo, British Official: Crown Copyright*

Gialo oasis will not, presumably, affect the communications of Rommel's main forces, but it may have upset his plans if he contemplated an attempt to recover Kufra.

Both the Tobruk and Benghazi raids are a welcome indication of the offensive spirit at Middle East H.Q., although they were mainly harassing operations.

FAR EAST

The landing of small contingents, evidently intended to reinforce parties which had taken refuge in the hills, was followed by a larger scale Japanese attempt to recapture the Guadalcanal aerodrome.

The attempt was defeated, but if it had succeeded it would probably have provided an opportunity for a still heavier counter-stroke. The appearance of a strong Japanese naval force, and its retreat when attacked from the air, is not easy to explain; but it seems probably that it was in the neighbourhood ready to take action if the recapture of the aerodrome had been effected, thereby depriving the Americans of a near-by shore-based umbrella. As it was, failure to capture the aerodrome may have made the Japanese unwilling to take risks with their fighting ships.

Japan has lost the temporary liberty of action she secured at Pearl Harbour, and I believe her strategy henceforth will be

Allied counter-offensive operations, and not a step towards invasion of Australia.

The attempt on Port Moresby has been checked for a time at least. The old theory that mountain passes are best defended at

IN MAJUNGA, the important port on Madagascar's west coast, which capitulated to our forces after little opposition on Sept. 10. British officers are seen chatting with the wounded commander of the Vichy garrison, after the civil and military authorities had arranged the surrender of the place. PAGE 259 *Photo, British Official: Crown Copyright*

Madagascar's Capital Now in British Hands

FRENCH COLONIAL TROOPS in Madagascar, some of whom are seen above, very largely composed the strength of the Vichy forces at the disposal of M. Annet, the Governor-General. Right, Gen. Sir William Platt, G.O.C. East Africa, who was in command of the British forces.

ANTANANARIVO, the chief objective of the British thrusts, was occupied on Sept. 23rd ; below is a view of the city, with the old palace in the centre. Right, airport at Majunga, captured on Sept. 10.

Map, The Daily Express. Photos, Paul Popper, Sport & General, Assoc. Press

Between the Japanese and Port Moresby

IN NEW GUINEA, the Owen Stanley range constitutes a barrier through which the Japanese are attempting to drive down towards Port Moresby on the coast. Allied fighters have heavily attacked the vital trail between Buna and Kokoda.

Devastating air attacks have slowed up Japanese operations in the enemy's thrust towards Port Moresby, capital of New Guinea. Tracks, wharves and supply dumps have been repeatedly pounded. Americans are seen (top) pushing a B25 bomber across an airfield near Port Moresby. In the background are Airacobra fighters. Allied Army trucks plunge down a primitive road, centre left.

Photographed at their Port Moresby base, Australian Bren gun-carriers, each normally manned by four men, are seen, right, ready to go into action. On Sept. 22 it was stated that the difficult supply problem for the enemy had been aggravated by our raids, and that mopping-up operations in Milne Bay had been completed.

Photos, Keystone, Associated Press

PAGE 261

Reds and Nazis in the World's Greatest Battle

SCENES FROM THE RUSSIAN FRONT give a vivid picture of the Caucasus and Stalingrad battlefields. 1, P. Kurkin, 64-year-old Cossack, armed with sub-machine gun, has been awarded the Order of the Red Banner for his bravery. 2, Russian 120-millimetre trench-mortar battery in action. 3, Column of German prisoners captured in N. Caucasus fighting. 4, One of the huge guns with which the enemy bombarded Stalingrad. 5, German troops display the Swastika to intimate to the Luftwaffe that the surrounding area is in Nazi hands and so avoid being bombed by their own airmen.

Photos, British Official: Crown Copyright; Planet News; Topical Press, G.P.U., New York Times Photos

Bombs, Bombs, Yet More Bombs On Stalingrad!

LUFTWAFFE OVER STALINGRAD. An air blitz of the most devastating kind was launched upon the great Volga city in mid-September. Top, picture taken by a German cameraman of the suburbs on the bend of the river; the city itself is in the far distance. Bottom, the city seen from an enemy plane through the smoke of bursting bombs; note the racquet-shaped railway about the hill, and lines running north to Moscow and west to Rostov. The Volga is on the right.

Photos, Associated Press, Keystone. Plan, News Chronicle

THE WAR IN THE AIR

by Capt. Norman Macmillan, M.C., A.F.C.

THE strategic and tactical employment of air forces for the prosecution of war on land has at present reached a stage of stabilization; although their methods may differ slightly the aim of the use of air power is, with all the belligerents, alike.

In Western Europe British air power is employed mainly to deplete the enemy's war resources in materials and plant. The shooting-up of locomotives by cannon-firing fighters in the occupied area of France and the Low Countries coincides with the German demand for railway engines for military purposes and with Bomber Command's heavy night raids on the locomotive-building plants of Kassel; during this period the American Army Air Force in the United Kingdom raided railway yards in France and Holland by day. It will be clear that these interlocking activities are co-ordinated as the result of preliminary intelligence reports.

But, in the main, the ever-lengthening activities of Bomber Command are directed to the diminution of the submarine menace to the sea communication lines of the United Nations; while Coastal Command is almost entirely engrossed in the more direct pursuit of this object in a hunt for U-boats on patrol.

The present small-scale retaliatory German air attacks against the United Kingdom appear to be linked with their U-boat warfare; their object is apparently as much to attack the supplies for the population as to attack war objectives. That is the most rational explanation of the types of air attacks which the Luftwaffe has made against the United Kingdom during recent months.

THUS it can be said that more than fifty per cent of the air activity over Western Europe is directly concerned with the submarine war. At the same time, air pressure upon Germany has far-reaching effects, for, if Germany is to maintain submarine war at its peak level, other war industries must be depleted to make good the losses sustained by the heavy industries working on the German submarine-building programme. So, indirectly, Allied air pressure on Germany and occupied Europe assists Russia by adding to the strain of German industrial effort; and it aids Russia directly by reducing German power to interfere with sea convoys bound for Russian ports.

Much of the sea-mining of German-controlled waterways is aimed at curtailing submarine activities, although it simultaneously affects German waterborne lines of surface communication.

When regarded in this light, it will be seen that the air war over Western Europe is a war of attrition whose results affect every theatre of war, every sea-lane and every ocean.

In the fighting zones aircraft concentrations are essential. In quiet periods there is a demand for continuous reconnaissance for intelligence purposes, and there is the need to maintain strategic bombing to endeavour to disorganize the enemy rear bases of supply and lines of communication. Although called strategic bombing, these operations are only strategic in the limited sense of their relation to the disposition of the land forces; by the use of the term "strategic" they are distinguished from the tactical operations which engage from the air the actual front-line or immediate reserve fighting units.

The employment of air power on the fighting fronts has acquired a stabilized technique, but the increasing use of bomber aircraft as army "artillery" and of fighter aircraft as armed "cavalry" has created as great a demand for air power for ground forces as the demand for gun-power in the Great War. Indeed, so great has this demand become among the German forces that it has outstripped the supply of aircraft which the Luftwaffe and German aircraft factories can produce. In consequence, some zones must be left relatively weak to make it possible to strengthen others. The battle for Stalingrad has absorbed a force of about a thousand first-line German aircraft, or about one-fifth of the total first-line strength of the Luftwaffe. That leaves Germany with about 4,000 first-line aircraft to cover the 2,000 miles' length of the Russian front, meet

fighter aircraft. Now Germany has applied the lessons. A new version of the Messerschmitt single-engined fighter, the 109G, has been reported from Russia; it has a service ceiling of about 41,000 feet; it is armed with three cannons and two machine-guns. A new version of the Junkers 86 bomber, fitted with two semi-diesel, turbo-supercharger Junkers engines, has been produced which can climb to within two or three thousand feet of 50,000 feet.

THE employment of means to attain great heights will vitally affect the defence, for interceptors may be unable to reach the bomber's operating height fast enough to engage them, and, in addition, bombers flying in the rarefied atmosphere are likely to be considerably faster, and will travel above the effective level of fire of current anti-aircraft guns. But to give them full effect, means will have to be devised to enable the bombers to carry heavier loads than are at present possible at such heights.

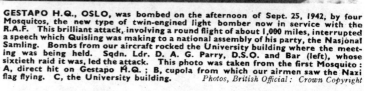

GESTAPO H.Q., OSLO, was bombed on the afternoon of Sept. 25, 1942, by four Mosquitos, the new type of twin-engined light bomber now in service with the R.A.F. This brilliant attack, involving a round flight of about 1,000 miles, interrupted a speech which Quisling was making to a national assembly of his party, the Nasjonal Samling. Bombs from our aircraft rocked the University building where the meeting was being held. Sqdn. Ldr. D. A. G. Parry, D.S.O. and Bar (left), whose sixtieth raid it was, led the attack. This photo was taken from the first Mosquito: A, direct hit on Gestapo H.Q.; B, cupola from which our airmen saw the Nazi flag flying. C, the University building. *Photos, British Official: Crown Copyright*

requirements in North Africa, the Mediterranean, Western Europe, and in the Battle of the Convoys. This is a tenuous force to cover such huge military requirements, and to that fact alone can the people of the United Kingdom ascribe the relatively small-scale nature of the raids which they have suffered for many months.

It is certain that this air situation is a serious one for Germany; her only way out is through the defeat of Russia. Hence the ferocity of the struggle in the great plains and among the foothills of the Caucasus.

It seems to me that in this present stage, almost of equilibrium, in the total air war, three important developments are apparent. Two concern the technical development of aircraft. The first of these developments is the struggle for height of operation. The earliest air fighting in France took place mostly below 25,000 feet. Today air fighting takes place up to between 30,000 and 35,000 feet. The turbo-superchargers of the Fortress bombers have enabled them to operate above the most efficient fighting level of German

The second technical development is the use of larger and heavier bombs. So far the R.A.F. is ahead of the world in dropping 8,000-lb bombs. But the latest Heinkel 177 heavy bomber can carry at least 8,000-lb bomb load, and it is to be expected that it will be converted to carry a bomb of that size for retaliatory purposes.

CARRYING of greater loads and flying at greater heights are opposed conditions. British search for the first and German search for the second indicate to my mind determination to attack upon the part of the R.A.F., and endeavour to evade upon the part of the Luftwaffe. This is again a pointer to the changing conditions of the ratio of air power. At the same time the R.A.F. cannot ignore the value of high altitude flight.

The third, and tactical, development is the increasing use of fighter aircraft to protect convoys when they are out of reach of land-based fighter protection. The Sea-Gladiators have already done well from carriers and from merchant-ships' catapults. They helped the Malta and the Murmansk convoys. Their work is as vital as that of the bombers who blast the submarines and mine enemy waters.

American 'Sky-Troopers' Try the English Air

U.S. ARMY PARATROOPS are among the most rigorously trained fighting men in the world. Numbers of them have been trained in Britain, where their commanding officer is Lt.-Col. E. D. Raff. Their uniform includes ankle-length boots, into which the trousers are tucked, and they wear a silver badge in the form of an open parachute. They carry automatic weapons, mortars, grenades, bayonets and combat knives. They are here seen about to enter Douglas troop-carrying planes.

Photo, New York Times Photos

55 Men (And One Woman) to Fly a Stirling

LOADING-UP FOR A RAID ON GERMANY, a giant Stirling aircraft (above) waits for its freight of firebombs. The bomb-train has moved into position, preparatory to its load being fitted into the plane. Members of a ground crew (right) are seen "handling" one of the Stirlings. Some idea of the size of these formidable aircraft can be gained by comparing the height of the men with that of the landing wheel. Stirlings have inflicted enormous damage on enemy war industry.

PERSONNEL OF FIFTY-SIX maintains, services and flies a heavy bomber of the Stirling type: I, Air crew: Captain, 2nd pilot, air-gunner-bomb-aimer, flight-engineer, observer (navigator), wireless operator, two air-gunners. 2, Flying control officer. 3, W.A.A.F. parachute packer. 4, Meteorological officer. 5, Flight maintenance (12 men). 6, Ground servicing (18 men). 7, Starter battery operated by crew shown at 5. 8, Bombing-up team (11 men). 9, Bomber tractor driver. 10, Petrol bowzer (tank lorry) driver (corporal) with aircraftman 2nd class. 11, Oil bowzer driver.

Photos, British Official: Crown Copyright; Planet News

Yet Again Düsseldorf Was Burnt and Blasted

DÜSSELDORF, a vital centre of Germany's war machine, became a veritable furnace on the night of Sept. 10-11, 1942, when R.A.F. bombers made the heaviest and most successful raid yet achieved by Bomber Command on a moonless night. R.A.F. crews are seen (top) before setting off; with them are members of the ground staff. Düsseldorf's main station was severely damaged. On the left of the reconnaissance air photograph above are seen the wrecked railway line and station buildings. Damage is clearly visible over a wide area.

Photos, British Official

UNDER THE SWASTIKA

What of 'Morals' Under the 'Master Race'?

Nazism is not a pagan creed (argues PAUL TABORI in the article that follows), for the pagans had a clean, decent joy in life and love. It is, as far as its moral aspects are concerned, the philosophy of the pimp and the stud-farm—an evil blight which must be stamped out if it is not to spoil the life of future generations.

NEVER perhaps have the standards of religion and morality been assailed with such ferocity and systematic brutality as in the man-made hell of Nazi Europe. The old standards must be destroyed ; the ideals which Christianity has established in the field of sexual behaviour, maternity and marriage must be dragged into the mire of an obscene and obscure philosophy of Blood and Race.

Though the Nazi " thinkers " may talk highfalutin nonsense about the " eugenic mission " of the Herrenvolk, there is a very good reason for the extraordinary laxity of morals in Germany and the countries she rules. Every aspect of human life has had to be regimented, every commodity to be rationed. In the Third Reich only sex is unrationed. Pornography has been let loose in magazines, newspapers and books—because the shrewd devils who rule most of Europe have realized that they must give an outlet to the people's passions and desires, and this has seemed to be the cheapest and simplest way. Also, the Aryan master race must multiply and increase ; if married couples cannot provide this increase, let the conventional traditions of wedlock and decency go overboard. You need only look at the German magazines like the Simplicissimus or the Kladderadatsch, read a few sentences in Der Schwarze Korps or Der Stürmer, to realize what has happened to Germany's morals. And this pernicious cancer is attacking other countries ; wherever the ideas of Nazism are spreading, the moral dissolution follows. The *Gnadentod*, the " mercy killing," the compulsory sterilization of hundreds of thousands, the system of houses of ill-fame into which thousands of Polish, Czéch, Serbian and Russian women have been herded—a hundred similar details show that Christian ethics have indeed suffered grievously at the hands of the Nazis.

No wonder that even the Schwarze Korps, the S.S. newspaper, finds it necessary to pillory certain young ladies—the Misses Evelin Bienial of Ratibor, Olga Schmechtig of Berlin, and Waltraut Moldt of Hamburg—who have written letters to " unknown soldiers " on the Russian front. Fräulein Evelin asked her nameless pen-friend to bring her " some figured silk, nice shoes, or anything nice." Fräulein Olga informed him that she wore the smallest size in combinations and petticoats. Fräulein Waltraut needed " a lot of stockings and dresses." In other words, they encouraged these distant friends to loot for their sake. And what did they offer in exchange? Fräulein Waltraut explained that she had a " fiery temperament " and liked " kissing and the rest." Fräulein Olga promised to do her best to " compensate " her pen-friend when he came on leave from " the cold of Russia." Fräulein Evelin made it clear that she had no moral scruples " in love." Not one of the three ladies mentioned marriage in her letter, but Fräulein Olga confessed that she would be prepared to bear the child of a " fair-haired, blue-eyed hero " without the blessing of the Church.

This readiness to dispense with conjugal ties has been put into the German mind by careful propaganda. But the same principle is being forced upon other nations with callous brutality. According to the Swedish Social Demokraten Hitler has recently signed a decree which arranges for the " disposal " of illegitimate children of Norwegian and

'WED BY PROXY.' A member of a German Panzer unit having decided to get married while on service in Russia, he sits (extreme right) at a rather sparsely-furnished wedding breakfast without the bride. Such a marriage may be inspired by the desire to legitimize a child about to be born. Sometimes for the same reason a girl in Germany is wedded by proxy to a soldier already killed at the front.

Dutch women by German soldiers. Germany, magnanimously, pays the expenses of the birth and education of these children which are to be brought up in German State Homes for Infants. Even more magnanimously, the women are to be protected by German law against " all inconveniences of their unmarried status." This is little better than legalized prostitution designed to increase the Reich's population ; for the birth-rate of the Herrenvolk has been declining for some time in spite of all inducements to have children.

By encouraging sexual laxity, the Nazis have completely forsaken their original slogan for German women : *Kirche, Kinder, Küche* (Church, children, kitchen). They are drafting women into war industries by the million, and are angry with those who still live for pleasure. A small paper in Western Germany fulminates against women who appear in public " in men's trousers and even in bathing costumes, showing their painted toenails, wearing big cowboy hats, and smoking cigarettes. By their behaviour they give offence to women working hard in the fields." Kreisleiter Woll thundered in Constance against women " who still have the time to enjoy prolonged sun-bathing every day." Apparently the Nazis do not realize that German women, in order to console the " tired heroes " and reach the " happy stage of motherhood," want to make themselves attractive and refuse to become drudges if they also must be " ladies of pleasure."

German women must bear children to increase the master race. Foreign women of " Nordic race " are permitted to do the same. But women of " low blood " are not allowed to " mate " with the Herrenvolk. The Voelkischer Beobachter complains bitterly about the " sentimental fools " who dare to fall in love with foreign women workers in the Reich, especially with those who belong to the conquered peoples and those " who are still at war with us." The paper continues : " The German Michael still harbours romantic ideas of blond youths conceiving true passions for fiery maidens. We would rather stick to the unromantic truth that no people—and least of all a conquered people—will send its daughters into the bedrooms of others, and that as a rule it is only the human refuse which goes beyond the limits of natural decency."

THIS moral hypocrisy is especially disgusting if we consider the statistics—sadly incomplete—about the thousands of Polish, Serbian, Russian girls who have been sent to soldiers' brothels in the occupied territories. Within the Reich the " purity " of the race has to be defended ; outside it the sexual brutality of the conqueror is given full scope.

And the cancer spreads. General Palangean, the Police Prefect of Bucharest, the capital city of Rumania, has been forced to issue a decree forbidding " obscene language in public." General Antonescu broadcasts a furious talk in which he states that " the prodigality of entertainments and the dissolute life provoke the soldiers." The Rumanian quisling has ordered the internment of woman " who behave indecently by wearing their hair in shocking coiffures or by using rouge or wearing short skirts. Also . . . men who, excusing themselves by the heat, walk about with open collars or in shirt-sleeves or cause scandals. Juveniles found smoking will be arrested."

Even in Finland—sober, industrious Finland—morals are on the decline. A letter in the Uusi Suomi, signed " a very angry woman citizen," declares that there are " incessant attacks on women in the streets of Helsinki after nightfall."

BUT perhaps the most tragic case of enforced immorality comes from Hungary, where recently an anti-Jewish law was passed forbidding " respectable " Christian girls to marry Jews or to live with them outside conjugal bonds. Of the hundreds of Gentile girls engaged to, or in love with Jews, the majority have decided to live with their fiancés or lovers, declaring under oath that as the man is keeping them, they are not " respectable." As these cases have increased daily, the Hungarian Government has passed another decree, maintaining that the mere fact of accepting money or presents from a man did not rob a girl of respectability, and that only " licensed prostitutes " could be considered to belong to the class exempt from the original law. Thereupon most of the girls registered as prostitutes rather than give up their lovers. Recently many Gentile girls embraced the Moslem faith in Hungary, as this is another way of marrying a Jew without infringing the law.

What could be more tragic than this desperate farce ? True love having to accept disgrace, ostracism, shameful humiliation—because it is the only way to live with the beloved ?

Hitler Has the Best of Laval's Exchange

FRANCE UNDER GERMANY'S HEEL. Top, men of Laval's "Légion Tricolore" during a parade at Vichy. In Nice a bicycle taxi (inset) does the work of a car. At the beginning of September the Germans had released only 1,000 French prisoners in exchange for about 25,000 workmen sent from France to work for the Reich. A poignant scene at Compiègne station (above) shows the arrival of French soldiers released from prison-camps in Germany. Those welcoming them are French workers destined for slave labour in Nazi war factories.

Photo, Planet News, Keystone

New Links in the Chain of Panama's Defence

Early in September it was announced that Ecuador, although not actually in the War, had agreed to the establishment in the Galapagos Islands, in the Pacific Ocean south-west of the Panama Canal, of strategic bases and airfields for use by the armed forces of the U.S.A. The importance of this concession will be obvious from the following account of the defensive "apron" now surrounding the canal.

Is the Panama Canal better guarded, more strongly defended, than was Pearl Harbour a year ago? We may well hope so, since two bombs on the Culebra Cut (declared a German writer in the Essener National Zeitung a few months before the War), in the mountainous centre of the Isthmus, would render the whole waterway unusable inside ten minutes.

Two bombs! Ten minutes! And the shortest route between Britain and the east coast of North America on the one hand, and the Pacific coast of *all* the Americas, Australia and New Zealand on the other, would have been destroyed. With the Panama Canal closed, if only for a few weeks, shipping would have to take the infinitely longer, and hence more dangerous, route round Cape Horn. (The Panama Canal shortens the route from New York to San Francisco by 6,000 miles, and 3 weeks in time.) More ships, more escorts, more men, *more time*—all these would be required. So let us hope that Panama is not caught napping, like Pearl Harbour, like Clark

(see Vol. III, p. 277). By the Anglo-American Naval Agreement of Sept. 3, 1940, it will be recalled, fifty U.S.A. destroyers were traded for bases—or rather for land on which bases could be established—in Newfoundland and Bermuda (in these cases, the land was a gift, "generously given and gladly received"), the Bahamas, Jamaica, St. Lucia, Antigua, Trinidad and British Guiana, in all of which the territories required were leased for 99 years, free of all charges save the necessity to pay reasonable compensation to private property interests. Within a few months of the Agreement 75,000,000 dollars had been allotted to the work of improving the newly-acquired bases, and much of the programme, we may well believe, has been carried to completion. Details are not readily available, for obvious reasons; but it is understood that in Jamaica, for instance, the fleet anchorage at Portland Bight, the Port Royal Dockyard, Galleon Harbour—where 33 square miles, including Goat Island, were comprised in the grant—and airfields in many parts of the island have received attention. The

America, are all American protectorates to a greater or lesser extent. What has been described as the chief American base in the Caribbean is, indeed, at Guantanamo, at the south-eastern tip of Cuba, which is held on lease from the Cuban government. Then as further links in the Caribbean chain there are the islands of Puerto Rico (American by right of conquest, following the defeat of Spain in the war of 1898) and the Virgin Islands of the U.S., purchased from Denmark in 1917 for 25,000,000 dollars.

On the Caribbean side, then, the Panama Canal would seem to be adequately furnished with a chain or "apron" of protective bases. But what of the other side—that facing the Pacific? Here the most noticeable difference is that there is no great fringe of islands such as links Florida with South America: indeed, the map reveals only one archipelago, the Galapagos Islands, lying on the Equator some 600 miles out from the coast of Ecuador, to which country they are politically attached. They number several hundred, but only twelve are of any size. Albemarle—the largest, 75 miles long—has 600 inhabitants, Chatham 300, and Indefatigible about 100; for the most part the people live on fruit, fish, and game. Dense jungles of mangrove fringe the southern beaches, and elsewhere there are rugged cliffs of grey lava. Inland the country rises to volcanic peaks reaching to nearly 5,000 feet.

According to John Gunther, mail reaches the Galapagos once a month or so; there are no shops, no newspapers, no hotels, no money, no radio. Only naturalists have found it a perfect paradise, so full is it of strange and rare beasts and birds: its name is derived from the Spanish *galápago*, a tortoise, of which there are giant forms in the islands. Hardly a tourists' mecca, it is obvious; but there are harbours in plenty and stretches of fairly level ground which may be converted into airfields. Thus it is that for years past the Americans have had in mind the establishment of bases in the group; Japan is reported to be well aware of their existence and their potentialities; and in 1940 the Sedta airlines, a German-controlled concern in Ecuador, proposed—but the suggestion was turned down, to run a weekly air service between Ecuador and the Galapagos. In May 1941 an agreement was reached for the transfer to Ecuador of several small ships of the U.S. navy which were to be used in patrolling the waters between the Galapagos, Ecuador, and the Panama Canal; but it was only last month that the U.S.A. was granted the right to establish bases and airfields in the archipelago.

Still the American defence chiefs are not altogether happy. They have yet other plans up their sleeves, and a most interesting one was revealed the other day: the construction of a great highway connecting the southern borders of Mexico with the Canal Zone via the Central American states of Guatemala, El Salvador, Honduras, Costa Rica and Panama—all of which have already given their consent to the project. Strategically, the Panama Road or Highway will be invaluable, since it will permit direct motor transport from the U.S.A. to Panama, incidentally freeing a good deal of American and Allied shipping now plying between the ports in the Caribbean. Some 625 miles of new road have to be constructed, and there is a very tough proposition facing the American engineers in the Darien jungle; but, as the New York Times put it the other day, "We *do* know how to build roads."

THE PANAMA CANAL, one of the most vital waterways of the United Nations, is now defended by a vast ring of bases established, as this map shows, on American and British islands in the Caribbean. Now the Galapagos group is being brought into the system. *New York Times*

airfield and Cavite naval base in the Philippines; or unprepared, like Singapore . . .

No one outside the inner circles of the American High Command can say how many guns are pointing skywards along the canal's fifty miles by ten, how many ships of the American fleet are patrolling the ocean approaches to the all-important waterway. But the facts of political geography cannot be so easily hidden, and it is comforting to know that during the last year or two a great protective "apron" of bases, from and to which the American bombers can operate, has been stretched far out into the Atlantic, thus countering that most menacing and dangerous of war's possibilities—surprise.

Rather more than two years have passed since the Roosevelt-Churchill deal of American destroyers for British bases was announced

Bahamas were scheduled as an auxiliary or emergency aeroplane base. British Guiana was described as having harbour potentialities ripe for development.

But these bases acquired from Britain tell only part, and that not the most important part, of the story. For many years past—since, indeed, the birth of "Yankee imperialism" at the turn of the century—the U.S.A. has maintained a number of strategic outposts in the Caribbean; and although the "dollar diplomacy" of Roosevelt I has given place to the "good neighbour policy" of Roosevelt II it is still not very wide of the mark to say that the nominally independent republics of Cuba, Haiti and the Dominican Republic in the island of Santo Domingo (Hispaniola), and Nicaragua and Panama in Central

Stalin's Own City in the Caucasus

Capital of the Georgian Socialist Soviet Republic, Tiflis—or Tbilisi as the Russians know it—stands on either side of a rocky gorge carved out by the River Kura. It is the terminus of the Georgian Military Highway crossing the mountains from Ordjonikidze, and through it run the railway and the oil pipeline from Baku on the Caspian to Batum on the Black Sea.

'Twixt the Black Sea and the Caspian

Tremendous mountains—there are eleven peaks higher than Mont Blanc—terrific gorges, forest-clad slopes, make up the Central Caucasus. (1) a view in the Aragva valley. The old town and the new of Tiflis are contrasted in (2) and (3), and another glimpse of Stalin's own city is shown in (4); in the higher regions the country is a formidable wilderness (5).

Mountain Barriers to Hitler's Progress

Framed in the schoolhouse window overlooking Kubachi, in Daghestan, these Caucasian
schoolgirls are doing their lessons (6); only a few years since theirs would have been a life
of ignorance, seclusion and subjection. In (7) we have an aerial view of the cowsheds
attached to a collective farm near a Daghestan village—another sign of the Soviet Revolution.

273

Russia's Great Oil Metropolis

Photos, Keystone. E.N.A., Associated Press

Baku, on the shores of the Caspian Sea, is the oldest and still the most important centre (producing in peacetime 75 per cent of the output) of the Soviet's oil industry. As will be seen from (1), and the nearer view in (2), the town is a forest of derricks. At work in the oily fluid (3), and a few of the tanks in which the precious fluid is stored before export (4).

VIEWS & REVIEWS Of Vital War Books

Liddell Hart on This Expanding War

As a military critic Capt. Liddell Hart is sometimes right, sometimes wrong (though less often wrong than right); but he will have his place in history as the man who did his best to make the War Office understand the importance of mechanized warfare —and was defeated by the serried ranks of senior officers still thinking in terms of 1914.

IN Spain they speak of "the Generals" when they mean the fossil-minded reactionary section of the Ruling Class. We had our Generals in this sense too. Two years in advance of the present war Capt. Liddell Hart wrote in a review article on the defence of the Empire that our first problem was to reduce our needs in military man-power by " remodelling our forces on a new design and seeking to develop new types of force which have more force than the old in proportion to their size." What he had in mind was a New Model army, such as Oliver Cromwell created when the value of cavalry in new conditions of warfare was recognized. Again there were new conditions, created this time by the petrol motor. Again there was urgent need to understand and take advantage of these. Machines must to a very large extent take the place of men.

But our Generals did not like machinery. They had grown up before the civilized world fell under its domination. Their traditions were of the barrack square, the hunting field, the " steadily shoulder-to-shoulder " type of battle. Mr. Hore-Belisha as War Minister listened to Liddell Hart, took his advice, and tried to carry it out. He met with polite, but obstinate resistance. The Generals won.

IN his new book This Expanding War (Faber, 12s. 6d.) Liddell Hart shows how the few men who were keen about tanks received very little encouragement—were, indeed, discouraged, and some of them penalized. It was hoped that Lord Gort, when he became Chief of the Imperial General Staff, replacing a man of antiquated ideas, or of none, would take up a more progressive attitude. He had seemed to favour giving mechanized experts the task of re-modelling the Army. But the prospect was not fulfilled. Officers of the mechanized arm were not promoted to posts where their knowledge and keenness would have been of value. These posts remained in the hands of men with 1914 minds.

They had to do a little in the way of preparing to try out the machines they so heartily detested, but, as Liddell Hart puts it, the War Office behaved like the old families which hated the change-over from broughams and dogcarts to motor-cars and, when at last they were forced to make it, " tried to turn their old coachmen into chauffeurs." Young men " who had grown up in the mechanized arm " were needed as leaders. They could have been found, but no search was made for them. The War Office would not " face the fact that successful commanders of the mobile arm have almost always been young men."

When Seydlitz, that most dynamic cavalry leader of Frederick's wars, was promoted general, his view of the essential conditions of mobile command was shown in his curt comment: "High time, if they wanted more work out of me. I am already thirty-six." If our new army is to be similarly dynamic, the War Office will have to swallow a dose of " Seydlitz powder."

THAT was written nearly a year ago. The lesson is perhaps being learned—but slowly. Quickening the pace of warfare from 2-3 to 20-30 miles an hour " is apparently too large a change for its logical implications to be recognized. The handling of mechanized forces is a radically different technique from that of handling old-style forces. Unwilling to admit the existence of the gulf and leap across it, the Army has preferred to tumble into it."

After Lord Gort's appointment in 1937 the ratio of two armoured divisions to four infantry divisions completely motorized was agreed upon " in principle." This had been very strongly urged upon Mr. Hore-Belisha. He was in favour of it. Lord Gort was believed to be.

Unfortunately a more conservative attitude prevailed ; the reorganization and expansion of the armoured units was postponed, and a decision was taken against the complete motor-ization of the infantry divisions—instead of all the divisional infantry being mounted in handy-sized trucks, lorries were provided on a scale adequate to move only one-third of them at a time. And when the war came the second armoured division was still only in embryo.

So with our partly Old Model we came up against the Germans, who had their entirely New Model, and we have been suffering for it ever since.

We have suffered, too, from the stupidity of the Baldwin-Chamberlain Government in

HITLER'S MILITARY SUICIDE ?

IT still seems to me that the prospects of invading the Continent successfully depend, apart from other conditions, on our capacity to create a " New Model " army, radically different from the present pattern—and on our resourcefulness in providing it with new types of sea transportation that will partially free it from dependence on ports.

In default of such a master-key to open the gate, our hopes must rest with the leaders of Germany and their capacity to destroy the strength and morale of the German Army in vain attack—in unavailing pursuit of the victory that they deemed so certain in 1940. They did that in 1918. As Mr. Churchill pointed out in The World Crisis, his analysis of the last war—" It was their own offensive, not ours, that consummated their ruin. They were worn down not by Joffre, Nivelle, and Haig, but by Ludendorff." So there is ground for hope that they may do so again. And the course of the campaign in Russia has given encourage-ment to that hope. Going farther back, we can at least find a hopeful omen in the fact that this is the same theatre where Napoleon committed military suicide.

What a warning to aggressors it would be if history were not only to repeat itself thrice, but to repeat itself twice in the same place.—This Expanding War.

refusing to tackle seriously the Three-in-one Staff Brain Problem, as Liddell Hart calls it. He means the necessity for a supreme com-mand, such as General Wavell had in the Pacific zone, of sea, air, and land forces. Combination of effort and aim is essential to victory. In The Times, whose Military Correspondent he then was, Liddell Hart wrote soon after British rearmament began (1935) a succession of articles putting this view forward. It received support from many quarters, and was pressed upon Mr. Baldwin so firmly that he was compelled to appoint a Minister for the Co-ordination of Defence.

But in thus yielding to the public demand he subtly evaded its real point by a clever side-step —too clever to be good for the country's interest. In this vitally important new post was placed the Attorney-General, Sir Thomas Inskip (now Lord Caldecote), which implied that a knowledge of law should suffice to unravel the complex problems of future war. It might have been a good choice, if war had been as slow to change as the law.

That appointment, and the other one of Mr. Burgin to be Minister of Production, handi-capped us heavily in the race to be ready for war. When it came, we were not ready. We were woefully behindhand with our prepara-tions. We have been straining ourselves to catch up ever since.

The Germans jumped to the idea of a Three-in-one Staff Brain—perhaps got it

Capt. B. H. LIDDELL HART, says Who's Who, " informally collaborated with Mr. Hore-Belisha (War Minister) 1937-8, suggesting a programme of reorganization and reforms, of which some 60 were achieved, though many were delayed—in particular measures for the increase of mechanized forces."
Photo, Howard Coster

from us, for at the very time when the scheme was here reduced to a shadow, they made a striking advance in the same direction. Planning of their combined operations is carried out by a group of specially trained officers, some 30 in number, between the ages of 35 and 50. They go through army, naval and air force training, also through the war production workshops. If they do not give satisfaction they are ruthlessly dispensed with. They planned the combination of the three arms which so quickly and competently completed the conquest of Norway. We worked in separate compartments and were thrown out of the country.

I feel, as I read Liddell Hart, that quickness of mind, that receptiveness to new ideas, that unprejudiced readiness to welcome change if it promises improvement, which in the past has been so lamentably lacking in our army commanders—since the days of Welling-ton. It was deficiency in imagination that made them hostile to the use of aircraft. When Blériot had flown the Channel in 1909 and the value of an air arm was urged on the War Office, they objected that, even if it turned out to be valuable—which they strongly doubted—" it would destroy the cavalry's function and spoil a great tradition." And we had no statesman big enough to tell them not to be such fools. Or perhaps I should say, no big statesman sufficiently interested in war to stand up to those who were supposed to be professionals at it.

IN that supposition lay the trouble. Few of them were professionals. Men like Wolseley and Roberts were rare. Even Kitchener was more ready to talk about excavations or old china or High Church ritual than about soldiering. They wanted the world to stand still. That is why " the desert of Service history is strewn with the skeletons of pioneers." That is why drill, which once taught soldiers what they would have to do in battle, became " formal or ceremonial, losing touch with reality," and teaching them what they would never have to do except on parade-grounds.

We are changing all this. We have made many advances in the past three years under the lash of bitter experience. But with Ham-let we still plead, "O, reform it altogether ! "
HAMILTON FYFE

Sweeping for Mines in the Egyptian Desert

SOUTH AFRICAN ENGINEERS are constantly engaged in the Western Desert in the dangerous occupation of laying, sweeping, and detecting the presence of mines. 1, One man is digging out an enemy mine while his colleague continues searching with his detector. 2, Using the detecting apparatus. 3, An engineer has detected the presence of a mine and is pointing out its position to an officer. 4, Sappers advancing through heavy fire and creating a safety lane for troops and tanks by locating mines with their bayonets and then removing them. Minefields have played a great part in the recent fighting.

Photos, British Official

'To the Island Fortress ~ the George Cross'

MALTA was awarded the George Cross by King George on April 17, 1942. On Sept. 13 the medal was presented to Sir George Borg, the Chief Justice, by the Governor, Viscount Gort. At the time of its award Malta had had more than 2,000 raids and alerts. I, The ceremony amid the bombed debris of the Grand Master's Palace in Valetta. 2, Sir George Borg receives the case containing the medal. 3, Written in his own hand, H.M. the King's letter to Malta. 4, Men of Malta's A.R.P. and the special constabulary.

Photos, Sport & General

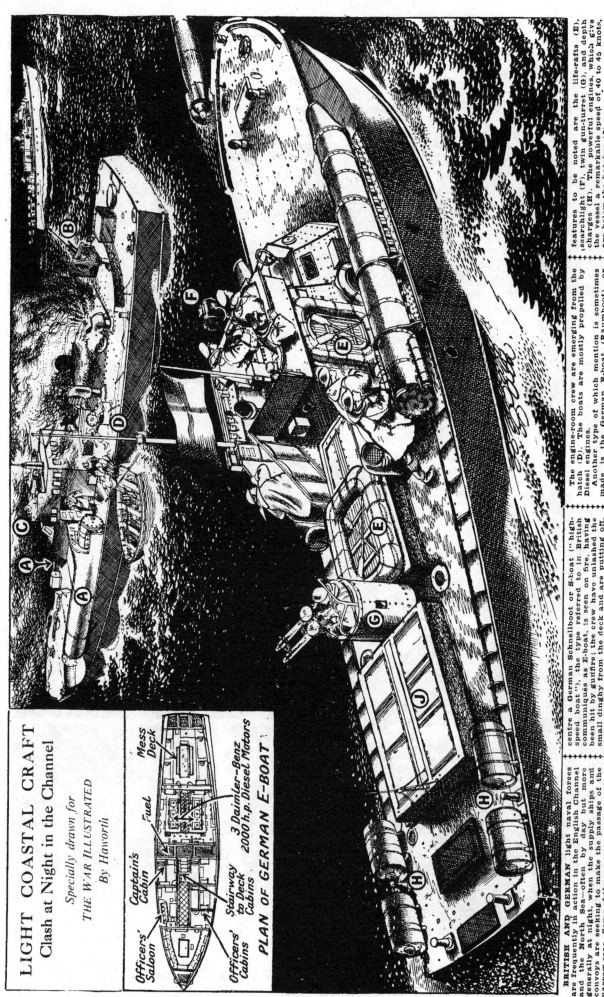

LIGHT COASTAL CRAFT
Clash at Night in the Channel

Specially drawn for
THE WAR ILLUSTRATED
By Haworth

PLAN OF GERMAN E-BOAT

Officers' Saloon
Captain's Cabin
Fuel
Mess Deck
Stairway to Deck Cabins
Officers' Cabins
3 Daimler-Benz 2000 h.p. Diesel Motors

BRITISH AND GERMAN light naval forces are frequently in action in the English Channel and the North Sea—often by day but more generally at night, when the supply ships and convoys are seeking to make the passage of the narrow seas. Some of the more recent encounters are described in page 246: an attack by British patrols on a German supply ship bound for Cherbourg, a similar action in the Straits of Dover, and a series of clashes off the Dutch coast.

This drawing gives an impression of such a night action, and of the craft engaged. In the centre a German Schnellboot or S-boat ("high-speed boat"), the type referred to in British communiqués as E-boat, is seen on fire, having been hit by gunfire; the crew have unlashed the small dinghy from the deck and are putting off. These vessels are 106 ft. long and broad in the beam. The two torpedo-tubes (A) are the main striking power, but one or two 20-mm. cannon are mounted (B), and the small shells from these can be very damaging to the light hulls of this type of craft. The bridge and navigating cabins are at (C). Accommodation for captain and officers is forward below—see plan inset.

The engine-room crew are emerging from the hatch (D). The boats are mostly propelled by Diesel engines.

Another type of which mention is sometimes made is the German R-boat (Räumboot), or motor-minesweeper.

In the foreground a British M.T.B. is seen travelling at speed and discharging one of its torpedoes. These motor-boats are rather similar to the Schnellboote, but are usually about 70 feet in length and capable of greater speed. The captain and crew are seen tensely watching the result of their manoeuvre. Interesting features to be noted are the life-rafts (E), searchlight (F), twin gun-turret (G), and depth charges (H). The powerful engines, which give the vessel a remarkable speed of 40 to 45 knots, are below the hatches (J).

In the background is seen a British motor-gunboat of a later type. These are of similar length to the German S-boats, but less beamy; they mount a heavy armament of pom-poms and machine-guns.

A third type, not illustrated here, is the British motor-launches; these are used chiefly for coastal convoy work.

THE WAR AT SEA

by Francis E. McMurtrie

IN attacking the convoy which reached North Russia last month the Germans for the first time on that route made use of torpedo aircraft, besides large numbers of other types. In spite of this exceptional concentration of force, the convoy got through to its destination with losses which cannot have been unduly severe, since it has been officially stated that it delivered to Russia the largest quantity of munitions yet transported in a single voyage from Britain and the United States.

Moreover, there is no doubt the enemy's losses were very heavy: indeed, even the Berlin commentators described them as "painful." This was undoubtedly due to the exceptional strength of the escort provided. Not only did it comprise 75 warships of all types, from battleships and aircraft-carriers down to destroyers and minesweepers, but the Fleet Air Arm contingent included a number of Sea Hurricanes. These, it is understood, resemble the Hurricane in their main features, but have folding wings and a modified undercarriage to enable them to operate from aircraft-carriers. They did great execution amongst the enemy air squadrons, while their own losses were light. Only four fighters became casualties, and the pilots of three were saved.

New badge now worn by all officers and warrant officers qualified as Observers in the Fleet Air Arm.

Comment on these facts has not always been well informed. It has been suggested that "lack of understanding" of air power in the Royal Navy has been the cause of inferiority of equipment in the Fleet Air Arm.

No one who is in touch with naval affairs as they are administered today is likely to accept that view. On the contrary, the Navy is only too eager to utilize all the improved equipment that it can get; but up to now the demands for aircraft for other purposes —bombing Germany in particular – have been paramount. It is to be hoped that the supply to the Fleet of Sea Hurricanes is merely an example of what may be expected now that the production of aircraft is mounting towards a level where the requirements of all the Services can be met without stint.

Experience with convoys in this war, both in the Mediterranean and on the route to Russia, agrees with the lessons taught in former conflicts. As enemy attacks become more formidable, so must the strength of the escorts be increased, until a point is reached where the assailants lose so heavily that they are likely to be deterred from venturing near a convoy unless weather or other circumstances are exceptionally favourable.

It is only recently that we have had enough warships to spare to give really adequate protection to every convoy. Even now it must place a strain on the available force to provide escorts in the required ratio.

IN the raid on Tobruk, on Sept. 13, our naval losses included two big destroyers with fine fighting records—H.M.S. Sikh and Zulu—two motor torpedo-boats and a motor launch, besides a party of Royal Marines who were landed to carry out demolition work. In default of a completely detailed account of the operation, one must be sparing of criticism, but it is devoutly to be hoped that the destruction done ashore

was such as to be well worth the losses incurred. It is to be feared that until the Army is able to regain its lost ground and drive the enemy back to Benghazi or beyond, any naval undertaking within close range of the North African coast must be a hazardous one. Apparently the " air umbrella " cannot in present circumstances be relied on to keep off all enemy attacks, though, compared with Crete, cooperation has vastly improved.

It is worth while speculating on the difference that a really big Naval Air Service, such as existed up to April 1, 1918, would have made to the fortunes of the present war at sea. It was not until July 30, 1937, that the unfortunate decision taken in 1918 was to some extent reversed, and the responsibility for the administration of all ship-borne aircraft restored to the Admiralty. To this day, however, responsibility for the supply of aircraft and equipment rests with another department.

WHEN war began the newly emancipated Fleet Air Arm was still very far from fully developed. Immense credit is due to its gallant and highly efficient personnel for the wonders achieved with machines and equipment which in quality left much to be desired. In Norway a magnificent fight was made against heavy odds. As the Rear-Admiral commanding Aircraft Carriers reported at the time, " our fleet aircraft were outclassed in speed and manoeuvrability, and it was only the courage and determination of pilots and crews that prevented the enemy from inflicting far more serious damage."

At Taranto on Nov. 11, 1940, the Fleet Air Arm gave the enemy a still more striking demonstration of its capabilities, the Italian fleet being crippled by a torpedo attack made in the moonlight by aircraft from H.M.S. Illustrious and Eagle. Six months later it was aircraft from the Victorious and from the Ark Royal that struck at the Bismarck in weather which in normal circumstances would have been regarded as too bad for flying, and disabled her to an extent that determined the issue. At the battle of Cape Matapan our battle squadron would

never have overtaken the Italians had they not been delayed by the attacks of naval aircraft from the Formidable.

Had not the natural development of the Royal Naval Air Service been arrested in 1918, we might by 1939 have had an adequate force of first-line aircraft carriers, with the necessary aircraft, equipment, and personnel. With such a force at our disposal the damage inflicted on the enemy navies might well have been decisive, while disasters such as the sinking of the Prince of Wales, Repulse, Hermes, Cornwall, and Dorsetshire need never have occurred.

OUR great ally, the United States, and our most formidable foe at sea, Japan, have each been wise enough to maintain a powerful Air Service as an integral part of the fleet. It was this that enabled the Japanese to carry out the shattering attack on the U.S. fleet at Pearl Harbour last December. Similarly, the American recovery from this blow and the swift counter-strokes off Midway Island and elsewhere are to be attributed to the possession of an Air Arm which is both heavy and far-reaching. These facts are nowhere better appreciated than in the Royal Navy, which does not despair of obtaining, before the War ends, the additional air strength which it lacks.

ON H.M.S. FORMIDABLE'S FLIGHT DECK—Grumman Martlet aircraft are ready for taking off. Completed in 1940 the Formidable belongs to the Illustrious class, and has a displacement of 23,000 tons. This famous British aircraft-carrier's complement is 1,600, and she carries sixteen 4·5-inch (dual purpose) guns.   PAGE 279   *Photo, British Official: Crown Copyright*

Grand Fellows, the Men Who Guard the Convoys

CONVOY PROTECTION as seen from some of the guardian ships. 1, A corvette is passing through the Straits of Gibraltar. 2, Looking down from the "crow's-nest" of an escort vessel to the captain's bridge, where an officer keeps watch. 3, Weighing out the crew's meat rations aboard an escort ship. 4, Enemy submarines have been sighted; these men are at "action stations." 5, One of the U-boats, having made an attempt upon a merchantman, is attacked with depth charges.

Photos, Planet News

'Your Destroyers—Gee, They're Swell!'

ESCORT DESTROYERS, part of the naval force of 75 ships which, under Rear-Adm. R. L. Burnett (inset), protected recent convoys to and from Russia : H.M.S. Fury is leading, followed by H.M.S. Ashanti. "Where would the convoy have been, but for the destroyers ?" asked Reuter's Special Correspondent, who watched them in action throughout the six days' battle. And. he quoted this tribute to the Royal Navy by an American sailor : "You talk snooty, but you're great guys. And your destroyers—gee, they're swell !"   *Photos. British Official: Crown Copyright*

THE HOME FRONT

by E. Royston Pike

At Waterloo one day this week—London's Waterloo, not Liverpool's—I noticed a porter (or should it be porteress?) wearing a beautifully fresh, altogether spick-and-span white silk blouse. On the same day I happened to come across a remark by Mr. Justice Archer : " No one is a lady or gentleman now," he told a witness at Lewes County Court who had described an assistant at a laundry as a young lady ; " we are all men and women." Maybe there's no very obvious connexion between the blouse and the aphorism, unless it is that they are both signs of change in this old country of ours, change in the ways of doing things, change in the ways we look at things, at people and events. Such signs—slight in themselves, but massively imposing 'in the aggregate—of the ferment of time and circumstance are to be found on every hand. Britain and the British are changing, and changing fast.

" Stop me and buy one " is an exhortation which has become very familiar to us of recent years since Messrs. Walls, Eldorado, and Lyons have endeavoured to make us as ice-cream-conscious as the Americans. But we are not likely to see it again, at least until after the war. Lord Woolton has decreed that ice-cream is a luxury, and that the labour and equipment employed in its production may well be put to better uses. However strong our partiality for bricks and cornets, we are unlikely to quarrel with the decision. If it has been criticized it is on the ground that ice-cream vendors—there are about a hundred thousand retailers of the luscious stuff, if the forty thousand stall-holders and street-corner men are included—are to receive no compensation. True, in many cases ice-cream parlours are a side-line of confectioners and tobacconists, but there are many small people in the trade who have been entirely dependent upon the production and sale of ice-cream for their livelihood. Theirs would seem to be a hard fate ; they join the other small shopkeepers whose businesses are to be counted among the economic casualties of the war.

So far as we consumers are concerned we shall accept this further deprivation with a good grace. After all, we are getting used to restrictions now. Recently in the House of Lords, Lord Portal, Minister of Works and Planning, quoted some figures showing the extent to which civilian consumption has been cut down. The supply of clothing has been cut to 45 per cent of the pre-war level ; coupon rationing and the Limitation of Supplies Order have reduced the use of textiles to no more than a quarter—indeed, of household textiles only about 10 per cent of pre-war supplies are being produced, and some furnishing fabrics are not being produced at all. Lord Portal went on to describe the important part played by salvage in the conservation of essential raw materials. An average of 26,000 tons a week of iron and steel scrap is being collected by his Ministry, and a further 6,500 tons by the local authorities. Since the beginning of the year the weekly collection of wastepaper has increased from 12,500 tons to 18,000 tons. The most important material to be salvaged at the moment is rubber, the supply of which has been reduced to less than half of what it was before the war. If he were speaking on behalf of the Minister of Production (concluded Lord Portal), he would say " use less " ; if

on behalf of the Minister of Food, " eat less," and if on behalf of the Chancellor of the Exchequer, " spend less." Their lordships cheered.

All the same, there still seems to be quite a lot of people who do not realize the gravity of the state—almost a state of siege—in which the fourth winter of the war is finding us. In July, the last month for which figures are available, the Ministry of Food prosecuted 3,205 wholesalers and retailers for various contraventions of the Food Control Order, and of the prosecutions, just under 90 per cent were successful. In most of the cases small fines were inflicted ; in only 260 cases did the fines exceed £20, and in 121 cases sentences of imprisonment were imposed. These figures are the highest to date, but in every

'ON THE ROAD' in S. Wales, Lewis Casson, husband of Dame Sybil Thorndike and well-known actor and producer, drives one of the Old Vic vans which carry scenery and props from one mining village to another. Taking the theatre to the people is one of the many praiseworthy activities of C.E.M.A., described in this page. *Photo, British Official*

month since the beginning of the war there have been a large number of prosecutions of " food-hogs " and " black marketeers."

Surely one of the sillier slogans is the " Is your journey really necessary ? " that is so prominently displayed on the railway stations, since it is hardly to be believed that the train will be taken off if the questioning placard should send us conscience-smitten from the booking office empty away. If the powers-that-be want to stop us travelling, then (the great public quite reasonably argues) they should cut down the facilities. And that is what they are now doing—at least in some small measure. From Oct. 5 ordinary cheap-day tickets and cheap tickets for various classes of pleasure travel were discontinued throughout the railway system ; and during the six winter months, October to March inclusive, free tickets or reduced fare vouchers issued to parents or relations visiting evacuated children in the country, to evacuated or transferred Civil Servants, and men and women in the Services, are all being cut down. Then the Green Line coaches of the London Passenger Transport Board have also been withdrawn, together with most of the long-distance coach services. No doubt many people are feeling distinctly inconvenienced, but for a long time it has been difficult to see the necessity for running

motor-buses and coaches from London to places on the South Coast, for instance, served by a most up-to-date system of electric railways.

More travel restrictions are likely in the not distant future ; in the meantime the public are urged to avoid all unnecessary journeys, to walk or bike short distances, do their shopping between 10 a.m. and 4 p.m., and support schemes for staggering working hours. What is needed, says the Ministry of War Transport, is a complete change of outlook. Frequent shopping and social visits to the nearest large town must come to an end. Every urban district and suburb must become a self-contained unit, supplying its own interests. A self-sufficient countryside, local *autarky*—this is what the Ministry's plea would seem to mean.

It was echoed the other day by the Minister of Agriculture when he addressed a Diocesan assembly in Salisbury. Mr. Hudson's opening theme was 1942's harvest, one of the heaviest that England has ever known, but from a well-deserved pat-on-the-back for the farmers and farm workers he went on to paint a picture of rural Britain as it ought to be, might and must be. After the war, he said, we shall build a new rural civilization.

In many ways a village is or should be an ideal community. It is just large enough for everyone to know nearly everyone else, to raise a cricket and a football team and run a tennis club, whist-drives and dances, without being so small that cooperative life is impossible, or so big that one feels lost in it and belongs to no one. But we have got to make village life like that. We cannot just sit down and hope for it to happen.

Towards the building up, in Mr. Hudson's words, of " a sum of good life upon the land that will make the villages of the future blossom and shine again with the spirit that is in them," a grand work is being done by C.E.M.A.—the Council for the Encouragement of Music and the Arts, of which Lord Keynes is the chairman. Those who know something of what C.E.M.A. has done of recent years will never be in the least sceptical of the public response to " unaccustomed forms of beauty, in sound and thought and design "—to lift a phrase from the recent report of the Pilgrim Trust, which has contributed £50,000 to C.E.M.A.'s funds. In two years C.E.M.A.'s art exhibitions have attracted more than half a million visitors. A million and a half have attended plays given under its direction, and the number of its concerts in all parts of the country has almost reached 8,000. Music and drama have been taken to the people—to war workers and evacuees, to factories and military units in remote rural districts.

Most notable of its recent ventures is the guaranteeing of the Old Vic Theatre Company—what a nostalgia the name gives rise to, what memories of that most homely and intimate of London's theatres, down there in the Waterloo Road !—against financial loss. Thanks to this timely assistance the Old Vic has presented Shakespeare and Shaw, Euripides and Tchekhov, to crowded, eager audiences not only in towns still possessing theatres but in places where the " living theatre " had not been seen for years, if ever —in the mining villages of Northumbria and South Wales, in industrial Scotland and in the cotton towns of Lancashire. In all, fifteen companies of professional players have worked in association with C.E.M.A.

The good work goes on. Every day new bricks are being added to the house in which we all, town-dwellers and villagers alike, will have an opportunity of developing the technique of the " good life," after the war.

The Battle of Britain: Two Years After

SOME OF THE FEW. The photograph shows, left to right : Sqdn.-Ldr. A. C. Bartley, D.F.C. ; Wing-Cmdr. D. F. B. Sheen, D.F.C. and Bar (Australia) ; Wing-Cmdr. R. Gleed, D.S.O., D.F.C. ; Sqdn.-Ldr. Max Aitken, D.S.O., D.F.C. ; Wing-Cmdr. A. G. Malan, D.S.O., D.F.C. ; Sqdn.-Ldr. A. C. Deere, D.F.C. (New Zealand) ; Air Chief Marshal Sir Hugh Dowding, G.C.B., C.M.G. ; Flt.-Offr. Elspeth Henderson, M.M. (one of the first service women to be decorated for bravery) ; Flt.-Lt. R. H. Hilary, D.F.C. (Sydney) ; Wing-Cmdr. J. A. Kent, D.F.C., A.F.C. (Canada) ; Wing-Cmdr. C. B. F. Kingcome, D.F.C. ; Flt.-Lt. D. H. Watkins, D.F.C. ; and Wt.-Offr. R. H. Gretton.

AT the time of the Battle of Britain in the autumn of 1940, the chief of Bomber Command was Sir Hugh Dowding. He is now retired, but on the eve of the anniversary of his Command's greatest day he made his first public tribute to the pilots who achieved so great an air victory. Here are points from his speech :

" It was a battle designed to break down our fighter strength and to pave the way for invasion. The invasion was mounted and waiting for the word 'Go.' But that word was never given because Britain's fighter defences were never overcome.

" My own contribution to the battle had been made weeks and months before, and I could leave most of the tactical work to subordinate commanders and the dauntless fighter pilots who achieved so much.

" Here I am proud and happy to be surrounded by these pilots—two years older, with more rings on their sleeves and more ribbons on their chests, but if they had what they deserved their chests and sleeves would be completely obliterated with embroidery.

" Let us remember with sorrow and affection those R.A.F. men who did not survive that great battle, and above all let us never forget those who were broken in this war. Let the many be mindful of their debt to the few."

AT STEPNEY, in the playground of Single Street School, a large crowd gathered on Sept. 15 to pay tribute to " the courage and high enterprise of the men of the Royal Air Force and the steadfastness in the face of death and destruction of the people of London." The service was conducted by the Rector and Rural Dean of Stepney, and with him were the Mayor of Stepney and other East End mayors, men of the R.A.F., Civil Defence workers, nurses, and over 600 East End men and women, some of whom are seen in the photograph above.

The band of the Grenadier Guards played as the crowd gathered round a platform set in front of the school entrance, where there are now neither doors nor windows, and the banner of Stepney and flags of the United Nations fluttered gaily among the ruined beams and rafters.

Photos, New York Times Photos, Keystone, Daily Mirror

Round and About Goes Our Roving Camera

CAMPS FOR THE U.S. ARMY IN BRITAIN are being constructed in various parts of the country, most of the materials used throughout being British. Above are seen U.S. engineers erecting huts at a camp in the Home Counties.

Adm. Sir William James, C.-in-C., Portsmouth, was admitted on Sept. 15 to the honorary freedom of that world-famous naval centre. He is seen, right, being presented with the casket by "Pompey's" Lord Mayor, Sir. D. Daley.

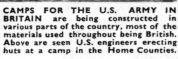

TWO V.C.s, one awarded post-humously for outstanding bravery in the Western Desert, were announced on Sept. 11.

Private A. H. Wakenshaw (left), of the Durham Light Infantry, served as a member of the crew of a two-pounder anti-tank gun. On June 27, 1942, near Mersa Matruh, his left arm was blown off, but Wakenshaw crawled back to the gun, loaded it with one arm and fired 5 rounds at an enemy gun. He was wounded again, but kept up the fight until he was killed by a direct hit.

Sergt. Q. G. M. Smythe (right) took command of a platoon when his officer was wounded during an enemy attack in the Alem Hamza area on June 5, 1942, and stalked and destroyed an enemy machine-gun nest, capturing the crew. Though badly wounded, he continued to lead the advance.

TRAFFIC LIGHTS are being restricted as part of the economy drive. Above, one of the lights in Oxford Street, London, suspended for "the duration."

Some of London's well-known statues have been removed to Berkhampstead. Among them are (right) The Burghers of Calais and Lord Wolseley.

Photos, British Official: Crown Copyright; L.N.A. Topical Press, G.P.U., Sport & General

I WAS THERE! Eye Witness Stories of the War

From the Zulu I Saw the Sikh's Last Fight

The spectacular joint raid on Tobruk on the night of Sept. 13-14, and the sinking of the destroyers Sikh and Zulu, are described here by the only British correspondent with the expedition, John Nixon of Reuter's, who was on board the Zulu.

CMDR. R. T. WHITE, D.S.O. with Bar, who was in command of H.M.S. Zulu, one of the two destroyers sunk in the raid on Tobruk. He was among those saved.
Photo, London and Northern Studios

WE left our base in darkness early one morning to the pipe of "action stations." All day we sailed through the Mediterranean without sighting a single enemy aircraft and without any U-boat alarm.

Just a few hundred British soldiers were to grapple with a mixed garrison of some thousands of Germans and Italians, with the prospect of having to cope with an additional thousand Germans encamped near the port. But that night, as the ships raced through the pitch darkness towards Tobruk, the men sipping their cocoa were in high spirits.

As they took up their positions on the deck in the star-studded darkness, the men were walking arsenals. Like their officers, they wore khaki shorts and shirts, steel helmets, and heavy suède boots with thick crêpe soles for silent walking. Armed to the teeth with tommy-guns, Bren-guns, machine-guns and rifles, every man was also bristling with grenades, sticky bombs, and guncotton. Each man responsible for demolition had 20 lb. of guncotton. The ships themselves had been converted into floating arsenals. Besides huge boxes of ammunition of various kinds on our decks and tied to our forecastle, were several red and green boxes containing sufficient gelignite to blow the average city sky-high.

We could see our bombers having a great time as we swept in towards the shore. Huge bursts of lurid flame on the skyline followed by thuds told us that their "eggs" were falling as arranged. Two huge fires were visible when we were

Badge of H.M.S. Zulu
By permission of H.M.S.O.

still many miles away. We steered towards them. They resembled at that distance a couple of powerful car headlamps, but when we got nearer we could see the flames leaping high into the sky.

One fire periodically burst out into a strange pink glow, shedding a lurid radiance far over the sea. Streams of coloured tracer bullets shooting up from the flames, punctuated by violent explosions, suggested a large munition dump had been hit. Flashes broke the darkness at other points as A.A. guns vainly tried to keep off the bombers, which were dropping some of the heaviest bombs. Searchlights vainly probed the black ceiling, and when we got close to the shore one or two occasionally swept down and across the water, making us blink with their bluish glare. But apparently the shore defenders failed to spot us.

MEANWHILE, the troops had landed from their motor torpedo boats. Punctually at two o'clock came the message we were all waiting for—that our forces ashore had succeeded in their mission of putting certain guns out of action. Finally, secret papers were burned in the ward-room. Then we all went on deck to embark in the landing craft. It was now three o'clock. According to plan, the bombing ceased.

Men silently lining the decks got into boats which were slung out with faint creaks and lowered into the water. Then there occurred a fantastic piece of ill-luck, which delayed the

entire landing by nearly an hour and a half and probably had an important effect on the operation. At the last moment a hook used in handling the boats came adrift and took a considerable time to repair. Then one of the towlines parted just as the boats were leaving, and the whole party had to wait until this had been remedied. We were encouraged by the sight of the vast clouds of smoke discernible in the glow of the searchlights, showing that much destruction had already been done.

Then, when all was ready, "flights" of troops in craft towed by power boats crept silently away to the shore, looking like convoys of black beetles on a black sea. As they went our captain called out: "Good luck to you all." They had to find a stretch of beach only 50 yards long and completely invisible in the darkness. The ship's navigator had done his best to ensure we were in the correct position to the nearest yard.

NOTHING much happened to us after that for almost an hour. Anti-aircraft fire ashore ceased and the searchlights went out after a last final tired sweep of the sea and sky. Then Tobruk disappeared in utter darkness and became as silent as a dead city. We spent some time wondering what was happening to the boys in the landing craft.

Suddenly, just after five o'clock, a searchlight or two flickered on and began waving across the sea as if seeking something. Apparently the alarm had been given on land. We had not long to wait for this to be confirmed. Bright flashes flickered against the blackness, followed by thumps, and then the eerie moan of shells came to us on the bridge. The shore batteries were firing at us.

Within 10 minutes the Sikh's guns were replying, and a minute later our own ship was rocked as her salvos screamed into Tobruk. A searchlight now had us pinned uncomfortably in its sickly glare. The whine of shells passed close overhead and others could be heard splashing alongside us.

Shattering news came through our small wireless receiver at 5.30 a.m. The Sikh said that her steering had gone—almost the worst thing that can happen to a ship apart from being sunk—and one of her engine-rooms was also out of action. She said she could steam at 10 knots to a position out of range

of the shore batteries and then we could take her in tow, but she made such slow progress that it was decided to take her in tow sooner.

The next hour was the most terrifying I have ever experienced. With searchlights on us we edged up to the stationary ship and began the operation of taking her in tow. By now the batteries had the range of Sikh, and all they had to do was to keep on firing to score hits with practically every shell. As we got to within a few feet of her shells began to hit us, too. One landed at the base of a ladder not more than four feet from where I was standing, but by a miracle I was unhurt. I moved to the other side of the ship. A second later a second shell burst a few feet to my left with a shower of brilliant sparks. A cloud of acrid smoke enveloped me. I was convinced my last moment had come.

AT our stern men were trying to connect the two ships while shells were bursting all round. They succeeded, but then occurred a further stroke of almost unbelievable misfortune. A shell by a million to one chance severed the steel towline, and the operation of passing a new line had to be begun. Meanwhile shells were raining down on both ships unceasingly, but, as I afterwards found, our casualties were surprisingly light.

It was now 6.35 a.m. and the Mediterranean dawn was just beginning to break, revealing the yellow cliffs of the coastline. The captain was giving orders ceaselessly, but

H.M.S. SIKH, sunk on Sept. 13 during the combined operations off Tobruk, belonged to the Tribal Class and was a sister ship of the Zulu. Both were completed in 1938, had a displacement of 1,870 tons, and carried eight 4·7 guns. When last seen H.M.S. Sikh was ablaze, but her guns were still firing.
Photo, Wright and Logan

one I remember came through at this moment: "Run up the battle ensign at the mast-head," he said.

We were persevering with the plan to tow Sikh despite the deluge of shells. At 6.50 a.m. it was decided that the situation was getting too hot, for now a couple of bombers had appeared and were joining in the attack. The senior naval officer in Sikh ordered us to withdraw, and we replied "God bless you." Back came a final message, "Thanks, cheerio."

We sped away, making a smokescreen, but even then we did not give up the idea of saving the Sikh's crew, for a little later our captain suggested to Sikh that we have one last try to take them off, but he was told that he must withdraw. The sun was now well up. Both ships were perfectly visible from the shore. While we were trying to take Sikh in tow we were only just over a mile from land so that the batteries could hardly miss.

With heavy hearts we turned out to sea and raced away. There were still a few landing-craft round Sikh, but it was impossible to tell whether these contained further instalments of troops who were to land, or some who had returned from shore. For the next 10 minutes the batteries continued to fire at us and shells whistled down fairly close, but now we were moving at high speed and every second getting farther away.

No further hits were scored on this ship, but I fear that Axis gunners had the easiest target of a lifetime in the Sikh. While we were racing away, and until she slipped out of sight below the horizon, shore guns continued to fire at her. I could see the columns of water leaping up on all sides of the stricken vessel, and smoke pouring from her. But Sikh refused to give in. For every flash from the shore guns, I saw a defiant

answering flash from the guns of the crippled ship. I could still see those flashes when she was nothing more than a tiny speck at the base of a huge column of dirty grey smoke.

As we were leaving, we saw four British motor torpedo boats speed in our direction. We flashed to them that we were hurrying on and that they were to follow us.

For some hours now we knew that we should be a lone ship and we expected the Luftwaffe to give us almost undivided attention. We had not long to wait. Just before nine o'clock a twin-engined bomber suddenly screamed down out of the sun, its stick of bombs falling close as our captain neatly turned the ship aside. After that we were bombed at frequent intervals until nightfall. Altogether some 70 bombers must have been sent against us.

Time after time the Junkers and Stukas planted bombs all round us, but we dodged them all, thanks largely to the skill of our captain. I lay on Zulu's deck with rubber ear plugs in my ears, my tin hat jammed down tightly, and my "Mae West" lifebelt inflated, as the ship squirmed past the bombs and the planes roared down. Some of the planes had sirens which gave an unearthly screech as they dived.

A cup of soup hurriedly gulped down was all we had for lunch, and then we settled down again to bombing. During the middle afternoon we were hit. At least seven dive-bombers attacked one after another, and as the final one shot past there was a loud thump and the deck kicked beneath me.

The ship heeled over at once. All except essential personnel were transferred to another ship, which had joined us. We leapt from one heaving ship to another. Our wounded were handed across. Then the Zulu was taken in tow by a third ship, but sank later.

Singapore was a pathetic sight. No civilians to be seen. Just isolated groups of exhausted troops and machine-gun posts. Buildings and cars in flames ; many planes overhead. A desolated and deserted city. The docks were on fire and no one knew the way. For nearly an hour we dashed about trying to find an entrance that was not burning. Finally we found it and scrambled on board a ship with 2,500 passengers, mostly troops and R.A.F.

Next morning we were on our way, but so were the Japs. For four hours we had raids. The last was one of fifty-seven planes which did a great deal of damage and caused many casualties. We were busy attending to the wounded and improvised three small sick-rooms. All the nursing sisters lived down below in the hold where the huge cargoes of frozen meat were normally carried. We slept on the deck. Meals didn't exist, but the officers gave us what they could —Army biscuits and corned beef, and buckets of tea which we drank out of cigarette tins.

Washing was almost impossible, and those who had no luggage had to remain in the clothes in which they had sheltered in the sewer. We were glad when we reached Batavia, where I bought a little uniform. Then I sailed for Bombay in a troopship.

And here is an extract from the letter of another nurse employed in an Army hospital in the Far East :

Between 100 and 200 nursing sisters left ... on the small steamer Kuala. There were many other women and children on board, besides certain Government technical officers. This ship was heavily bombed and sunk near an island. Casualties were heavy, both from wounds and from drowning, and I am afraid scores of nurses were killed. Most of those who escaped managed to get ashore, where some hundreds of people had collected.

While the Kuala was sinking, a lifeboat picked up 39 people from the water, including Army sisters. Owing to the strong tide and currents this boat could not reach the island, and so had to head out to sea, eventually reaching another island at dusk. I happened to be in this boat.

For three days we were marooned with no food of any kind, only about a gallon of

We Nurses Were in the Front Line of Fire

Wherever our soldiers serve, women of the military nursing services are there to tend the sick and wounded. Something of the dangers and hardships they have endured is told in these letters from nurses in the Far East. Singapore is the scene of the first—and probably also of the second.

At the end of Jan. 1942 the enemy had drawn so close that it was decided there was no hope of holding the Malayan mainland. The hospital had orders to evacuate to the Gordons' barracks at Changi, Singapore.

The place was filthy, and there were no servants. Fortunately we had no patients for a few days, and all turned to and made the place presentable. Then the patients arrived and everyone was busy ; soon the wards had a professional appearance, while the operating theatre was a marvel to behold in a barrack square.

In spite of large red crosses on all the buildings and barrack square, the Japs dive-bombed and machine-gunned us frequently. It was terrible to see the shell-shocked patients as the bullets fell around us. All sisters donned their tin hats (mine became my dearest possession), and if the bombs were dropping too near we also dived under the beds. I can see Matron now, after one of our worst raids (during which one V.A.D. was killed), jumping up from under a bed and rushing out into the open, with bombs still dropping, to find out if the night sisters had been hurt.

The situation now became desperate. We were in the front-line of fire from the enemy's guns on the Johore coast, and in front of our own front-line troops. This went on for forty-eight hours.

The next night Matron told us to be ready at daybreak to be moved to Alexandra Hospital. We were relieved to hear that we were not to be handed over to the Japs— as we had been previously told that evacuation was impossible. Another sleepless night

at Alexandra Hospital. In the morning the Principal Matron sent a message that 80 of us were ready to go to the docks with hand luggage only. On the way to the docks we had to shelter in a sewerage drain with a group of Indian troops.

FROM THE QUAY AT SINGAPORE women and children mounted the gangway to the ship which would evacuate them to a safer zone. Events moved with a terrible swiftness after the Japanese had swept down the Malayan peninsula. They first set foot on the island on Feb. 9, 1942 ; six days later Singapore fell.

Photo, British Official

fresh water, and no dressings for the wounded except torn-up pieces of clothing. A doctor of the Malayan Medical Service and two or three civil nursing sisters had been picked up also, and they all did magnificent work.

After three days we were rescued by a Chinese junk, which took us to a small island farther south where there was a tiny native

village. From this island we moved on south by native boats by night from island to island, dodging the Jap aircraft and surface patrols until some reached an island with a military hospital. That was the last I saw of them as I took another route in a native boat, and it is possible that all these sisters were captured by Japs a few days later.

In this page is told how a rubber dinghy saved yet another of our airmen forced down at sea. This pilot awaits rescue by Walrus Amphibian aircraft. *Photo, Keystone*

On the 13th Day I Killed and Ate a Seagull

This is the story told by Pilot Officer Holbrooke Mahn, 23-year-old American member of the Royal Canadian Air Force, who spent 14 days in a small dinghy in the North Sea following the crash of his Hampden bomber.

WHILE we were flying off the Frisian Islands at about 200 to 300 feet the port engine of my kite suddenly failed. We did not have time to jettison the bombs before the crash. The dinghy had been successfully released and a gunner and I hoisted the dazed navigator into it. The tiny craft was full of water, but we dared not bale it out for fear of losing what gear we had in the dark. All our iron rations, pigeons and other gear had gone down with the aircraft.

At sunrise the weather was fairly sunny, and we managed to get our feet and clothing dry, but we found our food was contaminated by petrol. The water, however, was intact. We had two containers of approximately one quart each. We put out a sea marker and estimated a drift of eight miles to the north-west on the first day. We all felt fairly comfortable, including the navigator, who was fairly well recovered by this time.

We drank no water at all on the first day, and decided to ration our small supply to one sip each in the evening. Two quarts won't go very far among three men. The first night was quite calm. We tried out the flares, but they, like the food, had been too much damaged for use by the force of the crash.

The second and third days were much the same as the first. We all felt fairly cheerful, but on the fourth day things got worse.

A high north-north-west wind sprang up and the heavy swells soaked us to the skin. For the next six days I got very little sleep—we baled continually. We had to drink more water than the sip we had agreed to, and we finished our first bottle on the fifth day.

On the evening of the eighth day, about two hours before sundown, our spirits were suddenly revived. A Junkers 88 circled our craft. Thinking our rescue was near, we drank the last of our water. But then a Beaufighter dived to the attack and the Junkers headed for home. As the Beaufighter dived low over our dinghy, we waved, but it made off and we never saw it again.

Shortly after sundown the navigator died.

The ninth day was cloudy and rough, and there was an easterly wind which drove us away from the Dutch coast. At about four to five o'clock four Hudsons came over us on a parallel course, at about 600 to 700 feet, but our tiny dinghy was not spotted. The Hudsons came and went for about an hour or an hour and a half and then went away.

Now the gunner lost hope. He was much weaker than I, and next he began drinking sea water. I took away the can and threw it into the sea. I had no desire to drink sea water, I did not want to die that way. About this time it began to rain and I tore off a piece of canvas from the dinghy and caught some

of the rainwater. I tried to persuade my companion to drink some, but he would not do so. I therefore drank it all—several tablespoonfuls.

Soon after drinking the sea water the gunner became delirious, and two hours later he died. It was quite a struggle, in my weakened condition, to remove his body from the dinghy. On the 12th day, however, I had to stop baling entirely owing to weakness.

On the 13th day I had my first food since the day of the crash. A seagull alighted on the edge of the dinghy. It stuck its head under its wing. I grabbed it, cut off its head, and sucked the blood. I also ate the fish in its guts. I was not struck with repulsion, but had only a desire to get something to eat. The bones and feathers were found in the dinghy when I was picked up. Barely had the 14th day of agony begun—it was 12.45 in the morning of June 18—when help arrived and I was rescued.

OUR DIARY OF THE WAR

Sept. 16, 1942, Wednesday 1,110th day
Sea.—Admiralty announced the loss of destroyers Sikh and Zulu in raid on Tobruk on Sept. 13-14.
Air.—R.A.F. made heavy raid on the Ruhr, Essen being the main target.
Russian Front.—W. of Stalingrad the Germans gained some ground.
Africa.—On the night Sept. 15-16 our desert forces attacked Gialo oasis. They occupied the position for some days, destroying ammunition and supply dumps.
Indian Ocean.—Governor-General of Madagascar asked for an armistice.
U.S.A.—Navy Dept. announced that on Sept. 14 American heavy bombers attacked Jap shipping at Kiska, Aleutians.

Sept. 17, Thursday 1,111th day
Russian Front.—Heavy street fighting ended in the repulse of Germans who had penetrated into Stalingrad.
Africa.—Heavy night raid on Tobruk by Allied bombers.
Indian Ocean.—French plenipotentiaries in Madagascar refused to accept our terms, and operations continued.

Sept. 18, Friday 1,112th day
Russian Front.—Fierce fighting in the north-western outskirts of Stalingrad.
Indian Ocean.—Fresh British landing on east coast of Madagascar.

Sept. 19, Saturday 1,113th day
Air.—R.A.F. bombers over southern and western Germany in strength, made Munich chief target.
Russian Front.—Street fighting in Stalingrad went in favour of the Russians. Moscow announced that von Kleist had been killed on Mozdok front.
Africa.—Allied bombers again raided Tobruk.
General.—Paris theatres, etc., closed and curfew on non-German civilians from 3 p.m. Saturday to Sunday midnight, following shooting of 116 "Communist terrorists."

Sept. 20, Sunday 1,114th day
Sea.—Destruction of U-boat in West Atlantic by Canadian destroyer Assiniboine announced. Admiralty announced loss of H.M. submarine Unique.
Russian Front.—Hand-to-hand fighting continued in N.W. Stalingrad.
Africa.—Tobruk raided by Allied aircraft for seventh time in eight nights.

Sept. 21, Monday 1,115th day
Sea.—Canadian Navy Minister announced loss of destroyer H.M.C.S. Ottawa through enemy action in the Atlantic. Admiralty announced loss of H.M. trawler Waterfly.
Russian Front.—German attacks repulsed in the Stalingrad area, on the Mozdok front and in the area of Sinyavino (Leningrad).
Indian Ocean.—In Madagascar our forces closed in on Antananarivo.
Australasia.—Mopping-up of Japanese in Milne Bay area of New Guinea reported to be complete.

Sept. 22, Tuesday 1,116th day
Air.—R.A.F. bombers made daylight attacks on power stations and industrial buildings in Lille-Lens area.
Russian Front.—Hand-to-hand fighting continued inside Stalingrad; in the main battle on the N.W. of the city the Russians were on the offensive.
Africa.—U.S. heavy bombers attacked Benghazi at dusk; night raid on Tobruk by R.A.F. and R.A.A.F. bombers.
Australasia.—Allied air force kept up raids on enemy installations at Buna, Kokoda and Rabaul.

Sept. 23, Wednesday 1,117th day
Sea.—Admiralty announced arrival in North Russian ports of an important convoy of British, American and Russian

ships, in spite of heavy attacks by enemy aircraft and U-boats.
Air.—R.A.F. raided submarine yards at Flensburg.
Africa.—Announced that on night of Sept. 13-14 our desert forces operating behind the enemy lines raided Benghazi and Barce.
Russian Front.—Timoshenko began counter-offensive N.W. of Stalingrad in attempt to relieve city.
Indian Ocean.—British forces entered Antananarivo, capital of Madagascar.

Sept. 24, Thursday 1,118th day
Russian Front.—German attempts to penetrate to centre of Stalingrad repulsed.
Australasia.—U.S. army bombers attacked Jap transports in Western Solomons, scoring three hits.
U.S.A.—Heavy bombers attacked Jap installations at Kiska, Aleutians.

Sept. 25, Friday 1,119th day
Sea.—Admiralty announced loss of destroyer Somali and minesweeper Leda during passage of convoys to and from Russia; at least 40 German aircraft were shot down and six U-boats sunk or damaged.
Air.—R.A.F. Mosquito bombers made daylight raid on Gestapo H.Q. at Oslo.
Russian Front.—Russians made some progress inside and outside Stalingrad.

China.—U.S. aircraft attacked aerodrome at Hanoi, Indo-China.
Australasia.—Allied fighters and bombers attacked Kokoda; Buna and Rabaul.
U.S.A.—U.S. and Canadian aircraft attacked shipping at Kiska, Aleutians.

Sept. 26, Saturday 1,120th day
Russian Front.—Russians continued to make progress N.W. of Stalingrad.
Mediterranean.— Admiralty announced that British submarines had sunk or damaged eight enemy supply ships.
China.—American aircraft made successful attack on Jap supply columns on the Lungling-Chefang road.
Australasia.—Japs withdrew their outposts in Owen Stanley area of New Guinea.
U.S.A.—New aircraft-carrier Lexington launched one year ahead of schedule.

Sept. 27, Sunday 1,121st day
Sea.—Admiralty announced loss of H.M. submarine Thorn.
Russian Front. — House-to-house fighting in Stalingrad; German attacks repulsed N.W. of the city.
Africa.—American Liberator bombers made heavy raid on Benghazi.
Australasia.—Japanese bombers and fighters attacking U.S. positions at Guadalcanal suffered heavy losses.

Sept. 28, Monday 1,122nd day
Russian Front.—On the N.W. outskirts of Stalingrad superior German forces made a tank penetration in one sector.
Africa.—R.A.F. again bombed Tobruk.
China.—American bombers raided Jap installations on the China-Burma border.
Australasia.—Twenty-three out of 25 Jap bombers were shot down over Guadalcanal, making a total of 42 aircraft destroyed in four days by U.S. planes without loss.

Sept. 29, Tuesday 1,123rd day
Russian Front. — Repeated heavy attacks on Stalingrad were repulsed. On Rzhev front Russians made some progress.
Indian Ocean.—Our forces occupied the port of Tulear in Madagascar.
Australasia.—In the Owen Stanley area of New Guinea our troops launched an outflanking attack on the enemy.

★━━━━━━━━━━ *Flash-backs* ━━━━━━━━━━★

1939
September 17. Soviet troops entered Poland. H.M.S. Courageous sunk.
September 27. Surrender of Warsaw, capital of Poland.

1940
September 18. R.A.F made fiercest attack on German "invasion ports" on the Channel.
September 27. The Tripartite Pact

between Germany, Italy and Japan signed in Berlin.

1941
September 16. Riza Khan, Shah of Iran, abdicated.
September 21. Russians announced evacuation of Kiev.
September 28. Lord Beaverbrook and Mr. Harriman in Moscow for Three Power Conference.

Editors Postscript

THE magnitude of the task which that truly great man Franklin Delano Roosevelt had to achieve in order to bring America into the War against Germany, with no fewer than 15,000,000 persons of Germanic origin inhabiting the United States, must never be forgotten when we consider the part America is now fated to play in the world fight for freedom. Theodore Dreiser is an eminent American journalist and writer of fiction, born in the "Hoosier" country of Indiana, but his name betrayeth his mental provenance, just as his obsession with those underlayers of society, where "things perverse, obscene, abominable" are bred, indicates a gloomy and distorted view of life, as reflected in his many "powerful" novels, and especially An American Tragedy. He is an isolationist and violently anti-British. Yet this man, at this time, recently unburdened himself in Toronto of the most subversive and ignorant stuff about Great Britain that puts Lindbergh's scatterbrained attacks quite in the shade.

IF Russia were defeated this man Dreiser hoped that the Germans would invade England and rid the world of a nation that has gone pappy by allowing itself to be ruled by a horse-riding (shootin', huntin', and fishin') aristocracy. The typical ignorance of this fictionist in all that concerns the life and genius of the British people may, in some measure at least, be attributed to the English habit of self-depreciation, by contrast with an opposite American propensity that need not be emphasized. Another alleged gem from Dreiser's lips at Toronto runs: "England has done nothing in this War thus far except borrow money, planes, and men from us." Listening to such iniquitous untruths one's heart goes out to Mr. Roosevelt, knowing what a job he has had, and still has, in bringing the minority of American-born but foreign-thinking citizens into line. A half-hour's broadcast talk by any of the intelligent and patriotic American flying leaders now in England would show up Dreiser's dicta for the unmitigated drivel they are.

THE timidity of the British propaganda in America in face of the whole-hearted and full-blooded boosting of American achievements in the U.S. press, can be blamed for the prevailing ignorance which Dreiser, thanks only to his reputation as a writer of fiction, has been able to shout into wider and louder notoriety. Last August Alastair Cooke, the New York correspondent of The Daily Herald, was apprehensive of the effect of the "headliners" in a too free and irresponsible press shouting the odds on American effort while singing small about the British. He wrote:

"The consequences can hardly be guessed. As long as the war goes on Americans will have a vague, but exaggerated, notion of the actual fighting power and presence of Americans on the European and Asiatic battlefronts. I doubt if ten Americans in a hundred have any notion that the Polish force in Britain has far surpassed, and perhaps still does, that of the Americans. Or that Canada has sent more than twice as much food to Britain as the United States. Or that of the fifteen thousand men of Wednesday's heroic (Dieppe) raid, most of them were Canadians and Britons."

THE Dreiser folly, which must have warmed the cockles of what serves Goebbels as a heart, is also symptomatic of the lengths to which the clamour for a second front can reach—for Dreiser was upbraiding Britain for not doing enough to succour Russia. When all the facts are available the world will be astounded to know the sacrifices which Britain has made to assist her brave Soviet allies of today and to protect from Nazi domination America herself, by bearing the brunt of the Germanic onslaught after France had crumbled, by keeping the struggle for Freedom alive while America was only in the preliminary stages of her preparations for defence, let alone any planning for her offensive. But the shouting for a second front in 1942 has been overdone. Foolish youths are chalking it up on the blasted walls of London, I observe. The best time for a second front was away back in 1939, but Stalin in his own wisdom chose to let Hitler have one front then—and oh the difference to the world of freemen that did make!

THERE is much that one could say on this topic; but now is not the time for saying it. What matters to us (if we are "realists") is the situation that exists. And I would point out that to use a fleet of seventy-five men-o'-war to take one convoy to the Soviets, when that great fleet might have been employed in strengthening our reserves in the Middle East, where in truth we are holding a second front, is some slight evidence of the extent to which we are supporting our Soviet Allies. Britain has achieved marvels of self-sacrifice in helping her allies. But for the honouring of our obligation to Greece the story of the Middle East might have taken a very different turn. We have had more than enough of self-depreciation and ignorant criticism. The time has come to stand up for ourselves.

WHAT a pleasant old chap Dr. Joseph Parker, of the City Temple, would seem to have been when you got him on the subject of tobacco! I recollect him as an aggressive and self-assertive preacher, with something of the crudities of certain of Israel's minor prophets. Reading today a paragraph which he wrote just fifty years ago in a monthly symposium of The Idler for Nov. 1892, I think I know why I didn't cotton to the man. Here is the paragraph:

"I hate smoking. From end to end it is a nuisance. It ends in cancer, apoplexy, bad temper, bankruptcy and almost in hydrophobia. It is an invention of the devil. It is the pastime of perdition. No dog smokes. No bird pines for tobacco. No horse is a member of a pipe club. No intelligent person ever puts a cigar in his mouth. The whole idea and practice of smoking must be condemned as atheistical, agnostical, and infinitely detestable. Smoking has been abandoned by all reputable persons, and left to ministers, editors, poets, and other intellectual confectioners."

BELIEVE it or not, the man who wrote that was filling the City Temple (he built it in 1874) twice every Sunday up to his death in 1902, and had been for many years in the big money of the religious world as both preacher and writer. These stupid, ill-couched phrases, nearly all expressing untruths, were typical of the man, yet had wireless been invented in his time he would almost certainly have been the star performer on the air, where his lusty invective, his wild and whirling words would have had many admirers. And yet I'm sorry that the Temple he laboured so well to build and filled so long with his crude eloquence should at last have gone up in fire—and smoke. No dog smokes, indeed, and one might add that no horse ever asks for a pink gin or a bottle of Chateau Yquem. Which "ministers" did Parker mean to associate with editors? Surely not prime ministers!

AMONG the worst offenders in paper-wasting are the numberless organizations that bombard the charitable—i.e. known subscribers to charities—with frequent circular letters. I have been able to add to my stock of miscellaneous unused envelopes many a score, sent to me by these "appeal secretaries." One importunate institution has sent me no fewer than four "repeats," each consisting of (1) the containing envelope with a 2½d. stamp, (2) a printed reply envelope unstamped, (3) a four-page imitation typewritten letter with actual signature, and (4) a pictorial leaflet with subscription form. That is typical of scores of appeals that come to my desk and soon after go into my salvage bin, except for the envelopes, which I save for using with pasted over address slips. The flood of such appeals, to which I have long been accustomed as a humble subscriber to more charities than I can now assist, does not seem to have lessened greatly in the drive for paper-saving. It must involve a high percentage of waste on the sums collected, quite apart from the valuable paper, so much of which, despite the ingenuity of the appeal secretaries, falls on stony ground. There is a case here, I think, for investigation.

AIR MARSHAL W. A. BISHOP, V.C., D.S.O. and Bar, world-famous British air "ace" of the First Great War, and now Director of Air Force Recruiting in Canada, in the cockpit of a Spitfire while on a visit to a R.C.A.F. squadron in England. With him is Sqdn.-Ldr. Norman Bretz, D.F.C. *Photo. Fox*

Printed in England and published every alternate Friday by the Proprietors, THE AMALGAMATED PRESS, LTD., The Fleetway House, Farringdon Street, London, E.C.4. Registered for transmission by Canadian Magazine Post. Sole Agents for Australia and New Zealand: Messrs. Gordon & Gotch, Ltd.; and for South Africa: Central News Agency, Ltd.—October 16, 1942. S.S. *Editorial Address:* JOHN CARPENTER HOUSE, WHITEFRIARS, LONDON, E.C.4.

Vol 6 The War Illustrated Nº 140

Edited by Sir John Hammerton

SIXPENCE

OCTOBER 30, 1942

ONCE GREAT AND LOVELY STALINGRAD is now (says Reuters Moscow Correspondent) a gigantic inferno. "Street after street burnt or blasted to smithereens ; gaunt smokestacks rising out of mounds of rubble ; dead bodies lying in gruesome attitudes, waiting for burial which the living have no time to perform. A pall of acrid smoke hangs over the city like a funeral shroud . . ." This photograph, radioed from Moscow, shows an unhappy Russian woman retrieving a few of her household goods from the ruins of her home.
Photo, U.S.S.R. Official

ALONG THE BATTLE FRONTS

by Our Military Critic, Maj.-Gen. Sir Charles Gwynn, K.C.B., D.S.O.

LAST year October saw the opening of Hitler's offensive towards Moscow, which he announced would result in the final destruction of Russia's capacity to wage war effectively.

In spite of the Germans' initial successes, which undoubtedly have reduced Russia's offensive power, October this year found them still far short of that achievement. Russia's defence is as stubborn as ever, and her capacity for offensive action remains formidable. In the Middle East there is the same record of frustration after initial success; and in the Far East it would seem that Japan has been compelled to abandon, or indefinitely postpone, her most ambitious projects. The thoughts of the Axis Powers and Japan must now be mainly directed towards maintaining possession of what they have conquered.

The Allies have had little enough to claim of positive success, but that the enemy is showing signs of fear that the initiative is passing from them, and that they must henceforward think in terms of defence, is clear. Hitler has spoken of establishing an invulnerable defensive position in Europe; Italy talks of General Alexander's coming offensive; and the Japanese have already had to give ground for defensive reasons. Though this may be the general trend of developments, the immediate course of action that may be adopted in the various theatres is still obscure.

RUSSIA

In my last article (*see page 258*) I suggested that Von Bock might contemplate the abandonment of attempts to capture Stalingrad by assault, and might adopt slower and less costly methods which would enable him to release troops for other tasks. Shortly after I wrote, Hitler's declaration: "Stalingrad will be taken" (though, cautiously, he did not say when) seemed to imply a continuance of assault methods. But the military spokesman at Berlin, a few days later, using much the same arguments as I had suggested, spoke of overcoming the final resistance of the great

city by the slow process of bombardment. A difference between Hitler's views and those of the German General Staff seemed clearly indicated; and Goering, in a speech that followed, took care to [throw responsibility for decision on to Hitler. Since then there has been no marked slackening in the German assaults, but I suspect that the General Staff

CROSSING A RIVER IN THE CAUCASUS, Soviet troops are seen mounting a gun on pontoons to transport it across the water. Thwarted at Stalingrad, the Germans intensified their drive towards the Grozny oil-fields and the Caspian to secure a decision before winter should set in. Fighting developed fiercely in the Mozdok area. *Photo, Planet News*

in the long run will have their way, though without openly opposing Hitler's view.

The most recent major attacks have all been directed on the north of the city, apparently with the primary object of securing positions on the banks of the Volga from which the ferrying of reinforcements across the river could be prevented. These attacks, while meeting Hitler's views to some extent, may also be a necessary preliminary to the adoption of a policy of investment and bombardment, which would have little chance of success so long as the defence was receiving fresh troops to replace casualties and relieve the exhausted. Pressure on other parts of the city has been maintained, but apparently by slow infiltration methods; and the attack from the south, which at one time seemed so dangerous, has apparently lost weight.

That Von Bock had contemplated a switch of his main effort to the Caucasus front is suggested by the intensification of attacks in the Mozdok region and a renewal of the attempt to reach Tuapse by the road over the mountains, as well as by the coast road from Novorossisk. The strengthening of the attacks in the Caucasus may account for the slackening of the attack on Stalingrad from the south, for the railway communications of

both run through the Rostov bottle-neck and probably are inadequate to meet the requirements of intensive operations on two fronts.

Meantime, the steady though slow progress of Timoshenko's relief offensive north of Stalingrad, together with his subsidiary relief operations to the south of the city, must tend to aggravate German difficulties of supply and of finding fresh troops for offensive operations. I should not be surprised if the Germans found it necessary to stage a large-scale attempt to inflict a heavy defeat on Timoshenko's relief army, instead of the counter-attacks so far carried out mainly with the object of checking its progress. If such an attempt is made, it would almost certainly mean a relaxation of the attack on Stalingrad and might very probably affect operations on the Caucasus front as well.

Russian defence in the Mozdok region and in the Western Caucasus has stood up admirably to the recent intensification of German attacks. German complaints of the difficulties they are encountering from snow and rain is an admission of disappointment.

THE operations in the Mozdok region are not easy to follow, but apparently the Germans are engaged in a two-prong attack. One prong is directed up the Terek valley towards Ordzhonikidze, where the military road across the mountains to Tiflis starts. The other is attempting to advance by the Baku railway towards the Grozny oil-fields. The object may be to develop a pincer movement on Grozny, but the capture of Ordzhonikidze would also provide flank protection for the communications of a major advance on Baku, preventing Russian forces which might threaten them from using the military highway as a line of supply.

On other parts of the Russian front there has been little change in the situation, but at Leningrad it is evident that the Germans had to undertake considerable counter-offensive operations to relieve pressure on their positions encircling the city; and it is claimed that they were compelled to draw reinforcements from the southern front for the purpose.

The approach of winter almost certainly negatives any major German operation in the north and centre, but it is still an open question whether offensive operations will be continued in the south throughout the winter. If Hitler seriously contemplates the

ENEMY THRUSTS IN S.E. RUSSIA were slowed down as the result of Stalingrad's tremendous defence. German movements in the elbow of the Don were hampered by Timoshenko's counter-blows. Shaded portion on the above map shows the German-occupied areas in mid-October. *Courtesy of the News Chronicle* PAGE 290

U.S. FORCES IN THE ALEUTIANS are in occupation of islands in the Andreanov group. On Oct. 4, 1942, it was stated that an airfield had been established from which to attack the Japanese in the western tip of the island chain ; enemy-held Kiska, 125 miles from the most westerly island occupied by the Americans, was vigorously attacked. This photograph shows U.S. troops unloading equipment on a lonely beach. The convoy, which included several transports, was the largest that had yet sailed in the North Pacific. *Photo, Keyston*

establishment of a self-sufficient European defensive block, as he suggests, then access to Transcaucasian oil would be of increased importance, for it would be required for the development of the economic resources of the occupied territory in Russia.

EGYPT The first two weeks of October saw no break in the lull on the El Alamein front. The Italian press, however, evidently expected General Alexander to take the offensive, and reported extensive preparations behind the Allied lines. Intensification of air attacks on Axis supply lines, forward positions, and aerodromes also indicated that a major move by one side or the other was imminent.

Rommel's visit to Germany may have been for reasons of health, but it is probable that he used the opportunity to make a personal appeal to Hitler for further reinforcements. The intensification of the air attacks on Malta that began on Sunday, Oct. 11, suggests that he is being given them. But Malta's magnificent defence makes the cost heavy ; in five days 94 Axis aircraft were shot down, and scores more damaged. That Rommel will be back at the front before the next storm breaks we may regard as certain, whatever the state of his health may be.

FAR EAST It is evident that the recapture of the Tulagi area in the Solomons is still the main immediate Japanese object. They have been able to continue to land reinforcements on Guadalcanal, but at a cost in shipping and aircraft which imposes caution. Troops and transports are apparently assembled at bases in other islands, near enough to take advantage of favourable opportunities, but also evidently near enough also to be subjected to Allied bombing attacks. So far the American Marines—magnificent troops—appear to have had no great difficulty in repelling Japanese attacks ; and in the air Allied aircraft have had much the better of exchanges. Barring some unforeseen naval misfortune, there seems no reason for anxiety.

IN New Guinea I had felt little concern about the situation near Port Moresby, but I admit I was surprised at the Japanese retreat without fighting. If, however, they relied on natives for porterage of supplies, as seems to have been the case, it is not surprising that air attacks on their communications proved decisively effective. The failure of the enemy air force to make any attempt to interfere with the attacks is interesting, and seems to indicate that Japan's output of aircraft has limitations which compel strict economy.

But whether all available aircraft are being concentrated for operations in the Solomons, or are being held in reserve in case the Australian advance should offer opportunities for counter-attack, remains to be seen. The Australian troops have re-established contact with the enemy, but it is improbable, with such a difficult line of supply, that they will make any attack in force across the mountains. There is a distinct possibility that the Japanese will withdraw the bulk of their troops from New Guinea, where they can effect so little, retaining only sufficient numbers to protect aerodromes from which Darwin and Port Moresby can be attacked.

THE withdrawal of the Japanese from the islands they had occupied in the Aleutians, with the exception of Kiska, is presumably with a view to economizing strength and to minimize exposure of shipping and isolated detachments. The establishment of an American air base within short range of Kiska will, in any case, make communication with that island precarious, and will probably mean an increased wastage of Japanese shipping. Dutch Harbour provides the new base with a second line, both for offensive and defensive purposes, which should give it a distinct advantage in case of bombing exchanges with the Japanese at Kiska.

HONOURED FOR BRAVERY IN BATTLES ON MANY A FRONT

Trooper K. ANDREWS, R.A.C., a dispatch rider, has been awarded the M.M. for outstanding bravery in rescuing wounded men under heavy fire from the enemy.

Trooper A. J. MANSELL, R.A.C., awarded the M.M. for taking charge of a tank during an enemy attack. He drove the tank, whose crew were wounded, to a protected position.

Wing-Cdr. G. R. HOWIE, awarded the D.S.O. for gallantry displayed in the execution of air operations. He has served in the Italian, Syrian, Iraq, Greek and Libyan campaigns.

Lt. A. T. ALMOND, R.A.C., whose courage in saving the driver of his tank and carrying on for 10 hours despite being wounded has won for him a well-deserved M.C.

They Covered Themselves with Glory at Dieppe

After the great raid on Dieppe of August 19, 1942, it must have proved a difficult and somewhat invidious task to decide which of the thousands engaged were most worthy of having their bravery recognized. In the event, scores of decorations were awarded, and in this and the facing page we give photographs of some of the recipients, with extracts from the official citations.

VICTORIA CROSS

Lt.-Col. Charles Cecil Ingersoll Merritt (above), the South Saskatchewan Regiment, showed matchless gallantry and inspiring leadership while commanding his battalion during the raid.

From the point of landing, his unit's advance had to be made across a bridge in Pourville which was swept by very heavy machine-gun, mortar, and artillery fire; the first parties were mostly destroyed and the bridge was thickly covered by their bodies. A daring lead was required; waving his helmet, Lt.-Col. Merritt rushed forward, shouting: "Come on over. There's nothing to worry about here."

He thus personally led the survivors of at least four parties in turn across the bridge. Quickly organizing these, he led them forward, and when held up by enemy pillboxes, he again headed rushes which succeeded in clearing them. In one case he himself destroyed the occupants of the post by throwing grenades into it. After several of his runners became casualties he himself kept contact with his different positions.

Although twice wounded Lt.-Col. Merritt continued to direct the unit's operations with great vigour and determination, and while organizing the withdrawal he stalked a sniper with a Bren gun and silenced him. He then coolly gave orders for the departure, and announced his intention to hold off and "get even with the enemy." When last seen he was collecting Bren and tommy guns and preparing a defensive position which successfully covered the withdrawal from the beach. He is now reported to be a prisoner of war.

To this commanding officer's personal daring the success of his unit's operations and the safe re-embarkation of a large portion of it were chiefly due.

Capt. (temp. Major) Patrick Anthony Porteous, R.A. (right), was detailed to act as Liaison Officer between the two detachments assaulting the heavy coast defence guns.

In the initial assault, working with the smaller of the two detachments, he was shot at close range through the hand, the bullet passing through his palm and entering his upper arm. Undaunted, Capt. Porteous closed with his assailant, succeeded in disarming him and killed him with his own bayonet, thereby saving the life of a British sergeant on whom the German had turned his aim. In the meantime, the larger detachment was held up, and the officer leading

this detachment was killed and the Troop Sergeant-Major fell seriously wounded.

Capt. Porteous, without hesitation and in the face of a withering fire, dashed across the open ground to take over the command of this detachment. Rallying them he led them in a charge which carried the German position at the point of the bayonet. Though shot through the thigh he continued to the final objective, where he eventually collapsed from loss of blood after the last of the guns had been destroyed. His most gallant conduct, his brilliant leadership and tenacious devotion to a duty which was supplementary to the role originally assigned to him, were an inspiration to the whole detachment.

DISTINGUISHED SERVICE ORDER

Brig. Sherwood Lett, M.C., E.D., as officer commanding a Canadian Infantry Brigade, by splendid leadership and the highest kind of personal courage provided not only fine direction to, but a most stirring example for, the troops under his command.

He personally spent long periods at the wireless sets sending and transmitting orders and reports, under heavy M.G., mortar and shell fire. During one of the most intense periods of enemy barrage, while working at an exposed

wireless set, he was seriously wounded. In spite of this he continued to direct his brigade for the rest of the action, his thought being entirely for the units and individuals of his command.

His soldierly handling of a difficult situation and cheerful, confident and effective leadership under stress were decidedly noteworthy and impressed all ranks.

Brig. Clarence Churchill Mann was the Military Commander

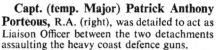

aboard the second H.Q. ship. Although this ship was repeatedly attacked and hit, Brigadier Mann continued to carry out his duties with a coolness and efficiency which were an inspiration to all about him, and which exercised a most valuable influence upon the course of the action.

Brigadier Mann's work in preparing the detailed military plans for the Dieppe enterprise was most exceptional. At no time, either before or during the operation, did he spare himself. To his great ability, indefatigable energy and steady courage is due a great part of the credit for the success obtained on this occasion.

Lt.-Col. Dollard Menard, Fus. M.R., while in command of his battalion displayed the highest qualities of courage and leadership. Landing with the first attacking parties, he was wounded almost from the beginning, but he continued to direct the operations of his unit by wireless under constant machine-gun, mortar and artillery fire.

Later, in order to gain a better point of vantage, he crept forward to higher ground, but was again wounded. When finally taken on board an L.C.T., although wounded for the fifth time, he still insisted on organizing A.A. defence and looking after his men. He set an example in the best tradition of the service and was an inspiration to all ranks in his battalion.

Wing Cdr. W. E. Surplice, D.F.C., was the pilot of the leading aircraft of a formation of bombers detailed to release smoke bombs to screen the landing of troops on the beaches near Dieppe. On the accuracy of this depended not only the success of the subsequent smoke-laying operations by following aircraft but, in a great measure, the safety of the entire combined operation. Wing Cdr. Surplice, skilfully guided by F/O Ruther-

ford, flew in to the target at a low level and, defying an intense barrage from the ground defences, dropped his smoke bombs with precise accuracy.

Maj. (now Lt.-Col.) Douglas Gordon Cunningham, Camerons of Canada, A/B.M. of a Canadian Infantry Bde., set an outstanding example. He manned the rear link set to Force H.Q. Ship from the beginning of the operation at 04.30 hours until the evacuation was

Heroes of the Great Raid on Hitler's Bastion

completed at 12.00 hours, allowing neither his own danger nor heavy damage suffered by the L.C.T. on which he was serving to interfere with his devotion to the interests of his battalions. His calmness and utter disregard for his personal safety were a constant inspiration to his men.

Major Cunningham had played an essential part in the preparations for the raid, and this, combined with his courage and determination, constituted a very important contribution to its success.

Maj. (now Lt.-Col.) Arthur Hayward Fraser, P.P.C.L.I., Brigade. Major of a Canadian Infantry Brigade, displayed the greatest coolness and steadiness under heavy fire.

When the destruction of his No. 19 wireless set left him without contact with Force H.Q., he transferred himself, his staff, and his No. 18 set to the L.C.T. carrying H.Q. of a Canadian Infantry Brigade, and thus re-established touch between Force H.Q. and the units of his own brigade. On this L.C.T., although under intense fire from the shore and bombardment from the air, he maintained contact with his battalions, and was mainly responsible for the successful re-embarkation from Green Beach.

His cool courage had a great steadying effect upon those serving under him and his initiative and determination contributed in very large degree to the success of the operations.

Maj. Andrew Thompson Law, Camerons of Canada, was second in command of the regiment during the operation. The commanding officer having been killed immediately on landing, Major Law took over the unit, and despite very heavy enemy fire reorganized it and proceeded to direct its attack. He successfully and efficiently fought his unit approximately two miles inland, inflicting heavy casualties on the enemy.

On the order for withdrawal being given, Major Law fought a rearguard action to the beach, and so effectively controlled the battalion that approximately 80 per cent of the personnel were intact at this time. The cool and steady manner in which Major Law directed the action throughout, while continually under fire, was an inspiration to the whole battalion, and to him goes the major portion of the credit for the fact that a comparatively large proportion of its personnel was withdrawn.

Maj. James Earl McRae, South Saskatchewan Regiment, was second in command of the regiment during the operations. His ability and initiative in moving Battalion H.Q. out of enemy mortar and artillery fire, but in maintaining communications and in passing information to the companies and to Brigade H.Q., contributed immensely not only to the tactical success of the operation but also to the reduction of casualties.

During the withdrawal to the beach, Major McRae continued to exercise his inflexible control, although under intense and continuous enemy fire. He encouraged the wounded to carry on and directed the flow of men under cover of the wall. On reaching the L.C.A., although in deep water and exhausted he assisted the wounded aboard before permitting help to himself.

Temp. Maj. Peter Young, M.C., second in command of No. 3 Commando. The L.C.T. in which Major Young's party was accommodated was the only one to land on the beach assigned to the assault party. The detachment, however, consisted only of Commando and Troop Headquarters personnel (20 all ranks), the majority of whom were runners, signalmen, or mortar detachment numbers.

With this small and inadequately armed force Major Young set off unhesitatingly to undertake the task originally assigned to the whole fully armed Commando. They scaled a precipitous cliff, penetrated elaborately wired and mined defences, advanced intrepidly on the German gun positions, defended by upwards of 200 of the enemy, and so harassed the enemy as to render the gunfire ineffective.

After 3½ hours of continuous fighting Major Young fought a successful rearguard action back to the beach. Major Young, another officer and an exhausted private were the last to embark, being towed by life lines from the L.C.T.

Capt. William Denis Whitaker, R.H.L.I. Captain Whitaker landed with the first wave, directed the cutting of both rows of wire on the beach and organized the necessary covering fire for B Company's advance on the Casino. He himself then proceeded to the Casino with his party, where, after clearing the building and organizing a defence against counter-attack, he led a large party of all elements of the battalion towards the town. Later he directed the withdrawal of a great portion of the battalion from the town and Casino to the beach and supervised their re-embarkation.

Captain Whitaker was at all times cool and collected, and displayed great courage and initiative in the command of his troops. Captain Whitaker was an inspiration to all.

BAR to D.F.C.

Group Capt. H. Broadhurst, D.S.O., D.F.C., A.F.C., in the combined operations against Dieppe flew with great distinction. Although he was several times engaged by

hostile aircraft, one of which he destroyed, he displayed great skill and furnished much valuable information regarding the trend of the air operations. In the course of his duties he flew alone for some eight hours in an area where hostile patrols were in great strength.

NORWEGIAN CROSS

A./Wing Cdr. F. D. S. Scott-Malden, D.F.C., R.A.F.V.R. During the past six months

this officer has led the wing on a large number of sorties. In this period it has destroyed 49 enemy aircraft and probably destroyed or damaged many others. During the operations at Dieppe the wing destroyed 21 enemy aircraft and many others were damaged. Wing-Cdr. Scott-Malden led the wing on three of these sorties. For his leadership of the Norwegian wing he was awarded the Norwegian Cross by King Haakon, and his D.S.O. was announced on September 11.

DISTINGUISHED CONDUCT MEDAL

L/Sgt. George Alfred Hickson, R.C.E., was in charge of a group charged with destroying the main telephone exchange in the Post Office. Finding the fire on the beach too heavy to move directly to his target, he assisted an infantry platoon in mopping up enemy M.G. positions, and destroyed a 3-inch gun by detonating a 3-lb. charge on the breech.

When the Platoon Commander and most of the senior N.C.O.s were put out of action, Hickson assumed command and led the platoon to the Casino, where strong enemy opposition was nullified. Using explosives, he blew his way through the walls to reach a large concrete gun emplacement, then with another charge blew in the steel door, killing a gun crew of five. He then destroyed the 6-inch naval gun and two M.G.s after infantry had cleared the post.

L/Sgt. Hickson then reorganized his platoon, and despite heavy enemy opposition led them into the town as far as the St. Remy Church. Unable to find Brigade H.Q. and being without support, he withdrew his party to the Casino. L/Sgt. Hickson throughout the day showed determined leadership and high qualities of initiative, and was among the last group to evacuate.

Pte. James Maier, Essex Scottish, in a day filled with incidents of heroism set a fine example of courage and initiative and soldierly leadership. Under heavy fire he engaged enemy positions with an L.M.G. Although wounded he persisted in his attack. Wounded a second time more seriously, he nevertheless used an A.Tk. rifle with telling effect against two posts which had defied small arms fire. Both of these he silenced. He continued to snipe successfully with this weapon until the time of withdrawal, when he collapsed from wounds and loss of blood. Believed to be dead, he was thrown overboard, but recovered and was picked up from the water by another craft. His actions throughout showed the highest devotion to duty and were an inspiration to his comrades.

MILITARY MEDAL

Cpl. Franklin M. Koons, U.S. Army Ranger Battalion, showed conspicuous gallantry and admirable leadership, continuing to carry out his duties with very marked success under heavy fire, which eventually caused the almost total destruction of the building from which he and his men were sniping.

Photos, British Official; New York Times Photos, Keystone, Fox

Through New Guinea Runs Australia's Front Line

In their aggression against Australia the Japanese landed in New Guinea last March, but so far their progress has been slow and intermittent. This chapter tells of the scene of the fighting in what has been described as the most secret front line in the world-wide war.

HALF a century or so ago New Guinea possessed a very unsavoury reputation as a home and haunt of tribes of savages, cannibals many of them, living on the lowest rungs of the human ladder. There are still headhunters and cannibals in the remoter and more inaccessible parts of the great island, but in many districts, if not in most, the nearly naked warriors who fought each other with bows and arrows, with axes of polished stone and with daggers made from crocodile bone, have given place to peaceful horticulturists growing coconuts and bananas, yams and sago, fishermen skilled in the use of net and spear, and employees of the trading firms, plantations, and goldfields of the white man.

But of late war has come back to New Guinea. There is slaughter once again in the mountain passes, in the steaming swamps and tangled vegetation of the forests. But this time the war is not between tribe and

islands, second only in size to Australia and Greenland. Of its 300,000 square miles almost exactly half is taken up by Netherlands or Dutch New Guinea—a vast area almost entirely undeveloped, very largely unexplored, and whose coasts are not yet fully charted. In the dense forest of the interior continue to exist (so it is reported) tribes of headhunters and cannibals, few of whom have ever seen a white man and fewer still have had any experience of the advantages, and disadvantages, of the white man's civilization. The Dutch settlements are dotted here and there along the coasts, and the white officials and traders are a mere handful compared with the 200,000 or so of natives. At Fak Fak the Dutch Assistant Resident has his headquarters; politically, Dutch New Guinea is part of the Moluccas, a group of islands lying between New Guinea and Celebes in the Netherlands East Indies.

So far as the other half is concerned, New

siderable economic development. Coconuts and rubber are produced on the plantations; goldfields are worked, and a railway has been constructed from Port Moresby to some promising copper deposits. By steamer and aeroplane the Territory has regular communication with Australia. Something has been done to raise the natives above that primitive existence to which long ages have accustomed them; the proceeds of a hut tax are largely devoted to native education, in the development of which the missionary societies have played an honourable part.

CAPITAL of Papua is Port Moresby, which, with its coral reefs, its foreshore fringed with coconut palms and tropical flowering shrubs, its background of high, jungle-covered mountains, is generally described as one of the beauty spots of the Pacific.

Before the war Port Moresby's white population was only a few hundreds, but today it is the centre of a large military camp. The offices and bungalows of the officials have been taken over by the military authorities, who have also assumed the work of the native administration. " During my recent stay," wrote a Special Correspondent of The Times on Sept. 14, " I did not see one civilian or one woman. The white women were all evacuated to Australia long ago, and the native women have betaken themselves to villages in the interior. A certain number of their fuzzy-haired menfolk are working as stevedores at the docks and as porters on the overland route, but the little native village close to the port, a cluster of thatched wooden huts resting on piles driven into the sea, is completely deserted." Along the road to the interior are camps and military establishments simply described as Eighth Mile, Seventeenth Mile, and so on, according to the number of miles they are from the port.

American Negro engineering and constructional units have been employed; but, to quote from The Times correspondent again, " Papuan men, their heads often crowned with huge golliwog mops of black hair, are doing good work as porters and as stretcher-bearers bringing back seriously wounded men from the front line. There have been several cases where pilots who have crashed or baled out over the jungle have met with great assistance from the natives, who fed them and guided them back to Port Moresby."

NEW GUINEA, the world's third largest island, lies just south of the Equator. Its tropical climate is modified somewhat by the mountains in its interior, however. Land of exuberant Nature and savage men, it is now a battlefield in the war of White v. Yellow.

tribe, but between white men and yellow, men possessed of guns and bombing planes; and the slaughter and devastation puts into the shade anything that was once laid to the charge of the miserable savage.

FOLLOWING the Japanese landing at Rabaul, the former capital of New Guinea, but situated in New Britain in the Bismarck Archipelago off the north-eastern coast, the Japanese crossed the dividing waters and effected landings on New Guinea itself at Lae and Salamaua on or about March 8. Some four months later they carried out a fresh series of landings in the Buna and Gona area, on the northern coast across the mountains from Port Moresby, and promptly began to fight or filter their way inland. On August 15 they seized Kokoda airfield, and on Sept. 8 were within a few miles of the vital gap in the Owen Stanley Range. But three weeks later they were reported to be in full retreat, having altogether failed to overcome the Australian-American resistance. A landing at Milne Bay was also repulsed at the end of August.

Thus it came about that a new war zone was opened up; from being one of the world's backwaters New Guinea became front-page news. For the first time the many millions of the general public came to know more about the island than that it was peopled by a lot of fuzzy-wuzzies.

Rather to their surprise they learnt that New Guinea is one of the world's biggest

Guinea is included in the British Commonwealth. There are two main divisions: Papua, the south-eastern part, and the Mandated Territory of New Guinea to the north.

This Mandated Territory was declared a German protectorate in 1884, but in 1920, after the Great War, it was mandated to the Australian Commonwealth by the League of Nations. It has an area of 69,000 square miles with a population of at least half a million natives, 4,000 whites, chiefly British, and 2,000 Chinese. Rabaul, in New Britain, was the capital until August 1941, when, following a volcanic eruption, the administration was transferred to Lae, on the mainland, the principal base for aeroplanes carrying machinery and native labour, etc., to the goldfields of Wau and Bulolo in the interior.

PAPUA has an area of about 90,000 square miles, and in 1940 it was estimated to have a population of 337,000 Papuans and 1,822 Europeans. Following the annexation of western New Guinea by the Dutch in 1848, the Australians feared that the whole of the island might ere long come under Netherlands rule, so in 1884 a British protectorate was proclaimed over this south-eastern portion, and in 1888 it was annexed to the Crown. Then in 1906 it was transferred to Australia as the Territory of Papua, and since then has been an integral part of the Commonwealth. Under Australian rule there has been con-

BROADLY speaking, however, the native population of New Guinea is not sufficiently numerous nor sufficiently developed to play any considerable part in the struggle now being waged across the island's mountain backbone. And who can blame them? Among the most juvenile of Nature's children, they have found it difficult enough to put away their spears and knives, to cease decorating their housetops with the dried heads of their enemies. Now they are amazed to witness this new kind of war, one far more ferocious and deadly than that which they or their fathers have ever known. Bewildered and terrified, they have taken to their heels into the bush—into that bush where things change little for many, many moons, where the ghosts of their ancestors hold potent sway, and the sorcerer with his potions and spells is a power behind the throne.

So it is that the Australians and Japs now waging desperate war in the dense forests and rugged valleys of the monster island have the battlefield to themselves. No native war-drums throb through the forest. Crouching in his hut of straw and palm leaves, the trembling savage listens from afar to the white man's fury. **E. ROYSTON PIKE**

Martial Array in a Giant Island of the Tropics

Australian soldiers walk down the main street of a typical village in New Guinea. On either side are native huts of poles, coconut matting and thatch.

ON THE NEW GUINEA FRONT. Supplies for Allied troops fighting in the Owen Stanley Range are carried on the shoulders of native porters (top right). These men carry about 40 pounds of food and equipment apiece. Australian ground defence unit (centre left) operates a searchlight during a Japanese night raid. Circle, dumping supplies to Allied forces in the Kokoda area from a transport plane. Below, the airfield at Port Moresby, chief Allied air base in New Guinea, after a Japanese raid. Australian and U.S. troops clear up such damage as has been done while an American aircraft circles low.

Photos, Paul Popper, Planet News, New York Times Photos

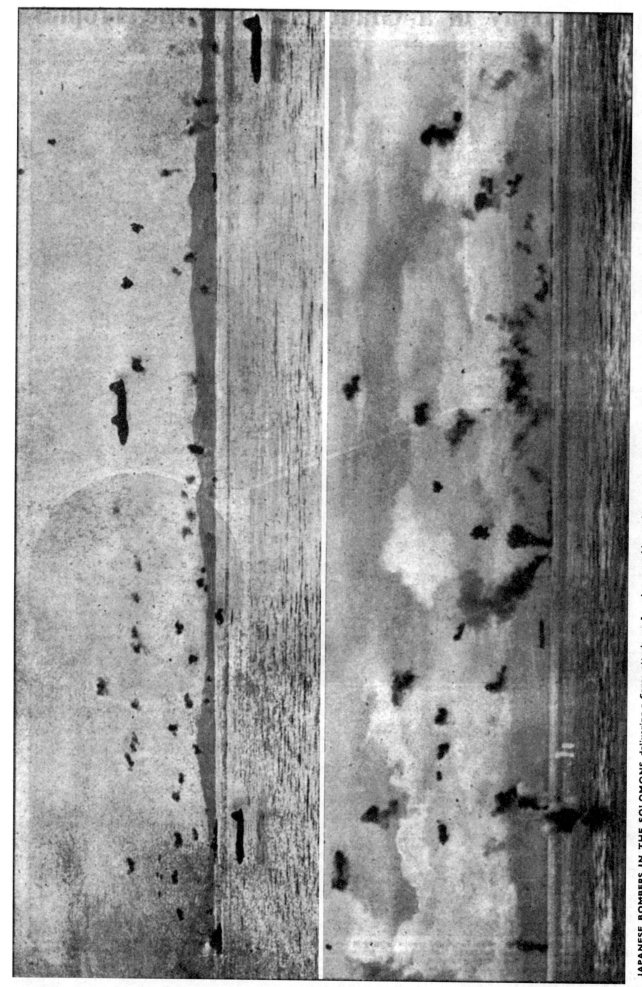

JAPANESE BOMBERS IN THE SOLOMONS delivering a fierce attack on American warships and transports. At the beginning of August 1942 American Marines landed on three islands in the Tulagi area, and in spite of strong enemy opposition, both on sea and in the air, managed to consolidate their positions. The top photograph shows four Japanese bombers, three of them flying so low as almost to skim the water; they are sweeping in for a low-level attack on the U.S. ships, some of which are seen on the extreme left. In the lower photograph, taken during the same action, one of the Jap bombers, visible just above the water line, dives to attack through the terrific barrage put up by a formidable concentration of American guns.

Photos, Central News

THE WAR AT SEA

by Francis E. McMurtrie

RECENT enemy utterances provide evidence that things are not going so well with our foes as they had hoped and expected earlier in the year.

Apart from the much-publicized speeches of Hitler and Goering, the tone of which was unusually subdued, the President of Tokyo University, Mr. Kunijiko Okura, delivered a remarkable broadcast to the Japanese people during the last week in September. In this he admitted that :

Contrary to expectations, our enemies seem to be hitting back at us and regaining their footing. They are now fighting with all their hearts, and if we do not face the situation with renewed determination we shall be confronted with a terrible end. Is there not some evidence that people are looking at this war with the easy feeling that victory is a certainty, just because we hear of successes day after day ? But China is not the old China, and the Chinese Army is no longer a despicable opponent. In addition, America is now standing up and mobilizing her vast resources in materials. We must not continue at ease as we have been in the past.

FOR such firm believers in " saving face " as the Japanese, the above remarks are a notable confession of alarm. Obviously they are designed to stimulate the Japanese public into renewed efforts, and may be regarded as the prelude to fresh attacks on Allied positions. These so far have taken the form of fresh landings on the island of Guadalcanal, from which it is imperative that the enemy should expel American Marine forces if the Japanese are to retain their grip on the Solomon Islands and adjacent groups.

Vice-Admiral Robert L. Ghormley, who commands the United States naval forces in this area, is fully alive to the situation, and may be depended on to use every exertion to counter the enemy moves. It is true that during the first week in October Japanese troops in Guadalcanal were reinforced under cover of darkness, but the warships which covered the landings did not escape unscathed. One destroyer was sunk on the night of Oct. 5, and three nights later a 7,000-ton cruiser of the Kako type was torpedoed and set on fire by bombs. She was still burning when sighted by air reconnaissance planes the following afternoon.

Without constant reinforcement and renewal of their supplies of ammunition, food, etc., the Japanese in Guadalcanal can hardly hope to maintain their foothold, let alone drive out the well-entrenched U.S. Marines, who hold the aerodrome which gives the island strategical importance. Fortunately, the Allies have now established air superiority in this region, and should be able to detect and break up further attempts to disembark fresh troops. At the best, therefore, the Japanese can hardly hope to do more than delay the progress of Allied arms in the Solomons.

Japanese Threat to India

IT is not to be expected, however, that Japan will remain quiescent elsewhere. In my opinion, her next target will be India, which, owing to the general unrest caused by the Congress party, offers a tempting bait. To deliver a serious attack on India, enemy possession of Malaya and Burma is not enough. Control of the Bay of Bengal must also be obtained.

Last April a Japanese fleet appeared in this area. From its aircraft-carriers raids were made on the British naval bases at Colombo and Trincomali, in Ceylon, and three British warships were sunk. These were H.M.S. Hermes, an aircraft-carrier of

10,850 tons launched in 1919, and two 10,000-ton cruisers, the Dorsetshire and Cornwall. Having accomplished this destruction, the enemy force seems to have retreated to its base at Singapore.

It may be assumed that the British Eastern Fleet, now operating in the Indian Ocean under the command of Admiral Sir James Somerville, is fully prepared to meet a second incursion into the Bay of Bengal by Japanese naval forces. When it comes—as it must, if the Japanese are to continue the struggle with any hope of success—it is to be hoped that the defeat inflicted on the enemy will be a salutary one. It is fortunate that, out of the nine aircraft-carriers with which she entered the war, Japan has lost five. Of the four survivors, only two are big modern

ITALIAN SUBMARINE COBALTO, attacking one of our Mediterranean convoys last August, was rammed by the British destroyer Ithuriel. This photo, taken shortly before she sank, shows the huge hole in her conning-tower ; some of her crew are seen in the background struggling in the water, while others still on board scramble towards the bows, whence they were rescued.
Photo, Associated Press

carriers, the loss of which she cannot afford to risk except in the direst emergency.

Official photographs released on Oct. 8 illustrated the destruction of the Italian submarine Cobalto by two British destroyers, H.M.S. Ithuriel and Pathfinder. This occurred during the Malta convoy action on August 12. None of the three vessels mentioned was afloat when war began. It is probable that the Cobalto is one of half-a-dozen submarines ordered in 1939 of a type resembling the Perla class, each armed with six torpedo tubes and a 3.9-in. gun.

Recently Italy has been shedding her submarines rather rapidly. Not only have a certain number been lost in the Mediterranean, but the Germans have been insisting on more being sent to the Atlantic to support U-boat attacks on Allied convoys. That they have accomplished much in this direction is to be doubted, in spite of the extraordinary claim that the Barbarigo, of 941 tons, had sunk the United States battleship Idaho off the West African coast. An equally fantastic claim to have torpedoed an American battleship

was made several months ago by the same submarine, then stated to be operating off the coast of Brazil.

Official announcements made in Rome on August 26, Sept. 2, 17 and 28 admitted that certain Italian submarines were missing and must be presumed to have been lost. One of these may have been the Pietro Calvi, rammed and sunk by H.M.S. Lulworth.

How Many U-Boats at Sea ?

OF course, it is the German submarine flotillas that provide the backbone of the underwater campaign against Allied shipping. Red Fleet, the official organ of the Soviet Navy, recently devoted some space to an analysis of the German strength in submarines. This is estimated at over 300 units, which agrees fairly well with a recent Swedish assessment. At the start of the war there were 71 in service, and it is believed that over 400 have been built since. Losses must therefore have approximated to 200 U-boats, or as many as were destroyed and surrendered during the whole of the last war.

Taking the last war's record as a guide, I am of the opinion that about 80 is the average number of German submarines at sea, operating against commerce, at the present time. Recently, according to Berlin, the bulk of this force has been diverted from the Western Atlantic—no longer a profitable hunting-ground—to the route by which our armies in Egypt and the East are supplied—down the West African coast and around the Cape.

IT would seem that Japanese submarines cruising in the Mozambique Channel—especially now that the ports of Madagascar are no longer open to them—have accomplished less than was hoped. On Sept. 24 it was announced simultaneously in Berlin and Tokyo that " Japanese naval units " had joined forces with other Axis forces in the Atlantic. It is clear that this amounts to little more than a gesture for propaganda purposes. One or two Japanese submarines are doubtless in the Atlantic, based on French or German ports, but the practical effect of this on the general situation is of little importance.

Dianthus Sent a U-Boat to the Bottom

Watching out for lurking U-boats during the passage of an Atlantic convoy, H.M. corvette Dianthus sighted an enemy submarine and immediately gave chase. After a three-hour pursuit the U-boat was blown to the surface with depth-charges and rammed four times by the corvette. The action was a grim one, for every rifle and revolver that the corvette's crew could muster was used with deadly effect against the enemy. Just before she sank the U-boat's bow reared up and crashed upon the deck of the Dianthus.

A number of German prisoners were picked up and taken aboard the British ship, and then the corvette rejoined her convoy to rescue survivors from torpedoed merchantmen. Right, superficial damage caused by the U-boat's final lunge against bows of Dianthus. Centre right, reloading a depth charge thrower aboard the corvette.

Lt.-Comdr. C. E. Bridgeman, R.N.R. (smoking pipe), captain of the Dianthus, who directed the corvette's action against the U-boat, photographed upon his ship's bridge.

BEARDED U-BOAT PRISONERS (left) seen on arrival at a British port. They have just disembarked from H.M.S. Dianthus, and are listening intently to the instructions of their captors. The crew of the Dianthus (right), lined up on the deck of their ship after reaching their base receive the congratulations of Admiral Sir Percy Noble, C.-in-C., Western Approaches. The officers and men of the little warship were highly commended for the redoubtable fight they put up against the German submarine and for the valiant part each of them played in a remarkably successful action.

Her Thunder Meets the Thunder of the Sea

H.M.S. DUKE OF YORK was laid down in 1937 and completed in 1941 ; her first " mention " was in Jan. 1942, as the ship which took Mr. Churchill to America. She belongs to the King George V class, her sister ships being King George V, Anson, Howe, and Prince of Wales. The Duke of York has a displacement of 35,000 tons, and carries a complement of 1,500. Her armament includes ten 14-in. and sixteen 5·25-in. guns and 4 multiple pom-poms. She is here seen firing a salvo from her after 14-in. guns.   PAGE 299   *Photo, British Official*

Never in History Such Street Fighting as This

BIG FACTORY BUILDING ON OUTSKIRTS OF STALINGRAD HELD BY RUSSIANS AS A FORTRESS

GERMANS ATTEMPTED TO BURN DOWN THE CITY

GERMAN TANKS MEET HEAVY FIRE

FALLEN MATERIAL ONLY STRENGTHENS THE STRONG POINT FROM WHICH GUNS FIRE ON ADVANCING TANKS

Stretching for many miles along the Volga, Stalingrad ranks among Russia's greatest industrial cities ; today it is one great battlefield. The drawings in this page give an extraordinarily realistic picture of fighting conditions in the outer suburbs and inside the city. Above, a great factory building on the outskirts has been converted into a formidable fortress, while in the foreground debris serves as a strong point blazing defiance at advancing German tanks. Below, an impression of fighting in the city's centre ; in the same building different floors are held by the one side and the other.

GERMANS HOLD FLOORS IN THIS BUILDING

CROSS FIRE ABOVE STREET

BUILDING HELD BY RUSSIANS

WRECKED GERMAN TANKS

STRANDED GERMAN TANK

OVERTURNED TRAMCAR

RUSSIAN TANK

'THE BATTLE OF STALINGRAD is unique,' says General Dietmar, the Nazi military spokesman. "The Russians have done everything that could be done to fortify the city, and their talent for fortification is well known. For the first time in modern warfare the Germans are confronted with the task of fighting right through a great city which is being systematically defended. Street fighting in a town of 500,000 people is indeed a phenomenon." These vivid drawings tell their own story. *Drawings by E. Byatt ; courtesy of The Sphere*

In Stalingrad Every Ruin Blazed Defiance

STALINGRAD'S ORDEAL has been a terrible one under the enemy's mass attacks. Top photograph, gutted buildings in one of the main squares ; on the right is a group of statuary. Centre : Two women carry supplies to the heroic defenders against a background of blazing buildings. Bottom photograph, from a German source, two Nazi soldiers cautiously advancing along a ruined street. "The battle of Stalingrad," wrote a Nazi war correspondent, "has become a war between human moles."

Photos, News Chronicle, Planet News & G.P.U.

Stalingrad's Name Is Written In Blood

Stalingrad has been called the Soviet Verdun, but not even Verdun at the height of its agony
was so blasted and burnt as has been the great centre of Russian industry on the Volga. Verdun
was a great and powerful fortress : Stalingrad has found its principal defence not in guns and
fortifications, but in the spirit of its defenders.

WHEN in August 1942 the enemy drew near to the very gates of Stalingrad, the city committee of the Bolshevik Party issued a stirring call to arms :

Once again, as twenty-four years ago (the reference is to Stalin's successful defence of Stalingrad, then called Tsaritsyn, against the Whites), our city is experiencing trying days. The bloodthirsty Nazis are pushing towards sunny Stalingrad, towards the great Russian river Volga. People of Stalingrad ! Do not surrender the city to be defiled by the Germans. Rise like one man in defence of our beloved town and our homes. In the grim days of 1918 our fathers saved Tsaritsyn. We will do the same in 1942. All who are capable of shouldering arms, defend your city, your home !

To this appeal the people responded with patriotic eagerness and heroic zeal. Those who through age or infirmity could play no useful part were evacuated across the river ; others, men and women alike, took up arms and devoted themselves to keeping up a steady supply of munitions and rations to those in the firing line, and to repairing tanks and guns damaged in the fighting. And though the battle was raging on their very doorsteps, the war factories, the great tractor factory in particular, kept on working at full blast. Sometimes when the Nazis broke through the workers downed tools, took up their rifles, and hurried to the combat. Then, when the danger was averted, back to their benches they went, to their lathes, their furnaces.

So the great city—Stalingrad stretches over an area on the western bank of the Volga some twenty miles by ten, as big as eighteenth-century London and composed, as London was then, of a built-up heart surrounded by chains of suburbs and straggling villages—became a battlefield. The Soviet High Command took the deliberate decision to defend the city to the last street, the last house, the last floor. There was not a street that was not made into a tank obstacle, not a block of flats or office buildings that was not converted into a nest of pillboxes, not a factory but had its garrison of resolute fighters.

THE Germans were surprised ; soon their surprise was tinged with amazement, with ever-deepening horror. They expected, having broken through the outer ring of defences, to march in triumph through Stalingrad's streets as they had marched in triumph through so many cities in the length and breadth of Europe. How they were deceived ! Stalingrad was no Paris. Stalingrad was defended as not even Warsaw or Belgrade, Kharkov or Rostov, had been defended. The assailants had to face fire from every angle, every corner, every roof-top. The street fighting was the fiercest ever to be witnessed. Grenades and fire-bottles rained down on the German tanks from roofs, through windows. Thousands of the city dwellers joined in the struggle. Never in history has a great industrial city been exposed to such an assault, devoted to such destruction, defended in such a fashion.

By the end of September a great and terrible battle was being waged inside the city between small groups of desperate men armed to the teeth. " Every man uses an automatic weapon," reported The Times Special Correspondent in Moscow, "and enemies jostle one another on staircases and in corridors. Never before in military history has so much fire-power and weight of material clashed in so small a space." He went on :

It is a war à outrance. You may lose the hall of a building and from the staircase you may see the enemy pour across the threshold. But there can be no surrender. From the first-floor windows your machine-guns try to keep more men from entering, while troops with tommy-guns wait for the enemy to climb higher. And if you lose the first floor there is one above it.

Soon, of Stalingrad's thousands of buildings only the stone structures remained, and many of these were reduced to ruins by the German pattern-bombing. The vast areas more or less covered with the wooden shacks and shanties, strongly suggestive of a pioneer settlement in America's Wild West, went up in flames or were crushed beneath the Nazi tanks or wiped out by the incessant hail of bombs. But the great business buildings, blocks of flats, and factories were made into strong positions, connected below ground by tunnels which provided excellent cover for the defenders taking such tremendous toll of the men in field-grey. Some of the fiercest engagements took place at street crossings and in the adjoining blocks, between small groups of tanks, shock troops, and grenadiers. Powerful barricades were built across the streets composed of heavy furniture, massive safes from the offices, mountains of sandbags filled by thousands of eager workers toiling hours without end. Reported The Times correspondent :

The noise of the battle is said to be appalling. It is compounded of the harsh din of heavy tanks, the ceaseless chattering of machine-guns, and the unabating zoom of hundreds of aeroplanes fighting large battles in formation. Only in the infrequent lulls do the screams of the dying and the whimpering of the battle-crazed reach the ears of the soldier.

Inside the city Von Bock's panzers were almost useless, since their progress across the piles of shattered masonry was so slow ; his bombing planes, too, had their drawbacks, since looking down on that extraordinary battlefield it was impossible to detect where amid the shell-pocked ruins the Germans lay and where the Russians. But outside the city the tanks raged and roared across the steppes, over the hillocks and down the ravines, through the melon fields and in and out of the windmills still waving their arms above the plain. Now and again a hundred or even two hundred tanks were formed into a massive battering-ram and flung against the defenders within the built-up area ; every gun that could be brought to bear pounded the Red positions, and through the gaps the Nazi infantry filtered. But time and again Timoshenko's men rallied and retrieved what had been a desperate position.

THOUSANDS upon thousands fell ; little was reported of the wounded's fate, but every account spoke of the dead piled in horrible heaps. " German infantry at Stalingrad no longer has the old striking power," cabled a correspondent of a Berlin newspaper ; " regiments have shrunk to skeletons of their former selves, and it is almost incredible that these men who have scarcely had a wink of sleep for days or even weeks can continue to fight against the Red Army's ferocious resistance."

Nazi commentators and war reporters vied in their descriptions of Stalingrad's inferno.

Fighting in the city, so far from slackening, increases in fury every hour (cabled another German eye witness). During the day Russian and German tanks are locked in battle often little more than ten yards apart. They are engulfed in a thick grey mist from the shattered buildings and the smoke of their own cannon. At night, infantry fight hand-to-hand engagements in darkness lit by leaping flares, exploding bombs, and the glow of burning buildings. Fighting through these streets is a matter of creeping from shell-hole to shell-hole, over barricades made of beams and planks from ruined houses. Snipers occupy every remaining roof-top and window. Russian sharp-shooters lie hidden behind walls or in pits scooped in the earth. The Germans must face fire from every direction at once.

ONE more quotation from a man who saw the battle at its height, at quarters uncomfortably close. It is a German Propaganda Corps war correspondent speaking.

The German infantry is now very tired. It is impossible to imagine what it means to remain exposed in open day and night fighting perpetually. The Russian artillery fires unceasingly. Batteries fire from the centre of the city, and amid thick vegetation on the Volga's farther bank one can see flashes of guns. Anti-tank guns blaze away at us from the heights which surround our positions. Tanks fire at us from all sides. Russian aeroplanes bomb us. There is literally a rain of shells creating an inferno through which our infantry must pass.

" Fierce as was the enemy," went on the correspondent, " he is less numerous now." But the Germans, too, had had losses. " There are German graves all over the steppes of the Don, and the dry brown soil is carpeted with the bodies of those who have died heroically for Germany. *The soldier no longer fears death—he regards it as his destiny.*" In thousands of German homes those words must have struck like a knell of doom. And that was the battle of Stalingrad—the city which, says the German spokesman, Gen. Dietmar, the Russians raised into the symbol of victorious resistance.

FIGHTING AT STALINGRAD in the central sector of the factory district, the Germans were forced to bring up artillery to smash the resistance of the defenders. This photograph from a German source shows the bombardment of a factory which is being used by the Soviet troops as a base for counter-attacks. *Photo, Keystone*

At Rostov They Fought in the Streets

In the Russian cities every street is a battlefield, every house a fortress that has to be stormed
at terrific cost. Artillery and tanks must be brought up to subdue the desperate resistance
of the defenders. These photographs taken by a Nazi cameraman when Rostov was captured
by the Germans last July are evidence of the grim character of the struggle.

303

Photos, British Off
News, G.P.U.

In All History's Many Centuries . . .

Time and again the Red Armies have been " annihilated "—did not Hitler himself say a
year ago that " Russia has already been broken and will never rise again " ?—but still their
oft-claimed triumph eludes the invaders. So far from being worsted, the Russians return to
the attack (1), recapturing towns, e.g. Vereya, S.W. of Moscow (2), befouled by the Nazis.

... *No Battle So Vast as This*

After a year of siege Leningrad still stands fast : (3) a Russian scout in the outposts.   At
Rzhev the Nazis have rushed up reinforcements (4) to check the Russian counter-thrust ;
and siege guns have had to be brought up at Stalingrad (5), as field pieces were at Rostov (6).
"We are faced with the devil himself," recently complained a Nazi commentator.

Journey's End in the Caucasus

Photos, Topical Press, Keyston

For many weeks and months the Germans have been fighting their way towards the oil-fields that lie on either side of the mountains whose snow-capped peaks look down upon the column of Russians seen marching to the front in the top photo. And where as at Maikop (below) the Nazis have reached their objective, they have found the wells engulfed in flames.

VIEWS & REVIEWS Of Vital War Books

Will Air Power Decide This Global War?

When an air ace, with proved capacity in modern aircraft design and large-scale production, confronts the American and British nations with a reasoned statement that Victory Through Air Power (the title of Major Alexander Seversky's book, Hutchinson, 9s. 6d.) is the quick, the final and the only means to achieve victory, he forces upon us a reconsideration of basic principles obscured by long controversy.

THE bomber is to be supreme and will strike across oceans and round the world. No land or sea operations are possible without air control. Navies are no longer lords of the seas. Battleships will be consigned to museums of outlived weapons. Unity of command, long recognized on land and sea, applies with no less force to the air.

These are far-reaching doctrines—destructive of all older and many current ideas of strategy. But they are advanced with weighty arguments by Major Seversky, and there is every reason why they should be considered with care. For it may be that, though they are destructive of older ideas, they are of constructive importance in the phase of the war which we have now entered. That our own and the American Bomber Commands are working on somewhat similar lines was seen in the recent statements of Brig.-Gen. Eaker, commanding the 8th Bomber Command U.S. Army Air Force, now in Britain: "Air power is the most powerful means we have to win the war," said the General ; and "there are enough aerodromes built and building in the British Isles to accommodate all the Allied air forces needed for the destruction of Germany."

Major Seversky puts the cat among the pigeons when he makes the statement that in a very few years we shall see inter-hemisphere air fighting direct across the oceans.

The range of military aviation is being extended so rapidly that the Atlantic will be cancelled out as a genuine obstacle within two years, the Pacific within three years. After that, in five years at the outside, the ultimate round-the-world range of 25,000 miles becomes inevitable.

It is of little use to object that we are not immediately concerned, in the war against the Axis, with what may happen in five years' time, even in three. If, in so short a period as five years, round-the-world air fighting were proved to be practical and not the dream of an air-intoxicated visionary, then its earlier developments must affect air strategy immediately. Already range, power, and altitude of bombers and fighters are increasing.

SEVERSKY'S revolutionary thesis is concentrated in his eleven basic principles on which air power is to be developed, eleven "air-power lessons for the Allies." Briefly they are as follows :

1, No land or sea operations are possible without first assuming control of the air above.

Control of the skies is paramount for strategic jurisdiction of any land or water surface. National dominance, in war or peace, must be measured with the yard-stick of air power. Anywhere within striking distance of enemy aviation an adequate air umbrella is a minimal condition today for surface warfare.

2, Navies have lost their function of strategic offensive.

A fleet today can approach an enemy shore only under the shield of a powerful umbrella of land-based air power. In short, in the struggle for possession of coast lines, the initial offensive action is the function of aviation, not of navies. This theme is developed in Seversky's fifth "lesson."

3, The blockade of an enemy nation has become the function of air power.

Britain has learned the hard way, says Seversky, that blockade, heretofore a task of sea power, has been taken on in a very much larger measure by air power, which is destined to be the only effective type of blockade. Given enough properly-armed aeroplanes of adequate range, the enemy's supply lines can be wrecked. The first objective of aerial blockade, therefore, is conquest of the skies.

4, Only air power can defeat air power.

A.A. artillery, balloons, and other land and ship defences offer supplementary hazards to attackers, but are at best palliatives and not a cure. Despite first-class A.A. fire, H.M.S. Illustrious was put out of action by bombing planes, the Bismarck could not ward off aerial torpedo attacks, and both British and Japanese battleships have failed to avert destruction by their own A.A. fire.

5, Land-based aviation is always superior to ship-borne aviation.

WHILE navies will always carry their own auxiliary aircraft, Seversky considers that naval aviation is a temporary expedient, marking the transition of military aviation from short to long range. When this is achieved the aircraft-carrier will no longer be essential. He goes so far as to state that the time is approaching when the phrase "sea power" will lose all real meaning. Navies will still fight other navies, but the issue, like all military issues, will be settled by air strength. In the Coral Sea and Midway Islands battles the Japanese were defeated without the warships coming to grips.

If battleships venture into hostile waters without an air umbrella equal or superior to the total enemy aviation, they court destruction. And even then, he holds, this kind of convoy is uneconomical and illogical. A country with air power sufficient to guard a battle fleet in enemy waters should unloose that power at the heart of the enemy instead of wasting it to shield a less effective force.

6, The striking radius of air power must be equal to the maximum dimensions of the theatre of operations.

It is here that Seversky develops his theory of global air control—a theory so startling in its logic that it paralyses, he says, the imagination of the people unprepared to accept the facts. In the development of military aeronautics air power, for maximum effectiveness, must function directly non-stop from home bases. It must strike at the enemy anywhere in the world without intermediate stations. The mind stands appalled in contemplating the end possibilities of his basic proposition that a plane with a 15,000-mile range and a striking radius of 6,000 miles can give to air power total world dominance. And in the Douglas B 19 America already has a bomber of 7,800 miles range.

IT was because the Luftwaffe suffered from deficiency of range that Hitler had to occupy one nation after another in order to bring his air force within striking distance of his main objective, whether it was Britain, the Mediterranean, or Russia. In Russia his handicap of short range showed up sharply.

7, The factor of quality is relatively more decisive than the factor of quantity.

Goering counted on overwhelming the R.A.F. by sheer weight of aviation, but a 25-mile edge in speed, plus greatly superior fire power, decided the Battle of Britain. Similarly, long-range bombers with good fire power can accomplish greater destruction and brush off enemy fighters (for example, the newer Fortresses). In the Pacific, says

ALEXANDER SEVERSKY, a Russian air ace born in Russia 48 years ago, was a U.S. test pilot in 1918. He founded the Seversky Aviation Corporation in America in 1931, and designed the first fully automatic bomb sight.
Photo, New York Times Photos

Seversky, U.S. aviation was actually inferior in quality, as well as quantity, to the Japanese. In fact, counting heads in the air without taking quality into account is a mere delusion, and the quick obsolescence of aircraft may leave the mass producers at a heavy disadvantage. Hence the superiority of the R.A.F. at the very beginning.

8, Aircraft types must be specialized to fit not only the general strategy but the tactical problems of a specific campaign.

THE argument here is supported by German failures. The Heinkels and the Dorniers were used as all-purpose bombers and 2,300 of them were lost in the futile attacks on London. It is essential that we should out-think as well as out-build the enemy, and our military leaders must have technological foresight as well as strategic and tactical foresight.

9, The destruction of enemy morale from the air can be accomplished only by precision bombing.

This is a vital lesson that has surprised even air specialists. Panic expected from random bombing is shown to be a myth. The people's will to resist can be broken only by destroying the essentials of their lives, and this demands precision bombing. Industrialization affords perfect concentrated targets.

10, The principle of unity of command long recognized on land and sea applies with no less force to the air.

All the author's previous argument builds up to this conclusion. The conquest of the air is a separate enterprise in a different sphere and must have a unified command.

11, Air power must have its own transport.

It is ludicrous for an air force moving at 300 miles an hour to be dependent upon transport at 10 or 15 knots. Aerial transport won the Battle of Crete and the lack of it handicapped the defence of Hawaii and the Philippines. The main advantage of the air weapon is that it ignores surface obstacles.

Throughout this thought-provoking volume Major Seversky enforces his arguments and builds up his theories by detailed examination of the air history of the present war. If the prospects he offers us have their terrifying aspects—for both sides are surely thinking on similar lines ; even if we think him extreme and reject half of what he has to say—there still remains a hard core of ideas and facts which only needs a simple analysis of the air mistakes made by all the Powers to demonstrate their vital importance.

S. G. BLAXLAND STUBBS

Mr. Kaiser's the Man to Beat the U-Boats

Can Hitler's U-boats sink the ships of the United Nations faster than the shipyards in Britain and America can turn out new vessels ? On that question the fate of this island, and, indeed of our common cause, may well depend.

TEN days to build an ocean-going cargo ship ! In the last war the record time for building a similar ship was 212 days. In this war the time has been steadily reduced. On August 24 the shipbuilding record of 35 days was established. It stood for exactly 5 days : on August 29 a similar vessel took the water 24 days after its keel was laid. Then, less than a month after, Sept. 23, yet another 10,500-ton Liberty freighter took the water. She was launched 87 per cent complete ; and on Sept. 27—13 days 23½ hours after her keel had been laid—she was delivered ready for service to the United States Maritime Commission. All these record-breaking ships have been turned out from the shipbuilding yards of Mr. Henry J. Kaiser, a middle-aged contractor who a few months ago was practically unknown even to his fellow citizens in the U.S.A., although today he enjoys a world-wide reputation. Henry J. Kaiser is the man who knows how to build ships—and build them quick.

Little more than a year ago fourteen merchant vessels were launched at various American ports on the Atlantic, the Pacific, and the Mexican Gulf. One of the fourteen was called Patrick Henry, after the famous orator and statesman of the period of the American War of Independence—the man who in 1775 at a revolutionary convention in Virginia supported the proposal for arming the militia by a speech with the dramatic peroration, "I know not what course others may take, but as for me, Give me liberty or give me death ! " Because of this association, the 312 ten-thousand-ton freighters, of which the Patrick Henry was one, were called Liberty ships.

THAT was on Sept. 27, 1941. Twelve months later 327 Liberty ships, as well as some 160 cargo vessels of other types, tankers, etc., were already in use and many more were on the stocks ; and the anniversary of that first launching was celebrated throughout America as Liberty Ship Sunday. The highlight of the celebrations was a message of thanks from Mr. Churchill to the shipyard-workers and merchant-seamen of the U.S., broadcast from London by Mr. Winant, the American Ambassador, in which the Prime Minister declared that the completion of nearly 500 large ocean-going cargo vessels in the short space of twelve months is "a master-stroke in Freedom's cause."

Who was the man chiefly responsible for this tremendous effort ? America seems to be unanimous in answering with the name of Henry J. Kaiser. Little seems to be known about him : at least, little has been cabled across the Atlantic concerning his life before he took up shipbuilding. For the most extraordinary thing of the extraordinary story is that Mr. Kaiser was until quite recently—since the war in fact—an absolute tyro in shipbuilding. He was a public works contractor, and he had a very large share in the construction of the Boulder Dam and other great concrete engineering works which are among the outstanding monuments of Mr. Roosevelt's New Deal. When the war began Mr. Kaiser had never built a ship, and we are assured that he knew nothing about shipbuilding. But, like many other up-to-date Americans, he knew a great deal about machinery ; and the secret of his success would seem to be that he knew how to apply machinery in the production of ships just as Mr. Ford applied it in the production of motor-cars. During the last year or two he has secured control of six shipyards on America's Pacific coast—in one or two cases he has actually built the yard ; and he was granted contracts for the building of 679 Liberty ships, each of 10,500 tons. Swiftly he got down to the job ; one after another, in successive batches, the ships poured out of his yards.

IN the House of Commons last July Mr. Oliver Lyttelton, Minister of Production, in referring to the United States shipbuilding programme as one of the most "fascinating, almost fantastic, industrial achievements that could be imagined " went on to refer to Mr. Kaiser, " who never made a ship before but is now turning them out at an almost unbelievable rate. One can see the superstructure of a ship, with the captain's shaving glass and the carnations and everything else, being lifted in like a child's toy. Somebody says, ' What is missing ? ' Somebody else says, ' The bows are,' and then they are lifted in to make the thing complete."

How does Mr. Kaiser do it ? Pre-fabrication seems to be the answer. To Mr. Kaiser a ship is not like a building, something that has to be raised slowly, step by step, in stage by stage, from its foundation ; rather it is a unit composed of a number of parts, all of which are manufactured separately but simultaneously and then put together. His

MR. H. J. KAISER, " the World's No. 1 Shipbuilder," seen with his wife at the launching of one of his 10,500-ton Liberty cargo ships. He is a man of 60, living in Oakland, Cal.
Photo, New York Times Photos

method of working has been described by Mr. Robert Waithman, News Chronicle correspondent in Washington :

First he builds a model. Then he takes the model and divides it into convenient parts. Steel plates arrive to make the full-scale parts, and welders are waiting for them. On vast sub-assembly platforms plates are cut, bent and welded until they become a ship's bows or part of a deck-house. Seventy-two-ton cranes pick them up and move them on. Eighty-five-ton trailers drag them down to the slipways. They are welded to the other sections. In days instead of weeks there is a ship ready for launching.

It moves into the water and is tied up at what we used to call the fitting basin, only there never was a fitting basin like it. Hundreds of engineers, plumbers, electricians, painters and carpenters descend upon it ; in a week-end it is fitted and furnished. They have built a Liberty ship, starting with the laying of the keel and finishing with the making of the captain's bed, in 46 days.

That was around last July ; since then, as we have seen, Kaiser has smashed his own record time and again, and is now turning out a ship in ten days. And he has not finished yet. He is confident he can do better. Nothing is impossible, he declares.

U.S. SHIPBUILDING has broken world records. On Sept. 25, 1942, it was reported that 488 cargo ships had been completed within the previous 12 months; of these 327 were Liberty ships. By Jan. 1943 American shipyards will be turning out more than 4 ships a day. Above is seen one of the largest vessels of war to be launched in U.S. inland waters. Bearing the slogan " Forward to Victory, America," this ship is the first of a fleet of landing craft for tanks.

Photo, Keystone

All Records Broken by America's Shipyards

A LIBERTY SHIP IN TEN DAYS! In one of the Pacific Coast shipyards of Mr. H. J. Kaiser, the world-famous American shipbuilder (see opposite page), workmen are engaged on the bottom of a Liberty ship (top). Five days later the freighter is well on the way to completion (centre right). Then, on Sept. 23 she takes to the water (bottom photo, radioed from America), 87 per cent complete. Three days later, 13 days 23½ hours after her keel was laid, she was handed over to the U.S. Maritime Commission.

Photos, Associated Press, Keystone

THE WAR IN THE AIR

by Capt. Norman Macmillan, M.C., A.F.C.

New technical developments current in the air war are primarily aimed towards two ends. One of these is to enlarge the cubic area of the atmosphere within which flight to attack can be made. The other is to increase the weight of attack by the concentration of heavier loads of bombs, and by reducing the time intervals between attacks around the twenty-four-hour clock.

These developments concern the offensive type of aircraft, namely, the bombers. The purpose behind them is the age-old military object of seeking to penetrate the defences ever more efficiently.

Enlargement of the cubic area of the atmosphere is effected by the employment of surface-level bombers and sub-stratosphere bombers, so that the enemy anti-aircraft gunners and defensive fighters can never be certain at what height they may have to go into action. This forces the Luftwaffe (which controls and mans guns as well as aircraft) to duplicate all defences everywhere over the areas within which such attacks can be made, for the same guns and fighters are not suitable for both high- and low-level defence.

This new characteristic of the United Nations' air offensive over Western Europe must throw a still greater strain upon German industry and the whole enemy defensive organization from, say, Stavanger down to St. Nazaire, although the full weight of the new tactical development has been felt so far only between Oslo and Lille.

R.A.F. Attack on Oslo

Twin-engined Mosquito bombers, capable of high speed at low-flying levels, attacked the Gestapo headquarters in Oslo from roof-height on Sept. 25 (see page 264). That was their first public demonstration.

The tactical method adopted for the attack was interesting. The four planes flew east of Oslo, about ten miles inland from Oslo fjord, and then turned to attack, heading on the course for home. There are two aerodromes close to Oslo—Fornebü and Kjeller. Focke-Wulf 190 fighters rose to meet the British raiders. The German fighters got one of the Mosquitos, just before it reached the city. Squadron Leader Parry saw it go down into the fjord with its port engine smoking and a Focke-Wulf on its tail.

But the three remaining Mosquitos bombed the centre and the east and west sides of the Gestapo H.Q. and saw debris and dark-red dust and smoke thrown up. As they bombed they photographed. No better confirmation of the accuracy of the bombing could be obtained. It must be borne in mind, however, that such photographs indicate only the effect of the bomb-hit on the buildings and not the explosion when the delayed-action fuses fire the bomb after the aeroplanes have flown out of the danger zone.

How to 'Read' Air Photos

I have heard people say that they cannot understand air photographs, and that the photographs of the bombing of the Gestapo headquarters in Oslo were particularly ineffectual in conveying to them a true idea of the value of air attack. I know why they are puzzled. Bombs released when flying low travel forward at the same speed as the aeroplane, and hit the objective at the same moment as the machine passes over it. In consequence, the photograph must be taken after the aeroplane has crossed the target. It is taken not as the pilot sees his target, but as the rear gunner sees it, looking backward down the tail. In all probability

the bomb may have hit a side of the building hidden by the one shown in the photograph, so that all one sees is a small cloud of dust thrown up by the impact of the bomb upon a part of the building which does not seem to be distinguishable in the print. Anyone looking at such photographs and imagining that the view is that of the pilot must be misled, and I can well understand their bewilderment. But with this explanation the reader will, I trust, be better able to understand such photographs, and to appreciate

RAID ON OSLO of Sept. 25, 1942 : the arrow shows smoke from bombs exploding on the Gestapo H.Q. The photograph was taken by one of the British aircraft ; another photo appears in page 264 (see text).
Photo, British Official : Crown Copyright

their true value—which is to confirm the accuracy of the bomb-hits.

The three Mosquitos shook off the Focke-Wulfs thirty miles from Oslo. The boss of one airscrew of one of the Mosquitos was hit, but the aeroplane flew on smoothly. That was all the damage the F.W.s did to them in a thirty miles' chase.

Air photography is also used to assess the effect of night raids. Photographic flash-bombs of about 50 million candle-power are dropped with the bombs. A blinding light lasting about one-tenth of a second illuminates the target, which is then automatically photographed by a camera with an open shutter. Accuracy of night bombing is thus disclosed to air intelligence. The series of photographs, taken by succeeding bombers, builds up the story of the effectiveness of the raid as each successive film shows increasing numbers of fires ; and in the later films

perhaps the whole target is seen to be ablaze. This method of night aerial photography was first developed in the United States some years before the war. Major Albert Stevens, well-known American air photographic expert, who flew to 72,000 feet in the stratosphere balloon Explorer II, made many early experiments.

On Oct. 2 Mosquitos bombed Liége iron and steel works in daylight, and four days later a factory and power station at Hengelo. Before Hitler came to power the Germans had a factory at Hengelo (just over the German frontier), where range-finders for warships and other technical equipment for naval ships were made.

On the upper side of the atmospheric cube, U.S. Army Air Force Fortress bombers have proved more than a match for Germany's best fighter aircraft. On one occasion they shot down twelve German fighters without loss to themselves when raiding a target in Holland without escort.

Since then large combined fighter-bomber attacks have been made. On Oct. 2 Fortress bombers bombed the former Potez aircraft factory at Meaulte, near Albert, used as a maintenance and repair base by the Luftwaffe, while other Fortresses bombed the German fighter aerodrome at St. Omer-Longueness. The 80 bombers were assisted by 400 fighters, including British, Canadian, New Zealand, Polish, Norwegian, Belgian, and American squadrons, which swept an area of 160 miles from Le Havre to Nieuport, penetrating to a depth of 50 miles.

Great U.S. Raid on Lille

On Oct. 9 a force of 115 U.S. Fortress and Liberator (mentioned for the first time in a European action) bombers, assisted by 500 fighters, bombed the Fives-Lille locomotive and steel works in daylight. The fighters shot down five German aircraft without loss to themselves. The bombers shot down 48. Four bombers were lost ; the crew of one were saved.

This remarkable bomber achievement must be attributed to the splendid quality of American air crews and their equipment. The Fortress, with turbo-supercharger car-buretted engines, can fly higher than the most effective operating height of Focke-Wulf fighters—Germany's present best. The speed of the Fortress at height is as great as that of the F.W. The Fortress carries 13 half-inch machine-guns which shoot bullets about four times heavier than rifle-calibre bullets ; these have a penetrative quality greater than the resisting power of current German fighter aircraft armour (which was doubtless intended to give protection against the rifle-calibre bullet-stream of Hurricanes and Spitfires). The half-inch machine-gun has a greater range of fire and a flatter trajectory than the rifle-calibre machine-gun and a far more numerous succession of projectiles than the cannon-gun.

The operating height and armament of these aircraft are a technical surprise for the Luftwaffe. German endeavour to armour fighters to resist the half-inch calibre bullet will tell against their performance. The present relatively small bomb-load of the Fortress is to be increased.

Add to these factors the load-carrying capacity of British night bombers (about double that of Germany's best Heinkel 177), and it will be apparent that around the cube and around the clock the United Nations are now pressing heavily upon German air defences in Western Europe. Our first great victories against Germany are taking place now in the air. And with the tactical air offensive again surpassing the tactical air defensive, just as it did seven to ten years ago, the period is decidedly favourable to the United Nations, who are now approaching a phase of rising air superiority.

How to Recognize U.S. Fighters & Other Craft

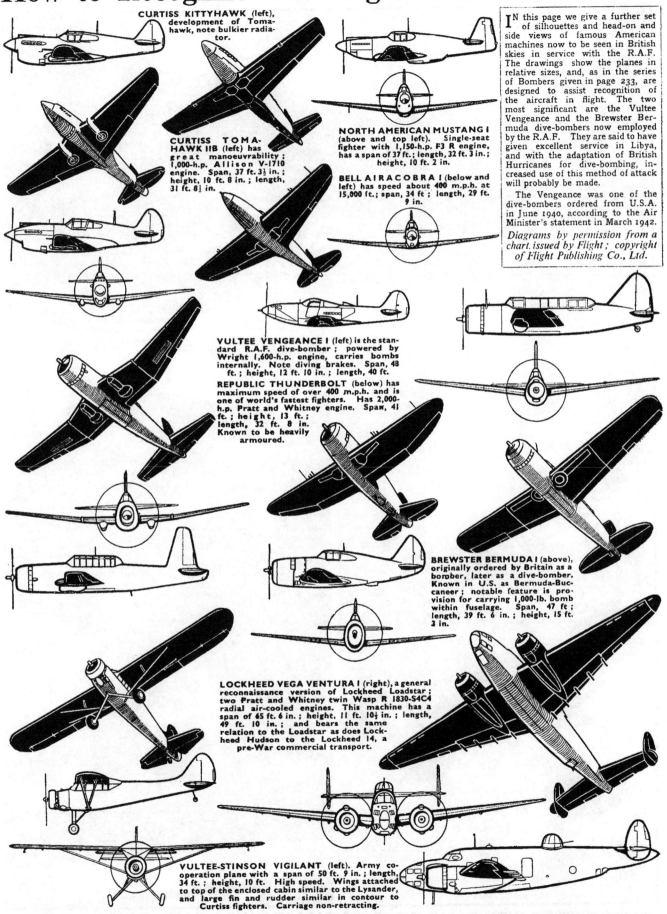

CURTISS KITTYHAWK (left), development of Tomahawk, note bulkier radiator.

CURTISS TOMAHAWK IIB (left) has great manoeuvrability; 1,000-h.p. Allison V-1710 engine. Span, 37 ft. 3½ in.; height, 10 ft. 8 in.; length, 31 ft. 8½ in.

NORTH AMERICAN MUSTANG I (above and top left). Single-seat fighter with 1,150-h.p. F3 R engine, has a span of 37 ft.; length, 32 ft. 3 in.; height, 10 ft. 2 in.

BELL AIRACOBRA I (below and left) has speed about 400 m.p.h. at 15,000 ft.; span, 34 ft; length, 29 ft. 9 in.

IN this page we give a further set of silhouettes and head-on and side views of famous American machines now to be seen in British skies in service with the R.A.F. The drawings show the planes in relative sizes, and, as in the series of Bombers given in page 233, are designed to assist recognition of the aircraft in flight. The two most significant are the Vultee Vengeance and the Brewster Bermuda dive-bombers now employed by the R.A.F. They are said to have given excellent service in Libya, and with the adaptation of British Hurricanes for dive-bombing, increased use of this method of attack will probably be made.

The Vengeance was one of the dive-bombers ordered from U.S.A. in June 1940, according to the Air Minister's statement in March 1942.

Diagrams by permission from a chart issued by Flight; copyright of Flight Publishing Co., Ltd.

VULTEE VENGEANCE I (left) is the standard R.A.F. dive-bomber; powered by Wright 1,600-h.p. engine, carries bombs internally. Note diving brakes. Span, 48 ft.; height, 12 ft. 10 in.; length, 40 ft.

REPUBLIC THUNDERBOLT (below) has maximum speed of over 400 m.p.h. and is one of world's fastest fighters. Has 2,000-h.p. Pratt and Whitney engine. Span, 41 ft.; height, 13 ft.; length, 32 ft. 8 in. Known to be heavily armoured.

BREWSTER BERMUDA I (above), originally ordered by Britain as a bomber, later as a dive-bomber. Known in U.S. as Bermuda-Buccaneer; notable feature is provision for carrying 1,000-lb. bomb within fuselage. Span, 47 ft; length, 39 ft. 6 in.; height, 15 ft. 3 in.

LOCKHEED VEGA VENTURA I (right), a general reconnaissance version of Lockheed Loadstar; two Pratt and Whitney twin Wasp R 1830-S4C4 radial air-cooled engines. This machine has a span of 65 ft. 6 in.; height, 11 ft. 10½ in.; length, 49 ft. 10 in.; and bears the same relation to the Loadstar as does Lockheed Hudson to the Lockheed 14, a pre-War commercial transport.

VULTEE-STINSON VIGILANT (left). Army co-operation plane with a span of 50 ft. 9 in.; length, 34 ft.; height, 10 ft. High speed. Wings attached to top of the enclosed cabin similar to the Lysander, and large fin and rudder similar in contour to Curtiss fighters. Carriage non-retracting.

AMERICAN FIGHTERS, DIVE-BOMBERS, with a Bomber Reconnaissance plane and an Army Cooperation machine. These are all working with the R.A.F. in Britain and overseas. A machine of which much is expected is the P.47, Seversky or Republic Thunderbolt, described as America's fastest fighter, exceeding 400 m.p.h. It stood up to 680 m.p.h. in diving tests. In America it is known as an Army pursuit plane with six machine-guns. The N. American Mustang is now supplied to a British Army Cooperation squadron; it is of very high speed with four machine-guns.

In Libya We're Bombing Them All the Time

HAMMERING ROMMEL'S BASES in Libya and the Western Desert the R.A.F. Middle East have given no respite to the Axis-occupied ports and vital centres of communication. The top photograph shows the remains of a street in Benghazi after a heavy raid. Supply lines serving Rommel's forces in the desert have been ceaselessly attacked. Below left, bombs are bursting on a number of enemy motor transports during an attack by our light bombers. Vehicles which escaped the full force of the salvo are shown by minute specks. Right, bombs being unloaded from the hold of a ship which has just arrived in port with fresh supplies.

Photos, British Official: Crown Copyright; Keystone

On a Village School the Nazi Dropped a Bomb

SCHOOLBOY VICTIMS OF A GERMAN RAIDER were buried with their headmaster (Mr. Charles Stephenson), and a woman teacher, in a common grave on Oct. 3. Their school, situated in the little town of Petworth, in Sussex, received a direct hit on Sept. 29. 1, All that was left of the school building. The headmaster stayed on till the end, getting out as many boys as possible. 2, This boy received head injuries ; he is seen with his mother. 3, Army lorries carry 26 coffins to the graveside. 4, Scene at the graveside. In all 32 were killed. *Photos, The Daily Mirror, Sport & General*

UNDER THE SWASTIKA

In Paris They Have a Way with the Boche

For two years and more the "City of Light and Laughter" has been a city of darkness and depression; through the streets once filled with carefree crowds move the Nazi soldiery and officials, still bumptious and bullying, though not perhaps quite so swaggering as in the first days of their easy triumph. In the article that follows, written by a French Correspondent, we are shown something of present-day life in Paris.

DESPITE the enemy hanging around, the streets in the residential parts of Paris are not very much different from what they were in peacetime—at least, if you look at them superficially. Of course, the Quartier Montparnasse has lost all its cosmopolitan glamour, and as it has become one of the favourite haunts of the Boche, the Parisians have also deserted the well-known cafés such as the Dôme, the Coupole and the Rotonde, whose spacious "terrasses" encroaching so largely on the broad sidewalk used to be crammed with crowds of artists and would-be artists come from the four corners of the earth.

But if you walk up under the double rows of trees that shadow each footway of the Boulevard Raspail and reach the Place du Lion de Belfort, you find things very much as usual. Here begins the populous "Petit Montrouge" included in Paris since 1860; it is situated a thousand feet above the level of the Seine, and every morning a large part of its population "go down" to Paris, as the old inhabitants still say, to work in offices, stores, workshops and workrooms. Very decent people all of them—hard working, thrifty, steady and well-behaved, who like at their moments of leisure to take their children round for a walk along the broad avenues edged with trees.

ON the platforms they will join the crowd that gathers around a performer, a singer, male or female, with musicians playing concertinas or accordions or even scraping on a fiddle, crooning some sentimental "romance" or giving full value to the hints and innuendoes of a comic song. The boys are eager to go a little farther on, where they are sure to find, when the weather is fine, the well-known Jules Lefort, an acrobat in tights, bare arms showing his enormous muscles, ready to perform some feats of strength, to lift weights or dumb-bells or any other tricks. But he will not begin before enough money is down; he wants it in cash; he estimates his feat of acrobatics at thirty francs: "Just the price of a horse-flesh steak at the next cook-shop," he will banter. He has the gift of the gab, and his patter is sparkling with sallies and quibbles which make the onlookers shake with laughter. There are sure to be some double-meaning quips, hinting at the unwelcome guests, the *fridolins* (Fritzies) or the *doryphora* (potato beetles) as they call the Boche; and the audience will look round with sarcastic grins on their faces and hatred in their souls to see whether there is a field grey around there.

THE other day Jules Lefort's eloquence was interrupted by a shrill voice coming from the corner of a street where is the branch of a well-known food store, to which in peacetime housewives used to flock to obtain at cheap prices all kinds of eatables and victuals, although now the windows and stalls are empty. A woman has been hoisted

on a trestle outside, and as she throws handfuls of leaflets among the disappointed customers she cries: "How long are we going to stand it? When are we going to revolt as the British and the Americans tell us to do?" Two policemen and several Germans in uniform rush up and drag the woman down. Across the street, apparently resting idly against the banisters of the tube station, with their hands in their pockets, are a group of men; now of a sudden they stretch out their arms, shots ring out, policemen and Boches fall, the woman and the men vanish among the crowd and nobody

RESERVED FOR GERMANS. France's best railway coaches, like most of the other good things in that unhappy country, are reserved for the use of the conquerors. Old, dilapidated wooden compartments are considered good enough for the French people by the Nazi authorities.
Photo, Keystone

will see them again. The incident will soon be radioed all over the world, but soon Jules Lefort has an audience again, and while the ambulance carries away the casualties he continues with his performance.

AMONG the restrictions imposed as the result of German requisitions and pillage the shortage of wine is one of the hardships French people find it most difficult to bear. Ordinary wine is drunk by all classes at meals—and a very healthy drink it is, too. Before the war you could buy a litre, not far short of two pints, for a franc (say, 2d.), and for three francs you could get a bottle of Médoc or Beaujolais. Now it costs four or five times as much, and it is rationed, each adult being entitled to one litre a week —when it is to be had in the shops. But in the case of wine, as of nearly all other foods, there is a black market, and if you know where to turn with enough money you can drink as much wine as you can afford. The fact was once more disclosed by a scandal that was lately exposed at Amiens, where in a single week a profiteer disposed of 5,000 gallons at 50 frs. a gallon to retailers who sold it by the glass, charging 7 or 8 frs. for a small glass. At the inquest the warehouseman made a clean breast of it and admitted that he was hand-in-glove with the requisitioning German authorities, sharing the spoils with them; even so, he confessed to having made twenty million francs since

the armistice, going halves with the German peculators.

The people who wallow in wealth are not all profiteers. The industrialists who manage to get coal and raw materials from the Boche and to keep their factories working full-time, are certainly making large profits, but they are not stuffing their coffers with the marks the enemy is paying them with, and whose final value they mistrust. They turn it into more solid possessions, into land, houses, farms. For less ambitious investments, people with fattened wallets will go to the Hotel des Ventes, the only place in Paris where auction sales can take place, whose official name is Hôtel des Commissaires-priseurs, from the name of the official valuers who alone are entitled to proceed to auction sales. Some of the sales are widely advertised, and on sale days not only all the well-known dealers and amateurs, but the Boches, flock to the Hôtel Drouot; the latter are always well supplied with specially-printed marks, whose exchange rate is arbitrarily fixed at twenty francs to the mark, so that everything comes cheap to them. All the same, as often as not the "bande noire," the "black gang," may be quietly operating against them, so that a few nods will make them pay according to the real rate of exchange.

A LITTLE while ago a very small water-colour by Manet had been very much admired before the sale by a group of on-lookers, all with close-shaven heads and obviously Teutonic. When it was put up to auction they began to bid eagerly, only to be outbid time after time by two or three men who were obviously frequenters of the room, and known to the auctioneer. Their quiet nodding soon seemed to kindle the wrath of the Boches, who looked daggers at their competitors, but went on bidding angrily, and when it reached the enormous price of 320,000 frs. the Frenchmen prudently let it be knocked down to the close-cropped amateurs —who looked very happy at securing a "triumph," when in fact they had come a really awful cropper.

Here is another incident. A wine sale is proceeding. Many close-shaven skulls are nodding. Two bottles of Pommery 1911 go for 920 fr. Six magnums of Ruinard 1928 reach 5,720 fr. and ten bottles of Grand Marnier 9,200 fr. Then, with his tongue in his cheek, the auctioneer announces three bottles of White Horse whisky, *cachet d'or*; and with a prepossessing look towards the Boches he adds: "They are well worth a thousand francs each. Not easy to get more. You'll have to wait for the invasion of England." The Boches do not demur, the French smile. The auctioneer goes on: "*C'est dit. Je mets à prix à trois mille.*"

IMMEDIATELY, before any of the Teutons has had time to speak, one of the Frenchmen says *Quatre!* Then, in close succession, *Cinq! Six!* from two Frenchmen. The tussle clinches. *Sieben!* from one of the Germans. *Sept!* repeats the auctioneer. *Acht!* raucously blares out an apoplectic Boche. *Neuf!* announces the auctioneer, catching a nod from a French bidder. The Boches remain silent in spite of the appealing shakes of the head of the auctioneer: "Going, going, gone!" And the hammer falls on the desk while the bookkeeper, who seems to be familiar with the bidder, gives him a wink and writes his name in the register.

'So, You Would Force Us Greeks to Kneel!'

GREEK DEFIANCE of the Axis reached its climax on March 25, 1942, on the occasion of the Greek National Independence Day celebrations. This day, of great significance in modern Greek history, commemorates the country's liberation from the domination of the Ottoman Empire brought about by the Greek War of Independence (1821-1833). Now once again Greece suffers under a tyranny in comparison with which the barbaric systems of the past fade into insignificance. Greek love of freedom is uncrushable, as the Germans and Italians have found to their cost.

Students of Athens University (left), bearing the national flag and singing patriotic songs, paraded the streets on March 25.

With Teutonic brutality the German inscription on the wall below declares: "We will force you to your knees."

IN ATHENS, on Mount Lycabettus, the students crowned the bust of Xanthos, the Hellenic patriot whose efforts among his countrymen abroad from 1814 to 1821 did much to further the Greek War of Independence. One of the students is seen above placing a laurel crown upon the bust. The latter stands in the square Philike Hetaerea (Association of Friends).

Having returned from the ceremony, students are rounded up by Axis troops in the streets of Athens A group (right) fearlessly watches the efforts of the soldiers to deal with demonstrators. Patriotic fervour on the part of the Greeks has grown as the Axis has to resort increasingly to repressive measures.

Photos issued by the Greek Government in London

Here and There with Our Roving Camera

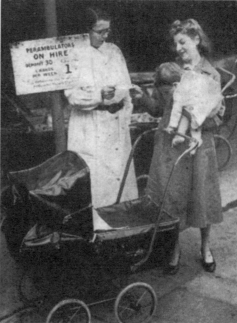

MAHARAJAH JAM SAHEB OF NAWANAGAR, a member of the War Cabinet and Pacific Defence Council, spent a day recently with an airborne division of the Home Forces. He is seen on the right of the above group, while on the left is Capt. E. M. Egan, the first padre of British paratroops. Paddington Borough Council have enabled mothers to hire prams on the instalment system. The first pram is seen, right, leaving the Welfare Centre.

SGT. KEITH ELLIOTT (above), fifth New Zealander to win the V.C. in this war—his award was announced on Sept. 24, 1942—displayed outstanding bravery at Ruweisat in the Western Desert on July 15. Wounded four times, he led survivors of his company, numbering 19, and captured 130 prisoners, five machine-guns, and an anti-tank gun.

N.F.S. 'SHOCK TROOPS' are now training on Commando lines. Volunteers for Mobile Columns must be prepared to go anywhere at any time. Part of their training includes a special "assault" course, modelled on Army pattern. Such a course demands the utmost toughness from these National Fire Service volunteers, who must be proficient in the arduous technique of crossing rivers, etc., in full kit. Above, some of them are seen doing exercises at their camp.

BOSTON BOMBER'S 'SOUVENIR.' Making a low-level attack on an industrial target in Northern France, a Boston's wing struck a steel mast. A section of tubing broke off and remained wedged in the ripped wing. The aircraft reached home safely. Miss C. McGeachy (right), attached to Mr. H. Butler's staff at the British Embassy in Washington, is the first woman to attain British diplomatic status.

Photos, British Official: Crown Copyright; Topical Press, Daily Mirror

I WAS THERE! Eye Witness Stories of the War

'Were You Frightened, Reuter? So Was I, Very!'

A great Allied convoy battled its way through the Arctic seas with vital supplies for Russia (see pages 279, 281). Here is an eye witness account of the tremendous adventure by Arthur Oakeshott, Reuters Special Correspondent with the Home Fleet.

THE largest convoy ever taken to Russia is feeling its way through the danger belt north of Scandinavia. All hands are at " Action Stations "—keyed up for the inevitable clash. We know a powerful German attack force is lurking in wait. Then loudspeakers crackle. Tension breaks. The words we have been expecting blare their warning . . . " Large group of enemy aircraft approaching on starboard bow."

Beside me the yeoman of signals, binoculars to eyes, counts them aloud : " One, two, three . . . Ten, fifteen. . . . Forty-two coming in, sir ! Where's me bloody tin hat ? I can never find it when I wants it."

So it started—a prolonged and concentrated assault, the " worst torpedo bombing attack of the war." They are coming in. Fifty-two roaring streaks of streamlined death, each carrying two torpedoes. Some are Ju 88s. Others are Heinkel 111s—all twin-engined heavy bombers. They come in a long line, only a few feet above the surface of the water, fanning out as they approach.

The vast convoy stretches out on either side of the Scylla, protected by the largest destroyer escort ever known. Battle was joined while the enemy were still many miles from the merchant ships. We heard the flash and roar of big guns from the outer screen of destroyers, followed immediately by the staccato rattle of the multiple pom-poms— the " Chicago pianos."

SHELL bursts were soon joined in the Arctic air by long streams of cerise-coloured tracer shells from the Oerlikon guns. Then, as the planes zoomed over the destroyer screen, hell breaks loose. Nothing else can describe it. The port guns of the destroyers open up, followed immediately by every gun in the convoy, from the smallest merchant ship to the " big stuff " aboard the Scylla—heavy pom-poms, Oerlikons, anti-aircraft guns of every description, machine-guns, Bren guns.

From then on the battle becomes a whirling maelstrom of shells, bullets, tracers, black, blue, brown and grey smoke-bursts. The zoom of aircraft, the crashing of bursting shells, adds to the din. From time to time we hear the crash as torpedoes find their mark—there were losses, but nothing like what the Nazis hoped. Columns of smoke rise up into the low-hanging clouds. Bursts of flame spout forth and yells of triumph rise as plane after plane hits the sea and sinks.

I shall never forget the extraordinary sensation of looking down from the flag deck—I repeat, down—on the Heinkels and Junkers as they roared past the ships and

Rear-Adm. R. L. BURNETT, commanding the naval force which (as told in this page) escorted the convoy to Russia, photographed as he was transferred to a destroyer from his flagship H.M.S. Scylla. *Photo, British Newsreel*

B. J. COFFEY (left) and Chief Steward P. GREY (right) displayed outstanding courage when their ship went down. The former, who was first cook, stayed to tend injured comrades and was later rescued ; Russia awarded him the Order of the Red Star. Mr. Grey, who assisted three men to a raft, received the George Medal.
Photos, Daily Mirror, Topical

turned sideways to launch their loads, while the merchant ships kept steadily on their course without the slightest deviation.

Now the battle takes on a new phase. Hurricanes roar off from the flight deck of an aircraft-carrier to do battle with the enemy, and, within less seconds than it takes to write this, dog-fights are going on above the clouds, below the clouds, in breaks through the clouds, or low over the sea.

I hear a yell, and, looking to port, see one Junkers roaring up into the cloud with smoke pouring from it and another Hurricane hot after it. " He's hit ! " roars the signalman. So is another, nearer to Scylla. I am just in time to see only its tail protrude above the icy waters of the Barents Sea. Farther away still more aircraft stream in. The excitement on the flag deck becomes deafening, only to be stilled by the stentorian voice of that yeoman of signals : " Shut yer ruddy jaw ! Can't you see that destroyer's lamp calling up ? Go on, get on to it ! "

Nothing perturbs Yeoman White, who controls everybody in that small space with a vocabulary such as beats any sergeant-major I ever heard, even during my Army days. Even more unperturbed is the First Lieutenant, affectionately known as " Number One." Lieutenant-Commander J. A. H. R. McKean, R.N., microphone in hand, wanders from side to side of the bridge, keeping up a running commentary on the battle for the benefit of the ship's company. He scorns a steel helmet, wearing just a fur-lined cap that he picked up in North China, and a brown woolly coat. He is calmness personified. His voice scarcely showed excitement even when at a later stage an attempt was made to sink the Scylla.

GRADUALLY the noise of battle dies away as the surviving Germans, having dropped their loads, streak for home, followed by myriads of shells. Those that dive low to the sea to avoid a high burst are followed with cunningly placed cerise Oerlikon tracer shells that ricochet off the water and plunk into fuselage and cockpit. I saw at least one Junkers come to a sticky end as a result.

It seems hardly any time before the calm voice announces that there are twenty-five more Junkers 88s or Heinkels coming at us. This time they carry bombs as well as torpedoes—but they have miscalculated. They are met, before they reach the convoy, by a drove of Hurricanes which completely breaks up the formation, so that they have to come in singly, and consequently are

When their ship was sunk in the attack on the Russian convoy, these sailors lost their possessions. The Red Cross provided them with new outfits, and here they are seen receiving warm clothing. Thrilling episodes of the memorable sea and air fight in the Arctic are recounted in this page.
Photo, British Official: Crown Copyright

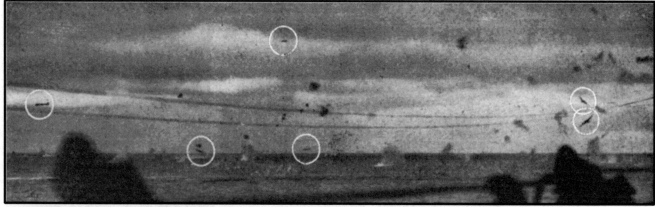

During the four-day attack upon the largest Allied convoy yet dispatched to Russia, our ships, as related in this page, battled through a terrific bombardment of bombs and torpedoes. Above, an aircraft-carrier is being attacked by enemy planes. German aircraft are ringed in white. Below, an escorting British warship puts up a powerful barrage. *Photos, British Newsreel*

easier targets for the guns which once more roar into action. The attack comes from high level, low level and sea level. Torpedoes speed towards the Scylla, but the brilliant seamanship of the skipper, Captain I. A. P. Macintyre, C.B.E., R.N., who turns the ship with the rapidity of a motorist swerving a car, causes the " tin fish " to drift harmlessly past our stern.

Then comes the warning: " Bombers ahead ! "—" Keep a sharp look-out ! "

The Scylla gives the Jerries everything she's got. Suddenly there comes a whistle, and four bombs speed towards us out of the clouds. Again the skipper whips his ship round, and they splosh harmlessly into the sea. That is seamanship !

Another short breather. Then the alarm goes again—but not before a seaman has time to approach an officer and say : " Please sir, can we borrow some darts to pass the time away ? " That is one of the men Hitler cannot understand !

Dashing back to the bridge I met the P.M.O. (Principal Medical Officer). He tells me that when the alarm sounded all the patients in the sick bay leapt from their beds to their action stations at the guns, and when the situation eased they returned to their beds—to be waited on hand and foot. One of them who had some badly damaged ribs, manned a gun forward. After the first attack he was asked by the P.M.O. how

he felt. " Bit of a headache, sir. I could do with a couple of aspirins," he replied.

The all-too-brief Arctic night gives us a spell of rest, but next day sees Jerry hard at it again. Our aircraft-carrier is singled out for special attention by a bunch of Heinkels and Ju 88s. In all, 17 torpedoes, to say nothing of a shower of bombs, are flung at her, but she comes through unscathed.

And then I see something that will always live in my memory. The carrier seems to shake herself like an outraged angry hen, but instead of her chicks hiding in her wings for protection they—the Hurricanes—roar off her deck in pursuit of those who have upset their mother's equanimity—and did they give it to those Jerries ! Later she makes a signal that she has had " the honour of being the sole object of attack," claiming four planes for certain and three "probables."

Attacks continue through Monday. The day is notable for an amazing feat of seamanship ! The minesweeper Harrier comes alongside and, although we are travelling at considerable speed, she lashes herself to us and lands some 80 survivors from a torpedoed merchant ship. This is a difficult feat in peacetime in a smooth sea, but in a high sea with an icy wind and the enemy overhead—well, words just fail one.

This happens again later when H.M.S. Sharpshooter transfers to us more survivors, amounting to well over a hundred in all.

All through the hell of bomb and torpedo the convoy steamed steadily on, keeping position, never turning aside from the course

set them by R.A.D. (Rear-Admiral Destroyers) and the convoy commodore. Each day and night until we reach the area of comparative safety our ship is shaken by the thunder of depth charges released by the destroyers forming the escort screen.

Now that we have passed the danger zone it is decided Scylla had better go on ahead with the survivors, seeing that she has served her purpose as an anti-aircraft ship, leaving Rear-Admiral Burnett to continue with the convoy until it is " in the quiet waters."

His flag is therefore transferred to a destroyer, and to do this an operation is performed which must be unique in this war at least. The destroyer comes alongside, a rocket line is fired over her bows, and she is lashed to the Scylla. All the time both ships are keeping the same speed as the convoy.

Then a crane gets to work and transfers the admiral in a slung chair over the " drink " and aboard the destroyer. True to the R.N. tradition, six seamen rise to their feet in a boat hanging from the davits and solemnly pipe the admiral over the side while the crew stand to attention and officers salute. The destroyer then speeds away with the admiral's flag at the masthead.

We lower the admiral's flag from our own mast and put on a terrific speed into the gathering dusk alone, but not before we have seen that the destroyer screen is already in action against submarines.

Before he left, Rear-Admiral Burnett, in an interview he gave me on the bridge, said : " Well, Reuter, were you frightened ? "

I replied, " Yes, very, sometimes."

" So was I," he said, " very. And any man who says he was not is a B.F. ! "

One Evening I Crossed the Volga to Stalingrad

In all history no city, not even Verdun, has been more fiercely defended than Stalingrad. A perilous visit to this "city of dreadful night" is here described by Konstantin Simonov, the well-known Russian author; it is reprinted here by courtesy of the Soviet War News.

One evening this week I crossed the Volga to Stalingrad. The battlefield stretched ahead in the brief southern dusk—smoking mounds, burning streets. The enemy's white signal flares shot into the sky.

The Volga at Stalingrad is not the Volga we have known. Its banks are pitted with craters. Bombs that miss their targets and fall into the river send up heavy swirling columns of water. Heavily laden ferry-boats and other light craft ply across to the beleaguered city. The din of battle echoes over the dark waters. The blaze of burning houses lights up the whole horizon. The artillery thunders incessantly and the crash of bombs is heard day and night. There is no such thing as a safe spot in Stalingrad today. But this no longer bothers the people. The very pattern of many of Stalingrad's streets is obliterated. Others are so churned

up with bombs as to be nearly impassable. Such women and children as have not been evacuated shelter in the basements or in caves dug in the ravines leading to the Volga. The wreckage of Nazi bombers piles up in the streets. A.A. shells endlessly punctuate the sky.

Yes, it is difficult to live in Stalingrad today. The sky is on fire. The very earth staggers. There is no time to bury the dead. On the Volga beach lie the charred corpses of women and children burned to death when the Germans bombed a steamer that was taking them to safety. Night brings no relief. The air hums and throbs as German bombers circle the city with their loads.

Seated beside me on the ferry was a 20-year-old Ukrainian girl, an army doctor's assistant. It was her fourth or fifth trip to the city, helping to evacuate the wounded. Red Cross nurses and doctors' assistants work in the very front line. They arrange for the wounded to be carried to the far end of the city, to the quayside, where there is a shuttle service of ferry-boats and other craft which convey the wounded to the opposite bank.

" I ought to be used to it, I suppose," the girl suddenly said as we approached the Stalingrad bank. " Yet every time I come I'm a bit afraid to land. I've been wounded twice—once quite seriously. But I never once thought I'd die, because I've seen so little of life yet."

HER wide-open eyes were sad. I knew what she must feel to be 20 years old and twice wounded, to have been at war for fifteen months and to be making her fifth trip to Stalingrad. In a quarter of an hour she would be threading her way through blazing houses, forcing a passage through side streets blocked with debris, heedless of shell fragments, seeking the wounded and carrying them away.

The headquarters of Stalingrad's defence is situated deep underground, where the enemy cannot smash it. The faces of those who direct the battle are grey as ashes ; their eyes are fevered with lack of sleep. While I talked with them I tried to light a cigarette. It was no good. Match after match went out. There was too little oxygen in the air.

The commanding point is situated in an unfinished factory. A street leading north towards the German lines is under constant trench-mortar fire. It is a dangerous post.

The day breaks and the sky pales to blue. We make our way to an observation point in a key sector. Make yourself comfortable ! Here is a well-sprung armchair ! For this post is located in what was a well-furnished fifth-floor flat. We can see German motor-cars moving past at the extreme end of the street. German motor-cyclists and infantrymen come into view. Mines

burst near by and a car jolts to a stop in the middle of the road below.

We leave the post and go on to a near-by factory which has a tank repair shop. At the gate armed worker-volunteers in leather jackets, cartridge belts wrapped round their bodies, carefully inspect our documents.

SHOT DOWN IN STALINGRAD, this German bomber is one of many destroyed by the heroic defenders of the great Russian city. The wrecked machine lies amid the debris of building spounded by the enemy. *Photo, Planet News*

We go down to one of the underground workshops.

A few days ago these workers heard that German tanks had pierced the defences and were making straight for their factory. The directors and the repair shop superintendent called the workers together. A number of tank crews were selected. Then repairs were speeded up on a few tanks that were nearing completion. When the job was done the workers jumped into the tanks and set off to meet the enemy, followed by several armed detachments of their comrades. They intercepted the Germans at a stone bridge across a narrow ravine. The tanks confronted each other across the bridge and a furious gun duel ensued. Meanwhile, German tommy-gunners began to clamber down the bank in an attempt to reach the other side. The factory workers engaged them. Barricades were built in all the streets leading to the bridge. As during the Civil War, the wives carried ammunition to their husbands. Young girls moved about the advanced positions, bandaging the wounded and dragging them to safety. Many died ; but the workers held the Germans until darkness fell and Red Army reinforcements arrived to plug the gap.

I STOOD on this bridge and gazed along the ravine. It was an extraordinary sight. The steep banks hummed like an ant-heap. They were honeycombed with caves. The entrances were covered with boards, rags—anything the women of Stalingrad could lay hands on to protect their families from the rain and wind. The sight of those sorrowful human nests, that had replaced the bustling streets of a lively city, filled me with bitterness. But the citizens of Stalingrad, men or women, young or old, have the confident smile and steady hand of a soldier. Theirs is a fight for life itself.

OUR DIARY OF THE WAR

SEPT. 30, 1942, Wednesday *1,124th day*
  Russian Front.—Germans made advance in factory district of Stalingrad.
  Africa.—Preceded by artillery barrage, our troops opened limited attack on the Egyptian front. Heavy raid on Tobruk.
  U.S.A.—U.S. heavy bombers attacked Jap ships in Kiska harbour, Aleutians.

OCT. 1, Thursday *1,125th day*
  Air.—R.A.F. attacked chemical works in Holland and oil refineries near Ghent by day. Night raid on Flensburg and other Baltic ports.
  Russian Front.—After five attacks had been beaten off, Germans gained some ground N.W. of Stalingrad.
  Australasia.—In New Guinea our troops occupied Nauro. U.S. army fighters raided Jap ground forces and shipping at Guadalcanal in the Solomons.

OCT. 2, Friday *1,126th day*
  Air.—Four hundred Allied fighters and strong formation of British and U.S. bombers made daylight sweep over N. France. R.A.F. made night raid on Krefeld and other Rhineland towns.
  Russian Front.—Large enemy attacks repelled by Russians, who made some progress in one sector at Stalingrad.
  Burma.—U.S. bombers destroyed railway bridge on Myitkyina line.
  Australasia.—Jap bombers raided Guadalcanal in the Solomons.
  General.—M. Edouard Herriot, former French Premier, arrested by Vichy Govt.

OCT. 3, Saturday *1,127th day*
  Russian Front.—Germans made some headway towards Volga N. of Stalingrad.
  Australasia.—Jap bombers attempting to raid Guadalcanal turned back by U.S. fighters and A.A. guns. During night of Oct. 3-4 U.S. dive-bombers attacked Jap warships landing reinforcements.
  U.S.A.—Navy Dept. announced that U.S. troops had occupied Andreanof Is., in Aleutians, and established air bases.
  General.—British made small-scale Combined Operations raid on Sark.

OCT. 4, Sunday *1,128th day*
  Russian Front.—Six German attacks on Stalingrad repulsed.
  Indian Ocean.—In Madagascar our troops occupied Antsirabe.

OCT. 5, Monday *1,129th day*
  Air.—Strong force of R.A.F. bombers raided Western Germany.
  Russian Front.—German offensive in factory district of Stalingrad met with some success.
  Australasia.—Attack by U.S. carrier-borne aircraft on Jap shipping and base in Solomons resulted in sinking of one destroyer and damage to another.
  U.S.—American bombers raided Jap camp at Kiska.
  General.—State of siege proclaimed in Trondheim following acts of sabotage.

OCT. 6, Tuesday *1,130th day*
  Air.—Mosquitos of Bomber Command made daylight attacks in W. Germany and Holland. Osnabrück was main target of night raid by R.A.F.
  Russian Front.—Russians regained lost positions in factory area of Stalingrad.
  Mediterranean.—R.A.F. raided aerodrome at Maleme, Crete.
  Africa.—Allied aircraft made widespread attacks on German camps.
  Australasia.—In New Guinea Australians advanced towards Owen Stanley gap.
  U.S.A.—American bombers raided Kiska.
  General.—Ten Norwegians shot at Trondheim for alleged acts of sabotage.

OCT. 7, Wednesday *1,131st day*
  Russian Front.—Russians repelled all German attacks at Stalingrad.
  General.—Fifteen more Norwegians executed at Trondheim. Seventeen French shot at Lille for " Bolshevist activity."

OCT. 8, Thursday *1,132nd day*
  Russian Front.—Germans captured two streets in factory area of Stalingrad.
  Australasia.—U.S. dive-bombers attacked Jap ships covering landing operations at Guadalcanal, damaging a cruiser.
  General.—Germans fettered 1,376 British prisoners taken at Dieppe as reprisal for tying of hands of Germans during raid on Sark.
  Nine more Norwegians executed at Trondheim.

OCT. 9, Friday *1,133rd day*
  Sea.—Admiralty announced loss of anti-aircraft cruiser Coventry.
  Air.—More than 100 U.S. bombers made daylight raid on Lille, destroying 48 enemy aircraft for certain and probably 38 more, for the loss of only four bombers.
  Russian Front.—N.W. of Stalingrad the Russians improved their positions.
  Africa.—Allied aircraft made heavy bombing attacks on enemy landing grounds and supply columns.
  Australasia.—Allied bombers made

heavy attack on Rabaul. Our troops made contact with Jap patrols in New Guinea.
  U.S.A.—American heavy bombers again raided Kiska.

OCT. 10, Saturday *1,134th day*
  Russian Front.—Renewed German infantry assaults repelled at Stalingrad.
  U.S.A.—American heavy bombers kept up raids on Kiska.
  General.—Canadian Govt. ordered fettering of 1,376 German prisoners of war in Canada.

OCT. 11, Sunday *1,135th day*
  Air.—R.A.F. bombers made daylight attack on Hanover.
  Russian Front.—At Stalingrad German tanks and infantry showed no activity.
  Mediterranean.—At least 15 enemy aircraft shot down in attacks on Malta.
  Australasia.—U.S. cruisers and destroyers engaged Jap warships off Solomons, sinking one heavy cruiser, four destroyers and a transport, and damaging a cruiser and destroyer.
  Home Front.—Sharp air raid on N.E. coast.

OCT. 12, Monday *1,136th day*
  Sea.—U.S. Navy Dept. announced loss of heavy cruisers Quincy, Vincennes and Astoria on August 9 in naval battle off Solomons.
  Air.—R.A.F. bombed industrial targets in N. Germany by night.
  Russian Front.—Comparative lull at Stalingrad broken by one German infantry attack which was repelled.
  Mediterranean.—In renewed raids on Malta 24 enemy aircraft destroyed.
  Australasia.—Japs bomb Guadalcanal airfield. U.S. reinforcements landed.

OCT. 13, Tuesday *1,137th day*
  Air.—R.A.F.'s heaviest attack on Kiel.
  Russian Front.—Comparative lull on Stalingrad front continued.
  Mediterranean.—Twenty enemy aircraft destroyed over Malta ; over 1,000 aircraft now destroyed in battles round the island.
  Australasia.—On night of Oct. 13-14 Jap warships shelled Guadalcanal and landed reinforcements.
  General.—Gen. Smuts in London.

★━━━━━━━ *Flash-backs* ━━━━━━━★

1939
October 1. Garrison of Hel Peninsula, Poland, surrendered.

1940
September 30. R.A.F. made four-hour raid on Berlin.
October 7. Heavy German raids on London ; 27 aircraft destroyed. German troops entered Rumania and occupied the oilfields.

1941
October 7. " Mercy ship " plan for exchange of wounded prisoners of war cancelled.
October 8. Russians announced evacuation of Orel.
October 12. Briansk evacuated.
October 13. Evacuation of Vyazma announced by Russians. German threat to Moscow developing.

THE Expanding Universe was the title of a fascinating book by Sir A. S. Eddington which I read nine years ago, and Captain Liddell Hart has made a happy adaptation of the title for his latest book, This Expanding War ; but an equally interesting thesis, if not for a book, certainly for a study, might be This Contracting World. Every day with the astounding development of aeronautics the world is becoming a smaller place to live in, and I was not surprised when recently a friend who runs a prize stock farm in Sussex told me that he was negotiating for the purchase of a large area in Kenya with the idea of developing it as a great ranch for the breeding of livestock after the War. " You see, it will be quite an easy matter for me," he said, " to run the two places in conjunction, as it will be possible to pop over to Kenya by aeroplane every few weeks ; in fact, it won't be much more difficult to run my place in Sussex and another in Kenya than it would have been before the War to run one in Devon and another in the North of Scotland."

AND during the last week or two I have been receiving quite a number of letters from correspondents in far parts of the Empire, telling me chiefly about how they have found THE WAR ILLUSTRATED wherever they have gone. Ceylon, Eritrea, and various places in East and West Africa I have heard from. Among these an airgraph came from Cape Town and was lying on my desk a very few days after it had been handed in at the post office in South Africa. As some of my readers may not have seen one of these latest products of modern ingenuity I print it in facsimile, which shows the size of the document when received by the addressee, but while it is on its air journey it is only a tiny piece of film the size of a man's fingernail, and has to be enlarged on arrival.

THE anomalies of the salvage campaign are without number. It seems almost a waste of time to draw attention to some of them, but anyone who has the misfortune to live near places of military concentration with daily evidences of unrestricted waste in the matter of food and petrol, must have difficulty in keeping his blood from touching boiling point when he reads of a man being fined for baiting a fishing hook with a bit of bread while endeavouring to catch a fish for the breakfast-table, or the vicious fine inflicted on some wretched tradesman who had acquired a gallon of petrol without a coupon, when one sees petrol wasted daily by joyous lads in khaki making detours from their lawful routes just to pull up at out-of-the-way pubs for a drink.

I AM also told by a friend, just returned from a brief holiday on the Yorkshire moors, that he was astounded to observe the vast tonnage of massive and mainly ugly iron railings available up there, whereas he had witnessed iconoclastic destruction of beautiful old ironwork in his own residential district, attributable only to the undiscriminating zeal of the local bureaucracy. In one case mentioned some light and graceful iron gates that had cost about a thousand pounds were taken away from the front of a fine house during the absence of its owner. They could have produced only a fraction of the metal he had seen available in some hideous railings at a Yorkshire farmhouse. There is, of course, no redress and no equality of treatment possible so long as the bureaucrats are in the saddle and permitted to ride at their own sweet will.

ONE of my recent correspondents, the Rev. O. Manby, of Diss, Norfolk, tells me that he formed the habit in the last War of

AIRGRAPH from South Africa referred to in this page

various small economies which have been urged upon us all today, such as the reversing of used envelopes, never writing a letter where a postcard would do, sifting the cinders, saving old razor blades and cartridge cases. Some of these economies he continued after the War, and a friend to whom he wrote on one of his reversed envelopes regarded this as an act of meanness, almost an insult, so that he sent him a large packet of new envelopes, hoping to break him of the habit ! He also mentions his amusement in listening to the announcers on the B.B.C. as to the saving of rubber washers, corks, string and the raking out of fires, details of which " we are told as if we were children."

THE trouble is that, taking the public by and large, that is just what they are. And the shameless waste that goes on wherever the military forces are concerned may be ascribed to the same cause : the childish attitude of mind, which is naturally disposed to wastefulness. In times of peace I do not consider this is entirely an evil, as it cannot be denied that to go through life carrying thrift to the extreme must have a constricting effect on character and will result eventually in a meaner way of life than the abundance of the earth really warrants. But faced as we are today with the cutting-off of so many of our sources of supply, we must be " mean " in the use of everything that has any War value, and probably the only way to enforce a general level of war-time thriftiness is to impose penalties for breaches of regulations, but to administer these with discretion. It is unfair, however, that every form of waste for which the civilian population can be sharply punished seems to go on unchecked so long as the culprits are dressed in khaki.

SOME of the regulations concerning the austerity clothing of men and women are really more suitable for comic comment than for serious consideration. A friend who is a tailor with a large business in a northern city tells me that his life has been made a burden by the ill-considered restrictions imposed upon the trade, and he is very doubtful that economies of any real value to the War effort will be effected, even when the present confusion has been cleared up. I am quite without information in detail as to what this confusion may be, but I am very ready to believe that it exists from the evidences I have seen elsewhere of the indiscriminate application of hastily decided regulations which, on paper or in the cross-talks of the committee-room, appear to be workable and are found to be impossible only when put into practice. I noticed the other day that some regional scheme for paper-saving and other salvage had elicited something like 20,000 letters of appreciation, congratulation, and promise of help !

THE prohibiting of the turned-up finish to trouser-legs and the shortening of shirts may be regarded as quite sensible regulations, for many of us had worn out numerous pairs of trousers long before p.t.u. became the mode and trousers worn with morning coats have never had the permanent turn up. So far as shirts are concerned American men have always worn a much shorter garment than the English, because their habit has been to wear belts rather than braces. The popular song of the last War celebrated " those saucy soft short shirts for soldiers Sister Susy sewed," and I suspect that in the shortening of the shirts that has now been decreed those of the military will be the first to suffer abbreviation. There is one good thing about the long-tailed shirts of the British, however : it is that in this time of stress the tails can furnish sufficient material for re-fronting shirts in which the points of the popular turned-down collars have rubbed holes. I have just had half-a-dozen from my own stock that were showing signs of wear repaired in this way, and made " as good as new." I am told that in the domestic economy classes throughout the country practical demonstration of how to effect this very real economy has been going on for some considerable time.

Printed in England and published every alternate Friday by the Proprietors, THE AMALGAMATED PRESS, LTD., The Fleetway House, Farringdon Street, London, E.C.4. Registered for transmission by Canadian Magazine Post. Sole Agents for Australia and New Zealand : Messrs. Gordon & Gotch, Ltd. ; and for South Africa : Central News Agency, Ltd.—October 30, 1942. S.S. Editorial Address : JOHN CARPENTER HOUSE, WHITEFRIARS, LONDON, E.C.4.

Vol 6 | The War Illustrated | Nº 141

Edited by Sir John Hammerton

SIXPENCE

NOVEMBER, 13, 1942

THE 'FIFTY-FIRST' IN ACTION AGAIN! Although in the brief campaign in France in the summer of 1940 the 51st (Highland) Division suffered grievous losses in the rearguard action and at St. Valery, where most of the division were made prisoners, its spirit lived on, to " fight another day." Reconstructed and re-equipped, on Oct. 23, 1942, the 51st went into action again, this time with the 8th Army in Egypt. This photograph shows Highlanders in the Western Desert shortly before the great Allied offensive began. *Photo, British Official*

NO. 142 WILL BE PUBLISHED FRIDAY, NOVEMBER 27

ALONG THE BATTLE FRONTS

by Our Military Critic, Maj.-Gen. Sir Charles Gwynn, K.C.B., D.S.O.

THE last week of October found the general situation tense on all the principal war fronts. Stalingrad had passed safely through a desperate crisis, but there was no assurance that another change in the weather might not revive it. The Eighth Army offensive started on the night of October 23 with good hopes but with little expectation of securing rapid decisive results. In the Solomons a major Japanese attempt to recapture Guadalcanal was brewing and might start at any moment.

The development of the strategic situation depended therefore on the unforeseeable results of tactical encounters which seemed likely to extend over a considerable period, for in each case there was little scope for manoeuvre, but rather a probability of repeated frontal attacks on strong defensive positions in which the processes of attrition would largely affect the issue.

EGYPT

No one, I hope, underestimated the difficulties General Montgomery had to face when he launched the Eighth Army against Rommel's strongly-entrenched position. With practically no possibility of manoeuvre there seemed every probability that a prolonged battle of attrition was inevitable.

The depth of Rommel's position, immense, carefully-sited minefields and masses of wire negatived the probability of rapid penetration, and until penetration was effected armoured units would have little chance of finding scope for their most formidable potentialities. The over-estimate of the power of defence, at one time current, should not blind us to its very real advantages in such circumstances as these.

Nor because "attrition," after the last war, was by many considered the last resort of the incompetent, should its importance be discounted. Determined pressure on his fighting troops and incessant attacks on his supply lines may prove the only means of breaking down Rommel's resistance and of opening the way for manoeuvre. His long and vulnerable supply line is Rommel's heel of Achilles, but it cannot be interrupted altogether; and without forcing him to expend his resources, attacks on it could not have decisive results. But premature attempts to effect a breakthrough with armoured forces might result only in weakening our power to exploit success.

In a battle of attrition morale may be the first thing to wear down, and constant bombing is likely to prove a severe test of Italian nerves, which must be a source of anxiety to Rommel. Before these notes can be published much may, however, occur to falsify my expectations.

WAR IN WEST

The daylight attacks on Lille and the Schneider works at Creusot, and the day and night attacks on Northern Italy, show a marked advance both in the technique and range of the Allied bombing offensive. The attack on Creusot

is of special importance, and should prove one of the heaviest blows yet struck at German-controlled war industry.

The raids on Genoa were evidently closely associated with the opening of offensive operations in Egypt and should, combined with the failure of Axis attacks on Malta, make Rommel's prospects of receiving the material he evidently considers he badly needs, distinctly poorer.

The recent attention Bomber Command has been giving to the German transportation system probably goes far to account for the warnings given in Germany that there will be a transport crisis during the winter. Suspension of offensive operations in Russia would not reduce materially the strain on German railways, and a continuance of active operations there, defensive or offensive, would almost certainly make it more acute. I should be surprised if we do not hear much more about German transportation difficulties before the winter is out.

WEST AFRICA

The strategic importance of West Africa is immensely greater now than in the last war. Our main line of communication with the East has been diverted from the Mediterranean to the Cape route. Added to that, the increased range of enemy U-boats

enables them to operate in West African waters. In the last war, after the German Colonies of Togoland and the Cameroons had been captured, practically the whole coast from Morocco to the Congo was in Allied hands. Today great stretches of Vichy French territory separate British possessions, complicating defensive measures. The need for protection is now greater, yet the forces and bases which provide it are fewer.

APART from the increased importance of the Cape route, the status of West Africa as a producer of raw material for war industries has grown. Manganese ore from the Gold Coast (shipped in quantities from the new port of Takoradi), palm oil, tin, and many tropical products entail a volume of coastal traffic which is further increased by the necessity of importing stores for a greatly expanded European population and military establishments.

An entirely new development has, moreover, added to West Africa's strategic importance. Since the French Chad province and Equatorial West Africa joined General de Gaulle it has been possible to open a trans-African route to the Middle East for aircraft and motor vehicles. Aircraft shipped to West Africa and flown across the continent reach their destination with much greater speed than when it was necessary to ship them round the Cape. With the development of roads, trans-African traffic by land is also likely to increase.

Freetown in Sierra Leone, which, like the French port of Dakar, fronts Brazil across the Atlantic at its narrowest part—here less than 1,700 miles wide—is strategically the most important point in Allied hands. Possessing a good harbour, it forms a well-placed base for protective operations, and for the assembling of convoys. For many years Freetown was a naval coaling station and armed against cruiser attack.

U-boats have recently been active in this focal region, and probably had established secret bases in the adjacent negro republic of Liberia, whose government lacked the means to exercise effective control. This can now be provided by American troops.

The little Gambia colony, some 500 miles to the north of Sierra Leone, is of no great importance; but it provides the northern edge of the air umbrella which, with the occupation of Liberia, is now complete as far as the Congo.

RUSSIA

Last year the third week of October saw the great German offensive against Moscow brought to a standstill by Russian tenacity, rain and mud. This year at Stalingrad the same factors produced the same result.

On Oct. 14, presumably on Hitler's orders, the Germans launched what was evidently intended to be a decisive attack on the northern districts of the city in order to secure a footing on the Volga banks from which a movement southwards would isolate the remainder and bring about surrender.

MEDITERRANEAN WAR ZONE. Set at a rather unusual angle, this map shows the vital area from Malta to Alexandria, whose fate may well be determined by the battle that began on Oct. 23. Inset, the Egyptian battlefields on a larger scale. *By courtesy of The Daily Telegraph*

THE BATTLE FOR STALINGRAD continued without respite throughout the autumn of 1942. The enemy attacks were particularly heavy in the vital factory district, N.W. of the city. Black arrows show German thrusts at the end of October.

By courtesy of The Daily Telegraph

The attack, aided by terrific, concentrated bombing and artillery support on a narrow front, made considerable progress. Some of the main Russian centres of resistance were captured, and some mechanized units may have reached the Volga. In any case the Russian position was dangerously reduced in depth, air attacks destroyed bridges by which reinforcements previously crossed the river, and the situation looked desperate.

But the Russians were not beaten ; clinging to every yard of ground, and still receiving reinforcement by boat, they slowed down the German advance. Then providentially the weather at last broke ; the Luftwaffe was grounded, and tanks and infantry became bogged in the mud. By Oct. 17 the momentum of the attack was lost ; and though, after a short lull, local attacks, of varying strength, were continued, they were met by counter-attacks and made little or no progress.

If the Germans are to avoid the necessity of withdrawal it is almost essential for them to capture the city, if only to obtain shelter, for the bitter winds of the steppes may prove even less bearable than the lower temperatures of the Moscow region. But can the Germans, from their experience to date, have any confidence that they will be able to overcome Russian resistance without maximum assistance from the air ? And can that now be provided ?

During the dry weather improvised landing-grounds could be multiplied, and the probabilities of the air crews developed to the fullest extent. But, possibly through over-confidence of rapid success, or because communications did not suffice to maintain a requisite supply of labour, airfields, usable in all weather, have evidently not been constructed ; and it seems more than doubtful whether, even in frost, many of the improvised landing-grounds will again become serviceable.

Yet I believe that the Germans are now too deeply committed to abandon attempts to take the city by storm. To leave it undefeated would expose their troops to desperate hardships, and be a shattering blow to prestige. Moreover, Timoshenko is pressing heavily on their northern flank and withdrawal, which could not be carried out

without immense loss of men and material, might become necessary.

In the Caucasus, on the Mozdok front, weather has also brought relief to the Russians, and the defence seems as firm as ever. Towards Tuapse the Germans have made some, if slow, progress, but here also they complain of difficult conditions. Should, however, the Germans elect to abandon offensive operations during the winter they appear to be in a better position to stabilize the front in the Caucasus than at Stalingrad. Elsewhere on the Russian front there have been no special developments.

The Germans are showing anxiety about Russian concentrations between Rzhev and Lake Ilmen, which they assume are preparations for a large-scale offensive.

FAR EAST In New Guinea the Australians continue to make satisfactory if slow progress, and there has been sharp fighting. It must be realized, however, that the advantages of defending the exits of a mountain defile will now be with the Japanese, who, as they are driven back to lower ground, may have more scope

for the employment of artillery—if the country is not too completely jungle-covered.

At the time of writing, the situation in the Solomons remains tense, and a heavy Japanese attack with the object of recapturing the Guadalcanal aerodrome is expected. Allied aircraft have, however, been taking a considerable toll from Japanese shipping, which has evidently been lurking in the vicinity. The naval forces on both sides are apparently unwilling to engage in major operations which would expose them to air attack. Should the Guadalcanal aerodrome be put out of action, either by capture or in consequence of the rainy season, now due, the Japanese fleet would probably act with more boldness.

The situation is the more critical because it is evident that American reinforcements cannot reach the island without considerable risk to transports and their escorts. The same to some extent applies to the Japanese, but their fleet in the Solomons has no line of communication to protect of immediate importance comparable to the line between the U.S.A. and Australia, so they can afford to take greater risks.

BRITISH OFFENSIVE IN EGYPT. Launched on Oct. 23, 1942, by the Eighth or Desert Army, this took the form of a frontal assault on Rommel's strongly defended position before El Alamein. Top, a line of Axis prisoners, first of the 1,450 captured up to Sept. 25. Lower photo, British infantry charging through the smoke and dust of battle to attack Rommel's advance posts.

Photos, British Official : Crown Copyright

Aussies & Americans Side by Side in New Guinea

GEN. MacARTHUR, Supreme Commander of Allied Forces in S.W. Pacific, and Gen. Sir T. Blamey, C.-in-C. of Allied Land Forces in Australia, on a tour of a vital battle area (left). Gen. MacArthur stands in the foreground with Gen. Blamey on his right. On Oct. 19, 1942, it was reported that Allied forces in New Guinea were only 8 miles from Kokoda, the important base from which the Japanese have been operating against our troops fighting in the Owen Stanley Range.
Photo Exclusive to THE WAR ILLUSTRATED

AUSTRALIAN A.A. guns and crews in one of the Allied forward positions in New Guinea (below). The crew operating the gun in the foreground are from Victoria. On the gun barrel are the words " Haifa Horror," a reference to the Italian air raid on the Palestinian port, Sept. 1940,

U.S. TROOPS (circle) queue for their dinner on the New Guinea front. A delayed-action bomb (above) explodes near an Allied base.
Photos, Central Press, Sport & General

From Summer into Winter Stalingrad Fought On

AFTER TWO MONTHS of ferocious assault, Stalingrad still defied the Nazi hordes. 1, Soviet defenders rush along the railway track serving a factory during one of the fiercest phases of the battle for the city. 2, Red Army defenders sniping at the enemy during house-to-house fighting. 3, Ammunition and arms being ferried across the River Volga to the besieged city. 4, An industrial suburb of Stalingrad. The devastation. in the foreground testifies to the violence of the contest.

Photos, U.S.S.R. Official ; News Chronicle, Keystone

Setting the Stage for Action in West Africa

From many points in West Africa come indications of activity on an unprecedented scale.
American landings in Liberia, U-boats active off the coast, feverish preparations by the Vichy
French at Dakar, troop movements in the Sahara . . . all go to show that something is afoot.

WHEN the news of the landing of American troops in Liberia was published in the middle of October, the German press and radio went into ecstasies of excited and sublimely hypocritical denunciation. "The American assault on Liberia," said one commentator, " is in line with the other acts of violence by Britain and the United States against small countries such as Iceland, Persia and Iraq "; and another declared that " the occupation of Liberia is pure rape of a free state."

Seemingly the American troops amounted to a " task force " of a division or so, that is, between 10,000 and 18,000 men; and the purpose of the landing was not the suppression of that rarity in the African continent, an independent native state, but the securing of bases for the air patrol engaged in countering the German U-boats which, judging from recent sinkings in the Gulf of Guinea, have been operating to some effect. So far from resenting the occupation of their country, the Liberians might be expected to give the "invaders" a hearty welcome. This is understandable enough when we remember the close association of Liberia with the United States from the very day of its inception.

Liberia was founded by a handful of white American philanthropists in the eighteen-twenties as a place of refuge for freed American negro slaves. In the early days of the colony a number of negroes did indeed migrate across the Atlantic and found a chain of independent settlements; in 1846 they proclaimed Liberia as a sovereign state, and set about organizing their republic on the lines of the American constitution. But there was no flood of migrants, and after a few decades even the trickle showed signs of drying up. So it comes about that today, of the total population of about one-and-a-half millions the number of Americo-Liberians is considerably less than twenty thousand. These constitute the upper class, the superior caste; they are the descendants of negroes and mulattos—freed slaves for the most part. For the rest, the population is pure African; and with the exception of some sixty thousand coast negroes they are tribes-folk, passing their days in the most primitive kind of existence.

THE two sections of the population have mixed hardly at all. The Americo-Liberians live for the most part in the capital, Monrovia, named after the U.S.A. President who also gave his name to the Monroe Doctrine. Along the coast there is a row of little towns—nine ports are usually listed; and a number of others are situated in the immediate hinterland. But most of Liberia, a country of about 43,000 square miles, is scrub, jungle, and dense forest; indeed, Liberia is described as the forest country *par excellence* of West Africa.

Economically, Liberia must be regarded as a " colony " of the American empire. The greatest industrial interest in the country is the Firestone Corporation, which in 1926 received a concession from the Liberian Government of a million acres of land at an annual rent of six cents an acre. The *quid pro quo* for the concession was a loan of five million dollars, the 7 per cent interest on which is charged against the customs duties and head money received from the tribes in the interior. The Firestone Corporation

laid it down that half the loan should be expended on public works, and the other half on debt repayment; and the new roads and harbours that have been built as a result have facilitated the export of the rubber produced on the Corporation's plantations to the U.S.A.

Some ten years ago the " Black Republic " achieved a most unpleasant notoriety when the shocking ill-treatment of the native tribes by officials, chiefs and slave traders called for the dispatch of a League of Nations Commission. The Commission's report was filled with horrors, but following its publication the Liberians did their best to put their house in order. A new President, Mr. Edwin Barclay, was elected, and his administration has proceeded along progressive lines. Corruption in the Government services has been cleaned up, agriculture has been stimulated, something has been done for education, and the finances have been put on a sound footing. Throughout, President Barclay has kept in close touch with the U.S.A.; and Mr. Roosevelt's representative, Mr. Lester Walton, a negro journalist, has been a power behind the scenes.

Liberia's armed forces comprise a militia numbering 4,000 and a frontier force of about 750 regulars. Navy there is none, just as there are no railways and only 180 miles of road suitable for light motor traffic. All the same, the accession of Liberia to the United Nations has its value in that it reduces to

half the gap of some 600 miles between the British colonies of Sierra Leone and the Gold Coast; and the other half, represented by the Ivory Coast, a French colony still under the influence of Vichy, may now be spanned by R.A.F. planes operating from east and west. This should be a factor of considerable importance in the war against the U-boats operating off the coast.

But even with Liberia as good as an ally, only about half of the coast line of the West African " bulge " is under the control of the United Nations. North of Dakar, between that outpost of Vichy and Tangier in Morocco over against Gibraltar, there are 1,800 miles of French and Spanish territory; nominally, this vast stretch is neutral, but its neutrality has a tendency to tip the scale against the Allied cause.

DAKAR is the chief danger-point—Dakar, with the best natural harbour on the whole West Coast and only 1,800 miles to Brazil. Submarines based on Dakar could work havoc with the Allies' communications with South Africa and the world beyond the Cape; aircraft from Dakar's aerodromes could bomb ports on the opposite side of the Atlantic. Dakar is a commercial centre, a fortress, and an important naval base all in one; within its harbour are reported to lie the great battleships, the Richelieu, three cruisers (Gloire, Montcalm, and Georges Leygues), three modern destroyers (Terrible, Fantasque, Malin), a dozen submarines, the submarine supply ship Jules Verne, and a number of minesweepers and other small craft. Rumour has it that this fleet is short of oil, but all the same it still constitutes a formidable fighting force. Of late weeks there have been many Axis-inspired rumours that Dakar was about to be attacked; if attack does come, then more likely than not it will be by way of the land, since, like Singapore, Dakar is chiefly strong against the sea approach.

A hundred miles to the south is the narrow little strip of territory forming the British colony of Gambia; its capital is Bathurst, at the mouth of the Gambia river. Another 350 miles—Portuguese Guinea and French—and we come to the British colony and protectorate of Sierra Leone; Freetown, the capital, has a harbour described as the best in West Africa, and from it runs a narrow-gauge railway reaching almost to the Liberian frontier.

On the east of Sierra Leone is Liberia, and after Liberia comes the French Ivory Coast—a vast area, reaching from the Gulf of Guinea to the borders of the Sahara. The chief town is Abidjan-Port-Bouet, but the whole coast is dotted with the names of other important centres of industry and commerce.

NOW we come to the Gold Coast, another prosperous example of British rule. French Togoland and Dahomey come next; and then we are on the borders of the great British colony of Nigeria, and after Nigeria looms up the even vaster bulk of French Equatorial Africa. This has declared for General de Gaulle; and it constitutes a corridor along which planes, trucks and men may proceed to the Sudan, Egypt and the Middle East. That corridor, we are left in little doubt, has been very busy of late; soon it may be busier still.

LIBERIA, situated on the West Coast of Africa between the British Colony of Sierra Leone and the Vichy-controlled Ivory Coast, has a seaboard of some 350 miles. Monrovia, capital of the Negro Republic, is also the chief port.
Courtesy of The News Chronicle

Now Liberia Is Ranked Among Our Friends

IN THE NEGRO REPUBLIC OF LIBERIA, where, it was announced on Oct. 17, 1942, U.S. troops have arrived. 1, A street scene in Monrovia, capital and chief port. 2, Warriors of the Kru tribe, seen during a visit to the capital. 3, Mr. Edwin Barclay, President of Liberia since 1932. 4, Bridge constructed of lianas, tropical climbing plants which abound in the dense Liberian forests. 5, Native worker gathering rubber fluid (latex) on one of the great plantations of the Firestone Corporation.

Photos, Dorien Leigh, Planet News, New York Times Photos, Associated Press, G.P.U.

THE WAR AT SEA

by Francis E McMurtrie

ON the eve of Trafalgar Day 1942 the First Lord of the Admiralty, Mr. A. V. Alexander, disclosed that since the beginning of the war more than 530 Axis submarines have been sunk or damaged by Allied attacks. This does not include attacks by the Russians, or any by the French Navy prior to June 1940. It includes some made by the Americans, but does not pretend to be up to date in this respect.

On the analogy of the last war, it seems unsafe to reckon on more than one-quarter of the 530 attacks having been completely successful. Even so, the loss to the enemy is a heavy one. Still, it has not stopped the U-boat menace by any méans ; and until the battle of the Atlantic is undisputably won the end of the war will not be in sight. All our operations depend upon the safe transport by sea of the vital munitions, supplies, and reinforcements needed to keep our land and air forces in action. As the First Lord put it, behind every bomber sent into enemy territory the Navy must maintain the petrol supplies to enable it to fly.

IN the last war the number of U-boats destroyed was 178. Of these, 44 succumbed to mines and 38 to depth-charge attack ; 19 were torpedoed by British submarines ; 16 fell victims to gunfire ; 14 were rammed ; 12 were surprised by decoy ships ; six were sunk by aircraft ; six were caught in nets of various kinds before being finished off by mines or depth-charges ; five were destroyed by high-speed sweeps ; four were lost accidentally ; one was captured ; one was wrecked ; and the exact fate which befell the remaining 12 is unknown.

Germany had altogether 372 submarines in service in 1914-18. Apart from the war losses catalogued above, 15 were scuttled and the remainder surrendered or otherwise disposed of, e.g. by cession to the Austrian Navy, etc. In November 1918 there were 226 U-boats under construction.

At the start of this war the enemy already possessed 70 submarines, as compared with 30 in 1914. Moreover, there is no doubt that far more extensive building facilities existed in 1939 than at the earlier date. It is pro-

bable, therefore, that the figures contained in the Russian estimate quoted in page 297 are not very wide of the mark.

In the Solomon Islands the situation does not seem to be regarded as satisfactory by our American allies. At least that is the only reasonable explanation of the supersession of Vice-Admiral R. L. Ghormley, hitherto in command of the South-West Pacific area, by Vice-Admiral W. F. Halsey. At the same time the subordinate flag officer in charge of the actual operations in the Solomons, Vice-Admiral H. Fairfax Leary.

Vice-Admiral Halsey was in command of the successful raid on Japanese posts in the Marshall and Gilbert Islands at the end of January, as well as of attacks on Marcus Island on Feb. 24 and Wake Island on March 4. Vice-Admiral Leary is an able and energetic officer who has for some time been regarded as a coming man. He was Assistant Naval Attaché in London a few years ago.

Reasons for the replacement of the officers responsible for the conduct of operations in the Solomons are not announced. They may be connected with references in New York newspapers to " costly and unnecessary losses," attributed to " over-caution and the defensive complex." At the same time, the experience of Pearl Harbour and the Java Sea battle prove that in dealing with the Japanese a certain amount of caution is essential. It can hardly be supposed, however, that the U.S. Naval authorities have been influenced by Press criticism in making these changes. It may be assumed that they have been undertaken with the concurrence and probably on the recommendation of the Commander-in-Chief of the Pacific Fleet, Admiral Chester W. Nimitz.

EVERY sympathy should be felt both for the superseded admirals and their successors in the difficult task with which they are faced. One of the main obstacles is the distance between Guadalcanal, in which U.S. Marines still hold the Lunga airfield, and the nearest Allied base. The latter is understood to be in the island of Espiritu Santo, the largest of the New Hebrides, fully 550 miles away.

Vice-Adm. H. F. LEARY (left), who, it was announced on Oct. 25, 1942, had succeeded Vice-Adm. W. S. Pye as commander of a secret Pacific task force. Right, Vice-Adm. W. F. HALSEY, whose appointment as C.-in-C. naval forces, S.W. Pacific, in succession to Vice-Adm. Ghormley, was announced on the same date.
Photos, Sport & General, Associated Press

In this respect the Japanese are better situated. Apart from their headquarters at Rabaul, in New Britain, there are sundry subsidiary bases in various convenient harbours in the Solomon Group, notably in Ysabel Island, and at Gizo, off the west coast of New Florida. It is this advantage which has enabled the enemy to land reinforcements and guns in Guadalcanal under cover of darkness.

FOR a time the Americans appear to have relied on their air forces to deal with these fresh incursions, but, having failed to stop them by this means, U.S. warships were last month ordered to intervene. In their opening brush with the enemy on Oct. 12 losses were suffered by both sides. The Japanese are believed to have lost a 10,000-ton cruiser and four destroyers, while American ships sunk include the destroyers Porter, Meredith and O'Brien.

Judging from the action of August 8, in which H.M.A.S. Canberra and the U.S. cruisers Astoria, Quincy and Vincennes were lost, the Japanese have made a careful study of night tactics, and are imitating the methods of the British Mediterranean Fleet as exemplified at the Battle of Cape Matapan. Approaching at high speed the Japanese squadron appears simultaneously to have switched on its searchlights and opened fire, with the disastrous results already recorded. Retreat seems to have been effected immediately, before closer action could ensue.

Then on October 26 it was announced by the U.S. Navy Department that the U.S. aircraft-carrier Wasp had been sunk on September 15 by an enemy submarine attack ; and the fleet tug Seminole lost off Tulagi on October 5.

IN the Bering Sea there have been few developments of note. Certain islands of the Aleutian chain have been occupied by U.S. forces, and Japanese warships and transports at Kiska have been bombed and in some cases destroyed. It seems evident that in occupying Kiska and other islands the enemy intended merely to create a diversion which it was hoped would draw American ships and aircraft away from the more important theatre of operations in the South-West Pacific. At the same time the apparent threat to Alaska, though illusory, was bound to excite uneasiness in the uninformed minds of the American public.

NAVAL BRUSH IN THE SOUTH SEAS. The U.S. auxiliary transports, Colhoun and Little, carried out vital operations in the Solomons at the beginning of Sept. 1942. On Sept. 5 Colhoun was attacked by Japanese bombers off Guadalcanal ; she is seen on the right of the photo as she goes down. Her sister ship, the Little, whose loss was announced on Sept. 24, is outlined against the smoke from the doomed vessel. PAGE 328 *Photo, Keystone*

More Gallant Chapters in the Sea War's Story

ADRIFT IN THE ATLANTIC. 43 Allied seamen whose ship was torpedoed by a U-boat in the Atlantic owe their lives to a Flying Fortress of the R.A.F. Coastal Command, which sighted them—some on rafts, others in a lifeboat 500 miles out at sea. Rations and life-jackets were dropped by the aircraft and wireless messages sent giving positions. The following day the survivors were picked up by destroyers and corvettes. Men are seen (right) waving to the plane from their lifeboat.

Below, members of a U-boat crew clambering aboard a rescuing ship in the Mediterranean.

RETURNING FROM RUSSIA, these American gunners, on board a merchant ship bound for a British port, are well protected against Arctic conditions. Their furs were obtained during their stay in Northern waters.

When a Stuka dived to make a low-level attack on a British warship, skilful handling on the part of the ship's crew brought the vessel safely through her ordeal. Although bombs exploded close to the ship, the gun crews were able to drive off the enemy. On the left the crew are seen firing a multiple pom-pom at the plane.

Photos, British Official: Crown Copyright; G.P.U., Keystone Planet News

The Story of a British Boy's Grave in Malta

IT is good to know that in the midst of the most savage and inhuman war in the world's history and at a spot where its terrors are possibly concentrated to a degree that is not reached at any other point of the conflict, the humanities which make life tolerable and which have ever been associated with the British character and with the races that have gladly accepted the way of life which has made Britain the great civilizer, still persist, and cannot be destroyed by all the bombs that Germany may rain upon it. A little story, which should have a peculiar interest for THE WAR ILLUSTRATED readers, will serve as well as many far more important that might be told.

In August last one of our readers, Mrs. Williams, of Normanton, Yorkshire, wrote to the Editor to tell him that her only son, First Class Boy Ronald D. Williams, who "gave his life taking things to Malta that it needs from England," had been killed on the island during one of its thousands of air raids. "We ourselves," wrote the mother, "will never probably see the cemetery or look on his grave, but we should love to possess a picture of it." How was this to be achieved ?

FORTUNATELY, as our readers will be aware, we have a large number of enthusiastic followers of THE WAR ILLUSTRATED in the Isle of Heroes, and several young Maltese—than whom there are none more enthusiastically British—have written from time to time to the Editor. One in particular, John Mizzi, has had the honour of several appearances in our pages ; his latest contribution being included in No. 138 at page 253, and it occurred to the Editor that here was a likely medium whereby the sorrowing mother in Yorkshire might be put in possession of the much-desired memento of her boy's last resting-place in that Mediterranean island, with whose dust any Briton might be glad to think his own might mingle, for Malta is surely as much a part of Britain today as Yorkshire itself. John Mizzi quickly responded to our appeal, and by the middle of October we had the satisfaction of sending to Mrs. Williams the photographs which appear in this page, together with a larger one of the individual grave.

Shaded by cypress trees, on a hillside near Capuccini overlooking the sea, are the last resting-places of British seamen in Malta's Protestant Naval Cemetery. But there is no peace here—there is no peace anywhere in Malta. Even the headstones are shell-splintered.

For this, thanks go first to the enterprise and enthusiasm of our seventeen-year-old correspondent in doing this fine service for the sake of the dead boy of his own age whose grave is one of the many additions to those of the British sailors that lie in the Naval Cemetery of Malta. The Editor is taking this way of expressing his thanks to his gifted young correspondent and would also make special mention of the kindly consideration with which Major Wells of the Malta War Graves Commission received the suggestion and granted every facility for the taking of the photographs. These will bring comfort to many mothers other than that of First Class Boy Ronald Williams, in the knowledge that wherever their sons have made the great sacrifice for Britain, and the British way of life, they are certain to be honoured in their death if fortunate enough to meet it on territory where British control is effective. It will not escape the reader's notice that in the view of the Malta cemetery reproduced above, with its suggestion of the free-shaded "God's acre " of our homeland, the cemetery itself has suffered inevitably in the bombing of the Island.

The foregoing must on no account be taken to imply that THE WAR ILLUSTRATED can undertake similar inquiries for other readers, as that would be quite impracticable at this time.

The grave of First Cl. Boy Ronald D. Williams is seen at left ; it is the first of the middle row of three, nearest to shrub in the centre of the picture. Completion of these graves in the Naval Cemetery awaits the cessation of hostilities.
Photos, Public Relations, Malta

New Airfields Built on the Canadian Prairies

CANADA'S ALASKAN ROUTE AIRFIELDS, some of which are already in use, form a chain which largely dictated the course of the 1,600-mile Alaska highway. 1, This repair-shop services tractors used in the construction of Watson Lake airport, situated midway between Edmonton, Alberta, and Fairbanks, Alaska (see map p. 332). 2, Levelling up after the ground-clearing crews have finished their work. 3, A grader puts the finishing touches to the runway; U.S. planes in the background.

'America's Burma Road' Finished in Six Months

Like many other far-distant corners of the world, Alaska seemed until only the other day at the very back of beyond. Now, however, for reasons given in the article that follows, it is the scene of intense military and engineering activity, and ere long it may be playing a great part in the deciding of the war against the Japanese in the Pacific.

WHEN the U.S.A. bought Alaska from Russia in 1867 there were few in America who were not of the opinion that the Russians had had the best of the deal. Seven million-odd perfectly good American dollars ! Paid for what ? For a territory which, big as it was—as big as Germany, France and Italy added together—was still believed to be nothing more than a wilderness of mountain and frozen soil. In fact, however, the purchase turned out to be an excellent investment, since before long Alaska was producing great quantities of gold and other minerals, furs and timber. And valuable as it has proved to be in peacetime, Alaska is proving to be even more valuable now, when the U.S.A. is at grips with Japan.

Alaska is the nearest U.S. territory to Japan, if the Philippines be excluded; from the airfields the Americans have been busily constructing in Alaskan territory it should be possible before very long to bomb Tokyo and the other great cities clustered so closely on the Japanese islands. Moreover, Alaska provides a substantial base for the chain of American outposts reaching out to Dutch Harbour and along the Aleutians. Then Alaska is next door to Asia ; at its narrowest the Bering Strait is only some 50 miles wide—indeed, it is said to be possible to paddle a canoe from island to island, from America to Asia. Lastly, Alaska provides a short route for American supplies to Russia ; and not only to Russia, but still more to China. Indeed, now that the Burma Road is closed this route across " the top of the world " is practically the only route left open whereby the Allies can convey material aid to their hard-pressed ally in Chungking.

OF course, Alaska's great drawback is its inaccessibility. Between it and the continental U.S.A. is a great mass of Canadian territory some 800 miles wide, which in the northern part is almost bare of roads. There is a route by sea along the coast from Seattle to the little ports on the Gulf of Alaska ; another is by air across Canada. But in wartime the ships that might be employed in making the Alaskan passage are badly needed elsewhere, and the carrying capacity of planes is very limited. It is hardly surprising, therefore, that the long-discussed plan for linking the U.S.A. to Alaska by road should have been brought out of cold storage.

Years before the war the project was frequently discussed, and there were many to advocate it, both for commercial and tourist reasons, and also for the strategic consideration that a road connexion would facilitate the defence not only of Alaska but of the whole of the North American continent. In 1939 a joint Canadian-American commission was appointed to investigate and report upon the possibility of constructing a highway to Alaska and the Yukon Territory, and two routes were considered : one running north-

ward from Hazelton on the Skeena river, and the other from Prince George, in the valley of the Fraser, high up in the Rockies. The Joint Defence Board established in 1940 rejected both routes, the one because it lay so near to the coast as to be vulnerable to air attack, and the other because its course through the Rockies involved immense engineering difficulties. As an alternative it proposed a third route, one which ran along the eastern side of the Rockies much farther inland than the others ; this would not only be far easier and so speedier to construct, but would also serve as a link between the aerodromes (see map) which have been constructed by the Canadian Government of late years in Alberta, British Columbia and Yukon.

FROM U.S.A. TO ALASKA a great new highway has recently been constructed under the direction of American military engineers. Its route is clearly shown on this map ; and the Canadian airfields, to link up which was a deciding factor in the planning of the route, are also indicated. (See illus. p. 331.)
By courtesy of The Manchester Guardian

This third route, the one adopted, is an extension of the road which runs from Edmonton to Dawson Creek in B.C., where the new road begins. From Dawson Creek it proceeds in a northerly direction to Fort St. John and Fort Nelson. Turning then to the west, it enters the Yukon Territory just south of Watson Lake, proceeds to Whitehorse, and there connects with the railway above Skagway. From Whitehorse it continues north-west to Boundary—a well-named township situated where the Canadian territory joins American—and thence to Big Delta, where it links up with the 75-mile stretch of road connecting that township with Fairbanks, the capital of Alaska.

Until fairly recently Canadian opinion was not too enthusiastic about the project. The great stumbling-block was the expense, but

that was removed when Mr. Roosevelt's Government let it be known that America was quite prepared to shoulder the entire expense, while agreeing that at the end of the war the road should be incorporated in the Canadian national road system. The U.S. Administration officially approached the Canadian Government on February 13, 1942, with the suggestion that the road should be constructed forthwith. Mr. Mackenzie King's Government immediately agreed, although there were some critics who declared that the route was not the best that might have-been selected. Thus Mr. George Black, M.P. for the Yukon, informed the Canadian House of Commons that for the most part the route ran over tundra (the rolling treeless plain of Arctic regions) and muskeg (rocky basins filled with leaves, marsh, moss and other unstable material)—ground which would be both difficult and expensive to traverse.

BUT the scheme went through, and very shortly Colonel William Hoge, an American Army engineer from Missouri, had arrived at Dawson Creek, where he established his first working base. A second base was established at Fort Nelson, and a third at Whitehorse.

The Army engineers, it was expected at the outset, were to build a pioneer road which would be " passable but not much else." When this had been built it would be turned over to the Public Roads Administration of the U.S., which would proceed to convert it into a standard 24-ft. highway with foundations of crushed rock.

The summer months went by. The American Army engineers and their gangs of navvies—10,000 soldiers divided into seven engineering regiments, and 2,000 civilians—toiled and sweated, dug and blasted their way across the wilderness. Now they were working in a temperature well below zero ; now it was in almost tropical heat, and the men had to wear gloves and head-nets to ward off the swarms of mosquitoes. To such good purpose did they work—16 hours a day, progressing 8 miles in every 24 hours—that on Sept. 24 Mr. Stimson, U.S. Secretary for War, said that the highway, the greatest engineering feat since the construction of the Panama Canal, would be in use by Dec. 1, many months ahead of schedule. Moreover, so far from being just a rough track, it was a well-graded and drained highway, admitting two-way traffic on much of its length.

EVEN this prophecy was soon out of date. On Oct. 29 Mr. Stimson proudly announced that the corps of soldiers and civilians under the direction of the Public Roads Administration had actually finished the job—1,671 miles of new road 24 feet wide, involving the bridging of 200 streams, constructed in slightly over six months. That week, he said, trucks were starting to carry munitions and material to the U.S. troops in Alaska.

Beside the Rockies Runs the Alaskan Highway

THE ALCAN HIGHWAY, as the 1,671-mile-long road linking Alaska across Canada with the United States is styled, runs through grandly beautiful scenery, as this photograph of a typical stretch shows well. After the War it will draw, no doubt, a great host of pleasure motorists. Today, however, it echoes to the rumble of military trucks, carrying supplies and men to the Canadian airfields and the bases now in course of being established by the Americans in Alaska.

Photo, Sport & General

What Britain Has Done For Russia

Of late months vociferous demands have been made in this country, in America and in Russia, that a second front should be opened in the West to relieve the terrific strain on the U.S.S.R. In this article, however, we are concerned not with such questions of high strategy but with the almost as vital question of material aid for the armies and people of our valiant but hard-pressed ally.

Oᴺʟʏ a few hours after Hitler launched his troops against Russia, Mr. Churchill, in a broadcast from London, made the promise : " We shall give whatever help we can to Russia and to the Russian people." He went on, " We have offered to the Government of Soviet Russia any technical or economic assistance which is in our power and which is likely to be of service to them . . ." That was on June 22, 1941 ; a few months later, on Sept. 9, the British Prime Minister told the House of Commons that we should be prepared for serious sacrifices in the munitions field in order to meet the needs of Russia. It should be remembered " that everything that is given to Russia is subtracted from what we are making ourselves, or in part at least from what would have been sent to us by the United States "; that time and geography were limiting factors, and that there were also limitations of transport, harbour facilities, and, above all, of shipping.

At the end of that same month of Sept. 1941 Mr. Churchill assured the House of Commons that the interval which had elapsed since he and President Roosevelt had sent their message to Stalin from their conference in the Atlantic had been used in ceaseless activity. Now British and American representatives had gone to Moscow with clear and full knowledge of what they were able to give to Russia, month by month. " It is not only tanks," said the Premier, " the tanks for which we have waited so long, that we have to send, but precious aircraft and aluminium, rubber, copper, oil, and many other materials vital to modern war, large quantities of which have already gone . . . The veriest simpleton can see how great is our interest, to put it no higher, in sustaining Russia by every possible means."

Tʜᴇ Moscow conference was in session from Sept. 29 to Oct. 1, and at its conclusion it was announced that an agreement had been reached to place at Russia's disposal virtually every requirement for which the military and civil authorities of the Soviet Union had asked (see Vol. 5, page 202).

These are the promises: what of the performance ?

On his return to London from the Moscow conference Lord Beaverbrook declared in a broadcast on Oct. 12, that " out of the resources of Britain and U.S.A., each bearing a full share of the burden, the Russians are now being supplied with much that they asked for. And certainly with all that at present we can give them. As for tanks and aircraft, the numbers that Stalin asked for have been promised. The full numbers promised for October have been provided . . ." A fortnight later Lord Beaverbrook announced that a considerable quantity of wheat had been sent from our own stocks in Canada and large quantities of sugar from our own stocks in Britain. Moreover, we had given tanks to such an extent that we should have to have an immense increase in output. Then at the end of November, Lord Beaverbrook, who was still Minister of Supply, told a meeting of Glasgow shop-stewards that everything we had promised to Russia for delivery in November had been dispatched ; and he went on to read a telegram from Stalin.

Beaverbrook—Let me express my gratitude for the sending of aeroplanes and tanks. Some of these British-made aeroplanes and tanks are already in action in the front line. The reports of our commanders on the British-made tanks are favourable. The Hurricanes are greatly appreciated. We would like as many Hurricanes and tanks as you can send . . .

LEAVING LONDON FOR RUSSIA these crates, packed with vital war supplies, represent part of Britain's aid to our gallant ally. Actual figures are not usually available—how the enemy would like to know them !—but there is good reason to believe that substantial assistance has been, and is being, afforded.
Photo, Fox

The news that hundreds of British aircraft had been sent to Russia was announced by Mr. Churchill in the House of Commons on Sept. 11, and a few days later it was officially stated in London that an R.A.F. wing had arrived on the Russian front. The wing was ere long withdrawn, but a large number of Hurricanes, as well as American Airacobras, were by then being flown by airmen of the Red Air Force.

HELP THE RUSSIAN WOUNDED !

Since Mrs. Churchill launched her Red Cross " Aid to Russia " Fund, 2,571 tons of medical stores, etc., have been shipped so Russia. They include, in addition to motor and portable X-ray units and ambulances :

530,000 Blankets	200,000 Ampoules
50,000 First Aid Pouches	Strophantin
50,000 Children's Coats	50,000 kg. Lanoline
40,000 „ Breechettes	15,000 kg.Sodium Brom.
2 Tons Chloroform	180,000 Scalpels
2 Tons Ether	60,000 Surgical Scissors
10,000 kg. Sulphanilamide	11,000 Sterilizers
150,000 Dissecting Forceps	324,000 prs. Surg. Gloves
63,000 Hot-water Bottles	523,000 yds. Rubber
50,000 kg. Chloramine	Sheeting
77,000 Hypodermic Syges	54,000 Tourniquets

Subscriptions to the Fund should be sent to Mrs. Churchill at 10, Downing Street, London. S.W.1.

(On Oct. 28, 1942, it was announced that the R.A.F. was again in Russia ; Coastal Command planes and pilots helping in convoy protection.)

By the opening of 1942 there were widespread suspicions that deliveries to Russia were not up to schedule. But on Jan. 27 Mr. Churchill told the House that, in spite of the still-present threat of invasion of these islands, we had sent " Premier Stalin exactly what he asked for." Yet on Feb. 15 in his Singapore broadcast the Premier admitted that " it is little enough that we have done for Russia, considering all she has done to beat Hitler and for the common cause." Then, in the House of Lords on Feb. 12 Lord Beaverbrook, now Minister of Production, declared that we had fulfilled all our obligations to Russia up to Jan. 21, except for one tank. British tanks, he revealed, had played a great part in the successful defence of Moscow.

Aѕ the year wore on the Government's spokesmen continued to maintain that the promises were being fulfilled.

To the questions, " Have we fulfilled the actual contract which we entered into with Russia for delivery of supplies, and have we sent all the tanks and aircraft which we promised them ? " Mr. Oliver Lyttelton, Minister of Production, answered on July 18 with an emphatic " yes." " We have been shipping tanks to Russia at the rate of 50 a week [2,000 in all by early July]. By the end of May we had actually shipped 11 per cent more aircraft than we had promised up to the end of June. For every 100 aircraft we promised we have shipped 111. These supplies we have sent in spite of the urgent demands of our own armies in the Middle East and the preparations of the field force in this country. So we may fairly say that in the matter of equipment we have done everything that we could do to assist our Russian allies."

In September the greatest convoy to leave these shores for Russia battled its way through, escorted by 75 warships, to North Russia (see pp. 279, 317).

" We must send supplies to Russia," said Mr. A. V. Alexander, First Lord of the Admiralty, on Oct. 20, 1942, " although I think that often too little credit is given for what we have already done in that respect." We had put hundreds of supply ships into Russia since the war started, running into a tonnage of millions. On the same day Mr. Hugh Dalton, President of the Board of Trade, told the Commons that last year we sent Russia more than 500,000 blankets and more than 400,000 woollen garments, and the supplies we were about to send would be greater still.

But the criticisms grew. Nor were they unaffected by the answers made by Mr. Stalin on Oct. 4 to certain questions put to him by an American journalist, Mr. Henry Cassidy. " As compared with the aid which the Soviet Union is giving to the Allies, by drawing upon itself the main forces of the German Fascist armies," said the Soviet leader, " the aid of the Allies to the Soviet Union has so far been little effective. In order to amplify and improve this aid, only one thing is required : that the Allies fulfil their obligations fully and on time."

Britain Delivers the Goods to Russia

On a railway siding at one of Britain's monster Ordnance factories a trainload of Matilda tanks are receiving the final inspection. Soon they will arrive at the port of embarkation, there, together with a consignment of Hurricane fighters each contained in a crate as big as a bungalow (lower photo), to be put on board a transport. And so (see page 338) to Russia.

Not All Hitler's Might and Malice . . .

Photos, Brit
(ci

With Russia bearing the full weight of Germany's military machine, it was vitally important that the convoy, one of the greatest to leave Britain's shores, should get through to Russia. And get through it did (see pp. 279, 317). Our upper photograph (1) shows one of the many exciting moments in its passage : a Nazi bomber has secured a near miss on a carrier.

. . . Could Stop the Flow of Allied Aid

Not all the ships in the convoy got through, however; in (2) great clouds of smoke billow to heaven from a stricken merchantman. That the climatic conditions of the Arctic passage are extreme indeed is evident by (3). Escorting the convoy was a British force of 75 ships, some of which are shown in (4); in the van are H.M.S. Fury and H.M.S. Ashanti.

Photos, U.S.S.R. Official; Associa

The Tanks Arrive and Speed to Action

At Murmansk the convoy, after battling through frozen seas, after enduring all the malice
and might of an alert and powerful foe, has put into harbour. Allied sailors and Russian
stevedores with eager speed unload the freight, more precious in the present hour of extreme
danger than mountains of gold; and soon the tanks from Britain are charging the foe.

VIEWS & REVIEWS Of Vital War Books

by Hamilton Fyfe

VERY few people here, even among those who study the war, seem to think of a direct attack on the United States as likely, or even possible. The Americans themselves, however, are thinking of it a good deal. One of the writers who have been discussing the possibility is Mr. William B. Ziff, who was over here to get acquaintance with our air problems not long ago. His book, The Coming Battle of Germany (Hamish Hamilton, 7s. 6d.), has been selling in very large numbers in America. It is easy to understand why.

Mr. Ziff brings the actualities of the war before his readers in clear-cut terms, emphatic language, and a grip that holds attention all the time. He sees the struggle, not in a number of separate compartments (which is the way many of us have seen it—and still do), but as a whole. The United Nations cannot afford to regard the defence of Britain as one necessity, the defence of the United States as another. They must not suppose the operations in the Mediterranean are local and bear no relation to those in the Pacific. Above all, they must not get muddled in their minds by thinking this war is like wars of the past, or that it can be won by methods belonging to the past.

He tells his countrymen they are in danger of being invaded. He also tells them that their safeguard against invasion up to now has been, and still is, " the continued existence of Great Britain, pointed like a pistol at the very heart of the German giant." That is very useful talk indeed. It not only disposes of the silly idea in so many American heads that Britain has done little or nothing so far. It shows how necessary it is for the United Nations to learn to fight the war as one conflict and to direct it in a bold, adventurous spirit.

IN every respect save one the Germans " have an overwhelming superiority to anything we can offer in the way of organization, instruments of war, effective numbers, position and communications." Our one advantage over the enemy is " our power to strike at the heart of the Axis war effort, that is, at Germany proper, through the air."

Here is the value of Britain as a safeguard against invasion of America. The British Isles are only a few hundred miles from the German heart. They can be used as " a forward base for the operations of the United States," and this gives the United Nations " a technical superiority certain to bring to collapse the entire German war effort with fierce, unmerciful blows, after American

technological science has succeeded in evolving the proper instruments and technique of action."

That may strike us at first as arrogant and unfair. Haven't we been evolving these things ? Must we learn from America ? Well, I am afraid we have to admit the Americans can teach us a good deal we haven't learned before. I read the other day an article by Major Oliver Stewart, showing how they plan their raids mathematically and how valuable this innovation is. In construction, too, American plane designers look ahead without any blinkers on, and can get their suggestions considered more easily.

=== THE ===
Coming Battle
of Germany

Mr. Ziff gives an example of British unreadiness to adopt new techniques : the two-men submarines used by the Japanese at Pearl Harbour are, it appears, the development of an invention by a British submarine commander (Colin Mayers), which the Admiralty " turned down as fantastic."

DON'T suppose, though, that Mr. Ziff thinks American ways leave nothing to be desired. He says, for instance, there is too much in his country as well as here of what Napoleon called " seeking wisdom in debates and conferences." That, Napoleon said, led to prudent decisions being made, which were " the worst possible." Mr. Ziff agrees.

It is the unusual and the extravagant which win wars, not the stolid and the commonplace. They cannot be won by committees. They cannot be won by politicians directing the course of military affairs, not even by the greatest and most inspired.

To quote Napoleon is not by any means conclusive. He made plenty of mistakes, although he had the " absolute command and energetic decision " which he declared to be essential. But Mr. Ziff puts the case for unity of command with forcible good sense. We had to come to it in 1918. How much longer shall we be hampered by its lack ?

It was only when President Lincoln gave dour old Ulysses S. Grant complete and undivided authority over the conduct of the Civil War that the North began to win battles.

If the United Nations would use the one advantage they possess over the chief enemy, Hitler, Mr. Ziff believes that " air power alone could certainly gain the decision." The conventional military view that an enemy must be defeated on land and his territory, or some of it, occupied, is " not supported by a study of the last war, which was lost by a nation whose armed forces had not been beaten and were standing on foreign territory on every front at the moment of capitulation." And Germany almost won, it is added, through the use of submarines with no occupying power whatever !

WHAT the R.A.F. have done in the way of hampering German industry is not overlooked. The destruction of the immense Heinkel plant at Rostock gets special mention. But what the book urges is the creation of an American bombing force which would make it possible to keep up continuous systematic attacks (such as have been made day and night since it was written) by as many as 5,000 aircraft at a time, weighing up to 300 tons each and with a speed of 400 m.p.h.

A sky battlefleet of the proportions proposed, coupled with a readiness to write off 2,500 of the craft a month, would for the first time constitute an aerial body capable of delivering an attack in force so as to be able to compel an absolute decision with no other important supplementary factors operating.

Then would be the time to drop leaflets. At the start they were of no use. It was foolish to imagine they would be. When the Germans are shell-shocked, when their cities are falling about them, then they will feel the effect of "cold, inexorable phrases" telling them that the materials for this terrible attack were mostly coming, not from Britain, where they could bomb factories in return, but from the United States, " whose productive energies were not being sapped by any counter-assault," and that the punishment would go on, becoming always more and more devastating, until they cried " Hold, enough ! '

ALREADY there are types of plane which could do most of what is proposed, but new types will no doubt be perfected, since " the striking power of aircraft is just at the beginning of its development, and it is certain that before this war is over there will be startling new forms of design and radically altered tactics, infinitely more efficient and deadly than any now known." An eight-engine bomber with a speed greater than that of fighters is being projected. Such a machine would not only outstrip the interceptor combat planes sent against it : it would outgun them: "it would have the air to itself."

" Sheer wishful thinking ? " Perhaps. But it is the combination of imaginative looking forward with an assembly of hard facts that makes Mr. Ziff's pages so attractive.

U.S. FLYING FORTRESSES, whose performances have been described as " exceeding even the fondest expectations of their American proponents," are here seen at one of their operational stations in Britain. These machines, whose exceptionally heavy armament protects them against fighters, have scored outstanding successes in the great daylight raids over Europe ; and their achievements may be held to reinforce the arguments advanced by Mr. Ziff in the book reviewed in this page. This photograph shows Fortresses taxi-ing across the tarmac. *Photo, Planet News*

Americans Have Been With Us Since 1939

AMERICAN NURSES, attached to a U.S. hospital in Britain, chatting to a patient (left). The first American to be killed in this war—P O W. M. L. Fiske, who gave his life in the cause of liberty when serving with the R.A.F. during the Battle of Britain in August 1940—is commemorated by a plaque in St. Paul's Cathedral, London (right).

AMERICA'S FIRST TWO YEARS, by Mrs. Anthony Billingham (John Murray and The Pilot Press, 6s.), gives a vividly informative picture of the many and varied contributions made by U.S. citizens and organizations to the British war effort from 1939 to 1941. These voluntary activities have included service in the Flight Ferry Command, established in Sept. 1940, in which more than 25 per cent of the pilots are Americans over fighting age, and the famous Eagle Squadrons, founded by Col. Charles Sweeney, which flew at first with the R.A.F., but in Sept. 1942 were handed over to the U.S. Air Force.

More than £6,000,000 was contributed for relief during the first two years of war by the American Red Cross. In addition, gifts were sent ranging from 152 ambulances, over 13,000,000 surgical dressings, nearly 5,000 litres of blood plasma for emergency transfusion, to many thousands of parcels of clothing and shoes.

Another source of supplies is the "Bundles for Britain" organization founded by Mrs. Wales Latham, which has sent us 4,000,000 garments, 500,000 blankets, £30,000 for canteens, day-nurseries and air-raid distress, and over £70,000 to various hospitals. There are two U.S.

hospitals established in this country, the American Hospital in Britain (Churchill Hospital), specializing in orthopaedic surgery, and the Harvard Hospital for communicable diseases. The U.S. British War Relief Society has sent money to the value of over £3,000,000, used in part to establish homes for bomb-shocked children, rest home for nurses and help for London firemen, and a variety of gifts, including 264 motorized ambulances.

Among the social centres which contribute to the comfort of servicemen or of blitzed civilians are the English Speaking Union, the American Women's Club and the Eagle Club.

Then mention may be made of the American unit of the Home Guard, founded in July 1940. "We started the American unit," said its commander, Brig.-Gen. W. H. Hayes, a World War I veteran, "because our homes are here, and we wanted to show that we were ready, with the British, to share the responsibility of defending their soil."

These are just some of the many interesting facts assembled by Mrs. Billingham in a volume which, in word and photography, excellently portrays the incomparable assistance given to Britain during the two crucial years before America herself entered the war as a combatant.

FROM THE U.S.A. Red Cross supplies arrive in this country in vast quantities. Month by month fresh consignments travel across the Atlantic and reach British ports after running the tremendous risks of the war at sea. One such consignment is seen above on its arrival at the London Docks.

Right, group of airmen of the U.S. Eagle Squadron, seen at an R.A.F. fighter station. First formed in Oct. 1940 from American volunteers, the Eagle Squadrons developed into a formidable force. Their first C.O., Sqdn.-Ldr. W. E. G. Taylor, who has seen service in the U.S. Marines as well as the Royal Navy, is fourth from the left.

Photos, Fox, Associated Press, L.N.A., Keystone

How Lease-Lend Speeds the Goods to Britain

RUSHING THROUGH BROADWAY in the centre of New York go the vans carrying the precious machines to the dockside. Being Lease-Lend vehicles they are accorded the same privileges as ambulances and fire engines and are escorted by motor-cyclists. So the brilliantly lit streets of the American metropolis are left behind.

AT WASHINGTON, Edward Stettinius, Junr., U.S. Lease - Lend administrator, and his colleagues in the Lease-Lend conference room have decided to grant priority to Great Britain in the all-important supply of U.S. multiple gear-cutting machines essential for the production of tanks. Swiftly the momentous decision is carried into effect.

ACROSS THE ATLANTIC moves the convoy in which is the ship carrying the vital machines. There was a " spot of trouble " from U-boats, but in due time the cargo reached its destination in Britain. On the right the machines are seen hard at work, having been installed in one of the many great factories where British workers are turning out hundreds of tanks. The photographs in this page are stills taken from the film, We Sail at Midnight.

PAGE 34?

THE WAR IN THE AIR

by Capt. Norman Macmillan, M.C., A.F.C.

THE changing character of the air war is becoming more apparent in current operations. The greater part of German air operations is concerned with short-range, concentrated attacks. The major part of the United Nations air operations is devoted to attacks which cover a steadily increasing area.

The difference between the methods of Germany and of the United Nations arises from the different geographical outlook of the opposing peoples. Britain and America have always had to face great oceanic crossings, demanding range of operation. Germany has been wrapped up with European considerations, where distances are short, frontier barriers frequent, and long range in aircraft could not be employed effectively either before the war, or for the type of campaign which Germany envisaged after the war began.

The restriction on aircraft imposed by European conditions was vividly brought home to me when I flew from England to Finland. Although I was flying a slow-speed trainer I passed over three complete countries in a flight of three hours and forty minutes. Faced with such conditions the Luftwaffe, air instrument of the German Army, devised a policy of close cooperation with the ground forces, which in turn produced the demand for relatively short-range aircraft. For three years this policy proved successful in most campaigns, but the conditions of the war have now turned, and are less favourable to German policy and more favourable to United Nations policy.

AERO-ENGINE developments providing greater power for each engine unit have enabled our aircraft designers' four-engined bombers to transport greater bomb-loads over longer distances at only fractionally slower speeds than the shorter range German bombers ; the larger Allied types of aircraft are more heavily armed than the smaller German craft.

The United Nations air forces are so equipped that " air battleships " play an important part in their operations, whereas the Germans have concentrated on the " cruiser " type of aircraft for their principal offensive air weapons. There is less diverg-ence in principle between the belligerent forces in regard to the lighter types, the small bombers, fighter-bombers, and fighters.

The other great difference between the Royal Air Force and the Luftwaffe lies in their distinctive organization. The German force is composed of Air Fleets, each fleet detailed to cover a particular area. This method provides for close cooperation with surface forces, and it also enables full advantage to be taken of the inherent mobility of aircraft. The Royal Air Force, on the other hand, is organized on a functional basis, in a series of Commands, each concerned with a duty rather than an area.

NOW that the R.A.F. has expanded to a size comparable with that of the Luftwaffe it is possible to compare the two methods of organization on a fair basis. The advantage lies with the R.A.F. now, although it did not do so when the numerical advantage heavily favoured the German air force in a four-to-one ratio. For this reason, the flexibility of R.A.F. functional organization today enables Commands to combine for a given operation or series of operations with but slight disturbance of their normal activities. The Luftwaffe method of organization means that increased air pressure can be applied in one direction or area only at the expense of reduced pressure elsewhere.

The German method is at its best in attack. The R.A.F. method is equally good in defence or attack. Once again the meticulous, cast-iron military organization of the Teuton mind will be overthrown by the more flexible mind of the Anglo-Saxon.

American air support could not have dove-tailed into the German plan for organization as smoothly as it dove-tailed into the R.A.F. plan. It is a straightforward proposition for the American air forces in the United Kingdom and abroad to operate functionally together with the British on a basis of mutual cooperation. Already the collaboration has been brilliantly successful, in the Australasian area, in the Atlantic, in Western Europe, in the Mediterranean.

The whole North Atlantic is patrolled by aircraft of the British and American forces. An R.A.F. Coastal Command squadron is based on the U.S. Atlantic coast. Recently a U.S. Navy Air Corps Catalina flying-boat operating from Iceland made its first U-boat kill from that base. The submarine was caught on the surface and so damaged by bombs before it could submerge that it later sank ; 52 prisoners were picked up by a fishing boat and taken over by a destroyer called up by the Catalina's radio.

From bases in the United Kingdom, North Russia, and the west coast of Africa aircraft of Coastal Command search the waters for the under-water enemy.

The whole pattern of the anti-U-boat warfare is closely interlocked from America to Europe, from the Arctic Ocean to the Equator. The sea and air patrol is a contiguous and continuous effort, in which one must mention the notable work of an Australian squadron based in Britain.

While the Germans have thrown their short-range aircraft against Stalingrad, to maintain a continuous round-the-clock offensive, staking 3,000 aircraft in the effort to subdue heroic Russian resistance by weight of metal and explosive dropped from the sky, fired from guns, and driven against the defence positions in the guise of tanks, the far more flexible R.A.F. and United States air forces have been engaged over wide areas, bringing perceptibly nearer, by action after action, the time when United Nations air supremacy will be universal.

Bomber Command struck at the Schneider-Creusot works and Henri-Paul transformer station in Central France with 94 Lancasters just after sunset on Oct. 17, concentrating the whole attack into seven minutes' assault. Flying without escort, low over France, the force suffered the loss of only one Lancaster, possibly blown up by its own bombs dropped from a few hundred feet. This 287-acre factory is the French equivalent of Krupps. Its whole output was destined for Germany.

NOTE that Schneider-Creusot works are conveniently situated to supply Rommel's forces in North Africa, and that Bomber Command's next big attack was against Genoa on the nights of Oct. 22 and 23. Genoa is the main outward port for the Axis Europe-Africa communication line ; it contains Italy's " Krupps "—the Ansaldo works. Savona and Turin were also attacked on the night of Oct. 23 ; on Oct. 24 Lancasters bombed Milan in daylight, and Stirling, Halifax and Wellington bombers continued the attack after dark. Contrasting with these two British attacks were the heavy Axis air attacks on Malta, all indicating air preparations for the battle in North Africa begun on Oct. 23.

THEY BOMBED MILAN BY DAY. Lancaster bomber crews are here seen on their return from the great daylight attack of Oct. 24, 1942. It was Milan's sixth raid, and the first time that our home-based bombers had crossed the Alps in daylight to attack Italy—a round trip of 1,700 miles. Flying very low across France the raiders were enthusiastically greeted as they flashed over. Most of our aircraft dived down below the level of Milan's balloon barrage to release their bombs, and the attack was concentrated into a matter of minutes. Before the last of the crews had reached home, a night attack upon Milan was developing.

Photo, G.P.U.

Learning to Glide to Battle from the Sky

AIRBORNE TROOPS of the British Army train at Army Cooperation Stations where R.A.F. instructors teach N.C.O.s of the Glider Regiment of the Army Air Corps to pilot troop-carrying gliders. 1, Airborne troops entering a glider for a training flight. 2, Photographed from an accompanying aircraft, Hotspur gliders being towed by planes. 3, Men of the Glider Pilots Regiment receiving tuition from the R.A.F. instructors. Map-reading and some navigation are included in the curriculum.

Photos, Planet News, Daily Mirror

THE MOSQUITO, officially described as a reconnaissance bomber, is a product of the de Havilland Aircraft Co., those chiefly responsible for its design being Capt. Geoffrey de Havilland and Messrs. C. C. Walker, R. E. Bishop, and R. M. Clarkson. Believed to be the world's fastest bomber, it is a twin-engined monoplane and—a sensationally novel feature this—is made of wood. It carries a crew of two, and its armament may be four 20-mm. cannon and four 303 machine-guns. It has a span of 54 ft. 2 in., height 15 ft. 3 in., and overall length 40 ft. 9½ in. Mosquitos were first reported in operation on Sept. 25, 1942, when four of these planes bombed the Gestapo H.Q. at Oslo (*see* page 264). This photo (by J. H. Yoxall of *Flight*) of a Mosquito is the first to be released of this aircraft.

Photo, British Official: Crown Copyright

'In This Spirit We Will March to Victory'

OPENING with an acknowledgement of "the honour you have done me and your affectionate welcome," Gen. Smuts in his speech at Westminster on Oct. 21 referred to the presence of Mr. Lloyd George and Mr. Churchill, "the two great actors in the continuing drama of our age." But, he went on, there is a third, and greater, actor—the British people.

The people of this island are the real heroes of this epic world-wide drama, and I pay my small tribute to their unbending, unbreakable spirit . . . I remember this smiling land, recovered and rebuilt after the last war, where a happy people dwelt securely, busy with the tasks and thoughts of peace. And now I have come back to a country over which the fury of war has swept, whose people have had to face in their grimmest mood the most terrible onslaught in its history.

Many of the ancient monuments are damaged or gone for ever. The blitz has passed over cities, ports, churches, temples, humble homes and palaces, House of Parliament and Law Courts. Irreplaceable treasures of a thousand years of almost uninterrupted progress and culture and peaceful civilization have disappeared for ever. War—the horror people still call war, but in its modern scientific form something very different from what passed under that name before—war has come to this favoured land and attempted its worst. Much has gone which is lost for ever.

But one thing is not lost—one thing, the most precious of all, remains and has rather increased. For what will it profit a nation if it wins the world and loses its soul ? The soul remains.

AFTER paying tribute to China, the little nations of Western Europe, Serbia, and "the new glory of Greece which has so effectively dimmed the tinsel grandeur of Mussolini's Rome," Gen. Smuts turned to Russia.

The resistance and magnitude of Russia's resistance have surprised not only Hitler but probably everybody else. Probably no such losses on both sides have ever been suffered in the history of war. If the Russian losses must be terrible, it is equally true that the German Army is bleeding to death in Russia . . . The course for the Allies to follow is clear. Whatever help in whatever form we can give to Russia to sustain her in her colossal effort should be given in fullest measure and with the utmost speed. She is bearing more than her share of the common burden . . .

We have now reached the fourth year of this war, and the defence phase has now ended. The stage is set for the last, the offensive phase. Once the time has come to take the offensive and to strike while the iron is hot it would be folly to delay, to over-prepare, and perhaps miss our opportunity.

GENERAL SMUTS then turned to emphasize the deeper significance of the struggle on which we are engaged. "It is no ordinary political issues that are at stake . . . This at bottom is a war of the spirit, of man's soul."

Hitler has trampled under foot the great faith which has nourished the West and proved the greatest dynamic of all human history and made Western civilization the proudest achievement of man. He has trampled on the Cross and substituted for it the crooked cross, fit symbol for the new devil worship which he has tried to impose on this country and the world. Nietzsche's superman is substituted for the Man of Nazareth as the new leader of the human race and the human advance . . . The real issue has now been made clear. There is a challenge to all we have learnt to value, and to prize even above life itself. Behind all the issues of this war lies the deeper question now posed to the world : which do you choose—the free spirit of man and the moral idealism which has shaped the values and ideas of our civilization, or this horrid substitute, this foul obsession now resuscitated from the under-world of the past ?

This in the last analysis is what this war is about. At bottom, therefore, this war is a new crusade, a new fight to the death for man's rights and liberties, and for the personal ideals of man's ethical and spiritual life. To that Nazi fanaticism we oppose this crusading spirit which will not sheathe the sword till Nazidom and all its works have been purged from this fair world.

And in that spirit the United Nations will march forward to victory and to the world which will follow this victory

THE HOME FRONT

by E. Royston Pike

THAT new London, that new England, that new world! The plans are being poured out now for the things to come after the War. Some are so fanciful as to border on the fantastic, others seem to have little or nothing to do with the everyday needs of the ordinary man, while yet others seem to be inspired by nothing more than the determination to undo and replace everything that the centuries, the scores of active generations, have done. Why, for instance, should the Planning Committee of the Royal Academy, a number of whose designs for the new London are on exhibition now at Burlington House, think that St. Paul's would be improved by having *two* deaneries, *two* chapter-houses, and that Hyde Park Corner would look finer if there was an Apsley House on both sides of Park Lane? Are there to be, then (one is tempted to ask), two Deans of St. Paul's, two Dukes of Wellington? Why, moreover, should Sir Edwin Lutyens and his team of planners favour so decidedly a style of architecture that historically is associated with the blue skies of the Mediterranean, and fill in the gaps of their Italianate creations with monster boxes of steel and concrete such as are among the most vital expressions of American genius? If these plans go through, London, we are assured, will be the world's most beautiful and majestic capital. That is as taste may have it; far more probable is it that the new London would have lost that air of intimacy, that tradition-soaked atmosphere, that easy adaptation of the old to the ever-changing needs of the present, which today give it so much distinction and charm.

BUT it is all to the good that architects and engineers, artists and writers, local councillors and the men in the street should be giving their time and attention to the rebuilding on firmer and fairer lines of the structure blasted by the storms of war. Not that planning is sufficient in itself; it is a delightful exercise, but as Lord Reith said the other day in the House of Lords, when urging the setting up of a Ministry of National Planning and the immediate adoption of the most urgent recommendations of the Scott and Uthwatt Committees, " I am tired of lip-service to dreams of New Jerusalems in what little is left of a once green and pleasant land. New Jerusalems never have and never will come down from heaven, and in no item of very high significance, social, economic or physical, will anything come unless we start building now . . ."

What are the two Committees referred to by Lord Reith? What do they recommend?

The first to report was that presided over by Lord Justice Scott (Report of the Committee on Land Utilization in Rural Areas: Cmd. 6378, H.M.S.O., 2s.). Visualizing the establishment of a central planning authority, the Committee declare that " the land of Britain should be both useful and beautiful." By equalizing economic, social, and educational opportunities in town and country, those who prefer country life will no longer find themselves and their children at a permanent disadvantage; while the growth of industry should be fostered in those areas " where the greatest balance of advantage will result both to the prosperity of industry and to the nation as a whole." As a rule factories should not be established in the villages, although rural trades and crafts should be encouraged. There should be no more building on good agricultural land. Rural housing is a matter of the very first importance; every village should have its playing fields, its social centre, its services.

Also concerned with the proper use of Britain's land was the Committee on Compensation and Betterment, which derives its name from its Chairman, Mr. Justice Uthwatt.

In their Report (Cmd. 6386, H.M.S.O., 2s. 6d.) they do not propose any scheme of nationalization since, in their opinion, this is not a policy to be embarked upon lightly and would arouse political controversy, the financial operations involved might be out of the question in the immediate post-war period, and it would need complicated administrative machinery. But they recommend that the State should acquire all rights of development in land outside built-up areas on payment of fair compensation. No further development would

BRITISH WOMEN WORKERS are urged in this striking poster, issued as part of a safety-at-work campaign, to follow the example of Russian women and wear caps while at work in the factories. *Courtesy of the Ministry of Labour and National Service*

then be permitted without the consent of the State. Thus the development value for all time would be acquired, and compensation would no longer be the hindrance to proper planning that it has been so often and so generally in the past.

So much for the future. But what of the immediate present? We see a Britain well in the stride of war. Never in our history have there been so many people as now engaged in productive employment: as long ago as last June out of a population of thirty-three millions between 14 and 65, twenty-two millions were full-time workers in industry, the armed Forces or Civil Defence. Yet, withal, there is still work for more hands if the hands can be found, somehow, somewhere. Boys of 18 are to join the Army; married women are being steadily drafted into the war factories, and there is talk of taking them for the Services. Labour, announced Mr. Lyttelton, Minister of Production, on Oct. 14, is to be made much more mobile: labour is to be transferred

from less heavily burdened areas to those which can no longer supply from their own local resources the workpeople needed for essential production. Doubtless this may involve inconvenience, hardship and strain, but workpeople (went on Mr. Lyttelton) should remember that all these inconveniences are not to be compared with those which have to be put up with by the soldier. To be transferred from, say, Nottingham to Northern Ireland is not the hardship that a soldier endures when he finds himself transferred to Basra or Cairo.

THEN there is the question of absenteeism. In the past, much of the talk of " those lazy miners " and the like has come from persons who have never handled a pick or shovel in their lives, and to a considerable extent the criticism of industrial absentees is just as ill-conceived. On a rough estimate it is believed that of the six million employees covered by the Essential Work Order about 600,000 may be absent on any one day for various causes, but of these probably two-thirds are away owing to sickness or accident. Transport difficulties are responsible for another considerable section of involuntary absenteeism, although there are innumerable cases of women with children travelling up to three hours a day to their work and another three hours to get home again. Probably, we are told, only two per cent of the absenteeism may be classed as voluntary. And this is now receiving attention.

Talking of accidents, fatal accidents in British factories in 1941 numbered 1,646, an increase of 20 per cent over 1940, and non-fatal accidents numbered 269,652, an increase of 17 per cent. Among adult women workers the approximate accident rate was 18 per thousand women, nearly double the preceding year's figure. The most distressing of these accidents were stated to be those caused by the hair of the women and girls becoming entangled in moving machinery: in 1941 there were 179 accidents due to this cause. Unfortunately, says the Chief Inspector of Factories in his recently issued Report, the modern style of hairdressing does not blend itself to the hair being carefully covered as with a cap, and the fluffy curl still protrudes. Even after a minor scalping accident the same girl was again found without her cap: she said she preferred to have an accident rather than to look a fright. But women are not naturally more prone to accidents than men—rather the reverse. The rise in the figure of women's accidents is attributable to the increased number of women employed, and to their increased share in dangerous processes.

UTILITY furniture is in the news again. From November 1 it is the only kind of furniture that may be manufactured, and the only designs are those which have been registered with the Patent Office by the Board of Trade. Unlike clothing, utility furniture may be bought without coupons, but permits must be obtained, and preference will be given—and altogether rightly—to persons who have been " bombed out " and to newly married couples. Prices of the new furniture have not yet been fixed, nor has it been decided whether purchase tax will be imposed. In its construction only home-grown timber is available, and no plywood could be used, metal springs are scarce, and paints and varnishes are strictly limited. Most of the material used is hard board—a compressed paper and wood pulp mixture, veneered on both sides. The new furniture is not expected to be as durable as that of pre-war production, but it combines strength with a design that is neat and pleasing, and thoroughly in line with the " functionalism " of modern planning.

'Utility' Finds Fresh Fields to Conquer

UTILITY CROCKERY made by Wedgwoods, and so designed as to eliminate unnecessary labour, is devoid of ornamental detail. Each piece can be adapted to serve more than one purpose. Unhandled beakers (left) fit neatly one inside the other. Teapot and jug (above) are so designed as to minimize the risk of breakage.
Photos, Courtesy of Josiah Wedgwood and Sons, Ltd.

WOMEN'S SUITS, designed by the London Society of Fashion Designers, displayed by four mannequins at a Board of Trade show (above): the third from the left is an original West End model, the fourth its mass-produced Utility counterpart. On the left is a Utility stewpan-kettle.

MEN'S SUITS, cut on smart but economical lines, have been shorn of some customary sartorial features. Made in various shades, these suits range in price from 50s. to 5 gns. As will be seen above, the jacket is single-breasted and has no outside breast pocket nor buttons at the wrists. The waistcoat has two pockets, but no buckles. The trousers have no turn-ups or front pleats. "Austerity furniture" is designed on clean, simple lines. Left, a dining-room suite, recently on exhibition at the Building Centre in London.

Photos, Sport & General, Keystone, Topical Press, New York Times Photos

On the Home Front with Our Roving Camera

TRAFALGAR DAY—Oct. 21—was celebrated as usual this year by the Navy League in Trafalgar Square. Adm. Sir. L. Halsey, the King's Naval Equerry, is here seen before the microphone. Behind him stands the First Sea Lord, Adm. Sir D. Pound. British and Allied representatives laid wreaths at the base of Nelson's column.

Mr. Hy. MORGENTHAU, Jnr., Secretary to the U.S. Treasury, who in October came to Britain on an official visit. A publisher by profession, he has occupied the key post in the American financial system since 1934.

3rd Officer Pamela GRACE, a 22-year-old Wren, to whom the award of the M.B.E. (Military) was announced on Oct. 20, 1942. She saved the lives of 30 W.R.N.S. ratings during an air raid on her station.

Maj. G. LLOYD GEORGE, the Minister of Fuel, talks to miners at the Whitburn Colliery during his recent visit to the Durham coalfields. After conferences in Glasgow he declared on October 14 that the coal output was rising and that the decline in coal production, which was noticeable at the beginning of the year, had definitely stopped. Meanwhile, London's winter coal reserves are being accumulated ; on the right is seen a large dump piled up under the trees in Regent's Park.

Photos, Fox, G.P.U., Daily Mirror, Evening News

I WAS THERE!

I Slaved for the Nazis in the Channel Islands

*Just escaped from German tyranny in the Channel Islands, a Frenchwoman,
Mlle. Raymonde, has a revealing story to tell of the hardships endured
by herself and by English civilians under Nazi rule—or rather misrule.
It is reprinted here from The Daily Mail.*

A SHORT time ago I was peeling potatoes for German workers building the defences in the Channel Islands. Now that I have escaped, I can tell my story of life in the only English possession under German rule.

Let me first say how I came to be there. I lived in Eastern France, and had been put by the Germans into one of their clothing factories to make Army uniforms. It was very tiring work. One day in February I saw an advertisement calling for cooks to work for the German authorities in Brittany (in Brittany, you will note, and not the Channel Islands). The payment offered was about 6½d. an hour.

I answered this advertisement, and in due course went to the local commissariat in the town where I lived and signed a contract to work as a cook. I left by rail, and when I reached Brittany I found 16 other women there who had answered the same advertisement. The German authorities met us, and conducted us to a house specially set aside for us. We were given straw palliasses, and a meal of soup and bread, and told to wait further instructions. About ten o'clock, as we were going to bed, German officials of the Todt organization broke into the house and told us to get dressed again as we were going away immediately.

We were then crowded into a German Army lorry and driven through the night for several hours. We finished the journey at a military barracks, where we were kept under guard for the rest of the night. Then, next morning, to our amazement, we were sent to Jersey by boat.

The people I had to cook for were the German labour corps who were building the island defences. They lived in special huts which were built for them, and that is where I cooked. There were about 800 workers, as far as I could tell, with 100 German overseers. In the cookhouse the head chef was a German, helped by two Dutch women, three Spanish women, four English, and twelve French girls.

When I had finished work, which was usually at seven in the evening, I used to go to see two English friends—one of them was a fisherman and the other grew tomatoes.

Jersey Under the Nazis

ANY English people who knew Jersey as a holiday centre would hardly recognize the place today. The holiday hotels are, of course, occupied by the Germans and about every other shop has shut down. Though the English are nominally free, and the young men have not been conscripted, the tempo of life has become very slow and melancholy.

There are still a few English policemen in the streets, and cases which concern the Channel Islanders rather than the Germans are dealt with under peacetime law.

There are very few cars—most of them German—and if you want to travel on the railway you have to show that you are on urgent business. Of course, there is a black-out, and curfew from 10 p.m. to 6 a.m.

There is very little meat, and bread is not too plentiful. The German workers get a bread roll, measuring about a hand's span, to last them three days, and about an eighth of an ounce of butter a day.

My English friends live on potatoes, some fish, and tomatoes, and a few grapes. The English still have more or less the same newspapers to read as they did in peacetime, but they are censored. You can listen only to the German radio because the death penalty threatens anybody who has a private set, so people have to go up to the German post to get any news.

As it happened, none of the Germans in my kitchen could speak French, so I used to tune in to what I said was Radio Paris. It was really the B.B.C. news in French.

THE English get a little tobacco—40 cigarettes and about one-sixth of an ounce of pipe tobacco to last them a fortnight. Milk is short, and fuel is even more so. There is a £5 fine if you pick up a piece of wood in the street.

I am told that the cost of living in the Channel Islands used to be very low. I do not know whether that is still true, for I did not have very much money to spend; but I do know this—that the English in the Channel Islands do not escape income tax these days. They pay tax to the Germans. Moreover, a lot of their villas have been requisitioned. I myself slept in one—on straw spread on the floor.

I was sleeping there on the night of the Dieppe raid. We heard in the evening a rumour that the British had landed at Dunkirk, Dieppe, and Boulogne. I was very excited about this because I was in Dunkirk at the time of the evacuation.

When the Germans first heard about the Dieppe raid they lost their heads, and started issuing contradictory orders. They put the curfew forward by two hours. I talked over with my girl-friend what we should do, and when I came into the streets I wore a little French flag on the lapel of my coat, but put it on upside down to make it look more like the British flag—red, white, and blue instead of blue, white, and red.

A German officer stopped me. "Why are you wearing that?"

"I am French," I said, "and it is the French flag."

"It looks more British than French."

"Anyway, it's better than the swastika!"

At that he tore it off my coat and stamped on it. I made as though to do the same with his badge, and then he struck me, but this wasn't the end of the incident. I complained to the Commandant, and he admitted, "Even if the British invaded the whole of Europe there would still be no excuse for a German hitting a woman."

Meanwhile, the Germans—armed with machine-guns and rifles—were patrolling all the streets and quays. They kept this up until the next day, and gave out that in the event of the English invading they would leave the islands and take the entire population back to Germany with them. I determined there and then to escape. I persuaded a fisherman to get me a seat in his boat.

In the cookhouse we were all working harder than ever. Up at six in the morning, working twelve hours a day with only a quarter of an hour break for lunch, and constantly under the surveillance of armed guards. For lunch we had soup made from

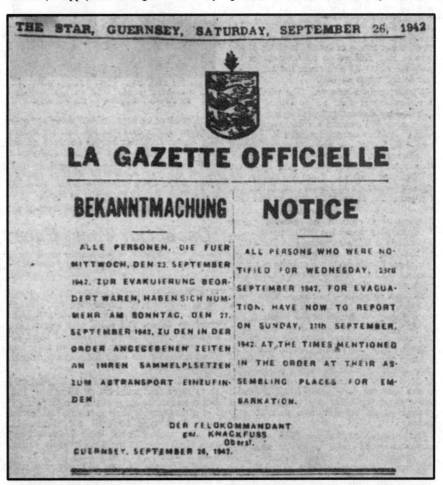

GERMAN PROCLAMATION brought back by Commandos after a small-scale raid on Sark on Oct. 3, 1942; it affords irrefutable proof of the Nazis' compulsory deportation to Germany of many Channel Islanders. This raid, carried out by 10 officers and men, confirmed suspected ill-treatment of British residents. As told in this page, conditions in the Channel Islands have steadily deteriorated since the Nazi occupation.   PAGE 349   *Photo, British Official*

water and a few vegetables. For supper more soup, which was supposed to have meat in it, but I never saw a piece of meat at all in the kitchen where I worked.

One evening I had a message that my fisherman friend would be sailing for England next morning. I got up before dawn, went down to the coast and sat and waited on a rock until he came. He had a nine-foot boat with a small auxiliary motor. We were fifty hours at sea. The weather was very rough,

but I had no time to begin to feel sick, for I was too busy baling water out of the boat. We were eventually spotted by an Air Force launch some miles from the English coast. They came along and picked us up. They gave us some hot meat and dry clothes, and soon we had arrived safely at one of the English ports.

Now I am in the Fighting French Forces, and soon will go to one of your A.T.S. camps to learn to be a driver.

'It Made Me Feel as if I Were in the Abyss of Hell'

Here is the story of how the crew of a torpedoed British tanker were rescued by a Polish freighter during a U-boat attack on an Atlantic convoy. Told by a Polish junior officer on board the freighter, it constitutes a grimly realistic chapter in the long epic of the Atlantic battle.

WE were sailing from America to Britain with a cargo of food and arms. A mid-September night found us somewhere in the North Atlantic, sailing 60 strong in formation. There was another Polish ship in the convoy and a number of Allied ships, but the greater number of the vessels were British.

After my watch I went to my bunk and though I tried not to go to sleep it was not long before I dozed off. As it was an emergency period I slept in my clothes. Only the jacket of my uniform and my life-waistcoat were lying alongside the bunk, so placed that I could jump into them both at once in an emergency.

Suddenly a detonation rent the air. The wall of my cabin trembled. Then a second detonation. A new shaking and more whistling of sirens dragged me to my feet. I shot out of the cabin and fell into the arms of the wireless operator, who was running to wake me up. The first mate and two men, blowing sharp blasts on their whistles, were rushing along the men's quarters. The explosions, the roar of the engine and of the waves, the prospect of being blown up at any moment and sinking to the bottom of the ocean the next—all this made me feel as if I were in the abyss of hell.

It lasted only a minute. The whole crew were standing at their action stations. The Commodore's order, repeated by our master, was short : " Powerful U-boat attack from several points simultaneously ! " In the glare of the fire of our gun salvos we glimpsed the silhouettes of the ships in the convoy. Once more the main attack was from the left, but this time also from the centre. A moment before we had been right in the line of attack, but fortunately they missed us.

SUDDENLY a column of greenish-yellow flame shot up on the left of the convoy, followed by a hollow explosion. We turned our field-glasses in that direction. By the light of the flames we saw a column of smoke shooting up to a height of some 1,000 feet. " It's the tanker Bulysses—she's torpedoed. The cargo of motor spirit is on fire!" was the report of our master. The fire shot up like a geyser. It began at the bowsprit and the forecastle. The after-deck and stern were still all right, and we could see people swarming aft. They were already beginning to lower the lifeboats and to throw out the rafts, and they were signalling accordingly. We were about a thousand yards from them. At this moment the Commodore signalled a course sharp right for the convoy, with a separate signal for us. We were to stay behind.

The engines slowed down. The last of the convoy steamed past. Now to the port side, towards the burning tanker. More explosions. Columns of fire pour into the water, mingle with the waves, or advance in flaming combs. I never lived through such a terrible experience, though I had my baptism of fire at Dunkirk. The wind was

blowing gently, luckily for us, towards the burning vessel and not from it.

Now we could see, on a background of flame, the men leaping into the water. Now the fire began to die down every few minutes, and then to burst out again with a blinding effect. We got quite close to the doomed tanker. We had to go carefully, as in the

Capt. B. LAMB of the ill-fated tanker Bulysses. As recounted in this page, he was rescued by a Polish freighter in the Atlantic.

blinding glare we kept losing sight of the men. We strained our eyes into the swirling waters. The flames from the tanker gleamed on the crest of the waves, but the hull still cast a large shadow. In that blackness we perceived the red flashes of electric torches. Every sailor has a watertight torch, to facilitate finding him in the water at night.

Our orders were to rescue the crew of the

tanker. We lowered the storm-traps overboard. At that moment their lifeboat came alongside. It was a gleaming mass of little red lights, and was obviously overloaded. The master gave orders for the reception of the survivors on board our freighter. One by one they came up the storm-traps. I counted 47 of them, most of them British, but a few Chinese among them. Some of them were wounded, some of them burnt.

We were supposed to take the whole crew on board, but it was easier said than done. Our ship had accommodation and supplies for a crew of 35, and here we had already 47 extra men on our decks. We had to share out our bedding, bunks, food and first-aid supplies. Our first mate was a " hospital " in his own person. We sent off the cook and two men to prepare meals, also tea and rum. We took the tanker's empty lifeboat in tow. The survivors informed us that their crew comprised 61 officers and men. So there were 14 still missing on board the tanker or in the water, including the captain.

WHILE we were pulling the survivors up the storm-traps, in constant fear of a fresh attack, the engines of a plane suddenly roared overhead. It circled round, alarming us considerably, but the wireless officer reassured us : it was a British plane assisting us in looking for survivors. It dropped several flares, and in their light we saw the tanker's second lifeboat and their raft with some people on board. They were drifting with the wind towards the hull of the tanker, although they were making a terrific effort to get away from her. Then some of their crew climbed up on the deck in the hopes of dropping a rope to the raft and dragging it against the wind and out of the smashing blows of the waves. Our master then gave orders to lower our motor-boat. With the greatest difficulty we managed to take off the men both from the lifeboat and the raft.

There were ten of them altogether, including the captain of the tanker, seriously wounded, and a Chinese sailor who was badly burned. It turned out that four members of the crew had perished : the first mate and three Chinese seamen. A torpedo below the watermark had struck the first mate's cabin, and he must have been killed in his sleep, for the captain, who was immediately above him, had barely escaped with his life.

The next day we had to make up lost time and get back to the convoy, when we were able to procure medical assistance for the tanker's survivors. After that fateful night we had ten more days of difficult but uneventful passage before we arrived in Britain.

One of Our Tanks Gave Jerry the Shock of His Life

Typical of the smaller engagements which continually take place in the Western Desert is the following description of a raid on a small desert-fortress as given by L.-Corp. C. J. Wilson.

WHEN the time came for the attack, we went in with fixed bayonets, between our tanks and Bren carriers. We had crept up during the night and had waited impatiently for first light. Isolated machine-gun nests tried to stop us, but we soon had them bolting from their hide-outs with their fingers crossed.

The " Ities " were a scruffy-looking lot and there were fair numbers of Germans, too. But it seemed to me that the " smart guys " had already made their getaway, leaving the slow-witted type to shift for themselves. Without their armour these Nazis seemed very much down in the dumps. Only a party with a machine-gun in a high tower in the centre of the fort kept up any resistance, until a direct hit by a shell stopped their larks.

My section passed through the litter of burned-out enemy tanks and lorries, enlivened

by occasional incidents, when some of the enemy went to ground in odd corners, but we winkled them out and passed them back to other sections detailed to take care of them. About half-a-mile north of the position, we halted in readiness for the counter-attack, but the ground was very rocky and all we could do was to pile up little heaps of stone for cover.

About eight o'clock in the evening the enemy came straight across our front firing high-explosive shells, tracer and incendiary bullets, while his artillery laid down a creeping barrage. Our tanks were in a defensive circle behind us, all round the fort and our field-guns and anti-tank two-pounders banged back shell for shell with interest. Stuff was flying in all directions, but most of the enemy's hits were scored on his own abandoned lorries and dump. For two hours they hammered away and got nowhere, and during the night they suddenly withdrew. When things were quiet six of our men went out with an officer on reconnaissance. They reported considerable moving of guns and transport, so we knew we were for it.

All through the night we watched the enemy's flares put up to keep us under observation, and to guide his planes bombing our transport. During the small hours a weary Italian wandered into our lines, glad to be made a prisoner. At dawn the enemy made another counter-attack, but our tanks gave them such a reception they soon got out of it.

SUDDENLY we spotted four German tanks only 400 yards away coming straight for us. Our chaps were heavily armed with Bren guns, hand grenades, anti-tank grenades, daggers and rifles, so we were confident of giving them a hot welcome. The Jerry tanks stopped, opening fire on a British " I " tank which was standing about forty yards behind us. Their first shell struck the turret and the next three were direct hits, broadside on. Not a sound came from our tank. Everybody inside seemed to be dead. So we settled down to wait for the main effort by the Jerry infantry.

To our astonishment our tank opened up with all he had. The Jerries were evidently as surprised as we were, for they started to withdraw, but our chap stopped two of the enemy retreating machines dead in their tracks, and at 900 yards scored another direct hit on a third, setting it alight. We could hear our tank commander quite plainly, giving the range and fire orders to his gunner. Then we saw the German crews scrambling out of their helpless tanks, and we opened fire on them. Meanwhile, the remaining Jerry tank hopped out of it. Our " I " tank had given them the shock of their lives. It had suffered no serious damage, and all the crew were unharmed. Later one of our officers went over

WRECKED GERMAN TANKS, the result of a fierce engagement such as the one described in this page, litter the sandy wastes of the Western Desert. In the background a Bren gun-carrier crosses the battlefield in the wake of the enemy.
Photo, British Official ; Crown Copyright

to inspect the wrecked German tanks, and found two of the crew dead.

That seemed to discourage Jerry, and the rest of the day passed with nothing but artillery fire from both sides. At night there was the usual display of flares, and some enemy planes came over and bombed not only us but also their own lines, which was all right by us. Next morning, there was no sign of Jerry & Co. on our front. At intervals

long-range shells came lobbing over, and during the morning eighteen German dive-bombers with fighter escort came down out of the sun, giving us a birthday, but they did little damage, and one of the planes, a Messerschmitt, was cut in two by our A.A. fire. As the pilot baled out we noticed two carrier pigeons fly out and make straight back for the enemy's lines. So we had a nice pigeon and bully-beef stew for supper.

OUR DIARY OF THE WAR

OCT. 14, 1942, Wednesday 1,138th day
Sea.—U.S. Navy Dept. announced U.S. submarines had sunk 8 Jap ships in Far East.
Russian Front.—No large-scale engagements on the Stalingrad front ; Germans bombed Grozny area of Caucasus.
Mediterranean.—Over Malta 23 enemy aircraft were destroyed and 30 damaged.
Indian Ocean.—In Madagascar our troops occupied Ambositra.
Australasia.—Jap aircraft twice attacked Guadalcanal airfield, losing 9 bombers and 4 fighters. During night of Oct. 14-15 U.S. positions on Guadalcanal were shelled by Jap warships.
U.S.A.—Liberator bombers raided Kiska.

OCT. 15, Thursday 1,139th day
Air.—Strong force of bombers made night attack on Cologne,
Russian Front.—Fierce fighting again broke out in workers' settlement of Stalingrad.
Mediterranean.—Fourteen enemy aircraft destroyed over Malta.
Australasia.—Jap transports landing large reinforcements on Guadalcanal were attacked by U.S. aircraft.

OCT. 16, Friday 1,140th day
Russian Front.—After heavy German attack, Russians evacuated a factory settlement at Stalingrad.
Mediterranean. — Announced that British submarines had sunk 3 enemy supply ships and torpedoed four others.
Australasia.—Heavier fighting in Owen Stanley area of New Guinea.
U.S.A.—Announced that American ground troops had occupied another of the Andreanof Is. in the Aleutians.

OCT. 17, Saturday 1,141st day
Air.—R.A.F. Lancaster bombers made heavy daylight attack on Schneider armament works at Le Creusot.
Russian Front.—All German attacks at Stalingrad were beaten off.
Africa.—Announced that U.S. troops had arrived in Liberia.
Australasia.—U.S. warships bombarded Jap positions on Guadalcanal.

OCT. 18, Sunday 1,142nd day
Russian Front.—Strong German attacks held at Stalingrad.

Australasia.—Allied Flying Fortresses raided Jap base on Bougainville Is.
U.S.A.—Liberator bombers raided Jap base at Kiska.

OCT. 19, Monday 1,143rd day
Russian Front.—Germans captured block of buildings in Stalingrad.
Africa.—Allied aircraft heavily raided enemy landing grounds and concentrations in Western Desert.
Australasia.—U.S. aircraft bombed Jap installations on Guadalcanal.

OCT. 20, Tuesday 1,144th day
Sea.—Announced that new battleships H.M.S. Howe and H.M.S. Anson had joined the Fleet.
Russian Front.—Two violent German attacks repelled at Stalingrad.
Africa.—Allied air activity in the Western Desert continued on a heavy scale.

OCT. 21, Wednesday 1,145th day
Sea.—U.S. Navy Dept. announced loss of destroyers Meredith and O'Brien by enemy action off the Solomons.
Air.—Mustang fighters raided W. Germany ; U.S. Flying Fortresses bombed submarine base at Lorient.
Russian Front.—Russians reoccupied several buildings in Stalingrad.
Mediterranean.—Announced that British submarines had sunk four Axis supply ships.
Australasia.—American troops repulsed Jap attacks on their positions on Guadalcanal.

OCT. 22, Thursday 1,146th day
Air.—Strong force of R.A.F. bombers raided Genoa by moonlight.
Russian Front.—No fresh ground gained by Germans at Stalingrad. German attempt to land on island in Lake Ladoga routed.
Africa.—Allied air offensive continued against enemy supply columns.
Australasia.—In New Guinea the Australians advanced on Kokoda.

OCT. 23, Friday 1,147th day
Air.—R.A.F. again raided Genoa by night. Savona and Turin also bombed.
Russian Front.—Renewed German attacks beaten off at Stalingrad.
Africa.—During the night Oct. 24-25 the Eighth Army launched offensive at El Alamein.
Australasia.—Allied bombers sank or damaged ten Jap ships at Rabaul.
U.S.A.—Liberator bombers raided Jap submarine base at Kiska.
General.—Mrs. Roosevelt arrived in London.

OCT. 24, Saturday 1,148th day
Air.—Lancaster bombers made daylight raid on Milan, followed by night raids on Milan and other N. Italian cities.
Russian Front.—Germans made slight advance in one sector of Stalingrad.
Africa.—Advanced elements of the Eighth Army penetrated enemy's main positions.
Australasia.—Jap tank and artillery attacks repelled on Guadalcanal.

General.—Bomb explosions in Warsaw killed several German officers.

OCT. 25, Sunday 1,149th day
Sea.—Admiralty announced loss of H.M. trawler Lord Stonehaven.
Russian Front.—Germans occupied two streets in Stalingrad.
Mediterranean.—Announced that British submarines had sunk or damaged 12 Axis supply ships.
Africa.—1,450 Axis prisoners taken in Western Desert fighting.
China.—Allied aircraft bombed Hong Kong.
India.—Jap aircraft raided Chittagong and U.S. aerodromes in Assam.
Australasia.—Japs launched land, air and sea attack against U.S. positions at Guadalcanal.

OCT. 26, Monday 1,150th day
Sea.—U.S. Navy Dept. announced that aircraft-carrier Wasp was sunk by torpedo on Sept. 15 off Guadalcanal.
Russian Front.—Germans drove wedge into Stalingrad defences, but were forced to withdraw after five hours' fighting.
Africa.—Eighth Army extended the area they had occupied in the enemy's defences.
China.—U.S. bombers again raided Hong Kong.
Australasia.—In sea and air battle off Solomons, 2 Jap aircraft-carriers, 2 battleships and 3 cruisers were damaged and 100 aircraft destroyed : U.S. destroyer Porter and aircraft-carrier sunk.

OCT. 27, Tuesday 1,151st day
Air.—Mosquitos of Bomber Command made daylight attack on shipbuilding yards at Flensburg.
Russian Front.—The battle for Stalingrad grew in violence.
Mediterranean. — Allied heavy bombers raided aerodromes in Crete.
Africa.—A tank encounter in the Western Desert resulted in considerable loss to the enemy. German counter-attacks beaten off during the night.
China.—Chinese bombers and fighters raided Jap airfield at Yuncheng.
Australasia.—Japs again pierced American lines in Guadalcanal, but U.S. Army and Marines successfully counter-attacked.
General.—Fifty hostages taken and curfew established in Warsaw as reprisal for bomb attacks.

★ ═══════ **Flash-backs** ═══════ ★

1939

October 14. H.M.S. *Royal Oak* sunk by torpedo in Scapa Flow.

October 16. Cruisers Southampton and Edinburgh and destroyer Mohawk damaged in bombing raids on Firth of Forth.

October 17. Announced that 1st

British Army Corps in France had taken over sector of front.

1940

October 26. Liner *Empress of Britain* bombed and sunk.

1941

October 20. State of siege proclaimed by Stalin in Moscow.

AN interesting point is raised in a letter from a reader (G. W. Hitchings of Deptford), one of several that wrote to me in August 1941 about my article entitled Air Views of Hamburg—What Do They Show? As I expected at the time, my unreadiness to accept, on the strength of two photos released by the M.O.I., the assessment of the "great damage" that had been caused by our raids, was put down to my being no expert in the interpretation of air photos, though I had made microscopic examinations of those in question and applied a fairly observant eye and at least an average intelligence to them. Mr. Hitchings was one of the inexpert critics who agreed with my conclusions and he has recently been reading Assignment to Berlin (Michael Joseph), by Harry W. Flannery, the American correspondent, in which there is a description of Hamburg soon after the raids whose results these two photographs illustrated. Here is Mr. Flannery's impression of the very area as he saw it at that time with his own eyes :

" Before I went to Hamburg I had heard that the damage from bombing was great, and credible witnesses who had been there a few months before said many hits had been made near the railway station, but I saw almost no effects of the R.A.F. raids. The damage near the station had been repaired ; there were no more than half a dozen places damaged around the Binnen Alster and Aussen Alster, and but little evidence of British bombs in that part of the harbour that I could see in a day's ride down the Elbe."

As my correspondent remarks, this would seem to confirm my inexpert reading of the photos ; but, on the other hand, it might also be a tribute to the efficiency of the German camouflage. I still think those particular photos were unconvincing as to the nature of the damage, but I have since examined many later ones of other bombings with much greater satisfaction on account of the unmistakable evidence of damage and, in my opinion, that's the only kind worth publishing. So far I haven't seen as many as I should have liked of the havoc wrought by our thousand-bomber raids, but it may well be that often the scenes where destruction has been greatest are just those most difficult to photograph, since a good result depends so greatly on weather conditions and the lapse of time before the photos can be taken. The Germans are as clever, I'm sure, in concealing the damage as they admittedly are in camouflaging untouched areas.

OF late I have noticed that the old punctilio of saluting is not so much in evidence in the London streets. With the coming of the Americans perhaps the practice is declining through some sort of mutual understanding, or, it may be, that some modification has been tacitly agreed to. I do not know. I can speak only from casual observation. But I do know that the English captain whom I saw this morning in St. James's Street carrying a lady's hat box and two parcels in addition to his swagger stick, which was tucked under his left arm, while his stylish young, high-heeled wife minced along beside him, was in no condition for being saluted by any inferior. I suppose that when an officer turns himself into a lady's lackey his only recourse, should he be about to meet some of the rank and file, is to look the other way ! But I have actually seen a naval officer carrying his cap in his left hand taking the salute from juniors as he walked along Pall Mall in one of the recent rare blinks of sunshine. That seemed to me extremely irregular.

I WONDER if there has been anything at all in the nature of profiteering under the 5s. limit set upon meals in restaurants and hotels. The very considerable "house charge" beyond the 5s. which the West End restaurateurs were officially allowed to charge was taken advantage of to the extreme in some cases. 5s. for dinner and 7s. 6d. house charge simply made a farce of the regulation. But I notice that the Food Control have been looking into this with fairly obvious results here and there. Meanwhile, I have been hearing enthusiastic praise of a certain restaurant known to me in a certain seaside town known to many, where a lunch consisting of a soup, joint, three vegetables, and sweet, is available at 3s. The dinner costs a total of 4s. 6d. And the viands supplied are equal, if not superior to those of the very best West End restaurants. The fare provided at the restaurant in question —and I may say that my informants are connoisseurs—for 3s., compares favourably with an 8s. 6d. lunch in any part of the West End. Even allowing for all the heavy overheads which have to be borne by London restaurants, and the snaffling by income-tax sleuths of all their excess profits, the margin of difference remains considerable, but I will not say excessive.

I HAVE watched with amusement the sudden popularity of the word "allergic." It has been freely (very freely) used in America for some years, but only now is it finding its way into the dictionaries, and meanwhile it is having a jolly time in the vocabulary of many who like to use it but have not troubled to make quite certain of its meaning. A recent example occurs in an explanation by Lord Strabolgi of his ill-considered attack on the high command of the British Army. Lord Lovat's suggestion that a dip in the nearest horse pond would have been a good sort of answer to his fellow peer may have been applauded by some, but Lord Strabolgi might have proved allergic to the dip ! Himself, he says that the clique which controls the British Army is " intensely conservative, allergic to all change and innovation."

HE obviously uses the word here as a synonym for antagonistic or opposed. It is not. Properly it implies a reaction peculiar to a particular individual. Whereas we can most of us eat strawberries, eggs, pork, bananas, and fish without any but good effects, there are certain individuals who react to the point even of illness if they touch one of these foods to which they have developed a perhaps dangerous *allergic* sensitiveness. (It is of topical interest that the Commander of the 8th Army, Gen. Montgomery, is forbidden pork and certain other foods, quite probably because he is allergic to them.) The transfer of the term from the strictly medical sphere to popular use has widened and thereby weakened its application. That proposed dip in the horse pond might have been entirely to Lord Strabolgi's liking, refreshing and invigorating, or it might not. He can hardly be regarded as allergic to it, however, for anyone else might react in the same way to it. The growing popularity of the word will be worth watching, but it looks as though it will wind up in popular usage as a needless substitute for opposed or antagonistic, as used by Lord Strabolgi. But that is the common way of words, for black is originally derived from a word meaning white !

ANOTHER recent letter from South Africa comes from a youthful reader, George Doxey, who is now sixteen and in the matriculation form at his school at Rondebosch, Cape Province. He has been getting THE WAR ILLUSTRATED ever since its first number and tells me that most of the senior boys at his school are regular subscribers. Some of them have even dared to read it during school hours ! "I was witness last week to an amusing sight," he goes on; "a master, noticing a boy trying to conceal something which he had been reading, went to investigate and found it was a copy of THE WAR ILLUSTRATED. But to our amusement, instead of destroying it, as is the fate of all magazines read during class-time, he himself began to read it, evidently thinking that a publication of such interest ought not to be destroyed." It is a further testimony to the efficiency of the protection of the Royal Navy and our postal system that out of all the copies issued at the time of his writing, when No. 132 [July 10] had arrived, only two of the preceding numbers had failed to reach him at Rondebosch on account of enemy action.

'AMERICA'S FIRST LADY,' Mrs. Eleanor Roosevelt, who is not only the wife of her husband, but is famous in her own right as a newspaper columnist and as a wise and witty personality. On Oct. 23 she arrived in London for a short visit. *Photo, Topical Press*

Printed in England and published every alternate Friday by the Proprietors, THE AMALGAMATED PRESS, LTD., The Fleetway House, Farringdon Street, London, E.C.4. Registered for transmission by Canadian Magazine Post. Sole Agents for Australia and New Zealand : Messrs. Gordon & Gotch, Ltd. ; and for South Africa : Central News Agency, Ltd.—November 13, 1942. S.S. *Editorial Address :* JOHN CARPENTER HOUSE, WHITEFRIARS, LONDON, E.C.4.

Vol 6   *The War Illustrated*   Nº 142

Edited by Sir John Hammerton

SIXPENCE   NOVEMBER 27, 1942

CHARGING TO VICTORY IN EGYPT—a photograph taken amid the dust and noise of the terrific battle that began on Oct. 23, and radioed to London from Cairo. It shows Australian troops, covered by a smoke screen, advancing to the assault of an enemy strong-point which has put up a stubborn resistance. Attacked on all sides, taken too by surprise, the defenders surrendered before it came to the bayonet.

Photo British Official : Crown Copyright

NO. 143 WILL BE PUBLISHED FRIDAY, DECEMBER 11

ALONG THE BATTLE FRONTS

by Our Military Critic, Maj.-Gen. Sir Charles Gwynn, K.C.B., D.S.O.

NOVEMBER has again proved to be a black month for Germany and her partners. The amazing victory of the 8th Army, which, at the time I am writing (some three weeks ahead of publishing day), had already achieved outstanding strategical results—securing the safety of the Middle East and laying for ever apprehension of a great pincer attack—promises to have a still greater effect on the general situation. If, as it is justifiable to hope, it will lead to the occupation of the whole of Libya, the effect on sea communications and shipping problems will be far-reaching and therefore immensely improve the capacity of the Allies for offensive action.

Then, at the moment when Rommel had just reached the Libyan frontier in his desperate attempt to concentrate the remains of the Afrika Korps and check pursuit, came the news of the landing of the American Expeditionary Force in Algeria which promises to render Rommel's plight still more hopeless and to extend the effects of the 8th Army's victory over all North Africa.

But it is not only in Egypt that the situation has improved. In Russia, both at Stalingrad and in the Caucasus, the Red Army has shown its power of resilience, and the German offensives which looked so dangerous are becoming festering sores in her outstretched arms.

In the Far East the Australians have won a remarkable success in New Guinea ; and in the Solomons, Japan's attempts to recapture Guadalcanal have entailed losses of ships and aircraft she can ill afford, and have diverted her forces from other theatres, where the Allies can make use of the consequent respite to build up their offensive strength. The situation in the Solomons is still critical, but every week that the Japanese attack can be held relieves tension. Events in Egypt may well have important repercussions in the Far East before even they are fully felt in the European theatre.

EGYPT When I last wrote, the 8th Army offensive had just opened in full blast, though it had actually begun weeks earlier with persistent attacks on Rommel's communications and air force. What was accomplished in the preliminary stages we recognize in the hard disputed air supremacy that has been established, and in the fact that no tanker had reached Libya for six weeks before battle was joined. Furthermore, the full fruits of these activities have not yet been gathered.

I confess that, although I had good hopes that Rommel would be driven out of his defensive lines, yet I did not expect that it would be accomplished so speedily or with such decisive results—results which promise to be even more shattering and far-reaching in their effect than the most sanguine imagination could have pictured.

How was it done ? Speaking broadly, the attack was admirably planned, the staff work above criticism, and the fighting qualities of the troops in courage, dash, and trained skill above praise. The enemy, tied to the defensive, was never allowed to regain the initiative, but was forced to conform to his opponent's moves.

Yet that would not account for the completeness of his defeat, for a skilful general—as Rommel undoubtedly is—can, as a rule,

escape disaster by retreat if he has plenty of room behind him. I cannot help thinking that Rommel, having himself failed to break out of El Alamein bottle-neck, assumed that Montgomery would similarly fail, and, being confident that he would retrieve any temporary loss of ground with his armoured " fist," postponed retreat till too late. Montgomery's tactics, and the superiority of his air arm, however, prevented the " fist " coming into effective action.

It is interesting to compare Montgomery's tactics, when confronted by a position having secure flanks, with those so often employed in the last war. Haig strategically adopted a policy of attrition of Germany's total strength ; but tactically in most of his offensives, until the final stages of the war, he started with an attempt to effect a break-through. When that failed he fell back on tactical attrition. Montgomery, on the

other hand, started his offensive with tactical attrition, reserving his main blow till he had worn through his enemy's defences, and reserved his strength for a final break-through, when it would have decisive strategical results.

There is another point worthy of notice in this connexion.

I have often seen it stated that the good general will look for a soft spot in which to deliver his decisive attack. I have argued that this is seldom true, and that the good general tactically aims at making a soft spot in the place where his decisive attack will produce the most far-reaching result ; and that will seldom be where tactical resistance is likely to be weakest. In this case, Montgomery made his soft spot at the part of the enemy's front tactically strongest, and delivered his decisive attack when the soft spot had been made by preliminary action.

To follow the battle till it became a question of pursuit. At 10 p.m. on Oct. 23, after an all-day bombing of the enemy's airfields and a half-hour hurricane artillery bombardment, the initial attack was launched at a number of points on the whole of the enemy's front—sappers and infantry clearing roads through minefields to enable tanks to get forward to assist in the capture of the enemy's posts and in repelling counter-attacks. A footing in Rommel's forward positions was practically everywhere gained, and the ground captured was consolidated. Objectives were limited, and no attempt at a decisive break-through was made, though tanks in the northern sector, where penetration was deepest, on Oct. 24 went some distance forward.

During the next and following days our troops were mainly engaged in consolidating ground won, in repelling local counter-attacks, and extending their hold by minor operations, generally carried out by night. The weight of the attack was in the north, where the 9th Australian and the 51st Divisions succeeded in making a deep bulge in the enemy's position. This drew the enemy's main armour to the north. On several occasions they threatened to counter-attack in force, but under heavy air and artillery bombardments dispersed.

All this time the enemy were kept under continuous bombardment from air and ground, suffering heavily. No considerable clash of armoured forces took place, though there were some long-range exchanges of fire.

On the night of Oct. 30 the Australians, now deep in the enemy's position, struck northwards to the sea, cutting off the enemy regiment on the coast, and successfully repelled counter-attacks and attempts to

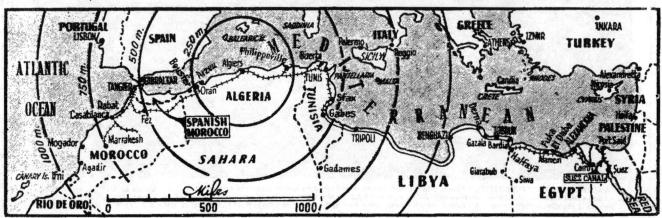

NORTH AFRICA. The scene of vast Allied operations, French Morocco and Algeria became the focus of world attention on Nov. 8, 1942, when numerous and well-equipped U.S. forces, supported by the Royal Navy and the R.A.F., landed at strategic points along the North Atlantic and Mediterranean coasts. Algiers fell on Nov. 8, Oran on Nov. 10, and Casablanca on Nov. 11. Tunisia was invaded by the British 1st Army before the week was out. Thus Rommel's retreating troops were threatened from the rear.

By courtesy of News Chronicle

withdraw the troops in the pocket. What their ultimate fate was we were not told at the time, but probably they found their way to a prisoners-of-war cage.

By now the enemy's defences had been weakened. His reserves had been forced to concentrate on a threatened flank, and his minefields had been penetrated. The time had come for a decisive blow to break through and open a gap through which our armour could pass.

On the night of Nov. 1 the decisive attack was launched, some ten miles south of the coast. By dawn on Nov. 2 the last minefield had been passed and our main armour moved into open country through the gap. Little has yet been told of the tank encounter which then occurred. Apparently, Rommel attempted to concentrate armour and anti-tank guns to close the gap, but was unable to prevent our armour breaking through to the south, where it isolated the whole of the right of Rommel's position, held by five Italian divisions. The attempt to close the gap failed, therefore, and merely offered a target to aircraft and guns.

On Wednesday, Oct. 4, the world heard that Rommel was in full retreat with his transport and wheeled vehicles of all sorts streaming west along the coast road, presenting a target all airmen must dream of—an army in retreat through a congested defile.

Rommel for a time attempted to form an armoured rearguard to cover his retreat, but allotted the duty to the Italian armour; and, abandoning the Italian divisions in the south to their fate, withdrew his badly shattered Afrika Korps at all speed.

Probably he hoped to retain a fist which might strike at his pursuers if they outran their supplies. At least it would form the nucleus of a force which, with reinforcements, might defend Libya. His return to Libya has been faster even than his advance into Egypt, but he will find Libya bare of supplies, especially of petrol, and his air arm and transport services are shattered. Alexander and Montgomery are unlikely to be overawed by Rommel's reputation as a turner of tables. They have far to go before the fruits of their victory can be fully gathered, but their pursuit will lack nothing in vigour nor be checked by any lack of foresight in preparation.

When all have done so magnificently, it would be invidious to offer bouquets; but it should be realized that the foundation of the victory was the infantry who, by closing with the enemy, compelled him to open vulnerable targets to the other arms and confirmed the effects of their action. The infantry's task was the hardest, entailing the greatest risks and the most continuous and arduous effort.

RUSSIA So long as the Germans have a
.... footing in Stalingrad, and show a determination to capture the city at any cost, the danger that they may succeed remains. Yet the danger is no greater and to some extent may be less than it was a fortnight ago. Renewed attacks have been made both in the north-west suburbs and against the city itself; some have been on a small and some on a considerable scale with fresh troops, but none has gained ground permanently. Russian counter-attacks have been more vigorous than ever, and have even recovered positions previously lost. Rein-

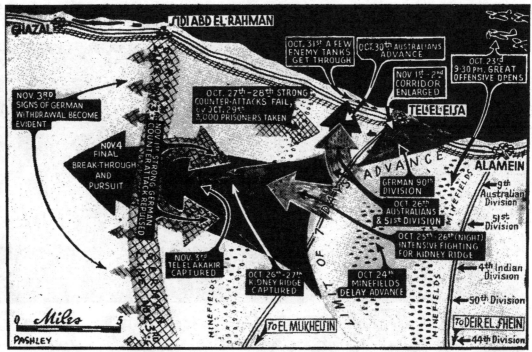

THE BATTLE OF EGYPT, as Mr. Churchill named it in his Mansion House speech on Nov. 10, was "a remarkable and definite victory." Not only were the German and Italian forces thrown out of Egypt, but the enemy's hold upon the whole of N. Africa was threatened. This map shows, as accurately as may be so far ascertained, the successive stages of the Allied drive from El Alamein between Oct. 24 and Nov. 4, 1942.   By courtesy of News Chronicle

forcements have been steadily reaching the garrison, and in some instances have been landed at points where they were able immediately to attack and surprise the enemy. The relief armies continue to maintain pressure and to gain ground.

The German failure to make progress is difficult to explain. It may be that part of the Luftwaffe has been diverted to the Caucasus front, or that there is some shortage of artillery ammunition. One cannot, however, help suspecting that disappointed hopes and the desperate scale of losses have taken some of the fire and determination out of the Nazi troops, while the Russians, knowing that they have time and again stopped the enemy, continually gain confidence that they will do it again. And, moreover, experience has taught them how it can be done.

In the western Caucasus the situation has improved even more than at Stalingrad, for not only has the German drive to Tuapse been halted, but it has lost ground. In the

central Caucasus the situation in the Terek valley looked serious when the Germans launched a new offensive from a point south-west of Mozdok against the weakly held Russian left flank at Nalchik. The attack seems to have come as a surprise, and not only was Nalchik captured but considerable progress was made towards the important town of Ordzhonikidze, the terminus of the great military road across the Caucasus.

It is inconceivable that the Germans intended at this season to attempt to cross the mountains by this road which leads to Tiflis or by the other road leading to Batum on which they gained a footing, for both passes reach an altitude of 9,000 ft., and are already snowbound. On the other hand, the occupation of the Upper Terek valley would have deprived the Russians of a valuable base of operations and source of supplies; and it would provide the Germans with winter shelter. The drive made in formidable force pressed back the Russians, who fought stubborn rearguard actions, until the arrival of reinforcements enabled them to bring it to a standstill. The critical situation now seems to have passed, since, although the Germans in the Mozdok area renewed their attacks, they made no progress.

In the centre and north of the vast Russian front autumn rains have evidently made operations on a large scale by either side impracticable, but when frost sets in there are likely to be developments.

FAR EAST The Australian drive
.... across the Owen Stanley Mountains and their capture of Kokoda was a remarkable achievement, and the prevention of the Japanese attempt to land reinforcements at Buna is an indication of a weakness in Japan's whole strategic situation—the vulnerability of her lines of communication.

In the Solomons Japanese attempts to recapture the Guadalcanal aerodrome have failed, and the American Marines have counterattacked successfully, but the situation cannot be considered entirely satisfactory so long as the Japanese are able to land reinforcements. The Allied air arm is, however, compelling the Japanese fleet to act cautiously.

It was welcome news that the French in Madagascar had at last accepted the inevitable, and agreed to an armistice. General Platt's force has done its work admirably, and its achievement makes a substantial contribution to the general improvement in the strategic situation.

LT.-GEN. S. F. ROWELL, commander of the Allied forces which recaptured Kokoda, New Guinea, on Nov. 2, 1942. On Nov. 8 it was stated that his forces controlled all Papua except areas around Buna and Gona.
Photo, Keystone

Watch the 8th Army Assail Rommel's Lines

The Western Desert sky brilliantly illuminated during the mighty artillery barrage which preceded the great advance on Oct 23.

VIVID and dramatic are the scenes of the Egyptian battle-front which appear in this and the opposite page; they were taken by a corps of 25 sergeant-photographers, members of the A.F.P.U. (Army Film and Photographic Unit). Despite desperate hazards these men roam the battlefields on motor-bicycles, carrying "still" cameras. Most of them were recruited and trained in Britain, and some were newspaper photographers in civil life. Going right into the thick of battle, they have unrivalled opportunities to "shoot" troops in action.

In the earlier campaigns in N. Africa photos were flown to England, and so rapid was the development of "news" that some of these photos became out of date before their arrival. Now, however, radio-transmission is installed in Cairo, and the processes of taking photos on the battlefield, rushing them to the base, developing, printing, captioning, transmitting and distributing them are completed in less than 48 hours. From Cairo there are direct transmissions to London and New York. Inset, A.F.P.U. badge.

THE 8TH ARMY'S ADVANCE IN EGYPT was maintained at tremendous pressure as the shattered enemy columns retreated towards the Libyan frontier. Centre, Allied lorried infantry thrusts relentlessly forward through an Axis minefield in spite of intense shell-fire. Below, a formation of Baltimore bombers, seen through the lower gun-hatch of another aircraft, is leading a violent attack against Axis ground positions. Air pursuit of the enemy greatly contributed to our success.

Photos, British Official

'Action' Photographs Taken at Deadly Hazard

BATTLE-LINE SCENES FROM EGYPT. As a result of the 8th Army's magnificent drive against the Axis forces in the Western Desert, it was stated in Cairo on Nov. 8, 1942, that the number of enemy tanks captured and destroyed possibly reached the total of 500. In the top photograph the survivor of a knocked-out Panzer is surrendering to British infantrymen. Below, our troops are taking shelter behind another wrecked German tank.

Photos, British Official: Crown Copyright

Montgomery to Our Air Forces: 'Quite Magnificent'

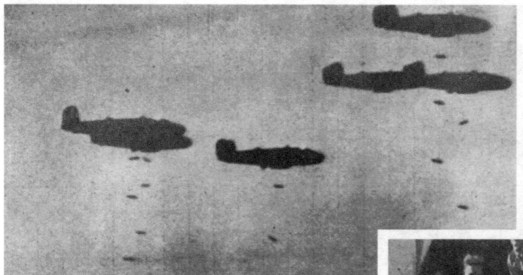

"In this battle," said Gen. Montgomery on Nov. 6, "the 8th Army and the R.A.F. in the Western Desert are a complete entity. Throughout the battle we have been one fighting machine, and that machine has been such that we have finished the Germans here." Left, a formation of R.A.F. B.25s (U.S. Mitchell bombers) drops a shower of bombs with deadly precision.

Although the enemy did his best to challenge our air supremacy over the Egyptian battle area, Air Vice-Marshal Coningham's planes were ever "on top." Below, men of an R.A.F. Fighter-Bomber Squadron discuss their triumphs with the aid of diagrams drawn in the sand. In two days this squadron's "bag" amounted to 11 Stukas destroyed and several more severely damaged.

In the Battle of Egypt heavy toll was taken of Axis aircraft by the Allied air force, on the ground as well as in actual combat. Centre left, cannon shells enter the tail of a Ju.52 military transport plane which has been forced down on an enemy airfield in the desert, and its starboard engine is on fire. A member of the crew is lying on the ground beside it.

Taken from one of the attacking aircraft, the photograph on the left shows an enemy supply train with twenty-six trucks blazing furiously as the result of a devastating swoop by R.A.F. long-distance fighters and S.A.A.F. light bombers behind the enemy's lines in Egypt. An ammunition truck was blown to pieces and the locomotive set ablaze, as our fighters raked the train with cannon fire.

Photos, British Official

How the Correspondents Saw Rommel Crack

When the great Alexander-Montgomery offensive was launched on Oct. 23, the Press correspondents at the front in Egypt had a grandstand view of the tremendous battle. But for days their cables were severely censored (and very rightly). Here, however, we print a number of selections from their dispatches, which leave nothing to be desired in dramatic reporting.

THE evening of Oct. 23, 1942. "Britain's vast new desert Army is looking on at an unforgettable sight," cabled Ralph Walling, Reuters special correspondent; "beneath a bright moon and across the path of the sun, it is seeing score after score of British and American aircraft of the great air striking force fly over the short 70-mile gap separating the Nile Valley and the El Alamein front, and hearing them pound and strafe the enemy." Then the enemy lines were deluged with metal.

Only a few hours ago I saw the beginning of the heaviest concentration of British artillery fire since the battle of the Somme in the last war. A thumping chorus of thousands of shells, fired from hundreds of 25-pounder, medium and heavy guns, is still roaring around us . . .

Ralph N. WALLING (left) and Richard McMILLAN, Special Correspondents of Reuters and B.U.P. in the Western Desert.

Passing through the British lines while all was yet calm, I drove slowly between columns of men muffled to their ears in greatcoats against the sharp desert winter night. As we came nearer the front we seemed to be driving into a massive arc of fire, spurting against the dim skyline with remarkable clarity. There was no smoke to be seen from this distance, only the flashes running along the horizon to and fro as in a tropical storm of unparalleled frenzy.

Twenty minutes after this the infantry went forward, Greeks and Fighting French marching shoulder to shoulder with British forces . . . It was a proud and determined Eighth Army which went into the battle with a resolute spirit.

AND here is a passage from an account by Christopher Buckley, The Daily Telegraph special correspondent.

It was precisely at 9.40 on Friday night that, with a crack and flash, all round the horizon the British guns burst into life. It was an awe-inspiring experience. I was standing outside the Highlanders' H.Q. Zero hour for the infantry was 10 p.m. As I waited, column after column of khaki-clad figures tramped past me in the moonlight. They had packs on their backs and they carried trenching tools. Their bayonets were fixed. Surprisingly, bayonets do not "gleam in the moonlight." Here and there one carried a large square tin which would be used for containing a flare. They moved forward grimly, silently. There wasn't a word spoken as they passed.

From the sea to the Qattara Depression the battle was joined. F. G. H. Salusbury of the Daily Herald vividly described the infantry assault.

They all walked forward behind their screen of fire under the moon into a wilderness of mines and a venomous welcome of bullets and shells. Some of the mines were touched off by unlucky men; others staggered under the lash of projectiles, fell, and rolled over in the sand, spilling their lives and blood. And the artillery rolled on . . .

Perhaps the most dramatic moment of the night was when I encountered a force of our tanks taking up their positions. They came at me out of the moon haze with a whisper of sound that swelled to a roar and the peculiar dry rattle of tracked vehicles on sand ; and they went by like monstrous horses with men riding high on them, and leaning back out of the turrets as if they were in saddles.

A dramatic detail was given by Richard McMillan, the British United Press correspondent, who advanced with the crack 51st Highland Division.

The skirl of bagpipes playing "Highland Laddie" and "Wi' a hundred pipers and a'" sounded in the moonlit night just before our attack opened on the German lines at El Alamein. The pipes were suddenly drowned by the biggest blast ever heard on this front as the British barrage opened with a terrifying roar from hundreds of guns . . .

FOR days the battle continued as Montgomery's infantry fought their way forward, step by step. On Oct. 30 there was another full-scale assault, preceded by another terrific artillery barrage rivalling that which opened the offensive a week before. William Munday of the News Chronicle wrote :

I had driven at dusk into what had previously been enemy lines. The scenery here was never very much, but now the landscape was ripped and torn as if a million madmen with steam shovels had been let loose there during the night. That is what our guns had done.

Germans and Italians had lived here until, at 10 p.m., the desultory crack of a gun here and there suddenly roared into a tornado of splintering steel right back behind the forward enemy troops, putting a curtain of death between them and retreat.

Gradually the guns shortened their range, and every bursting shell shepherded enemy troops nearer and, finally right into the arms of those holding the front opposite them. Meanwhile, others of our units were sweeping around behind them to chop off the salient.

Came a pause, a brief lull ; then, in the early hours of Nov. 3 the infantry went over the top again to break through Rommel's defences, to establish a bridgehead in the coastal sector.

I watched the battle begin, said Edwin Tetlow, Daily Mail's special correspondent, from hastily dug cover in the bare desert near Divisional Headquarters, from which units of our shock

William FORREST (left) and William MUNDAY, war correspondents of the News Chronicle at the front in Egypt.

troops were being directed into battle. The barrage was more concentrated than any we have yet put up, and that is concentrated indeed. . . . It would have been a great tonic for the arms workers of Britain, America, and other armament countries if they could have been here as the moon rose this morning and watched the magnificent results of their labours in the workshops. Three parts of the horizon around this spot became studded from zero hour on with leaping tongues of yellow flame. The desert shook with a succession of cracks and rumblings, and the air echoed the whistle and whine of scores of shells per minute passing towards the enemy's positions around. This nerve-deadening noise and amazing sight went on unbroken for five hours.

Meanwhile, towards the west, our highly-trained shock troops—sappers and lorry-borne specialists—were boring across No-Man's Land and beating out a path for our armour. . . . As the battle developed during the hours before dawn, the struggle with the enemy became ever more fierce, when he rallied from his surprise and began sternly to dispute possession of every inch of defended ground . . .

Rueters Ralph Walling was there, too, watching our tanks tunnelling forward.

The armoured formation—this *corps d'élite* of the British Army—was a formidably impressive sight, moving forward along the desert tracks almost wheel to wheel and gradually emerging on to the edge of the battlefield. A steady artillery fire which had opened up some hours before the advance was pricking the dark clouds to westward. As our leading armoured giants followed up, the Axis forces sent up chandeliers of flares into the sky to catch a glimpse of what was happening.

Edwin TETLOW (left) and F. G. H. SALUSBURY, representatives of the Daily Mail and the Daily Herald respectively.

Beneath their pale glare the infantry wormed forward, tearing and hacking at the fresh and hastily-placed wire, while engineer companies prodded and searched for scattered mines . . . The bridgehead was cut in one final sweep by our infantry after the gallant Australians had driven a salient northwards towards the coast . . . just deep enough and no more. It is a dusty, smoky hell on both sides and at the far end, where no one is welcome who has not a job to do with knocking out German tanks and anti-tank guns.

On Nov. 3 a break-through of the enemy lines proper had been achieved after very hard fighting against a very stubborn enemy, wrote Eric Lloyd Williams, Reuters Special Correspondent at a forward aerodrome.

First signs of the Axis rout were reported back to this aerodrome early this afternoon when a message flashed from the Eighth Army's land forces announced that the enemy was beginning to fall back towards the west. It was the moment for the Allied forces to strike. The call went to the squadrons to "send in every available bomber and every available fighter . . ."

Great dust plumes rose as one plane after another took off heading west with throttles wide open. Down on the aerodromes tired ground crews, the sweat running down their faces grimed with oil and dust, paused for a few seconds in their work to give the "thumbs up" sign to the pilots. Everyone was in on this great show. British airmen, Americans at their aerodromes where the stars and stripes fluttered in the dust clouds, Australians, South Africans—every squadron mustered every possible plane, loaded them with bombs and sent them in to pound the enemy . . . One British fighter pilot, newly returned from strafing a road, said : There's very little future in being a German this afternoon.

AFTER the break-through, General Montgomery was able to spare a few minutes to tell the correspondents something of how the victory had been won. The meeting was described in vivid phrases by William Forrest of the News Chronicle. Coming out of his tent with a tank beret on his head, General Montgomery told the pressmen that "the Boche is completely finished. Those portions of the enemy's forces which have not got away are trying to do so. They are in full retreat. Those that cannot, are facing our troops, and the whole lot will soon be in the bag . . . When the battle began I hardly hoped for such complete victory after only twelve days of fighting, but there it is—he's absolutely finished."

BATTLESHIPS IN MINIATURE, as corvettes have been aptly termed, are among the 800 warships and auxiliaries which are engaged in the grim struggle to keep our merchantmen plying back and forth with their vital cargoes. Sturdy little escort vessels built on whale-catcher lines, the corvettes are fast and well armed, particularly seaworthy, and comparatively quickly and cheaply built. In this page a vessel of the corvette type is shown carrying out a job of work.

A torpedo-carrying Heinkel III has been shot down during an attack on the convoy. As the merchant ships press onwards, the escort vessel stops to lower away a boat, which will pick up the German airman, whose inflated rubber dinghy has become swamped (1).

During the lull the messman carries round to the gunners and lookouts a pail of hot tea (2). He is seen dishing it out to the crew of the forward 4-in. gun. This is a dual-purpose weapon, and the shells to feed it can be seen ranged on racks on the semi-circular gun platform (3). On the high lookout platform two sailors keep watch against a fresh attack, whilst a third changes ammunition drums on the A.A. machine-guns (4).

Below this group is the signalling platform leading from the navigating bridge. Here is seen the ship's captain as he keeps watch (5). Within the square superstructure are wheel-house, chart-house, compass platform, etc., and on either side are other A.A. machine-gun posts manned by steel-helmeted, duffle-smocked mate-lots (6). The tea is brewed in the galley, the position of which is revealed by the tall "stove pipe," between bridge and funnel (7). On the forward face of the funnel can be seen one of the twin sirens used for signalling, etc. Ventilator cowls (8) are

from the engine-room down below, where the oil-burning furnaces are located. Aft of the funnel is the searchlight platform, then the Jack-staff with White Ensign and the Carley floats (9) ready to be launched down the curved runners should emergency demand. The crews of the two pom-pom guns are on the alert (10). Note the ammunition lockers (11), between which a gangway descends to the deck. Here can be seen a minia-ture edition of the "Chicago Pianos" on large warships. This one is a multiple A.A. M.G. (12). When a U-boat is detected the crews swing a depth-charge on to the thrower (13), and many more can be seen stacked in the stern chute (14).

Specially drawn for THE WAR ILLUSTRATED *by Haworth*

THE WAR AT SEA

by Francis E. McMurtrie

NEWS of the first importance was received from French North Africa on Nov. 8. Under the protection of the Royal and the U.S. Navies American troops have occupied the principal ports of Algeria and French Morocco. They may now be expected to advance through Tunisia to attack Rommel's army in the rear. Though French warships and coastal batteries at Casablanca and Oran offered some resistance, this was overcome and both ports surrendered.

This successful undertaking has been one of the greatest feats of organization in British naval history, involving as it did the secret assembly and safe escort to their destinations of hundreds of transports and supply ships. Everything was accomplished promptly to schedule. Yet the Germans seem to have imagined that our shipping losses had been altogether too severe for such an enterprise to be feasible. This gives a clear illustration of the value of sea power. It has enabled fresh military forces to be thrown suddenly into action at points where their arrival could not have been foreseen, thus giving the inestimable advantage of surprise.

IT is to sea power also that we owe our resounding victory over the Axis armies in Egypt. Without the Royal Navy that victory could never have been achieved. Every soldier, every tank, every gun, and every ton of ammunition used by General Montgomery to defeat Rommel ; and all the petrol and most of the aircraft employed by Air Marshal Coningham to the same end, had to be transported to the theatre of operations by sea.

Except for a small proportion landed at a West African port to find their way across the continent, the bulk of these troops, planes and supplies had to be brought to the ports of Egypt via the Cape of Good Hope, a route fully 11,000 miles in length. In vain have German, Italian and Japanese submarines tried to stem this steady stream of traffic. Losses there doubtless have been, but their importance has not been such as to interfere with the programme. Without the protection afforded by the Navy it would have been a hopeless enterprise to dispatch troops and supplies over such an immense distance. Recently German commentators have endeavoured to make the most of U-boat attacks upon shipping on the Cape route, suggesting that they have misgivings as to their efficacy.

With the surrender of the last remnant of Vichy's troops in Madagascar, all prospect of Axis submarines making further use of the ports of that island has vanished. It is understood that the islands of the Comoro group, at the northern end of the Mozambique Channel, have also been brought under British control.

In these circumstances it is questionable if the enemy can find a secure lurking-place anywhere on the African coast south of the Equator. Suggestions that use might be made of such remote and desolate spots as Gough Island or Bouvet Island, on the fringe of the Antarctic regions, carry no conviction. It is far more likely that U-boats are seeking to maintain themselves on these distant stations with the aid of supply ships hiding in the less-frequented sections of the South Atlantic and Indian Ocean, well away from the trade routes. In the past such ships have occasionally been intercepted and destroyed by British cruisers, which may be relied on to hunt them down in time.

In the Mediterranean the work of British submarines in stopping supplies on the short sea routes from Italy and Greece to Libya has been beyond all praise. It has been stated that for six weeks only a single enemy tanker succeeded in getting through, and she was bombed and sunk on arrival at Benghazi.

H.M.S. LIGHTNING. Though destroyers of the Lightning class have been in service for 18 months or more, this is the first photo of the type to be released. In general appearance this design is an enlargement of that of the Javelin type that preceded it. Displacement has gone up from 1,690 tons to 1,920 tons, and dimensions compare thus : Lightning type, length 354 ft., beam 37 ft., draught 10 ft. ; Javelin type, length 348 ft., beam 35 ft., draught 9 ft. Part of the extra weight is absorbed by the gun mountings, the main armament of six 4·7-in. weapons being housed in turrets of more massive pattern than the Javelin's. As will be seen, these can be used with a high angle of elevation. Bigger boilers and more powerful turbine engines are another factor that absorbs weight. The Lightning can develop 48,000 shaft horse-power, equal to 36·5 knots, as compared with 40,000 S.H.P. and 36 knots in the Javelin. *Photo, Central Press*

Aircraft of the Fleet Air Arm and R.A.F. have also done their part in attacking enemy convoys bound for North Africa.

There are indications that shortage of petrol and oil fuel had an important bearing on the Axis defeat, and these are probably well founded.

Increasing Threat to Italy

IF the campaign continues to progress as favourably as it has done so far, it looks as though it would not be long before the Germans and Italians are expelled from North Africa. We shall then be free to concentrate our energies on attacking Italy in earnest, and it is difficult to imagine that the junior partner in the Axis will long be able to stand the strain.

With all the landing-fields they need on the southern shores of the Mediterranean, our aircraft will be able to make ceaseless attacks on the ports of Sicily and Southern Italy and on coastal shipping. Taranto, the harbour in which the Navy's torpedo aircraft crippled the flower of the Italian Navy in a night attack two years ago, will become untenable, and Italy's fleet will either have to proceed to sea and fight for its existence, or retreat into the recesses of the Adriatic.

Malta, the "unsinkable aircraft carrier " as our enemies have termed it, will be relieved of the pressure which it has so long withstood, and will be in a position to retaliate on its attackers. In the natural course of events we shall be enabled to resume regular sea traffic through the Mediterranean, greatly shortening the time of transit of troops and supplies bound for India and for Russia via the Persian Gulf.

Our foes are perfectly well aware of the consequences which are likely to flow from their final defeat in North Africa ; and we must be prepared to meet the most desperate efforts to avert such a contingency.

Struggle for the Solomons

IN the Pacific the struggle for the Solomon Islands continues without any decided advantage having accrued to either side. In the sea and air action fought to the eastward of the Stewart Islands on October 26 severe damage is believed to have been inflicted on the Japanese aircraft carriers Syokaku and Zuikaku, of 20,000 tons, both being hit repeatedly by heavy bombs. Two enemy battleships and three cruisers also received hits on this occasion. In further fighting, two and possibly three Japanese destroyers were sunk.

On the other hand, in an encounter off the Santa Cruz Islands, some 50 miles or more to the eastward of the Solomons, an American destroyer, the Porter, was sunk, and an aircraft-carrier torpedoed. Having been severely damaged below the waterline, the latter ship was too badly damaged to be saved, and was therefore sunk by order from the Commander-in-Chief of the U.S. Navy in Washington, Admiral Ernest J. King. Her name had not been published up to Nov. 8, but she was presumably either the Ranger, of 14,500 tons ; the Hornet or Enterprise, each of 20,000 tons ; or the Saratoga, of 33,000 tons.

That damage almost if not quite as severe was inflicted on the enemy aircraft-carriers on the same day may be inferred from the fact that the bulk of the Japanese forces withdrew from the scene of action and have not displayed equal activity since.

In Mid-Ocean a Tanker Was Set Ablaze

TORPEDOED IN THE ATLANTIC by an enemy submarine, the crew of an American tanker fought a desperate battle indeed. In order to keep the vessel on an even keel, oil was pumped into the sea, and after a long and dangerous struggle the fire was subdued. The tanker was then towed by a U.S. warship to an American port. Top left, two members of the crew pumping oil into the sea. Top right, ship's carpenter fighting oncoming flames. Below, the tanker enveloped in smoke.

Photos. Planet News

Where the Americans Landed in North Africa

FRENCH N. AFRICA was invaded by American troops on Sunday, Nov. 8. One of the places seized was Rabat (left photo) ; on Nov. 9 it was stated that the airfield had been captured by U.S. forces. Right, Algiers harbour, into which on Nov. 9 an Anglo-American naval force sailed and landed reinforcements of U.S. infantry and R.A.F. personnel, the latter taking over airfields captured in earlier landings. The three photos (top inset) show prominent U.S. commanders in the N. African campaign. Left to right : Lt.-Gen. D. D. EISENHOWER, C.-in-C. Allied forces ; Lt.-Gen. M. W. CLARK, Deputy C.-in-C. ; Brig.-Gen. J. H. DOOLITTLE, Commanding General, U.S. 12th Air Force, Allied Expeditionary Force.

PRESIDENT ROOSEVELT TO THE FRENCH PEOPLE

MY FRIENDS, who suffer day and night under the overwhelming yoke of the Nazi. I speak to you as one who was in France in 1918 with your army and your navy. I have preserved throughout my life a profound friendship for the whole French people. I retain and carefully cherish hundreds of French friends in France and outside France . . . I salute again, and I declare again and again my faith in liberty, equality, and fraternity . . .

We are coming among you to repulse the cruel invaders who wish to strip you forever of the right to govern yourselves, to deprive you of the right to worship God as you wish and to snatch from you the right to live your lives in peace and security. We are coming among you solely to crush and destroy your enemies. Believe us, we do not wish to do you any harm. We assure you that once the threat of Germany and Italy has been removed from you we will immediately leave your territory . . . Do not, I beg of you, hinder this great purpose. Render your assistance, my friends, where you can. Long live eternal France !

ORAN harbour (above). Following a number of U.S. landings east and west of the naval base at Oran, Vichy reported on Nov. 9 that the port was "almost encircled," and on Nov. 10 it surrendered.

CASABLANCA (left), French naval base on the Atlantic, was attacked by the Anglo-American armada on Nov. 8. French naval forces put up a strong resistance, but this ceased when a number of small ships had been sunk and the battleship Jean Bart hit by dive-bombers and left a burning hulk. On Nov. 11 the town capitulated.

Photos, Sport & General, Planet News, Associated Press, E.N.A., Paul Popper

What the Germans Have Won in Russia

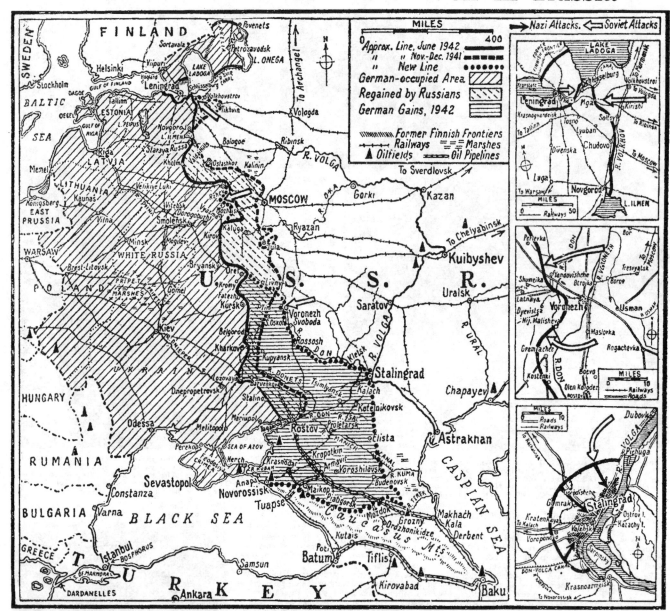

IN RUSSIA DURING 1942, though the Germans gained considerable territory, particularly in the south-east, their successes were not to be compared with those they achieved in the previous year. In this map the horizontally shaded areas show the enemy's advance from June 1942 up to mid-Oct. 1942. A key to the shaded areas is inserted: the "German-occupied area" is that overrun by June of this year. In the three larger-scale maps on the right, arrows mark the direction of the German and Russian attacks on the Leningrad, Voronezh, and Stalingrad fronts. During the autumn of 1942 the enemy's main thrusts were concentrated upon Stalingrad and the Caucasus.

By courtesy of Free Europe

REINFORCING THE DEFENDERS OF STALINGRAD who hold the front line in the battered city, these Red Army troops are seen marching through a street that is partially blocked by debris from devastated houses. Stalingrad's streets rapidly became a series of "communication trenches" leading to the actual fighting line. The desperate battle for the key-city on the banks of the Volga which opened in August 1942 has seen the bitterest fighting of the war.

Photo, News Chronicle

Battle in the Snowbound Passes of the Caucasus

IN S.E. RUSSIA. 1, Red Army automatic riflemen on patrol among the snow-covered heights of Northern Caucasia. 2, Russian infantry in action near Mozdok, through which runs the oil pipe-line from Grozny to Rostov. 3, Weary units of a German advance column entering a Soviet village. 4, Russian prisoners of war transporting munitions and supplies over the mountains for their Nazi captors. 5, Soviet ambulance on the Georgian Military Highway.

Photos. 1, Exclusive to THE WAR ILLUSTRATED; 2 and 5, U.S.S.R. Official. 3, Associated Press, 4, Keystone.

Anson and Howe: Our Two Newest Battleships

With the release of their photographs, the fact has been made public that two sister-ships of
H.M.S. King George V and H.M.S. Duke of York are in full commission with the Royal Navy.
Below FRANCIS E. McMURTRIE provides a descriptive appreciation of these latest and most
powerful additions to our sea power.

THERE is little prospect of H.M.Ss. Anson and Howe being used in a full-scale naval action such as Jutland. Germany's resources in capital ships do not amount to much, comprising merely the huge Tirpitz, the battered Scharnhorst and Gneisenau (both under refit), and the so-called "pocket battleships" Lützow and Admiral Scheer, which are really glorified armoured cruisers. As the ill-fated cruise of the Bismarck demonstrated, the enemy plan is to use these powerful units as commerce destroyers, if and when they can slip out of port unobserved.

This in turn implies that our own capital ships will be employed to a large extent as heavy escort vessels. It is understood, indeed, that the Anson formed part of the escort under Rear-Admiral R. L. Burnett which took an important convoy through to North Russia in September. It will also be recalled that when the Bismarck made her dramatic appearance in the Atlantic in May, 1941, at least two British battleships, the Rodney and Ramillies, were officially stated to have been engaged on convoy duties.

Future Role of Capital Ships

A similar situation existed in 1918, when the Germans, after raiding Norwegian convoys first with destroyers and then with cruisers, threatened to employ capital ships in such attacks. This threat was promptly countered by adding battleships to the escorts. There is, however, this difference in the present position. In 1918 there was still a possibility, though remote, of another fleet action. Such a contingency can hardly be envisaged today.

When this war is over there is no doubt that a new conception of the capital ship will have been formulated. So long as the battleship combined the strongest offensive qualities with the maximum degree of passive defence, there was no need for any radical alteration in design. But the fate of H.M.Ss. Prince of Wales and Repulse has shown clearly that battleships cannot be regarded as invulnerable to air attack with torpedoes unless they can be afforded fighter protection. Clearly, therefore, a new type of capital ship is required. This may embody, in addition to certain existing features of the present type, the ability to carry its own fighter escort.

Armament and Armour

Without probing further into the future, the fact remains that the Anson and Howe are large and powerful fighting ships, which can be relied on to give a good account of themselves in action. In design they are identical with King George V and Duke of York, all having been laid down in 1937; but they include sundry improvements in detail dictated by recent experience.

On a displacement of 35,000 tons, each ship mounts a main armament of ten 14-inch guns. Eight of these are in two quadruple turrets, one forward and one aft. The remaining pair are carried in a smaller turret immediately abaft the big forward turret, but on a higher level, so that there may be no interference with their field of fire. This ingenious disposition of the heavy guns effects a considerable saving in weight as compared with either eight guns in four turrets, as in the Tirpitz, or nine in three turrets, as in the Scharnhorst design. Desire to save weight also influenced the choice of the 14-inch calibre. Though it fires a lighter projectile, this gun has an effective range greater than the 15-inch mounted in earlier ships, as measured by the perforation of any given thickness of armour.

As secondary armament there are mounted in pairs on either beam a total of sixteen 5·25-in. guns. These are what is known as "dual purpose" guns, meaning that they can be employed either at low angles against targets on the same level, or at high angles against aircraft. It carries four multiple pom-poms and a number of machine-guns, etc.

A special feature of the design is enhanced defence against air attack, in the shape of more extensive distribution of deck and side armour, more elaborate subdivision, and an improved system of under-water protection. It has been stated unofficially that the total weight of the armour is over 14,000 tons, and that its thickness on the waterline is 16 inches.

Four aircraft and a catapult are included in the equipment. Propelling machinery consists of geared turbines of the Parsons type, driving four shafts. The total shaft horse-power is 152,000, equal to a speed of over 30 knots. Steam is provided by oil-fired watertube boilers of the Admiralty three-drum type.

Originally the Anson was to have been named Jellicoe, but the name was changed in Feb. 1940 after H.M.S. Duke of York had assumed her present name instead of Anson. At the same time the Howe was given that name in place of Beatty, the one first assigned to her.

Ansons of Bygone Days

Both names have considerable history behind them. The first Anson was launched at Bursledon, Hants, in 1747, a 60-gun ship. The second was a 95-ton cutter, and the third a 64-gun ship which fought under Rodney at the Battle of the Saints in 1782. Reduced to a frigate in 1794, she served with credit during the next dozen years, including the action in which a French squadron was destroyed by Sir John Warren off Tory Island in 1798. She was wrecked in Mounts Bay in 1807.

Another Anson, of 74 guns, was launched in 1812 and lasted until 1851. She was succeeded by a steam 90-gun ship launched at Woolwich in 1860, which was later re-named Algiers. The sixth ship was a battleship of 10,600 tons, launched at Pembroke in 1886; she was sold for scrap in 1909.

All these ships were named in commemoration of the services of the old sea-dog Admiral of the Fleet George, Lord Anson (1697-1762), who, as a commodore in the Centurion, took a squadron into the Pacific to attack Spanish possessions there. With indomitable resolution he carried through this enterprise in the face of great misfortunes, which involved the loss of all his ships but the one named above. After harrying the Spaniards in South America, he captured the Acapulco galleon, full of treasure, and returned by way of the Indian Ocean and Cape of Good Hope, having circumnavigated the world. He later defeated the French at the Battle of Finisterre, and for the last dozen years of his life was First Lord of the Admiralty.

Admiral of the Fleet Richard, Earl Howe (1726-99), affectionately known as "Black Dick," gave his name to three ships previous to the present one. These were launched in 1815, 1860 and 1885 respectively, the third being a sister ship of the sixth Anson. It was Howe who won the victory over the French on "the Glorious First of June" in 1794.

In the Royal Navy tradition counts for more than in any other Service, and names such as these do much to perpetuate it.

MEN WHO BUILT H.M.S. HOWE are seen leaving the battleship on her completion. As recounted in this page, the Howe and her sister ship, the Anson, both belonging to the King George V class, are two of Britain's latest and most powerful warships.
Photo, British Official: Crown Copyright

Since 1747 the fame of the old seadog Admiral Lord Anson, whose portrait by Reynolds is on the left, has been kept green by a succession of ships bearing his name. Above is the sixth H.M.S. Anson, a battleship of 10,600 tons, launched in 1886

Anson: Latest of a Glorious Line

Laid down in July 1937, the seventh H.M.S. Anson was built by Swan Hunter on the Tyne; the news that she was at sea with the Fleet was released on Trafalgar Day 1942. She is what is called a "Chatham ship," but included in her complement are men from all parts of the world. Circle, her commanding officer, Captain H. R. G. Kinahan, C.B.E., R.N.

The Incomparable Air Photograph of the War!

One Saturday afternoon in October, 94 R.A.F. Lancasters set out to bomb the Schneider armament works at Le Creusot, 170 miles south-east of Paris. In this photograph—one which merits, if ever photograph did, the adjective " unique "— taken from one of the Lancasters engaged, 47 of the raiding force may be counted as they roar over the pleasant little town of Montrichard, on the Cher, a tributary of the Loire, less than thirty minutes' flying time from their target.

Lancasters Carrying Destruction to Le Creusot

At 6.9 p.m. they were due over Le Creusot. At 6.9 the first of them arrived, and at intervals of 4½ seconds one after another of the giant aircraft went in to bomb. Never in daylight had such a raid been attempted before; rarely has a raid been so successful. In seven minutes one of the world's greatest armament works, one of Hitler's most vital war factories, was a blazing ruin (*see* photo in page 375). Only one of the 94 aircraft taking part in the raid failed to return.

Like the Anson, H.M.S. Howe commemorates a famous sea captain of the past—Admiral Earl Howe ; his portrait by Copley is on the right. The first Howe was launched in 1815 ; above is No. 3, a sister-ship of the 6th Anson, launched in 1885.

Howe: Inheritor of a Grand Tradition

A month before her sister ship the Anson, H.M.S. Howe was laid down in the yards of the Fairfield Shipbuilding and Engineering Co. on the Clyde ; it is now revealed she is actually in commission. Circle, her commanding officer, Captain G. H. L. Woodhouse, C.B., R.N., who commanded the Ajax at the Battle of the River Plate in December 1939.

*Photos, British Official ; Rischgitz Studios.
Badge by permission of H.M.S.O.*

Churchill Reveals Secrets of the Battle of Egypt

When the House of Commons assembled on Nov. 11 for a new session Mr. Churchill delivered a review of the dramatic changes which had so recently transformed the whole aspect of the war. He spoke of Russia and North Africa, of France and the Second Front, but for the most part his inspiring utterance was devoted to an account of the great victory in Egypt. From this portion of his speech the following most impressive passages are extracted.

I HAVE to tell the House about the great battle of Egypt, a British victory of the first order. There are three points which must be duly examined in matters of this magnitude and violence—first, the time required for preparation ; secondly, the need of combination and concert ; and thirdly, the importance of surprise.

Taking the question of the time, it is not generally realized how much time these great operations take to mount. For instance, the British divisions which have reinforced the Eighth Army for this battle left England in May or early June. Most of the 6-pounders we are now and have been using in so many hundreds were dispatched before the fall of Tobruk. This also applies to the more heavily armoured British tanks and the more heavily gunned British tanks.

As for the American tanks, the admirable Shermans, they came to us in the following way : On the dark day when that news of the fall of Tobruk came in I was with President Roosevelt in his room at the White House. Nothing could have exceeded the delicacy and kindness of our American friends and allies. They had no thought but to help. The President took a large number of their very best tanks, the Sherman tanks, back from the troops to whom they had just been given. They were placed on board ship in the early days of July and they sailed direct to Suez under American escort. The President also sent us a large number of self-propelled 105mm. guns which are most useful weapons for contending with the 88mm. high-velocity guns of which the Germans have made so much use. One ship in this precious convoy was sunk by a U-boat, but immediately, without being asked, the United States replaced it with another ship carrying an equal number of these weapons. All these tanks and high-velocity guns played a recognizable part, indeed an important part, in General Alexander's battle . . .

Thus you will see that the decision taken by the President on June 20 took four months to be operative, although the utmost energy and speed were used at each stage.

Records were broken at every point in the unloading and fitting up of the weapons and in their issue to the troops, but it was indispensable that the men should also have reasonable training in handling them.

We recreated and revivified our war-battered Army, we placed a new army at its side, and rearmed it on a gigantic scale. By these means we repaired the disaster which fell upon us and converted the defence of Egypt into a successful attack . . .

Another important point to remember is the need of combining and concerting the operations of the various allies and making them fit together into a general design, and to do this in spite of all the hard accidents of war and the incalculable interruptions of the enemy.

I can now read to the House the actual directive which I gave to General Alexander on August 10 before leaving Cairo for Russia. It has at least the merit of brevity :—

1, Your paramount and main duty will be to attack or destroy at the earliest opportunity the German-Italian army commanded by Field-Marshal Rommel, together with all its supplies and establishments in Egypt and Libya.

2, You will discharge, or cause to be discharged, such other duties as appertain to your command without prejudice to the task described in paragraph 1, which must be considered paramount in his Majesty's interest.

I think that the General may very soon be sending along for further instructions.

General Alexander and General Montgomery set up their headquarters in the desert, and Air Vice-Marshal Coningham, who commands the air forces in the battle there, was in the same little circle of lorries, wagons, and tanks in which they lived. In a very short time an electrifying effect was produced upon the troops, who were also reinforced by every available man and weapon.

Our attack had to fit in harmoniously with the great operation in French North Africa, to which it was a prelude. We had to wait till our troops were trained in the use of the new weapons which were arriving and we had to have a full moon on account of the method of attack. All these conditions were satisfiable around Oct. 23.

When I spent a night on August 19 with Generals Alexander and Montgomery in their desert headquarters, General Montgomery, with General Alexander's full assent, expounded in exact detail the first stages of the plan which has since been carried out.

It was an anxious matter. In the last war we devised the tank to clear a way for the infantry, who were otherwise held up by the intensity of machine-gun fire. On this occasion it was the infantry who would have to clear the way for the tanks to break through and liberate the superior armour. This they could only do in the moonlight, and for this they must be supported with a concentration of artillery more powerful than any used in the present war. On a six-mile front of attack we had a 25-pounder gun or better every 23 yards.

It was necessary to effect a penetration of about 6,000 yards at the first stroke in order to get through the hostile minefields, trenches, and batteries . . .

For the purposes of turning to full account the breach when made, an entirely new corps, the 10th, was formed, consisting of two British armoured divisions and a New Zealand division—that "ball of fire," as it was described to me by those who had seen it at work. This very powerful force of between 40,000 and 50,000 men, including all the best tanks—the Grants and the Shermans—was withdrawn from the battle front immediately after Rommel's repulse in the second battle of Alamein, and it devoted itself entirely to intensive training exercises and preparation. It was this thunderbolt, hurled through the gap, which finished Rommel and his arrogant army.

The success of all these plans could not have been achieved without substantial superiority in the air . . . In Air Marshal Tedder and Air Vice-Marshal Coningham we have two air leaders of the very highest quality, not technicians, but warriors who have worked in perfect harmony with the generals.

It is impossible to give a final estimate of the enemy's casualties. General Alexander's present estimate is that 59,000 Germans and Italians have been killed, wounded, or taken prisoners; of these 34,000 are Germans, and 25,000 Italians. Of course, there are many more Italians, who may be wandering about in the desert and every effort is being made to bring them in. The enemy also lost irretrievably about 550 tanks and not less than 1,000 guns.

Our losses, though severe and painful, have not been unexpectedly high, having regard to the task our troops were called upon to face. They amount to 13,600 officers and men. They were spread over the whole army. Fifty-eight per cent of them are British troops from the United Kingdom, with a much larger proportion of officers.

The speed of advance of our pursuing troops exceeds anything yet seen in the several ebbs and flows of the Libyan battlefield. Egypt is now clear of the enemy, we are advancing into Cyrenaica . . . The battle of Egypt must be regarded as an historic British victory, and in order to celebrate it directions are being given to ring the bells throughout the land next Sunday morning, and I should think many who listen to their peals will have thankful hearts.

MAKERS OF AMERICA'S NAVY. The life of Admiral W. S. Sims and his great work for the U.S. Navy have just been made the subject of a new book in America. He is seen in this historic photo with Mr. F. D. Roosevelt, the latter then Assistant Naval Secretary. Admiral Sims stated in a London speech at the end of the last War that "without the British Navy not a single U.S. regiment could have set foot in Europe." Mr. Roosevelt and his brilliant naval and military leaders of today are equally ready to recognize that without the magnificent support of the British Navy America's splendid cooperation in Egypt and North Africa would not have been possible. Our Navy remains the pivot of all successful operations in the Mediterranean—and elsewhere. *Photo, Topical Press*

Across Africa the Allies Have a Highway

When our convoys to the Middle East were forced to take the long route round the Cape instead of through the Mediterranean, the value of the Free French colonies in Equatorial Africa was realized as never before. In this article—a companion study to that on West Africa in page 326—we give an account of the recent development of this vast and vital area.

SOME sixty years ago a French explorer, Count Savorgnan de Brazza, then engaged in staking out a claim for France in the vast unexplored territory of the Congo basin, reached the great river at Stanley Pool and founded a settlement which in due course received the name of Brazzaville. For a long time the place was nothing more than a small colonial station, but of late the imperative needs of war have developed it into a large and flourishing township.

Today Brazzaville is indeed the centre of the Free—or, more correctly, the Fighting—French Empire in Equatorial Africa. It is the seat of Governor-General Eboué, the famous negro from the French West Indies who by sheer native merit secured the position of Governor of the Chad, whence he was transferred in 1940 by General de Gaulle to become Governor-General of the whole of French Equatorial Africa. Here, too, is the station of Radio Brazzaville, most important of the propagandist agencies of the Fighting French movement ; every day it sends out fifteen news programmes in all the leading languages of the world, and its broadcasts can be picked up in England, America and, even more important, in France. Just outside the town is Camp d'Ornano, the "St. Cyr of Fighting France," where officers are trained for General de Gaulle's army. For the rest, Brazzaville has its administrative buildings, a variety of schools, a hospital and Pasteur Institute, and a few factories engaged in producing equipment and supplies for the French troops.

AN English girl who has worked there recently described Brazzaville in La Lettre de la France Combattante :

She sketches the market-place as a " flowing colour pattern flashed on a screen," where are to be seen Hausa merchants, in long robes and picturesque head-dresses, carrying bundles of wares wrapped in a sheet slung over their shoulders. "They will sit crosslegged on the floor and spread out for your inspection a fascinating array of snake, leopard and antelope skins ; multi-coloured leather and aigrettefeather cushions, ivory elephants, crocodiles, birds, quaint wooden figures, knives and spears, and every conceivable variety of leather goods. In the village school," she goes on, "the native children, the merriest in the world, are yelling a French recitation at the top of their voices . . . Down by the river a group of negroes are loading cotton on to the boats . . . A motor-bicycle ridden by a smartly dressed negro in a khaki sun-helmet comes rattling by, on the pillion a plump negress in gaudy colours . . . At the Commissariat of Police opposite the 'Mairie,' black policemen are discussing the war, and groups of young soldiers are talking wistfully of France . . ."

Opposite Brazzaville, on the eastern bank of the Congo, is Leopoldville, capital of the Belgian Congo and the commercial centre, where rubber and tin and other native products are treated and shipped on the way to being added to the resources of the United Nations. The whole of this vast area, French and Belgian, has an economic wealth beyond all measurement, but it is even more important as a corridor of communications, since across it runs a land, air and water highway from the Atlantic to the Sudan.

East Africa and Egypt and thence to the whole of the Middle and the Far East.

Even before the war the French in Equatorial Africa were busily building roads through the largely trackless jungle, but since 1940 the work has been greatly intensified. As will be seen from the map, great roads now link the ports in the Gulf of Guinea, Lagos, Duala, Pointe Noire, and the rest, with the valley of the Nile, the Red Sea and East Africa.

Through these ports, over these roads, vast quantities of supplies and large numbers of men have been transported during the

HIGHWAYS ACROSS CENTRAL AFRICA, marked on this map by black dotted lines, have opened up hitherto inaccessible regions and offer limitless possibilities to the United Nations in their fight against the Axis. This is not the least of the contributions made by the Fighting French to the common cause. *By courtesy of The Evening Standard*

last year or so to the British armies in Egypt, the Fighting French in Libya, and the bloc of states controlled by the United Nations between the Mediterranean and the Bay of Bengal. Not only is the road shorter—it represents a saving of some 7,000 miles over the sea route round the Cape—but it represents a great saving in time (perhaps as much as three or four months), it economizes shipping, and also, of course, it is far less dangerous since it runs not only where no U-boats can penetrate, but also far from the nearest Axis air bases.

BUT this corridor across Africa is not only a road-link : it is also an air route—indeed, it was as such it was developed immediately after the fall of France. It was a tremendous enterprise, establishing aerodromes and emergency landing-grounds in the jungle and bush and desert of Central Africa, but with the help of many thousands of native labourers the job was done, and done quickly. For more than two years now Allied pilots have

braved the perilous journey, one of the most difficult and dangerous in the world. At the end of last month it was stated that more than a thousand aircraft had been flown to the Middle East over this West African route —Blenheims and Hurricanes, American Marylands and Tomahawks—with a loss of only two per cent on the way. They came in crates to the West African ports from Britain and America, were speedily assembled and then flown across Africa by British, American, and Polish pilots. (Most of the Poles, we are told, went down with malaria as soon as they arrived, but they quickly recovered, and in between their flights managed to find time to attend daily classes in English.) Each journey takes over twenty-four flying hours, excluding putting down at the various landing-grounds en route, where the aircraft are refuelled and the engines inspected. The fighters carry additional petrol tanks, as otherwise they could not make the long hops between the landing-grounds. At first only two or three convoys of aircraft made the trip each week, but latterly the convoys have been a daily occurrence.

MOST of the pilots who inaugurated the system are now convoy leaders, and one of them recently gave this description of his job.

Everything is so easy and simple now, but it was very different two years ago. Then it was dangerous flying indeed. Now the meteorological service and improved landing-grounds have helped a lot, although sometimes a storm will suddenly spring up and make flying a real nightmare. There have been accidents naturally, and men have wandered for days in the jungle or in the desert before being picked up. Sometimes they have not been picked up. But there have been few aircraft which failed to arrive on schedule. As for the trip itself we have to cross a huge forest where it would be impossible to find a landing place should anything go wrong.

I remember that in the beginning we had to put up in native huts if we stayed for the night, and that was not a very pleasant experience. The landing-grounds, too, were pretty rough and primitive at one time, but they have been smoothed out. We also cross what is, I believe, one of the most interesting stretches of country in the world, crammed full of lions and other wild animals. But I prefer to stay in the air.

The most boring part of the trip is a stretch of more than two thousand miles over the Sudan and nothing but barren desert all the way except for two stopping-places. Once we get to Khartoum we reckon the trip as good as over, for after that it is a straight run up Egypt to our destination.

NOT only convoys of bombers and fighters use this "reinforcement road" across Central Africa : on all days of the week aircraft carrying official and urgently-needed personnel or cargoes of valuable freight may touch on one or other of the aerodromes which British engineering skill and American muscle have created in the heart of what not long ago was "Darkest Africa." Once these regions were high on the list of those which possessed the reputation of being the white man's grave. Today they are no longer a grave, but a channel throbbing with the notes of victorious effort.

Over Jungle and Desert They've a Skyway Too

Photos, *Associated Press*

FROM THE ATLANTIC TO THE NILE has been constructed one of the most important of Allied routes to the Middle East (see opposite). Along it passes an almost continuous stream of U.S. aircraft which have played a great part in the triumph in the Battle of the Western Desert. 1, Flagging in a transport at a U.S. base. 2, Laden with bricks, this camel assists in the construction of an airfield. 3, A clerk checks a list of United Nations' officers bound for the Middle East. 4, African natives work on the foundations of a building.

THE WAR IN THE AIR

by Capt. Norman Macmillan, M.C., A.F.C.

I**N** New Guinea Australian troops, continuing their advance across the Owen Stanley mountains and pushing along the 55 miles that lie between Kokoda (already captured) and the Japanese base at Buna, received invaluable air support. In this difficult jungle and mountain country transport of special supplies by aircraft was an essential part of swift-moving action. Without air transport of supplies (dropped in special containers attached to parachutes where no landing-grounds are available) white troops would have found it difficult to maintain themselves, and either the advance would have slowed down, or the attacking force would have been reduced in strength by having to operate within the capacity of surface transport commissariat possibilities.

In this area of the global war American troops were landed by air transports in the Buna area, while reinforcements and heavy supplies were sent by ship. This is the first time that large numbers of United Nations troops have been conveyed by air transport to a fighting zone. Its success demonstrates the foresight of the Americans, who planned a large proportion of all their multi-engined military aircraft to be built as transport craft.

The combined Australian advance and the American air landing leave the Japanese holding only a coastal strip around Buna-Gona in the Papuan section of the great island of New Guinea.

The importance of this success against Japanese forces in the Far East is overshadowed by the triumphant outcome of the El Alamein battle in Egypt, but it must not be overlooked, for it indicates beyond doubt that possession of air superiority by the United Nations will play a chief part in the strategy of the offensive against Japan.

In Egypt the air has contributed magnificently to the success of Generals Alexander and Montgomery over Field - Marshal Rommel. It is clear that advocates of a triple service organization of sea, land, and air forces have been justified. The success of the battle of El Alamein could have been no greater if all the aircraft employed had been under the control of the War Office in army units (as many reactionaries wanted). Indeed, the success might have been less important, for the training for air war follows a technique different from that of sea or land war, even if it is subservient to the same general principles.

'Composite Pattern' in Egypt

It is the cooperation of all services—land, sea, and air—in one fighting force that finally counts. The prior organization and training of each service are a specialized procedure ; in consequence, the command of each service in the zone of action should also be in the hands of a specialist acting under and in unity with the supreme strategic and tactical commanders of the combined force.

S**UCCESS** in Egypt sprang from this flexible but strong organization, and in the air, United Kingdom, American, South African and Australian units flew and fought in one composite pattern, denied Rommel petrol supplies for six weeks, knocked the Luftwaffe out of the sky, and with the cooperation of the air defences of Malta, the ground defences in Egypt, and paratroop and ground attacks (including one by the R.A.F. Regiment) on enemy-held aerodromes during the course of the battle, gave the German air force the severest blow it has sustained in any campaign.

The complete air superiority which has been wrested by the United Nations along the North African stretch of the Eastern Mediterranean has created a situation which must render Rommel powerless unless he can receive swift air reinforcements. These he can be given only at the cost of weakening defence positions elsewhere along the enormous German-held perimeter, which is now defensive.

And by the continued strategic disposition of United Nations air power, German ability to attack must continually shrink to ever-narrower sectors of her perimeter.

U**NITED NATIONS** landings in French North Africa from Algiers to Casablanca have a vital parallel significance. Initiated by sea and air power, their complete success would enable the land and air forces under General Eisenhower and those under General Alexander to secure complete control of the whole south Mediterranean coast (with the exception of Spanish Morocco) by effecting a junction in Tunisia after the defeat of Rommel.

Tunisia was not made an initial objective, presumably because it lies too close to the German-Italian air forces in Sicily, and too far from Gibraltar. Instead, the method of advance towards Tunisia is one of coastal progression towards an objective to secure lines of communication, obtain air protection from shore-based aircraft, and create the opportunity to push a protective and aggressive fighter aircraft force within striking distance of the enemy strong-point where the Mediterranean narrows. Any attempt to make Tunisia an initial objective would have exposed landing forces within a zone of local enemy air superiority from the Sicilian aerodromes.

Possession of the aerodromes along the French North African coastal zone will provide air protection for United Nations shipping convoys through the Mediterranean, shorten the supply line running to the Middle East, Russia, and India, and will create an unbroken Allied air line from the Arctic Ocean through Archangel, in one great sweeping curve, via Iran, Iraq, Palestine and North Africa to the Atlantic, hemming in the Axis partners of the west, and forcing them to face the ever-growing air power of the nations ranged against them.

U**NLESS** the Japanese and the Germans can break through and effect a junction, the global strategy of the war may soon present a picture of two vast beleaguered areas of the world wherein the separated members of the Axis will be pinned. The duration of the struggle will then be dependent upon the two factors, of time for strangulation of the besieged enemy and of time required for organization of the United Nations' full air striking power (as a fractional part of which Bomber Command again attacked Genoa on the nights of November 6 and 7) to enable the final victory to be achieved with certainty and the minimum loss to the forces of the United Nations.

R.A.F. RAIDS ON GENOA during October and November 1942 caused great devastation in the dock area and in the centre of the city. This reconnaissance photo shows damage done in the Ansaldo fitting-out yards. A, long shed gutted over three-quarters of its length ; B, damage caused by fire at west end of an important workshop ; C, the roof of another which received a direct hit.

Photo. British Official: Crown Copyright

What the Lancasters Did to Le Creusot

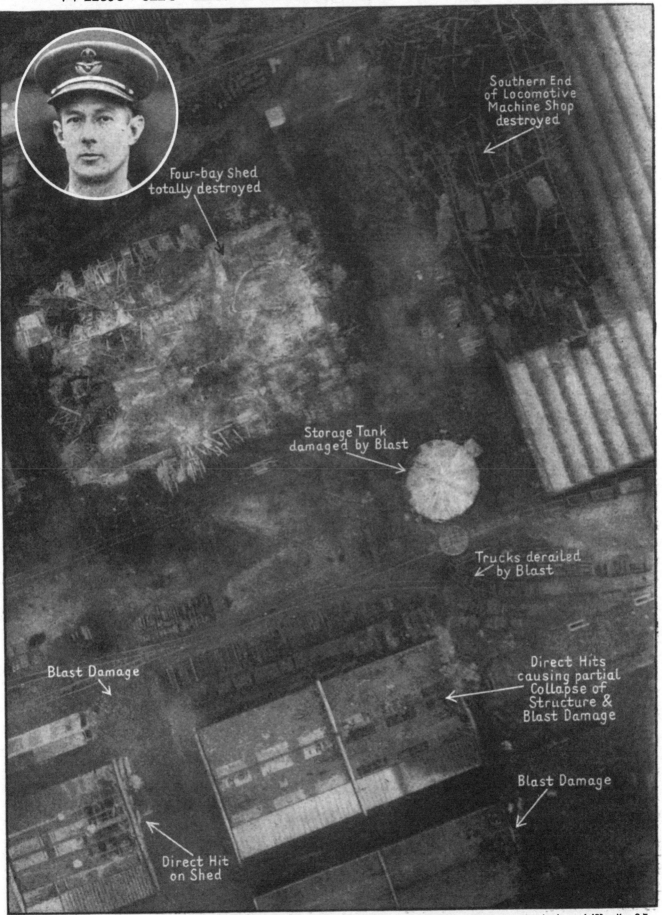

Four-bay Shed totally destroyed

Southern End of Locomotive Machine Shop destroyed

Storage Tank damaged by Blast

Trucks derailed by Blast

Blast Damage

Direct Hits causing partial Collapse of Structure & Blast Damage

Blast Damage

Direct Hit on Shed

LE CREUSOT—the " Krupps of France," as it is called because it is the home of the vast Schneider armament works—is situated 170 miles S.E. of Paris. On Oct. 17, 1942, it was attacked by 94 Lancaster bombers (see photograph in pages 368-69), and although they were over the target for only seven minutes many tons of bombs were dropped with devastating effect. This reconnaissance after-the-raid photo shows a general view of the destruction at the Processing Works. Wing-Cmdr. L. C. Slee (inset) led the Lancasters, and on Oct. 31 it was announced that he had been awarded the D.S.O.

Photos, British Official : Crown Copyright, News Chronicle

Fierce Is the Struggle for Guadalcanal

IN THE SOLOMONS fighting developed fiercely during October and November, 1942, when the Japanese strove hard to land reinforcements on the island of Guadalcanal. 1, U.S. howitzer battery blazes at enemy positions on the Matanikou River. 2, Maj.-Gen. A. A. Vandergrift, commander of U.S. Marines, directs operations. 3, American troops move up through the jungle. 4, Marines crouch in a jungle nest, while overhead roars a U.S. Navy scout plane. 5, U.S. amphibian patrol bomber lands on Lunga airfield. PAGE 376 *Photos, Keystone, Planet News, Associated Press*

In New Guinea the Allies Stormed Kokoda

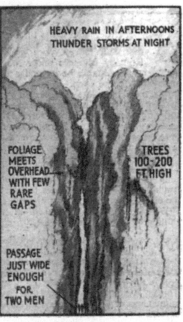

THREE months' heavy fighting by the Allied forces against the Japanese in New Guinea culminated in the recapture of Kokoda on Nov. 2, 1942. The Allies (largely Australian infantry, supported by Australian and U.S. aircraft) forced their way to the summit of the Owen Stanley Range. The drawing above shows a typical narrow path constructed of matted roots through the jungle. Map (top centre) shows the Kokoda section of the Port Moresby-Buna road. The mileage figures refer to the distances from Port Moresby.

NEW GUINEA roads are seldom wide enough for more than two men to walk side by side. Tracks run steeply either up or down hill, and the most difficult rivers are bridged with tree-trunks. As the Allies approached the Kokoda Gap they encountered primitive trails, of which the above drawing shows a cross section through the jungle. The trees rise 100 to 200 ft. on both sides and the foliage meets overhead. Wherever possible horses are used to transport supplies to outlying districts, and on the left Australians are seen loading up.

ON THE JUNGLE ROAD TO KOKODA progress was necessarily slow for heavily-laden native carriers. This drawing indicates something of the difficulties encountered in crossing the gap in the Owen Stanley Mountains (see map above). Supplies are divided into loads, each sack or box weighing from 60 to 80 lb. carried on the back or suspended on poles. On Nov. 10 the Japanese rearguard at Oivi was outflanked by the Australians.

Drawings by courtesy of The Sphere; photo, Sport & General

THE HOME FRONT

by E Royston Pike

At the time when France fell a hundred thousand sheep were grazing on Romney Marshes under the eye of the enemy, a valuable booty and a dreadful nuisance. In the event of an invasion they would have been like refugees on the road. So they had to be moved *en masse* by road and rail. And moved they were. For nineteen days a thousand lorry-loads of sheep were taken off and distributed over England, in double-decker trucks, the lambs on the top storey and the ewes beneath. There were only six casualties. So runs the story, one of many such, contained in Transport Goes to War: the Official Story of British Transport, 1939-1942, recently published at a shilling by the Stationery Office.

Only now are we beginning to realize the tremendous burden of dangerous responsibility that was so successfully shouldered by our transport workers in the months of blitz. Things which we only guessed at, happenings of which we may have had some slight observation, are only now being brought into the full light of day. Somehow or other the trains went through, the lorries and the buses, the barges on the canals. Brave deeds were two-a-penny, heroes (and heroines) "did their stuff" and went to work the next morning, just as they have done every morning since.

Through the murk of those dreadful nights we catch a glimpse of the train which for twelve miles was pursued by a flare falling low in the sky. "It seemed to be following us. I put on speed to get away from it, but it kept on following. I reckon it was the suction of the train drawing it after us. I was glad to see the last of it." We see the lorry driver on "Coventry's evil night" who, refusing to follow an infuriating 80-mile diversion down country lanes, gave the "toadstools" (Toadstool=what crops up suddenly in the night=policeman) the slip and drove through the city as it burned. We meet the station-master of a big London terminus who, when a time-bomb dropped on the bridge over the lines, was told that the station would have to close. "But we have cleared one line," I told them, "let me run one train. Let me run that little local over the bridge." "You can't do that," they said. "Yes, I could. I'd like to. To keep the station open" He argued and argued with them, until at last they said, "All right. You can run a short one if you like." "And," says the station-master with a touch of mischief and pride, "we did. We can say now that we didn't close down on April 17. We ran a short one."

One of the biggest jobs carried out by the transport services was the evacuation of the early days of Sept., 1939, when 607,000 people were taken into the country by London Transport alone. In August 1940, when the Battle of Britain began and everyone was telephoning to their relatives, the "2nd book of Exodus" was started. Not such a fat book as the first, but 127,000 people were moved out of London, and many other towns could tell a similar tale. In Bootle, for instance, a town of dockers which had been badly raided, the officials got a large number of people out at a few hours' notice. The telephones had gone, so instructions were sent out by lorry. The order to evacuate was not given until 4 p.m., but by 11 o'clock that same night the people had been taken away. The men who did this work were mainly dockers who had to be back on the job in the morning. And back they were . . .

Thousands of children—mothers, too—who were evacuated in those early days of the war are still living in their country billets, but many more have returned to their homes (at least, those of them who have homes to return to) in the towns. In London so many children have returned indeed that the Government decided that no more children were to be evacuated after Nov. 10, 1942. At the end of September there were still 225,000 London children in reception areas, but during the past eighteen months, although

YOU HAVE BEEN WARNED! This poster, designed in bright colours, has been officially distributed for display in schools and elsewhere. By its means it is hoped to diminish the number of casualties in rural areas due to the chance discovery of unexploded bombs, grenades, and shells.

800 a week have been sent on an average to the reception areas from London, some 2,000 have returned. For the past three months only about 50 children a week have been sent out of town, and the Ministry of Health has decided that, in view of the tremendous amount of work involved in organizing these small parties, it is not justified, quite apart from increasing difficulty in finding billets.

The decision has not come as a surprise, since there have been many complaints of children (or their parents) who simply make a convenience of the country folk. There have been cases of children who have been evacuated, come back to London, and have then been re-evacuated six or seven times.

Whilst still on the subject of transport, we can record the decision of the Ministry of War Transport to bring under its control long-distance road transport as a wartime measure. One of the principal objectives of the new plan is, of course, by cutting out unnecessary journeys to save oil and tires.

And, talking of tires, at the end of October the Ministry of Supply issued a statement requiring owners of "any laid-up vehicle with rubber tires which is unlicensed, or for which no fuel allowance has been granted for any period after Oct. 1942" to complete form T.C.1. giving particulars of the vehicle and more particularly of its tires.

To those people who like an English Sunday, the English Sunday is a very nice institution indeed. It is admitted, I believe, that Sunday Schools have their warmest supporters amongst parents who are delighted that Sunday Schools for the youngsters enable *them* to spend a pleasantly somnolent Sunday afternoon. But many people do *not* like the English Sunday, and amongst these may well be included a great majority of the men and women of the Services who are forced to spend Sundays in towns or villages where they know next to nobody. It is hardly surprising, then, that demands for Sunday concerts, Sunday cinemas, even Sunday music-halls, are being expressed far more loudly, more generally, than ever before.

But there is not only the English Sunday, there is also the English law—and the law, as Mr. Bumble maintained, "the law is a ass." In many places Sunday cinemas are now permitted, although sometimes a benighted local council refuses to give its permission. Concerts are permitted, too, as a rule, particularly "sacred" concerts. But under no manner of circumstances may you put on a public stage show or a series of variety turns. For if you do you are likely to be reminded of the existence of the Sunday Observance Act, passed in 1672, when "good King Charles" of many spaniels and more lady-loves was on the throne.

This ancient statute is appreciated by none so much as by the Lord's Day Observance Society. A few weeks ago a variety show was to have been given at Sevenoaks, Kent, under the patronage of Sir John Laurie, Lord Mayor of London, and the proceeds were to have been given to the Prisoners of War Fund. At the last moment it was reported that some of the artists were going to don music-hall garb. Whereupon the Lord's Day Observance Society intervened. Since there could be no scenery, no costumes, no make-up, the show was not held, the prisoners of war did not benefit, and the soldiers who would have been in the audience were *not amused*.

But against this Sabbatarian triumph we may note that the freer air of today has blown away an even more ancient practice. Some 1,900 years ago St. Paul wrote (1 Cor. XI, 5-10) that "every woman that prayeth or prophesieth with her head uncovered dishonoureth her head . . ."—a hard saying which has confounded the commentators. One interpretation has it that man's high dignity as the image and glory of God forbids him wearing a head-dress, while woman's subordinate position as the glory of man requires her to do so. Professor Peake goes on to suggest that the phrase "because of the angels" means that an unveiled woman when praying or prophesying in ecstatic mood would be particularly exposed to the lustful advances of the "angels," as were the "daughters of men" in Genesis VI, 1-4. But whatever the origin of the custom, the Archbishops of Canterbury and York have now decreed that "we wish it to be known that no woman or girl should hesitate to enter a church uncovered, nor should any objection to their doing so be raised." So we shall no longer have the spectacle of women and girls hurriedly searching for handkerchiefs and scarves in the church porch. It takes a war to bring about such great changes as this.

Raids or No Raids, Transport Sees It Through

BRITISH RAILWAYS IN THE BLITZ performed a magnificent job of work. This L.N.E.R. tunnel, heavily damaged by a bomb, is undergoing repairs, while rubble is being removed.

THE TRAIN GOES THROUGH on completion of the repair work. Strong timber balks have been put in to support the damaged tunnel, and the choking debris has been cleared away.

ROAD TRANSPORT CARRIED ON, and the horse on the left was rescued with its companion after having been trapped for eight days in a wrecked London stable. Mr. B. Kennedy, stable foreman, saved the lives of these two animals; he is here seen leading one of them to safety. Right, London tram-car severely damaged as the result of a daylight raid. Owing to petrol shortage, canal transport is increasing. Centre, traffic jams such as this are apt to occur in a narrow reach.

Photos, Topical Press, Daily Mirror, Planet News

Round and About Goes Our Roving Camera

LONDON BUSMEN, veterans of the London Passenger Transport Board's service, are giving instruction to Army lorry drivers in the handling of heavy motor vehicles. Right, Mr. J. Latham instructs Pte. J. D. Haldane of Toronto.

JOHN GRIX, aged 14½, who received the George Medal at a recent investiture, showed the utmost bravery and devotion to duty during a raid on Norwich.

LADY MacROBERT, whose three sons, Sir Alasdair, Sir Roderic, and Sir Iain MacRobert, have been killed while serving with the R.A.F. In 1941 Lady MacRobert gave £25,000 for a Stirling bomber, to be named "MacRobert's Reply." On Sept. 16, 1942, it was announced in Cairo that she had presented 4 Hurricanes to the Middle East Air Command, to be used where they could be of most assistance to Russia. Three of these planes are named after her three sons; the fourth is called "MacRobert's Salute to Russia." The MacRobert fighters are included (right) in a formation of Hurricanes serving in the Western Desert.

MR. CHURCHILL and GEN. SMUTS addressed some 2,500 representatives of the mining industry on Oct. 31, 1942, at a giant meeting held in London. One miner from each of the 1,300 pits in Britain was present, and coal-owners and management were also represented. Mr. Churchill is here seen making his address. On his left are seated Maj. Lloyd George, Minister of Fuel, Gen. Smuts, Mr. Attlee, Sir Stafford Cripps and Mr. E. Bevin.

Photos, British Official: Crown Copyright; Planet News, Topical Press, Associated Press

We Knocked Out 37 Axis Tanks in Egypt

Described by their Corps Commander as " one of the finest actions of the war," a company of 8th Army riflemen, cut off by the enemy in the Western Desert, fought on for 36 hours and with their 6-pounder guns knocked out 37 Axis tanks. The story of the engagement is told by Sergt. Charles Calliston and is reprinted here from The Daily Telegraph.

WE moved up to occupy a post at night. There was a very bright moon, and as we advanced we came in for a spot of bother from some German anti-tank guns. Our post was on a small diamond-shaped ridge. The enemy started machine-gunning us and sending over mortar bombs. A thousand yards away I could see the lumpy shape of a leading German tank.

They came rumbling on, spurting at us with their machine-guns, backed by shells and mortar bombs. There were 50-odd tanks and a staff car leading them. I let go at 150 yards. You could not miss. All our guns seemed to be firing at once. My target burst into flames, but came on another 50 yards before halting. Over on my left one blew up at 200 yards.

We were giving them hell, but we were not by any means getting away with it. Our position was rather exposed, and they let us have everything they had got. They even attacked us with lorried infantry, but the main battle was our guns against the 50 tanks. When they about-turned and retired we knew that for the moment our guns had won.

Some enemy tanks tried to hide by mixing up with the knocked-out tanks and derelict vehicles, but we were used to most of Jerry's tricks. The crew of one tank tried to repair it on the spot ; we picked them off with rifles. I heard an 88-mm. gun banging away at us on the flank. Then there was silence as one of our guns scored a direct hit.

ALL this time the enemy never let up ; nor did we stop. My gun had smashed up five tanks in the first attack, and I only count those that were burned out. Some of our guns were out of action. Some had run out of ammunition.

The thing that sticks out in my memory is our company commander saying we were cut off and there wasn't anything that could get through to us. We could fight it out, and keep on fighting as long as we had a shell or bullet or bayonet. Yes, we understood. There was no rest. When you had time to listen you realized we had fewer and fewer guns firing.

Two of my crew crept out on their bellies right into the open to get some ammunition under enemy fire. Then the platoon commander decided to reach a jeep which had four boxes of ammunition on board. God knows how he got to it—they were machine-gunning him the whole way.

They hit the jeep and it caught fire, but he kept on driving it on. We got the " ammo." off and then I had a funny idea. We had naturally been unable to light a fire, but here was a perfectly good one. So I put a can of water on the burning jeep, and it brewed up well enough for three cups of tea.

OUR colonel kept going from gun to gun. How he inspired us ! The enemy tried to shift us with infantry attack, but we sent them on their way with our Bren carriers.

When the next tank attack came the colonel was acting as loader on my gun. He was wounded in the head—it was a nasty wound, and we wanted to bind it up, but he would not hear of it. Keep on firing—that's what he wanted, and we did not pause. When the colonel was too weak to refuse attention we bandaged his head and put him behind some scrub.

He called out that he wanted to know what was happening, and my officer kept up a running commentary. We hit three tanks with three successive shots, and the colonel said " Good work—a hat-trick ! "

Another gun got two tanks with one shell— they were one behind the other, and so the shell passed right through the nearest into the other, knocking out both. The

Sergt. Charles Calliston, M.M., of Forest Gate, London, is the author of the lively account of a tank battle given in this page.
Photo, British Official ; Crown Copyright

ground in front of us was littered with broken tanks. Our officers were all working on the guns with us.

Suddenly I realized my gun had only two rounds of ammunition left. We took a line on two tanks and got both. Then came an order to make our way back to our own lines as best we could. We had to go under fire the whole way for two and a half miles.

We removed the breech-blocks and sights from our guns. We had men with tommy-guns leading us, and we carried the wounded in the centre. I had one of the wounded on my back. It took us four hours to reach our lines. Today we heard that some of our troops are back on our position. I hope they have our guns. We still have the breech-blocks, you know !

I'm Priest of a Church at 'Hell-Fire Corner'

How the citizens of Dover, England's ancient gateway on the Straits, stand up to shelling by German long-range batteries is described below by a priest whose services are often punctuated by the roar of shell-fire. His story is reprinted here from the Daily Mail.

THEY'VE been shelling us here in Dover again. It began as it always does—as it began, in fact, on a Sunday morning I shall always remember. Dover on a Sunday morning is a quiet town, so quiet that in the old parish church the cries of gulls outside can clearly be heard.

Their cries became raucous and annoyed at that first sudden explosion. It was a strange sound, an enormous " bang," followed by a " wump " and a series of rumbling echoes passing up all the little valleys around like the shutting of doors.

There is no longer any mystery about that odd noise to Dover people. It means that some German battery commander 20 miles away on the French coast has given harsh orders, that one of his guns has elevated its barrel, that shell-lifting tackle has

clankingly hoisted to the breech a large missile, and that, sped by a charge so powerful that it is hurled over the sea at an altitude of six miles, the shell falls vertically on to English soil upon the other side of the Narrows.

Since the shot takes a minute to do the 20 miles over sea, the gun will have finished recoiling and the crew be moving through the fumes to clean it before the first siren sounds in Dover. After a pause it will sound again, giving the " double warning," which means bombardment, and makes the Dover air-raid wardens write in their log books, " Shelling warning, red."

The congregation who have attended morning prayer go soberly home, unhurried, unmoved. They make a very civilian, un-impressive sight moving up the street.

IT is very quiet again in the church, where from the walls memorials of generations of English folk look down on to the deep and hallowed peace of the place. It is nearly a thousand years old and very beautiful. At the altar the verger is carefully putting out the lighted candles.

There have been four more explosions, very heavy this time, which means that a full battery has now come into action. Past the church door a warden in a white steel helmet cycles towards a sound of tinkling glass. The church clock chimes ; it is half-past twelve.

DURING THE BATTLE OF EGYPT at the end of October an isolated company of British riflemen made a magnificent stand against Rommel's armour. Above are officers and N.C.O.s of the gallant company.
Photo, British Official   PAGE 381

ON 'BRITAIN'S FRONT LINE FARM' near Dover (see p. 156) works Miss G. Harrison, a member of the W.L.A.—indeed she has received the B.E.M. for her devotion to duty there. She is seen carrying a bath filled with shell splinters—the result of the firing of German long-range guns, such as that shown in the photo below. An account of these bombardments is given in the accompanying text. *Photo, Associated Press*

There is a man digging in his garden at the foot of the hill. He looks up briefly as another salvo lands, marks the bursts, then turns again to his digging. He turns up another row, and then a fresh salvo crashes down and he pauses, a hand on the stock of his spade.

THAT lot fell in the town in a tightly packed spot behind the shoulder of an intervening hill. It will be nasty—an ambulance scoots off down the road into the town. The man in the garden rubs his chin.

Dimly, subconsciously perhaps, he will be reassuring himself, drawing instinctively upon his long history. Fundamentally unchanged, his race and kind have outlasted, often against the probabilities, all those who have ever come against him. It is he who has invaded the world, not the world which has invaded him. He has had many ups and downs. But it will pass. They always have passed.

In the meantime, he doesn't enjoy it ; but he sticks it. He would be a fool if he did enjoy it, and he is not a fool, this stubborn man of Kent, this modest sharer, with the inhabitants of Malta, of Stalingrad, of Moscow, of Chungking, of Corregidor, in freedom's grim stand against tyranny. And he knows that the day of release from battle, murder and sudden death will be the day of final victory, and that day only.

And so he waits, noting often the R.A.F. swarm out across the sea, where for long he saw the enemy roar blackly in. Soberly, without demonstration, he lifts up his heart. He starts to dig another row.

From the dawn of English history Dover has been a fortress watching the Narrows, and this morning it looks the part. Here the Romans landed, here the Normans came. On its rock the great castle crouches, a Union Jack flying above the keep. This flag flaps loosely, for there is little wind, and the chimneys of the town at its foot send their blue smoke straight into the air.

Then on a swell of down a gout of black smoke appears. Then another, and another. It takes quite a time for the sound to arrive.

with no means of ventilation already packed with a dozen young Spanish "reds," all miserable human skeletons, some sentenced to death, others to prison for life. The atmosphere was filthy.

We slept, like the others, on the damp paved floor. No blankets, no soap, no towel, no possibility of washing. A most horrible soup twice a day. Permission to communicate with our Consul was refused. Our poor Spanish fellow-prisoners tried to be kind and helped us all they could.

After eight days in that prison we were taken to the no-less-filthy concentration camp of Mirandade Ebro in the mountains, where Franco gathers all " foreign undesirables." We were placed in packed, dirty quarters— no sanitary installations, no means of having a proper wash ; we slept on the floor. Most of the prisoners, including very old men and boys of 15, all with heads shaved, were in rags covered with vermin. The whole camp was an appalling nightmare.

Twice a day we stood for hours in long queues to get a ladleful of a disgusting liquid they called soup, and a small piece of bread made of maize, millet, and beans. We had to work long hours without rest, carrying stones and sand for new buildings in the camp. All the prisoners, many of whom could hardly stand on their legs, were thin, pale, and haggard. And no way out—no hope of escape from this hell ; there were armed sentries every ten yards day and night.

AFTER three and a half months of this horrible life I was lucky to find myself one morning in a group of 20 prisoners and escorted to the French frontier where French gendarmes took charge of us. Horribly dirty, dressed in filthy rags, our bodies covered with vermin, handcuffed and chained to

My Year's Struggle to Join General De Gaulle

Imprisoned, half-starved, handcuffed and chained—these were some of the trials suffered by a Frenchman fired with the resolve to rejoin the fight for France's freedom. His story is reprinted here from the News Chronicle.

I WAS a sergeant of the Reserve in the Colonial Infantry. I was wounded early in the Battle of France. I left hospital at Bordeaux as German troops arrived there, got promptly demobilized, and returned to my post on the administrative side of an important factory in the Bordeaux region.

Eight months later the Nazis ordered our factory to resume, under their control, the production of war material. I told my director that on no account would I work for the Boches, handed in my resignation, and said I had decided to join the fighting forces of General de Gaulle. He congratulated me, gave me 1,000 francs and said that I could return to my job when victory comes. Having sold all I had and obtained a loan from a friend, I found myself with 5,000 francs— quite enough, I thought, to get to some British port. But how to do it ?

I had mixed up with patriotic organizations of resistance, but they were unable to give me the practical assistance I wanted. I decided

to venture the risky trip across Spain, and was glad to find a companion for it.

We left Bordeaux on April 2, 1941, on our way to Spain. At the foot of the Pyrenees we managed to slip across the French border at night under the noses of German sentries and their dogs and beams from dozens of Nazi searchlights.

It took us two days and two nights to walk across the Pyrenees through secret paths known only to helpful smugglers we met at the early stage of our journey. Our guides were so good that we did not meet a soul all the way. But when we got to our destination in the early morning we were confronted at a street corner by two Spanish gendarmes, who levelled their rifles at us.

My companion and I were taken to prison, where everything—money, papers, even our toothbrushes—was taken from us. In fact, the only things they left us were the clothes we wore, but they emptied the pockets. We were thrown into a small, dark basement cell

NEAR CALAIS, on the coast of France opposite Dover, is this German long-range gun— one of a number used by the enemy to bombard from time to time the English shore. *Photo, E.N.A.* PAGE 382

one another, our pitiful group had to walk through the streets of Pau. We cried like children.

When we appeared before the court the Public Prosecutor pointing at us exclaimed, " Look ! Here is the De Gaulle army ! " As none of us admitted having crossed the frontier to join the De Gaulle forces we were sentenced to only one month's imprisonment.

DESPITE the fact that our French gaolers were kind and the food relatively good, I was a wreck on leaving prison. In Spain I had lost 38 pounds in weight. But I was more determined than ever to join De Gaulle.

I got a free railway ticket to Marseilles, where a De Gaullist gave me 100 francs and a brilliant " tip ! " The result was that to join the Fighting French I enlisted for two years in the Vichy Colonial forces. The idea was that on the way overseas there was a good chance that our vessel would be stopped by a British warship and then I could escape.

After four months in a military camp, where I found that 70 per cent of the men who had re-enlisted were De Gaullists, a couple of hundred of us left for Dakar at the end of last December. In my group alone there were 20 N.C.O.s anxious to join the Fighting French. From Dakar newcomers were sent to various posts in West Africa. I pleaded for Dahomey, where I had once worked, and my plea was granted.

I managed to get sent to Kandi, 300 miles inside the country. Then I found a companion for the journey to the Nigeria frontier, which was about 80 miles away, in wild country with no road, no villages. I copied a map of the region and on April 2 we left Kandi with our two Senegalese servants under the pretext of a hunting expedition in the bush. We had a compass, our rifles and some food and water.

We walked three nights and two days—

FIGHTING FRENCH marching past Gen. de Gaulle on the occasion of his visit to Pointe Noire in French Equatorial Africa a few months ago. The adventures of a French sergeant filled with the determination to " do his bit " for France's freedom are told in this and the previous page.
Photo, Forces Françaises Libres

sleeping between mid-day and four when the sun was too fierce. When our water supply was exhausted we had to drink any kind of water we found. How we did not kill ourselves I don't know ! We were in a lamentable condition on reaching the Nigerian border. On arriving at a village near Illo in Nigeria, the chief gave us food and a

pair of horses to go to the first British post, where we got a warm welcome. Since then we have been treated magnificently by the British authorities.

Now I am happy, having been able to do what I have been wanting to do for over a year : I have joined the Forces of General de Gaulle, the gallant Fighting French.

OUR DIARY OF THE WAR

OCT. 28, 1942, Wednesday *1,152nd day*
Egypt.—Minor tank engagements in Western Desert ; enemy on defensive.
Russian Front.—At cost of heavy losses Germans advanced along two streets in Stalingrad. Soviet Marines raided German positions E. of Novorossisk.
India.—Jap aircraft raided U.S. aerodromes in Assam.
General.—Fifty-five hostages executed in Warsaw as reprisal for sabotage.

OCT. 29, Thursday *1,153rd day*
Mediterranean.—Allied heavy bombers raided Crete.
Egypt.—Our troops extended their gains in ground and took more prisoners.
Russian Front.—German attacks held at Stalingrad ; fierce fighting round Nalchik.
U.S.A.—Mr. Stimson announced that the Alaskan Highway was open for its entire length.

OCT. 30, Friday *1,154th day*
Sea.—Admiralty announced loss of destroyer H.M.S. Veteran.
Egypt.—Enemy counter-attacks on our new positions were beaten off.
Australasia.—Announced that Jap fleet had retired from battle of the Solomons. U.S. troops held all their ground on Guadalcanal.

OCT. 31, Saturday *1,155th day*
Egypt.—Our troops made a further advance and took a number of prisoners.
Russian Front.—Heavy fighting in the Caucasus, where the Germans made some progress at Nalchik and the Russians at Tuapse.
Australasia.—In New Guinea Allied forces occupied Alola. U.S. heavy bombers damaged Jap battleship and aircraft-carrier at Buin.
Home Front.—Nine German aircraft brought down in daylight raid on Canterbury, and four more destroyed during the night.

NOV. 1, Sunday *1,156th day*
Egypt.—Our infantry began a new attack against enemy positions.
Russian Front.—In the Caucasus Russian troops withdrew in the area of Nalchik.
Australasia.—U.S. Marines made two-mile advance on Guadalcanal.

NOV. 2, Monday *1,157th day*
Sea.—U.S. Navy Dept. announced that

American submarines had sunk seven enemy ships in Far Eastern waters.
Egypt.—By dawn a lane was breached in the enemy minefield for our armoured formations to advance.
Russian Front.—Evacuation of Nalchik in the Caucasus announced by the Russians.
Australasia.—In New Guinea Allied forces recaptured Kokoda. Japs landed fresh reinforcements on Guadalcanal.

NOV. 3, Tuesday *1,158th day*
Air.—Stirling bombers made daylight raids on industrial and railway targets in Western Germany.
Egypt.—Armoured battle developed following infantry advance.
Russian Front.—Fresh German attacks on Stalingrad were beaten off.
Australasia.—U.S. land forces made further progress on Guadalcanal.

NOV. 4, Wednesday *1,159th day*
Egypt.—British H.Q. in Cairo in special communiqué announced that Eighth Army had won magnificent victory, and Axis forces were in full retreat.
Russian Front.—German attacks by infantry and tanks were repulsed in several sectors of Stalingrad.
General.—Fifty hostages shot in Slovenia as reprisal for killing of German official.

NOV. 5, Thursday *1,160th day*
Egypt.—Eighth Army continued its pursuit of the enemy throughout the day.
Russian Front.—All German attacks held at Stalingrad and in the Caucasus.

Madagascar.—Hostilities ceased and an armistice was signed.
Australasia.—Allied ground forces in New Guinea continued their advance from Kokoda towards Buna. U.S. troops on Guadalcanal repulsed Jap counter-attacks.

NOV. 6, Friday *1,161st day*
Air.—R.A.F. bombers made daylight raids on Osnabrück and other places in N.W. Germany. Two hundred Spitfires engaged in one sweep over Northern France. Heavy night raid on Genoa.
Mediterranean. — Admiralty announced that our submarines had sunk six enemy vessels.
Egypt.—Remnants of Rommel's Panzer army driven west of Fuka ; mopping up of Italian divisions in progress.
Russian Front.—Fierce fighting continued in the area of Stalingrad.

NOV. 7, Saturday *1,162nd day*
Air.—U.S. heavy bombers raided docks and submarine base at Brest by day ; other raids on factory and railway targets in France, Belgium and Holland. R.A.F. made another night raid on Genoa.
Egypt.—Eighth Army's pursuit of Rommel's Panzer army continued ; Hellfire Pass and Buq Buq heavily raided by our bombers.
Russian Front.—In the Stalingrad area Russian troops consolidated their positions.

NOV. 8, Sunday *1,163rd day*
Air.—U.S. Fortresses made daylight raids on steel works at Lille and airfield at Abbeville.

North Africa.—United States Army, Navy and Air forces, supported by Royal Navy and R.A.F., started landing operations in French North Africa, round Algiers, Oran and Casablanca. Algiers surrendered.
Egypt.—German rearguards at Mersa Matruh capitulated ; many more Italian prisoners taken.
Russian Front.—In Stalingrad Germans were ejected from several buildings in the factory area.
Australasia.—Announced that Allied forces (including Americans brought by air from Australia) controlled all Papua except beach head in Gona-Buna area.

NOV. 9, Monday *1,164th day*
Air.—U.S. Liberator and Fortress bombers made daylight raid on docks at St. Nazaire ; R.A.F. Bostons attacked Havre. Heavy night raid on Hamburg and other places in N.W. Germany.
North Africa.—U.S. forces landing to E. and W. of Oran made progress against stiff local resistance. Gen. Giraud in Algeria cooperating with Allied forces.
Egypt.—Enemy rearguards engaged in Sidi Barrani and Sollum areas.
Russian Front.—German attack in area of Mozdok was repulsed.
U.S.A.—Army bombers attacked Jap aircraft and shipping at Attu and Kiska, in Aleutians.
General.—Vichy Govt. broke off diplomatic relations with United States.

NOV. 10, Tuesday *1,165th day*
Air.—R.A.F. Bostons, accompanied by 200 Spitfires, raided docks at Havre ; other fighter squadrons made sweeps from Cherbourg to Fécamp.
North Africa.—Oran captured by U.S. troops ; resistance continued at Casablanca, where American dive-bombers and warships bombarded the harbour. Announced that British troops and R.A.F. had landed in North Africa.
Egypt.—Our forces advancing on the coast road drove the enemy from Sidi Barrani and engaged his rearguard at Buqbuq.
Russian Front.—German attacks were repulsed at Stalingrad and round Nalchik ; Russians made progress at Tuapse and on the Leningrad front.
Australasia.—In New Guinea the Jap main forces were ejected from Oivi with heavy losses. On Guadalcanal U.S. troops continued to attack.

★═══════ *Flash-backs* ═══════★

1939

November 8. *Bomb explosion in Buergerbrau beer-cellar in Munich shortly after Hitler had been speaking there.*

1940

October 28. *Italians launched attack on Greece from Albania.*

November 3. *Announcement made*

that British troops had landed in Greek territory.
November 5. *Roosevelt re-elected President of the United States for a third term.*

1941

October 29. *Russians announced evacuation of Kharkov.*

November 9. *Establishment of U.S. base in Iceland announced.*

I REJOICE in the success that is attending Mr. Noel Coward's splendid film In Which We Serve. I went to see it on the second or third night of its opening week and shared to the full the enthusiasm of the audience. As I saw it unfold a story of a ship of the Royal Navy I felt that here Noel Coward was performing a service to the British War effort equal, if not superior, to that which he had done for the British way of life in Cavalcade. It made me regret that so much of his time during the earlier period of the War had been frittered away on less vital work ; but that is only in character with most of our War effort ; we fumble about a little blindly before we get really started, yet once we have started we can " show the world." Nothing finer in the way of visual propaganda has been conceived in America, and if In Which We Serve gets the great run it deserves throughout the American cinema world it cannot help being a contribution of the most persuasive nature (and much needed) to the better appreciation over there of Britain's effort. To have conceived, written, produced, and played the leading role in this inspiring film is surely a highwater mark in Noel Coward's uniquely distinguished career.

SITTING in the lounge of a well-known hotel the other night and regarding a group of young naval officers, I was interested to observe that four out of the five were so baldheaded that the day was not far distant when they might qualify for that condition once satirized as an " egg." One of them, indeed, was well advanced in egghood. It made me reflect on the stupidity of generalizing on baldheads, for I had read that very afternoon that some youthful world-reformer had stated publicly that there was no longer any place in the active services for baldheads and old crocks, the latter presumably a reference to age. But I have not seen it urged anywhere that General Smuts ought not to be leading the Union of South Africa or taking the eminent part that is his in the War Council because he is now 72 years of age. This question of age presents many difficulties ; there is no yardstick by which it can be measured ; there are " young seventies " and " old forties." " Go up, thou baldhead " is an indication that even in Bible times the lack of hair on the cranium was regarded as derogatory ; but it is worth remembering that it was youngsters who used the phrase, whereas it was, I think, one of the energetic younger members of Parliament who made the remark that led to my taking special note of that clutch of young naval baldheads.

THIS week I have had no fewer than three instances in which the hasty decisions made by some examining doctors for War Service have cost the national exchequer quite a bit of money. No. 1 is the case of a personal friend, a young man who had undergone some years ago a critical ear operation, which should have barred him from active work in any of the Services. The doctor thought otherwise, passed him for the Navy, and the

young man, being particularly intelligent, had no difficulty in qualifying for a commission. But he had not done a month's active service before it was discovered that he was really physically unfit to bear the strain, and he is now discharged to pursue his professional studies with a pension for life. No. 2 was that of a young man, known to me, who had quite recently suffered from a bad attack of rheumatic fever and otherwise was not physically fit for any harder job than that of a bookseller's assistant, in which he was quite efficient. A few brief months of service in the ranks, and he is now going about so crippled with rheumatism that it is doubtful if he will be fit enough at any time to resume his old job. Naturally he, too, has a small pension to draw.

MAJ.-GEN. H. LUMSDEN, D.S.O., M.C., Commander of the British Tank Forces (30th Corps) in the Middle East. His succession to the late Lt.-Gen. Gott was announced on Aug. 18, 1942. One of the " discoveries " of the War, he did brilliant work at Dunkirk.
Photo, British Official : Crown Copyright

THE third case is that of a brilliant staff officer who in his youth had suffered an alarming accident to one of his eyes, which has in no wise impaired his general efficiency, as he has a splendid physique. When he first stripped for his medical he was instantly allocated to the Infantry, his general health was so obviously good. And this although he had mentioned his eye injury. But on starting a course of musketry he proved totally unable to aim correctly at the target, and thereupon he was immediately transferred to the Artillery. I mention these cases because all three have come under my notice within the last few days, and also because they must be typical of many thousands throughout the country. Surely it would seem that a little more discrimination on the part of examiners might save future taxpayers a considerable burden in pensioning the unfit who, in the first two cases mentioned, were able to give so little real war service and have themselves suffered from their particular

disabilities having been so cursorily dealt with at their medical examinations.

HAVING had to vacate my seaside home some time ago and move inland to a country cottage, I have realized that the re-directing of letters and circulars must involve extra work at the Post Office, and latterly I have been trying to avoid this as far as possible by sending out notices of the changed address as permanent. These usually bring a confirming acknowledgement, but I was amused the other day to receive one assuring me that the change of address had been " duly registered in the books of the Company," the said acknowledgement being sent to the old address ! Such indications of clerical carelessness must, I think, be attributed to War conditions which tend to lower the mental alertness of all who are not directly engaged in actual War work, where the exciting interest of the job may sharpen one's wits . . . Or does it ?

THE change that has come over the treatment of the Press not only since the War of 1914, but since the beginning of the present conflict, is very noticeable in the marvellously interesting photographs that have recently been coming through from the Middle East. These are taken by intrepid cameramen who face all the risks of the front line soldiers and make their pictures amid every conceivable battlefield danger. Some of the results are astonishingly effective, and the reality of the incidents which they represent is conveyed with all the sense of movement which an artist's drawing could suggest, but with the added conviction that here is actuality. These heroes of the camera who, I understand, have been organized into a definite unit and go about their work with all the freedom enjoyed by the war correspondents themselves, are doing a public service no less valuable than that of their brothers of the pen, and it is a pity that the public should not know their names.

A DAY or two will carry us into "drear-nighted December," so I'll cheer up my readers once again with a quotation from my entertaining friend Old Moore. He (at least my particular Old Moore) promises us both " good news " and " a happy Christmas " in this delightful forecast :

" December brings good news for the general public in Great Britain. Reports come through of further settlements of International relationships (!). The world is beginning to settle down to the new era (!) and Christmas arrives with real hope in our hearts that our children and our children's children will never again have to suffer—and still to some extent are suffering —the disturbed conditions which war, long after peace is declared, must always cause . . . Hope is again arising and man marches forward with reviving confidence in his heart. A big religious revival takes place on somewhat unorthodox lines."

We shall soon be able to check up this prophetic picture of December 1942. I look forward to Christmas to settle an account with a formerly optimistic friend of mine who has twice postponed and twice doubled his bet " that the War would be over before next Christmas." I am now more optimistic than he. I have never thought of the end being in sight before Christmas 1943, with a possibility of final victory by Christmas 1944.

Printed in England and published every alternate Friday by the Proprietors, THE AMALGAMATED PRESS, LTD., The Fleetway House, Farringdon Street, London, E.C.4. Registered for transmission by Canadian Magazine Post. Sole Agents for Australia and New Zealand : Messrs. Gordon & Gotch, Ltd. ; and for South Africa : Central News Agency, Ltd.—November 27, 1942. S.S. *Editorial Address :* JOHN CARPENTER HOUSE, WHITEFRIARS, LONDON, E.C.4.

Vol 6 · # The War Illustrated · Nº 143

Edited by Sir John Hammerton

SIXPENCE

DECEMBER 11, 1942

AGAIN THE UNION JACK FLIES OVER TOBRUK. By Friday, Nov. 13, 1942, this Axis fortress was for the second time in our hands, South Africans being the first to enter. Taken during Gen. Wavell's advance in Jan. 1941 Tobruk withstood eight months' siege from April to December of that year, when it was relieved by our second Libyan offensive. On June 21 this year it was retaken by the Germans, but following Gen. Montgomery's decisive victory in the Battle of Egypt, the Nazis made no attempt to hold it.
Photo, British Official

NO. 144 WILL BE PUBLISHED THURSDAY, DECEMBER 24

ALONG THE BATTLE FRONTS

by Our Military Critic, Maj.-Gen. Sir Charles Gwynn, K.C.B., D.S.O.

WHEN I wrote a fortnight ago the general strategic situation of the Allies had clearly immensely improved, especially in the Mediterranean theatre. Since then not only has the improvement in the Mediterranean been well maintained, but it has spread to all other theatres of war. It is now evident that the Japanese defeat in the Solomons amounted to a naval disaster, and the plight of their land forces on Guadalcanal and in New Guinea reveals the dangers which threaten all their widely dispersed detachments once their air and naval strength is challenged.

In Russia, too, although the defenders of Stalingrad have still to face a critical period, there is clear evidence that the initiative is passing to the Red Army, and that the Germans are facing another winter in circumstances little, if at all, better than those of last year—particularly in the south where shelter and secure positions will be hard to find. The defeats they have suffered in the Caucasus give assurance that the Red Army and its leaders are capable of exploiting their opportunities, and that its offensive power is still formidable.

Perhaps the most encouraging aspect of the situation is that the Axis, during the coming winter, will have little chance of recuperation. Italy especially is bound to suffer from air attacks of a violence which no other country has yet experienced—even if she is not invaded. And the temporary respite from bombing Germany is enjoying, at the expense of her partner, will probably not last long. There is, of course, the practical certainty that in the near future a struggle for air supremacy over the central Mediterranean will develop on an unprecedented scale, and that there will be a concentration of U-boat warfare in the Mediterranean and at the approaches to the Straits of Gibraltar.

IN both instances the initial surprise effected in the invasion of French North Africa gave to the Allies advantages tantamount to winning the first round; and General Alexander's great victory will have far-reaching effects on the air situation. The Allies may have heavy losses of shipping and material while developing their initial successes, but there is no reason to fear that these will seriously cripple the enterprise—whereas the Axis losses may go far to undermine its capacity to retain its grip on con-

GEN. NOGUES (left), who was Resident-General in French Morocco, is here seen with Gen. Juin in Algiers after armistice terms had been signed between the latter and Gen. Eisenhower on Nov. 8, 1942.
Photo, Associated Press

quered territory. The battles have, however, still to be won, and there is no justification for easy optimism or relaxation. The spirit in which General Montgomery has driven the 8th Army forward must be shared by all concerned in the War effort.

NORTH AFRICA
The speed of the 8th Army's pursuit, in spite of rain and mud, has beaten all records, and the R.A.F. has kept pace—convincing proof of administrative foresight as well as of tactical drive in both Services.

Egypt has been cleared, and Cyrenaica, with its all-important airfields, is now once again in our hands. Rommel, writing off immense losses and exploiting the elusiveness of mechanized forces, has so far escaped with the remnants of his Afrika Korps. He has, no doubt, been able to replace some of his lost vehicles and other material from his former bases in Cyrenaica, but he is evidently desperately short of petrol, with little prospects of obtaining adequate fresh supplies.

At the time I am writing, it seems probable that he will make a stand in his old defensive position at El Agheila ; but I expect that his object will be to delay the advance of the 8th Army rather than risk decisive battle there. Defeat at El Agheila with its long line of communication to his Tripoli base would spell final disaster for him ; whereas, if he can delay the final issue it would prevent a considerable part of the Allies' Middle East air forces from intervening in the air encounters in Tunisia which promise to be of paramount importance. It is possible that Rommel will continue his retreat to Tripoli leaving only rearguards at El Agheila in the hopes of either evacuating as much as possible of his Army from Tripoli, or of causing dispersion of the Allied armies in Tunisia by an attempt to join the Axis forces there.

I DOUBT, however, whether he has at the moment any clearly defined object beyond delaying the 8th Army's pursuit. He presumably expects that Montgomery, with his ever-lengthening line of communication and consequent supply difficulties, would not, without a pause, be able to develop the full strength required to overcome opposition.

The advance of the Allies into Tunisia has proceeded favourably and as fast as could be expected. Up to the time of writing, contact has been made only between strong reconnaissance groups, with the Allies gaining minor successes in the resulting clashes. There can

FIELD MARSHAL ROMMEL (left) with Gen. Nehring. The latter was reported on Nov. 16, 1942, to have been appointed C.-in-C. of the Axis forces in Tunisia. *Photo, Associated Press*

be no certainty as to the strength of the forces the enemy has succeeded in landing, but the estimate of 10,000 men with few tanks may well be too low. A number of small ships as well as transport aircraft are apparently making the passage from Sicily, which might mean the presence of a force of considerable numbers, though probably one deficient in transport and heavy weapons.

SUCH a force might offer stubborn resistance in defence, although it would have little counter-attacking power or mobility. Owing to the shortage of petrol and few aerodromes it would probably have to depend for air support on aircraft based on Sicily or Sardinia. There is likely to be some hard fighting, for, although the Axis Powers can have little hope of retaining their footing in Tunisia for long, they may hope to gain time for the re-grouping of their armies. The more the Allies are compelled to expend their resources the greater will be the strain on their communications and the greater the exposure of their shipping to air and U-boat attack.

Evidently the battle for air supremacy may become of greater importance than that on

ALLIED THRUSTS IN LIBYA AND TUNISIA constitute a vast pincer movement directed against the Axis forces in French Tunisia and Italian Libya ; its ultimate object may be seen as their complete ejection from North Africa. On this map arrows show the extent of our advance by Nov. 21, 1942. *By courtesy of The Times*

STALINGRAD AREA. By Nov. 23, 1942, the Russians had taken Kalach, 50 miles W. of Stalingrad, thus cutting the German link between the Volga and the Don.
By courtesy of The Daily Telegraph

land, and it seems likely to develop under conditions which have not yet occurred in this war. On other occasions, e.g. in the Battle of Britain, one side has definitely been on the defensive, but in the coming battle of the Mediterranean both sides will have great opportunities of exploiting both offensive and defensive action. Both can employ great concentrations of air power, and the main arena is highly centralized. Quality rather than numbers will be, I believe, the main factor in deciding the issue.

It must be realized, however, that the maintenance and expansion of Allied forces in North Africa implies a constant exposure of shipping to attack, and the risks may not be less than those incurred on the Axis communications with Libya. Fortunately Oran and, to a lesser extent, Algiers are ports outside the extreme danger zone of air attack and afford fairly safe bases connected with Tunisia by good railway and road communications. To reach them, however, ships will run the gauntlet of concentrated U-boat attack till that menace is brought under control—a process which Admiral Cunningham encourages us to believe is well in hand.

RUSSIA
Stalingrad has still to pass through a critical period, because till December the Volga will not be frozen sufficiently to bear traffic and in the meantime ice-floes prevent the passage of boats. Supplies and reinforcements therefore cannot reach the city. During the recent lull in the fighting it is, however, believed that substantial reinforcements were thrown in. Certainly the garrison has been meeting German attacks, both large and small, with great success, and has recovered some lost ground. The enemy's air attacks have been on a greatly reduced scale, probably in part owing to transfers to other fronts, in part to landing-grounds having been put out of service by the weather. Though Stalingrad may still be in danger the prospects of the Germans, if they fail to capture the city, are rapidly deteriorating. Winter has set in, and without shelter and with precarious communications the enemy is not to be envied.

In the Caucasus the Russian position has immensely improved. The German drive through Nalchik towards Ordzhonikidze, which looked so threatening, has not merely been checked but has met with a major defeat, involving apparently the destruction of at least one Panzer division, a number of other units, and much transport. The Russian counter-stroke was evidently made with much skill and determination, but equal credit may be due to the troops which, by stubborn rearguard actions, delayed the German advance until the weather finally brought it to a standstill and made it impossible to maintain petrol supplies. The victory deprives the Germans of all hopes of reaching the Grozny oilfields this year, and leaves them without an organized winter position and with indifferent communications.

In the Western Caucasus there seems little prospect of the Germans reaching Tuapse. Russian counter-attacks have been vigorous and effective, and though the Germans have not suffered a major reverse they have been compelled to adopt a defensive attitude in a terrain unsuitable for winter occupation. They have, moreover, notably failed to eliminate the Black Sea Fleet, and are therefore unlikely to be able to make much use of sea communications to relieve their supply difficulties.

Their great offensive would appear to have brought them not a drop of additional oil, for the Grozny field has not been reached, and the Maikop wells, according to reliable reports, are likely to be out of production till well into next year.

Indications from both German and Russian sources are that Stalin intends to launch another winter offensive and, judging from the amazing resilience of the Caucasus army, which at one time seemed to be in a shattered condition and cut off from supplies and reinforcements, the Germans are justified in feeling apprehensive that the Red Army is still capable of striking hard.

On the whole, great as its achievements have been and alarming as its progress was, the German offensive has practically everywhere failed to reap the fruits of success. It

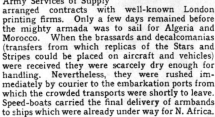
has inflicted much damage on Russia, but has notably failed to improve the strategic or economic situation of the Axis.

★ I HAD written the above paragraphs before the B.B.C. announced on Sunday evening, Nov. 22, the Russian offensive which has begun with such astounding success. I prefer not to attempt to revise what I had written, for I believe it was then a fair picture of the situation when the counter-offensive was launched. It is evident that Stalin has timed the offensive not only to save Stalingrad at a critical moment, but also to take full advantage of the dislocation of German dispositions caused by the situation in the Mediterranean. It would be premature to estimate the probable effects of the counter-offensive, but evidently we are on the eve of a new phase in the war. It may, however, confidently be assumed that Stalingrad is now safe, and that the army which threatened it is facing the possibility of crushing disaster. I have in previous articles emphasized the precarious nature of its communications, especially under winter conditions, and it would seem that they have now been cut by the capture of Kalach.

It is probable that the Russian offensive will not be limited to the Stalingrad front. The whole of the German army used in their great offensive may stand in danger, and the armies investing Leningrad are also in no secure position. Much is likely to happen in the next fortnight. We may be sure that the Germans will fight with the fierceness of rats

in a trap, but meanwhile it may be noticed that for the first time the Russians have announced the capture of a large number of prisoners. This makes it improbable that the break-through became possible because the Germans, having warnings of the coming blow, had already commenced the withdrawal whilst continuing minor attacks on the city to conceal their intentions.

FAR EAST
In the naval engagements which began on the night of Nov. 13–14, and continued for several days, the Americans won a notable victory which is likely to have far-reaching results. Its immediate effect is to make their hold on Guadalcanal secure, and this will probably mean the liquidation of the Japanese troops in the island.

A remarkable feature of the encounter was the non-participation of any Japanese aircraft-carriers despite the fact that some of their capital ships were engaged and that their shore-based aircraft had already proved incapable of providing an adequate umbrella. This must be a clear indication that Japan now finds herself short of a type of ship on which she had placed special reliance, and which is essential to the conduct of any amphibious operation carried out beyond the range of shore-based fighter aircraft. Her offensive capacity is in consequence immensely reduced, and her capacity to protect her sea communications from air attack is also affected. Presumably she is husbanding her remaining carriers for cooperation with her main fleet should it be brought to battle.

In New Guinea the advance of the Australians across the Owen Stanley Mountains was a remarkable feat; and now that an American force has appeared to cooperate, there are good prospects that the Japanese base at Buna will be captured. The appearance of the American force evidently came as a surprise to the Japanese, and we have not yet been told where it assembled or how it reached its assembly position. Part of it seems to have been transported by air. The Japanese are fighting hard in defence of their bridgehead positions, and have the advantage of possessing artillery, whereas the attackers depend on mortars and machine-guns owing to lack of roads for vehicles. It is clear that the Japanese feel their position critical, for they brought up destroyers in an attempt either to land reinforcements or to evacuate their troops. The attempt failed, and cost them some destroyers from air attack.

The operations here and in the Solomons tend to show up the essential weakness of the dispersed Japanese detachments depending on long lines of sea communication. It is more than evident that control of sea communications by sea and air power is the vital factor in the Far Eastern situation. This can only be gained by a step-by-step process, but the first steps have been taken and the pauses between steps are likely to become shorter.

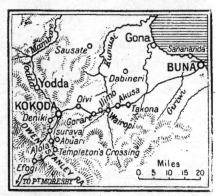

NEW GUINEA FRONT. It was announced on Nov. 24, 1942, that Australian forces had entered Gona, 12 miles from Buna. At the latter place U.S. troops were closing in on the Jap defenders. *By courtesy of The Times.*

Up the African Beaches Goes 'Old Glory'

ALLIED OFFENSIVE IN N. AFRICA. 1, Flying the Stars and Stripes, U.S. troops land at Surcouf, a small village 14 miles E. of Algiers. 2, Maj.-Gen. Lloyd R. Fredendall, U.S. commander of the Allied forces which captured Oran on Nov. 10, 1942. 3, German members of the Armistice Commission arrested at Fedala, Morocco, on their way to an internment camp under armed guard. 4, In Algiers about 200 Italians belonging to the Commission ran the gauntlet of jeering crowds as they were driven away in U.S. trucks. *Photos, British Official; Associated Press, Planet News*

Triumphant Progress for the Allied 'Invaders'

CAPTURE OF AIRFIELD AT ALGIERS. The important Maison Blanche aerodrome was occupied on Nov. 8, 1942, soon after the landing of Allied forces. 1, Headed by " Old Glory," American troops march towards the objective. 2, Men of the R.A.F. Regiment on their way to take part in the capture. 3, Maj.-Gen. C. W. Ryder who commanded the assault forces at Algiers. 4, R.A.F. ground crews seen after the occupation of the aerodrome which was almost at once taken over by Allied fighter squadrons. PAGE 389 *Photos, British Official: Crown Copyright; Topical Press, Associated Press*

To the Rescue of Wounded Men and Machines

WITH THE TANKS in the Battle of Egypt. 1, Transporter belonging to the tank recovery section of the Royal Electrical and Mechanical Engineers Corps carries a damaged Sherman tank from the battlefield to the repair-shop. 2, R.E.M.E. crew pause for a welcome smoke while a dogfight rages overhead. 3, Heavy British tank narrowly escapes destruction by a near miss. 4, Ambulance men gently lift a wounded member of a tank crew through the turret.

Photos, British Official: Crown Copyright ; British Newsreels

'Clearing-Up' in the Eighth Army's Wake

AIR ONSLAUGHT ON ROMMEL. 1, Our bombers attacked Mersa Matruh harbour by day and night, and on Nov. 8, 1942, the 8th Army entered the town. A German seaplane which crashed on the quay is seen in the foreground. 2, An Allied fighter photographed near the wreck of a Messerschmitt 110 on a captured enemy landing-field in the desert. 3, Air Chief Marshal Sir A. Tedder, G.C.B., A.O.C.-in-C., Middle East, visits a long-range fighter squadron. He is seen (left) with Wing Comdr. Bragg, the squadron's C.O. 4, A ground crew servicing a fighter. *Photos, British Official*

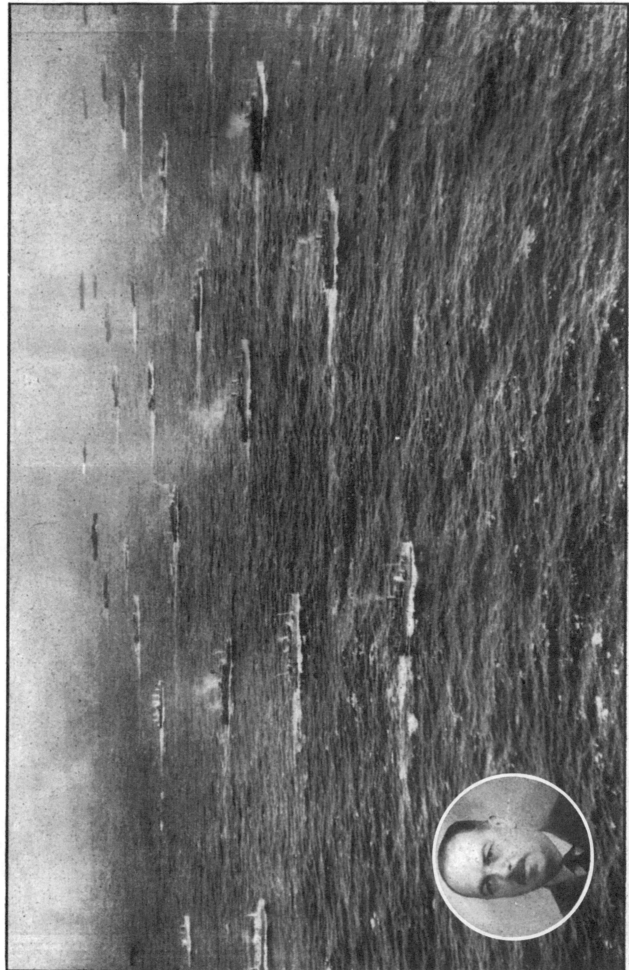

'THE GREATEST ARMADA IN HISTORY' was no exaggerated claim for the vast assembly of ships that carried Anglo-American forces to French N. Africa. There were 850 vessels, 500 being in convoy, and as many as 350 warships escorting the expedition. Ahead of schedule the Royal Navy landed thousands of men off Algiers and Oran (more than 200 miles apart) at the same time on Nov. 8, 1942. Here is a section of the enormous convoy, seen from one of the R.A.F. Coastal Command aircraft that formed a unit in the protecting air umbrella. Air Vice-Marshal Douglas Colyer (inset) was responsible for this great air operation, in the course of which the R.A.F. flew over 1,000,000 miles and 8,000 flying hours.

Photos, British Official: Crown Copyright; Bassano

THE WAR AT SEA

by Francis E. McMurtrie

IN a series of closely contested actions, mostly fought at night, the United States naval forces in the Solomon Islands area, under the command of Vice-Admiral W. F. Halsey, inflicted a severe defeat on the Japanese Navy on Nov. 13-15, 1942.

Though full details have (at the time of writing, some three weeks ahead of publication date) yet to be received, it is evident that the enemy, having failed in previous attempts to dislodge U.S. Marines from the island of Guadalcanal with its important airfield, assembled an exceptionally heavy force in the expectation of crushing all opposition. The core of the attacking fleet is reported to have been formed by the battleships Kongo, Haruna, Hiei and Kirisima, which are the oldest in the Japanese Navy, having been launched in 1912-13. They had been extensively modernized, the armoured decks being thickened as a protection against attack from the air. Mounting a main armament of eight 14-in. guns on a displacement of 29,330 tons, and steaming at 26 knots, they made quite formidable opponents.

In the earlier stages of the fighting the heaviest American ships engaged were heavy cruisers of 10,000 tons, armed with 8-in. guns. In spite of the odds against them, these seem to have stood up well to their more powerful opponents, though two U.S. flag officers (Rear-Admirals Norman Scott and D. J. Callaghan) lost their lives. In the concluding part of the action, Admiral Halsey threw his own battleships into the struggle. Their presence appears to have been unsuspected by the enemy, and thus the American victory was ensured.

ALTOGETHER the Japanese lost in this action two battleships (one of which may actually have been a heavy cruiser, perhaps one of the new vessels of the "pocket battleship" type), eight cruisers, six destroyers, eight troop transports and four cargo vessels carrying stores and munitions. No effective aid appears to have been rendered to the Japanese military forces in Guadalcanal, who are now very hard pressed by their adversaries. It is reckoned that some 20,000 or more Japanese sailors and soldiers must have been drowned in this vain attempt to dislodge the Guadalcanal Marine garrison.

American losses were comparatively light, considering the importance of the success gained. They amounted to two cruisers and seven destroyers sunk. No aircraft-carriers appear to have taken part in the action, both sides having lost so heavily in this category that they are naturally unwilling to risk the few precious survivors.

In its effects, this battle is clearly of much greater significance than the

Japanese defeat off Midway Island in June. With Guadalcanal firmly in American hands, the Japanese invaders of New Guinea in desperate straits, and the time factor operating against them, our Oriental enemies have sustained the heaviest shock that has yet been administered to their sea power, upon which all else depends. To replace in full their naval losses is beyond the capacity of Japanese shipyards, while the United States Navy is adding daily to its strength. Short of another and even more desperate attempt to retrieve the position by throwing in forces hitherto kept in reserve, it is difficult to forecast the enemy's next move. It would be in keeping with the Japanese character to strike a fresh blow in quite a different direction; but the possibility of this will naturally have been taken into account by the Allied commanders, and preparations made accordingly.

UP to the conclusion of the landings the Allied invasion of French North Africa was entirely a naval operation, organized in advance so far as the British part of it was concerned by the same flag officer who conducted the famous Dunkirk evacuation in 1940—Admiral Sir Bertram Ramsay. Allied naval forces employed, numbering over 350 warships, were under the chief command of Admiral Sir Andrew Cunningham, former Commander-in-Chief in the Mediterranean, and more recently Head of the British Admiralty Delegation in Washington.

It was the Navy's task to ensure the safe arrival at the appointed hour, at the various landing points, of some 500 ships of varying tonnages and speeds, ranging from large liners to trawlers and tugs. Over 3,000 miles had to be traversed by some of the ships, with the possibility of submarine attack ever in view. Never before in history has a seaborne expedition been successfully launched so far from its starting points without advance bases being provided.

Three main forces had to be landed: one in French Morocco, around Casablanca, under the immediate escort of American warships under Rear-Admiral H. K. Hewitt, U.S.N.; one at Algiers, under Rear-Admiral Sir Harold Burrough; and the third at Oran and neighbouring ports, under Commodore T. H. Troubridge, R.N. At all these points troops were landed at 1 a.m. on Nov. 8.

Obviously, the success of these operations was dependent on a high standard of navigation and the skilful handling of the large number of ships concerned, as well as on perfect understanding between all the units engaged, so as to obviate any unnecessary signalling which would have given warning of approach. That every ship should have disembarked its assault troops punctually, except one that was damaged by torpedo and thus delayed slightly, is the most eloquent tribute that could be paid to the efficiency of the Allied Navies and the merchant shipping under their guidance.

BRITISH capital ships and aircraft-carriers, under the command of Vice-Admiral Sir Neville Syfret, with Rear-Admiral Lyster in charge of the carriers, covered the Mediterranean landings; and U.S. capital ships under Rear-Admiral Robert Giffen performed a similar function at Casablanca. Only at the last-named port was there any formidable French naval opposition. This came chiefly from the half-completed French battleship Jean Bart, of 35,000 tons, mounting three 15-in. guns. Shells from the 16-in. guns of the American battleships set her on fire, and her discomfiture was completed by torpedoes from naval aircraft. Now the Jean Bart is a battered wreck, lying half-waterlogged in the naval harbour. Some smaller French warships, mostly destroyers, were sunk or forced to beach themselves, the only vessels to escape being submarines.

At Oran, though two British sloops (former U.S. Coast Guard cutters) were lost, a French destroyer and two torpedo boats were driven ashore, another destroyer and a submarine scuttled, and a second submarine escaped to Toulon. Two other submarines are stated by Vichy to be missing.

Practically all the resistance came from the French Navy, who were also in control of coastal batteries which had to be silenced.

As an impressive illustration of the influence of sea power on the course of a war, the expedition to N. Africa can hardly be paralleled.

JEAN BART, French battleship which was left blazing in Casablanca harbour on Nov. 10, 1942, as the result of resistance by French ships to U.S. naval forces. Belonging to the Richelieu class, she had a displacement of 35,000 tons and carried a complement of 1,670.
Photo, Associated Press

Navy's Work in the Mediterranean

ADM. SIR A. CUNNINGHAM, G.C.B., D.S.O., Naval C.-in-C, Allied Expeditionary Force, which covered the Allied landings in N. Africa in November, 1942.

ENTERING ALEXANDRIA harbour after successful operations in the Mediterranean, this British submarine flies the "Jolly Roger" as a sign that she has sent an enemy ship to the bottom. She is greeted by a "postman" with letters from home.

The task of convoying some 500 ships to N. Africa was brilliantly performed by the Royal Navy. A destroyer comes alongside to receive the Admiral's final instructions. The message is passed by line from ship to ship.

ADM. SIR B. RAMSAY, K.C.B. (above), made the preliminary plans for the vast seaborne expedition to French N. Africa. After 40 years in the Navy he was placed on the retired list in 1938, but in June 1940 it was stated that he had planned and directed the evacuation from Dunkirk. Now his work has been highly praised by Gen. Eisenhower. Sir Bertram Ramsay is 59.

AMERICAN RANGERS carried out the U.S. Army's first operational engagement in the occupation of N. Africa. Supported by the R.A.F. and the Royal Navy, the Rangers landed at strategic points on the Atlantic and Mediterranean coasts of Morocco and Algeria. Right, landing-craft at a beach W. of Oran. This French naval base was occupied on Nov. 10.

Photos, British Official: Crown Copyright; Keystone, News Chronicle

The Battle of Alamein as the Axis Saw It

Taken by Axis cameramen, the photos in this page show scenes behind Rommel's lines at the beginning of the Battle of Egypt, when the 8th Army penetrated his main position in the El Alamein sector on Oct. 24, 1942. Right, German patrol seeks cover as a British shell bursts just ahead.

Reports of the progress of the El Alamein battle were hardly calculated to cheer Rommel, who is seen below, standing with folded arms, in glum converse with some of his Italian allies. A captured S.A. fighter pilot who saw the German commander and later escaped, described him as "a red-faced man with a jutting jaw and a look of sheer arrogance, almost truculence."

Axis troops suffered the full fury of a combined land and air assault. Enemy lines of communication were strafed unremittingly by day and night, and so effective was our air superiority that the Germans were deprived of the Luftwaffe's protection. Above, Axis soldiers crouch under a ridge as they seek shelter during a fierce phase of the tremendous battle.

Italian tanks on the edge of the Qattara Depression move towards the battle (left). The retreating Germans abandoned the Italians to their fate, and thousands of the latter gave themselves up as our prisoners. The enemy description of this photo reads : "Germany and Italy have drawn still closer to each other in their struggle for living space and freedom."

Photos, Keystone, G.P.U.

Tunisia, the Key Country of North Africa

This brief account of the more interesting historical and topographical facts about Tunisia, which has suddenly become the centre of the struggle for the Allied command of the North African shores, has been expressly written for this publication by M. HENRY D. DAVRAY, the eminent French publicist, who has had much personal experience of that enchanting land.

THE British and American troops now fighting the Axis forces in Tunisia find the country greatly different from that which the French Zouaves and Spahis—foot and horse—first entered in 1880. They had crossed the Algerian border to put an end to the forays of the Kroumir tribes then overrunning their neighbours after the harvest, robbing them of their grain and their cattle. The Bey of Tunis was utterly unable to impose his authority on the highland chieftains ; he had borrowed money from France, Britain and Italy, and was no more in a position to pay the interest than to refund the loans, his whole country being in a complete state of anarchy.

The chief of the French Government was then Jules Ferry, a real statesman with broad views. He deemed the time ripe to put the Bey's house in order, the incessant raids of the Kroumirs providing an excellent pretext. After a short campaign the Berber tribes submitted and a treaty was signed with the Bey at his Bardo Palace, a few miles from Tunis. He accepted the French Protectorate, but remained the " Sovereign and Owner " of the Regency of Tunis, such being the designation of the country.

The first Resident-General was M. Paul Cambon, who was later to become Ambassador of the French Republic to the Court of St. James's and remain in London for twenty-two years, playing an important part in effecting the Entente Cordiale. In Tunis he did excellent work, comparable with Lord Cromer's in Egypt. M. Cambon entirely reorganized the Bey's administration, over which he superimposed French officials. The working of the reorganized Treasury was so efficient, and the prosperity of the country developed so rapidly, that within a few years the Resident-General could refund the foreign loans, beginning with the Italians in order to allay their blatant requests. Henceforward, the budget was balanced and remained so even during the four years of the First Great War.

The Regency being a Protectorate, with the Bey as its own " Sovereign and Owner," the electorate has never sent representatives to the Paris Parliament, unlike Algeria, which is administratively incorporated into France, and depends on the Ministry of the Interior. In Tunis the Resident-General and his French staff have been appointed by the Ministry of Foreign Affairs.

ALTHOUGH agriculture is highly developed in French North Africa, there is practically no heavy industry in spite of the fact that the subsoil is rich in many deposits. Iron, for instance, is to be found all along the mountainous chain that runs from the Atlantic to Bizerta, and specially in Algiers. But those Algerian deposits are not exploited, although enough iron ore could be extracted for smelting steel and casting guns and shells for a hundred years' war or for the more desirable implements of peace. All this mineral wealth remains unused. Why ? Because the concessions were granted to companies formed by the same people who

own the rich mines of Lorraine, and who, anxious to avoid competition, were clever enough to exclude from their agreement a clause compelling them to work their mines.

In Tunisia, however, M. Cambon was not caught napping, and when deposits were discovered in the Regency he imposed on the concessionaires the same " articles and conditions " as they have to accept in Australia. So the phosphate and iron mines in Tunis have been properly worked. Needless to say, there was no fear that the zinc and manganese deposits would remain unexploited. As it is, the immense phosphate

TUNISIA, now invaded by the British First Army and by Axis forces under Gen. Nehring, is rather smaller than England. The west side is flanked by the Algerian mountains ; the east coast is flat. Bizerta and Tunis are northern keypoints. From Gabes, terminus of an electric railway, a coastal road runs S.E. towards Tripoli.

Specially drawn for THE WAR ILLUSTRATED *by Félix Gardon*

deposits of Metlaoui and of Redeyef yield annually about twenty million tons, which are carried by two railway lines to the ports of Sfax and Sousse ; these have modern equipment for loading, surpassed only by Casablanca, for the Kourighat phosphates of Morocco. In the valleys of the north, between the well-wooded slopes of the hills and mountains, there are very fertile wheat land and vineyards ; the plains of the south, which were bare desert sixty years ago, are now covered by immense plantations of olive trees that expand fan-like, specially around Sousse and Sfax. They number more than 18 millions.

One gets an idea of the increase of value of the desert when one knows that an acre of bare land can be secured for five francs and, fifteen years after, when the trees bear an average crop, the same piece of land changes hands for four hundred francs.

The population of Tunisia is prosperous. There are two million Moslems, Arabs and Berbers, mostly attached to the soil that provides them with ample resources. The Jews number 52,000, living in the towns mostly, and the majority have acquired French nationality. Europeans, chiefly French and Italians, including a good many Maltese, number 200,000 ; and, whatever the Fascist propaganda may brag, the majority of these are French. One must admit that the Italians follow near, but quality is not on their side. The Italian colony is composed largely of a rabble of street-porters, dock-hands, unskilled labourers who live in conditions inferior even to the poorest natives. It is certainly not to them that the economic development and the increase of land values in Tunisia are due.

WHEN the French troops invaded Tunis in 1880 there were neither roads nor railways, only tracks and trails. The only metalled road they found was four miles long and connected the Bardo Palace to the capital ; it had been finished only the year before. The Bey Mohammed es Sadok had visited the Paris Exhibition in 1878, where he bought a gorgeous horse-carriage. When he took delivery of it there was nowhere to drive it ; so he had a road made for the purpose ! Now a network of over 2,000 miles of metalled roads connects the various towns and regions of the Regency ; and over sixteen hundred miles of broad-gauge railways have been built, linking up with the Algerian system and farther on with the Moroccan railways, so that it is now possible to travel by rail all the way from Gabes to Marrakesh.

At first, all commercial exchange had to be carried by sea, and there were no ports. The French dug a deep canal through the Tunis lagoon giving access to ships of big tonnage to the quays of La Goulette. The eastern coast is formed of bottom reefs to a distance of several miles out at sea, making navigation in territorial waters often impossible and always difficult and dangerous ; however, two clear passages allow access to the ports of Sousse and Sfax, which are among the best-equipped in the world. As to Bizerta, it is the finest harbour of North Africa, and one of the best sheltered. It is a very strong naval base, and is also well-equipped as a commercial port.

After Rome destroyed Carthage in 146 B.C. the province of Africa, as the country was now called, thrived under the " Pax Romana," and it has since known many invasions : the Vandals devastated it ; several successive hordes of Arabs swarmed over it with fire and sword ; the French king Saint Louis died besieging Tunis in 1270, and then in the second half of the 16th century the Turks conquered it. Now for more than half a century the Regency has thrived under the " Pax Gallica." Let us hope that the Nazis, those modern Vandals, will soon be expelled before they can bring devastation to this fair and not unprosperous land.

For These Allies and Axis Are Now At Grips

NORTHERN TUNISIA is of immense strategical importance in the Allied drive for the control of the Mediterranean. There are good road and rail communications with Algeria, and well-equipped military aerodromes at Bizerta and Tunis. Grouped round these centres are many other valuable landing-grounds. Southern Tunisia is the crucial region in the campaign against Tripolitania. The main obstacles on the road to Tripoli are the crossing of the Tunisian desert and the passage through the Mareth Line (built during the late 'thirties when an Italian invasion seemed imminent). 1, A modern house in the oasis of Gabès in Southern Tunisia. 2, A view of Sfax ; the large building on the right is the town-hall. (*See* maps pp. 396 and 407.)

BIZERTA AND TUNIS, principal port and capital of Tunisia, are situated in the N.E. corner of the country. 3, Quayside and harbour of the great naval base of Bizerta ; only 150 miles from Sicily, it has a population of 25,000, and the largest warships can enter the inner basin. 4, General view of Tunis showing the harbour in the background. A well-planned modern city, it lies about 145 miles from Sicily, and some 250 miles from the British island of Malta.

Photos, Press Topics, Associated Press, P. G. Luck

How They Prepared to Invade North Africa

In a congratulatory message to General Eisenhower, the Allied C.-in-C. in North Africa, Lord Louis Mountbatten, Chief of (British) Combined Operations, referred to it as "the greatest combined operation of all times." Some conception, albeit necessarily inadequate, of the preparations involved may be had from what follows.

SHORTLY before Christmas 1941, when the Japanese onslaught on Pearl Harbour was still a recent and exceedingly painful memory, President Roosevelt and Mr. Churchill sat down in Washington to discuss the desirability and possibility of an offensive against the Axis. Various offensives were discussed (revealed the President a year later, at his Press conference on Nov. 11), especially a large frontal attack from England across the Channel. Expert military and naval opinion was that this would be feasible, and a good deal of preliminary work was done with this offensive in view. " But the more it was studied the more it became apparent that because of physical limitations such an offensive could not be carried out with a reasonable chance of success in 1942."

Some months passed ; and by the early summer, in May and June 1942, the question of an offensive was viewed in a somewhat different light. Now the issue lay between a large-scale offensive about the middle of 1943 and one on a smaller scale in 1942. All the possibilities of this small limited offensive were surveyed, and by the end of June an Allied offensive had been agreed upon. At the end of July the fundamental questions—the points of attack, the numbers of men involved, the shipping problem and the production problem —had all been surveyed. Thus it was that when a little later people were beginning to talk about a " second front," this second front, in the shape of a descent on French North Africa, had already been determined upon by the two Governments.

In July Gen. Marshall, head of the U.S. Army, came to London with Admiral King, C.-in-C. of the U.S. Navy, and had consultations with Mr. Churchill ; and the decision to " hold the enemy on the French shore and strike at his southern flank in the Mediterranean through North Africa," to quote Mr. Churchill's words, was taken with the full concurrence of the War Cabinet and the staffs. By the end of August the approximate date of the attack had been decided. " So for several months," remarked the President, " Mr. Churchill and I had to listen with a smile—or shall I say, had to ' take it on the chin.' "

But to use the President's homely simile, a " tailor-made offensive cannot be purchased in a department store." An offensive which was not planned properly *might* succeed, given lots of luck ; but since hundreds of thousands of lives were involved, it was imperative that there should be a great deal of study, co-ordination and preparation of all kinds.

TROOPS were available in Britain and America, but they had to be trained for a particular kind of offensive action. The crews of naval carrier-borne aircraft had to learn the art of cooperation with the Army as well as with the Navy. Communications, too, had to be worked out to the last detail. Hundreds of warships, transports and supply ships had to be made available and assembled with the minimum interference with the passage of the normal convoys. Ships had to be fitted out to carry landing-craft, men, fuel for the landing-craft, ammunition, cased petrol for quick transport to captured landing-grounds for the air forces, and even coal to enable the North African railways to be put into immediate commission in the Allied service.

THERE had to be rehearsals, and these had to be conducted with the greatest secrecy ; where they were held is even now not disclosed. The enemy was kept guessing ; indeed, it may be said that there have been few war secrets so well kept as this. Now we can see why it was decided not to publish our shipping losses. The Germans and Italians were deceived by their own lies ; according to their own account they had sunk so many British and American ships that it would be quite impossible for the Allies to mount so huge an expedition.

U.S. TROOPS IN N. AFRICA make friendly contact with the inhabitants. As told in this page, the majority of Algerians and Moroccans ardently wished to cooperate with Britain and America, and thus to remain free from Axis domination. *Photo, British Official : Crown Copyright*

WHILE these operations, so vast and so varied, were afoot, a secret mission was sent to North Africa to prepare the way for the invading host, so that the expedition should meet with the minimum of resistance and the maximum of welcome and support. Highly dramatic were the circumstances ; in fact, the story of the mission as told from Allied H.Q. in North Africa on Nov. 12 reads like the plot of an Oppenheim thriller.

The Anglo-Americans, said Gen. Eisenhower, Supreme Commander of the Allied Forces in North Africa, knew full well that the vast majority in French North Africa was anxious to avoid Nazi domination and eager to cooperate with Britain and America. So it was decided to send a little party of British and American Army officers " to get the reactions of North Africans, because it would be crazy to proceed in the dark." General Clark, at 46 the youngest general in the U.S. army and now General Eisenhower's deputy, was head of the party, and here is his story of the mission.

I went to Algiers after a certain group of people in North Africa had asked for a conference with an American general ; to get there I used planes, trains, ships, submarines, canoes, automobiles—everything but mules.

Arrived off the Algerian coast, they were landed from a British submarine under the command of Lieut. N. L. A. Jewell, R.N., who had received verbal instructions from his flotilla captain. To continue the story, as told in The Daily Telegraph.

At one point on the coast they had to look for a light which would be shining from the window of an isolated house, where they were to talk with French leaders. The light failed to appear. The mission thought that it had been trapped. It waited for 24 hours. Finally, late one night, they saw the light shining through the darkness. They cautiously made their way towards the light and entered a gloomily-lighted house, where they were greeted warmly. The owner of the house had sent his wife away on a holiday. He had told the Arab servants to take a few days off, as they would not be needed because of his wife's absence.

The Arabs became suspicious. They later told the police of mysterious movements in the house, which nearly put the party in the hands of the local authorities, loyal to Vichy. The police raided the house. There was just time for the brightly-uniformed French officers to make a quick change into civilian clothes. " I never saw such excitement in my life," General Clark said. " Maps disappeared like lightning. The French general changed his clothes in a minute. I last saw him going out of the window."

General Clark and his staff gathered their papers and guns and hid in an empty wine cellar for an uncomfortable two hours. The Vichy police search, plus the protestations by the pro-Allied French officers, " sounded in the cellar like a riot." The tall angular general crouched in the cellar with a revolver in one hand : " If the police came down I was undecided whether to shoot them or bribe them." After the mission had spent an hour in hiding the police left, partly satisfied. The mission decided that there was no time to waste. Gathering their papers, they departed. It was then that they lost their trousers, shirts and almost everything else when their two boats upset. " We lost almost every stitch of our clothes and £4,500," said General Clark.

The party scrambled ashore with only their papers and underclothes and hid in the woods during the day, alternatively walking and shivering. Finally they reached a secret destination whence erelong they were whisked out of North Africa. Even then their mission remained secret, as they could not be recognized anywhere until they reached London, eight days after their start.

Those accompanying General Clark on his perilous mission were Capt. C. Courtney, Capt. R. P. Livingston, and Lt. J. P. Foot, British Commando officers, and Brig.-Gen. Lyman Lemnitzer, Col. Archelaus Hamblen, Col. Julius Holmes, all of the United States Army ; and it is small wonder that all were recommended for American decorations.

" The fact that resistance was not terrifically great anywhere and that we did not have to land in a place where opposition was great," said General Eisenhower, " testifies to the success of the mission." It should be added that the Fighting French had their agents and emissaries active, too, in every part of North Africa, and these contributed largely to the eventual success.

AT last all the preparations were complete : the vast armada had been assembled, the men were taken aboard, the guns, the planes, the tanks, vast quantities of war material of every kind, even a specially-printed supply of bank-notes. The expedition set sail—the greatest land-sea-air expedition that history records. By Nov. 7 it was within sight of the coast of Africa. On the next day, Sunday, Nov. 8, the first troops were put ashore ; before the week was out French resistance, spasmodically fierce though it had been, had come to an end in Algeria and Morocco. The Allies' supremely audacious coup achieved the success that the genius and toil that went to its making deserved.

Victor of the Battle of Egypt

Hard on the heels of Rommel's shattered columns, the 8th Army's commander watches the pursuit from his tank turret. Thirty-four years have passed since Bernard Law Montgomery joined the Royal Warwickshire Regt. as a subaltern. In the last war he served three years on the Western Front; in this he took the 3rd Division to France, and brought it back from Dunkirk. Now he is concerned to see there's no Dunkirk for the Afrika Korps.

Where Now Is Rommel's 'Arrogant Army'?

"At last," said Mr. Churchill in his Mansion House speech on Nov. 10, "the Germans have received that measure of fire and steel which they have so often meted out to others." After twelve days of terrific grappling amid the minefields facing Alamein, much of Rommel's armour lay broken and derelict (1), his guns were beaten into silence, their crews slain (2), and tens of thousands of his soldiers were on their way to the prisoner-of-war cages (4).

'V' For an Historic British Victory!

" This is not the end. It is not even the beginning of the end. But it is perhaps the end of the beginning."
In these pregnant phrases the Prime Minister summed up the Battle of Egypt. The spirit of the attackers
is symbolized by this Tommy giving the " V-sign " to two captured Nazis (5); their mortars blasted the
enemy's resistance (3), and their tanks, seen here (6) entering Mersa Matruh on Nov. 8, kept the foe on the run.

In This Battle the R.A.F.'s on Top

Puffs of smoke, dark against the tawny of the desert, mark the explosion of the " eggs " dropped by a Baltimore bomber amongst the tanks and transport—black specks in the photograph—of Rommel's once so proud and powerful an army. In the upper photograph we see the remains of a hundred or so German planes strewn over the bomb-pitted floor of El Daba airfield, forward base of the Luftwaffe.

UNDER THE SWASTIKA

How the Nazis Treat Their Prisoners-of-War

From time to time information leaks out from Hitler's Europe of the way of life of the hundreds of thousands of Allied soldiers who, by the fortune of war, have fallen into the hands of the enemy. In this article PAUL TABORI builds up a picture which depresses when it does not horrify.

THERE have been protests in this country against the chaining of German prisoners, declaring that this game of reprisal and counter-reprisal was unworthy of the United Nations. But putting a few hundred prisoners of war into irons is really the least and lightest of the crimes which the Nazis have committed and are daily committing on thousands of defenceless men, in open violation not only of international law but the laws of common humanity.

" The Germans use prisoners-of-war for loading and unloading boats, but avoid using them on foreign boats," a Swedish seaman told the editor of *Trots Allt!* after a recent visit to Germany. " They do not arrive at their work under guard, but are accompanied only by a civilian boss, for if they tried to escape they would starve. They are clothed in the remains of their uniforms with the addition of rags made of sacking and they are utterly weak . . . Once I saw a Frenchman lifting a weight which a ten-year-old boy could have lifted, but he retched and collapsed ; he was assisted to his feet with kicks by the overseer. When I pointed out that his treatment was not suitable for a sick human being, the German replied : He is not a human being, he is worse than an animal . . . While we were eating our meal nothing could stop the prisoners from gathering outside the messroom. Once I saw a prisoner take the garbage pail, containing dish water, potato peels, etc., and eat the contents. When I asked them how much food they got, they answered by forming a small circle between thumb and first finger—a little soup in the morning, consisting without exception of potatoes and water. They were paid eight marks daily in slips which were valid only in the camp and therefore were usually thrown away as valueless . . ."

THIS is a grim picture, but the fate of the Russian prisoners-of-war is infinitely worse. The Germans argue that the U.S.S.R. has not signed the Red Cross Convention of 1929 at Geneva, and therefore Russian prisoners-of-war are not entitled to any protection. So horrible is their fate that often the civilian population takes pity on them —a sentiment which the Germans try to check with cold-blooded severity.

Outside a large Russian prison camp near Tromsoe in Norway the inhabitants gathered to help the prisoners, in spite of their own food shortage. The Germans simply shot a number of these Norwegian Good Samaritans. Next they issued a proclamation which declared : " 1. Any contact with persons belonging to a foreign power is espionage and will be punished by the death sentence. 2. Any communication with Russian prisoners by speech, signs or other means is prohibited. Women especially are forbidden contact with prisoners. Anyone infringing this order will be court-martialled. 3. Anyone approaching prisoners or found in the vicinity of the camp will be shot. 4. Expressions of sympathy for prisoners will have the most serious consequences."

But not only Norwegians are "guilty" of the crime of humanity. A Breslau paper complains bitterly that there had been numerous cases where German women and girls had to be sentenced to penal servitude for having had contact with prisoners-of-war. At their places of employment bartering with prisoners occurs frequently; and on several occasions Germans have forwarded letters for prisoners. Apparently prisoners-of-war in Germany are not allowed to walk on the pavement (the same humiliating restriction applies to non-Aryans !) but only in the roadway—yet Germans have committed " the grave crime " of inviting them to come up to the pavement. " This is an interference with military regulations which cannot be tolerated."

The same regulations demand that Russian prisoners should be stripped of their warm clothing immediately upon capture and given a thin, shabby coat and trousers, *ersatz* shoes with wooden soles, but no socks or

ENEMY PRISONERS IN THE WESTERN DESERT live in camps, of which the one here shown is a typical example, until arrangements can be made for their dispatch to more permanent quarters in Egypt or India. In the foreground men are seen lining up for a meal. On the extreme left rises an altar, surmounted by a cross, where religious services are held. *Photo, Associated Press*

underwear ! The same regulations employ Russian prisoners in the immediate operational zone, contrary to all international law, where they are often killed by the barrage of their own artillery. Sometimes whole columns of prisoners are mown down on the roadside and left unburied. Now and then bullets are considered to be too precious for the massacre ; the prisoners are bound together and German tanks crush their bodies. Polish, Greek and Serbian prisoners-of-war are treated just as brutally.

AT the same time chaos seems to grow inside Germany, in spite of the Gestapo and Nazi efficiency. I found querulous articles in a Bremen and a Karlsruhe paper both complaining about prisoners-of-war who " desert the posts entrusted to them and are roaming about." A stern warning has been issussed to managing directors of factories not to employ "escaped prisoners-of-war " but return them to their former place of work. This warning reveals more of the disjointed economic life of Germany than any other piece of information coming from the Third Reich. Evidently these harassed managers, driven by the Nazi warlords, are willing to employ anyone without

bothering to ask where he comes from, so great is their need of manpower. And Hitler can apparently spare fewer and fewer men to guard his prisoners, thereby making their escape comparatively easy.

We all know the shameful bargaining which Laval carries on over the bodies and souls of Frenchmen. The " releve " aims at bringing back half a million prisoners in exchange for 150,000 skilled workers. But though the French are threatened with conscription and with decreased rations, they have refused to a large extent to have any part in this immoral transaction. Paris sources admit that though 600,000 French prisoners have returned from Germany (mainly because the Reich could not feed them) less than 20,000 French workers (skilled and unskilled) have gone to the Nazi paradise.

INTERNATIONAL law determines with great detail in what work prisoners-of-war can be employed. It bans any job connected with the armament industry. Yet according to a circular recently drafted jointly by the German High Command and the Reich Propaganda Ministry, " all war prisoners will to the fullest extent be employed in our production process. Prisoners-of-war must be treated in such a way that their full capacity will be available to our industry and agriculture. Unwillingness to work will be condignly punished by the Wehrmacht." And the circular adds the usual warning against the least human impulse : " War prisoners fought against Germany and are therefore our enemies. German women who cohabit with war prisoners thereby expel themselves from the national community and will receive the punishment they deserve. Every appearance of fraternization must be avoided."

Italian papers have hinted at a large-scale escape of British airmen from an internment camp in Unoccupied France. Once the truth of this escape is known, it will certainly make one of the greatest stories of the war. The Giornale d'Italia quotes the Italian-language paper Il Nizzardo and says: " Fifty-seven British fliers escaped. The episode reveals a vast net of accomplices, as the escape could not have been successfully managed without outside help. The French persist in keeping British prisoners in the immediate vicinity of the Armistice line. Does Vichy not understand the considerable inconvenience which this entails ? "

As a rule, Britishers are infinitely better off than any other nationality. German industrial papers complain that " of all the prisoners-of-war the British are the worst workers," but as the percentage of escapes has been highest among the Britishers, this may explain why they are comparatively seldom employed outside the camps.

Cyprus Guards the Gate to the Middle East

R.A.F. IN CYPRUS has maintained a vigilant watch over this British outpost in the Eastern Mediterranean, and the few Axis planes which have approached the island have received a very warm reception. The photo on the right shows members of the ground staff overhauling a machine. In the background, beyond the arid plain, the mountains of Cyprus rise sharply against the skyline. Below is seen a general view of Nicosia, the capital; the minaret is a reminder of former Turkish rule. Nicosia has a population of about 23,000.

AFTER the capture of Crete in the early summer of 1941 the defenders of the island of Cyprus—a British protectorate since 1878 and annexed from Turkey in 1914—lying in the Eastern Mediterranean some 60 miles off the coast of Syria, made ready for an imminent assault. English troops and Indian, R.A.F. units (including a squadron which had distinguished itself in the Battle of Britain) and the local Volunteer Force, whose members were filled with the same spirit as the Cypriots who fought at Dunkirk, in Greece and Crete, made up a well-prepared and resolute garrison. Towns round whose medieval walls Crusaders and Turks had once fought were now defended by heavy guns and mechanized units. The opening of the Allied N. African front and the defeat of Rommel in Egypt in Nov. 1942 brought the war yet closer to Cyprus, as the struggle for control of the Mediterranean was still further intensified.

BRITISH AND CYPRIOTS are included in this group of A.A. gunners listening to an impromptu concert (left). The primary system of arterial or main roads in Cyprus totals 862 miles. Above is a section of a mountain road, one of many built recently for military purposes.

Photos, British Official: Crown Copyright; Topical Press.

Stalingrad Spells Colossal Defeat for the Nazis

Winter's approach on the Stalingrad front saw the Germans falling back before a series of heavy Russian counter-attacks. Fighting continued to rage fiercely in the city's streets in the middle of November, 1942. Left, an abandoned anti-tank gun in a street leading down to the Volga.

Stalingrad's defenders led by the brilliant Siberian Gen. Chuikov daily inflicted enormous losses on the enemy. Attacks were concentrated mainly in the N.W. factory region. Below, a wrecked tank lies in the great Red Square. The devastated buildings in the background are all that remain of this once busy centre.

BATTERED BUT UNDEFEATED, Stalingrad withstood repeated blows launched by the enemy on a narrow front ; and on Nov. 23 Moscow announced that Timoshenko's armies had broken through the besiegers' lines. Above, German field-howitzer in action against Soviet street positions. Right, a Red Army advanced patrol moves towards an enemy strongpoint. *Photos, Associated Press, Planet News*

THE WAR IN THE AIR

by Capt. Norman Macmillan, M.C., A.F.C.

STRATEGIC and tactical handling of United Nations air power has demonstrated in a series of actions the importance of superimposing air activity upon surface and submarine activities. In the Pacific zone surface-ship fighting for possession of the approaches to the Solomon Islands was aided by air reconnaissance on behalf of the American fleet; this air contribution was stated to have played an important part in the resulting victory, when sixteen Japanese warships were sunk. Air cooperation in New Guinea assisted the ground forces to reduce the area held around Buna by the Japanese to a 12-mile beach; Fortresses bombed and sank a Japanese cruiser and destroyer with 500-lb. bombs on Nov. 19 off Buna and Gona. American bombers continued their action against the Japanese

(There are, of course, air bases outside this area and outside the Pacific triangle, situated farther south in Africa and farther west in the Americas, as well as those sited in India, Australia, New Zealand, and elsewhere, some of which serve as stations for the waging of bombing war: for example, Indian aerodromes whence attacks are launched against Akyab, Rangoon, and other places in Japanese hands, and those of Northern Australia which cover the southern islands of the archipelago overrun by the Japs.)

WITHIN the great western combative area aircraft are employed for four main purposes, viz. (1) tactical fighting with the forces in the field; (2) strategic operations in connexion with the general plan of campaign; (3) transport of troops and supplies

The preliminary to the occupation of French North-West Africa was the successful outcome of the El Alamein battle in Egypt by the British Eighth Army. In addition to British supplies, 1,000 aeroplanes, 20,000 trucks, and hundreds of pieces of artillery were shipped from America to Egypt during the nine months from Feb. to October 1942 inclusive. These figures indicate but a fraction of the transatlantic transport problem. The landing of the United Nations' forces under General Eisenhower in North Africa entailed the employment of a huge convoy of 500 transport vessels and more than 350 warships. To provide air cover for this great sea fleet, Coastal Command of the R.A.F. flew more than 1,000,000 miles and 8,000 flying hours in just over three weeks. Petrol consumption for this air cover probably averaged about 2¼ miles to the gallon, so that this air operation alone required about 400,000 gallons of aviation spirit.

Diversionary strategical requirements of the operation reduced air attacks against Germany, introduced more attacks against French and Italian factories, brought Bomber Command into strong action against the port of Genoa, while the Mediterranean Command of the R.A.F. attacked targets in Sicily and Sardinia, and Coastal Command waged bomber and fighter war against the submarines over the Bay of Biscay, and U.S. Army Air Force bombers bombed the submarine bases at St. Nazaire and Lorient.

While the Middle East air forces under Air Vice-Marshal " Mary " Coningham harried the retreating Axis forces speeding along the coast road through Egypt past Halfaya Pass into Cyrenaica, the great convoy approached the Gibraltar Strait under its air cover, accompanied by aircraft-carriers of the British and United States navies, and protected further by aircraft based on Gibraltar.

(Viscount Trenchard visited the R.A.F. units in Egypt just before the battle of El Alamein. Although not the inventor of the " air umbrella " he was the originator of the " air curtain " over the Battle of Messines in June 1917, when a screen of protective aircraft held the sky all day from zero feet to 20,000. I remember flying in that screen. We never saw an enemy aircraft approach it.)

AERIAL RING OF THE UNITED NATIONS. As is stated in this article, the whole of the area enclosed by the heavy line on this map is now brought within the sphere of operations of Allied aircraft. In this " western combative area " there is a fourfold demand on our air power.

force in Kiska, in the Aleutian Island chain. All these actions are in the nature of long-term operations aimed at denting the Japanese-held perimeter in the Pacific with a view to further constrictive action. The importance of this great theatre of war, extending from the Solomon Islands to Ceylon as the base of a vast triangle which finds its apex in the Aleutian Islands in the Bering Sea, will increase; but for the moment the main operation in the global war is concerned with closing the line of encirclement round the Axis partners in the west.

THE western theatre of war operations lies within an immense land and water area whose boundaries are at present delineated by straight lines joining Natal (Brazil), Suez (Egypt), the south end of the Caspian Sea, Archangel, thence bending round the North Cape to Iceland, Greenland, Labrador, and finally encompassing the great curve including the Western American coastline including the Sargasso Sea, the Gulf of Mexico and the northern stretch of the South Atlantic Ocean to the relatively narrow (1,800 miles wide) channel between Natal and Dakar. Over this vast area of the earth's surface aircraft are in constant operation from bases in North, Central and South America, West Africa, Gibraltar, the United Kingdom and Northern Ireland, North Russia, and Iceland, in addition to those actually concerned with the focal points of fighting.

in strategic connexion with focal fighting centres; and (4) protection of seaborne and overland communication lines.

The inter-relationship of the four principal demands upon United Nations' air power is not constant. It therefore follows that the allocation of aircraft for the several duties must alter from time to time as changing situations warrant. This master handling of the air situation is the responsibility of those engaged in the highest strategic direction of the war, and the penultimate decision would rest with Mr. Churchill and President Roosevelt advised by their Chiefs of Staff. Until such time as the United Nations possess sufficient aircraft to execute all requirements with maximum pressure there must be occasions when effort in one direction will be relaxed to enable the aircraft necessary for greater effort in another direction to be made available. This is the explanation of the apparently variable character of the strategic air war waged against Germany, which, rising to its peak last May and June with the three plus-1,000 bomber raids on Cologne, Bremen, and Hamburg, has since fallen both in numbers of aircraft and continuity of raids. In other words, strategic air war has been forced to give way to meet the needs of tactical air war (and the lesser strategico-tactical raids in and around the Mediterranean) for the United Nations' offensive operations in North Africa.

AMERICAN landings made at Oran on Nov. 8 were supported by Fleet Air Arm aircraft bombing and machine-gunning aerodromes. American paratroops left England on the evening of Nov. 7, flew the record air invasion distance of 1,500 miles in Douglas Dakota transports, and landed to take part in the attack on Oran. More paratroops (mostly British) left England on Nov. 10 and landed at Maison Blanche (Algiers) aerodrome next day, and on the following day dropped and took Bône aerodrome. By Nov. 11 Spitfires and Hurricanes were operating from the Algiers aerodromes.

On Nov. 11 Axis fighters and dive-bombers were reported to have landed at El Alouina (Tunis) and Sidi Ahmed (Bizerta) airports. German air transports and Italian ships brought troops to Tunisia, and a German airborne tank division was reported to be landing 12-ton tanks by air.

While General Anderson's British First Army marched eastward towards Tunisia, United Nations' paratroops were flown far ahead of the ground forces and dropped to engage the German airborne troops who had entered the strategic French central Mediterranean zone opposite Sicily, and R.A.F. aircraft began the bombardment of the Axis-held Tunis airport; continuing its offensive against the southern end of the Axis, Bomber Command attacked the Fiat works in Turin on the nights of Nov. 18 and 20. Four big raids were completed against Italian cities without the loss of a single aircraft. Raids against Britain almost ceased, indicating the transfer of Luftwaffe aircraft to other fronts.

Who Holds This, Holds the Mediterranean

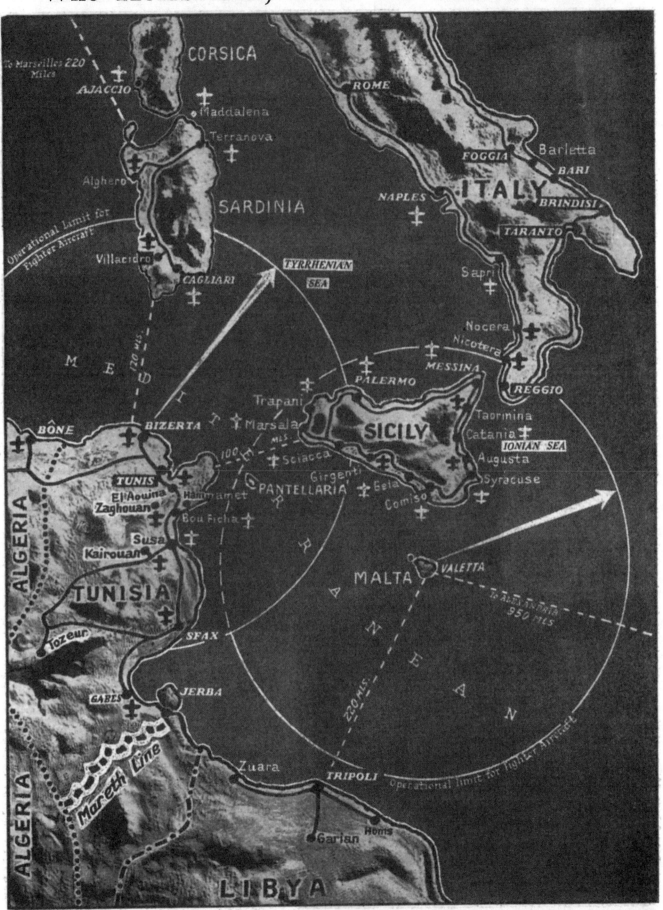

STRATEGIC IMPORTANCE OF BIZERTA is clear from this map. The great base is but 120 miles from Sardinia, and about 150 from Sicily, and dominates the Sicilian Narrows, through which all our fleets and convoys have to pass on their way to and from Malta, Egypt, and the Near East. Moreover, air mastery will almost certainly decide the land issue in Tunisia; and it is obvious from his reinforcement of the Luftwaffe in both Sicily and Sardinia, followed by heavy attacks on Allied bases in N. Africa, that the enemy fully realizes this. (Air bases are indicated above by a conventional aeroplane symbol.

'Do We Intrude?' Let the Nazis Answer!

SETTING OUT ON AN 'INTRUSION' RAID, this Boston aircraft is about to take off from its home base. The enemy has learned to fear these attacks that strike at important airfields used by him in France and elsewhere.

'INTRUDERS'—in other words, night-fighters (operating under Fighter Command) whose special task it is to destroy enemy bombers over their home aerodromes in the Occupied Territories—have seriously hampered Axis activities by their persistent attacks. Not only are enemy machines destroyed, but railways, trains, factories and road transport have been shot up and severely damaged. The photograph above, specially taken for The War Illustrated, shows Wing Commander B. R. O'B. Hoare with his mascot, "Tadzee." A description of this pioneer intruder's work is given in this page.

Right, an example of the conditions with which the night-fighters have to contend. A Boston aircraft is caught in the light of bursting shells as it flies above an enemy target.

'THERE'S WHERE WE CAUGHT JERRY' . . . Members of the crew point out on the map a record of the night's destruction as they make their report to the Intelligence Officer on their return to their base.

Photos, British Official : Crown Copyright ; Topical Press   PAGE 408

WING CMDR. B. R. O'B. HOARE, D.S.O., D.F.C. and Bar, was one of Fighter Command's first pilots to go "intruding" at night over enemy territory, shooting down enemy raiders over their own bases as they took off for raids on Britain or returned after their night's work.

He began in Jan. 1941 and was largely responsible for evolving Fighter Command's present "intruder" technique. His first sorties were made in a Bristol Blenheim carrying eight small bombs and armed with five machine-guns fired by the pilot. Soon afterwards his squadron was re-equipped with the more modern American-built Havoc fighter-bombers.

Before his first "intruder" operation, which was to the Lille area, Wing Cmdr. Hoare had flown at night only in peacetime. Now he has destroyed at least six enemy aircraft on night patrols (the types including the Heinkel 111, Junkers 88, and Dornier 215) and damaged others, not counting those bombed on the ground.

Once he pressed home his attack to such close range that when the enemy bomber, with one engine already on fire, made a steep turn and "seemed to stand still on one wing," as the Wing Commander put it, there was a collision and the Blenheim came home with pieces of the bomber embedded in its wing. On another occasion, to make sure of his victim, he dropped his bombs from so low that splinters punctured a tire of his aircraft, made a hole in one wing and almost severed some of the controls.

Wing Cmdr. Hoare was awarded the D.S.O. on Oct. 9, 1942, the citation mentioning his "excellent leadership" and adding, "he has inspired confidence in those under his command." He had then completed over 80 intruder flights over occupied territory. This veteran "intruder" is now with one of Fighter Command's operational training units, where he is busy training young night-fighter pilots in the methods of which he is so able an exponent.

Born at Brighton in 1912 and educated at Harrow and Wye Agricultural College, Wing Cmdr. Hoare joined the R.A.F. in 1936.

On Tunis Airfield Nazi Crosses Made a Target

AXIS AIRCRAFT AT TUNIS, photographed from a Beaufighter the day following a heavy attack on this important aerodrome. Five German Ju.52 troop-carriers are seen with the burnt-out remains of an Italian S.M.81. Above the latter's wreckage is another S.M.81 with German markings. Following the Anglo-American landings in Morocco and Algeria on Nov. 8, 1942, the Germans poured troops into Tunisia from Sicily, and these carriers are evidence of the Axis design to convert Tunis itself into a stronghold. Inset, Air Marshal Sir W. Welsh, in command of the R.A.F. with the Allied Forces in N.W. Africa.

Photos, British Official; Crown Copyright; Associated Press

THE HOME FRONT

by E. Royston Pike

For two years and more they had been silent, since those dark and desperate days of Dunkirk when the enemy across the Channel seemed very, very near. That was in June 1940; now it was Nov. 1942, and from cathedral belfries, from the towers and steeples of churches throughout the land, the bells rang out " in celebration," to quote a message issued from No. 10 Downing Street, " of that success granted to the forces of the Empire and our allies in the Battle of Egypt and as a call to thanksgiving and to renewed prayer." At the stroke of nine on Sunday, Nov. 15, the B.B.C. broadcast Coventry's bells pealing above the shattered and roofless cathedral. A little later they rang again, and with the bells of Westminster Abbey and of St. Cuthbert's, Edinburgh, of the cathedrals of Armagh and Llandaff, and of the village church of Prestwich in Lancashire, were broadcast throughout the world. Millions heard them in the free countries and in those groaning under Hitler's yoke. " Did you hear them in occupied Europe ? " asked the announcer. " Did you hear them in Germany ? After noon today they will be silent again, except for warning of invasion if needed, till they ring out for final victory." Never was the music of the bells more welcome, never had it been heard with such grateful hearts, in sober pride—unless it was in 1588 when to city and town and village came the news that Philip of Spain's mighty armada had been shattered beyond recovery, and to St. Paul's —it was on a November day too— Queen Elizabeth went in state to return thanks for a great and glorious victory.

But not from all Britain's churches came the victory peals: some 1,200 have been wrecked or severely damaged by bombs, or the towers have been made unsafe. These stand in grim reminder of the hurricane of fire which not very long ago scorched our towns and pleasant countryside; in that hurricane the temples of God and the homes of men were alike engulfed.

Only recently has it been revealed by Mr. Ernest Brown, Minister of Health, that just over 2,750,000 houses in England and Wales have been damaged by bombs since the outbreak of war—more than one out of every five houses in the country. (In some London boroughs three houses out of every four.) Of course, included in this figure is a very large proportion of cases of minor damage where the people have not had to leave their houses at all, but houses which suffered nothing more than broken windows are not included ; the figure also relates only to houses and not to shops or business premises. Of this massive total, 2,500,000 have been repaired by the local authorities and are once more occupied ; while of the balance of 250,000 fewer than 150,000 have been subsequently torn down and not repaired, while nearly all the remaining 100,000 have received first-aid repairs, but for various reasons are not yet inhabited. Moreover, against this loss of 150,000 some 135,000 new houses which were in course of construction at the outbreak of war have been completed and brought into use, so that the net loss is only about 15,000.

That same Sunday when the church bells rang was Civil Defence Day, a new addition to the British calendar. As Mr. Churchill said in a special message, it was a piece of good fortune, it was symbolic, that the day, " a witness and reminder of the great defensive effort of two years ago, should fall in the midst of our first great offensive success over the Nazi enemy. While we rejoice

in the deeds of the Navy, the Army and the Air Force in Africa, we remember those other days, when the deeds of Civil Defenders did so much to keep our will to victory invincible." That was well said, and the day was well kept. In all parts there were special church services and Civil Defence parades, and in London the King, prior to attending a service at St. Paul's Cathedral, took the salute as 1,500 heroes and heroines of the Blitz marched past. A contingent from Dover headed the procession, since Dover was the first of our towns to experience raids on a large scale ; after them came a detachment from heavily-punished Coventry, and then group after group each carrying a board with the name of its much-raided town or city. That night the postscript to the 9 o'clock news was given by Mr. Herbert Morrison, the Minister of Home

LORD WOOLTON, Minister of Food, holding the special Victory Loaf presented to him at a display of 7,000 loaves made by master bakers all over Great Britain with a view to discovering the most nutritious bread for the nation. *Photo, Sport & General*

Security. The fighting qualities now seen in the triumphant attacks of our citizen soldiers on the African battlefields were first visible, he said, in the deeds of Civil Defenders in our city streets, under the bombers' moon. " You entered it for a principle," he told the great civilian army. " You have fought it like crusaders. History will name you the spearhead of humanity on its onward march. After the War, whatever may happen to the body of Civil Defence, its spirit will not die . . ."

Winter has come again—the fourth winter of the War—and the Ministry of Health has launched its usual health campaign. Attack on the careless cough and sneeze is being renewed, and we shall be seeing posters with last year's rather uninspired slogan, " Coughs and sneezes spread diseases—Trap the germs in your handkerchief." Generally speaking, public health seems to be pretty good, but a note of warning was sounded by a Birmingham doctor, Dr. A. J. Brown, at a conference organized by the British Medical Association.

In the industrial areas, at least (he said), doctors' consulting-rooms are becoming fuller and fuller, and their time is being more and more occupied by men and women suffering from a host of minor ailments. Food is adequate, he went on ;

workers can supplement their rations by canteen meals, black-out conditions have not altered, bombing has been less severe—yet there is increased illness. Why ? " I suggest the obvious cause is fatigue, industrial fatigue due to excessive working hours, often under poor conditions, particularly of light and ventilation." Dr. Brown quoted a passage from a report by the Chief Inspector of Factories, that the long hours being worked are " in the nature of a concession to a section of outside opinion, which is prone to associate reasonable hours with personal slackness or with alleged waste of man-power . . ."

There's one disease that is increasing—one which always increases in time of war, when men and women are living unnatural lives, far from their homes and friends and exposed to temptations which in normal times would have small appeal.

Venereal disease before the War was steadily decreasing, Sir Wilson Jameson, Chief Medical Officer of the Ministry of Health, said recently ; but whereas in 1939 the number of new infections of syphilis was 5,000, in 1940 it was 5,600 and in 1941 it was 7,300—an increase of 50 per cent during the war years and, if infections in the Services in this country are included, of 70 per cent. And since last year there were about 60,000 new cases of gonorrhoea, the total venereal infections among civilians is nearly 70,000. Everything necessary for the cure of these diseases is at hand, said Sir Wilson Jameson, and facilities for free and confidential diagnosis and successful treatment exist in all parts of the country. But because of the old hush-hush tradition the public does not know what it ought to know. "Let's get rid of this taboo. I believe that the people of Britain, who have stood up to far worse things in this way, are ready to face up squarely and seriously to the problem of V.D. Once they do that, we are well on the way to solving it. The moral aspect will be dealt with by others ; to me, venereal disease is just another medical and public health problem, like diphtheria, scarlet fever and consumption ; and I know it often spreads to men and women who are in no sense guilty parties, and to unborn babies."

By propaganda it is hoped to persuade sufferers from these diseases to submit to early treatment, but notorious cases may now be dealt with under a new Defence Regulation, 33b. If at least two separate patients under treatment for V.D. name the same person as the suspected source of their infection the local Medical Officer of Health may require the person named to submit to medical examination and if necessary to attend for treatment by a specialist until free from infection. Failure to do so will be punishable with up to three months' imprisonment, or a fine of £100, or both.

All the same, some critics of the Order have argued that it will work unfairly against women. (This was the argument, it may be recalled, advanced by that brave Victorian lady, Josephine Butler, in her long fight against the Contagious Diseases Acts passed in the middle of the last century to regulate prostitution in the neighbourhood of military garrisons.) But the charge of unfair sexual discrimination could be brought much more reasonably against the D.O.R.A. Regulation 40d of 1917, which made it a criminal offence for a woman suffering from venereal disease to communicate it to a member of H.M. Forces or to solicit him. At least it may be claimed that 33b applies both to men and women, and it is said to avoid other features which made the regulation of the last war objectionable. True, it represents an invasion of the liberty of the subject ; but only the most fanatical devotee of laissez faire would advance that here.

But there's one instance of sexual discrimination about which there is no doubt : the rates of war injuries compensation paid to women are only two-thirds of the men's. Why ? No one seems to know, unless it be that women usually are discriminated against in pay and pensions. But Mrs. Tate, M.P. for Frome, wouldn't take that for an answer ; and on Nov. 25 her "equal compensation" amendment to the Address was defeated only by 229 votes to 95.

Women Shipbuilders Out to Beat the Record

IN BRITAIN'S SHIPYARDS women and girls are greatly contributing to the high-speed production of merchant vessels. These photos were taken at a Northern yard where women are employed as riveters, welders and painters. 1 and 2, Women painters at work on the hatches of partially finished vessels. 3, This girl carries a plate which marks where rivets have to go. 4, A 7,000-ton merchant ship completed within three weeks. American Mr. Kaiser must look to his laurels!

Photos, L.N.A., Planet News

On a Sunday in November the Bells Rang Again

CIVIL DEFENCE DAY—Nov. 15—appointed by the King to honour the Civil Defence services, coincided with the nation's desire to mark the Battle of Egypt. Fifteen hundred "civil defenders" from the principal bombed areas of Britain marched past the King and Queen outside St. Paul's, London. This photo shows women drivers of the British-American ambulance sections, members of the staff of London Transport, nurses and ambulance women passing the saluting base at the south portico.

F./O. L. T. MANSER, R.A.F.V.R., captain and 1st pilot of a Manchester aircraft, took part in the Cologne raid of May 30, 1942. Although his plane had been hit and was on fire, he pressed home his attack and enabled his crew to bale out before he perished with his machine. It was announced on Oct. 24 he had been awarded a posthumous V.C.

VICTORY BELLS rang out from cathedrals and churches on Nov. 15, 1942, in thanksgiving for the Allied successes in Egypt. The joyful clangour of the bells (silent since June 1940) was broadcast to the world. Above, bellringers at Westminster Abbey sounding the opening peal. Right, members of the Ancient Society of College Youths releasing the ropes and greasing the bells of St. Paul's Cathedral in readiness for the occasion.

I WAS THERE!

Off Algeria We Fought Waves of Nazi Bombers

How the landing of the British First Army in Bougie Bay on the Algerian coast, at dawn on Nov. 11, was successfully accomplished, in spite of ferocious attacks on our troopships by the Luftwaffe, is told below by Charles Wighton, Reuters correspondent with the Navy in North Africa.

I AM alive to write this story because the great troop-transport in which I am travelling was saved by the audacious seamanship of a Dutch captain and the lean-faced British Naval officer who stood beside him on the bridge through twenty-four hours of incessant, nerve-racking bombing by Junkers planes.

Our liner was the main target in a last great all-out attack when more than fifty German dive-bombers rained 21 near-misses around the ship in 65 minutes. Today we are safe at last from the screaming bombers and the whistling aerial torpedoes. For this we thank the gun-crews, who maintained an unbelievable barrage in the dusk and the dawn in their open turrets above the decks.

There was no opposition from the French authorities when our detachment of the 1st Army was landed. But within two hours of the London radio announcement that the port had been occupied three-engined Italian Cants roared over in a terrific high-level bombing assault.

Intense A.A. fire drove them off. Then 20 or 30 Ju.88s came diving from the low clouds on the shipping about Bougie Bay. One bomb smashed through a lifeboat hanging on one of the ship's davits and destroyed a motor landing craft alongside. The crew were killed and there were other casualties among small craft moving between the ships. Dusk was shadowing the coast when 50 Junkers in relays of five weaved their way through the fierce criss-cross anti-aircraft fire from the 6,000-ft.-high mountain tops.

I WATCHED this raid lying flat among timber on Bougie Pier. Soon I was on a landing craft racing to take off the troops still aboard the transports. As the raid opened a ship put to sea. In the thickening darkness the bombers spotted her. For an hour the Junkers trailed her remorselessly as she steamed westward along the coast at 20 knots, hammering her with bombs and torpedoes.

Hit by heavy bombs, she sank in flames a short distance offshore. Less than half an hour after the first torpedo hit most of the vessel had disappeared—but not before all on board had been taken off in small craft. Three hundred were transferred to our liner.

Our dark grey shape merged into the deeper colours of the mountainous coast wall as we waited for the inevitable dawn attack. If we had been hit, everyone could have got ashore. As the fine Dutch sailor said to me during this night of waiting : " If I had taken this ship so near the shore in peacetime I should have been sacked. But I have my duty to the hundreds of people I have aboard."

MORNING light was growing stronger when we heard the hum across the waves. There, camouflaged by the mountains, we watched the new attack—spectators for once. We appeared to be perfectly concealed from the attackers. Ships which had not taken similar precautions, and were still at anchorage, were the targets of the bombers and torpedo-carriers that thundered across the bay.

When the fierce attack ended we could see British fighters streaking out to sea after the retiring enemy, and we all thought, " It will be the end. The Spitfires are here." We returned to the bay and once again started unloading Army transport vehicles for the troops landed the day before. For three hours we had peace.

But we were obviously the main target for what might come. Our Dutch captain and the cheery British senior Naval officer who was always at his elbow decided it was suicide for us to stay. We signalled ashore for permission to leave with our cargo partly unloaded. The reply was still awaited when the attack came.

FLYING high they came at us, waves of three or four every few minutes. Around us were freighters and small naval ships, but we were the target. The Luftwaffe were determined to wipe out the troop transports. If they had anything to do with it, we should not leave Bougie.

For an hour that fleet of at least 50 aircraft pounded at the shipping—with three-quarters of the bombs directed at us. And we were never hit. Never once did we call on the medical officers, who risked their lives by remaining near danger spots. Around the decks were the usual light A.A. guns and two heavier ones. They were manned by the Army and Navy and by the Dutch crew.

At the height of the raid I saw the barber and the bar attendant banging away at diving bombers as though they had been gunners all their lives. The Oerlikons rattled, and those

below knew that another wave was determined on our destruction. Throwing up everything we had in that wild kaleidoscope of multi-coloured shell, the gunners concentrated on the end of the dive.

Time after time, at the exact moment before Nazi thumbs tightened on the bomb-release buttons, that devastating fire made the reckless airmen waver—and their bombs screeched into the water anything from 15 to 100 yards from the ship. Great cascades of water ringed the liner as they came in at us from port and starboard, ahead and astern.

EVERY time the ship shuddered with the shock of near-by explosions, everyone asked, " How long can we stand it ? " Still those Germans came at us, and still the naval craft in the harbour gave us all the support of which they were capable. But we were fighting our own battle. Wave after wave— sometimes they made two runs across the ship to straddle us with their bombs, two to port, two to starboard. Again and again the gunners made them falter at the final second. The water was brown all around with mud churned from the bottom by exploding bombs. An intense fire of yellow, green and

BOUGIE, Algerian port at which troops of the British 1st Army landed on Nov. 11, 1942, lies 120 miles E. of Algiers. In the aerial view of this town (upper photo) six squadrons of seaplanes are to be seen in the outer port. Lower photo, tracer shells sent up by ships of the Royal Navy against enemy aircraft that sought to interfere with the Allied operations, as described by Reuters Correspondent in this page.

Photos, British Official; E.N.A.   PAGE 413

red streamed through the bombers' fuselage. We did not see any of the attackers go down —though almost certainly some did not survive the swirling steel curtain of explosives, and many may have failed to reach their Sardinian bases.

This could not go on. No ship could hope to stand up to such punishment and escape every time. Four bombers straddled us. Two of the bombs screamed over the wireless aerial to plunge 20 yards to the port side. The aircraft banked and made for home. For over an hour we had endured this rain of high explosives. With a fatalistic shrug of their shoulders, the resolute couple on the bridge raised their glasses to watch for the next wave. They watched and waited. It did not come. From the shore came a signal : " Proceed to base."

ON the faces of our 300 survivors from the sunken ship was a look of infinite relief. But we were still faced with the trip to our base. As we rounded the point another alarm sounded. We escaped the bombers' notice. Determined to save the hundreds on board if we were hit, the captain kept close inshore and made up his mind to run aground if we were bombed and set ablaze. With the engineers driving the motors faster than they had ever turned during the voyage, the captain tore along the Algerian coast as near as he dared.

One, two, three hours passed. We were lined up on the deck carrying out emergency drill. Jocularly, the ship's sergeant-major suggested that he and I might share a Carley float. Over the water came the low note of aircraft. Far away we spotted the machine approaching over the waves—a torpedo-bomber taking up position.

Gun crews raised their still-hot guns—and cheered. Chugging towards us was a Fleet Air Arm Walrus. Looking for all the world like a tramcar adrift in the sky, it passed close by and kept a watchful eye on our ship and escort for some time.

Gradually, Bougie Bay with its terrible

ON ROMMEL'S RAILWAY this train, running between Sidi Barrani and Mersa Matruh, has been set on fire by a low-flying plane. Above, shooting-up ammunition on the anti-aircraft truck ; below, shells bursting on the engine. As told in this page, Axis supply lines to the front in Egypt suffered non-stop attacks from our aircraft. *Photos, British Official : Crown Copyright*

memories slipped behind. Had the Junkers and Dornier crews reported that we had received direct hits and had probably sunk ? Again the faint whine of aircraft motors came. Two Spitfires streaked past. From then until darkness, several hours later, small groups of fighters shepherded us closely every few minutes.

The red African sun slipped below the waves. Back on the bridge after his first brief sleep for many hours, the captain searched the gloom through his glasses. Darkness blotted us out. In less than half an hour we were at anchor in our base.

We Blitzed the Nazi Convoys from 10 Feet Up

Beating-up Rommel's supply columns on the coastal road to Tobruk was " Great fun ! " for British fighter pilots but nightmare for the Nazi lorry drivers, says a young wing commander who was in charge of convoy-smashing operations in Egypt. His lively story is given below.

HONESTLY, beating up that road is great fun. You cannot help feeling just like a small boy in school with a pea-shooter. We just race along, 10 ft. up in the air, and shoot up everything we see—petrol lorries, troop-carriers, everything. And you can't imagine the scene. Drivers leap off without stopping, the vehicles and lorries run into each other, and roll off the road.

And then we shoot-up the troops with our machine-guns as they run across the desert. We fly well out to sea and then sail in over the enemy coast, just above the beach. We try to be as cheeky as we can, and just pop in anywhere. Often we fly so low that we go beneath the telephone wires, but we have to rise a little for the attack as we must dive down to open fire.

We have to keep a look-out for explosions in the vehicles just below us. I have seen a lorry wheel floating by me through the air. The damage done to enemy transport along the road is colossal, and what is more satisfactory is the fact that, since we really went for this road in earnest early in October, my squadron hasn't lost a single aircraft.

Jerry brought heavy A.A. guns up to the road to try to spoil our fun. But even then we managed to fool him. He would launch one barrage at about 50 ft. right across the road. Then, about a mile farther on, there would be another at about 150 ft. His idea was that we would try to jump over the first

barrage and run into the second. But we fooled him beautifully by going in beneath the first barrage and knocking the hell out of everything from about ten feet up.

Shooting-up trains is a sort of sideline which crops up every now and again. Once when we shot up the locomotive of a train there was no opposition—so we went back and just sprayed the whole train from one end to the other methodically and set it on fire.

I Watched the General Decorate Our Heroes

Some were quiet-looking little men you would expect to see at home behind shop counters, on office stools, taking fares in buses—but each was a hero. This account of the simple ceremony of a desert battle-front investiture comes from Clifford Webb, the Daily Herald special correspondent.

THE Corps Commander had fixed fifteen hours thirty as the time for the distribution of awards, and at fifteen hours a rectangle about 60 yards by 30 had been pegged out on the desert plateau.

At fifteen hours, four soldiers armed with Bren guns posted themselves at each side of the rectangle. A small table was brought from a near-by caravan and placed inside what was now hallowed ground.

Officers began to drift towards the scene, and away in the distance two columns of marching men swung steadily towards us. For a moment I was puzzled. Then I remembered. That was it. For the first time I was watching men march in formation

in the desert. I had seen men in tanks, in trucks, on foot in dispersed formation about to go into action, but never before in close marching order.

It was a brave spectacle. Somewhere in the distance bagpipes skirled. They had nothing to do with the ceremony, but had crept in most appropriately as off-stage noises sometimes do.

The columns swung down each side of the rectangle, were halted and turned to face inwards by officers who had probably not shouted so loud in months.

" By the right, dress. Up a bit No. 4 in the rear rank ! " The good old parade ground stuff out here in the blue. A mere couple of miles away the heavy guns snarled angrily, but nobody gave a sign they heard anything. "Stand at ease!"

An officer advances to the centre of the rectangle and addresses the men:

"In the event of an attack by hostile aircraft, you will about turn, disperse and double to cover as fast as you can."

THE medal winners, a thin line of officers and men, ranged themselves at the open end of the rectangle opposite the table. And now the General himself, dapper in shorts and bush shirt, steps down from his caravan, acknowledges the salutes of his officers, and walks into the hollow square.

"You probably think it a bit of a nuisance," he says, "having to come here to be decorated, but I wanted to thank you and to congratulate you personally. Medals are not won easily in the British Army, and you may be sure any man who gets an award has earned it.

"I read all the recommendations for awards. They make magnificent reading. They form the complete answer to any suggestion that this race of ours is decadent. We have here today officers who rallied their men when all seemed lost, gunners who stuck by their guns though wounded, and in desperate danger, anti-tank men who held their fire in the face of murderous enemy shelling until such time as the German tanks came near enough to be wiped out with direct hits."

The General goes back to the table where an officer is handling the new, brightly-coloured medal ribbons. The ordeal of the brave men begins—the D.S.O. for Brigadier G. W. J. E. Erskine, Military Crosses for captains and lieutenants, D.C.M.s and M.M.s for sergeants, corporals and troopers,

That awkward walk up to the table between admiring lines of comrades. The smart salute, the handshake and the mumbling, halting words of reply to the General's congratulations—I see the stuff of which

GEN. SIR B. L. MONTGOMERY presenting the V.C. ribbon to Sgt. K. Elliot, of New Zealand, for outstanding bravery at Ruweisat on July 15, 1942. An account of a similar investiture in the desert is given in this page.
Photo, British Official

heroes are made, and I realize more than ever before that there is no physical pattern for a brave man.

Some of these medal winners are timid, inoffensive-looking little men you would expect to see at home behind shop counters, on office stools, taking fares in buses. I feel somebody ought to cheer, but nobody bats an eyelid.

Lance-Sergeant McNeill, a bow-legged, granite-like little Scot, marches awkwardly to the table and performs a quick two-step in his embarrassed anxiety to come smartly to attention before saluting. But he grins happily as the General pins the ribbon to his shirt, and talks back confidently enough.

Rifleman Willis wears glasses, and a bandage on one leg, but comes to attention readily enough despite his limp. He looks to me like the kind of man who could and would pick up a dog that had been run over and injured without getting bitten.

Gunner McMullen can only extend two fingers for his handshake. The others are hidden under bloodsoaked linen. And so the desert ceremony comes to an end.

NO enemy aircraft had made dispersal necessary, but all through the guns had rumbled and roared.

"*Will Company Officers dismiss their men.*"

The staccato orders are given. The men turn and move away. The Brigadier representing the medal winners turns to salute the General, then moves easily across to congratulate his fellow heroes. Would they join him in a cup of tea?

They would. That's fine. The big tent across the way. And as I walk with them I inquire with a newspaperman's curiosity when and how they will get the medals that go with the ribbons just received. A sergeant looks blankly at a trooper, who shakes his head. "Blowed if I know!" he grins.

OUR DIARY OF THE WAR

NOV. 11, 1942, Wednesday 1,166th day
North Africa.—Darlan ordered all French commanders in Algeria and Morocco to cease hostilities. British 1st Army and U.S. troops occupied Bougie. Axis aircraft landed in Tunisia.
Russian Front.—Soviet troops made progress N.W. of Stalingrad.
General.—German and Italian troops began occupation of Vichy France and Corsica.

NOV. 12, Thursday 1,167th day
North Africa.—British and U.S. paratroops captured aerodrome at Bône. Tunis airfield raided by Allied aircraft.
Libya.—Allied fighters strafed enemy columns W. of Tobruk; six troop-carriers full of German troops shot down.
Russian Front.—Fresh German assault on Stalingrad resulted in slight advance.
Australasia.—Naval engagement off the Solomons began on night Nov. 11-12.
General.—Germans announced that Toulon would not be occupied.

NOV. 13, Friday 1,168th day
Air.—R.A.F. Lancasters and Stirlings raided Genoa by night without loss.
North Africa.—Eastern Task Force under Gen. Anderson occupied Bône.
Libya.—Tobruk again in British hands; Sollum and Bardia also occupied.
Russian Front.—Many German attacks repelled at Stalingrad.
Australasia.—Off Guadalcanal Jap fleet tried to cover large-scale landing of reinforcements.

NOV. 14, Saturday 1,169th day
Air.—U.S. Fortresses and Liberators made daylight raids on La Pallice and St. Nazaire U-boat bases.
North Africa.—New Allied contingents landed at Bône. Allied raid on Tunis aerodrome.
Libya.—Our forces cleared retreating enemy from Cyrenaica as far as Tmimi and Gazala.
Australasia.—In New Guinea Australians captured Wairopi and advanced on Buna.

NOV. 15, Sunday 1,170th day
Sea.—Admiralty announced loss of H.M. submarine Talisman.
Air.—R.A.F. bombers again raided Genoa without loss.
Libya.—Eighth Army occupied landing-

ground at Martuba. Enemy losses by casualties and capture now estimated at 75,000 Germans and Italians.
Russian Front.—Soviet troops continued to advance S.E. of Nalchik.
Burma.—R.A.F. bombers made day and night attacks on Jap aerodromes at Akyab and Magwe.
Australasia.—In New Guinea Australian and U.S. troops joined forces and converged on Buna.

NOV. 16, Monday 1,171st day
Australasia.—U.S. Navy Dept. ann. that off Guadalcanal on Nov. 13, 14 and 15 American fleet sank two Jap battleships, 8 cruisers, 6 destroyers and 12 transports for the loss of 2 U.S. light cruisers and 7 destroyers.

NOV. 17, Tuesday 1,172nd day
Air.—U.S. Fortresses and Liberators raided submarine base at St. Nazaire.
North Africa.—Allied bombers from Libya raided Tunis aerodrome; nine enemy aircraft destroyed in attacks on our forces between Bône and Tunisian border.
Libya.—Announced that our troops had occupied Derna and Mekili.
Russian Front.—Soviet forces on defensive at Stalingrad, but attacked S.E. of Nalchik.

NOV. 18, Wednesday 1,173rd day
Air.—U.S. Fortresses and Liberators bombed submarine bases at La Pallice and Lorient. R.A.F. bombers raided Turin.
North Africa.—Announced that advanced elements of British 1st Army, British and U.S. paratroops, and French forces had entered Tunisia at several points. U.S. bombed airfield at Bizerta and R.A.F. attacked aerodrome at Tunis.
Burma.—Wellington bombers from India raided Jap aerodromes in Burma.
General.—Pétain gave Laval power to make laws and issue decrees.

NOV. 19, Thursday 1,174th day
North Africa.—Tank and infantry engagements in Tunisia between British and enemy; engagements also took place between French and German units.
Russian Front.—Special communiqué announced that Russians had routed a strong German force in the Caucasus and removed threat to Ordzhonikidze.
Australasia.—Jap cruiser and destroyer sunk off Solomons by Fortresses.
Burma.—R.A.F. Blenheims attacked Jap aerodrome at Pakokku.

Australasia.—Announced that Gen. MacArthur had taken the field in New Guinea.

NOV. 20, Friday 1,175th day
Air.—R.A.F.'s night raid on Turin was heaviest yet made on Italy.
North Africa.—Enemy mechanized columns driven back by Allied advanced elements in Tunisia. R.A.F. and U.S. bombers raided airfields at Tunis and Bizerta; enemy aircraft bombed Algiers.
Libya.—Our troops occupied Benghazi.
Burma.—U.S. heavy bombers operating from India raided Mandalay.

NOV. 21, Saturday 1,176th day
North Africa.—British advance units in Tunisia inflicted heavy damage on German armoured column.
Mediterranean.—Trapani and other aerodromes in Sicily raided by R.A.F.
Russian Front.—Germans announced that Russian attacks N.W. and S. of Stalingrad had "assumed the nature of an offensive."
Burma.—R.A.F. attacked Jap airfields at Mingaladon and Toungoo.

NOV. 22, Sunday 1,177th day
Air.—R.A.F. bombers raided Stuttgart.
Russian Front.—Special communiqué announced that in offensive N.W. and S. of Stalingrad Soviet troops had advanced 40 to 50 miles and taken 13,000 prisoners.
Burma.—R.A.F. and U.S. bombers raided Akyab, Magwe and Mandalay.

NOV. 23, Monday 1,178th day
Air.—U.S. Fortresses and Liberators attacked submarine base at St. Nazaire.
North Africa.—Darlan announced from Algiers that French West Africa had put itself under his orders.
Libya.—Our forces occupied Jedabia and Jalo.
Russian Front.—Soviet troops continued to advance N.W. and S. of Stalingrad, recapturing five more towns and taking 11,000 more prisoners.
Australasia.—In New Guinea Australian forces entered Gona.

NOV. 24, Tuesday 1,179th day
North Africa.—In S. sector of Tunisia Allied paratroops repulsed enemy mechanized column and took prisoners. Bizerta, Tunis and Gabès attacked by our aircraft.
Russian Front.—Red Army advancing N.W. and S. of Stalingrad captured three German divisions and took 12,000 more prisoners. N. of Stalingrad Russian troops joined hands with city's defenders.

★══ *Flash-backs* ══★

1939
November 13. *Bombs dropped for first time on British soil, in the Shetlands.*
November 18. *Sinking of Dutch liner Simon Bolivar in North Sea marked opening of German magnetic mine campaign.*

1940
November 11. *Libreville, capital of Gaboon, occupied by Free French.*
November 12-13. *Fleet Air Arm attacked Italian navy at Taranto.*

November 14-15. *Heavy raid on Coventry from dusk to dawn.*

1941
November 14. *H.M.S. Ark Royal sank off Gibraltar after torpedo attack on previous day.*
November 18. *Eighth Army under Gen. Cunningham launched attack in Libya.*
November 20. *Germans opened large-scale attack on Moscow.*
November 22. *Germans claimed capture of Rostov-on-Don.*

O N June 30, 1940, I wrote a special article in THE WAR ILLUSTRATED which began with these words: "At the moment of writing the only hope of a France resurgent would seem to lie in Africa." After giving in some detail my reasons for so thinking, including a reminiscence of travel with a high official of the Algerian army, I finished thus: "That France's colonial empire may save her from sinking to the status of a minor power if it acts in full accord with the British Empire is still a possibility." For nearly two years and a half the impotent Vichy government—impotent for all but mischief—appeared to be bent on a prolonged form of national suicide: not only tolerating the spectacle of its country degenerating into a vassal state, but willing that in the process it should bring ruin upon a faithful ally.

S OON, indeed, the men of Vichy were fallen so low that at the bidding of the conqueror they abjured the principles on which the Third Republic had been founded and for Liberty, Equality, Fraternity—the very battle cry of Democracy—substituted Work, Family, Country, a meaningless trio of words when so grouped, designed only to bring once glorious and independent France into the framework of an inchoate 'New Order' where all established ideals of justice and humanism were ruthlessly to be suppressed. A deplorable derogation of all greatness, the free institutions of a nation of splendid achievement and noble ideals being abrogated for the capricious rule of a feeble old man surrounded by the political adventurers whose selfish ambitions and rivalries had been the main cause of the Republic's downfall.

T HE first, perhaps the worst, betrayal of her own people and her former allies was allowing Japan to establish bases in many parts of the strategic land of Indo-China there to begin preparations for the eventual conquest of the Philippines, Malaya, Burma, and the South Pacific: Indo-China, the key that unlocked the door to all that followed Pearl Harbour, was handed over by Vichy's representatives almost without a shot; but when Britain had to secure Syria in order to protect not only her own vital interests in the Near East but also to prevent the further deterioration of the French colonial empire, that bitterly anti-British colonial High Commissioner, General Dentz, put up an energetic though futile resistance. And the British efforts to save important elements of the French fleet from falling into the hands of the Nazis were as bitterly opposed by order of the Vichy servitors of Hitler at Dakar and Oran, as though the ally they had so recently betrayed were bent only on their destruction.

T O look back on these events, to find fallen France valiant only in facing at every turn her old ally, whose dearest wish was to succour her, is not a pleasant thing, but history will show that after the Vichy set-up the worst enemy of France was the debased and bewildered government of Pétain in which almost without exception Frenchmen who were noted for their anti-British opinions had access to the key positions. Darlan and Laval are two names that will long be remembered by the French people with strangely mixed feelings. Darlan, as head of the French Navy, was notoriously out of step with Britain even before the débâcle and did not hesitate to give stronger expression to his prejudice when he rose

to power in Vichy as head of both her military and naval forces in the Pétain government. Laval, the foulest figure in the malodorous mess of modern Paris politics, eventually pushed himself into the prime position behind the simulacrum of power named Pétain and the anti-British Darlan suddenly found himself playing a lesser role as naval chief behind the glorified gangster. "Envy's a coal comes hissing hot from hell": Darlan was envious, and disgruntled. The mean rivalries of her leaders which brought France to her knees may yet lift her to her feet: a consummation devoutly to be wished.

A FTER France had been made to play Hitler's game in many ways, she was sinking deeper in the mire of treachery until our Eighth Army had made its fine start with the destruction of Rommel's forces

What Think Ye of DARLAN?

in North Africa, what time the greatest armada in all history was secretly assembling in the western approaches of the Mediterranean: an armada designed to save Laval-led France from her corrupt and feeble government as well as to restore that vital seaway to the control of the United Nations. That Laval helped by any deep-laid treachery to his Nazi colleagues to facilitate this, double crosser though he be, is unbelievable; that Darlan did may not be so far outside credence. For although he may hate Britain from the traditional impulse of Trafalgar and from mean personal reasons, it may be that he dislikes Laval more than he dislikes Churchill; that he loves Hitler less than either. And in common with many other Frenchmen (again influenced by tradition) he would rather salute Old Glory than the Union Jack. Thus we begin to see how his presence in Algiers when the U.S. Army made its surprise attack may have been less accidental than it appeared. He was placed in a position that enabled him to do a good turn for the United Nations and for France herself while feeding a deep personal grudge.

A S the one high Vichy official present in Algiers at the moment of the Anglo-American surprise attack his decision to cease hostilities and surrender to the American army (carried there thanks mainly to the Royal Navy and the R.A.F.) enabled him to do a great day's work for France, for the United Nations, while doing a bad one for Laval. The human vanities: how they can affect the course of history! But there was a further and a worthier influence at work: General Noguès, Resident-General of Morocco, was there also as it happened, and he and Mittelhauser were outstanding among all the French Colonial leaders in June 1940 in urging that the Colonial Empire should remain in arms against the Hun

and so help the mother country to recover from her defeat. Noguès had been over-ruled by Vichy, just as General Mittelhauser had been in Syria, but while the latter eventually lost his job Noguès has held on "through chance and change" in Morocco and may well prove a force for French resurgence in view of the *fait accompli*: he, at least, has never been a willing collaborationist in a Nazi-ruled France. So we may yet see great good come out of evil.

W HILE it is unlikely that the British could ever again regard Darlan as a clean-handed ally, as Mr. Churchill treated him in Paris in November 1939 and again in London in the following spring (how pathetic to look now on these old pictures of the little French naval chief who was so soon to be branded pro-Nazi!), strange things happen in War and a double-crosser should not be ignored if eventually the fortunes of the conflict throw him back into the arms if not the hearts of those he once left in the lurch.

T HERE remains the possibility that some of the anti-British propaganda emanating from Vichy since the Pétain government moved there in 1940 may have been eye-wash to deceive the Nazi overlords. It is conceivable that men who are not at heart defeatists may under duress assume that antic disposition while hoping that things might so fall out that they would after all be able to take part in a real come-back and see the invader ignominiously ejected from their midst—just a possibility, not much more. Nothing can change the spots of those leopards Laval, Doriot, Déat, Bergery, and many others who were avowed defeatists long before the War. Only a man of great courage and unswerving public rectitude, like M. Herriot, could live "among the faithless faithful only he" . . . There may not be many Herriots inside France today, but there are millions who hate the Boche more than ever in the past, and they will have the last word one day.

A S I write it is not easy to get a clear idea of the situation in North Africa. Pétain denounces Darlan before the world as a traitor, and it might be thought that we were witnessing the old game of the pot calling the kettle black. But the persistency with which Darlan, in throwing in his lot with the United Nations, claims to act under the authority of Pétain is significant. We must not exclude the possibility that there may be a ruse of war in the confusion of voices. Neither Pétain nor Darlan has ever shown himself callous about the fate of France. Mistaken, misguided, antipathetic to Britain as both have been held to be, their desire that France should somehow survive may have been honest enough, whereas Laval's foul record of political chicanery leaves no doubt that he would wallow in dishonour if his ill-gained wealth could be saved and possibly augmented thereby. The entry of America has helped Darlan to a decision for which we must be grateful, though it will yet involve some delicate negotiation as between our true and tried friends the De Gaullists, and their more dubious fellow-countrymen. In enlisting aid from any available source that can further our cause in the new and enlarging prospect of the Axis doom, the fortunes of war demand that we profit to the utmost from such cooperation. Not even with heroic Stalin have we always walked hand-in-hand.

Printed in England and published every alternate Friday by the Proprietors, THE AMALGAMATED PRESS, LTD., The Fleetway House, Farringdon Street, London, E.C.4. Registered for transmission by Canadian Magazine Post. Sole Agents for Australia and New Zealand: Messrs. Gordon & Gotch, Ltd.; and for South Africa: Central News Agency, Ltd.—December 11th, 1942.   S.S.   *Editorial Address:* JOHN CARPENTER HOUSE, WHITEFRIARS, LONDON, E.C.4.

Vol 6 *The War Illustrated* Nº 144

Edited by Sir John Hammerton

SIXPENCE

DECEMBER 26, 1942

RED ARMY ON THE OFFENSIVE. From Russia there comes every day news of the hammer-blows delivered by Stalin's armies against the Nazi invader. This photograph shows just one corner on the 2,000 mile long front, stretching from the frozen wastes of the Arctic to the almost equally bleak slopes of the Caucasian heights. Automatic riflemen of the Red Army are speeding the enemy's departure from yet another " inhabited place," as the villages are styled in the Russian communiqués.

Photo, U.S.S.R. Official

NO. 145 WILL BE PUBLISHED FRIDAY, JANUARY 8, 1943

ALONG THE BATTLE FRONTS

by Our Military Critic, Maj.-Gen. Sir Charles Gwynn, K.C.B., D.S.O.

WHEN, in the first week of November, I wrote that the month had again proved to be a black one for Germany, I little expected how black it would become before its close. Germany and her partners have received a series of shattering blows; and though their full effects have not yet been realized, they threaten even more devastating results. The issue in several instances still hangs in the balance, and for the present it is better to take encouragement from what has been achieved than to indulge in optimistic speculation.

The scale and initial successes of Mr. Stalin's counter-offensive are particularly heartening, for obviously it is in Russia that the greatest results can be obtained.

In North Africa the Allies have made a good beginning, but it is clear that the Axis Powers will not be dislodged easily or quickly from their foothold in Tunisia. They are well placed to conduct a determined struggle for air supremacy, and it must be realized that the Allies, depending on a long and vulnerable line of sea communications, cannot without considerable delays develop their full strength. Until the enemy is evicted few of the strategic fruits of the great enterprise can be gathered. Even then the Mediterranean route will not be fully opened. Though convoys could be given a much more effective air umbrella and protection by light naval vessels, they would still be exposed to heavy attacks.

Meanwhile, in the struggle for air supremacy over the Tunisian battlefields, the Allies should be able to establish an advantage when their forward air bases are developed, for the Axis will find it difficult in a cramped area to operate bases for short-range aircraft.

ROMMEL is likely to put up a stubborn fight at El Agheila, but he can have little hope of retrieving his disaster. His chief object would now seem to be to prevent the concentration of all the Allied forces for the further development of their plans. General Alexander evidently does not underestimate the strength of Rommel's position; and, avoiding premature action, he intends to attack with the greatest force he can muster.

In the Far East Japan's naval losses continue to mount in her efforts to recapture lost ground; and the manifest inferiority

of her aircraft is an encouraging feature of the situation. Her army, however, remains at full strength; and the tenacity with which her troops will fight in the most forlorn situations has been clearly proved.

NORTH AFRICA

Official communiqués on events in Tunisia have been marked by

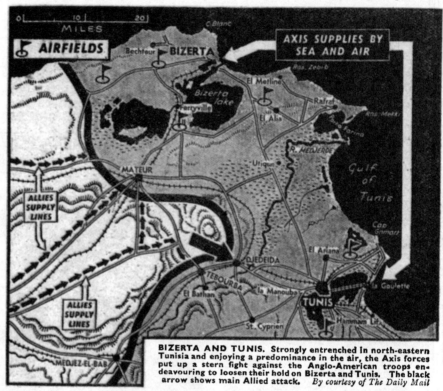

BIZERTA AND TUNIS. Strongly entrenched in north-eastern Tunisia and enjoying a predominance in the air, the Axis forces put up a stern fight against the Anglo-American troops endeavouring to loosen their hold on Bizerta and Tunis. The black arrow shows main Allied attack. *By courtesy of The Daily Mail*

reticence, and unofficial reports throw little light on the importance of what has happened in initial operations. Apparently the Allies thrust their advanced guards boldly forward in order to pen the Axis into a restricted area, and to secure the mountain passes for the passage of the main army. This seems to have been successfully accomplished, but naturally the advanced guards

met heavy counter-attacks and suffered some reverses—though how severe was not made clear. The fighting evidently was sharp with both sides having considerable losses.

In these advanced guard actions the Allies suffered from lack of air protection, and the enemy's Stuka dive-bombers—even if, as we are told, they are an obsolescent weapon—are still formidable when fighter protection cannot be given. It was obvious that in the earlier stages in the struggle for air supremacy the enemy would hold the advantage, having fully equipped aerodromes in Sicily and Sardinia in addition to such as he could use in Tunisia. The Allies, on the other hand, had in the first instance to bring all their fighter aircraft and ground organization by sea, and no doubt the first consignment of

ANZACS IN BARDIA. On the same day as Tobruk was reoccupied by men of the Eighth Army, the little port of Bardia, between it and the Egyptian frontier, was captured by Imperial troops for the third time in the Libyan campaigns. This photograph shows a Maori patrol of the New Zealand forces advancing down the town's main street. The church, it will be seen, is still little harmed, but the houses on either side are pitted with shell and bomb splinters.

Photo, British Official: Crown Copyright

RUSSIAN CENTRAL FRONT. In this sector the Red Army has maintained its pressure on Rzhev, and broken deeply into the German defences. This map shows the battle line at the beginning of Dec. 1942 and arrows indicate the direction of Soviet attacks. *By courtesy of The Times*

machines and first aerodromes to be equipped were those required for the protection of the further processes of disembarkation. Not until fresh consignments of aircraft had arrived and been disembarked could forward air bases be established for the protection of the advanced elements of the army which had moved out of fighter range of the base ports.

Obviously the building up of the Allies' air power must be a gradual process—perhaps even more gradual than the building up of the armies' transport and supply depots. Eventually the Allies should be able to establish superiority in short-range aircraft, since it would seem improbable that the Axis would be able to maintain aerodromes in effective operation in the restricted area they hold.

Meanwhile, it is of the first importance that our advanced forces should retain their hold on the ground they have secured for the deployment of the main army, whose advance is likely to be considerably slowed down by air attacks. Its heavy armaments and transport services are bound to present vulnerable targets. Fortunately, the long-range bombers of the Middle East Air Force, fighter bombers from Malta and the Navy can evidently do much to prevent the enemy rapidly developing counter-offensive potentialities.

The more we are told of the original landing in North Africa the greater must be our admiration for the part played by the Navy, and perhaps especially for the secrecy which was maintained. It will now be on the R.A.F. that the chief responsibility for opening the way for final success will fall, even though it will be the Army that will have the hard task of gathering the fruits. That it is not going to be an easy matter to evict the enemy from Tunis and Bizerta is, however, all too clear.

In Libya, while I write, Alexander is still closing up Montgomery's army for a new encounter with Rommel. Before this is published (some fortnight from now) we shall know how far he has succeeded, and what Rommel's real intentions are. Whether he intends to fight a decisive or merely a delaying action is at present uncertain; but it is hardly conceivable that he stands a chance of retrieving his disaster by any form of counter-stroke, though he may exact a heavy price from the 8th Army.

RUSSIA

Hoth's army, encircled in front of Stalingrad between the Don and the Volga, is still in danger of complete annihilation, but it has recovered from the first shock of surprise and has organized strong defences. It has evidently no intention of attempting to cut its way out of the ring, but means to hold its ground in hopes of relief.

It is improbable that the Russians will make further large captures of prisoners or material unless lack of supplies and munitions brings about wholesale surrender. They appear, however, to be maintaining their attacks and to be steadily, if slowly, gaining ground. Such pressure would tend to exhaust German supplies; and the efforts being made to send in reinforcements and supplies by air seem to indicate a real shortage. In view of their many attacks on Stalingrad it is improbable that the Germans can have accumulated great reserve stocks, and they probably have lost some of their main depots at Kalach. Dumps in forward areas in the outskirts of the city would, however, presumably be large; possibly it was to protect them that attacks were continued, after it must have been evident that they would be futile.

Timoshenko evidently intends to secure a position which a relief army would find it difficult to break through, and he seems to have made much progress westwards along the railways on both sides of the Don. The situation here, is, however, rather obscure, for there is little to indicate what is the strength or organization of the German forces he is encountering. They may be the nucleus of a relief army. Kotelnikovo on the Stalingrad-Novorossisk railway is a centre where one such might form.

On the Caucasus front German reports speak of Russian counter-attacks developing into a major offensive, but the Russians make no such claim. Any pressure that they are exercising certainly complicates the German problem; and should a collapse occur at Stalingrad the German position in the Mozdok region in particular would become precarious.

Zhukov's offensive on the Rzhev-Velikiye Luki front makes slow progress, but it has had remarkable success considering that it is attacking probably the most strongly entrenched part of the German front. German counter-attacks have been numerous and vigorous, but have obviously entailed the employment of important reserves and have been more costly than successful.

Clearly the Germans intend to hold Rzhev at all costs. Its capture would remove the block on the Moscow-Riga railway, the use of which would be of immense value to Zhukov, especially when heavy snow paralyses road transport. The lack of railway communications behind his front may make it difficult for him to maintain the weight of his offensive if Rzhev continues to hold out. The town is held by a large force, and must have ample supplies; so even if its communications have been cut it has great possibilities of prolonged defence.

The situation on this front also is obscure, but evidently it is causing the Germans great anxiety. Much is likely to depend on how the sheer fighting efficiency of the German troops is maintained under winter conditions after the experiences of last year. A major Russian success at any point would shake the stability of the whole German front.

THE FAR EAST

The persistent attempts by the Japanese to reinforce their detachments on Guadalcanal and at Buna have had practically no success, and have cost them further serious losses; loss of ships, both naval and transport, is, of course, a heavier blow than the loss of troops, though the drowning of large numbers from sunken transports may have its effect even on Japanese nerves.

The attack on Buna has evidently been greatly handicapped by lack of artillery, and the arrival of two howitzers by air may serve to expedite matters. Though the number is too small to produce crushing effect, they may help in the successive capture of small localities.

Now that we have been told the full extent of the Pearl Harbour disaster, its shattering effect on the whole Far Eastern situation will perhaps be more fully understood in this country. It gave Japan a completely free hand, though fortunately only for a limited time.

WINTER IN THE CAUCASUS brought some relief to the Soviet forces fighting for possession of the Georgian Highway. On Nov. 19, 1942 it was announced that the Germans had suffered a heavy defeat at Ordzhonikidze, some 5,000 of their men being slain, and an even greater number wounded. Red Army troops are here seen clearing a mountain road preparatory to their comrades' advance. PAGE 419 *Photo, U.S.S.R. Official*

With the Allied Forces in French North Africa

IN CASABLANCA, great seaport of French Morocco, General Noguès, French Resident-General, and Maj.-Gen. G. S. Patton, commanding U.S. Western Task Force, attend a ceremony held in memory of American and French soldiers who had fallen in battle (top). Spahis (Moroccan troops) form a picturesque guard of honour. Inset, left to right, Maj.-Gen. L. R. Fredendall, commanding U.S. Central Task Force; Lt.-Gen. M. W. Clark, second-in-command to Gen. Eisenhower; Brig.-Gen. J. H. Doolittle, commander of U.S. Air Forces in N. Africa. Below, American motorized column drives eastward through Algeria.

Photos, Keystone, Planet News

When the Luftwaffe Hit Back at Algiers

AIR WAR IN ALGIERS. Although the Axis ground forces were unable to contest the Allied landings in Morocco and Algeria, the Luftwaffe was soon in action. German dive-bombers attacked Allied transports in Algiers harbour, and top photo shows a smoke-screen being laid by naval craft to protect the Allied armada. Inset, Sir A. Tedder, Vice-Chief of Air Staff (left), and Maj.-Gen. L. H. Brereton, commanding U.S. 9th Air Force. Below, enemy bomb damage in Algiers.

Photos, British Official; Keystone

What So Precious as Water in the Desert?

FRESH WATER FOR THE TROOPS constitutes a major problem in desert warfare. But during the 8th Army's pursuit of Rommel's retreating forces the Royal Navy took a hand, and at Sollum (on the Egypt-Libya frontier) landed 33,000 barrels brought from Alexandria. Below, part of this welcome shipment being run ashore, and (top right) rolling one of the barrels up the beach ; each barrel contained 44 gallons of water. Top left, Royal Engineers relaying the water pipe-line near El Daba.

Photos, British Official : Crown Copyright

Speed the Supplies to Montgomery's Men!

IN PURSUIT OF ROMMEL the 8th Army pressed hard on the shattered Axis forces from Egypt into Libya. This photograph shows a huge convoy of British supply and ammunition lorries streaming westward along the road which runs beside the railway from the Nile Valley to near Tobruk. Strongly indicative of Allied air supremacy is the close grouping of the vehicles. By the beginning of Dec. 1942 Rommel had withdrawn to El Agheila, almost on the border of Cyrenaica and Tripolitania.

Photo, British Official: Crown Copyright

THE WAR AT SEA

by Francis E. McMurtrie

Capt. W. G. AGNEW, C.B. (left), and Lt. Cmdr. A. P. H. NOBLE, D.S.C., commanders respectively of the cruiser Aurora and destroyer Quentin, which played a prominent part in smashing an Axis convoy in the Mediterranean on Dec. 2, 1942. *Phillips, Keystone*

By borrowing a leaf from the German book and scuttling their ships at Toulon, the French disappointed Hitler's hopes of seizing them. From the rapidity with which a strong force of troops was thrown into the town, immediately making its way to the dockyard, it seems evident that the decision to take over the French fleet was not a sudden one. Fortunately, French plans were also of long standing, and, as far as can be ascertained, the only German prize of any value was a group of three destroyers which happened to be lying in a basin some distance from the rest of the fleet. Two cruisers also appeared from the air to be intact, but may have been damaged under water.

It is sad to reflect that had Vice-Admiral de Laborde and his officers taken their courage in their hands a fortnight earlier, they might have sailed for African waters and so placed themselves in a position to offer more than passive resistance to the invaders who hold France in subjection.

Various statements have appeared concerning the condition of the sunken ships. Obviously, any reliable report would need to be preceded by a thorough examination of the wrecks, for which purpose divers would have to be employed. It would appear that some ships were blown up, while others merely foundered or capsized. It seems to be generally accepted that the water in which they lie is comparatively shallow, so salvage should not be unduly difficult. But to refloat and refit so many ships full of complicated mechanism is bound to be a long job, occupying a considerable amount of labour and material. It must be concluded, therefore, that although the French ships cannot be written off as total losses, they are unlikely to be ready for active service for a very long time. If Hitler was counting upon them to reinforce his enfeebled allies in the Mediterranean, he must now be faced with a fresh problem.

It is generally believed that Mussolini, while ready to risk his light ships in escorting convoys to Tunisia and Tripolitania, regards his battleships as too precious to send to sea. On the rare occasions on which they have been sighted, they have invariably retired to port again at the first sign of danger.

In spite of this, three of them were put out of action at Taranto in the famous moonlight torpedo attack made by the Fleet Air Arm on November 11, 1940. Two years later, on December 5, 1942, American aircraft delivered a heavy bombing attack on Naples, another important naval base. A cruiser of the Attendolo type capsized, and a battleship received damage, though it is improbable that she was hit in a vital spot.

Should the situation become sufficiently desperate, Hitler may insist on the Italian battle fleet proceeding to sea to protect the convoys, on the arrival of which German troops in Africa depend. There are no German warships available for the purpose, the few that remain in service being either in Norwegian waters or in the Baltic. The squadron based on Trondheim, comprising the Tirpitz, Admiral Scheer, Lützow, Prinz Eugen and Admiral Hipper, has shown few signs of activity since it proceeded northward in July with the object of intercepting a convoy bound for Russia. A Soviet submarine claimed to have torpedoed the Tirpitz on that occasion, though there is no certainty that she was damaged.

In view of the fate of the Bismarck in May 1941 it is improbable that another sortie will be made into the Atlantic, for the chances of any considerable success in this direction are far less today than they were then.

The Navy and North Africa

It was revealed recently by Mr. A. V. Alexander, First Lord of the Admiralty, that the expedition to North Africa was organized in three separate forces. One, which sailed from the United States, was entirely an American responsibility ; it was this unit that occupied Casablanca and other ports in French Morocco, disabling or sinking the battleship Jean Bart and other French warships which opposed the landings. The other two units, comprising both British and American troops, sailed from this country under the protection of the Royal Navy, with aid from ships of the Royal Canadian, Polish, Royal Norwegian and Royal Netherlands Navies, and proceeded to Oran and Algiers.

British warships lost in the course of the operations were the auxiliary aircraft-carrier Avenger, the destroyers Martin and Broke, the corvette Gardenia, the sloops Ibis, Hartland and Walney, the minesweeper Algerine, the depot ship Hecla, and the anti-aircraft escort vessel Tynwald. The Dutch lost a destroyer, the Isaac Sweers, and the Americans five naval transports. Compared with the results achieved, these losses must be regarded as trifling.

Though the Germans have contrived to assemble some 20,000 troops in Tunisia, they have suffered heavy loss in transporting them there. Not only have many ships been sunk by H.M. submarines, but twice in 48 hours convoys were intercepted by our surface warships.

Shortly after midnight, December 1-2, 1942, a force under Rear-Admiral C. H. J. Harcourt, comprising H.M. cruisers Aurora, Sirius and Argonaut, and the destroyers Quentin and Quiberon, practically wiped out an enemy convoy proceeding from Italy to Tunisia. Although the convoy scattered and sought to cover its retreat with smoke-screens, four merchant vessels, at least two of which were troopships, and three destroyers were set on fire and destroyed. Admiral Harcourt summed up the whole situation afterwards when he made the signal : " Well done, everybody ; I think we have helped the 1st Army."

On the night of December 2-3 light forces under Captain A. L. Poland, R.N., came in contact with another south-bound convoy which had been shortly before by torpedo aircraft. In the earlier encounter two ships of mercantile type were destroyed, and in the second an Italian torpedo boat was sunk.

These engagements were no mere matter of chance, but were the fruit of careful planning and skilful leadership.

The United States Navy Department's official report on the Pearl Harbour disaster, made public on December 6 last, is a most interesting document. Out of eight battleships lying in port on December 7, 1941, Japanese torpedoes from the air so severely damaged five that they were either sunk or put out of action for some time, while the remaining three also received damage. Only one of these battleships, the Arizona, has had to be written off as a total loss, and with the exception of two destroyers, whose main and auxiliary machinery have been recovered, the various other warships sunk or damaged by the enemy attack have either been salved and repaired, or are now under salvage. Those ships which have been taken into dockyard hands for refit after salvage will be modernized before rejoining the fleet.

It is proof of the fine quality and spirit of the United States Navy that it should have recovered itself in so short a time from such a heavy blow. Moreover, in the last few months it has taken the initiative.

SEA-AND-AIR BATTLE OFF THE SOLOMONS. On the right an American aircraft-carrier is making a sharp turn to avoid Japanese attacks during a fierce engagement which began on Oct. 26, 1942, near the Santa Cruz Islands. In the centre an enemy plane is crashing on to a U.S. destroyer. On Nov. 1 the U.S. Navy Dept. announced that an aircraft-carrier and a destroyer had been lost in this battle. *Photo, New York Times Photo-*

Out of Toulon's Smoke France Will Rise Again

ADM. DE LABORDE (above) gave the order to scuttle the French fleet at Toulon on Nov. 27, 1942, when the Germans were at the gates of the naval base. By so doing he vindicated the honour of France and also deprived the Axis of a powerful concentration of warships. On the next day the Fighting French Navy observed a one-minute silence in honour of their countrymen who were lost with their ships at Toulon. Flags were flown at half-mast; right, French sailors lowering the tricolour in London.

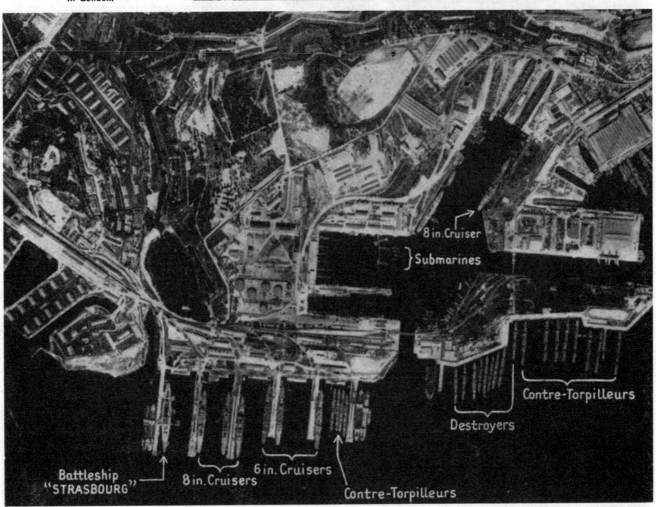

8 in. Cruiser

} Submarines

Contre-Torpilleurs

Destroyers

Battleship "STRASBOURG"

8 in. Cruisers

6 in. Cruisers

Contre-Torpilleurs

THE FRENCH FLEET AT TOULON consisted of some 60 ships, including the battleships Dunkerque, Strasbourg, and Provence; four 10,000-ton cruisers, three light cruisers, a seaplane-carrier, about 28 destroyers and *contre-torpilleurs* (a slightly larger type of destroyer); and some 20 submarines. This air view of the harbour, taken before the Axis occupation on Nov. 27, shows many of these ships in their berths. "From the flames and smoke of the explosions at Toulon," said Mr. Churchill on Nov. 29, "France will rise again."

Photos, British Official: Planet News, Sport & General

'Occupy All France!' said Duce to Fuehrer

THE GERMAN OCCUPATION OF VICHY FRANCE, which took place on Nov. 11, 1942, destroyed the last vestiges of Hitler's pretence that this part of France was a "free zone." 1, German infantry passing through the Arc de Triomphe in Marseilles. 2, The Italians were permitted by their German masters to make an excursion along the Riviera: a motorized detachment pauses on the road to Marseilles. 3, German vehicles on the famous Cannebière in Marseilles. 4, Enemy tank in Toulouse.

Photos, Associated Press

In New Guinea They've Got the Japs on the Run

AUSTRALIANS AND AMERICANS IN NEW GUINEA, following their recapture of Kokoda on Nov. 2, 1942, were swift in their pursuit of the retreating Japanese. Australian troops entered Gona on Nov. 23 while U.S. forces hammered at Buna, the last remaining enemy stronghold on the coast. Top, cheery Australians wounded at Kokoda make their way back to the rear for treatment. Below left, Allied troops examining a captured Jap tank; and (right) an enemy landing-barge.

Photos, Associated Press

A Second Winter's Tale of Dreadful War

Winter's coming has brought no cessation of hostilities on the vast Russian front. On Nov. 19 the Red Army launched an attack in the Caucasus; three days later it went over to the offensive at Stalingrad, and on Nov. 28 a third offensive was launched on the Moscow front.

L AST winter was bad enough for the German armies in Russia; this winter may well be worse. Not only are the Russians fighting with still tremendous, seemingly undiminished, strength, but they are nerved to greater efforts by the consciousness of victories already won. The myth of Hitler's invincibility has been blown to pieces by Montgomery's guns in Egypt, by Timoshenko in the Caucasus and before Stalingrad, and by Zhukov in Central Russia.

How near the Germans were to defeat, even to disaster, in the campaign of last winter has been revealed by Hitler himself. In a speech to the Reichstag last April he admitted that "neither the German soldier, nor tanks, nor locomotives, were prepared for such intense cold." Nerves were at breakingpoint, obedience wavered, and a sense of duty was lacking—these are all Hitler's own expressions—and in a few cases it was necessary for him to intervene. So "we mastered a fate that broke another man Napoleon 130 years ago."

Goering, too, dilated upon the enormous difficulties which confronted the Germans. In a speech last May he spoke of the time when, after Hitler's "unheard-of victories, after the Germans had penetrated 1,500 kilometres and more into Russian space,"

"A new enemy fell upon us. Not the Russian divisions, not the Russian armies, not the Russian command, but the elements rose against us. Almost suddenly winter fell upon us, producing immense cold within three days—such a winter as has never probably been experienced in the history of such struggles. Rivers were frozen, swamps and lakes; one white blanket of death was spread over the limitless country . . . The Russian was in our rear in the north, in the centre, in the south. Partisan detachments blew up everything. Maddening cold almost froze our troops. The cold hindered railway transport and the lines cracked with the cold, the locomotives could no longer move. For days the front remained without supplies, without ammunition, without food and without clothing. Out there the brave musketeer stood in the icy snow, his hands numb. When he touched the barrel of his rifle the skin of his fingers stuck to it. The motors failed, could no longer be started. Tanks got stuck in the deep snow. One thing piled on top of another . . ."

T HAT is Goering's picture of the winter war of 1941, in its main essentials it is a picture of that of 1942. True, so far the climatic conditions have not equalled those of last year, while Hitler's propagandists have maintained that the lessons of last year's campaign have been well learnt—that this year the preparations have been much more complete. Barracks have been built in many parts of occupied Russia. Huge quantities of furs have been purchased (or stolen) in all parts of Europe. Tens of thousands of skis have been bought to send to the Russian front: white hoods and cloaks, too. Vast quantities of bread, meat, fats and potatoes are being supplied every week by General Wietersheim, Hitler's First Quartermaster, who has been boosted as the "Ludendorff of the New Army." One fact we can be sure of; that the German soldier at the front will be given the best of everything that Germany can produce. It is the civilians who will go short, and the civilians of the occupied countries will go shortest of all: they can starve so far as Hitler cares.

All the same, it is a bleak prospect for the Germans. In the north and central sectors they have towns and cities in which to winter, but their hold on these would seem to be uncertain, following Zhukov's offensive. In the south, in the Stalingrad sector, there are no cities, and most of the villages have been destroyed. In large measure the prolonged onslaught on Stalingrad was dictated by the necessity of obtaining winter quarters, since otherwise the attackers would be condemned to spend the winter in the empty, icy steppes. But Stalingrad still stands; and the Germans are now falling back through a devastated countryside in which there is no warmth, little food, and less shelter. And everywhere the partisan detachments are active throughout the long winter nights. Behind the German lines there are millions of Russians, and every one of them is a foe made desperate and relentless by ferocious treatment.

But for the Russians, too, the prospect is of a bleak and hungry winter. Throughout

WARE SNIPERS IN STALINGRAD! Reproduced from the Berliner Illustrierte Zeitung, this photograph purports to show German shock troops looking up to detect any sign of Russian presence in the upper storeys of the largely demolished houses.

the country (reports Reuters Correspondent) the slogan is "everything for the front," and this means that the civilians in the rear must tighten their belts still more. At times they must go hungry; they must do without central heating since all the fuel is required for the army and war industries; they must do without comforts, even many of what we should call the necessities of life. Last year the Russians lost the Ukraine; this year they have had to abandon the Kuban, richest remaining source of foodstuffs. These losses have but spurred them on to ever-greater effort. Nothing has been spared the Red Army. Vast quantities of skis and sledges have been turned out by the factories for the new ski army; winter clothing, also, and heating equipment for gun-sites, dug-outs and billets. And all this not for "static hibernation" but for a vigorous and victorious offensive in the depths of winter.

In Moscow the Muscovites all through the summer have been collecting fuel, and in the squares there are great stacks of birch logs. In the allotments people have been working by moonlight to get the potatoes up before the frosts come. Although Moscow's young men have gone into the Army, although great numbers of its population are working now in factories hundreds of miles away in the Russia of the Urals and beyond, the capital city of the Soviets is still palpitating with life. Everywhere the mood is a confident one.

Much the same can be said of Leningrad, now preparing for its second winter siege. Old wooden houses have been dismantled for fuel; each citizen has been required to prepare for the winter four cubic yards of wood for himself and two more for the community. Dozens of repair squads are active; plumbing has been overhauled, substitute glass put into windows, methods of saving fuel publicized. "Winter is coming! Prepare for frosts!" comes from the radio at frequent intervals. Last winter the Leningraders suffered horribly from cold and privation: they are better prepared this year.

O N the whole, then, the Russians have the advantage: most important, they are fighting to liberate their own soil and on every hand they see signs that the tide of war is at last turning in their favour. The contrast between the invader and the invaded has been well depicted by A. T. Cholerton, The Daily Telegraph's correspondent in Moscow, in a dispatch published on Nov. 27. He writes of that new feature of war on the Russian front—the taking of large numbers of Nazi prisoners. They were astounded, he says; they were in despair over their defeat. They were real fighting-men, and it would have been moving to see them had one not remembered "their cold, hard arrogance and their way of treating even the grand Don Cossack villagers as people of a lower race—slaves and chattels to be worked out, starving to death in trench and road building, and then flung out to die in the snows on the wide gale-swept steppes."

These arrogant "lord folk" of Hitler's grand army (went on Mr. Cholerton) may have been a bit troubled in their minds at not taking all of Stalingrad before the winter, and at being left out to face its icy gales in the naked steppe. But they seem to have felt very sure of themselves while out chasing the old Cossack men, young boys and women, and they did themselves pretty well in the matter of billets, making the ruined houses quite cosy with stolen mattresses and eiderdowns. They covered their own backs, too, with filched sheepskin coats and women's furs. Underneath they wore female shawls, jumpers and pullovers. In they roll, these prisoners, in their thousands and tens of thousands, often without escort and led by their own officers, some still trying to swagger.

A S they march by to the prisoner-of-war camps they are watched by their victims and pre-ordained slaves.

In those little local crowds of peasants, who have been first strafed from the air, then fought over, and then ignobly dragooned in the past four months, there are armed partisans whose brothers have been tortured and then hanged and strangled by the neck without any merciful six-foot drop. There are Russian regulars, too, armed with tommy-guns, and feeling big, broad and at ease in their sheepskin caps, their sheepskin coats, their big, clumsy felt high-boots—providential equipment, wearing which one knows one can march to hell without getting frostbite, unless one is left out in the open wounded.

It speaks well for the Russian "tommies" who, except in the heat of battle, are rather easygoing, habitually rather humble-minded folk, that they have taken prisoner and left alive so many scores of thousands of these cocky Prussians.

And to think of it, that "these wretches, at least their airmen, have during the past few weeks dropped down millions of leaflets telling the Stalingrad garrison and the huge adjacent Russian armies that they were all utterly encircled and destroyed!"

Grim Battle in Russia's Snowbound Landscape

THIS RUSSIAN MARKSMAN, a member of an anti-tank crew defending positions from a blockhouse, maintains a vigilant watch, never taking his eyes from his gunsights during a prolonged attack by the enemy. In front and behind him are stores of ammunition.

SOVIET INFANTRYMEN, led by one of their comrades carrying a light machine-gun, clear an enemy trench during patrol activity on the central front. Heavy snowstorms in this sector at the beginning of Dec. 1942 added to the Germans' difficulties.

RUSSIANS ADVANCING to the N.W. and S.W. of Stalingrad in Nov. 1942 cut off large German forces which had long been hammering at that city. By the first week of December the enemy had lost many important heights, and the trapped Nazi divisions were reported to be clinging to every position favourable to defence.

Right, Russian tanks going in to attack an enemy position near Stalingrad. In their efforts to extricate themselves from the giant Soviet trap between the Volga and the Don the Germans improvised sledges, for frost and snow paralysed mechanical transport. Above, the retreating enemy moving across the snow with their sledges —a picture suggestive of Napoleon's retreat in 1812.

Photos, U.S.S.R. Official ; Planet News, Keystone

In Italy Is Fascism Riding for a Fall?

Will Italy crash—and when, and how? These are questions that men are asking everywhere, following the crushing defeats of her armies in Abyssinina and in Libya and the series of devastating air raids on Genoa, Milan, Turin and Naples. In this specially contributed article Dr. EDGAR STERN-RUBARTH endeavours to interpret the writing on the wall.

IT is said that when Mussolini finally agreed in 1934 to grant Hitler an interview at Venice, he placed the Fuehrer, when they came to be photographed, in such a position that the Hebrew letters on the Decalogue Tables held by the Lion of St. Mark appeared just over the head of the world's Jew-baiter No. 1. Today Il Duce no longer dares to make jokes of any kind about the man he then despised as his imitator. He allowed himself to be tied hand and foot when he jumped on France's back.

What then appeared to be an easy racket for squeezing a New Roman Empire out of a Nazi-conquered world has since been transformed into the greatest disaster to befall a would-be world power for the last thousand years. Yet, such is the present attitude of the United Nations that there is still a loophole by which Italy, if not Mussolini and his Blackshirts, may escape; and both the Fascists and their Italian opponents within and outside Italy know it. This is the fact behind all the unrest, all the moves and counter-moves, observed in Rome of late, ever since Mussolini began to "liquidate" or cashier such men as Balbo, Badoglio and Cavagnari, and started to "purge" his own party, evicting from it in the summer months of this year no fewer than 66,000 members. Many of the victims were high officials—among them more than two-thirds of the 94 prefects (provincial governors), judges, civil servants and provincial secretaries of the Fascist Party. His purge did not stop at some of the greatest industrialists, landowners and nobles of the kingdom; the Duce even tried to "cleanse" the Forces. But there he encountered opposition too strong for a deflated dictator . . .

This opposition was not provoked by disagreement with the bitter necessity of uprooting graft, corruption, profiteering and all the other ugly phenomena of a system of wanton rule. It was due to other considerations. When Crown Prince Umberto recently wrested his A.D.C., Colonel Granuzzi, from the clutches of the O.V.R.A. (secret police) which wanted to shoot him and other high officers for "high treason," it was obviously because a large and increasingly influential portion of the Italian leadership and people has begun to interpret high treason in terms diametrically different from those of the orthodox Fascists. In conformity with the 600,000 Italians in the U.S.A. now freed from the stigma of enemy status, who are preparing another Garibaldi Legion for the liberation of their homeland, and with other hundreds of thousands elsewhere, they see Italy betrayed by "one man," the ambitious would-be Caesar and his minions.

THEY have good reason for adopting that attitude. In Rome, near the Piazza del Popolo, one of the most famous barracks is occupied by a German regiment; visitors at the Palazzo Venezia must obtain first a German permit, after passing close scrutiny by Hitler's Gestapo; the German Embassy, with four departments representing the main functions of a government, rules over all but the provincial administration of the country; Field-Marshal Kesselring, Goering's deputy, commands the air all over the "Mare Nostrum" and Italy herself (leaving Italian

MR. CHURCHILL TO THE ITALIANS

OUR operations in French N. Africa should enable us to bring the weight of the war home to the Italian Fascist State in a manner not hitherto dreamed of by its guilty leaders or, still less, by the unfortunate people Mussolini has led, exploited and disgraced. Already the centres of war industry in N. Italy are being subjected to harder treatment than any of our cities experienced in the winter of 1940. But if the enemy should in due course be blasted from the Tunisian tip—which is our aim—the whole of the south of Italy, all the naval bases, and all the munition establishments and other military objectives wherever situated will be brought under a prolonged, scientific and shattering air attack. It is for the Italian people, forty million of them, to say whether they want this terrible thing to happen to their country or not.
—*From the Premier's broadcast, Nov. 29, 1942.*

cities and industries denuded of A.A. guns); and Rommel was forced on the Italians as Supreme Commander over the whole Mediterranean sphere only a few weeks ago, at the height of his triumph. Gestapo officials sit in every central and local government department; Sicily is wholly in the grasp of the Nazi Luftwaffe; and since Allied blows have begun to fall on the other side of Italy's waters, Nazi generals, headed by the German Army Chief, Keitel, have appeared in Rome itself in order to tighten their grip.

ITALY's economic life had long been completely in the German grasp, depending as it does on a regular flow of at least 12 million tons of coal a year from Germany—under peace conditions—and forced to yield hundreds of thousands of skilled workers to Germany. Resistance on the part of Italian industrialists was hopeless from the beginning. Under a cleverly devised system of contracts, they had to let all their modern, efficient plants fall under Nazi domination. Numerous world-famous Italian plants (the Ansaldo, Montecatini, Brescia, Caproni, Breda, Pirelli, etc.) have fallen into the maw of Goering's huge combine, the Ruhr magnates and the German Dye Trust, who either took them over outright by obtaining the majority of the shares or relegated them to the position of spare-part-making subsidiaries. In some cases, as had been done already in France, whole factories, with their engineers, foremen

and workers, were transferred to Germany. The Nazis have requisitioned the repair shops of Italy's railways. They have stolen so much of Italy's agricultural produce that on her rich soil rations have to be lower than anywhere except in starving Greece and Poland. Italy has even to go begging for timber in Finland, again giving foodstuffs in exchange, since her armies failed to subdue Yugoslavia whence she used to import it.

It is to be expected that, in these circumstances, there is not much love lost between the Italian people and the masters whom Mussolini's megalomania has foisted upon them. But after the loss by Rommel of what little had remained of Italy's African Empire, after the invasion by an Anglo-American armada and air force of her own waters, what can Italy do about it?

THAT question was pondered, and answered, long before the blow fell. Loosely knit at first, a *camarilla* had developed, centring on the Royal House: the generals and admirals, the nobility, estate owners, financiers, industrialists and, with the exception of the Archbishops of Naples and Milan, the high clergy, had all come to the conclusion that Fascism spelt ruin—either way; and now a second opposition group is forming among the "Traditionalists" and Youthful Radicals of the Fascist party itself. With a victorious Axis, Italy would come under Hitler's heel, as a mere puppet-state, run and exploited by the "Great Ally"; with a defeat of Hitler, she would have to share his doom . . . Unless, of course, she could desert the Axis cause in time. Quite a number of peace feelers have been put out during the last year, by way of Vatican circles favouring the "Latin Bloc" idea, anti-Fascists in exile, and relatives of the Italian royal family.

There seemed, however, to be no silver lining on the clouded horizon while Mussolini lorded it inside the country. Yet, Italy's army leaders have made a move that may have far-reaching consequences: when the new Mediterranean situation arose they declined all German help for the defence of their own soil. Forming new armies—Italy desires to defend herself alone, if need be by withdrawing from the Dalmatian coast, and even leaving Sicily and Sardinia unprotected but for the Luftwaffe. Yet Hitler, as afraid of his "unprotected" allies as of the enemy, is pouring divisions across the Brenner.

To be on the safe side, however, a few weeks ago tens of thousands of workers of his Todt Organization began to build a "South Wall"—along the Italian border. The Fuehrer may envisage an Allied assault somewhere on southern Italian territory after the ultimatum delivered by the R.A.F., whose blows have been felt by Genoa, Milan, Turin, and Naples, and among other disasters provoked sanguinary clashes between a powerful underground movement and Fascist gunmen. He may fear a revolution that would smash the whole Fascist machinery and resurrect a humane, democratic Italy who would turn against her seducer. His assumptions may well be correct. Certainly a large part of the Italian population already sees not us but him as the enemy; they may soon be the majority.

HUNGRY ITALY cultivates every inch of her soil, and even the flowerbeds in Italian cities are being utilized to produce food. This photo shows wheat growing in the Piazza del Municipio, one of the main squares of Naples.

Photo, Keystone

Leader of Britain's 'Crusaders'

In command of our First Army in North Africa is fifty-year-old Lt.-Gen. Kenneth Arthur Noel Anderson, C.B., M.C. The First Army has for its badge the "Crusader" flash. To quote from the Order of the Day issued when it was introduced last summer, "Just as of old the Crusaders wore on their shields the sign of the Cross . . . so we carry this emblem to show our unity of purpose in the dedication of ourselves to the rescue of Europe from the grip of barbarism . . ."

431

North Africa Invaded by the Allies

In all history there has been no such armada as that which landed General Eisenhower's Allied Army on the shores of Morocco and Algeria. 1, Guns carried inshore by landing-craft being man-handled up the beach near Algiers. 2, Above an old fort blasted into surrender by dive-bombers of the U.S. navy, "Old Glory" flies in triumph. 3, British 1st Army paratroops all smiles at Algiers.

Photos,
Co

They Came to Conquer, Remain as Friends

Fortunately, French resistance to the Anglo-American invasion was short-lived, and the good accord that was erelong established is witnessed by this scene (4) of the American and British flags being hoisted over Allied H.Q., while a French guard of honour salutes. 5, One of the 500 transports which brought the troops across the Atlantic. 6 and 7, American troops coming ashore at Arzeu, near Oran.

America Comes to Africa

Along the dusty highway skirting the Atlantic coast, American soldiers march from Fedala to Casablanca, the great naval base which, after some stiff fighting, surrendered to the Allies on Nov. 11, 1942. Arabs on mules and a very superior-looking camel give an oriental touch to the scene. In the lower photograph more of General Eisenhower's warriors move out to battle up a cactus-fringed road.

434

VIEWS & REVIEWS
Of Vital War Books

by Hamilton Fyfe

LORD CHATFIELD, whose book The Navy and Defence, reviewed in this page, was Minister for the Co-ordination of Defence, 1939-40. *Photo, Sport & General*

I N 1886, when Admiral of the Fleet Lord Chatfield joined the Royal Navy, the British nation considered its first line of defence perfect. A few years before it had been shouting, in defiance of Tsarist Russia :

We've got the ships,
We've got the men,
We've got the money, too !

If it had known the truth about our ships and men as it is revealed in Lord Chatfield's book The Navy and Defence (Heinemann, 15s.), it would not have slept so well o' nights.

In half a century great changes have been made. It is due to Lord Chatfield and a few more like him—never very many—that those changes have almost all been improvements. The Navy has been transformed since he passed out of the Britannia. It certainly needed transformation. He tells the story in a straightforward, sailor-like style, throwing in frequent references to his domestic life, telegrams announcing births of children, troubles with furnished houses ; and telling often, too, how he got a little bit of shooting or stuck pigs or made a century at cricket. All of which makes it a pleasantly human record as well as one of historical value.

The bearded men who commanded our ships in those days had plenty of individuality. They were, many of them, " powerful personalities," but few of them were mentally alert. When they combined intellect with character, they tended to be intolerant and quarrelsome, as Jacky Fisher and Percy Scott were. To those two Lord Chatfield gives the chief credit for " changing the whole fighting outlook of the Navy " ; but he admits that Fisher was too headlong in his methods, sometimes even brutal, and that Scott " had a cocksure manner which brooked no argument and added to an unpopularity created by a forceful ' manner ' of pushing his wares."

Naval officers at that period were mostly inclined to suspect and dislike innovations. They felt uncomfortable if it was suggested they should get out of their old ruts, use their minds, alter their methods. One cause of this was that in general they drank too much. When, as a young gunnery officer, Lieut. Chatfield introduced many much-needed reforms in a ship which had an inefficient captain and an antiquated second-in-command, he received a certificate, not commending his good work, as he expected, but merely saying he had " conducted himself with sobriety," as if that was very unusual.

W HEN he got his first ship as midshipman, the hard drinking that went on in the gunroom was " not untypical." The sub-lieutenant in charge was " not infrequently drunk," and the other officers the same. The boy's first evening taught him what to expect. After dinner another sub-lieutenant rushed in, " pursued by the Captain's orderly whom he had just insulted. His first act was to raise his walking-stick and sweep all the tumblers, wine-glasses and decanters off the table. Glass flew in all directions. He then called to the waiters in a drunken voice to open the trap-hatch to the pantry, a small opening about two feet square. With a cry to the frightened mess-boys in the pantry, ' Catch me or I'll kill you,' he then ran and dived head foremost through the trap-hatch, amazingly without hurting himself severely."

With such examples before them, the seamen for the most part drank hard, broke their leave, and committed petty offences against discipline. When shore leave was granted patrols had to be landed to keep order, stop fights, arrest drunken men. " It is good to

compare the fine yet imperfect material of those days with the highly-educated, self-respecting seamen that have now been developed—to me the finest representatives of our countrymen. Drunkenness is almost unknown among them, and leave-breaking is looked down upon (instead of being almost the fashion) and occurs comparatively seldom."

This has largely been brought about by the change in the ships. The type of man who " went aloft in a gale at night or hauled on the main brace or sheet without encouragement because his life depended on it " has become a skilled seaman-mechanic, able to use and repair delicate machinery. The

THE
Navy & Defence

" trusty carthorse has given place to the Derby winner." This has made it necessary to alter methods of handling the lower deck and the spirit in which they are led and trusted. " The modern seaman may be more critical of those who command him, require greater care, attention and comfort, but well handled you can get more out of him because he has more to give."

Y ET Lord Chatfield recognizes that " to live a sailor's life in a ship of war is hard and trying. He has none of the comforts known to the civilian, or indeed to the other fighting Services. His work is unregulated by the clock, because he must cope with weather and emergencies which happen only on the seas. No sailor can go to his hammock with certainty that he will not be roused in the night. Returning from wet and cold work in a boat, no hot bath and armchair await him, nor does the barrack gate stand ajar for him to join his family in the evening. He sits at meals on a hard wooden form at the wooden mess-table . . . No individual could live a contented life under the White Ensign unless he was trained to it from boyhood, and had the spirit of comradeship and unselfish service impressed on him in his malleable teens."

The A.B. is good-tempered, " because ill-temper in a ship does not pay and speedily

NAVAL CADETS at the Royal Naval College, Dartmouth, receiving instruction in a model of the rigging of the battleship H.M.S. Nelson's mainmast. *Photo, Topical Press*

leads to ruin." He is cheerful and optimistic " because he must so often live on hope." Lord Chatfield has found it of absorbing interest to command seamen. He knows they like " a firm but just hand over them, the unruly punished, the well-conducted rewarded." The portrait he draws does equal credit to them and to him.

There has been change too in the relations between the Navy and the Admiralty. Even in 1919 they were " poles apart." The Board seemed to be separated altogether from the sailor, it was " a body that wore top-hats and was his permanent enemy." That was improved by making our Navy Department less bureaucratic, substituting naval private secretaries for civil servants, creating a better understanding between the latter and the men in the ships.

Some very grave and dangerous defects in the Admiralty system during the 1914 war Lord Chatfield exposes in his account of the poor-quality shells supplied to the Fleet and used with weak effect at the Dogger Bank and in the Battle of Jutland. Our gunnery was better than that of the Germans, but they said our shells were " laughable," and they were right. The officials in Whitehall stuck to it that there was nothing wrong. Only when trials had proved the contrary could they be made to give the Navy shells that would pierce armour as those of the enemy did.

S OMEONE ought to have been hanged for this. Beatty wrote a letter to be published if he was killed, telling where the blame lay. But he was not killed, and the letter did not appear. A report made by Lord Chatfield raised the question whether an inquiry should be held and those who had so grossly failed in judgement brought to book. It was decided to let the matter rest, since " an inquiry would inevitably drag into its list of witnesses all kinds of personalities." So, to save a few prominent people, the folly which had lost so many lives and ships was overlooked. Social considerations overcame national. The guilty escaped scot-free.

The Admiralty erred also when it announced during the first stage of Jutland that the German Battle Fleet was not at sea ; but this did not much affect the course of the battle, though some ships came under very heavy fire and suffered severe damage. Lord Chatfield's account of the engagement is vivid and exciting, though there are points in it which make me feel a little uneasy. For instance, he attributes to chance the silhouetting of our ships against a clear sky and the enveloping of the enemy's in the gloom of a dull grey sky. Surely there was more than chance in this ? Again, he mentions that an order given by him to alter course was " misheard." Alarming to think such a thing could happen during a critical action !

Bizerta's Significance in Tomorrow's Strategy

Very much in the news is Bizerta, the great French base in Tunisia which was seized by the Axis in mid-November. Some conception of its importance to the one side and the other is provided by this article by Capt. FRANK H. SHAW.

UNLIKE tragic Singapore, Bizerta—the most important port between Algiers and Alexandria—is strongly defended against attack from the landward side as well as from the sea; and the slowing-up of our First Army's advance to the occupation of Tunisia was not surprising in view of the circumstances. The French have always been masters of fortification, and when Admiral Muselier was put in supreme command of the defences of this vital base, he employed excellent craftsmen to make it as nearly impregnable as might be. Heavy batteries—their guns having a range of over 25 miles—command all land approaches from south and west. Similar weapons dominate the narrows between this pointing finger of territory and Sicily. Attack from the sea by the United Nations might be costly in a high degree: it is an accepted fact that ships are almost impotent against fixed defences.

"Was *this* the face that launched a thousand ships?" he quotes. To gain a correct impression of the outstanding value of Bizerta, however, one must look beneath its mediocre surface. It is far more vital to Mediterranean strategy than ever Singapore was to the Pacific, for it commands one of the most important stretches of sea-water in the world, one that is next in importance to the English Channel. Admiral Muselier transformed it into a most formidable arsenal, for not only was this distinguished French sailor responsible for its naval efficiency, but he was placed in supreme charge of its air facilities; and the present war is proving daily that sea-power is dependent on air-power for continued potency. He worked well, and established airfields of unique value. Many of these are already in Allied hands: each fresh capture must bring added qualms to Axis hearts. Once we have secured air-supremacy in this

Any surface fleet desirous of denying this passage to the Axis forces would be liable to relentless attack by U-boat and from the air, by U-boats based on Bizerta itself and the Sicilian ports, by aircraft flying not only from Sicilian and Southern Italian airfields but also from Pantellaria—the rocky islet lying roughly midway between Malta and Bizerta. Pantellaria is to Mussolini what the Maginot Line was to France: a strategic certainty.

But with Bizerta and Tunisia as a whole in Allied hands Pantellaria loses all its value: it can be dominated night and day, winter and summer, by Allied forces. So, too, do the Sicilian airfields lose their value: Allied aircraft operating from Bizerta's spacious fields might blast these strongpoints out of existence, and so annul all previous threats to the seaborne traffic of the United Nations.

Once Bizerta and Tunis fall into our hands, the systematic subjugation of all South Italy and Sicily becomes inevitable. Turin, Milan and Genoa have proved the material as well as the moral value of concentrated air-attack. Assuming that Mussolini has transferred his humiliated navy—or what fragments still remain—to Venice and the Adriatic ports, these harbours are brought within easy range of our heaviest bombers. Taranto automatically loses whatever value it had as a haven; and Palermo and Messina, Syracuse and Catania, are—judged by modern ideas of distance—within easy pistol-shot of Bizerta-based aircraft.

BIZERTA is, indeed, the most vital citadel of all the Middle Sea. It is good for defence; but its capacity as a taking-off place for attack cannot be overestimated. No wonder Hitler is stripping his Eastern Front to bolster up its defence! By striking a ruthless blow at Tunisia the Allies have sealed the Fuehrer's death-warrant in Russia. In aiming to hold both the Russian line and Tunisia he stands to lose both, as events are proving.

Naval control of the Mediterranean is likewise dependent on the possession of this area. With the Italian surface navy practically confined to its harbours, Axis sea-strategy can consist only in the employment of submarines. Valetta, in Malta, was the only harbour open to Allied warships between Gibraltar and Alexandria until the recent occupation of Morocco and Algeria; and the ports of these countries are not much better than open roadsteads. Malta, until Sicily is subjugated, is a precarious haven at best. But if Bizerta be overcome and safely in our hands, an overwhelming antisubmarine flotilla can be based there in complete safety. Conceivably, before surrendering, the Axis will apply a "scorched earth" policy to Tunisia; but even so, the skeleton of a great and invaluable harbour will remain. Admiral Muselier saw to it that the port of Bizerta was prepared for practically all eventualities. It has dry docks capable of holding the greatest battleships. It has repair shops in adequate supply. It has superbly designed and protected submarine docks. All the destroyers and corvettes and "mosquito craft" necessary to overwhelm the Axis U-boat flotillas can harbour in the port or its spacious approaches. From its airfields not only can bomber-attacks be launched at the vulnerable belly of Europe, but sea-patrolling aircraft, equipped to tackle the submarine threat, can operate with ease.

No wonder that, to secure possession of this unique stronghold, General Anderson and his Allies are taking infinite pains!

BIZERTA, key-point of N. Tunisia, was occupied by Axis troops, largely airborne, following the Allied occupation of Algeria. By the end of November it was reported that some 20,000 of the enemy had reached the Bizerta-Tunis area. This photo shows the waterway that connects the outer harbour with the inner lake. (See diagram opposite.) *Photo, E.N.A.*

But Bizerta and the adjoining country form a prize worth winning—and winning quickly. This very considerable naval base and airport is nothing less than a pistol pointed at Italy's heart. With Bizerta and Tunis—which latter city possesses at Goletta a notable harbour—in our hands, Mussolini's position would become well-nigh desperate.

NOT that, at first glance, Bizerta impresses an observer as being anything extraordinary: it is a typically shabby French colonial city. The French are not—they never were—really good colonists; and this town which at present commands the whole world's interest is uninspiring. It is the usual North African blend of east and west: tawdry, dishevelled, none too sanitary; where veiled women rub shoulders with ex-Parisian cocottes parading their slightly bedraggled finery along neglected streets. None the less, it is the focal centre of some of the richest territories along the entire North African littoral: Tunisia is a rich country, and, properly handled—the French only exploited it—its mineral and vegetable wealth would be incalculable.

Even so, a first glance makes for disappointment. Kipling, in his Village that Voted the Earth was Flat, expressed amazement that any place that had made so much history as Huckley should be so mean.

vicinity, the annihilation of Italy, as an Axis accomplice, follows as a matter of course. The narrows between Bizerta and Sicily are roughly 150 miles wide; and with the exception of the negligible Straits of Messina, form the only channel between the Western Mediterranean and the Eastern.

Every ship steaming east and west between Gibraltar and Port Said must negotiate this narrow stretch of water, which is seldom rendered unobservable, especially from the air. By virtue of its narrowness, this short stretch can easily be crossed by Axis sea-transport under cover of darkness; and were Axis shipping available, which it is not, to reinforce Bizerta and all Tunisia by wholesale, would be a comparatively simple matter. That is why haste is the essence of the contract in our attempts to subjugate the region. Working frantically, running a shuttle service from Palermo to Bizerta, loading and unloading at top speed, an entire army with its heaviest equipment might be thrown into Tunisia in a dog-watch almost. The port is equipped to deal with such an inrush: Admiral Muselier and his consultants saw to that. Its dock facilities are almost unique; and the approaches to the port itself lend themselves to a baffling tactical use: the whole entrance can be mined and boomed without great difficulty.

Finest Harbour on the North African Coastline

TUNISIA'S CHIEF PORT, Bizerta, lies at the head of the Gulf of Tunis. The harbour works were begun in 1891, when the lakes were dredged and channels constructed to admit warships. At Ferryville are situated the arsenal and naval establishments. Two large aerodromes have recently been built, one on the shores of the Lake of Bizerta, and the other near the outer harbour. Top, right, Bizerta station on the railway to Tunis and Sfax. Top left, scene at a bazaar.

Photos. Dorien Leigh. E.N.A. Drawing by courtesy of The Sphere

THE WAR IN THE AIR

by Capt. Norman Macmillan, M.C., A.F.C.

THE hard core of the air war has crystallized over the area surrounding the broken, natural central bridge of the Mediterranean, where land, which has since subsided, once joined Europe with Africa and divided the inland sea into two great lakes. Across this bridge the prehistoric monsters fought their way southwards to escape from the rigours of the European Ice Age. Today, modern monsters in the shape of tanks have crossed from Europe, using ship and aeroplane where the sea has covered the missing span.

Everywhere the tempo of the air war is rising, for it is the speed of aircraft which gives them their advantage over all other weapons of war and vehicles of war transport.

Above the narrow stretch of water that separates Cape Bon from the nearest part of and gave the Luftwaffe the opportunity to deploy dive-bombers against the front-line troops of the First Army without having to face the fury of the Spitfires.

It may have been partly the local air superiority which the Axis forces enjoyed in the air over the advanced battle area that enabled them to force the slight withdrawal of the advanced elements of the First Army to more favourable positions where cover was easier to improvise.

In this situation it is possible to perceive the clear lesson of modern tactical warfare, namely, that the movement of surface forces, either by land or sea, without the air cover of the most effective types of fighter aircraft is fraught with grave risks when such movement takes the forces concerned into a zone where enemy aircraft can operate in force.

The most important reinforcement to any

British Advanced Air Striking Force; and again during the Battle of Britain. The effect of such action is too temporary, unless overwhelming surprise is achieved, as was the case when the Luftwaffe bombed the Dutch and Belgian Air Forces before dawn on May 10, 1940, with no declaration of war.

With these past examples known, there was no reason to assume that bombing the aerodromes at Bizerta and Tunis would be effective in reducing Axis air superiority over an advanced fighting zone to a degree which could compensate for the absence of short-range United Nations fighters.

THE mileages involved are of special interest. Bône to Bizerta is 120 miles, to Tunis 136 miles; Malta to Tunis is 236 miles; Marsala (Sicily) to Tunis is 142 miles. The front-line fighting at Mateur is 22 miles south-west of Bizerta; in the Tebourba sector it is 20 miles west of Tunis.

The crucial part of the ground operations is associated with the Axis possession of two important advanced aerodromes, and the United Nations lack of them. Small wonder, then, that Mr. Churchill, speaking at Bradford on Dec. 5, indicated that it would be no easy task to drive the Axis completely out of Tunisia. It will be a hard fight, its course dictated by the situation in the air.

Realizing this, the Axis have sent many of their latest aircraft to North Africa. Among them are Messerschmitt 109Gs and Junkers 86Ps, substratosphere fighter and bomber respectively. One of the few large Blöhm and Voss 6-engined, 45-ton flying-boats possessed by the enemy was shot down off the Tunisian coast; originally designed for transatlantic air transport, it was converted into a troop-carrier, and believed to accommodate 80 troops.

THE advantage the Americans are securing from their policy to build 25 per cent of all multi-engined aircraft as air transports is beginning to show to advantage in the Pacific war zone. A complete field hospital, flown into the Papuan area of the island of New Guinea in ten large transports, was working south of Buna the day after its arrival. Two-ton 105-millimetre guns were flown 1,500 miles from Australia to the Buna-Gona area, where the Japanese are hemmed in against their beachhead; each gun, with its crew

ROYAL DUTCH STEEL WORKS at Velsen, near Ymuiden, photographed after a recent attack by two unescorted Boston bombers during a daylight raid on German-occupied Holland. A, Probable burst near transporter crane serving foundry basin. B, Smoke from explosion near coke-oven plant. C, Bombs bursting among tanks of benzol by-product plants. *Photo, British Official: Crown Copyright*

the Sicilian coast must wage an air battle for mastery of the sky. For that stretch of ninety miles is within the range compass of the swiftest and most deadly fighters—those of the Hurricane, Spitfire, and Messerschmitt classes; and whoever holds aerodromes on both sides of the broken span of the bridge holds an important military advantage. Indeed, no advance into Europe through Sicily by United Nations forces can be contemplated until British and American fighter squadrons can operate from aerodromes in Sicily in addition to those at Tunis and Bizerta.

The British First Army advanced eastward from Algeria after the union of French North Africa with the cause of the United Nations. Paratroops were dropped in advance to seize points ahead of the army and to deny them to the Axis forces. The advance of the First Army was rapid in the direction of Bizerta and Tunis. It carried troops far in advance of the forward airfield at Bône, and close to the Axis-held airfields at Bizerta and Tunis.

That advance stretched the Allied front in Tunisia almost beyond the effective range of Spitfire short-range fighters based on Bône, tactical advance is that given by short-range fighter aircraft, which are at once the fastest, most manoeuvrable, and swiftest climbing aircraft, and are therefore capable of dominating the day sky over which they operate.

It was therefore important that advanced landing-grounds should have been constructed quickly in the rear of the line of advance of the First Army to enable the short-range fighters to maintain cover over the troops engaging the enemy. Undoubtedly, the mountainous country in North Tunisia is not favourable to the swift construction of aerodromes; and in the first stage of the action the alternative course of bombing the Axis-held forward aerodromes at Bizerta and Tunis was adopted.

THERE has been repeated proof during the course of the War that the bombing of aerodromes is not a satisfactory method of reducing enemy air power. This was demonstrated during the Norwegian campaign when Stavanger aerodrome was one of Bomber Command's principal targets; during the German attack on France when the Luftwaffe failed to knock out the squadrons of the and tractor, was carried from Australia to New Guinea in a Fortress, but the last lap over the Owen Stanley Mountains was made by smaller transport aircraft better able to use the forward landing-ground, each one carrying half the load borne by a Fortress. The guns were in action soon after their arrival in the fighting zone.

The R.A.F. has no substantial number of air transport aircraft yet, but this is a gap which must be made good.

On Friday, Dec. 4, American Liberator bombers made the first United States attack on Italian metropolitan territory by appearing suddenly over Naples in daylight, and scoring direct hits on a battleship and other targets.

Two American pilots have power-dived the Thunderbolt fighter to a speed of 725 m.p.h., probably the fastest speed yet attained by man. German aircraft have been discovered to be using phosphorus-loaded bullets; one British air navigator, wounded by one, died of phosphorus poisoning six days after an operation successfully extracted the particles of metal. The R.A.F. must remember this when the day of reckoning comes. In air fighting this is foul play.

Mustangs Are the Eyes of the Army

MUSTANGS are the product of North American Aviation, Inc., of Inglewood, California, and have appropriately been termed the "eyes of the Army." Used extensively by Army Cooperation Command of the R.A.F., these powerful fighters are now cooperating with Fighter Command and have scored outstanding successes over the Continent. Among their many targets have been railway engines, gun posts, bridges and important lines of communication.

These machines have a wing span of 37 ft. 3 in., a length of 31 ft. 3 in., and are fitted with a single 1,150 h.p. engine. A distinguishing feature is the shallow radiator aft of the wings. The tapered fin and rudder has a square apex, and the cockpit cover is comparatively short. Mustangs habitually fly at what the R.A.F. calls "o feet," that is, skimming the sea and tree-tops, in their long-distance trips to attack enemy targets. Their first big test came with the Dieppe raid on August 19, 1942, and subsequent attacks were made on other vital centres with such success that an American air expert, Maj. T. Hitchcock, declares that the Mustang will prove the "best fighter for 1943."

WORLD'S FASTEST ARMY COOPERATION AIRCRAFT. Mustangs have made history by attacking targets in Germany by daylight—the first time that single-engined fighters based in Britain have reached the Reich. Top left, a pilot of Army Cooperation Command of the R.A.F. receives instructions from the Air Liaison Officer at an operational station. Top right, climbing into his Mustang on the airfield. Below, making a low-level attack on an armoured car: a training photograph.   PAGE 439   *Photos, L.N.A., Planet News, Central Press*

Halifaxes Respond Well to Hospital Treatment

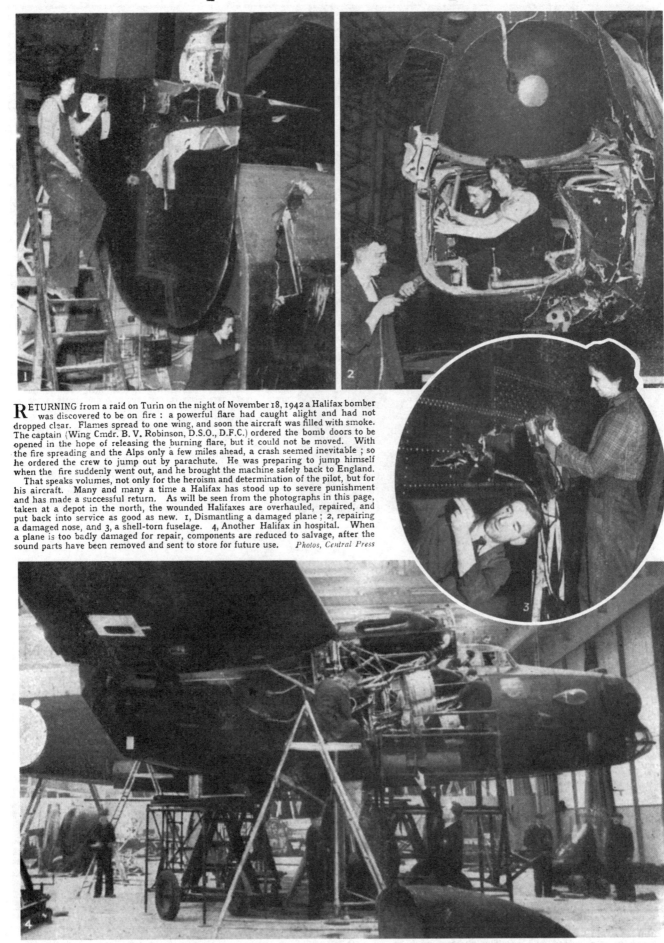

RETURNING from a raid on Turin on the night of November 18, 1942 a Halifax bomber was discovered to be on fire : a powerful flare had caught alight and had not dropped clear. Flames spread to one wing, and soon the aircraft was filled with smoke. The captain (Wing Cmdr. B. V. Robinson, D.S.O., D.F.C.) ordered the bomb doors to be opened in the hope of releasing the burning flare, but it could not be moved. With the fire spreading and the Alps only a few miles ahead, a crash seemed inevitable ; so he ordered the crew to jump out by parachute. He was preparing to jump himself when the fire suddenly went out, and he brought the machine safely back to England.

That speaks volumes, not only for the heroism and determination of the pilot, but for his aircraft. Many and many a time a Halifax has stood up to severe punishment and has made a successful return. As will be seen from the photographs in this page, taken at a depot in the north, the wounded Halifaxes are overhauled, repaired, and put back into service as good as new. 1, Dismantling a damaged plane ; 2, repairing a damaged nose, and 3, a shell-torn fuselage. 4, Another Halifax in hospital. When a plane is too badly damaged for repair, components are reduced to salvage, after the sound parts have been removed and sent to store for future use. *Photos, Central Press*

For the Third Time We March into Benghazi

BENGHAZI, capital of Cyrenaica, occupied by the 8th Army on Nov. 20, 1942, was first taken by British Imperial forces under Gen. Wavell on Feb. 7, 1941. Subsequent evacuation by our troops and occupation by the Germans were announced a few weeks later, on April 3. In Nov. 1941 the second British drive into Libya began, and by Christmas Eve units of Gen. Ritchie's army had swept into Benghazi, having covered the 250 miles from Derna in five days. Again the tide of war turned, and on Jan. 29, 1942 the British withdrew. Advancing from Jedabia, Rommel occupied the town; and during the ensuing months constant bombing attacks were made by Allied planes operating from Egypt.

Men of the 8th Army in lorries (top photo) passing the wreckage of Axis motor transport as they entered the place on Nov. 20, 1942. Immediately above, keenly-interested inhabitants watch Australian infantry marching through the streets on Feb. 7, 1941. Right, the crew of a South African armoured car column enjoy their Christmas fare on the Cathedral Mole at Benghazi—a photo taken on Dec. 24, 1941.

Photos, British Official: Crown Copyright

THE HOME FRONT

by E. Royston Pike

WHEN did you last see the "drunken sailor" of the convivial chorus—or a drunken soldier, airman or civilian? More beer is being drunk, and more people are drinking it. But very seldom do we see nowadays the rolling drunkard who, according to G. K. Chesterton, made the rolling English road, going home trailed through the gutter by his bedraggled wife (complete with black eye) and quiverful of sniffing, ragged little urchins. Few there are who, visibly at least, take "one over the eight." Maybe it is because to reach the eighth round is an expensive business, taxation being what it is; it was very much easier to escape from Hogarth's London when the gin shops established above their straw-strewn cellars used to advertise: "Drunk for a penny, dead drunk for two pence, straw for nothing." Maybe it is because the composition of present-day beer is such that a cup of tea brewed so that a mouse could dance on it is a much more harmful beverage. Long before the eighth glass we have had more than enough of—water. Or it may be that we are constitutionally more temperate than our fathers were, and know better when to stop.

PUBS, too, have changed a lot. Those dazzling establishments described by the English reformer J. A. Roebuck a hundred years ago—"splendid windows, brass rods and ornaments, a fine showy counter, immense tubs of spirits and gay damsels ready to serve it"—these are as dead as the "spit and sawdust" bars once favoured by the proletariat. The public house is now a very respectable place—so respectable, indeed, that it is ceasing to be a man's sanctum. This is one of the conclusions reached by Dr. Ernest Barker, who after a lifetime spent in the study and teaching of political thought has recently devoted his attention to an analysis of our drinking habits during the war. Writing in the monthly bulletin of the Fellowship of Freedom and Reform, he notes that the "local" has been quietly but successfully invaded by women; it has become the "gossip-shop of both sexes," with darts and other diversions jointly shared. He regards this as an inevitable development; women are working everywhere side by side with men: they naturally come to sit by their side, and drink by their side, in times of leisure. And, indeed, he sees some good in it. Women may bring a breath of fresh air into a frowsty atmosphere, he says, and sweeten and humanize the pubs. There may also be some evil, but "as long as beer is the drink the evil is a possibility rather than a fact."

DR. BARKER is not so happy, however, about the drawing of the young—of both sexes and particularly young boys still in their teens—into the public house. They have money burning in their pockets; they have been working by the side of grown-ups to earn the money; they want a fling. In spite of the efforts of "the Trade" to maintain discipline there is a good deal of noisy display; and "to spend 9s. a week on beer would seem to be moderation in the view of lads who are earning £3 or £4 a week." To continue my quotation:

"Reflection suggests that it is in no way surprising that drinking should have increased. The unemployed have ceased to be unemployed, and they can now get their pint of beer (that, I confess, makes me happy). The community generally is earning good wages and in these days of restricted supplies it has few things on which it can spend. It turns to beer—beer and tobacco—and tobacco even more than beer." From reports received lately it would seem that the lad who spends 9s. a week on beer will spend 18s. on cigarettes; indeed, one observer records that "it is not far from the truth to say that for every shilling spent on beer most adolescents spend four on cigarettes." How shall we judge of this habit? "When I drink a glass of beer (which is rarely) or smoke a pipe of tobacco (which is far more frequently) I say to myself, 'I am paying my taxes; and this is a painless and indeed a pleasant mode of extraction.' When a community at war, under a system of high indirect taxes, drinks and smokes it is not going to the dogs."

SIR WM. BEVERIDGE, whose Report on Social Insurance and Allied Services was published on Dec, 1, is a "social engineer" of the first rank. Born in 1879, after pioneer work as a Civil Servant in establishing Labour Exchanges and National Insurance, he was Director of the London School of Economics from 1919 to 1937, since when he has been Warden of University College, Oxford. *Photo, Topical*

Anyhow it smokes far more than it drinks, and beer is an innocent compared with tobacco."

IN truth it is all to the good that "pubs" have changed, since there are still plenty of places where the Sabbatarians do their best to ensure that the choice shall still lie between "gloom and drink," as those penetrating and authoritative writers on English social history, J. L. and Barbara Hammond, put it in their book, The Age of the Chartists. A century ago the English Sunday was a fearsome institution. Sunday theatres were frowned upon; W. Friese-Greene had not invented his moving-picture camera; public transport was in its infancy, and even excursion trains were condemned by the more strait-laced since women making day-trips to the country and seaside were exposed to the temptations of vice . . .

To quote from the Hammonds again, "For the masses of the working classes there was only one day in which they were free of the discipline of mill and workshop. On that day they were refused recreation of mind or body, music or games, beauty of art or nature." In the London of Little Dorrit "There was nothing to see but streets, streets, streets; there was nothing to breathe but streets, streets, streets." That was a century ago; are things very much better today?

Recently there was published a letter above the signatures of Mr. Leslie Henson and seventy other leading actors and actresses stating that "owing to the persistent action taken by the Lord's Day Observance Society in upholding the law passed in 1677 and never repealed or adjusted to modern requirements" they regretted that "we are not allowed to give stage performances for any charity, or performance to which money is subscribed, on any Sunday."

WHILE making it clear that actors and actresses will still be happy "to give their services for the free entertainment of His Majesty's forces, the Lord's Day Observance Society having no jurisdiction over these activities," Mr. Henson declares that:

"We are not going to wangle round the law any longer, although it is being wangled all over England by selling tickets through clubs. We cannot perform for charity on Sundays unless the money is taken through clubs, although cinemas everywhere are open, and the B.B.C. broadcasts plays every Sunday. At a Sunday concert Mr. George Robey, who has raised thousands of pounds for good causes, may not put on his eyebrows. Recently at a Sunday show at the Coliseum, because the frock worn by a soprano looked like a crinoline the show was stopped and the singer had to change into street clothes before being allowed by the L.C.C. representative, sent there by the Lord's Day Observance Society, to continue."

MUCH the most important development on the Home Front of recent days has been the publication of Sir William Beveridge's report on Social Insurance and Allied Services. A document of over 100,000 words, it must be read to be appreciated; it is published by His Majesty's Stationery Office (Cmd. 6404) at 2s. Its proposals affect every man, woman and child living in the country today, and millions yet unborn; it is the greatest thing of its kind since Mr. Lloyd George's Health Insurance Bill of 1911. And as likely as not it will give rise to as vast a volume of controversy. But about the spirit in which it is framed surely there can be no quarrel.

"The proposals of this report represent, not an attempt by one nation to gain for its citizens advantages at the cost of their fellow-fighters in a common cause, but a contribution to that common cause. They are a sign of the belief that the object of government in peace and in war is not the glory of rulers or of races, but the happiness of the common man." And again, "the Plan for Social Security is submitted by one who believes that in this supreme crisis the British people will not be found wanting, of courage and faith and national unity, of material and spiritual power, to play their part in achieving both social security and the victory of justice among nations upon which security depends."

AMONG the other reports that have seen the light of day within late weeks is that of Lord Kennet's Committee on Manpower in Banking and Insurance.

At the outbreak of war there were employed in banking about 66,000 men and 19,000 women. Some 55 per cent of the male managerial and clerical employees have been called up, and in the clearing banks women represent 42 per cent of the present labour force; of the 4,353 men of military age left almost all are over 35 and occupying positions of some responsibility. But Lord Kennet's Committee thinks that more men might be released. It rejects the amalgamation of separate banks as a means of releasing man-power, but recommends that banks should close at 2.30 p.m.; more branches, too, might be closed, although by May last 1,742 branches out of 8,469 whole or part-time offices had been shut.

The Committee recommends similarly that the staff of the insurance companies (industrial and ordinary) should be combed further.

Salvage P.S. "Thousands of tons of bones are being lost annually through being buried by dogs."—*Letter to The Times*

Striking Page from Story of London's Ordeal

THE NIGHT OF MAY 10, 1941 marked the climax of the Luftwaffe's prolonged and savage attack on the metropolis. Front Line, 1940-41, the official story of this grim period of the war (recently issued by H.M. Stationery Office at 2s.), tells of the heroic deeds performed by countless men a women in defence of their city. "May 10 saw nine conflagrations and a further 21 major outbreaks. It was a night that must have graven on many a fire-fighter's heart the words ' no water,' " so many were the mains broken by the bombs. This remarkable photo shows a building crashing in Queen Victoria Street.

By permission of the Commissioner of Police, City of London

Wartime Faces & Places seen by our Roving Camera

'BACK-YARD FARM,' of 2½ acres in Surrey, produces most of the food for a household of eight. Milk is provided by goats, while ducks, chickens, and about 60 rabbits complete the livestock. Mr. P. Lyne, owner of the farm, is seen above turning a furrow with his 3½-h.p. motor plough. Left, Allied Army and Ministry of Supply officials receiving the first shipment of U.S. UTILITY LOCOMOTIVES which have been built to conform to both British and Continental systems.

THANKSGIVING DAY, Nov. 26, was celebrated in London by U.S. forces when thousands of them attended a special service in Westminster Abbey. The Stars and Stripes flew from one of the Abbey towers for the first time in its centuries-old history. Above, an American sergeant carries Old Glory along the central aisle.

MEN OF THE BOOM DEFENCE guard the anti-submarine and anti-torpedo nets that form curtains of steel mesh at the entrances of our harbours. The nets are kept in position by spherical floats on the surface and heavy sinkers on the sea bed. Constant attention is needed to keep these booms in order, and the boom defence ships carry out repairs on the spot.

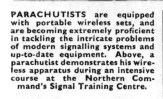

PARACHUTISTS are equipped with portable wireless sets, and are becoming extremely proficient in tackling the intricate problems of modern signalling systems and up-to-date equipment. Above, a parachutist demonstrates his wireless apparatus during an intensive course at the Northern Command's Signal Training Centre.

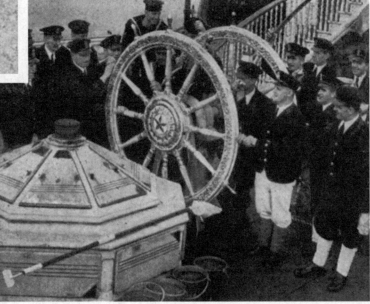

VICTORIA AND ALBERT, the King's 43-year-old yacht, which was due to be broken up before the War, is acting as an overflow accommodation ship for a Royal Naval gunnery school. Right, trainees examine the picturesque handwheel and binnacle. The handwheel came from the old man-of-war, H.M.S. Royal George.

Photos, Planet News, E. W. Tattersall, Keystone, Associated Press, Fox, G.P.U.

MAJOR (T/Lt.-Col.) V. B. TURNER, of the Rifle Brigade (Prince Consort's Own), displayed the most conspicuous gallantry on Oct. 27, 1942, in the Western Desert. He led a battalion to an objective where 40 German prisoners were taken, after which he organized the captured position for all-round defence. Later in the action he was wounded. On Nov. 20 it was announced that he had been awarded the V.C.

I WAS THERE! Eye Witness Stories of the War

Back from Stalingrad We Chased the Nazis

Here is a dispatch from the Stalingrad front of the tremendous battle waged between Gen. Chuikov's Russians and von Hoth's Nazis. Written by Soviet war correspondents Kuprin and Akushin, this dramatic piece of war reportage is reprinted here by courtesy of the Soviet War News.

ALONG the path of our offensive leading to the west over the level steppes of the Don are trenches, blockhouses, dugouts, deep anti-tank ditches, massively-fortified gun sites, abandoned by the enemy. Droves of lost horses wander over the plains, cropping the dry, prickly grass. They have been deserted by their masters, who preferred to trust to their own legs. The ground is thickly strewn with black and green German helmets, gas masks, broken shell- and mine-cases, enemy bodies and dead horses.

Here is a shell-torn height, its slopes covered with scraps of twisted metal and burnt-out machines. The remains of enemy trenches and blockhouses are barely recognizable. The wide tracks of our K.V.s (Klim Voroshilov tanks) are clearly visible in the earth. The heavy machines swept to the west, destructive as a huge torrent, wiping out everything in their path. Rifles and machine-guns are embedded in the crushed trenches. In this area the enemy resisted madly and was exterminated. Traces of hand-to-hand fighting can be seen everywhere. Farther on are abandoned guns, some of them put out of action by our artillery and tanks, some in full working order, complete with large supplies of shells. Salvage companies are loading them on lorries and carting them away to the rear.

BEYOND the height is a place known as "the ravine of death." Its slopes are furrowed with fortifications. It was the enemy's second defence line. It is shattered. The defenders' bodies in their green uniforms lie mouldering everywhere. Burnt-out lorries and planes with Nazi markings block our path. We try to count the abandoned transport lorries and guns. It is hopeless. There are hundreds of them.

West of the ravine it is the same—the road blocked by smashed vehicles, the verges littered with helmets, guns and other equipment. The enemy attempted to get his supply columns away, but failed. Our mobile units rushed into the breach and caught up with the fleeing beast. Cases of shells and mines, cartridges, broken bicycles,

motor-cycles, staff documents, are mixed up with the carcasses of horses and dead Nazis. Here is a huge pair of *ersatz* felt boots, their soles stuck with straw and paper. The enemy was busy preparing for the Russian cold, but for him it became too hot. He dropped his boots and ran along barefoot; but even so he was caught. Our men were merciless to those who resisted.

Farther west is the wreckage of a heavy artillery regiment sent by the enemy to hold his defences at the village of Plodovitaya against our advancing troops. Long before it got there it was attacked by our mobile units. The K.V.s encircled the Nazi gunners, who were wiped out before they had any opportunity to get into fighting formation and use their weapons.

PRISONERS moving east block the roads—thousands of them, escorted by groups of Red Army men. The cold wind blows through their thin uniforms. They are wrapped up in looted blankets and scarves. One column consists of 2,800 prisoners—the entire strength of an infantry regiment, captured together with their colonel.

West again, through a liberated village. The country people greet the Red Army men with tears of joy, begging them to come into their houses, to warm themselves and eat. For three months these villagers have suffered under German occupation. The Nazis butchered their cattle, took away their grain. Everywhere is devastation. The soldiers, smoking pungent cigarettes, listen grimly to the terrible tale of a grey-haired collective farmer.

It used to be a wealthy, well-run village. Now it is in ruins. On house walls and fences are German notices, road signs and posters. The people are scraping them off, or painting them over. The signposts are being re-lettered in the Russian language. There are two big cemeteries in the village. The graves of the Nazi "conquerors" are marked by a forest of crosses. Those are the dead of the hot August days and still hotter battles when the numerically superior enemy forces were pressing on towards Stalingrad.

Advanced units of the Red Army firing at the retreating enemy N.W. of Stalingrad. In this page Soviet war correspondents give a vivid account of the Russian offensive before the great Volga city. *Photo, Planet News*

Beyond Abganerovo railway station, towards Aksai, the railway line is blocked with stranded trucks and engines, goods trains crammed with food and ammunition, guns and military supplies. The enemy did not have time to move them before the Red Army struck. Our vanguard groups destroyed the bridges, blew up the track, cut off all lines of retreat. Near by hundreds of disabled and burnt-out German tanks are stacked in an immense scrap-heap.

To the west rolls an endless line of lorries carrying food and supplies, Soviet artillery and cavalry units, reserve regiments and battalions. The offensive continues.

THE BATTLE OF STALINGRAD was long and bitter, but by Nov. 25, 1942 the Germans were in retreat in all sectors of this front, and six enemy divisions were reported to have been cut off. Above, a radioed photo shows ruins of the city when Soviet guardsmen—one of them is seen on right—were repulsing an enemy attack. On the turret of the Russian tank which is firing into the ruins are two roughly painted words which in translation mean: "For the Fatherland." As told in this page, the Germans suffered crippling losses as the Russians, in spite of desperate enemy resistance, continued to advance. *Photo, News Chronicle*

The 'Eyeties' Begged Us to Give Them a Lift

With the victorious Eighth Army in pursuit of Rommel's beaten hordes, T. E. A. Healy, war correspondent of the Daily Mirror (from which this story is reprinted), drove through 70 miles of Nazi wreckage. He tells of amazing scenes in the Egyptian desert, and of forlorn enemy troops anxious above everything to give themselves up.

I AM writing this dispatch on notepaper of Rommel's crack lorry-borne infantry division, the 90th Light. The paper was taken from a German lorry overturned by an R.A.F. bomb outside Fuka. Can you imagine what today has meant, to advance seventy miles in one hop with our Eighth Army?

Continuously to the left, right, and ahead the desert has been strewn with enemy transport wreckage, enemy tanks burnt, bombed and blown up. I've looked on death and destruction till I'm sick of it. It has told me eloquently just how completely we've smashed the Axis in Africa. We went across the battlefield of the last ten days, driving gingerly over mined ground and past the wreckage of German and British tanks.

Beside a cluster of German Mark III tanks I came on a grave marked by a cross made of pieces of a jam box, on which a British soldier had written : " Here lies unknown German soldier," and had propped up on the grave the soldier's knife, fork and comb, leaning them against his tin helmet. There were photos about of German wives and children to whom their husbands and fathers will never return. There were letters home and letters from home blowing about in the dust. Up the track we came across still greater masses of guns and ammunition and tanks abandoned.

I NOTED that over only a few graves the swastika of Nazism was inscribed. Others bore the Black Cross of the Kaiser's Germany. Above one grave protruded one of the propeller blades of a Spitfire. It was the grave of a Canadian buried by Germans. Near the graves was a pile of new enemy overcoats and boots which soldiers were fitting on. The scene reminded me of Caledonian Market. One soldier looked up from boot-fitting and said : " Wouldn't der Fuehrer be derfurious ! "

As we went westwards the destruction and havoc wrought by the R.A.F. intensified. In a swath almost 200 yards wide enemy transport lay charred and battered. The scene was eloquent of fear and panic of the worst kind. Many vehicles were blown up on their own mines, for the road on either side was mined a foot off the tarmac.

Movement up the narrow road was slower as we got farther westward because the traffic problem was further complicated by the arrival of a stream of prisoners, mainly German, in huge German and Italian lorries.

We knew there was something peculiar about the procession and couldn't make out what it was. Suddenly someone shouted : " Gosh, they're driving themselves to prison ! " They were, and only in the front vehicle and in the last was there a guard.

Fully 2,000 prisoners passed in one hour. They seemed, even for Germans, utterly unconcerned, and when one of their trucks broke down they clambered out and watched British mechanics repair it.

WHAT a sight for the prisoners it must have been, this immense column of British transport, British tanks and men filing their way forward! Perhaps at that moment as they looked at it they realized why they were beaten and in the bag. Every British transport vehicle bore some girl's name. How many girls in Britain—Dorises, Eileens, Annes, Jeans, Betties, Evelyns—have been driven in spirit into captured enemy towns in this campaign? Tankmen always give their vehicles fighting names like Thunderer, Valiant, Defiant, etc. One man broke the rule and named his Mother. We drove past cars abandoned in hundreds, guns left with piles of ammunition, huge heaps of clothing and ground-sheets.

While we had lunch we saw soldiers prodding the roadside for mines, which are like round covered pudding dishes, with the charge an inch wide in the centre. Soldiers were digging them up like turnips.

A FEW miles farther on I got out of a car with another reporter near a group of twenty-eight forlorn and desolate Italians. They came up, saluted, and said they wanted to surrender but could not find anyone to take them prisoner. Everyone was in too much of a hurry.

One spoke French and asked whether we could take them. We accepted their surrender. We stopped a lorry driven by a young Scot. He did not want to cart " ruddy Eyeties " to a prison camp, but said he would hand them over to the military police. The prisoners brightened up considerably at this, but took so long explaining to themselves that everything was settled that the Scot said angrily : " Well, bloody well get cracking or I'll leave you behind."

They quickly got on the truck, and as the truck moved away the Italians thanked us profusely and said there were some of their mates farther down the road. Would we be so kind as to help them too ? But prisoner groups were too many and we were in too much of a hurry to bother. They were popping out of holes all over the desert and looking for someone to take charge of them. I saw them begging lifts to prison from our lorries and even tanks. Some at least of them were covered in vermin.

Over the Alps We Flew to Bomb Genoa

Another smashing success was scored by the R.A.F. on the night of November 7, when home-based bombers inflicted on Genoa, Italy's great naval base, its heaviest raid of the war. Impressions of this sensational 1,300-mile flight are given below in the form of extracts from the log of a " novice "—a R.A.F. Public Relations Officer who flew in a Stirling.

FIVE-ELEVEN in the afternoon : I'm airborne, but didn't know it. I poked my head up the astro-dome to find out how the take-off was getting on, and discovered that we were about 500 feet up— so smooth had been the getaway. Several other Stirlings are circling around, gaining height and preparing to set course.

6.5 p.m. We cross the coast. It is still light enough to observe that, owing to the state of the tide, the white line of sea breakers does not at all conform to the map. There is a fine sunset to the starboard beam as we cross the Channel. Long streaks of cloud are lit by a fading red. I go down into the bomb-aimer's hatch to try to spot the moment when we cross the coast of France. But the dark blue on the windows imperceptibly changes to cloud and I can smell the mist in the aircraft. And so the only news I get that we are over France is the gentle evasive action of the pilot. No flak comes up.

6.50 p.m. We are passing through a rain storm.

7.30 p.m. St. Elmo's fire round the propellers. Now again in the astro-dome I can see the circles of flame round the propellers, and the front-gunner reports blue darts on his gun barrels and flame trickling around the metal of the turret. This lasts about ten minutes. We are climbing for the Alps, and the flight-engineer switches on oxygen. The smell and feel of the mask are strange at first and rather like an anaesthetist's apparatus.

8.14 p.m. I am lying flat over the bottom blister. Though there is no moon, the Alps come into view—surfaces of a grade of purplish-white peppered with black. The captain suggests that if I come forward again I shall soon see Genoa. I take several deep breaths of oxygen and then plug out to struggle forward. Though the Stirling is a huge aircraft, it seems that nothing could

be big enough for me, a novice, to move gracefully in. As I climb towards the nose my dangling inter-com. winds itself around everything from the automatic pilot to the flight-engineer's neck. Just visible in his macabre red light, the captain looks up, grins, and shouts " How are you feeling ? "

" Fine ! " I say. " Liar," says he. " Don't worry, it's always the same on your first trip. If we are worried, think what those poor silly Eyeties must be feeling. Look over there. That's Genoa. No fun being in Genoa on a night like this ! "

We are the first aircraft to approach the target, but searchlights are wandering frantically across the sky while we're miles away. The flak is not as expected. At first, all I can see are masses of white gun-flashes on the ground. As we circle over the Mediterranean in towards the target, I begin to see the light stuff coming up and some red fireballs ascending.

9.5 p.m. Now it becomes frightening. There appears to be no way through the wall of searchlights and flak. The front-gunner goes down into the bomb-aimer's hatch and the captain starts violent jinking. From the astro-dome I can see the glow of our exhausts, and the great hump of the outer engines rising up and descending again against the vivid light of the flashes and the beams. As we wind our way along, the giant humps on either side continue to rise.

9.16 p.m. " Open bomb doors ! " comes through the inter-com., and then " O.K., bomb doors open ! " I lift my oxygen mask and bite into a small English Newtown apple. For some reason it gives me great pleasure to munch an English apple over Genoa. As we get over the searchlights I am less scared. Down below the gun flashes reveal the blocks of buildings. Searchlights wander across our propellers, edge the wing

DRIVING THEMSELVES TO PRISON ! Left to their fate by Rommel, thousands of Italians gave themselves up, not at all unwillingly. Some (like those here) even drove in their own lorries to the surrender points.
Photo, British Official : Crown Copyright

tips, flick the tail, and, fantastic as it seems, never catch us. But the flak comes nearer, and the red fireballs closer as the captain levels out for the bombing run and calls to the bomb-aimer, "O.K., remember the precise target!" We are dead steady for a mighty long 20 seconds before the bomb-aimer reports, "Bombs gone!" And now the thinking begins again.

The lattice-work of searchlights which from a distance I thought we would never penetrate now seem to have the most comforting wide spaces between them. Then down below I can see our incendiaries, the first fires in Genoa on Saturday night. The rear-gunner proudly points out that those are gold and broad, which means that the bombs have turned into real fires. Incendiaries on their own are silver, glittering, and sharp.

As we come out of it flak increases. It comes up towards us and then they try to shoot out the flares which now illuminate the town and the bay. Within ten minutes of the first flares Genoa is alight. So far as I can see the main huge fires are near the coast-line and harbour. A bomb flash adds to bomb flash, and before we are out of sight not one solitary searchlight remains on. I step down to allow the wireless-operator to have a look. He watches for a moment, grunts "It looks good!" and we change places. I peer again at the glorious view of the Alps under the stern, and then slowly, once more, the scene merges into the cloud over the plains of France.

Static electricity again brings a kind of dangerous beauty to the Stirlings, and then hail beats on our windows. Near the coast of France cloud gives out, and the flak and searchlights appear.

01.36 a.m. I can see the very comforting light of our flare paths back at base. "O.K.,

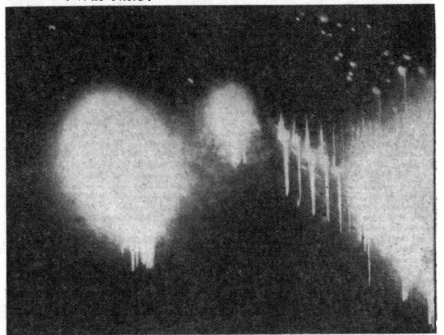

SATURDAY NIGHT IN GENOA. "It looks good!" said the wireless-operator in the accompanying story, when he looked down on the dock area strewn with scintillating pockets of fire. In this photograph, taken on the occasion of the raid of Oct. 22, scores of fires are burning; the vertical streaks are descending flares.
Photo, British Official: Crown Copyright

V for Victor," says base. "You can land now." And so we land and wander into the interrogation-room and people make the usual jokes, such as "You can identify an Italian fighter because he is always going the other way!"

And so to the operational breakfast with bacon and egg and hot tea and the "line book" already waiting on the table. My statement about thinking our incendiaries were Italian searchlights goes straight into the line book. But I'm forgiven, being a novice.

OUR DIARY OF THE WAR

NOV. 25, 1942, Wednesday 1,180th day
Russian Front.—N.W. and S. of Stalingrad Soviet advance continued; 15,000 more prisoners taken.
Burma.—R.A.F. made day and night attacks on Jap airfields and railways.
China.—U.S. aircraft attacked Jap shipping at Canton and Hankow.
Australasia.—Two Jap destroyers sunk off New Guinea in attempts to relieve troops at Buna.

NOV. 26, Thursday 1,181st day
N. Africa.—Enemy driven from Medjez-el-Bab, 30 m. S.W. of Tunis.
Mediterranean.—Allied bombers attacked aerodromes in Sicily.
Russian Front.—Red Army in Don bend took 12,000 more prisoners.
Siam.—U.S. heavy bombers made first attack on oil-refinery at Bangkok.
Australasia.—Flying Fortresses raided Jap aerodrome near Buin.

NOV. 27, Friday 1,182nd day
Air.—Mustangs and Spitfires attacked railway and water transport targets in France and Low Countries.
N. Africa.—First Army entered Tebourba, 15 m. from Tunis.
Mediterranean.—U.S. aircraft attacked docks at Leros, Dodecanese.
Russian Front.—Soviet counter-offensives continued round and in Stalingrad.
China.—U.S. bombers attacked Jap shipping and aircraft at Canton.
General.—German troops entered Toulon; French warships scuttled by order of Adm. de Laborde.

NOV. 28, Saturday 1,183rd day
Air.—R.A.F. made heavy raid on Turin.
N. Africa.—Allied forces repulsed counter-attacks at Tebourba. Bizerta and Tunis bombed by Allied aircraft; Bône twice raided by Axis.
Libya.—Tripoli raided by our heavy bombers.
Mediterranean. — Announced that British submarines had sunk nine enemy supply ships bound for Tunisia.
Russian Front.—New Soviet offensive launched on Central front, E. of Velikiye Luki and W. of Rzhev.
General.—Fighting French forces landed on Réunion Island in Indian Ocean.

NOV. 29, Sunday 1,184th day
Air.—R.A.F. again raided Turin.
N. Africa.—Our forces occupied Djedaida, N.E. of Tebourba, in Tunisia.
Libya.—U.S.A.A.F. made daylight raids on Tripoli.

Russian Front.—Soviet troops broke enemy lines on E. bank of Don.
U.S.A.—Announced that Japs had re-occupied Attu in the Aleutians.

NOV. 30, Monday 1,185th day
N. Africa.—German counter-attack on Allied positions in Djedaida. Two French submarines from Toulon reached Algiers.
Russian Front.—Further Russian advances on Central front and round Stalingrad.
Indian Ocean.—U.S. heavy bombers raided Andaman Is. and Rangoon.
Australasia.—U.S. fleet intercepted Jap convoy off Guadalcanal, sinking six destroyers and three transports for loss of one U.S. cruiser.
General.—Announced that Reunion Island had joined Fighting French.

DEC. 1, Tuesday 1,186th day
N. Africa.—Allied air attacks on Tunis, Bizerta, Gabès and Sfax.
Libya.—Enemy artillery successfully engaged by our forces at El Agheila. Our heavy bombers raided Tripoli.
Mediterranean.—Navy sank two Axis destroyers and four supply ships bound for Tunisia; destroyer Quentin sunk by enemy aircraft.
Russian Front.—Red Army continued to advance on Stalingrad and Central fronts in face of increased resistance.
Australasia.—In New Guinea Allied ground forces cut Jap lines between Buna and Gona.

DEC. 2, Wednesday 1,187th day
Air.—Frankfort and other places in W. Germany bombed by night.
N. Africa.—Allied troops beat back big German counter-attack with tanks and dive-bombers in Tebourba area.
Mediterranean.—Two Axis supply ships sunk by torpedo aircraft and Italian torpedo-boat sunk by light naval forces off Tunisia.
Australasia.—Arrival of U.S. troops in New Zealand announced.

DEC. 3, Thursday 1,188th day
N. Africa.—Another enemy counter-attack repulsed near Tebourba. Bizerta docks and Tunis airfield raided by Allies.
Australasia.—Allied airmen shot down 23 Jap fighters and drove off naval convoy attempting to reinforce Buna-Gona area of New Guinea. Off Guadalcanal, U.S. aircraft scored hits on two Jap cruisers and one destroyer.
General.—Announced that defence pact between U.S.A. and Liberia was signed on March 31.

DEC. 4, Friday 1,189th day
N. Africa.—Axis forces recaptured Djedaida; hard fighting proceeding in triangle Tebourba-Djedaida-Mateur.
Mediterranean. — U.S. Liberators bombed Naples by daylight without loss, doing much damage to warships and port.
Libya.—Allied heavy bombers raided Tripoli by night.
Russian Front.—Russian offensive continued inside and outside Stalingrad.

Burma.—R.A.F. and U.S. bombers raided Jap shipping and supply columns.

DEC. 5, Saturday 1,190th day
N. Africa.—Enemy mechanized and infantry units entered Tebourba; our troops regrouped on surrounding heights.
Russian Front.—Soviet troops on offensive round Stalingrad, near Tuapse; and on Central and Leningrad fronts.
India.—Jap bombers and fighters made brief attack on Chittagong area of Bengal.

DEC. 6, Sunday 1,191st day
Sea.—Admiralty announced loss of H.M. submarine Unique.
Air.—Nearly 100 light R.A.F. bombers attacked Philips radio works at Eindhoven, Holland. U.S. Flying Fortresses and Liberators raided Fives-Lille locomotive works and airfield at Abbeville. R.A.F. night bombers raided S.W. Germany in bad weather.
N. Africa. — German attack in Tebourba area of Tunisia penetrated one of our positions.
Russian Front.—Red Army offensive continued on Central front and in Stalingrad area.
Australasia.—In New Guinea U.S. troops broke through at a fresh point in Buna-Gona beachhead.

DEC. 7, Monday 1,192nd day
Air.—Whirlwinds and Mustangs attacked railways and shipping in France, the Low Countries and Germany.
N. Africa.—After counter-attack by one of our armoured units the enemy withdrew in Tebourba area.
Libya.—Our heavy bombers attacked Misurata and aerodromes near Homs.
Russian Front.—Many German counter-attacks repulsed on Central front and N.W. of Stalingrad.
Australasia.—In fierce air fighting over New Guinea 20 Jap aircraft were destroyed. Allied bombers attacked Lae and Jap bases in New Britain.

DEC. 8, Tuesday 1,193rd day
Air.—Mosquitoes attacked industrial and railway targets in Holland and N.W. Germany. Turin again raided by night.
Russian Front.—Soviet troops continued to make progress in and around Stalingrad and on Central front in spite of violent German resistance.
Australasia.—Allied ground forces at Buna threw back enemy counter-attack; Allied bombers drove off six destroyers attempting to relieve Jap forces.

★═══ *Flash-backs* ═══★

1939

November 26. *Admiralty announced sinking of armed merchant cruiser Rawalpindi by Deutschland on November 23.*

November 30. *Russia launched land, sea and air attack on Finland.*

December 7. *Polish submarines Orzel and Wilk escaped from Baltic and joined British Navy.*

1940

December 8. *Greeks occupied Argyrokastro in Albania.*

1941

December 6. *Russians began counter-offensive at Moscow.*

December 7. *Japan declared war on Gt. Britain and U.S.A. Pearl Harbour bombed.*

December 8. *Japanese troops landed in Northern Malaya.*

Editor's Postscript

I AM sure that on Christmas Eve, when this number of THE WAR ILLUSTRATED will be on sale, many of my readers will be delighted to know that next month "huge stores of food, clothing, etc., will pour into Great Britain from America, and large stocks will be diverted to help sustain the famished section of Europe and Norway, freed from direct Axis intervention." But we are warned that it will not be "roses, roses all the way," as Japan will still fight on tenaciously. This, it would appear, is known to those who are aware that "the eventful year of 1943 opens under the influence of Saturn, combined with the determination of Capricorn the Goat." But as I am not one of those who know anything more about goats than that they are the most odoriferous of domestic animals, I can only pass this cheering information on with due acknowledgement to my entertaining old friend the prophet "Old Moore," from whom I have so often culled words of cheer in these pages.

SOME day I feel sure that his persistence will be rewarded; though the stars may at times be a year or two fast as he reads them, events must at some time or another catch up with the forecast. While I am offering some odds against that taking place in January 1943 I have a profound conviction that when we have said good-bye to 1942 we shall be stepping into the most momentous year of the War, before the end of which we may well have listened to the death knell of Nazidom in Europe and be turning to the cleansing of the eastern hemisphere from the yellow stain with which the Japs have soiled it. Still, the path ahead of the nations struggling for freedom is beset with thorny thickets and prickly pitfalls and only simpletons will expect to go primrose-gathering even in 1943. And as for roses, let's remember they have thorns when we go gathering them. "Out of this nettle, danger, we pluck this flower, safety"—I remembered Neville Chamberlain quoting this when I heard it again from the lips of Hotspur (Henry IV) at the Westminster Theatre the other week. And I'm sure we shall do so, if not in 1943 certainly in 1944.

ONE of the many lessons we have learnt in these War years is the reassessment of values : things we have long cherished suddenly seem worthless, what we have despised turns precious. The value of transport is not likely again to depreciate, since War conditions have emphasized its supreme importance in every concern of modern life. Though I have done my best from time to time to illustrate this in these notes, I confess that not until last autumn had I become so transport-conscious as I found myself when, confronted with an abundant crop of lovely apples, I had to see the orchard becoming ankle deep with windfalls. Nobody wanted to buy them, few were willing even to take the crop for the pulling. They could not all be stored for lack of accommodation, and many of them, though splendid specimens, were not "good keepers."

THANKS eventually to some enterprising young people associated with the Y.W.C.A. and other organizations, I had the satisfaction of seeing something like two tons of this rich harvest cleared from the orchard and transported for use in certain schools and canteens, whence letters of keen appreciation for the gift were received. But it was really no gift ; merely the removal of what, owing to the sheer abundance of the fruit, had become an embarrassment. And yet in some parts of England, and in London, as I myself had frequent occasion to observe, apples in no way comparable with any in the numerous sackfuls joyously picked by Boy Scouts, Girl Guides and members of the W.V.S. from my orchard of little more than an acre, were selling freely at 8d. per pound. I know of many other instances where "apple acres" in the same district were in similar plight, and I have no doubt they could be multiplied by the thousand throughout the country, so that when produce which does not fetch even a penny a pound on the trees cannot be bought under 8d. at a distance from its place of origin, it is worth remembering that the true value resides not in the article but in its transportation from where it is abundant to where it is scarce.

IN looking at a news reel of Mr. Wendell Willkie some little time ago, I made a note: "remember Big Bill Thompson of Chicago." I came across this note last night, and after a little cogitation it struck me that I must have seen some fanciful resemblance between the intrepid Republican leader and Chicago's aggressive mayor of twelve years ago. Then I remembered that Big Bill aquired some momentary fame from warning King George V "not to put his snoot into Chicago." Why Big Bill did this I forget ; but I can conceive no advice ever so needlessly offered. It is possible that, as Mr. Willkie had just started to "prod" Great Britain to open a second front (without knowing that in closest alliance with the official American leaders we were just about to do a bit of prodding in North Africa which will stand in history for centuries to come) the thought struck me, while watching the self-satisfied Mr. Willkie on the news reel and listening to his voice, that his advice was just about as apposite to the case of Britain's leaders at this day as Big Bill's was to the least aggressive and most tactful of British monarchs, whose qualities are so eminent in his son today. Perhaps our Press has given too much space to the utterances of the said Mr. Willkie, who, in my estimation, was making nothing more than political capital out of the great opportunity provided by the generous gesture of Mr. Roosevelt when he sent his political opponent to report on aspects of the War on all fronts. His ungenerous use of this opportunity to feed an ancient Republican grudge against the British Empire should, in my opinion, reduce the interest of his name as a headliner on the front pages of the British Press, even though we have no counterpart of Big Bill Thompson in England who would be so free of speech and so impolite as to tell Mr. Willkie to keep his snoot out of the British Empire.

NOT a week goes by that I do not have occasion to marvel at the way in which Malta carries on, despite its thousands of air raids, as I am continually receiving letters from readers there, although I can give only occasional mention to any of them. One from a reader named Eddie Gauci (if I do not misread his signature) of B'Kara, took only about ten days to arrive in London and contained an order for the binding cases for Volume V, as he has all the others safely bound, and while congratulating me on the recent changes in the character of our contents, he adds : "I hope you will continue to publish THE WAR ILLUSTRATED in this way, or in any other way, as in it you are performing a splendid work for all of us who are proud to be members of the British Empire although we cannot all have an opportunity of visiting its capital city."

THE foregoing I had written some weeks ago and the Malta scene has changed meanwhile. The island that could take it is now the fortress that can give it ! And here I might mention as still further evidence that "Britain delivers the goods" a letter just to hand from Geo. W. Crossan, of Hamilton, N.Z. Not even a single number has failed to reach what he calls "this farthest outpost of Empire," as he had received every issue up to No. 130 when he wrote to me in September.

LOOKING through an old stage journal of 1892 today, I notice that its letter from America is headed "Across the Pond"— the facetious name for the Atlantic current in the 'nineties. But how appropriate to the contracting world in which we are living, when eight hours suffice for its aerial crossing ! Many a true word spoken in jest.

ADM. SIR MAX K. HORTON, K.C.B., D.S.O., whose appointment, as C.-in-C. Western Approaches, in succession to Adm. Sir P. Noble, was announced on Nov. 9, 1942. He had been in charge of British submarines since the beginning of the War, and was succeeded as Flag Officer Submarines by Capt. C. B. Barry, D.SO.
Photo, Topical Press

Printed in England and published every alternate Friday by the Proprietors, THE AMALGAMATED PRESS, LTD., The Fleetway House, Farringdon Street, London, E.C.4. Registered for transmission by Canadian Magazine Post. Sole Agents for Australia and New Zealand : Messrs. Gordon & Gotch, Ltd. ; and for South Africa ; Central News Agency, Ltd.—December 24, 1942   S.S   *Editorial Address :* JOHN CARPENTER HOUSE, WHITEFRIARS, LONDON, E.C.4.

Vol 6 *The War Illustrated* Nº 145

Edited by Sir John Hammerton

SIXPENCE

JANUARY 8, 1943

AXIS SHIPS IN BENGHAZI HARBOUR were still blazing as the result of the non-stop attack by Allied bombers on Rommel's chief Libyan port when the 8th Army entered the town on November 20, 1942. Two Indian soldiers in the foreground are enjoying the interlude in the hurricane of war. Immediately after our recapture of Benghazi the harbour was speedily cleared up, and by mid-December was again in working order.

Photo, British Official: Crown Copyright

NO. 146 WILL BE PUBLISHED FRIDAY, **JANUARY 22**

THE BATTLE FRONTS

by Maj.-Gen. Sir Charles Gwynn, K.C.B., D.S.O.

'MARBLE ARCH,' a pretentious Italian monument marking the half-way line between Tripoli and Egypt, stands near what was the Axis forward fighter base before Rommel retreated from El Agheila. *Photo, Daily Mail*

THE retreat of Rommel from El Agheila on Dec. 13, 1942, and the capture of Buna the next day, were highly satisfactory events. It would have been more satisfactory if Rommel had given Montgomery an opportunity of gaining a decisive victory, but his retreat from such a strong position affords convincing proof that his losses at El Alamein were not exaggerated. It is also an indication of the inability of the Axis Powers to reinforce him owing to the number and serious nature of their other commitments. The recognized strategy for armies compelled to act on exterior lines is to maintain relentless pressure at a number of points in order to prevent the enemy concentrating his forces where he is most threatened, or has opportunities for a counter-stroke. This strategy is now in operation, and its effect in causing the enemy to disperse his resources and in counteracting the inherent advantages he possesses of rapid movement on interior lines can be seen.

The comparatively small size of the forces engaged in New Guinea should not make us under-rate the importance of the achievements or the difficulties that were overcome. The passage of the Owen Stanley range, and the attacks on Buna itself under appalling conditions, have shown once again the adaptability of Australian troops to all sorts of warfare and their fighting qualities. The desperate fight made by the Japanese adds to the brilliance of the achievement.

In Russia and in Tunisia the situation continues to develop favourably, although it is yet too soon to indulge in expectation of immediate sensational results.

NORTH AFRICA

Information as regards operations in Tunisia has been so meagre that at the time of writing (in the middle of December) the situation is somewhat obscure, especially in the southern regions. On the whole, it seems fairly satisfactory, especially since there are indications that in the struggle for air supremacy the Allies are by degrees depriving the enemy of his initial advantages. So long, however, as he can operate short-range aircraft from the airfields of Tunis and Bizerta decisive supremacy over the battlefield is not likely to be achieved. The Allied advanced forces have had to deal with a number of counter-attacks; and though they do not appear to have suffered any serious reverses, they have been compelled to withdraw from their most forward position and to shorten their line. They have, however, inflicted considerable losses on the enemy, and hold positions covering the deployment of the main army.

Weather has been unfavourable, and the movement of transport columns through the mountains has been difficult, and will probably be the main reason for delay in opening major operations. The enemy's strength is undoubtedly growing, though at the price of heavy losses on his lines of communication inflicted by the Navy and the Middle East air force.

The possibility that Rommel may abandon Tripolitania and attempt to join hands with the Axis forces in Tunis exists; but should he attempt to operate in Southern Tunis it is difficult to see how he could be adequately supplied. He would have no established bases to work from, and his sea and air communications would become increasingly precarious.

ROMMEL'S retreat from El Agheila without attempting serious resistance naturally raises the question: Why did he retreat so precipitately to that point if he did not intend to make full use of the defensive potentialities of the position? I think it is safe to assume that he hoped to receive there substantial reinforcements, and that his hopes were disappointed. It may be that he also hoped that Montgomery, flushed with success, would attack him with weak advanced forces, and without proper preparations—thus exposing himself to counter-attack. If that were so, Montgomery's deliberate procedure made the hope vain.

I DO not think that Rommel gained much time by his halt at El Agheila, since in any case the 8th Army was bound to pause to close up, to bring the port of Benghazi into operation, and in general to reorganize its lines of communications before embarking on a further advance of over 400 miles into Tripolitania. His halt and final retreat have done little more than reveal fully the weakness of the force Rommel now has at his disposal.

It is now generally assumed that Rommel will make a stand at Misurata. But would his prospects there be much better than they were at El Agheila, unless in the meantime reinforcements are poured into Tripoli? Misurata is a weaker position than that at El Agheila; and though its communications with Tripoli are shorter, that disadvantage would not be great unless Tripoli is a well-stocked base. Is it likely to be well stocked? I should imagine it is not; for while Rommel was in Egypt it seems almost certain that whatever material and supplies were landed or were in stock, at Tripoli, would have been sent forward into Cyrenaica or to even more advanced depots. I should be surprised if Tripoli, since Rommel entered Egypt, has held stocks much in excess of those required for Italian outlying posts in the south. Since the Battle of Egypt the increasing risks of the sea passage and the competing demands of Tunisia make it improbable that deficiences, if they existed, have been made good.

The chief advantage the Misurata position has is that the 8th Army would again be strung out in its advance, and that its line of communication would be long and difficult, with water supply a particularly difficult problem. Still, it must be remembered that, when we were in occupation of Cyrenaica, Rommel at El Agheila was able to

STALINGRAD AREA saw considerable gains for the Russian forces during Nov. 1942. This map shows the extent of Soviet thrusts S.W. of the city by Dec. 6. *By courtesy of The Times*

maintain and build up a strong striking force under much the same difficulties of communication and with less assistance from sea transport than we may expect.

RUSSIA

The statistics of losses inflicted on the Germans in the first three weeks of the Stalingrad offensive and in the offensive on the Moscow front are very impressive, and there seems no reason to doubt their substantial accuracy. I note that Mr. A. T. Cholerton, the very well-informed Moscow correspondent of The Daily Telegraph, evidently considers them reliable. An organization exists apparently in the Red Army for recording accurately enemy losses. Claims of prisoners taken on

8th ARMY'S ADVANCE TOWARDS TRIPOLI was made possible by hundreds of Allied bombers and fighters which operated from Libyan bases S. of Benghazi. Enemy airfields which follow the Tripolitanian coastline were heavily strafed by our planes. The arrow shows the direction of our advance after the network of minefields had been crossed in the El Agheila region in mid-December 1942.

By courtesy of the Daily Mail

GERMAN OFFICER, his Iron Cross prominently displayed, his head bowed and hands raised in token of submission, gives himself up to Allied troops in Tunisia.
Photo, Associated Press

MISURATA, on the coastal road to Tripoli and situated some 300 miles N.W. of El Agheila, has a population of about 45,000. By Dec. 17, 1942 the fleeing Afrika Korps was nearing the town. This photo shows Italian troops in the main street. *Photo, E.N.A.*

number of reasons would seem more likely to stand the strain on their morale. The Germans in general are better placed as regards railway communications; but where, as at Stalingrad and Rzhev, railways have been lost, the strain on the Luftwaffe transport service is clearly becoming great, and the destruction of transport aircraft a very serious matter, made all the more serious by the diversion of transport planes to the Mediterranean.

On the Stalingrad front, though Russian progress has been slowed down, the situation for the Germans shows no sign of improvement. There are few indications that they have mustered a relief army sufficiently strong to break through the Russian ring. Though a fairly powerful force appears to be forming at Kotelnikovo, its main object at present is probably to check a further Russian advance towards that important centre: Kotelnikovo would evidently provide an advanced base for any attempt made from the south to re-establish communication with the encircled army.

IF relief operations are undertaken, they will most probably be from the south, with the Novorossisk-Kotelnikovo-Stalingrad railway as their axis. The Russians on that side, lacking good communications and not easily reinforced, can hardly be in great strength. Moreover, the obstacle of the Don would be avoided. Relief operations by the railway on the north bank of the Don are less likely, for in addition to having to force the passage of the Don they would be exposed to a flank attack by powerful Russian forces from the north. Further-

the Moscow front are very moderate, nor have additions to the numbers taken in the first break-through on the Stalingrad front, when mass surrenders took place, been large. With the Russians steadily gaining ground the numbers of killed should also easily be ascertainable, and Mr. Cholerton states that no estimates are made of the considerable numbers of killed behind the German front. In the heavy fighting in those parts of the front where attack and counter-attack are constantly being delivered without much gain of ground, the mortality rate on both sides must be very high, and the process of attrition rapid; but the Russians for a

more, the Germans are anxious about a threatened Russian offensive south of Voronezh, and are probably holding reserves in readiness to meet it should it be launched. The whole situation on the Stalingrad front is made the more obscure because it is never made clear whether German counter-attacks reported have been made from outside the ring or by troops within it.

STRIPPED FOR ACTION, this New Zealand machine-gunner opens fire at a Stuka during the Libyan fighting. The snake-like ammunition belt moves at great speed through the gun. *Photo, Associated Press*

On the Moscow front the fierceness and frequency of German counter-attacks show the enemy's determination to hold on to positions threatened with isolation, and to avoid at all costs a withdrawal to straighten his front—a determination based no doubt on the recollection of just how disastrous the withdrawals made last winter really were.

FAR EAST The taking of Buna points to the elimination of the Japanese foothold in Papua, but it also reveals the fanatical courage Japanese troops can display. If the same spirit prevails throughout the Japanese army, the prospects of a quick recovery of our lost territory would be poor indeed.

But the Japanese have been known to crack, and there is reason to believe that the garrison of Buna was a picked force. It must be realized, too, that the attacking troops were desperately handicapped by ground and weather conditions, and were unable to develop superiority in armament.

In the Solomons the situation seems to be satisfactory, especially in the air; and the Japanese have lost more ships in fruitless manoeuvres. Papua, New Britain, and the Solomons have a heavy rainfall at all seasons, but November to April (summer in those latitudes) is the wet season; and extensive operations will presumably be postponed till the drier conditions may be expected.

TRIPOLI, capital of Tripolitania, has for the past two years been the chief port through which Axis forces in N. Africa have drawn their supplies. Allied air attacks were concentrated on the docks and military buildings. Tripoli's population of about 110,000 is equally divided between Italians and Arabs. Here is an aerial view of the city. On the right, jutting into the harbour, is the old Castle.
Photo, Keystone

Hard and Bitter Is the Battle for Tunisia

FIERCE FIGHTING IN NORTHERN TUNISIA developed towards the end of Nov. 1942 as the 1st Army advanced in the direction of Bizerta and Tunis. Top, knocked-out German tank at Mateur, key-point S.W. of Bizerta. Circle, the gun of a U.S. General Lee tank receives a pull-through after taking a prominent part in the capture of Medjez-el-Bab. Bottom, Italian tank taken in the course of the fierce fighting near Tebourba being examined by a British soldier.

No 'Picnic' for the Men of Anderson's Army

IN THE FIGHT FOR TEBOURBA, some twenty miles W. of Tunis, a battalion of the Hampshire Regiment covered themselves with glory. For four days they held up a largely superior German force in the most advanced of the First Army's positions in a wood beside the Jedeida-Tebourba road, but after charging the enemy time and again and defeating many a counter-attack, they were at length compelled to withdraw on Dec. 3, 1942 from their foothold in Tebourba's outskirts. Top, bomb damage in Tebourba; circle, British officers in the vicinity; below, 1st Army Bren gunners in the line near Mateur.

Photos, British Official: Crown Copyright

'Blood Banks' Save Lives for the 8th Army

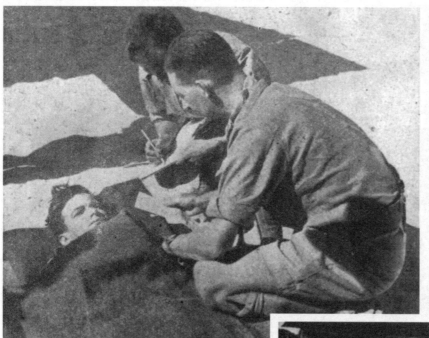

BADLY WOUNDED MAN (left) at a Casualty Clearing Station. To enable him to withstand an operation, a blood transfusion is ordered. Above, a dispatch-rider sets out for the "blood bank."

Into the dispatch-rider's pack a medical orderly attached to a "blood bank" places a bottle of blood of the correct group. With this the rider returns at speed to the C.C.S.

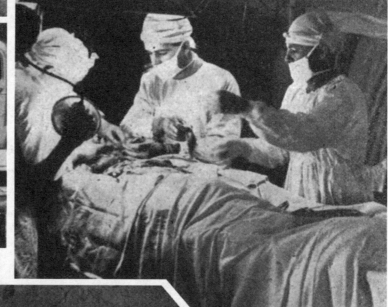

IN LIBYA "blood banks" are proving an invaluable adjunct to the medical officers accompanying the 8th Army. They are established in the fighting areas to supply dressing stations and mobile operating theatres. Blood transfusion has been the means of saving the lives of many men who, owing to loss of blood, would not have had the strength to undergo surgical treatment. Above, a major operation is in progress in one of the desert theatres. Left, patients convalescing in the ward of a tent hospital in the desert. This hospital is operated by a New Zealand unit.

Photos, British Official: Crown Copyright; Associated Press

Montgomery Drives On Along the Road to Tripoli

SIDI BARRANI, abandoned by Rommel's fleeing troops by Nov. 11, 1942, was a mass of ruins when the 8th Army entered the town. Left, the wall of a shattered building provides an appropriate setting for humorous slogans. Above, a British anti-tank gunner in Barce armed with a welcome assortment of bread-rolls.

SMASHING AT ROMMEL IN THE WESTERN DESERT, a 4·5-gun of an R.A. Field and Medium Battery is seen in action. This gun, one of the latest developments of our field artillery, has been used with deadly effect in forward areas; and has caused great damage to tanks and transport in the enemy's rear positions. The 4·5 has concertina-like compensators which assist in absorbing recoil, and has proved a formidable counterblast to the German 88-mm. gun.

Photos, British Official; Crown Copyright; Sport & General

THE WAR AT SEA

by Francis E. McMurtrie

PUBLICATION of air photographs of the naval dockyard at Toulon, taken the day after the French fleet was scuttled, has provided the first actual evidence of its state. Some of the ships were still on fire, and others were obviously semi-submerged. Of the two modern battleships, the Strasbourg was lying alongside a pier, apparently aground, while her sister-ship, the Dunkerque, could be seen in dry dock, where she had evidently been placed to enable the under-water damage inflicted by torpedoes at Oran in July 1940 to be repaired.

Though some vessels appeared in the photograph to be intact, it is impossible to be certain that there is no under-water damage. Personally, I am of the opinion that there are very few vessels of any fighting

WORLD'S BIGGEST BATTLESHIP, U.S.S. New Jersey, one of 10 new ships launched in American east coast yards on Dec. 7, 1942, the first anniversary of the attack on Pearl Harbour. Belonging to the Iowa class, she will displace 52,000 tons, full load, her length is 880 ft., and her main battery will consist of nine 16-in. guns.

Photo, Keystone

value at Toulon that could proceed to sea without more or less extensive refitting.

In answer to an inquiry from an American correspondent, Admiral Darlan has declared very definitely that he hopes all available French warships will now be employed in operations against the Axis Powers. In this hope he categorically included not only ships at Dakar, Casablanca, Oran and Algiers, but also those immobilized at Alexandria, under an agreement made in July, 1940 between Admiral Sir Andrew Cunningham and Vice-Admiral Godefroy.

THOUGH they have been laid up in a demilitarized condition, in charge of nucleus crews, ever since, these ships are believed to be in good condition, though probably their machinery would require some overhauling after the long period during which it has been idle. The ships comprise the old battleship Lorraine, the cruisers Suffren, Duquesne, Tourville and Duguay-Trouin, the destroyers Basque, Forbin, and Le Fortuné, and the submarine Protée.

At Casablanca are the half-completed battleship Jean Bart, the cruiser Primauguet, one or two destroyers and possibly some submarines, all more or less damaged. It would be necessary to patch up the Jean Bart and Primauguet to enable them to be taken to a fully equipped dockyard in this country or the United States for complete refit before they would be of the slightest use for fighting purposes.

There are several destroyers at Oran and Algiers, aground or in a semi-wrecked state, together with some smaller craft of little importance, and the submarines Le Glorieux, Casabianca and Marsouin, which escaped from Toulon and are in sound condition.

At Dakar are the cruisers Georges Leygues, Gloire and Montcalm, with at least three destroyers and some submarines, all presumably in a seaworthy state, as well as the disabled battleship Richelieu, which, like her sister-ship Jean Bart, would require to be taken to a dockyard for extensive repair before she could be regarded as serviceable.

Leaving out of account the disabled units, there would be available for operations in the near future seven cruisers (assuming the Alexandria ships can be counted), one or perhaps two flotillas of destroyers, and a flotilla of submarines. For escort purposes the cruisers and destroyers would be most valuable; and there is no reason why the submarines should not engage in harrying enemy communications between Italy and Tunisia, as British and Greek submarines have done so successfully in the past.

There is, of course, the question of manning these ships, since it is not certain whether full crews of trained Frenchmen could be found for them all. Of the desire of the majority to avenge the indignities inflicted

on their country by the Germans there is little doubt; and there is every reason to suppose that they would be equally ready to fight the Italians, whom they heartily despise.

IN the race to replace lost aircraft-carriers the United States is making rapid strides, and is likely soon to outdistance Japan. Of those with which they started the war, neither combatant has more than three first-line units remaining in service. There are a number of auxiliary aircraft-carriers in the U.S. Navy of the Long Island and Charger types, but these are not suitable for operating with a fleet. Similarly the Japanese are rumoured to have improvised some make-shift carriers, to which the same remark would apply.

During the second half of 1942 there have been launched from American shipyards three new aircraft-carriers of 25,000 tons, the Essex, Lexington and Bunker Hill, and three of 10,000 tons, the Independence, Princeton and Belleau Wood. The latter trio were laid down as cruisers, but were altered during construction and should not take so long to complete as the bigger ships. When all six are in service some time in 1943, they should accelerate the pace of the war in the Pacific.

Ten more aircraft-carriers of the 25,000-ton type and possibly as many of the 10,000-ton class are under construction, and some of these should also be delivered during 1943. In the vast Pacific, with its immense distances, a preponderance in first-line carriers should give the United States a tremendous advantage, which should hasten Japan's defeat.

Even as it is, American torpedo aircraft and dive-bombers from the airfield at Guadalcanal continue to inflict loss and damage on the Japanese Navy. A comparison of casualties over many months reveals clearly that in the air the Americans have decidedly the upper hand. This must have seriously depleted the number of trained Japanese airmen, so that as time goes on the situation in this respect should still further improve.

THERE was a smart little action in the Channel on the night of December 11-12, 1942 not far from Dieppe. Light naval forces —an expression comprising anything up to a destroyer—under the command of Lieut.-Commander A. A. F. Talbot, R.N., intercepted a westbound enemy convoy of two medium-sized supply vessels with four escorting ships. One of the supply vessels and at least one if not two of the escorts were sunk. Our casualties were light, and only minor damage was done to our ships.

There is nothing novel in this type of encounter, which has been occurring at intervals for many months past. What it does show is that, despite the risk involved, the enemy still find it worth while to try to relieve the burden on their overtaxed land transport by sending supplies by sea.

British submarines continue to take heavy toll of enemy supply lines to North Africa. Admiralty communiqués have detailed various exploits, such as the sinking of an armed merchant cruiser, a tanker and sundry supply ships. On one occasion an Italian railway-train was shelled and half-wrecked; on another, lighters trying to land supplies for Rommel's retreating forces were sunk inshore. A submarine of the Royal Hellenic Navy participated in one of these exploits.

There are no braver or more determined men in the Royal Navy than the personnel of the submarine service. A conspicuous example was afforded by H.M.S. Truant, which recently returned to this country after an absence of 2½ years. During this time she covered more than 80,000 miles in the Mediterranean, Indian Ocean, and Java Sea, and was responsible for sinking or damaging over 20 enemy vessels. She went to the United States in May 1941 for a refit, but was soon back on patrol against Italian supply lines. In the Far East the Japanese claimed to have sunk her, but she escaped.

Life or Death Struggle in the Submarine War

IN THE MEDITERRANEAN recently, British submarines have taken heavy toll of Axis supplies en route for Tunisia and Tripoli. On the left a submarine crew is seen coming ashore at Alexandria. Complete with kit, these men have just disembarked for well-earned leave. Their vessel entered the harbour with the "Jolly Roger" fluttering from her flagstaff as a sign that she had sent an Axis ship to the bottom.

Below, the end of a U-boat. Brought to the surface by depth charges and then bombed by a Coastal Command Liberator operating from Iceland, this submarine received a direct hit. Fragments of metal thrown up are ringed with white. Periscope standards, jumping wires and deck are clearly visible.

IN MID-ATLANTIC a German long-distance aircraft of the Condor type hovers over a U-boat lying in wait for Allied convoys. During the closing months of 1942 the Battle of the Atlantic swung heavily in our favour.

BRITISH SEAMEN who spent 12 days in open boats ran ashore on a desolate part of the African coast. They were found by natives and given hospitality. Meanwhile, they traced an S O S in the sand, and their signal was spotted by a British reconnaissance aircraft which reported to the nearest naval base. A trawler was then sent out, the castaways were transferred from shore to ship in native canoes, and subsequently returned to Britain to man another vessel. Left, British sailors, in scanty tropical kit, help one of the exhausted survivors to reach the rescuing trawler's deck.

Photos, British Official: Crown Copyright; Associated Press

Deep Snow Covers the Russian Battlefront

IN THE DEPTHS OF WINTER the Red Army has launched a series of powerful offensives—in the central sector, at Stalingrad, and on the Middle Don. The top photograph shows Soviet light artillerymen transporting their guns along a frozen road ; ammunition is hauled on sledges. Below, a detachment of sappers serving with a Russian Guards regiment listens intently to a lecture on recent offensive operations given by their commanding officer at a camp on the northern front.

Photos, Planet News

Through the Wintry Forest Speed the Red Guards

CLEARING A WOOD IN THE CAUCASUS. Having knocked out a German tank, a detachment of Russian Guards dash forward past the blazing machine to attack the enemy in the middle of this snow-covered wood on the Caucasian front. It was a Guards division which, under Gen. Alexander Rodimtsev, won undying glory in the defence of Stalingrad. German attempts to advance north-east of Tuapse failed in the face of strong Soviet opposition during mid-December 1942.

Photo, Planet News

Why the Solomons Battle Is So Important

Five hundred miles to the east of New Guinea lie the Solomons, a group of islands which since last summer have been a battleground for Americans and Japanese. As the following account makes clear, what is at stake is not just the ownership of a South Seas paradise, but a position of immense strategical importance.

WHEN the Spanish navigator Alvaro Mendaña first set foot on them in 1567 he thought that he had discovered the source of King Solomon's treasure ; apparently he mistook the iron pyrites visible in the outcropping rocks for traces of gold. It was not gold ; and from whatever quarter the fabulously wealthy Hebrew monarch may have derived his riches, it was certainly not from this far-distant and inaccessible corner of the earth. But the name that Mendaña bestowed in his hour of ignorance stuck : *Islas de Salomon* he called them, and the Solomon Islands they are to this day.

When the Spaniard sailed away the very existence of the archipelago was practically forgotten ; in Madrid they hushed up the details of Mendaña's narrative so as to

themselves here and there in the group. As recently as 1927 missionaries were killed in the Solomons.

Politically, all the archipelago is British ; Guadalcanal, Malaita, San Cristobal, New Georgia, Choiseul, Isabel, Tulagi and some smaller islands were annexed in 1893 when the British were busily engaged in painting red any vacant places on the map, while Bougainville and Buka, German from 1893 to their occupation by an Australian force in 1914, were assigned to Australia by the League of Nations as a mandated territory in 1920. The area of the British Solomons protectorate is about 15,000 square miles, with a population of about 500 whites and 100,000 Melanesians ; in the Australian (mandated) portion there is a native population of about 50,000 in an area of 4,100

informing the headman of the native settlement of the quota of foodstuffs that he will be expected to provide in future for the Japanese overlords, have quietly withdrawn. Other of the islands, however, have a Japanese garrison. These include New Britain and New Ireland, lying off the north-east coast of New Guinea, and the most northerly of the Solomons—Buka, Bougainville, Shortland, Fais, Gizo, and Florida. Then in the monster island of New Guinea, while the Allies hold Papua and the Gona and Buna area of the mandated north-eastern region, the Japanese hold most of the island's northern coast from Salamaua westward, and they have also established their positions in the Dutch south-western portion.

As for the Allies, they hold a multitude of islands to the south and east—the New Hebrides and New Caledonia (Fighting French, this), Nauru and Ocean, Samoa and Fiji—together with the south-eastern tip of New Guinea.

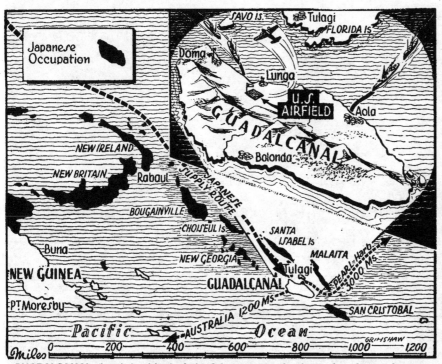

GUADALCANAL (inset), key-island of the Solomons, saw the destruction of many Japanese planes and ships during Sept.-Dec. 1942, when Allied air and sea power took a heavy toll of Jap reinforcements. This map shows Guadalcanal in relation to enemy-occupied islands in the S.W. Pacific.
By courtesy of Reynolds News

discourage aliens from following in his footsteps and securing the wealth for themselves—that wealth which must be Spain's or nobody's. Just two hundred years passed before the Solomons were discovered afresh, by the Englishman, Philip Carteret, and the Frenchman, Louis de Bougainville (after whom one of the islands is named, as well as the tropical plant). In 1769 another Frenchman, de Surville, made a lengthy stay in the archipelago, and gave to a number of the islands the names they still bear. New Georgia was named by Lieut. Shortland in 1788. So the tale continues. But then for many years the peaceful record of discovery was followed by one of bloodshed and rapine. The natives were no carefree children of Nature, but fierce cannibals, and their manners were not improved by contact with traders, whalers and ruffianly "black-birders" who derived their livelihood from kidnapping natives for labour on the plantations of Fiji and Queensland. The white man, bringing with him depopulation and disease, earned the black man's hatred ; and it is hardly surprising that generations passed away before the missionaries could establish

square miles. Bananas, coconuts, rubber, sweet potatoes, and pineapples are grown.

The Resident Commissioner of the Protectorate has his seat in Tulagi, a little island off the coast of Florida—the Solomons' Florida, of course ; Kieta in Bougainville is the chief town of the mandated islands. One of the most important of the islands is Guadalcanal or Guadalcanar, as it is also spelled. About the size of Devonshire, it is, like most of its fellows in the archipelago, volcanic, rugged, and mountainous.

GUADALCANAL lies near the limit of Japan's expansion to the south-east. To the north and west her conquests have been widespread since the collapse of Allied resistance in the Netherlands Indies at the end of February 1942. On a number of the myriads of islands and islets that dot this vast area of the Pacific her troops have effected landings, even if they have not found it worth their while to make a prolonged stay. Some have been visited merely by a Japanese launch containing a mission of a handful of army officers and a civilian or two who, after

FROM this survey it will be clear that Guadalcanal occupies a key position, *the* key position, in this great war zone. Hence the bitter and prolonged fighting that it has seen of recent months. It was on August 7, 1942 that a body of American Marines seized the harbour of Tulagi, with the islets of Gavutu and Tanambogo commanding its entrance, and the aerodrome recently constructed by the Japanese above the beach at Guadalcanal. Although taken by surprise, the Japanese recovered swiftly, and on the next day struck back at the Americans, inflicting severe losses on their fleet. But the Marines held their ground with the utmost resolution, and soon from Henderson airfield on Guadalcanal American planes were operating against the Japanese in the islands and their accompanying fleets. Six large-scale attempts have been made by the Japanese to drive out the Marines. All have failed, and not only have the Americans held their ground, but they made the enemy pay dearly in warships and transports. The story of the struggle for Guadalcanal is indeed a page of history of which America and her Allies have every reason to be proud.

When the Americans occupied their beachhead on Guadalcanal they were acting on the defensive ; the move was dictated by the desire to prevent the Japanese from penetrating farther to the south-east in the direction of the vital sea-passage from America to Australia that runs past the New Hebrides to Brisbane. But it was soon demonstrated that the move had an offensive aspect as well : the possession of the airfield at Guadalcanal and the harbour at Tulagi not only removed the threat of Japanese invasion from the islands to the south, but it helped in large measure to make possible an Allied countermove along the Solomons towards Japan's important base at Rabaul in New Britain and her mandated islands in the north-east.

But any such move would be imperilled by an attack on the flank from the Japanese in New Guinea. Thus we can realize now the strategical implications of the Allied drive across the Owen Stanley Mountains from Port Moresby to Buna (reported taken by General MacArthur's troops on December 15, 1942). Once, and only if, the Allied western flank in New Guinea is made secure, it should be possible to push on along the four-hundred-mile-long chain of the Solomons to assail the Japanese in the strongholds of their power in the central Pacific. Guadalcanal is a pistol pointed at, if not Japan's heart, at least one of the most menacing of her ugly, far-reaching tentacles.

Guadalcanal, Cockpit of the S.W. Pacific

WAR IN THE SOLOMONS. 1, Japanese prisoners captured by U.S. Marines are seen after their arrival at one of the detention areas on the island of Guadalcanal. 2, This ridge, guarding Henderson airfield in Guadalcanal, was the scene of fierce fighting at the beginning of Nov. 1942, when the enemy made repeated attempts to dislodge Marines entrenched here. The Japs suffered heavy losses. On Nov. 24 Washington stated that all Guadalcanal airfields were in U.S. hands. 3, With guns manned and ready, amphibian tractors from the American transport in the background bring welcome reinforcements to the "Leathernecks." PAGE 461 *Photos, Paul Popper, Keystone, Fox*

Japan's Fanatical Belief that She Can Win

"Far too many people in this country," writes Sir Robert Clive, British Ambassador to Tokyo from 1934 to 1937, "simply cannot believe that to defeat the Japanese may be an even tougher proposition than to defeat the Germans." Hence the importance of this article—"I agree with every word and should like to see it widely circulated," says Sir Robert—by Alex. H. Faulkner, The Daily Telegraph's New York Correspondent, published in that newspaper on December 10 and reproduced here by courtesy of the Editor.

IN the broadcast which he made on the eve of his birthday Mr. Churchill lifted a corner of the curtain that hides the future when he discussed the possibility that the war in Europe may come to an end before the war in Asia.

This warning that Japan is a formidable foe was well-timed, for even in the United States, which is much nearer to Hitler's Asiatic ally than Britain is, there are still many people who are inclined to under-estimate the enemies to whom they scornfully refer as "Nips."

There is one man who suffers from no illusions about Japan's toughness. Since his repatriation, Mr. Joseph Grew, the former United States Ambassador to Tokyo, has been speaking and writing continuously in an effort to correct what he considers fallacious thinking on the part of a large proportion of Americans about the war with Japan. Now, when the first anniversary of Pearl Harbour has come round, he has published Report from Tokyo, which sums up his convictions.

Mr. Grew is one of America's most polished diplomats, but this report is written in a forthright style that the most able of journalists might envy. Without disclosing any diplomatic secrets he nevertheless makes it clear that his own Government had been fully informed about the dangers that threatened it. He repeatedly warned it, especially during 1941, reporting that Japan might strike "with dangerous and dramatic suddenness," as in fact she did, at Pearl Harbour.

Writing to a Japanese friend on Sept. 1, 1941, Mr. Grew said without reservation that :

We believe that the Nazis seek to control and alter our whole way of life. Therefore, as a reasonable and sensible measure of self-defence, we determined to help Great Britain to avoid defeat.

In another passage he stated :

The British began to fight this war as amateurs, perhaps, but at least like gentlemen. They trusted like gentlemen to Germany's pledged word.

Elsewhere he asserts :

The British people forgot their rights—they thought only of their duties and their capacities. To the British people our debt is incalculable.

ALMOST immediately after Japan's declaration of war on the United States and Britain, police closed and locked the American Embassy's gates and "from that moment we were regarded and treated as prisoners." A group of Japanese radio experts then immediately came and "went through all our houses with a fine tooth comb, taking away all short-wave radio sets." American missionaries, teachers and newspaper correspondents and business men were ill-treated and "subjected at times to most cruel and barbaric tortures."

Such incidents emphasize the vast differences between the Japanese and more civilized codes of conduct, but Mr. Grew's principal theme is the problem of defeating a country which, in his opinion, is far stronger than the Western peoples realize. He contrasts Japan with Germany as Mr. Churchill by implication did in his broadcast.

I know Germany. I lived there for nearly 10 years. I know Germans well ; truculent and bullying and domineering when on the crest of the wave, demoralized in defeat. The Germans cracked in 1918. I have steadfastly believed and I believe today that when the tide of battle turns against them, as it assuredly will, they will crack again.

I know Japan. I lived there for 10 years. I know the Japanese intimately. They won't crack morally or psychologically, or economically, even when eventual defeat stares them in the face.

They'll pull in their belts another notch, reduce their rations from a bowl of rice to half a bowl of rice, and fight to the bitter end.

Again he says :

Germany and Italy possess groups of unknown size and power which await only time and opportunity to revolt. In Japan there are no such groups:

Mr. Grew tries to make it clear that to the Japanese there was nothing reckless or foolhardy about challenging the might of the United States. They had previous successes to encourage them. They had defeated the gigantic Manchu empire of China, they had defeated the empire of the Tsars, and finally they had fought against Germany and seen Germany surrender before she was invaded. They unquestionably count on making the United States surrender without necessarily being invaded.

JOSEPH C. GREW, American Ambassador to Tokyo from 1932 until the outbreak of war in Dec. 1941. He is at present Special Assistant to Mr. Cordell Hull, U.S. Secretary of State.
Photo, Topical Press

The Japanese may not intend to take New Orleans or San Francisco or Vancouver or Toronto —in this war. They do intend and expect in dead seriousness to conquer Asia, to drive us out, to force us to make a peace which will weaken us and cause us to grow weaker with time. And then later, in five years or ten years or fifty years, they would use a thousand million men of enslaved Asia and all the resources of the East to strike again.

HE holds that there is no limit to the Japanese desire for conquest. Given this desire, given their estimate of the United States, the attack on Pearl Harbour was a logical development. He holds that Washington was aware of this.

Insisting in another passage that Japanese leaders think they can win, Mr. Grew declares that " they are not suicidally minded incompetents—history will show they have made miscalculations, but they have miscalculated less than most of us suppose."

He seeks to give a clear picture of Japanese strength. He emphasizes that not for one moment should the idea be entertained that the failure of the Japanese forces in China has

discouraged the Japanese people. It has merely served to steel them for greater sacrifices. He points out, moreover, that in any case the published Budget figures show that only 40 per cent of the appropriations voted for the Defence forces was expended on the conduct of hostilities in China. Sixty per cent was used to prepare the armed services and industrial plants for the greater emergency to come. Further, only one-fiftieth of the materials and weapons furnished to these services was sent to China, the rest being used to expand and modernize the armies and fleets held in reserve.

ALREADY Japan has conquered an area ten times that of the Japanese empire as it stood a year ago, and obtained control of populations aggregating three times the population of the Japanese empire. Here is a huge aggregate of human beings the majority of whom are docile and capable of tremendous toil.

Mr. Grew regards the fighting spirit of the Japanese soldiers as one of the greatest assets of the Empire.

We are up against a powerful fighting machine ; people whose morale cannot and will not be broken by economic hardships ; a people who individually and collectively will gladly sacrifice their lives for their Emperor and their nation, and who can be brought to earth only by physical defeat.

He speaks of the " cruelty, brutality and utter bestiality, ruthlessness and rapaciousness of the Japanese military machine which brought on this war."

Americans, he argues, have too long looked upon the Japanese as insignificant people, whose achievements are a poor imitation of American achievements. If, he warns his countrymen, they do not throw everything into the fight they will risk the danger of stalemate ; and Japan firmly in possession of the huge area her forces have already seized would constitute for the United States as grave a menace as Nazi Germany securely in control of the European Continent would constitute for the British Isles.

If we fail we pass into slavery and all the world passes into slavery with us ! But we will not fail.

THE former Ambassador thinks that the war against Japan will be won by progressively dislodging her forces from all the bases and areas they have occupied and by the gradual destruction of the Japanese Navy, Merchant Marine and Air Force.

The main designs of Japanese propaganda, ridiculous though they may seem to us, have so poisoned the mind of a nation that only complete and final military defeat will convince the Japanese people of their falsehood.

Mr. Grew, who learned to admire many things in Japan, is not bitter about the ordinary Japanese people. Canada and the United States, he argues, cannot stand apart from the destiny of peoples on the other side of the Pacific. But :

Once militant Japan is out of the picture there should remain no threat of further war in the Pacific area. Japan is the one enemy and the only enemy of peaceful peoples whose shores overlook the Pacific. We can hold out hope of a liberated Japan. A population as great as that of the German Reich waits to be freed not only from its militarist masters but from itself.

On this note, what Mr. Grew calls " a message to the American people " ends. What he has written is a stirring call to the United Nations to gird up their loins for what may well prove to be a last long pull before victory.

War Comes to New Guinea

To the monster island of the South Seas war has come again—war, not of native tribes, urged on by tribal feuds and cannibal lust, but of 20th-century man. Through the jungle, so dense and dark, so clammy and filled with every kind of creeping thing, American soldier-woodsmen have hacked a way for the jeeps and trucks, the tanks and guns that MacArthur's troops have used to such effect in their struggle to eject the Japanese invader.

On the Trail Through the Jungle

Impenetrable jungle is the geographers' term for the greater part of New Guinea's natural covering. But human brain and brawn have wiped out the adjective. With extraordinary resolution the Australians have dragged their 25-pounder guns (1, 2) through country which even for the infantry makes very hard going. 3, Gen. MacArthur drives in a jeep with the Australian G.O.C., Gen. Sir Thomas Blamey (back seat), to the fighting zone.

Photos, Sp.
Press, Pa

To the Front with General MacArthur

Over the natives of New Guinea the war has swept like some giant hurricane, engulfing their homes, disrupting their ways of life. Some, dazed and affrighted, have made off into the bush; others, however, have enrolled in the Allies' service. 4, Native canoes provide most useful river transport. 5, Allied A.A. gunners " jump to it " on the signal of enemy planes approaching. 6, U.S. officers inspecting a Jap tank ditched beside the trail.

Bombs in the Tropic War Zone

Photos, Associated Press, Sport & General

From a look-out post on an outlying height of the Owen Stanley range a trio of Aussies and a solitary steel-helmeted American watch Japanese bombers attacking Port Moresby. Bombs have been dropped, and the columns of black smoke tell of hits on the oil drums stacked beside one of the Allied airfields. The lower photograph affords a glimpse of a native village of straw-roofed huts raised on stilts. Through the bush in the foreground a team of packhorses carries supplies to the Allies.

UNDER THE SWASTIKA

Hungry and Cold Are the French This Winter

Since all France was overrun by the Nazi troops in the middle of November, news of how our former Allies are faring has been even sparser and more unreliable than before. This article, by M. HENRY D. DAVRAY, is based on information received prior to the pre-Toulon invasion.

GROANING under the burdens imposed by the occupation authorities, the French people are looking forward with something akin to terror to the trials of another winter.

It has been a lean year for agriculture, owing in some parts to the protracted drought and in others to an excess of rain. Then the lack of transport increases the difficulties. The Germans keep on requisitioning the locomotives and the rolling-stock of the railways—their own wear out rapidly in the service of their armies fighting in Russia ; and the R.A.F. is playing havoc with their constructing and repairing works, as well as destroying a large number of trains on the tracks and in the marshalling yards. The locomotives are its special targets in the northern system that serves the coal mines and the most industrialized part of France, where 80 per cent of her iron and steel works and textile factories are to be found. A large proportion of the supply of coal for town and country comes from Belgium and the Nord, and it is now severely hampered. It used to be carried on the waterways in big barges, but the R.A.F. is sinking the few that the Germans have not yet confiscated. Wood was also extensively used in France as fuel and transported on the waterways ; and you could see, before the War, long convoys of huge barges stacked high with logs, towed by sturdy little tug-boats coming down from the Morvan (about 140 miles to the south-east) along canals and rivers and converging on the Seine on the way towards Paris, where their loads were piled up along the quays, there to dwindle swiftly as the winter months slipped by. Now there is a shortage of lumbermen for the felling of trees, and a worse shortage of fuel-oil for the tugs. In big and small towns alike log and coal yards remain empty, and so will the fireplaces all through the cold season.

As for food, the problem is no less crucial. In such fertile regions as the Vexin, the Beauce, the Brie and the Limogne, where agriculture is highly developed, it has suffered seriously from the drought ; the wheatheads were light, the straw was short, clover and lucerne yielded no second growth, hay shrivelled in the meadows ; and there is sure to be a shortage of fodder for the cattle also.

At harvest-time townspeople went to help the farmers. Those who went to lift potatoes received, for two weeks' work, 60 lb. of potatoes, and 140 lb. for four weeks ; married men received in addition 60 lb. for their wives and the same weight for each child. On the big farms and on the large estates in the occupied area the Germans confiscated 40 per cent of the agricultural and cattle produce as soon as it became available. Another 40 per cent is requisitioned by the French authorities to assure the adequate nourishment of the population, which leaves to the farmer only 20 per cent to dispose of or use.

France is a country whose land is parcelled out between nearly ten million owners, all of whom dig their gardens, however small, and sow and plant, making use of every patch in order to get a plentiful crop that can allow a " swop " with the neighbours. But the season has been bad, and the crops are scanty. In Normandy and in Brittany, along the Channel coast, rain has spoilt the potatoes ; they are very small when they are

not diseased, the biggest not larger than an egg, and plants have yielded less than a pound each. Tomatoes and beans did not mature. In other provinces, e.g. Touraine and Burgundy, dry weather was the cause of the trouble. Vegetables were *cuits sur place* (cooked on the ground), even weeds ; and people who breed rabbits, to make up for the lack of butcher's meat, had to feed them with tree-leaves. Goats found nothing to graze upon along the side-paths of roads or lanes where they are usually chained.

SOUTH of the Loire, certain parts of the country have enjoyed more favourable weather. An old lady from Paris, who owns an estate in Berry and has lived on it since the war, has managed to grow a sufficient crop of oats and barley for her horse and grain for her poultry, although her gardener and her farmer are prisoners-of-war in Germany. At harvest-time the difficulties began ; but she succeeded in hiring 18 persons to help with the threshing, and she even managed to gather enough victuals to feed them according to custom. The meals were composed of rabbits and vegetables, washed down with wine and an inferior kind of brandy, these latter not being served everywhere, as owing to the drastic German requisitions wine is rationed, a family of four receiving about one gallon a week. As to alcohol, it is confiscated for industrial use.

THERE is a constant struggle between producers and the German officials. The cunning French farmers contrive to outwit the enemy in order to keep as much of their produce as they can for themselves and to dispose of it for the benefit of neighbours, the people of the village or the inhabitants of the next market-town, who roam about on bicycles in quest of some " grub." Maximum prices are fixed for everything, but they are no use for these cash dealings, which reach from 5 to 15 times the official tariff.

A friend of mine, perched on an old crock, with one or two baskets of fruit, goes out in the open country early in the morning ; and after riding for miles he will, if he is lucky, bring back a few ounces of butter, an egg or two, some lard, which he exchanged for his apricots or his peaches. He may bring back a pint of milk or, as the other day, a duckling ! You may also see him sturdily treadling uphill, carrying on his back a bundle of fodder or a sack of grain for his rabbits and his fowls. And there are tens of thousands like him all around towns in France.

RATION-BOOKS entitle you to a certain quantity—a very small one—of various foodstuffs ; but they do not guarantee that you will be able to buy them in the shops. You may go for several weeks without meat, milk, butter, cheese, fats, if you have only the shops to rely on. French people use a large quantity of oil not only as dressing for green salads, but also for cooking and for frying ; the ration is two and a half ounces per month—but they seldom get any. Things you have to do without, ration or no ration, are soap and writing-paper, body linen, household napery, woollens, socks and stockings, mending-wool and darning-cotton. Shoes, boots and slippers are nowhere to be

LES HALLES, the great central market of Paris, presents a tragic spectacle under the German occupation. Hungry Parisians are confronted by rows of empty barrows and depleted stalls in what was once one of Europe's busiest and most thriving centres. German police control the streets, and all available food is sent to the Reich. *Photo, Associated Press*

found, and when you take your old ones to the cobbler to be re-soled, he will tell you that he has no nails or no leather. In the cheap restaurants of Paris and big towns they manage to cook dishes of turnip or carrot tops without any kind of fat, *Ça vous emplit le bidon, mais ça ne vous nourrit pas*, as a skinny journeyman said (It fills your drum, but it does not feed you).

The Germans have two reasons at least for resolving that the land shall be stripped bare. One is their fear of an invasion ; they don't want the invading armies to find any supplies, so that the Allied commissariat will be compelled to bring all provisions across the sea. The other is that they want to compensate the shortage of rationing in Germany. In his recent harvest thanksgiving oration on that subject, Field-Marshal Goering put it very clearly. Under the New Order the *Herrenvolk* are entitled to deprive the occupied peoples of their essential food and send it to Germany. The Germans are taskmasters for whom others must slave and starve. Whoever starved, said Goering, the Germans would not ; and French people are beginning to think that very little indeed will be left when the Hitler devotees have had their fill this winter.

The War Comes Very Near to Sicily

With the Allies striving their hardest to eject from Tunisia Axis forces which are being constantly reinforced from across the Sicilian Channel and supported by aircraft operating from Sicilian airfields, Sicily is, already playing a considerable part in the War. That part may soon be greater yet, as HENRY BAERLEIN suggests in the article that follows.

IN Mussolini's programme—carefully considered, but not quite carefully enough—a star role was reserved for Sicily : from her aerodromes the Regia Aeronautica was to sail forth ruthlessly for the destruction of Malta, an operation that was to take about half-an-hour. Something went wrong, however ; and in due course the Sicilian aerodromes have been receiving a number of visits from the R.A.F. These aerodromes will now be more battered than ever, as the war moves in Sicily's direction. "They intend," says the Italian wireless, "to attack even the sacred soil of our country "— though it is a little difficult to see why Italy's

The coast to the west of Syracuse offers landing facilities, although there is no harbour to speak of till we reach Trapani. Round the corner at Palermo is the best-equipped harbour, for which reason it has been attended to on various occasions by the R.A.F. To the north of Syracuse we find the roomy seaplane base, Augusta ; and still farther north there is Catania, whose commercial harbour is not to be despised. But for the landing of troops Syracuse and the coast to the west of it would as likely as not be chosen.

All round the island there are aerodromes which are easily accessible to bombers and

rigorous steps that were taken against the Mafia, that confraternity of brigands which dominated Sicily for many a year ; part is attributable to the discontent caused by absentee landowners, who prefer to live in the towns of Sicily, even in Naples or Rome, rather than on their estates.

IN considering Sicily from the strategic point of view one must naturally take into account the probable attitude of the population to an invading force. Under the rule of the last sovereigns of Naples and Sicily—those Bourbons of infamous memory, who after being ejected during the Napoleonic regime were restored by the Allies after Waterloo in 1815—the people were so oppressed that they received Garibaldi and his thousand heroes with open arms when they landed at Marsala on May 11, 1860. That is not to say that a similar welcome awaits the armies from Tunis today, but there will be many Sicilians who will be moved by the wireless admonitions that are being addressed to them from New York by Giuseppe Luchis, a compatriot of theirs and a veteran of the last war.

SICILIAN AIRFIELDS have been greatly developed by the Luftwaffe during the past two years, and the majority of the heavy raids on Malta were launched from these bases. This photo shows a German-occupied airfield in the island. In the foreground bombs are ready to be loaded on to the waiting planes. A map of Sicily's air-bases will be seen in the opposite page.

Photo, Presse Diffusion, Lausanne

"The American armies of Liberation," he has told them, "will shortly be coming to your island . . . They are not coming to sack or pillage your towns. Hold out friendly hands to them. Take up your arms and join these armies in the struggle against Fascism . . . Sicily will shortly become the centre of operations in this terrible war." Luchis knows very well that while the average Sicilian is a prudent and patient person, resigned to his lot—*come Dio vuole* is his equivalent of *kismet*—he can break out into the most terrific passion.

soil is more sacred than that of any other country, unless it be because it is the home of that *sacro egoismo* of which we used to hear so much.

YES, Sicily will have to bear a heavy burden. It is the most convenient part of Italy for the Allies to invade, seeing that the distance from Tunis is little more than ninety miles. It so happens that the southern and western shores are generally flat, whereas those to the north and east are steep and rocky, rising in many places to very considerable heights direct from the sea. And in the south is a most convenient harbour, that of Syracuse, from where in other days the daily ship to Malta used to sail, the distance being about the same as that which divides Tunis from the west of the island. Syracuse stands at the end of a large arm of the sea, the land at either side almost enclosing it. If we decide to make for Syracuse we shall be following the excellent example of the ancient Greeks—who came, of course, by sea and captured the place. They liked it so well that they built temples, theatres, and so on in the city and its vicinity ; one at least of the undying plays of Aeschylus had its first performance in a theatre at Syracuse.

most of them even to fighters from Tunis or Malta. Of course, they are equally accessible to planes coming from Calabria on the Italian mainland ; and unless Italy capitulates the R.A.F. will have to advance by stages.

Some have thought that it would be advisable to by-pass Sicily, and make for Sardinia, which is at the same distance from Tunis. But Sardinia is an inhospitable island, with far fewer facilities than Sicily, which is the largest, the most populous, and the most fertile in the whole Mediterranean. It has quite a good railway system ; and from Messina it is only a mile or two across to the mainland, whereas Sardinia is much farther removed. (*See* map, page 407).

BUT what of the interior of Sicily ? For the most part it is so mountainous that it is likely to be avoided in military operations. Isolated and poverty-stricken, the people there are very lukewarm in their adhesion to Fascist principles. But indeed, all over Sicily we find that the present regime is not regarded with much enthusiasm, notwithstanding Mussolini's slogans painted in huge black letters on many a whitewashed structure. Part of this lack of enthusiasm is due to the

out into the most terrific passion.

Strategically speaking, Sicily is involved in both of the two triangles based on Tunis—the first stretching from Tunis to Sardinia and Sicily, the other from Malta to Sicily and back to Tunis. The former is likely to be the scene of an intensive air and naval struggle, even if the United Nations succeed in rapidly occupying the port of Bizerta. Of course, the possession of Bizerta will vastly assist in removing the menace from ships passing between Tunis and Sicily. In the midst of the second triangle lies the small Italian island of Pantelleria, which has been strongly fortified by the Italians (who in recent years, like the Japanese in their mandated islands, prohibited all visits, even of the civilian population) ; it is said to have submarine nests hollowed out of its flanks. Although its harbour is only large enough for one or two destroyers, it has an aerodrome which has caused us a certain amount of inconvenience.

Before it is rendered harmless, before we can secure a Sicilian base, there will have to be a good deal of fighting, for the agents of the Gestapo are everywhere ; and though the population be inflamed against them they will not find it an easy matter to shake off their evil domination.

Italian Island Now a Base of the Luftwaffe

STRATEGIC POINTS OF SICILY. 1, General view of Catania from the harbour with snow-capped Mount Etna in the background. This port has a population of about 245,000. 2, Sicilian air strongholds. Names underlined indicate aerodromes with full facilities and concrete runways. "S" implies seaplane or flying-boat accommodation, often in addition to the airfield. Apart from the places named, there are numbers of auxiliary airfields which can be used by the Luftwaffe. 3, Shipping in the Bay of Palermo ; this famous city lies under the shadow of Monte Pellegrino. 4, Rising in picturesque confusion, Messina faces the Italian mainland.　　　PAGE 469　　*Map by courtesy of The Daily Telegraph. Photos, Fox, Dorien Leigh*

THE WAR IN THE AIR

by Capt. Norman Macmillan, M.C., A.F.C.

NORTH AFRICA continued to be the main theatre of war in the world, marked by more movement and a sense of urgency on both sides—characteristics which differentiated it from the heavy bludgeon-blows given and taken by both sides in Russia, and from the bantam-weight sparring in the Australasian zone. Then in the India-Burma area activity was confined to patrols and air raids ; warnings were given to look out for the dropping of Japanese parachute-borne spies in India, labelled appropriately para-spies—a reward of £375 was offered for the live capture of such enemies.

North Africa fighting is divided into two kinds : one, the westward drive along the coast through Libya, and the other the holding fighting in Tunisia. Both zones have been objectives of important air support within the tactical fighting areas and within the wider strategical circle which reaches right up to Northern Italy.

DEALING with the Libyan action first : Rommel's retreating columns of vehicles of all kinds were pounded mercilessly by the R.A.F. from El Alamein to El Agheila. When Rommel halted at El Agheila, the R.A.F. began to bomb, cannon-shell and machine-gun the areas behind the bottle-neck defences held by the reorganized formations of the Afrika Korps. Principal target was Marble Arch, a desert landing-ground 40 miles behind the Rommel front. The attack was so continuous that the Luftwaffe was unable to maintain its aircraft at Marble Arch and German fighters were forced to retreat 50 miles to Nofilia aerodrome.

That decided the issue. With the nearest fighter aircraft situated 90 miles behind his surface fighting front, Rommel could not maintain an effective air covering force, and his position at El Agheila became untenable. Before the Eighth Army units on the ground did more than " probe " Rommel's positions by reconnaissance raiding forces, the commander of the Afrika Korps packed his troops into lorries and fled westward under cover of dark on the night of Dec. 12-13, 1942. The attack upon Marble Arch began nine days earlier ; its neutralization was completed in six days. For three days before the German evacuation of El Agheila, R.A.F. and Allied fighter-bombers flashed un-hindered all over the German advanced ground positions, bombing, machine-gunning, and cannon-shelling every available target. So well dug-in and widely dispersed were the German forces that it was almost impossible to use medium bombers against them with advantage. But on Sunday, December 13, Allied fighter-bombers made 300 sorties during the day—a record for any theatre of war—bombing, shell-riddling, damaging and firing vehicles on the road west of El Agheila.

ROMMEL'S fleeing columns will get no rest from the attentions of the air power of the United Nations grouped within the tactical requirements of General Montgomery's Eighth Army. Almost for the first time during the course of the war the Axis troops are learning the meaning of air superiority. What their aircraft did to the occupants of the crowded roads of Europe, the R.A.F. and the Allied and Dominion air units are doing to them ; but this time there are no refugees—those pitiable victims who gave the Luftwaffe " sportsmen " such easy targets. Every target along the coastal road of Libya is a uniformed enemy, the remains of Mussolini's " Roman " legions and their friends the Huns.

The importance of the advance from El Agheila from the British point of view is that our forces have now passed the most southerly point of the North African Medi-terranean coastline. Every mile advanced brings them nearer to Malta and to the British First Army in Tunisia. Malta is 460 miles from El Agheila, 340 from Sirte, 240 from Misurata, 220 from Homs and Tripoli. Misurata to Gabès (Tunisia) is 300 flying miles ; Gabès to Malta is 300 miles. Thus, if Rommel retreats to Misurata, he must pass into a zone wherein enfilade air attacks can be brought to bear upon him from Maltese airfields by long-range fighters and bombers, able to operate safely under the air cover provided by the tactical fighter units at-tached to the Eighth Army.

FROM the air point of view Rommel's retreat is not proceeding westwards to a safer zone. Actually he is retreating to a more dangerous zone. The strategy behind his retreat is therefore bound up with the military situation of the Axis forces elsewhere—probably in Italy and Sicily. His delaying action is slight, just enough to distinguish his movement from precipitate flight—and per-haps just enough to give the Axis defence forces in Sicily and Metropolitan Italy time to construct stout defences, which again is the indicated purpose behind the Axis operations in Tunisia.

In Tunisia the situation has not been so favourable to the British First Army, for there the Axis forces have had the advantage of short lines of communication and a number of advanced airfields, some within five minutes' flying-time of the surface fighting forces. In consequence the zonal superiority in the air over the fighting units has assisted the German troops and ham-pered the British.

Airfields cannot be conjured out of nothing overnight. They require time for construc-tion. The high-speed aircraft of today demand room for take-off and alighting, and it is useless to begin to use a forward landing-ground too soon if the result is to be but crashes. But, almost coincident with the advance from El Agheila, Allied advanced landing-grounds came into use in Tunisia, scratched out of any flat ground among the mountains, and from them American Light-ning twin-engined fighters and British Spitfires have been flying, so that the Luftwaffe has had to fight for its results more frequently than when the United Nations' flying-fields were too far back to permit of patrols of more than short duration over the fighting zone. Soon it should be possible to bring the slight German advances in Northern Tunisia to a halt, and then advance.

The contrasting lessons of ample and of insufficient air power have been written clearly in the skies of Libya and of Tunisia. The United Nations need no further lessons in the all-important factor of air power. Air power is the spear-head of the forces which will drive the Axis out of Africa.

IN Europe nearly 100 day bombers at-tacked the Philips radio factory at Eind-hoven, Holland, on December 6, 1942, and set it on fire ; 12 bombers were missing. On the same day Fortresses attacked the Fives-Lille locomotive works, and Liberators the Abbeville-Drucat German fighter base. About 400 fighters provided diversionary sweeps and air cover. Karlsruhe and Pforzheim were bombed on December 6-7, Turin on the nights of December 8-9, 9-10, and 11-12. Naples was bombed by Medi-terranean air forces by day on December 11, and again the following night ; while Palermo was bombed on the night of December 12-13—all strategic raids connected with the war in North Africa.

In 1938 the U.S.A.A.F. had 1,800 officers and 20,000 men ; today they have over 1,000,000 ; by the end of 1943 they will have over 2,000,000. During 1942 America produced 49,000 war aircraft. From February 1 to December 5, 1942 the U.S. Army Air Forces destroyed 928 enemy air-craft and probably destroyed 276 ; they lost 130, and 104 are missing.

FLYING FORTRESS bombers, making 1,063 sorties against Germans, up to November 30 lost a total of 32 Forts, while they had destroyed 293, probably destroyed 150, and damaged 192 enemy aircraft.

Land and air fighting continued in the Buna area of Papua after the occupation of the Gona area by the Allies on December 10. Allied air power there is slowly wearing down Japanese sea transport power.

FLYING FORTRESS in service with the R.A.F. Coastal Command carrying out patrol duties over a large convoy. U.S. Fortress bombers are reported to have a ceiling of 40,000 ft. They carry a crew of 6-9, and their bomb load is from 4-5 tons. These powerful machines have a maximum speed of about 300 m.p.h. *Photo British Official : Crown Copyright*

On a December Day They Bombed Eindhoven

DAYLIGHT ATTACK ON HITLER'S CHIEF RADIO PLANT. On Dec. 6, 1942, nearly 100 R.A.F. bombers, unescorted by fighters, attacked the Philips radio works at Eindhoven, in Nazi-occupied Holland—Europe's biggest and most important radio-valve producing plant, now working for Germany. 1, A pre-War view. 2, Fires enveloping the buildings. 3, Boston bomber crews leaving their operational station on their return. 4, Map showing position and distance from London. 5, A closer view of the blazing factory. *Photos, British Official: Crown Copyright; E.N.A., Planet News*

Newcomers to Our Battle-line in the Air

VENTURA (left), Bomber Command's latest light bomber, is a Lockheed product, and is faster and stronger than the same firm's Hudson. It is powered by two Pratt and Whitney Wasp engines and carries a crew of four. The Ventura has a length of 57 ft. 6 in., a wing span of 65 ft. 6 in. and a swept up tail of 25 ft. 10 in. span. Guns in the nose and elsewhere protect all vital parts. These planes are now being mass-produced in America and a large number has already been delivered in Britain. Venturas took a leading part in the great attack on Eindhoven. (See p. 471.)

SPITFIRE, the world's most famous fighter, an improved type of which is seen on the right. This Vickers-Supermarine aircraft is now being used with deadly effect against the Luftwaffe. Speed, ceiling and many other features remain secret, though it has been announced that the new Spitfire has a Rolls-Royce Merlin 61 engine, instead of the Merlin 45 or 46. Armament is reported to be two cannon and four machine-guns housed in the wings. To take up the extra power a greater propeller-blade area was necessary. The height of the aircraft precluded any lengthening of the blades, so the problem has been solved by using four blades instead of two. The chief difference in appearance between this and previous types, apart from the longer nose, is to be seen in the wings. These have underslung radiators; there are also minor differences in the engine installation.

The Spitfire achieved immortal fame during the Battle of Britain in 1940, when great aerial conflicts took place over this country by day and hundreds of German machines were destroyed.

LOCKHEED LIGHTNING (P38), long-range fighter which has been in action in Tunisia. This machine is powered with two 12-cylinder 1,150 h.p. Allison engines, has a speed of over 400 m.p.h. and a high rate of climb. Its ceiling is between 35,000 and 39,000 ft. Armament consists of four machine-guns, and one 20 m.m. cannon in the nose. Wing span, 52 ft.; length, 38 ft.; height, 9 ft. 10 in. Easily identified by their twin fuselage; Lockheed Lightnings are here seen flying over their base in Britain.

Photos, Associated Press, G.P.U.

Germany's Biggest Plane Takes Troops to Tunis

BLOHM & VOSS B.V. 222
...PATROL FLYING BOAT & TRANSPORT

Span 150 ft. Length 112 ft.
Weight Loaded 100,000 lbs.
Six 1,000 h.p. Engines.
Speed 199 m.p.h.

GOTHA TWIN BOOM GLIDER & JU 52 TROOP CARRIER.

THE BLOHM AND VOSS BV222 is a giant six-engined type of flying-boat which the Germans have employed to carry soldiers and war material from Italy to Tunisia. Our long-range fighters shot down one of these machines between Tunis and Sicily at the end of November 1942. Designed by Dr. R. Vogt, the BV222 is reported to carry 80 men, and was intended to operate the transatlantic service before the War. The weight loaded is over 44 tons, the wing span is 150 feet, and the boat's length is 112 feet. The six B.M.W. engines develop 1,000 h.p. each, and the maximum speed is just under 200 m.p.h. Range is 4,400 miles at 170 m.p.h. Built at Hamburg, the first Blohm and Voss was completed in the spring of 1942. The armament consists of twin machine-guns in the fore and aft turrets, and either cannon or heavy machine-guns in port and starboard positions.

Seen inset are a Junkers JU52 troop- and freight-carrying aircraft and a Gotha GO242 twin-boom glider (see also photo below), both reported to have been in action on the Tunisian front. These latter are capable of carrying 21 fully-equipped infantrymen besides a crew of two, or up to two tons of freight. Doubtless petrol and small pieces of artillery can be ferried by the enemy across to Tunisia in this manner. These gliders have a span of 79 feet and a length of 52 ft. 6 in. As for the JU52, these were extensively used in Crete and Libya.

REINFORCEMENTS FOR ROMMEL ran the gauntlet of devastating Allied air power in the Battle of Egypt. Ports and landing-grounds received shattering attacks and many enemy airborne transports were destroyed. Left, German paratroops who succeeded in reaching their destination wearily tramp across the desert. Right, a Gotha glider, captured almost undamaged at an airfield in the El Daba area, is seen in its pen.

Diagram specially drawn for THE WAR ILLUSTRATED *by Haworth*

THE HOME FRONT

by E. Royston Pike

ONLY a short time after the Archbishops had graciously announced that women and girls may now enter a church uncovered, the Lord Chancellor has decreed that women need no longer wear hats in Court. The reason given is "a certain change in social habits," which suggests that the women have won a victory for common sense over the lawyers entangled in medieval thoughts and ways. But it is much more likely that there is an economic basis for the move. Indeed, Dr. Dalton, the President of the Board of Trade, is very concerned over the shortage of milliners' materials; and first their Graces of Canterbury and York and now the Lord Chancellor have been induced to agree that it is easier to abandon a long-cherished, if somewhat superstitious, practice than to release straw and ribbon, silk and felt for feminine headgear. After this concession by Church and Law, who will deny the supreme importance of the economic factor in our present-day lives?

FROM hats to Luton is no jump at all. Luton's sole claim to fame, indeed, is that it makes hats, hats of every kind, shape and size, and has made them for many a long year past. But a few days ago it seemed that the days of Luton hat-making were numbered. The Government, it was whispered, had a scheme in hand for the transference of the industry to the north-east coast. Before the War the industry employed some 16,000 men and women, but after the 140 hat-making firms have twice voluntarily cut their staffs, the number today is only 4,000, most of whom are women, or men over 50. But 4,000 skilled workers are worth a lot to Mr. Bevin; and, besides, Sir Thomas Barlow, Director-General of Civilian Clothing, is said to be keen on concentrating the clothing industries in certain parts of the country, of which Luton is not one. As soon as the rumour of the proposal got round, Luton rose as one man (and woman) in protest. Nor were the protesters mollified by the hint that the industry would come back to Luton after the War. Dr Leslie Burgin, Luton's M.P., led a deputation to the President of the Board of Trade on December 2; and the official statement issued after the meeting said that "there had been a misunderstanding of the real position," the Board of Trade "had not contemplated uprooting the hat industry from Luton. All that was intended was a wartime contraction, which would not injure Luton's position as a centre of the hat industry after the war."

After Luton's day of excitement it was Worcester's turn. The local 600-year-old glove-making industry was to be moved, it was rumoured; and the civic fathers and the leaders of the industry roundly declared that they would fight any removal scheme. Then a similar tale came from Birmingham, where not gloves but perambulators were the threatened industry. Birmingham makes half the country's output of prams—an article whose importance has been recently recognized by the Board of Trade to the extent of raising the annual quota of production from 250,000 to 300,000 perambulators. After all, how can we expect the people to go in for babies if there are not enough prams to put them in? Again and yet again the Board of Trade emphasized the purity of their intentions. What, shift so

old and important an industry from Worcester, from Birmingham? Nothing of the kind . . . "Mr. Dalton's young men at the Board of Trade are certainly learning something about industrial psychology," unkindly commented The Manchester Guardian.

WHILE the Beveridge Social Security proposals have provided many a meaty mouthful for the polemics of platform and press, it is good to know that our social progress has continued. If a list could be prepared of the social reforms that have been carried out since the War, said Mr.

STATIC WATER TANKS, since the blitz a feature of the wartime urban landscape, are now being fitted with strong wire mesh —so many have been the children drowned in them and so vast the accumulation of litter of every kind of which they have been made the receptacle.   *Photo, Planet News*

Ernest Brown on November 20, it would be seen to be a remarkable one. The Economist has compiled such a list:

In the social services aiming at preventing destitution, the rates for unemployment assistance and supplementary pensions have been raised, the test of personal need has been substituted for the household means test, and the machinery for paying supplementary pensions has been transferred from the public assistance authorities to the Assistance Board. The maximum for worker's compensation has been raised from 30s. to 35s. per week, and children's allowances have been added. In 1940 compulsory unemployment insurance, and at the beginning of 1942 National Health insurance, were extended to non-manual workers earning up to £420 a year instead of £250 as heretofore; and sickness and disablement benefit and unemployment benefit have been raised by 3s. and 2s. a week respectively; the pensionable age for wives of men covered by the contributory pensions scheme has been lowered from 65 to 60; and the pensionable age of all women insured in their own right has been lowered to 60. Among health reforms, specialist treatment has been made more easily available, a national rehabilitation and resettlement scheme

for the disabled has been launched, and a national scheme for the care of the tuberculous has been adopted. A factory and welfare department has been established in the Ministry of Labour, and a beginning made with an industrial health service. Among the reforms associated with food policy are the provision of free or cheap milk to all nursing and expectant mothers and to children under five, and of free or cheap fruit juices and cod-liver oil to small children; the increase in the Exchequer grant for the milk in schools service and for the provision of school meals, and the extension of factory canteens. Children have also been granted priority in certain rationed foods, and war nurseries have been established.

But, as The Economist points out, many of the so-called reforms are really social necessities, dictated by wartime increases in the cost of living or by wartime shortage.

Some, e.g. factory canteens, are by no means nation-wide; and even today less than a quarter of the elementary school children in England and Wales have a dinner at school. Moreover, there is a very considerable debit in the shape of social evils: the break-up of families, due to evacuation and war service; the breakdown of education, which has not yet fully recovered from the disastrous effects of closed schools in the early part of the war; the growth in juvenile delinquency; the increase of certain diseases, such as tuberculosis and venereal disease; and the suspension of pre-war social reforms, such as shorter working hours—especially for children —holidays with pay, the raising of the school-leaving age, and the new Criminal Justice Bill.

VENEREAL disease provided the House of Commons with the subject for a remarkable debate on December 16. Dr. Edith Summerskill moved that an Address should be presented to his Majesty, praying the annulment of Regulation 33B (*see* page 410), on the ground that it was a third-rate measure.

Yet it was designed to deal with an insidious disease more devastating to health and happiness than Hitler's bombs, one from which the casualties last year were greater than those during the blitz. "The Minister of Health has approached this problem like a Victorian spinster bred in a country parsonage and sheltered from the facts of life." Another woman Labour M.P., Mrs. Hardie, similarly described the Regulation as objectionable and useless, opening the way to the blackmailer, the informer, and the poison pen. Seeing that most of the victims are young men between 19 and 23 (she went on) it was clear that there was something very wrong with our educational system. Promiscuous immorality was due to the extension of drinking facilities—a view which Lady Astor hastened to support, while urging that the number of women police and doctors should be greatly increased

A FRESH note was struck by Mr. Boothby: not enough emphasis is being laid on prevention as against cure, he maintained.

In time of war it was not to be expected that promiscuity would be entirely stopped. "It is well known that prophylactics are to a large measure effective in preventing the spread of the disease. The time has come when preventive packets should, under proper regulation and safeguards, be available at proper chemists up and down the country." In his view compulsory notification and treatment were inevitable. Dr. Haden Guest supported the Regulation from his experience as medical officer on the staff of one of the Home Commands, and he pointed out that infection took place not only from professional prostitutes: he instanced two well-to-do women of 35 or so who had set up house near an R.A.F. aerodrome, entertaining the officers and infecting four or five of them. "They were not professionals, but women who wished to lead that kind of life."

Mr. Ernest Brown, replying to the debate, said that the Regulation was part of a planned programme embodying public education, adequate free treatment, and indirect action to discourage promiscuity. Dr. Summerskill's "prayer" was rejected by 245 votes to 31.

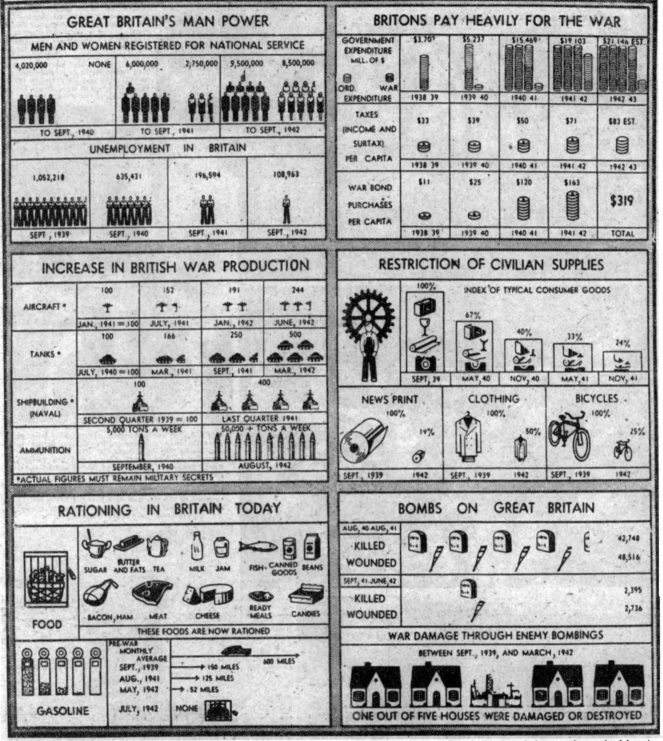

BRITAIN AFTER THREE YEARS AT WAR

"WE British need not apologize to anyone for our three years' part in the war," said the Home Secretary, Mr. Herbert Morrison, on October 30, in a speech to his constituents at Hackney. "We are mobilized for war. We have flung our man-power into the scale to the limit, and are now scouring the last corners for what little may remain. We are turning out war goods at a greater rate in proportion to our population than any country in the world, bar none. Our people, millions upon millions of them, are travelling during the black-out, working long hours, shivering more than a little at times, and yet going on their way serenely with no more than the minimum human amount of grousing and grumbling.

"Whatever glories future months and years may hold in store for this page of Britain's history, the tale of three years' war thus far inscribed upon it reveals a people united in the love of their native land and not afraid to dare the full, overwhelming might of tyranny, and today standing unconquerable in the strength of their honest and constructive purpose."

So that Britain's war effort shall be brought home to the people of America, the above chart has been prepared and is now being widely distributed throughout the United States.

In the caption to the diagram it is stated that : " These cold figures barely hint at the three years of fighting sacrifices which the British people have devoted to smashing the Axis. British income tax starts at an income of $440. The standard rate is 50 per cent ; with surtax it rises to 97½ per cent. War savings include nearly $200,000,000 which Britons have voluntarily lent their Government without interest. The growth of British war production has to be shown by percentages based on 100 rather than by actual figures which are secret. The chart shows only a few examples of the restrictions placed by law on the supply of consumer goods—and even the limited supplies permitted are not always available to the shoppers. Many foods not rationed are completely unobtainable. Thus the whole people contributes to victory."

Diagram by the Ministry of Information

Our Roving Camera Tours the Commonwealth

SIR O. A. PREMPEH II, K.B.E., Paramount Chief of Ashanti (West Africa), is seen below in his ceremonial robes. He was photographed during a recent inspection of the Ashanti Home Guard (left) at the capital, Kumasi. In a stirring broadcast, he called on his people to remember their traditions as a great warrior race. Inspired by his example the people of Ashanti have subscribed large sums to Spitfire and bomber funds. The Chief succeeded his late uncle, Nana E. A. Prempeh I, in 1931, and was knighted in 1937. He is 50 years of age, and is Hon. Lt.-Col. of the Home Guard.

E.N.S.A. (Entertainments National Service Association) provides a regular service of cinema and living entertainment in war zones as far apart as Iceland, West Africa, and the Middle East. Members of the Forces derive considerable enjoyment from these first-class "shows." Three E.N.S.A. girls are seen (left) during an afternoon performance on an improvised stage on the summit of the Rock of Gibraltar, 1,400 ft. above sea level. An appreciative audience of troops follows their every movement.

ASBESTOS FIRE-FIGHTING SUIT (left) worn by one of a party of naval ratings from a British warship in the tropics, who went ashore to practise the most modern methods of fire-fighting. They left their ship to avoid endangering the vessel. The contraption is an object of deep interest to the natives. A CANADIAN LAND GIRL (above) holding one of the great knives used for topping sugar beet, a crop which has done exceedingly well of late on the Canadian prairie.

Photos, British Official; Crown Copyright

I WAS THERE!

They Were Jammed Like Sardines in Naples Harbour

Flying in a U.S. Liberator bomber at dusk on Dec. 4, 1942, Henry Gorrell, British United Press correspondent, helped to unload huge bombs on Naples harbour. The "bag" included an Italian cruiser sunk, a battleship and another cruiser crippled. His story of this devastating raid from North Africa is given below.

I SAW our small group of Liberators—only a small part of the whole force—drop thousands of pounds of bombs in the area of the Porta de Massa quay and the Angioino mole, covering about 700 square yards in the Naples dock area. In this area there were battleships, cruisers and destroyers. Every bomb hit something. I did not see a single ripple of water. They were all hits.

Flying at an altitude of several miles, in temperatures below zero, our bomb-aimers pin-pointed their targets. I saw one battleship hit dead in the centre and giving off a column of smoke that rose a couple of thousand feet into the air. There were also two large fires, one of which, with hundreds of fiery red particles flying in every direction, looked like Vesuvius in eruption.

And we were just the leading group of the attacking force. It will take some time to patch up the damage done to Naples harbour, which has been used as the main supply depot for the Axis forces defending Bizerta, Tunis and Tripoli.

THE Italian people have partly their fleet to blame for whatever death and destruction may have been caused by stray bombs in Naples. The Italian surface ships and submarines jammed like sardines in the harbour were one of our chief objectives. They hadn't come out for weeks, so the United States bombers went in and hit them in their hiding-places.

With well over 200 anti-aircraft guns, including several scores on the warships and on several anti-aircraft ships in the bay, the Italians were certainly in a position to defend themselves. Yet not one of our bombers was even holed.

The only previous raid by U.S.A. heavy bombers from North Africa to compare with this was a recent one on Tripoli, in which 90 per cent of the bombs dropped connected with shipping and harbour works. The U.S. Army Air Force here has pictures to prove it.

I flew in The Chief, commanded by Captain Lee C. Holloway, from Alabama.

The huge bomber had been holed at least 75 times and had run into trouble on her last eight missions, but had always successfully delivered the goods.

The first few hours were uneventful. We flew low over the water through clouds, and there was a slight drizzle. Before we put on our oxygen masks I spotted a horseshoe hung up in the cabin and touched it for luck.

As the navigator clocked off the altitude, we got into fur-lined flying suits and adjusted our oxygen masks. Soon we were at an altitude that would kill a man in 15 minutes if he didn't have a mask on. One of our waist gunners had his eyelashes frozen together from the steam coming out of the top of his mask, and had to pull them apart. One bomber had to turn back because a waist gunner's mask had frozen and he couldn't breathe.

Now we are approaching the target, and coming lower. Suddenly I see Vesuvius far below, looking like an inverted ice-cream cone except for the trail of white vapour. I am on the alert, because the pilot says that if the bomb bay doors fail to open I am to push the hand lever.

The clouds disappear, and there is Naples below us, bordered with mountains and looking very sleepy. The pilot motions to me. Sure enough the bomb doors are stuck. I push a lever and a gust of freezing wind rushes in. My knees are knocking, and it

The crew of a U.S. Liberator inspect the bullet-riddled tail of their machine on returning to their N. African base from a raid over enemy-occupied territory.
Photo, Associated Press

seems to me a lifetime before the bombs drop.

I can see the Naples dock area thousands of feet below, but it is so cold I don't care whether it is Naples or Timbuctoo. I grit my teeth and hold on to the lever. At last the huge bombs, on which most of the boys have written their names and "The Season's Greetings," go down. I close the doors and shut out the cold.

Our bombs were answered by the flashes of A.A. guns and the red balls of flaming onions. Soon the plane seemed to be wading through the A.A. fire. The Italians, taken by surprise, "went crazy," firing pom-poms which could not reach higher than 6,000 or 7,000 feet. The shells exploded below the bomber, looking like lights on a Christmas tree. On the way back the island of Capri spat fire from heavy A.A. batteries.

We Rammed Oran's Boom to Land Our Troops

To facilitate the landing of Allied assault troops at Oran the concrete boom across the harbour entrance had to be smashed and defences immobilized. The part H.M.S. Hartland played in this perilous action on Nov. 8, 1942, is described by two of her officers in the Reuter story below.

H.M.S. HARTLAND hit the breakwater outside the harbour on the first run in, but afterwards passed through to her scheduled spot under a hail of machine-gun fire, with one boiler out of action and liable to blow up at any moment. Lieut. Hickson said the plan was to take the Hartland to the most easterly jetty, at the

head of which they found a French flotilla leader and a French tug.

As it was difficult to get the Hartland between the two ships the captain gave orders to get a wire on to the tug. The Frenchmen seemed rather to resent this, but we got a wire across to her and started to disembark what was left of the boarding parties and troops,

NAPLES, the great port of Southern Italy, has been raided more than once by Allied bombers since the establishment of the Anglo-American bridgehead in North Africa. An account of one of these attacks is given in this page. This photo shows the harbour crammed with submarines lined up for a naval review when Mussolini still boasted of "our sea."

Photo, Associated Press

ALLIED ASSAULT FORCES AT ORAN on Nov. 8, 1942, encountered stiff resistance. Two ex-U.S. coastguard cutters, H.M.S. Hartland and H.M.S. Walney, broke into the harbour but were destroyed. Hartland's part in this great naval episode is told by two of her officers in this and the preceding page. Two days later Oran surrendered, when a U.S. infantry and tank column, covered by Adm. Cunningham's warships, entered the town. This photo shows a destroyer laying a smoke-screen round one of the transports during the landing operations.   *Photo, British Official*

British and American, among whom a lot of casualties had been caused by machine-gun and battery fire.

By this time the ship was on fire fore and aft, one side of the bridge had gone and she was liable to blow up at any moment. Just as we started the slow job the captain said "abandon ship." Everyone had lifebelts, and one by one they went over the side. Once ashore they were taken prisoner.

Even before we went into the harbour Commander Billot had been wounded. He was on his hands and knees when he took the ship alongside. He was also blinded in one eye. He had his shoulder smashed and a machine-gun bullet in his leg. Nevertheless he said, "I am going through." When we got alongside the jetty and were abandoning ship he refused to leave until he was convinced that every member of the crew,

both wounded and unwounded, was ashore.

Eventually he lowered himself over the side with his one sound arm and got into a rowing-boat with the idea of pulling out of the harbour and reaching a British ship outside, though he was obviously in need of medical attention. The French, however, picked him up in the harbour.

The attack was made just before 3 a.m. Lt. R. B. Bilborough, chief engineer of the Hartland, said:

Almost straightaway we were hit in the boiler-room. All the fire and repair parties were knocked out. A moment later at almost full speed we hit the concrete breakwater. There was little hope that anyone could be alive in the boiler-room.

The ship was on fire almost entirely fore and aft. There was no further hope of saving the ship. Some got away by swimming a quarter of a mile to a floating dock. At about 7.30 a.m. on Sunday the Hartland blew up.

From above, the attack presented other features. To quote Lt. Hickson again :

Machine-gun fire was opened. It was extremely inaccurate, and we thought it was token resistance. Afterwards we found we were wrong. The Hartland was repeatedly hit. We were caught by a searchlight and became an easy target. At the jetty, which was our objective, a flotilla leader opened fire at us at 50 feet. Every shell hit us.

I Spent Three Days in a German U-Boat

Mrs. Blanche Allen, her husband (a sergeant in the Hussars) and their six-year-old son Michael were sailing home from Durban when their ship was torpedoed. Their subsequent adventures, as told to Geoffrey Simpson, provide one of the strangest stories of the war; it is reprinted here from the Daily Mail.

I WAS changing into evening clothes for the ship's dance when the torpedo struck home. The ship lurched over, and we were ordered to our boat stations.

I climbed into a lifeboat in my thin evening dress, with Michael, while my husband went back for his Army greatcoat to keep the two of us warm. Our boat pushed off and we were all together. That was something—and we were glad of that coat later. There were 50 of us in the open boat, and it was bitterly cold. On the third day poor Michael was unconscious from exposure.

Then suddenly six German U-boats and an Italian submarine surfaced around us. One of the U-boats ordered us alongside. The commander was a tall, fair, good-looking man of about 35. He ordered his crew to distribute hot coffee, cigarettes, food and water to the men in the boats.

He spoke to us in excellent English. He said he would take the women and children aboard, but he regretted that he must leave the men to fend for themselves. I was terrified, but my husband insisted that I should go. I kissed him good-bye and entered the conning-tower.

The other women with me were Mrs. Davis, Miss Davison, Mrs. Atkins, Mrs. Sarnsum, and Mrs. Frain. There were two other children, aged eight and eleven.

It was stifling inside—a long oven-like corridor of winding pipes, wheels and dials. The U-boat captain went out of his way to reassure us. " I am deeply sorry you have been torpedoed, ladies," he said. " Please make yourselves comfortable, and be sure I will see you to safety."

They gave us coffee and biscuits, and chocolate for the children. Later they supplied cooked meat and vegetables. Sailors gave up their bunks for us. I shared mine with another woman. We were too scared to be alone. In any case it was hard to sleep, because of the noise and the heat.

The crew played a radiogram for most of the day. They played the Blue Danube and Red Sails in the Sunset. The tunes made me think of home and my husband.

Then the captain came to see us again. He asked us if we would like to listen to the B.B.C. We said we would, and he switched on Bruce Belfrage reading the 9 o'clock news.

THE last day was dramatic. The crew suddenly became tense and strained. We were diving. An American bomber, they said, had sighted us. Everything was very quiet now, but then came two distinct crumps of falling bombs or depth charges. It shook all of us, and I was glad Michael was sound asleep. We remained submerged for two hours—two of the most anxious hours I have ever spent.

One of the crew—they called him Hans— played a lot with Michael. He produced a photograph of his own little boy—and I knew why. Others in the crew showed us pictures of their wives and families.

Some hours after the bombing attack we cruised up to a Vichy destroyer and I and the other women and children were transferred. The U-boat captain, still a model of courtesy, again apologized for the inconvenience caused us, and wished us a safe return.

A day later we were put aboard a Vichy cruiser. We were well treated aboard her, too. We sailed in the cruiser for a week, eating well and having comfortable quarters. She took us finally to Casablanca.

There we were transferred again—this time to an internment camp under Vichy guards. Oh, what a difference ! By comparison with our treatment in the U-boat and the French warships we were badly dealt with by those

RELEASED FROM INTERNMENT, this happy group of British women and children, victims of U-boats and taken as captives to Morocco, were photographed at Gibraltar on their way home. Mrs. Blanche Allen, whose adventures are described in this page, is seen with her little boy, second from the left.
Photo, British Official

people. For two months we were on semi-starvation rations. These consisted chiefly of watery lentil soup and eggs. Yes—eggs and eggs and eggs, until we felt that our stomachs would revolt at the sight of them.

How glad we were when the Americans came to North Africa. The guards came and told us. They had the impudence to say, " Tell the Americans when they arrive that we looked after you properly."

My relatives tell me I have lost weight as a result of my experiences, but that does not trouble me. All that I am anxious for now is news from my husband. My last sight of him was of a waving figure in an open boat while I stood on the deck of a German submarine. The ending is a happy one, for Mrs. Allen has now been rejoined in England by her husband. He had been picked up by a French cruiser and taken to Morocco.—Ed.

OUR DIARY OF THE WAR

DEC. 9, 1942, Wednesday 1,194th day
Air.—Turin again raided by strong force of bombers.
North Africa.—Docks at La Goulette and Tunis airfield raided by Allied aircraft.
Russian Front.—Germans counter-attacked round Stalingrad and Rzhev, but failed to hold their ground.

DEC. 10, Thursday 1,195th day
North Africa.—Enemy tank and infantry attacks in direction of Mejez-el-Bab beaten back ; Tunis docks bombed.
Libya.—Allied aircraft attacked Marble Arch landing ground, W. of El Agheila.
India.—Jap bombers and fighters raided Chittagong, Bengal.
Australasia.—Announced that Allied forces had completely occupied Gona area of New Guinea.

DEC. 11, Friday 1,196th day
Sea.—Admiralty announced loss of minesweeper H.M.S. Cromer ; Greek submarine Triton also lost.
Air.—Turin again raided by R.A.F.
N. Africa.—Our forces in Tunisia beat off two enemy tank and infantry attacks.
Libya.—Nofilia landing-ground, W. of El Agheila, attacked by our aircraft.
Mediterranean.—Naples raided by U.S. aircraft by day and by R.A.F. at night ; Palermo docks also bombed.
Russian Front.—German counter-attacks between Don and Volga thrown back.
Indian Ocean.—American bombers renewed their attacks on Rangoon docks and on Port Blair, Andaman Is.
Australasia.—U.S. dive-bombers hit five out of 11 Jap destroyers heading for Guadalcanal.
U.S.A.—U.S. bombers attacked Jap shipping at Kiska, Aleutians.

DEC. 12, Saturday 1,197th day
Sea.—U.S. Navy Dept. announced sinking by mine of liner President Coolidge, transport in S. Pacific.
Air.—American bombers and Allied fighters attacked Rouen ; 23 enemy fighters destroyed.
N. Africa.—Enemy attempts to infiltrate N. and S. of Mejez-el-Bab stopped. Tunis docks bombed by U.S. Fortresses.
Libya.—Our forward troops continued to probe enemy defences before El Agheila. Tripoli raided by our bombers.
Mediterranean. — Palermo harbour raided by Allied bombers.

Burma.—Blenheim bombers attacked Mandalay.
Australasia.—U.S. warships engaged Jap destroyers heading for Guadalcanal and sank or damaged three.
Home Front.—Sharp raid on N.E. coastal area.
General.—German prisoners in Britain and Canada unshackled following Swiss Govt.'s appeal to Britain and Germany.

DEC. 13, Sunday 1,198th day
Sea.—Admiralty announced loss of destroyer Penylan and trawler Jasper.
N. Africa.—Heavy U.S. bombers attacked docks at Bizerta and Tunis by day ; R.A.F. raided Tunis and La Goulette at night.
Libya.—Eighth Army turned Rommel out of his strong positions at Mersa Brega, E. of El Agheila.
Russian Front.—S.W. of Stalingrad strong German attack beaten off.
Burma.—R.A.F. Wellingtons bombed aerodrome at Magwe.
Australasia.—In New Guinea Japs began fresh landing operations at Mambare, between Gona and Lae, under heavy Allied air attack.

DEC. 14, Monday 1,199th day
N. Africa. — Eight raids by Allied bombers on docks at Tunis and Bizerta on Dec. 13-14.

Mediterranean.—Heavy bombers from Libya raided Naples.
Russian Front.—At cost of heavy losses Germans made wedge in Soviet lines in Kotelnikovo area S.W. of Stalingrad.
Australasia.—American troops in New Guinea captured Buna village.
General.—Agreed that Madagascar to be administered by Fighting French under Gen. Legentilhomme.

DEC. 15, Tuesday 1,200th day
N. Africa.—Allied bombers raided Sfax, Susa, Bizerta, Tunis, and La Goulette.
Libya.—Eighth Army, hindered by mines, continued pursuit of Axis forces W. of El Agheila.
Russian Front. — German advance halted S.W. of Stalingrad.
India.—Two Japanese raids on Chittagong.

DEC. 16, Wednesday 1,201st day
Sea.—Admiralty announced loss of H.M. submarine Unbeaten.
N. Africa.—In Tunisia Allied bombers and fighters attacked enemy troops and railway near Mateur.
Libya.—Our advanced forces reached Wadi Matratin and cut off portion of Rommel's rearguard.
Australasia.—U.S. dive-bombers attacked Jap shipping off New Georgia Is.
Home Front.—Single enemy aircraft

attacked towns and villages in S. and S.E. England ; two raiders shot down.

DEC. 17, Thursday 1,202nd day
Air.—R.A.F. bombers raided N.W. Germany in bad weather ; 18 aircraft lost.
Russian Front.—Soviet troops continued to make progress on Stalingrad and Central fronts.
Burma.—British troops advanced about 30 m. into Burma and occupied territory N.W. of Akyab without opposition.
U.S.A.—Liberator bombers attacked Jap bases on Kiska, Aleutians.

DEC. 18, Friday 1,203rd day
N. Africa.—Allied bombers attacked docks at Bizerta, Tunis and La Goulette.
Libya.—Axis forces evacuated Nofilia.
Burma.—R.A.F. bombers raided Akyab.
Australasia.—U.S. bombers raided Jap base at Munda, New Georgia.

DEC. 19, Saturday 1,204th day
N. Africa.—French troops in Tunis occupied Pichon, W. of Kairouan.
Libya.—Allied aircraft attacked enemy transport columns at Buerat, W. of Sirte.
Russian Front.—Announced that Russian troops had launched fresh offensive in Middle Don area, recapturing 200 places.
Burma.—Allied bombers raided aerodrome at Toungoo.
Australasia.—U.S. dive-bombers and Fortresses again attacked Jap base at Munda, New Georgia.

DEC. 20, Sunday 1,205th day
Sea.—Admiralty announced loss of H.M. trawler Ullswater.
Air.—U.S. Liberator and Fortress bombers made daylight raid on aircraft repair works at Romilly-sur-Seine ; 44 enemy fighters shot down ; six U.S. bombers lost. R.A.F. raided Duisburg by night.
Libya.—Our forward patrols in touch with enemy round Sultan, 30 m. E. of Sirte.
Russian Front.—Russians made further progress in new advance on Middle Don.
India.—Enemy aircraft made first raid on Calcutta area. Chittagong also bombed.
Indian Ocean.—British naval force made heavy air attack on Sabang, Sumatra.
Burma.—Allied bombers raided Rangoon and Magwe.
Australasia.—After heavy fighting in New Guinea U.S. and Australian troops captured Cape Endaiadere, S.E. of Buna.

★ ═══════ *Flash-backs* ═══════ ★

1939
December 13. *Battle of River Plate between Graf Spee and Exeter, Ajax and Achilles.*
December 17. *Graf Spee scuttled outside Montevideo.*

1940
December 9. *Wavell's offensive opened against Italians in Western Desert.*
December 16. *British occupied Sollum and Fort Capuzzo.*

1941
December 9. *Japanese landed in Luzon, Philippines.*
December 10. *Prince of Wales and Repulse sunk off Malaya. Japanese captured Kota Bahru aerodrome, Malaya.*
December 11. *Germany and Italy declared war on U.S.A.*
December 15. *Russian offensive continued ; Kalinin recaptured.*
December 19. *Derna occupied by Eighth Army under Gen. Ritchie.*

THERE are times in this fourth winter of black-out when "I am aweary, aweary," but never one when I go the whole way with Mariana of the moated Grange, and "would that I were dead!" Never. Life at its longest is so brief a business, especially when you contemplate the millions of years that had passed before you were conscious of living and the possibility that you will be quite a long time dead, that I think we ought to regard every hour of it as precious. That is why I am inclined to resent the feeling of weariness that descends upon me when the black-out blackens and the sleepy feeling, induced by no sunshine, that comes upon me too often. Thinking that advancing years might not unreasonably account for this, I have discussed it with many persons of all adult ages and find, to my solace, if not to my encouragement, that it is the common experience of those who are twenty or thirty years my juniors. Surely those who order our way of life ought to realize this by easing their restrictions wherever that can be done with safety and without hurt to our war effort; for a lively and good-tempered public is in itself an essential to waging a total war. Yet there are those among our bureaucrats who take a fierce, sadistic joy in making loyal and well - meaning citizens miserable by unsympathetic consideration of cases of hardship resulting from the blind, mechanical application of a general rule to differently conditioned individuals.

IT is hardly necessary to detail any of these, as every living Briton has suffered from the form-filling mania that is common to every department of our bloated bureaucracy, and must have discovered by now that the real purpose of many of the forms we are asked to fill up is not to help us in any way to a fair share of obtainable necessities so much as to disgust us with the plaguy process of acquiring our due. We then decide to do without it, even to the point of lessening our individual ability to help in the national effort. This very common sense of frustration is, I suspect, not unconnected with the weary feeling I have mentioned, which might be counteracted in some degree at least by a more general recognition from officialdom that those swanking around, clothed in a little authority, are not really a different class of human beings equipped to make the lives of another class, the burden bearers, needlessly hard and gloomy, but that they are creatures "of like passions" whose function ought to be one of helpfulness to their fellows. It would have been jolly if some of these restrictive departments had made a New Year's resolution to be helpful in 1943 rather than harassing to the ordinary decent folk whose labour is paying their wages. I think I hear someone say wearily, "You have a hope !" Still, the right time for a hopeful heart to beat a little stronger is at the beginning of a new year. I am even finding a crumb of comfort in the minutely lengthening daylight which in another three months will banish once again those black-out blues !

DISCUSSING with a friend of his the other day, a journalist who long since laid down his pen and passed into the shadows, I recalled that on one occasion during the last War when he had some part in my own activities, we were together at an entertainment in a certain well-known London club one Saturday evening, when my old friend Lyle Johnstone contributed a new song entitled "Never Again with the Likes o' These." Personally, I found its sentiments entirely acceptable and it was set to a rollicking tune which ought to have given it a greater vogue than I think it ever attained. "These" were naturally the Huns of 1914, but my journalistic friend, who went through life enunciating a sort of mushy idealism and just fell short of being a pacifist, was so indignant at the vigorous anti-German feeling of the song that he endeavoured to leave the room in protest, and would no doubt have done so had it not been the custom then in that particular coterie to have the door locked out of respect for the vocalists, so that they should not suffer from members barging in in the middle of their efforts. But probably this was the only time that the locked door stood in the way of a sentimental soul whose kindly feelings for all mankind made him uneasy at the prospect of our never again grasping the hand of the Hun in fellowship. I have thought of him in noticing that a Never Again Society has recently been formed in England, and I wonder if they know of the existence of the composition in question, which might serve them as a theme song. At any rate, I can commend it to their attention, as I believed in it then and more strongly approve its sentiment today.

As one who has always taken a keen amateur interest in astronomy I have noted with some surprise the announcement that a new planet, sixteen times larger than Jupiter, was discovered at the end of November 1942 by a Swedish astronomer named Dr. Strand, who calculates that the object of his discovery must have a weight of some 5,000 times that of the Earth. This will give one a faint idea of the amount of space still available outside the tiny Solar System in which this Earth of ours has a very minor position. For Jupiter is the largest of the planetary masses that have their orbits round the Sun, which in its turn is one of the smaller of the millions of suns burning within the immeasurable vastness of space. Jupiter is 1,312 times larger than the Earth and is attended by no fewer than nine moons, while we are struggling along with one, but the density of Jupiter is much lower than that of our planet, so that its weight is not relatively greater than that of the Earth.

THAT an unknown planet 18,000 times bulkier than the Earth has evaded the ceaseless investigations of astronomers from Galileo to Sir James Jeans would be a bit of real news if we were not so occupied with the War that is raging on our own pumpkin of a planet at present. Meanwhile, I have my doubts about it, though I had none concerning the last authentic discovery of another planet in the Solar System, since Pluto (as it was christened) has a diameter only half our own. There would be at least one consolation if Earth were as enormous as Jupiter: a World War on it would be impossible, as a century might go by before the news that its northern inhabitants were exterminating each other had reached as far south as its Australia !

OUR friends down south, especially the Diggers who write to me, must be a breezy lot. One of the raciest letters I have had of late, the spelling of which would have done credit to Josh Billings or Artemus Ward, comes from farther south, Tasmania, and tells me that the writer has been reading THE WAR ILLUSTRATED since it began and is so pleased with it that he urges me to keep it going "War or no War." Personally, I think that we shall all be fairly fed up with the War, as a war, by the time it is ended, but as a period of great adventure and marvellous events it will yield material for thousands of publications in the years to follow. I like this correspondent particularly because he is so frank about my own gossip, which he tells me is sometimes "very tame" and occasionally "just mush." But some of the things which he, as an old soldier (his name, by the way, is Patman, and he writes from Moonah, Tasmania), says about our Blimps I would not dare to quote. Evidently my own particular bête noire of the B.B.C., those dreadful boomings of Big Ben at nine o'clock, have a value more appreciable in the far reaches of the British Commonwealth than in the British Isles, for this cheery critic finishes up his letter by saying that "all is well, as I have just heard Big Ben striking . . . and now we will hear some of the Colonel Blimps from the B.B.C. studio, which is full of them."

FAMOUS FIGHTERS OF THE R·A·F

WING CMDR. D. R. S. BADER, D.S.O., D.F.C., renowned "legless" pilot. He was taken prisoner on Aug. 9, 1941, after having brought down 22½ German planes (the last being shared) in the Battle of Britain of 1940, and in daylight sweeps over N. France, 1940-41.
Drawn by Eric Kennington: Crown Copyright reserved

Printed in England and published every alternate Friday by the Proprietors, THE AMALGAMATED PRESS, LTD., The Fleetway House, Farringdon Street, London, E.C.4. Registered for transmission by Canadian Magazine Post. Sole Agents for Australia and New Zealand : Messrs. Gordon & Gotch, Ltd. ; and for South Africa : Central News Agency, Ltd.—January 8, 1943.   S.S.   *Editorial Address :* JOHN CARPENTER HOUSE WHITEFRIARS. LONDON. E.C.4.

Vol 6　　The War Illustrated　Nº 146

Edited by Sir John Hammerton

SIXPENCE　　　　　　　　　　　　　　　　　　　JANUARY 22, 1943

GENERAL GIRAUD was appointed High Commissioner for French North Africa after the assassination of Adm. Darlan on Christmas Eve, 1942. A renowned French military leader, he would have become generalissimo in the Battle of France, in succession to General Gamelin, had he not been taken prisoner in May 1940. This recent photograph shows him reviewing U.S. troops in N. Africa. An account of his dramatic career is given in page 486.　　　　　　　　　　　*Photo, Planet News*

THE BATTLE FRONTS

by Maj.-Gen. Sir Charles Gwynn, K.C.B., D.S.O.

At the beginning of 1942 it was generally expected that the year would see the major crisis of the war; but during the first nine months there was little to show that the crisis would be successfully passed. For the Empire the months had been marked by failure of hopes and by disasters the most shattering in its history. Russia, too, had received a terrible buffeting, and if still unbeaten it was difficult to believe that she possessed a reserve of offensive power. Anyone who had in September forecast that the end of the year would see the initiative passing to the Allies and both Germany and Japan on the defensive would have been scoffed at as an absurd optimist.

The defeat of Rommel in what he deemed to be an impregnable position brought relief and hope, but few could have expected that in a few weeks Russia would have won even more remarkable victories. It is true that last winter Russia had made a wonderful recovery, but that was because Hitler's rash challenge to the Russian winter presented Stalin with a fleeting opportunity which he was ready to seize. But the blow he struck was with light forces against an exhausted army already in retreat, and not a prearranged offensive delivered at a selected time and place. When it met strong, organized defences the blow had not sufficient weight behind it to overcome them. This winter, on the other hand, the offensive was fully prepared and admirably planned, and because it had of necessity to be delivered against fully organized positions, its achievements have been beyond all comparison greater than those of last year, and admit of further exploitation.

RUSSIA In my last article (see page 450) I wrote that there was no expectation of immediate sensational results on the Russian front. The Russians appeared to be engaged in strengthening and deepening their ring encircling the German 6th Army at Stalingrad, and in maintaining pressure on the Rzhev–Veliki Luki front in order to prevent transfer of German reserves to the Lower Don, where it seemed probable that the Germans might assemble at Kotelnikovo a force for the relief of the 6th Army. The Germans were aware that there was a Russian force east of the Middle Don below Voronezh, and it seemed probable that they had reserves disposed to meet the threat.

That picture did not allow for the full scope of the masterly plans Zhukov (who we now know is in direct control of the Russian operations) had laid, nor did it anticipate German mistakes. Sensational results have most certainly been achieved, which, moreover, have revealed that, despite its losses in the past year, the Red Army retains offensive power far exceeding all expectations. To underrate it was the fundamental German mistake.

Zhukov's plans have been described officially by Moscow in the stages of their development.

There was first the November two-pronged attack north-west and south-west of Stalingrad which encircled the 6th Army. Measures were then taken to consolidate the positions of the encircling ring against attacks from outside, involving especially an advance towards Kotelnikovo from which relief attacks were expected.

It was at this stage the Germans seem to have made two fatal mistakes, possibly unavoidable. They made a rescue attempt before they had assembled an adequate force, and they delayed dispatch of reinforcements to the Middle Don front.

When by early December they had assembled at Kotelnikovo a striking force of three Panzer and three motorized infantry divisions, they launched an attempt on December 12 to break through to the 6th Army. The force constituted, of course, a very powerful spearhead, and it drove deeply into the Russian positions. But the

spearhead lacked a shaft—an infantry force to hold the sides of the corridor which the spearhead was attempting to form. The Russians counter-attacked, enveloping the flanks of the thrust; and after some days of hard and critical fighting the Germans were in full retreat, having suffered great losses. In three days they lost all the ground they had gained in twelve; and with the Russians in pursuit they were unable even to retain their hold on Kotelnikovo. Kotelnikovo was captured on Dec. 29 with great quantities of booty, and not till they were well west of the town could the retreating enemy make a stand.

Meanwhile, the Germans had made their other fatal mistake. They had seen the

threat on the Middle Don growing, and had set in motion formations to strengthen the line, held there mainly by Italian troops. But before the reinforcements arrived the storm broke. Possibly it was thought the ice was not yet solid enough to carry heavy traffic across the Don, or the weight and speed of the assault were unexpected.

Under a terrific artillery bombardment the Russian infantry carried the meticulously-prepared defences, and mechanized columns penetrated rear positions, leaving isolated centres of resistance to be mopped up in turn. The speed of the Russian advance in spite of snow was amazingly well maintained, and the breakthrough was complete over a wide front. The Voronezh–Rostov railway—the supply line for the whole Middle Don front —was overrun, and depots of supplies of all sorts, well-stocked for the winter, were captured.

The Nazi retreat became a rout, which the reinforcing divisions coming up could not check. Some of the towns on the railway, prepared as centres of resistance, were rushed at once, others held out for some days; but it was not until the important railway junction of Millerovo was reached that the Russian progress was checked and German resistance was stiffened by the arrival of further reserves. Millerovo, though almost surrounded, could not be rushed; but farther south the Russian Middle Don army joined hands with the army north-west of Stalingrad, mopping up the enemy still holding positions in the Don loop and on the railway leading to Stalingrad.

It was an amazing feat in a snow-covered country and without railway communications for the Russians to maintain the impetus of their offensive for over one hundred miles, but the pace was bound to slacken and a pause was necessary to bring up supplies and to deal with centres of resistance which had been by-passed. Moreover, the network of railways within the Donetz basin enabled the

RUSSIAN ADVANCE. At the end of Dec. 1942 the plight of the isolated German forces before Stalingrad became desperate. The Red Army continued to advance in the mid-Don area, and in N. Caucasus the recapture of Mozdok on Jan. 3, 1943, and of, Nalchik on Jan. 4 were major victories. Shaded portions of this map show Russian-held territory at the beginning of January.
By courtesy of The Evening Standard   PAGE 482

RUSSIAN TANKS, supported by artillery, are shown rolling forward to victory on the Central front. This photograph was taken shortly before the Soviet forces succeeded in dislodging an important enemy-held position in the Veliki Luki area, and subsequently wiped out an entire German infantry battalion. It was announced on Jan. 1, 1943 that Veliki Luki itself had been recaptured by the Soviet troops as a result of this decisive attack.
Photo, U.S.S.R. Official

Germans to rush up reserves. Millerovo, as I write, is holding out, and German resistance east of Donetz is stiffening.

The immediate German aim must obviously be to hold the line of the Donetz covering the approaches to Rostov and to the centres in the Donetz basin such as Voroshilovgrad and the important railway junction at Likhaya. Four railways cross the Donetz on a front of one hundred miles, which may enable the Nazis to maintain strong forces east of the river; and if Millerovo holds out it will tend to break up the continuity of the advancing Russian wave. It would be premature, therefore, to assume that the Russians have immediate prospects of reaching Rostov or the Donetz basin.

But Zhukov had still further plans. Following the example of Foch in 1918, when a thrust in one direction seemed temporarily to have exhausted its impetus, he struck at a new point. By an astonishingly swift advance southwards and westwards he overran the comparatively weak German forces in the Ergeni hills and Kalmuck Steppes bypassing the town of Elista, which the Germans were compelled to evacuate hurriedly. This movement, still in progress, seriously threatens the communications of the Germans in the Terek valley, who, at the same time, are being counter-attacked by the Russians who have for so long successfully opposed them. It is not surprising that under this double threat the Germans

have withdrawn from Mozdok and Nalchik, abandoning their winter shelter and all hopes of capturing the Grosny oilfields.

The net results of these offensives have been disastrous to the Germans. They have lost over 300,000 effectives killed or prisoners, and immense quantities of material. Their 6th Army in front of Stalingrad is in a desperate position, and the fact that it made no attempt at a sortie to join hands with the relief force from Kotelnikovo proves how completely it is immobilized and without hope of cutting its way out of the net. The steady and increasing pressure which is being applied to it seems to indicate moves preparatory to dealing it a death-blow.

What can the Germans do to retrieve the situation? A merely defensive attitude would almost certainly mean the acceptance of the inevitability of further disasters. Yet they have already learnt that a premature and inadequate counter-stroke only adds to their

losses. If they have reserves available their position on the Donetz does, however, appear to afford an opportunity of concentrating a powerful offensive force; and the Russians opposing them, without railway communications, may have difficulties when snow deepens. I feel sure that the Germans would wish to postpone counter-offensive operations to the spring, trusting to the ability of isolated hedgehog centres to survive attack; but the fall of Veliki Luki (claimed by the Russians on Jan. 1, 1943) may have shown them that hedgehog centres are not invulnerable to the forces and weapons Russia can now bring against them. They may feel compelled, therefore, to attempt a counter-offensive unprepared as they probably are for mobile winter operations.

The capture of Veliki Luki, apart from the evidence it gives of the vulnerability of hedgehog centres, is of great importance. It exposes the Leningrad-Kiev railway, the chief German line of lateral communications, to immediate attack at Sokolniki, where it is joined by the line from Riga; and it of course liberates strong Russian forces and heavy weapons for further action.

Warned by the fate of Veliki Luki, the Germans, it seems possible, may attempt to withdraw their garrison from Rzhev even though that would open railway communication

from Moscow to Veliki Luki and give the Russians a much needed supply line. If it can maintain its supplies during the winter the Russian central offensive may yet achieve successes comparable to those in the south.

NORTH AFRICA
In Tunis operations are still confined to the activities of covering troops and to air attacks on the enemy's bases and communications. Weather conditions have delayed the development of major operations.

In Tripoli the 8th Army has advanced steadily and has passed the Wadi el Kebir, encountering only mines and light rearguard opposition. The enemy, however, seems to intend to hold the Wadi Zemzem strongly, and General Montgomery is not likely to attack the position seriously until his army is closed up and his communications are well established.

Rommel has been reinforced, but it is still uncertain whether he means to fight a decisive action or merely to delay the advance of the 8th Army as long as possible. It is a situation in which Montgomery is bound to exercise caution.

FAR EAST
Attrition of Japanese air power and shipping resources proceeds steadily, and the isolated detachments in Guadalcanal and at Buna are fighting fanatically in a hopeless situation. There is no indication, however, that, either in Burma or elsewhere, the Allies are ready to undertake major offensive operations.

The advance towards Akyab in Burma is probably intended merely to deprive the Japanese of a base conveniently situated for harassing air attacks on India, and to secure an advanced air base for ourselves.

ON THE N. AFRICAN FRONT. Axis forces evacuated Nofilia, half-way to Sirte, on Dec. 18, 1942. A British 8th Army vehicle is seen (upper photo) approaching a signboard in the centre of the town. Below, First Army guardsmen seen during fierce fighting last December on Long Stop Hill, N.N.E. of Mejez-el-Bab. *Photos, British Official: Crown Copyright.*

Through Tripolitania the Enemy's Flight Continues

"MARBLE ARCH" (below), through which a convoy of 8th Army transport units is seen advancing, is situated on the coastal road about halfway between El Agheila and Nofilia. It was built by the Italians in the days when they dreamed of emulating the ancient empire of Rome. Right, the shadow of an Allied sentry with fixed bayonet falls across these exhausted Axis prisoners in the Western Desert.

ENEMY REARGUARD STANDS in Libya, devised to facilitate the escape of Rommel's main forces, were swiftly dealt with by the Allied troops. Left, the British crew of a 6-pounder anti-tank gun flatten themselves upon the sand during enemy counter-fire. Above, an Eighth Army observation-post under shellfire near El Agheila.

Battle Is Joined Between Anderson & Nehring

ADVANCING ON THE TUNISIAN FRONT, men of the First Army, supported by American light tanks of M3 type, move across the countryside in open order to attack enemy forward positions.

AT AN R.A.F. STATION in Northern Tunisia, a canteen has been improvised out of a dump of petrol tins. We may imagine that the men needed no urging to "kew upp" for "English Beer." R.A.F. ground staff on the right are examining Sten guns.

IN TUNISIA fighting was mainly concentrated in the Jedeida, Tebourba and Mejez-el-Bab areas during the closing weeks of 1942. By Jan. 1, 1943 our most advanced forces were reported to be some 60 miles from Tunis. The rainy season, which continues until February, rendered the ground unsuitable for tank operations in the north, and during November French troops made considerable progress against immobilized Axis forces. Above, Axis prisoners, captured during the First Army's offensive, are being marched through the docks at Algiers, preparatory to embarkation. Right, gunners of the First Army guard the approaches to Mejez-el-Bab. They have converted their A.A. gun for use as a field gun.

Photos, British Official; Keystone

General Giraud Writes Another Page of History

Of all the great personalities thrown up by the War there is none perhaps who has had a more dramatic career than the 63-year-old French general who succeeded Admiral Darlan in his present authority in North Africa. Below we give the high-lights of a story that is still far from told.

CHRISTMAS EVE in Algiers. A few minutes after 3 p.m. Admiral Darlan, High Commissioner of French North Africa, drove up to his office in the Summer Palace, passed between the Spahis guarding the entrance, and began to walk along the corridor to his room. Then a door opened. A young man stepped out—a young man with a pistol. There were shots, and in a few seconds the Admiral lay mortally wounded. He died half an hour later as the car to which he had been carried entered the hospital gates.

Saved with difficulty from the Spahis' swords, the assassin was rushed away for interrogation. The next day he was tried by a French court-martial and condemned to be shot; at dawn on December 26, 1942 the sentence was carried out. A few hours

de Guerre. But in 1913 he was back in Africa as a captain of Zouaves, and soon after the outbreak of war in 1914 he was in action on the Belgian frontier.

At the battle of Charleroi Giraud was wounded as he led his men in a bayonet charge and was left on the field as dead. But during the night he was picked up by a German ambulance and taken away to hospital behind the enemy lines. As soon as he could get about, he and Captain Schmitt, a fellow prisoner, made an attempt to escape. They were captured, but on November 15, 1914, they escaped again and reached St. Quentin, where they were harboured by the mayor and by a pork butcher who kept an hotel. Giraud was for some time a stable lad and after that employed by a coal merchant, while Schmitt was a washer-up in a restaurant and then a butcher's assistant. But things got too hot for them at St. Quentin, and the two, aided again by many friends at the risk of their lives, got a job in a

builder's staff. During the terrible Rifl campaign he was Lieut.-Colonel of the 14th Regiment of Tirailleurs. He fought in six battles and, according to his seventh mention in dispatches, " gave repeated proofs of his energy, his ardour in action, and a personal bravery beyond all praise." In 1936 General Giraud was appointed Governor of Metz, and in 1939 he was given a seat on the French Supreme War Council.

AT the outbreak of war in 1939 he received the command of the French 7th Army; but when General Corap's 9th Army was swept away at Sedan in May 1940 General Georges chose Giraud to replace Corap. To quote from the citation of the Grand Cross of the Legion of Honour that Pétain gave him, he " galvanized the troops by his presence among them, utterly ignoring the constant bombardments. He drove through the enemy lines, personally organizing the creation of strong points: He imparted to all his fiery energy and succeeded in stemming for several days the German armoured advance, inflicting severe losses. He was taken prisoner while still commanding the last centre of his army's resistance."

For two years he was a captive. Then on April 25, 1942 the German radio announced that General Henri Giraud had escaped from the fortress at Koenigstein in Saxony ; a reward of a hundred thousand marks was offered for his capture. Three days later it was reported from Switzerland that the General had entered that country under an assumed name on April 21 and left on April 25. On May 4 Vichy made the surprising announcement that Giraud was in Unoccupied France, that he had attended Franco-German talks at Moulins, on the frontier of the Occupied and Unoccupied zones, on May 2, and had since returned to Vichy from Lyons. It was made clear that he was wholly free, and had not been confined or handed over to the Germans. Giraud apparently remained in Unoccupied France until November. He was not inactive, however, and must soon have been in touch with the Allies. How otherwise can we account for the next chapter in his story ?

For several nights in early November (says Reuter) a British submarine, under the command of Lieut. L. A. Jewell, with whom was an American officer, Captain Jerauld Wright, lay off the French Riviera coast, coming to the surface only at night.

GENERAL GIRAUD, appointed French High Commissioner in N. Africa on Dec. 26, 1942, in succession to Adm. Darlan, was captured by the Germans in France in May 1940. This photo, reproduced from the Nazi-controlled paper La Semaine, shows him as a prisoner (left) at Koenigstein Castle, in Saxony, before his dramatic escape to Switzerland in April last year.

On November 4 orders were received to proceed, submerged at 60 ft., into a certain harbour. As the periscope broke surface a lamp on the shore was observed signalling " Wait one hour." After a second message had been received a rowing-boat was seen approaching, and the watchers in the submarine were able to identify General Giraud, his son, and other officers. General Giraud was about to step on to the slippery deck of the submarine when a wave caught the small boat. He lost his balance and fell into the water, but almost immediately was rescued by members of the submarine crew. The submarine then submerged and made for the open Mediterranean.

Next morning it made contact with a flying-boat according to plan. General Giraud and his companions then transferred to the waiting aircraft, and a few hours before the Allied expeditionary force landed he was with General Eisenhower, the Allied Commander-in-Chief.

On November 8 the Anglo-Americans landed in North Africa, and during the morning General Giraud, describing himself as Commander-in-Chief of the French Forces in North Africa, broadcast from Radio Algiers an appeal for cooperation with the Allies.

Six weeks later fate gave another twist to his fortunes when his colleagues of the Imperial Council in Algiers elected him to the place made vacant by an assassin's bullet.

later Admiral Darlan's body was borne with stately ceremony to the grave. Before the day was out the Imperial Council, appointed by the Admiral a few weeks earlier to exercise authority in French North Africa, elected General Giraud as Darlan's successor. The choice was well received. Particularly significant was General de Gaulle's reference to Giraud as " the renowned French military leader " who, had he not been taken prisoner by the Germans during the Battle of France, would have been appointed Generalissimo in Gamelin's place.

WHO is this Giraud ? Certainly he is no new-comer to the headlines. All the world knows him as the man whom no German prison has been able to hold. First, however, let us note some of the details of his long and brilliant career in the French army.

Henri Honoré Giraud comes of old bourgeois stock. Born in Paris in 1879, he entered the French military college of St. Cyr when he was nineteen, and in 1900 received his commission as a Sous-Lieutenant in the 4th regiment of Zouaves. So began his connexion with North Africa. He saw garrison duty at Bizerta and Tunis, but after seven years he returned to France and graduated as a Staff officer at the Ecole

travelling circus which took them as far as Brussels. Giraud was the conjurer.

One day a man addressed him : " Should I say mon Lieutenant or mon Capitaine ? " " I know you—you are a deserter from the Legion," Giraud flashed back. " You will not leave my side or I'll blow your brains out." " Yes," the man confessed, " I am a Legionary, but at the moment I am helping Englishmen and Frenchmen to escape. First of all let me take you to a doctor." Giraud, whose wounds had not properly healed, was for a week under the care of a practitioner who introduced him to Nurse Edith Cavell. She confided him to the care of the Jaunart family, who arranged his passage and that of Schmitt into Holland. All went well for Giraud, but his companion was hit by a rifle shot and torn on the barbed wire. Giraud picked him up and carried him. Eventually they arrived at Flushing, whence they were sent to England.

February 1915 found Giraud once more in France ; he was decorated by Joffre, and placed on the staff of the 5th Army. But in 1917 he rejoined his 4th Zouaves, and again distinguished himself in action ; then until the end of the War he was Chief of Staff to General Daugan of the Moroccan Division. After the armistice he saw service in Constantinople and the Rhineland, but in 1922 Marshal Lyautey called him to Morocco, where he joined the great empire-

French Troops Fight Beside the Allies in Tunisia

SOLDIERS OF GEN. GIRAUD'S ARMY have been fighting side by side with the Anglo-American forces from the opening of the campaign in November 1942. Top, in the foreground, French soldiers are manning a machine-gun while their British allies are ready for action at their Bofors. Centre right, a British lorry crosses a bridge which is guarded by the French. Below, a train of pack-mules loaded with equipment passes through the ruins of a Tunisian village en route for the front line.

Photos, British Official: Crown Copyright: Keystone

FIERCE BATTLE OFF GUADALCANAL. On Nov. 12, 1942 U.S. naval forces bombarded Japanese shore positions on this important island of the Solomons, and during these operations the enemy lost 30 out of 31 aircraft sent to attack the American ships. This photo shows a Jap plane plunging to destruction after it had dropped a bomb near the U.S. cruiser San Francisco (centre) and had been shot down by intensive A.A. fire. It was shortly after this engagement that the San Francisco was slightly damaged and 30 men killed, as the result of a disabled enemy plane crashing on her. It was later announced that among those killed were Rear-Adm. D. J. Callaghan (flying his flag in this ship) and Capt. C. Young, the San Francisco's commander. (See illus. p. 393.) In the foreground is a U.S. cargo transport.

Photo, Associated Press

THE WAR AT SEA

by Francis E. McMurtrie

EVEN on the basis of their own communiqué, the German attack on a convoy bound for North Russia on the last day of the old year seems clearly to have been a failure. In view of the present military situation on the Eastern Front, the enemy must be desperately anxious to stop further supplies reaching the Soviet forces, but their efforts were evidently abortive.

The Admiralty announcement on the subject stated that a German destroyer was sunk and a cruiser damaged. The enemy admit the loss of the former ship, and on the other hand claim to have accounted for a British destroyer, which sounds like a mere counterblast for propaganda purposes. Otherwise, the only claims made are of damage by gunfire to our escorting cruisers and destroyers, and torpedo hits by a U-boat on four ships of the convoy. As it is added that weather conditions precluded observation of results, these claims amount to very little.

AT this time of year the hours of daylight in the region of Bear Island, where the encounter took place, are very few ; and in addition the weather seems to have been so bad that visibility during those hours must have been intermittent. Aircraft were prevented from operating, which must have handicapped the enemy attack considerably.

Although the Germans have for months past maintained a strong naval force in Norwegian waters, comprising all their available heavy ships, our convoys have continued to get through to Russia in spite of efforts to intercept them. Losses have sometimes been incurred, but the average deliveries of war material have been important, and must have contributed not a little to recent Soviet successes.

Battleships in the Pacific

As the result of the completion of the remaining four ships of the 35,000-ton Washington class, the United States Navy is now much stronger than it was before the Pearl Harbour disaster. Of the five battleships sunk or put out of action on December 7, 1941, three have been refitted and are again in service. Only in aircraft-carriers is there a temporary shortage, but as Japan has suffered still more severe losses in this category, here also the balance remains on the right side. It is true that six cruisers have been sunk, yet Japan has lost a greater number ; and

several new American cruisers have been commissioned, and more are due for delivery shortly.

REPORTS of Japanese battleships of 40,000 to 45,000 tons being on the point of completion continue to appear with suspicious regularity. Up to now there has been no evidence that any such ships have been put into service, and it is likely that their construction has been delayed. On the other hand, two or three vessels of an improved "pocket battleship" type are believed to have been added to the Japanese fleet. Their names are somewhat uncertain, but may include Takamatu and Titibu, previously assigned by rumour to two of the big new battleships mentioned above.

As time goes on, Japanese losses in cruisers and destroyers must have a serious effect on the balance of types composing the fleet, since it is hardly possible for battleships to operate successfully without a due proportion of cruisers and destroyers.

The Italian Navy is likely soon to be in a similar position. This all goes to show the futility of treating capital ships as a sort of hidden reserve, not to be risked until the last. Had we been as cautious with our battleships, we might not have lost the Barham, Prince of Wales, or Repulse—but we might very well have ended by losing the war.

German Raider Sunk

For reasons which are not entirely clear, the German propaganda department have issued a somewhat highly-coloured account of the sinking of the armed raider Atlantis by H.M.S. Devonshire in the South Atlantic on November 22, 1941. In announcing the destruction of this ocean pest, the Admiralty described how, when first sighted, the Atlantis was stopped, with a boat lying off containing oil drums. There is no doubt she was engaged in re-fuelling a U-boat, the presence of which was later established.

After the Atlantis had been set on fire, the crew took to their boats. Later her magazine blew up, and she sank. In view of the nearness of an enemy submarine, no attempt was made to pick up survivors. According to the German account, the boats were taken in tow by the submarine and those in them were transferred by degrees to other U-boats, so that most of them got back to Germany.

Several Nazi ocean raiders have been intercepted from time to time. As a rule, their victims have been few, as they cannot afford to remain on a trade route for any length of time without grave risk of being caught. They are not to be confused with blockade runners, endeavouring to get through to Germany with selected cargoes of rubber and other products of which the enemy is in great need. Three such cargoes have been stopped by the Royal Navy in recent weeks, one in the Indian Ocean and two in the Atlantic.

Though very little is heard of its activities, the presence in the Indian Ocean of a strong Eastern Fleet under the command of Admiral Sir James Somerville has had a deterrent effect on the enterprise of the Japanese Navy. Since April last Japanese warships have scarcely been heard of in the area outside the Strait of Malacca, though there is believed to be a fleet of some size based on Singapore.

Royal Navy in the East

It seems probable that the port of Sabang, at the northern extremity of the island of Sumatra, is being used by the enemy as a minor naval base. On the night of December 20-21, a British naval force operating in the Bay of Bengal carried out a heavy air attack on this place, causing damage to various objects of military importance. Large explosions, followed by fires, were observed.

As a matter of historical interest, it may be observed that during the hard-fought struggle for command of the Indian seas in 1782-83 the French Admiral Suffren made use of this same locality—the northern end of Sumatra—as a winter base before renewing his battles with Admiral Sir Edward Hughes.

Undoubtedly the greatest task which confronts the United Nations in 1943 is the defeat of the U-boat menace. Though shipping losses are less than they were, the leeway in merchant tonnage has not yet been made up, and the numbers of the enemy submarines continue to increase. It is true that it is hardly possible for trained crews to be provided in equal degree, but even so the danger of our operations in North Africa being hampered by U-boat depredations is too serious to neglect.

IT is essential therefore that no pains should be spared to hunt to death every enemy submarine that is detected. For this purpose it is understood that priority is now being given to all the material which the Royal Navy requires to amplify its anti-submarine measures. This presumably is one of the results at which Field-Marshal Smuts was aiming in his warning words on the U-boat menace last year.

BRITAIN'S EASTERN FLEET. A warship is seen steaming through a heavy smoke-screen during manoeuvres. Such practices are of vital importance for the successful prosecution of naval actions, such as that of Dec. 20, 1942, when aircraft-carriers comprising part of a British force made an intensive attack on the Japanese at Sabang, on Sumatra.

PAGE 489 *Photo, British Official: Crown Copyright*

Wounded from Libya Are Her Passengers Now

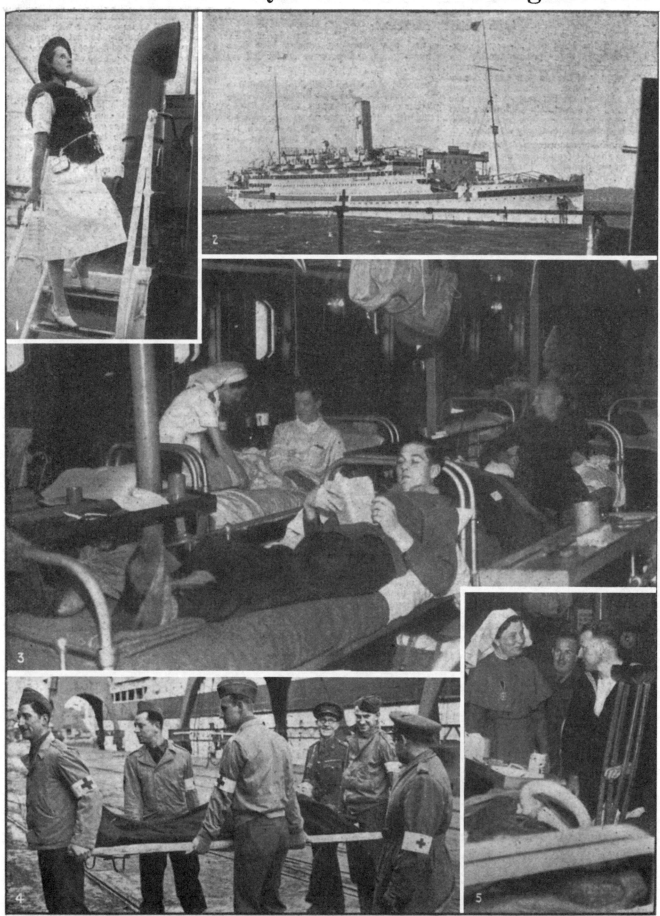

BRITISH HOSPITAL SHIP ATLANTIS—formerly a luxury liner—recently returned home from the Middle East with sick and wounded men from the 8th and other armies. 1, Sister Christina Hobbs in the life-saving jacket and steel helmet provided for use in case of emergency. 2, The Atlantis homeward bound. 3, A corner of a surgical ward aboard the ship. 4, U.S. ambulance men help to disembark casualties. 5, Miss M. F. Northrope, R.R.C., the ship's matron, says good-bye to some of her charges. PAGE 490

Inside Germany in the War's Fourth Year

OUTSIDE A BERLIN FACTORY (1) offers of employment to girls and women witness to Germany's increasing labour shortage. 2, Ploughing a lawn in the Gendarmenmarkt, the centre of Berlin. 3, According to the German caption, these men are armament workers training with an A.A. gun. 4, "I work my fingers to the bone to save my nation:" Hitler addresses his old party members in Munich on Nov. 8, 1942. Pudgy and dishevelled, this is a very different Fuehrer from the sleek boaster of years gone by.

Photos, British Official: Crown Copyright; Pictorial Press, Keystone, Associated Press

Calcutta's Civil Defence Meets the Challenge

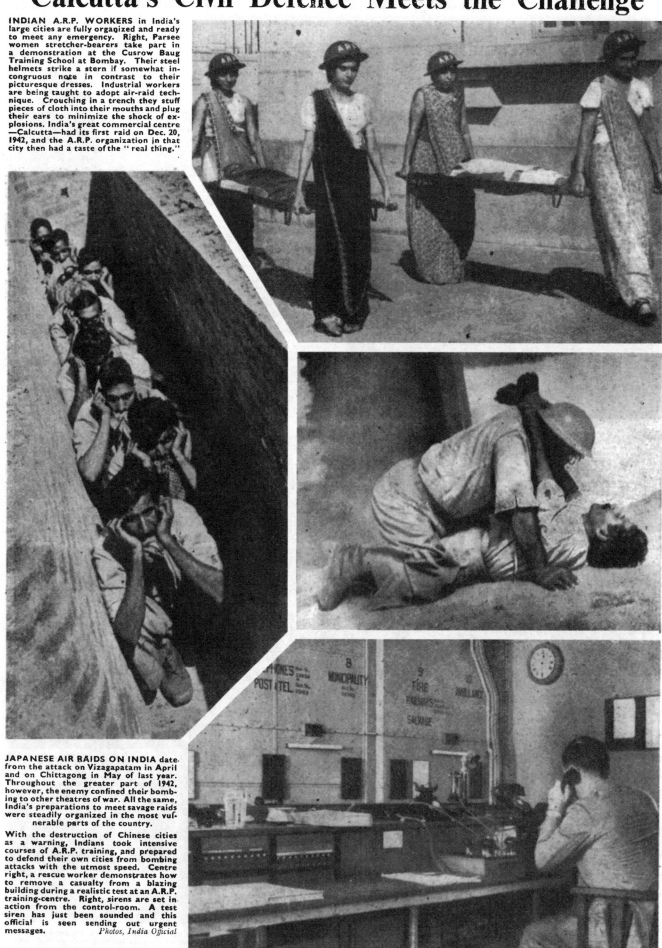

INDIAN A.R.P. WORKERS in India's large cities are fully organized and ready to meet any emergency. Right, Parsee women stretcher-bearers take part in a demonstration at the Cusrow Baug Training School at Bombay. Their steel helmets strike a stern if somewhat incongruous note in contrast to their picturesque dresses. Industrial workers are being taught to adopt air-raid technique. Crouching in a trench they stuff pieces of cloth into their mouths and plug their ears to minimize the shock of explosions. India's great commercial centre —Calcutta—had its first raid on Dec. 20, 1942, and the A.R.P. organization in that city then had a taste of the "real thing."

JAPANESE AIR RAIDS ON INDIA date from the attack on Vizagapatam in April and on Chittagong in May of last year. Throughout the greater part of 1942, however, the enemy confined their bombing to other theatres of war. All the same, India's preparations to meet savage raids were steadily organized in the most vulnerable parts of the country.

With the destruction of Chinese cities as a warning, Indians took intensive courses of A.R.P. training, and prepared to defend their own cities from bombing attacks with the utmost speed. Centre right, a rescue worker demonstrates how to remove a casualty from a blazing building during a realistic test at an A.R.P. training-centre. Right, sirens are set in action from the control-room. A test siren has just been sounded and this official is seen sending out urgent messages. *Photos, India Official*

Wavell Assumes the Offensive in Burma

ADVANCING INTO BURMA from Assam, Allied forces, it was announced on Dec. 19, 1942, were pushing steadily forward into the interior. By Dec. 29 a British force had penetrated into the Chindwin valley, about 50 miles N.E. of Arakan—scene of the memorable fighting withdrawal by our troops in May last year. This advance had been preceded by heavy bombing raids on Japanese bases in Burma.

Lt.-Gen. J. W. Stilwell (right), U.S. Commander of Chinese forces in Burma, addresses part of the Chinese army he has helped to build up in India. Known as "Uncle Joe," Gen. Stilwell, who was former Chief of Staff to Marshal Chiang Kai-shek, speaks Chinese fluently.

Gen. Wavell, C.-in-C. India (promoted to the rank of Field-Marshal in the New Year Honours, 1943), is seen below with Lt.-Gen. N. M. S. Irwin, Commander of India's Eastern Army. This photograph was taken during Gen. Wavell's visit to our forward positions on the Indian N.E. frontier, before he crossed into Burma.

CHINESE GUN CREW—members of Gen. Stilwell's highly efficient and reorganized army —being instructed by a U.S. artillery corporal in the operation of a 155-mm. howitzer, one of America's most modern weapons.

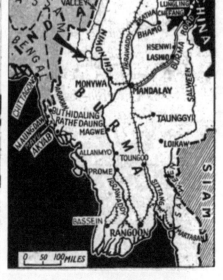

ON THE N.E. INDIAN FRONTIER, Gen. Wavell inspects a detachment of his troops on the eve of the Allied advance into Burma from Assam. Heavy arrow on the map (right) shows direction of our main thrust towards the Chindwin river. Smaller arrow above indicates positions in the Kabaw valley also occupied by our troops. The first clash with the Japanese in Western Burma occurred on Dec. 27, 1942 in the neighbourhood of Rathedaung. After an exchange of fire the enemy broke off contact and it was reported that the bulk of his forces had fallen back against the port of Akyab. Rangoon, Mandalay, Monywa, Magwe, and other important Jap bases were repeatedly bombed by the R.A.F. All communiqués emphasized the encouraging effect which these attacks had on our troops. Enemy aircraft which raided eastern Bengal in December encountered a spearhead of British fighter defence at Chittagong.

Photos, Indian Official: Copyright reserved; Keystone

It's the Same War All the World Over

Opening the newspaper of a morning, listening to the news bulletins of the B.B.C., one has an impression of a great number of different fronts, widely separated in space and varying greatly in importance. Yet as the famous writer, BOYD CABLE, explains in the article printed below, the War is one, a Total War indeed.

OUTSIDE the few trained specialists and experts in strategy there are few today who realize how closely related are the numerous fronts in this Total War, or how the results of a battle fought by a few thousand men or a score of warships may have reactions which affect a front half the world away and a battle between millions of men.

While the Battle of Britain raged in the skies over England the whole world looked, listened, heard the broadcasts or read the newspapers in much the same way as we used to listen to the round-by-round commentary on a heavy-weight contest, or read from edition to special edition the reports of a Test Match. The experts knew then how much hung on that battle; but in America, in our own Dominions, throughout the world, not one in a thousand had the faintest under-

strips of beach no longer than the Brighton promenade. There were sea battles fought at Midway and the Coral Sea which seemed isolated from all the other fronts. Yet if the Allies had not succeeded in checking and holding the Japs in those distant Pacific seas the Germans might today have been in Stalingrad and the Caucasian oil-fields, or we might have been suffering in England worse bombing raids than ever we have known.

We know that there is a neutrality pact between Japan and Russia; and we also know well that Japan would (or will) break that pact the moment it pays her to. Japan wanted that pact until she could at least establish full control of all the islands down to Australia, if not go to the length of an Australian invasion. If Australia could have been blocked off, and the islands north of it

which may some day and in some way prove of value in the war. But the fact that America has firmly gripped her Aleutian base and denied to Japan more than the merest toe-hold on the tip of the island chain, has played an important part in that same need for Japan to abstain from any attack on Russia. The bringing into use of the Alaskan Highway well ahead of programme has also helped.

Progress in North Africa

The Allies' occupation of French North Africa had an immediately helpful result for Russia, because the Germans were forced to bring a mass of aircraft from Russia to attack our African convoys and to ferry troops across to Tunisia. Now against the danger of an Allied attack from Africa on " the soft under-belly of the Axis " Germany has had to stretch and strain her military strength to garrison and fortify the whole length of the North Mediterranean shores. This could only be done by weakening the Russian front, or by using reserves required for it.

The fighting now going on to take Bizerta and Tunis will have repercussions which will vibrate through Russia, India, Burma and China. When we have taken those two bases and established airfields round the coast of Tunis, the Allies will have a short convoy route under the umbrella of air fighter protection along the Mediterranean to Egypt and Syria. This means the ability to transport men and munitions rapidly to Russia and India and Persia, so blocking any attempt at junction between German and Japanese forces and building up strength to attack Burma, free the Burma Road, and thus bring into action millions of Chinese troops now almost immobilized by lack of equipment.

Even if such a happy result cannot be accomplished for months or years, the mere threat of it should hold Japan back from that attack on Russia, and in time may easily lead to the Chinese sweeping clear enough of their coast to establish fleets of bombers to strike at the heart of Japan itself.

Malta's Magnificent Defence

The gallant and unswerving years-long defence of Malta has excited the admiration of the world; we have all thrilled to the stories of the convoys fighting a way through with vitally necessary oil and supplies. But it is quite wrong to suppose the Battle of Malta is only a stirring episode, little (or not at all) likely to affect the broad results of the war. The " unsinkable aircraft-carrier " has been of the highest importance in its interference with Axis transport across the Mediterranean during the fighting in Libya and Egypt. Its importance will continue, or even increase, when we begin to move our convoys through the Mediterranean.

Fortunately for us, all these apparently separate and disconnected actions on far-apart fronts have been deliberately planned and carried out as a strategic whole. The collapse of France and the first overwhelming success of the Japs must have thrown all previously conceived strategy of the Allies in the fire. But ever since we touched bottom in our losses—as I believe we did touch bottom when America lost a fleet at Pearl Harbour, her Pacific bases and the Philippines; we lost Malaya and Burma; the Dutch lost Java and the East Indies; and the Russians were hurled back hundreds of miles—it is now becoming evident that new and bold strategic plans were drawn up. Now they are being carried into effect, and the scattered jigsaw puzzle pieces are being collected and fitted together in an interlocking world-wide front.

MALTESE CHILDREN, undaunted by savage and prolonged Axis air attacks, are here seen recounting their experiences to a group of sailors on a quayside. Large supplies of bombs for the valiant island's counter-offensive were unloaded shortly before Christmas from a convoy that ran the gauntlet of the Mediterranean front line.

Photo, British Official : Crown Copyright

standing that the fate of all mankind for generations to come hung on the issue of the battle.

It is only since that we have learned from Crete what can be done with airborne troops after the destruction of a defending air force and the completion of the occupation of its aerodromes. Now we do begin to understand how airborne Germans might have seized a bridgehead on our shores and rushed tanks and guns across the Channel, even as is now being done from Italy into Tunisia.

The Battle of Britain was an outstanding and exceptional example of how every battle-front on land and sea depended on a single front and the outcome of one battle. But an understanding of this has not been enough to bring full realization of how closely inter-locked are all the world war fronts of today, and of how success or failure of far distant and at the moment apparently unimportant battles may affect many or all other fronts.

In New Guinea and the Solomons men who can be numbered in tens compared with the thousands on the Russian front have been fighting for months to take and hold an air-field and circle of surrounding jungle or a few

built into a strong wall of sea and air bases against possible Australian-American attack, Japan would have deemed it safe to play her usual stab-in-the-back act against Russia. Russia, knowing this, had to keep a tremendous force along her Far Eastern front.

Japan on the Defensive

But Japan has failed to secure her island chain of protection, and indeed must now face the possibility of a leap-frog series of assaults from island to island under land-based air fighter protection. Consequently, Russia was reasonably free to bring reinforcements from the Far East to launch those shattering blows from which the Germans are now reeling. The Luftwaffe has needed all its strength in Russia, and has had nothing to spare for the bombing of Britain, as it might have had last autumn and this winter if the Germans had been able to dig themselves into " hedgehog " positions in Russia.

The Aleutian Islands have not had much of the limelight up to now, and the completion of the Alaskan Highway (*see page 332*) is vaguely regarded as a great engineering feat

Dread Winter Reigns in Russia

With January's coming the Russian winter approaches its bitter climax, so that mobility is reduced to a minimum. But to this problem, as to so many another, the Red Army has found the solution. " Every infantryman must be a skier." is now the slogan. Top, a patrol of Russian ski-troopers on the Leningrad front. Below, a number of Nazi tanks captured on the same front have been repaired, and are here seen moving into action against their former owners.

Ghostly Warriors in a World of White

Although the weather has been indescribably cruel, the Russian armies have continued their gigantic offensives. In these actions a big part is played by specially-trained ski-soldiers, a detachment of whom—parachute troops, camouflaged in white and armed with tommy-guns—is seen in (1). Tremendous losses have been inflicted on Hitler's armies, both in men and material : 2, a Nazi tank photographed at the moment of touching off a mine in the Voronezh area.

Photos, Br
U.S.S.R. C

Arctic Conditions on the Eastern Front

Over snowbound ground, in and out of the icicle-festooned trees of the gloomy Russian forest, German troops (3) plod wearily and warily along, garbed in overalls which once were white so as to make them invisible to the snipers of the Red Army.   In (4), a photo taken on the Stalingrad front, Red Army sappers are clearing a road of mines.   As the Germans retreat they leave behind them vast quantities of war material ; here (5) are some of a batch of 150 Nazi motor-cycles.

War in Russia's Gloomy Forests

Photos,· Associated Press, Planet News

But for the " dzots " Hitler's invasion of Russia would have ended ere now in disaster. What, then, is a dzot ? The word is formed from the initials of the Russian words for " wood earth firing point."   That the name is apt will be apparent from our photo (top) of one of them in a forest. Below, a Russian casualty clearing station just behind the line ; a wounded soldier of the Red Army is receiving attention from a medical orderly and one of that brave regiment of women, the Soviet nurses.

VIEWS & REVIEWS

Of Vital War Books

by Hamilton Fyfe

WHEN you read now and then about the guerilla war that is being carried on against the Nazis in the mountains of Serbia, and about the leader of the brave men who are fighting for their country's independence and freedom, how do you picture this General Mihailovich to yourself?

With some knowledge of Balkan *comitadjis*, as the bands of turbulent mountaineers who have disturbed the region called Macedonia for so many years are called, I supposed him to be a man of tough, even ruffianly appearance—not young by any means, full of courage, but not very brainy. I was surprised to discover from the photograph of him in George Sava's new book, The Chetniks of Yugoslavia (Faber, 10s.), that he has a face in which intellect as well as character are plainly discernible. This is how the London doctor (born Russian, now British) who calls himself for literary purposes Sava, describes the General :

A man in the late forties, of medium height and with striking eyes of a bright mountain-flower blue, and fairish curly hair. But his physical details were dominated by his presence. It was that of the born natural leader. Here was a man, one said at once, in whom one could place one's entire faith, a man to die for. Yet there was nothing aloof about him ... He put no gulf between himself and us, such as an officer puts between himself and his men and even more so between himself and irregulars.

" Irregulars " though they are, these Yugoslavs know more about the sort of warfare that is going on in the region between their country and Montenegro, Albania and Greece, than any of the scientifically-trained German staff officers. Mihailovich had a training of that kind himself. He was in the army, served as a lieutenant in 1914-15, then as military attaché in Sofia and Prague. He had a command in 1941, but found it impossible to stand up against the enemy's tanks and artillery with the poor equipment he was given. When the order to capitulate reached him, he had only a few battalions of Chetniks left. With them he moved into the mountains, ignoring the instruction to surrender, resolved to " carry on the war to the victorious conclusion and show that Serbia still lives."

Now, who are the Chetniks? They do not seem to be a race or a tribe. The term is used apparently to describe people who live in a certain part of the wild country on the Yugoslav border. Anyway, they are showing the Germans what the spirit of Yugoslavia is.

Their task was to collect together the scattered fragments of the army which refused to surrender, so that they might reform to make a new fighting force in the heart of the land . . . From all parts peasants came to the centres of resistance, bringing with them old guns and hunting-rifles, some of them muzzle-loaders complete with ramrod and powder-horn. Trains of mules dragged small century-old cannon, for which no ammunition could be procured. And against these weapons the Germans used all the resources of a modern army. They bombed and machine-gunned from the air. Their heavy tanks lumbered about.

But it must have seemed to them that for every one Yugoslav they crushed, two more made their appearance. During one month the Chetniks killed 12,000 Nazis, blew up 200 bridges, set fire to between three and four hundred petrol, ammunition, and store dumps, wrecked seventeen trains. They made the Germans jumpy, never knowing where they would strike next or what they would do.

Their methods were ingenious. One was to make thermometers with a very powerful explosive in them, and put them up in railway stations, public buildings or hotels-frequented by German officers. No one took much notice of them until they went off. The Italians were particularly scared. It was said they would not for months let thermometers be put into their mouths in hospital for fear they might be blown up !

THE Chetniks of Yugoslavia

When an Alpine regiment, trained in the highlands of Bavaria, was sent against them, the Chetniks showed them they were up against men who knew every crag and cranny on the barren heights. They were decoyed up to a mountain from which there were only two ways down—one the road they used, which was promptly closed behind them, and a sheer abyss of 2,000 feet. None of that regiment escaped.

THERE is a rough humour about the Chetniks. They captured eighty Germans by derailing a train loaded with ammunition. What should be done with them ? Mihailovich asked. " We won't hang them for the crimes they have committed on our people. We must teach them a lesson. We've got to frighten these bullies. We'll pull their trousers down and write on their backsides, ' Show yourselves to the garrison of Belgrade. The next we capture we shoot.' "

They actually did that, tattooing the message with an indelible vegetable dye, putting the prisoners into coffins, loading the coffins on wagons, and driving the wagons into the heart of the capital. They were taken to the doors of the German headquarters ; there the drivers decamped. In a few minutes the men in the coffins began to wriggle, then to put their heads up. Their comrades came out and released them. " Fear struck deep into their hearts. Many of these soldiers, no more than boys, turned pale and began to cast hurried glances about them, while they fingered their triggers nervously."

With the Chetniks are a number of British soldiers who made their way into the mountains after the disastrous end of the campaign in Greece in the spring of 1941. They taught their hosts how to use anti-tank rifles and other modern weapons ; and they repaired tanks captured from the enemy, which the Serbians had not been able to do anything with. Their chief difficulty was getting accustomed to the food and to the small amount of it. But in villages where there were pigs and poultry they managed to " initiate the Serbs into their favourite breakfast dish, eggs and bacon."

THAT the Germans would like very much to keep their grip, which is growing weaker, on Yugoslavia is obvious. It is a country of vast potential riches. It has, for instance, the largest deposits in Europe of bauxite, which is necessary to the making of aluminium for aircraft construction. It has zinc and iron ore, lead, silver and marble; immense forests, enormous numbers of pigs and sheep.

Little has been done to develop these possible sources of wealth. The great mass of the people are without any kind of formal education. Their rulers have been more anxious to make themselves prosperous than to bring prosperity to the nation. Large districts are inhabited by people who have scarcely advanced in the arts and ideas of civilization during the last two thousand years. The Nazis do not allow that they have " any value as human beings," they are " so much cattle, ripe for exploitation."

After the War some federation of the Balkans must be formed for mutual protection. So far the system there has been "all against all." I remember being one autumn in a little town near which are the frontiers of Bulgaria, Rumania and Yugoslavia. I made friends with a Russian who had been an admiral in the Tsar's Navy and was now by an odd turn of fortune commanding a gang of desperadoes who carried hand grenades in their pockets and lived on the country like bandits—though they didn't like being called bandits. They called themselves patriots.

I have many amusing recollections of them. One is of a supper-party the admiral gave, at which performed an orchestra of three musicians looking, I thought, rather nervous. When after supper the *comitadjis* began firing their revolvers at the ceiling and the pictures on the walls, I understood why. I got my feet up on the seat of my chair when the man next to me fired into the floor, and I left soon afterwards. But I was glad of the experience, for it showed me what sort of people prevented the Balkans from becoming civilized. Subjected to the discipline of an ordered, peaceful society, these desperadoes would have been fine fellows. Perhaps if Gen. Draza Mihailovich comes through and leads his countrymen in peace as boldly and cleverly as he is leading them in war, we may see such a society.

YUGOSLAV PATRIOTS have done much to frustrate Axis plans for the subjection of their country and its incorporation in the Hitlerite system. This photo shows members of a guerilla band being marched away after having been captured.   PAGE 499   *Photo, New York Times Photos*

Meet Some of Norway's Young Fighter Pilots

From time to time HENRY BAERLEIN has contributed to these pages articles descriptive of the Allied contingents who have found in Britain a home from home and a base from which they may sally forth to do battle with the common foe. In this article we are told something of the Norwegian airmen who have arrived from across the North Sea to fight side by side with the R.A.F.

RECENTLY I have visited Norwegian fighter pilots at a camp in this country. They are under the famous Riiser-Larsen, the first man to sail in a dirigible over the North Pole, after having tried with Amundsen to reach it by plane. Riiser-Larsen is one of the world's most renowned airmen, who received his flying training in England during the last war; he has the physical frame which the Nazis call "Nordic," and as a rule is a huge, silent Norseman. But he can on occasion talk, as when he alludes to "Little Norway," the camp in Canada which he helped to establish. "It took us barely three months to get going down there. The air-field with its pea-green huts was soon finished with the help of local labour. It is the most up-to-date thing anyone can imagine, right down to the camp kitchen. Training machines were available just as soon as we needed them, for our Government had ordered them a long time beforehand. And everything for the Norwegian armed forces is paid for by Norwegian money." That is a matter of which all the Norwegians are rightly proud.

'Neither Quislings nor Spongers'

It may be thought that this has nothing to do with the Norwegian Air Force. But one cannot be for long with these happy-go-lucky, broad-shouldered Norse airmen and be unaware of the psychological effect produced by the knowledge that they are paying their way. "We are neither a race of Quislings nor a race of spongers," said one of them.

They had various adventures in their travels from stricken Norway to "Little Norway." For instance, one to whom I talked had been an airman in his country's small pre-War force. At that time they had at their disposal Glosters from England and Focke-Wulfs which were built under licence in Norway. When the Germans suddenly invaded Norway there was as much resistance as was humanly possible. Some of the pilots developed, as one of them told me, a new technique of doing without bomb-sights—for the very good reason that they had to. After the capitulation of the country they obeyed the voice of King Haakon on the radio and made their way to Sweden, where they were interned, as a matter of form, for a few days. Subsequently they obtained visas and departed for Moscow, where they were splendidly treated, and then they went via Japan to America. There they were joined by many young Norwegians who had managed to get away in fishing-boats to Britain and thence to Canada.

ONE sturdy fellow said that people looked down their noses at him because he had never liked to kill birds, but he had no objection at all to killing Germans. And now this young man has had his heart's desire, for he takes part in hedge-hopping expeditions over France, Belgium and Holland.

"It made me laugh a lot," he said, "when I came out of a cloud in Belgium the other day and shot up a number of German soldiers who were on the roof of a barrack building."

"Oh, well," said a friend of his, "there's room for some laughter even in Norway nowadays. I was at home for fifteen months after the Germans had arrived, and they told us they were only resting on the way to England. They used to say that Britain would fall to them like a piece of cake. We have the same expression in our language,

et stykke kake. At first they didn't listen much to the B.B.C., but when I left—like many others, in a fishing-boat—they not only were listening but were believing what the B.B.C. told them."

To bring the conversation back to matters of the air I mentioned Dieppe, where (I had been told by others) the Norwegians did particularly well. The two fighter squadrons of the Royal Norwegian Air Force which took part in the raid accounted for 14 machines definitely destroyed, four probably destroyed and 13 damaged, while the Norwegians lost two airmen. Their most successful pilot was one, aged 19, from Oslo, who destroyed two German aircraft and probably a third.

"I was luckily among the first (he said) to meet the Germans in the air. I saw a Focke-Wulf 190 tailing a Spitfire. I warned the pilot by radio, but the German was too quick and he shot the Spitfire down. His victory was short-lived, as a

NORWEGIAN 'WRENS' attached to a Norwegian naval squadron are learning to handle and fire rifles as part of their training at a naval depot in England. *Photo, L.N.A.*

few moments later I sent him spinning through the air to crash 200 yards from where the Spitfire had fallen. Then I saw three more Focke-Wulfs which were coming in to attack me, so I turned on them, damaging one, which was later credited to me as a 'probable.' As my ammunition was now exhausted I returned home." The moment his machine was refuelled he went back into the battle zone. This time he took part in a fight with eight Dornier 217s, accounting for one of the six which were shot down.

One of the Norwegian pilots told me that he had been a mechanic for six months. He had gone with his parents to the United States as a small boy, and before the States were officially in the War he had gone across the frontier to Canada and been accepted in "Little Norway." His special task has been to attack shipping; and according to him it is not too difficult to hit a ship even when you are going at some 350 miles an hour.

"To be in those sweeps over France, Belgium and Holland (he said) is very exciting and great fun. It is more like a sport than anything else. The other day when I was escorting Flying Fortresses some ack-ack exploded not far underneath me and my machine bumped 25 to 50 feet. But one gets used to that kind of thing. When I said that our job is sport I should have added that, like real sportsmen, we have rules that we

keep. For instance, when we make for a train we are careful to hit the engine only, if there is any fear that civilians are in the compartments."

Some of these airmen have had a trying time in getting across to Britain in small ships of every kind.

"I could stand it no longer in Norway (said one of them, a corporal), so I left my wife to look after my garage, where I had been obliged to repair German cars. They told us at first that they had come to protect us from the terrible British onslaught. We didn't answer that sort of thing, but merely looked at them, and it works very well. It was some time before five of us could get hold of a little boat, and as we put to sea it was fairly rough, but there were no German planes about and we were picked up by a patrol-boat with Scottish people on board. How nice they were to us, and how white was the bread they gave us!"

One husky young man told me that he and some friends of his found a lifeboat, rigged a sail, and made for the open sea, with hardly any provisions, a meagre supply of water, and always the anxiety that they would be spotted by German patrols and shot at sight.

"One morning (he said) we saw a tiny speck on the horizon. It turned out to be a British destroyer. Never shall I forget how we danced with joy in our cockle-shell of a boat; it nearly turned over. This meant England, liberty and—what we hoped for most and were now likely to get—revenge."

Two of the company had to thank the skill of a cook, for when some German airmen left their plane at a certain place in the south-west of Norway and sat for a longish time enjoying an excellent meal, these two young men seized the opportunity and the plane, in which they reached Britain without any incident. There probably was some incident when the Germans had to report to their superiors, but that is a matter of surmise.

ANOTHER man I met was at the time of the German invasion of his Motherland a truck-driver in western Canada, at a place where all the people were of Norwegian origin. Even the storekeeper, he mentioned, was Norwegian; but the children were learning English at school and the older folk could talk it pretty well. Among themselves they used Norwegian, but if other people were around they spoke English. "We didn't want to offend a fellow," said the ex-truck-driver, "if we could help it, and it is kind of nasty hearing a language you can't understand. I had applied for naturalization, but when the War broke out I went to the Norwegian consul, and that was the first step to my getting to the camp of 'Little Norway.'"

"When you go back to Canada after the War," I said, "back to your truck . . ."

Hedge-hopping over Europe

His rather stern face dissolved into smiles. "I shall be able to tell them," he said, "about a different sort of driving a machine. For example, hedge-hopping over in France and Belgium. One day I was told to look for some shipping near Ostend, but there was none, so I went on into a cloud and then came down; and while I was hedge-hopping I came on to a canal and got some German barges, and ten minutes after that there was a town where they started shooting at me, but my friend—we were in sections of twos—was a little hit in the tail, not much, and I not at all. So it goes on day by day, and I don't just know whether I'd like it to go on for ever. But I dare say I'll get used to my truck again when we've won this war and peace returns to the world."

Norway's Sons Never, Never Will Be Slaves

Photos, Norwegian Official

FREE NORWEGIAN FORCES in the British Isles are greatly contributing to the cause of the United Nations. Ever since June 7, 1940—the day that King Haakon and his Government sailed to England, there to continue the struggle against the Germans—the ranks of the Norwegian Army, Navy and Air Force serving with the Allies have been steadily increasing. In the air, redoubtable squadrons are ceaselessly on the offensive. Top left, members of the ground staff serving with a Norwegian fighter squadron in the North of England. Above, amid scenes that recall the snowclad hillsides of his native country, this Norwegian soldier practises musketry against the day when he will help to throw out the enemy from his homeland.

THE ROYAL NORWEGIAN NAVY is now the fourth largest of the Allied fleets. The majority of Norway's warships and other vessels were sunk in resisting the German invasion of 1940, but since that date rebuilding has been going on apace, and today this new fleet comprises some 5 destroyers, 4 corvettes, submarines, 36 minesweepers, 10 smaller fighting ships and 2 harbour service vessels. Many thousands of Norwegians (numbers of whom escaped after the German occupation of their country) are serving in the R.N.N., which has its own training centres in Britain and Canada. The photograph above was taken aboard a Norwegian corvette escorting an Atlantic convoy. An enemy submarine has been located, and preparations are being made for depth charging. Right, a Norwegian ski-ing patrol is shown putting up a tent at one of the training camps established in Scotland.

Photos, Norwegian Official

THE WAR IN THE AIR

by Capt. Norman Macmillan, M.C., A.F.C.

Three pointers to United Nations' supremacy in 1943 are: (1) Britain now has numerical superiority in aircraft over Germany and Italy combined; (2) Russia has numerical superiority in aircraft on the eastern front; (3) the United States built 48,000 warplanes in 1942, thereby exceeding the combined production of Germany, Italy and Japan.

Supplies have reached China by air since the Japanese closed the Burma Road, but the British southward move into Burma from India is the first sign of territorial redressment of Chinese isolation from the increasing supplies coming off the production lines in Britain and America. British and American aircraft execute combined operations against the Japanese in Burma, some of the latter from Chinese territory.

Now is the time to press forward in that area, for as summer approaches the heat becomes oppressive; and when the monsoon breaks the humidity becomes a torment, and minor ailments, such as prickly heat and dobi's rash, torture one's skin. To aircrews, subjected to differing temperatures and pressures when flying at varying altitudes, any skin irritation becomes doubly noticeable, especially after alighting from a flight. Heat on the ground feels more oppressive after the relative coolness of the upper air. And although airframes, engines and airscrews are vastly superior to those we used in the days when I was the first pilot to cross India in the monsoon, crews still have to fight their way through storms of wind and rain, and thick, dense clouds that come down sometimes to ground level. But the monsoon does not break until May or June (the date varies from year to year); until then air forces have the most favourable weather for operations.

Wellingtons and Blenheims concentrated largely on attacking Japanese air-fields in Burma. Many are reclaimed from rice-fields; their construction and maintenance demand heavy and constant coolie labour for draining, levelling, road-making, and the construction of shelters. R.A.F. bombs churn up parts of the surface to the consistency of paddy-fields and hamper the operations of the Japanese army air force. Bombers have been escorted by Hurricanes. Sometimes fighters have made the attacks.

Calcutta was raided by Japanese bombers for the first time on December 20, 1942. Other raids were made on December 22, during the night of December 22–23, and on Christmas Eve. About nine tons of bombs were dropped in the four raids—a light weight judged by British standards. The raiders were met by anti-aircraft gunfire and night fighters; one bomber was shot down by night fighters on Christmas Eve. In the first three raids 25 persons were killed and fewer than 100 injured. There were only three Japanese aircraft in the third raid; two were damaged by night fighters.

Allied air pressure has been exerted against the Japanese on their southern perimeter in the Solomons (Guadalcanal and New Georgia) and in Papua where the yellow-skinned soldiers were driven back to a small beach-head; Japanese attempts to land reinforcements by sea transport and parachute were defeated, largely by air power.

Bombs by Parachute

When bombing this restricted beach-head American bombers have used parachute bombs to ensure accuracy. These bombs must not be confused with land-mines dropped by the Luftwaffe on British cities. The land-mine, a special bomb containing a high explosive content, is dropped by parachute so that it will explode on or slightly above the surface to secure the maximum blast effect. The parachute bombs used by the Americans are ordinary bombs dropped from a very low height. The parachute checks the forward speed of the bomb, thus causing it to fall upon the object over which the bomber flew at the instant of release; during the bomb's fall the aeroplane flies on and is out of the danger area when the bomb explodes. The R.A.F. use the delayed-action bomb to achieve similar safety. Advantages of the parachute bomb are that it makes sighting easy—release when over the objective—and prevents the bomb from bouncing, as often happens when a delayed-action bomb is released from a low level; some of the latter have bounced over three rows of houses before exploding. I have known one bounce off a field and explode at about 50 feet, almost destroying the Messerschmitt 109E that dropped it.

It is rather surprising that the American parachute bomb was not used earlier in this war. The American Armament Corporation tried to interest London in it about 1937–8. I was privileged to see a very hush-hush film of the bomb in action on a bombing range at that time. The R.A.F. did not take it up. Now the Americans are using it, apparently with success, in Papua.

On the northern horn of the Japanese perimeter American bombers have again attacked Japanese ships. On December 30 two cargo boats were bombed in Kiska Harbour with uncertain results. The American bombers and escort of twin-boom Lightning fighters were intercepted by Zero floatplane fighters; one bomber, two Lightnings and one Zero were shot down in the resulting fight. Next day American medium bombers scored three hits on one ship and two on another and lost no aircraft. Weather plays a large part in the results of air operations in the Aleutians.

On Christmas Eve 1942 the largest mass heavy-bomber raid yet made in the Pacific zone was delivered by U.S. Army A.F. four-engined aircraft (probably Fortresses and or Liberators) against Japanese-occupied Wake Island (and adjacent Peale Island), former American possession and part of the air route island chain from San Francisco to Hong Kong. This was the third air assault on Wake Island. More than 75,000 lb. of bombs were dropped. All the bombers returned, presumably to Midway Island 1,200 miles distant, or to Honolulu 2,000 miles away.

In their full-scale counter-offensive the Russians have employed aircraft extensively, both with the Red Army and the Black Sea Fleet air arm. Parachute troops dropped from transport planes on a German-occupied airfield in the dark and threw the enemy into confusion, after a bomb attack by heavy bombers and Stormoviks. Russian air superiority makes it impossible for the Luftwaffe to withdraw many aircraft for other fronts. German aircraft losses in Russia, apart from accidents, are at the rate of between 5,000 and 10,000 a year.

Activity in the Mediterranean

Following Axis evacuation of Nofilia on December 18, 1942, Allied air pressure in Libya was directed around Sultan on December 20, and against Hon airfield next day. Sirte fell to the 8th Army on Christmas Day.

Meanwhile, Malta, supplied by convoys, increased its value as an air base. December 1942 saw Malta's heaviest air offensive, bombing Tunis port with 4,000-lb. bombs (Wellingtons), sinking two ships in a convoy of four off Sicily with "tin-fish" (Albacores), and bombing Sicilian aerodromes.

In North Africa from November 8 to December 27 the Allies destroyed 277 enemy aircraft for a loss of 114.

On December 20, 1942, Fortresses and Liberators attacked the German-occupied base at Romilly-sur-Seine, and shot down 46 German fighters for a loss of six bombers. On December 30 they attacked the submarine pens in Lorient.

Bomber Command raided North-West Germany on December 17, Duisburg on December 20, and Munich on December 21, losing 18, 11, and 12 aircraft on the three raids.

NORTH AFRICAN AIRFIELDS, taken over by the Anglo-American forces in Morocco and Algeria, have provided the Allied airmen with excellent bases from which to launch intensive air war against the Axis. Nevertheless, new ones have to be constructed, and this photograph shows men of the Royal Engineers laying a portable metal runway.

Photo, British Official Crown Copyright

America Guards the Sky Above Midway

AMERICA'S NAVAL BASE IN MID-PACIFIC, the little island of Midway, was first raided by the Japanese on Dec. 8, 1941. The U.S. garrison put up a determined resistance and held out successfully. On June 4, 1942 the enemy launched a full-scale attack and suffered crippling air and naval losses. This photo shows U.S. Douglas Dauntless dive-bombers maintaining a vigilant watch around Midway's shores. From Pearl Harbour in Hawaii to Midway is about 1200 miles.

Photo, Keystone

Nazi Planes 'Under New Management' in Libya

CAPTURED GERMAN AIRCRAFT, a large number of which fell into Allied hands in Libya, were made serviceable, whenever possible, and given test flights. 1, This signboard, propped against a re-painted JU 87D, aptly sums up the situation. 2, "Writing-off" a swastika to be replaced by R.A.F. markings. 3, Bearing R.A.F. roundels, this repaired ME 109 takes off on its test flight. 4, Heavy bombs on sleds abandoned by the enemy at Benina airfield, near Benghazi.

Photos. British Official: Crown Copyright

Britain's 'Crusaders' in Action in North Africa

CRUSADER TANKS, greatly contributing to our Libyan victory, are being used with deadly effect in Tunisia. 1, Tank men of the 1st Army read their mail during a lull in operations. 2, The Fighting French have formed an armoured unit known as Fighting French Flying Column No. 1, which works with a British Armoured Brigade; men of this column are here shown boarding a Crusader. 3, British workers who helped to build Crusaders discuss technical details over a model with a major of the 8th Army. The Crusader is a 15-ton tank, now armed with a 6-pounder gun, and has a speed of 30 m.p.h. 4, Crusaders go into action in Libya.

Photos, British Official : Crown Copyright

THE HOME FRONT

by E. Royston Pike

WHO is Private Tom Snooks? He is the "ordinary man," explained Lord Nathan to the House of Lords in a debate on post-war reconstruction on Dec. 16, 1942. He is, of course, a soldier; his wife is evacuated and is doing part-time war work, his daughter is in munitions, his son is an aircraftman, and his two youngsters have been evacuated to Devonshire. The house in which he and his family lived and the little shop which provided them with a livelihood have been bombed. And Tom Snooks, like Rosa Dartle, "wants to know."

Some of the airy generalizations about reconstruction, said Lord Nathan, are like an escapist's paradise.

"What the ordinary man—Tom Snooks—wants to know is what is going to happen to him after the war—to him, his family, and his job. Tom Snooks is a private just now, but he wants to get back to lead an ordinary family life. The first aim of reconstruction is to give Snooks independence for himself and security for his family. That is all the aim of Democracy. We must have a housing policy to give Snooks a home; a full-time employment policy to keep all the Snookses employed practically all the time; an education policy for his children; and a policy to bring Snooks and his scattered family all back together again. Snooks has fought for this: he expects this, and if he does not get it there will be trouble. For myself, I affirm a passionate faith in the Snookses of this country. It is Snooks's wants and needs which are the real war aim."

Revolution in Finance

ON the same day there was a debate in the House of Commons on war finance. It was opened by Mr. Pethick-Lawrence, one of Labour's financial experts, with a review of the financial revolution of the last two or three decades.

This revolution he attributed to (1) the fact that the gold standard is not only dead but damned; (2) the State has regained supremacy over currency; (3) the volume of credit, though nominally controlled by the banks, is, as Mr. McKenna recently pointed out, decided by Government policy; (4) the price of credit, both long and short, although apparently arrived at by mutual bargaining, is in reality dictated by the Government; (5) the general level of prices, including the cost of living, is today regulated by the Government; and (6) it has been discovered that that which was economically possible cannot be financially impossible. "It is still true that we have got to cut our coat according to our cloth, but the cloth is an economic cloth and not a financial cloth as it used to be thought."

On the whole, Mr. Pethick-Lawrence was optimistic: "I am not despondent about the position after the War."

If we can avoid the extremes of inflation and deflation, then, with the power of production freed from the restricting bed of Procrustes imposed upon it by the gold standard, and with a wise national policy in foreign, imperial, and domestic affairs, we should be able to have full employment and use to the utmost the knowledge and technique acquired during the twentieth century. If, coupled with this, we had a more equitable distribution of wealth, he saw no reason why, a few years after the War, we should not be able to double our pre-war output and reach a national income of £10,000,000,000 instead of the £5,000,000,000 before the War. On that basis, with the banishment of want and idleness and with a reducing burden of taxation, we could build up a community of free and healthy men and women in a prosperity hitherto unknown.

REPLYING to the debate, Sir Kingsley Wood, Chancellor of the Exchequer, revealed that in the first three years of the War 42 per cent of the total expenditure was met out of revenue, and for the current financial year 50 per cent would be met in this way. This war is being fought on a much more economical basis than the last; loans, exclusive of the floating debt, have cost only 2½ per cent as compared with 5 per cent in 1914 to 1917. The gross cost to the taxpayer of borrowing a given sum has been one-third of what it was in the last war. The "heavy and painful" demands which have been imposed have a double purpose of keeping borrowing to a minimum and reducing the increase in purchasing power which, if given free play, would produce serious inflation.

One of the most striking facts of financial history, the Chancellor of the Exchequer went on, has been the universal acceptance of the burdens of war taxation.

"We find that some 9,500,000 black - coat workers and others with small incomes have made a contribution of some £270,000,000 per annum in order that we may achieve victory." The result of the National Savings campaign in the last three years has also been most remarkable. "It has yielded £4,600,000,000 in all, an average of £30,000,000 a week since the beginning of the War. The total is made up of £2,900,000,000 from large market securities and £1,700,000,000 from small savings." Sir Kingsley Wood described this as a monumental corporate effort which would have tremendous social consequences in the future. "It is a striking fact that one-third of the population of the country now hold Savings Certificates."

But it may be doubted whether, the Chancellor was altogether pleased with the spectacle of Christmas week, when the people's spending was reported to be breaking all records. This was evidenced by the tremendous number of £1 and 10s. currency notes that were required to be put into circulation. During the last five weeks of 1942 over £53,000,000 worth of notes were put into circulation, bringing the total number of notes issued to the new high record of over £923,000,000. Only during the Munich crisis in 1938 and in the fortnight before the outbreak of war were there so many new currency notes demanded by the public from the banks and post offices.

'SAFETY HAT' for women factory workers—the winning design in a £50 competition organized by Rootes of Piccadilly, to find a hat which women workers would wear. Of brown linen and netting, it protects the hair from machinery, while the peak obviates glare. Last year there were 179 scalping accidents in British factories. *Photo, G.P.U.*

AT the end of 1939 there were £555,000,000 in circulation; three years later, in Dec. 1942, the figure had grown by nearly £400 millions. In large measure this huge increase has been made necessary by the tremendous increase in employment. There are more people "gainfully employed" in this country than ever before in our history. Quite apart from the men and women in the Services, there are at least 18,000,000 men and women, youths and girls, working in civilian jobs. Unemployment has dropped to a mere fraction of what it was in the years between the Wars. From 1919 to 1939 there was never a year when there were fewer than a million registered unemployed, but the latest return of the Ministry of Labour showed that there were fewer than 95,000 persons wholly unemployed in Great Britain and Northern Ireland. Thus for every worker receiving unemployment benefit there are 182 in employment. And what with wage increases and overtime their pay envelopes usually contain more money than three years ago.

Millions of New Coins

NOT only notes but coins are in big demand at the present time, affording yet further evidence of bumper employment among those classes of the community who receive their pay weekly in cash. Since the beginning of 1939 our metal money has increased by £20 millions, so that there is now more coinage in circulation than ever before. Yet there are reports that coins are scarce, particularly pennies. This is understandable, since in order to save 800 tons of copper a year for munitions, no new pennies have been struck since June 1940. True, many millions of pennies formerly locked up in automatic machines are now in constant circulation; but, on the other hand, millions more are immobilized in slot meters (since the gas and electricity companies are short of collectors to empty them as often as they used) or are kept in the tills of Service and civilian canteens. But the Royal Mint is not concerned overmuch. There are some 3,000,000,000 bronze coins in circulation, and 60 coppers a head of the total population *should* be enough!

THEN there is the new threepenny-bit, of which over 60 million were minted in 1941; this is now a very popular coin, doubtless because of the dwindling purchasing-power of the penny. The War is responsible for the increased number of halfpennies and farthings that have been struck: think of the 1½d. minimum fare on London's transport and the odd farthings that appear in so many prices as a result of the Purchase Tax and the various rationing schemes. And another coin that owes much of its popularity to wartime needs is the two-shilling piece or florin: 24 million were issued in 1941.

TWO OF THE 18 MILLION. Never have there been so many people at work in Britain as now. Thousands of men and women have been drafted from less essential work into the armament factories. Above, Eileen Justice, aged 17, formerly a clerk, learns while she works beside her father at a London training centre for munition workers. *Photo, G.P.U.*

Guns & More Guns for Britain's Armies Overseas

IN A ROYAL ORDNANCE DEPOT, one of many now functioning in Britain, weapons of all calibres are being turned out for shipment overseas. These photographs were taken in the armaments section of one R.O. factory. Top left, welder at work in the machine-shop. All types of equipment are examined, stripped down, tested, built up again and crated for dispatch. Top right, A.T.S. girls getting ready 3·7 A.A. guns for breaking down. Below, some of these guns being prepared for dispatch.

Photos, Central Press

On the Record by Our Roving Camera

COMBINED OPERATIONS COMMAND has a new shoulder badge (above) incorporating an eagle (to symbolize the part played by the Americans), tommy-gun and anchor. Red on a blue ground, it is worn by sailors attached to Combined Operations, naval beach commando men, Royal Marines serving with the Command, R.A.F. officers and men trained for Combined Operations duties, and all soldiers working with the Command.

MR. H. MACMILLAN, M.P., Under-Secretary for the Colonies, whose appointment to the freshly-created post of Minister Resident at Allied Headquarters in N.W. Africa was announced on Dec. 30, 1942.

MR. W. S. MORRISON, M.C., K.C., M.P., new Minister-Designate for Town and Country Planning, had been Postmaster-General from 1940. He was Minister of Agriculture from 1936 to 1939.

MR. H. G. STRAUSS, M.P., who, also on Dec. 30, 1942, was appointed Parliamentary Secretary - Designate for Town and Country Planning. He is Chairman of Scapa and a member of the National Trust Executive.

COASTGUARDS on Britain's shores are doing splendid work. In addition to their ordinary duties they watch for enemy planes, surface ships and submarines approaching the coast. Here are two stalwart members photographed in front of their post.

A.T.S. GO OVERSEAS. Britain's armies abroad are making increasing demands on the mother country, and at home the ranks of the A.T.S. are experiencing changes as the result of many members of this efficient corps having been posted overseas. Above, A.T.S. girls with their equipment are shown during an inspection parade before they leave Britain. They are part of the largest A.T.S. contingent ever sent to "an Allied theatre of war."

'POTATO PETE'S XMAS FAIR,' organized by the Ministry of Food, attracted thousands of children (and parents) to Oxford Street, London, during Christmas 1942. Opened on Dec. 15, on the bombed site of Messrs. John Lewis, the fair covered 15,000 sq. ft., and was held under a huge marquee which protected it from the weather. The Fair, which included special features such as the "Tunnel of Surprises," the "Hall of Distorting Mirrors," a cinema, "Cookery Nook," and a "Sink-a-U-boat" shy, was completed within 14 days. Right, Lord Woolton, Minister of Food, photographed with "Potato Pete" himself.

Photos. British Official: Crown Copyright; Planet News, Howard Coster, Elliott & Fry, L.N.A., Topical Press

I WAS THERE!

Our 80,000 Miles in the Triumphant Truant

Recently arrived at a base in Britain after an 80,000-mile cruise, lasting two and a half years, in the Mediterranean, Indian Ocean, and Java Sea, H.M. Submarine Truant has to her credit the sinking or damaging of more than 20 Axis ships. Something of her sensational story is told below by two of her officers.

As she came slowly alongside the depot ship she was displaying the skull-and-crossbones success flag of the submarine service. On the flag were four stars to indicate successful gun actions, and sixteen white bars—one for each ship torpedoed. Her exploits included : going into an enemy harbour on the surface, because it was too shallow to enter submerged ; getting stuck on the bottom and unable to move, while enemy destroyers steamed overhead searching for her ; running the gauntlet of Japanese destroyers when the Dutch East Indies fell ; sinking two out of three ships in a Japanese convoy: The Commanding Officer of H.M.S. Truant during all these exploits was Lt.-Commander H. A. V. Haggard, D.S.O., D.S.C., R.N., son of Admiral Sir Vernon Haggard, and a nephew of Rider Haggard, the novelist. He is 6 ft. 5 in. tall, being one of the tallest officers in the submarine service.

One of her early successes was a daylight gun action against an enemy ammunition ship which she blew to pieces. She carried out this action under fire from enemy coastal batteries on the North African coast less than half a mile away.

When the Truant was patrolling in the Adriatic she sighted an Italian convoy, crawling, as usual, up the coast within half a mile of the shore. The Truant went in to attack, and torpedoed a tanker. But she was so close inshore that, when she turned round to come out again, she grounded with only a few feet of water above her. The escorting destroyers, roused by the torpedoing, were thrashing up and down overhead.

"We sat with all our machinery shut off, keeping as quiet as we could," said Lieutenant K. S. Renshaw, D.S.O., R.N.R., torpedo officer of the submarine. "Each time a destroyer passed over us it sounded like an express train going through a station. Then,

as the sounds died away, the Captain went ahead and astern to try to dislodge us. We felt our position very much.

"If a depth charge had been dropped anywhere near us it would have finished us for certain, and we must have been clearly visible from the air. After an hour the Captain managed to get the boat away and we cleared off."

British submarines have to work close inshore in enemy waters, but the Truant actually entered an enemy harbour on the surface—on the coast of Cyrenaica, which the Germans were using to supply Rommel's Army. It was too shallow for the submarine to enter submerged, so, at dusk one evening, she surfaced just outside the entrance and steamed in. Because of the tricky entrance due to sandbanks it was impossible to make the attempt in the dark.

When she got inside she fired two torpedoes at a ship alongside the quay. Although they passed under the ship they damaged the quay. To get out again Truant had to back and reverse. The harbour was so small she could not get round in one turn. While manoeuvring, she came within a few yards of the ship she had tried to torpedo, but she had so surprised the enemy that she was able to get away without a shot being fired. One man

appeared on deck and shouted at her. Lt.-Commander Haggard shouted back, waved and disappeared into the growing darkness.

In May 1941, after nearly a year patrolling in the Mediterranean, the Truant went to the United States for refit, but she was back again on her old hunting grounds in October. Then in January 1942 she was ordered to Singapore. Before she arrived Singapore fell, and she was diverted to the Dutch East Indies. She operated from Sourabaya with Dutch submarines until the Japanese invasion. Just before the port was captured she sailed for Colombo. She had to pass through the Sunda Straits, which were heavily patrolled by Japanese destroyers. She made the passage by night and was attacked constantly. There were over half-a-dozen separate depth charge attacks, but she got through all right. From March to September she operated in the region of the Malacca Straits. One night the Japanese thought they had got her.

"The night was pitch black," said Lieutenant C. A. J. Nicoll, R.N., the First Lieutenant, "and we suddenly saw a dark object very close. A searchlight flicked on and caught us right in its glare. It completely blinded us and we did a crash dive. Depth charges started to explode round us. I counted twenty. Some of them were pretty close.

"We switched off all machinery and lay as quietly as we could. There was dead silence in the boat. After half an hour things calmed down and we were able to creep away. When we got back to port we read in the papers a Tokyo communiqué claiming to have sunk two submarines. It must have been us—both times ! "

Actually, Truant lived to sink two out of three supply ships in a Japanese convoy. She torpedoed them on a moonlight night.

Gona Beach Was Strewn With Japanese Dead

Gona, one of the Japanese strongholds in Papua, was stormed by the Australians on December 9, 1942. When the victors entered the village a horrible scene met their eyes. This grim account was cabled from New Guinea by The Times Special Correspondent the same day.

I ARRIVED at Gona in the early afternoon. There were fantastic scenes in the village. It was littered with Japanese dead in every stage of decomposition, some newly killed, others already skeletons in uniforms and helmets. The Japanese had made no

effort to bury their dead, and the stench was nauseating.

I noticed the corpse of a Japanese soldier who had pointed a rifle at his head and had then pulled the trigger with his toe. Other bodies were washed by waves on the beach. Many Japanese last night took to the water and tried to swim out to a wreck off the shore. They were betrayed by phosphorescence in the water and were picked off by our riflemen.

The western part of the village was a scene of complete devastation. There were craters made by bombs, by 25-pounder shells and mortar shells. Some Japanese trucks and Australian bicycles captured by the Japanese and one ammunition carrier were burnt out and fretted by bullets.

The buildings of the Gona mission had been razed to the ground. Japanese dead lay in craters. The tops of coconut palms had been lopped off by shells. Their bark was pitted, and the fibre was beginning to break out like horsehair from an old sofa. Only the white cross of the Gona mission remained unscathed, as if to underline this desolate scene. And behind the trunks of palms there stretched the peaceful vista of this beautiful Papuan coastline.

The Japanese had strong dug-in positions on the beach at Bast and among the roots of some huge, gnarled trees which overhang the shore. Two hundred and fifty yards from the beach there was a perimeter of out-posts well dug in and roofed, with excellent fields of fire. Communication trenches joined the various posts. It was a system of defence based on mutual support. Whenever our men attacked one post they came under fire from others. Snipers used to hide in the tops of trees. Before making an attack we would

H.M.S. TRUANT, as recounted in this page, flew the skull-and-crossbones as she came alongside her depot ship on her return home after 2½ years' absence. This photo shows a group of her officers and men proudly displaying their " victory " flag. The white bars indicate ships sunk, the stars successful fights. *Photo, British Official : Crown Copyright*

always comb the trees with Bren-guns and fire several hundred rounds into them.

What prompted the Japanese to make this desperate suicidal bid for freedom ? They had masses of rice in straw bales, plenty of ammunition, and an abundance of medical supplies and they could easily obtain water by sinking a well. Undoubtedly conditions were becoming so bad that even the Japanese could not endure them. Small wonder that they had been seen wearing gas masks.

Moreover, our encircling ring had been gradually closing in on them. Two days ago they were dive-bombed again. Yesterday 25-pounders pumped 300 shells into them and our infantry made further important gains ; our troops attacked from the east along the beach, and gained about 50 yards. Last night the Japanese garrison attempted to break through to the east. This morning in front of every post there was a pile of Japanese dead. Others lay in the long grass and scrub, armed with hand grenades. They were mopped up during the morning, and our troops secured the entire length of beach.

Even so Japanese resistance continued. A small group of wounded Japanese fought from a patch of timber 200 yards from the beach. They rejected an invitation to surrender and were killed to the last man. Only at 5 o'clock were the Australian troops on the beach joined by their fellows who had advanced through wooded country from the south, combing the undergrowth for Japanese.

Among the interesting trophies which have fallen into our hands were Samurai swords of Japanese officers and a small package containing many envelopes, each holding nail clippings, a piece of hair, and the name and address of a dead Japanese soldier. The Japanese were carrying paper notes, printed

SIGNPOST AT KOKODA, pointing in the direction of Oivi and Buna, was a welcome sight to the Allied forces when they entered Kokoda on Nov. 2, 1942. A description of the fighting round Gona, one of the last enemy strongholds in New Guinea, is given in this and the preceding page.
Photo, Sport & General

by the Japanese army, in rupees, Straits dollars, guilders, pounds, pesetas, and other currencies. Rarely has a victory been more hardly fought for. Every foot of Gona and its surroundings has been fiercely contested. Small cemeteries of Australian dead along the beach testify to the cost of victory.

which the " All Clear " was never sounded.

Some of its buildings have been destroyed and rebuilt four and five times. Because of the likelihood that there will have to be a sixth and seventh reconstruction they have not been re-erected with any idea of permanence. Such brick buildings as remained repairable have almost all been taken over by military and Government bodies. The better dwelling houses are of mud and bamboo, roofed with thatch. Tens of thousands of people are living in homes that are a patch-work of salvaged timber and matting.

I Found Both Gaiety and Gloom in Chungking

No city has suffered such continuous bombing as Chungking, yet its people can still smile. The following description is condensed from two articles contributed to The Daily Telegraph by Martin Moore, its Special Correspondent in the capital of Free China.

CHUNGKING is the gayest and gloomiest place I have ever visited. Gaiety is in the faces and bearing of the people. Gloom is in the grim, grey, shattered city, a ruined slum rising on steep cliffs above the confluence of two muddy rivers. Over Chungking hangs a leaden sky. Only twice in the past three weeks has the sun shone.

Europe can show no devastation to compare with that to be seen in Chungking. Coventry and Rotterdam have had more shattering raids, but no city has suffered such continuous punishment as China's wartime capital. It has been destroyed piecemeal, not once but several times. One of its raid alarms lasted day and night for two weeks, during

The streets were shattered with the houses, and though main thoroughfares have been repaved many are only tracks of trodden earth which turns to ankle-deep mud after a shower. The infrequent motor-buses, running on vegetable oil, are yet frequent enough to keep the windless air constantly heavy with the sickly odour of their exhaust. There are no trams and no taxis. The few cars to be

CHUNGKING, China's wartime capital and headquarters of Marshal Chiang Kai-shek, has suffered terribly from Japanese bombers. As recounted in the accompanying article, some of the city's buildings have been repeatedly rebuilt. Left, the roof of an office-block being covered with layers of bamboo. This ingenious construction lessens the impact of bombs. Right, an entrance to one of the fine air-raid shelters on the city's outskirts. These tunnels have been drilled into the solid rock of Chungking's cliffs.
Photos, Planet News

BUILT UPON ROCK, and standing at the junction of the Kia-ling-ho with the Yang-tse-Kiang, Chungking had a pre-war population of about 425,000. As told in this page, even the most savage raids by the Japanese were unable to crush Chungking's heroic spirit. Here is shown a general view of the steeply-built city.
Photo, Planet News

as well as a ventilating shaft, through which electric fans draw fresh air. Every resident in the locality has his appointed place in the tunnel, and there is a special section for passers-by or strangers. A long-range warning system gives people several hours' notice of impending attack, so there is no excuse for anyone not to go to his proper place in his own shelter.

Mr. Wu told me that while there are half-a-dozen of these huge shelters, the later policy has been to dig smaller caves accommodating 500 people. Even the smallest has two entrances, because in the early raids on Chungking debris often blocked the doors and people were imprisoned until a way could be dug through. Apart from these public shelters, most offices and Government departments have their own dugouts. Altogether there are about 700 tunnelled into the hillside.

LIKE London, Chungking has had a long respite. It is more than a year since it had its last air raid. But, though danger is not imminent, and may never come again, the A.R.P. organization with its 20,000 volunteers is kept in a state of constant readiness. At an hour's notice bakeries can be turned on to produce millions of special "iron ration" cakes in case the city's population should be confined for days on end in the shelters.

In the main street of Chungking one day I saw a man riding a bicycle—a rare treasure he was lucky to possess. He ran over a brick and the bicycle frame snapped in two. In a country where a second-hand bicycle costs the equivalent of £50 to £100 this was more than a misfortune. It was a tragedy. Yet the gathering crowd laughed—and no one laughed more heartily than the victim as he picked himself up out of the mud.

That scene seemed to typify the new China. Devastation and want and war hang over her like Chungking's unlifting cloud, but underneath she is smiling.

seen belong to Government officials or foreign diplomats.

Most people walk. The alternative is some aged rickshaw, its parts tied together with bits of string and wire. Rickshaws are expensive, and a few fares a day enable a coolie to earn as much as a university professor. Many of Chungking's roads are too steep for a rickshaw, and the conveyance is a litter, carried by two coolies.

The most remarkable feature of the Chinese capital is its famous system of air-raid shelters. The hillsides are honeycombed with tunnels, which can accommodate the entire population. The 39-year-old Mayor, Mr. K. C. Wu, who is head of the A.R.P. organization, showed me 'round one of the largest of these dugouts, where 6,000 people sit in perfect safety, with 100 ft. of solid rock between them and the Japanese bombs. The cave has three entrances

OUR DIARY OF THE WAR

DEC. 21, 1942, Monday *1,206th day*
Air.—R.A.F. heavy bombers raided Munich by night.
Libya.—Axis bombers raided Benghazi.
Australasia.—U.S. tanks in action against strong-points at Buna.

DEC. 22, Tuesday *1,207th day*
Air.—R.A.F. fighters made night attacks on railway targets in N. France.
India.—Enemy raids in Calcutta area by day and night.
Burma.—R.A.F. and U.S. bombers raided Akyab and Rangoon.

DEC. 23, Wednesday *1,208th day*
Mediterranean.—Announced that large convoy had reached Malta safely.
Pacific.—Heavy U.S. raid on Japanese-occupied Wake Island.

DEC. 24, Thursday *1,209th day*
Russian Front.—New Soviet offensive launched in Central Caucasus.
India.—Another Jap raid on Calcutta.
Burma.—Two enemy attempts to re-take positions in Arakan were repelled.
Australasia.—Announced that mine-sweeper H.M.A.S. Armidale sunk near Timor by enemy air action.
General.—Admiral Darlan fatally shot at Algiers.

DEC. 25, Friday *1,210th day*
N. Africa.—Heavy fighting, involving units of the Guards, for hill N.E. of Medjez-el-Bab.
Libya.—Eighth Army occupied Sirte.
Australasia.—U.S. Fortresses from Guadalcanal bombed shipping at Rabaul.

DEC. 26, Saturday *1,211th day*
Sea.—Announced that destroyers Fame and Viscount, Norwegian ship Acanthus and other escort ships sank two U-boats and damaged several others in four-day attack on Atlantic convoy.
N. Africa.—French forces repulsed enemy attack at Pichon, Tunisia.
Libya.—Fighting French forces from Chad in contact with enemy in the Fezzan.
Russian Front.—In Middle Don Russians occupied Tarasovka and penetrated into the Ukraine.
Burma.—R.A.F. long-range bombers attacked Jap aerodrome at Heho.
U.S.A.—Lightning fighters raided Kiska.
General.—Gen. Giraud succeeded Adm.

Darlan as High Commissioner in French N. Africa.

DEC. 27, Sunday *1,212th day*
Russian Front.—S.W. of Stalingrad Soviet troops captured rly. stns. of Zhutovo and Chilekov.
Siam.—U.S. bombers raided Bangkok.
Australasia.—Flying Fortresses and Liberators bombed Rabaul, wrecking four large Jap ships. Lightning fighters in action over Papua for first time.

DEC. 28, Monday *1,213th day*
N. Africa.—Tunis and Susa bombed by Allied aircraft from Libya.
Russian Front.—Soviet troops occupied Chertkovo on Middle Don front.
Australasia.—Jap warships off New Guinea bombarded Buna village.
General.—French Somaliland adhered to United Nations as part of Fighting France.

DEC. 29, Tuesday *1,214th day*
N. Africa.—Announced that our troops had withdrawn from hills N.E. of Medjez-el-Bab.
Russian Front.—Kotelnikovo, on Stalingrad-Novorossisk railway, captured by Russians.

DEC. 30, Wednesday *1,215th day*
Air.—U.S. heavy bombers made daylight raid on submarine base at Lorient.

Mediterranean.—Heavy allied raid on aerodrome at Heraklion, Crete.
Australasia.—Allied raids on Munda and Rekata Bay in Solomons and Lae in New Guinea.
U.S.A.—American bombers again raided Kiska.

DEC. 31, Thursday *1,216th day*
Sea.—Admiralty announced that in naval engagement in northern waters, enemy cruiser and destroyer were damaged.
Air.—R.A.F. raided W. Germany.
N. Africa.—Allied aircraft bombed Sfax, Susa and Gabès ; enemy bombers raided Casablanca.
Libya.—Fighting French from Chad routed enemy motorized column in the Fezzan. French planes bombed enemy aerodrome near Murzuk.
Burma.—R.A.F. raided aerodrome at Shwebo and port of Akyab.

JAN. 1, 1943, Friday *1,217th day*
Sea.—Admiralty announced loss of destroyer Blean.
N. Africa.—Tunis raided by Allied aircraft ; enemy raid on Bône.
Mediterranean.—Large-scale Allied air attack on Crete by night ; Palermo also bombed.
Russian Front.—Veliki Luki on the Central front and Elista, S. of Stalingrad, occupied by Soviet troops.

Australasia.—U.S. dive-bombers raid Jap H.Q. on Guadalcanal.

JAN. 2, Saturday *1,218th day*
Sea.—Enemy blockade runner in Atlantic intercepted and scuttled.
N. Africa.—Heavy Allied air attacks on La Goulette, Susa and Sfax ; enemy bombers twice raided Bône.
Mediterranean.—British and U.S. aircraft made first daylight raid on Crete.
Australasia.—Allied troops occupied Buna mission. Heavy bombers attacked Jap armada at Rabaul.

JAN. 3, Sunday *1,219th day*
Sea.—Admiralty announced loss of corvette Snapdragon.
Air.—U.S. heavy bombers attacked St. Nazaire. R.A.F. bombed Ruhr by night.
N. Africa.—Enemy attack on French troops in Tunisia repulsed.
Russian Front.—Mozdok and Malgobek in Caucasus captured by Soviet troops.
Australasia.—Flying Fortresses raided Jap shipping at Rabaul and new Jap airfield at Munda.
Home Front.—Raid on Isle of Wight caused fatal casualties.

JAN. 4, Monday *1,220th day*
Sea.—Admiralty announced loss of destroyer Firedrake.
Air.—R.A.F. again raided the Ruhr.
Russian Front.—Nalchik, in the Caucasus, and Chernyshkovsky, S.W. of Stalingrad, captured by Russians.
Burma.—R.A.F. and U.S. aircraft bombed railway yards at Mandalay.
Australasia.—Allied air attacks on Lae and Gasmata.

JAN. 5, Tuesday *1,221st day*
Sea.—Admiralty announced sinking of another blockade-runner in Atlantic.
N. Africa.—British units drove enemy from high ground W. of Mateur. Announced that Canadian troops had arrived in N. Africa.
Libya.—Eighth Army at Buerat, 60 m. W. of Sirte.
Russian Front.—Prokhladnaya, rly. junction W. of Mozdok, and Tsimlyanskaya on Don front occupied by Russians.
Australasia.—Nine Jap ships sunk at Rabaul by Allied bombers. U.S. warships bombarded Jap airfield at Munda, New Georgia.

★════ *Flash-backs* ════★

1940
December 23. *Greeks announced capture of Chimara.*
December 29. *Night fire raid on City of London : Guildhall and other famous buildings destroyed.*

1941
December 22. *Japanese launched major attack on Philippines.*
December 24. *Japanese captured Wake Island in the Pacific.*

Eighth Army entered Benghazi.
December 25. *Hong Kong garrison surrendered to Japanese.*
December 27. *Commando raid on Norwegian island of Vaagso.*
December 30. *Kaluga, on Moscow front, recaptured by Russians.*

1942
January 2. *Eighth Army took Bardia. Manila and Cavite, in Philippines, occupied by Japanese.*

ON the whole, although recently there has been a renewal of censorious criticism of the British censorship, my own feeling is that for the last three years or so it has worked very efficiently. It is notorious that the abuse of censorship by the French military authorities contributed substantially to the collapse of France in the lowering of public morale; and so far as I can gather, the American censorship is not being handled so efficiently as the British. Naturally, there are occasions when one might well be irritated by official decisions for which no sound reason can be discerned. Only a week or two back a very instructive broadcast on the European News Service, which I greatly wished to print in THE WAR ILLUSTRATED, was vetoed by the Naval censorship, although the B.B.C. most courteously put it at our service. I am still unable to determine why some information that was officially supplied to and broadcast by the B.B.C. to some millions of listeners, could not be reprinted in our pages without danger to the State. Equally I cannot see that the reproduction of a number of significant quotations from Continental journals, copies of which are certainly filed in Dr. Goebbels' Berlin bureau, could prove a source of danger to the Allies' war effort; but although I have had my attention drawn to this officially under a certain regulation I am still uncomplaining, realizing as I do that there may be some hidden danger which an alert censorship might detect that would be less obvious to those of us who are guided by nothing better than common sense.

TALKING of common sense, I bought at a bookstall the other day a copy of Irish Freedom, a monthly publication printed in Derbyshire and published in London, although so far as I could gather from a glance through this 8-page newspaper, it is devoted to the cause of a " united Ireland " —in other words, a separate or completely non-British Ireland —and a cartoon on its front page would seem to suggest that the means of achieving the union lies with the Irish workers; that is to say, the friendly industrial north is to shake hands with the unfriendly agricultural south and bring the whole distressful island under the benign rule of—Mr. de Valera! This newspaper performs at least one good office, so far as I can judge, in proving that at a time when Great Britain and Northern Ireland are fighting for their way of life against an implacable enemy, and Eire is the one scrap of the British Commonwealth not actively assisting in that fight, British toleration allows this propaganda sheet to appear regularly, placing British transport at its service for paper supply and distribution. Meanwhile, there is a strict censorship of all war news. Even news reels illustrating the achievements of British forces in the world fight for freedom—Irish freedom as well as British and American, Russian and Chinese—are subject to censorship and suppression in the freedom-loving south of Ireland!

THE recent festive season (if such a phrase may still be used) raised afresh the question of tipping. A friend of mine who never, never tips " on principle," for he alleges it is a degrading habit—unlike mercy, it degradeth him that gives and him that takes!—was holding forth against it at a Christmas dinner. With far more experience of the practice, I demurred. Even paying 15 per cent for service on hotel bills does not solve the matter, as out of the total accruing for division, some of it goes to members of the staff who have never done you any service. So I take the risk of degrading those whom I have found especially helpful by tipping them individually despite the 15 per cent impost. Why not?

When I hand a specialist £3 3s. for examining my eyes and telling me there's really nothing wrong with them, or give a porter a shilling for carrying my suitcase from the train to the taxi, I am giving something for service rendered, and I am sure the ophthalmist is no more conscious of being degraded in the act than is the porter.

BUT tipping should be reasonable—neither too much nor too little. In a "luxury" restaurant the other night I took note of the couples dining on each side of me. The gentleman on the left, a " regular," left two sixpences on his plate—" sixpence a head," the meanest conceivable tip; and he on my right, a " casual," left two half-crowns; far too much. Half-a-crown is adequate where the total bill, drinks included, is somewhere about a pound and less than thirty shillings. In these days of grossly inflated prices for drinks there is no occasion to step up tips in accord with the total bill; the

viands have not gone up excessively, and a waiter does no heavier work in serving a bottle of wine at 25s. (pre-War 8s. 6d.) than a bottle of lemonade at 1s. 6d. But those who grouse about tipping " on principle " always leave me with the feeling that they want to give the least possible reward for a service they are the readiest to command.

HERE is one of those innumerable little incidents that find no record in the newspapers, yet speak eloquently for the British temperament that has made this little island of ours the real bulwark of liberty in withstanding the aggression of power-mad tyrants and their dupes. In a certain town where an air raid took considerable toll of life and did some material damage recently, while the rescue parties were still at work among the dusty ruins a queue was forming for the cinema within sight of the bomb craters! The urge of life is strong enough in most European peoples to produce a measure of stoicism in face of danger and death; with the Japanese their willingness to die for their god-emperor would probably minimize the celerity of their collapse under bombing; but on the other hand their populous cities are so largely made of inflammable material that their destruction, when once the Allies set about it, will be so complete that in that fine Bismarckian phrase the inhabitants will be left only their eyes to weep with! No other race among our enemies more richly deserves that fate, and no race would more wholeheartedly approve it than Bismarck's countrymen, who for the moment are profiting from their unnatural alliance with non-Aryans—always provided, of course, that the Hun was no longer able to use the Jap to his own ends.

AMONG the latest gems from the brain-box of the B.B.C. which I have accidentally picked up or heard about are Chile, pronounced to rhyme with guile, Ek-you-aye-dor for Ecuador (properly pronounced Ekwadór) and Tok-eye-o for a well-known city in far Japan, which five minutes later was given its familiar pronunciation by Mr. John Morris in a brilliant description of the Japanese. Mr. Morris's broadcast was one of the best I have listened to: he ought to be able to write an extremely valuable book on Japan from the intimate knowledge he gained during his years as a professor at the Bunrika University, Tokyo. I have had so much and such rarely broken disappointment as a listener-in through 1942 that I have practically given up switching on anything but the nine o'clock news, and limit myself to the more important broadcasts.

I AM often surprised at the omissions in quite pretentious atlases and know only too well how easily these occur; but I happened to turn to an atlas produced since the start of the War and issued by a certain " national daily " in which the total space devoted to the northern part of Tunisia is less than a half-inch square; neither the name nor the " town stamp " of Bizerta is given. The compilers were evidently lacking in vision, as the work contains only a few scraps of the Mediterranean area from which it is impossible to gather any idea of the extent or shore lines of the region in which the Second Front of 1942 had to be opened.

FAMOUS FIGHTERS OF THE R·A·F

WING CMDR. B. ('PADDY') FINUCANE, D.S.O., D.F.C., 21-year-old fighter ace and victor of 32 air combats, whose death was announced on July 17, 1942, was one of Britain's most daring airmen. A brief account of his career is given in p. 104 of this volume.
Drawn by Captain Cuthbert Orde: Crown Copyright reserved

Printed in England and published every alternate Friday by the Proprietors, THE AMALGAMATED PRESS, LTD., The Fleetway House, Farringdon Street, London, E.C.4. Registered for transmission by Canadian Magazine Post. Sole Agents for Australia and New Zealand: Messrs. Gordon & Gotch, Ltd.; and for South Africa: Central News Agency, Ltd.—January 22nd, 1943. S.S. Editorial Address: JOHN CARPENTER HOUSE, WHITEFRIARS, LONDON, E.C.4.

ON TOP IN TUNISIA! Sergt. R. Sumner, a Londoner, recently distinguished himself in a remarkable exploit in the fierce fighting with Nehring's Nazis. During an attack on the enemy positions he charged a machine-gun nest single-handed, capturing two Germans with their light machine-gun and 3,000 rounds of ammunition. While he was using the gun later it jammed, but he persuaded one of the prisoners to adjust it, and held down enemy fire until his ammunition was spent. Sergt. Sumner is here seen with the captured gun.
Photo, Planet News

NO. 148 WILL BE PUBLISHED FRIDAY, FEBRUARY 19

THE BATTLE FRONTS

by Maj.-Gen. Sir Charles Gwynn, K.C.B., D.S.O.

DURING the first half of January 1943, although there were no major developments in other theatres, the German situation in Russia continued to deteriorate rapidly. Zhukov's great southern offensive showed no sign of losing its momentum. It is true that on certain parts of its front the advance was slowed down or even temporarily brought to a standstill. That was only to be expected where, as on the Donetz and Lower Don front, the Germans had special facilities for bringing reserves into action and where it was vitally important for them to hold every foot of ground. Yet even on these comparatively static parts of the front the Germans are suffering heavily. They have been forced to counter-attack constantly, purely as a defensive expedient and not in the hope of initiating a counter-offensive on a scale which would retrieve the situation. The counter-attacks have been costly in men and material. They have contributed to the high rate of attrition of man-power resources which is giving Berlin much anxiety, and they have not removed the threat to vital centres. On the Caucasus front there is no question of the offensive losing momentum, and here undoubtedly the Germans have to face the possibility of disaster on a scale as great as that which threatens the 6th Army at Stalingrad.

In view of the situation in Russia, will the decision to send an army to Tunisia prove a disastrous embarrassment for the Axis coming on top of the necessity to retain strong forces in the occupied countries? The decision cannot be reversed; and Hitler may be compelled to treat an ulcer in Tunisia as serious as the Spanish ulcer was to Napoleon.

GERMAN TRANSPORT difficulties in Russia are acute. Here are Nazi soldiers dragging shells along in sledges improvised from ammunition containers. *Photo, Associated Press*

RUSSIA

By the middle of January the Russians had accomplished so much that it was less their day-to-day achievements that excited interest than the vista that was opened. What would be the fate of the defeated German armies, and what would be the strategic policy of the German High Command?

The army of the Middle Caucasus was in full retreat, having abandoned masses of material in what almost amounted to a rout; all pretence that it was an orderly withdrawal in order to shorten the front became absurd. Russian pursuit was too vigorous, and on too broad a front, to permit even a temporary stand on the Kuma river. The retreat continued, and sporadic rearguard actions did little to check pursuit, though in some localities they resulted in fierce encounters.

The immediate question, then, was whether the defeated army would be able to rally on a position covering the railway junction of Armavir? If it could not, the Maikop oilfield would have to be abandoned, and the forces operating against Tuapse would be forced to undertake a difficult retreat. The Upper Kuban and the important centre of Voroshilovsk seemed to indicate a possible rallying position; but the pursuit was hot and threatened to turn the position from the north before it could be firmly established.

Moreover, another threat was developing which would seal the fate of the retreating army if it attempted to stand. The Russian drive from Kotelnikovo down the Stalingrad-Novorossisk railway was making steady if not very rapid progress. It had reached the line of the Manych river, and on its right the lower reaches of the Sal. German resistance, though stiff, was being steadily overcome; and the important town of Salsk, with direct railway communication with Rostov, was closely threatened. Even more important: if the advance could not be stopped, Tikhoretsk, through which the communications of the Middle Caucasus army and the Maikop forces run, would be in danger. It seems probable, therefore, that the Germans may be forced to retreat to cover Tikhoretsk and to avoid the danger of becoming completely isolated. They would have long distances to cover; and an early decision whether to stand to cover Armavir or to retreat on Tikhoretsk must be taken. If Tikhoretsk were captured or closely threatened it might well lead to a withdrawal of all German forces in the Caucasus.

WHILE the Germans in the Caucasus were being hard pressed, the Russian advance north of the Don had been slowed down and in some places stopped by numerous counter-attacks. The Germans were evidently determined to hold the line of the Donetz at all costs in order to cover the approaches to Rostov and the important towns and railway system of the Donetz basin. But although the position gave them great facilities for bringing up reserves the counter-attacks failed to do more than bring temporary relief, and were very costly.

By the middle of the month the Russians began again to make progress and actually reached the eastern bank of the Donetz. It seems improbable that anything amounting to a break-through will be achieved; but, on the other hand, the attrition of German reserves is likely to be an important contribution to the general progress of the offensive. Now as I write (in the middle of January) has come the news of the new break-through south of Voronezh—an event of the first importance. Apart from the casualties inflicted and booty captured, it will clear the Voronezh-Rostov railway as far as Millerovo and open prospects of cutting communication between Kharkov and Rostov. The fall of Millerovo, announced by the Russians on Jan. 17, coupled with the capture of the railway farther north, must immensely improve the communications of the Russians on the Donetz front.

The news from Stalingrad is equally important. Although the Nazi General Paulus has refused to accept terms of surrender, it is clear that his troops are in no condition to resist the Russian exterminating attack and they will probably take the law into their own hands. Paulus was, of course, justified in refusing to surrender, however hopeless his position, because evidently it is of first importance to the Russians to open railway communication through Stalingrad and to secure the release of their investing

FLOODS IN TUNISIA held up military operations during the greater part of January this year. Roads were converted into running rivers and became impassable for transport. This photograph shows a German motorized column halted by a large expanse of flood-water. One lorry has already been marooned in a venturesome bid to make the passage, and the rest of the column waits upon the bank in the background, completely immobilized. *Photo, Associated Press*

army as soon as possible. Every day's delay may have important consequences.

The situation on the Moscow front has changed little since the capture of Veliki Luki. The Germans have been counter-attacking furiously in the hopes of retaking it, and their long refusal to admit its fall was due probably to the hope that success would make admission of such a reverse unnecessary. Russian progress in exploitation of the removal of this hedgehog has not been marked, but the rate of attrition of German reserves must have been greatly increased by fruitless counter-attacks.

Up to the time of writing, Moscow has been silent as regards operations which the Germans report the Russians have started for the relief of Leningrad, but these may obviously produce very important results.

ON the whole, the situation in Russia has improved beyond all expectation, and there is every reason to hope that it will improve still further.

The recovery by the Russian air force of the ascendancy it achieved last winter is likely to prove of great importance, for it will have more chances of exploiting its superiority than it had then.

The amazing results achieved by Russian war industries during the past year which, in spite of the necessity to make good heavy losses and expenditure, has enabled reserves to be built up for the offensive affords a heartening assurance that the summer will not find the Red Army with its material resources exhausted. How many tanks and aircraft supplied by the Allies are being employed in the present operations we have not been told ; but there seems little doubt that the most effective weapons in winter warfare are of Russian manufacture. It has still to be proved whether the weapons are of an order which will enable the offensive to be maintained during the worst of the winter. So far, the season appears to have been exceptionally mild ; and on the Caucasus front mud rather than snow has hampered rapid movement. In any case, the Russians retain their superiority in cavalry and ski troops, and their guerilla bands will probably have greater opportunities than ever of effective action as German reserves are drawn into the main battle area.

STALINGRAD AND N. CAUCASUS FRONTS. Arrows show direction of main Russian thrusts at Jan. 19, 1943. The shaded areas are those recaptured by the Red Army in the course of the previous fortnight. Note the German 6th Army enveloped at Stalingrad, and Rostov menaced from north and east.

By courtesy of The Times

GEN. PAULUS, commander of the German 6th Army trapped in the Stalingrad area. On Jan. 8, 1943 he rejected a Russian ultimatum that he should capitulate.

Photo, New-York Times Photos

It is too early yet to speculate on whether the disasters the Germans have suffered will compel them to attempt a drastic general withdrawal in order to shorten their communications and to establish a straighter front. Such a course was contemplated last year, but it was realized that it would be too desperate an undertaking to carry out in mid-winter. This year it would probably be even more difficult, but the alternative of holding on at all costs might be even more disastrous if the momentum of the Russian offensive is maintained.

NORTH AFRICA

Operations in Tunisia no doubt appear to many disappointingly slow. We should realize, however, that we have been told nothing as to the actual progress of the deployment of the main Allied forces. We have had the frank admission of the failure of the original attempt to anticipate the Axis forces in the occupation of Tunis and Bizerta, and we have had some account of the encounters in which the advanced force which made the attempt have since been engaged. Difficulty of operations in wet weather, difficulties on the lines of communication, and difficulties in establishing aerodromes have also been described.

All this has suggested the idea that someone has blundered, and some criticism has been excited. It has been suggested, for instance, that it was a mistake to undertake the operation at all in the wet season, and that the conditions encountered should have been foreseen. Such criticism rather ignores the probability that the operations were designed to synchronize with a Russian winter offensive, and also with the 8th Army offensive which could not well be postponed indefinitely or till the heat of summer.

It would not be surprising, moreover, if the state of the roads in Algeria and Tunisia, or what the effect of rain would be on the ground, were not well known. We now know that the roads have been neglected since the collapse of France, and that rain produces mud conditions very hampering to military operations. But how could such information have been obtained ? French North Africa has been closed to Allied agents for the last three years, and in pre-war years there was no reason for collecting detailed information about the territory of a friendly Power which did not even adjoin British possessions. I doubt whether even residents in the country would have appreciated the effects of rain on military operations, since none had ever taken place in the country—certainly not since the days of mechanization.

In Tripolitania, Montgomery as I write has again started to move, and apparently Rommel has not risked a decisive encounter. The main fact is that after its long pause the 8th Army should be in a good state to follow through and maintain pressure.

FAR EAST

The very difficult and expensive Papuan operation is practically ended. It is to be hoped that a valuable base for operations against Rabaul and Japanese footholds farther north in New Guinea has been secured to reward troops who have done so splendidly.

Pioneer Corps Handle Vital Supplies in N. Africa

MEN of the Pioneer Corps are doing a fine and vitally important job of work in North Africa. Many of them were rejected for Regular Army service on account of poor eyesight and other physical disabilities; but in spite of such handicaps which precluded them from fighting in the first line, they are now unloading and reloading goods on trains and lorries in 12-hour shifts, night and day. Five tons of material per man are handled in each shift, and during an emergency as much as seven or eight tons per man is maintained.

The Pioneers also build camps and roads, and stack goods at ordnance and supply depots. Organized into pioneer aerodrome companies, they are hard at work on constructing badly-needed airfields for the R.A.F. They can finish an airfield and have it ready for use in thirty-six hours. A number of European refugees recently released from internment camps in Algeria, have offered their services to the Pioneers. One company, composed principally of Austrians and Germans—victims of Nazi oppression—has already been formed, and many North African natives are also enlisting to swell their ranks.

IN Algiers harbour (left) British and American troops are being disembarked from a large transport; evidence of the Pioneers' activity is afforded by the stores piled in the foreground. The photograph below, taken at Bône, E. of Algiers along the Mediterranean coast, shows small-arms ammunition being transferred from ship to quay by means of rollers, an ingenious method that saves both time and labour.

Photos, British Official: Crown Copyright

Skirmishing Activity Amid the Tunisian Hills

IN Tunisia both the Allies and the Germans were building up their forces at the beginning of January 1943. Except in the south, where French troops, with U.S. support, beat off enemy raids on their positions, the weather held up operations. On Jan. 8 it was disclosed that the Coldstream Guards, Grenadier Guards, Northamptonshire Regt., Hampshire Regt., Lancashire Fusiliers, and East Surrey Regt. were among British units in this theatre of war. As regards the contribution of French troops, numbers steadily increased. On Jan. 13 it was reported that an additional contingent of some 6,000 men had been placed in the firing line, bringing the number of French troops in the field to well over 50,000.

Meanwhile, the military situation remained obscure. It was reported that Axis reinforcements were reaching Tunis at the rate of 1,000 men a day, and that the garrison of Tunis itself had been greatly strengthened.

THE photographs in this page show men of the Allied armies in the Tunisian front line. 1, A medical outpost, effectively camouflaged among a pile of rocks. A U.S. soldier, wounded in the arm, is being attended by a doctor. 2, Men of a Guards Battalion holding a front-line slit trench. 3, British parachute troops set off on patrol duty in the Beja area. 4, German tank blazing as the result of a duel with U.S. and British anti-tank units in the Medjez-el-Bab region, 40 miles west of Tunis.

Photos, British Official: Crown Copyright ;
Keystone, Planet News

PAGE 517

Commanders Have to Keep Up With the War

In the First Great War the headquarters of the rival commands were often in palatial châteaux in some town conveniently situated behind the front, e.g. the Kaiser's H.Q. was at Spa in Belgium, while Haig's was for years at Montreuil. But, as ALEXANDER DILKE explains below, in the campaigns of today mobility is the key-word, and the generals, too, have to be "mobile."

IT was recently revealed that when General Eisenhower was in Britain working out the strategy of the Allied invasion of North Africa, he used a "sleeper" which had been part of the Night Scotsman and Aberdonian expresses. Converted into a work-room by removing the berths, the sleeper became a hive of activity as it moved secretly round Britain, taking General Eisenhower to each of the many commands that had to be consulted. Probably no great campaign has been launched from such a small and modest headquarters. The mobile conference-room measured only 20 ft. by 6 ft., but in it were taken some of the biggest decisions of the war.

The speed and nature of modern warfare are forcing generals more and more to avoid the great country mansion or luxury hotel which was once the typical headquarters. Not only does the speed of war call now for mobility, but also the big houses form too easy a mark for bombers or even parachutists. A friend writing of our retreat in Malaya told how Japanese bombers always made the largest building in the town, the club or the racecourse buildings, their first mark, convinced that this was where the British would set up their headquarters. But the British had learned ; and in their retreat the H.Q. of this unit found comparative peace by choosing very ordinary native houses in which to work.

Hitler's Armoured Train

"The Fuehrer's Headquarters" has become a familiar phrase. It is from this spot that the biggest German claims are made. It is probably purely a propaganda place, for from it flows with equal ease news of air, naval and military operations. The German High Command, of course, has headquarters, and Hitler has his specially-constructed armoured train which becomes his "headquarters" when he visits the front. In fact, the Russians, who have been at great pains to discover the sleeping-place of Hitler and have no inhibitions about bombing him, are convinced that the train has never been nearer than 400 miles from the front. The military could not guarantee immunity from attack by guerillas at a less distance.

Hitler's train is heavily armed and armoured. It is particularly well equipped with light A.A. guns—and not without good reason, for Russian airmen have bombed it at least twice, although it does not seem certain that they knew who was in it. According to reports, it does not move a great deal. Indeed, with its elaborate telephone system it would be difficult for it to do so.

THE German G.H.Q. train consists of a number of specially-built coaches providing offices, conference-rooms, sleeping accommodation, wireless car and, in fact, everything required by a considerable staff. The wireless car is equipped with teleprinters, and both the world's news and private information flow in day and night. The accommodation is luxurious by active service standards. The kitchen cars, for instance, can provide not only meals for several hundred people, but dinners fit for the distinguished foreign visitors who are occasionally invited to the Fuehrer's headquarters—and the light pastries which are Hitler's weakness.

This mobile headquarters is something of a "stunt" to give the atmosphere of the front line to visitors and, for that matter, to Hitler himself. Big as is the accommodation, it is not sufficient to house anything like the organization required in controlling the huge German armies. The real work is done in extensive buildings converted for the purpose. They are believed to be in East Prussia, but their whereabouts is one of the most closely-guarded of German secrets.

Because of the menace of air or land raids, all armies must now keep the nature and position of their headquarters secret. Rommel learned his lesson in November 1941, when Commandos led by Lieut.-Col. Keyes attacked the villa he was using as headquarters at Sidi Raffa near Tobruk. This headquarters seemed far from the fighting-line, but submarines and the skill and courage of the raiders took them to it. Only the unlucky chance that Rommel was away at the time saved his life ; several of the officers on his staff were killed.

Specially-equipped aircraft are used by generals as mobile headquarters, enabling them not only to cover considerable distances

GEN. K. A. N. ANDERSON, Commander of the 1st Army in N. Africa, photographed in the armoured car in which he travels and directs operations in Tunisia.
Photo, British Official: Crown Copyright

rapidly, but also to work while travelling. Britain has mobile offices with every required type of equipment, including miniature printing-presses to enable the administration to keep up with the army.

Curiously enough, Air Force H.Q. do not require quite the same mobility—an air force moves forward in jumps rather than continuously. In the Western Desert miniature underground "cities" were excavated for R.A.F. headquarters ; there was one at Maaten Bagush, for instance, known as the "rabbit's warren," complete with operations-rooms, orderly-rooms, accounts sections, etc.

FOR working out a big operation, safety is more important, perhaps, than mobility. For this reason, when he went to Africa, General Eisenhower put the finishing touches to his plans in a tunnel specially hollowed out of the rock at Gibraltar. Visitors to Allied Forces headquarters had to walk a quarter of a mile underground before reaching it, and pass so many guards that there was little chance of a surprise attack even by exceptionally cunning or resolute men. The actual rooms used as headquarters were concreted to keep out the damp ; and in them generals, admirals, and air marshals worked all day, coming up only to sleep.

Montgomery's Desert Caravan

General Montgomery has used a specially-fitted caravan as his mobile headquarters during his great advance in the Western Desert. It is austerely but efficiently furnished, and, of course, camouflaged. The caravan can keep pace with the fastest fighting vehicles, and in the unique conditions of the desert has the advantage of providing shelter and "office" at any convenient spot, quite independently of the "inhabited places," which are not only few and far between, but magnets for bombers. Gen. Montgomery does not travel in the caravan, but in a small car.

A "fitting" of the caravan which always calls forth comment from visitors is a large photograph of General Rommel. Probably this is the only headquarters in the world where a photograph of the enemy general is prominent. General Montgomery explains that he captured his life-size photograph and has ambitions to capture the "original."

MOBILE NERVE CENTRE in the Western Desert. This Armoured Command Vehicle enables staff officers of the 2nd Armoured Brigade of the 8th Army to keep in touch by wireless and telephone with every phase of the swift-moving campaign. A Brigadier is seen leaving the A.C.V. during a halt in the desert. PAGE 518 *Photo, British Official: Crown Copyright*

Tripoli Added to the Eighth Army's Prizes

THE 8th ARMY ENTERED TRIPOLI on January 23, 1943; here are scenes in Mussolini's "jewel city." 1, The splendid bay and embankment. 2, Roman triumphal arch, built in A.D. 163, in honour of the Emperors Marcus Aurelius and Lucius Verus. An Arab mosque rises in the background. 3, Sixteenth-century Castle of Tripoli, overlooking the harbour. 4, The Corso Vittorio Emanuele, fashionable shopping centre. An Italian seaplane swoops low over the white buildings

Photos, Pictorial Press

U-BOATS are now more concentrated than before, said Mr. A. V. Alexander on Jan. 20, 1943; new U-boats are being used, with new tactics. It is computed that the enemy has now some 700 submarines which can be employed against our shipping. The enormous output of U.S. shipyards and the drive in British naval construction are the United Nations' answer. Top, diagram showing a standard ocean-going U-boat of 740 tons. Left, photo taken from a Coastal Command Whitley aircraft during a depth-charge attack on a U-boat, showing a standard ocean-going was taken—in the Caribbean Sea.
Diagram by courtesy of The Daily Express: photos British Official: Crown Copyright: Associated Press

THE WAR AT SEA

by Francis E. McMurtrie

No excuse is needed for reverting to the U-boat menace. It is unquestionably the most dangerous weapon which Germany wields, a fact of which our enemies are only too well aware. Though our shipping losses from this cause may not be so serious as they were six months or more ago, they are still far too heavy to be regarded with equanimity ; and there is unfortunately every prospect of their increasing in the spring, when our foes are bound to strain every nerve to interrupt our vital seaborne supplies.

We have been officially informed that the rate of construction of U-boats still exceeds the rate at which they are being destroyed. Until this position is reversed we cannot afford to abate our efforts one iota ; indeed, we must augment them in every possible way.

To accelerate the speed of merchant ship-building in this country and on the other side of the Atlantic is not a solution of the problem. It is only a palliative, especially if the shipping is turned out faster than the warships and aircraft required for its protection. To provide additional targets for U-boats without a corresponding increase in the number of escorts would tend to play into the enemy's hands.

It is, in fact, the multiplication of the escorting warships which is the most important object to keep in view if we are to bring about a bigger slaughter of U-boats. As recent accounts of the defeat of attacks on Atlantic convoys make plain, these ships are doing magnificent work in guarding our supply routes across the ocean. But the scale of these attacks is clearly very heavy, as they are often renewed day after day, showing that the number of enemy submarines employed is considerable.

Though they cannot fly in all weathers, and are unable to afford succour to survivors of ships sunk, aircraft afford very valuable collaboration with convoy escorts. Indeed, one of the most useful types employed in convoy work today is the auxiliary aircraft-carrier, whose planes can scout around a convoy's track, in order to spot submarines on the surface and force them to submerge to avoid bombs or depth charges. This greatly reduces a U-boat's efficiency, as its speed on the surface may be anything from 16 to 20 knots, while under water this is reduced to 8 or 9 knots. Moreover, it is not possible to maintain this speed indefinitely while submerged without using up the stored electricity driving the motors.

Shortage of Naval Aircraft

Undoubtedly, an increase in the number of naval aircraft available for convoy work would be of material advantage. Both the First Lord of the Admiralty and Lord Hankey have recently expressed concern that the Royal Navy, which is charged with the task of keeping our life-line open, is still short of aircraft of up-to-date type for this work. If ever there was a case for priority being given, irrespective of other less vital needs, this is one.

Though bombing submarine bases such as Lorient may do something to hamper the regular routine of reliefs on which the U-boat war on commerce is dependent, it is hardly credible that any damage can be done to the vessels themselves, protected as they are by 15 feet or more of solid concrete above the shelters in which they lie when in port. Nor can it be hoped that the morale of the submarine crews—the weakest link in the U-boat chain—will be affected by occasional bombing raids on bases.

Neither is it likely that submarine building and assembling yards will be put out of action by such raids. Not only are there far too many of them, scattered all over Europe, but a shipyard is not a particularly vulnerable target, as our own experience in 1940-41 goes to show. If more aircraft could be directed to the actual location and attacking of U-boats at sea, it would be far more valuable than bombing bases and shipbuilding establishments.

It has been a subject of comment from time to time that, compared with the Royal Air Force, the Royal Navy achieves less publicity than is its due, having regard to the vital importance of its war operations.

An appointment announced on January 13, 1943 is designed to remedy this situation. Admiral Sir William James, Commander-in-Chief at Portsmouth from 1939 to 1942, and a former Deputy Chief of the Naval Staff, has been selected for the new post of Chief of Naval Information. He will be entrusted with the planning and co-ordination of all forms of naval publicity. For this task he is well fitted, as Press representatives who have had to approach him during his tenure of the Portsmouth command can testify. From another point of view his choice for the difficult task of explaining the Navy's work to the public would seem to be a very happy one. He is a talented naval historian, able to describe in vivid words the deeds of naval daring which saved our country in the past, as readers of his books The British Navy in Adversity and Blue Water and Green Fields will unhesitatingly agree.

No new machinery is being set up for the publication of naval announcements, which will continue to be issued through the Press Division of the Admiralty and its Naval Affairs section, located at the Ministry of Information.

Ships Lent to Our Allies

H.M.S. Dragon, a cruiser of 4,850 tons, launched in 1917, has been lent to the Polish Navy. She is by far the biggest warship so far turned over to any of our Allies.

It is not generally realized how many of H.M. ships have thus been made available to our Allies. Apart from certain corvettes and trawlers transferred to the United States Navy last year to aid them in stamping out the U-boat pest on their Atlantic coast, over 40 vessels have hoisted Allied flags.

Besides the Dragon, the Poles have taken over the destroyers Piorun, Slazak, Krakowiak, Kujawiak (since lost), and Garland, and the submarines Sokol and Dzik. The Norwegians have manned the destroyers Eskdale, Glaisdale, Bath (lost), Lincoln and St. Albans, and the corvettes Rose, Acanthus, Eglantine, Montbretia (lost), and Potentilla.

The Dutch recently acquired two large destroyers, the Jan van Galen and Tjerk Hiddes. The Greeks have obtained four destroyers, the Pindos, Adrias, Kanaris, and Miaoulis, and four corvettes, the Apostolis, Kriezis, Sachtouris and Tombazis ; they will shortly add to these two more destroyers, the Nearchos and Themistocles. The Fighting French were last month given a destroyer, La Combattante, having previously been possessed of a number of corvettes, including the Commandant d'Estienne d'Orves, La Malouine, Roselys, Alysse, and Mimosa, the last two of which have been sunk. Even the Belgians, whose available personnel is not very numerous, are manning a corvette and an examination vessel. All these ships are operating in close and cordial conjunction with the Royal Navy.

LA COMBATTANTE, recently-launched destroyer of the Fighting French Navy, was built in a British shipyard. Some of her crew are shown aboard their new vessel. Fighting with the Royal Navy are many units manned by our Allies (see accompanying text). Inset, a Polish bosun is seen with his pipe.

Photo, Fighting French Official, L.N.A.

Scylla and Bengal Sink Two Enemy Ships

GERMAN BLOCKADE RUNNER, sighted in the Atlantic by an R.A.F. Coastal Command Wellington, was sunk in the Bay of Biscay by H.M.S. Scylla (5,450 tons), it was announced on Jan. 5, 1943. After a 200-mile pursuit the Scylla was within 20 miles of the enemy when a Sunderland aircraft reported the position of the German vessel. The latter fell to the Scylla's guns and torpedoes and subscquently sank. Top, she is seen going down. Above, Capt. MacIntyre, C.B.E., D.S.O., R.N., Scylla's commander. Right, the torpedo crew which sent the enemy ship to the bottom.

NAVAL ACTION IN INDIAN OCEAN. On Nov. 11, 1942 it was announced that H.M.I.S. Bengal, a minesweeper, and Ondina, a Dutch tanker, had engaged two Jap commerce raiders S.W. of Java, destroying the leading enemy ship. Left, two shells pierced the tanker's bow and exploded inside. Above, canvas sign attached to gun-barrel aboard the tanker shows victory record. (The aircraft were on the raider.)

Photos, British Official: Central Press, Sport & General

Through the Smoke of Battle Surge the Anzacs

NEW ZEALANDERS under the command of the famous V.C. General Freyberg, charge across broken, rocky ground, through dust and smoke, as they make a surprise attack on enemy positions at Nofilia, 90 miles W. of El Agheila, about ten days before Christmas. An outflanking movement carried out by the New Zealanders at Wadi Matratin accelerated the already speedy retreat of the Afrika Korps in the direction of Tripoli; Nofilia was abandoned by the enemy by Dec. 19, 1942.

Photo, British Official: Crown Copyright

Russia's Cruel Winter Grips Retreating Nazis

Left, German soldier, ill-clad against the cold, warms himself at an improvised stove. Above, enemy field-gun crew take a hasty meal amid the snow during their retreat.

RETREAT ACROSS THE STEPPES. Intense cold and heavy snowstorms made the "return journey" extremely hazardous for Hitler's poorly shod troops on the Don front. Loss of vital bases, severance of communications and supplies, rendered their plight an unenviable one. The Fuehrer's boast that the winter of 1942-43 would see his armies splendidly equipped against the elements proved to be as false as have so many of his announcements. Left, sheltering from the icy wind, German troops huddle behind a snowdrift. Above, terrible plight of a German prisoner brought in by Russian scouts. Ice has formed on his eyebrows, and the moisture from his breath has frozen into a thick coating of ice on the scarf, worn as protection against the cold.

Photos, Associated Press, Keystone, Planet News

Neither Cold Nor Nazis Stay the Red Army

COLD FEET are greatly troubling Hitler's troops in Russia. A captured pair of ersatz overboots are here much amusing Soviet tank personnel of whose own practical footwear they are a poor copy.

ARTILLERY OBSERVERS of the Red Army, armed with tommy-guns, are seen above climbing to their post in the mountains of the N. Caucasus. Russian successes assumed ever greater proportions on this front in January 1943, when their forces pushed on from Georgievsk towards Armavir. Left, Soviet mortar team drag their heavy weapon and ammunition on improvised sleighs as they go into action. They are well protected against the cold.

' AEROSLEIGHS ' (right), used by the Soviet troops in the winter fighting are wingless planes, bristling with machine-guns, which hurtle over the vast snowfields of the Russian front at a speed of 70 m.p.h. Numbers of these terrifying machines have been employed with good effect in the Don and Donetz regions, the enemy being forced to fall back from many fiercely defended places. Soviet thrusts in the Donetz basin threatened to deprive the enemy of his direct lines of communication with Rostov and Kharkov military district, and on Jan. 16, 1943 it was reported that German forces trapped between the Don and the Volga had been reduced from 200,000 to 78,000.

Photos, U.S.S.R. Official; Planet News

Epic Exploit of the New France in Fezzan

The conquest of the Italian Fezzan by the Fighting French constitutes, said General de Gaulle in a broadcast on January 13, 1943, an exploit which will rank among the finest in French history. "Once more the enemy has seen the French flame of war surge forth, that flame which he believed extinguished by disaster and treason, but which has not for one day ceased to burn . . ."

THEIR advance timed (we may well believe) to coincide with General Montgomery's drive into Tripolitania from the east and with General Anderson's march into Tunisia from the west, Fighting French under General Leclerc moved out from Fort Lamy in the Chad Territory in French Equatorial Africa against the Italian positions lying more than a thousand miles to the north in the deserts of southern Libya.

This General Leclerc—the name is reported to be a *nom de guerre*—has made swift

IN S.W. LIBYA, Fighting French columns striking N. from Fort Lamy, far to the south in the Chad Territory, occupied Italian Fezzan in January 1943. At the same time French troops from Tunisia attacked outposts in the west of the Italian territory. Arrows show the French, Fighting French and British advances.
By courtesy of The Daily Telegraph

strides up the ladder of fame. A soldier of the French regular army, he is still under 40. In the Battle of France he fought as a captain, was wounded, and taken prisoner. Carried to a hospital which had been taken over by the Germans, he managed in spite of his wounds to escape to a neighbouring château owned by some relatives of his. The Germans were in possession, and in one of the salons they were making merry over the contents of the cellar. Leclerc, however, managed to avoid them, and changed from his French uniform into a suit of "civvies." Then he walked through the front door and found a German soldier riding his wife's bicycle, which he asked to be given back. The Nazi handed it over, and Leclerc made off for the coast. Eventually, after an adventurous journey he reached London, where he joined General de Gaulle's forces.

WHEN his wounds were barely healed he was sent—now a major—by General de Gaulle to the Cameroons to help organize the resistance to the Vichy authorities who were then still in control. Leclerc succeeded ; and de Gaulle promoted him to the rank of Lieut.-Colonel and gave him command of the Fighting French forces in the Chad Territory. Ere long he captured the oasis of Kufra, and for this received the French Order of Liberation and the D.S.O. Vichy passed a sentence of death on him *in absentia*, whereupon General de Gaulle made him a colonel.

At the beginning of December 1942 General Leclerc's forces began their march. Writing from Fort Lamy to the Daily Express on Dec. 3, Colin Clair revealed that some of the garrison were already on their way to Tibesti in Libya ; from Garoua and Fort Archam-

bault and other military posts in the French Cameroons and Equatorial Africa long convoys were moving northwards. Though their ultimate destination was still an official secret, officers and men (he wrote) were heartened by the knowledge that they were advancing towards the vast North African battlefield, where they could justify their claim to the title of the Fighting French. Hitherto their life had been for the most part one of boredom in a lonely outpost ; many of the men had been stationed in the Chad for several years, without news of their wives and families in France—lonely, and a prey to malaria, blackwater, and other fevers and diseases which life in the Saharan climate entails. In peacetime eighteen months was the longest that a soldier had to serve without leave, but many of General Leclerc's men had spent four years in the desert because no relief had been possible.

The Chad troops were the first to rally *en bloc* to General de Gaulle after the armistice in June 1940, and as the months passed they were joined by other officers and men of the French Army who felt they could not serve under Vichy. In the remote outposts they had not been idle. Although little war activity had come their way, save the brilliant long-distance raids against enemy outposts at Murzuk and Kufra (Jan. 11 and Feb. 7, 1941, respectively), the *Tchadiens* had trained large numbers of African troops in modern war.

NOW the contingents were pushing north-wards across the desolate, burning desert in which there were no roads but only caravan tracks used from time immemorial by the Arab slave traders. For the first 300 miles north of Fort Lamy the march lay through a country of high plateaux and tall grass, country which affords good grazing for cattle and is reasonably well watered. But after passing through Sahel the columns entered the Tibesti area, a vast expanse of stony,

GEN. LECLERC, who is in command of the Fighting French forces invading Libya from the Chad, is here seen decorating a French N.C.O. Murzuk, capital of the Fezzan, was reported on Jan. 12 to have been occupied by his troops.   *Photo, Keystone*

sandy waste, in which the sand is so fine and soft that lorries often sink axle deep. Here their supplies had to be most carefully husbanded, since they were advancing ever farther into a desert where there was neither food nor water. The nearest oasis was at Murzuk, some five hundred miles across the frontier in Tripolitania.

ON the last day of 1942 General Leclerc reported that his motorized forces were advancing in the southern Fezzan, while the Bretagne squadron of bomber-reconnaissance planes had attacked the Italian aerodrome of Sebha, north-east of Murzuk, destroying a number of enemy planes ; from this it was apparent that the invaders were outflanking Murzuk, with a view to cutting off stragglers. On the next day came the news that advanced elements of the Fighting French had encountered and put to flight an enemy motorized column ; Fighting French bombers had again attacked the Italians in Murzuk and the neighbourhood. Then came the news that Oum-el-Araneb, main Axis outpost in Fezzan, 65 miles east of Murzuk, had been attacked by land and air by a column of *Tirailleurs Senegalais du Tchad* under the command of Colonel Ingold, and after a three days' struggle taken by storm, some 100 prisoners and much booty being captured.

Following these successes, a flying column of *Meharistes* (French Camel Corps, mounted not on camels but on motor-trucks) detached themselves from the main body of Leclerc's forces and swooped on the Axis outpost of El Gatrun, south-east of Murzuk. Covering a great distance at record speed, a Tibesti Meharistic detachment, under the command of Captain Sarazac, stormed the post, capturing 177 officers and much war material. In the same communiqué it was reported that the Bretagne squadron had razed to the ground the hangars and workshops at Sebha.

By Jan. 9, 1943 General Leclerc was able to report that the enemy's retreat was becoming a rout. Fighting French advanced elements had taken Brach, one of the most vital cross-roads in the Sahara, some 200 miles north of Murzuk, and Murzuk itself was reported to be encircled. Leclerc's supply problem was considerably eased by these captures, since Oum-el-Araneb and the rest afforded him advanced bases for his air arm, petrol dumps and water wells.

THE remaining enemy resistance was soon overcome. On Jan. 12 news was received from General Leclerc that Colonel Ingold's troops had occupied Murzuk and Sebha, in both cases capturing almost the entire garrison. A force of 110 attempted to escape to Ghadames, near Tunisia's southern tip, but they had gone only some 20 miles across the desert when, pursued by a single Glenn Martin aircraft, they vigorously waved a motley collection of white flags. A handful pressed on, but they too were herded up by the Glenn Martin and ushered back to where the Fighting French armoured cars were waiting to escort them back to Murzuk.

"The conquest of the Fezzan is now achieved," claimed General Leclerc. Thus within little more than six weeks the Fighting French had made their way from Fort Lamy in Chad to within two hundred miles or so from the Allies in North Africa, a distance altogether of about 2,000 miles. From three sides Rommel's sole remaining base was definitely threatened—by Montgomery, by Anderson and by Leclerc. By the middle of January the semicircle was closed ; Leclerc was in touch with both flanks and Col. Ingold had reported to General Montgomery.

Salute to the Animals in the War

Although this war is the most mechanized that history recalls, it is only too true that a host of unoffending animals has become involved in Homo Sapiens' bloody quarrel. Chief amongst them, of course, is the horse, which in spite of armoured " cavalry " plays a great role on the battlefield and behind it. Top, Russian scouts on the Middle Don front. Below, Germans employing a horse team to drag one of their cars through the Russian mire.

527

Man and Bird and Beast Together . . .

From riding the whirlwind—and how it can blow in the Atlantic in mid-winter !—R.A.F. pilots in Iceland enjoy a " spot " of pony-riding (1). Another wintry scene (2) is of a Red Army patrol in their dog-drawn sleigh. Amusing indeed is this photograph (3) of an American Army corporal finishing well in front of the field in a donkey race in Tunisia. Then in (4) Russian scouts are setting out with the dogs which serve not only as faithful companions but as swift carriers of a message.

*Photos, British
Planet N*

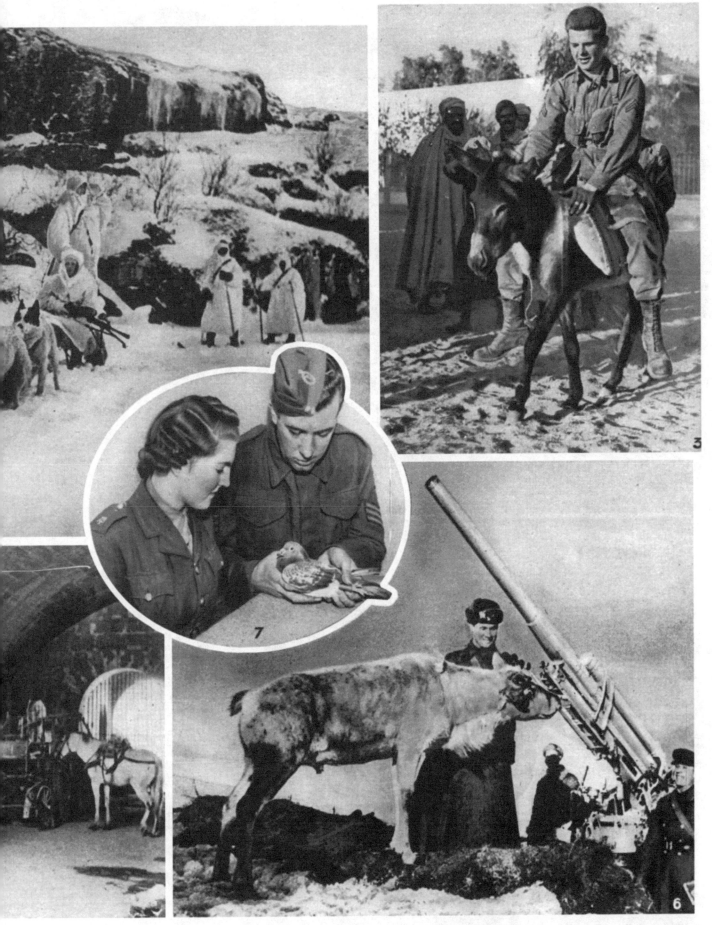

... Share the Endless Toils of War

Malta's ponies, the beasts of burden of the George Cross island, have stood up to the persistent bombing with characteristic imperturbability : here are some (5) sheltering beneath the Porto Reale in Valetta during an air raid.   A Russian A.A. battery on the Murmansk front has for its mascot a reindeer which makes a morning round of the guns (6).   And here (7) is Beachcomber, one of two pigeons dispatched from Dieppe beach with the first message of the landing on August 19, 1942.

Still in the Martial Train!

In the days of old of which the Bible tells and whose life is sculptured on the walls of the Egyptian tombs, camels and asses were the means of transport most valued alike by the patriarchal chieftain and the all-conquering pharaoh. And all down the ages these humble, patiently-plodding beasts have continued in their career of usefulness. Thus today, as the photograph above shows, through the dry and dusty heart of Tunisia heavily-laden camels and donkeys take provisions and ammunition to the Allied troops about to attack down a mountain pass; while on the left we see camels harnessed to the supply-drays of American troops who have arrived in India. But what would Abraham or Rameses have made of the motor-trucks whose drivers, we may well imagine, are luridly critical of the slow-moving creatures taking up so much of the road?

Photos, Associated Press, Pictorial Press

UNDER THE SWASTIKA

Nazis Scour the Continent for Factory Slaves

In another of his studies in the social and economic aspects of the Hitler regime in Germany and the German-occupied countries, PAUL TABORI writes here of the efforts to obtain workers for the Nazi factories. Cannon-fodder or factory-fodder—these are the grim alternatives Hitler offers to Europe's unhappy millions.

NAZI Germany has evolved the most gigantic system of plunder ever known in history. She is systematically and rapidly depriving the countries under her sway of raw materials, food, and armaments. But her most strenuous efforts go towards the kidnapping of millions of men and women. It is the greatest and most fatal weakness of the Third Reich, her Achilles heel, and it may prove in the end her doom, that her industries cannot keep up with the demands of the armed forces.

Today, according to an official estimate, there are (including prisoners of war) six million foreign workers in Germany and this means that every fourth worker in Hitler's Hell is a non-German. The other day it was pointed out that this represents the biggest "sixth column" on the side of freedom which we have ever known. Yet the six million men and women are still insufficient. The shortage is in skilled workers, and it is growing daily. This desperate situation explains why Hungarian factories are closing down, why Laval is involved in a sordid bargaining over French workmen and French prisoners of war why Denmark has been presented with an economic ultimatum, why the Reich has adopted a more conciliatory attitude towards Polish, Czech, and Serbian skilled labour. The whole of Europe has been turned into one gigantic slave market in which Germany is the only buyer.

YET the foreign workers represent a constant danger and worry. In Graz, for instance, the Police President announced recently that all foreign women workers must be housed in camps instead of hotels, boarding-houses, and inns. New arrivals are allowed to stay in such places only forty-eight hours, and if someone does not register his or her foreign lodgers, the punishment is a large fine and three months' imprisonment. Germany is afraid that these foreign women will "contaminate" the "sturdy Germanic spirit" which her own workers seem to lack more and more.

Laval declared proudly some weeks ago that the so-called Sauckel decrees which conscripted skilled workers all over Europe would not apply to France at all. But a few days later the Vichy Government was forced to announce that this concession was only a temporary one. By Oct. 15, 1942 some 150,000 skilled French workers should have left for Germany or at least signed their enlistment, but by the middle of September only 12,000 "specialists" had gone. In October, however, "recruiting" was intensified, and just before Christmas the Nazis claimed that 115,000 French specialists had gone to Germany. France has taken stringent measures to keep her "specialists" easily available for forcible deportation to Germany—last September they were warned by a proclamation of the French Secretary of State for Labour that they may not change

their place of work without "explicit and correct authority"—so that they can be seized and sent abroad whenever Laval has to offer a new sacrifice to the German Moloch.

Shortage of skilled workers is spreading everywhere. In Bulgaria, for instance, there is a great lack of well-trained technicians, and though four training schools have been opened at Sofia, Bitolj, Xanthi and Varna, it will be a long time before these produce sufficient graduates. Holland, though she is practically denuded of vital workers, must also contribute to Germany's immediate war effort. Dr. Boening, of the Social Management Department of the Reichskommissariat,

FRENCH YOUTH FOR THE REICH. In July, 1942 5,000 out of 1,400,000 French prisoners of war in Germany were released in exchange for workers from France. These two young Frenchmen are here seen registering to work for Hitler's war machine. The poster declares: "Young men help to free your elders." *Photo, Associated Press*

made an announcement which was cynically frank : thirty thousand metal workers must be transferred to Germany within the next three months. " It is necessary for Germany to make use of the skilled workers from Dutch factories," Dr. Boening declared, " and of those who can be trained in Germany . . . It cannot be denied that for the most part Dutch workers have not yet reached the German level of efficiency and therefore we must make greater use of the so-called compulsory labour regulation." This regulation means, among other things, that all Dutchmen born after Sept. 30, 1924, can be transported to Germany or German-occupied countries and used as it pleases the conqueror.

NATURALLY, Germany is making use of skilled technicians within the occupied countries. And this use means a total disruption of social and labour legislation. Vichy, for instance, has tried to combat unemployment by a reduction of working hours ; but the 48-hour week was suspended in the metal industry of Unoccupied France, as well as in the factories engaged in machine construction, the fine mechanical industry

and the railway repair shops. Overtime is paid at ten per cent above the normal rate—a ridiculously low wage. A Swiss newspaper described a recent health inspection in French factories which showed that "a large proportion of the workers, owing to under-nourishment, are incapable or barely capable of supporting a slack rhythm of work, and any measures not taking account of this situation arouse serious doubts." Naturally, Germany is little concerned with the well-being of her slaves, and keeps them steadily at starvation level.

NO wonder that there are constant attempts to escape this slavery. A Ghent newspaper published recently a leading article describing a visit to the Labour Exchange. The quisling journalist expressed great indignation because the skilled workers recruited for Germany "cannot be found " when the time comes for their transfer to the Reich, "thereby endangering the good relations between the Fuehrer and Belgium." Many of these workers escape to France, where they manage to hide at least for some time from the Gestapo and Sauckel's recruiting minions. The Germans seem to have the same trouble in Norway, where they are openly complaining that Norwegian technicians employed on fortification works fail to return after their leave has expired. More than two hundred have recently been sent to a concentration camp for this offence, and "much sharper measures are threatened."

From Holland come reports of widespread sabotage in industry, in which foremen collaborate with skilled workers. The output of the Dutch mines has sunk to 40 per cent of the pre-war standard in consequence of this sabotage. Miners "have refused to do any Sunday work. They mix stones with the coal, and regard that as both sabotage and wage adjustment."

Italy is even worse off in the matter of skilled workers than Germany. Workers are being removed from one province to another to act as stop-gaps if production is threatened with a complete breakdown. Even soldiers on leave are pressed into industrial work ; women and children are employed in ever-growing numbers.

Within Germany the lot of both foreign and native workers is not at all enviable. The German worker has to pay thirteen different kinds of taxes—including the "voluntary contributions." His wages are severely controlled ; and while the purchasing power of money has been greatly lowered, there are fewer and fewer things to buy.

LONG hours, small wages, complete lack of freedom—these characterize the life of the German and foreign skilled worker in Hitler's Europe. Not even his private life is safe from strict regimentation. The other day the Wuppertal Labour Court sentenced a woman worker to three years in prison—because, while the Fuehrer's latest speech was being broadcast, she went on reading a love story ! " This is such a serious crime," the court said, " that the worker could not be tolerated in our community. The decisive factor is not a breach of the 'peace of labour' but the lack of respect towards the Fuehrer. Considering that she is forty, she should have known how irreverent it was to read a cheap story on such an occasion." Poor woman, she sought refuge from the Fuehrer's spate of eloquence in a love story. She was punished, and the Fuehrer goes on ranting while German workers toil like slaves.

America's Hundred Billion Dollar Budget

In the U.S.A. the opening weeks of 1943 were marked by two presidential utterances which not only gave a vivid picture of the immense strides taken by the Republic along the road to Total War, but presaged even greater steps to be made in the immediate future. From these speeches of President Roosevelt it is clear that Uncle Sam is indeed taking off his coat.

No prophet of smooth things did President Roosevelt reveal himself in his Message on the State of the Union and his War Budget Message to the new Congress ; yet, as old Isaiah would have put it, the things he spoke of were the *right* things.

"This 78th Congress," he said in his Message of January 7, "assembles at one of the great moments in the history of this nation. The past year was perhaps the most crucial for modern civilization. The coming year will be filled with violent conflict—yet with high promise of better things." In brief sentences, closely packed paragraphs, he spoke of the great events of the year that had gone : of Russia's magnificent defence, of Japanese advances, of Britain's counter-attacks in Libya, of China's heroic contribution. America

farmer had raised the greatest amount of food ever made available in a single year of the country's history.

Of course, there had been dislocation, inconvenience, even some hardship ; there had been mistakes, too many forms and questionnaires. But they would learn from their mistakes, improve by their experience. 1943 would not be an easy year for them on the home front : in many ways they would feel in their daily life the sharp pinch of total war. But—to quote one or two of the President's most forthright sayings—" We do not intend to leave things so lax that loopholes will be left for traitors or chisellers or for the manipulators of the black market," and " fortunately there are only a few

amounted to $2,000,000,000, a figure which may be easier to grasp if we refer to it as two billions, since an American billion is a thousand millions. (An English billion, by the way, is a million million.) At the beginning of 1943 it exceeded six billions a month and during the coming fiscal year it will average more than eight billion dollars a month—say, a hundred billions a year (at $4 = £ ; £25 thousand million).

This enormous expenditure is bound to have the most serious effects on American ways of life. It involves the total mobilization of all America's men and women, all America's equipment and materials. During 1943 approximately 6,000,000 people will be needed above present requirements for the armed Services and war production.

Production of less-needed commodities must be reduced, while the production of commodities for war and essential civilian use must be increased. " That may hurt our taste, but not our health."

During the coming year American civilians may expect to be able to purchase about 500 dollars' (£125) worth of goods and services ; this represents an average of nearly 25 per cent below the record level of 1941.

" Total war demands the simplification of American life. By giving up what we do not need all of us will be better able to get what we do need. We must assure each citizen the necessities of life at prices he can pay. By concerted effort to stabilize prices, rents, and wages we have succeeded in keeping the rise in the cost of living within narrow bounds. We will continue those efforts and will succeed."

U.S. TANK OUTPUT is being greatly accelerated by Ford mass-production methods now used to produce 32-ton M4 medium tanks. This photo shows workmen putting finishing touches to tanks as the machines roll off the assembly lines.

pays tribute, he went on, to the fighting men of all the United Nations, to the fighting leaders of America's allies ; he revealed something of the magnitude and diversity of America's own military activities. " As I speak to you, approximately one and a half million soldiers, sailors, marines and flyers are in service outside continental limits all through the world."

Where will the next blow fall, when are the United Nations going to strike in Europe, and where ? The President refrained from prophecy, but this he could and did say : " We are going to strike, and strike hard . . . We believe that the Nazis and the Fascists have asked for it, and they're going to get it. . . ."

Progress in the field depends upon progress on the production front, and on the whole Mr. Roosevelt seemed to be satisfied with what had been achieved.

In 1942 they had produced 48,000 military planes—more than the production of Germany, Italy, and Japan put together ; in last December alone 5,500 military planes had been turned out, and the rate of production was still rising. In 1942 they had produced 56,000 combat vehicles, 670,000 machine-guns, 21,000 anti-tank guns, ten and a quarter billion rounds of small-arms ammunition, 181,000,000 rounds of artillery ammunition . . . " I think the arsenal of Democracy," commented the President, " is making good." And while this " miracle of production " was in process of achievement, the American armed forces had grown from two millions to over seven millions, and the American

Americans who put appetite above patriotism."

For the rest, the President was concerned with the " State of the Union " *after* the war ; and here he took the wind out of the sails of those of his critics (particularly the Republicans in Congress who had recently won their seats and felt that they had a mandate to be independently critical) who had anticipated that we would " out-Beveridge Beveridge " in his plans for the post-war world. He submitted no detailed set of blueprints of the America that is to be when the war is won, but contented himself by repeating those broad generalizations drawn from his liberal philosophy which almost all Americans have approved as they have fallen from his lips, and which there is every reason to believe they still approve.

Four days later the President presented his war budget message to Congress, what he described as " a maximum programme for waging war." America was waging total war, he said, because her very existence is threatened. " Total war is a grim reality. It means the dedication of our lives and services with a single objective—victory . . . In total war we are all soldiers, whether in uniform, overalls, or shirt sleeves."

Just before Pearl Harbour, America's monthly expenditure for war purposes

How is the vast programme to be financed ? In the first place, by the reduction of non-war expenditure from six and a half billions in 1939 to four billions in 1944. Henceforth 96 cents of every dollar expended by the U.S. Federal Government will be used to pay war costs and interest on the public debt, leaving only 4 cents for all the so-called non-war purposes. An extra sixteen billion dollars is to be collected by taxation or savings, thus enabling the State to meet approximately 50 per cent of the coming year's war expenditure.

In brief, in the current twelve months to next June, United States war expenditure will be 77 billion dollars ; in the succeeding twelve months it will be around a hundred billion dollars. The figures are so huge as to seem, as Mr. Roosevelt says, fantastic. Yet it may be doubted whether with an expenditure of 100 billion dollars the United States will be devoting any larger proportion of its resources to the prosecution of the war than this country or Canada.

As Mr. Oscar Hobson has pointed out in The News Chronicle the cost of certain manufactured war products in America is in dollars much higher than four times their cost in pounds here. (It should be explained that for purposes of comparison the pound is now usually taken as four dollars). It is known that the ratio of wages of workers doing comparable work is nearer $8 = £ than $4 = £. Again, the American private soldier gets something over 8s. a day against the British Tommy's 3s., giving an equivalent rate of exchange of $10 or $11 = £.

Without attempting to minimize America's effort in the least, concludes Mr. Hobson, it would be a more accurate measure to take the dollar at about six to the pound, and to say that America's 1943-4 war expenditure will be not £25,000 millions, or five times ours, but £15,000 millions, or three times ours. The population of the U.S.A. it may be noted is about 132 millions, as compared with Great Britain's 48 millions.

Uncle Sam Rolls Up His Sleeves for War

AMERICA'S TOTAL WAR. 1, Members of a Los Angeles unit of the Women's Ambulance Defence Corps replace men on a Californian ranch, where thousands of tomatoes have to be picked. 2, Luncheon in the Combined Chiefs of Staff building at Washington. Left to right : Adm. E. J. King, C.-in-C. U.S. Fleet; Gen. G. C. Marshall, C.-in-C. U.S. Army; Adm. W. D. Leahy, Chief of Staff to Pres. Roosevelt ; Lt.-Gen. H. H. Arnold, commanding U.S. Army Air Force. 3, On Nov. 22, 1942, at Kluane Lake, Yukon, members of the Canadian Cabinet cut the tape on the Alcan Highway—the 1,671-mile-long road linking Alaska across Canada with the U.S.A. (see pp. 331-333 of this volume). 4, Synthetic rubber ready for shipment in paper drums. Each drum holds 200 pounds. 5, Troops demonstrate how to remove ice from a tank tread at the Arctic testing laboratory at a U.S. Army post. 6, Workers of a U.S. rubber company fasten bolts in a metal case designed to hold the self-sealing tank of a dive-bomber.

Photos, New York Times Photos, Associated Press, Keystone, Sport & General, Pictorial Press

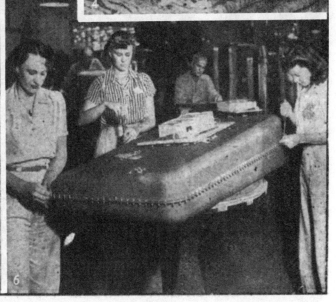

HANDLEY - PAGE HALIFAX four-engined bombers have played an outstandingly successful part in our bomber offensive against the enemy. Here one of these powerful machines is shown making its attack. The great aircraft is flying straight and true on the "run-up" to the target; and, crouched on his padded cushion, the bomb-aimer (2) watches the target below come into his sights. Then he presses the switch in his right hand, thus releasing the huge bomb; which particular part of the enormous load of bombs to be released is first

selected on a switch panel seen at his right hand. The large bomb doors (18) have already been opened.

Sitting tensely at the controls, the pilot and captain of the aircraft (5) has followed the bomb-aimer's directions until the bombs have been "got away." As the bomb crashes on to the target it is automatically photographed.

The navigator (3), whose daring skill has enabled the plane to reach the target area, is seated at his desk, preparing to give the pilot a bearing for the journey home. Near by is the wireless operator (4). The engineer (8) is using the astral-dome (9) to spot for night fighters. It is his job to control—at the direction of the pilot—the functions of the four 1,175 h.p. Merlin engines. This he does by means of his instrument panel (10), which actuates the covered-in controls to the engines (11).

The front twin-gun turret (1) and the mid-upper turret (15) are shown, as is the method

of supplying ammunition from the magazines (16) to the rear four-gun turret by means of tracks (17), down which the ammunition is hydraulically fed. In this manner a greater weight can be carried because the balance of the aircraft is not upset. Fuel tanks are situated in the wings, while the heating system (12) is operated by hot air from the engines. Folding seats for the second pilot and engineer, and bunks for the crew are seen at (6) and (13), while oxygen bottles (7) and a supply of flares (14) are also shown.

Specially drawn for THE WAR ILLUSTRATED *by Haworth*

THE WAR IN THE AIR

by Capt. Norman Macmillan, M.C., A.F.C.

IN most sectors of the global war areas attack is now the keynote of United Nations policy.

The Ruhr industrial district was bombed eight times by aircraft of Bomber Command during the nights following January 3, 4, 7, 8, 9, 11, 12, and 13, 1943. Bombs weighing up to 4,000 lb. were dropped during these raids. In the last raid more than 100 tons of high-explosive and incendiary bombs were dropped in 12 minutes by four-engined bombers which got through in spite of violent anti-aircraft gunfire. Seventeen bombers were lost in these raids.

Essen was the principal target—the main centre of Krupps armament firm, which produces more of Germany's heavy naval, coastal defence, and mobile railway guns than any other concern. With Germany known to be increasing her coastal defences as rapidly as possible in fear of a United Nations' assault upon Europe, Krupps is a desirable strategic target for R.A.F. bombers from the British point of view.

The Germans tried to defend Essen with night-fighters in addition to anti-aircraft gunfire. Shots were exchanged between British and German aircraft, but there were few serious encounters. One Lancaster captain reported after the fifth raid : " Our aircraft were still bombing when I left, and fires were springing up all over the target. I could still see the glare when I was a hundred miles away." During the sixth raid a pilot circling the target area made a steep bank. Suddenly he found his Lancaster upside down. " Apparently I had done a half roll," he reported ; " I should hardly have thought it possible in a Lancaster. One engine cut out, but it picked up again once we were straight and level."

A JUNKERS 88 night-fighter attacked a British bomber during the eighth raid. The first warning to the crew of the bomber was the impact of bullets from dead astern. The rear gunner was wounded in the leg. Another burst tore a large hole in the port wing, and released the rubber dinghy, which shot into the air. The dinghy wrapped around the tail of the bomber. The aircraft became uncontrollable and fell 2,000 feet. During its fall the Junkers lost it. The pilot regained control, came home with the hydraulic system out of action, the rudder and elevator damaged, and holes in the fuselage and rear and mid-upper gun turrets.

After eight right punches at Germany's Ruhr in 11 days, Bomber Command suddenly landed a hard left, right on the heart, Berlin, which a strong force bombed on the night of Saturday, January 16. The 1,200 miles' journey was made through and over wind cloud. But there were clear patches over Berlin. High explosive bombs up to 3½-tons weight were dropped and many thousands of incendiaries fell on the city. Large fires were seen. Only one bomber was lost, despite the defence zones of searchlights and severe flak. This the 54th raid on Berlin, was its heaviest. Indeed, many early raids on the German capital were made by a mere handful of bombers, of types unable to load up the weight or sizes of bombs now carried almost every night to some part of Germany.

The 53rd raid took place on November 7, 1941, when Mannheim and Cologne were also raided. Russian bombers raided Berlin during the subsequent interval.

BRITISH bombing policy changed greatly during this interval. The column of single machines, with wide time intervals between each bomber, gave place to the present method of concentrated bombing. The new method does more damage in a briefer time, and so makes it more difficult for A.R.P. personnel to reduce the extent of the damage. Indeed, it has been reported that German A.R.P. personnel keep under shelter during concentrated raids, and emerge to fight the fires when the bombers have gone : a policy adopted to cut down the casualties in trained personnel due to the rain of bombs. The number of bombers simultaneously over the target area confuses the locater crews, whether operating acoustically or by electrical apparatus, and gives additional protection against shellfire and night-fighters, for neither gunners nor fighter pilots can engage more than a few of the bombers.

Renewed Raids on London

The 54th raid on Berlin provoked the Luftwaffe into retaliation against south-east England and London on the following night ; the Luftwaffe made two attacks with a considerable time interval between, indicating that the same aircraft may have been used. Ten German bombers were destroyed. During this night the R.A.F. were again over Berlin. Weather favoured defence during the long trip across Germany ; there was bright moonlight all the way, no cover from cloud except over the target ; 22 bombers were lost from a strong force.

On January 20 about 90 enemy fighters approached the south-east coast of England. Some 25 Me. 109 and FW. 190 fighter-bombers flew inland and fanned out over

FLT.-SERGT. R. H. MIDDLETON, R.A.A.F. (No. 149 Sqdn.), was on Jan. 13, 1943 awarded the V.C. for " devotion to duty in the face of overwhelming odds unsurpassed in the annals of the Royal Air Force." He was captain and 1st pilot of a Stirling detailed to attack a Turin factory in Nov., 1942. His plane was hit and though badly wounded, he bravely carried on and brought his aircraft back to British waters, though he died in the attempt.

Photo, British Official : Crown Copyright

Kent and Sussex. About six reached the London area. Fifteen enemy aircraft were shot down that day by defending British aircraft of Fighter Command, five by the Hawker Typhoon 400 m.p.h.-plus fighter, which has been in operation since the Dieppe raid. The Typhoon is the world's most heavily armed and armoured fighter. Its Napier-Sabre engine develops about 2,400 h.p.

The Russian advance has continued. Presumably air bombardment assisted the capture of Millerovo, important rail town between Rostov and Voronezh. German air losses continue at a high rate. Russia reports latest German aircraft losses as 255 in one week against 133 Russian. The Russians have stormed the aerodrome used by the Germans to supply troops cut off in the Stalingrad area. Its capture will force the Luftwaffe to supply the remainder of the garrison by parachute, a less efficient method than landing air transports.

In the Mediterranean strategic bombing was applied against targets in Sicily, Lampedusa, and Tunisia, and Allied aircraft have been pasting Rommel's fleeing columns. The air arm tore the German supply system to shreds by the bombing of Tripoli, Bizerta, Tunis, and every North African port open to the use of enemy shipping, and ports on the European side of the Mediterranean, too.

STEADY pressure has been maintained against the Japanese in Burma and the Far East. In Burma, British and American fighters and bombers attacked land, sea and river targets everywhere ; U.S. bombers sank one ship in a Japanese-escorted convoy far to the south of Rangoon.

Japanese bases throughout New Guinea were subjected to air attack. U.S. forces are securing their Solomon Islands aerodrome by advancing slowly in Guadalcanal.

The Air Ministry has released photographs of the R.A.F. 2,000-lb. parachute blast bomb, which is dropped by medium and heavy bombers on industrial area targets to secure maximum effect by blast. It should not be confused with the parachute-check bomb which I referred to in page 502 as in use by the Americans in Papua ; the latter is an anti-personnel bomb used to attack troops and similar front-line targets, against which our fighter-bombers employ delay-action bombs.

BACK FROM BERLIN. Lancaster aircraft are here seen after their return from the heavy R.A.F. attack on the German capital on Jan. 17, 1943. The previous night also saw a devastating raid on Berlin, and on both occasions a great load of bombs, including 8,000 pounders, was dropped. *Photo, G.P.U.*

Allies Reach Last Stage in New Guinea Battle

JAPS' LAST STAND IN NEW GUINEA in the Sanananda region was extremely tenacious after the Allied occupation of Buna and Gona during the closing weeks of 1942. 1, Australian machine-gunner; whose post is effectively hidden amid foliage, goes into action. 2, Papuans bringing in a wounded American. 3, U.S. soldiers building an operating-table at a medical post in the Buna area. 4, Australians crossing the Kanusi river by means of "flying foxes."

Photos, News Chronicle, British Newsreels, New York Times, Sport & General

How Our Men Pass the Time in Captivity

BRITISH PRISONERS OF WAR in Germany are housed in camps (see map, Vol. IV, p. 101) which are divided into various categories: Oflags (officer camps), Stalags (for other ranks), Dulags (temporary camps), Luftlags (for airmen), Marlags and Milags (for naval ratings). By international convention prisoners have certain rights which are safeguarded by the International Red Cross Committee at Geneva. The chief of these rights are: food on the same scale as the captor country's backline troops; clothing, underwear and footwear; medical attention; correspondence, parcels of food and reading matter. Right, photo from an enemy source showing British soldiers captured at Dunkirk in 1940 enjoying a circus which they have built at their camp. Below, Xmas card received from an officer camp in 1942.

TO DEFEAT BOREDOM, our men organize exhibitions and games. Above, a boxing contest. Below left, model built from drawings and descriptions contained in letters sent home by British captives, of their living quarters at a camp for airmen prisoners.

Window Removed to Show Interior

Food Locker

Room 26 E
STALAG LUFT 1

"IT is amazing how clever some of the fellows are with such limited resources," wrote a British prisoner of war from Stalag Luft III. In his letter, which was recently received by the British Prisoners of War Relatives' Association, the writer was referring to an arts and crafts exhibition organized by some of his comrades at a camp in Germany. "About ten barracks have been converted into exhibition halls and the general effect is astonishing," wrote another prisoner. "For four hours I wandered round this exhibition, forgetting that I was in a Stalag."

THIS is indeed a bright side to the picture, and it shows that our men are turning their captivity to good account, for prison-life in Germany would be unbearably monotonous without some such organization among the prisoners themselves, deprived as they are of most of the things that make life worth living. Therefore, every effort is made to supply lacking material wants. Parcels containing clothing, reading matter and games of all kinds provide a few of the prisoners' pressing needs. How greatly these are appreciated is shown by thousands of letters and messages from the innumerable camps throughout Germany. Food parcels, which are dispatched at the rate of one per week per man through the Red Cross, are, of course, extremely welcome. Prisoners who are ill are the special care of an Invalid Comforts Section of the Red Cross and receive invalid food and other necessities.

'Photos, Planet News, Keystone, Daily Mirror

THE HOME FRONT

by E. Royston Pike

KNOCKERS-UP—or rather the lack of them—caused a strike in the L.M.S. railway yards at Nottingham on January 11. For the benefit of those not acquainted with this species of human fauna, a knocker-up is a man whose job it is to rouse whether by a fierce rat-a-tat on the front door or by a handful of gravel thrown at the bedroom window) those workers who have to report for duty long before it is light. Before last winter there were eight knockers-up in Nottingham who used to call the locomen detailed for duty between midnight and 7.30 a.m. But on November 2 they were withdrawn owing to labour shortage, and the locomen were left to their own devices. Some of them had alarm clocks; others would like to have had them, but found that you cannot get one now for love or money. Still others relied on their wives to wake them . . . But sometimes she " fell down " on the job, and a loco-man, arriving late at the depot, found that his train had gone. He was sent home and lost a day's pay in consequence.

EARLY in January the locomen held a meeting and resolved to strike at midnight on the following Sunday unless knockers-up were provided ; and when that midnight came 600 drivers, firemen and guards stopped away from work, and 17 local passenger trains and a number of goods trains did not run . . . During the day negotiations with the L.M.S. and the local Ministry of Labour officials were resumed, and in a few hours a settlement was reached. The knockers-up were put back, men who had lost time through not having been called were to have their payment made up, and there was to be no victimization. The men agreed to provide their own knockers-up for the present, but it was left to the Ministry of Labour to find them permanently.

Alarm clocks would have prevented the locomen from oversleeping, but of alarm clocks the shops are bare. Before the War they used to come in large quantities from the U.S.A. and Switzerland. Now these channels of supplies have been cut off, and English clockmakers are busy making munitions. In London it was reported from one of the big stores that they had a waiting-list for alarm clocks at 55s. each ; even at that price a hundred a day could be sold—if they could obtain them.

ANOTHER and more vital necessity of wartime life is the electric torch, and from all parts of the country complaints have come in of the scarcity of batteries. The battery for the convenient pocket-torch is in very short supply, because the Board of Trade has decided that no more cases of this size are to be manufactured (although a limited number of batteries will continue to be made for those torches already in use). But scarcer far are the batteries for cycle lamps. I do not know how many millions of cyclists there are on British roads at the present time (how pleasant it is cycling nowadays even on the great arterial roads which once were death-traps for the humble cyclist !), but to ride a bike after dark without a light is to court trouble.

From various districts there come reports of large-scale prosecutions by the police of workers who have been found going to work or home in the black-out minus a light. To take a case in point, the Swadlincote magistrates were nonplussed when they had brought before them a number of miners from the South Derbyshire coalfields, summoned for cycling to work in the early morning without rear lights. In defence it was urged that it was impossible to buy batteries, and this the police admitted. Coal production would be gravely affected if the men had to walk four miles from their homes to the pits and then another two to the coalface. Neither oil nor acetylene lamps were available, and public transport there was none. All the cases where it was proved a battery was unobtainable were dismissed on payment of costs, and it was stated that Mr. Lloyd George, Minister of Fuel and Power, was trying to speed up the delivery of more batteries.

UTILITY FURNITURE, free of purchase tax, may be bought only by bombed-out citizens and newly-wed or engaged couples. Permits have to be obtained, and these incorporate a " points " system. Here is shown a well-designed Utility kitchen cabinet of stained beech.
Photo, Topical Press

AT the beginning of January the Board of Trade announced that the Utility Furniture scheme was in operation. The furniture, it was explained, could be supplied only to those obtaining an official permit, and those permits will be issued to : (1) people who are about to set up a home for the first time, provided they have married since the beginning of 1941 or intend to marry within two months of applying for the permit ; (2) people who wish to set up a home because they are going to have a child ; (3) people who have lost their home through enemy action. Only in special circumstances will exceptions be made, e.g. for the purchase of a bed for a child growing too big for his cot, or for the purchase by a newly-married couple of furniture for a bedroom in the house of parents. Permits, however, are not required for nursery furniture (i.e. cot, play-pen and child's chair).

That reference to engaged couples gave rise at once to some speculation. A Daily Express reporter who made inquiries at the Board of Trade discovered that there is to be an elaborate system of checking and confirmation. Are the couple really engaged ? When is the wedding date, and where is the marriage to take place ? Have either of the young couple any furniture of their own already, or are they living with their parents ? These are some of the preliminary questions which have to be satisfied before the permit is issued. Then, in due time, inquiries are to be made as to whether the wedding took place ; if it did not, why not ? If the engagement has been broken, then the permit is cancelled and any furniture bought must be returned.

NONE of the furniture is as yet available for inspection. It must be ordered from a furniture dealer from a catalogue, copies of which can be obtained (price 9d.) from any bookseller or newsagent or direct from H.M. Stationery Office. No purchase tax is levied, and the maximum retail prices which have been fixed cover free delivery within a radius of 15 miles. Hire purchase terms are to be made available. The maximum number of units is 60 in the case of a married couple setting up a home, and up to 15 more will be allowed for each child. Specimen charges, with the " cost in points " given in brackets, are :

Dining table, £4 13s. 6d. and £5 15s. 3d. (6 points); dining chair, £1 3s. to £1 10s. (1) ; easy chair, £3 12s. and £6 10s. (6); sideboard, £7 6s. 6d. and £10 7s. (6); double bed, £3 10s. 9d. (oak) to £4 11s. (mahogany) (5); wardrobes, £13 2s. 9d. to £17 4s. 9d. (12 or for 3 ft. size, 10) ; 3 ft. dressing chest (with mirror), £8 11s. to £10 10s. (8) ; kitchen table, £2 14s. and £3 8s. 6d. (6, or for smaller one 4) ; kitchen chair, 12s. 6d. and 14s. 3d. (1).

RECENTLY the Select Committee on National Expenditure issued their report (H.M. Stationery Office, 4d.) on The Health and Welfare of Women in War Factories. In the three years since mid-1939 rather more than one-and-a-half million women have taken up fresh jobs in industry. The Committee comment unfavourably on the fact that, except in the case of Royal Ordnance Factories and certain private undertakings, there has been no selective medical examination before the intake of women into industry, with the result that many women sent from a considerable distance to work at a factory have been found on arrival to be suffering from an illness or mental disability which made it impossible for them to be accepted for employment. It is urged, therefore, that the Government should give close attention to the problem of securing a satisfactory industrial medical service, and that greater use should be made of women doctors.

Physical amenities are also criticized. In some factories, it is stated, an inadequate time is allowed for meals, and if service in the canteen is not too good, girls have to bolt their food ; in others, workers still eat a snack at their machines or worktables. Insufficient attention is devoted in some factories to personal cleanliness and the prevention of industrial dermatitis. Washing-rooms are generally unattractive, and often badly lighted. Then many factories, particularly the medium-sized and smaller establishments, leave much to be desired in the way of lighting and ventilation.

HOURS of work, too, are the subject of unfavourable comment. Although the Ministry of Labour advised employers two years ago that the number of hours worked by women should vary only between 48 and 56 per week, cases were reported of women who are working 12 hours a day, spending two or three hours travelling, and on top of this undertaking household duties. Small wonder is it that in these circumstances sickness and absence from work are reported to be more frequent among women workers than among the men.

London's Little Streets Have Kept Their Courage

LONDONERS IN THE BLITZ (1940-41) behaved with proverbial courage. The retaliatory night raid on Jan. 17, 1943, launched by a few German aircraft in reply to our heavy bombing of Berlin the previous night, was the Metropolis's first big raid since May 1941 ; two days later the capital was attacked in daylight. This photograph shows a woman warden minding a baby whose parents are salvaging their furniture from their bombed-out home.

Photo Topical Press

At Home and Abroad With Our Roving Camera

H.M.S. ROYAL EAGLE in peacetime carried thousands of Londoners to N. Kentish resorts. Two years ago she was commissioned as a warship of the Royal Navy. During this period she has spent 520 nights and 132 days at sea, covering a mileage of 25,000. She has been in action 52 times against enemy aircraft, and has destroyed two for certain and many probables. Among the honours awarded to her crew are two D.S.C.s, four D.S.M.s, and 13 mentions in dispatches.

This record is apart from her fine achievement at Dunkirk, when the Royal Eagle (not yet on the Navy's strength), brought home nearly 3,000 men, one of her most distinguished passengers on that historic occasion being Gen. Pownall. Each man of the ship's company who was on board at that time carries a silver penknife inscribed " Royal Eagle, Dunkirk 1940," presented by men of the Cheshire Regt. whom she brought safely back. Below, polishing the ship's paddle-wheel. Right, ratings fill pom-pom ammunition belts aboard their redoubtable vessel.

AUSTERITY COBBLING has been brought about owing to shortage of leather. On Jan. 1, 1943, patchwork repairs for shoes, with two-piece repair for heels over 1¾ in. in width or length, and heel reinforcement at the point of wear in rubber or iron, became compulsory. Repairs will henceforth be rough-finished, but adequate. A wartime code for treatment of footwear has been given by the Board of Trade. Important points are ; examine your shoes each evening ; have them repaired as soon as the top layer of leather has worn through ; clean them regularly. This photograph shows how the new repair work will be carried out.

NEW ARMY OVERCOAT. The Regular Army and the Home Guard are being issued with winter overcoats of utility cut. Instead of brass, these coats have khaki-coloured plastic buttons, and are of a slightly thinner material than hitherto. A pleat runs from the top to the bottom at the back, thus giving greater freedom for the arms. In previous issues the pleat ran only from the belt to the bottom of the coat. Such changes in Army uniform designs are under frequent review.

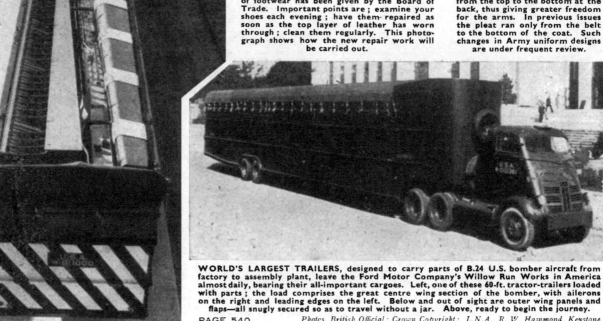

WORLD'S LARGEST TRAILERS, designed to carry parts of B.24 U.S. bomber aircraft from factory to assembly plant, leave the Ford Motor Company's Willow Run Works in America almost daily, bearing their all-important cargoes. Left, one of these 60-ft. tractor-trailers loaded with parts ; the load comprises the great centre wing section of the bomber, with ailerons on the right and leading edges on the left. Below and out of sight are outer wing panels and flaps—all snugly secured so as to travel without a jar. Above, ready to begin the journey.

Photos, British Official: Crown Copyright; L.N.A., R. W. Hammond, Keystone

I WAS THERE!

We Got the Convoy Through the U-Boats

Attacked 35 times by U-boats in the Atlantic, an armada of merchantmen recently reached this country. The part that a Liberator of the Coastal Command played in this battle lasting four days and nights is told below: the story is reprinted from The Daily Telegraph.

"WE had been over the convoy only about half an hour," said Sqdn.-Ldr. Bulloch, "when we sighted the first submarine. There was a hailstorm at the time and in the early morning light visibility was bad.

"But this U-boat was on the surface about 11 miles behind the convoy. It was travelling fast to catch up with the ships. I circled to attack. It sighted us and started to crash-dive, but I got it just as it was disappearing, and the depth charges went down on top of it."

Flyg.-Off. Michael S. Layton, Bulloch's Canadian navigator, had a "grandstand" view of what happened then.

"I looked back from the astrodome," he said, "and saw about 40 feet of the submarine sticking out of the water at an angle of 30 degrees. The depth charges exploded right along the track of the U-boat and the spray completely smothered the stern."

A patch of oil nearly 800 yards long spread on the surface of the sea and was followed seconds later by debris. The Liberator signalled a corvette to the scene. When it arrived it disturbed a flock of seagulls which were hovering over the debris. The corvette signalled Sqdn.-Ldr. Bulloch, "You certainly got him." Another signal read, "You killed him." And a third, "Dead bodies seen."

Three hours later the squadron-leader sighted two U-boats 300 yards apart going like mad for the convoy.

"There was oil coming from one of them," he said. So they attacked it and the depth charges were well placed. A couple of seconds after the explosions had died away a terrific spout of water shot us into the air.

The Liberator had now no more depth charges, but it continued its patrol. The crew settled down to the routine jobs and one of the gunners cooked a lunch of steak and potatoes on a paraffin stove.

"I was sitting in the cockpit with a plate on my knee, with ' George '—the automatic pilot—in charge," Sqdn.-Ldr. Bulloch said. "I was going to enjoy that steak, but another U-boat popped up.

"The plate, with its steak and potatoes, went spinning off my knee as I grabbed the controls and sounded the alarm. There was a clatter of plates back in the aircraft as the rest of the crew jumped to it, forgetting how hungry they were.

"We dived on the submarine and opened up on it with cannon and machine-gun fire. We couldn't do anything else. But the U-boat didn't know that, and as soon as it saw us coming it got under quickly. Our lunch was ruined, but that U-boat didn't get within torpedo range of the convoy."

Twenty minutes later another one was sighted, and Sqdr.-Ldr. Bulloch began to wonder if the whole German U-boat fleet had congregated in that part of the Atlantic. They attacked again with their cannons, and again the U-boat dived in a hurry.

Another half-hour and the squadron-leader sighted a sixth submarine ; 50 minutes later a seventh ; and in another 25 minutes the eighth. All three were attacked with cannon fire and forced to crash-dive.

SQDN.-LDR. BULLOCH, D.S.O., D.F.C. (left), whose story is told in this page, has received a bar to his D.S.O., and Sergt. McColl (right) the D.F.M. The awards were announced on Jan. 10, 1943. *Photo, British Official*

It was only when darkness was beginning to fall that the Liberator headed back to base. It landed safely after a patrol of nearly 17 hours and after attacking U-boats from dawn to dusk.

We Were the Cat Among Rommel's Pigeons

Armoured cars of the Royal Dragoons executed one of the 8th Army's most spectacular manoeuvres when they broke through Rommel's lines on Nov. 2, 1942, and in four days destroyed 200 vehicles, captured and destroyed at least 30 guns, and cut many phone lines. The story is told here by a leader of one of the armoured squadrons.

WE attribute the luck which attended our initial break-through to the splendid work of the infantry and the artillery, which paved the way. We left our location and passed through the mine-fields in single file. No shot was fired at us. The only impediment to our progress occurred when the first car ran into an 88 mm. gunpit filled with dead Germans. One or two more cars, including three petrol replenishment

ESCORT SHIPS OF THE ATLANTIC CONVOY that battled against enemy submarines in early Dec. 1942 (see accompanying text) included those of the British, Polish and Norwegian navies. 1, H.M.S. Fame, British destroyer, and 2, Norwegian corvette Rose, which sighted and engaged two U-boats. 3, Norwegian corvette Eglantine, which successfully attacked three of the German submarines in two successive actions. 4, Polish destroyer Burza chased a U-boat and attacked it with depth charges.

Photos, British Official : Crown Copyright

lorries, got stuck in slit trenches, but most of them pulled out when dawn broke and fought their way up to us.

The enemy was too astounded to do anything as we came through, or else the Italian section thought we were Germans and the German section thought we were Italians. They waved Swastika flags at us with vigour, and we replied with " Achtung ! " and anything else we could think of, which, with a wave and answering wave, would get us through their lines.

As it grew lighter they stared and blinked at us. Although a warning artillery barrage had been going on all night they couldn't believe their eyes. They would goggle at us from short range, see our berets, bolt away a few yards, pause as if they didn't think it was true, and come back to take another look. We passed within ten yards of the muzzles of an entire battery of field artillery. Right down the column we went with Germans standing by their guns and fortunately failing to let them off. One of them would suddenly see we were British, and run a few yards to tell somebody else. Then both of them would stare unbelievingly.

We Woke the Quartermaster!

As the dawn broke we passed a man in bed. From the mass of vehicles and equipment surrounding him he was obviously an Italian quartermaster. We woke him up by tossing a Verey light into his blankets. He broke the record for the sitting high jump ! Into one of his lorries we heaved a hand grenade. The results on the lorry were most satisfactory, but they scared the second-in-command who, following in his armoured car, had failed to see us toss the grenade.

Picking our way through trenches and gun positions we came upon what was evidently a " permanent " headquarters. Lorries were dug in, men were asleep everywhere They were surprised to wake up and see their lorries go up in smoke one by one. We were now some miles behind their lines, and their astonishment had been so colossal that we hadn't had one shot fired at us. It was full daylight, and getting amongst the " soft " transport our work of destruction began.

In the first quarter of an hour the two squadrons destroyed forty lorries by simply putting a bullet through the petrol tanks and setting a match to the leak. The crews of lorries which had got bogged in the breakthrough transferred themselves to German vehicles holding petrol. Spare men climbed aboard Italian vehicles mounted with Breda guns, and on we pushed across the desert.

Germans panicked from their lorries into slit trenches. We had no time to take prisoners. We just took their weapons and told them to commence walking east. Only those who refused were shot. Few refused. The majority were most anxious to oblige us in every way, and readily assisted in draining vehicles we thought fit to immobilize.

The Italians asked for far greater consideration. They wanted to come with us, clinging to the sides of our armoured cars as they fought each other to come aboard. To stop these poignant scenes a troop-leader asked for one of their officers. Half a dozen men stepped forward. We explained we couldn't take them all and, skimming off the cream, pushed on with a colonel and two majors clinging for dear life round the muzzles of our two-pounders.

' Bumped ' by Bombs from the Air

Up till now we had had no casualties, except three petrol lorries and one armoured car jammed way back in the minefields. The commander of the armoured car surprised our headquarters by returning to our own lines the following morning unarmed and driving thirty Italians before him. The columns of smoke climbing up from the lorries we burned attracted the attention of tanks and aircraft. We managed to dodge the tanks, but the aircraft pestered us throughout the next four days.

The German pilot adopted a novel form of bombing. He had probably grown tired of aiming at the small target offered by an armoured car and, attaching a bomb on a piece of rope suspended from his Me.109, flew over us hoping to bump the bomb into our turrets. After 24 unsuccessful attempts the bomb hit the ground and exploded, causing irreparable damage to his piece of rope. The armour of our cars was excellent, and the only casualties inflicted on us from the air were on the German lorries we shanghaied to come along with us. We had one personal casualty—one of the Italian majors swinging round a turret was shot off by one of his own planes. After that we allowed the other two Italians to walk it.

Then the two squadrons parted, one continuing due west, the other going south-west. In the south we cut the Axis telephone lines connecting the left and right flanks of their Alamein line, and added a little more to the general confusion. For the remainder of the first day we sat astride their lines of supply, holding up and destroying lorries as they arrived to supply front-line troops. This highway robbery continued for another three days without variation, except that instead of burning vehicles and so attracting aircraft, we merely rendered them useless.

Ever since we raided the headquarters we had had reprisals sent out after us. Slow-flying reconnaissance Torches came after us. We shot one down. We also came upon some aircraft, a marvellous target for our bombers, and sent back the information that they were waiting on the airfield to be destroyed. In an astonishingly short time our bombers were over—and so were their aircraft. There was an amusing incident when we came across a South African pilot who had been ground strafing. He was shot down practically under the wheels of one of our armoured cars. Expecting to be man-handled so far behind the enemy lines he couldn't believe his eyes when he realized we were British.

And so we stayed fifteen miles behind Rommel's lines. The only real battle we had was on November 2, when our break-through took place. We heard later, when told that the British tanks had broken through, that Rommel's reply had been, " Oh, yes. I know about that," in reference to our armoured cars. At the time our tanks really had broken through.

Having waylaid a number of vehicles containing retreating German troops, we met up with several 50 mm. anti-tank guns. Things looked black for us when we met the Fighting French coming west. Fortunately for us mutual recognition came quickly, and together we compelled the enemy to leave behind many anti-tank guns and some field guns which he had in tow. With this our job was over. There was no need to return. The Eighth Army had come out to meet us.

My Night of Tense Expectancy in the Russian Lines

Written by Boris Yampolsky, well-known Soviet war correspondent, this
account of preparations in the Russian lines for the great November offensive
is reprinted from Soviet War News.

From a desolate height in the front line, battle-orders ring through the night air. The gun crews jump from their trenches. Soon columns of black smoke and earth mark the explosions of Soviet shells in the German lines.

A few seconds after the first salvo, searchlights stab up in all directions. Soon they have grasped their prey—a Focke-Wulf. The machine-guns spit into action to supplement the A.A. guns. A dispatch rider jumps from his horse, trying to help bring down the enemy plane with his rifle. Drivers, too, stop their lorries and let the German have it. A sapper and a signaller, the sentry at headquarters and a team of roadmenders join in. Even the cook grabs a rifle and blazes away. But the F.W. disappears and is followed by Heinkel bombers which drop their screaming loads around our

BRITISH ARMOURED CAR reconnaissance patrol advancing in Libya. An account of a spectacular break-through by a raiding column of these vehicles is given in this and the preceding pages.
Photo, British Official

positions. Uprooted trees blaze like rocket flares. Meanwhile, the artillery pounds away more heavily than ever. The Germans reply with heavy but poorly directed fire.

Trench digging under fire is difficult. Fortunately, the earth hereabouts is generously equipped with craters made by German land-torpedoes. These make excellent premises for headquarters, observation posts, radio stations, munition dumps and gun crews. It is a kind of underground city, stretching back many miles through forests and swamps. There are underground repair shops and garages. A printing-press is installed in what was once a bear's den. The post office still works in the open. Every now and again a shell fragment cuts a hole in the stack of letters. There is an underground bath-house to which the Red Army men come direct from the firing-line. Seldom have I seen a barber work so quickly and dexterously.

No one sleeps at night. Traffic pours along the roads leading to the front line. A kitchen squad makes its way along a dark path, carrying flasks of hot cocoa for the tankmen. The regimental postman hunts out addresses in a maze of trenches and barbed wire entanglements. Lorries unload cases of cartridges and hand-grenades, which are immediately rushed forward to the front line.

There is a sinister quiet in the direction of the German trenches ; but suddenly a mortar shell hisses through the still night, followed by a storm of German artillery fire. The munition-carriers move about noiselessly. They never stop for a moment. They can tell by the sound of the shells where the danger lies. Red-hot shell fragments stream like fireworks through the dark. The men lie low, protecting the cases of bullets with their bodies. These dangerous

GREAT SOVIET DRIVE on the S. Russian front continued with unabated speed in Jan. 1943. This photo shows Russian infantry attacking enemy positions in the Don area. Preparations for the Soviet offensive are described by an eye-witness in the accompanying text.
Photo, Planet News

nights are a commonplace to them. They know exactly when to leap into a crater for shelter. The mortars shift their fire to new sectors, and the men leave the craters to advance from tree-stump to tree-stump, now crawling, now making a wild dash for it. A tall fir burns like a candle and illumines the entire forest. Some distance away trees are crashing to earth, burying men beneath them. We can hear faint groans.

Meanwhile, the munition-carriers move deeper into the night, through raging fire and burning brushwood, until they reach the battle-line, which is brilliantly lit by German flares. They crawl from trench to trench, sometimes up to their necks in water.

' Everywhere men are on the alert. Even those who are off duty sleep with a rifle or grenade clutched in one hand. The munition convoy creeps ahead in a dazzling glare which dies down momentarily, leaving a dull, dark landscape. Snipers' bullets rip through the air around them. Some fall ; others pause to find out whether they are dead or only wounded. The wounded are quickly bandaged and hidden in craters. Men on their way back from the front line will carry them to the nearest dressing station.

OUR DIARY OF THE WAR

JAN. 6, 1943, Wednesday   *1,222nd day*
  North Africa.—Enemy counter-attacks dislodged our troops from hills W. of Mateur.
  Libya.—Gen. Leclerc's Chad forces captured outpost of Oum-el-Araneb in the Fezzan.
  Mediterranean.—Aircraft from Malta bombed La Goulette and Tunis.
  Burma.—R.A.F. bombers attacked Jap positions near Akyab.
  Australasia.—U.S. bombers raided airfield at Munda.
  U.S.A.—Liberators bombed Kiska.

JAN. 7, Thursday   *1,223rd day*
  Air.—R.A.F. raided the Ruhr.
  Libya.—Fighting French flying column captured El Gatrun in the Fezzan.
  Mediterranean.—U.S. heavy bombers raided Palermo in daylight.
  Australasia.—U.S. aircraft bombed Bougainville and Rekata Bay in Solomons.
  U.S.A.—Liberators again raided Kiska.

JAN. 8, Friday   *1,224th day*
  Sea.—Admiralty announced that in sea battle off North Cape on Dec. 31, destroyer Achates was sunk and Onslow damaged ; convoy reached Russian ports without loss.
  Air.—R.A.F. again raided the Ruhr.
  North Africa.—U.S. aircraft attacked Axis concentrations at Kairouan.
  Russian Front.—German Sixth Army trapped before Stalingrad rejected Russian ultimatum demanding surrender. Soviet troops occupied Zimovniki.
  Australasia.—Three Jap transports in convoy bound for Lae sunk by bombers.

JAN. 9, Saturday   *1,225th day*
  Air.—Essen and the Ruhr bombed by R.A.F.
  Libya.—Gen. Leclerc's Chad troops captured outpost of Brach in the Fezzan.
  Russian Front.—Heavy German counter-attacks repelled at Velikie Luki.
  Australasia.—In attempt to land reinforcements at Lae 130 Jap aircraft were destroyed or damaged.

JAN. 10, Sunday   *1,226th day*
  Sea.—Admiralty announced loss of submarine Utmost.
  Libya.—Bombing and machine-gun attacks on Axis troops between Tripoli and Misurata.
  North Africa.—Daylight raid on La Goulette by Allied bombers.
  Burma.—R.A.F. made day and night

attacks on Akyab ; U.S. aircraft wrecked Myitnge bridge over Irrawaddy.

JAN. 11, Monday   *1,227th day*
  Air.—R.A.F. heavy bombers again attacked the Ruhr.
  North Africa.—German attacks on French troops in Tunisia were repulsed.
  Mediterranean.—Daylight raid on Naples.
  Russian Front.—Soviet troops occupied Georgievsk, Mineralniye Vody, Pyatigorsk and Kislovodsk in the Caucasus.
  Australasia.—During night Jan. 10-11 U.S. torpedo-boats torpedoed two Jap destroyers and drove off others attempting to reinforce Guadalcanal.

JAN. 12, Tuesday   *1,228th day*
  Air.—Another R.A.F. raid on the Ruhr.
  North Africa.—U.S. Flying Fortresses attacking Castel Benito air base, Tripoli, destroyed 16 enemy aircraft in the air and 20 on the ground.
  Libya.—Murzuk, capital of Fezzan, and Sebha, military base, occupied by Gen. Leclerc's Chad forces.
  Mediterranean.—Targets in Crete, Sicily, and Lampedusa Is. attacked by Allied aircraft.

JAN. 13, Wednesday   *1,229th day*
  Sea.—Admiralty announced loss of corvette Marigold.
  Air.—British and American bombers

made daylight raids on Lille, St. Omer, and Abbeville ; Essen and the Ruhr had concentrated night raid.
  Russian Front.—Soviet troops in Stalingrad broke through to the western suburbs and consolidated their positions.
  Australasia.—Allied bombers and fighters made heavy raids on Lae and Salamaua, New Guinea, and Gasmata, New Britain.

JAN. 14, Thursday   *1,230th day*
  Air.—Heavy night raid on U-boat base at Lorient.
  Russian Front.—Soviet troops continued to advance in Caucasus and on Lower Don.
  Burma.—R.A.F. raided Akyab area by day and night.
  Australasia.—Allied troops broke through Jap positions at Sanananda in Papua.

JAN. 15, Friday   *1,231st day*
  Sea.—Admiralty announced loss of destroyer Partridge.
  Air.—R.A.F. raided Cherbourg by day and Lorient by night.
  Libya.—Eighth Army started offensive at Buerat.
  Mediterranean.—Our submarines sank three enemy supply ships and damaged three more.
  India.—Three Jap aircraft shot down by one fighter pilot in Calcutta district.

  Australasia.—Widespread raids by U.S. aircraft on Jap bases in Solomons.

JAN. 16, Saturday   *1,232nd day*
  Air.—Strong force of R.A.F. bombers raided Berlin; one aircraft lost.
  Libya.—Announced that Gen. Leclerc's forces had made contact with Eighth Army.
  Russia.—Soviet H.Q. announced opening of new offensive south of Voronezh ; town and rly. centre of Rossosh captured.
  Australasia.—Five Jap ships sunk or damaged by Allied bombers at Rabaul.
  General.—Iraq Govt. announced itself at war with Germany, Italy and Japan.

JAN. 17, Sunday   *1,233rd day*
  Sea.—Admiralty announced loss of trawlers Horatio and Jura.
  Air.—R.A.F. again raided Berlin in strength; 22 bombers missing.
  Libya.—Castel Benito, air-base of Tripoli, heavily raided by Allied bombers.
  Russian Front.—Soviet troops captured Millerovo, on Voronezh-Rostov rly.
  India.—Enemy aircraft raided airfield in Chittagong area.
  Australasia.—Jap bombers and fighters raided Milne Bay, Papua.
  Home Front.—In two night raids on London and S.E. England ten enemy bombers were destroyed.

JAN. 18, Monday   *1,234th day*
  North Africa.—In Tunisia Germans gained some ground S.W. of Pont du Fahs.
  Libya.—Eighth Army advancing on Tripoli passed through Misurata and reached Zliten ; Castel Benito air-base again heavily bombed.
  Russian Front.—Soviet troops occupied Sinyavino and Schlüsselburg and raised the siege of Leningrad.
  Australasia.—Sanananda village in Papua captured by Allied troops.

JAN. 19, Tuesday   *1,235th day*
  Libya.—Our forces advancing towards Tripoli closed in on Homs and Tarhuna ; Axis airfield at Castel Benito again bombed.
  Mediterranean.—In night operations on Jan. 17, 18 and 19 our destroyers sank 13 enemy vessels.
  Russian Front.—South of Voronezh, Soviet troops captured Kamensk and rly. junction of Valuiki.
  India.—Small-scale enemy air raid on Calcutta area ; two bombers destroyed.
  General.—Announced that M. Marcel Peyrouton was appointed Governor-General of Algeria.

★ ═════════ *Flash-backs* ═════════ ★

1940

January 8. *Russian 44th Division routed by Finns at Suomussalmi.*

January 13. *R.A.F., in longest reconnaissance raid to date, dropped leaflets at Vienna and Prague.*

1941

January 10. *Cruiser Southampton lost, aircraft-carrier Illustrious damaged by Axis air attack in Sicilian Channel. Klisura in Albania taken by the Greeks.*

January 19. *Kassala, Sudan, re-occupied by British troops.*

1942

January 10. *Japanese invaded Celebes, Dutch East Indies.*

January 11. *Japanese entered Kuala Lumpur, Malaya.*

January 12. *South Africans captured Sollum.*

January 13. *In Libya, British troops occupied Jedabia, on Gulf of Sirte.*

January 19. *Russians recaptured Moiaisk, on Moscow front.*

Editor's Postscript

A CORRESPONDENT who signs himself "Fairplay" sends me a postcard from Harrow saying: "Why is it that you are always boosting Scotch, Australian, Canadian, Indian, South African and other oversea and foreign soldiers, sailors and airmen to the detriment of Englishmen who are doing the bulk of the fighting by sea, land, and in the air?" I can assure him that we of THE WAR ILLUSTRATED are conscious of no offence in this respect, nor can I regard his complaint as a fair one. We are all with him in agreeing that Englishmen are doing the bulk of the fighting. He might have some cause for complaint if he had access to the American newspapers, but he doesn't accuse us, it will be noticed, of giving undue prominence to the Americans! The fact is that we attempt no discrimination—which too readily leads to recrimination—in recording the news of the fighting as that reaches us from official and other sources. It stands to reason that as Scotland has a population of some 5,000,000 and England has some 41,000,000 there must be more Englishmen than Scotsmen in arms. Of all races the English have ever been the least given to national self-assertion and the readiest to give, without any trace of jealousy, honour where it is due. Clearly the major part of the British fighting by land, sea, and air must be done by Englishmen and perhaps that's why too often "it goes without saying." Personally I deprecate all "boosting" of fragmentary elements in the grand total of united British effort, which is the rigid, unbending backbone of this fight for freedom.

T HE things they say! I was reminded of the feature I run with this title in World Digest by the glossary of American terms given in a leaflet issued by the Navy, Army and Air Force Institutes—N.A.A.F.I. for short—for the guidance of those members of its staff who may be called upon to serve American soldiers, sailors and airmen, whether in canteens, messing stores or offices. In When You Meet the Americans, Miss N.A.A.F.I. is warned that she must be prepared for surprises. "The first time that an American soldier approaches the counter and says, 'How'ya, baby?' you will probably think he is being impudent. By the time several dozen men have said it you may have come to the conclusion that all Americans are 'fresh.' Yet to them it will be merely the normal conversational opening, just as you might say, 'Lovely day, isn't it?'"

T HIS understood, she is conjured to "try not to appear shocked at some of their expressions. Many of these may sound remarkably like swearing to you, but in fact they are words in everyday use in America. It will not occur to the lad from Ohio that you are not accustomed to hearing them used in front of girls." What those words are is (tantalizingly) left unstated. N.A.A.F.I.'s young ladies are told, however, that Hot Dogs are fried sausages in split rolls, and Hamburgers are savoury rissoles in split rolls or between slices of bread. They are informed that Americans call a biscuit a cracker, while to them biscuits are scones or tea-cakes. When they want grilled meat they ask for it broiled. Chocolate and sweets are candy; chipped potatoes are french fried (to them chips are potato crisps); porridge is known as oatmeal; a kipper is a smoked herring, and vegetable marrow is known as squash. What we call beer or bitter, they call ale; beer to them means lager, while if they ask for their change in bills they will expect it in notes. Braces are suspenders, sock suspenders are garters. And if the young lady behind the counter is informed by a solicitous customer that she has got a "run" she will know that it refers to a ladder in her stocking.

CAPT. R. ST. V. SHERBROOKE, D.S.O., R.N., of H.M.S. Onslow, who won the V.C. for valour in defence of an important convoy bound for N. Russia on Dec. 31, 1942. "Never was there anything finer in Royal Naval annals," declared Mr. A. V. Alexander, First Lord of the Admiralty.
Photo, Janet Jevons

A T the end of the leaflet are some Do's and Don'ts. "Don't make fun of the American accent or vocabulary," Miss N.A.A.F.I. is told. "Your own accent and words probably seem just as odd to them." "Don't snub an American unless he has really deserved it." "Be a little more friendly than you normally would." "Don't talk about Chicago gangsters as if they represented 90 per cent of the population of America." And "Most important of all, remember that every time you lose your temper with an American, or refuse to understand his point of view, you are fighting Hitler's battles for him. Germany's propaganda at the moment is directed mainly to the task of separating Britain from America. *Don't help Hitler!*"

" T HE picture that sank a battleship" is one of the 130 photographs contained in Coastal Command, prepared for the Air Ministry by the Ministry of Information and recently published by H.M. Stationery Office at 2s. You may have guessed that the battleship in question was the Bismarck, and the photograph that sealed her fate was taken by an aircraft of Coastal Command on May 21, 1941. In the course of a reconnaissance of the Norwegian coast the aircraft had flown as far north as Bergen, and there, reconnoitring the approaches to the port, the pilot discovered two warships, one of large size, at anchor in a small fjord. On his return to his base he made a cautious report of what he had seen to one of the station intelligence officers. They soon were sure where he had surmised. The Bismarck and the Prinz Eugen were out.

Y OU know the rest of the story. We devoted about a dozen pages to it in Volume 4 (see pp. 580–583, and later). But you will not be averse to reading it again. Moreover, certain details are now published which could not be revealed two years ago. Then, of course, there are many other thrilling stories in Coastal Command. How could it be otherwise, when we are told that in fulfilment of their duties aircraft of Coastal Command between Sept. 3, 1939 and Sept. 30, 1942 escorted 4,947 merchant convoys, attacked 587 U-boats, and flew some fifty-five million miles? Much of the Command's work is unspectacular; most of it is carried out hundreds of miles from land, beyond sight of witnesses, and leaves no record of stirring adventure, of thrilling escape. One has to take the somewhat stereotyped and colourless reports of the men who fly the aircraft—unassuming heroes every one of them—and read between the lines. Sometimes (we are reminded) there is no report. A plane flying on its solitary reconnaissance has not returned . . .

N O author's name appears on the title page of Coastal Command, but I understand that it is by Mr. St. George Saunders, who was also responsible for those previous best-sellers The Battle of Britain and Bomber Command. Some 3,750,000 copies of the first were sold, and 1,250,000 of the second. The first impression of Coastal Command ran to 400,000, heavily over-subscribed before publication, and a second is in course of preparation. Even before the War such figures would make the mouth water. But now, when our paper ration is but a fraction of what it was three years ago, well . . .

W ITH your appetite whetted by the official story, you may like to turn to Coastal Command at War, a well-illustrated book which takes us behind the scenes—into the H.Q. Operations Room, the Group Headquarters, the stations, the aircraft themselves. Published by Jarrolds at 7s. 6d., it is by "Squadron Leader Tom Dudley Gordon"; according to the Evening Standard's Londoner, "Tom" is Squadron Leader Guthrie, "Dudley" is Squadron Leader Barker, and "Gordon" is Wing Commander Gordon Campbell. Vividly written, the book contains a mass of information concerning not only the Coastal Command's operations, but its principal personalities and those details of everyday life which must be of particular interest to those who have to stay at home and wait. It carries the story a year later than the point reached in Coastal Command.

Printed in England and published every alternate Friday by the Proprietors, THE AMALGAMATED PRESS, LTD., The Fleetway House, Farringdon Street, London, E.C.4. Registered for transmission by Canadian Magazine Post. Sole Agents for Australia and New Zealand: Messrs. Gordon & Gotch, Ltd.; and for South Africa: Central News Agency. Ltd.—February 5, 1943. S.S. *Editorial Address:* JOHN CARPENTER HOUSE, WHITEFRIARS LONDON. E.C.4.

Vol 6· # The War Illustrated Nº 148

SIXPENCE

Edited by Sir John Hammerton

FEBRUARY 19, 1943

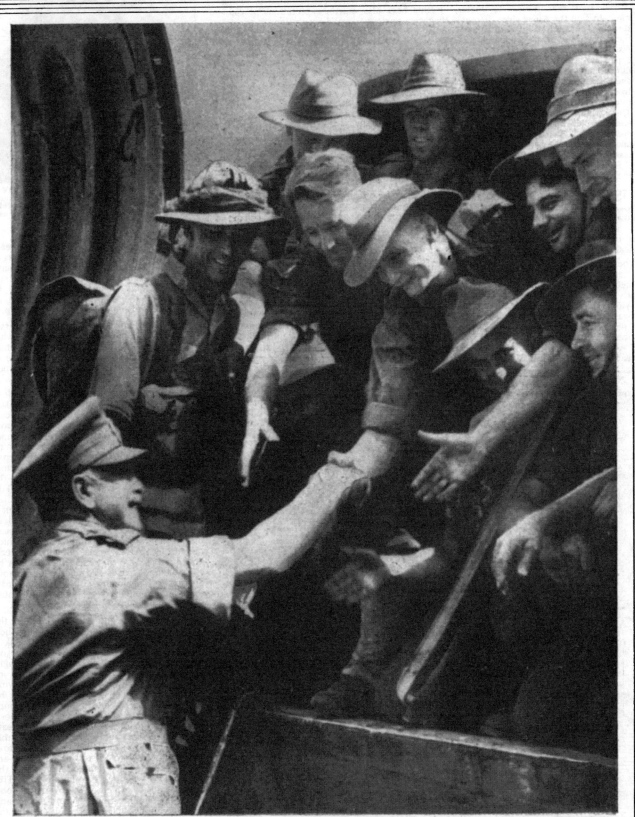

GOOD LUCK, AUSSIES! Gen. Sir Thomas Blamey, C.-in-C. Allied Forces, Australia, gives these cheerful "Diggers" a cordial send-off as they set out on their journey for the New Guinea front. They were among the first Australian soldiers to reach the battlefield by air; and, as the enemy was soon to know to his cost, they have given a splendid account of themselves in the Papuan fighting.

Photo, Sport & General

NO. 149 WILL BE PUBLISHED FRIDAY, MARCH 5

THE BATTLE FRONTS

by Maj.-Gen. Sir Charles Gwynn, K.C.B., D.S.O.

COL.-GEN. KONSTANTIN ROKOSSOV-SKY, commander of the Russian forces on the Don front which compelled the capitulation of the German 6th Army. He began the war as a colonel, and even now is only 38.
Photo, Pictorial Press

DURING the last half of January 1943 the situation of the Axis continued to deteriorate at a pace that compelled German propaganda for home consumption to switch from reassurances to threats. Events have also outrun expectations of commentators on the Allied side. Possibly they were anxious to avoid accusations of wishful thinking, but up to the time Paulus was offered terms of surrender the possibility or even the probability that his encircled army might hold out till relieved in the spring was discussed. A general slowing up if not a complete arrest of the Russian offensive was expected. In Africa, too, it was thought that the capture of Tripoli would prove a difficult undertaking even if Rommel were not strong enough to risk decisive battle. How over-cautious such views were is now apparent. Paulus' army has been wiped out. Far from being brought to a standstill, the Red Army continues to go from success to success, to open new fronts of attack and threaten the German line at its most vulnerable points. The Germans admit that their front must be shortened, but it will be under compulsion and to avoid, if possible, further catastrophes—not as a deliberate, well-planned strategic operation. It will have to be carried out under the most difficult weather conditions and at a time when railway communications, already over-taxed, have the additional task of replacing vast quantities of lost material.

In Africa Alexander has brought the Libyan campaign to a triumphant conclusion and is ready with the 8th Army to play his part in Tunisia.

RUSSIA Since I last wrote announcements of Russian victories have followed each other with bewildering rapidity. Here are some of the main events of the last half of January, approximately in chronological order:

The relief of Leningrad; the capture of Kamensk, giving a bridgehead across the Donetz; exploitation of the break-through south of Voronezh, leading to the capture of Valuiki and other towns on yet another railway of vital importance to the Germans on the front covering Kharkov; on the Caucasus front the capture of Voroshilovsk and Armavir—where it was thought the army retreating from the Terek Valley might stand in order to cover the Maikop oil-fields and the communications of the force operating across the Caucasus towards Tuapse; the opening of railway communications through Stalingrad as a result of the progressive annihilation of Paulus' army; the crossing of the lower Manych and the capture of Salsk, followed by a two-pronged advance along the railways leading to Rostov, and to the vital railway junction of Tikhoretsk; the advance of the Russians from Tuapse in pursuit of a retreating enemy and the re-occupation of the Maikop oil-fields; the continued pursuit of the Germans from Armavir and Voroshilovsk, leading to the capture of the important railway junction at Kropotkin; and, finally, the great break-through at Voronezh with the capture of the strong hedgehog town of Kastornaya on the direct line of approach to the still more important bastion of Kursk; to be followed in the south by the capture of Tikhoretsk and the occupation of Maikop.

THAT is an amazing record of successes spread over an immense front, but what are their chief strategic implications? Cumulatively they imply a threat to the whole of the great salient formed by the German front south of Kursk.

To examine them in detail from south to north: The German armies of the Caucasus, estimated to amount to 250,000 men, are in immediate danger. Two groups, those from the Terek Valley in the east and from Tuapse in the south, are in full retreat, abandoning vast quantities of material and having heavy losses. The line of retreat of the former group towards Rostov has been cut by the drive from Salsk which has captured Tikhoretsk. Some elements may have extricated themselves before the town was taken, but a great part of the force appears doomed to annihilation. The main line of communication of the Tuapse and Maikop group, which ran through Armavir, has already been cut, and the only way of escape open to it is by cross-country roads through mountainous districts to Krasnodar. In winter, retreat by this route would be very difficult and entail the abandonment of all heavy equipment.

AT the western end of the Caucasus the Germans appear still to be holding their position from Krasnodar and Novorossisk—the lower Kuban here gives them a defensive position facing south. They have brought up reserves to hold a bridgehead east of Rostov on the railway to Salsk, and are trying to stop the Russian advance on that line by counter-attacks. Whether they will attempt to link up with Krasnodar as a rallying position for the troops retreating from the east is still not clear; but it seems more probable that they will be compelled to fall back to a line much closer to Rostov because they are threatened by converging attacks from the directions of Salsk, Kropotkin and Tikhoretsk, all of which will now have good railway communications. Many troops and heavy weapons will also be released by the annihilation of the Paulus army to reinforce the drive from Salsk.

A small bridgehead may be established east and south of Rostov, but it seems inevitable that the whole of the Caucasus will have to be abandoned, and that a great part of the army that has been operating there

RUSSIAN GAINS ON SOUTHERN FRONT. Arrows show the principal Russian thrusts at Feb. 1, while the lines showing the front at that date, a fortnight earlier, and before the beginning of the Russian counter-attack last November, demonstrate the complete reversal of fortune in this field of war.

By Courtesy of the Times

VELIKI LUKI, important railway junction on the Russian Central front, was re-occupied by the Soviet forces on Jan. 1, 1943. The scene of fierce street fighting, the town was reduced to ruins before the German garrison was finally overcome. This radioed photo shows the Soviet flag flying in triumph above a scene of devestation. *Photo, Planet News*

will be lost, together with enormous quantities of material and equipment.

North of the Don the Germans are still trying desperately to hold the line of the Donetz, but the Russians have secured footholds across it ; moreover, having now control of the railways from Stalingrad and Voronezh, their communications have been greatly improved and reinforcements from Stalingrad will also be available. Meanwhile, farther north, the progress of the Russian drive south of Voronezh threatens to cut the communication between Kharkov and the Donetz and is approaching the Upper Donetz. The Donetz basin, in fact, seems likely to become a dangerous salient under attack from three directions. There is therefore a possibility, though it is still remote, of which the German people have been warned, envisages a withdrawal from the Donetz when everything has been done to save the armies of the Caucasus.

MEANWHILE, the success of the breakthrough at Voronezh has produced another critical situation. It will mean further heavy demands on German reserves, and it threatens to interrupt the railway from Kursk to Kharkov, which is one of the main lateral routes by which reserves can be moved. Moreover, this thrust has proved once again that the Russians are now capable of breaking through the most strongly defended positions and that hedgehog towns are liable to prove traps rather than defensive assets.

In the centre and north there has been no great change since the capture of Veliki Luki and the relief of Leningrad, but at both of these points dangers threaten which tie up German reserves.

The German soldier continues to fight hard, but he cannot, after a series of disasters and retreats, be the man he was when full of confidence. The numbers of prisoners captured may be symptomatic of some loss of morale. The satellite armies, which have for so long served a useful purpose, have almost ceased to exist, and such remnants as remain can have little military value. Will the Germans be able to replace their immense losses ? They may by superhuman exertions replace material and fill up their depleted ranks with young and partly-trained men. But they cannot make good the loss of fully trained and war-experienced men, especially officers and non-commissioned officers.

Apart from victories gained, territory recovered and railway communications reopened must immensely improve the Russian situation. But, on the whole, the best reason for optimism is the new standard of tactical efficiency now manifest in the Red Army.

NORTH AFRICA

The sound of the pipes in Tripoli gave cheering proof that the last page of the last chapter of the history of the Libyan campaigns had been reached.

For all-round brilliancy it would be difficult to find an equal of Alexander's campaign. With all three services pulling their weight, and with the administration organization performing as brilliantly as the fighting forces, it was a wonderful exhibition of team work of the highest order.

Rommel, if he hoped to throw Montgomery out of his stride at Zem-Zem, was disappointed, and the resistance offered by his rearguard there did practically nothing to delay the advance of the 8th Army and cost him casualties. Thereafter, he relied mainly on mines to slow down pursuit which has now reached the Tunisian frontier.

Will Rommel attempt to bar the advance of the 8th Army into Tunisia either on the Mareth Line or at the Gabès defile ? That he will hold one or both as strong rearguard positions is practically certain ; and, as at Zem-Zem, Montgomery, before attacking, will probably have to pause to close up his army, reconnoitre and get his supply services

well established. The time required to make the port of Tripoli reasonably usable is likely to affect the development of the situation. I find it hard to believe, however, that the Germans will attempt to hold Southern Tunisia permanently. It would mean spreading their troops over a very wide area and the maintenance of a much larger force than their precarious sea communications could be relied on to keep fully supplied. Moreover, the defensive Mareth and Gabès positions would be exposed to attack from both front and rear.

IT seems more probable, therefore, that they will concentrate on holding the more important northern half of the country. Rommel certainly may stand in the south till Montgomery is in a position to attack, and he may be reinforced there in the hopes that an attempt to interpose on his line of retreat might offer an opportunity for one of his characteristic counter-strokes. Axis reports indicate that an American army is threatening to interpose, and Rommel may believe that an inexperienced army may offer opportunities which the experienced 8th Army never presented.

On the whole, however, the situation in Tunisia is full of uncertainties and is veiled by secrecy. Yet it is not unreasonable to believe, with the situation in Russia going from bad to worse, that the Germans will try to keep their commitments in Africa to the minimum which will meet their main object of keeping the Sicilian Channel closed to our convoys.

THE FAR EAST

With the final extermination of the Japanese in Papua operations for the time being are almost exclusively confined to air attacks on advanced Japanese bases. The Papuan operations afforded a convincing proof of what white men can accomplish in the most trying tropical surroundings and weather. It was a desperate test of courage and endurance brilliantly passed.

In Guadalcanal the Americans are extending their area of occupation and by degrees mopping up the remaining Japanese.

What the assembling of a large Japanese convoy in the more northern islands means is not yet clear, but it is costing the enemy heavy losses in aircraft and shipping.

UNION JACK FLIES OVER TRIPOLI. On Jan. 23, 1943 two Lanarkshire men of the Eighth Army, Sgt. D. Grant and Pte. W. Clark—both Gordon Highlanders—proudly hoisted the British flag from a fort that overlooked the harbour of Tripoli. The following day it was announced that the Eighth Army was driving in pursuit of Rommel.

Paving the Way for Victory in North Africa

ROYAL ENGINEERS IN TUNISIA have been busily constructing new roads and bridges for the needs of the First Army and of our Allies. 1, Men of the R.E.s at work on a road intended for military transport. 2, A mobile crane is employed in bridge-building operations to place concrete base blocks in position. 3, The bridge is here shown almost completed. It is 130 ft. in length. A bridge over the River Medjerda, with its two approach roads, was built by the sappers in 4 days.

Photos, British Official: Crown Copyright

Just What and Where Is the Mareth Line?

IN 1938, when Mussolini threatened to occupy Tunis, the French constructed the Mareth Line. Running for 30 miles from the Mediterranean to the Matmata Hills in S. Tunisia, these defences take their name from Mareth, an inland village which forms the pivot of the whole line. Built on the pattern of the Maginot, the Mareth defences consist of three lines, each with a series of fortresses cut into the desert rock or built of reinforced concrete. Underground sleeping quarters, guns which can be lowered out of sight, telephones, underground water supplies drawn from the Mareth Oasis are some of the most important features of this Tunisian Maginot.

The defences stretch for a depth of from nine to ten miles, filling in the whole of the gap between the hills and sea. In 1940 Vichy agreed to dismantle them, but to what extent demilitarization was carried out it is impossible to tell.

It is estimated that 40,000 men are needed to take over the defences at full strength. The only good road from Tripoli to the S. Tunisian plain runs through the Mareth Line. The photographs in this page were taken in 1938, when the defences had just been completed.

STRONG POINTS OF THE MARETH LINE. 1, The Le Bœuf redoubt, a typical example of a Mareth fort. 2, Military roads link the chain of small forts that stretch across the rocky Matmata plain. This photo was taken from a hill-cave. 3, A native soldier guards the imposing entrance to the post of Djenein. 4, French tanks assembled outside a village. 5, One of the innumerable pill-boxes in the defence zone seen through barbed wire entanglements.

Photos, New York Times Photos; Keystone; E.N.A.

Into Tripoli Montgomery Marched in Triumph

Crowning the splendid achievement of the 8th Army in its 1,400-mile advance from within the Egyptian frontier was the capture of Tripoli, last surviving capital of Mussolini's "Roman Empire." This account is based for the most part on the dispatches of Reuters correspondents, Eric Lloyd Williams, George Crawley and Dennis Martin.

As dawn was breaking General Montgomery stood on the Gebel heights and watched his victorious troops stream down the precipitous mountain roads into the streets of Tripoli, last remaining city of Italy's once extensive colonial empire. It was a great moment, the crowning achievement of a magnificent piece of generalship. From the very beginning of the campaign Rommel had been hopelessly outgeneraled, his men outfought. Before the offensive was launched, war correspondents at the 8th Army's H.Q. were told that Tripoli would be in Allied hands on January 22 ; and sure enough, the British columns were outside Tripoli before nightfall on the appointed day—this, in spite of some of "the wildest-ever advance." He pictured British tanks and gun columns racing through a vast wilderness of hills and deep, wide ravines looking like mountains of the moon. One minute they would be seen going across a flat tableland covered with black basalt rocks ; the next, the whole column would disappear. You would not see it again until you came to the steep edge of some wadi ; and there, with the leading tank many miles away, just dust in a mirage of distorted distance, you would see the column picking its way through a great ravine. So they went on, bouncing along across wide rocky plains, then creeping through basalt-dotted hills, descending into sand-filled wadis where no road had ever been made, churning along

MONTGOMERY TO HIS MEN

LEADING units of the Eighth Army are now only about 200 miles from Tripoli. Tripoli is the only town in the Italian empire oversea still remaining in their possession. Therefore, we will take it from them ; they will then have no oversea empire.

The enemy will try to stop us ; but if every one of us, whether a front line soldier or an officer or man whose duty is performed in other spheres, puts his whole heart and soul into this next contest, then nothing can stop us.

Nothing has stopped us since the Battle of Egypt began on October 23, 1942. Nothing will stop us now. Some must stay back to begin with, but we shall all be in the hunt eventually.

On to Tripoli ! Our friends in the home country will be thrilled when they hear we have captured that place.—*Jan. 12, 1943.*

FIRST BRITISH TANK TO ENTER TRIPOLI—a Valentine—is here seen being admired by some of the inhabitants of the city. Among the men of the victorious Eighth Army who are riding in triumph on the tank is the piper of the Gordon Highlanders, who piped the tanks through the city. See also p. 551.
Photo, British Official: Crown Copyright

the heaviest going in North Africa—while behind them streamed a great caravanserai of trucks, carrying hospital equipment, water, food, shells, repair units, bridge-builders, tank-recovery units, and all the other equipment needed for running a modern army.

The 8th Army's final advance on the doomed city was made from three directions : two columns of armoured units and New Zealanders charged through the desert to the south, while the infantry; the Highlanders of the 51st Division, mopped up along the coast road. No minefields were found in the desert, but along the coast road the enemy used his old rearguard tactics of mines and booby-traps. Every conceivable device was adopted to delay the advance ; every culvert and bridge was demolished and the road surface was pitted with holes blown in by the retreating enemy. Armed resistance, however, was slight. The last engagement with Rommel's panzers before the city's fall was fought at Azizia, a few miles to the south, when the crack 7th Armoured Division were in action.

It was an amazing performance. Eric Lloyd Williams of Reuters, who was with one of the armoured columns, described it as

through the great seas of sand until finally they climbed up through the tumbled peaks of the Tripolitanian mountain ridge guarding the town on the Mediterranean shore.

GATHERED in their three columns in the fields surrounding the city walls, the British assault troops awaited General Montgomery's order to advance. When this was given, the three columns converged and moved on the town. This was at 5 a.m. on January 23. One column came from the east ; a second force, which had streamed down the mountain pass the night before along the road from Tarhuna, moved in from the south ; the third column rumbled in through the western gate.

Just after six a.m. on Saturday, January 23, reported Alexander Clifford of The Daily Mail, when the eastern sky was still only faintly pale with dawn, a British tank called Dorothy (after the driver's sweetheart in Liverpool) clattered into the main square. Seven Gordon Highlanders and a sapper clung to the tank as it felt its way cautiously through the still streets. But the first British troops to scout the city were a patrol of 11th Hussars who were nosing up into the southern

suburbs as early as 4 a.m., and an hour and a half later drove in through the streets and out again. "If anybody deserves the honour of being first into Tripoli," wrote Clifford, "it was these Hussars, who have been so long in the desert that they glory in the nickname of 'the Desert Rats.' The Gordon Highlanders, then, were the first infantry in. Dorothy was the first tank. Seaforth Highlanders, who fought so gallantly at El Alamein, singing machine-gunners of the Middlesex Regiment, and men of the Buffs—the Royal East Kent Regiment—and the Queens—the West Surreys—followed."

AT noon General Montgomery, standing in the sun at the Porto Benito cross-roads just without the city wall, officially received the surrender of the city. To him, standing between an interpreter and one of his brigadiers, approached the Lord Mayor of Tripoli ; Commandatore San Marco, Vice-Governor of Libya ; and the Prefect. The Italians were in full uniform, glittering with medals ; Montgomery made an interesting contrast, in his battledress, tank beret and two sweaters of different colours. The delegates listened carefully to his demands, said Mr. Clifford. "The Vice-Governor's nose twitched once or twice as though he wanted to blow it, but didn't quite like to. Then they all turned and frowned. But at the end they had no questions to ask." Commissariat and police were to remain Italian responsibilities, said the General. "There's a very big population here. I have nothing against the civilian population, provided it remains orderly. My war is against the Italian and German armies." At the same time he uttered a stern warning against any treachery or espionage.

As General Montgomery with his senior commanders entered the town, Arab and Italian civilians lined the streets and cheered. Before them marched British infantry to the skirl of the Highlanders' bagpipes, and the General took the salute in the main square. Then as column after column of British troops swept by, the Union Jack was broken at the masthead over Tripoli Town Hall. A few hours later General Montgomery spoke to the correspondents. "I have nothing but praise for the men of the 8th Army," he said, "they have done what I expected of them."

In the city itself there was never a sign of resistance, few signs even of hostility to the conquerors. But in the harbour area the effects of repeated pounding by the R.A.F. were plentiful. Wrecked ships dotted the bay and the warehouses lay in ruins.

Soon life in Tripoli was back almost to normal. Shops began to open, and the hotels filled up with military personnel. In the square the citizens listened with growing appreciation to the roll of drums, the strange music of the pipes.

The Roman Wolf Hears the Conqueror's Pipes

FUNERAL MARCH OF THE ITALIAN EMPIRE. On Jan. 23, 1943 Tripoli was entered by the Eighth Army. Marching behind their Pipers to the accompaniment of their famous battle tune—Cock o' the North—these men of the Gordon Highlanders are seen in the chief city of Mussolini's now vanished African empire. In the background lies the harbour, dominated by the monument of the wolf which, in ancient legend, nourished Romulus and Remus, the founders of the Roman state.

THE WAR AT SEA

by Francis E. McMurtrie

NEWS was received at the end of January 1943 of the supersession of the supreme Chief of the German Navy, Admiral Raeder, by one of his subordinates, Admiral Doenitz. Previously the latter had been in charge of the Nazi submarine service.

Whatever the underlying reasons for this change, it is obvious that, like the wholesale dismissal of German generals each time the Army fails to achieve its objects, it is designed to provide a scapegoat under the gospel that the Fuehrer himself is infallible.

Probably the immediate cause of Raeder's downfall, though he has doubtless been slipping from favour for some time past, was the failure of the German fleet to stop British convoys getting through to North Russia. Without the arms and munitions that have poured in by this route, it is improbable that the Soviet armies could have accomplished a tithe of what they have done recently. Apart from this, there is reason to suppose that Hitler is by no means satisfied with the progress of the submarine campaign. Though fantastic figures have been broadcast by Berlin of the alleged sinkings of shipping by U-boats, the fact that the Allies were able to land their armies in North Africa with such small opposition must have been a bitter disappointment to the enemy.

It is of course quite possible that Raeder showed himself to be a lukewarm supporter of the submarine as the principal naval weapon. In pre-war days he strongly advocated the sending out of surface raiders to prey upon commerce. His belief in this method of attacking seaborne trade has been shown by the persistency with which heavily armed ships of mercantile type have been let loose on to the trade routes, to say nothing of the Graf Spee's ignominious end and the loss of the Bismarck. Several of the mercantile type raiders also failed to return, such as the Atlantis, sunk by H.M.S. Devonshire on November 22, 1941; the Kormoran, sunk in action with H.M.A.S. Sydney in the same month; the Pinguin, sunk by H.M.S. Cornwall in May 1941; one sunk by H.M.S. Dorsetshire in December 1941; and yet another which was recently reported to have been destroyed by U.S. Naval forces in the South Atlantic.

Raeder himself is understood to have said that he was relieved of his duties at his own request, " on account of the state of his health." That excuse is unlikely to deceive anyone who has studied Hitler's methods of dispensing with the services of those who do not satisfy him.

DOENITZ, in an order of the day to the German Navy, stated that he will continue in personal charge of U-boat operations. He must call for " unconditional obedience, supreme courage and sacrifice," he concluded. This may be taken as further evidence that in the coming spring a supreme effort to sink more shipping will be made by the Axis submarine flotillas.

It is now clear that in a broadcast ten days earlier the Nazi authorities were leading up to Doenitz's new appointment. It was then announced that he had " established a wireless network across the ocean to track Allied convoys," adding that the submarine war against shipping " is first and foremost in the mind of Admiral Doenitz." This, in view of what has since happened, sounds as though Raeder were being blamed for not devoting more attention to submarine warfare. According to enemy reports, Doenitz recently went as far as Madagascar in a submarine, in order to confer there with the Chief of the Japanese Naval Staff.

TRIPOLI'S Importance as a British Naval Base in the Mediterranean.

What effect will the occupation of the port of Tripoli have on the battle for Tunisia? This must depend to some extent on the time it takes to clear the harbour of wrecks and to repair the damaged moles. From experience at Benghazi, it is evident that this can be done much more rapidly than the enemy supposed when the work of blocking and demolition was executed.

Once in working order, the port can be used freely by our supply vessels, which will relieve the long land lines of communication of the Eighth Army of much of the task of keeping it reinforced, fed and munitioned. Moreover, cruisers, destroyers and smaller craft of the Mediterranean Fleet will be able to use Tripoli as a base from which to attack the seaborne supplies of the Axis armies in Tunisia. Already those supplies have been suffering from the incessant attacks of our submarines and aircraft, the former based on Malta. Recently the enemy have made increasing use of schooners, which can creep along the coast unobserved after making the crossing from Sicily by night. Not only are they less conspicuous targets than bigger ships, but to lose one is a less serious matter in the present depleted state of Italian shipping.

A foretaste of what is to come was given at the beginning of December 1942, when British cruisers and

ADM. DOENITZ, appointed C.-in-C. of the German Navy in place of Adm. Raeder on Jan. 30, 1943. Hitherto chief of Hitler's U-boat Command, he was a U-boat commander in the last war. *Photo, Sport & General*

destroyers under Rear-Admiral C. H. J. Harcourt sank four supply ships and two escorting destroyers in a smart action. With Tripoli available as a base, operations of this kind will be much easier to carry out; and the Royal Navy can be trusted to miss no opportunity of striking. In time shortage of supplies must gradually weaken the enemy in Tunisia to an extent which will render his defeat inevitable.

The Admiralty have to be congratulated on their latest appointments in connexion with the Fleet Air Arm. Rear-Admiral Denis W. Boyd, who has had war experience in command of aircraft-carriers, has been appointed Fifth Sea Lord, a post which has been temporarily vacant since Vice-Admiral Lyster went back to sea in the early part of last year. His secondary title, instead of " Chief of Naval Air Services " as in Admiral Lyster's case, is " Chief of Naval Air Equipment."

CAPTAIN R. H. PORTAL, hitherto Director of the Air Division of the Naval Staff at the Admiralty, becomes Assistant Chief of the Naval Staff (Air), with acting rank of Rear-Admiral. Though he will not himself be a member of the Board of Admiralty, he will be responsible to the Chief and Vice Chief of the Naval Staff, both of whom are on the Board. Rear-Admiral Portal has had long experience of naval flying, in which he graduated during the last war. He is a younger brother of the Chief of the Air Staff, Air Chief Marshal Sir Charles Portal, no inconsiderable asset when it is remembered how often the two Services have to co-operate. Admiral Sir Frederic Dreyer, who has been Chief of Naval Air Services at the Admiralty since the departure of Vice-Admiral Lyster, will continue his good work with the new designation of Deputy Chief of Naval Air Equipment. The post of Assistant Chief of Naval Air Services, hitherto held by Vice-Admiral R. B. Davies, V.C., has been abolished.

This reorganization, together with the news announced by Mr. A. V. Alexander, the First Lord, in an address in London on January 13 of a general speeding-up in the production of new types of aircraft for the Navy, is welcome and timely in view of the need for augmented air defence against U-boat attacks on shipping. Another welcome piece of news released by the First Lord was that the Navy is expecting early delivery from the United States of a number of new dive-bombers.

REAR-ADM. D. W. BOYD, whose appointment as Fifth Sea Lord, with the additional title of Chief of Naval Air Equipment, was announced on Jan. 22, 1943. He commanded the aircraft-carrier Illustrious at Taranto in 1940, and was given command of an aircraft-carrier squadron in 1941. *Photo, Associated Press* PAGE 552

They Got the Convoy Safely Through to Malta

CAPT. C. R. MILL, O.B.E.
His ship destroyed 3 enemy aircraft before being sunk herself.

E. E. HAYES, B.E.M.
Greaser of a torpedoed vessel, he displayed great skill and courage.

F. FOTHERGILL, B.E.M.
His cool and accurate gunfire helped to destroy a U-boat.

C. R. B. GOODMAN, M.B.E.
As 2nd Officer he showed exceptional ability in convoy duties.

CAPT. W. HARRISON, C.B.E.
He handled his vessel with exceptional skill and daring.

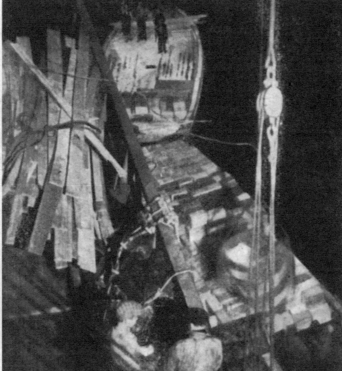

J. L. WILLIAMS, M.B.E.
As Fourth Officer he showed outstanding ability and courage.

CAPT. H. PINKNEY, D.S.O., M.B.E. **CHIEF ENG. L. BENTLEY, D.S.C.** **2nd OFFICER R. BETTESS, D.S.C.**
Like their fellows of the Merchant Navy whose photographs appear above, these three Mercantile Marine officers helped to defend an important convoy which reached Malta in August 1942. They were among those of the Merchant Navy to win naval honours for the first time in history. Centre, unloading the precious cargo at the docks by night.

Photos, British Official : L.N.A., Wm. J: Jones (Malta)

Coastal Command Keeps Watch and Ward

COASTAL COMMAND 1939-42. (H.M. Stationery Office, 2s.) Published in Jan. 1943 the Air Ministry account of the work of Coastal Command contains a number of photographs not hitherto released : here are some of them. Top left, Wellington fitted with special attachments for exploding magnetic mines before ships were equipped with degaussing gear. Top right, U-boat under fire from a Sunderland flying-boat. Below, German invasion barges massed in Boulogne harbour in 1940.

Photos. British-Official : Crown Copyright ; Fox

Great Achievements Recalled by the Camera

TRIPLE TASK OF COASTAL COMMAND, working in cooperation with the Royal Navy, is " to find the enemy ; strike the enemy ; protect our ships." These photographs are some of those included in the recently published Coastal Command, 1939-42. Top, an Anson aircraft maintains vigilant watch over a convoy. Below, the men who do the job—1st and 2nd pilots (background) of a Catalina flying-boat with their navigator (right) and radio operator.

Photos, British Official : Crown Copyright

Premier and President Hold Council of War

'THIS IS A HISTORIC MOMENT.' For ten days in mid-January 1943 the President of the United States and the Prime Minister of the United Kingdom were in conference at Casablanca, French naval base on the Atlantic coast of Morocco. During his stay in N. Africa Mr. Roosevelt visited U.S. troops and (1) shows him seated in a Jeep as he makes his tour of inspection. The President and the Prime Minister occupied adjoining villas at Anfa, a small resort near Casablanca, and (2) they are seen in the garden of a third villa in which their talks were held. Gen. Giraud, High Commissioner for French N. Africa, and Gen. de Gaulle, leader of the Fighting French (3), shake hands in the presence of the two great democratic leaders, who simultaneously exclaimed, " This is a historic moment." *Photos, British Official: Crown Copyright* PAGE 556

THE Casablanca Conference—the fourth occasion on which Mr. Churchill and President Roosevelt had met since the beginning of the war—may prove to be one of the most momentous events in the history of the present conflict.

It was on January 27 that the world learned that the great leaders of the two nations had been in consultation at Casablanca (whither they had gone by air) since January 14. Great Britain and the United States were thus active participants in the " unconditional surrender " meeting—so named by the American President in a Press conference to denote that the unconditional surrender of Germany, Italy and Japan was the only assurance of future world peace.

Gen. de Gaulle and Gen. Giraud also met and discussed plans for the unification of the war effort of the French Empire ; and on January 27 they issued a joint statement. " We have met. We have talked (it read). We have registered our entire agreement on the end to be achieved, which is the liberation of France and the triumph of human liberties by the total defeat of the enemy. This end will be attained by the union in the war of all Frenchmen fighting side by side with all their Allies."

The Conference came at a crucial time for the Axis, and the news of its holding filled the peoples of the United Nations and of the oppressed European countries with renewed hope and assurance as they looked towards the campaigns of the coming year. In London and Washington the great gathering was accepted as a council of war —a sure sign that increased pressure would be brought to bear upon the Axis, involving a concerted plan of the utmost significance.

MR. ROOSEVELT flew 5,000 miles to N. Africa. It was the first time that any President of the United States had left his country during a war, and the first flight made by Mr. Roosevelt since 1932. He flew by Clipper to a point in N. Africa, where he transferred to a four-engined bomber which had been specially fitted out for the journey. On his return journey the President, travelling via Liberia, visited President Vargas of Brazil at Natal, called in at Trinidad, and arrived back in Washington on January 31. Mr. Churchill went from Casablanca to Cairo, when he proceeded to Adana, in Turkey, for consultations (January 30-31) with President Inonu and his ministers. Having paid a brief visit to Cyprus, he returned via Cairo and Tripoli, arriving in London on February 7.

History in the Making at Casablanca Meeting

"THE President of the United States and the Prime Minister of Great Britain have been in conference near Casablanca since January 14," said a communiqué published on January 27. "They were accompanied," it went on, "by the Combined Chiefs of Staff of the two countries, and a number of other high-ranking officials and officers from both countries. For ten days the Combined Staffs were in constant session, meeting two or three times a day and recording progress at intervals to the President and the Prime Minister. The entire field of war was surveyed—theatre by theatre, throughout the world, and all resources were marshalled for the intense prosecution of the war by sea, land, and air. Nothing like this prolonged discussion between two Allies has ever taken place before.

"Complete agreement was reached between the leaders of the two countries and their respective Staffs upon the war plans and enterprises to be undertaken during the campaign in 1943 against Germany, Italy, and Japan, with a view to drawing the utmost advantage from the markedly favourable turn of events at the close of 1942.

"Premier Stalin was cordially invited to meet the President and the Prime Minister, in which case the meeting would have been held very much farther to the east. He is, however, unable to leave Russia at this time on account of the great offensive which he himself as C.-in-C. is directing. The President and Prime Minister realized to the full the enormous weight of the war which Russia is successfully bearing along her whole land front, and their prime object has been to draw as much of the weight as possible off the Russian armies by engaging the enemy as heavily as possible at the best selected points. Premier Stalin has been fully informed of the military proposals.

"The President and the Prime Minister have been in communication with Generalissimo Chiang Kai-shek. They have apprised him of the measures which they are undertaking to assist him in China's magnificent and unrelaxing struggle . . .

"The occasion of the meeting between the President and the Prime Minister made it opportune to invite Gen. Giraud to confer with the Combined Chiefs of Staff and to arrange for a meeting between him and Gen. de Gaulle . . .

"The President and the Prime Minister and the Combined Staffs, having completed their plans for the offensive campaigns of 1943, have now separated in order to put them into execution."

AT THE CASABLANCA CONFERENCE. Top photograph, taken at a Chief of Staff conference in the Anfa Hotel, near Casablanca, shows : 1, Adm. E. J. King, C.-in-C., U.S. Navy ; 2, Gen. Marshall, Chief of Staff, U.S. Army ; 3, Lt.-Gen. Arnold, commanding U.S. Army Air Force 4, Field-Marshal Sir J. Dill, head of British Joint Staff in Washington ; 5, Sir. C. Portal, Chief of Air Staff ; 6, Gen. Sir A. Brooke, C.I.G.S.; 7, Adm. Sir D. Pound, First Sea Lord; 8, Lord Louis Mountbatten, Chief of Combined Operations. Below, Mr. Churchill (3) is seen with the British representatives. 1, Sir C. Portal ; 2, Adm. Sir D. Pound ; 4, Field-Marshal Sir J. Dill ; 5 Gen. Sir A. Brooke ; 6, Gen. Sir H. Alexander ; 7, Lord Louis Mountbatten ; 8, Maj. Gen. Sir H. Ismay ; 9, Lord Leathers ; 10, Mr. MacMillan, Resident Minister at Allied H.Q., N. Africa.

'Mines Were Laid in Enemy Waters'

Become almost a commonplace in the news bulletins over the past few months, this announcement hides one of the most interesting and one of the quietest offensives of the war—an attack in which the air and naval arms of the United Nations have combined their strength in striking hard blows at the Axis transport system. This article is contributed by J. ALLEN GRAYDON.

THE attacks by Bomber and Fighter Commands upon Germany's transport system have forced the Nazis to utilize more than ever before the coastal ships they constructed before the War. This fleet has been strengthened by the inclusion of craft commandeered from France, Norway, Belgium, Holland and Denmark.

R.A.F. MINELAYING AIRCRAFT repeatedly drop mines in enemy waters. This photo was taken at a station from which Canadian and British planes operate. One of the mines is about to be loaded into the waiting Hampden. *Photo, Central Press*

With this coastal fleet at their disposal the Germans hoped to ease their overworked railway system.

But the R.A.F. and Royal Navy, by splendid cooperation, as I have seen for myself, have cut deep into Hitler's reserves of coastal shipping—and the mines they have laid in enemy shipping lanes have played a major part in this success.

In The First Great War the Royal Navy, in four years of war, laid 128,652 mines in enemy waters. Already, in cooperation with Bomber Command, the Senior Service has exceeded this figure. From Norway round to Toulon our minelayers go quietly about their work ; and to talk with these men who carry out one of the most secret of our many offensives makes you appreciate all the more the greatness of their achievement.

DURING the course of the last thirteen months Bomber Command, in some cases calling upon the giant Lancasters, Halifaxes and Stirlings, has flown 3,000,000 miles on operations concerned with minelaying. Last month 500 of these "eggs of death," as pilots call them, were dropped in enemy shipping lanes. We have good reason to believe that for every German vessel sunk as the result of mines, the loss of which is made public, yet another is destroyed and kept secret by the Axis authorities. German U-boats, too, slinking close inshore, are reported to have suffered serious damage as the result of hitting British mines.

"I suppose you think minelaying a daredevil job," a young pilot officer, captain of a Lancaster, said to me when I sat in an R.A.F. mess a short time ago. "You're wrong. It's one of the most monotonous jobs in the world. You take your orders from the Admiralty, fly for hours in the dark, reach the ' target area,' drop the mine, then go back home. No thrills. No bangs. Just monotony."

I might add that this young pilot was once caught in the beam of German searchlights

on the coast and had his wrist-watch shot off by an enemy night-fighter ; yet he kept to his course and " placed " his mines in the spot the Admiralty " brains behind the scenes " had selected.

Even the famed Kiel Canal, and other waters hitherto thought closed to our minelayers, have been " visited " by Bomber Command. In fact, since the R.A.F. and Navy joined hands in this attack our successes have increased day by day.

It is interesting to watch mines being loaded aboard our flying giants. I have seen the " eggs," after being loaded aboard trollies by crane, hauled along by a tractor, driven by a young W.A.A.F., to the machines. Always a naval expert is present to fuse the mines, and to see how closely he works with the R.A.F. ground crews makes you appreciate just how well the Senior and Junior services are working.

The Germans, in their efforts to reduce the efficiency of our aerial minelayers, have introduced night-fighter patrols, together with anti-aircraft ships, to cover their coastal waters. Powerful searchlights have also been mounted, but the minelayers, although the danger has increased, continue to force home their attacks. When I was in Germany just before the War I heard talk of a new " speedboat minesweeper " the Reich Fleet had introduced. Today we know it as the R-boat. It is a speedy vessel and was put into commission to sweep up our mines in the shortest possible time. The German seamen do not relish being drafted on to these craft, but the British mine offensive is causing the Nazi transport system to creak.

Nazi merchantmen and tankers forced out of their normal lanes by our mines have to run the gauntlet of Royal Navy " light coastal forces." Motor torpedo boats, protected by the motor and steam gunboats, as I have seen when out in the English Channel and North Sea, take a terrible toll. During recent months these light forces have destroyed over a score of merchantmen and tankers, and severely damaged forty-five. And the mines forced the Germans, against their wishes, into our trap.

Royal Navy motor launches, under cover of darkness, also play a big part in this most secret war. I have seen them, under cover of darkness, put their bows into the open sea, " slide " quietly

into waters close to the enemy, unload their T.N.T., and just as quietly set a course for home. The Germans, knowing the daring of these men, many of whom I found to be members of the R.N.V.R., have strengthened their patrols by including among the armoured trawlers the speedy Schnellbootes, more commonly known as " E-boats." (*See* Haworth diagram of British and German light coastal craft in page 278).

ONE young commanding officer, formerly a solicitor, with whom I have talked, told me how, on one particularly dangerous mission, they passed clean through the middle of a German convoy. Every man aboard the motor launches wanted to fire upon the Hun, but they held their fire while the Germans passed but a few yards away. One German ship passed within twenty yards of a motor launch, and the Germans aboard were so surprised that they could only let off—a rocket ! By the time the alarm had been given the British craft were laying their mines. This task completed, they withdrew from the areas and watched the Germans fighting it out among themselves !

On another occasion a rating was injured when a German fighter attacked. But he refused to allow anyone to tend him until the minelaying had been completed. During another " trip " our minelayers were so close to the German-held coast that a sentry, on anti-invasion patrol, hailed them, but fortunately without disastrous results.

Today the enemy, to assist their own surface craft, as well as planes, to locate and destroy British minelayers, have mounted some of the most powerful searchlights in the world in various coastal areas. I have been blinded by those facing Dover, and had the experience of being caught in their beams when in the Straits of Dover. By using them the Hun would appear to think that he will at least keep our minelayers away from his shores.

But the men who conduct one of the most important offensives, an attack which must remain for the most part on the " secret list," still take their war into the enemy's shipping lanes—and have given Hitler a headache he cannot shake off !

M.T.B. CREW LOADING A TORPEDO into their ship. Motor torpedo boats play a great part in the hazardous work of protecting our coastal waters, and have scored many successes against the enemy

Photo. Central Press

Malta, Island of the George Cross

Would she, could she, survive ? That was the question asked in the summer of 1940, when Malta was exposed to the full fury of Axis strength in the Mediterranean. Two and a half years have passed, and not Malta but Tripoli has fallen. Always Malta has roared defiance—thanks to her people's gallantry, the R.A.F. and the Royal and Merchant Navies which have kept them supplied with arms and food. Top, convoy on its way ; below, unloading a supply ship in the docks.

Photos,

In the World's Most Bombed Island

Deep in the rocky heart of Malta functions the H.Q. of the island's Command.   To the Coastal Defence
Room (1) news is flashed of the approach of enemy raiders, and from it the orders proceed to the
answering guns and fighters.   During 1942 alone Malta's planes and A.A. guns shot down 955 Axis
raiders ; our photograph (2) shows Maltese children playing amongst the remains of a German bomber.

Malta Rises Above the Smoke of Battle

Only twenty minutes' flying time from Axis aerodromes in Sicily, Malta has experienced about 3,000 air raids. Last year the enemy dropped 12,000 tons of bombs on the island, and among the many buildings of historic interest that have been damaged is St. Publius's church in Valetta (3). In St. Julian another bomb has dropped (4), while in (5) we see Maltese folk clearing a pile of rubble.

' Unsinkable Aircraft-Carrier' in Action

Photos, British Official : Crown Copyr.

During 1942 aircraft based on Malta's airfields dropped 1,500 tons of bombs on enemy bases in North Africa and Sicily, while scores of enemy ships were hit with bombs or torpedoes by planes of the R.A.F. and Fleet Air Arm. Top, a naval pilot running to take off in his Hurricane, standing ready and bombed-up on a Malta airfield. Below, searchlights and enemy flares light up the night sky above Floriana cathedral as the island experiences yet another raid.

UNDER THE SWASTIKA

Ominous Cracks in the Facade of Hitler's Fortress

In spite of all that Himmler and his Gestapo can do to suppress every whisper, criticism, every symptom of unrest, it is clear that things are far from well in the Nazi world. The article that follows is contributed by Dr. EDGAR STERN RUBARTH, the prominent anti-Nazi German publicist who has previously written in our columns.

HAD Hitler confined his ambitions to the German tribe, to the Germans in the widest possible interpretation of the word, he might have got away with it, as he got away with the tearing up of treaties, rearmament, and the incorporation of Austria and Sudetenland. But his megalomania induced him to attempt the conquest of Europe, even the world ; and in so doing he raised up the opposition which will eventually destroy him.

There are three more or less organized centres of resistance : the military, the holders of material power ; the Churches and social leaders, supporters of tradition ; and the oppressed—the conquered peoples as well as dissident groups within Germany, fighting for their liberty in underground movements. Those comprising the first and second centres went with Hitler part of the way, hoping to use him and his gang for their own ends : the first, in order to regain their old Prussian supremacy and privileges within the State, glory and booty around it ; the second in order to fight Bolshevism, rationalism, Trade-Unionism and other developments threatening the overthrow of an old order and a caste-system. These Hitler did little to destroy ; he even favoured them, while concentrating upon the annihilation of the third. The Churches, the big industrialists and financiers, the heads of the civil service, the large estate owners— these began to separate themselves from, even to stand up to, Hitler when they discovered that this kind of brown bolshevism was rather worse, since it was more wanton and subtle, than the red. But the soldiers, pampered and spoiled and favoured as never before, not even under the Hohenzollern soldier-kings, went further than any with Hitler. He could have relied on them until the end had he, the ex-lance-corporal, the drummer, not yielded to the ambition of playing Napoleon and, as their "war lord," not made at least five major mistakes.

WHAT were these mistakes ? In the first place he did not attack Britain when, in the summer of 1940, he might perhaps have overpowered her. Then he assailed Russia after having given her two years to prepare. Like his hapless predecessor, Kaiser Wilhelm II, he dragged America into the war. Next he squandered his best troops for the sake of prestige when he disregarded the generals' demand for a withdrawal from the most exposed positions in Russia at the outset of last winter. Finally, he debased all favours and advantages previously granted to his officers' corps by forcibly permeating it with his Nazi Party gangsters who were granted ranks for which generals of the old school had had to work hard for decades, under exacting professional and social rules. Of all Hitler's mistakes, this, last is most likely to accelerate his doom, even beyond all that the mounting power and experience of the United Nations can do.

Hitler got away with his first grave mistake in this connexion : he had merely to apologize for the murder, on June 30, 1934, of General von Schleicher, his predecessor as Chancellor, and his wife. He was able to dismiss von Blomberg, his own docile War Minister, in February 1938, when he got the first faint scent of military opposition, and assumed his role himself, while substituting Keitel and Brauchitsch for his able C.-in-C., General von Fritsch. Then and subsequently

between 50 and 100 staff officers, denounced by his hangman Himmler as being involved in the "plot," were done away with, strict secrecy being imposed upon their mourners ; but he had to wait for the war before being able to have Fritsch assassinated without the risk of a revolt. Though neither Hitler nor Himmler shrink from this simple way of overcoming opposition, the latter had to warn the Fuehrer against that "usual method" when giving him the next and most dramatic piece of news about the generals' junta. For this news was of a more powerful, more far-reaching, and more

HITLER'S 'INTUITION' AT WORK. Hitler is here shown planning the two summer offensives of 1942, both of which were doomed to utter failure. Keitel is seen on the Fuehrer's right, while Von Bock is on the extreme right of the photo. The latter was stated to have been dismissed some three months later for his failure to take Stalingrad. *Photo, Associated Press*

popular move than all the previous ones— nothing less than a challenge by most of the men he had made field-marshals and national heroes, of his decision to go on with his Russian offensive through the bitter winter of 1941.

YET he dismissed von Brauchitsch, von Rundstedt, von Bock and not a few others ; he made himself Supreme Commander in fact as well as in name and tackled the opposition within the army's brains, the General Staff. He had to recall in the spring of 1942 Field-Marshal von Bock, that ruthless Prussian nobleman and soldier whom the army calls "Der Sterber" (the "Die-er"), in order to launch his southern offensive—the result of a compromise with the General Staff which, more correctly than the amateur strategist, gauged Germany's remaining resources ; but he had dismissed since von Leeb, unsuccessful besieger of Leningrad, von Manstein, who had squandered his divisions in the Crimea and failed in the Caucasus approaches, and many others. And, stubbornly insisting upon not only equal but privileged rank for his private S.S. gunmen-force and its gutter-snipe leaders, he favoured the few Nazi upstarts among the regular officers. "If only I had two Rommels ! . . ." he is known to have exclaimed occasionally.

Yet even had he a dozen of the Rommel stamp it would but help him to win a few

battles, never to win a great war. For that is the task of extremely difficult, hard, persistent team-work by organized brains, for which Hitler—the Bohemian, the "inspired" leader—has but sneers. So it is that after dismissing generals right and left, after giving amateurish battle-orders painfully translated into strategic language by his private "Fuehrer Staff" under General Jodl, Hitler finally decided upon being, not only his own Supreme C.-in-C., but also his Chief of Staff.

THAT fatal decision welded together a military camarilla inspired by individual disappointments, hatreds, revenges, and ambitions. It centres around Brauchitsch and Bock, the latter dismissed for the second time, on October 4, at Stalingrad. Dismissed—or so Hitler is made to believe. He is hardly aware yet that all the generals to whom he has "given the boot" wanted and got his "boot" to get an alibi for the army leadership in case of a stalemate, for which they hoped— or a defeat, which they now fear. Their technique is simple : when called to his sumptuous H.Q. and confronted with reproaches or demands, they arouse the Fuehrer to one of his famous fits of maniacal fury, then tender their resignation before he has time to calm down. Always weak politicians, their purpose would seem to be the creation of a nucleus of power representing an alternative to Hitler and his gang (who would be sacrificed willingly enough to the Allies—"liquidated" by the Army) ; in return for this, and for the liberation of the West, they would hope with the help of reactionary elements in our midst, to persuade us that the Prussian army must be spared to some extent, with the generals and Junkers at its top, as a bulwark against the tide of Bolshevism threatening to engulf all Europe.

MAYBE their aims are narrow-minded, but the results are far-reaching and should, ultimately, prove disastrous for the Nazis. For their example and their arguments—often more outspoken than those of civilians— spread throughout the country and encourage resistance, not merely in other traditionalist circles, but also amongst the workers and peasants.

The iron monster the Fuehrer is driving across Europe is still colossal ; but it has proved to be cast-iron. The first cracks in its structure—at Voronezh and Stalingrad, in the Caucasus, in N. Africa, and in his western air defences—have shown by now ; and cast-iron breaks suddenly and completely once hammer-blows encounter fissures, however slight.

Leningrad's Epic of the Unknown Civilian

What London was in 1940, so was Leningrad from 1941 to 1943—an Epic (as a writer in the London Zeitung put it) of the Unknown Civilian. Below we tell of the sixteen months' siege, and of the final battle which lifted the dreadful shadow from the lives of the long-suffering but most valiantly enduring Leningraders.

WHEN Captain Fyodor Sabakhin and Captain Demidov met on the snow-covered, corpse-littered battlefield outside Leningrad they first exchanged the passwords so as to identify themselves. Then, as is the fashion of demonstrative Russians, they gave each other three kisses on the cheek, and flung their arms round each other's shoulders. Their men, too, coming up did likewise. Then for a brief interval they sat on the snow, "swopped" tobacco, and talked for a while of the things they had seen and done.

Just an incident in the years of war. And yet that meeting had an historic importance. For Sabakhin was commander of an infantry battalion of General Govorov's army *in* Leningrad, while Demidov was one of General Meretskov's men fighting their way *to* Leningrad from the Volkhov front to the south-east. Their meeting signalized the junction of the besieged and their deliverers: in other words, the siege of Leningrad had been raised.

For sixteen months Leningrad lay under the menace of imminent capture by the Hitlerites. It was on August 21, 1941 that the Germans under Von Leeb began their onslaught, and by September the siege proper had begun. For some weeks the city was entirely cut off from the rest of Russia, but in November 1941 General Meretskov's troops on the Lower Volkhov front drove the Nazis from the southern shore of Lake Ladoga except for a small stretch at Schluesselburg—and even here the fortress on an island off-shore continued to be held by a handful of Red Marines from the Baltic fleet.

THENCEFORTH communications with Russia were maintained across Lake Ladoga. During the ice-free months light craft and tugs towing barges dashed across the great lake—it is about the size of Wales—to a branch-line of the Murmansk railway ; then in December 1941, when the cold was so intense that birds dropped dead on the wing and the life of the city was at its lowest ebb, a double-track highway, complete with traffic-lights, service-stations and bomb-shelters, was brought into operation across the ice. Even so, this was but a slender and precarious route to a city of three million people (not to mention several millions more in the neighbourhood).

What saved Leningrad was the active defence policy of its garrison under Govorov. Always the Russian planes were in action against the Germans in front of the city and their bases on the Finnish coast and in Estonia ; always the Russian ground forces nibbled at the Nazi defences so that they could never be properly consolidated. The Red Fleet, too, sailed out when ice permitted to attack the German supply-routes in the Baltic, while in the winter, when the Gulf of Finland was ice-bound, the naval gunners went ashore with their big guns and went into action with them on the land front. Even when, in the depth of last winter, all municipal transport ceased, the water-supply failed, and workers in the factories toiled in Arctic temperatures in overcoats and felt boots—even then the supply of shells, mortars and guns continued to flow from the great armament works inside the city.

AT the outset the city's food stores were considered to be adequate for a long siege, but what with German bombing and the appalling difficulties of transportation across the ice, Leningrad was brought to the verge of famine. Aeroplanes were used to fly provisions into the beleaguered city until the route across the ice had been properly developed. To quote a passage from a brilliant dispatch from the Special Correspondent of The Times in Moscow :

They were the days when people were dragged dead through the streets on sledges . . . when workers arriving at the factories fell into a coma on the floor by their benches ; when it was not rare for someone telephoning to hear the voice falter and cease and to find out afterwards that the speaker had fallen dead ; when, save for the sound of battle, the life of the city was stilled and in streets festooned with tangled wires (the Germans dropped pieces of rail to cut them), littered with broken glass and deep in uncleared snow, scenes of desolation occurred.

But even in those hard and terrible times Leningrad showed its fighting spirit. Thousands of its workers went to the front, women taking their places at the furnaces and lathes in the suburbs under shellfire. Although it was so cold that the ink froze in the ink-wells, 100,000 children attended the schools ; and after the day's lessons were over the boys and girls alike " did their stuff " as messengers, first-aiders and postmen. Wooden houses were torn down for fuel. Communal feeding-centres were organized. On May Day last year, so as to have their share in the national celebrations, 150,000 volunteers set about an immense spring-cleaning of the city with such excellent results that during the summer Leningrad could boast that she was the cleanest city in Russia. Every patch of ground was cultivated, and the heart of the city was transformed into an immense vegetable garden. Most symbolic, perhaps, of Leningrad's spirit was the performance on April 5 by a scratch orchestra to an audience muffled in fur coats in the Pushkin Hall, of Shostakovitch's Seventh Symphony, specially dedicated to the heroic city.

So for sixteen months it went on. Always there was fighting, in winter and summer alike, fearful and bloody ; inside the city the people drew in their

RELIEF OF LENINGRAD. On this map the dotted line shows the German corridor which after 16 months was obliterated by the Russians in Jan. 1943 ; the subsequent front is indicated by the heavy black lines.
By courtesy of The Times

belts notch by notch, suffered terrible privations, died of hunger and cold. In the autumn of last year Meretskov launched an offensive with a view to taking Sinyavino ; and once they cut down the German corridor from eight miles wide to three. But they could never get through the bloody swamps to the Neva.

THEN on the morning of Tuesday, January 12, 1943, Meretskov and Govorov struck together. Following an artillery bombardment of unprecedented weight, Red Army infantrymen equipped with climbing-irons slid down the northern bank of the Neva and sped across the ice-covered river to the steep southern bank. As they crossed German shells tore up the surface, but in less than ten minutes the first wave of Russians had made good their foothold on the southern bank. Hard on their heels came the second wave, pushing field-artillery before them, and the guns were hoisted by ropes up the bank. Soon the battle was joined in the network of concrete forts which German military engineering science had created south of Schluesselburg. Next the Russians brought heavy tanks across the river by pontoons ; and these, aided by the low-flying Stormoviks and the infantry with bayonets and automatics, thrust the Germans out of their massive fortifications to the edge of the forest. Meanwhile General Meretskov had smashed his way through to Ladoga and now pushed southwards towards Sinyavino, so as to link up with Govorov across the German corridor. And all the time the guns of the Schluesselburg fortress and of the Baltic fleet kept up a terrific pounding of the slowly narrowing belt between the two armies.

GERMAN resistance was of the most embittered kind ; particularly violent was the fighting between Sinyavino and Schluesselburg and 10,000 Germans were reported to be killed there. Then Schluesselburg was stormed by units of the Leningrad army, aided by ski-troops from the Volkhov front who, crossing the canal, reached Lake Ladoga behind the town and so surrounded the garrison. The Nazi ring was broken.

But all the generalship, the bravery and devotion of the Red Armies could not have maintained Leningrad for the Soviet if it had not been for the ordinary men and women who for so many long and terrible months within its ring of forts lived and worked and fought and died.
— **E. ROYSTON PIKE**

CHILDREN IN LENINGRAD, playing in a sunlit street of the hard-pressed Second City of the Soviets, appear to be happily unconscious of the grim struggle which their parents waged against the enemy for many a tragic month. *Photo, U.S.S.R. Official*

Speedy Progress Along the Road to Rostov

RUSSIAN DRIVE TOWARDS ROSTOV-ON-DON was further accelerated by the Red Army's recapture of Salsk, on Jan. 22, 1943. From this important railway junction the Soviet forces advanced to capture Tikhoretsk and Kropotkin in an attempt to cut off the enemy fleeing from Armavir. A Russian armoured car patrol is here seen pushing forward across the snow-covered ground under fire of German mine-throwers in the Lower Don area. A mine is exploding as the cars advance.

Photo. Planet News

THE WAR IN THE AIR

by Capt. Norman Macmillan, M.C., A.F.C.

Towards the end of January 1943 it was reported that the German police were to enforce the carrying of gas-masks by German civilians throughout the Reich. It is curious that this report should coincide with the increasing misfortunes of the German armies in Russia and North Africa. Under the prevailing conditions of continuing victories there is no reason for the United Nations to resort to aerial gas warfare. Moreover, Britain has stated without equivocation that we will not be first to use the gas weapon.

The objective of this enforcement order might be to frighten civilians in Germany and make them more ready to toe the line to the most stringent Government decrees ordaining harsher terms of living. If this is the reason it might be good United Nations propaganda to use aircraft to drop leaflets containing an official assurance that the United Nations will not use gas unless Germany or one of her allies first uses it. This would defeat the German object of instilling fear into the people to make them obedient to the crack of the whip. The alternative objective of the order might be to prepare for the consequences of an Axis resort to gas warfare as a means to try to turn defeat on land into victory. That is a possibility against which the United Nations must be prepared. We should not forget that Italy is the only Power ever to have used gas from the air as a weapon of war, and that she used it without pity against Abyssinian tribesmen, who were completely defenceless against this form of war because they had no defence against gas and no defence against aircraft.

Let us hope that air war on the scale on which it is waged today will not take this additional horrible turn. But even if this were to happen I cannot conceive that it would bring victory to the Axis. The end of the air war, and of the war as a whole, is already written in the waning power of the Axis in the air and the waxing power of the United Nations in that element. British aircraft output in 1942 was 50 per cent greater than in 1941.

The forward troops of the Eighth Army entered Tripoli early on January 23. The advance of the Army over the 1,400 miles from El Alamein was made under the continuous cover of the R.A.F. The Luftwaffe was unable to play a big part in the campaign because its aircraft and supplies were often smashed on the ground. From October 1 to January 22 fighters, bombers, and ground-fire of the United Nations destroyed in the air 507 enemy aircraft for a loss of 335 Allied aircraft. Successive campaigns in the Middle East have cost the Axis about 4,000 aircraft lost in flight and about 2,000 on the ground. Yet only recently has the Axis had to face a great accumulation of air strength.

DESERT Landing-Ground Prepared in 3 hours as 8th Army Advance

During the 8th Army's advance fighter squadrons' ground personnel moved up almost within sight of the enemy, striking forward in mobile columns to occupy evacuated enemy airfields or create new ones out of desert scrub. One landing-ground 1,200 yards square was serviceable three hours after advanced ground parties had selected

the site. That was in the Bir Dufan area, fewer than a hundred air miles from the town of Tripoli. Fighter formations, including an American pursuit group, moved forward into this area in one hop of 140 miles.

R.A.F. ground staff, with their supply and transport columns, attached units of Royal Engineers, and airfield graders, were protected by the Allied fighters. Ahead of Rommel's rearguard German and Italian ground units were constantly harried from the air. Rommel's supply position was rendered precarious by air attacks against shipping and ports on both sides of the Mediterranean and Junkers 52 air-transports in flight. The citation to the award of a Bar to the D.F.C. to Wing Commander S. B. Grant showed how Rommel tried and failed to get supplies by air. It reads : " In December 1942 this officer flew the leading aircraft of a formation acting as escort to a force of fighter-bombers. During the flight 63 enemy air transports escorted by five twin-engined fighters were intercepted. Leaving the fighter-bombers to attack the transports, Wing Commander Grant led his formation in an

CASTEL BENITO AIRFIELD, outside Tripoli, was heavily strafed by Allied bombers as Gen. Montgomery's forces drew near the capital. A sapper of the 8th Army is here seen removing a mine from the landing-ground. Behind him is another sapper at work with a detector. Wrecked hangars are shown in the background.
Photo, British Official: Crown Copyright

attack on the enemy fighters, all of which were shot down . . ." That left the Junkers transports as easy prey. Aircraft based on Malta played a big part in these interceptions of transport aircraft and shipping.

Rommel's defeat must be ascribed in part to the failure of General Field-Marshal Albert Kesselring's 2nd Air Fleet of the Luftwaffe (of which the 2nd Air Corps was commanded by Colonel-General Bruno Lörzer, well-known Great War fighter pilot, and first President of the German Air Sport Association—Deutsche Luftsport Verband—founded in 1933 by the Nazis as the foundation of the flying section of the forbidden air force) when operating from Sicily against Malta. For months this Air Fleet pounded away at Malta, but could not break the spirit of the George Cross Island—greatest " aircraft carrier" in the world. Curiously enough, Kesselring and Rommel were not friends. Now Malta has done much to smash Rommel.

In page 470 I referred to Rommel's retreat westward, pointing out that it was by no means a retreat to safety. He is now open to

air attack from the advanced airfields around Tripoli, from Malta, and from air squadrons in Tunisia, and Algeria ; from the air he is outflanked and surrounded ; his way of escape is, as ours was from Greece and Crete, by sea, or else by air. The *dénouement* of the African battle against Rommel and Von Arnim has yet to come, and it may hold surprises.

From the United Kingdom the Fortress and Liberator bombers of the U.S. Army Air Force 8th Bomber Command attacked Germany for the first time on Wednesday, January 27, from bases in the United Kingdom. Principal target was Wilhelmshaven naval base, on which bombs were dropped from a great height through cloud-gaps. The Liberators shot down 22 German fighters. Other of their daylight targets lay in North-West Germany.

MOSQUITOES Raid Submarine Diesel Engine Works at Copenhagen

On the evening of the same day Mosquitoes of Bomber Command, led by Wing Commander Hughie Edwards, V.C., D.S.O., D.F.C., attacked the submarine Diesel engine works in the shipbuilding yards of Durneister and Wain at Copenhagen. After passing through banks of cloud and rain the crews found ideal weather over The Sound. Speeding in at dusk between 50 and 300 feet up, the pilots dodged the chimneys and many spires of the Danish capital, and then the masts of

ships in the harbour, and reached the island east of the city where the yards stand. Everything made there goes to the enemy. In face of intense flak from shore and ships " the great bulk of the bombs went in," and flames roared up to a hundred feet.

From the night of January 18 until the morning of January 28 Bomber Command raided heavy industries, factories, oil installations, railway communications, submarine bases and docks in the Ruhr, at Hengelo, Terneuzen, Lorient, Flushing, Bruges, Bordeaux, Copenhagen and Düsseldorf, laid mines in enemy waters, and bombed airfields at Maupertuis (Cherbourg), Abbeville and St. Omer. Coastal Command was also concerned in the attack on Bordeaux. The raids were made by day and night. Twenty-two bombers were lost.

American Mitchell B.25 284 m.p.h. medium bombers were officially mentioned for the first time as part of the force which bombed the French airfields on January 22. These bombers were named after the late General William Mitchell—the great, and in his life time despised, American protagonist of air power.

Losing only one aircraft, the R.A.F. bombed Berlin in daylight for the first time on Saturday, January 30. To celebrate Hitler's tenth accession anniversary they made it a double. Darting out of cloud cover, Mosquitoes bombed at 11 a.m. and 4 p.m., the 56th and 57th raids by British aircraft on the Reich capital. A.A. was negligible ; flak-crews were dispersed to hear loud-speaker speeches by Goering and Goebbels. Bomber Command made Hermann one hour late on the microphone. Emden was also raided that day. Hamburg got a tough half-hour during the succeeding night from 8,000-lb. and 4,000-lb. bombs and tens of thousands of incendiaries ; five bombers were lost in this raid.

Air war in New Guinea, New Britain, the Solomon Islands, and the surrounding territories continued against military and naval concentrations.

At Home in a Land of Scrub and Sand

WITH THE R.A.F. IN N. AFRICA. 1, Bargaining with a native vendor in a village street. 2, Intelligence Officer listens to pilots' accounts of an operational raid over enemy territory. 3, This tent-pole serves as a scoreboard, and testifies to the squadron's bombing efficiency. 4, Armourers of a fighter-bomber squadron busily loading a Hurricane for an attack on Axis positions. 5, These pilots have just returned from a raid. Their machines are seen in the background.

Photos, British Official: Crown Copyright

Help from America for Hard-pressed China

U.S. AIRCRAFT IN CHINA. 1, Clearing the ground to enlarge an airfield, these Chinese women and children are busily at work with hoes and scythes. **2,** U.S. airman indicates his score of four destroyed Jap planes to a comrade who also has one to his credit. **3,** Chinese soldier mounts guard as repair work begins on a fighter plane. The huts serve as camouflaged hangars. **4,** Transport planes of the India-China Ferry Command loading-up with Chinese troops on their way to the front.

Photos, Keystone, Associated Press

Did He Want His Bombs to Drop Just Here?

BOMBS ON A LONDON SCHOOL. Soon after midday on Jan. 20, 1943 enemy aircraft dropped bombs on the south-eastern suburbs of London. An L.C.C. school in Lewisham received a direct hit, 39 children and 5 teachers being killed, and 60 children severely injured. 1, The demolished wing. 2, A clergyman assists Civil Defence workers. 3, Despite her injuries this child manages to smile. 4, A policeman directs the search for the missing. 5, Wreckage of one of the raiders—an F.W.190 which was shot down. On his return to Berlin one of the Nazi airmen, Capt. Stuhman, broadcast an account : " We dropped our bombs where they were to be dropped."

Photos, Daily Mirror, Planet News, Associated Press, G.P.U.

Alamein to Tripoli: 1,400 Miles in 80 Days

"Today," said Sir James Grigg, Minister of War, in a broadcast delivered on Saturday, January 23, 1943, "we have the news of the fall of Tripoli. To all intents and purposes this completes the destruction of the Italian Empire in Africa." In what follows we tell something of the magnificent organization which lay behind a great feat of arms and which, coupled with brilliant generalship, military skill and bravery, made the triumph possible.

ON October 23, 1942 Rommel's army and Montgomery's faced each other across the wire and trenches of El Alamein. The one was still flushed with triumph, boasting of the next stage which would inevitably carry it to the Nile and beyond. The other, with defeats to avenge, was quietly confident in its new-found strength. At dawn on that fateful day the Eighth Army attacked. For a while there was fierce battle, but from the first Montgomery secured and maintained the mastery. By November 4 Rommel's Afrika Korps and his Italian allies were streaming back along the road they had come. The Eighth Army had begun that advance which was to carry it across 1,400 miles to Tripoli, and past Tripoli over the border into Tunisia—as great a distance as from Leningrad to Paris, as from New York to New Orleans.

IT was not an unopposed advance. All the time (as Sir James Grigg emphasized) there was skirmishing between the light armoured forces which headed our columns and the tanks and guns which shielded Rommel's rear. Sometimes, as at Fuka and Matruh, the fighting was on a bigger scale; and twice, at El Agheila and at Buerat, Rommel halted and dug himself in, making at least a show of serious resistance. But General Montgomery profited by these enforced delays to bring up the innumerable stores and supplies by which an army lives and fights; and as soon as the stores were in hand he gave Rommel that extra kick which drove him on once more in flight.

Nor was it easy going. There was no railway beyond that which runs from the Nile Valley to Tobruk. There was only one good road with an asphalt surface, the one which runs the whole distance through the coastal region; and that had been blown up in scores of places by the enemy. Thousands of mines, too, were strewn in the path of the advancing troops. But when causeways had been blown, when minefields hidden under the dusty tarmac of the single road made it impassable, our cars ploughed their way across the desert until such time—often it was a matter of hours only—as the engineers had cleared the obstacles and made a safe passage for the lorries following each other bonnet to tail for mile after mile along the line of march.

WORKING to an imperative time-table over some of the worst going in the world, faithful always to the rule "the supplies must get through," the swarms of vehicles kept up their steady progress. Well might the War Secretary pay tribute to the work of the Quartermaster-General's staff under Lieut.-Gen. Lindsell, and to those vitally necessary but so often unnamed services, the Royal Engineers, the Royal Army Service Corps,

the Royal Army Ordnance Corps, and the Royal Electrical and Mechanical Engineers. As the army advanced it was accompanied by an elaborate gradation of aid detachments and workshops which retrieved cripples and made them fighting fit again.

Constant labour was required to improve and repair the surface of the coastal road, and to make passable the rough, ill-defined tracks across the desert which constituted the shortest route. The railway from Alamein to Tobruk was soon working with the punctuality of a British railroad, bringing up scores of thousands of tons of supplies. What quantities of ammunition had to be handled may be gathered from the fact that in the course of the barrage that preceded the attack at El Alamein the field guns alone fired 1,000 tons weight of shells in an hour. In one week at a late stage in the advance over three million gallons of petrol were delivered at the front, and over 8,000 tons of ammunition. On an average, each man required 5 lb. weight of food (and containers) per day, as well as 50 cigarettes and 2 boxes of matches a week.

Most important of all the stores was water. From El Agheila to the hills south of Tripoli fresh water is altogether lacking. The Army needed more than 5,000 tons of water a day and half of it was brought from the Nile, along a pipe-line to Tobruk; 1,500 tons, still from the Nile, were shipped to Benghazi daily, 300 tons were landed on beaches from lighters, and the balance of 700 tons came from local wells. From Tobruk to Benghazi the water was carried to the forward troops by water companies operating with specially-constructed tank wagons or metal containers holding four gallons each.

A GREAT part in the advance was played by the Royal Navy, whose preparations began months before, not at Alexandria, but (cabled George Crawley, Reuters special correspondent) at the ends of the earth, where warships herded together the vital convoys which flowed unceasingly to the Middle East.

After the great push began the Navy was charged with tremendous and hazardous tasks in feeding and supplying the Army as it advanced along the Libyan coast. One ton of supplies delivered by sea to the advanced posts was worth (it was estimated) ten sent along the hundreds of miles of over-crowded roads between Alexandria and Tripoli. Most of the petrol required—millions of gallons—was sent by ship to Tobruk or Benghazi. Before the opening of the Alamein battle Naval advance parties were organized in detail: complete units for Sollum, Bardia, Tobruk, Derna, Benghazi and Tripoli were waiting at Alexandria for the word to go,

LT.-GEN. SIR W. G. LINDSELL, in charge of the Middle East Administration since August 1942. In 1939-1940 he was similarly responsible for the provisioning of the B.E.F. in France.
Photo, Associated Press

long before each of the ports fell in turn. Not a single item was left unprovided for. Minesweepers for the opening up of the captured ports, small patrol craft for the essential harbour duties, tugs and tank-landing craft—all were ready and complete with supplies and equipment. As a result, petrol and water were landed at the captured ports almost before the dust of the rearmost Axis vehicles had settled.

All the way from Egypt to Tripoli the R.A.F. spread its covering wings around and above the Eighth Army; but perhaps its biggest contribution to the triumph was the unrelenting and shattering blows dealt at the enemy's air-bases and supply-lines. There was scarcely a day or night on which the Axis lines were not bombed, raked with fire from cannon, machine-guns, left shattered. Far in the rear their personnel was demoralized. From the beginning of the battle air superiority was secured, and that meant much more than superiority of air power over just the battle area: it meant soundness of directing power at the top, efficient means of supply and maintenance. Then it may be added that R.A.F. transport aircraft were used on a much larger scale than ever before; huge quantities of ammunition, petrol, rations and water were flown to the troops composing the vanguard. Bombers taking supplies to the front brought back wounded. In return the Army seized and made ready new advanced landing-grounds which enabled our fighters to keep up with the retreating enemy.

IN spite of everything the average rate of advance of the Eighth Army was 17 miles a day; if we exclude the major pauses at El Agheila and Buerat it was 30 miles a day. In eighty days Montgomery's men stormed their way from Egypt to the borders of Tunisia; Cyrenaica was overrun, Tripolitania captured, Tripoli entered in triumph. In those same eighty days Rommel's Afrika Korps suffered 80,000 casualties in killed, wounded and prisoners; 500 of his tanks were destroyed or captured, 1,000 pieces of artillery, and tens of thousands of his vehicles.

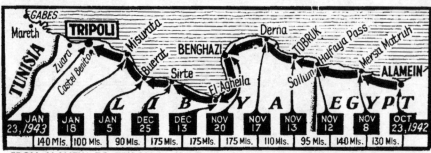

FROM ALAMEIN TO TRIPOLI in 80 days is the proud record of the 8th Army. On Nov. 4, 1942 Gen. Montgomery's forces began their pursuit of the Afrika Korps in Egypt; on Jan. 23, 1943 the 8th Army occupied Tripoli, having covered a distance of nearly 1,400 miles. This map shows the stage-by-stage progress of our troops along the Mediterranean coast.
By courtesy of the Daily Herald.

A 'Most Useful Weapon' Mr. Churchill Called It

'THE PRIEST,' as the Allies' latest self-propelled gun has been nicknamed by the 8th Army, is a 105-mm. gun-howitzer known to the U.S. Army as the M. 5. As Mr. Churchill disclosed on November 11, 1942, it is a most useful weapon in contending with the German 88-mm. anti-tank gun. 1, Side view; note the one-pounder A.A. gun amidships. 2, Mounted on an M. 3 Gen. Grant tank chassis, the 105-mm. gun is here seen ready for action 3, A "Priest" in the background passes a burning enemy tank. PAGE 571

Photos, British Official: Crown Copyright

By Land and Sea With Our Roving Camera

H.M.S. BRAMBLE, British minesweeper forming part of a convoy to N. Russia, was announced on Jan. 20, 1943 to have been lost. She made an enemy sighting report on the morning of Dec. 31, 1942, and a study of reports received later makes it clear that the Bramble endeavoured most courageously to do what she could to protect the convoy, and went down fighting.

FUR COATS FOR A.T.S. Operational A.T.S. have recently been issued with winter clothing. Here are seen two members of an A.A. battery well protected against the cold.

STATION RAILBAR (right), recently opened by the L.M.S. at Euston, has been designed to take the place in wartime travel of withdrawn dining-cars on trains.

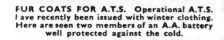

UNDERWATER FIGHTERS. Before crews set out on their first submarine operational patrol they are given a rigorous training. The instructor is here seen helping pupils to descend the steel ladder into the practice tank.

'POTATO KING OF ARRAN.' Mr. D. MacKelvin, M.B.E. (right), and two of his helpers inspect seed potatoes before planting. He has cultivated over 3,000 seedling varieties on his trial grounds in the Isle of Arran. *Photos, Central Press, Sport & General, Topical Press, E. W. Tattersall* PAGE 572

I WAS THERE!

Eye Witness Stories of the War

These Men Juggle with Death on the Home Front

Our fighting men are dependent on the perilous work of Home Front civilians who daily juggle with deadly little grains of powder at the risk of instant destruction to themselves. Here is " Rear-ranker's " story of his recent visit to one of these factories somewhere in the country.

THE gatekeeper took my pipe, tobacco and matches. Then they fixed me up with rubber goloshes over my shoes, and the turn-ups of my trousers were carefully swept clean and left turned down. My guide explained. Trouser turn-ups can carry match-heads and all sorts of things which may ignite chemicals. Shoes have nails and metal pieces which may grind a particle of explosive to danger heat. As he put it, " Some of the stuff round here goes off if you raise your eyebrows at it."

Single-storied wooden huts are separated by high grassy mounds of earth, to localize explosions or fires. There are no hanging lights, no electric switches, no metal fittings. The wooden swing-doors have no handles and no latches. Their hinges are on the outside and the doors pull open with a knotted rope. The lighting comes from bulbs shining inwards through small thick glass screens in the inner wall. Fire-extinguishers, fire-hydrants and hoses are everywhere.

THERE'S a white line painted along the centre of the gangways. It isn't there for fun. For you meet men carrying little red boxes by rope handles. And, believe me, those boxes aren't just full of ice-cream. So you walk on the left of the white line— and stay walking there. The heavier stuff is gently pushed around by hand in small wooden wagons on little brass wheels. The wood is dovetailed together to make those boxes and wagons. There isn't a steel nail anywhere.

Experienced middle-aged men do the mixing, and work the hydraulic presses— at 3 tons a square inch—that squeeze this sensitive stuff into tiny pellets with a terrific kick in them. Half a dozen men will be standing at a little counter almost touching each other. Each will be doing just one— or maybe two—delicate, unhurried filling operations. So many tiny pellets, and then a wafer-thin paper washer, placed in a container by one man—so much powder, carefully weighed, and a little wad of felt by the next, and so on.

Finally, the last man in the row gently pushes the container on to the tray of a vertical flash-tight half-cylinder let into the wall. Then he pulls a lever which turns the cylinder—just like the revolving doors at a hotel entrance. The man waiting on the other side of the wall takes out the container and carefully places it ready for the hydraulic press.

THEN my guide took me off to a small hut all by itself. He turned me over to its only inhabitant, who examined my pass and took off my cuff-links and wrist-watch. I had to put on one of the workmen's coats—he didn't like my buttons. Inside the hut a smooth wooden counter ran the full length of one of the walls. On it were a few tiny straggling heaps of reddish powder. Innocent-looking stuff. It arrives, mixed with water, in small red-painted kegs.

While the powder's wet it wouldn't hurt a fly. But on the counter in this hut the grains are drying—and there's a special trap to keep that fly out, and any other insect which might get in. For if one of them picked up a single dry grain and flew around and dropped it in the hut, you, and the fly, and quite a slice of the surrounding countryside would never be seen again. There's even a fine mesh net hung below the

ceiling to catch any tiny splinters that might fall. As usual, the lighting comes from electric bulbs behind glass in the walls. Even the sunlight is dangerous.

He showed me a wooden egg-spoon. It was nice and smooth, he said, for picking up the powder. Less chance of accidentally squeezing a grain against the counter. Slowly and gently he started filling a minute glass tube. Marvellous to watch how skilfully he made those deadly little grains run with the minimum of friction against each other.

A POLISHED leather case, about the size of a 1-lb. tin of tobacco, stood at the end of the counter. It was deeply padded with cotton-wool, lined with fine silk. Inside it, four of the little glass tubes, already filled, stood upright in their holes. He finished the fifth tube and put it in. Then he put the leather cap on the case, slipped his wrist through the silk thongs which ran right under it, and we walked out of the enclosure to the mixing hut.

He put the case on a counter in the mixing hut, whistled to George the Mixer, shook my hand and said good morning. Then he walked off to do the same thing tomorrow— and the day after—and the day after that. And you would think that he had just brought round a box of cigarettes, instead of the potential destruction of half a dozen enemy ships. I never saw such cold nerve and skill—for he's under no illusions as to what may happen if he should make one mistake.

GEORGE showed me his polished brass mixing bowl, about a foot in diameter. It's mounted on a pedestal, waist-high for him. Close against one side of the bowl is a strong curved shield, bolted to the floor, and reaching up well above his head. In the shield there's a thick glass window at his eye-level.

In the mixing bowl lay a tiny silk bag, about the size of one of those old-fashioned ring purses. It was wide open and he showed me the other powder inside waiting to be mixed with the dangerous red one. Properly mixed, he explained, they can be handled with absolute safety. Then he stationed me behind the entrance wall, where I could put my head round and watch. He took one of the little glass tubes of red powder and went behind his shield. Putting his arms round inside the shield, and watching

DANGER—T.N.T.! This Canadian worker wears a face-piece to prevent inhalation of poisonous fumes. A graphic description of work in a British explosives factory is given in this page. *Photo, Fox*

through his glass pane, he emptied the red powder very gently into the bowl. Then he gathered the neck of the bag together with a silk draw-cord, which he hooked over a wooden lever on the machine which does the mixing.

All is now ready for mixing, and we leave the hut. George then pulls the machine's starting lever. We wait in silence, for this is the critical moment. It either mixes as usual—or it goes off. George knows the timing to a split second. All's well—we go back—and now the stuff is as safe as houses. With grim humour he shows me how the wall of the hut on the opposite side of his shield is fitted to blow out with the least trouble and expense.

NOW the powder mixture goes into detonators, which give the kick that explodes the big fillings of guncotton, or T.N.T., in torpedoes, mines, and shells and bombs. You can handle these big fillings with no more ceremony than so many hundred-weights of cheese. Put a detonator the size of your little finger in the middle of them, and—well, you've seen photographs of what's happening to Axis ships and factories.

His Operating-Theatre was in Mid-Atlantic

One of an escort group fighting off a U-boat attack on a convoy, a corvette has been hit and has several badly wounded men needing immediate medical attention. A young surgeon aboard a destroyer receives the corvette's signal. What happens then is told by the Naval Reporter of The Evening Standard, from which the story is reprinted here.

HUNDREDS of miles out in the Atlantic a British destroyer momentarily slackens speed as a small boat is quickly lowered away. The ratings, in their cumbersome cork life-jackets, pull lustily as the boat rides like a cockle-shell up and down the deep troughs of the waves. In the after-part of the boat sits a solitary figure clutching a case and with a heavily-laden haversack slung over his shoulder.

The destroyer gathers speed again and swings round in a wide protecting circle as the boat - approaches a smaller warship. The loaded figure scrambles agilely aboard as the boat is tossed up a matter of some ten or twelve feet on an almost oily swell.

PAGE 573

" Good," says the destroyer captain, who has been watching from his bridge. " The doctor has made it. Now we must get cracking."

The smaller warship is a corvette flying the flag of the Norwegian Navy. Not long before she, and other ships of the escort group, fought off a U-boat attack on a convoy. The convoy is safe, but the corvette has been hit and has signalled that she has several badly wounded men who require immediate attention. The young surgeon at once collects his instruments and dressings and goes to their aid.

Aboard the destroyer, in a north-west port, I have just met the surgeon. His story is one that is typical of the men who wear bright

A NORWEGIAN CORVETTE during a patrol in the Atlantic. On such a small ship as this the "Doc." referred to in the accompanying story performed a number of ticklish operations, while his "theatre" rocked and rolled with the ocean swell.

Photo, Norwegian Official

red between the gold rings on their arms. He is an R.N.V.R. surgeon lieutenant in the early twenties. When war came he was completing his medical studies at the London Hospital. He took an appointment at the hospital and grew old in experience during six months of heavy raids in the East End. Then the doctor—he is an Irishman, with crisp, curly hair and grey eyes which alternate between deep seriousness and twinkling mirth—joined the Navy.

"Sometimes for weeks on end it seems a waste," he told me. "There is little for me to do except act as a glorified chemist's shop. Then there comes a time when I need every bit of skill I have as a surgeon, and there must be no hesitation because men's lives are at stake."

"Doc.," as the wardroom knows him, has been across the Atlantic 14 times. "Life in a destroyer which is crashing about the Atlantic in all weathers can be extraordinarily uncomfortable," he confided. "But for some reason which I cannot define, I enjoy it.

Before the war began I had planned to go round the world as a ship's doctor. Well, I've travelled many thousands of miles at sea—but it has hardly been a world tour." Of his work he would only tell me one instance. He knew that I had heard most of the story.

"When I arrived in the Norwegian corvette," he said, "I knew that I was under strict orders from my own captain to return to the destroyer in five hours, just before darkness fell.

"There was no sick bay in the corvette, so we rigged up an emergency operating theatre in one of the flats (small open spaces) near the galley. I had to perform three major operations and several minor ones.

"Often, as the ship rolled, I had to prop myself up against a bulkhead. An R.N.V.R. lieutenant, British liaison officer in the ship, who had never seen an operation before, helped me. He kept up the supply of hot water and held the patients on the 'table.' I finished with twenty minutes to spare."

'All Hell Seemed to be Let Loose Beneath Us'

Several newspaper correspondents accompanied the R.A.F. on the great bombing raid on the German capital on the night of January 16; Colin Bednall of The Daily Mail (from which this story is reprinted) tells how the Lancaster bomber in which he went to "the party" was brought home.

WE were just turning in on the last leg of our journey and preparing for the run into the heart of Berlin when all hell seemed to be let loose beneath us. We had sailed right into the middle of a barrage. The guns kept quiet until we were in the middle of it, and then they all opened up in one bewildering, shattering crash.

The whole world, it seemed to me in my greenness, was suddenly spread with horrible flashes. Shells were exploding everywhere. The pilot took violent evasive action, throwing the aircraft around like an aerobatic fighter. This went on for minutes, but still there were shells everywhere.

Then, suddenly, I heard over the inter-com. just about the worst thing I ever wanted to hear. The aircraft had shuddered from a burst right beside us, and the pilot shouted in rage: "Damn! Blast it! I'm hit!" He called for the air bomber. I heard him say, "Come up here, quick!"

But there was no reply from the air bomber, and I remember wondering what was to happen next. We all thought he must have been hit even more seriously than the pilot. After an interval that seemed like years, with the plane swinging over in a steep down-ward turn, the air bomber's voice came through on the inter-com. as sweet as life itself. "Yes, sir," was all he said, in a voice

that was as quiet and restrained as that of a waiter in a West-End restaurant. Then I heard the pilot say he was bleeding rather badly and he would have to see how much worse it was likely to get. Then the pilot did what obviously seemed nothing extraordinary to him, but to me was little short of incredible.

We were still in the middle of the barrage with "dirt" flying everywhere, and before he decided on his next 'action he calmly circled round, studying the flow of blood from the wound and calculating whether he could afford to continue to Berlin.

The air bomber by this time was up in the cockpit beside the pilot, and had clamped a dressing on to the wound. The blood came through this as if it were paper, and so a second dressing was placed on top of the first. For a minute or two it looked as if the pilot would be unable to take us out of the barrage, let alone get us to Berlin or far-off England.

"I am sorry, Bednall," said the pilot, "I am afraid we will have to cut the party short." At that moment I did not much care what he did so long as we got away from those guns around us. Turning away from the main raiding force meant that the whole of the defences we encountered could concen-

trate on us alone. We started off on a lone course that took us away.

Judging by the opposition we met on the long, rambling journey home there are many gunners in the German Army who could tell the next part of our story better than I can. The flak was bad enough going out, but it was now many times worse. Everywhere we turned there seemed to be a new barrage waiting for us.

ALL the time the pilot was flying with one good hand and the only sound he made was to curse his "bad luck" at not being able to take S for Sugar just exactly where he had planned. The air bomber wanted to put a tourniquet above his shattered forearm, but the pilot refused this, saying it might make it impossible for him to carry on. He told someone standing beside him not to lift his eyes off him for a second.

"If I go out to it," he said, "you'll just have to shove me out of the way and take over." He must have suffered agony, as time after time the plane had to be put into violent evasive action to avoid the flak.

We were all now expecting to see any minute a stream of enemy fighters coming in to complete the "kill." The clouds, against which we were pinned like a fly on the ceiling of a room if we went beneath them, provided a magnificent background also for sighting by fighters when we were above them.

For some hours we were the only Lancaster within hundreds of miles and should have been "easy meat" for the Junkers 88 boys. The crew said afterwards it must have been the weather, causing severe icing at high altitudes, which kept them away.

At least three times on the way back we were caught in barrages as heavy as that bad one in which the captain was hit. The captain got us out of the worst of them. We seemed to gather strength the farther we went, and after a while the routine aboard went on almost as if nothing was amiss.

OCCASIONALLY one of the crew would bring up a fresh article of clothing to wrap around the pilot's arm, and then go quickly back to his job. After what seemed an eternity we finally got out once more over the North Sea with nothing more serious than a few flak-ships to cope with on the last really hazardous stage of our journey.

The closest watch, however, had to be kept for fighters until we were out beyond their maximum range. All four motors were going beautifully on a pretty full throttle, however, and, sliding down from altitude in a steady descent, we did eventually reach lovely England long before we had dared hope.

The captain landed us at our base without giving us much worse than a bit of a jolt. Only he knows just what it took out of him to do so. As we were approaching the base, the wireless operator sent a message that we had been hit and the pilot was wounded. A fire-tender, an ambulance, and the ever-watchful doctor were waiting beside the plane as it finally came to rest at the end of its landing.

Much to everybody's surprise the captain jumped out of the aircraft almost without assistance. The doctor, however, whisked him off to hospital, and he was being operated upon within an hour of landing.

The doctor said another hour in the air would probably have found the captain helpless. As it was we had been in the air for seven hours, and for more than half that time the pilot had been flying the machine in a condition which very few would like to meet in the air, let alone over the heart of the most heavily defended country in the world.

the time we were right way up again he'd hit the ground and was blazing away.

Then came Dornier number three. Again I got in a long burst amidships. There was a yellowish explosion and down he went. As he did so he fired about a second's burst, two streams of red tracer, but they went nowhere near us. Number four was a Junkers 88, and the most spectacular of the night. We found him somewhere in the Croydon area. My cannon-shells set both his engines on fire and flames spread along the wing and back to the fuselage. They lit up the sky so clearly that we could see his black crosses. And we saw four of the crew bale out, one after the other. As it went down you could see all the streets lit up, and when it hit there was a terrific flash.

Well, that was that. Four in a night. Home we went; pleased, but wondering what luck the rest of the squadron had had.

In Six Hours I Shot Down Four German Raiders

On Sunday, January 17, 1943, following the great R.A.F. raid on Berlin, the Nazis came to drop bombs on London. Wing Commander Wight-Boycott, in the air for six hours, in a Beaufighter, tells here how he shot four of the raiders out of the night sky.

THE curious thing about the first one I shot down was that although London was throwing up a terrific amount of flak and there were any number of searchlights about I don't remember seeing anything of them at all. I was looking up all the time to find the enemy silhouetted against the bright moonlit sky.

We'd just popped above a thin layer of cloud and there was the Dornier, a sort of grey colour. I fired a long burst and saw an explosion behind the pilot's cockpit. It seemed to go straight down and I tried to follow, so steeply that my observer came out of his seat. When the Dornier crashed, three brilliantly white blobs appeared to jump out of the ground. That was Dornier number one. The next patrol nothing happened at all, except my observer complaining about the hardness of his seat.

We got Dornier number two during the second alert. It must have been about four in the morning. He was travelling very fast and jinking violently. He didn't keep a straight course for more than a few seconds at a time. But there was no cloud about now ; it was a good night for interception, and I managed to get in a fairly long burst.

He caught fire and slowed up very quickly. I got so close to him that I was caught in his slipstream and rolled on to my back, but I managed to avoid colliding with him. By

WING CMDR. C. M. WIGHT-BOYCOTT, commanding an R.A.F night-fighter squadron, is here photographed with his observer, F/O. A. M. Sanders (left). In the accompanying text he gives a vivid description of how he brought down four of the German raiders on the night of Jan. 17, 1943. His D.S.O. was gazetted on Feb. 5. *Photo, British Official*

OUR DIARY OF THE WAR

JAN. 20, 1943, Wednesday 1,236th day
Sea.—Admiralty announced that mine-sweeper Bramble went down fighting on Dec. 31 in protection of convoy to Russia.
North Africa.—Enemy forces advanced seven miles S.W. of Pont du Fahs.
Libya.—Our troops occupied Homs and Tarhuna.
Russian Front.—Rly. centres of Proletarskaya and Nevinnomysk occupied by Soviet troops.
Home Front.—Daylight raid on S.E. England and London ; L.C.C. school in Lewisham bombed with death-roll of 39 children and five teachers.
General.—Chilean Govt. broke off relations with Germany, Italy and Japan.

JAN. 21, Thursday 1,237th day
Air.—Venturas and Bostons raided airfields at Caen and Le Havre ; Cherbourg and Flushing docks also bombed. Night raid on Ruhr.
Russian Front.—Soviet troops occupied Voroshilovsk (Stavropol) in Caucasus.

JAN. 22, Friday 1,238th day
Air.—Large-scale daylight raids on airfields and oil installations in N. France.
Libya.—Eighth Army occupied Castel Verde, 35 m. E. of Tripoli.
Russian Front.—Soviet troops occupied Salsk S.E. of Rostov and Mikoyan in Caucasus.
Australasia.—With mopping-up at Sanananda, Jap resistance ended in Papua.

JAN. 23, Saturday 1,239th day
Sea.—Admiralty announced loss of submarine Traveller.
Air.—U.S. Fortresses bombed Lorient and Brest by day ; R.A.F. raided Lorient and W. Germany by night.
Libya.—Eighth Army entered Tripoli.
Russian Front.—Armavir, on main Caucasus rly. to Rostov, captured by Soviet troops.
Australasia.—U.S. air and naval forces bombarded Kolombangara Island, New Georgia. Jap aircraft raided Pt. Moresby.

JAN. 24, Sunday 1,240th day
North Africa.—In Tunisia enemy occupied hill E. of Ousseltia valley.
Mediterranean.—U.S. aircraft bombed shipping at Palermo and Messina.
Russian Front.—S. of Voronezh, Soviet troops occupied Starobielsk.

Burma.—Allied bombers attacked Rangoon, Shwebo and Akyab.
Australasia.—Waves of U.S. aircraft raided Munda, New Georgia.

JAN. 25, Monday 1,241st day
Air.—Bostons bombed Flushing docks.
Libya.—Our troops occupied Zauia, W. of Tripoli. Gen. Leclerc's troops reached Tripoli.
Russian Front.—Soviet troops occupied whole of Voronezh, from which Germans had withdrawn.
Australasia.—U.S. troops captured Kokumbona on Guadalcanal.

JAN. 26, Tuesday 1,242nd day
Sea.—Admiralty announced loss of trawler Kingston Jacinth.
Air.—R.A.F. again attacked Lorient by night ; Bordeaux also raided.
North Africa.—In Tunisia Allied forces regained ground in Ousseltia valley. In raid on Algiers six enemy bombers were shot down.
Russian Front.—Only two small groups of German Sixth Army still holding out at Stalingrad.
Australasia.—Allied heavy bombers attacked Rabaul and other Jap bases.

JAN. 27, Wednesday 1,243rd day
Air.—U.S. bombers in England made first raid on Germany, attacking Wilhelmshaven in daylight ; 22 German fighters shot down. Mosquitoes bombed shipyards at Copenhagen. Short, heavy night raid on Düsseldorf.
Russian Front. — Advancing from Tuapse, Soviet troops captured Apsheron on way to Maikop.
Australasia.—U.S. aircraft bombed Kolombangara, New Georgia.
General. — Announced that Mr. Roosevelt and Mr. Churchill had been in conference at Casablanca since January 14 ; Gen. de Gaulle and Gen. Giraud also present.

JAN. 28, Thursday 1,244th day
Russian Front.—Soviet troops captured Kastornaya, on Voronezh-Kursk railway.
Australasia.—Attacks by Allied aircraft on Jap air bases and shipping in Timor, New Britain, New Guinea and New Georgia.
General.—Mr. Churchill conferred with Service chiefs in Cairo.

JAN. 29, Friday 1,245th day
Air.—Another night raid on Lorient.
Libya.—In patrol operations our forward troops crossed Tunisian frontier.
Russian Front.—New Soviet offensive W. of Voronezh, Novy Oskol occupied ;

Kropotkin in N. Caucasus also captured.
Australasia.—Strong Jap patrols repulsed near Mubo, New Guinea.

JAN. 30, Saturday 1,246th day
Air.—Mosquitoes made two daylight raids on Berlin on occasion of tenth anniversary of Hitler's accession. Heavy bombers attacked Hamburg by night.
North Africa.—In Tunisia German tanks, infantry and artillery pushed through Faid Pass on road from Sfax.
Mediterranean. — U.S. Liberators made daylight raid on Messina harbour.
Russian Front.—In Caucasus Soviet troops captured Tikhoretsk and Maikop.
Australasia.—Sea and air battle began off the Solomons.
General.—Mr. Churchill arrived in Turkey for two-day conference with Pres. Inonu. Adm. Doenitz, U-boat chief, appointed C.-in-C. of German Navy.

JAN. 31, Sunday 1,247th day
Sea.—Admiralty announced loss of submarine P 222.
Libya.—Eighth Army occupied Zuara.
Mediterranean.—Allied heavy bombers again raided Messina.
Russian Front.—Field-Marshal Paulus and 15 generals of German Sixth Army captured at Stalingrad.
U.S.A.—Jap aircraft bombed U.S. shipping in W. Aleutians.
General.—Mr. Churchill visited Cyprus on way back from Turkey.

FEB. 1, Monday 1,248th day
North Africa.—U.S. counter-attacks failed to retake Faid Pass.
Russian Front.—Svatovo, 100 m. S.E. of Kharkov, and Zernovoy, 30 m. from Rostov, captured by Russians.
Australasia.—Fighting continued in Mubo-Wau area of New Guinea. U.S. troops made progress in Guadalcanal.

FEB. 2, Tuesday 1,249th day
Air.—In night raid on Cologne R.A.F. bombers dropped one hundred 4,000-lb. bombs in less than twenty minutes.
Libya.—Our troops occupied Zelten.
Russian Front.—All remaining German forces at Stalingrad capitulated ; eight more generals captured.
Australasia.—Allied aircraft bombed Jap supply dumps at Kaukenau, Dutch New Guinea.

★ ═══════ *Flash-backs* ═══════ ★

1940
February 1. *Russians launched violent attack at Summa in Mannerheim Line.*

1941
January 22. *Australians under Wavell entered Tobruk.*
February 1. *Agordat, Eritrea, captured by Allied troops.*

1942
January 21. *Rommel began to advance from El Agheila.*

January 22. *Japanese landed at Rabaul, New Britain.*
January 23. *Rommel recaptured Jedabya.*
January 25. *Japanese landed at Lae, New Guinea.*
January 26. *American troops landed in Northern Ireland.*
January 29. *Rommel recaptured Benghazi.*
January 30. *British forces withdrew from the mainland of Malaya to Singapore Island.*

Editor's Postscript

A CORRESPONDENT of mine writing from Port Said tells me that he has been subscribing to THE WAR ILLUSTRATED since No. 1, and that, despite the fact of his newsagent being bombed out in one of the raids on that town, he has been able to gather a complete series up to the time of his writing, when No. 124 had arrived, which is pretty good going. I am interested to know that some of the newspapers published in Egypt make frequent use of our articles without acknowledgement, which is, of course, a reprehensible practice in journalism ; but as the first concern of us all is the winning of the War, we can afford to ignore such informalities, and I am sure that the Egyptian papers are helping in that direction, even when they quote THE WAR ILLUSTRATED without acknowledging the source of their information. All the same, one would prefer an occasional " credit title," as the film producers and their many associates ever eager for their individual, efforts to be recognized, phrase it.

AMONG the letters on my desk the other morning was one of New Year's greeting from the Royal Norwegian Government. It was stamped with the first Norwegian postage stamps to be issued by the Norwegian Government since its temporary departure from Norwegian soil on June 7, 1940, and was mailed from Free Norwegian territory—in other words, it was posted on the high seas on one of the more than seven hundred vessels belonging to the Norwegian Mercantile Marine which, in spite of severe losses, are continuing to transport men, munitions and food in the service of the United Nations. The stamps form a series of six, and together they provide a symbolic representation of Norway's fight against the German invader. Each of them bears the symbol " H 7 " surmounted by the royal crown—a symbol which has been chosen by the Norwegians to demonstrate their continued loyalty to King Haakon VII and to the fight for freedom and independence which he personifies. Specially interesting is the 20-öre stamp which shows the Norwegian home front slogan *Vi Vil Vinne* (we will win)—Norway's adaptation of the V-sign—painted on a Norwegian country road. All of us will echo most heartily the Norwegian Government's wish " that in the year 1943 it may prove possible to transform *Vi Vil Vinne* into *Vi Vant* (we have won)."

ONE day in mid-August last year Wing-Commander A. B. Austin, who had already achieved some distinction with his book Fighter Command, received a single ticket from London to a place on the south coast and the brief summons : "Waterloo Station tomorrow at 0900 hours. Bring one suit of battledress and the minimum of luggage. Tin hat and gas-mask, of course." That was the beginning of days of arduous and frequently dangerous adventure. It hardly needs to be said that that adventure was the combined attack on Dieppe, and what took place on that long-to-be-remembered August 19 has been described by none more vividly than Mr. Austin, who represented ten national newspapers on that historic, occasion. In our own pages we quoted some passages of brilliant narrative from his story of the Commando attack on the German positions above the cliffs west of Dieppe. (*See* page 197.) Now Mr. Austin has written a much fuller account. In We Landed at Dawn (Gollancz, 7s. 6d.) he describes not only the events on the day of battle, but tells something of the long preparations, of the Canadian soldiers he came to know, of many a deed of heroism, of many an incident touched with humour.

CPL. J. A. FRENCH, of the Australian Infantry, to whom the posthumous award of the V.C. was announced on Jan. 14, 1943. He destroyed 3 Jap machine-gun posts at Milne Bay, Papua, last September, but was killed after he had silenced the third post.
Photo, Planet News

MANY a reader will be amused, and not a little moved, by his story of the concert on board ship as they crossed the Channel on the eve of their desperate adventure : of the Rabelaisian monologue, of the Canadian soldier singing The Road to Mandalay, and the sailor who obliged with Round Her Knee She Wore a Purple Garter, after which an A.B. rendered The Longshoreman in an Edwardian voice (whatever that is)—of the petty officer who in a most remarkable strip-tease act gave an impression of " a young lady, a very young lady, very tasty, very sweet, getting into, and having her bath . . . ' Gee, don't he know a lot,' murmured a boy behind me from Toronto.'' It is this spirit that the " foreigner " finds it so difficult to understand ; the spirit that is so typically—English, British, whatever adjective you like to select to include that strange race of beings who are ourselves.

BUT then so much that we do must amuse those who are not of our lineage and language. That debate in the House of Lords the other day, for instance—the one initiated by Lord Brabazon, who, having done his job of work at the Ministry of Aircraft Production, is now concerned with the importance of phonetics in democratic education. Strange that we should find time for such things in the midst of the greatest war in history ! And yet not so strange, since so many people profess to be able to fight better if they have a promise of something better to fight for. Lord Brabazon emphasized his point by drawing a delightful little picture of Lord Simon and Lord Cranborne, dressed in sweaters and corduroys, chatting with the " locals " in a pub in Wapping. In three minutes, he said, the people would be calling Lord Simon " sir," not because he knew more about racing and football than they did, but because his voice was different : it was a cultivated voice. But Lord Brabazon was not at all pleased that this should be so, since in his view the working classes are kept down because they do not speak with the same accent as the professional classes. So he urged that all extreme types of English should be " jumped on " in early life.

LORD STRABOLGI disagreed ; he put in a plea for the provincial and local dialects. Even Lord Simon, who must have smiled at the story of his imaginary visit to the riverside hostelry, thought that a vast amount is added to the value and effectiveness of human conversation if certain varieties in speech, derived from the area from which people came, should be preserved. The school must never dream of despising or denouncing local habits, manners, and modes of speech, he declared, although at the same time it must use its influence to discourage mere mumbling, slovenly and down-trodden language. As for the Oxford accent, the Lord Chancellor considered it has no more to do with Oxford than the Oxford Group. " Announcers do admirably," he went on ; " but my own experience is sometimes that when I turn on the wireless to hear the news I am compelled to listen to backchat between performers who, I understand, are technically known as ' comics,' by whom the English tongue is debased almost beyond recognition. Sometimes one has to endure noises produced by the human voice which certainly are neither music nor even in tune. The technical name for those noises is ' hot rhythm.' I cannot see why we should have to endure it. There ought to be a close season for such performances.'' But for my part, I am not at all sure that the " comics " are any more debasing than those mouthers and mumblers whose names the placards outside the theatres print in the biggest letters that the stars of the stage can command.

YET again I have to greet the publication of another Stationery Office publication. This time it is The Battle of Egypt, which has been prepared for the War Office by the Ministry of Information, and costs but 7d. In its 32 large pages there are 80 excellent photographs, many of them published for the first time, taken by the Staff of No. 1 Army Film and Photo Section, attached to the Public Relations services in the Middle East. There is also a double-spread diagrammatic map in two colours, illustrating the course of the great battle which decided the fate of the Italian Empire in North Africa.

Printed in England and published every alternate Friday by the Proprietors, THE AMALGAMATED PRESS, LTD., The Fleetway House, Farringdon Street, London, E.C.4. Registered for transmission by Canadian Magazine Post. Sole Agents for Australia and New Zealand : Messrs. Gordon & Gotch, Ltd. ; and for South Africa : Central News Agency, Ltd.—February 19, 1943.   S.S.   *Editorial Address :* JOHN CARPENTER HOUSE, WHITEFRIARS, LONDON, E.C.4.

Vol 6 · *The War Illustrated* · Nº 149

Edited by Sir John Hammerton

SIXPENCE

MARCH 5, 1943

WELCOME HOME TO 'A GREAT ENGLISH GENTLEMAN'! Mr. Churchill is here seen outside No. 10 Downing Street on his safe return to London on Feb 7, 1943, from his momentous air-journeyings to Casablanca, Cairo, Turkey, Cyprus, and Tripoli. In a broadcast a few days later, President Roosevelt referred with intense satisfaction to his consultations with "a great English gentleman," which had shown that Britain and the U.S.A. were in complete accord in their determination to destroy the forces of barbarism in Europe, Asia and Africa.

Photo, Keystone

THE BATTLE FRONTS

by Maj.-Gen. Sir Charles Gwynn, K.C.B., D.S.O.

DURING the first half of February war news as regards land operations came almost exclusively from Russia. But how amazing and heartening the news has been ! Practically all the dangers with which in my last article I suggested the Germans were threatened have matured ; many unforeseeable disasters have overtaken them ; others appear inevitable ; and others still greater are rapidly entering the category of possibilities.

It is not, however, the recapture of towns or the reoccupation of territory that matters so much as the damage done morally and physically to the German war machine and the proof given of the superiority of Russian generalship. There are some observers outside Russia who apparently still retain some of their belief in the Reichswehr's power, speaking of a great new German offensive when the snow has gone, and hard ground facilitates manoeuvre. I think that in the main they are unduly nervous, although I admit that, till it surrenders, the Reichswehr, like a wounded animal, will always be dangerous.

I suggest that while the Germans held the initiative they were able with great efficiency to carry out their carefully-prepared plans for a blitzkrieg war, and they had forged an admirable instrument for the purpose. But since they lost the initiative they have fumbled and made mistake after mistake.

RUSSIA By the beginning of February 1943 the Russians had practically accomplished the first two objects of their offensive. On Feb. 2 the 6th Army's surrender (*see* p. 595) marked the end of one of the most dramatic episodes in military history. Hitler and his myrmidons have attempted to veil the gross mistakes which brought about the disaster by raising the undeniably gallant fight of the 6th Army into a supreme example of self-sacrifice which achieved all it intended. Self-sacrifice there undoubtedly was ; but how far it was willing or how far it resulted from docile obedience to orders may be questioned. It is more certain that the sacrifice was made in vain, and had little or no effect on the development of Russian plans.

At that date, too, the Germans were still in full flight from the Caucasus, and it was only a question of how much of their Army in that region would find temporary safety at Rostov or in the Crimea. By February 5 the way of escape through Rostov had been closed ; and a week later all the small ports on the Azov coast to which railways lead were in Russian hands. The remnants which had not escaped, and which still clung to Krasnodar and Novorossisk, had become practically innocuous, and were in danger of annihilation. By February 13 Krasnodar had been retaken after stiff but futile resistance ; and a force landed by the ever-active Russian Black Sea Fleet threatened to cut off the garrison of Novorossisk from all hope of retreat.

How much of the Caucasus armies has escaped immediate annihilation is still uncertain ; but even those elements that have escaped may yet become involved in dangers that threaten the armies of the Donetz Basin and the Crimea—unless they have been sent far to the rear for reorganization.

DEVASTATING as these German disasters have been, they represent the first fruits only of Zhukov's offensive. Since the beginning of February, while the army which originally broke through the German positions on the Middle Don and that which had encircled Von Paulus were steadily closing on Rostov and on the Germans established on the loop of the Donetz, Zhukov's right wing was making sensational progress. In my last article (*see* page 547)

I suggested that the break-through south of Voronezh, the one that had captured Valuiki, was threatening to cut the communications between Kharkov and the Donetz Basin, which might then become a dangerous salient. I also suggested that, farther north, the drive from Voronezh itself, that had captured Kastornaya and threatened to interrupt the communications between Kharkov and the important bastion of Kursk, would make heavy demands on German reserves to protect this main avenue for lateral movements. The great improvement in Russian railway communications, the lack of which had previously threatened to handicap the maintenance of the impetus of the offensive, had also been noted as a result of successes gained.

THE way success has been exploited has, however, far exceeded my most sanguine expectations. The two thrusts not only linked up to clear the whole length of the railway from Moscow through Eletz to Valuiki, but the northern one pushed on to capture the great " hedgehog " of Kursk.

The southern thrust has had even more sensational success. Wheeling southwestwards, it captured Kupiansk and other important centres, severing all communications from Kharkov and Poltava to the Donetz Basin. Pressing on, it captured Lozovaya, cutting communications between Kharkov and the Crimea. Even more important, it has cut the railway from the Donetz Basin to Dnepropetrovsk, the direct and main line of retreat from what had indeed become a dangerous salient, containing a great army almost completely encircled. This was an audacious manoeuvre, for it not only involved the crossing of the Upper Donetz and the capture of strongly defended towns in the face of counter-attacks from within the salient, but it also risked an attack in flank from Kharkov.

As a main base centre, presumably strongly garrisoned and with ample railway communications by which reinforcements could arrive, Kharkov appeared an obvious point of assembly for a counter-stroke. It was probably quite as much to guard against this danger as to bring about the capture of the place that Russian attacks were directed towards the city and its communications, while the thrust towards the south-west passed across its front.

That no offensive movement developed from Kharkov, combined with the rapid fall of Kursk, was a clear indication that the

ROSTOV-ON-DON, capital of N. Caucasus, whose recapture was announced by the Russians on Feb. 14, 1943, was first taken by the Germans on Nov. 22, 1941, but 6 days later the Russians drove out the enemy. In July 1942 the city fell again to the Germans. This photo shows a street scene shortly before the enemy entered Rostov last year.

Photo, E.N.A.

Germans had few reserves unexpended. It seems probable that most of those available were rushed forward in order to check the earlier Russian drives, to form the bridgehead east of Rostov, and to hold the line of the Lower Donetz.

From within the salient the Germans made fierce if somewhat piecemeal counter-attacks in attempts to stop the thrust at their line of retreat, but these were ineffective. Meanwhile, Kharkov was threatened with encirclement, and its garrison incapable of offensive action.

Loss of the initiative and the rigid character of the " hedgehog " defence system have no doubt combined to make it difficult for the Germans to assemble any large force for a major counter-stroke. " Hedgehog " centres absorb large numbers, and if garrisons are reduced the " hedgehogs " lose their quality of impregnability.

It would seem from the fate of Kursk and other centres that in their search for reserves the Germans have been forced to this fatal compromise, and have fallen between two stools—weakening their defences without obtaining a mobile force of adequate power.

While the threat to the base of the Donetz salient developed, the Russians increased their pressure at its apex. At the time of writing (mid-February) they have crossed the Donetz and the Don delta, and Moscow has just announced the recapture of Rostov and Voroshilovgrad. Fighting has been fierce, but there are indications that the Germans have decided that retreat is inevitable. If that is their decision it is belated ; and it will require desperate rearguard and flank guard actions to save any large part of the army from complete catastrophe.

Danger still threatens the Germans in the centre at Veliki Luki and in the north at Leningrad, so that on the whole the prospect of their being able to establish a stabilized front on a shorter line before spring mud affords a respite is far from hopeful.

NORTH AFRICA

In the period under review (first half of February 1943) there was little serious fighting on land. The 8th Army advanced steadily into Tunisia, driving back fairly strong delaying detachments but without encountering any definite rearguard position. Bad weather, mines, and demolitions have slowed down the pace of advance ; but there was no object in attempting to increase the speed until communications through Tripoli could be well established.

On the 1st Army and American front there was little change, though there were some stiff local engagements with varying fortune. The air situation, however, continued to improve with the arrival of reinforcements

RUSSIAN SOUTHERN FRONT in mid-February 1943. Arrows represent the main thrusts by the Red Army. By Feb. 15 the Russians had recaptured Rostov, Voroshilovgrad and Voroshilovsk ; Kharkov was almost encircled (it fell the next day) ; and in the Caucasus the Nazis held little more than a bridgehead behind Taman.
By Courtesy of The Times

in Algeria, the improvement in airfields, and the advance of the 8th Army's bases.

The unification of the whole Allied North African force was evidently a necessary step, and the solution arrived at should prove satisfactory. It closely resembles that of 1918 with General Eisenhower assuming Foch's position and General Alexander that of

Haig, though with a different title. If the arrangement should not work smoothly— and there is no reason to fear that it will not—I am convinced it will not be General Alexander's fault, for no one better fitted temperamentally for loyal and tactful co-operation could have been found.

FAR EAST

In the Pacific and on the Burma front the record is mainly of increasing Allied air offensive operations. Of the naval engagements in the Solomons area we have as yet been told little, but the Japanese decision to withdraw altogether from Guadalcanal is an indication that the Japanese claims to a considerable success were, as usual, grossly exaggerated, if not altogether unfounded.

The withdrawal certainly implies the admission of a notable failure involving heavy losses in ships and aircraft and the abandonment of offensive projects which the recapture of the island would have facilitated.

In New Guinea the failure of the Japanese to capture the airfields at the Wau goldfields is another rebuff. The situation there must be unique : a force dependent entirely on air communications defending itself against another operating through almost impenetrable jungle. Nevertheless, possession of the airfields may have considerable importance in future operations.

U.S. TANKS IN NEW GUINEA recently took part in successful actions in one of the most difficult fighting terrains in the world. These two light American tanks are forcing their way through a coconut grove near Cape Endaiadere. The crews have just given the machines a quick overhaul.

PAGE 579

Photo, Associated Press

On the East Front Nazis Suffer Blow after Blow

ON THE S. RUSSIAN FRONT, said Moscow radio on Feb. 16, "the beaten German armies are rolling back in ever-increasing disorder."   Left, a cine-camera, operating beside a Soviet sniper in Stalingrad, recorded this swift sequence of events as a German soldier emerges from cover and falls victim to accurate marksmanship.   Top : Armed with a tommy-gun, a Russian girl helps guard German prisoners near Veliki Luki.   Below, this Nazi gunner has fired his last round.

Photos, U.S.S.R. Official ; British Newsreels, Associated Press

All Along the Line Victorious Russia Marches On

RUSSIAN GENERALSHIP AND RUSSIAN VALOUR have defeated the enemy, not only on the rapidly-crumbling Southern front, but also on the Northern and Central battlefields. Top, Russian troops, crossing a frozen stream, drag their machine-guns and equipment with them in boat-shaped sledges; this photograph was taken near Leningrad. Below, Soviet anti-tank guns, with their crews on caterpillar tractors, are moving up to reinforce the advancing Red Army on the Central front.

Photos, Planet News

Gen. Giraud's Army Takes Shape in North Africa

MESSAGES BY CARRIER PIGEON are still a feature of modern warfare. Grouped round a table these French officers are preparing important messages for dispatch to other sectors of the line.

FRENCH TROOPS IN TUNISIA have shown their splendid fighting qualities in many actions against the enemy. Maj. Durix (above, with map), of the Tunisian Tirailleurs, gives instructions to his officers.

Fighting on the Bou Arada front presented considerable difficulties for both sides. The French fought with great determination and, despite intensive opposition, held on to their positions against superior enemy forces. Right, a French 75-mm. field-gun in action.

Below, a British sergeant instructs French recruits as they fire Bren guns on a range. These men wear British uniforms, but retain their casques and forage caps. On the latter they wear a red and blue flash for Britain.
Photos, British Official: Crown Copyright; Associated Press

IN an Order of the Day published on February 11, 1943, Gen. Juin, commanding French troops in Tunisia, announced that French forces in this vital theatre of war were to be re-equipped and rearmed. Ultra-modern weapons and equipment had already poured into Tunisia, and the arrival of fresh Allied troops at the front made it possible for certain French contingents to be relieved at the front line in order that they could go to areas in the rear to receive intensive training with these latest weapons.

In making this important announcement Gen. Juin declared with emphasis : " The French forces will finish the job that has been started so well.

The three upper photographs in this page show men of a French cavalry regiment who joined forces with a British unit on the Bou Arada front. Many of them were familiar with the country in which they were then fighting, having lived in Tunisia most of their lives.

In Tunisia the 'Gallant 50th' Rout the Italians

THE QUEEN'S OWN ROYAL WEST KENT REGIMENT recently distinguished itself in the Tunisian fighting. Men of a battalion of this famous English county regiment took up their positions at Siliana on the fiercely contested central front, and then moved east through Robaa to relieve a hard-pressed French unit. They advanced, "C" Company vigorously maintaining contact with retreating Italians. The latter were subjected to heavy shelling by our 25-pounders. Again the enemy retreated, and on Jan. 29, 1943, the Royal West Kents lost contact. The positions which had thus been regained were then handed over to another French unit. The photographs in this page show various phases during this operation. 1, New Vickers water-cooled heavy machine-gun in action. 2, A 3-in. mortar—one of the most effective modern weapons—in position on the bed of an almost dried up wadi. 3, Amid rocky surroundings a 25-pounder goes into action. Left, Badge of the Royal West Kent Regiment—the White Horse of Kent with motto Invicta (Unconquered). Among the nicknames applied to the Regiment or to individual battalions are Gallant 50th (the Regiment is a merger of 50th and 97th Foot), The Dirty Half-Hundred, The Celestials, and The Devil's Royals.

Photos, British Official : Crown Copyright

ATTACK ON A JAP MERCHANTMAN as seen through the periscope of the United States submarine which sank the enemy ship. The heavily-camouflaged 9,000-ton merchantman is seen lying in the unidentified harbour where she was sighted by the submarine. Three torpedoes found their mark. A small boat pulling away from the vessel is ringed in white.
Photo, Associated Press

THE WAR AT SEA

by Francis E. McMurtrie

WITH news of fresh defeats leaking out daily, the German public is sorely in need of some comfort. One after the other its generals have been discredited, the fame even of Rommel having been extinguished by his summary expulsion from Egypt and Libya.

In these circumstances the Nazi propaganda department is trying to persuade the world that it still possesses a trump card in the U-boat offensive which has been prepared for the spring. Admiral of the Fleet Karl Doenitz, the newly appointed commander-in-chief of the German Navy, has announced that officers and men who are at present serving in surface vessels must now be prepared to undergo training for submarine duties.

It would be mere wishful thinking to draw from this the inference that the increased rate of destruction of U-boats, referred to by Mr. Churchill on February 11, is putting any serious strain on the available reserve of submarine personnel. It is safer to conclude that an unusually large number of new submarines will be commissioned during 1943, and that fresh crews are to be trained in advance in order to maintain that reserve at full strength.

AT the same time it is useful to recall that early in 1918, when the institution of the convoy system and the provision of an ample supply of depth-charges had caused U-boat casualties to rise from two in the month of April 1917 to an average of about eight in the last four months of that year, a shortage of experienced engineers and petty officers was beginning to be experienced. To make good these deficiencies, some of the best ratings were taken from the High Seas Fleet to serve in submarines. It is quite possible that a similar course is now being followed, as Doenitz is less concerned than his predecessor to preserve the efficiency of his surface ships, whose record has been disappointing.

On the other side of the Atlantic there appears to be considerable apprehension concerning the likely effects of the coming U-boat offensive. That serious shipping losses will be sustained is highly probable. But it is unlikely that they will be as heavy as in the first half of last year, when the Germans found a fresh field for their depredations in the Western Atlantic. Memories of those disastrous days are still fresh in the minds of the American public. Fortunately, the United States Navy has gained greatly in experience and in the numbers and equipment of its anti-submarine vessels during the past year.

These were amongst the facts which Mr. Churchill had in mind when he expressed his confidence that the U-boat campaign would fail to avert the defeat of the Axis Powers. It may delay it, but that is all. He declared that any increase in the numbers of U-boats would be countered by a corresponding addition to the strength of the convoy escorts. For this reason greater emphasis is now being thrown upon the construction of escort vessels, equipped with "every new device of anti-U-boat warfare." What these devices are we have not been told, but the recent upward trend of U-boat destruction suggests that they are very effective.

How different is the present situation from that which confronted us twenty-six years ago! At that date we were so short of escorts that it was not until reinforcements were received from the United States Navy that the convoy system could be put in force. This was in May 1917. During the preceding month the total of shipping losses reached the appalling figure of 881,000 tons. For the whole of that critical year the losses due to enemy action, according to the records of Lloyd's Register, amounted to 2,734 ships, of 6,350,362 tons. Such figures in themselves convey little; but the position is made plainer when it is added that during the terrible month of April 1917 out of every 100 vessels leaving these shores, 25 never returned. Nothing so serious as that has been experienced in the present conflict; and in view of our infinitely improved anti-submarine organization today, there is good reason for the confidence expressed by the Prime Minister in the ultimate issue.

SCIENTISTS Have Their Part in Sea-War Developments

Science is playing an increasingly important part in the present war. It has already provided antidotes to various enemy devices, such as, for example, the magnetic mine, the acoustic mine, etc.

Radio-location, which had advanced beyond the experimental stage before the war, was employed at an early date for detecting the approach of enemy aircraft. It can also be used at sea, in the detection of aircraft by ships and of ships by aircraft; as well as in the detection of ships by other ships. So far it has not been possible to use radio-location under water, which wireless waves cannot penetrate. Very long wavelengths can be received through a foot or two of water, but no more. It is therefore impossible for U-boats while submerged to employ radio-location for the detection of vessels on the surface. Nor can submerged submarines be detected by this means from ships or aircraft.

AS the result of six months' hard fighting by the U.S. Navy and Marine Corps, aided towards the close by the Army, Japanese forces have been expelled from the island of Guadalcanal. During the last few days of organized resistance enemy officers of the higher ranks appear to have abandoned their men, hastening to take the first available places in the boats which came in at night to evacuate as many as possible of the surviving troops. Two or three enemy destroyers were sunk in the course of the evacuation, which only brought away about 1,500 troops.

GUADALCANAL — a Severe Blow to Japanese Prestige

It is estimated that fully 20,000 Japanese lost their lives in Guadalcanal, while 30,000 more were drowned during attempts at reinforcement. Japan holds human life very cheap, so this means nothing to the military dictatorship in Tokyo. At the same time, the blow to enemy prestige is a severe one. Undoubtedly, some fresh move will soon be made in an endeavour to restore it. Already mobilization of the whole population of Japan, other than those engaged in war industry and other vital occupations, has been ordered. More than 70 per cent of the textile mills will close, so that the mill-hands may be transferred to work of greater importance to the war.

There are still numerous Japanese forces in the Solomon Islands area, with airfields wherever favourable sites exist. It will not be easy to drive them out, but the cleaning-up of the Guadalcanal situation is a big step forward.

Rabaul, in the island of New Britain, is the principal Japanese base. If it could be taken the minor positions would fall more easily, and the entire clearance of these islands would be in sight.

The United States Navy would then be faced with the task of seizing fresh bases nearer to Japan itself. Two of which the strategical value is outstanding are Truk, in the Caroline group, and Guam, in the Mariana Islands. The latter was in American possession until it was captured by the Japanese in December 1941. It has sometimes been called the key of the Western Pacific, and would be extremely useful as an advance base for an attack on Japan.

Bombs on the U-Boats in Their Concrete Lairs

LORIENT, great enemy submarine base on the N.W. coast of France, has been so heavily attacked by our home-based bombers that the Germans ordered the evacuation of the entire civilian population on Feb. 8, 1943. 1, R.A.F. bombs actually bursting on the base. 2, Inside a U-boat—an extract from a captured German news-reel. 3, U-boat returning to its concrete pen. 4, U.S. officer questions a member of a captured U-boat at Oran.

Photos, British Official; New York Times Photos, Associated Press, E.N.A.

Smashing Defeat for the Japs in the Solomons

JAP WITHDRAWAL FROM GUADALCANAL was announced on Feb. 10, 1943. During the six months' fighting the enemy lost 50,000 men and 800 planes in addition to many ships. 1, U.S. Marines man a 75-mm. gun. 2, Flying Fortresses on Henderson Airfield amid the wreckage of enemy fighters. 3, Burning Jap transports—remnants of a destroyed invasion force. 4, Men and supplies being landed from a U.S. transport. 5, Enemy tanks abandoned at the mouth of the Matanikau River.

Photos, Keystone, Associated Press, Planet News, Fox

More Tanks from the Canadian War Factories

CANADA'S WAR SUPPLIES are to be shared by the United Nations on the basis of strategic needs without financial consideration. In making this announcement on Feb. 8, 1943 Mr. Ilsley, the Canadian Finance Minister, stated that the Dominion Parliament would be asked to authorize a further £225,000,000 for that purpose. This photograph shows a trainload of tanks arriving at a Canadian port to be loaded aboard ships bound for Britain and the U.S.S.R.

Photo Associated Press

VIEWS & REVIEWS Of Vital War Books

by Hamilton Fyfe

GERMAN PARACHUTISTS, whose exploits are referred to in this page, are here seen at their camp after the enemy invasion of Crete in May 1941. *Photo, Associated Press*

SEVEN years ago I went to a party at the Russian Embassy in London. A propaganda film was shown. Included in it was a sequence of soldiers dropping from aircraft by parachute. There were hundreds of them, coming down on a vast airfield. Some of the spectators at the Embassy were merely amused. "Very enterprising and ingenious," they commented, "but—not war!" Others went away thoughtful.

That same year there were Red Army manoeuvres attended by the military attachés of the Moscow embassies. They saw two battalions of troops with a number of light field guns dropped in eight minutes; their task was to occupy a small town. They occupied it.

This was in 1936. From that time on the Russians and the Germans both gave a great deal of attention to this new form of warfare. Our War Office and headquarters staff looked on. You won't blame them so much perhaps if you remember that Tom Wintringham in his book on Army Reform, published early in 1939, did not mention airborne troops. We did not take the new development seriously. It was new.

The first jolt we got was in April 1940, when the Nazis landed 3,000 men in an hour close to Oslo and took the Norwegian capital by surprise with little opposition. They lost heavily because they did not allow time enough between the arrivals of troop-carriers. Waves of five came at intervals of only three minutes. There was not room for them to land, so that a number were wrecked. But the operation succeeded, and the Germans profited by the lesson their losses had taught them. They allowed more time for the transport aircraft to be emptied.

THESE were not parachutists, and therefore the title of Capt. F. O. Miksche's new book, in which the incident is described, is not quite accurate. He calls it Paratroops (Faber, 10s. 6d.), but most of it is about troops taken to the field of battle in planes. It is as sound and stimulating as readers of the Czech captain's Blitzkrieg will expect. It both tells what use was made of airborne troops up to the Battle of Crete two years ago and discusses in a most interesting way their value, training, handling, and probable future.

If the troops carried through the air are needed to reinforce an army engaged in battle, no parachutists are required. But if the aim is to capture an airfield or a small town, parachute troops go first to make preparations for the landing of the large numbers who follow in transport planes. To land many parachutists at the same time is a hazardous operation. When 1,200 men of the German 3rd Parachute Regiment were dropped in Crete, we disposed of half their number. Nevertheless, the rest managed to do what they had been sent to do. Most of the land fighting on the island was done by the airborne battalions. Gliders towed by bombers were used to a large extent. This surprised the British commanders: "They had not taken the possibility of gliders into account."

From gliders the troops usually descend by parachute. They are too easy a mark if they come down to earth to land their passengers, and they do not land well; many were destroyed in Crete. But if they can be manoeuvred so as to discharge their crews on the ground, a great advantage is gained: the men "are under the immediate control of their section leader at the moment of landing—so that the platoons and companies will be assembled for combat in a shorter time." A glider that costs £500 can take a load of weapons and ammunition up to 2¼ tons. Some larger ones the Germans have which carry as many as 140 men. With these it is possible "to launch whole companies at once in the enemy's rear."

BUT that is not a method which can often be followed. Admitting fully the effect on the nerve of a force which knows there are enemy troops behind it, it can be of small value unless there is full support from the air arm, and unless the units landed from the air act in close cooperation with the rest of the ground forces. As a rule, Capt. Miksche seems to think airborne troops

Airborne Troops In Modern Warfare

will be used for the attainment of some particular purpose, such as the capture of an airfield, the silencing of enemy guns, or the destruction of some building, waterworks, power-station, or factory on which the enemy depends.

In May 1940 the Belgian fortress of Eben Emael was silenced by Germans deposited on the top of it by gliders. Its guns were preventing the invaders from crossing the Maas river by the only two bridges they could use for tanks. This had been foreseen. During the winter of 1939-40 a model of the fort had been made in Germany, and the

BRITAIN'S PARATROOPS were first mentioned as having been in action in a raid on Southern Italy in Feb. 1941 (see Vol. 4, p. 217); some were flown recently to N. Africa from Britain. This photo, showing paratroops collecting equipment from a parachute-dropped container, was taken at a demonstration by an Airborne Division. PAGE 588 *Photo, British Official*

attack rehearsed over and over again. So when the time had come for the real performance the performers were ready and knew their parts.

The men on top of the fort had plenty of explosives with them. They threw these into the gun cupolas, into the muzzles of the guns, into the ammunition hoists. The garrison could not go on firing. The road for the German tanks was now clear. What the party on the roof would have done if their comrades on the ground had not soon got into the fort is doubtful. They were in their risky position for some thirty hours till the attackers below relieved them.

WHERE an enemy is retreating through mountain passes or on narrow paths through a region of lakes and streams, troops dropped to contest these may do most valuable work. If the French had been in a position to use two or three airborne divisions against the 45,000 road vehicles, mostly lorries, that brought up the German army from Cologne, Bonn, and Coblenz in such overwhelming strength to the French frontier the advance might, suggests Capt. Miksche, have been dislocated. A year later, in the great battles on the Russian front in May 1942, the Germans stopped Marshal Timoshenko's move towards Kharkov in just this manner.

SO numerous have been the transport planes destroyed lately by the Russians, by the Americans in the Pacific, and by us over the Mediterranean, that some readers may think Capt. Miksche goes too far in considering airborne troops and material an important factor in warfare today. If the transporters are not protected by aircraft, they certainly run serious risks. Their use must be most carefully regulated and staff work must be perfect; even then the danger will be great. But the risks will be taken, the danger defied.

The airborne land force has taken its place as an instrument of modern war. So the more we know about it the better.

Invasion Fears Haunt the Nazis in Norway

NORWAY UNDER THE GERMAN HEEL. 1, German Marines acting as infantry during anti-invasion exercises near Narvik. 2, Furniture being removed from Oslo flats "commandeered" by Germany. 3, Yet another German officer has committed suicide in a Norwegian village. Above his body a Quisling poster reads (ironically enough): "Europe is Conquering Bolshevism." 4, A roll-call at an interment camp established by the enemy for Norwegian professional men.

Photos, British Official : Crown Copyright ; Norwegian Official, Keystone

Stalingrad: Symbol of Unconquerable Russia

"The city is tired, the houses are tired, the stones are tired," said a Red Army man one night during the long and bitter battle for Stalingrad; "but we are not tired." And so it was that the great Russian city, which Hitler had boasted time and again was his, became in the end the graveyard of the flower of the Nazi Army.

ACTING upon your order, the troops of the Don front at 16.00 o'clock, February 2, 1943, completed the defeat and annihilation of the surrounded enemy group at Stalingrad." So ran Operational Report No. 0079, addressed to Comrade Stalin, Supreme C.-in-C. of the Armed Forces of the U.S.S.R., and signed by Marshal of Artillery Voronov, delegate of the H.Q. of the Supreme Command, and Col.-Gen. K. K. Rokossovsky, Commander of the troops of the Don front.

It was a historic document, issued at a historic moment. Its few words, its laconic

GEN. F. M. VON PAULUS (extreme right), G.O.C. German 6th Army, whose surrender with the remnants of his force at Stalingrad on Jan. 31, 1943 was a major Russian triumph, is here shown during his interrogation by his captors. Left to right: Col.-Gen. Rokossovsky, Russian G.O.C. Don Front, Marshal of Artillery Voronov, and Maj. Dyatlenko, interpreter. *Photo, U.S.S.R. Official*

phrasing marked the close of the gigantic battle for Stalingrad, the greatest and most bloody battle of this war, one of the greatest and bloodiest battles of all wars.

When after three weeks' bombardment the first Germans thrust their way into Stalingrad's streets on September 12 last year, the huge city, sprawling for miles along the Volga bank, must have seemed ripe for the plucking. Yet they were met by an intense fire, and had to fight their way from street to street, from house to house, floor to floor, even room to room.

IN Stalingrad was the Soviet 62nd Army, commanded by 42-year-old Lt.-Gen. Chuykov, part of Col.-Gen. A. I. Yeremenko's Stalingrad army. They were not fresh troops, yet with devoted, self-sacrificing enthusiasm they obeyed Chuykov's injunction, "Everyone must be a stone of the city." One by one their strongpoints were overwhelmed, foot by foot they were forced back, ever nearer to the Volga's bank; and at the end of September the Germans seized the Mamaev Kurgan, a ridge dominating the city and the river beyond. At this moment of extreme danger a fresh division of crack Soviet troops— Major-Gen. Alexander Rodimtsev's 13th Division of the Guards—arrived by a series of forced marches on the east bank of the Volga opposite Stalingrad and, crossing the river in small boats or on rafts—there was no bridge—flung itself into the city. They managed to retrieve what was threatening to prove a desperate situation. The front was re-established; yet in spite of all, by the end of October the Russians were separated by a wedge of German troops, occupying a five-mile front on the Volga itself. Practically the whole of the city and its outskirts was in enemy hands, so that Hitler was not too far from the truth when on November 8 he

boasted that "we have got Stalingrad save for some very small parts."

"The bloodiest day of all was October 14," said General Chuykov, "when the Germans brought in five new or re-manned divisions, with two tank divisions, and hurled them into a front only three miles wide. They had an incredible number of guns, and their planes were making 2,500 flights a day. The noise was so tremendous that one could not hear the shells and bombs exploding, nor see more than five yards because of the smoke. The whole city shook as if in an earthquake. The vibration was so intense that if a glass were put down on the table in my dug-out it was smashed to atoms. The Germans put everything they had into their blows . . . The two armies were locked in a deadly grip: neither side could disentangle itself . . . Some big buildings changed hands twenty times between the beginning of October and the middle of November. On that bloody October 14, I had 61 officers of my staff of 83 killed or wounded . . ."

But Chuykov's and Rodimtsev's men justified Stalin's confidence, and held on while the great Russian offensive was being prepared. They could be given little air support, though gallant pilots of the Red Air Force lived through an ordeal even grimmer than that of the R.A.F. in the Battle of

Britain. Neither long-range artillery nor the Luftwaffe were able to close the supply-line across the Volga, where creaking old ferry-boats, fishing-boats and improvised rafts, manned by old pensioners, peasant-women and fishermen, crossed under the protection of units of the Red Fleet.

Then, in the second week of November, the tide began to turn. Two Russian relief armies—Col.-Gen. N. F. Vatutin's army of the south-west and Col.-Gen. Rokossovsky's army of the Don—began to close in on the city from north and south, gradually encircling the German 6th Army under Paulus, comprising 21 divisions, about 300,000 men, so inextricably entangled with the troops of Yeremenko's army. On November 22 a special Russian communiqué stated that an offensive had been launched at the approaches to Stalingrad. In three days of heavy fighting the Russians had advanced nearly 40 miles, occupying Kalach and Abganerovo; at Kalach they joined hands, and Paulus's host was encircled. The besiegers were now the besieged; with the linking-up on November 25 of Chuykov's men in Stalingrad with Rokossovsky's attacking from the north the siege of Stalingrad was in effect over.

DRIVEN ever farther to the west, the Germans under von Manstein made a desperate attempt in mid-December in the area north of Kotelnikovo to break through to the rescue of beleaguered Paulus. The attempt failed. The gap between Paulus and his would-be deliverers widened daily: he and his 6th Army were in a bag whose neck was being inexorably drawn tighter. On January 8 the Soviet High Command presented him with an ultimatum with a view to avoiding unnecessary bloodshed.

"All hopes for the rescue of your troops by a German offensive from the south and south-west have fallen through (it read). The German troops which hastened to your assistance have been routed . . . The German transport-planes which supplied you with miserable quantities of food, ammunition, and fuel are frequently compelled to change their aerodromes, and cover long distances to reach the positions of your surrounded troops. They suffer tremendous losses in aircraft and crews. The position of your encircled troops is desperate. They are experiencing hunger, disease, and cold.

(Continued in page 595)

CAPTURED GENERALS AT STALINGRAD. Left to right: Gen. Dimitriu, 20th Rumanian Infantry Division; Lt.-Gen. von Daniel, 376th Infantry Division; Lt.-Gen. Schlemmer, 14th Armoured Corps; Maj.-Gen. M. von Drebber, 279th Infantry Division, and a lieut.-general. Twenty-four Axis generals in all were taken. PAGE 590 *Photo, U.S.S.R. Official*

To the Immortal Glory of Stalingrad

In the city of gardens as well as of factories that the Russians built on the Volga's banks after the Revolution, the Square of Fallen Heroes (top) commemorated the siege of 1918, when, under Stalin's leadership, Tsaritsyn beat off the Whites. Tsaritsyn became Stalingrad, and now Stalin's City has seen another horde recoil from its walls. Gaunt and grim as are the ruins to which its people are returning (lower photo), they have a glory which will endure as long as Russia lives.

Yesterday: Triumph of Soviet Planning

One of the supreme achievements of the First Five-Year Plan was the great tractor factory (1) at Stalingrad, opened in 1930. In peacetime its output was 60,000 tractors a year, and more than 10,000 workers—in (2) some of them are seen at a change-over of shifts—were employed there. Came the War; tractors gave place to tanks, and the factory itself became a battleground. Amongst the final gains of the Nazis in Stalingrad, it was their last stronghold.

Today: Graveyard of Hitler's Vaunted Might

For five months Stalingrad was bombed and bombarded by Hitler's guns and planes so that it blazed and smoked to heaven (4). " It will be taken," swore the Fuehrer on Sept. 30; and on Nov. 8 he boasted that it was his " except for some very small parts." It never was taken, however, thanks to the superb bravery of its defenders, some of whom are seen in (6). At the height of the fighting stray animals roamed the ruins (3), while their owners found safety across the Volga (5).

593

Friend and Foe in Stalin's City

Photos, Keystone, Associated Press, Planet News

All through the siege some of Stalingrad's 800,000 populace remained in the city to give what help they could to the armed defenders. For the most part they lived below ground, in cellars, dug-outs and caves. Sometimes they were unearthed by the Nazis (top left) as they mopped-up amid the shattered buildings (top right). Most of the people were evacuated across the Volga, however; and now they are returning, to " swop " their experiences with their gallant liberators.

The Battle of Stalingrad

(Continued from page 590)

The bitter frost, the cold biting winds, and the snowstorms have yet to come. Your men have not been supplied with winter uniforms, and live in appalling, unhygienic conditions. You as the commander realize full well that you have no real possibilities of breaking the ring of encirclement. Your situation is hopeless, and further resistance is useless.''

Followed the terms for an honourable capitulation, which, however, the German general ignored. So on January 10 the work of systematic destruction of an entire German army was resumed.

As January wore on the plight of the encircled Germans grew worse and worse. No Junkers loaded with supplies reached them now. They were reduced to eating horse carcasses, and their bread ration was down to 4 oz. a day. Tens of thousands were killed, tens of thousands gave themselves up. By January 26 only two small scattered enemy groups totalling no more than 12,000 haggard, typhus-ridden, frost-bitten, half-starved and hopeless men, had so far escaped annihilation—one of them north of Stalingrad and the other nearer the centre of the city. Both were doomed ; but as a salve to wounded German prestige they were ordered to hold on to the end. Broadcasting on January 29, the Berlin military spokesman Dietmar said :

" The last defenders of Stalingrad are resisting heroically the savage onslaughts of the enemy. Since November these men have been fighting to the last cartridge, and to the last drop of blood. Their accommodation is so bad as to be almost non-existent. Their clothing consists of rags ; they have no more food, no ammunition—no hope at all. Although abandoned and knowing it, they fight.'' Then comparing the Germans with the Americans at Corregidor, Dietmar said : '' But while MacArthur took a plane, General Paulus remains at his post ;'' and other messages from Berlin pictured him as a truly German hero, directing the battle from his dug-out with two revolvers and a bottle of poison at hand if things came to the worst . . .

On January 31 a special statement from Hitler's headquarters read over the radio announced that Paulus had been promoted General Field-Marshal. At 7.37 p.m. the same day Berlin gave out that he and his battle group had been overwhelmed.

Paulus's last stand was in the ruins of a big store in Stalingrad's central square. The Russians surrounded the building, and after fifteen minutes' blitz shelling Lieut. Fedor

IN LIBERATED STALINGRAD. Grim and unforgettable reminders of the titanic struggle litter the devastated streets. This radioed photograph shows Stalingrad citizens walking through the snow. A dead horse lies in the foreground, and on the right stands a derelict tram-car.
Photo, Planet News

Yelchenko of Col. Burmakov's motorized sharpshooter brigade was about to rush the building with his men when out popped a German officer carrying a white flag and accompanied by an interpreter. The little 21-year-old lieutenant presented himself. In his own words, reported by A. T. Cholerton, The Daily Telegraph's correspondent :

" They asked for a big chief to meet their big chief. I said, ' I am the nearest here. What do you want ? ' He said ' Surrender.' I said, ' Right-ho.' ''

Impatient Russian sharpshooters trying to rush the iron-grilled gateway leading down to the inner yard were warned by German soldiers that the gateway was mined ; so during the lull Yelchenko, with fifteen of his men, made for the basement by another entrance. They pushed their way past several hundred Germans who were packed tightly in the underground corridors. Into " that beast's lair '' as he called it, Yelchenko made his way with a couple of his men. He was received by Lt.-Col. von Rasske, who asked for terms of surrender. Yelchenko replied that they were those contained in Col.-Gen. Rokossovsky's ultimatum.

" Rasske behaved like an officer (went on Yelchenko), without fear or special arrogance. He and Paulus's chief of staff, von Schmidt, kept going over to the bed where Paulus was lying. I didn't have to talk to him, but took a good look at him ; he didn't look ill, but sort of unhappy. Rasske asked me if I had any questions to put to Paulus personally. I said No, because the position was clear enough to me. They had explained already that Rasske and not Paulus commanded that last German knot in central Stalingrad. Rasske asked me to prevent Paulus being man-handled, or treated like a tramp. In fact, we got him a good car with a good guard to take him to our H.Q. Only half an hour later we took away his little automatic pistol, leaving him his pocket-knife . . . No, we didn't search him for poison.''

Only one little pocket of Germans now remained—that in the north of Stalingrad where the remains of the 11th Army Corps held out under Col.-Gen. Strecker. At dawn on February 2 the Soviet guns deluged the position with fifteen-minute barrages. Then the guns would be silent for five minutes as an invitation to the Germans to give up the fight. The invitation was readily understood, and during each pause groups of dazed and dirty German soldiers crawled out of the debris waving their shirts

as flags of surrender. What may have been the final blow against the Germans in Stalingrad was delivered by one Sergeant Ozerov, who crept up to the last nest of resistance, a shattered house, and sprayed the windows with his tommy-gun, thus allowing his comrades to make the final assault.

So the Battle of Stalingrad came to an end. In Germany the news was made the occasion for a veritable orgy of patriotic mourning, extending by official order over three days. The 6th Army was hailed as '' the bulwark of a historical European mission '' which had sacrificed itself so as to give the German command time to take the counter-measures on which depended the fate of the whole Eastern Front. The truth came from Moscow :

" The Sixth Army,'' said the announcer, '' did not fight to the last bullet. Some of its units did, but not all. And the German generals did not fight at all. Of the 330,000 German officers and men of the 6th Army, 90,000 soldiers, over 2,500 officers and 24 generals surrendered. For every surviving general 10,000 German soldiers had died . . . According to Goebbels the generals died heroes' deaths. In reality, however, they are all alive and prisoners of war.''

After the battle Stalingrad was revealed as a city of desolation—a vast wilderness of masses of broken machinery, twisted rails, wrecks of giant planes, frozen bodies, and street after street of gaunt, wrecked houses. " Around me everywhere,'' cabled Harold King, Reuters special correspondent, " as far as eye could see, was a desolation I could never imagine, even in a hideous dream. For two days I walked and walked, covering about 30 miles from the north of the city to the south and then to the west. I saw the bombing of London, but the worst scenes in London, Coventry, and Plymouth are overshadowed by the almost fierce grimness of Stalingrad.'' Yet in the debris-covered streets there was a strange holiday feeling. Men and women were coming back to rebuild their shattered homes, while streaming along all the roads to the west moved the triumphant divisions of the Red Army. " Five days ago,'' said Lt.-Gen. Gurov, one of Stalingrad's defenders, on February 6, " the Germans were only three hundred yards away. Now they are nearly three hundred miles to the west.''

" And what a devil of a way it is,'' commented a staff-officer as he lifted his eyes from the map spread out before him.

STALINGRAD MEDAL presented to the city's heroic defenders. Obverse (above), '' For the Defence of Stalingrad ''; reverse, '' For our Soviet Land.'' Similar medals were struck for Leningrad, Sevastopol, and Odessa.
U.S.S.R. Official

Britain's Premier and Turkey's President Meet

TURKEY IS OUR ALLY, OUR FRIEND

FROM the conference at Casablanca, with the full assent of President Roosevelt, I flew to Cairo and then to Turkey. I descended upon a Turkish airfield at Adana already well equipped with British Hurricane fighters manned by Turkish airmen ; and out of the snow-capped Taurus Mountains there curled like an enamel caterpillar the Presidential train, bearing on board the head of the Turkish Republic and Prime Minister, the Foreign Secretary, Marshal Chakmak, and the party leader ; in fact, the high executive of Turkey

HITHERTO Turkey has maintained a solid barrier against aggression from any quarter, and by doing so even in the darkest days has rendered us invaluable service in preventing the spreading of the war through Turkey into Persia and Iraq, and in preventing the menace to the oil-fields at Abadan, which are of vital consequence to the whole Eastern war.

It is of important interest to the United Nations, and especially Great Britain, that Turkey should become well-armed in all the apparatus of the modern army, and that her brave infantry shall not lack essential weapons which play a decisive part on the battlefield of today. These weapons we and the United States are now for the first time in a position to supply to the full capacity of the Turkish railways and other communications to receive.

We can give them as much as they are able to take, and we can give them these weapons as fast as or faster than the Turkish troops can be trained to use them.

AT our conference I made no request to Turkey except to get this rearmament business thoroughly well organized, and a joint military mission is now sitting in Angora, a British and Turkish mission, in order to press forward to the utmost the development of the general defensive strength of Turkey, improvement in communications, and by the reception of new weapons to bring its army up to the highest pitch of efficiency.

Turkey is our ally. Turkey is our friend. We shall well wish to see her territories, rights, and interests effectively preserved, and we wish to see in particular warm and friendly relations established between Turkey and our great Russian Ally to the northwards, to whom we are bound by the 20 years'. Anglo-Russian Treaty.—*Mr. Churchill in the House of Commons, Feb.* 11, 1943

THE PRIME MINISTER IN THE NEAR EAST : I, Mr. Churchill and President Inonu of Turkey at Adana during their consultation on Jan. 30-31, 1943. 2, The Presidential train in which the momentous conference took place. A Turkish soldier keeps guard. 3, Cairo was a vital port of call for the Premier. He is here seen with Air Chief Marshal Sir Sholto Douglas, A.O.C.-in-C., Middle East, on his arrival. 4, Mr. Churchill returned to England on Feb. 7 in a Liberator bomber named "Commando"—the same machine in which he flew to Russia last year. This photo shows his baggage being unloaded from the aircraft after his safe return.

Photos, British Official: Crown Copyright

Mr. Churchill Greets the 8th Army in Tripoli

Mr. Churchill in House of Commons, Feb. 11, 1943

TALK ABOUT SPIT AND POLISH!

FROM Cairo I proceeded on my magic carpet to Tripoli, which ten days before was in the possession of the enemy. Here I found Gen. Montgomery. I should like to say this: I have never seen troops march with the style and air of the Desert Army.

Talk about spit and polish! The Highland and New Zealand Divisions paraded after their ordeal in the desert as though they had come out of Wellington Barracks, and there was an air on the face of every private and a look of that just and sober pride which come from victory and triumph after toil.

I saw the same sort of martial smartness and the same punctilio of saluting and discipline in the Russian guard of honour which received me in Moscow six months ago. The fighting men of democracy feel they are coming into their own.

Let me also pay my tribute to that vehement and formidable general, Gen. Montgomery—a Cromwellian figure, austere, severe, accomplished, tireless, his life given to the study of war, who has attracted to himself in an extraordinary measure the confidence and devotion of his army.—

PREMIER WITH DESERT VICTORS: 1, Having landed at Castel Benito aerodrome on Feb. 3, 1943 the Prime Minister drives through Tripoli to the saluting base. 2, Greeting Gen. Montgomery at Castel Benito. 3, Taking the salute as the pipe band of the 51st (Highland) Division marches past.

Photos, British Official: Crown Copyright

THE WAR IN THE AIR

by Capt. Norman Macmillan, M.C., A.F.C.

THE outstanding recent events in the war were the defeat of the Japanese in Guadalcanal Island (announced on February 9) and the continued surge forward of the Russian armies out of the steppe country into the industrial area of the Ukraine. In both cases air activity played a considerable part in the pressure which forced the enemy withdrawal.

The effectiveness of the American air and naval blockade of the Japanese forces on Guadalcanal was a decisive factor. The alleged evacuation of the island (according to the Japanese) is a significant admission of defeat. But it must be remembered that this was a relatively small-scale operation. The numbers of combatants engaged on both sides in the island battles of the South-West Pacific have nowhere been large, because of the difficulties of supply over sea communications stretching for thousands of miles, and a final difficult porterage over tropical and, in some places, mountainous country, to the actual fighting areas.

The Pacific Ocean, dotted with islands, is provided by Nature with a great number of " fixed aircraft-carriers " which can be used by the United Nations in the war against Japan in much the same way as Malta was used in the Mediterranean against the Axis. And undisputed possession of Guadalcanal Island, with its aerodrome (*see* illus. p. 586), must be of great tactical value to the American air forces operating in the Solomons zone.

Under the conditions obtaining in the Pacific Ocean the mobility of the aeroplane reaches full significance. It can bring up urgent reinforcements of men and materials. Its inherent power as a fighting weapon against surface forces and against the submarine can be brought to bear upon an enemy fighting under conditions where the only alternatives are withdrawal or surrender. The success of the American air forces in the Solomons is a sure pointer to the ultimate defeat of Japan, whose communication line from factory to front is but one-half the length of the American air communication line from factories in South California, and one-third of that from factories on the Atlantic coast.

A REMARKABLE feature of the air fighting in the S.W. Pacific lies in the difference between the Japanese method and the American in attacking ships. The favourite Japanese method (as we found out in the case of the Prince of Wales and Repulse) was by airborne torpedo; the usual American method is by bomb. Under the conditions of anchorage found among tropical islands, the bomb attack may be easier to carry out than the torpedo attack, for the first can be made either from high-level flight or a steep dive, but the torpedo can be launched accurately only when the conditions are peculiarly favourable to this form of attack. It is, however, too soon to attempt an analysis of the relative value of the two forms of attack, but it is probable that this is already earnestly engaging the attention of the air and naval technical staffs.

The Russian Air Force achieved a technical surprise in the employment of the rocket-propelled bomb. The Stormovik has often been called a dive-bomber, but this is an erroneous description. It is really a low-level bomber, employing the rocket-propelled bomb, which, because of the velocity imparted by the rocket, travels in a straight line from aeroplane to target instead of following a curving trajectory. The impact force of this type of bomb is greater than that of the gravity-propelled bomb, and it is therefore a more useful projectile to employ against tanks, if the standard of aim can be raised to an accuracy sufficient to provide direct hits.

FLYING-TANKS and Anti-tank Aircraft Foreshadowed

It is therefore probable that the future will see more urgent development of anti-tank air attack, for if the aeroplane can be provided with the appropriate projectile it becomes the most mobile anti-tank weapon. For such attacks the aeroplane must fly low. It must therefore be heavily armoured. Two developments in air-land warfare are thus probable: the production of (1) transport aircraft able to carry large tanks to their field of action, and (2) flying-tanks to defeat the land-tanks. Only a reduction in the duration of the War, coupled with the difficulties of introducing new productions in wartime, will prevent such air transports and weapons from being employed in the course of the present war.

The achievements of the Red Air Force, which have been mainly responsible for stretching the Luftwaffe to its limit, have surprised those who did not before the War study closely the trend of Russian air technique. The Russians were designing and building extremely clean and aerodynamically efficient aircraft many years before the War began; while their special long-distance record-breaking aircraft were remarkable in possessing cantilever wings (these are wings with no external bracing) with a greater aspect ratio (that is relation in length of wing-span to fore-and-aft wing-chord) than had been believed to be possible.

It was one of Hitler's serious blunders to underestimate the Red Air Force. But he was not alone in this. Many Britons did the same.

Bomber Command maintained its offensive against Germany, Italy, and occupied Europe, day bombing railway yards near Bruges on Feb. 2 and Abbeville on Feb. 2 and 3, St. Omer aerodrome on Feb. 3, railway yards at Caen on Feb. 10 and at Roosendaal (Holland) and Serqueux (N. France) on Feb. 11, and in N.W. Germany on Feb. 12. Night attacks were directed against Cologne (Feb. 2); Hamburg (Feb. 3); Turin, Spezia naval base, Lorient, and Ruhr (Feb. 4); mine-laying and Rhineland (Feb. 6); and Lorient and Ruhr (Feb. 7); Wilhelmshaven (Feb. 11); Lorient and W. Germany (Feb. 13); the Cologne, Hamburg, Turin, second and third Lorient raids were especially heavy; 48 bombers were lost in these day and night raids, 16 in the Hamburg raid. Germany has ordered the evacuation of all persons but essential workers from Brest and Lorient; it is probable that the reasons are scarcity of housing and desire for maximum dispersal of workers to give greater security from raids.

Coastal Command aircraft have continued to meet and fight Junkers 88 aircraft over the Bay of Biscay. One was shot down by a Halifax, and three by Beaufighters. These German patrol aircraft endeavour to protect the submarine lanes in and out of the Bay.

APPROACHING Battle for Supremacy in the North African Sky

Fighter and Army Cooperation Commands continue to make sweeps over Occupied France and the Low Countries, attacking aircraft, trains, locomotives, lorries, barges, and coastal shipping.

German fighter-bombers have continued to make scattered day raids on South and East Coast English towns and villages. One raid on Feb. 10 was made by Dornier 217 bombers. Objectives appear to be the larger buildings, which involve schools, hospitals, churches, stores, and restaurants.

THE war in N. Africa has been quieter. Consolidation of command under Gen. Eisenhower in preparation for the Battle of Tunisia sees Air Chief Marshal Sir Arthur Tedder in strategic command of all British and American aircraft, with Air Vice-Marshal Sir Arthur Coningham in tactical command; these two are the successful Egypt-Libya battle team. The battle for Tunisia will be waged fiercely in the air. All the fighters the Luftwaffe can spare from Western Europe and Russia have been sent there. The first part of the struggle must be for mastery of the sky, just as it was in Egypt. Large-scale ground fighting must await the end of the rainy season, which terminates in March.

Award of ten decorations to crews who, day-bombing Berlin on January 30, upset the broadcasts of Goering and Goebbels, confirms that each of the two raids was made by three aircraft. The squadrons who made the raids were Nos. 105 and 139. Other notable awards include two D.F.C.s and three D.F.M.s to the surviving members of the crew of eight in No. 149 Squadron's Stirling bomber which attacked the Fiat works in Turin on November 28, 1942, under the captaincy of Flight Sergeant R. H. Middleton of the R.A.A.F., who lost his life at the end of the return flight and was posthumously awarded the V.C. (*see* photo, p. 535).

LORIENT was one of the principal targets of Bomber Command in Feb. 1943. This photo shows the attack on Feb. 7-8 : A, two bombers over target ; B, sticks of incendiary bombs burning ; C, concrete submarine pens ; D, radial slips turntable ; E, smoke from large fire. (See also illus. p. 585).

Photo, British Official

Lancasters over Hamburg : High Level of Daring

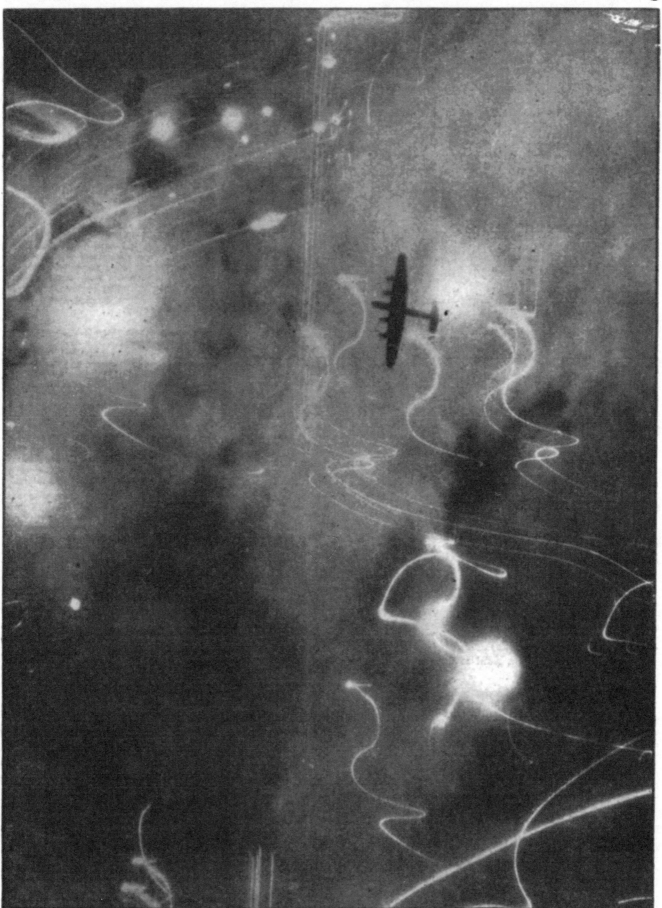

CROSSING THE NORTH SEA IN A GALE, one of the worst for many years, R.A.F. bombers on Jan. 30, 1943 raided Hamburg for the 94th time. In 30 minutes a great weight of 4,000 and 8,000 lb. H.E.s was "cascaded" on the dock and U-boat yards, which stretch for 9 miles along the Elbe, and huge fires were left raging. This photo gives a vivid impression of the raid as it appeared to the crew of a Lancaster. Another Lancaster is seen silhouetted against a background of fire and flak.

Photo, British Official : Crown Copyright

On the Way It's Packed A Life May Depend

Sailing down through the air, the airman who has just escaped from his blazing plane, and the paratroops descending from the aerial troop-carrier, are sustained by their parachutes until they reach Mother Earth with never a broken bone, not even—most likely—a sprained ankle. In the article printed below, ROBERT DE WITT gives some interesting facts concerning this vital new appliance in the equipment of modern war.

THE parachute is no longer simply the "lifebuoy" of the air, saving the life of an airman in a crashing plane. It is used deliberately by hundreds, even thousands, of men every day in the airborne divisions. Paratroops nearly always jump from a low level ; and for them, perhaps, even more than for airmen the instantaneous opening of the parachute without a hitch is a matter of life and death. This opening depends upon the huge circle of silk and

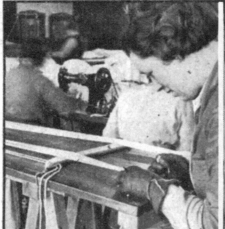 

PACKING PARACHUTES is a highly skilled and responsible job. Left, this parachute-maker is fastening cords to metal rings fitted to harness. She ties them with a special knot. Right, a member of the W.A.A.F. prepares parachutes ready for packing.

Photos, British Official ; Pictorial Press

hundreds of feet of fine cords being correctly packed. The thousands of men and women engaged in packing parachutes have, therefore, exceptionally responsible work, a life depending literally on every movement of their dexterous fingers.

The layman presented with the billowing folds of a parachute and told to pack it in the canvas holder would probably wrestle for an hour or two with the cords and silk, and end up with a roll several times too big for the pack ! But in the hands of the experienced W.A.A.F. silk and cords seem to fall almost naturally into place, and it is only ten minutes before the parachute has been folded into a long triangle of silk, the cords separated and placed in their retainers. The triangle is folded until it seems to fit neatly into the pack.

THIS skill comes only with intensive training. The student packer is shown how to hold the "peak" of the parachute in place on a hook at one end of the 40-foot-long table provided, and then separate the panels and cords. The standard parachute has 96 panels made of some sixty yards of silk, and 24 silk cords joining it to the harness. Little bags of shot help to keep the soft silk in position on the table as she works, her eye open for the slightest flaw in any part of the parachute as her fingers smooth the folds. The seams are numbered to facilitate getting an even number on each side. It will be seen that the packer has to start with number 13 on one side going up to 24, numbers 1 to 12 being on the other side. But skill matters in this task, not superstition.

All the time it is impressed upon the packer that the slightest carelessness may result in a serious accident or even a death. "Always think that it is your husband or your fiancé that is going to wear this para-

chute," one instructor says to his pupils. The fact that parachute accidents due to faulty packing are almost unknown shows that the girls are fully alive to their responsibilities. Indeed, more than one parachutist has remarked to a packer that he would rather make a dozen jumps than pack a parachute for someone else—much too responsible a job !

Before the student is "passed out" and licensed to pack parachutes, there is a severe test. A parachute must be packed in a given time—half an hour, but it is not so much the time that counts as absolute accuracy. Before the War a licence to pack parachutes was prized. Very few women were qualified, and the work was done by non-commissioned officers in the R.A.F. Today hundreds of W.A.A.F.s have qualified for the work. Anyone who makes a mistake may have the licence revoked. I have not heard of any instances in Britain, but not long ago the licence of a parachute "rigger" in the U.S. was revoked "for inspecting, repacking and certifying as airworthy a parachute when in fact it was unairworthy."

MAKING sure that the parachute and harness are in perfect condition is a not less important part of the packer's work than actually packing them. Every inch of the silk and cords is inspected, and the slightest fraying or weakness results in the parachute being put aside for repair—a new silk panel inserted or a new cord attached. Small repairs are done in the packing room where sewing machines, etc., are installed.

Damp is the parachute's greatest enemy. The packing-rooms at large air

stations are air-conditioned, the warmed and dried air circulating round the canopies hung from pulleys in the ceiling and looking like monstrous ghosts. Every time a parachute is packed it gets an air of from ten to forty-eight hours. The difficulty of drying is increased at some stations in notoriously damp parts of the British Isles. At aerodromes just behind the front it is not always possible to get these ideal conditions. Then either large buildings like barns are converted into packing-rooms, or the packing may be done in the open on gigantic waterproof sheets spread on the ground.

Whether it is used or not, the rule is that every parachute must be examined and re-packed at least once a month. What a contrast with the old days when few airmen "believed" in parachutes and sometimes did not unpack them for a year or more. Incidentally, although such extreme care is rightly taken in correct packing, it is by no means certain that a badly-packed parachute would fail to open.

EVERY parachute when it comes from the manufacturer has been severely tested at every stage of its manufacture, and when passed it is given a number and a "log book." In this log is recorded its final test and then, week by week, every incident in its life. All repairs are noted. A diagram of the parachute facilitates instructions for major repairs without actual marking of the delicate silk of the parachute itself. A "live" jump is recorded in red, and if the parachute has been used in wet weather this is recorded. Every time it is packed the packer signs the log. This brings home and emphasizes the responsibility for another person's safety.

Between the men and women who pack the parachutes and the men who use them there is often a very real comradeship. Airmen who have jumped and saved their lives often come into the packing-room and thank the W.A.A.F. who packed the parachutes. After the Battle of Britain one packer whose parachutes had saved the lives of some dozen pilots in the course of two months was presented with a cigarette-case engraved with the autographs of all the grateful pilots.

CORPORAL 'JEAN,' 19-year-old W.A.A.F., receives Sergt.-Pilot J. R. McLeod's congratulations on the efficiency of her packing. He could speak with feeling, since it was to this that he owed his safety when he jumped by parachute from his blazing Spitfire. He is the fourth airman to thank this W.A.A.F. girl for saving his life. *Photo G.P.U.*

This Is What Our Heavy Bombers Did to Mainz

R.A.F. ATTACKS ON MAINZ, the Rhineland transport centre, on August 11-12 and 12-13, 1942, were among the heaviest blows delivered at that time by our bombers. The top photograph shows the area round the Municipal Theatre (large domed building) before these devastating raids. Below, the same area three months later. Clearance work has been done, and many buildings swept away. Seven out of every ten houses in Mainz were reported to have been wrecked.

Photos. British Official: Crown Copyright

THE HOME FRONT

by E. Royston Pike

SPRING is the season of hope, and this year there's a dash of optimism in the air which makes us think that it is not altogether untimely to give a thought to the things to come when the War has been won and has passed into history. At about this stage in the First World War there was much talk of Reconstruction, with a capital R, and not a little planning and preparation. Those who were internationally minded were busy paving the way for the League of Nations, already taking shape in the brains of Lord Robert Cecil and General Smuts, Lord Phillimore and President Wilson; while those whose fancy turned to things nearer home found abundant scope for their reforming zeal. Mr. Fisher was piloting his Education Bill through the Commons, and Dr. Addison was presiding over a special Ministry of Reconstruction. Plans, wonderful plans, were being drawn up for the building of a multitude of houses, those "homes for heroes" which, alas, became all too surely a synonym for broken promises. Women's suffrage was rapidly passing into law, and Arthur Henderson was overhauling the Labour Party machine in readiness for the coming battle of the polls.

LOOKING back on those days is no altogether pleasant occupation for those of us who belong to what may be called the disillusioned generation. Our hopes were great, our disappointment correspondingly great. There was a slump and then a boom, and then another and far greater slump. The fruits of the war had a bitter, bitter taste. Those were what Mr. H. G. Wells, with his customary pungency, has called the fatuous twenties and the frightened thirties. No, it is not pleasant to recall these things, those years so characterized by frustration, so filled to the brim with disappointed hopes, with schemes gone awry. And yet, if we have not become dry and wrinkled and completely cynical, we cannot fail to welcome the signs (and they are many) of another chance being given us, of another opportunity being afforded of doing what a generation ago we ought to have done, could have done, but in our stupidity failed to do.

ALTHOUGH little or nothing has been revealed as yet, it is understood that the Government are working on a number of projects which will soon be exposed to the parliamentary air. Mr. Butler has an Education Bill in preparation; Mr. Hudson is attempting nothing less than the putting of British agriculture on so firm a soil that it will never revert to that state of neglect that was one of the most disgraceful features of our pre-War economy; Mr. Brown is laying the foundations of a much healthier, and therefore happier, Britain; Sir William Jowitt, Lord Portal, Mr. W. S. Morrison—these and many another of their ministerial colleagues are deeply engaged in the fine art of political incubation. Then there is Mr. Bevin . . .

When, after much preliminary sparring, the Minister of Labour's Catering Wages Bill was introduced in the House of Commons, it gave rise to a debate marked by an outburst of opposition by a considerable section of M.P.s as remarkable as (in these days of national government) it is rare.

The Bill proposes to establish a Statutory Commission of seven members empowered to examine the arrangements for regulating the pay and conditions of work in the catering trades (generally alleged to be amongst the most unorganized in the country), to report where these are adequate or can be made adequate, and to make proposals for the setting up of Wages Boards where these are considered to be necessary. In moving the second reading on February 9, Mr. Bevin argued that the Bill was not controversial: it was simply the development of a policy that had been followed for more than fifty years—a reference in particular to the Trade Boards Act of 1909, when Mr. Churchill was at the Board of Trade. "I need the Bill for the War," declared the Minister of Labour; he could not order people to take up work in the catering industry under an essential work order if he were not satisfied that they would receive fair

MR. AND MRS. BEVIN join in a vigorous chorus with these men of the Merchant Navy during the Minister of Labour's recent visit to a N.E. area.
Photo, Daily Mirror

wages and would work under decent conditions. He needed it, too, for the peace; after the War "the first thing the people of Britain will want will be a holiday," and he wanted to ensure that it was a health-giving holiday. Then great numbers of visitors would be coming to this country, "to see battle-scarred Britain and the people who stood up to the blitz," and hotel-keeping might well become a major industry. Before the War about 500,000 people were employed in the catering trades; this figure might be doubled, if not trebled. But the industry must be organized. Drudgery ought to be wiped out; there ought to be a wage at the end of the week, and not just what the worker could get by way of tips. The industry must be made efficient so as to attract enterprise, opportunity and capital. "I am not socializing the industry . . . No one could make a better conservative speech than that . . ."

MOVING the rejection of the Bill, Sir Douglas Hacking denounced it as a "monster of bureaucratic autocracy," a distinct breach of the understanding not to introduce "controversial" matters in wartime. A hard-hitting debate ensued; deep feeling was displayed and given voice. On the one side were those who felt that the Bill was another step along the road to nationalization; on the other those who maintained that catering, at least in some of its branches, was a sweated industry. When the division was taken, 115 members (111 of whom were Conservatives) supported Sir Douglas Hacking; into the Government lobby there poured 285 (107 Conservatives, 138 Labour, and the rest Liberals, etc.). Mr. Bevin's opponents hailed the vote as a moral victory,

and urged him to drop the Bill. But this he showed no intention of doing, although, of course, there would be opportunities for its amendment on the committee stage.

Perhaps the most interesting feature of the debate was the marked division of opinion between those of whatever party who hanker after a policy of as little Government intervention as possible in the industrial sphere, and those who look on the State as the instrument of great social and economic change. This division gave rise, just a week later, to another battle when the Commons debated an all-party motion welcoming the Beveridge Report on Social Security. The motion was moved on February 16 by Mr. A. Greenwood who, when Minister without Portfolio responsible for the planning of post-war reconstruction, set Sir William Beveridge his task. No document within living memory had stirred such hopes, said Mr. Greenwood, or made such a powerful impression as the Beveridge Report. "The people of this country," he declared, "have made up their minds irrevocably to see the plan in its broad lines carried into operation." Sir John Anderson followed with the announcement that the Government accepted in principle the Beveridge Report, and promised that with as little delay as possible the scheme would be shaped and put into legislative form. But some of the younger Conservatives were not quite satisfied; they urged that a Minister of Social Security should be set up forthwith; and there was promise of considerable support for a Labour amendment urging "the reconsideration of the Government's policy with a view to the early implementation of the plan." However, Mr. Herbert Morrison, winding up for the Government, was able to convince many of the waverers that the Cabinet really did "mean business," and in the division the Government had a majority of 217—336 votes to 119.

ONE hundred thousand families are living in houses which were condemned as unsuitable for human habitation three years ago, revealed Mr. Ernest Brown, Minister of Health, in the House of Commons not long since. Practically no new houses have been built since the War; most of the builders have been called up, and materials have been urgently required for other jobs. Hundreds of thousands of houses have been destroyed or seriously damaged. In the country the housing shortage has become so acute that the Ministry of Health has launched what it describes as "a modest building programme." It is indeed modest, since it aims at providing 3,000 cottages this year. Of these Lincolnshire, which has the reputation of the blackest housing area in rural England, is to have 228, Yorkshire 218, Devonshire 116, and Norfolk 90. Not 3,000, but 30,000—some say as many as 250,000—rural cottages are required at once. And they must be at rents the farm-workers can afford to pay. Thirteen shillings a week, the rate proposed for the new cottages, is said to be too high; the rent should be nearer the 4s. or 5s. that is now the usual charge.

WHEN a few weeks ago some three dozen children in a London school were killed by a German bomb, the news was received with universal shock. And shocking indeed it was. But isn't it just as shocking that last year 1,315 children were killed on our roads? Perhaps even more shocking. We know that bombs are no respecters of persons, slaying the tottering patriarch and the baby in its cradle with a fine impartiality. Bombs are meant to kill; and now that war is a totalitarian business we are all in the front line. But those who die on the roads are the victims of human carelessness, of what is sometimes criminal negligence. Since the beginning of the blitz in September 1940 (notes The Economist) about 5,500 children have been killed in air raids; from the beginning of 1940 to the end of 1942 nearly 4,000 were killed on the roads. Of a truth we all need awakening to "the needless, senseless tragedy taking place on Britain's roads."

New Names on the R.A.F.'s Roll of Heroes

Actg. F/L. W. V. CRAWFORD-COMPTON, awarded a Bar to his D.F.C. for remarkable skill and daring. He has repeatedly led his flight on numerous operational sorties over enemy territory and, in addition to his brilliant leadership, he has destroyed 7 enemy aircraft.

Actg. S/L. H. J. L. HALLOWES, D.F.M. and Bar, awarded the D.F.C. for his unswerving devotion to duty. An outstanding and relentless fighter, he has brought down 19 enemy aircraft and has damaged many others. He represents the highest traditions of the R.A.F.

F/L. E. E. COATE, R.A.A.F., awarded the D.F.C. He has been engaged in operations both in the W. Desert and from Malta, and has destroyed many enemy machines. In Nov. 1942 he shot down a B.V. 222 in flames (see illus. p. 473.) and damaged a Dornier 24.

A Mosquito makes a low-level daylight attack on the Hazemeyer electrical plant at Hengelo, Holland. Enemy A.A. gun opens fire from a flak tower.

Actg. F/L. A. D. FRECKER, R.A.F.V.R., awarded the D.F.C. An exceptionally able pilot, he took part in many attacks on enemy shipping, and has destroyed 4 German aircraft. He was born in 1913, and joined the R.A.F.V.R. two years before War.

P/O. C. H. HARRIS-ST. JOHN, awarded the D.F.C. last Oct. for brilliant reconnaissance photography which proved invaluable to our daring combined operational raid on Dieppe on Aug. 19, 1942.

F/O. A. H. BURR, whose award of the D.F.C. was recently announced. He attacked 15 enemy bombers menacing a convoy bound for Russia and hit three of them. The rest of the enemy fled.

Actg. S/L. R. P. BEAMONT, whose award of a Bar to his D.F.C. was announced on Jan. 22, 1943. In five weeks he damaged 12 enemy locomotives. He won the D.F.C. in 1941.

Photos, British Official: Crown Copyright; Fox, G.P.U. Topical Press

Round the Country with Our Roving Camera

NATIONAL GALLERY ART TREASURES are stored in air-conditioned subterranean caves in which the temperature and humidity are scientifically controlled. Housed in six separate " buildings," they are immune from air attack inasmuch as the underground working in which they are stored has between 200 ft. and 300 ft. of rock cover. Machinery controls the temperature and the ¼-mile of miniature railway.

Right, packed in a special sealed container, pictures are seen on their way to the studio, hewn out of rock in the heart of the mountain. Below, canvases ready for inspection. To save space oblong paintings are placed on end.

BRITAIN'S LARGEST VILLAGE GREEN—at Great Bentley, near Ipswich—has now been ploughed up so that potatoes may be planted on its 50 acres. Above, village children are watching their centuries-old green being ploughed by 18 year-old George Bennett, driving a tractor.

' SAFETY FIRST.' Police throughout the country are cooperating with education authorities in an effort to reduce the number of road accidents to children. Below, a police officer demonstrates the Safety Code on a blackboard, with the aid of charts and posters.

BRITISH ENGINES FOR RUSSIA. This L.M.S. 2-8-0 locomotive seen in course of construction was designed to haul heavy freight trains. Many of these engines have gone abroad, notably to the U.S.S.R., where they are contributing in no small measure to our Ally's magnificent war effort.

Photos, Keystone, Fox, Topical Press

My Escape from Germany—by General Giraud

Captured in 1940 during the Battle of France, and imprisoned in Castle Koenigstein, in Germany, Henri Honoré Giraud—now French Civil and Military Commander-in-Chief in Africa—tells G. Ward Price (War Correspondent of The Daily Mail, from which the astonishing story is reprinted) how he escaped from his cell and eventually reached North Africa to fight again. (See also page 486.)

GEN. GIRAUD (left) and Gen. Noguès, en route to a military parade in French N. Africa. Gen. Giraud's own story of his escape from Germany is told in this page.
Photo, Planet News

FOR eight months after I fell into German hands my old wounds kept me a cripple, walking on two sticks. But in January 1941 I began to plan my escape.

Like my fellow French prisoners I was allowed to take daily exercise in the castle garden. From its parapet one looked down a 150-ft. precipice on to rough ground covered with bush. I discovered a corner of the garden which was out of sight of the sentry on the watchtower. This was the point I chose for my escape.

I began to make systematic plans for it which took me the whole year. For months I secretly collected every bit of cord and string I could lay my hands on, to make a rope. Working only at night, I twisted and spliced them into a rope of nine strands, about as thick as two fingers. I would make a piece about two yards long, and then hide it in the garden.

IT was soon evident that I couldn't make the rope strong enough to bear my weight, 13½ st. Fortunately I had an old friend in France with whom I had arranged a simple letter-writing code in case I should be taken prisoner again.

I used this to write and ask for lengths of rubber-insulated copper telephone wire to be sent to me hidden in tins of jam. As this gradually arrived I wrapped it round my rope to strengthen it and give it a better grip. And I requested my wife to send me large quantities of chocolate at frequent intervals. She had no suspicion that I wanted it to sell through another prisoner to Germans at half the market price. In this way I accumulated 600 marks as funds for my escape.

With some of this money I bought secretly an old pair of civilian trousers and a battered raincoat, which I hid in my cell. Meanwhile I used my code to arrange, months ahead, for a daring French agent to be sent to meet me at a rendezvous a few miles from Koenigstein on the day I planned to attempt escape.

I also managed to get hold of a blank German identity card. This I filled up with a description of myself as a commercial traveller in artificial silk. Meanwhile I saved up enough food from parcels to last me three days. I had biscuits, cheese, sugar, and a bottle of brandy.

At last the day came. I had to make the attempt in broad daylight as I couldn't reach the garden at night. Every quarter of an hour a German N.C.O. patrolled it, so at 9.45 that morning, when I was waiting near my buried rope, I made a joke with him as he passed.

The instant he was out of sight I dragged my rope from its hiding-place, fastened it to a convenient staple in the wall, climbed the parapet, and began to slide down. I had to go slowly for fear of losing my grip. It took me four minutes to descend 150 feet. Then I hid in a clump of bushes and looked up at the parapet. No sign of any excitement, so I shaved off my moustache, put on a pair of dark glasses, threw away my general's uniform, and dressed myself in the civilian trousers and raincoat I had brought down with me.

Then I walked quite openly along the road towards the rendezvous I had fixed for my friendly agent to meet me with complete civilian outfit. At the prearranged place a workman, carrying a small suitcase, met me. "Morgen, Heinrich," he said. It was my confederate.

In the nearest wood I changed into full civilian kit, complete with hat, and walking boldly to the next station I took the train for Breslau. I knew the Germans would expect me to make for France, so I deliberately headed east.

IN the course of a week I saw several newly posted placards on the walls offering a reward of 100,000 marks for my arrest. They contained a photograph of myself, which, fortunately, was a very bad one. Only once did I nearly get caught.

My train stopped for a long time at a wayside station, and it was evident that a specially strict examination of identity papers was going on. In the 2nd-class carriage in which I was travelling was an officer of one of Rommel's panzer divisions. He had the words "Afrika Korps" on his sleeve and wore the Knight's Cross of the Iron Cross, so he was evidently a distinguished person. As the examiners approached, I engaged this officer in conversation. Though doubtless a good soldier he did not look particularly intelligent.

NEVER was Rommel so lauded to the skies as by me in that talk, which secured for me the indulgent attention of my fellow-passenger. The result was that when the Gestapo man arrived in my compartment he scrutinized everyone else's papers, but didn't venture to demand to inspect those of a civilian who was apparently on intimate terms with the highly-decorated German officer.

At last I reached a point near the Swiss frontier. I knew the ground well, having been there to shoot in peacetime. But the border was closely guarded. There was a sentry every 100 yards, with patrols constantly passing between.

By night I crept into the heart of thick bushes a few yards from the frontier and lay there from one o'clock in the morning till six. I was unable to stir a hand or a foot as two of the sentries came and stood within a few yards of me. I could hear them talking. Improbable as it sounds, they were actually discussing my escape. I lay as still as a corpse. At last, nearing six in the morning, when I was aching with cramp and almost

KOENIGSTEIN CASTLE, Saxony, the scene of Gen. Giraud's imprisonment by the Germans, towers picturesquely over the little town of that name on the River Elbe. Gen. Giraud spent many months in this inaccessible fortress, and the dramatic details of his subsequent escape make fascinating reading. He arrived in Switzerland on April 21, 1942, and reached Algeria in a British submarine just before the North African campaign began in November last year.

Photo E.N.A.

exhausted, one said to the other : "Well, he hasn't come. Perhaps we shall have better luck this evening. It's time to get breakfast."

A quarter of an hour later I was in Switzerland. When I eventually got back to France the Gestapo shadowed me everywhere for six months. I lay low in various places, but all the time I was in touch with the Americans.

Finally, on November 2 last year, I got a secret communication telling me of the Anglo-American landing due to take place in N. Africa six days later. Would I come over by submarine to cooperate with the Allies ?

Then started another series of adventures. With my son and three officers who were with me I rowed out over a rough sea by night to meet, a mile off shore, the submarine sent to fetch me.

We could just make out its dark shape lying on the surface. We exchanged pre-arranged recognition signals with flashlamps.

As I was boarding the sloping hull I slipped, but didn't fall into the sea. I was seized and pulled on board when the water was up to my knees. Much more difficult was the transfer next morning from the submarine to a seaplane which met us out in the Mediterranean.

The only means of getting from one to the other was by a rubber dinghy paddled by two young Commandos whom the submarine had brought, specially chosen for their skill and strength. This light craft danced like a cork on the steep waves. The commander of the submarine thought I would never do it, but at 63 I am still pretty supple, and I just managed to scramble in.

When we got to the seaplane a burly young Canadian leaned out and called : " Stretch out your arms and I'll catch you by the wrists." I did so, and as the dinghy shot upwards on the crest of the wave he by sheer strength swung me on board.

In Malta We Went Nearly Mad with Joy

From a Malta "intoxicated with good news" comes this joyous letter to the Editor. Our young Maltese correspondent, John Mizzi, has sent us many vivid communications during the dark months of the George Cross island's travail. Here he records the excitement when news came that Tripoli had fallen, and Malta's long siege was raised. Mightily changed conditions are indicated by the fact that his letter was only 15 days in transit.

I HAVE many a time written about Malta under fire ; now, at last, I can write about Malta as we knew it before the war, happy and proud ! I am typing this by the light of a small paraffin lamp on the evening of January 23, from a Malta intoxicated with good news. Tripoli at last has fallen ! We in Malta toiled, suffered, some of us died, but at last our struggle has borne fruit. We are nearly all mad with joy. For two long years have we waited for this day, two years of death, destruction and hunger.

> Say not the struggle naught availeth,
> The labour and the wounds are vain. . .

How far away seems June 1940 ! As I look back to the dark months through which we have passed, especially to those fierce days of 1942, how proud I feel ! I can picture the German planes criss-crossing across the blue sky, weaving in and out of A.A. puffs, scattering bombs right and left. But they are only pictures now. We are top dogs at last. Those days of March, of April, and of May will go down in history and there they will remain. Those days, those moments of fears and havoc will never darken the pages of humanity again !

Hour by hour, for three days we waited for news of Tripoli's fall. As each day passed our hopes rose higher, higher till this morning . . . At midday today the news of Tripoli's fall flashed across the Island. The 8th Army had done it !

Nowhere in the world was the news more anxiously awaited, more heartily received than in Malta. The siege had been lifted, a siege in all its horrors : death, ruin. Malta cried as the news spread, not tears of sorrow, but hot tears of pride and uncontrollable joy. Even the ruins of buildings seemed majestic as they reminded us of the "days that have been," days that are no more. History will record the day in sparkling letters.

AT midday, whilst I was at the office, a friend of mine came running in, beaming and eyes wide open. "It's ours !" He forced the words through a radiant mouth. We all turned round as if by magic, for we all knew what he meant. I closed the book I was reading and ran out of the office into a coffee-shop near by, which was crammed full of people listening to the B.B.C. news. I chose a likely victim, disfigured my face with a broad smile, and blurted out " Ours ?"

" Yes, sir ; at last," he replied, " it is ours. Tripoli ! Tripoli is in our hands ! "

His voice trailed away as I ran into a near-by club, where in solitude a man was sitting near a radio, smiling and rubbing his hands. I went and sat near him. He smiled at me, and I returned his smile. The B.B.C. reporter in Egypt in a steady voice was giving the latest news from the front. Tears of happiness sprang into my eyes as emotion got the better of me. The Maltese announcer on the local broadcasting station was shouting, " *Tripli taghna. Ifirhu!* I repeat, Tripoli is ours. Rejoice ! "

As I hurriedly left the club I saw a flag scaling a flagpole to flutter to the rhythm of the breeze and happy Maltese hearts. The men around me, and those children playing at soldiers, oh, how they have suffered ! But now they will suffer no more. Malta, we have not failed thee !

I HAVE just come from Valetta, where, amidst the ruins of the buildings, the flags of the United Nations present a striking contrast. The air vibrates with relief. The narrow streets are canopied with flags of Malta with a George Cross superimposed. Under these walk the common men and women of Malta, mere actors in this world drama, but principal actors none the less. Navy, Army and Air Force uniforms flitter here and there, and on many a breast rests the ribbon of a medal. Planes flit across the sky on the way to or from Tripolitania and Tunisia. Yes, they are striking out in defiance, not hitting back in defence. Verily, " the pages of scrapbook turn."

By the time this letter is published perhaps the enthusiasm may have died out, but the effect of today's events will for ever be felt. Malta has been relieved, thank God ! You in Britain may have given a thought to us in Malta as you heard the news. I thank you, and before I end this letter may I wish you all the best.

REJOICINGS IN MALTA over the Eighth Army's triumphal entry into Tripoli on Jan. 23, 1943 marked the lifting of a shadow which had loomed over the island for many a long and weary month. Now, however, Malta's nightmare was over at last. Maltese children, carrying the flags of a number of the United Nations, are shown in this photograph parading the streets of the sorely-blitzed Valetta.

Photo, British Official

I'm One of the Dutchmen Lent to the British Navy

Serving with our Royal Navy, a young Dutch seaman tells here of his
experiences in a cruiser escorting a convoy to North Russia—of how hell
suddenly broke loose for the Nazis diving from the sky, and why he twice
" shook hands with himself."

I WAS a landlubber; they made a sailor out of me. I'm proud of it. Now I have been lent to the British Navy to gain experience. I am pleased about that. The food is different from the food in our ships, but food is not so important ; they could serve me stinging nettles, so long as I can see German aircraft drop into the water.

I have been to Russia with a convoy— you know, the kind that never arrives; according to the Germans ! I was in a cruiser. Just before we joined the convoy the Commander discussed the whole thing with us, telling us what we were going to do, how long the voyage would take, what attacks we might expect, and other details. The first part of the voyage was rather quiet, except for U-boats and the noise of depth charges exploding day and night. There must have been a noise in those Huns' heads in their U-boats as well.

Whenever something important happened the first officer's quiet voice told us all about it through a loudspeaker. It was as exciting as a football match broadcast by Han Hollander at home. Only Han Hollander used to get excited when a goal was made, whereas these ice-cold English do these things in their own quiet way. You heard him say : " There are six planes coming along at low altitude on port, now there are only five, now there are four . . ."

We stood at our alarm-posts all the time. For many days there was no hot food— when the British fight they all fight, the cooks as well. But even then those chaps found time to bring everyone his food at his post. The broadcasting officer would say : " If So-and-so will go to the port anti-aircraft gun he will find his sausage, and if he is quick he will find it hot."

Then the real fun began—torpedo-bombers, high-level-bombers, dive-bombers. The first day with those Hun torpedo-bombers was worst for me—I had to get used to them. It is a weird experience to hear over the loudspeaker that 42 of those things are coming straight at you over the water. The first look at them was rather sickening. But then our own guns began to fire, and hell broke loose for the Huns.

The last torpedo-bomber had not gone before the high-altitude-bombers came along. Those rats had the advantage of low clouds, so that one seldom saw the planes. Suddenly we heard two terrific explosions, and the unmoved voice of the officer at his loudspeaker announced that two thousand-pound bombs had been dropped 15 metres to starboard. I swallowed, and shook hands with myself. I shook hands with myself again when I heard that the destroyer had sunk a U-boat, and that there was a lot of wreckage and oil and fresh vegetables floating about amid the ice. When the Commander asked if the destroyer was quite sure, she answered that the vegetables could not possibly come from her as she hadn't seen any for two weeks.

Finally we handed over the convoy to our Russian friends, who had come to meet us.

IN CONVOY TO RUSSIA. Some idea of the risks taken by our U.S.S.R.-bound ships may be had from the accompanying account. Our photo shows an A.A. rocket being loaded in anticipation of a dive-bomber attack (see p. 188). *Photo, Associated Press*

I am glad I went on the trip. We gave the Huns a beating, and I'm pleased to think I, as a Dutchman, had a hand in that. My comrades and I, we all work for the good cause, in Dutch submarines or destroyers or minesweepers, or flying Dutch planes, or serving with the Merchant Navy.

OUR DIARY OF THE WAR

FEB. 3, 1943, Wednesday 1,250th day
Air.—R.A.F. and U.S. aircraft raided Abbeville and St. Omer. Heavy night raid on Hamburg.
North Africa.—British troops in Tunisia captured a ridge of Jebel Mansour.
Russian Front.—Soviet troops occupied Krasny-Liman, in Ukraine, and Kuschevka, S. of Rostov.
General.—German radio announced three-day mourning for 6th Army at Stalingrad.

FEB. 4, Thursday 1,251st day
Air.—U.S. bombers made daylight raid on N.W. Germany ; 25 German fighters destroyed at cost of five bombers. Night raids by R.A.F. on Turin, Spezia, Lorient and the Ruhr.
Russian Front.—Kupiansk in the Ukraine and Shchigry and Tim, E. of Kursk, captured by Soviet troops.
Burma.—R.A.F. Liberators made heavy raid on Rangoon docks.
Australasia.—U.S. Fortresses again bombed Rabaul ; Lae, Gasmata and Buin also raided.

FEB. 5, Friday 1,252nd day
North Africa.—Under enemy pressure our troops withdrew from Jebel Mansour in Tunisia.
Mediterranean.—Palermo harbour raided by Allied bombers.
Russian Front.—Stary Oskol, W. of Kursk, and Izyum in the Ukraine occupied by Soviet troops.
Australasia.—Japanese troops evacuating Guadalcanal under cover of air attacks.
General.—Mussolini became Italian Foreign Minister in place of Ciano appointed ambassador to Vatican.

FEB. 6, Saturday 1,253rd day
Russian Front.—Lisichansk and Barvenkovo in Ukraine, Bataisk, S. of Rostov, and Yeisk on Sea of Azov occupied by Russians.
Australasia.—In air engagements over Wau, New Guinea, 41 Jap aircraft were destroyed or damaged.
U.S.A.—U.S. aircraft raided Kiska, Aleutians.

FEB. 7, Sunday 1,254th day
Air.—Heaviest raid yet on U-boat base of Lorient.
Libya.—Eighth Army in contact with enemy W. of Pisida, on Tunisian frontier.
Mediterranean.—Large-scale daylight

raids on Naples and Cagliari, Sardinia ; night raids on other airfields in Sardinia.
Russian Front.—Soviet troops captured German base of Kursk, Kramatorskaya in the Ukraine and Azov, at mouth of Don.
Burma.—R.A.F. Liberators made heavy attack on Rangoon.
General.—Mr. Churchill arrived back in London.

FEB. 8, Monday 1,255th day
Mediterranean.—Heavy daylight raid on Messina ; Palermo bombed by night.
Russian Front.—Korocha, N.E. of Byelgorod, occupied by Soviet troops.
Australasia.—Dutch and Australian bombers raided Dobo in Aru Is.

FEB. 9, Tuesday 1,256th day
Mediterranean.—U.S. bombers attacked aerodromes in Crete.
Russian Front.—Byelgorod, N. of Kharkov, captured by Soviet troops.

FEB. 10, Wednesday 1,257th day.
Sea.—Admiralty announced loss of submarine P 48.
North Africa.—Eighth Army in contact with enemy E. of Ben Gardane in Tunisia.
Mediterranean.—Allied air attacks on Palermo and railways in Sicily.

Russian Front.—Volchansk and Chuguyev in Ukraine captured by Red Army.
Australasia.—U.S. commander on Guadalcanal announced that the island was free of Japanese organized forces.
General.—Paris radio announced that Lorient and Brest were to be evacuated.

FEB. 11, Thursday 1,258th day
Air.—R.A.F. made heavy night raid on Wilhelmshaven ; arsenal blown up.
Russian Front.—Lozovaya rly. junction, S. of Kharkov, captured by Russians.
Australasia.—Japs continued to withdraw in Wau area of New Guinea.
General.—French warships, including battleship Richelieu, arrived in U.S. ports for refitting.
Announced that Gen. Alexander to be deputy C.-in-C. to Gen. Eisenhower in N. Africa.

FEB. 12, Friday 1,259th day
Russian Front.—Krasnodar in the Kuban, Shakhty, N. of Rostov, and Krasnoarmeisk and Voroshilovsk in the Ukraine captured by Soviet troops.
Burma.—U.S. bombers again attacked Myitnge railway bridge and also raided Rangoon.

FEB. 13, Saturday 1,260th day
Air.—Docks at Boulogne and St. Malo

and iron works at Ymuiden, Holland, attacked by day ; two night raids on Lorient.
North Africa.—Rommel's rearguard withdrawing towards Ben Gardane in S. Tunisia.
Mediterranean. — U.S. Liberators bombed Naples harbour by day ; aerodromes in Crete raided by night.
Russian Front.—Soviet troops captured Zolochev, on rly. between Kharkov and Briansk, Novocherkassk, N.E. of Rostov, and Likhaya, N. of Rostov.
Australasia.—U.S. aircraft attacked Jap shipping in Shortland Is. area of Solomons.
U.S.A. — Liberator and Mitchell bombers raided Kiska, Aleutians.

FEB. 14, Sunday 1,261st day
Air.—Mosquitoes attacked railway workshops at Tours ; heavy night raids on Cologne, Milan and Spezia.
North Africa.—In S. Tunisia Germans launched attack from Faid and Sened on U.S. positions round Gafsa and Sbeitla.
Russian Front.—Russians announced capture of Rostov and Voroshilovgrad.

FEB. 15, Monday 1,262nd day
Air.—U.S. aircraft bombed docks at Dunkirk.
North Africa.—Eighth Army occupied Ben Gardane in S. Tunisia ; Axis troops entered Gafsa, evacuated by Americans.
Mediterranean.—U.S. bombers again raided Naples.
Burma.—R.A.F. long-range bombers raided Heho airfield.
Australasia.—Allied aircraft attacked Rabaul, Amboina, Kolombangara, Munda, and Dilli, Portuguese Timor.

FEB. 16, Tuesday 1,263rd day
Sea.—Admiralty announced loss of trawler Stronsay.
Air.—U.S. bombers made day raid on U-boat base at St. Nazaire. R.A.F. bombed Lorient at night, while intruder fighters patrolled over German territory.
North Africa.—In S. Tunisia heavy fighting continued between Americans and Germans round Sbeitla.
Mediterranean.—Fortress bombers raided Palermo harbour by day ; heavy bombers attacked Heraklion, Crete, at night.
Russian Front.—Kharkov captured by Red Army after fierce street fighting.
Home Front.—House of Commons began to discuss Beveridge Report on social security.

★════ Flash-backs ════★

1940
February 13. Russians captured advanced positions of Finnish Mannerheim Line.
February 16. H.M.S. Cossack rescued British from Nazi prison-ship Altmark, in Norwegian fjord.

1941
February 6. Benghazi surrendered (1st time) to Australians and British under Gen. Wavell.
February 7. French forces from Chad captured Kufra.
February 10. British paratroops captured in Southern Italy.

1942
February 9. Japanese landed on N.W. coast of Singapore Island.
In Burma, Japanese crossed Salween River.
Japanese landed at Gasmata, New Britain.
February 12. Scharnhorst, Gneisenau and Prinz Eugen dashed from Brest through Straits of Dover to German ports.
February 15. Singapore fell to Japanese.
Large-scale Japanese landing in Sumatra, Dutch East Indies.

Editor's Postscript

WHY is it that when the great mass of the public, of every class and profession, creed, politics and economic circumstance, are working as never before to contribute all in their power to the national war effort, why is it that we should find apparently increasing evidence of the existence in our midst of persons who can be described by no other word than saboteur? I am not referring only to the "black marketeers"—those who never let an opportunity go by of turning a dishonest penny or of getting more than their fair share of a limited supply. Rather I have in mind those destructive maniacs who when nobody is looking damage and destroy public property, and those petty pilferers who seem to think that the railway companies (to take one of their particular victims) are fair game for the exercise of their thievish propensities.

WHEN the Nazis bombed south-east London the other day—it was the raid in which 39 little children and several of their devoted teachers perished—there was an immediate outcry because the public shelters in some districts were found to be shut. In fact, as Mr. Ernest Brown, Minister of Health, made clear in the House of Commons, keys were available at the nearest Wardens' posts, so that it was unlikely that there was any dangerous delay in opening the shelters. But *why* were they shut? Because of the difficulties arising from a "small but very active body of saboteurs." It is general knowledge that not in one or two places, but in many, the public shelters have been raided by thieves and deliberately damaged. Thousands of electric light bulbs have been stolen or broken, seats have been smashed, telephone and lighting wires wrenched away, locks forced, doors splintered; and the shelters have been used for other purposes that need not be described. In the light of such facts, who could blame the authorities for keeping these little buildings, designed and constructed solely for the public's own safety, under lock and key?

PILFERING on the railways has assumed proportions which would be almost incredible if the allegations were not supported by official statistics. I am informed that during 1942 on the trains—workmen's for the most part, but not by any means entirely—of the London, Midland and Scottish railway, 40,000 electric light bulbs were smashed, 8,600 windows broken, 10,000 electric light shades removed, 19,000 window and door straps removed or mutilated, 65 parcel racks damaged, and 100 ventilating frames broken. Prior to their withdrawal from the train-lavatories there was a tremendous loss of towels by all the railway companies, as I mentioned on the authority of a railway director two years ago. These figures constitute a simply appalling reflection on the morals—I use the word in its proper and not in its merely sexual sense—of the travelling public, which would seem to be much the same as the hooligan-minded public that abuses the A.R.P. shelters. One is inclined to ask where are the fruits of the tree of Popular Education that has been nurtured at such great expense for the past seventy years?

OF the many periodicals now issued in London by or with the help of Allied Governments, the latest to appear is The Norseman, published at 2s. 6d. every two months by Lindsay Drummond, Ltd. The first number lies before me, and it makes interesting and instructive reading. Most of the articles are, of course, by Norwegians or have a Norwegian subject. Mr. Nygaardsvold, who has been Prime Minister of Norway since 1935, opens with a contribution on Cultural Continuity; the famous Norwegian novelist Sigrid Undset describes some of her adventures during the first days of the war in Norway in April 1940; and Arne Ording writes on Norway and International Co-operation. Other contributors include the distinguished Soviet journalist, Ilya Ehrenburg; President Benes gives us some of his thoughts on the Peace, and Harold Nicolson a study of Winston Churchill. Then Dr. Wilhelm Keilhau, an Oslo professor, makes a plea for the adoption of English as the official language for the Commonwealth of Free Nations which we hope will be established after the War. If such an alliance is to be workable, he argues, it must possess a common language for the quick, practical and businesslike conduct of its affairs, and he favours English because of its tradition as the world's oldest democratic language.

RECENTLY the survivors of the Suffragette movement met in London to celebrate the silver jubilee of the Royal Assent to the first measure of women's suffrage—the 1918 Act which enfranchised women of 30 and over. (Votes for women on practically the same terms as men came ten years later.) So short a time ago; and it was seriously argued by men—and by women—in all parties and of every class, that because women were the "weaker sex" they were unfit to be entrusted with the Parliamentary franchise. It took a world war to give women the vote, as Lady Astor emphasized at the celebration at Friends' House. Because women showed what they could do at the munition benches, on bus platforms, and in many other jobs which hitherto had been male preserves, they were given the right to put a cross on a ballot paper. What shall they be given after this war, in which many of them have actually entered the firing-line? They have deserved much; and, no doubt, much will be given unto them. But I think Lady Astor is right when she says that it would take an earthquake to give women equal chances with the party machines, a tornado to put them on the Bishops' Bench, and a land-mine to blow them into the House of Lords!

SUCH is the way of things in Britain; but in Germany, as a Berlin radio commentator, one Hans Schwartz von Berg, put it the other night, "We don't talk about war and politics to German women if it can be avoided." But it cannot be avoided any longer, Herr Hans went on, "we are all in danger." So he had some quite nasty, harsh things to say to Frau and Fräulein. Apparently some German women are doing their best to dodge the call-up. The total mobilization recently decreed by Hitler (he said) "was certainly not meant to send some young lady looking for her long-forgotten sketching-pad and then to march to take an academy course, on the pretence that this is an important or at least sensible activity. Neither were the decrees imposed to remind hundreds of young girls that moulding busts or making vases or pretty figures for dear auntie's birthday is an interesting profession. Nor does it mean registering hastily for a course of gymnastics in the hope of being sent in six months' time to dance beautifully before the German troops in Paris, or rushing to take up the job of secretary to a good friend who has never had one before. Nor because five years ago you took a few lessons in Japanese will you now be given three years to perfect your knowledge with a view to becoming an interpreter."

MANY a German woman used the vote which the Weimar constitution gave her to put Adolf into power. He promised them, each one of them, a husband and a home; he ordered them out of industry, since that was no place for a woman. Gretchen and Maria used to scoff at the poor British and American women who had to go out to work. They don't scoff now. "Women in Germany are back where they were when Hitler asked them for power," said Rebecca West in a recent broadcast, "only far worse. Hitler cheated women, if only because he said: 'Every woman will have a husband for herself,' and did not add, 'but he will probably be a dead one.'"

FAMOUS FIGHTERS OF THE R·A·F

GROUP-CAPT. A. G. MALAN, D.S.O. and Bar, D.F.C. and Bar, who has destroyed 32 enemy aircraft in addition to many probables. A South African, he played a leading part in the Battle of Britain, and commanded one of London's Spitfire squadrons in 1941.
Drawn by Capt. Cuthbert Orde: Crown Copyright reserved

Printed in England and published every alternate Friday by the Proprietors, THE AMALGAMATED PRESS, LTD., The Fleetway House, Farringdon Street, London, E.C.4. Registered for transmission by Canadian Magazine Post. Sole Agents for Australia and New Zealand: Messrs. Gordon & Gotch, Ltd.; and for South Africa: Central News Agency, Ltd.—March 5, 1943. S.S. *Editorial Address:* JOHN CARPENTER HOUSE, WHITEFRIARS, LONDON, E.C.4.

Vol 6 # The War Illustrated № 150

Edited by Sir John Hammerton

SIXPENCE

MARCH 19, 1943

H.M.S. ILLUSTRIOUS, one of Britain's most famous aircraft-carriers, has taken a leading part in many thrilling actions, notably at Taranto in 1940. In 1941 she beat off nearly 100 enemy planes which attacked her in the Sicilian Channel (see Vol. 4, p. 108). This photograph shows Capt. R. L. B. Cuncliffe, R.N., taking the salute during Sunday divisions on the flight deck. In the centre is the lift trap through which aircraft are hoisted from their hangars.

Photo, British Official; Crown Copyright

NO. 151 WILL BE PUBLISHED FRIDAY, **APRIL 2**

THE BATTLE FRONTS

by Maj.-Gen. Sir Charles Gwynn, K.C.B., D.S.O.

THE period under review (the second half of February) was marked by fluctuations of fortune rather than by steady progress; and, writing on the last day of the month, it is impossible to assess positively the effect of gains and losses. In Russia the period opened with the brilliant capture of Kharkov, and it was followed by the renewal of the advance from Lozovaya towards Dnepropetrovsk. These successes, coming on top of the great victories earlier in the month, tended to excite undue expectations of further rapid progress. When, therefore, towards the end of the month, German resistance stiffened and Moscow had no sensational advances to announce, some disappointment was felt—no doubt accentuated by Rommel's initial success in Tunisia.

Actually, the Russian situation, though in places somewhat obscure, seems at the time of writing as satisfactory as could be expected, making due allowance for unfavourable weather and for the difficulty of maintaining uniformly the impetus of a great offensive movement. The factors that must be considered are analysed in more detail below.

In Tunisia it cannot be denied that Rommel, taking advantage of his interior lines position, inflicted a heavy reverse on the Allies. Fortunately, he would seem again to have been lured by success into attempting more than his resources justified, and he has paid a heavy penalty for vaulting ambition. It remains to be seen, however, which side has gained most in the exchanges. Below I have given my reasons for believing that on the balance the advantage rests with the Allies, although it would certainly be premature to claim an outstanding success.

TUNISIA

Some readers may remember that in page 547 I suggested that Rommel, while delaying Montgomery's advance to the Mareth Line, might receive reinforcements which would enable him to make a characteristic counter-stroke against the Americans who were a menace to his rear. The delaying potentialities of the Mareth position and the mobility of Rommel's force seemed to offer opportunities for exploiting an interior lines situation. I did not expect, however, that he would attempt a major operation against the communications of the 1st Army and that his object would be limited to forcing the Americans back and depriving them of capacity to cooperate with Montgomery.

This view is confirmed by what Sertorius, the German radio spokesman, is reported, in The Daily Telegraph of February 27, to have said in speaking of Rommel's retreat; it reads, "with his successes, *which went far beyond his original estimates,* Marshal Rommel can be content. Any attempt to expand further would have required *far larger forces* than had been foreseen for these operations in the general plan for the defence of the Axis Tunisian bridgehead."

The American troops appear to have been holding a wide front in no great strength; and it is not surprising that their positions were penetrated by Rommel's formidable assault. Through lack of war experience, and also because of the necessity of protecting advanced air-fields, their defence may have been over-rigid and counter-attacks fell into traps. It was a difficult situation for untried troops, particularly as they came under concentrated air attack without having much air support or strong A.A. protection. The men evidently displayed great gallantry, and have acquired valuable experience, but at a heavy price, as has happened before now with British troops.

Having captured or destroyed much material and temporarily broken the cohesion of the Americans, Rommel had certainly achieved his primary object, even to the extent of depriving the Allies of important aerodromes. But he was tempted by the magnitude of his success to exploit it beyond the limitations of his resources. It was repetition of his attempt to reach Alexandria in his pursuit of the 8th Army, but this time possibly with less justification. For if he really tried to attack the main communications of the 1st Army, General Anderson had stronger reserves to meet him than Auchinleck had at Alexandria. Moreover, the 8th Army remained a menace to his defensive force on the Mareth position.

I can hardly believe that he hoped to do more than to disturb the dispositions of the 1st Army and to extend the area of destruction of its advanced depots. Nemesis was slow in overtaking him at El Alamein; this time it came quicker, but probably less decisively.

An American correspondent (Mr. William Stoneman, in The Daily Telegraph of Feb. 27) gives General Alexander the credit for the speed and vigour of the counter-stroke at Thala. He writes, "The position of our forces was at danger-point when General Alexander instilled 'attack' rather than 'retreat' spirit into them." Be that as it may, there was evidently for two days a dangerous situation with fierce fighting in which both sides had heavy losses. As I read the information that has come to hand, neither side succeeded in establishing a clear mastery; but Rommel, realizing that his weakened and tired force had no chance of achieving further success, decided on retreat—which apparently was carried out in good order, though it probably suffered considerable losses from vigorous air pursuit.

THE question of the moment is, How far will Rommel retreat? Personally I believe he will withdraw the bulk of his striking force right away, to reorganize and re-equip in readiness to deal with Montgomery's advance; and, trusting to having robbed the Americans for the time being of much of their offensive power, will leave only rearguards to hold them in check, probably on the line from which his offensive started.

Rommel has been roughly handled, but it may not take him long to make good his losses. Losses of personnel can probably be replaced quickly by air transport; but much depends on how far the Axis have been able to build up a reserve of tanks and motor vehicles. Captured vehicles might be used to make good temporary deficiencies. It would be a mistake, therefore, to assume from the speed of his withdrawal that Rommel has suffered a crushing defeat.

Meantime, Montgomery is evidently faced with a formidable task on the Mareth Line if the Italians (who are reported to form the bulk of its garrison) fight with the determination they are sometimes capable of displaying. Italian artillery has generally fought well, and the defences were constructed on an artillery framework. We can be sure, too, that Rommel has made liberal use of mines and wire.

I still believe that Rommel will use the Mareth Line essentially as a delaying position, and would be unwilling to risk decisive action with the Gabès defile in his rear on which his line of retreat would converge. If he risks decisive action at all it will be, I think, at the Gabès position, where a powerful armoured reserve might have exceptional opportunities of counter-attacking a force that broke through. Moreover, retreat to

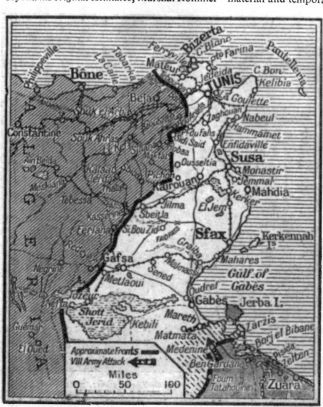

TUNISIAN WAR ZONE. Allied recapture of the Kasserine Pass by Feb. 23, 1943 frustrated enemy attempts to capture Tebessa. This map shows the Allied line at Feb. 26. The arrow marks a heavy drive against the Mareth defences by the 8th Army.

By courtesy of The Times

join Von Arnim in the north would be very much easier from Gabès than from the Mareth position; and that, it can hardly be doubted, is Rommel's ultimate intention.

The attacks which have been made on the 1st Army in the north do not seem to have been part of an original far-reaching plan, since they were not launched till Rommel's operation broke down. It is more probable that Von Arnim either intended to relieve pressure on Rommel or to take advantage of the situation to improve his own position.

RUSSIA
The capture of Kharkov on February 16, at the beginning of the period under review, especially as it involved the defeat of picked troops just arrived from Germany, made the situation of the Germans both in the Donetz basin and at Orel more than ever precarious. When it was followed by a renewal of the advance from the Lozovaya region towards the Dnieper bend, and a widening of this thrust towards Poltava, an outer ring of encirclement of the Donetz basin threatened to develop. Under these circumstances, and while snow conditions gave the Russians superior mobility, the Germans seem to have decided that retreat to the Dnieper was too dangerous to attempt. Material may have been evacuated by the one railway still open, but there have been no indications of a general retreat. There is a large army in the basin; with the contraction of the front it has probably built up considerable reserves, and with its many industrial towns the area it holds is highly defensible.

It seems therefore to be the Germans' intention to hold their ground in the Donetz basin, at Novorossisk and the Taman peninsula and at Orel, counter-attacking vigorously in order to check and exhaust the Russian attack, in the hopes that the spring thaw will finally bring it to a standstill. The fact that in the south thaw has this year begun exceptionally early has probably influenced German policy, and has accounted for some slowing down of Russian progress. The Russians are, however, maintaining pressure and are reported to have made preparations to continue to do so even in the height of the thaw

THE German bridgehead covering approaches to the Kerch Strait is growing smaller, and Novorossisk is isolated. At Orel, too, the ring is closing; and the railway to Briansk, the sole avenue of communications still open, is threatened. In the Donetz basin the struggle is at its height. German counter-attacks have been strong and fierce, directed chiefly towards the north-west against the flank of the Russian thrust which had penetrated to Krasnoarmeisk, cutting the main railway to the Dnieper and threatening to isolate the vital centre of Stalino completely. The situation is obscure. The Germans claim to have recaptured Krasnoarmeisk and some important towns on the railway to Poltava—claims probably to some extent true since they have not been specifically denied by the Russians. Meantime the Russian attack from Rostov and the east slowly advances.

The closely built-up industrial area of the Donetz gives both sides such exceptional

RUSSIAN FRONT. Great thrusts by the Red Army continued throughout February 1943, though enemy counter-attacks in the Donetz basin increased in violence towards the end of the month. This map shows the extent of Soviet advances between Feb. 16 and 27.   *By courtesy of The Times*

defensive opportunities that the battle which is raging is unlikely to produce a rapid decision; but it will make great demands on reserves of which Germany is short. If, in order to form an offensive reserve, the Germans intend to hold the shortest possible front, retreat from the Donetz sooner or later would be necessary. With the double purpose of preventing complete encirclement of the Donetz army, and of retaining the line of the Dnieper as a position to which it could withdraw, should more favourable conditions for retreat occur, the Germans are employing reserves brought from the west to counter-attack the Russian thrust towards Dnepropetrovsk. They have slowed down its progress, but have failed to remove the menace.

Will the Germans have sufficient reserves to withstand unrelenting pressure? Constant local counter-attacks are liable to lead to wasteful expenditure of fresh troops with only temporary results. It may be remembered that when they employed similar methods to hold the line of the lower Donetz the Russian advance was for a time checked, but eventually surged forward.

Meanwhile, the Russians have made marked progress north-west of Kharkov in the general direction of Kiev, and threaten to interrupt all direct communication between the German armies of the centre and south.

Russian offensives, about which little information has been given, are also, according to German accounts, developing on the Central and Northern fronts, where winter conditions still favour Russian tactics.

It is not surprising, under such continuous attacks that shortage of fighting reserves, and of man-power to maintain industrial production, is causing alarm, approaching to consternation, at Hitler's H.Q.

The Germans may still pin their hopes on being able to fight more effectively when summer hardens the ground, but I see no reason why the Russians should not in summer display the same new-found tactical and strategical skill that has been so marked this winter and to which their amazing successes must be largely attributed.

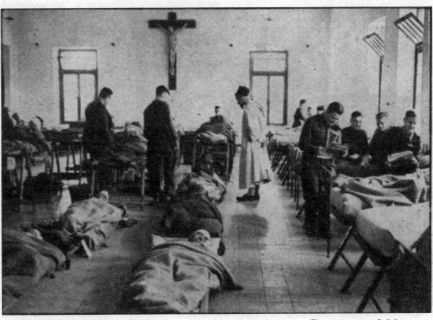

CASUALTY CLEARING STATION in a N. African battle area. There is one C.C.S. to a Division; the unit is completely mobile, carrying tentage for operating theatres and wards. Expert surgeons and medical staffs are employed, and 200 casualties can be treated at a time.
PAGE 611   *Photo, British Official: Crown Copyright*

Montgomery's Men Nearing the Mareth Line

8th ARMY'S ADVANCE INTO TUNISIA began on Jan. 29, 1943, when forward units crossed the border from Tripolitania. 1, R.A.F. and R.A.A.F. ground crews prepare a trackless stretch of desert for an airfield. 2, An airman walks a gangway plank from a waterlogged lorry at Allied Air H.Q. during the rainy season. 3, Lorries of the 51st (Highland) Division cross the frontier into Tunisia. 4, Gen. Montgomery, commander of the 8th Army, photographed with Gen. Leclerc in Tripoli. To reach the latter city Gen. Leclerc's Fighting French column trekked 2,800 miles from Chad Territory in the Sahara.

Photos, British Official : Crown Copyright

In North Africa the R.A.F. Has Its Commandos

AERODROMES CAPTURED IN THE N. AFRICAN FIGHTING are speedily put into operation by R.A.F. Servicing Commandos—men specially trained by Combined Operations Command to carry out dangerous tasks likely to be met with in the early stages of assault landing operations. 1, Servicing Commando airmen prepare a fighter to take the air. 2, Arrival by lorry of a fresh squad to support that already at work. 3, Unrolling tool-kits, with Sten guns handy. 4, Bisley light bomber, one of a squadron recently operating with the R.A.F. in N. Africa, lands at an advanced air-field.

Photos, British Official : Crown Copyright.

Tunisian Towns the Communiqués Have Mentioned

STRATEGIC POINTS OF SOUTHERN TUNISIA: 1, Medenine, occupied by the 8th Army on Feb. 20, 1943, is situated 40 miles N.W. of Ben Gardane, and forms a major outpost of the Mareth Line. 2, Native market at Gabès. This oasis port, situated just over 100 miles from the Tripolitanian border, has received shattering attacks from our bombers. 3, Gafsa, evacuated by American troops by Feb. 16, saw a fierce battle between our Allies and a force of some 130 German tanks. (See map, p. 626.)

Photos. Paul Popper, E.N.A.

Ancient Ruins the Background to Modern Battle

RECENT FIGHTING IN TUNISIA has raged around towns rich in Roman remains. 1, Street scene in the native quarter of Sfax, the port in the Gulf of Gabès which is the export centre of the world's largest phosphate region. 2, Ruins of the Byzantine Basilica at Tebessa—an important Allied base near the Algerian border, W. of the Kasserine Pass from which the Germans were pushed back in mid-February 1943. 3, Remains of Roman temples at Sbeitla—recaptured by U.S. troops on March 1.

Photos, Paul Popper, E.N.A.

AMERICA'S LARGEST SUBMARINE, the 2,710-ton Argonaut, was announced on Feb. 21, 1943 to have been lost when returning from patrol operations. Laid down in 1925 and completed in 1928, the Argonaut had a complement of 89 officers and men. Her armament comprised two 6-in. guns, four 21-in. tubes, and 60 mines. The submarine's engines were replaced in 1940-41, and at the same time the latest system of torpedo control was installed.

Photo, New York Times Photos

THE WAR AT SEA

by Francis E. McMurtrie

THERE has been a complete reorganization of naval commands in the Mediterranean as the result of Allied landings in French North Africa and the complete conquest of Libya by the Eighth Army.

Admiral of the Fleet Sir Andrew Cunningham, hitherto in command of Allied sea forces in the North African expedition, has now been appointed Commander-in-Chief in all that part of the Mediterranean coming within the scope of present operations against the enemy in Tunisia and Italy. This approximately corresponds to the Western basin of the Mediterranean and the Central area to a point beyond Malta.

Admiral Sir Henry Harwood, who relieved Sir Andrew Cunningham as C.-in-C., Mediterranean Fleet, when the latter went to Washington as Chief of the Admiralty Delegation last year, now becomes Commander-in-Chief, Levant and Red Sea, with headquarters at Alexandria.

Vice-Admiral Sir Stuart Bonham-Carter has relieved Vice-Admiral Sir Ralph Leatham as Flag Officer in charge at Malta. The latter has had a very strenuous time of it under Axis air attacks since he took up this post a year ago. For some months past he has been acting as Governor in the absence in this country of Viscount Gort.

Bonham-Carter is a name already well known in Malta. A kinsman of the new Flag Officer in charge, General Sir Charles Bonham-Carter, was Governor and C.-in-C. of the island from 1936 to 1940.

FRENCH WARSHIPS to Join the Allies' Battle-line

The French battleship Richelieu, of 35,000 tons, has arrived at the United States Navy Yard, New York, to have repaired the damage received at Dakar in July 1940. She was attacked first by a British motor-boat which blew off one of her propellers by dropping depth charges at the stern, and then by naval aircraft, which torpedoed her. She was thus immobilized until French West Africa threw in its lot with the Allies recently. Patched up sufficiently to cross the Atlantic under escort, she will now be completely refitted in order to take her place in the line against Axis battleships, should those elusive vessels ever elect to come out and fight. She should be a good match for one of the contemporary Italian battleships of the Littorio class, each being armed with eight 15-in. guns.

The cruiser Montcalm also made the passage from Dakar, proceeding to a Virginian yard for repair. Two destroyers have gone to another port. These, of course, are not by any means the only available French warships in African ports. There are besides the Richelieu's disabled sister ship, the Jean Bart, two or three more cruisers (one of them, the Primauguet, may be too badly damaged to be worth repair)—four destroyers and at least a dozen submarines—all of which can be most usefully employed as a reinforcement, the cruisers and destroyers in ocean patrol and escort duties, and the submarines in attacking Axis communications with Tunisia.

It is stated by Col. Knox, Secretary of the U.S. Navy Department, that negotiations are proceeding with Vice-Admiral Godfroi for the addition of the ships demilitarized at Alexandria. These comprise the old battleship Lorraine, four cruisers, three destroyers, and a submarine. Other ships that may be affected are the aircraft carrier Béarn and the cruisers Emile Bertin and Jeanne d'Arc, immobilized at Martinique and Guadeloupe, in the West Indies.

In a recent R.A.F. attack on the German naval base at Wilhelmshaven, the main explosive depot of the dockyard, containing ammunition for guns of various calibres, torpedo warheads, mines and depth charges, received a hit which destroyed 40 out of the 50 sheds in the depot, with an explosion which is described as " terrific." This is probably the most severe blow that has yet been dealt to Wilhelmshaven, one of the two principal naval bases in Germany. It is remarkable that this is the first time in several raids that such an important target has been found.

In the minelaying submarine Argonaut, of 2,710 tons displacement, reported overdue and presumed lost, the United States Navy has lost its largest under-water unit. The Argonaut has also been the biggest submarine in the world since the Surcouf, of 2,880 tons, manned by the Fighting French, was reported missing in April 1942.

Experience shows that very large submarines are seldom much of a success. The biggest British submarine ever built was the X 1 of 2,425 tons, which was scrapped some years ago after a comparatively short life, of which an undue proportion was spent in modifying and refitting the vessel. Our largest submarines today are the Severn and Clyde, of 1,850 tons ; the Porpoise and Rorqual, of 1,500 and 1,520 tons respectively ; and the numerous Thunderbolt class, of 1,090 tons.

So far as is known, none of the U-boats greatly exceed 1,000 tons, and the majority of those now at sea range from 500 to 750 tons. It is evident, therefore, that there is a limit to the useful size of the submarine as at present designed.

ALLIED VESSELS by the Hundred Cross the Atlantic in Safety

According to some figures recently supplied to the Press by Admiral of the Fleet Sir Andrew Cunningham, from the date of the first landings in North Africa on November 8 until the middle of February no fewer than 780 Allied ships, totalling 6,500,000 tons gross, arrived safely in Algerian and Moroccan ports. These included cargo ships from America which were under escort of the United States Navy, besides British convoys.

By no means such a cheering picture presents itself to our enemies, who have only succeeded in keeping their troops in Tunisia supplied at heavy cost. Week after week the Admiralty regularly reports lists of Axis supply vessels, ranging from big tankers and transports to schooners, which have been sunk or disabled by our submarines. In addition our light surface forces, including cruisers, destroyers, and motor torpedo-boats, and aircraft of the Royal Navy and the R.A.F., inflict quite a considerable amount of damage. No prudent underwriter would be eager to insure the ships which ply on this hazardous route.

Undoubtedly, the time will come when the Axis armies in Tunisia will find themselves forced to surrender or attempt an evacuation on Dunkirk lines. When that situation develops, it is very improbable that the Luftwaffe will be able to afford anything approaching an adequate " umbrella " to the evacuating ships. Nor is it probable that the Italians will be ready to volunteer to man small craft to fill the gap as our own amateur sailors did in May 1940.

France's Mighty Richelieu Arrives in New York

PAST NEW YORK'S SKYSCRAPERS glides the great French battleship Richelieu. She left Dakar in French W. Africa on Jan. 30, 1943 and arrived in America 12 days later, having been escorted in company with other French warships across the Atlantic by a number of U.S. destroyers. This 35,000-ton giant had been at Dakar since June 1940, when she was transferred there uncompleted from Brest. In this photo she has just passed under Brooklyn Bridge (see Vol. III, pages 33, 342).

Photo, Keystone

A British Trawler Met an Italian Submarine

H.M.S. LORD NUFFIELD, one of the Royal Navy's trawler fleet, has fought and destroyed an Italian submarine off the N. African coast (it was announced on Jan. 5, 1943). On sighting the enemy vessel—later identified as the Emo—the Italian fired depth charges, inflicting severe damage and so forcing the submarine to surface. A fierce duel ensued, during which the Emo's conning tower was hit; her crew then abandoned their rapidly sinking ship. They are shown (top) preparing to jump overboard. Below, survivors are swimming towards a rubber dinghy before being rescued by the Lord Nuffield. Only one man was wounded aboard the trawler as a result of this spirited action. The Emo had a surface displacement of 941 tons; her main armament was two 3·9 in. guns.

Photos, L.N.A.

American Troops Amid the Alaskan Snows

WITH THE U.S. FORCES IN THE FAR NORTH. 1, Supplies being unloaded at Skagway for dispatch by rail to the American troops. From this port a railway joins the Alaska-Canadian highway at Whitehorse in the Yukon (see page 332). 2, U.S. Marine stands guard at a naval operating base. 3, Wading through ice-blocked waters, members of a U.S. Navy ground crew guide a PBY patrol flying-boat to its base. 4, After the day's work these men listen-in to the latest war news.

Photos, Pictorial Press, Keystone

This Is the Red Army We Salute Today

"On this anniversary occasion," said Mr. Anthony Eden, Britain's Foreign Secretary, at a great "tribute to the Red Army" meeting at the Albert Hall, London, on Feb. 21, 1943, "we pay tribute to every department of the Red Army, to the High Command under the supreme direction of Mr. Stalin, to the generals in the field, to the junior officers, to the N.C.O.s and men for their stubborn endurance in adversity and the ardour with which they have swung over to the offensive."

WHEN the Red Army was born twenty-five years ago they were putting up the shutters in Russia. The Tsardom had fallen in bloody ruin, and it seemed certain that the Bolsheviks, too, would shortly fall in a ruin even bloodier. Yet as page after page of history has been turned, each has borne the record of some new enterprise by the people who, only a generation ago, were held to be amongst the most backward, the most dull-witted and stolid in their subjection. In Russia we have the spectacle of a hundred and ninety millions of the human race engaged in the greatest experiment of all time—nothing less than the achievement in a few decades of all that Britain and America and the western world as a whole have taken centuries to attain, even now are still attempting. In that great experiment the Red Army has played, and will continue to play, its part as its sure shield and buckler.

Originally the Red Army was formed out of detachments of workers and peasants (the original Red Guards), with some broken remnants of the Tsarist forces, who fought for

Another of the Russian soldier's outstanding characteristics is his intense patriotism. Patriotic motives (we learn from The Times correspondent) are probably more outspokenly expressed in the songs and literature of the Red Army than anywhere else in the world. Some of their rousing marching songs have the stirring quality of Hearts of Oak and John Brown's Body, and of all the British poets Rudyard Kipling has most readers in the Red Army. Very remarkable has been the growth of patriotic fervour during late years, a growth deliberately fostered by Mr. Stalin and his colleagues, but it is not patriotism of the "flag-wagging" variety. To quote another passage from the dispatch:

Rather has it been a discovery of all that is valuable and significant for the present time in Russia's heroic past; and the men who are fighting for the federation of Socialist republics have been made conscious that behind them, as they take their places in the trenches and gun emplacements, lie not only the great factories on the slopes of the Urals and wide cultivated plains in Siberia, Moscow with its still incomplete planning, a host of new cities beside the rivers

Stalin a few weeks ago—are young men in their thirties or early forties. Shaposhnikov is 60, Timoshenko 47, and Zhukov 46; but Chuykov, whose 62nd Army held Stalingrad, is 42, and Krylov, his chief-of-staff, two years younger. General Rodimtsev, whose guards played so fine a part in the Stalingrad battle, is 38—from a peasant's hut he joined as a private in 1927; while General Rokossovsky, in command of the army of the Don, is about the same age. General Golikov, whose troops stormed Voronezh and Kharkov, is 42; Gen. Malinovsky, who has twice recaptured Rostov, is 44; and Gen. Govoroy, whose most recent achievement has been the raising of the siege of Leningrad, is 46.

That the Russian commanding personnel was younger than in a number of other armies, in particular the British, was favourably commented upon by Field-Marshal Wavell as long ago as 1936.

SINCE the outbreak of war several highly significant changes have been made in the Red Army. In November 1941 infantry divisions which had particularly distinguished themselves in battle were renamed Guards, with special uniforms and double pay for rank-and-file and 50 per cent more for higher officers. Tank Guards were established in the following month, followed by Cavalry Guards and Air Force Guards. Epaulettes, once denounced as Tsarist foppery, are now permitted to the officers; and officers' rank is indicated by metal stars and braided stripes on the shoulder-straps instead of by discreet collar-tab identifications. Such terms as *offitzier* and *soldati* have returned into military parlance, replacing to some extent commander and Red Army man. Then the Revolutionary decorations, the Order of the Red Banner and the the Order of the Red Star, have been supplemented by new military orders for Red Army commanders who have distinguished themselves in the organization and direction of military operations and for success on the field of battle—orders named after heroes of the old eternal Russia, after Suvorov, Kutuzov (familiar to every reader of Tolstoy's War and Peace) and Alexander Nevsky, who captained the army of Novgorod against the Prussian Teutonic Knights in the great Russian victory of Lake Peipus in 1242. Among the first to receive the new Order of Suvorov were Marshal of Artillery Voronov and Marshal Zhukov. Here it may be mentioned that one-third of those decorated for valour during this present war have been neither Russians nor Ukrainians— but Mongols and Uzbeks, Georgians, Tartars, Armenians, Yakuts . . .

One more change must be noted: the conversion of the political commissars, reintroduced into military units a few weeks after the outbreak of war primarily as stiffeners of morale, into regularly commissioned Army officers. This does not mean that the political direction of the struggle is less important than before: on the contrary, the Red Army will be even more political, but there is no longer any necessity for a special corps of political watchdogs charged with the supervision of every officer to see that he keeps to the Party "line."

When Oliver Cromwell was raising his New Model army, the army which scattered the Cavaliers before them like chaff before the wind, he expressed a preference for "a plain, russet-coated captain that knows what he fights for and loves what he knows." The Red Army is filled with such, not only captains, but privates and generals too.

E. ROYSTON PIKE

RUSSIAN MILITARY LEADERS recently decorated at the Kremlin. Left to right: Lt.-Gen. Rokossovsky, Marshal Voronov, Lt.-Gen. Tolbukin (all of whom received the Order of Suvorov), and Lt.-Gen. Gromadin, who received the Order of Kutuzov. These are new decorations, named in honour of warriors famed in Russian history. *Photo, U.S.S.R. Official*

the Red Republic in Moscow and Petrograd in the autumn of 1917. By February 1918, when the Red Army, organized, directed and inspired by Leo Trotsky's demoniac energy, was formally constituted and halted the Kaiser's troops advancing on Leningrad, they numbered about 50,000; today they number— how many millions? Always they have been a highly disciplined force. So, too, was the Tsar's army; but there is one all-significant difference, that in the Russian armies of 1914-18 nine out of ten men were illiterate, while in those of 1943 nine out of ten have had at least a fair schooling.

As a portrait of the Red Army man of today we cannot surpass that drawn by The Times special correspondent in Moscow in a recent brilliant dispatch. The fighting-men of Britain and America, he writes, would not feel strangers beside him.

In company they would find the Russian soldier quieter, more reserved, more formal in his attitude towards his fellows than they are used to; and in intimacy more impulsive, articulate, and emotional. In moments of grief, anger, and triumph he is more exalted, but in the humdrum everyday experiences of life perhaps a little more patient. He smiles less, rarely laughs, but sighs more; cynicism is far from his nature; and his favourite songs, like the popular "Dug-out" and "Let's have a smoke," are wistful and tender, his thirst for education is unquenched by his experiences, and many go into battle with textbooks in their pockets; his taste is extraordinarily high . . . Their feeling for home is intense.

and on the forest edge of buoyant, aspiring, dogged workers and farmers of contemporary Russia, but also the cathedrals and the Kremlin and ancient tulip-domed churches; poets, musicians, and novelists, and those who fought for a land ordered by justice and reason, knowing no slavery—a Russia ever renewing herself by the fruitful talent of her much-enduring people.

That every soldier carries a field-marshal's baton in his knapsack was true of Napoleon's army in that at least some of his marshals rose from the lowest rank. But it is much more true of the Red Army. Trotsky had to find his leaders where he could find them, and in those early days of perpetual conflict many a man who had been a private in the Imperial Army was jumped to commissioned rank and rose high in the service. Marshal Zhukov, who, under Stalin, has been perhaps chiefly responsible for the recent victories over Germany's most experienced generals, served three years in the ranks under Tsar Nicholas and four as a subaltern under Trotsky. Marshal Timoshenko was another private in the Tsar's army; Marshal Budenny was a sergeant, and General Yeremenko, of Stalingrad fame, a corporal. Marshal Shaposhnikov was a colonel in the pre-Revolution army, but in 1917 retained his command by the vote of his men, and in 1918 was one of the first high-ranking Tsarist officers to join the Red Army staff. But most of the two thousand Russian generals— 450 new generals were commissioned by

Russian Cities Liberated by the Soviet Advance

THE RED FLAG FLIES AGAIN in many a Russian city from which the Nazi invaders have been hurled. 1, Joyful inhabitants of Krasnodar crowd round Maj.-Gen. Rosslov, commander of the Soviet force which freed them. 2, In Kharkov soldiers and citizens gather before the City Soviet building from which the Red Flag flies. 3, Russian A.A. gunners install themselves in Kharkov's Central Square, surrounded by the great semi-skyscraper blocks of buildings linked by covered bridges. 4, German troops, rounded up at Rostov, march off to internment. 5, Removing one of the many hated enemy signs in Byelgorod.

Photos, U.S.S.R. Official; Planet News

VIEWS & REVIEWS

by Hamilton Fyfe

I⊤ has long been a gibe against War Offices that they always prepare for the last war —some would say the last war but one —instead of getting ready for the next.

Certainly, if you look at the "defences" of our coast-line, you will be forced to conclude that those who put up miles of barbed wire and countless small blockhouses (as they were called in South Africa forty-two years ago) were thinking in terms of the Boer War of 1899 to 1902, and vainly imagining that what stopped irregular soldiers on the open veld would stop highly-trained German troops possessed of blasting machinery of immense power.

Again, the little concrete obstacles that were turned out by the million in 1940, when we began to realize that invasion was possible, were obviously ordered by generals who thought tanks were still in their last-war stage, and did not understand that invading forces would treat them as contemptuously as a charging rhinoceros might scorn a shower of public-house darts.

Gᴇɴᴇʀᴀʟ Sɪᴋᴏʀsᴋɪ, who is now both commander of the Polish army outside Poland and Prime Minister in the shadow Government which sits in London, is a soldier of unusual type. Perhaps I should say unusual among us. In European countries soldiering was taken seriously as a profession. The military art was studied by officers who wanted to rise high in the service, with the same assiduity that lawyers study law or those who aim at being famous doctors devote themselves to medicine or surgery. General Sikorski wrote a book some years before war came in 1939 to give warning that, when it did come, it would be " different from all past wars, not excluding the world conflict of 1914-18." This book, Modern Warfare (Hutchinson, 8s. 6d.), has been reprinted as it stood; and it says much for the General's foresight and quick-witted observation— what Mr. Churchill once called " intelligent anticipation of events even before they occur " —that the interest of what he wrote has not in the least diminished. Indeed, it is even more interesting, now that we can compare his forecast with what has actually happened, than it was in 1935, when to the majority of people most of his anticipations must have seemed rather far fetched.

I N one direction General Sikorski went wrong: he did not expect the seven months' "phoney war," as it was called, during which the opposing forces sat and looked at one another in France. He supposed the German lightning war (Blitzkrieg) would start at once. In Germany, he said, there were many experts in military affairs who maintained that the war would be a short one. He himself rather inclined to this view. To quote a passage:

It is certain that the technical means put at the disposal of the offensive by the progress of science have considerably increased since 1918. The speed of the transport of troops by motor-cars, the motorization of the units, the speed and power of the new tanks, the cooperation of the air force, the improvement of the radio—all these factors now favour the assailant to such an extent that a rapid attack would be much more redoubtable than it was in 1914.

Yᴇᴛ the rapid attack, which was made under much less favourable conditions in 1914, did not come in 1939. In war it is the unexpected that happens far more frequently than in most other human affairs. An outstanding example of this was the belief that the Maginot Line defending the frontier of France

would be impregnable. All General Sikorski says about this is that " the most solid fortifications do not constitute an absolute guarantee of security." That was proved also at Singapore. But Singapore might have held out if it had occurred to any of the various military and naval chiefs concerned in building that enormously important base that it might be attacked from the land. They anticipated sea attack only. A Maginot Line on the land side of the great naval base, one which would have been short and comparatively cheap to build, might have kept the Japanese at bay.

The use of air-borne troops, which I dealt with in my last article (see page 588), was foreshadowed by General Sikorski. He saw it would become possible " to transport to great distances small combative units destined for skirmishes or diversions in the rear of the

---

General Sikorski
on
Modern Warfare

---

enemy." This was done with all too terrible success at Rotterdam. He also suggested that " in order to transport a battalion of infantry (500-600 men) entirely equipped for battle, with provisions sufficient for a few days, some twenty aircraft of strong tonnage will be enough." The truth of that was proved in Crete two years ago to our discomfiture.

Wᴇʟʟɪɴɢᴛᴏɴ said once that the task of an army commander would be simple "if he knew what the enemy was doing on the other side of the hill." So it might have been in his day—if the enemy had not possessed the same advantage. Today both sides have it, through the use of reconnaissance aircraft ; but the difficulties of the army commander are as great as ever they were. General Sikorski rather overestimates the extent to

TEAR-GAS TEST in London : a newspaper-vendor carries on. General Sikorski, whose book is reviewed here, regards the use of gas by the enemy as still a possibility, even a probability.
　　　　　　　Photo, Sport & General

which secret movements would be made impossible by this means. General Montgomery was able to surprise the Germans at El Alamein last October ; the Russians have over and over again taken them unawares. The other day they caught a Nazi colonel in the act of shaving, and eight officers were unearthed from a dug-out drunk !

This Polish general does not write about war in the German manner—with relish and gleeful contemplation. He deplores the folly of it, the misery caused by it. But he is obliged to recognize that " from the time when men appear on earth and their history is recorded, war seems to have been one of the norms of their existence." He points out the only feasible method of stopping it—" the forming of a union of peaceful nations whose military preparation would be organized according to a common plan. Such a union would limit the military means of each member-country, and would be really capable of imposing peace by exercising an incontestable superiority only as a whole." This, he considered, in 1935, when he wrote, was not " politically mature."

It is worth recalling that Walter Page, United States Ambassador in London from 1913 to 1918, believed such a union could have been formed in 1913, when he declared his opinion that the only way to preserve peace was for all the peaceable nations to say to the Kaiser and his firebrands, " Stop it or we'll all make you ! " It could have been done. It was not done because, after the death, in 1924, of Woodrow Wilson, who shared Page's view, there was no statesman big enough to force the necessity for it on the attention of the world.

Wʜᴇᴛʜᴇʀ it will be done when peace next comes, no one can say. If it is not, then the plan General Sikorski sketches for anti-aircraft cities will probably have to be put in operation.

The buildings would be constructed entirely of reinforced concrete and erected in large blocks of flats, in order to diminish their surface and the efficiency of aero-chemical attack. Concrete terraces sufficiently resistant to the action of medium-calibre bombs would replace the present roofs ; underground gas-proof, watertight shelters would be under every building ; water, gas and electricity would be in armoured pipes.

Underground streets would serve as shelters during raids without interrupting traffic. The area covered by a city would be far larger than at present, with large open spaces, so that no closely-packed target would be offered to the bombers. The public buildings and services would not be centralized as they are now, but scattered. The important administrative centres, factories, and power-stations would be outside the city. Collective shelters would be planned, equipped with watertight doors, compressed-air apparatus and gas-masks, and in addition there would be private shelters in every house. But, in the General's opinion, "the only truly efficient defence against aero-chemical warfare would be the preventive action of the air force through operations which it might undertake against the enemy air force and its bases."

Tʜᴇ reference to chemical attack will have been noticed. General Sikorski was pretty confident that gas would be one of the principal weapons of this war. German professors have dwelt lovingly on the horrors of this method of attack, and predicted that it would shorten wars by terrifying the civilian populations. Well, as both sides would use it, the winners would be those who stood up to it most stoutly. For it is certain that, as the General says, victory " depends largely on the nerves of the nation, on its courage." We may have to brace ourselves for this ordeal yet.

Old Roads and New in Tunisia

Many an army has marched through the Tunisian valleys, but the roads and tracks that the Romans built, that the Arabs and the Turks and even the modern French have used—such a one, for instance, as is being negotiated by the dispatch-rider in our lower photograph—are altogether out of date in this age of mechanized transport. So the Royal Engineers have gone into action. New roads and bridges have been built, old roads made new (top right), even streams diverted (top left).

623

War in the Shadow of the Atlas

For the first time in history a British Army is fighting amid the Atlas Mountains of Tunisia, amid the hills covered with plantations of olive trees, the wheatfields and orchards, the vineyards, over the ploughed fields of rich red earth. Something of the landscape is suggested by these photographs recently taken in the 1st Army zone. 1, British paratroops just "come to earth"; 2, a patrol above a colonist's farm; 3, a distant glimpse of the German-occupied village of Mateur.

Photos, Cro

Where the 1st Army Are Engaged

Mud has been not the least of the hindrances to Gen. Anderson's progress in Tunisia, and the country shown in this photograph (4) of British infantry moving up under shell-fire to attack Bou Arada, would seem to make heavy going even in the sunshine. Over such a terrain mules have an advantage over trucks, and many are now included in the Allies' transport (5). But the road along which men of the R.A.F. Regiment are marching (6) looks first class—no doubt thanks to the R.E.s.

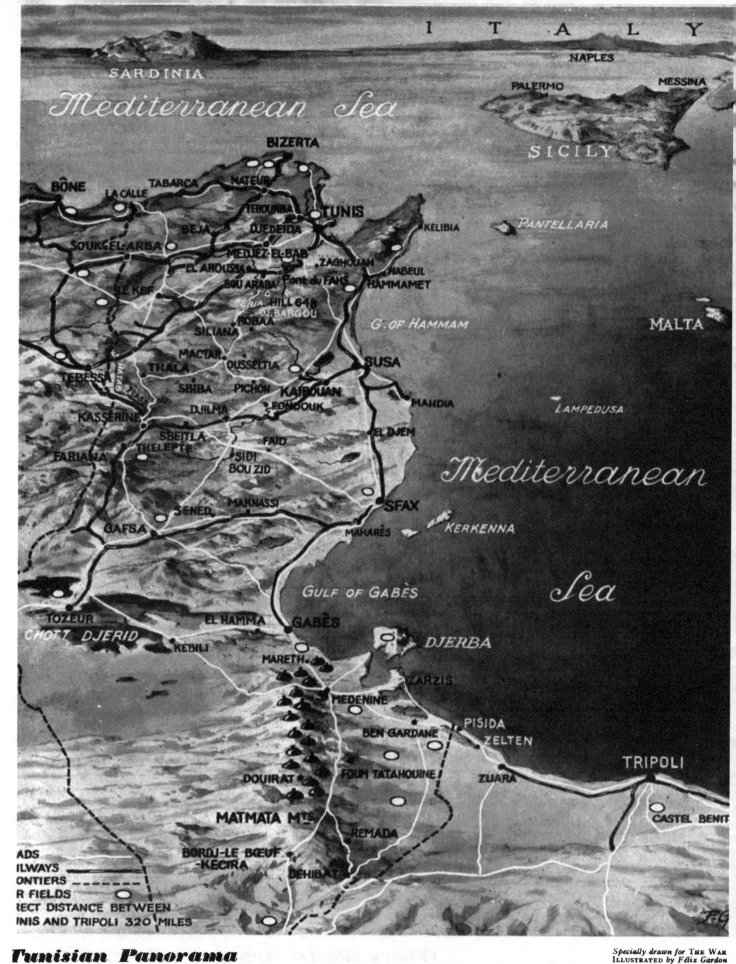

I T A L Y

NAPLES

SARDINIA

Mediterranean Sea

PALERMO
MESSINA

S I C I L Y

BIZERTA

BÔNE
TABARCA
LA CALLE
NATEUR
TEBOURBA
BEJA
DJEDEIDA
TUNIS
KELIBIA
PANTELLARIA
SOUK-EL-ARBA
MEDJEZ-EL-BAB
EL AROUSSA
ZAGHOUAN
NABEUL
LE KEF
BOU ARADA
Pont du FAHS
HAMMAMET
EBIBA HILL 648
DJ. BARGOU
G. OF HAMMAM
MALTA
ROBAA
SILIANA
MACTAR
OUSSELTIA
SUSA
THALA
TEBESSA
SBIBA
PICHON
KAIROUAN
MAHDIA
DJILMA
FONDOUK
KASSERINE
SHEITLA
FAID
EL DJEM
THELEPTE
SIDI
BOU ZID
Mediterranean
FARIANA
MAKNASSI
SENED
SFAX
GAFSA
MAHARÈS
KERKENNA
Sea
GULF OF GABÈS
TOZEUR
EL HAMMA
GABÈS
Sea
CHOTT DJERID
KEBILI
DJERBA
MARETH
ZARZIS
MEDENINE
PISIDA
ZELTEN
BEN GARDANE
TRIPOLI
DOUIRAT
FOUM TATAHOUINE
ZUARA
MATMATA MTS.
CASTEL BENIT
REMADA
ADS
ILWAYS
ONTIERS
BORDJ-LE BŒUF
-KECIRA
R FIELDS
DEHIBAT
RECT DISTANCE BETWEEN
NIS AND TRIPOLI 320 MILES

Tunisian Panorama

Specially drawn for THE WAR
ILLUSTRATED *by Félix Gardon*

Mountains cleft by narrow gorges, rolling hills and broad sweeping plains, salt lakes and palm-shaded oases, wadis that are now dry and now swept by tumultuous torrents, the whole enclosed between the Mediterranean and that other sea that is of the illimitable sands—this is Tunisia, now after many a long year the battlefield of warring powers.

What Sort of a Land Is This Tunisia?

When the Anglo-Americans first passed from Algeria into Tunisia we published an article on
the latter (see page 396) telling something of its history and its development under French rule.
The Tunisian campaign has been longer than was at first anticipated, and below we give some
further information concerning a country which is still a hotly contested battlefield.

Where the massive bulk of North Africa bulges out into the Mediterranean between Sardinia and Sicily is Tunisia. It is a land of rather less than 50,000 square miles, about the same size as Greece, about a quarter the size of France—a land of physical variety and abounding contrasts. For the most part it is rugged, but in the north it is definitely mountainous, since two spurs of the great Atlas range come down to the sea at Cape Blanc and Cape Bon. Towards the east and south the mountains gradually subside, merging first into a plateau, then into a low, sandy desert separated from the sea by a fringe of palm. The whole of the east coast, from Susa to Gabès, constitutes one big plain, Sahel it is called, low-lying and fertile.

In all this area, indeed in the whole of Tunisia, there is but one river, the Mejerda; for the rest, Tunisia is watered by mountain streams, torrents in the rainy season, but in the summer their beds are dried-up wadis. The Mejerda rises in Algeria and empties into the Gulf of Tunis. On either side of its broad, flat plain, covered with wheat-fields, groves of oranges and olives—the plain that has already seen so much hard fighting between Anderson's men and Von Arnim's, and will no doubt see very much more—are ranges of noble hills whose slopes are covered with vineyards, with forests of oak and cork. South of the Mejerda plain (writes Mr. E. A. Montague, The Manchester Guardian correspondent in Tunisia) it is Arab country. " Riding from farm to farm one may meet not only the ordinary Arab peasant, muffled in his robe striped with brown and dirty white, shuffling his bare feet in the mud, but grave, courteous men splendidly dressed, riding fine horses with embroidered saddle-cloths." Memorable things, Mr. Montague goes on, may happen to you in these hills.

" You may wake to see the tawny vineyards glowing brown and gold under the sunrise and the far northern hills clothed in all the colours of the opal, with a drift of mist drawn like a veil across their throats as the night's rain smokes upward from the plains. You may watch those same hills at sunset pass from red to royal purple and so into a deep glowing blue as the night closes around them. You may eat your lunch in a sunny upland glen beside a stream that was made for trout, and listen for a pastoral hour to a little Arab boy playing on his pipe as he watches his herd of sheep and goats."

A lovely and innocent land indeed, but to the south and east the scene changes. Here, to quote afresh from Mr. Montague's brilliant description : " You enter a country of savage hills and lonely plains ; or roads scarcely less primitive than the scattered Arabs whose squalid huts dot the waste ; an uncultivated land with no cover for the fighting-man except the solitary wild olive or deeply cut watercourse, or the occasional clump of cactus. This is no-man's-land and looks it ; and this is the country of the armoured car and motorized infantryman. They have their scattered headquarters in lonely villages, and at night they send out their patrols to range far and wide perhaps for days. Sometimes the dive-bombers sweep down on them, and then perhaps there is another burnt-out car to make a landmark beside the road, for cover is hard to find at need."

Separating Central Tunisia from the very different south is an almost uninterrupted

chain of salt lakes or *shotts*, swampy depressions from sixty to ninety feet below the level of the sea. This is a grim and gloomy region enough, and it would be even more depressing if it were not for the oases, palm-encircled pools of fresh water which are to be found here and there in the wilderness of mud and salt. To the west and to the south, to the east, too, the rippled dunes of the vast Sahara roll endlessly to the horizon. Here there are no villages, no settlements ; the only inhabitants are nomad Touaregs, wandering with their herds of camels and goats in search of pasture.

It is in this dreary, desolate region that the *Ligne Mareth* has its being. To call it a line is perhaps a misnomer. It would seem to be far less of a line than the famous Maginot, on whose pattern it is supposed to have been modelled. A line suggests a continuous zone of fortifications, a series of forts with never a gap between. But the Mareth Line is (it would seem) a complex of more or less isolated outposts, whose fields of fire, however,

MARETH LINE. With the occupation by the 8th Army of Medenine on Feb. 20, 1943 our troops were within a few miles of the Matmata Hills (seen in the background of this photograph), which constitute the western flank of the Mareth Line. Very different is this country from the flat sandy wastes of the Western Desert ; one slip on the rocky ground may cause a landslide, and tracks winding along dried-up river-beds and hugging the sides of mountain slopes put a severe test on drivers. *Photo, Fox*

are designed to overlap. Not being a well-defined line its actual location is difficult to define ; and in any case the French have not told everybody its secrets. It is generally stated to have its commencement at Zarzis, on the coast some 70 miles south-east of Gabès, and it runs in a south-westerly direction for some 60 miles to the Matmata Hills (up to 2,000 feet in places with many precipice-sided gorges) in the vicinity of the little township of Foum Tathouine.

With its left flank leaning on the sea and its right far out in a mountainous, waterless, and almost trackless desert, the Line possesses enormous natural strength ; and the French military engineers have done their best to supplement Nature by building their forts in reinforced concrete or cut out of the desert rock. Everywhere there are cleverly sited gun-emplacements, anti-tank pits, machine-gun posts, hundreds of miles of barbed wire, quantities of mines. The soldiers' quarters are underground for the most part, and they are reported to have tapped subterranean reservoirs of fresh water.

It was in 1938 that the French, made nervous by the shouts of " Nice, Corsica, Tunis ! " of the deputies in the Italian parliament, set about the construction of the Mareth Line ; at least Tunisia should be safe from an Italian invasion from Tripolitania. In the early months of this war, before the disasters of 1940, the Mareth Line was reported to be in a state of fighting efficiency, but after the armistice it was demilitarized. At least, the Nazis ordered that it should be demilitarized ; how far the Armistice Commission were able to enforce their terms is not known. Of late months there is reason to believe that the Line has been considerably strengthened by native labour working under *German* supervision.

Behind and in front of the Zarzis-Foum Tathouine line are other military posts and other systems of defence. Even a second line is spoken of, from Gabès to the shotts or salt lakes lying some fifteen to fifty (according to the season) miles to the west.

Mareth, after which the line is named, is an oasis, about twenty miles south of Gabès ; it is not even a village, but just a clump of palms beside a pool, with an estaminet, a store, and some shacks. Gabès is described as the base of the *Ligne Mareth* ; it, too, is an oasis, but one far larger—large enough to contain a fair-sized town, on whose outskirts are the military cantonments. It is the terminus, too, of the railway from Tunis via Susa and Sfax, and from it an extension is being built to Medenine—a bleak and dusty place composed of an Arab town and a French quarter, situated at an important desert cross-road (see illus. p. 614).

In the Matmata Hills lying to the west numbers of Berber tribesfolk live in pits or caves hollowed out of the easily worked rock. They are amongst the most miserable, the most poverty-stricken, the most squalid and diseased of Tunisia's peoples.

What are the reactions, one wonders, of these benighted barbarians to the soldiers garrisoned in the forts near by—to the sights and sounds of modern battle now being fought in the dusty plain beneath ?

UNDER THE SWASTIKA

The Balkan Powder-Barrel Awaits the Spark

For generations the Balkan countries have constituted one of Europe's chief storm-centres, and they are living up to their reputation. As Dr. EDGAR STERN-RUBARTH demonstrates below, they are either already in revolt or just waiting their moment.

IN the first documents betraying the Nazi plan of world conquest—Alfred Rosenberg's secret map of 1934 and his book The Myth of the 20th Century—Austria, Czechoslovakia and Hungary (with Holland, Belgium, Denmark, Switzerland, Alsace-Lorraine, Scandinavia, Finland, the Baltic States and the Ukraine) are shown as parts of one great German Reich; while the Balkans are also included as a " Protectorate." Albania and Greece, presumably preserved for Italy, are excluded.

Hitler's initial triumphs were due to his Fifth Column, propaganda, and bribery. Nowhere were the conditions more favourable for these preliminary activities than in the Balkans, an area slightly larger than France, yet split up into half-a-dozen national units, marked by ancient and furious antagonisms in race, language, religion, and economic interests; by unsettled frontiers mostly of recent date; and by a comparatively low state of education and technique.

THE FUEHRER had to fear but one element of resistance: the bond of Panslavism, uniting most of these units and linking them up with his Enemy No. 1, Russia. The realization of that potential danger, mitigated by Hungary's and, in part, Rumania's particular ethnical composition, may have affected his time-table in that he decided to subjugate the Balkans before he turned to attack Russia. But now that Hitler has suffered crushing reverses in Russia, that same danger crops up in the shape of unquenchable revolt in every one of the puppet-ruled or enslaved Balkan countries, of revenge for the brutal Nazi methods, mass-murder, pillaging, deportation and enslavement. By these methods the Nazis have succeeded in wiping out an old German, or at least Germanic, predominance and influence in all the countries concerned. Where a clever exploitation of the prevailing German language, Germany's buying power for agricultural products, and of the natural trend of all Balkan high-roads towards Europe's points-of-junction in Germany, might have led most Balkan peoples into the fold of a friendly and neighbourly Germany, whatever her regime (the Balkans themselves had mostly half-dictatorial ones still), the ruthless treatment meted out to the Balkan peoples by the Nazis has opened their eyes once and for all.

It hardly needed the refuge offered to their exiled governments, the help granted to them by Britain and her Allies, to make even the most backward peasant in the Balkans realize the everlasting threat to the very existence of smaller nations, and to make him turn towards new ideals—and also to fight for them, with all the undaunted spirit of old fighting races, rebels in turn against Turkish or Hapsburg rule, with more than a memory of the old law of the blood feud, and with every facility for guerilla warfare. That fight, ever since Hitler swept through the Balkans in 1940, has immobilized between 25 and 35 Axis divisions badly needed elsewhere; and now, when invasion of the Continent is menacing a weakened Nazi horde, it corrodes its armour from within. Post-haste, fortifications are being improvised all along the Greek coast of the Aegean, centring around Salonika, and on the isles surrounding the Peninsula, from Corfu in the west to Crete, the Dodecanese, Lemnos, Mytilene and Imbros in the east. Paratroops are kept in a state of readiness; protecting air forces, badly needed in the Western Mediterranean and on the English Channel, are held on the Greek islands, and the puppets—Bulgaria in particular, since she has stood out against being involved in the war with Russia—are pressed by all possible means into helping with the defence of the Balkan shores. Yet all the while a new menace develops: with the counter-offensive of the Russian armies, supported by their Black Sea Fleet, Rumania's and Bulgaria's coastline is being exposed; and

THE GREATER GERMAN REICH as envisaged in 1934 by Alfred Rosenberg, chief framer of Nazi political mythology. This is the map referred to in the accompanying text; it indicates the scope of the ambitions of the Nazis in Europe soon after Hitler's rise to power.

Hitler's one source of petroleum, Rumania's oil wells near Ploesti, is threatened. With armaments and, if need be, Allied forces guaranteed to Turkey (wooed in vain for years by Hitler and his sly envoy Von Papen), with the loss of Italy's North African bastions, the ring is closing.

IRRESPECTIVE of their separate ambitions and old rivalries, all the Balkan nations are now trying to escape the Axis net. They even make use of such rivalries to evade Hitler's demand for more troops, more workers: Rumanians and Hungarians respectively refer to their conflict over Transylvania, largely handed over to Hungary by his Vienna Award of 1940, in order to keep strong forces within their own borders. Hungary, openly defying Berlin, ordered all her workers who previously " volunteered " for Germany to report back at the beginning of this year, while dispatching her most ardent pro-Hitlerites, such as the Arrow Cross leader Imredy, to the fighting line in

Russia. Rumania did the same; imprisoning Iron Guards, her variety of Nazis, the fickle Conducator Antonescu ordered all Rumanians abroad—and most of them could only have been in Germany—to register for service at home by January 1, 1943. Bulgaria, where a sly and greedy king and a dictatorial government agreed readily enough to compromise with Hitler and take what temporary benefits could be reaped, mostly at the expense of her neighbours Yugoslavia and Greece, has proved even less inclined to shed her blood for Hitler's dream-empire, whether in Russia or in Turkey.

Methods of intimidation have failed just as completely as had previously bribery and cajolery. Old Admiral Horthy, under mysterious circumstances, lost his son and his son-in-law with Hitler's Air Forces; Antonescu, temporarily eclipsed by his so-called nephew, Mihail, lives under a permanent threat of being deposed, imprisoned, even killed by yet more docile elements; King Boris wriggles in the pincers of his Nazi-bribed Home Secretary Gabrovsky and his eighty-two-year-old father, Nazi-pensioned ex-Tsar Ferdinand.

None of them, however, can run much farther against their peoples' wills. With all their old rivalries, they are all equally striving to get away from Hitler and Mussolini, the smaller puppets—Croatia, Slovakia, Albania—not excluded. They find hardly a difference between their own treatment and that of their overwhelmed neighbours, Yugoslavia and Greece; and they are inspired by these neighbours' irrepressible resistance.

SOMETHING unheard of in the history of the Balkans has already resulted: Bulgarians and Rumanians, Hungarians and even Austrians, often enough in company or battalion formation under their own officers, have joined the ranks of the Yugoslav and Greek guerillas. Compared with that and its potential consequences, it is of minor importance that these Free Corps are somewhat disunited themselves, carrying regional and linguistic differences of former days into their present adventurous life and pledging their loyalty either to the Serbian General Mihailovich, or to the mysterious Croat "Tito," or to either of the Greek local captains, Katsokas or Hakaioi. The daring and the influence of these partisans turn the life of all Balkan quislings into a very hell. The Yugoslav Neditch, distrusted by his Nazi masters; the Greek Tsolakoglu, recently replaced by Field-Marshal List's ambitious niece and her husband, Logothetopulos; the Croat Pavelitch—hardly one of them who would not be glad to exchange his doubtful glory for a less transient, but secure, obscurity.

The Balkans used to be called a powder-barrel. More than ever before the description applies today when any spark of the war drawing nearer to the Peninsula might ignite it. But there is a new trend among the many races previously fighting none but one another—the feeling of a common brotherhood such as exists already among the ragged, half-starved warriors sweeping down from wooded mountains on Italian and German forces twenty times their numbers. The first tentative steps towards a Balkan Union, such as the Yugoslav-Greek federation agreed upon by the Governments-in-exile in London, may lead towards a better, a more united shape of Europe's south-east. And it may be that Hitler, willy-nilly, will have done something to forge that unity, to rekindle the Olympic fire from where, once, the flame of our civilization was lighted.

Brave Men of the Army: Some Recent Awards

Sgt. W. H. KIBBY (left), posthumously awarded the V.C. for displaying the utmost bravery on 3 separate occasions in New Guinea last Oct. He silenced enemy posts with hand grenades, and mended platoon-line communications, enabling mortar-fire to be directed against attacks on his Company's front. In wiping out a pocket of resistance behind enemy lines, he was killed by machine-gun fire as success seemed certain.

Pte. BRUCE KINGSBURY (right) of the Australian Army, posthumously awarded the V.C. During fighting in New Guinea last Aug. he cleared a path for his comrades by charging alone, Bren gun firing from the hip, through a network of Jap machine-gun posts. Coming through this ordeal unscathed, he swept Japanese positions with his fire, but was shot by an enemy sniper.

Capt. Rev. C. W. K. POTTS, of the Buffs, awarded the M.C. for displaying outstanding bravery and devotion to duty at El Alamein in the Western Desert last year. He showed fine qualities as a fighting officer. Originally an Army chaplin, he resigned to join up in the ranks, but he was soon commissioned again.

Lt.-Col. SMITH DORRIEN, of the Buffs, receiving the D.S.O. from Gen. Montgomery during the latter's visit to regiments of an Armoured Brigade in a forward position of the 8th Army. Many another officer and man was decorated at the same time for his share in the defeat of the Afrika Korps.

Sgt. E. J. GRAY, M.M., Royal Artillery, awarded the D.C.M. for saving his whole troop from a dangerous situation in Libya, by capturing 200 Italians in an enemy-held post. As he returned with his prisoners he was wounded. In the captured enemy post were found 3 anti-tank guns, 3 heavy machine-guns and many small arms.

Lt. C. G. ROB, R.A.M.C.; awarded the M.C. After a flight of 350 miles, he performed 140 surgical operations in Tunisia. He and his surgical team were under fire most of the time. Rob followed our parachutists dropped to capture an airfield during November last year.

Maj. R. G. LODER-SYMONDS, R.H.A., awarded the D.S.O. and Bar, also the M.C.—all three being won in Libya. The M.C. was gazetted in 1941, the D.S.O. in Feb. 1942, and the Bar came 6 months later. He displayed great courage at Tobruk in Nov. 1941.

Col. FROST, M.C., awarded the D.S.O. for courageously leading his paratroops under heavy fire in Tunisia and reaching his objective. Although surrounded he extricated a large part of his unit, and regained his lines after a trek of 50 miles. He won the M.C. at Bruneval in Feb. 1942.

Photos, British Official; Crown Copyright; Sheffield Newspapers, News Chronicle, Planet News, Central Press

THE WAR IN THE AIR

by Capt. Norman Macmillan, M.C., A.F.C.

On Sunday, February 14, 1943 German forces in Tunisia began a strong drive with armoured forces and lorry-borne infantry against the central front held by American troops who were thinned out lightly over the area.

The German air force in Tunisia had been strengthened by air units previously based in Tripolitania, and Luftwaffe strength was concentrated in support of the German ground thrust. A large proportion of the Luftwaffe's estimated first-line strength of 300 aircraft in Tunisia was thrown into the battle, and for a time the Germans had local air superiority.

On the first day about sixty dive-bomber sorties were made against the American forces by Junkers 87 Stukas, and about an equal number of fighter-bomber sorties were made by Messerschmitt 109 and Focke-Wulf 190 aircraft. (About 40 Stukas were employed.) On the second and subsequent days of the

American side was confined to fighter offensive patrols against the enemy.

Coincidentally with the German attack, modifications in the Allied Commands which had been decided at the Casablanca Conference between President Roosevelt and Mr. Churchill came into effect. Air Chief Marshal Sir Arthur Tedder arrived in North Africa by air from England on February 14, 1943 to take up his appointment as Commander-in-Chief of the Allied Air Forces in the Mediterranean ; accompanying him was Air Vice-Marshal Sir Arthur Coningham, who is to be responsible for operations in the field under General Carl Spaatz, U.S.A.A.F., who is responsible to A.C.M. Tedder for the direction of operations in North-West Africa.

The air forces attached to the British 1st and 8th Armies, the American Army, and those based in Malta, all came under Tedder's immediate command, and were swiftly con-

craft ; the first-line aircraft, originally organized in five divisions of 500 aircraft, have been reorganized into four divisions. The disposition of these divisions is given as : one in Manchuria, one in Burma-Indo-China-Siam-Malaya, half a division in China, and the remainder in New Guinea, Formosa, and Japan. The Japanese naval air strength is estimated at 2,600 first-line and 1,700 reserve aircraft. The total losses in the Japanese air forces during 1942 were estimated at 3,600 first-line and 3,500 reserve aircraft. Another estimate of Japanese air losses in all theatres of war gives the figure of 2,435 aircraft, between February 15, 1942 (the date of the fall of Singapore) and January 31, 1943.

Japanese output of warplanes is estimated in Chungking at about 2,400 a year. These figures indicate that the direct bombing of Japan proposed by President Roosevelt would have a rapid effect upon the front-line air power of Japan. The depletion of Japanese air power by the bombing of factories, in addition to the losses incurred in the field, would have a great effect upon the United Nations speed of attack, for it has been demonstrated in every theatre of war that air superiority enables strong defences to be broken down more swiftly and this permits ground and sea actions to be made at a faster pace.

LUFTWAFFE Losses in Russia Assume Gigantic Total

Air action on the Russian front continues in support of the opposing armies. The Luftwaffe is reported to be making considerable use of towed gliders for transporting supplies to the forward German troops, and it is thought that the serious losses in transport aircraft incurred by the Germans during the assault and defence of Stalingrad (and in the Mediterranean theatre of war) have caused a shortage of troop-transports. Gliders can be more quickly built, they are much less costly in labour man-hours, and they require no petrol, engine, or airscrew. In addition, their crews can be trained in a shorter time. Their extended use by the German army commanders indicates a compulsory economy due to pressure upon the German military machine from all directions. It is a sign that the all-round squeeze, by decimation on the fighting fronts, blockade by sea, and the bombing of Germany, is showing the trend of its ultimate and inevitable effect. Russia estimates that Germany has lost 4,000 aircraft in Russia since the summer of 1942. Meanwhile, Soviet bombers are bombing German lines of communication, breaking up the ice in the Kerch Straits, and combating the Luftwaffe in the air.

The day and night offensive against Germany is growing from United Kingdom bases, and it is probable that the early summer will see it rise to a new level of intensity. Fighter Command and Army Co-operation Command are taking an increasing part in the offensive.

VENTURA OVER HOLLAND. On Feb. 13, 1943 a force of Bostons and Venturas attacked the important iron and steel works at Ijmuiden during the day without loss to themselves. The target is shown in the bottom left-hand corner of this photograph.

Photo, British Official : Crown Copyright

attack the Germans laid more emphasis on the fighter-bomber attacks ; from this it is reasonable to infer that there were fewer stationary targets after the first day, for the dive-bomber, a highly-specialized type of aircraft, is relatively at its best against fixed or slow-moving objectives.

In the face of superiority in the air and superior forces on the ground the Americans were forced back. Gafsa was evacuated by February 16, and next day the aerodrome at Sbeitla and two other forward aerodromes at Thelepte (near Feriana) were overrun by German troops, after the Americans had destroyed or removed all the petrol stores and withdrawn to the rear all aircraft but those damaged beyond repair.

For a time it was not possible for the British armies and the Imperial and American air forces working with them to reach the area of fighting, and the Germans, continuing to advance, reached and captured the Kasserine Pass on February 20. Bad weather during this period of operations interfered with air activity which, on the Anglo-

centrated upon the fighting area in Tunisia. All types of bomber were employed—fighter-bombers, medium bombers, and heavy types (Liberator and Fortress)—to pulverize the concentration of German troops in and around the Kasserine Pass, their lorries, tanks, guns, and lines of communication. From a position close to the Algerian town of Tebessa and the border town of Thala the enemy were driven back and thrust southward through the three-mile-wide valley of the Kasserine Pass on February 25 after a six days' engagement, during which Allied air cooperation rose to a scale not witnessed in Africa since the battle of El Alamein. The course of this action is the first proof that superiority in the air will be the deciding factor in Tunisia : whichever side loses that superiority will suffer reverses ; to expel the enemy entirely from North Africa will demand a considerable concentration of United Nations' air strength.

Present Japanese army air strength is estimated by Chungking at about 2,000 first-line aircraft with about 1,300 reserve air-

Bomber Command attacked by day railway workshops and sheds at Tours (Feb. 14-15) ; targets in North-West Germany (Feb. 18) ; Den Helder docks (Feb. 19) ; Rennes rail yards and naval stores (Feb. 26) ; Dunkirk docks (Feb. 26 and 27) ; on these raids they lost three aircraft. Night attacks were made against Cologne, Milan, Spezia (Feb. 14-15) ; Belgium and West Germany (Feb. 15-16) ; Lorient (Feb. 16-17) ; Wilhelmshaven (Feb. 18-19, 19-20, 24-25) ; Bremen (Feb. 21-22) ; Nuremberg and W. Germany and minelaying (Feb. 25-26) ; Cologne (Feb. 26-27); N.W. Germany and minelaying (Feb. 27-28) ; on these raids 54 aircraft were lost. No aircraft were lost in the Bremen and last Wilhelmshaven raids; the last-named was made by a Canadian Bomber Group. Bombers of the U.S. Army 8th Air Force attacked Wilhelmshaven by day on Feb. 26, losing seven aircraft. Next day they attacked Brest without loss, but three covering fighters were lost.

Are the F.A.A. Planes Really Obsolescent?

FLEET AIR ARM planes have been criticized on the score of "obsolescence"; Mr. A. V. Alexander, First Lord of the Admiralty, recently said the work of their pilots, "with the old, slow, though pretty sound craft they have had, has been beyond reproach." Here are some of the machines with which the F.A.A. has already fought so magnificently. 1, An Albacore goes up in the lift from its hangar to the flight deck. 2, Martlet fighter about to land aboard the 23,000-ton Victorious. 3, Martlets stowed in the vast hangar below deck. 4, A Seafire fighter warms up. 5, Martlet taking off preparatory to a patrol flight. (See also illus. p. 609.)

Photos, British Official: Crown Copyright

From India Wavell's Men Move into Burma

WHY WE ARE INVADING ARAKAN

THE military operations in the Burmese maritime province of Arakan are the prelude to large-scale offensives to reconquer Burma, the key to the Orient. Since it occupies a highly strategic position in the Far East, Burma's reconquest is essential to the United Nations before any general counter-offensive can be launched against the Japanese on the Asiatic mainland. With Burma once again under the control of the Allied Powers, Japanese hold on the neighbouring countries would become precarious, the famous Burma Road would be reopened, and the Chinese would be free to complete the Burma-Yunnan railway, under construction at the time of the Japanese invasion of Burma last year. From Burma, combined American, British, and Chinese forces would be able to launch offensives against Siam and French Indo-China by way of the Kawkareik Pass and down southern Burma into Malaya.

Thus, as a preliminary to full-scale military operations to retake Burma, Field-Marshal Wavell has launched an attack against the Japanese in occupation of the Burmese coastal province of Arakan, which forms the eastern arm of the Bay of Bengal. Japanese forces in Arakan, with its strategic harbours and air bases, which are less than two flying hours away from Calcutta and the industrial centres of Bengal, where 70 per cent of India's war industries are to be found, constitute a threat to India, much more so than their presence in Northern Burma and the Chindwin Valley.

WAVELL'S immediate objective is Akyab, an important Japanese base situated at the mouth of the Kaladan River and only 65 miles to the south-south-west of Maungdaw, the Burmese frontier town, now in British hands. Several thrusts are being developed towards Akyab from Maungdaw and Buthidaung near the coast and on the Mayu River. But the main drive on Akyab is bound to be directed along the coastal track, supported by light naval forces from the sea, owing to the difficult nature of the country in Arakan, with ranges of forest-clad hills running north and south and sending out spurs and subspurs almost to the sea coast. The Arakan coastal strip is also intersected by a labyrinth of tidal creeks, and as a result has a highly developed system of inland waterways, which is the chief means of communication in this Burmese maritime province.

Seventy-five miles south-south-east by boat from Akyab is Kyaukpyu, situated on Ramree Island. Here the large expanse of water between Ramree Island and the mainland affords an excellent harbour, over 3 miles wide and 30 miles

STRAFING JAP AIRFIELDS IN BURMA, our bombers have recently scored many successes against the enemy. This photo was taken as bombs burst across runway intersections on an airfield at Pakokku. Two hits have been obtained on aircraft shelters. Black patches indicate cloud shadows.

long, large enough to take the entire Japanese fleet. It would be surprising, indeed, if Kyaukpyu harbour and the deep, narrow, salt water tidal creeks in the mainland opposite, which are ideal for submarines, are not being used by the Japanese as a naval base.

Occupation of Arakan, with its strategic air and naval bases at Akyab and Kyaukpyu, would not only remove the threat of a Japanese invasion of India; it would also serve as a jumping-off ground for an attack on the heart of Burma and her capital of Rangoon. Though Arakan is isolated by the Yoma mountains from the rest of the country, there are two mountain passes, the An and the Taungup, which lead into the interior of Burma. A 100-mile-long motor road, one which has been greatly improved by the Japanese, runs through Taungup Pass, 2,800 feet above sea level, from Padaung on the River Irrawaddy to the near coastal town of Taungup. From these geographical details the importance of the present operations in Burma can be appreciated.

OUR BURMESE OFFENSIVE demands formidable fighting qualities from British troops. Left, men of an English North Country regiment wade through a jungle stream during a reconnaissance patrol. The map of the Arakan Province in N. Burma shows main strategic centres. Heavy raids have been directed against the port of Akyab. Right, aircraft of a Blenheim bomber squadron, with escorting Hurricanes in the background, on their way to attack enemy targets.

Photos, British Official: Crown Copyright; Indian Official

Victory March of Malta's Unbeatable Defenders

'THE FINEST IN THE WORLD' was how Malta's C.-in-C. and Governor, Field-Marshal Lord Gort (recently on a visit to this country), described British infantry in Malta. This photo shows Brigadier K. P. Smith, O.B.E., standing in front of his camouflaged car, taking the salute as a long column of British troops in Malta marches past.

Photo, Associated Press

How an Invading Army 'Pays Its Way'

Not the least of the signs of the most careful preparation of the North African expedition was the printing of a special supply of Bank of England notes for the use of the "invaders" in their dealings with the local administrations and the native inhabitants. This and other aspects of the military use of money are given in this article by J. M. MICHAELSON.

BRITISH soldiers in the First Army in North Africa are now being paid in francs, the currency of the country, but during their first weeks in Africa they used special notes printed in England to prevent the Germans " unloading " Bank of England notes which they have kept for just such an occasion. Some of these notes in German hands have been captured, others looted from banks in occupied countries, and others again, no doubt, confiscated from people interned. The introduction of new notes, completely different in appearance,

'OCCUPATION MONEY' was specially printed by the Bank of England ready for issue to our landing-forces in N. Africa on Nov. 8, 1942. Notes ranged in value from a shilling to a pound, and at the time of issue the current rate of exchange was four American dollars to the pound or 300 Algerian francs. This shilling note bears the autographs of a landing-party at Oran.

effectively prevented the Germans getting rid of their notes and also made currency forgery, at which they are past masters, difficult.

The notes carried ashore by the invading armies were of denominations from one pound down to one shilling, the £1 and 10s. notes being of the same size as those used in Britain and the 5s. and 1s. notes rather smaller. The notes are freely changeable at 300 Algerian francs to the £ or four American dollars to the £. A 1s. note received in this country shows the chief feature is the device of a lion on a crown, familiar on our shillings. It bears in large letters the words Issued by the British Military Authority, and has the fine workmanship associated with British paper money. These notes had to be engraved and printed in the greatest secrecy some time in advance : and it is a testimony to the integrity of those engaged in this highly specialized business that, although the money must have passed through many hands before it reached North Africa, there was not even a hint of a rumour about it.

AN army entering a foreign country requires considerable sums to pay its soldiers. The Germans in all their advances have solved the problem with a simplicity only equalled by their unscrupulousness. They simply fix an arbitrary rate of exchange for the mark, impose the death penalty on anyone refusing to exchange or sell at this rate, and then dump unlimited quantities of notes on the country. Since the only " backing " these notes have is that of the press on which they are printed, and currency regulations prevent them circulating back

to Germany, it is a small matter what rate of exchange is fixed, although, in fact, the rate has always been fantastic. This is, of course, pure looting and does not differ in principle from putting armed soldiers at the door of a shop and proceeding to remove its contents.

In most countries shopkeepers have naturally been reluctant to part with goods for these " occupation marks." Within 24 hours of occupation the order has gone out that shops must open and must sell. To the unfortunate shopkeepers of Belgium, France, Yugoslavia, Greece and other countries, the alternative has been to lose all their goods for marks or to lose them for nothing, with a beating into the bargain.

An American businessman wounded in an air raid during the Greek campaign and left behind in Athens, recently told of an experience which illustrated the German method. When he had recovered and secured permission to leave for the U.S.A., he decided to give his car to a Greek aid organization. But, realizing that it would simply be confiscated by the Germans, he decided to sell it to them and then give the Greeks the money. He visited the officer in Athens in charge of Army purchases and was astonished when his high price was accepted without the car even being looked at.

" I am afraid that we have not such a large sum in cash at the moment," the German officer said, " but if you will wait half an hour I will have it ready." The money duly arrived, and the American paid some formal compliment about efficiency, even when the banks were shut. " Banks ! " exclaimed the German. " We don't need banks. We have a printing press in the basement." In fact, the German mechanized invasion columns include mobile printing presses for running off notes !

The Japanese have been equally unscrupulous. In the East Indies the advancing army secured considerable sums by forcing every man, woman and child to have a pass and pay 250 guilders for it, and in Malay and Burma the Japanese tried to get confidence for their notes by making them appear British.

The United Nations will never use such methods, for quite apart from the complete dishonesty of them, they are liable to recoil on the perpetrator. Germany is sowing the seeds of an eventual currency chaos even more disastrous than that which overtook her after the First Great War. The books made of 100,000,000 mark notes sold for a few pence by enterprising hawkers in Berlin as " souvenirs " of 1922 should have been a warning. A currency which has no backing but bayonets is liable to collapse when the bayonets are blunted.

THE methods used by the Allies to provide sufficient currency as one country after another is occupied will probably vary. But it is likely that they will err, if anything, on the side of financial orthodoxy. The U.S. forces in North Africa are also using specially printed U.S. currency to thwart the Germans. The notes were printed by order of the U.S. Treasury and cannot be used in any other part of the world. In addition, American pilots and the first troops to land carried gold coins from Canada and French francs for the persuasion of any who might be sceptical of the " almighty dollar " !

British troops in the East African campaign had a comparatively easy task in producing currency acceptable to the Abyssinians. The only coin universally used in Abyssinia has long been the silver Maria Theresa dollar, bearing the arms of Austria and the date 1780. It contains full value of silver. For many years the British Mint used to make these coins for Abyssinia. It was these dollars that British officers of secret " Mission 101 " carried into the country. But it is interesting to note that at one time they ran out and had to borrow 6,000 silver dollars from the Patriot leader, Dejasmatch Nagash.

It is not widely known that the British Mint in normal times used to make an average of 20,000,000 coins a year for various foreign governments, and British specialist printers were given large contracts for notes. One of the largest was that for 1,000 million banknotes for China in 1939.

In the First Great War the British Army used all kinds of currency, generally that of the country in which they were fighting. But in the 1919 campaign in Russia they had to print special rouble notes because the Germans had been up to their tricks and had flooded the country with worthless notes, making the ordinary rouble valueless.

INCIDENTALLY, soldiers have a habit of keeping special money as a souvenir. Many of the British notes in North Africa seem to have been autographed by landing-parties and will probably never circulate. British soldiers in the South African War of 1899-1902 sometimes amused themselves by " improving " the portrait of Kruger on a shilling, adding a hat and a pipe.

The travels of the British Army have given us some of our money slang. The "tanner," according to one account, comes from India, where the troops found the tanga, a rough equivalent of sixpence. The ticky got its name in South Africa from the fact that native labourers were given a threepenny-piece in exchange for their wage tickets. The guinea was first coined in 1663 by the Royal Company of Adventurers on the Guinea Coast of Africa. Soldiers fighting on the continent in the 14th century may have brought back the slang " bob " from the French coin *bobe*. And if we like to go back 2,000 years, Roman soldiers introduced the word money into our language.

To These Our Roving Camera Pays Tribute

LT. N. A. L. JEWELL (see pages 398, 486), captain of the British submarine which contributed to the success of the Allied N. African landings last November. In addition to valuable reconnaissance off the Algerian coast, he embarked General Giraud off the French shore, taking the French leader to the Mediterranean, where the General was transferred to a flying-boat.

DAME KATHERINE JONES, D.B.E., R.R.C., Matron-in-Chief of Queen Alexandra's Imperial Military Nursing Service, is the first nurse to be gazetted Brigadier in the British Army. Members of the Q.A.I.M.N.S. (and of the Territorial Army Nursing Service now merged into it) suffer all the hazards of war. Since 1941 its sisters have been accorded military rank as officers.

ADMIRAL AS SKIPPER'S MATE. A small vessel manned by a veteran crew of six has repeatedly carried out important coastal work. Former captain of the Renown, Sir Herbert Meade Featherstonhaugh serves as skipper's mate. Below, he is shown on the right; C. J. Burton, a dental surgeon (left), assists Capt. G. D. Begg, M.C., retired army officer, seen with broom, to "clean up the ship."

MRS. BEATRICE HARRISON drives an L.M.S. van in the London district, and gave up her job as a tailoress in order to devote herself to this war work. Every day she and her horse journey through London's streets, collecting goods for dispatch by the L.M.S. Mrs. Harrison gained experience during the last war as a railway van-driver.

ENGLAND'S OLDEST SWORD-MAKER, Mr. T. Beasley (centre), aged 82, has worked with the same firm for 56 years. He is at present busily engaged in making bayonets and Commando knives, an occupation to which he applied himself in the last war. The craft of sword-making has been handed down in his family for over 250 years. He is here shown engaged in testing a bayonet.

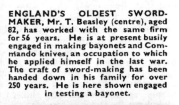

SIR STAFFORD CRIPPS, Minister of Aircraft Production, addresses workers at one of the Ministry's factories during a recent visit in the London district. Sir Stafford was appointed Minister of Aircraft Production in Nov. 1942, when he relinquished the Leadership of the House of Commons.

Photos, British Official: Crown Copyright; Topical Press, Central Press, Planet News, Daily Mirror

I WAS THERE! Eye Witness Stories of the War

I Had a Live Shell in My Leg—and Didn't Know It

One of the most extraordinary experiences of the War fell to the lot of H. J. Coates, of Islington. A 20-year-old Probationary Electrical Mechanic in the Royal Navy, he has written this story of his amazing escape from death specially for THE WAR ILLUSTRATED.

LIFE was placid enough at the training school in a South Coast town until that Monday morning when, having nothing in particular to do for a few minutes, I strolled along to the "local" and there met some of my pals. One of them had a telegram in his hand and joy written all over his face. The telegram announced that he had become a father—a fine bouncing boy. That called for congratulations and drinks, and we were about to celebrate when, above the buzz of talk, we heard the hum of a plane and the roar of A.A. gunfire.

Then came the shattering of glass and we flung ourselves flat to the deck, or rather the floor. There followed a short burst of what I took to be machine-gun fire and I felt a sudden sharp twitch in my right leg. Looking down, I was amazed to see a hole just above my knee. I thought I had been hit by a piece of flying glass or something, but I felt no pain—just the sudden twitch. I tried to get up, but my leg wouldn't work. I turned on my side to see if any of the boys had been hit : and there was my best pal, face downwards, with blood streaming from a big wound in the back of his head.

I let out one yell, and someone came along, lifted me on to a trolly and wheeled me to the sick bay. Others attended to my pal. In the sick bay, whilst they were dressing my leg and putting a splint on it, I asked what had happened to Andy, the proud father whose health we had been about to drink. They told me he had escaped without a scratch and that, fortunately, there were not many casualties. I still did not know what had happened to my leg, and no one told me.

The dressing completed, we—the casualties—were driven in an ambulance to the Royal County Hospital, Brighton. At the hospital they lost no time in getting to the bottom of my mystery. They took an X-ray photograph of my leg, and when they showed me the plate I got the shock of my life.

For I realized then that nothing so commonplace as a bit of flying glass had hit me. It wasn't even a bullet. It was an aero-cannon shell, about three inches long and three-quarters of an inch in diameter, buried deeply in the flesh. The officer in charge of a Bomb Disposal Unit, called in for consultation, identified it as of the armour-piercing variety

which explodes on impact ; there were suspicions that it might even be a sub-variety whose explosion is delayed. So I had been harbouring live ammunition in my leg for at least two hours ! I think the doctors were not a little astonished, too, but they made no fuss about it.

They wheeled me into the operating theatre and prepared me for the operation which would result in the safe removal of the shell, or—disaster. It was liable to explode at any moment. They told me afterwards that if it had exploded my leg would have been shattered and I might possibly have "gone West." The surgeon and his assistant, the anaesthetist and the nurses, all faced very considerable risk. At the least they might have been blinded. But they just ignored that and got on with the job. I've asked myself several times since if I would have had the pluck to do what they did.

I was under the anaesthetic, of course, and knew nothing of what was going on. They tell me the shell was lodged very tightly, near the knee joint, and that the surgeon had to do some cautious tugging to get it out. First he had to work down to the base of it, and then pull. It took him half an hour to complete the operation, described later by the Chairman of the hospital as " the most delicate and the most dangerous of his (the surgeon's) career." When at last the surgeon

Mr. H. J. Coates, [whose nerve-racking experience during a South Coast raid is told in this page. Skilful surgery and great fortitude brought him through his ordeal.

held the live shell in his hand it was passed over to the bomb disposal squad that had been standing by in readiness.

When I opened my eyes again I was in a big ward, in a nice warm bed, with a rather stiff right leg and a slight headache, but otherwise none the worse for the experience. My first thought was of my pal who had been wounded in the head. I asked how he was, and they told me he was very bad. Poor chap, he died in the hospital that night. I was the lucky one.

I Saw Our Shells Bounce off a German 'Tiger'

This " story in a nutshell "—an incident in the fighting between a British composite force of tanks guns and infantry, and Rommel's troops driving towards Thala—is told by Alan Humphreys, Reuters Special Correspondent on the Tunisian front.

WE held our positions on high ground north of the Kasserine Pass until dusk, when we were ordered to withdraw because the Germans were " winkling us out."

As we did so the enemy fired everything they had at us, including 105-millimetre guns. The shelling was very heavy and accurate. Later, undeterred by heavy rain, German tanks penetrated the pass and advanced towards Thala, some 40 miles to the north-west, headed by a number of " Tiger " tanks.

Though the moon was at full, rainclouds

had reduced visibility, adding to the difficulties of the anti-tank gunners. To ensure that he was not firing at our own tanks, the British battery commander went out ahead of our guns.

A tank approached along the road, but rattled to a stop at the British officer's command : " Halt ! " The officer then identified a German Mark VI (Tiger) tank. " Fire ! " he shouted to his battery, at the same time diving for a ditch. One man jumped from the Tiger tank and also dived into the ditch at the same moment as the British officer. Each went a different way

GERMAN 'TIGER' (MARK VI) TANK, referred to in this and the following page, is armed with an 88-mm. gun and two 7·92-mm. machine-guns. These photographs of one captured in Tunisia, show (left) the enemy practice of fixing old or spare tracks across the front of the tank to provide extra protection. Right, side view showing use of overlapping bogie wheels in suspension. The complete tank weighs over 55 tons.

Photos, British Official

however, the British officer dashing back towards his guns and the German racing to the tanks following up behind.

The battery, although only at 40 yards range, fired five rounds before the remainder of the crew of the Tiger tank jumped out.

One gunner, speaking of the action, told me : " The first shell from our six-pounder bounced off and went straight up in the air. I followed its flight, but I could not see the rest. I think several other shells also just bounced off the Tiger tank."

had got there before us. I did not answer and went back to the column, where an officer asked : " Who was it ? " I told him, and gave the order to keep going. We went on. We were challenged again, and still I did not answer.

Then machine-guns opened up and hit the middle of one company, who suffered about twenty-five casualties. The Germans began firing along the ditches, so the officer commanding the following company led his men down the middle of the road. All came through untouched.

We Were the American 'Lost Legion' in Tunisia

Surrounded by Nazi tanks in Southern Tunisia, a " lost " American battalion was led for more than nine miles through the enemy lines and back to its own base by Major Robert R. Moore, of Vallisca, Iowa, who told to Reuters Special Correspondent, Alan Humphreys, this story of how it was done.

W E were holding positions on the Djebel Lessouda—just north of Lessouda, about 25 miles east of Sbeitla—when the Germans threw more than 100 tanks round us in the dawn attack they launched on Sunday, February 7. We were well dug in, and for three days we stuck there. We beat off several attacks, did not suffer a single casualty, and captured some prisoners.

These included a German captain. " My comrades will soon come," he told me. " There is nothing for you to do except surrender." He is still a prisoner, and I should like to see his face now. By Tuesday evening we had eaten all our food. Ammunition was perilously short, when an American plane swooped over us and dropped a long yellow streamer. Inside was an order from the commander telling us to withdraw during the night to a point where protection and guides would be waiting.

The battalion moved out during the night and marched along a road. A sentry rose from a slit trench and challenged us at one place, but I did not answer. I just kept on, and he apparently assumed that such a large force so far behind the German front could only be Germans, and he got back

into his trench. I had given instructions to the leading troops not to fire in any circumstances for fear of prejudicing the chances of escape of those behind.

We reached the rendezvous and I was looking around when I was challenged. It was an unpleasant sound. The Germans

The next company had gone to the right and came past without even being fired at. Finally we caught up our protection and guides. I heard the familiar challenge, and asked " Are you American ? " The reply came back : " Are you that infantry outfit ? " I said " We are, and I'm glad to find you ! "

Hole No. 37 Was Her Address in Stalingrad

In a hole in the ground between two Armies lived one of the heroic women of Stalingrad - the washerwoman of No-man's-land. Her simple, tragic story is told by Paul Holt, War Correspondent of The Sunday Express, and reprinted here from that newspaper. For the story of the Battle of Stalingrad see page 590.

I REMEMBER it was just about the time I began to look at the ground as I walked along. When you are sick of a sight you look at the ground and that way it seems a quicker journey. A tired man does that. I was tired. Tired of looking at the savaged ruins of Stalingrad, tired of registering on the retina shock after shock of the power and terror and pity. The power of blast, the terror of the shapelessness of common things, the pity of scraps of household intimacies.

It was just about then that I noticed a stick standing upright in the rubble. It had a cardboard notice on it which said, very firmly and boldly, as if nothing had ever happened to Stalingrad, " Hole No. 37." You might imagine a postman trudging along as I was trudging, stopping and dropping in a letter at " Hole No. 37."

The road I was trudging was no road at all. It was a crooked, tortured track beaten out between shell craters and rusty iron sheets that might once have been tramped by the patient feet of an army under siege.

Tramping at night only, for this track lay between the Russian and German front lines, and led through a narrow No-man's-land between Stalingrad's great hill, the Mamai Kourgan, and the consumer goods building of the Red October factory, where Rodimtsev's Guardsmen fought the Battle of Garden Spades.

Just then a woman's head appeared beside the little stick that said " Hole No. 37." Behind her came two children, one a girl of three, all muffled up in a white woolly cap with flaps like a

Belgian rabbit's ears, another little girl, dark and solemn, about five. The woman went towards the washing that hung on the line, frozen stiff and flapping in the bitter breeze like three-ply boards in a gale. The little girls ran up towards a toy sledge.

We stopped and talked to the woman. She answered in monosyllables, and her voice had that tone that women put on when they talk of the imbecility of men. Yes, she had been there all the time. It was terrible. Yes, it was very difficult to live. Her husband was in the army. She had kept her children with her because there was no time to send them away.

But why did she stay ? Why did she live for five months in a hole in the ground between two armies, and why was it postmarked " Hole No. 37 " ? Her answer was very feminine. She was doing washing for the Red Army.

I said to the Red Army major who was our conducting officer : " This is Hole No. 37. How many such holes are there in Stalingrad ? " He shrugged his shoulders. There were many, he said. In that long walk to the Red October factory I did not see another.

The last Russian encyclopedia gave the population of Stalingrad as a quarter of a million. Since that date, with the growth of industrialization, the figure must have grown towards 400,000 by the time the Germans began to creep towards the Volga last summer.

H ow many are left ? There was, of course, in the early days before Stalingrad was " Rotterdammed " on August 23, 1942, evacuation. This was not an organized business of trainloads of people being taken to the rear. Those who wanted to go were ferried across the Volga, then set out to walk with their bundles, their children and their old folk, across the flat San Steppe, where only occasional mud-houses and little tin windmills of the artesian wells break the flat, brown expanse.

Many stayed—some to carry on working at the great factories, some because simply they did not wish to go. The workers joined home guard battalions and fought with the Red Army in the bad days of September and October.

Where have they gone ? In four days at Stalingrad, touring the city on foot and in ambulance lorries, I saw perhaps 50 people. I do not think there can be more than 500 people living there still. Those who do live have dug themselves into the sandstone

IN SOUTHERN TUNISIA, a U.S. " lost legion," fought against desperate odds in the Sbeitla region. Their experiences are recounted in this page. Here is the type of slit-trench, a "fox-hole," which formed part of their defences on the Djebel Lessouda.　　PAGE 637

WHILE THE BATTLE RAGED Russian women and children in the Stalingrad area, who had eluded German labour-camps, in many cases lived in damp, unlighted dug-outs and caves. As told in this and the previous page, living conditions were appalling, yet Stalingrad's heroic women battled on. This photograph shows a group of women and children calmly awaiting news during the fateful days of the great siege of the city.
Photo, Planet News

cliff along the Volga bank or into the deep sandstone ravines that run through the town.

There are three main ravines—Bath-house Gully, the Long Gully and Steep Gully. Looking down into these gullies, where some of the fiercest fighting of the whole battle took place, for they were royal routes for the Germans to the Volga, I saw a few clusters of cave homes with stoves smoking and washing hanging out.

The main impression I gained of those gullies is as if some bad-tempered giant had tipped up Father Christmas's sack, spilled

out all his dolls' houses, then stamped on them. When General Rokossovsky threw his ring around the German Sixth Army it stretched for 50 miles one way and 30 miles another. In that ring, so I learned from General Kotelkov, it was estimated that there were living 50,000 to 60,000 Russian civilians. Living in holes in the ground off food they had buried before the Germans came.

I asked another Russian officer what he calculated had become of those 60,000 Russian folk. He said : " We don't know yet how many have survived." And then he

said laconically : " At one place, just beyond Gumrak, when our men were driving forward, they came across a prison camp. It was just barbed wire and snow. In that camp they found 5,000 Red Army men and civilians dead from hunger and cold."

When the war is over this will be one of the crimes that will have to be answered by Hitler and his instrument, Field-Marshal Frederick von Paulus. And not the least of those either will have to answer will be the woman who stayed to do her washing in " Hole No. 37."

OUR DIARY OF THE WAR

FEB. 17, 1943, Wednesday 1,264th day
North Africa.—Feriana, Kasserine and Sbeitla in Central Tunisia occupied by forward Axis troops ; airfields at Sbeitla and Thelepte evacuated by U.S. forces.
Mediterranean. — Allied bombers raided airfields in Sardinia.
Russian Front.—In the Ukraine Soviet troops occupied Slavyansk.
Australasia.—U.S. aircraft attacked Munda and Kolombangara.
China.—Japanese landed in Kwang-chowwan, S. China, and attacked also in Hupeh, Kwangsi, Kwangtung and Kiangsu.

FEB. 18, Thursday 1,265th day
Air.—Mosquitoes raided Tours ; heavy night raid on Wilhelmshaven.
North Africa.—Troops of 8th Army occupied Foum Tatahouine in S. Tunisia and island of Djerba off the coast.
Russian Front.—Soviet troops captured Zalegoshch in Orel region.
Australasia.—Enemy aircraft flew over Sydney area.
U.S.A.—American warships shelled Japanese bases on Attu, Aleutians.
Home Front.—Labour amendment to Government statement on Beveridge Report defeated by 336 votes to 119.

FEB. 19, Friday 1,266th day
Air.—Den Helder docks attacked by day ; another heavy night raid on Wilhelmshaven.
Mediterranean. — Allied heavy bombers attacked airfields in Crete.
Russian Front.—Road and rly. from Kursk to Kharkov cleared of enemy.
Burma.—U.S. aircraft raided Lashio.
Australasia.—Fortresses and Catalinas raided Buin, Solomons.

FEB. 20, Saturday 1,267th day
North Africa. — Germans occupied Kasserine Pass in Central Tunisia. In the south, the Eighth Army occupied Medenine without opposition.
Mediterranean.—U.S. heavy bombers made daylight raid on Naples and Crotone ; Palermo harbour bombed by night.
Russian Front.—Soviet troops occupied Krasnograd and Pavlograd in the Ukraine.

FEB. 21, Sunday 1,268th day
Sea.—Admiralty announced loss of corvette Samphire. U.S. Navy Dept. announced that Argonaut, largest American submarine, was missing, presumed lost.
Air.—R.A.F. made heavy night attack on Bremen without loss.

North Africa.—Germans launched attacks through Kasserine Pass towards Thala, Tebessa and Sbiba.
Mediterranean.—Allied aircraft raided harbour of Melos, Greece.

FEB. 22, Monday 1,269th day
Sea.—U.S. Navy Dept. announced that 850 persons were missing from two U.S. liners torpedoed in N. Atlantic.
North Africa.—In Central Tunisia enemy launched another attack towards Tebessa, but were held by British and U.S. troops.
Burma.—British troops made raid from sea on Myebon, Arakan coast.
U.S.A.—American aircraft raided Jap positions at Kiska, Aleutians.

FEB. 23, Tuesday 1,270th day
North Africa.—U.S. and British troops forced enemy withdrawal in Kasserine area in Central Tunisia.
Russian Front.—Soviet troops occupied Sumi, W. of Kharkov, and Malo-Arkhangelsk, on Kursk-Orel railway.
India. — Enemy bombers attacked American air base in N.E. Assam.

FEB. 24, Wednesday 1,271st day
Air.—Wilhelmshaven again raided.
Russian Front.—Soviet troops continued to progress in N. Ukraine against heavier German resistance.
General.—Ribbentrop arrived in Rome on four-day visit.

FEB. 25, Thursday 1,272nd day
Air.—Nuremberg heavily bombed.
North Africa.—In Central Tunisia the Kasserine Pass was cleared of the enemy.
Mediterranean.—Liberators bombed Naples and Crotone.
India.—Japanese aircraft raiding aerodrome in Assam, lost 9 destroyed and 20 probably destroyed by U.S. fighters.
Australasia.—U.S. aircraft again bombed Rabaul and Kolombangara.

FEB. 26, Friday 1,273rd day
Sea.—Enemy tanker sighted in Bay of Biscay by Liberator of Coastal Command was sunk by H.M.S. Sussex. Admiralty announced loss of trawlers Bredon and Tervani.
Air.—U.S. Fortresses and Liberators raided Wilhelmshaven by day ; R.A.F. made three attacks on Dunkirk ; heavy night raid on Cologne.
North Africa.—In Northern Tunisia Axis attacked at many points along our front ; in the south, forward elements of the Eighth Army reached Mareth Line.
Mediterranean.—Docks at Cagliari, Sardinia, raided by Allied bombers.
Burma.—Enemy transports attacked and prisoners taken in small naval action off Arakan coast.

FEB. 27, Saturday 1,274th day
Air.—Dunkirk docks and airfield at Maupertuis, Cherbourg, raided by R.A.F., and Brest by U.S. aircraft in daylight.

North Africa.—U.S. troops occupied Kasserine in Central Tunisia ; in the north enemy attacks were held.
Mediterranean. — Allied fighter-bombers attacked Syracuse.
Russian Front.—Germans counter-attacking at Kramatorskaya and Krasnoar-meisk in the Donetz Basin.

FEB. 28, Sunday 1,275th day
Sea.—Admiralty announced loss of corvette Erica.
Air. — R.A.F. bombers again raided Maupertus airfield by day ; heavy night raid on St. Nazaire.
North Africa.—Enemy attack repulsed near Beja, in North Tunisia.
Mediterranean.—Flying Fortresses made daylight raid on Cagliari, Sardinia.
Russian Front.—Fierce battle round Kramatorskaya still in progress.

MARCH 1, Monday 1,276th day
Air.—Berlin had its biggest air attack of the war.
North Africa.—In Central Tunisia Sbeitla was re-occupied by Allied forces ; enemy attacks in the north died down.
Mediterranean.—Allied bombers raided Naples and made two attacks on Palermo.
Russian Front.—Announced that in new offensive Marshal Timoshenko had captured Demyansk and other places in Lake Ilmen region, on northern front.
Burma.—U.S. aircraft bombed Gokteik viaduct, on Mandalay-Lashio railway
Australasia.—Announced from Gen. MacArthur's H.Q. that air reconnaissance had revealed growing enemy strength in islands north of Australia.

MARCH 2, Tuesday 1,277th day
Air.—R.A.F. bombers raided targets in Western Germany.
North Africa.—New enemy attack developed in Sejenane area of Northern Tunisia. Allied aircraft bombed targets at Tunis and near Mareth.
Mediterranean. — Fighter - bombers from Malta attacked Lampedusa aerodrome.
Australasia.—Allied bombers began attack on Japanese convoy in Bismarck Sea off New Guinea ; four ships sunk or damaged. Jap fighters raiding aerodrome at Port Darwin were intercepted by Spitfires now operating in Australia.
General.—Italian Eighth Army returned home from the Russian front.

★ ══════ *Flash-backs* ══════ ★

1940
February 23. *Russians began heavy attack on Viipuri in Finland.*
February 25. *First squadron of Royal Canadian Air Force arrived in England.*

1941
March 1. *Bulgaria joined the Axis ; German troops marched into Sofia and Varna.*

1942
February 19. *First Jap raids on Port Darwin, Northern Australia.*

February 20. *Japanese invaded Bali, Dutch E. Indies, after sea and air battle.*
February 24. *In Burma Imperial forces withdrew across Sittang river.*
February 27. *Battle of Java Sea began ; Allies lost cruisers Exeter, Perth, Houston, Java and De Ruyter and six destroyers.*
February 28. *Combined Operations raid on Bruneval, Normandy.*
March 1. *Japanese landed at three points in Java, Dutch E. Indies.*

ONE of the first Nazi planes to cross the coast of Kent in the Battle of Britain in August 1940 dropped, not bombs, but a hundredweight of papers, copies of Hitler's Reichstag speech in which he made his " Last Appeal to Reason," urging Britain to cease hostilities. " I am not in the position of the vanquished begging pardons," he said, " but the victor speaking in the name of reason." That Nazi airman selected his target with a nice discrimination. The bale of papers fell on Barming Mental Hospital . . . For this delightful little incident I am indebted to a book written by a fellow scribe: Hell's Corner, 1940, by H. R. Pratt Boorman, Editor-Proprietor of the Kent Messenger (Kent Messenger, Maidstone, 7s. 6d.). Every Man of Kent and Kentish Man will be proud to read this first-hand, carefully documented, and excellently illustrated story of how the Garden of England became the Battlefield of Britain. Kent is fortunate in the possession of so able and painstaking an historian ; it is to be hoped that all the counties, all our battered cities and towns, will be so favoured. For this is the sort of history that matters, both to the men and women who have lived through these storm-flecked days and still more to the generations who are to come.

ON every page there is some hero's name, as often as not some heroine's. It does one good to read how the people, the ordinary people, of Kent stood up to the battle. Hundreds were killed or wounded ; nearly every town and village had its scars. But through it all "with patriotism and good humour they defied the enemy." Particularly notable are the tributes paid by Mr. Pratt Boorman to the transport workers, the railwaymen, the bus drivers, conductors and conductresses, many of whom were killed or injured. When Gillingham bus garage was heavily bombed a sailor did good work. He could not drive, but he got in a bus and started it up. Cannoning off one or two, he got the bus out ; but when he reached the road he could not stop. So he brought it to a standstill by running it into a telephone kiosk. Then he went back for another. After about fifty of the buses had been got out the unknown sailor disappeared into the night. Another of Mr. Pratt Boorman's vivid glimpses is of Coxswain Knight and his crew in the Ramsgate lifeboat crossing the Channel from Dunkirk, towing behind them wherries in which, in the course of forty hours' continuous service, they brought off about 2,800 men from that stricken beach. Coxswain Parker and the Margate crew in like manner brought off load after load, under continuous shelling, bombing, and aerial machine-gun fire. " An inspiration to us all as long as we live," was how the commander of a destroyer expressed it when he wrote his appreciation to the Lifeboat Institution.

HUNDREDS of planes crashed in Kent during those hectic weeks and thousands of bombs were dropped ; yet, taking it all in all, the casualties were by no means in proportion. Which reminds me of what a rural policeman told me the other day. In the area comprised by his " beat," a matter of some five or six miles square, containing ten or a dozen little villages, over 160 H.E. bombs have been dropped since the War began. Material damage was slight ; the only casualty 'one soldier home on leave who lost a leg !

So the old Cunard-White Star liner Majestic has been raised and brought inshore from the deep waters of the Firth of Forth in which she sank when she took fire some time ago. Already 13,000 tons of steel have been cut from her carcass, and at least another 25,000 tons will be salvaged. Many another sunken ship has been saved, the total. thus salvaged to date providing iron and steel sufficient (we are told) to build a dozen cruisers. One of the ships sunk off the west coast of Scotland had a cargo consisting in large measure of bottles of whisky. With a truly Scottish acumen, which I am quick to appreciate, the local crofters scented out the wreck before the salvage men could get there. The resulting atmosphere was highly

F/L. K. KUTTELWASCHER, D.F.C. and bar, intrepid Czech air-ace, whose exploits as a " night intruder " have achieved remarkable results over enemy territory. On July 30, 1942 he received the Czechoslovak War Cross for the fifth time.
Drawn by Eric Kennington, Crown Copyright reserved

convivial. But, talking of salvage, I could give directions how to reach a certain Sussex common where I saw some Bren carriers refuelling the other day, and passing later observed that they had kindly left nearly a score of empty two-gallon petrol tins which are still there—excepting only those that villagers may have put to better use as vessels for water carrying. I am told they are quite serviceable as pails when the top has been removed. But is this in accord with our ideas of salvage ? Should not our mechanized army be made to deposit its empties where they would be of use to the War effort, rather than turn rural commons into unsightly dumps of dirty tin cans ?

IN future, we are told, small cheque-books are to be the rule. A considerable saving in paper is anticipated, since many million cheques are made out in the course of a year. But the smaller cheque has at least one drawback in that the space for the payee's name is somewhat reduced. And how long some payees' names are ! In their nomenclature most of the banks have now attained to a sweet simplicity : we no longer have The London

Joint City and Midland, or the National Provincial and Union Bank of England. Some of the insurance companies, too, whose full titles tell of a history of amalgamation, have adopted shorter forms for the convenience of premium payers, although we still have a few such centipedes as The National Employers' Mutual General Insurance Association Limited. I don't know if the young ladies behind the shop counters pay their " dues " by cheque, but if so they must be hard put to it to compress National Amalgamated Union of Shop Assistants, Warehousemen and Clerks into 3¼ inches ; and I regard myself fortunate, if only in this respect, that I do not live in an area whose " juice " is supplied by The London and Home Counties Joint Electricity Authority. But I do have to write now and again to the Divisional Petroleum Officer, Divisional Petroleum Office, South-Eastern Division, The Pump Room, Tunbridge Wells, Kent. I can't help feeling that the Divisional Petroleum Officer, Tunbridge Wells, should suffice. Economy is a good watchword in wartime—economy in words as well as in things.

OUTSIDE your local cinema this week you may see an announcement of Desert Victory, the film of the recent Libyan campaign shot by Army Film and Photographic Unit and the R.A.F. Film Unit cameramen ; it should be worth seeing. Major David MacDonald, who was in charge of the A.F.P.U. in Libya, brought back to this country over 40,000 feet of film, which has now been knocked. into shape by the technicians at Pinewood Studios. Associated with Major MacDonald in this work have been Capt. Roy Boulting, who directed Thunder Rock ; Lieut. Jenkins, Asst.-Director for London Films at Denham ; and Sergeant Best, Asst. Editor of many peacetime productions at Pinewood Studios. An indication of the way in which the 30-odd cameramen of the A.F.P.U. kept up with the advance is evidenced by the fact that Capt. Geoffrey Keating and four sergeants of the Unit were in Tobruk for over an hour before the 8th Army occupied the town ; their photograph of the hauling down of the swastika flag and the hoisting of the Union Jack in its place is one of the high-lights of Desert Victory.

AT this very moment (Mrs. Amabel Williams-Ellis reminds us in her little book Women in War Factories ; Gollancz, 1s.) women are driving great steam hammers and travelling cranes, making the absurd barrage balloons reel and sing as they tape them, measuring and weighing, dipping something into a bath of boiling tin to test it, working with a pair of pliers screwed up in a gun-turret or the tail of a plane. They are also dishing out the soup in the canteens, travelling through the black-out, getting the worst of their housework done before they go to the factory. As Mrs. Williams-Ellis only too truly remarks, we, the general public, are not bothering our heads any too much about that great army shut away at their work behind the high walls or the electrified wire fences of the war factories and workshops. Yet these men and women " have stuck it for more than three years, and have done a job such as has never been done before in all history." We ought to know more about them and their work ; Women in War Factories will help to fill a gap in our knowledge of which we ought to be ashamed.

London Salutes the Ever-Glorious Red Army

IN THE ALBERT HALL on Feb. 21, 1943 an impressive pageant marked London's celebration of the 25th Anniversary of the Red Army. This photograph shows the vast assembly during the spectacular finale. On the platform the principal speaker, Mr. Eden, is seen in the centre. On either side, on the pedestals, are the narrators, Lt.-Cmdr. Ralph Richardson and Dame Sybil Thorndike. The huge backcloth represents a modern Russian city; and in front of the Soviet flag stands a Russian soldier on guard.

Photo, The Times

Printed in England and published every alternate Friday by the Proprietors, THE AMALGAMATED PRESS, LTD., The Fleetway House, Farringdon Street, London, E.C.4. Registered for transmission by Canadian Magazine Post. Sole Agents for Australia and New Zealand : Messrs. Gordon & Gotch, Ltd. ; and for South Africa : Central News Agency, Ltd.—March 19th, 1943.　　S.S.　　*Editorial Address :* JOHN CARPENTER HOUSE WHITEFRIARS, LONDON E.C.4.

Vol 6 *The War Illustrated* Nº 151

Edited by Sir John Hammerton

SIXPENCE

APRIL 2, 1943

INTO TUNISIA SWEEPS THE 8th ARMY. Where along the Mediterranean shore Italian Tripolitania meets French Tunisia there is a belt of marshland, of swamps which are sometimes lakes. But this natural obstacle was swiftly countered by the 8th Army's sappers, who flung a pair of wooden bridges across one of the lakes and so enabled the advance to continue. Pouring across the frontier, Montgomery's troops occupied Ben-Gardane, first of the Tunisian townships, on Feb. 15, 1943 : this photo shows Valentine tanks entering the town.

NO. 152 WILL BE PUBLISHED FRIDAY, **APRIL 16**

THE BATTLE FRONTS

by Maj.-Gen. Sir Charles Gwynn, K.C.B., D.S.O.

CITIZENS OF KURSK return to their homes. It was announced on Feb. 8, 1943 that the Red Army had recaptured this important town on the central front. *Photo, U.S.S.R. Official*

A T the time of writing (mid-March 1943) it is not yet certain how serious the reverses the Allies have suffered during the first two weeks of March will prove to be, or whether the notable successes they have achieved will have an even greater effect. The Germans have undoubtedly, for the time being at least, relieved the dangerous situation of their army in the Donetz; but it has yet to be seen whether the great efforts they are making to exploit that success will achieve results far-reaching enough to justify the expenditure of reserves incurred. If the attempt to recapture Kharkov has been made from motives of prestige and to offset their enforced abandonment of the Vyazma and Demyansk salients, it may prove a dangerously wasteful employment of their reserve strength, inconsistent with their announced strategic policy of shortening their front in order to recover their offensive power.

In spite of their reverses in the south, the Russians have had notable successes in the centre and north; they retain the initiative, but all the same have still formidable resistance to overcome before achieving results of decisive importance.

In Tunisia in the same period—the first half of March—the 1st Army, though it recovered almost all the ground overrun in Rommel's attack, has been pushed back, though not to a serious extent, in the north. On the balance it is improbable that it has yet fully regained its offensive potentialities. On the other hand, Rommel's costly failure to disturb Montgomery's preparations has probably weakened considerably his capacity to meet the 8th Army's attack when it comes.

RUSSIA During the first part of March it became evident that German counter-attacks in the Donetz basin and from the Dnieper bridgeheads were increasing in strength; and that German claims to have recaptured a number of towns taken by the Russian encircling thrusts were justified. It was, however, not till the end of the first week, when the Russians admitted withdrawal from eight important towns, that it became certain that the Germans had reopened the main railway communications from the Donetz to the Dnieper and Poltava.

At the same time it became evident that with reserves in the Donetz basin and with divisions which had reached the Dnieper from the west, the Germans had collected a force, amounting to twenty-five divisions, capable of staging a counter-offensive of considerable weight, and that they proposed to use it for the recapture of Kharkov. As I write, in the middle of the month, they have in fact achieved this object and may exploit their success further.

This undeniable reverse may be ascribed partly to the luck of the weather favouring the Germans, and even more to the fact that they possessed an intact railway system to facilitate the rapid concentration of reserves. The bold Russian thrusts which almost completely isolated the Germans in the Donetz owed their initial success to the rapid advance of armoured formations which caught the Germans unprepared. To consolidate their gains and to meet the inevitable counter-attacks, they needed the support of infantry and artillery masses. But without railways—those in existence could not be used till their gauge was changed—the Russians were dependent mainly on sledge transport; and when the unexpectedly early thaw came their main-bodies were largely immobilized. Heavily counter-attacked by superior forces and without hope of support, retreat of the armoured spearheads was inevitable, and in retreat they evidently suffered heavily. The Eastern pursuing force was checked by a defensive line formed on the Upper Donetz, but, concentrating a great mass of tanks to the west on a narrow front, the Germans penetrated the Russian rallying position in spite of fierce resistance.

That is what happened; but it is not yet clear what German intentions are. Their primary purpose was, no doubt, to remove the threat of encirclement, possibly only in order to permit the withdrawal of the army in the Donetz basin to the Dnieper, which would provide the shortest defensive line. The question is whether the recovery of Kharkov was undertaken only as an extension of their original plan in order to deprive the Russians of a base of great value for the continuance of their offensive towards the Middle Dnieper; or does it mean that the Germans now intend to retain their hold on the Donetz basin and to try to re-establish the defensive front they held last winter, running northwards from Taganrog to Kursk and Orel? Has there, in fact, been a change of plan to exploit the opportunity offered by an unexpected degree of success; and, if so, to what extent can exploitation be carried?

The tenacity with which the Germans are clinging to Orel in spite of the danger of its encirclement certainly suggests an intention to recover last winter's line. On the other hand, this would entail operations at a time when mud conditions are likely to become worse and in an area where recaptured railways would enable the Russians to bring up reinforcements, whereas the Germans would be dependent on motor transport.

A LREADY the Germans have had heavy casualties; and it must be questionable whether they are capable of a sustained effort under unfavourable conditions for mobile operations. The recapture of Kharkov for the time being may therefore be the limit of their immediate intentions. It may have prestige value and must undoubtedly affect the extension of the Russian offensive west of Kursk. These are points for consideration, but they do not provide a basis for definite conclusions.

Russian successes on the Moscow front undoubtedly offset to some extent reverses in the south. The capture of Rzhev—opening railway communications between Moscow and Veliki Luki—is of special immediate importance. It will enable greater weight to be given to the offensive which threatens the main line of German lateral communications. Its capture has also entailed what may be called the semi-voluntary abandonment of the rest of the great Vyazma salient. This on the one hand exposes Smolensk to attack, and on the other removes a potential

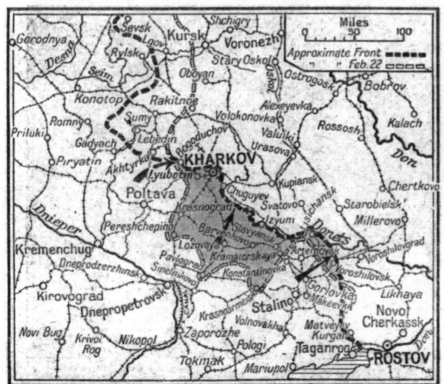

GERMAN GAINS AT KHARKOV. Retaken by the Red Army on Feb. 16, Kharkov became the target of a heavy enemy counter-thrust, and on March 14, 1943 the Germans claimed to have recaptured the great city, and the loss was admitted by the Russians shortly afterwards. This map shows the approximate front at Feb. 22 and at March 13, 1943; the shaded area is the territory regained by the Germans in their Kharkov thrust. *By courtesy of The Times*

TUNISIAN FRONT. In the north the 1st Army retired from Sejenane on Mar. 4th; in the centre the Anglo-Americans consolidated their gains to the east of Sbeitla; while in the south Rommel was meeting the 8th Army's attack on the Mareth Line. This map shows approximate battle-line at March 13.
By courtesy of The Times

easy, quick, or decisive victory can be expected. As at Alamein, it is likely to be a stage-by-stage affair, and Rommel has still sufficient armour to make formidable counter-attacks should opportunities arise.

How far the 1st Army now constitutes a real menace to Rommel's line of retreat it is impossible to judge. It is unlikely, with the growing threat of the 8th Army, that Rommel will be able to repeat his attempt to eliminate the menace if it exists. The possibility that he may strike at the Americans again cannot, however, be altogether discounted if Montgomery's attack is held up or delayed.

Von Arnim's attacks on the left of the 1st Army, although they have not achieved their main object of cutting lines of communication, have had rather disconcerting success. It seems clear that the nature of the country and weather conditions make defence of a long, lightly held front difficult. The enemy can always concentrate superior forces at a selected point, and the nature of the country favours the exploitation of infiltration tactics. Until General Anderson is in a posi-

MEDENINE, situated close to the Mareth Line, was taken by the 8th Army on Feb. 20, 1943, after it had been looted by the Germans. Here is a view of its wrecked buildings.
Photo, British Official : Crown Copyright

tion to undertake offensive operations on a large scale the disadvantages of defence must be accepted.

FAR EAST The total annihilation of the Japanese convoy that was attempting to reinforce New Guinea was, an outstanding achievement (*see page 662*). It shows the dangers any convoy runs, ours or the enemy's, when it ventures into waters covered by an effective umbrella.

General MacArthur has warned us that Japan, in spite of losses, can still concentrate a formidable armada, and that her air force especially should not be under-estimated.

It is satisfactory, however, that in the Pacific for a long time there have been no reverses to offset successes achieved.

threat to Moscow, which at all times tied down a considerable Russian reserve army.

In their withdrawal from the salient the Germans have had heavy losses of men and material, but have escaped disastrous defeat. Thaw will probably soon bring offensive operations to an end on this part of the front, but a lull in the fighting might be an advantage to the Russians, enabling them to restore railway communication in the recaptured area and to carry out such regrouping of their armies as may be necessitated by events in the south.

TUNISIA As I expected, Rommel withdrew, except at Gafsa, from the ground captured in his attack on the Americans and has re-established his flank screen in its original position. It was obvious that he would be compelled to use the bulk of his armour to meet the threat of the 8th Army. Characteristically he used it offensively, though probably with the object of gaining time by upsetting Montgomery's preparations rather than in the hopes of achieving any decisive success.

Once again he failed completely to catch Montgomery on the wrong foot, and suffered heavy casualties both in armour and, what may prove more important, in his picked infantry. The 8th Army's casualties, on the other hand, were light; and it is improbable that Montgomery's preparations have been delayed at all by the encounter. His counter-attacks were, however, purely of a local character, and the main battle remains to be fought.

The manner in which Rommel's attack was met should give us confidence in the result of this battle, though obviously no

ON THE OUTSKIRTS OF THALA, beyond the Kasserine Pass, the enemy made one of his most determined onslaughts. Two companies of Grenadier Guards crossed 10 miles of mountainous country in 5¼ hours to engage the 21st Panzer Division. But the latter, owing to the heavy losses they had incurred, had already beaten a retreat. Here are shown some of the Grenadiers with their Bren carriers.
Photo British Official

Up and Back Through Kasserine Went Rommel

THE KASSERINE PASS in Central Tunisia was the scene at the end of February 1943 of a German thrust against the Americans, followed by a swift withdrawal towards Feriana and Sbeitla as Gen. Anderson delivered a counter-stroke. Top, German positions under fire from Allied 25-pounder guns ; Axis troops were also heavily bombed during their flight. The Thala-Kasserine road was mined by the retreating enemy, and our armoured vehicles used cross-country routes as we advanced towards Kasserine itself. Meanwhile, Royal Engineers cleared the road ; below, men of an R.E. Field Company probing the highway for mines with bayonets. PAGE 644

British and U.S. Tanks Defeat an Enemy Thrust

MOVING UP TO KASSERINE, Sherman tanks (top) advance along a road in support of Allied infantry and an armoured force which cleared out the enemy from the Pass. On March 1, 1943 it was announced that both Kasserine and Feriana had been reoccupied by the Allies. Inset, German Mark III tank knocked out after a two-day battle. Churchill tanks (see p. 257) have played a vital role in the Tunisian fighting. In Feb. 1943 these tanks followed up our success on the Sbiba-Sbeitla front. They carried men of an R.E. Field Company (bottom) to lift mines and pave the way for a further Allied advance. See also opposite page. PAGE 645 *Photos, British Official: Crown Copyright*

Newspapers the Men of the 8th Army Read

How do the men in the battle line in North Africa keep abreast of the world's news—learn the rest of the history beyond that which they themselves are making? This article by LEIGH M. SCULLY gives the answer, telling as it does of newspapers, both amateur and professional, that have a wide circulation among our fighting men "out there."

As we wait eagerly for each daily, hourly scrap of news of fresh Eighth Army successes in North Africa, Eighth Army men are just as eagerly awaiting news from home. The men out there get it not only in airgraph letters, but also from home-made "newspapers" that cater for British and American Forces in the Middle East—some of these being written and printed within the range of enemy guns. There are four of these amateur news-sheets in general circulation—Gen (which is an R.A.F. slang word for information), Parade, Crusader (specially for the tank boys) and Eighth Army News, the last a proper newspaper with the most interesting story of the whole crowd.

It all began in a brown bell-tent in the desert, half hidden in a swirl of dust. They called the tent Fleet Street, and the news-sheet produced was the first official Eighth Army news-sheet. This news-sheet came about when the Army commander wanted a summary of the B.B.C. news brought to him every morning, this being done by the Information and Publicity Officers in the field. The single copy grew to several. An ancient duplicator was acquired, and the publication of local news from the battle front followed.

GRADUALLY the "premises" have grown. Here a tent replacement, there a lorry office. Maximum production was rushed on to the roads and into the battle areas by clerks in an old 8-cwt. Dodge, newsboys of the Eighth Army. Further progress in the news-sheet's life was the arrival of the Field Publicity Unit. The first printed issue of the Eighth Army News appeared in June 1942 in the middle of battle, the very time when it was most needed to get news to the troops.

More improvements followed. The F.P.U.'s three-tonner printing shop grew into three three-ton lorries, which, placed side by side, became one long room. There were now three presses and sixteen different types. Problems which arose when the new presses went into the desert were soon overcome; and there now exist on the spot efficient editorial offices and printing machines.

Publication of the first newspaper for Allied soldiers in North Africa is claimed by three soldiers, one of them Ivan Gore, a former News Chronicle artist. Called Allied Post, it is being printed on a small German press (possibly captured). Illustration blocks are cut with razor blades. The flags of Britain, America, and France are carried as a banner. Hasty block cutting resulted in the first number carrying the Stars and Stripes the wrong way round!

In addition to these Forces-only papers there are several local papers, some in French, some in English, that come out into the desert with lorry convoys. Probably the most widely-read of daily newspapers is La Bourse Egyptienne, also published by the Societé Orientale de Publicite, at a half-piastre, and circulating among the French-speaking population of Cairo and Alexandria. La Bourse—La Bourse is the cry you hear most often from the yelling Egyptian newsboys. Troops who know their French—and who are more accustomed to pay 1¼d. rather than 2¼d. for their newspaper—prefer it for up-to-the-minute news. Then there is Images, a large-size weekly picture paper, also published in French.

Most enterprising of the Middle East publishers are Societé Orientale de Publicité, who issue their various publications from the very modern offices and well-equipped press rooms in Cairo. Egyptian Mail and Egyptian Gazette are published by them—both English-language dailies.

EGYPTIAN MAIL comes out in the mornings; news editor now is a former Sunday Dispatch man, Lt. Alan Clarke; but till recently the Mail was hard-pressed for English staff, a couple having the job of supervising the spelling and lay-out. When they were off, or particularly busy on certain matters, readers were treated to a fair number of

howlers in headings and text. Egyptian Gazette was in much the same position, but, published in the evenings, it has a higher "class" reputation than the Mail. Outstanding feature in the Gazette has been the daily column "Passing By," written mainly by a red-headed American, Miss "Spencer" Brooke. Both papers cost one piastre each (2¼d.), and sell mostly to troops in Cairo and Alexandria.

THERE is, of course, no lack of skilled news-papermen serving out on the North African battle-fronts. Hugh Cudlipp, former editor of The Sunday Pictorial, is a War Office news officer in the Middle East, and is just recovering from an injury caused by a shell splinter received while he was on reconnaissance. Squadron-Leader G. W. Houghton has faced similar dangers as a Middle East Public Relations officer, and has just been mentioned in dispatches.

The best newspaper in the Middle East, copies of which are sent as far as Tunisia for the French and native troops, is Al-Ahram. Lads of the Eighth Army like it for the war pictures. Unfortunately they can't understand anything else in it, for it is printed in Arabic, reading right to left, so that even the positions and appearances of the pictures seem strange to our eyes.

THEY MAKE HISTORY—AND READ IT. General Montgomery's troops eagerly scan the news as they gather round this board in the desert. Among the papers here displayed are the Egyptian Mail and Eighth Army News (see accompanying text). In Tobruk Pte. Hayworthy returned to his pre-War occupation of newspaper-selling (upper photo). His papers, announcing the fall of the town, were soon sold out.

Photos, British Official: Crown Copyright

Calm before Storm along the Mareth Line

BEN-GARDANE, situated some twenty miles inside the Tunisian frontier from Tripolitania, was one of the Eighth Army's most important captures in the new war zone. In order to reach it they had to traverse a flooded area of marshland known as "the Causeway" (see p. 641), and in addition to contend with growing enemy resistance.

Right, a Bren-carrier of Gen. Montgomery's Army entering the centre of the town. Below, the driver of an Army lorry takes heed of this warning sign on the coastal road W. of Tripoli. Based on the once-popular "Confucius" joke, it indicates that care must be exercised in negotiating this road.

OFF FOR A DESERT 'JOY RIDE.' This strange-looking enemy vehicle (left) was one of the largest captured during the recent heavy fighting in the N. African theatre of war. It is a Mercedes-Benz, and was probably used by the Germans as a troop-transporter. Its caterpillar-wheels render it specially suitable for desert warfare. A party of Allied troops is here shown "going for a ride" across the sandy wastes.

When the Germans abandoned Ben-Gardane these two French gendarmes were left behind in the town to welcome the advancing British troops (above). They are seen amicably discussing an obviously absorbing topic with 2nd Lt. J. R. Probert, of the Royal Artillery.

Photos, British Official: Crown Copyright

PAGE 647

THE WAR AT SEA

by Francis E. McMurtrie

SUNDRY public utterances of late have tended to suggest that a new means of locating submarines under water has been put into operation. That the number of U-boats destroyed in the last few weeks has shown a welcome increase naturally encourages this belief.

Until a definite official statement on the subject is forthcoming too much should not be built on the above possibility. It is true, of course, that radio-location can be employed for the detection of submarines operating on the surface ; but water has been found impervious to this method. If indeed U-boats can now be detected more easily beneath the surface, it is more likely, that it is due to a further improvement of the well-tried "asdic" system, which the Royal Navy had developed to a high degree of reliability before the present war began ; though, on the other hand, some entirely new invention may have been perfected.

One thing is certain : there has been a considerable increase in the number of escort vessels, comprising destroyers, sloops, corvettes, and the larger editions of the last-named, which are now to be known as frigates (see illus. page 651). There are also more officers than there have ever been before with experience in anti-submarine methods. If U-boats are still being turned out faster than they are being destroyed, the same cannot be said of the personnel which will be required to man them. In this respect, therefore, those engaged in hunting submarines have a decided advantage.

In the week ended March 13, 1943 there were several encounters between our light forces and enemy coastal convoys in the Channel and North Sea. In one of these our forces under Lieut. J. S. Price, R.N.V.R., succeeded in sinking a German motor torpedo-boat, the loss of which was afterwards admitted by Berlin. In the second engagement our forces under Lieut. K. Gemmell, R.N.V.R., scored two torpedo hits on an enemy tanker, which was set on fire, as was one of the escorting vessels. Unfortunately we lost a vessel on this occasion, the enemy reporting that survivors had been picked up and made prisoners. This action was fought off the Dutch coast.

Next it was the turn of light forces manned by the Fighting French, under Capitaine de Corvette Muerville. Off the coast of Brittany an escorted convoy was sighted and attacked by these forces, a small supply ship being hit by a torpedo.

In spite of all this activity, the enemy attempted to pass a medium-sized supply ship through the Strait of Dover on the night of March 11-12. Intercepted by our light forces under Lieut. B. C. Ward, R.N., this vessel was torpedoed. In the following week two large supply ships were torpedoed off Terschelling by light forces under Lieut. D. G. H. Wright, R.N.V.R.

It is clear that, in spite of the vigilance exercised by our patrols, the Germans are finding the strain on their railways so intolerable that they are obliged to take the risk of sending supplies by sea.

AMERICA'S Vast Increases in Ships and Naval Planes

Some interesting facts and figures concerning American warship construction · were recently revealed by Col. Frank Knox, United States Navy Secretary (equivalent to our First Lord of the Admiralty). By 1945 it is hoped that the great majority of the new warships ordered during the past two years, totalling 5,675,000 tons, will have been completed. The number of private shipyards building vessels for the U.S. Navy is now 293, as compared with 108 a year earlier. Equally impressive is the output of new aircraft, of which the Navy's complement was increased last year from 15,000 to 27,500. Manufacture of guns and other weapons is keeping pace with these rapid developments. Only certain "large units,

upon which work has been suspended, due to material shortage and the length of time required to build," will be left outstanding after 1945. These are doubtless the five giant battleships of the Montana class, of 58,000 tons, and some if not all of the six 27,000-ton battle cruisers of the Alaska class.

To man the increased number of aircraft authorized, the number of U.S. Navy pilots was increased from 4,525 on June 30, 1941, to 11,240 a year later. Naval reserve aviators rose from 19,824 to 69,811 in the same period ; and men with aeronautical ratings increased from 12,432 to 31,106.

Colonel Knox also disclosed that a new type of destroyer, of about 1,300 tons, specially designed for transatlantic convoy work, was being produced in large numbers, exceeding 200. "Several score" of these vessels, he stated, had already been launched. It is understood that in their main features they resemble the later units of the British "Hunt" class.

A HEAVY blow was struck against the Japanese in the New Guinea area early in March. A convoy of 12 transports, escorted by three light cruisers and seven destroyers, was attacked again and again by Allied aircraft as it passed through the Vitiaz Strait (between New Guinea and the island of New Britain) and entered the Huon Gulf. It was carrying reinforcements for the Japanese garrison of Lae.

Sighted by Allied reconnaissance planes on March 1, the convoy was first attacked on the following day, four transports being sunk. During March 3 further attacks were made, destroying all but two destroyers, which were tracked down on the third day and sent to the bottom. Barges, lifeboats and rafts with survivors were also accounted for, so that not a single Japanese soldier is believed to have reached the convoy's destination. A few who landed on adjacent islands were killed or made prisoners. (*See* also page 662.)

This success is the more striking, since a strong air escort had been provided by the enemy. At least 59 enemy aircraft were brought down, and many more seriously damaged, in the course of the three days' operations. Allied losses amounted to one bomber and three fighters, convincing proof of the superior quality of our planes and pilots. More than 100 bombs were dropped on the convoy during one 24-hour period. American Mitchell bombers alone used 17,000 rounds of ammunition in firing on the enemy ships as they passed low over them. The attack was opened by R.A.A.F. Havocs, which scored 12 hits on six transports, most of them ships of about 6,000 tons gross. A Mitchell scored a direct hit on a 5,000-ton transport, which burst into flames and foundered a few minutes later.

THROUGHOUT the operations a strong force of Lightning fighters guarded our bombers. These were challenged by Japanese Zero fighters, but defeated them with heavy loss. Intense anti-aircraft fire was also encountered from the escorting enemy warships.

This highly satisfactory action shows very clearly that the Japanese failed to appreciate at its true value the lesson of Crete, nearly two years ago. In the Axis attack on that island our forces had practically no air cover, with the result that four British cruisers and six destroyers were sunk and many others damaged.

NORTH AFRICAN TRANSPORT, her decks crowded with troops—one of the many hundred ships which have carried men and supplies to the N. African ports since the Allied landings in Morocco and Algeria last November. Tanks are among the most important of the war material carried, the results of which have recently been seen in the vigorous fighting in Tunisia.   *Photo, British Newsreel*

Home from the Sea After a Year of Victories

H.M. SUBMARINE UMBRA recently returned to home waters after twelve adventurous months in the Mediterranean with 16 victories marked upon her skull-and-crossbones flag. The crew, under the command of Lt. S. L. C. Maydon, D.S.O., R.N., had many exciting stories to tell of their experiences. On one occasion they believe that the explosion caused by one of their torpedoes hitting an enemy supply ship was so great that it destroyed an escort plane diving above the blazing vessel.

Photo, British Official: Crown Copyright

Brave Men of the Royal Navy: Some New Awards

Cdr. J. M. HODGES, awarded the D.S.O. for displaying outstanding bravery during our operations in Madagascar last year. He is the son of Admiral Hodges.

Lt.-Cdr. H. HAGGARD, awarded the D.S.O. and D.S.C. for his gallant submarine actions in the Indian Ocean, Mediterranean, etc. He commanded the Truant.

Lt. D. COPPERWHEAT, awarded the G.C. An officer in H.M.S. Penelope, he scuttled a burning ammunition ship in Valetta harbour during a heavy raid.

SURVIVORS FROM H.M.C.S. OTTAWA and from a merchant ship, numbering 150, were picked up recently by a small corvette and taken to an Atlantic port. The Ottawa had rescued survivors from the merchant vessel when she was herself torpedoed. The corvette is here shown in port.

Lt. H. S. MACKENZIE, commander of H.M. submarine Thrasher, awarded a Bar to his D.S.O. for his daring exploits in raiding Axis supplies in the Mediterranean.

Art. R. E. MERRITT, awarded the D.S.M. on his return home after 2½ years' voyage in the Truant. His award was gazetted in Sept. 1940 for bravery in Norway.

Lt. W. TOMLINSON, awarded the D.S.C. for heroism. Commander of a motor-gunboat, he fought his ship through severe enemy air attacks in the Channel.

C.P.O. SAVAGE, awarded the D.S.M. and Bar. With him is Boy ROY DE MOUILPIED, awarded the D.S.M. Their ship, H.M.S. Penelope, was heavily bombed at Malta, and Mouilpied helped Savage throughout the gallant vessel's fourteen-day ordeal (see pages 22, 60).

Lt. R. H. MARRION (left) of H.M. minesweeper Fezenta, and Lt. R. H. PRATT, of H.M. minesweeper Welsbach, each awarded the D.S.C. They have been three years in minesweepers and are now group captains. They are so alike that they are often mistaken for each other.

Photos, Keystone, Fox, New York Times Photos, Planet News, Associated Press, L.N.A., News Chronicle, Central Press

Not Foe Nor Weather Stay the Ships for Russia

CONVOYS TO MURMANSK continue to get through despite Arctic conditions, severe bomber and U-boat attacks. Supplies from Britain to our Ally between October 1941 and December 1942 included 2,974 tanks and over 3,000 aircraft. Top, the enemy scores a hit on an ammunition ship; three of the attacking enemy aircraft were blown to pieces by the explosion. Left centre, H.M.S. Rother, one of Britain's frigates—a revival of a time-honoured description for a new type of swifter and heavier corvette. 3, Ice-encrusted heavy guns of a battleship operating in northern waters, before being prepared for action.

Photos, British Official; New York Times Photos

Always Ready to Save Is the 'Salvation Navy'

A band of brothers who find their work—and their happiness—in saving the lives of others : such is the Air-Sea Rescue Service whose work JOHN ALLEN GRAYDON describes in this article. Illustrations of the German rescue float will be found in Vol. 4, p. 134.

A scattered points around the coasts of Britain, at Malta, Gibraltar, and other parts of the Empire, in fair weather and foul, launches of the Air-Sea Rescue Service are always manned and ready to put to sea and rescue from a watery grave any fighter pilot, or bomber crew, forced to bale out when over the sea. For obvious reasons the number of pilots rescued by the " Salvation Navy " (as it is called) cannot be revealed, but many hundreds of men have lived to fight another day because of the gallantry and daring of the crews aboard the launches.

Measuring 63 ft. and capable of speeds well over forty-five miles an hour, the Air-Sea Rescue launches, which work in close cooperation with the Royal Navy, are, because of the increasing number of Fighter Command sweeps and attacks by aircraft of Bomber Command, busier than ever before in their history.

A short time ago I went out into the Channel aboard one of these launches. As we sped into mid-Channel hundreds of Spitfires and Hurricanes roared overhead, acting as escort to squadrons of Bostons and Havocs which were about to attack docks and stores on the French coast. When we were within two and three-quarter miles of the French coast, and our bombers dropped their loads, our launch " lifted " out of the water, so powerful were the explosives cased in our bombs !

Then a " dog-fight " between British and German fighters developed overhead, and the men aboard the launch prepared for action. We did not have long to wait.

After several of the German machines had turned towards base, smoke pouring from their tails, one of the Spitfires was seen to be in difficulties.

Our skipper turned towards the machine— not a moment too soon. Within a few seconds we knew the pilot had baled out, his white parachute standing out against the sky. Slowly he floated seawards, while comrades circled round to make sure that no over-anxious Huns attempted a little shooting practice.

Hardly had the man touched the water and was inflating his rubber dinghy (see illus. Vol 5, p. 71), when we were on the spot ; and, but a minute or so after he had entered the sea, that pilot was safe aboard our launch, drinking hot rum and changing into warm clothes.

" You fellows sure work fast," the airman, a young Toronto pilot, formerly a bank clerk and product of the Empire Air Training Scheme, grinned.

" So do you," I replied, for the Air-Sea Rescue ratings were too busy to engage in conversation. " That was pretty smart the way you inflated your dinghy. Been forced to bale out before ? "

" No," answered the Canadian, " but I reckon the training we have before taking the air, when we are taught in a special lake at training-school how to inflate our rubber boat under realistic circumstances, has saved many lives. It did just now, for I'm not a hot swimmer ! "

In the early days of the War the Air-Sea Rescue Service did good work, especially off Dover ; but it was not organized into the great body it is today. With the growth of the Royal Air Force, so has the " Salvation Navy " developed its own strength and called upon science to aid its brave men in the saving of life.

Around the coasts of Britain, for example, are special rescue floats. Painted bright yellow and red, they are moored at many points over which aerial combats take place with fair regularity. These floats are shaped like a boat and measure just over 30 ft.

Aboard them the pilot finds a complete change of clothing, preserved meat and vegetables, drinking water, tea, and rum. In addition to the necessities of life, there are clean towels, soap, a primus stove, and, most important of all, a signalling apparatus by means of which the marooned man can contact base and inform them of his position and the number of his float. By checking on their chart, the Air-Sea Rescue officers can immediately make for the float on which the pilot is stranded.

In the early days of the Service, despite the thoroughness of searchers, pilots were often missed by launches and aircraft sent to locate them. Scientists, however, commenced work, and developed yellow life-jackets and skull-caps, which when worn by the

NEW AIR-SEA RESCUE SERVICE BADGE shows a high-speed launch in white against a background of R.A.F. blue. It is worn on the right arm. *Photo, British Official : Crown Copyright*

crews are visible from the air and for a considerable distance on the sea. Smoke signals, too, have been developed. The smoke, which is of an orange colour, can be seen for over thirty miles, and I have seen no fewer than six pilots saved by this method. Fluorescine is also used to colour the sea a yellowish green, and men who pilot the Lysander and Walrus aircraft engaged in the hunts for pilots who have been reported shot down or in difficulties over the sea told me that this, as much as anything else, helps them.

One Walrus aircraft actually alighted on the sea within one and a half miles of the enemy coast and picked up a stranded Spitfire pilot. The man at the controls of the Walrus then discovered that the plane was in the centre of an enemy minefield ! By making his flying-boat " jump " over several mines the Air-Sea Rescue man managed to evade the enemy—and yet another well-trained pilot was taken back to the English shore to fight again another day.

At Malta one of the launches attached to the A.-S.R.S. based on the George Cross Island has saved nearly 70 airmen who have been forced to bale out over the sea in the course of the fierce air engagements that have taken place in this area.

The Germans used to pay respect to these launches of the " Salvation Navy," but since they have saved so many airmen's lives the Nazi has shown his true nature. Even when our men have been aiding shot-down German pilots, fighters of the Luftwaffe have swept over and machine-gunned friend and foe. At times our losses in launches and men have been heavy. Now the launches are mounted with guns—but the men aboard never use them until they are attacked. Unfortunately, they rarely get a chance of hitting back once the Hun, for no reason at all, has swept them with his cannons.

Despite this constantly-used method of " terror attack," the " Salvation Navy " continues to go about its work. And, as an appreciation of its personnel's great deeds over the past three years, the Air Ministry have awarded it a badge which will be worn on the right arm.

No Service, in its own quiet manner, has performed a more valuable role than the Air-Sea Rescue Service. A band of brothers who find their happiness in saving the lives of others.

U.S. FAIRCHILD AMPHIBIAN AIRCRAFT in the Western Desert, a type of machine extensively used by the Middle East Air-Sea Rescue Service. Inset, Spitfire pilot rescued off Mersa Brega (Gulf of Sirte) by one of these planes after baling out at 3,000 ft. Owing to an injured arm he was unable to paddle his dinghy and would probably have perished but for the " Salvation Navy."
Photos, British Official : Crown Copyright

Their Motto: 'The Sea Shall Not Have Them'

THE AIR-SEA RESCUE SERVICE has saved the lives of many airmen forced down round our coasts. 1, Sq. Ldr. R. F. Hamlyn, A.F.C., D.F.M., in command of an Air-Sea Rescue Squadron in the South of England. A veteran of the Battle of Britain, he has destroyed 13 enemy aircraft, 5 of them in one day. 2, Exhausted airmen come alongside the rescue launch in their dinghy. 3, This launch races to pick up airmen marooned in the North Sea. 4, British pilot signals to an A-S.R.S. crew from his dinghy. These compact little rubber boats are coloured yellow to make them more easily distinguishable at a distance.

Photos, British Official: Crown Copyright; Planet News

Bomber Command's Hammer-blows on Germany

Introducing the Air Estimates on March 11, 1943, Sir Archibald Sinclair, Secretary of State for Air, gave the House of Commons a most encouraging report. After announcing the establishment of an R.A.F. Transport Command, and reviewing the work of Army Cooperation, Fighter and Coastal Commands and the R.A.F. in North Africa, he came to Bomber Command's offensive against Germany. It is on this part of his speech that the following article is chiefly based.

Bombs on Germany! They are falling by day, they are falling by night, hundreds of tons at a time. At long last the German people are coming to learn what modern war really means. When it was London or Bristol, Coventry or Plymouth, that were getting the bombs, they were not at all concerned—many of them, indeed, openly gloated. But bombs on Munich, bombs on Nuremberg, Stuttgart, Cologne, Düsseldorf, Bremen and Hamburg, Essen, Berlin itself—that's a very different matter. The Nazis boasted of the destruction Goering's young airmen wreaked on Rotterdam and Belgrade, but now their newspapers are filled with moans about "British barbarism." Particularly hysterical were they when Nuremberg and Munich—"those unholy cities of the Nazi cult," Sir Archibald Sinclair called them in his speech in the House of Commons on March 11—were hit hard early in March. The Germans lyingly declared that the damage was confined to historic monuments, to medieval relics, to churches and museums: "the enemies of Europe and of European civilization, culture and art," said the Deutsche Allgemeine Zeitung, "are destroying systematically the most venerable monuments in Germany and Italy."

Such plaints do not ring true. No one on this side of the war will rejoice over the destruction of any part of Europe's cultural inheritance, of the little homes of the German people. But the Nazi Brown House at Munich (reported to have been damaged) is no monument of culture; and where military objectives are found in the midst of populous cities they can hardly be spared. In the debate following Sir Archibald Sinclair's speech Mr. R. R. Stokes protested "in the name of humanity" against what he described as our "merciless destruction of women and children." But it must be remembered, indeed it will never be forgotten, that it was the Nazis who initiated this savagery. Now they are reaping what they have sown. And verily they who sowed the wind are reaping the whirlwind.

In spite of bad weather, said Sir Archibald Sinclair on March 11, the tonnage of bombs dropped in January this year was only surpassed three times in 1942. In February with a delivery of over 10,000 tons of bombs, including three 1,000-ton raids, Bomber Command dropped more than half as much again as in any previous month. In the first 10 days of March more than 4,000 tons of bombs had been dropped. It was evident, Sir Archibald went on, from photographs taken following the attack on Essen on the night of March 5–6, that the German war industry had suffered in this raid its heaviest blow from our bomber offensive.

In the Krupps Works 13 main buildings had been destroyed or severely damaged and damage could be seen in at least 40 other factory buildings, sheds and workshops. The majority of those were in the steel works and included heavy damage to such key sections as furnaces, foundry and forges. In all, the severe damage to workshops and administrative buildings covered 136,000 square yards. There was a direct hit on the Essen power station, while damage to the gas works extended over an area of 3½ acres. Immediately to the east of the Krupps Works there was a total destruction of a built-up area of 160 acres, and it was estimated that there was a total of 450 acres where at least 75 per cent of the buildings had been demolished, or gutted. Two days after the attack fires were still burning. Some 30,000 people in Essen, most of whom were employed in the Krupps Works, had lost their houses, and many thousands in addition had been rendered temporarily homeless.

(Talking of photographs, surprised Berliners are reported to have remarked on the "incredible cheek" of a British reconnaissance plane which, following the last raid, came down so low to photograph the damage that the A.A. guns dared not fire!)

Bomber Command's operations have not been confined to Essen; elsewhere the destruction of Germany's industrial centres has been continued on a large scale.

The toll of devastation includes 118 acres in Wilhelmshaven, in Rostock 130 acres, in Mainz 135 acres, in Lübeck 200 acres, in Karlsruhe 260 acres, in Düsseldorf 380 acres, in Cologne 600 acres, together with a total of many thousands of acres of industrial property devastated in other towns.

In all, Sir Archibald calculated that Bomber Command's activities had caused the destruction of, or serious damage to, 2,000 German factories and industrial works.

Substantially more than a million people have been rendered homeless, not counting the large numbers who have been evacuated for fear of air attack, rendering towns in the eastern parts of Germany, Berlin among them, intolerably overcrowded. Direct damage to steel works in the Ruhr and Saar has caused a loss of 1½ million tons of steel, and the total loss of steel must be much greater. The daily output of coal in the Ruhr fell by 20 per cent in three months last summer, and in the latter half of 1942 coal exports to Sweden and Italy, partly through shortage of coal, and partly through dislocation of communications, were markedly diminished. Much working time has been lost in industry through absenteeism and the dislocation of transport.

Furthermore, the Air Minister pointed out, the three main Italian targets which had been selected for attack and so severely damaged by our bombers—Milan, Turin and Genoa—embraced practically two-thirds of the total industrial production of Italy.

Well might Sir Archibald Sinclair pay glowing tribute to those who are carrying out these operations, hazardous but tremendously important, terrifically devastating. He concluded:

Praise the men who are striking these hammer-blows at German might—fearless young men flying through storm and cold and darkness above the height of Mont Blanc, through the flak, hunted by the night fighters, but coolly and skilfully identifying and bombing these targets. They are sustained by the knowledge of duty well done, and of high achievement, and they deserve our thanks and praise.

Recently the Air Ministry published a survey of Bomber Command's activities during 1942. In this it is demonstrated that the trouble caused by our raids is more serious to Germany now than was Germany's air offensive against Britain two years ago, because we at that time still had plenty of fat and tremendous recuperative power. But Germany now is strained to the limit, so that a ton of bombs on Essen today is worth far more to us than was a ton of bombs on Birmingham to the enemy in 1940. The cumulative effect is even more important. One spanner in the works, such as the 1,000-bomber raid on Cologne, is not necessarily a very serious business, but a second spanner is harder to deal with than the first.

It is, however, a lengthy process to put out of action a machine as tough as the German industrial system. We know that the efficiency of German industrial production is falling, but we cannot say how much of its decline is due to bombing and how much to deficient food, foreign labour, and so on. The best method of dispelling doubts as to whether the bomber offensive is really worth while is to make a careful study of its development in 1942. During that year the total bomb-load of Bomber Command aircraft dispatched to Germany alone was 37,000 tons; what this means may be gathered from the fact that in the German attack on Coventry, on November 14, 1940, about 185 tons fell.

Finally, there is the question of morale. The German civilian, like the German soldier, is tough, and will not give up at all easily. But the Germans have been living under war conditions for much longer than we have, and they are now suffering military reverses such as they have never previously experienced. Under these handicaps the strain of repeated air raids is not easy to bear. It will take a lot to break the back of this particular camel, is the Air Ministry's conclusion. But no one who knows the facts of the bomber offensive against Germany in 1942, and considers the prospect for 1943, is likely to doubt the contribution which the British air offensive can make in the coming year.

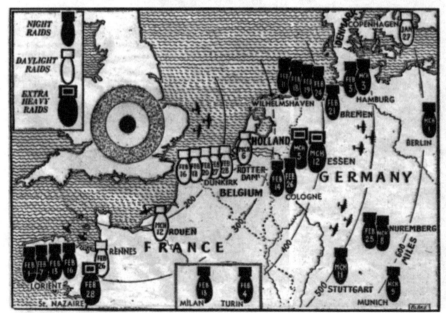

FOURTEEN THOUSAND TONS OF BOMBS were dropped by Bomber Command on enemy targets in six weeks, disclosed Sir A. Sinclair on March 11, 1943. Almost 2,000 factories, etc., have been destroyed or damaged in Germany during the whole offensive. Above are indicated the main R.A.F. raids during the period under review. *By courtesy of The Daily Express*

Bombs on Hitler's Europe !

Week by week, day by day, night after night, the weight of the Anglo-American air onslaught on the seats of Nazi power in the West grows and grows. Among recent targets most heavily "plastered" is the great naval base at Wilhelmshaven, where the toll of devastation has grown to 118 acres, including the utter destruction of the arsenal. Bombs of the 8th U.S.A.A.F. are here seen streaking down towards the recently-opened Adolf Hitler basin, on Jan. 27 last.

Day and Night the Offensive Continues

At a day bomber station the crews chosen for the next raid are being briefed (1); soon in their Douglas Boston IIIs, fastest twin-engined bomber the Americans have sent us so far, they will be blasting some bastion of "Fortress Europe." While they are away over Wilhelmshaven or Lorient the lands across the Channel will be swept methodically by our latest reconnaissance bomber (2)—the 270 m.p.h. Ventura, a product of the Lockheed Aircraft Corporation.

Photos: Top...
Photos,

Round the Clock in the Air War

New York Times
E. Brown

Afternoon comes, and perchance there are Nazis in the sky, a surface ship hugging the French coast, a U-boat making for home . . . These new and even better Spitfire IXs (3) will soon put paid to their account. Night, or rather early morning ; and back from the R.A.F.'s 58th raid on Berlin, the "thunderbolt" attack on March 1, there emerge from Z for Zebra, P.W/O C. S. Sanderson and his crew (4). Soon a new bomb will be painted up (5)—sign of another day's duty nobly done.

Destination Berlin!

Before it was light this morning the giant bomber touched down at the aerodrome, safe home after a raid on some city or port of Hitler's. But tonight she's due out again, so the ground crews are hard at it. Fitters and riggers are overhauling the engines (1), the fire-bombs are made ready (2), the ammunition belts refilled (3), and bombs—Lord Beaverbrook's big beautiful bombs—brought from the magazine (4). Maybe it's the Berliners who are going to have a bad night.

Photos, British Official : Crown
Copyright ; Charles E Brown,
Topical Press, Fox

UNDER THE SWASTIKA

An Englishman's Life in Pétain's France

In what follows HENRY DAVRAY writes of an old friend, an Englishman, "who loves France as much as I love Britain." This friend of his lives in France, and the story of his experiences in what until last November was Unoccupied France makes illuminating reading.

FOR the last forty years my English friend —let us call him John Taylor—has lived in France. When he first arrived in Paris he was on his way back to England after two years spent as a tutor in a noble family in Russian Poland. Paris made such an impression upon him that he never went any farther, and he was still living on the banks of the Seine when the First World War started. He decided to "stay put" and, as a large number of professors was being mobilized, he offered his services to the Ministry of Public Education and was appointed, for the duration, as teacher of English at one of the best renowned Paris lycées.

Few Parisians knew Paris as well as he did, and he had a special fondness for the old quarters, whose every house has a long history. He was equally allured by the countryside around Paris, the beautiful Ile de France with its rich fields and old market-towns. He scoured it on his old bicycle, sketching picturesque nooks, village churches and ancient manors, and making friends with the residents who invited him to stay with them at holidaytime. The parish priests specially, the curés, gave him a hearty welcome, and sheltered him as a guest in their roomy presbyteries.

About these spots in Paris and its environs he wrote a series of small books provided with maps and with a number of his own pencil-sketches. The curés became his zealous agents, displaying his elegant little volumes in literature stands in their churches, near the stoup, to tempt tourists motoring through the country.

Then my friend turned into a quiet and efficient propagandist for his own land and people, without any link or tie with officialdom. His idea was to issue a weekly paper in English for French schoolboys and schoolgirls who were learning English. He persuaded a well-known firm of publishers of schoolbooks to produce it, and thus The Briton knew an immediate success, which it enjoyed for many years until the collapse of France.

In these more recent years his sight worried him somewhat, and when he took medical advice he was told it was cataract and that an operation was becoming unavoidable. It was performed on one of his eyes, pending a second one on the other. To recuperate after that trial, he went to stay with some friends in the country east of Paris, and there he was when the Germans broke through the French defences on the Marne, and rushed down towards Paris.

WHEREUPON his adventures began. He was involved in a disastrous evacuation with some machine-gunning from the air thrown in. Then under heavy bombardment he lost sight of his friends and their car which was carrying all his worldly belongings. With the retreating forces he was swept along southwards across the river Loire, and at last stopped in a little village which, luckily, was not included in the occupied zone at the armistice. There the excellent curé took him in ; but when the curé's own relations began to flow in he could keep him no longer. So my friend went on to the next important town, which happened to be the chief town of a *département* in the right centre of France.

For three months he was looked after by the Little Sisters of the Poor. "They were very kind and considerate," he writes, " did not bother me about chapel and other observances, although I fancy they tacitly entertained the hope to convert me later on." In the meantime they rigged him out as best they could. "I suppose I had the proper down-and-out look, as a young man, one day, offered me 50 fr. in the street." All the time he was trying to get some job, but in a provincial town of 25,000 inhabitants, 175 miles away from Paris, it seemed hopeless. Still he went to the lycée ; and there, one of the lycée masters—" a saint, if there is such a thing," he writes, " now unfortunately for me transferred to the top of the educational tree in Madagascar "—helped him to find his feet again by getting him in a family, where for some time he earned part of his keep by looking after the son's Latin and other lessons. Meanwhile, some of his clothes straggled in from Paris, so that he was soon more presentable. He succeeded in getting a few pupils in English, and by this means was able to keep the wolf at a shortish distance from the door. Now he has " many good friends and some amusing acquaintances : a paralysed English woman who has made me her business man ; an old English jockey who can read but not write ; a sort of red Indian ; an Australian lady ; a Palestinian girl, etc." So his interests are varied.

Not long before the Nazis seized the whole of France the family he was living with moved into a new house where there was no room for him, and he looked in vain for another in a family or a *pension*. But the town was swamped with people from the Occupied zone, and he had to put up at a local hotel

whose landlord treated him as a friend. By a piece of luck he found among the refugees in the town the surgeon who had operated on his eye at the Rothschild Hospital in Paris, and who, being a Jew, had thought it advisable to shun the attentions of the Gestapo. However, my friend thinks it would not be wise, in the present unstable conditions, to undergo the second operation on the other eye. So, he writes, " I expect I shall have to worry through with one eye the rest of my days—not so many now, thank Heaven, but people are so kind that it is almost a pleasure to be 80 per cent blind."

THE rationing business he finds a weary affair. He goes to the baker himself and buys his bread for the day in the morning, and carries it about to places where one eats. He gets thin, but does not mind as he finds his general health keeps good enough. His morale keeps good enough, too. "It is no good being optimistic or pessimistic at this moment," he writes, " for we lack all the elements of a sound appreciation of the great problem. I don't take the papers (except for

FRENCH CHILDREN—victims of the appalling conditions brought about by the German domination of their country—visited Switzerland in large numbers recently. This photo shows some of a party of 1,000 returning to Lyons after their recuperative holiday in a land which stands out in honourable isolation as an island of freedom in the ocean of Nazi slavery. The article in this page gives a vivid impression of life in France just before its complete occupation by the Germans.
Photo, New York Times Photos

the crosswords) and I listen-in very irregularly. One feels, however, that something big, perhaps decisive, is preparing." So he replied last September to a friend in England who had inquired about his state of mind and how he managed his mental pabulum. " There is a goodish town library here," he wrote, " from which I take out books one day and hurl them back the next. I used to say that when I got old I would read no more but re-read ; and it was a silly thing to say. I cannot stand the old idols. Jane Austen even bores me . . . But on the other hand Galsworthy is about the only modern I can get away with. So I fall back on French."

THIS gives an idea of the kind of life an Englishman led in Unoccupied France for two years. Last autumn he wrote, " The people are doing all they can to make things easier for me, and when pupils begin to come back from their holiday, I hope to be rid of a part of my anxiety. So I decline to be pessimistic." As to the future, he has no doubts about it : " The present is gloomy, the future unreadable, but the past is our sure possession ; and I look back comfortingly to our long friendship, to all that we have been to each other, to all that we have done together. May we meet again, and take up something of the old life."

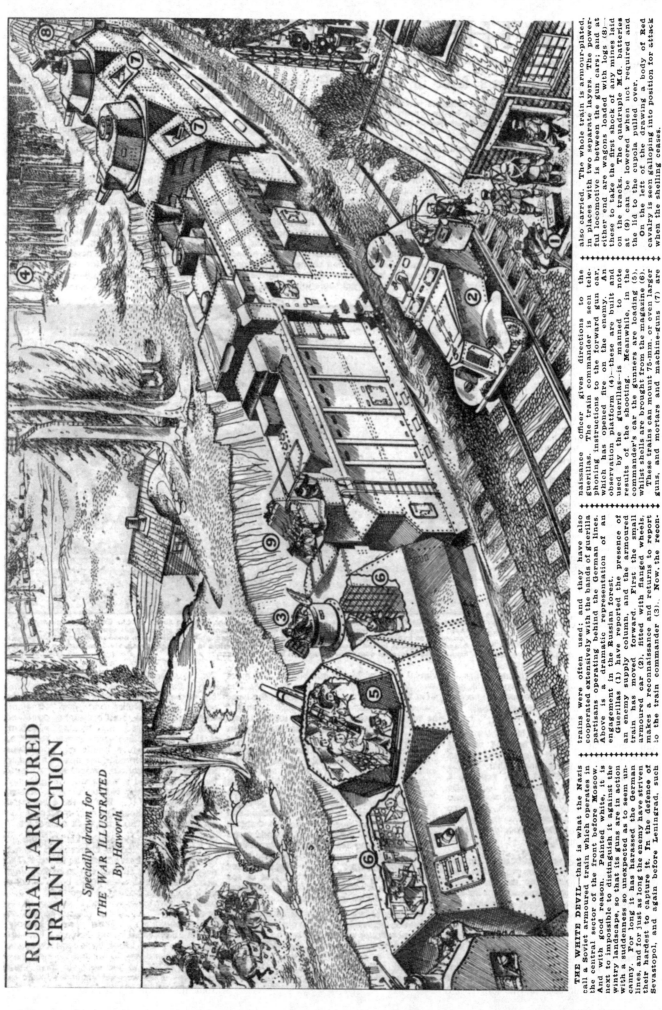

RUSSIAN ARMOURED TRAIN IN ACTION

Specially drawn for
THE WAR ILLUSTRATED
By Haworth

THE WHITE DEVIL—that is what the Nazis call a Soviet armoured train which operates in the central sector of the front before Moscow. And with good reason. Painted white, it is next to impossible to distinguish it against the wintry landscape, so that its guns are in action with a suddenness so unexpected as to seem uncanny. For long it has harassed the German lines, and for just as long the enemy have striven their hardest to capture it. In the defence of Sevastopol, and again before Leningrad, such

trains were often used; and they have also cooperated extensively with the bands of guerilla partisans operating behind the German lines. Above is a dramatic representation of an engagement in the Russian forest.

Guerillas (1) have reported the presence of an enemy supply column, and the armoured train has moved forward. First the small armoured car (2), fitted with flanged wheels, makes a reconnaissance and returns to report to the train commander (3). Now, the recon-

naissance officer gives directions to the guerillas. The train commander is seen telephoning instructions to the forward gun car, which has opened fire on the enemy. An observation platform (4)—these are built and used by the guerillas—is manned to note the results of the shooting. Meanwhile, in the commander's car the gunners are loading (5), whilst shells are brought from the magazine (6). These trains can mount 75-mm. or even larger guns, and mortars and machine-guns (7) are

also carried. The whole train is armour-plated, in places with two separate layers. The powerful locomotive is between the gun cars; and at either end are wagons loaded with logs (8)—these to take the first shock of any mines laid on the tracks. The quadruple M.G. batteries at (9) can be lowered when not required. Note the lid to the cupola pulled over.

On the left of the drawing a body of Red cavalry is seen galloping into position for attack when the shelling ceases.

Timoshenko Takes the Offensive in the North

SOVIET FORCES ENTER DEMYANSK. This photograph gives a vivid impression of the main street after the town's liberation by Marshal Timoshenko's troops. The Germans held on to the Demyansk region for seventeen months, following its capture by them in Sept. 1941, when they broke through the Russian defences S.E. of Lake Ilmen.

MARSHAL TIMOSHENKO, it was announced on March 1, 1943, had launched an offensive against the German 16th Army in the region of Lake Ilmen, and had captured the towns of Demyansk, Lychkovo and Zaluchye. During the eight days of fierce fighting that ensued the Russians relentlessly pursued the enemy and liberated some 302 inhabited places, clearing an area of 2,350 sq. km. (about 900 sq. miles). During these same eight days the Red Army captured 3,000 German officers and men and a large quantity of war material, including some 78 aircraft, 97 tanks, 289 guns of various calibres, and 711 machine-guns.

German resistance at Demyansk was stubborn. The enemy used massed artillery, mortars and machine-guns, furiously counter-attacking with infantry supported by tanks. In order to avoid encirclement he began a hurried retreat, abandoning strong-points, dug-outs and trenches which it had taken him many months to build. Some 40 German planes were captured on Demyansk aerodrome.

The Germans set great store by what they called the "Demyansk fortress" area, but they endeavoured to minimize its loss by admitting on March 2 that it had been evacuated, while stating at the same time that "the Soviet offensive front in the Lake Ilmen sector has been extended to the south." The Demyansk bastion was, indeed, second only to Rzhev in the whole German front between Moscow and Leningrad. Marshal Timoshenko smashed the vast German padlock, which the enemy had put on Russian offensive action between Leningrad and Veliki Luki.

ON March 6 the Russians recaptured Gzhatsk, an important German base S.E. of Sychevka (reoccupied by the Red Army two days later) and advanced in the direction of Vyazma—the remaining German "hedgehog" in the eastern part of the salient pointing to Moscow and the chief outpost of Smolensk, situated 140 miles west of the capital. Swiftly they fought their way along Napoleon's famous road of retreat in 1812, and on March 12 the Germans evacuated Vyazma. Thus the last enemy stronghold threatening Moscow was removed.

RUSSIAN COMMANDERS MAKE FINAL PLANS before leaving with their armoured train for a surprise attack on enemy-held positions on the Northern front. Commander A. Bulavin (centre) discusses the impending attack with his officers, Lt. P. Gorolov (left) and Lt. N. Gorodny. Behind them is their white-painted train. (See illustration in opposite page.)

CAVALRY OF THE SOVIET GUARDS reconnoitring a position during an advance by the Red Army on the S.W. sector of the front. These Cavalry Guards have won renown on many a battlefield, vanquishing the enemy when he was most sorely pressed during the fierce fighting at the beginning of 1943. The courage, daring and intrepid skill displayed by these men are beyond praise, and have contributed in no small measure to our Ally's remarkable achievements.

Photos, U.S.S.R. Official, Planet News

THE WAR IN THE AIR

by Capt. Norman Macmillan, M.C., A.F.C.

OUTSTANDING among recent events in the air war was the naval victory won by an Army general by the use of air power. The setting for this apparently anomalous action was the Bismarck Sea, the tropical waters in the neighbourhood of New Guinea and the archipelago of large and small islands lying to the north-east of that currently-contested island. The commander was General MacArthur, the first defender of the Philippines and, since his departure from that command, the supreme commander of the United Nations forces in the south-western Pacific.

Reconnaissance aircraft had been reporting for some time the gathering of Japanese forces and ships in Rabaul, the excellent harbourage of the capital of New Britain. On Monday, March 1, 1943 a Japanese convoy moving down the coast of New Britain was sighted by reconnaissance aircraft in spite of the bad weather which the enemy apparently hoped would cloak its movements. Fourteen ships were seen—three cruisers, four destroyers, and seven transports. They were shadowed. Because of the Japanese concentrations in Rabaul, General Mac-Arthur had meanwhile given instructions for the Allied (American and Australian) aircraft within the area to be concentrated into a striking force. On March 2 the longer range bombers—Fortresses and Liberators—flew out to the attack, and locating the convoy through heavy clouds, sank two transports.

On the succeeding day the convoy was observed to have been joined by another section of three destroyers and five transports. That day the air attack upon the convoy was intensified, and as the ships steamed within range of the medium bombers—Bostons, Mitchells, and Hampdens—these, too, flew to the attack, escorted by Lightning fighters, and followed up by Beaufighters.

Throughout the air-sea action Allied air attacks were made upon the principal Japanese land air base at Lae, and air fighting became fierce and frequent.

The superiority of the Allied forces was never in doubt. Some of the ships steamed on into the Huon Gulf, and there met their doom. Every ship in the convoy of 22 vessels was sunk between Rabaul and Lae, the latter enemy base in New Guinea being the intended destination of the convoy. Fifteen thousand men were killed or cast into the tropical waters. Those who attempted to reach the shore in barges and rafts (some of the rafts were reported to have been made from tree-trunks lashed together) were attacked from the air by fighters and bombers and decimated. Few can have escaped.

IN the air fighting over the ships and over the enemy aerodromes 102 Japanese aircraft out of a force of about 150 were shot down. The United Nations' losses were one bomber and three fighters, and a number of damaged aircraft which succeeded in returning to their bases. The victory was complete. There has been in history no more striking example of the power of the air weapon. Yet General MacArthur said that the forces employed in this air action were relatively small. Rather more than 100 tons of bombs

were dropped. In this running fight lasting several days only a fragment of the concentrated power which is unleashed over German targets when 500 to 1,000 tons are dropped within an hour was employed. It is a further indication of the inevitability of defeat for the Powers who are unable to secure superiority in the air.

BATTLES in the Pacific Won by Aircraft Alone

In this action it appeared that the Japanese fighters were not good enough for the Allied aircraft which were arrayed against them, either in bombers or fighters. Now Australia has received her first units of Spitfire fighters, manned by British and Australian personnel,

JAP CONVOY OFF NEW GUINEA was annihilated when attacked by U.S. planes, it was announced at the beginning of March 1943. Out of 15,000 troops 97 only survived the sinking of all the 22 ships of the convoy. Seen from a raiding aircraft, this Jap transport goes down in this Battle of the Bismarck Sea. *Photo, News Chronicle*

and defence in the Australasian zone will be correspondingly strengthened. These units were promised to Australia at an earlier date, but were diverted to North Africa in agreement with Mr. Curtin, Australia's Prime Minister, to share in the glory of the El Alamein battle and the subsequent driving of the Axis forces out of Egypt and Libya. That series of land actions demonstrated the absolute necessity of air support for land forces to achieve victory. Air Chief Marshal Sir Arthur Tedder, who commanded the combined air forces in the Middle East during their advance, said recently: " I never subscribe to the view that the air alone can win the ultimate victory . . . I hope, however, that events have forced home that the air is now the governing factor in war."

But in three battles, those of the Coral Sea, Midway Island and the Bismarck Sea, the Americans have demonstrated that aircraft *can* win battles alone and without a shot being fired from a ship or land.

There are, too, those who hold the view that Germany can be utterly crushed by air

bombardment alone, provided that the number of aircraft allocated for that purpose was sufficient. But the difficulty is that no action can now proceed to a sure end without air support, and the demands for aircraft from all the fighting fronts and from the ocean convoy zones increase every month, so that bombing power available to be used against Germany builds up slowly. To be catastrophic, the consequences of bombing must be greater than the power of recovery. That stage does not appear to have been reached in the bombing of Germany. The bombing of the Reich is therefore a part of the war of attrition. The demands of the field forces and the sea forces will determine whether in the course of this war it will be possible to prove the bombing theory that a nation's will and power to resist can be crushed from the air.

Meanwhile, Major-General Eaker, present Chief of the U.S. Air Forces in the United Kingdom, has said that an American bomber force in parity with Bomber Command will be built up in Britain to operate primarily by day.

I wonder how many readers have themselves heard the American Fortresses and Liberator bombers growling their way through the day skies to Continental targets ? They are splendid aircraft, and they have done fine work, albeit as yet on a small scale. The Fortresses pass through the sky like formations of fish through the water. Their side elevations are extraordinarily shark-like. When aircraft like these can duplicate by day what Bomber Command does by night, the climacteric of a German breakdown will indeed be near.

Weather has slowed down air action in the South-West Pacific; but in the north, American bombers have again been raiding Kiska, the most advanced Japanese base in the Rat Islands. In Tunisia, stroke and counter-stroke on land and in the air follow one another as the First and Eighth Armies prepare for combined action. The greatest air activity has centred over Western Europe.

Bomber Command maintained its day and night offensive. By day the following targets were attacked: factories at Hengelo and near Liége (Feb. 28); Knaben molybdenum mines, Norway (Mar. 3); rail centres at Le Mans and near Valenciennes (Mar. 4); rail targets at Lingen, Germany, Aulnoye and Tergnier in France (Mar. 8); Le Mans rail centre and Renault factory (Mar. 9); Cockerill's armament works near Liége (Mar. 12). Four bombers were lost in these day raids.

NIGHT targets were St. Nazaire and West Germany, over 1,000 tons bombs (Feb. 28–Mar. 1); Berlin and West Germany and mine-laying (Mar. 1–2); mine-laying and West Germany (Mar. 2–3); Hamburg and West Germany (Mar. 3–4); mine-laying and West Germany (Mar. 4–5); Essen, nearly 1,000 tons bombs (Mar. 5–6); mine-laying (Mar. 7–8); Nuremberg, South and West Germany (Mar. 8–9); Munich, over 500 tons bombs, West Germany, and mine-laying (Mar. 9–10); Stuttgart (Mar. 11–12); Essen, over 1,000 tons bombs (Mar. 12–13). In these night raids 106 bombers were lost.

The U.S. Army Eighth Air Force bombed Brest and Lorient by day on March 6, losing three bombers and two escorting fighters; Rouen on March 12 without loss; and targets in Northern France on March 13.

A new departure is the acquisition of helicopters by Britain for marine protection.

Albacores Over the George Cross Island

LIKE SOME MOSAIC PAVEMENT does Malta appear from the air. Hardly a tree is to be seen, but the countless stone walls, the carefully-constructed terraces, the villages dotting the plateau—all speak of many centuries of civilized order and growth. In the island's epic defence a great part has been played by the Fleet Air Arm. Here we see three of a truly gallant band—Albacores with their torpedoes " at the ready," speeding to engage enemy shipping.

Photo, Associated Press

Japanese Planes Shot Out of the Indian Sky

ENEMY AIR ATTACKS ON INDIAN CITIES have met with little success. 1, Flight Sergt. A. M. O. Pring, who intercepted Jap bombers during a night raid in the Calcutta area in Jan. 1943, shot down three in four minutes—a world record for night fighting. He received an immediate award of the D.F.M. 2, Indian youths view the wreckage of one of these bombers. 3, The charred remains of another. 4, Crowds gather round this smashed aircraft while pipers play triumphal music.

Photos, British and Indian Official

Abyssinia's King of Kings Opens His Parliament

CELEBRATIONS IN ADDIS ABABA. The Negus, Haile Selassie I, who returned to his capital on May 5, 1941, was crowned "Lion of Judah, King of the Kings of Ethiopia," on Nov. 2, 1930. On the eve of the first anniversary of his coronation following the freeing of Ethiopia by the Allies, the Emperor opened his parliament. 1, The Royal car with its picturesque escort en route to the Parliament House. 2, The Emperor (descending steps towards the right of the photograph) leaving after the ceremony. 3, Haile Selassie "picking up the target" during a recent inspection of modern army equipment.

Photos, Associated Press

THE HOME FRONT

by E. Royston Pike

"WHO goes home?" The ancient phrase, new in the days when M.P.s used to club together after dark to traverse the footpad-infested fields which lay between Westminster and Charing Cross, had a painfully sombre ring when the Commons dispersed on the afternoon of March 3. For while they were debating the Navy estimates the Deputy-Speaker (Col. Clifton Brown) left the Chair, the Serjeant-at-Arms removed the mace from the table, and the Clerk Assistant rose and said, "With extreme sorrow I have to inform the House that Mr. Speaker died this afternoon." For fifteen years Capt. E. A. Fitzroy had guided their deliberations with a suave but firm touch, a complete impartiality, an occasional touch of dry humour, and a complete dignity that nothing could ruffle. Now he was dead (the first Speaker to die in office since 1789), and the House rose forthwith. Since there was now no Speaker it could not function—not even under the Deputy-Speaker, since he is the deputy of the Speaker, and the Speaker was dead.

WHEN the House met on March 9, the day already appointed—their sitting could not be expedited since in law there was none to call them together at an earlier date—their first business was the election of a successor to Capt. Fitzroy.

Mr. Anthony Eden, Leader of the House, rose to state that the King had given leave to the House to "proceed forthwith to the choice of a new Speaker." As he sat down the Clerk to the House pointed to Mr. G. Lambert, who was first an M.P. in 1891. Mr. Lambert proposed that the Deputy-Speaker, the Rt. Hon. Douglas Clifton Brown, should take the chair as Speaker; Mr. Tinker, in his turn answering the beckoning finger of the Clerk, seconded. Several other members having spoken in support, Col. Clifton Brown declared his willingness, though in no spirit of self-congratulation or self-confidence, to occupy the most honourable post in the House. "I will try, and that is the only pledge I can give you. I do promise that always to the limit of my ability I will give you my level best, and on that I pledge you my word." Then Mr. Lambert and Mr. Tinker, approaching Col. Clifton Brown, pulled him from his seat, ignoring his attempts to push them away—a strange old custom this, dating back to when the Speakership was no coveted post but a dangerous responsibility—and pulled and pushed him towards the chair. Then the Serjeant-at-Arms replaced the mace on the table.

A little later in the day the new Speaker proceeded to the House of Lords, where a Royal Commission indicated the King's assent to his appointment. After which, to the cry of "The Speaker elected," he returned to the Commons, assumed his full-bottomed wig and robes of office, and took the chair. Once again the House of Commons was able to function.

AFTER the not very satisfactory debate in the House of Commons it was the turn of the Lords to discuss the Beveridge Report. This they did on Feb. 24 and 25; and, as is so often the case in these days, the speeches of their lordships compared not at all unfavourably with those in the House below.

The Archbishop of Canterbury gave his emphatic support to "an epoch-making and epoch-marking report." The serf of former years, he said, had security without freedom; to some extent the wage-earning classes in our country have had freedom without security. What is now proposed is to give social security compatible with freedom. A week later, at a great meeting in Westminster organized by the Liberal Party, Sir William Beveridge replied to certain criticisms of his Report. In particular he referred to the complaint that he had not shown how "full employment," one of his three "Assumptions," could be maintained. But, he pointed out, when he was asked to report on Social Insurance and Allied Services he wasn't asked to design a complete suit—only the trousers. "I've designed the trousers," he said, "and my advice is that we had better put them on at once so that with a free mind we can see about a coat as well as other parts of our reconstruction wardrobe."

ANOTHER of the criticisms levelled at the Beveridge Scheme is that contained in the question, "Can we afford it?" Sir William Beveridge estimates that the total of the Security Budget for the first full year of the scheme, assumed to be 1945, will be £697 millions, but the Chancellor of the Exchequer would have to find only £86

HIS MAJESTY — MUNITION WORKER
Dressed in engineer's overalls, on two evenings a week the King works at a bench in a small munitions plant staffed by members of the Royal Household, turning out with delicate precision tools special parts for a gun used by the R.A.F. Always interested in economic matters, his Majesty is now acquiring a practical knowledge of industry which cannot but make his questions—in this photo he is seen talking to a fifteen-year-old worker in a R.O.F. —even more to the point.   *Photo, Planet News*

millions over and above what the State is already committed to. Who dares say (urge Beveridge supporters) that this, less than a week's war expenditure, is a burden that cannot be borne? Besides, no account is taken of the possible—probable, nay certain —increase in the national income in the years after the war. Nothing stays put, as George Bernard Shaw has frequently reminded us; certainly not the national income, nor the industries from which that income is derived. After the War it will be a very different Britain—a vastly different business world.

Few people indeed realize the revolutionary changes in the technique of almost every sort of manufacture that are promised by recent scientific developments.

Some months ago there was published in The Times (Nov. 9, 1942) the report of an address delivered to a convention of the American Chemical Society by Dr. Charles M. A. Stine, adviser on research to the great Du Pont combine. Mr. Stine pointed out that the War is compressing into the space of months scientific developments which, without this spur of necessity, might have taken half-a-century to realize. Fuels, metals, and plastics are now ready to complete the revolution in transport begun early in this century. Measured by the old pace of development we are now technically in the 1960's of motor-cars; weights in future may be half what they are now, power may

be up, fuels may yield fifty miles to the gallon. Housing plastics, rustless steels, non-ferrous alloys, various types of composition board and synthetic finishes—all will be available in profusion. Stainless steel may be a common roofing material. We shall have glass that is unbreakable and will float, wood that won't burn, shoes containing no leather, machinery bearings containing no metal. So great is the amount of fertilizer chemicals that the new capacity for high-pressure synthesis of ammonia will be able to supply, that the basic trends of agriculture may be changed. The manufacture of chemical rubbers, aluminium, magnesium, and a hundred other products will be at a rate many times as great as before the War. Industry, concludes Mr. Stine, will emerge from the War with the capacity for making scores of chemical and other raw materials on a scale that only two years ago would have been beyond comprehension. He was speaking of America, but we may be sure that British manufacturers and industrialists are not going to be behindhand in this tremendous wartime revolution.

AMONG the preparations for the North Africa expedition (revealed Sir James Grigg, Secretary of State for War, when introducing the Army estimates in the House of Commons on February 25) was the moving from billets and depots to the ports in a period of about three weeks of 185,000 men, 20,000 vehicles and 220,000 tons of stores. This meant running 440 special troop trains, 680 special freight trains, and 15,000 railway wagons by ordinary goods services.

Such figures speak volumes as to the efficiency of the railways under the tremendous strains of the War. Yet before the War, as Sir Thomas Royden, Chairman of the London Midland and Scottish Railway Company, said at the annual meeting of the company on March 5, there was a fairly wide belief that railways were becoming, if indeed they had not already become, obsolete as the main means of transport—and this in spite of the fact that the passenger journeys on British railways represented some 20,000,000,000 miles of travel and the freight traffic 17,000,000,000 ton miles. These figures have been outstripped during the war period. Last year the passenger traffic increased by a further 10,000,000,000 passenger miles and the freight traffic by a further 7,000,000,000 ton miles compared with pre-War. Whatever the future may hold, the successive Ministers of War Transport have good reason for their recognition of the railways as the backbone of the country's transport system.

HAS anyone met a man in a Utility suit? Maybe there are some about, but it is rare indeed to find in a London street a man in a two-piece with no turn-ups to his trousers, no pleats, and a bare minimum of pockets.

It is not just male obstinacy or innate conservatism that makes the Utility suits unpopular; trousers with turn-ups last longer and there is always something to put in any and every pocket. When a Whitechapel tailor was charged the other day with making trousers with pleats, turn-ups and four pockets, a Board of Trade inspector told the Old Street magistrate, Mr. F. O. Langley, that it was the general opinion of the trade that the restrictions saved no cloth at all. That Mr. Langley was inclined to sympathize was obvious from the low penalties he imposed.

On the same day Mr. Dalton, when opening a "Count your Coupons" exhibition at Charing Cross Underground Station, gave a pledge "not to buy a new suit of clothes until the War is over." But it would be interesting to know how many suits the President of the B.O.T. had in the pre-coupon age—with or without turn-ups!

ARE cut flowers a necessity in wartime? The Ministry of War Transport says no, and last November it made an order forbidding the consignment of flowers by rail, and at the end of the year the sending of flowers by parcel post was also prohibited. The flower traders were not to be outdone, however, and soon men carrying bulging suitcases were remarked travelling from Penzance to Paddington. Whereupon the carrying of flowers to market by train passengers was banned. But still undefeated the traders proceeded to send their flowers by sea and by boy cyclists working in relays. Then it was announced that the rail ban would be lifted on March 25 for the summer.

Wings for Victory Above Our Roving Camera

POST-WAR CIVIL AVIATION is receiving close attention in Britain, where the enormous advances made at the spur of military necessity are fully realized. Above, long-distance flying-boats at a marine terminal airport of British Overseas Airways.

GAS PRODUCER BUSES (left) have recently made their appearance in London. On March 3, 1943 it was stated that three of these vehicles were employed on the Hither Green-W. Kilburn route, and that eventually some 550 would be put into service.

INVASION BELLS, it was announced on March 3, 1943, will be used in future as a local alarm signal for any form of attack by enemy troops, whether these come by sea or air. Right, troops carry out routine inspection of church bells.

LONDON'S 'WINGS FOR VICTORY' week opened on March 6, 1943. The target was £150,000,000, and by March 18 the total wss announced of £162,015,869. Below, crowds in Trafalgar Square gather round the Lancaster bomber placed there, as carrier pigeons are released bearing messages for 1,300 War Savings Committees.

Photos. Planet News, Fox, Associated Press, Sport & General

I WAS THERE! Eye Witness Stories of the War

We In France Honour the R.A.F.'s Glorious Dead

A citizen of a French village wrote the following moving tribute to our R.A.F. men who lose their lives while flying over that country. The message was smuggled out of France and was received by Fighting French Headquarters in London at the end of February.

IT was 8.40 p.m. The sky was full of the rumbling of many planes. Suddenly I saw a great red flame to the north of Louhans. It was a British bomber which had just crashed at Moncony, a small village six miles to the north. All the people who saw this were in a state of anguish ; we learned that it was a Halifax bomber No. 42,036. The plane had ten Britons aboard, nine of whom were killed. Only one baled out.

On the following day the catastrophe was the only subject of conversation at Moncony. The whole population was terribly upset. The funeral of the heroic victims was to take place on Sunday at 4.30. A crowd of ten thousand had come to follow the dead to their last resting-place, when an order—coming no doubt from Vichy—postponed the ceremony to the morrow ; the authorities were afraid of patriotic demonstrations.

On the Monday, at 2.30, the funeral procession left the village school towards the cemetery. The nine coffins were pulled by horses from neighbouring farms. The procession was led by a lieutenant from Bourg, representing the French Army. Military honours were rendered by a section of a local regiment, and then followed a crowd of two thousand carrying wreaths with the following inscriptions : " To our liberators," " To the Defenders of the World's Liberty," " To the Heroes who fell for us," " You are far from home but you are close to our hearts."

The massive oak coffins were covered with an avalanche of flowers, that of the C.O. of the bomber being draped with a big Union Jack which a young girl of Louhans had made by working all night. The coffins were lined up on the ground in the cemetery in front of a large ditch, then the *curé* of the parish uttered a last prayer and a last good-bye to the noble victims in simple, moving and Christian words.

We then saw an unforgettable thing—a choir of young girls from the village singing God Save the King slowly, majestically and perfectly executed, and then the Marseillaise which was taken up at once by the whole crowd. The eyes of all were filled with tears and we all thought of the families of the dead back in England, families who perhaps are still unaware of those for whom we were weeping. Let those families know that the entire population of the district gave the same honour and attention to their dead as they would have given to their own dearest relatives.

Let them know that their tombs—until the day when they may be taken back to England —will be daily surrounded by prayers and by flowers from real French men and women, those who do not forget. Before finishing, allow me to mention in the name of the innumerable patriots who attended the funeral, some of those who risked much and spent so much effort to see that the sad ceremony should be as dignified and impressive as the circumstances demanded :

Civil Servants of the district, the various groups who brought flowers and wreaths, the young girls of St. Germain-du-Bois who achieved the *tour de force* of learning overnight the words of God Save the King in English, and the unknown young girl who had so well made a British flag with the red, white and blue cloth which she had at home.

Finally, don't let us forget the thousands of people who covered twenty to thirty miles on foot or on bicycles in order to do their duty as good Frenchmen.

How London's Home Guard A.A. Greeted the Raiders

When German raiders came to bomb the capital on January 17, London's H.G. anti-aircraft gunners went into action for the first time. Edward C. Gayler Second Lieutenant in the Home Guard A.A. (and Finance News Editor of The Sunday Dispatch, from which this story is reprinted), tells what it feels like to fire Britain's secret barrage.

FOR months we have been on duty, practising our gun drill in the dark, having " dummy-dummy " turnouts in the middle of the night, yet never getting a chance to fire at the enemy. Indeed, we were approaching the dangerous state of boredom, which can only lead to inefficiency.

Very few of our men had ever seen the guns fired. Some of the lucky ones—mostly officers—had been down on the coast and had fired the guns, but then only in daytime and out to sea. No one really knew what to expect when all our guns were fired together.

Quite frankly, I, with my brother officers, had been hoping that some other officer would be on duty when the guns were first fired, but I would not have missed this opportunity for a fortune and I know that my colleagues would have been proud to sign the orderly book that night in my place.

I had been on the site barely five minutes when the bugle sounded our general alarm. Soon after the public alert was sounded and gunners poured on to the site anxious to have a crack at the enemy. But by then all our guns were fully manned by the duty men and dozens of volunteers had to be sent home again.

ALL the officers arrived to take charge of their own men and within a few seconds London's barrage began. Up till then I had been a little nervous as to what to expect and was all too conscious of my responsibilities. I went from troop to troop having a last-minute talk to the men.

Enemy planes were getting nearer and nearer, and we were able to trace their progress by the burst of Home Guard shells away to the south.

Those of us who knew what to expect recognized the burst of neighbouring batteries from the fancy patterns they weaved in the sky while the enemy was still some miles off.

Our orders were given. Not a man forgot his drill, although none had ever before received orders in the din of battle. The thud of the 3·7s and the 4·5s sounded monotonously in our ears, and through the barrage I heard the gun commanders repeat their orders " Stand by."

From my command post I heard " Fire ! " and instantaneously there swept across the gun site a terrible swish. The whole area around was lit by explosions. Our shells

'HEROES WHO FELL FOR US.' As told in this page, the entire population of a French country district paid homage to the memory of nine British airmen who lost their lives when flying over France. They were buried with full military honours at Moncony, and this photograph shows the oak coffins surrounded with flowers.
Photo. British Official

were on their way to the enemy planes above us.

In the crash of the explosions I hardly noticed the vivid flashes and the gunners were too engrossed in their job to feel the tremor which shook the earth. They know their job, those men. As soon as their first salvo was off they were busy reloading.

My first reaction was one of relief that things had gone off so smoothly. I had never seen such a sight before. Although I had been every night in the London blitz, this was something more terrible than I ever thought existed.

MY excitement was increased when a bombardier reported, "*We've hit one, sir!*" Although, for a variety of reasons, it may not be possible for the authorities to verify our claim, I know that our gunners did a good job and at least they can credit themselves with a hit. No doubt every plane which passed within range of the Home Guard battery was damaged.

When the lull came the men went off to supper and to rest, but, so keen were they to have another crack, that when the second alarm came some hours later they were at their posts in record time.

The effect on the morale of the Home Guard was better than months of training. They have been whetted by the blood of their first enemy aircraft, and they are anxious now to take on all comers. And what is true of my own site is true also of the many other Home Guard anti-aircraft batteries.

But here I must give a very necessary word of warning. Our shells are meant for the Nazi planes, but we cannot pump thousands of shells into the sky without a rain of metal below.

Compared with the number of shells fired the number which fall unexploded is infinitesimal. And though twelve people were killed by our barrage, it was due mainly to their own negligence. It was those Londoners who stayed in the streets or who

LONDON'S A.A. DEFENCES have now been taken over to some extent by the Home Guard. A graphic description of the intense barrage put up by a Home Guard battery during an air attack is given in this and the preceding page. This photo shows H.Gs. at a gun-post during practice.
Photo, Topical

stood on their doorsteps to watch the "fireworks" who were killed or injured.

If you do not take cover immediately you hear gunfire then you are asking to be a casualty. And remember that our civil defence workers have enough to do looking after the bomb casualties. Next time there is a night raid the more noise you hear the safer you will be, so stay indoors and don't expose yourself to a hail of metal by trying to see what is going on.

It isn't clever to look up into the sky now that London's air barrage is the heaviest ever known, and if you get hurt through staying out when you should be under cover it will be your own fault.

instructor: "Was that our big gun?" He said: "No, you mug, we've been hit."

Later, I was down in the T.S. (Transmitting Station to you). Then another crack blasted open the side of the hull. We tried to block the gap with a six-foot-wide bookcase, but it fell right through.

BY now it had occurred to most of us that it was time to seek pastures new, and we made for the deck. There was chaffing and singing going on to the last. A lot of us lay on the heeling hull until it was evident the old Achates must go. Before the action, some of us had had a turkey put into the refrigerator to have for Christmas dinner when we got to Russia. One wag, just before the Achates rolled over, bawled out: "What about our blankety turkey?"

Once you dived into the water you became numb in a few minutes. I thanked my lucky stars I'd been a competition swimmer. I had thought to rip off my duffle coat and heavy gear, and now struck out for the rescue trawler about half a mile away. I wasn't doing very well and was getting very tired of it all when suddenly someone tore past me at knots, doing the trudgeon stroke. I thought: "I can do that, too"—and beat him to the trawler, I never saw my unknown rival again. I hope I meet him one day. He probably saved my life.

I Was in the Achates When She Fought to the End

Ordinary Seaman Ted Cutler, who was the oldest man in the destroyer Achates, tells how his ship, fighting to the end against a German cruiser, was sunk during the defence of a convoy on the way to Russia, on the last day of 1942. His vivid story is given here by courtesy of the B.B.C.

FOUR months ago I had my elbows on the bar of my own pub at Colchester. You see, I'm 48, and up till then I'd imagined that this war was a bit beyond me. But in that old pub, first the Australians, then the Canadians and then the Americans came roaring in. This one had been to the Middle East; that one to Persia—they'd all done something worth while. I got tired of this, and suddenly I made up my mind to become the only bald-headed sailor in the Navy.

I must say I was rather proud when I was passed A1, although I have lost my early streamline. In no time I was drafted to a training school. Within ten weeks came the great news—a ship. My highest hopes had been a patrol vessel, until I suddenly knew I was drafted to the destroyer Achates.

GOSH—here was action! The rigorous, down-to-the-bone life in the destroyer shrunk the last traces off me of 25 years of easy living. I should say 60 per cent of my shipmates in the Achates were about 23 years old. I kept my ears open for any remarks about "Grandpa." I wasn't going to stand for that—although, as a matter of fact, I am one.

I have never been so excited as when the Achates in a line of destroyers tore northwards all-out to take charge of its convoy. That was life! It wasn't long before we struck interference. Some big German stuff had manoeuvred up near to

us in the darkness, and at 8.30 on the morning of December 31 the first salvos crashed out.

Our Achates was selected to make a smoke screen to shield the convoy, and the enemy picked us out for his early fire. We must have been conspicuous. The German cruiser got us the first time. It'll show you how green I was. I said to our gunnery

H.M.S. ACHATES went down valiantly defending a convoy to Russia on Dec. 31, 1942; the story of the destroyer's end is recounted in this page. She was completed in 1930, displaced 1,350 tons, and carried a complement of 138.   PAGE 669   *Photo, British Official.*

We Dropped Our Picks & Shovels to Fight the Nazis

In the battle area south of Medjez, Tunisia, men of the Pioneer Corps dropped picks and shovels and with a rifle and 50 rounds apiece held up the German onslaught until relieved by the Guards. Navvy-warriors' stories, as told to Alan Humphreys, Reuters Special Correspondent, and to Archer Brooks, War Correspondent of The Daily Mirror, appear below.

"IT was thrilling to think that the Pioneers got there before the Guards," said Corporal Norman Hampshire, of Sheffield. "We were working on a road, and the ration wagon was just coming up with dinner when an officer dashed up on a motor bicycle.

"'The Germans are breaking through at ——,' he said. 'Dump your tools anywhere and grab your rifles. Stop any transport going along the road, or march, but get into the front line. You have less than an hour and a half, and you have got to stick there at all costs.'

"We reached our positions during the afternoon. There was a tank battle and we saw several German tanks go up in flames. It rained in sheets throughout the night. Next morning we were heavily shelled, and later in the afternoon the enemy threw grenades at us. There we stayed until our tanks came along." Corporal Hampshire, who served in the Navy during the last war, in the Warspite, was for a time a radio operator at Malta.

With him in action was Corporal William Kirkpatrick, of Girvan, Ayrshire, who won the Belgian Croix de Guerre. "It was hot enough while it lasted," he said. "It put me back a good twenty-five years. I was in the Royal Scots and fought on the Somme, at Ypres and Passchendaele. I was a coal-miner. It was hard work and I thought I would take on something easier for a spell.

I don't like fireside soldiering. It is like the old times under shell-fire again. The tank shells are not like the Jack Johnsons and coal boxes the Jerry used to throw at us on the Somme, but they're nasty little things all the same. And I must hand it to these boys who were in their first 'do' for the way they stood up to it."

It was a new experience for Private Edward Burton, 37, of Pellatt Road, East Dulwich, a printer in peacetime, who said, "The shelling was a bit nasty. Six of us were playing nap in a trench when it started, and they were using shrapnel, which we had never seen before, but we soon got used to it, and went back to the game. When the Guards relieved us we fell back into the native graveyard, where the skulls and bones lying about gave us the shivers."

Private Alan Benford, whose home is at Highcross Road, Claybrook, Rugby, manned the company's only Bren gun. Alan is only 20, and he found it exciting waiting for Jerries to come into his gunsights:

"We had front seats for the tank battle: and did we cheer when the first Jerry tank went up in flames! I counted fourteen enemy tanks in action with ours and saw five out of them knocked out. We couldn't get any sleep in the night because of the rain."

Another veteran was Pte. Thomas Fagan, 49, of Dublin. He was at Mons in 1914.

MEN OF THE PIONEER CORPS (see accompanying text), Royal Engineers, and other units are here shown unloading ammunition and stores shortly after the opening of our Tunisian campaign. This photo was taken at an advanced base W. of Bizerta. *Photo, Keystone*

OUR DIARY OF THE WAR

MARCH 3, 1943, Wednesday 1,278th day
Air.—Daylight raid by Mosquitoes on molybdenum mines at Knaben in Norway. Heavy night raid on Hamburg.
North Africa.—Enemy attacks continued in Sejenane area of N. Tunisia.
Mediterranean.—U.S. aircraft made daylight raid on Messina.
Russian Front.—Soviet troops occupied Rzhev after prolonged battle.
Australasia.—Entire Japanese convoy of 11 transports and 10 warships sunk by Allied bombers in Bismarck Sea.
Home Front.—Two small-scale night raids on London ; accident at Tube shelter caused death of 173 persons.

MARCH 4, Thursday 1,279th day
Air.—U.S. Flying Fortresses raided Hamm and Rotterdam by day.
North Africa.—First Army troops retired from Sejenane to Tamera. French troops occupied Nefta in S. Tunisia.
Mediterranean.—Heavy bombers raided Naples by night.
Russian Front.—In Donetz Basin Germans claimed recapture of Proletarskaya and Slavyansk.

MARCH 5, Friday 1,280th day
Sea.—Admiralty announced loss of minelayer Welshman.
Air.—Heavy night raid on Essen.
North Africa.—In Central Tunisia Allied troops entered Sidi Bou Zid and Pichon.
Russian Front.—Soviet troops continued advance S.W. of Rzhev. Germans claimed recapture of Lisichansk on Donetz front.
Australasia.—U.S. warships shelled Jap positions in Solomons.

MARCH 6, Saturday 1,281st day
Air.—U.S. bombers made daylight raids on Brest and Lorient.
North Africa.—Attacks by Rommel's tanks and infantry were repulsed by Eighth Army in Mareth area.
Russian Front.—Gzhatsk occupied by Soviet troops.
Burma.—R.A.F. Liberators made heavy attack on Mandalay.
General.—Stalin awarded military title of Marshal of the Soviet Union.

MARCH 7, Sunday 1,282nd day
Sea.—Admiralty announced loss of trawler Lord Hailsham.
North Africa.—In Mareth region Rommel's forces withdrew N. of Medenine.

Australasia.—U.S. heavy bombers attacked enemy bases in Solomons.
U.S.A.—American bombers raided Kiska in the Aleutians.

MARCH 8, Monday 1,283rd day
Air.—U.S. Fortresses and Liberators bombed U-boat supply centre at Rennes and railway yards at Rouen. R.A.F. made heavy night raid on Nuremberg.
North Africa.—In N. Tunisia enemy attack was held near Tamera ; in the south French troops occupied Tozeur.
Mediterranean.—Allied bombers raided Palermo and Agrigento.
Russian Front.—Soviet troops captured Sychevka, N. of Vyasma, after stubborn fighting.

MARCH 9, Tuesday 1,284th day
Air.—R.A.F. made heavy raid on Munich.
Mediterranean.—Fighter-bombers from Malta attacked railways in Sicily.
Russian Front.—Soviet H.Q. announced evacuation of Krasnodar, Lozovaya, Pavlograd, Krasnoarmeisk, Kramatorskaya, Barvenkovo, Slavyansk and Lisichansk in the Donetz area.
Australasia.—Strong Japanese raid on Wau airfield, New Guinea.
U.S.A.—U.S. aircraft again raided Kiska, Aleutians.

MARCH 10, Wednesday 1,285th day
North Africa.—In S. Tunisia our troops repelled attacks at Ksar Ghilane with heavy loss to enemy.
Russian Front.—Soviet troops occupied Biely, in Smolensk region ; in the Donetz basin German threat to Kharkov increased.
Australasia.—Fortress bombers attacked Jap base of Wewak, New Guinea.

MARCH 11, Thursday 1,286th day
Sea.—Admiralty announced loss of submarine P 311.
Air.—R.A.F. made heavy night attack on Stuttgart.
North Africa.—In S. Tunisia French troops occupied Metlaoui, between Tozeur and Gafsa.
Russian Front.—Strong German attacks repulsed south and west of Kharkov.
General.—First official reports from H.Q. of French guerillas told of train-wrecking and other activities.

MARCH 12, Friday 1,287th day
Air.—Flying Fortresses attacked marshalling yards at Rouen and Mosquitoes bombed engineering works near Liége. R.A.F. made heaviest bombing raid on Essen.
North Africa.—Three enemy attacks repulsed W. of Sejenane.
Russian Front.—Soviet troops entered Vyasma, E. of Smolensk ; Russians retired W. of Kharkov.
Home Front.—German fighter-bombers made low-level day raid on

Greater London area ; five out of 24 FW 190s shot down by fighters of a Norwegian squadron.
General.—Announced that Mr. Eden had arrived in Washington.

MARCH 13, Saturday 1,288th day
Air.—American heavy bombers attacked railway yards at Amiens Abbeville and Poix.
Mediterranean.—U.S. Liberators made night raid on Naples harbour.
Russian Front.—Germans drove wedge into defences W. of Kharkov ; heavy attacks also delivered from north and south.
Australasia.—Allied aircraft attacked Jap convoy making for Wewak, New Guinea.

MARCH 14, Sunday 1,289th day
Sea.—Light coastal forces manned by men of Royal Norwegian Navy penetrated fjord and torpedoed two vessels in Floroe harbour, N. of Bergen.
Air.—Whirlwind bombers made daylight attacks on airfields at Abbeville and Maupertus.
Russian Front.—Germans claimed capture of Kharkov.
Burma.—Heavy fighting in Rathedaung area, where Japanese launched attacks.

MARCH 15, Monday 1,290th day
Russian Front.—Soviet troops evacuated Kharkov.
China.—Reported that Chinese had gained important victory in Yangtze River front W. of Hankow.
Burma.—U.S. aircraft attacked Gokteik railway viaduct between Mandalay and Lashio.
Australasia.—Allied aircraft inflicted heavy damage on Japanese transports off Aru is. Japs raided Port Darwin.
U.S.A.—American aircraft made six bombing attacks on Kiska, Aleutians.

MARCH 16, Tuesday 1,291st day
Sea.—Two large enemy supply ships torpedoed by light naval forces in North Sea.
Air.—Mosquitoes bombed railway workshops at Paderborn, W. Germany, in daylight.
Russian Front.—Soviet troops held enemy attacks S. of Kharkov and W. of Byelgorod.
Australasia.—Fortress bombers made heavy raid on Rapopo airfield, Rabaul.
U.S.A.—Three more raids by U.S. bombers on submarine base at Kiska.

★————— *Flash-backs* ————————★

1940
March 12. M. Daladier announced Allied expeditionary force of 50,000 ready to help Finland if appeal received.
March 13. Hostilities ceased in Russo-Finnish War.
1941
March 3. German troops reached Greek frontier through Bulgaria.
March 4. British naval raid on Lofoten Is., Norway.
March 6. Allied forces from Somaliland entered Ethiopia.

March 11. Lease-Lend Bill became law in U.S.A.

1942
March 3. Japanese air raids on Broome and Wyndham, W. Australia. R.A.F. bombed Renault works, Paris.
March 6. Japanese entered Batavia, capital of Java.
March 8. In Burma, Japanese occupied Rangoon.
March 11. Japanese landed at Buka in the Solomons.

Do they call it a bairn or a child in your part of the world? Do they speak of a brook or a beck, a biggin or a dwelling? Do they close their een and rest their heads on a cod? Do they do their courting in the gloaming, milk the kine, put on shoon, set traps for mousen or mouses, turn not the other cheek but the other wang? Do they say "I mun go" or "her told she" or "do ee give it to we"? Do they pronounce cup to rhyme with soup, and would with mud? The Association for Planning and Regional Reconstruction (32, Gordon Square, London, W.C.1) wants to know, and among the people to whom they have sent their questionnaires are (I learn from The Land Girl) the Women's Land Army.

Why the Land Girls? Because for the most part they are newcomers to the districts to which they are sent, and so, if they keep their ears open, they are likely to be struck at once by an unusual word, a novel turn of phrase. As often as not the villagers don't know that there are any unusual words in their vocabulary; they have always called a broom a besom, or said they were rad when they were afraid. The Land Girl tells of one W.L.A. girl in Hampshire who lived with a cowman and his wife. At first she could not make out what he meant when, sitting down to breakfast after milking, he used to say, "I feel that lear and cold." Apparently in that part of Hampshire the old word lear is still used to mean hungry or empty. That is the sort of information that the Association wants, and filling up the little questionnaires should help the Land Girls to pass the time—if they have any surplus time to pass. "Oh, oh, the farmer's girl!" writes Ola Trist in The Land Girl from a farm down in Cornwall:

Seven o'clock on a winter's morn
I start my little day,
And all day long I am tending cows
in a conscientious way . . .

I sit in the sun and consume a bun
when the morning's half-way
through,
Then go with a rush and madly
brush—I've got so much to do!
I clear the mud, and mop the blood
when the turnip knife misses its
way,
And walk for miles over hedges
and stiles for cows that have gone
astray . . .

Among my letters the other morning was one from a young man of nineteen who complains most bitterly that he has recently been turned down for air-crew duties in the R.A.F. on account of bad eyesight. "I am very eager to fly," he writes, "and I do not see why we unfortunates should be deprived of the main desire of our lives. Could not the Air Ministry find some possible means of allowing us the chance to fly? Why don't they allow us to wear glasses while flying, suitably fitted in the flying helmet? Is it possible to fly if one has the lens inserted in the eye? Would Ferry Command duties not be suitable for men whose eyesight is not the best? I am dying to fly and have a shot at the Germans, but I am afraid I shall have to sit back and watch." Only the Air Ministry can give the answers to these questions, but it seems a pity that so much youthful fire should be permitted to burn itself out. And I have noticed in a recent list of R.A.F. awards the name of Acting Squadron Leader G. B. Warnes, described as Fighter Command's only operational pilot wearing contact lenses—glasses fitting inside the eyelids.

Yet when Mr. Warnes (who before the War was an airman and has recently sunk an armed trawler, bombed a distillery, and made low-level raids on enemy airfields) first applied to join the R.A.F. he was told his eyesight wasn't good enough for flying duties. The Germans probably wish he didn't see so well.

From what readers tell me it is clear that they like to be informed of "War books" which are possessed of more than a merely ephemeral interest. Here are two which I can recommend. The first is The Fleet Air Arm by the novelist, Mr. John Moore (Chapman and Hall, 5s.). Mr. Moore writes from practical experience as an F.A.A. pilot, and his book describes both the history of the Fleet Air Arm from its

Wing Cdr. R. R. S. TUCK, D.S.O., D.F.C., and 2 Bars. By Feb. 16, 1941, when he was awarded a second Bar, he had brought down 27 enemy aircraft. He was reported a prisoner of war in 1942.
Drawn by Capt. Cuthbert Orde, Crown Copyright reserved

origins in the last war and its most outstanding achievements in the present struggle—from the sinking of a Koenigsberg class cruiser in the harbour at Bergen on April 12, 1940 (the first time in history that a major unit of any fleet had been sunk by air attack), to the great battle in the Channel nearly two years later, when the Scharnhorst and Gneisenau slipped out of Brest. There is a chapter on our aircraft-carriers, and another on the aircraft which the men of the F.A.A. know so well how to use—the Skuas, Rocs, and Gladiators, the Walrus and the Seafox, and these "Stringbags" which "looked obsolescent before the War and have remained obsolescent ever since, but have never become obsolete." Mr. Moore quotes the song made in their honour:

The Swordfish fly over the ocean,
The Swordfish fly over the sea;
If it were not for King George's Swordfish,
Where the 'ell would the Fleet Air Arm be?

My second recommendation is a book which has already received wide recognition—and very deservedly: They Were

Expendable, by Mr. W. L. White (Hamish Hamilton, 6s.). It is the story of the little band of very gallant gentlemen, the young officers of the U.S. Motor Torpedo-boat Squadron 3, who covered themselves with glory in the defence of the Bataan Peninsula and Corregidor in the great Philippines battle of a year ago. It was one of the four solitary survivors of the squadron who explained to Mr. White what "to be expendable" means in modern military parlance.

"It's like this" (he said). "Suppose you're a sergeant machine-gunner, and your army is retreating and the enemy advancing. The captain takes you to a machine-gun covering the road. 'You're to stay here and hold this position,' he tells you. 'For how long?' you ask. 'Never mind,' he answers, 'just hold it.' Then you know you're expendable. In a war, anything can be expendable—money or gasoline or equipment or most usually men. They are expending you and that machine-gun to get time. They don't expect to see either one again. They expect you to stay there and spray that road with steel until you're killed or captured, holding up the enemy for a few minutes or even a precious quarter of an hour."

So that's what to be expendable means: it's part of "that grim language of realism which the smug citizenry doesn't understand," the language spoken by "the sad young men back from battle who wander through those plump cities as strangers in a strange land . . . trying to tell of a tragedy which few enjoy hearing." But if their story is not one to be enjoyed it is, in its grim brilliance, in its reminder of others' sacrifice, one that we ought all to read, and remember.

But "War books," however admirable, however essential it is we should read them, should not be our only mental provender; and from many a quarter there come indications of a revived interest in the great books of the past. More than seventy years after his death Charles Dickens is still a very living force. Even the Brains Trusters who, when asked the other day to answer the question, "If you were a novelist, what book would you have been most proud to have written?" agreed with Dr. Julian Huxley in making Pickwick Papers their second choice (Tolstoy's War and Peace was their first, but then the broadcast version had come as a powerful reminder). In London and in many a provincial town, in Australia, New Zealand, Canada and the U.S.A., there are branches of the Dickens Fellowship in very active life, and The Dickensian still continues as a very readable quarterly. Well indeed is it that it should be so. Dickens is a mental tonic in these trying times; his characters put to rout those Nazi thugs, those Jew-baiters, those little yellow sadists of the Orient, who make the newspapers such nightmare reading.

From Mrs. A. V. Alexander, wife of the First Lord of the Admiralty, comes the intimation that a flag-day in aid of the work for seamen of six Sailors' Societies is being held in London on April 13—maybe in other places too. For over a hundred years these societies have served those who go down to the sea in ships, and today those men need more than ever the helping hand that these societies exist to hold out, at every port, after every shipwreck. It is impossible to do justice to the magnificent spirit of the men of the Mercantile Marine. Even in peacetime their lot was often a hard one, and now it is one long gamble with death. Buying a flag is surely the very least of our tributes.

In This Oasis a Spitfire Waits for Action

THE R.A.F. 'AT HOME' IN TUNISIA. Beneath the shade—welcome enough, however scanty—of a cluster of cactus trees in the otherwise barren desert the R.A.F. has established a forward aerodrome—one of many, it need hardly be said. A collection of petrol-tins marks the temporary workshop of the mechanics, and what is going forward is obviously full of interest to the Arab youth. An engine-starter battery, operated by the flight-maintenance crew stands on the left; and in the background is a Spitfire, ready to take the air. *Photo, British Official : Crown Copyright*

Printed in England and published every alternate Friday by the Proprietors, THE AMALGAMATED PRESS, LTD., The Fleetway House, Farringdon Street, London, E.C.4. Registered for transmission by Canadian Magazine Post. Sole Agents for Australia and New Zealand : Messrs. Gordon & Gotch, Ltd. ; and for South Africa : Central News Agency, Ltd.—April 2, 1943. S.S. *Editorial Address :* JOHN CARPENTER HOUSE, WHITEFRIARS, LONDON, E.C. 4.

Vol 6 *The War Illustrated* Nº 152

Edited by Sir John Hammerton

SIXPENCE   APRIL 16, 1943

'THE EIGHTH ARMY IS ON THE MOVE.' This significant announcement came at the end of Mr. Churchill's broadcast on March 21, 1943. The next day the world learned that Gen. Montgomery's forces had already begun their powerful assault on the Mareth positions; in little more than a week the whole Line was overrun. This photo shows the 8th Army's indomitable commander in a forward area in Tunisia, detailing his plans to members of his staff.   *Photo, British Official: Crown Copyright*

THE BATTLE FRONTS

by Maj.-Gen. Sir Charles Gwynn, K.C.B., D.S.O.

SINCE I last wrote in the middle of March 1943 the battle of Tunisia has begun. At the end of the month it is still in its early stages, and it will probably pass through many more. The need for secrecy prevents the release of definite information as regards the situation, and it has not yet advanced sufficiently to reveal with certainty the courses either side will pursue. The general strategic lay-out of the theatre of operations is clear enough, but it admits of development on several lines depending on the commanders' plans—and even they may be modified or drastically changed by the results of tactical encounters. All that can be foreseen with some certainty is a fierce struggle, probably prolonged over a period to be measured in months rather than weeks, and falling into a series of well-defined phases of which the battle for the Mareth Line is the first. Ultimate victory for the Allies is assured; but it is of importance to achieve victory in the shortest possible time—for time is essentially what the enemy is attempting to gain.

In Russia during the fortnight under review there has been much hard fighting on many sectors of the front, but thaw conditions have brought about something of a lull in major operations. Progress has slowed down, with attacks and counter-attacks aiming at local rather than at sweeping successes. It is clear that neither side is yet content to stabilize the front and wait for the ground to dry, and there is still the possibility of important developments before the summer campaigning season opens.

FIELD AMBULANCE of the Indian Medical Service rescues a member of a Gurkha battalion in Tunisia. This man was wounded when taking part in an attack on enemy positions in the Matmata hills.   *Photo, British Official*

NORTH AFRICA With the battle of Tunisia still in its initial stages, too much importance should not be attached to the first tactical encounters. It must be realized that the fight for the Mareth Line is only an opening episode, which may or may not prove to have a decisive bearing on final results, depending on whether Rommel is determined to attempt to hold his positions at all costs or whether he will, while his line of retreat is still open, join forces with Von Arnim in the north.

The general strategic position is clear. The Axis main object must be to retain their hold on Tunis and Bizerta. Von Arnim has the task of meeting any attack made by the 1st Army in the north; and that definitely prevents him from cooperating with Rommel in the south. Rommel has much the more difficult task. He has to hold off the attack of the 8th Army, and at the same time meet the threat of the French and American forces to his line of communications and retreat. He has had, it is true, in the Mareth Line a position very much stronger against direct attack than that which he failed to hold at El Alamein; but he lacks adequate numerical strength to meet both a direct attack and the threat to his rear.

Rommel's main advantage is that he possesses a powerful and mobile armoured reserve and a good road system by which it can be concentrated for counter-attack at the most threatened point, or against any one of the Allied columns which may give him an opportunity. His main object must be, by taking full advantage of interior lines, to prevent the Allied 1st and 8th Armies joining hands in a concentric close attack on the vital ports in the north.

General Alexander's problems are those of a numerically superior force acting on exterior lines. By maintaining unrelenting pressure at all points his opponent is prevented from concentrating reserves for counter-strokes to an extent that cannot be met by elastic defence at the point where counter-attacks are delivered. It may be necessary to give ground at such points while increasing pressure at others. Already we have seen this process in operation. Rommel has carried out counter-attacks at the most threatened points, but he has been forced to split up his reserves, with the consequence that counter-attacks have failed to achieve any considerable success and they are a wasting asset owing to losses.

Alexander's chief disadvantages are the long and difficult lines of communication, which probably limit the size and affect the composition of each of his attacking columns. This imposes a degree of caution. The main pressure on Rommel will probably have to be applied by the 8th Army, not only in its frontal attack but by the outflanking column which is threatening the Gabès gap at El Hamma. If the latter can maintain its position on the Jebel Tebaga ridge and can be reinforced—not an easy matter with such a long and difficult line of communications—it is very hard not to believe that Rommel will be compelled to withdraw to the Gabès position. An even more complete retreat would be unavoidable if the American thrust through Maknassi gains weight.

ROMMEL being attacked on such a wide front and from so many different directions must rely mainly on the mobility of his reserve fist. That reserve has already had heavy losses in its counter-attacks and is constantly harried from the air; it is therefore, as I have said, a wasting asset. The doubtful reliability in an emergency of some of his Italian troops must also be a source of anxiety to him. In the circumstances, the time must be drawing near for him to decide on retreat, or, deliberately, to face annihilation in order to gain time. A rapid, well-organized retreat might be combined with a heavy counter-attack possibly against the American Maknassi column.

I cannot believe that Rommel, who has so often saved himself from disaster by retreat, would deliberately allow himself to be enclosed in a trap. He probably realizes that he delayed retreat too long and expended his reserves too lavishly at El Alamein; and he must know that the loss of his army would leave Von Arnim in a desperate situation. His decision one way or the other cannot be long delayed; and I expect his retreat, probably covered by strong

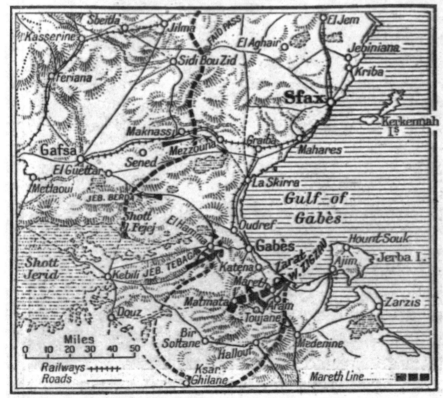

EIGHTH ARMY'S ADVANCE ON MARETH LINE. On March 29, 1943 it was announced that Matmata, Mareth and Toujane had fallen to Gen. Montgomery's troops, and that Rommel was falling back towards Gabès. This map shows (dotted) the Allied line at March 27. The solid black arrows indicate the American attack from Maknassi; Gen. Freyberg's left flanking movement on El Hamma; and the frontal assault on the Mareth Line.   *By courtesy of The Times*

counter-attacks, will have started before this article is published.

★Twenty-four hours after I had written as above came the news that the Mareth Line was in our hands. Once again Rommel had been out-manoeuvred and out-fought by the 8th Army. It may seem that Montgomery's outflanking attack on El Hamma which compelled Rommel to retreat was an obvious manoeuvre, and that his costly frontal attack was unnecessary. It should be realized, however, how audacious was the manoeuvre, for it involved dividing the 8th Army into two widely separated parts, and the attack, at the end of a long and difficult route, on an enemy strongly posted and possessing excellent and short lines of communication by which he could bring up his powerful reserves to counter-attack.

In view of the danger of defeat in detail the encircling attack was, in fact, only

RUSSIAN CENTRAL FRONT. On March 26, 1943 it was stated that the Red Army was only 25 miles from Smolensk. Arrows show direction of main Soviet thrusts.
By courtesy of The Times

If this pincer attack had succeeded it would almost certainly have entailed the loss of Kupiansk and of immensely valuable railway communications which the Russians had recovered. There was desperate fighting, with heavy losses on both sides ; but the Russian defence stood firm against repeated attacks, in which the Germans made prodigal use of reserve divisions, armoured and infantry, supported by great concentrations of aircraft. Not only did the Russians prevent the enemy getting a permanent footing on the left bank of the river, but they themselves retained a certain number of bridgeheads on the right bank.

Towards the end of the period under review, the ice on the river appears to have become too weak to take heavy weights, while it still prevented bridging operations. As a result, the scale of attacks diminished, though local attacks against the Russian bridgeheads across the river continue.

As their attempts against the Middle Donetz weakened, the Germans appear to have added to the weight of their drive north of Kharkov towards the Upper Donetz. Their capture of Byelgorod, on the right bank of the river, was a serious loss to the Russians, for it interrupted the railway from Kursk to Kupiansk and also implied a threat to the southern flank of the Russian offensive west of Kursk, which was also encountering increasing opposition on its front. The

Germans have without success made many attempts to cross the Upper Donetz in the Byelgorod neighbourhood, but both here and in the Orel region the situation is obscure and it seems probable that mud is hampering the operations of both sides.

Meanwhile, on the central front the Russians have retained the initiative and have made steady if slow progress westwards from Vyasma and southwards from the line of the Rzhev-Veliki-Luki railway, forcing and turning the line of the Upper Dnieper. The Germans have retreated fighting hard, and their resistance is stiffening ; but it seems improbable that they will stand to fight at all costs till the outer strong points of the Smolensk defences are reached. The Russians are getting very close to them now, and it seems probable that when they make contact with them they will not, at this time, attempt a further direct drive towards Smolensk itself. So far as ground conditions allow they may, however, continue their attacks in the more lightly defended fronts north and south of the Smolensk bastion.

The German counter-attacks about Zhizdra, north of Briansk, which were on the scale of a minor offensive of a forestalling or diversionary character, seem to indicate an attempt to frustrate some such plan. It may be noted, too, that the attacks met strong Russian forces and failed to make progress.

The early phases of the spring thaw are, however, already hampering Russian operations. Frost enables ski-troops to operate at night and in the morning, but by midday slush makes movement desperately difficult.

FARTHER north in the Ilmen and Leningrad regions the situation remains obscure ; but the Germans evidently expect the Russians to undertake further operations on a considerable scale before the winter is over.

In these recent operations along the whole front the Germans have made lavish use of reserves. This would seem to indicate that they have no intention of attempting any decisive offensive operations, in the early part of the summer at any rate, and that their main immediate object is to secure a favourably situated, stabilized front as a springboard for an offensive at a later stage, or from which a withdrawal, if events rendered that necessary, could be carried out without much difficulty when the state of the ground facilitates movement. But the winter war is not yet over, and much may happen before it closes.

JAP SUPPLIES moving up Burmese rivers have been heavily strafed by the R.A.F. Here is a typical target. The enemy vessel in the foreground has heeled over as a result of blast.
Photo, British Official : Crown Copyright

justifiable if the frontal attack was delivered with sufficient energy to engage a large part of the enemy's reserves, and if the communications of the force which delivered the flanking attack were secure from interruption. The first condition was fulfilled by the original frontal attack, and I suggest that the latter depended on the impassable nature of the Matmata hills on which Rommel had relied for the protection of his right flank, but which in practice protected the communications of the outflanking column. To Montgomery's promptitude in grasping the possibilities of the situation as it developed, and in modifying his original plans accordingly, his victory must presumably be attributed ; but it needed a magnificent response by his troops and the R.A.F. to the calls made on them to bring it to fruition.

RUSSIA
After the recapture of Kharkov —admitted by the Russians on March 14—the Germans drove eastwards towards Chuguyev, which stands at the elbow formed by the upper and middle reaches of the Donetz. At the same time they redoubled their attacks northwards in attempts to force a passage of the middle reaches of the river while it was still frozen.

HOME FROM MIDDLE EAST. The 9th A.I.F. Division, known as " Rats of Tobruk " owing to their long occupation of that fortress, recently arrived back in Australia. On March 23, 1943 Mr. Curtin announced that Mr. Churchill had sent a congratulatory message to Lt.-Gen. Sir L. Morshead, commanding the division. Here is a group of men singing as they are ferried to the homeward-bound ships.

Photo, British Official

Our Guns Stopped Them Dead in Their Tracks

ROMMEL'S TANKS IN S. TUNISIA made a violent assault on 8th Army positions on March 5, 1943. The attack failed, and the enemy was forced to withdraw to the hills N.W. of Medenine. Altogether 52 German tanks were knocked out, estimated at about half the total Axis force engaged, including eight of the new type Mark III's. Top, a six-pounder battery of an anti-tank regiment, which destroyed five Mark III's, shown in action. Below, three of the enemy tanks burning.

Photos, British Official, Crown Copyright

Opening Shots in the Great Battle for Mareth

EIGHTH ARMY'S FRONTAL ATTACK on the Mareth Line, concentrated on a 6-mile front between the sea and the Medenine-Gabès road, scored the opening round of the great battle which began on March 19, 1943. Furious fighting developed as the result of Rommel's counter-attack launched to restore the German main defence-line. Top, view from an observation-post outside Foum Tatahouine, southern bastion of the Mareth Line, which Gen. Montgomery's forces captured on Feb. 18. Below, a 4·5-in. medium gun contributes its quota to the great night barrage that heralded the 8th Army's assault.

Photos, British Official: Crown Copyright

Before the Big Push in Anderson's Sector

BATTLE OF TUNISIA. 1, Axis prisoners, captured by U.S. troops, shown en route to a prison camp. 2, Formidable 25-pounder gun mounted on a Valentine tank chassis. 3, Gen. Alexander, deputy C.-in-C., Allied forces in N. Africa, at the wheel of a " jeep " during a visit to an advanced Brigade H.Q. 4, Carriers wait to advance as a Bren gunner keeps watch (left). They are manned by men from a Home Counties regiment, supported by units of a Scottish regiment.

Photos, British Official; British Newsreels, Sport & General

Joyous Homecoming of Men Wounded in the War

FROM THE MIDDLE EAST these British soldiers, many of whom were wounded in the battles of Egypt, Cyrenaica and Tripolitania, crowd the rails of the white-painted hospital ship Atlantis as she arrives at a home port. The majority of the casualties had treatment in South Africa before embarkation. Nearly 2,000 sick and wounded men of the 8th Army—some of whom had been abroad for two years—recently returned to this country for rest and recuperation.

Photo, G.P.U.

THE WAR AT SEA

by Francis E. McMurtrie

Vice-Adm. SIR B. FRASER, whose appointment as C.-in-C. Home Fleet (with acting rank of Admiral), in succession to Adm. Sir J. Tovey, was announced on March 23, 1943. He is 55. *Photo, Vandyk.*

IN March 1943 the Admiralty announced a change in the command of one of our three principal fleets. Vice-Admiral Sir Bruce Fraser, aged 55, hitherto Second-in-Command, then relieved Admiral Sir John Tovey (aged 57) as Commander-in-Chief, Home Fleet. The latter, it is understood, relinquished this command by his own desire in order to facilitate the advancement of younger officers. He now becomes Commander-in-Chief at the Nore in succession to Admiral Sir George Lyon.

On the eve of Sir John Tovey's departure the King made a point of visiting the Home Fleet and paying a personal farewell to its Chief. Under Sir John Tovey its efficiency has reached a very high level, as demonstrated when the Bismarck and Prinz Eugen broke out into the Atlantic in May 1941. The former was hunted down and sunk within the space of six days, while the latter was driven into Brest, where she remained blockaded for nearly nine months.

Other changes in high naval appointments coincided with the alteration in command of the Home Fleet. Vice-Admiral Sir Henry Moore, Vice-Chief of the Naval Staff at the Admiralty, took the place of Admiral Fraser as Second-in-Command, and was himself relieved by Vice-Admiral Sir Neville Syfret, previously in command of " Force H," based on Gibraltar. The latter force was taken over by Vice-Admiral A. U. Willis.

Such changes in wartime are an excellent thing, as they ensure that officers at the Admiralty and at sea have had recent experience of each other's problems, enabling them to work together with greater efficiency.

MR. CHURCHILL made the definite statement on March 25 that the United Nations have afloat a substantially larger fleet than they had at the worst moment of the U-boat warfare, and that this improvement is continuing. This assurance may be taken to imply that, though the present intensified attack by enemy submarines on our convoys is causing serious losses, these are not up to German expectations. It has been reported from a neutral source that improved defence tactics have caused heavy U-boat losses, the best answer that could be made to the attack. Not until enemy submarines are being destroyed faster than they can be built

will it be possible to say that the menace has been mastered.

In the meantime Dr. Goebbels continues to make extravagant claims concerning Allied shipping losses. Invariably these are much exaggerated, but obviously he cannot afford to be moderate in his claims. The official view in this country, despite severe criticism, is that it would not pay us at this stage to disclose actual figures of mercantile tonnage sunk by the enemy, who would thus receive a useful guide to the progress of the U-boat campaign. For a similar reason no reports are made, save in exceptional cases, of the numerous enemy submarines destroyed; though it has been stated officially that of late the rate of destruction has shown a gratifying improvement.

MERCHANT NAVY Personnel Rescued from the Sea

Lord Leathers, Minister of War Transport, revealed recently that on the average 87 per cent are saved of ships' companies of cargo vessels sunk by enemy action. This is a high tribute not only to the life-saving appliances now in general use, but also to the diligence with which escort vessels and other merchantmen seek for survivors. It is, of course, obvious that in the Battle of the Atlantic the maintenance in adequate numbers of an experienced Merchant Navy personnel is even more important than the replacement of ships.

A GOOD example of the type of attack with which our convoys have to contend was contained in the official account of an action in the Atlantic in February. In this series of attacks, which continued for three and a half days, at least two U-boats were accounted for, one by the surface escort and one by Coastal Command aircraft which arrived on the second day.

The former enemy submarine was sighted on the surface seven miles away by H.M.S. Beverley, an ex-American destroyer commanded by Lt.-Com. R. A. Price, R.N. When the Beverley had approached to within two-and-a-half miles the U-boat dived, but the Beverley succeeded in keeping her under observation, while a second destroyer, H.M.S. Vimy (Lt.-Com. R. B. Stannard, V.C., R.N.R.), dropped a series of depth charges. After the third batch the U-boat

appeared on the surface again, and was instantly fired on by both destroyers. Her crew emerged and jumped into the sea just before the submarine started to sink by the stern. She went down vertically, her bow being the last part visible. Altogether 49 prisoners were recovered, four of whom died and were buried at sea.

Another U-boat was seen at this time, and during the night the attack was pursued by no less than five. Other vessels of the escort took active measures against the enemy, including H.M. corvettes Abelia, Mignonette, and Campanula, the U.S. destroyer Babbitt, and the Fighting French corvette Lobelia. To the last-named credit must be given for a second U-boat very seriously damaged, and probably destroyed. The Beverley also attacked several of the enemy submarines, damaging and possibly destroying at least two. Aircraft of the Sunderland and Liberator types finished off one U-boat and damaged four others.

Though the escort of three destroyers and four corvettes may seem fairly strong, it is evident that double this number of warships could have accomplished more against the convoy's assailants. Before the U-boat menace can be really scotched it will be necessary to have escort vessels available in much larger numbers than hitherto, as well as to devise some method by which aircraft cooperation can be afforded all the way across the Atlantic. Though the range of shore-based aircraft has been largely extended, there is still a considerable gap in mid-ocean which there seems no possibility of bridging at present. The provision of more aircraft-carriers for convoy work is an evident essential.

COLONEL KNOX, the United States Secretary of the Navy, doubtless had this in mind when he announced that dozens of American escort aircraft-carriers are now in service, with scores more under construction. So far the names of 13 of these vessels have been published, the U.S.S. Altamaha, Barnes, Block Island, Bogue, Card, Charger, Copahee, Core, Croatan, Glacier, Hamlin, Long Island, and Nassau. It is understood that all are ex-mercantile hulls of over 17,000 tons displacement, adapted for carrying up to 30 fighters or a smaller number of other types of aircraft. They are propelled by Diesel engines of the Busch-Sulzer type at a maximum speed of 16·5 knots and are armed with light anti-aircraft weapons and machine-guns. Though their low speed renders them unsuitable for work with a fleet, for escort purposes their value cannot be questioned.

H.M.S. VIMY, commanded by Lt.-Cdr. R. B. Stannard, V.C. (see Vol. 3, p. 222), was escorting her first N. Atlantic convoy when a U-boat pack attacked. The ensuing battle lasted for 3 days and nights, 2 U-boats being sunk and many others damaged. The destroyer Vimy sank one of the enemy submarines, the members of whose crew are shown coming ashore under escort at a Northern port. *Photo, British Official : Crown Copyright*

After 165 Years H.M.S. Victory Still Serves

H.M.S. VICTORY as she appears today in her dry-dock at Portsmouth : topgallant masts struck, topmasts and jib-boom housed, and yards lowered on deck. Below, left, commissioned and warrant officer candidates engaged in a discussion round one of the old-time guns ; right, tea in one of the broad-side messes. The deal table is slung from a beam. Capt. A Grant, C.B.E., D.S.O., is in command of the Victory. *Photos, British Official ; Crown Copyright*

NELSON'S FLAGSHIP in his last and greatest battle is now being used as a naval barracks. Fifty prospective Naval officers, studying for commissions and awaiting their Selection Board (they will become temporary sub-lieutenants, R.N.V.R., in the Special Branch), eat and sleep on the same mess-deck and in the same surroundings as did Nelson's men at Trafalgar in 1805.

These ratings live aboard from one to three months, and sleep in hammocks slung from the rails used by the Victory sailors, though they get more than the regulation 17 ins. of slinging width that was all that was allowed when the flagship's complement was 850 men —equal to that of a modern cruiser.

LAUNCHED in 1765 the Victory was not commissioned until 1778. She was paid off from active service in 1812, and since 1825 has flown almost continuously the flag of either the Admiral Superintendent of Portsmouth Dockyard or the C.-in-C. at Portsmouth. Placed in a special dry-dock at Portsmouth in 1922, she was restored to the same condition as at Trafalgar 138 years ago.

Mediterranean War Seen Through an Artist's Eye

'EAST OF MALTA, WEST OF SUEZ,' reviewed in page 684, contains several reproductions of naval paintings by Lt.-Cdr. R. Langmaid, R.N., who was attached to Admiral Cunningham's staff as official Admiralty artist. Here are three of the most striking. Top, Taranto, Nov. 11, 1940 : H.M.S. Illustrious (see opposite page) and her destroyer screen part company with the 3rd Cruiser Squadron. Centre, the monitor Terror and gunboats Ladybird and Aphis bombard Italian bases in Libya, Dec. 1940. Below, Matapan, March 27-28, 1941 : left to right, burning Italian cruisers Zara and Fiume, the Barham, Valiant and the flagship Warspite.

On Fire and Crippled, Illustrious Won Through

H.M.S. ILLUSTRIOUS, famous aircraft-carrier (see Vol. 4, p. 108), was singled out as the main target for enemy attacks in January 1941. Top, German dive-bombers begin their assault on Jan. 10. At that time the Illustrious was with the fleet, 100 miles W. of Malta. Centre, she is hit, and set on fire ; yet six hours after the attack she reached harbour. Below, while working parties repair her damage, the great ship becomes a target for further dive-bombing attacks as she lies alongside the dockyard at Valetta. On Jan. 23 the Illustrious left the island fortress, and was escorted to Alexandria.

East of Malta, West of Suez: The Navy on the Job

Describing the work of the Royal Navy in the Mediterranean from the outbreak of war in 1939 until the spring of 1941, East of Malta, West of Suez (H.M. Stationery Office, 1s.) is a naval story of the deepest interest and importance. Though no name appears on its title page, it was written by Paymaster-Captain L. A. Ritchie, known to fame as a writer of novels of the sea under the pseudonym of Bartimeus. Below is an appreciation of the book, and a number of illustrations from it are reproduced in pages 682 and 683.

SOME time in 1940 the billposters were busy in Italy pasting up on convenient wall-spaces large copies of a map of Italy, bearing the comforting heading E VULNERABILE L'ITALIA ? NO ! On the map were symbolic representations of Italy's military, naval and air might. The surrounding seas were shown to be securely held by a multitude of warships, and from the toe of Italy past Sicily to Bizerta was a great muster of Mussolini's navy. If the map were to be believed, the Mediterranean life-line of Britain's Empire was snipped through by the Italian scissors. "Is Italy vulnerable ? NO ! "

But Italy *was* vulnerable ; the Italian fleet was very far from being that sure shield that the propagandists portrayed. At first, however, things looked pretty bright from the Italian windows. In June 1940 the French armies were being ground beneath Hitler's tanks. The Mediterranean was closed as a supply route from the United Kingdom, so that British reinforcements for the Near East had to go round the Cape. Malta looked an easy prize. To use a naval colloquialism, it must have appeared to Mussolini like " money for old rope." We may be sure that if it hadn't, he would not have declared war at midnight on June 10.

Even to Admiral Cunningham, Britain's C.-in-C. in the Mediterranean, the outlook may have seemed pretty grim, yet from the very first hour of the new war he secured the initiative, and maintained it. On Mussolini's map-posters the Mediterranean was marked *Mare Nostrum*, but the Italian admirals showed no eagerness to make good the claim. Time after time in those first weeks and in all the months that followed, Cunningham trailed his coat before the Italian bases, hoping to entice Mussolini's ships out to battle ; but in spite of his superiority in numbers and armament, the enemy refused to venture all on the throw of a single sea fight.

The first clash came on July 8, when Captain R. C. O'Conor, in the Neptune, had the privilege of signalling " Enemy battle fleet in sight " for the first time in the Mediterranean since the Napoleonic wars. When the enemy battleships were engaged by the Warspite (flying the C.-in-C.'s flag) and the Malaya, they turned away under cover of smoke, closely followed by their attendant cruisers, and disappeared into the mist. The British ships, with the exception of the Gloucester, suffered neither damage nor casualties, but on their way back to Alexandria they were attacked almost continuously by Italian planes, nearly 400 bombs being dropped —without, however, any hit being scored. The action's chief interest lay in this revelation that Italy had decided to put her trust in the air arm as the weapon best calculated to defeat Britain's sea power.

For a nation which had air bases, actual or potential, straddling the central Mediterranean and stretching along the entire Libyan coast, this must have seemed the obvious strategy. By way of answer we had the aircraft-carrier and the Fleet Air Arm.

Until May 1940 the Fleet in the eastern Mediterranean had no carrier ; then the twenty-year-old Eagle (Capt. A. R. M. Bridge, R.N.) joined the Fleet from the East Indies. She brought with her two squadrons of Swordfish, and later acquired four Gladiators as the basis of a fighter squadron. To quote a passage from East of Malta, West of Suez :

There were no fighter pilots on board, but the Commander (Flying) of the Eagle, Commander C. L. Keighley-Peach, was an " old lag " of Fleet Air Arm fighters. ("Old lag" is their phrase —actually he was thirty-eight.) For a while he went up alone to defend the Fleet. Later he trained two of the bomber pilots as fighter pilots ; the three of them, until they were reinforced by more machines and pilots, were all the Fleet had in the way of air defence against bombers and shadowers. Between them they accounted for eleven enemy aircraft, and somehow contrived to preserve the Fleet from major casualty. On one occasion the " old lag " went up alone with a bullet still in his thigh from a previous encounter and shot down an enemy machine.

This grimly heroic episode has a companion in the story of the *four* Gladiators which were all that the R.A.F. had in Malta at the outbreak of war.

Wave after wave of bombers swept over the Island. They fought all day, coming down only to refuel and re-ammunition, taking on unimaginable odds. One machine was shot down, but the other three battled on in this fashion for two breath-taking months, when a squadron of Hurricanes came to their relief from England. Never before in its long history of assault had Malta seen so undaunted a defence : the inhabitants, peering out from the caves and tunnels at the three of them as they swooped against flights of ten, twenty and even fifty of the enemy, named them Faith, Hope and Charity.

Then we have accounts of engagements and incidents which have already been described and pictured in our own pages, e.g. the Fleet Air Arm's swoop on Taranto of November 11, 1940, the bombing of the Illustrious, and the Battle of Matapan in March 1941. Little is added in this new account that affects the main outlines, but there is an occasional detail which adds colour to the narrative.

By way of example, when in the early days of the war Commander H. St. L. Nicolson's four destroyers were being pursued by two Italian cruisers—they were hoping to entice the enemy to within range of H.M.S. Sydney's guns—the Hasty, who was last in the line, made a signal to the Hero, the next ahead. " Don't look round now," blinked her signal lamp, while Italian shells pitched round them in all directions, " but I think we are being followed."

Moving is the account of the end of the old monitor Terror, which had to be abandoned following tremendous dive-bombing attacks.

For two months her squat form had wallowed through gales and sandstorms in offensive bombardments off the Libyan coast, while she covered with her 15-in. guns her venturesome brood of gunboats (Aphis, Ladybird, Gnat) in their assaults. The rifling of her guns grew so worn that the ton-weight projectiles somersaulted about the enemy encampments like skittles in a bowling alley before they finally exploded. She had been a sort of Universal Aunt to the advancing army, acting as water-carrier, supply vessel and repair ship. In the swiftly occupied harbours, where all was improvisation, hers was the only effective defence against the Luftwaffe. Let it be her epitaph that she had endured all things and done well.

A few days later the C.-in-C. was promoted to be a Knight Grand Cross of the Most Honourable Order of the Bath. " I would rather," he said, when told of it, his mind on the little ships he had to send along that dive-bombed coast, " I would rather they had given me three squadrons of Hurricanes."

Cmdr. C. L. KEIGHLEY-PEACH, " lone " fighter-pilot, whose heroic performances against Italian dive-bombers in the Mediterranean in 1940 are described in this page.
Photo, Daily Mirror

VALETTA, capital of Malta, endured one of the most prolonged and savage onslaughts known to man. " Never before in its long history had Malta seen so undaunted a defence." Day after day, week after week, Italian aircraft dropped their bombs, but Malta became the world's most formidable fortress and, as the enemy knows to his cost, hit back with a vengeance. Here is a view of Valetta under a heavy air attack, great clouds of smoke rising above its ancient walls.

Photo, Times of Malta

Night and Day the Great Russian Battle Goes On

ALONG THE RUSSIAN FIGHTING LINE on the Central sector. I, Red Army men examine a German A.A. gun and standard, abandoned by a routed enemy unit. The photographs below were taken from an enemy source, and show phases of night-fighting. 2, Magnesium flare dropped from a plane reveals barbed wire entanglements in the No-man's land between Russian and German positions. In the foreground a machine-gun fires tracer ammunition. 3, The flash from a German howitzer illuminates the sky and snow-covered ground, providing sufficient light for the cameraman to photograph the scene.

Photos, U.S.S.R. Official ; Planet News

Carrier Pigeons Are Saving Our Men's Lives

Not the least of the many remarkable facts given in this article by J. M. MICHAELSON is that there are probably not less than a quarter of a million carrier pigeons now serving with our airmen and soldiers. Many have been wounded, many killed ; but these gallant birds are maintaining a fine record of devoted service.

THREE lines in the newspapers recently announced the arrival of a draft of pigeons at an African base for the Middle East pigeon service. They have gone to reinforce the Army Carrier Pigeon Post which has done great work with the Eighth Army in North Africa. Specially trained men of the Royal Corps of Signals have worked with mobile lofts, and the birds have flown as truly and faithfully in the desert as in the more temperate climate of their English birthplace. Many have fallen victims to shells and bullets in the air and on the ground, and it is no doubt to replace these as well as to meet the needs of an expanding army that the reinforcements have gone out.

All the ingenuity of inventors has not made the carrier pigeon, one of the oldest methods of speedy, long-distance communication, obsolete. Telegraph and telephone wires can be cut ; wireless transmitters can be damaged and, in any case, do not ensure secrecy. But the carrier pigeon will take a message quickly and secretly over a distance up to several hundred miles with almost unerring certainty. It was found that only five per cent of the many thousands of messages sent by pigeon in the First Great War failed to arrive.

The greatest enemy of the carrier pigeon is really bad weather. The homing instinct is so powerful that birds will struggle home against wind and rain, even if they fall dead in the loft. But sometimes they are beaten, and even in peacetime pigeon-races a percentage of birds was lost through bad conditions.

THE other enemies of the pigeon are hawks of various kinds, not very serious, and men with guns on the ground, whether enemy or friendly. The " friendly " man with a gun is usually a careless sportsman or a man with " trigger itch " who must shoot at anything that moves. It cannot be emphasized too strongly that the greatest care should be taken in shooting at pigeons to make sure first that they are not carriers. They are easy to distinguish. The wood pigeon is grey with a white ring round its neck. The carrier is light brown, blue or red and white. The carrier flies on a straight course and does not even deviate at a man with a gun, whereas every experienced shot knows that a wood pigeon will swerve away at anything strange on the ground. The carrier rarely alights to rest or feed. It is also a smaller bird.

There is really no excuse for mistaking the bird that is carrying a vital message for the pest of the countryside. But the error is made only too frequently, and casualties from guns in our own country are far heavier than from enemy action. Every person who goes shooting should know that thousands of carrier pigeons are flying over Britain every day. They are training, carrying messages

SAM, carrier pigeon attached to a Halifax bomber, was wounded in an R.A.F. raid over Berlin. A piece of A.A. metal pierced his canister and tore his beak. He is here shown with the damaged canister.
Photo, Daily Mirror

between the various headquarters or from aircraft or raiding-parties round the coast.

It is a crime to shoot a carrier and, I suppose, the average man when he finds he has made a " mistake " almost instinctively buries the evidence of his " crime." But by doing this he may imperil operations and lives. Anyone who shoots a carrier by accident or finds one dead or injured should take it to the police immediately. If it was an accident, no more will be said and, in any case, the police will be more concerned with seeing the message is delivered than with anything else. Undoubtedly airmen have lost their lives through carrier pigeons being shot down and the message never delivered.

When a pigeon has to fly over a battlefield there is always the chance of it being hit by bullets or splinters. But it takes a lot to kill a pigeon, and many struggle home with serious wounds. A curious fact is that they seem to take little notice of gunfire or—as in the Great War of 1914–1918—clouds of gas.

THE first news of the Dieppe raid last August was brought to Britain by a carrier pigeon. For reasons of secrecy, it was inadvisable to use wireless ; and two pigeons were set free on Dieppe beach, each with the first news of the operations. One pigeon was almost immediately shot down, but the other, Beachcomber, flew through the hail of fire and reached H.Q. It averaged 50 m.p.h. Beachcomber was bred by Mr. E. King of Ipswich (*see* photo, page 529).

There have been many instances of birds being badly wounded and living to fly home. Most famous of First Great War pigeons, Mocker, lost an eye by a shell fragment in the Battle of the Argonne in 1918, but delivered the message and lived another 20 years ! An R.A.F. pigeon named Sam was "mentioned in dispatches" for courage when wounded in a Halifax bomber over Berlin. A shell fragment penetrated the

metal container and tore the bird's beak, but Sam behaved well while being given first aid and will be on operations again soon.

Coastal Command aircraft have all carried pigeons since the outbreak of war. The success of the pigeon service led later to birds being carried on all bombers, and thousands are now engaged on this active service. Many pigeons, of course, make operational flights without even spreading their wings. They are not released except in emergency. Some have made up to 80 flights in aircraft, and are still fit and working. Others have been unlucky and killed or wounded severely by shell fragments while in the plane.

A typical incident showing the work of the birds with aircraft resulted in a bird called Winkie being awarded a bronze plaque. A Beaufort was forced down in the sea. As the crew scrambled into the dinghy, the wireless operator picked up the cage containing two pigeons. Somehow in the confusion one got away before a message had been attached. The other was released a few minutes later with a message giving the position. The bird carrying the message did not reach home. Perhaps it was shot down, perhaps it succumbed to the weather.

But the first bird reached its loft. When its owner, summoned by the tinkling of the bell rung automatically as a pigeon alights, found there was no message, he telephoned the number of the pigeon to the nearest R.A.F. station. They quickly identified the aircraft which had carried it, already overdue. Some clever calculating of the aircraft's probable course and the time of arrival of the pigeon resulted in an approximate area being marked on the map. Reconnaissance aircraft very soon spotted the dinghy ; and less than 24 hours after the accident the crew were safely ashore.

MANY thousands of pigeons were " demobbed " after the First Great War, but the R.A.F. maintained a nucleus of birds through the years of peace, and they did good work in bringing aid to disabled planes.

How many pigeons are now in service can only be guessed, but the number available is probably not less than 250,000. Early in 1939, when the threat of war began to loom, the 50,000 British pigeon fanciers (including H.M. the King, who has fine lofts at Sandringham) offered their birds to the War and Air Ministries through the National Homing Union. Young pigeons are hatched in the spring, but require careful and expert training before they are reliable "homers." The present extensive pigeon service would have been quite impossible without the help of thousands of enthusiastic amateurs.

The most recent development of the Carrier Pigeon Post Service is with parachute troops. The pigeons, in special containers that prevent them being harmed, are dropped with the men, and can be immediately released with news of the landing or other operations. Here again they have the great advantage of secrecy, as wireless might reveal to the enemy the position of troops whose landing was still unknown to him.

SPECIAL CONTAINER in which he carries a pigeon for taking messages forms part of this parachute trooper's equipment. As told in this page, pigeons prove of the greatest value in landing operations. *Photo, Sport & General*

With Anderson's Men in Tunisia

Down the boulder-strewn slopes of a little river-bed, now as dry as an ancient bone, Bren-gun carriers of the Grenadier Guards push on as fast as the terrain permits in the wake of the retreating Germans. A few days before, towards the end of February 1943, it was Rommel's men who were doing the advancing; up the Kasserine Pass they surged, almost to Thala. Then their onset was stayed by U.S. troops, a British armoured brigade, the Hampshires, Coldstreams and Grenadiers.

In a Cockpit of Sand and Rock

War in Tunisia is a strange mixture of big and little, of skirmishings and solitary patrols, of actions which can be described as battles. Our photographs reflect this military medley. 1, A German paratroop unearthed by a British Recce patrol. 2, Towing away a captured German 88mm. gun. 3, Churchill tanks of the 6th Armoured Division get ready to move to the support of the Guards near Sbiba. This action, fought on Feb. 2, 1943, was the Churchills' baptism of fire in North Africa.

Photos
Cr

Flashes of Life in the Forward Zone

Whatever the exotic appeal of Algiers, life at the front in North Africa has a toughness, a rude simplicity. Messing is no easy matter, and such additions to the diet as this sergeant at a forward R.A.F. airfield is negotiating with an Arab huckster (4) are very welcome. Life is dangerous, too, as well as earnest; in (5) we see stretcher-bearers bringing in a casualty from No-man's land, while in (6) we are inconveniently close to an R.E. sergeant and sapper digging out an enemy mine.

Old and New in North Africa

Illustrating just one of the many contrasts to be found nowadays in Tunisia, this tank passes a form of transport which might have been new generations ago. One of the many that have been repaired by the Royal Electrical and Mechanical Engineers at a mobile workshop belonging to this admirable service (see p. 692), the tank has been tested and is now being taken back to the front-line on a transporter by Reme's Delivery Squadron.

VIEWS & REVIEWS Of Vital War Books

by Hamilton Fyfe

To those who believe that nations have characters, the French at this moment present a difficult problem. France—that is the French Government, so far as there is one—lends Hitler aid in every way possible, not only from fear but (it would seem) from inclination. Outside France there are Gen. de Gaulle's Fighting French who stand with us and hate their Vichyite fellow-countrymen as heartily as they hate the Boche. Then there is the great mass of French people in France who seem to be little interested one way or the other, only wanting apparently to be left alone to follow their occupations and get what comfort they can. Which of these three so sharply divided sections represents the French national character?

Some light on this is thrown by two books by French writers just published by the Oxford University Press: one is France, by Pierre Maillaud, the other L'Autre Bataille de France, by Jacques Lorraine (each costs 3s. 6d.). The first is a rather complacent review of French culture, recent history, types of character, divisions of opinion. To M. Maillaud the collapse of his country is merely "an episode." He cannot disguise from himself that defeat was due to "total disruption of authority and organization"; he rightly defends the French private soldier from the charge of having "lost his fighting qualities." But he considers both the generals and the politicians guilty of incompetence in preparing for war, and incapacity in conducting it when it started.

But it will not do to say that a nation is "sound" when it allows intriguers and incompetents to lead it to disaster, any more than an allotment-holder can say his soil is good if his vegetables are poor. Leaders grow out of nations, as vegetables grow out of soils. If in Britain's darkest hour there had been among us politicians ready to treat with the enemy, generals like Pétain and Weygand who groaned that it was no use going on, admirals of the Darlan sort who were eager to knuckle down—can anyone who knows anything about us doubt what would have happened to them? They would have been hanged on lamp-posts all the way down Whitehall.

M. Maillaud is inclined to excuse many of the French high-ups who were ready to collaborate with Hitler. He defends their arguments as "bearing some relation to elementary logic." The policy of France had been for centuries aimed at preventing German unity, but this unity was nevertheless accomplished: why not, then, accept that fact and join with the Germans in setting up a new State, a new Empire of the West? But is that really a line of argument adopted by the men of Vichy? Are they not supporters of Hitler because they believe in Hitlerism? Do they not prefer Fascism to Democracy? Are not their actions based on what they believe to be self-interest?

M. Lorraine is very clear about this. He divides those who have betrayed their country to the Boche into two categories—collaborators and collaborationists. The former want Hitler to win; the latter wanted to save France from his vengeance when he had won. Both lots thought he would win; both lost heart as soon as the collapse began. The first lot wished this collapse to begin; they had done all they could to weaken their country's effort, and their sole aim was to prevent war from being prolonged. The second lot longed to see the Nazis beaten, but they lacked the vigour and determination to stand up to the traitors.

Laval was the chief scoundrel in the sordid drama that ended French resistance. M. Lorraine gives a spirited account of the way he stopped Herriot and Jeanneney, Presidents of the Chamber of Deputies and the Senate, from leaving Bordeaux for French North Africa with President Lebrun's authorization, to carry on the government from there—and of course, to continue the war. Lebrun meant to go to North Africa too.

Herriot, Jeanneney, with many senators and deputies, were on board the vessel that was to take them to North Africa. They found Lebrun was missing. He had at the last moment, after endless shilly-shallying, hesitated, procrastinated, stayed behind. They went ashore hastily to find him. The ship left without them. The opportunity had been lost. Laval had won. The wretched old Pétain was in his pocket.

The Fall of France In Retrospect

Laval took delight, it seemed, in declaring, "We have been thrashed. It's no use trying any more. We should only get a worse thrashing." Pétain agreed. At first he believed in his doting way that Hitler's terms were going to be "generous." It was put about by the Nazis that they had no wish to humiliate the French. Hitler supposed that, if he could stop French resistance, he could settle with Britain easily, and then turn to attack Russia. He had no idea of showing "generosity"; but it suited him to pretend that his terms would be reasonable, even easy. The French very soon found they were appallingly hard.

All who were their leaders at this moment, soldiers and politicians alike, believed that Britain was about to "have its neck wrung like a chicken." (You remember the Prime Minister's comment on that delusion in his speech at Ottawa—"Some chicken! Some neck!") When this did not happen, they did not say to themselves, "Now we must break loose from our bonds and stand up to Hitler again." They said on the contrary (M. Lorraine declares with justifiably savage indignation), "How can we help the Nazis to get the better of the British, in spite of their defeat in the Battle of Britain?"

Fortunately, they were not able to help a great deal. They did what they could, but they had the French traditional detestation of the Boche against them. A Nazi writer set out the advantages that the submission of France procured for his side. The French fleet was kept out of the war. North Africa could not be used as a base of Allied operations: that was, of course, before the landing there last November. The Americans were not installed at Bizerta. In addition, French workers produced enormous amounts of war material for Germany; and large numbers of skilled men went from France to work in German factories.

It is as refreshing to read M. Lorraine's fierce, biting French as it is disturbing to take note of the other writer's blindness to the lessons of the hour. M. Maillaud even hints that the disaster to the French army (which elsewhere he attributes correctly, as I have shown, to criminal unpreparedness and military folly) was due in some measure to British troops not being sent in large enough numbers. This, he adds, makes most Frenchmen feel that in giving up the fight they were not guilty of a breach of contract. Does he forget that the French Government gave an undertaking not to make a separate peace?

But M. Lorraine remembers this. He asks in poignant phrases what will be the fate of a France which has "lost the support and sometimes even the respect of foreigners, those foreigners who will tomorrow be setting the world in order." He urges the impossibility of "awaiting passively the victory of Germany's foes." The armistice, he shows, has done infinite harm, not only to us who were the allies of France but to the French themselves. For example, "hundreds of thousands of Frenchmen have died in prison camps of exhaustion, privations and hunger, and on French soil also." And all the torments the nation has suffered "have had only the result of postponing the defeat of the Germans and lowering France in the eyes of the world." There must come a moment, he declares, when the armistice will be "broken like glass."

The pretence of the Vichyites that defeat was necessary to end the decadence into which the French had been slipping, shows how low some members of this once proud and honourable people can fall. "Beaten, beaten, beaten!" wails the Victor of Verdun, yet he is still held in respect and veneration by the mass of the nation. Is it the French character which makes them judge men so perversely? Are they so simple as to be easily deceived? The whole "episode," as M. Maillaud calls it, is a riddle to which the answers are very difficult to find.

MARSEILLES VIEUX PORT has been blown up by the Germans to make room for "a new and clean district "—and also a U-boat base. This ancient quarter of France's great Mediterranean city housed some 40,000 people, and on Feb. 24, 1943 the enemy began their mass evacuation. This photo shows buildings being demolished. *Photo, Keystone*

Knocked Out?   Tanks Today Have Nine Lives!

Already in an earlier page we have described and pictured the work of the Royal Electrical and Mechanical Engineers (see page 251), but here follows from the pen of ALEXANDER DILKE a fuller account, incorporating what has been revealed of the Corps' work in the Battle of Egypt and the subsequent pursuit of Rommel across North Africa.

I F you have 400 tanks and 200 are knocked out, how many have you left? It seems a simple sum in arithmetic. But the answer may well be 300 instead of the 200 which arithmetic suggests. The key to the mystery is "Reemee," slang name for Britain's youngest army corps, the Royal Electrical and Mechanical Engineers, whose principal task it is to see that tanks knocked out are back in battle again as soon as possible. They had their baptism of fire in the Battle of Alamein and the pursuit that followed. Just how well they came through it is shown by the recently-revealed news that during the first month of the battle they repaired and put back in the battle no fewer than twelve hundred British tanks.

It is the ability of the modern tank to come back after being knocked out that explains why the figures for tanks put out of action given by both sides so often do not "add up." To avoid confusion, for instance, it should be explained that of the 1,200 tanks repaired and sent back into battle, many tanks appear more than once. They were repaired again and again after suffering damage from shells, mines, or simply breaking down through wear and tear.

In the earlier desert battles the advantage in this business of salving and repairing tanks was with the enemy. He had built up a fine organization—based upon British methods in the First Great War. On occasions after his armour had taken heavy punishment Rommel was able to strike back with surprising force because of his repair service. The lesson was learned by the British, and improved upon. Today "Reemee" works with a tenacity, skill and courage greater than the Germans have been able to show. None of the

German "blitzes" has shown tanks in first-class condition after a fighting advance of over 1,000 miles.

A "child" of the Royal Army Ordnance Corps, "Reemee" is responsible for all the work of repair and recovery of armoured vehicles, guns, wireless equipment, etc., in the field. It still depends upon the parent Corps for its supplies of spares, and this is no small business. There are 200,000 different items required for the repair of all types of tanks and vehicles, and 100,000 different items necessary for keeping in action and workable condition guns, wireless sets and engineering equipment. "Reemee" not only puts new caterpillars and engines into tanks on the field, but also repairs the most delicate optical equipment.

T HE work of repairing is echeloned backwards from front line to base, and is as carefully planned and organized as a modern factory. Working in the front line are men with mobile workshops on lorries whose task it is to do the minor repairs. A tank is a very robust vehicle, but it contains many delicate mechanisms and may be put out of action by a small defect which can be repaired by experts in an hour or two—if they are there to do it.

Any tank requiring larger repairs goes back to the brigade workshops, further behind the lines. Workshop is, perhaps, a misleading word. In the desert it generally consisted of well-dispersed lorries and folding canvas shelters. The brigade workshops are mobile also to the extent that they move forward in leaps as the army advances. Giant transporter vehicles carry back tanks unable to proceed under their own power. On many

occasions, the salvage and repair crews have shown great gallantry in pulling out tanks under the very nose of the enemy, often working in total darkness with nervous machine-guns sweeping the area.

Behind the brigade workshops are the divisional workshops. Here a tank can be fitted with a complete new engine, a new gun and, in fact, brought into battleworthy condition again after serious damage. Finally, there are base workshops, as solid and elaborately equipped as the factories that built the tanks. But comparatively few of the tanks go back beyond divisional workshops. Base workshops also do a big business in reconditioning batteries and tires. When every item has to be transported many thousands of miles through dangerous seas, the importance of salvage and reconditioning is vitally realized. Tanks so badly damaged as to be not worth repairing are stripped down for spare parts or, on occasions, two tanks are "synthetized" to produce a single new one.

Craftsmen and engineers of every kind are to be found in these workshops—welders, turners, blacksmiths, electricians, carpenters, radio engineers, armourers. And always they are working at top speed, for every hour that a tank or other vehicle is out of action means just so much less power to be brought against the enemy. In the heat of battle, tanks which can be rapidly got back into action get priority. Lulls give the men a chance to catch up on work on other vehicles.

I F there is a probability of a tank being put back into action in a matter of hours, its crew stay with it. But if it has to go back to divisional workshops, its crew leave it and are given another. When the tank is repaired it goes into the general "pool" from which tanks are issued.

The worst enemy of these men who have to keep the tanks moving has been not the Germans but the sand. It gets into everything; and although special precautions are taken against it, nothing can prevent the sand from causing certain parts of the tank to wear out very much more quickly than they do in Britain. Provision for this had to be made in estimating the number of spare parts required and sent out.

"Reemee," having come with flying colours through its first great battle, is now preparing for an even bigger one—the invasion of Europe. Thousands of armoured vehicles and tanks will take part, and it will be "Reemee's" task to keep them fighting fit. Far in advance, its staff must plan where it will set up its base, divisional and other workshops, and what machinery and spares it will need. Standardization has, to a degree, simplified the task, not only by reducing the variety of spare parts required, but also by limiting the variety of breakdown causes. Different tank types, like different makes of motor-car, tend to develop different defects in action, and the repair experts quickly get into the habit of looking for them.

The men who keep the tanks moving have played a very important if unspectacular part in the great victory in North Africa. They would be the first to say that they have been able to send the tanks in to fight again and again only because of the workmanship put into them in British factories. To those thousands of men and women in Britain engaged in making tanks it must be immensely satisfactory to know that they are maintained by a body of men who are as courageous and skilled as those who fight with them in battle.

R.E.M.E., as told in this page, has contributed magnificently to the fighting success of our tanks in Libya and Tripolitania. Thanks to this Corps' high speed repair service, 8th Army tanks and armoured vehicles pursued the Afrika Korps in a non-stop drive. Mechanics are here shown at work on a Crusader tank.   PAGE 692   *Photo, British Official*

Thanks to R.E.M.E. the Army Keeps On Moving

IN NORTH AFRICA the Royal Electrical and Mechanical Engineers (see page 251) have repaired some thousands of Army vehicles and recovered and "salvaged" scores of tanks since they began operations on October 1, 1942. These photographs illustrate some of R.E.M.E.'s activities during crucial phases of the fighting in the Western Desert and Tripolitania, in some of the worst conditions mechanized transport has ever been called upon to surmount.

1, Fitting hauling tackle to a disabled General Grant tank, preparatory to shifting it on to the transporter. 2, Removing a damaged tank in a Libyan forward area during heavy enemy air attacks. The tank has been safely hauled on to the transporter despite bombs bursting in the background. It was subsequently taken to a workshop, repaired and sent into action again.

DESERT WORKSHOPS of the 8th Army are fitted with the most up-to-date machinery, spare parts and repair equipment of every kind. Among the craftsmen whose job it is to repair vehicles are fitters, blacksmiths, turners, welders, armourers, instrument-makers, radio engineers, electricians, carpenters, etc. Each of these men is an expert at his particular job.

Above (3) is shown a busy scene at a blacksmith's shop. These craftsmen are hard at work all day. In addition to the pitiless glare of the desert they endure the heat of their furnaces as they labour at vital tasks of repairing guns and tanks. 4, The main workshop of this improvised blacksmith's shop is dug firmly into the sand, and effectively protected and camouflaged. The camouflage gives shade as well as protection.

Photos, British Official: Crown Copyright

THE WAR IN THE AIR

by Capt. Norman Macmillan, M.C., A.F.C.

Fortress and Liberator bombers of the United States Army Eighth Air Force based in Britain attacked with bombs in daylight the important submarine-building yards at Vegesack, near Bremen, on March 18, 1943. For this raid into north-western Germany the American bombers had to fight their way through Dutch and German skies. The engagement lasted two hours, probably the longest air battle of its kind in history.

The result was an operational triumph for American methods of day bombing. Only two bombers were lost. Fifty-two enemy fighters were destroyed, and 43 were probably damaged or destroyed. (See eye-witness account in page 701.)

This is a shattering blow for the Luftwaffe. They have been unable to prevent the growing night raids of the R.A.F. Here is a demon-

The F.W. 190 has a top speed of about 370 m.p.h. at 19,000 feet. The Me. 109F does about 370 at 22,000 feet, and the Me. 110 about 340 at 22,000 feet. The top speed of these fighters begins to fall above these heights, whereas that of the Fortress increases.

Even though the Fortresses do not travel at their top speed but cruise in formation, there can be only a slight speed advantage to the German fighters when they have to engage the American bombers above their own maximum efficiency levels. The ability of the German fighters to overhaul the bombers is reduced, their power of manoeuvre curtailed. If they are to close to accurate shooting range, the fighters must fly straight into the volume of fire from the whole bomber formation. Under these conditions,

FLYING FORTRESS of the 8th U.S.A.A.F. heading for a target in N.W. Germany ; just noticeable are the four separate condensation trails thrown off by the great machine as it speeds on its way. Daylight attacks by these formidable aircraft on enemy territory have been extraordinarily successful—one of the most remarkable being that inflicted on Vegesack (see pages 701 and 702.)
Photo, British Official : Crown Copyright

stration that they cannot protect the Reich in daylight.

The success of the American bombers is not due solely to their weight of fire from half-inch machine-guns (as many seem to think), and to the excellent shooting of the air-gunners. Part of their success must be ascribed to their technical design for the specific purpose of high-level precision bombing. They are equipped with turbo-supercharged engines, which give a high power-output at height. The Fortress II has the curved fin surface and enlarged tail of the stratoliner ; this alone indicates that it is a higher flying aircraft than the Fortress I, which had a maximum speed of 325 m.p.h. at 20,000 feet and a service ceiling of 36,700 feet. (The service ceiling is that height at which an aeroplane climbing at full throttle ascends at a maximum rate of 100 feet per minute.)

It has been stated in America that the 1941-type Fortress reaches 330 m.p.h. at 30,000 feet. Flying heights and speeds of aircraft vary according to the loads and kinds of equipment they are required to carry, but if these figures are anywhere near the true performance of the Fortresses when they raid Germany, it explains why they are able to defeat the German fighters in daylight as they do.

relative fire-power favours the bombers, for the Fortress carries eleven half-inch machine-guns against the contemporary German fighter's armament of eight rifle-calibre machine-guns or from two to four 20-millimetre cannon-guns and from two to four rifle-calibre machine-guns. The half-inch machine-gun's range is at least as good as that of the 20-millimetre cannon-gun. And it appears that at bombing height the German fighters are not fast enough to break through the fire-power of the American bombers.

It was one of Napoleon's maxims to choose the battle-ground that suited himself and offered disadvantage to the enemy. American military air strategists and aeronautical engineers sought this condition in the air, and the aircrews have demonstrated that it applies there too.

Attacking Wilhelmshaven naval base on March 22, the American bombers destroyed 28 German fighters, with a further 18 probably destroyed or damaged ; they lost three of their own aircraft.

Including the two raids mentioned, the Americans have made 51 raids since they first went into action, when they bombed Rouen with 12 machines on August 17, 1942. During this period they claim to have shot

down 356 German aircraft, for a loss of fewer than 90 bombers.

Technical improvements are in continued development, including new bombers able to carry four times the load of today, and a long-range fighter. In addition to the armour on the aircraft, personal armour is being provided to protect aircrews against flak and small-bore ammunition.

The American conception of the value of air power is summed up in the telegram sent by General MacArthur to Air Chief Marshal Sir Charles Portal, British Chief of Air Staff, who had telegraphed the congratulations of the R.A.F. to the American general on the victory of the Bismarck Sea. General MacArthur said : "The infinite possibility of the strategic application of air power is not even yet fully understood or comprehended. In proper co-ordination it opens up horizons of application not yet explored. Therein lies the way to victory, if we have sufficient constructive imagination to seize the opportunity."

What is described as one of the greatest battles of the War was fought during five days of February when twenty U-boats attacked a convoy in the North Atlantic. From bases in Iceland, North Ireland, and the Hebrides, Sunderland and Catalina flying-boats and Fortress and Liberator landplanes flew out in foul weather to act in close liaison with the escort ships of the Royal Navy, and the convoy was brought through "with comparatively small loss." Thousands of miles were flown in less than four days. Ten U-boat sightings and seven air attacks were made ; some U-boats were bombed from only 30 ft up. (See p. 680.)

WHIRLWINDS and Mosquitoes Haunt the Nazi Skies

Three De Havilland Mosquito long-range fighters encountered Junkers 88s over the Bay of Biscay, 60 miles out from the Gironde estuary, and destroyed both. The report of the encounter on March 22 was the first disclosure of the conversion of this fast day-bomber into a fighter. Fighter Command has recently been using its former Whirlwind fighter as a light day and night bomber. On March 14 Whirlwinds bombed Maupertus and Abbeville airfields ; on March 22 targets in Holland, rail targets near Armentieres, and canal barges near Lille ; on March 25 the railway yards at Abbeville ; on the nights of March 20–21 and 21–22 they bombed the Morlaix railway viaduct approach to submarine bases (see illus. p. 696) ; and on March 22–23 went for rail targets in Brittany. All attacks were made without loss. A British long-range intruder fighter was over Bremen on the night of March 23–24 ; this is an important development.

Meanwhile Bomber Command was handicapped by fog and mist. Aircraft laid mines on the nights of March 13–14 and 23–24, losing four aircraft. On March 22–23 St. Nazaire submarine base was attacked by nearly 300 four-engined bombers, one of which was lost ; the others had to be shepherded back by Flying Control, the R.A.F. ground organization responsible for the safety of aircraft in flight. On the night of March 26–27 the Ruhr (Duisburg) was bombed, and the following night Berlin received its heaviest raid to date with 900 tons of bombs.

Bomber Command day attacks (with Venturas and Mosquitoes) were made against St. Brieuc airfield (March 15) ; rail workshops at Paderborn (March 16) ; Maassluis, near Rotterdam (March 18 and 22) ; railway at Leer, N.W. Germany, by one Lancaster, and rail targets at Louvain by Mosquitoes (March 20) ; loco. works near Nantes (March 23) ; rail targets in N.-W. Germany (March 24).

Air activity increased in Burma following the Japanese attack and British counter-attack on the Arakan front. In Tunisia the Eighth Army offensive, begun on March 20, was accompanied by intense air activity.

The R.A.F. Celebrates Its 25th Birthday

OUR BIGGEST RAID ON BERLIN was carried out on March 27, 1943, when Lancasters, Halifaxes and Stirlings (nine of which were missing) dropped over 900 tons of bombs—double the tonnage unloaded in the enemy's deadliest attack on London on April 16, 1941. Great fires were left burning on both sides of the Spree. Here are pilots and crews of Lancaster bombers photographed after returning to their base. Another raid on the German capital was made two days later.

Photo, New York Times Photos

On Morlaix Viaduct Dived the Whirlwinds

MORLAIX, ancient town of Brittany, and in pre-War days a famous resort for artists, became an important target for Whirlwind bombers of Fighter Command on the nights of March 20 and 21, 1943. The picturesque little town is dominated by a two-tiered viaduct, 310 yards in length and 200 feet in height, carrying the main railway line between Paris and Brest (the latter being one of the most vital U-boat centres) over the rivers Que[ff]lent and Jariot. This viaduct was attacked by a force of Whirlwinds on both occasions.

In spite of intense flak the aircraft flew in low, and several effective hits were obtained on the target. After the first raid a fire was left burning on the viaduct, and during the second attack two railway bridges on a main German supply line in the area were also bombed with noticeable success.

WHIRLWIND fighter-bombers, which have scored so many successes against the enemy during ceaseless day and night raids, are as fast as the Spitfire and can blaze 600 shells a minute from their four cannon. Each machine carries two 250-lb. bombs under the wings. Enemy sources credit the Whirlwind with a top speed of 353 m.p.h. at 16,350 ft. It has a span of 45 ft., is 31 ft. 6 in. in length, and has a height of 11 ft. 6 in.

Powered by two Rolls-Royce Peregrine engines, this aircraft mounts formidable armament in the rounded nose of the fuselage in the shape of four 20-mm. Hispano cannon—a type which has been used with great effect against ground targets in France and elsewhere. During a period of six months a Whirlwind Squadron destroyed or damaged 37 goods trains in enemy-occupied territory.

GERMAN COMMUNICATION LINES were seriously disrupted by the Whirlwind bombers' attack on the Morlaix viaduct. 1, Whirlwinds flying in "box" formation. 2, Loading one of the aircraft with a 250-lb. bomb preparatory to the raid. 3, Part of the Whirlwind's effective armament ; loading up the four 20-mm. Hispano cannon. 4, The Place Thiers at Morlaix, with the viaduct—chief target of the Whirlwinds in their raids last March —spanning the town in the background.

Photos, P.N.A., Topical Press, E.N.A.

Invaders of Tomorrow Pass McNaughton's Test

ANOTHER 'BATTLE OF BRITAIN' was waged recently in the largest military exercise ever held in this country. Armies clashed in mock combat on a wide front in a scheme that presupposed a British-Canadian force, "Southland," commanded by Lt.-Gen. McNaughton, attempting to advance against the "Germans," represented by the "Eastland" Army. 1, Both sides had their own field newspapers. This Southlander scans The Advance Post. 2, Pilots of an R.A.F. Composite Group being interrogated after bombing operations. 3, Canadian infantry crossing the Thames at Oxford; the bridge was "destroyed" by the enemy. 4, Tank commander and driver check up a route before setting off. 5, A Canadian inspects bus passengers' identity cards. After the "battle" Gen. McNaughton said that it had been the finest possible training, and he was satisfied with the land operations. The bridging in particular was magnificent.

Photos, British Official: Crown Copyright

Youth in a Britain of Bombs and Black-out

For much of the information contained in this article we are indebted to a twopenny pamphlet, Youth in a City, recently published by the Board of Education, which describes an experiment of Youth Service in the Sherbourne Road district of Birmingham. Remarkable as it is, however, this venture is but one of many aiming, in general with very encouraging results, at the enlistment of the spirit of youth in the cause of national service.

BLACK-OUT time in a much-bombed district of Birmingham! As soon as it got dark, immediately after tea that is, it was the custom of the young people of those close-packed streets and alleys to take their pillows and blankets and queue up at the entrance to the public air-raid shelter. "Booking a place" for the family by parking the bedding, they waited till father and mother came to the shelter; then out they went into the dark streets to join their chosen mates. The boys hung about doorways or at street-corners, talking and fooling, the girls strolled from street-corner gang to street-corner gang; both made themselves a nuisance to the neighbours and passers-by, and often they joined forces in doing malicious damage, for which there was plenty of scope in a district which had been so heavily bombed—but this was not the worst aspect of black-out time. The really serious danger came later in the evening when the boys and girls paired off before going home. Morale and morals were reported to be exceedingly bad.

Altogether they constituted a serious problem; but fortunately there were those in Birmingham who had the guts and gumption to tackle it. Under the leadership of Mr. J. J. Hegan, principal of one of the city's evening institutes, a little band of social workers opened in May 1941 the Sherbourne Road Centre on the first floor of a redundant senior school. The immediate purpose was to provide a place where young people at a loose end could meet and also an opportunity for them to do something of value to themselves during their leisure, while at the same time developing their character and improving their morale. Classes were begun in singing, dancing, woodwork, and physical training, and clubs were started—a model aeroplane club, concert party, dramatic society—all managed by the members themselves and, so far as possible, self-supporting.

IN the first week 135 young people enrolled. The gangs responded reasonably well to the invitation to come in, but quite a number joined with the intention of wrecking the venture. And they almost did so. The first four weeks were a nightmare. Young rowdies climbed up the water-pipes, swung on the electric-light fittings and pulled them from the ceiling. Gang leaders expected to be permitted to break all the rules of the games or to have them altered so that they could win; when they lost the billiard-cue was flung to the floor, the table-tennis bat deliberately smashed. But Mr. Hegan and his stalwarts made good. Before very long these boys and girls from the dull and dingy little houses in those back streets were discovered taking the keenest of interest in all the varied activities of the Centre. The young gangsters worked off their surplus energy in boxing and wrestling, the street-corner girls learnt first-aid and nursing, homecraft and needlework. Some even took to reading books. The general reading level (we are told) was very low; few read at all, some read only the penny "comic"; only three had current City Library tickets, and eight were members of the twopenny libraries.

When the Centre first opened, most of the members were dirty, untidy and ill-mannered. Four girls and two boys, indeed, were excluded because they were verminous. Many came to the Centre in their working clothes, and few washed before coming. This was understandable since few of the members have baths in their homes, and they can't be bothered to wait in the queues at the public baths. Now the boys can take hot showers at the gymnasium in the Centre one evening a week, but the girls are less fortunate. The custom is for them to have a full wash in the kitchen on Friday evening, if and when fathers and brothers go out. The girls state that overtime and late

IN CORFE, ancient Dorset town of about 1,400 inhabitants—how different from the Birmingham described in this page!—children bring salvage to a dump under the hill dominated by the castle, ruined in the Civil War 300 years ago. *Photo Daily Mirror*

return cause the male movements to be erratic as to time, and if the coast is not clear—no bath! But soon it is hoped that the baths at the Centre will be open every night; it is hoped, too, that the members will bring their own towels.

BEYOND a doubt Birmingham is not exceptional in this matter of juvenile gangs (although it may be exceptional in the courageous way in which it was tackled). In every city, in every town, in many a village even, there are crowds of young people who have been cut or cast adrift from their moorings. School finishes at fourteen, and even this all too short schooling has been sadly interfered with by the bombing. Parental control has lessened. In hundreds of thousands of little homes Dad is in the Army, and Mum is on munitions. And when in their middle teens the young people go out into the world they are welcomed with open arms by employers willing and eager to pay 30s., £2, £3 a week for unskilled labour. From time to time there are reported in the papers cases of youths earning very much more than this; and an official at the Home Office recently spoke of

children walking in and out of jobs as though they were film stars with all Hollywood waiting to give them a contract. One child of fifteen was mentioned who had had 75 different jobs, as many as two in one morning. (Although, on the other hand, there are numbers of boys and girls working disgracefully long hours. Some come to the Sherbourne Road Centre utterly tired out, so tired that they cannot talk or read for some time. "A," for instance, age 18, who is at work at 4.30 a.m., reaches home at 4.30 p.m., has tea, then delivers newspapers and helps in his father's shop until about 7 p.m., when he goes to the Centre.)

IS it any wonder that juvenile delinquency is on the increase?

Comparing the year ended March 1942 with the last pre-war year the number of cases of larceny and other offences in which boys of school age were concerned increased over the whole country by 51 per cent; for London boys alone the increase was 14 per cent. For boys of over school age (14+ to 16+) the increase in London cases was 21 per cent, as against the whole country's 38 per cent. Cases of girls of school age increased 121 per cent in London, the increase for the whole country being 83 per cent; while the corresponding figures for girls over school age showed increases of 116 and 125 per cent.

Thousands of boys and girls are charged with larceny every year: thefts of articles from cars, thefts of bicycles, thefts from multiple stores. The London figures show that the number of offences was lowest in the 8-year-old group, increasing progressively with each year's age group until the peak is reached with the 16-year-old boys and girls. Nearly half the offences are committed by boys and girls of 15 and 16 years of age.

From the statistics it would seem clear that great numbers of young people of both sexes are running wild. That boys should do so is perhaps to be expected—"boys will be boys"—and the consequences in after-life may not be too serious or too lasting. But with the other sex it is different; and the deepest concern must be felt at the spectacle of young girls, the mothers of tomorrow, hanging about street-corners or on the outskirts of military camps and barracks. Perhaps it is the romantic appeal of uniform; perhaps war affects in some strange way the chemistry of the body. Whatever the reason, it is a fact that precocious girls of 15 or 16, even younger, constitute a danger to their own and to others' physical and mental health.

To put it in a nutshell, Youth is a handful. But we have learnt how to treat this problem in social hygiene. That Birmingham Centre we have described is on the right road; so, too, are the many Youth organizations which have been in being for many years—the Scouts and Girl Guides, for instance, the Boys' Brigade, the Church Lads' Brigade—and those which have been launched quite recently with a definitely military backing—the Air Training Corps, the Girls' Training Corps, and the Cadet Force. Given something to belong to, a uniform to put on, a "gang" one mustn't let down whatever happens—given these, and the Youth problem born of war conditions, bombing and the black-out, the evacuations and the broken-up homes, has found its answer. Britain's "dead-end kids" are becoming the good citizens of tomorrow.   E. ROYSTON PIKE

Our Roving Camera Roams the Home Front

NEW CAPS FOR NURSES of Queen Alexandra's Imperial Nursing Service have wide peaks and are light grey. They will replace the present Q.A.I.N.S. hats when the latter are worn out, and will save thousands of yards of material.

BRITAIN'S OLDEST LOCOMOTIVE on regular service, L.M.S. engine No. 20002, is 77 years old. Her mileage on Feb. 1, 1943 was 1,580,436. This veteran—in her day one of Britain's fastest engines—carried troops in the Boer War and during the conflict of 1914-18. She is now engaged in hauling loads of tanks and guns, and has achieved a fine record of work during the present war.

ROAST-POTATO STALL at Blackburn, Lancashire, does a brisk trade. War workers and schoolchildren crowd round Ivy Rossi, the owner of the stall. Until they were called-up her four brothers earned their living by selling roast potatoes. The Ministry of Food has urged everybody to "Eat more Potatoes," substituting them wherever possible for bread and thus releasing vital shipping space now taken up by imported wheat.

ROYAL SERVANTS at Buckingham Palace and other Royal residences have gone into "battledress." The King ordered a new style of livery to save materials. In place of tailcoat, waistcoat, stiff white shirt and collar, the servants wear dark blue "battle blouses." John Ainslie, the Palace steward, is shown above wearing the new livery; on his right is a Palace footman in the old attire.

GERMAN ANTI-PERSONNEL BOMBS, a number of which has been dropped recently in this country, are painted greyish-green or yellow, and may explode at the slightest touch. Each weighs about 4 lb. The casing, when open, expands into 4 hinged portions at the end of the wire (left); right-hand photo, bomb with its outer casing shut.

Photos, British Official; Keystone
Daily Mirror, Planet News

I WAS THERE! Eye Witness Stories of the War

We Formed Human Pyramids to Cross Wadi Zigzau

A young British major with a bullet embedded an inch above his heart continued to lead his men at the storming of Wadi Zigzau, in the first stage of the Mareth Line attack. Paul Bewsher, Daily Mail Special Correspondent with the Eighth Army, describes here his meeting with the gallant officer, and the major tells his own thrilling story.

BARE to the waist, he sat in the marquee of a field dressing station. All round him were unshaven Germans in dirty grey-green uniforms, receiving treatment. Tired and drawn, but still full of enthusiasm, this dark, lean-faced man from Taunton, Somerset, who won the Military Cross at El Alamein, described his men's heroism—without ever mentioning his own.

"Alamein was child's play compared to this," he said, as he drank hot tea and munched sardines and biscuits. "Our objective was a strong-point known as Ksiba Ouest just across the Wadi Zigzau. We knew from the maps and aerial photographs that it consisted of pillboxes with machine-gun nests round it, and we had rehearsed the whole operation as far as we could.

"After dark we gathered about half a mile this side of the wadi. While we were waiting we came under heavy shell-fire and machine-gun fire from both sides. Then to the second down came our own barrage, dropping heavy concentrations of shells on enemy positions right in front of us. For 20 minutes they came over. Then it was zero hour for our attack.

"Like clockwork those guns began laying a creeping barrage in front of us. It was a perfect, magnificent piece of work. Not one shell fell on our own men. Engineers had driven a path through the minefields, and we reached the near side of the wadi without meeting any enemy troops.

"It was full moon and very bright. The wadi is a very wide gully, with precipitous sides, and there were scaling ladders available if necessary. We all managed to slither down into the wadi. Crossing it was not very pleasant. Machine-gun fire and mortar shells came from both sides.

"But we got across all right. When we got to the other side we decided to climb to the opposite bank by forming human pyramids, which we had practised. You know —three sturdily-built men standing at the bottom, two more get on their shoulders, another man gets on top again, and the rest clamber over the top of the cliff. When everybody else is up except the pyramid men, they can be pulled up with rope if necessary.

"My men carried out this task splendidly, despite really fierce fire in the wadi. We went forward. Fire was coming at us from all sides. Then we had another obstacle to get through. There was a deep anti-tank ditch beyond the wadi, but we got across this by making human pyramids again.

"We found ourselves about 600 ft. to the left of Ksiba Ouest, our objective. The enemy opened very heavy fire with machine-guns and rifles from three concrete pillboxes. Gradually we worked towards them. The whole position was surrounded by a deep ditch, and barbed wire and mines were scattered about.

"We reached the wire, cut a way through, and dropped into the ditch." The speaker stopped, drank more tea, and said: "Hope I'm not talking too much. I've been having morphia, you know." I assured him he was not, and he went on: "Once we were in that ditch we started throwing hand grenades and put some pretty accurate rifle fire and machine-gun fire against those pillboxes.

"Suddenly they packed up. They just gave in. Out of the pillboxes men came pouring. We took 200 of them prisoners, and there were only 80 of us. The majority were Italians, but they included a number of Germans.

"They told us other Germans had driven away in the afternoon. One of the Italians was a doctor, so I let him dress my wound, which I had not had time to worry about before. Then we dug ourselves in all round the post. Men in my party put up a grand show. The whole job was done in three hours and we had very few casualties."

I asked him when he received that wound. "Oh, while we were waiting to start," he said casually. "But as I knew all about the job I thought I should go through with it."

At Hegra We Norwegians Held the Nazis at Bay

Three years ago, on April 9, Nazis landed at Trondheim and took the Norwegians by surprise. Not until now—upon the escape of Lieut.-Col. Holtermann—has the full story been told of how the beleaguered garrison of Hegra Fortress stood out, alone, for four weeks, against the might of the Wehrmacht. Here is the Commanding Officer's own dramatic story of the epic battle fought amid the Norwegian snows.

IT had originally been my intention only to occupy the camp west of the fortress in order to continue mobilization, as I assumed that the Norwegian forces in Inntröndelag, together with British and French troops, would soon advance southward in order to recapture Vaernes and Trondheim. It soon became clear, however, that that advance might be delayed and that I would be forced to stay at Hegra for some time. I therefore decided to occupy the fortress itself.

Hegra Fortress was built in 1907 as a frontier fort facing Sweden, but it was closed in 1926. It has a number of underground rooms hewn out of the mountain, and is surrounded by an open trench and also by a circle of barbed wire, but the latter could be crossed without difficulty at practically every point. The armaments consisted of four 10·5 and two 7·5cm. guns (made about 1898) in open positions, and also two old 8·4 field guns without recoil, but we managed to get them into some kind of working order. There were still comparatively large stocks of ammunition. Otherwise the fortress was practically devoid of equipment.

The greatest difficulty was caused by the fact that none of us had been at the fortress before. It took us some time to discover the outer works, which were snowed over. Several of the infantry trenches were also partly iced over, so that we had to break our way through. An important flank defence work on the north side was found only after the first infantry attack had taken place, and the well a few days before we had to surrender, but it was then so full of shrapnel and gunpowder residue that it was unusable. A great deal of work was also needed to clear away forest growth which had blocked the firing field of the guns.

We had hoped that the fortress would command Vaernes airfield, which was being used by the enemy. But our guns did not have the necessary range. We therefore constructed sledges for the old 8·4cm. guns with the idea of drawing them into a position on a mountain commanding the airfield from the south, but the enemy forestalled us by their attack.

For the first few days the enemy kept chiefly to Vaernes. In the afternoon of the 12th and the morning of April 13th, however, we observed signs which suggested that

SWEEPING FOR MINES in a forward area of the Tunisian battlefield, these sappers, under enemy fire, clear the way for the first units of the 8th Army to attack the Mareth Line. A dramatic description of the furious fighting that ensued is given in Paul Bewsher's interview with a young British officer printed above. *Photo, British Official*

important moves were pending. Planes could often be seen over the valley, and on the following day the Germans attacked our advanced guards. The guards at Maelen Bridge—numbering about ten men—were driven back at dawn. The forces at Hegra Bridge and railway station were attacked early in the morning, simultaneously from the north, across the river, and from the west, on the south side of the river. After a short but bitter fight the Norwegians were forced to withdraw to the south after Lieutenant Bergström and a number of his men had fallen. The bridge was blown up and most of the remaining troops later reached the fortress or the barricade guarding the approach.

In the afternoon the enemy by-passed the fortress and we were thus surrounded on the north and east, with only the ridge to the west and south still open. The next day the fortress itself was attacked from the east. Fortunately our guns faced this direction, and consequently fine work was done. The enemy approached to within 200 yards of the fort before they were halted : meanwhile the garrison were being pounded

to try to starve us into surrender. Some very heavy bombs were dropped, but the aim was bad. We defended ourselves as best we could from these air attacks with machine-gun and rifle fire and we succeeded in bringing down two planes and damaging one other.

The enemy bombardment lasted day and night, with short intervals only, from April 15 to May 4, and during this time our infantry suffered considerably. In the fort itself two guns were put out of action and a look-out tower was damaged. When the battle started we had food for ten days, plus a meat reserve of two live horses. But particularly pressing was the need for fresh supplies of bread. We had no Army Service Corps to depend on and had to fend for ourselves. The only solution was to break through the German lines and get help from the civilian population.

At first supplies were brought by ski patrols across the mountain from Leksdal—about six hours there and six hours back. But the Germans occupied Leksdal, destroying the depot and the farm where it had been established. We were then obliged to get our supplies from Selbu, the

During their ordeal at Hegra the heroic Norwegian garrison suffered terrible privations—the worst being lack of sleep. These men manage to rest for a few moments.

to the foot of the mountain, where it was collected by our patrols during the night. This continued until May 4, when we were told that there was no more flour left on the farms.

Lighting became a problem because of oil shortage, and this caused considerable difficulty in the darkness of the interior of the fort. There was too little room, and it was damp and wet everywhere. We had to sleep in our clothes the whole time and there was just a little straw to lie on. When the water supply was cut, snow had to be brought in and melted, and wood had to be collected during the night from outside the fort. Later, when the thaw began, we were able to secure all the water we wanted by placing vats in the fortress rooms and collecting the water which dripped from the roofs. The medical staff did wonders. Patrols had to be sent out to bring in the wounded and dead. The dead—and the badly wounded also—had to be taken through the German lines, across the mountain, and down to the village on the other side. It was impossible to operate at the fortress.

On the evening of May 4 we learned that the forces at Aandalsnes had capitulated on May 1, and the troops in North Tröndelag on May 2. We were thus alone in Southern Norway. It would have been possible to hold out for a day or two longer, but now there seemed to be little purpose in so doing. Consequently I paraded the whole detachment—everyone was in a bad state of health after the many privations—and told them that we would have to capitulate. On the morning of May 5, 1940, the white flag was hoisted. The Battle of Hegra was ended.

DEFENDERS OF HEGRA, as described by Lt.-Col. Holtermann in this and the preceding page, defied the might of the German Army for a month. Bombarded night and day, the Norwegians held out in the face of insuperable difficulties. This photograph, taken during the siege, shows a party of the defenders in a casemate.
By courtesy of the Royal Norwegian Government

by the fire of smaller enemy guns from the north side of the valley.

The next day the most dangerous attack we were to experience was launched. Two battalions attacked mainly from the north, and for a while the fate of the old fortress hung in the balance. Our gun crews were driven back by the enemy machine-gun fire, and we were afraid the fort would be stormed. To prepare for this eventuality we installed machine-guns in the passages of the fort, but this was not necessary because our men drove the enemy back again and reoccupied our positions. Our position was further helped when snow began to fall so that the German artillery and the Luftwaffe were hampered. It is also said that the German infantry troops lost their way in the difficult terrain and began to shoot at each other. On this day the fort's water supply was interrupted.

The Nazis gradually occupied the surrounding districts and established positions closer to the fort. From April 18 communications with the outside world could only be maintained by sending out patrols who sneaked between the German sentries at night. Now we were subjected to continual heavy bombardment by aircraft and artillery. It looked as though the enemy had decided

journey there and back taking twenty-four hours. But the Germans reached Selbu, and as a last alternative we had to descend the steep mountain side west of the fortress into the Stjoer Valley itself, about a mile away, and fetch our food from there. Captain Hofstad was sent down into the valley and arranged for the baking of bread in the neighbouring farms. He brought the bread

I Went with U.S. Bombers to Plaster Vegesack

On March 18, 1943, crews of the U.S. Army Eighth Air Force carried out a successful daylight raid on Vegesack, the U-boat "nest" near Bremen. Accompanying the raiders, in a Flying Fortress, was Wing-Comdr. N. J. Baird-Smith of the R.A.F. Bombing Directorate. Here is his story.

I WAS only a spectator, but as I was fairly far back in the formation, I had a grandstand view of the whole operation. It was a most impressive sight, especially when one realized that each of these aircraft had ten highly skilled men flying in it. The sky seemed to be full of Fortresses and Liberators. I think that this impression was increased by the close formation in which we were flying—a formation that was never broken. As we approached the enemy coast the fighters came up to have a look, but they

seemed very shy of attacking. They hung about, apparently waiting for an aircraft to stray out of the fold, and I felt that they disliked the idea of coming near the American "guns." In spite of pretty heavy flak, our pilot got on to his target all right and made a good bombing run—straight and level. It was evident that the bombs of the preceding aircraft had found their mark, for the whole target was already obscured by thick smoke.

You can judge a good deal about the crew of a bomber by its efficiency on the return

VEGESACK U-BOAT BUILDING YARDS suffered heavily when attacked by U.S. bombers on March 18, 1943. This daylight raid—an observer's account of which is given in this and the preceding page—brought congratulatory messages to Maj.-Gen. I. C. Eaker (commanding the U.S. 8th Army Air Force) from Mr. Churchill and Air Chief Marshal Sir C. Portal. This photo shows the target area as it appeared from one of the attacking U.S.A.A.F. bombers Numerous bursts almost obscure the Vulcan shipyards ; the power house area is shown by a circle.

Photo, British Official

journey. By this time they had been flying for quite a considerable time, and with the obvious strain such close formation flying imposed they became tired. I can say, however, that the formations returned as they had gone out—closely packed and ready to do battle with anybody.

The fighters were on the look-out for the lone aircraft homeward bound, possibly shot up by flak or disabled by fighters, thus being

unable to keep with the main formations. There were plenty of fighters and they attacked until we were a considerable distance from the enemy coast, but these attacks became less and less aggressive as they saw the German coast receding ; until just before they left us they were milling round in the hope that a Fortress or Liberator would straggle.

Our particular formation had all the answers ready. One more aggressive Ju.88

which came in too close was met by an intense volume of fire and blew up ; and I saw a FW.190 spinning out of control on its way down towards the sea. The meticulous planning of this operation, combined with the efficiency of the crews and leaders in carrying out this no mean task, seems to me to be the keynote to the successful bombing of Vegesack with such a small loss of aircraft to the U.S.A.A.F.

OUR DIARY OF THE WAR

MARCH 17, 1943, Wednesday 1,292nd day
North Africa.—In Central Tunisia U.S. forces captured Gafsa.
Mediterranean.—Fighters from Malta attacked railways in Sicily.
Russian Front.—In Chuguyev area, S.E. of Kharkov, Soviet troops drove Germans back and repelled six counter-attacks.
Burma.—Japanese pressure on the Mayu river led to withdrawal of our forces.

MARCH 18, Thursday 1,293rd day
Air.—U.S. Fortresses and Liberators heavily attacked U-boat yards at Vegesack, near Bremen, in daylight ; 52 enemy fighters claimed as shot down ; 2 bombers lost.
North Africa.—First Army troops withdrew from Tamera in N. Tunisia.
Mediterranean.—U.S. heavy bombers raided Naples by day and night.
Australasia.—Madang, Jap base in New Guinea, heavily raided by Liberators.
General.—French Guiana broke off allegiance to Vichy France.

MARCH 19, Friday 1,294th day
North Africa.—U.S. troops occupied El Guettar in S. Tunisia.
Russian Front.—Heavy fighting continued on the northern Donetz.
Australasia.—U.S. dive-bombers attacked Jap base at Vila, Solomons.
General. — Announced that Adm. Doenitz, C.-in-C. German Navy, had held three-day conference with Italian naval chief Admiral Riccardi.

MARCH 20, Saturday 1,295th day
Air.—Whirlwinds bombed railway viaduct at Morlaix, Brittany.
North Africa.—Eighth Army began attack on Mareth positions during night of 20th-21st.
Mediterranean.—Allied heavy bombers made night raid on Naples.
Burma.—British troops made progress towards Donbaik, N.W. of Akyab.

MARCH 21, Sunday 1,296th day
Sea.—Admiralty announced loss of destroyer Lightning.
North Africa.—In Mareth Line Eighth Army effected bridgehead across Wadi Zigzau ; flanking force approached El Hamma, north of Mareth Line. Americans occupied Maknassi.
Mediterranean.—Docks at Palermo heavily bombed ; night raid on Naples.

Russian Front.—Soviet troops evacuated Byelgorod, N. of Kharkov, but gained ground on central front and in Kuban.
India.—Japanese aircraft raided area of Chittagong.

MARCH 22, Monday 1,297th day
Air.—U.S. Fortresses and Liberators raided Wilhelmshaven by day ; 28 enemy fighters destroyed for loss of 3 bombers. R.A.F. made heavy night raid on St. Nazaire.
North Africa.—Germans launched counter-attacks on Eighth Army bridgehead in Mareth Line.
Russian Front.—Soviet troops captured Durovo, on Vyasma-Smolensk railway.

MARCH 23, Tuesday 1,298th day
Air.—Mosquitoes raided locomotive works near Nantes.
North Africa.—Germans regained greater part of 8th Army's bridgehead in Mareth positions, and attacked U.S. troops near El Guettar.
Russian Front.—Soviet troops captured Slavyanskaya in the Kuban.
India.—Enemy aircraft attacked airfield in S.E. Bengal.
Australasia.—Fortresses made heavy raid on enemy aircraft at airfields nr. Rabaul.

MARCH 24, Wednesday 1,299th day
North Africa.—Heavy artillery duels on Mareth Line.
Mediterranean. — Allied bombers made raid on Messina.
Russian Front.—In the Kuban Soviet troops captured Abynskaya, N.E. of Novorossisk.

MARCH 25, Thursday 1,300th day
North Africa.—Incessant Allied air attacks on enemy positions from Mareth to Sfax.
Mediterranean.—Malta-based aircraft attacked Rome-Naples railway.
India.—Jap bombers raided aerodrome in S.E. Bengal.
Australasia.—Allied aircraft made heaviest raid on Rabaul ; Amboina, Lae and Salamaua also attacked.
U.S.A.—American bombers made four raids on Kiska, Aleutians.

MARCH 26, Friday 1,301st day
Sea.—Admiralty announced loss of trawler Moravia.
Air.—R.A.F. made night raid on Duisburg and other targets in the Ruhr.
North Africa.—Attack by Eighth Army troops on positions S. of El Hamma forced enemy withdrawal from Mareth zone.
Australasia.—Liberators made heavy surprise raid on Nauru Island, S. Pacific.

MARCH 27, Saturday 1,302nd day
Air.—R.A.F. made heaviest raid to date on Berlin.
North Africa.—Fierce fighting continued in area of the Mareth Line. In Central Tunisia Americans captured Fondouk.
Burma.—Air battle over Arakan area resulted in 12 Jap bombers being shot down, ten by Hurricanes without loss.
Australasia.—Raids on Jap bases at Malahang and Lae.
General.—Hundreds arrested and curfew imposed following sabotage at Aarhus, Denmark.

MARCH 28, Sunday 1,303rd day
Air.—Daylight raids by U.S. heavy bombers on railway yards at Rouen and by R.A.F. Venturas on shipping at Rotterdam. Heavy night raid on St. Nazaire.
North Africa.—Eighth Army occupied Mareth, Toujane and Matmata.
Australasia.—Sixty Jap aircraft raided Oro Bay, New Guinea ; 25 shot down.

MARCH 29, Monday 1,304th day
Air.—Venturas attacked shipping at Rotterdam and railway yards at Abbeville by day. R.A.F. made another heavy night raid on Berlin and also bombed Bochum in the Ruhr.
North Africa.—In Southern Tunisia Eighth Army troops occupied El Hamma and Gabès ; in the north the First Army closed in on Sejenane.
Burma.—U.S. Liberators attacked docks and mining plant at Tavoy ; R.A.F. made night raid on Heho airfield.
Australasia.—Jap bombers again raided Oro Bay, New Guinea, U.S. fighters attacked seaplane base at Faisi in the Solomons.

MARCH 30, Tuesday 1,305th day
Air.—Mosquitoes bombed Philips radio factory at Eindhoven.
North Africa.—Vanguard of Eighth Army in pursuit of Rommel, occupied Metouia and Oudref, N. of Gabès ; in N. Tunisia the First Army recaptured Sejenane.
Russian Front.—Hard fighting continued on northern Donetz where fresh German attacks were repelled.
Australasia.—Japanese convoy bound for New Guinea was attacked and driven off by Allied bombers ; docks at Finschafen also bombed.

★══════════ *Flash-backs* ══════════★

1940
March 20. M. Reynaud formed Ministry in Paris following resignation of M. Daladier.

1941
March 24. El Agheila occupied by Axis forces ; first appearance of German Afrika Korps in Libya.
March 25. Yugoslav Premier and Foreign Minister signed Axis Pact.
March 27. Yugoslav Army under Gen. Simovitch deposed Govt. ; King Peter assumed power.
Agreement for lease to U.S.A.

of naval and air bases in Atlantic signed in London.
British captured Keren, Italian stronghold in Eritrea.
March 28. Battle of Cape Matapan.

1942
March 17. Gen. MacArthur arrived in Australia as C.-in-C. of United Nations in S.W. Pacific.
March 23. Japanese occupied Andaman Is., Bay of Bengal.
March 28. Combined Operations raid on St. Nazaire ; H.M.S. Campbeltown rammed dock gate.

STRANGE and wonderful is the language—I hesitate to call it English—written by our Whitehall scribes. But there is to be an improvement. Mr. Herbert Morrison has found time amid his innumerable cares and responsibilities to issue a circular, itself couched in concise and straightforward terms, urging the Civil Service to abandon their formal and cumbersome phraseology and express themselves in the English of everyday speech. Write in clear and simple language, is the keynote of the instructions. Keep your sentences short. Avoid officialese, and, above all, avoid clichés. Avoid ambiguity and do not hedge: if something is red, say so, and not "it appears to be of a somewhat reddish tint." Avoid stilted phraseology—"I am to," "I have to," and so on. Don't say "on the subject of" and "with reference to" when you mean "about" and "regarding." Time and trouble are well spent in seeing that circulars are clear and concise. If you have to turn down your correspondent's request, make it as clear as you can why you are turning it down.

SPEAKING recently at a luncheon given by the Waste Paper Recovery Association, Sir Andrew Duncan, Minister of Supply, said that since the beginning of the War nearly three million tons of waste paper have been salvaged. Generally speaking, the public have responded most loyally to the appeals to save paper, and a wonderful code of economy and recovery has been established. All the same, one can sympathize most heartily with the remarks made on the same occasion by Miss Megan Lloyd George, M.P. There would be greater confidence among the public in the salvage effort, she said, if they saw Government departments making greater efforts to save paper. "I think they might economize with great advantage in the use of forms," she went on. "The war effort would not be impeded, but greatly expedited if we could cut down a great many of those useless communications which are duplicated and sent out all over the country. It would be a great encouragement if it could be made clear that we are going to have a great and glorious clear-up of Whitehall to begin with."

WITH this Mr. Morrison would seem to agree, since another paragraph in his circular points out that "an enormous amount of the delay for which Government offices are blamed, particularly the really spectacular examples, is caused by the aimless circulation of paper in which no one will take an interest. So when a paper has been wrongly sent to you and you don't know whose job it is, keep on asking in likely places until you find out. Don't let the paper go until you have found out, and are sure you are passing it to the right quarter." Another injunction, and just as excellent, is that the newcomer to the Service should not jump to conclusions, become a slavish adherent to precedent and routine, but spend time and trouble in collecting and checking his facts. "This takes time, but it will be time well spent. Having surveyed your problem, make up your mind, and having made it up, stick to your view, unless it is later proved to be wrong. Don't haver!"

THIS last exhortation may prove a stumbling-block to some, as it has proved to A Scottish Civil Servant (Temporary), who has, written to The Manchester Guardian. "The circular is splendid," he writes, "though for a long time I was greatly puzzled by the passage which ends by advising the new Civil Servant not to haver. After long study I suddenly realized that the Englishman who composed this document did not know what 'haver' meant. It is as plain as day. He means 'swither.'" Possibly, but only on the principle that the greater includes the less. To haver just means to indulge in any sort of pointless turgid talk, to be verbose and also uncertain ; but to swither may be defined as "to doubt or hesitate, to be perplexed or undecided." There is really no obscurity in the wording of this Home Office circular, which is a most worthy document. Soon our Civil Servants ought to be writing with the sword-blade directness of our soldiers—of General Montgomery, for instance, some of whose phrases, like his recent "Rommel is

AIR VICE-MARSHAL A. H. ORLEBAR, A.F.C., whose appointment as Deputy Chief to Vice-Adm. Lord Louis Mountbatten, C.-in-C. Combined Operations, was announced on March 19; 1943. An expert on air defence, he evolved some of the fighter tactics employed in the Battle of Britain, 1940.   *Photo. British Official*

caught like a rat in a trap . . . We will, in fact, give him a very bloody nose," are examples of good direct idiomatic speech, compared with the periphrastic phraseology of your bureaucrat. But didn't Mr. Churchill issue a circular on similar lines not long ago—and where Winston failed can Herbert succeed?

LAURENCE BINYON, who died on March 10 in his 74th year, will live in men's memories as the author of the stanza :

They shall grow not old, as we that are left grow
old,
Age shall not weary them, nor the years condemn.
At the going down of the sun and in the morning
We will remember them.

Engraved at the doorway of the British Museum, where Dr. Binyon was for nearly forty years an official in the Department of Prints and Drawings, the lines form part of his poem, For the Fallen, which was originally published in September 1914, when the first casualty lists were bringing home the meaning of war's sacrifice. As every old

soldier knows, they have a prominent part in the simple ritual of the British Legion, and are often recited on those occasions when we are called upon to remember those who have died in order that England may live. Binyon's qualities as a poet were recognized even in youth, but it is not so generally realized that he was also an authority on the fine arts, more particularly on the art of Japan and China.

READING in one of the Sunday newspapers of the Nazis' latest pep-raising whisper, that they have nearly completed a tunnel under the Channel and that we in England cannot for the life of us discover where it is going to debouch—reading this reminded me of the Channel Tunnel proposals of earlier and happier days, when we in England thought it would be a distinct advantage to get to the Continent without the unpleasantness of mal-de-mer. Much more than a hundred years ago the idea was mooted by Napoleon I, and an actual scheme was submitted to Napoleon III in 1856 by a French engineer. Many on this side of the Channel supported the proposal, among them Queen Victoria and Prince Albert and the great engineers Brunel and Robert Stephenson, not to mention the politicians Gladstone, Bright and Lord Salisbury. On the other hand there was strong opposition, from those who feared the effect on Victorian ways and morals of holiday-making "Froggies," and also from the Blimps of the War Office. But a Channel Tunnel Company was formed, and from near Folkestone and near Calais preliminary tunnels were driven under the sea for a mile or so.

BUT beyond this nothing had been done when the First Great War broke out, and nothing has been done since—save that in 1922 Marshal Foch stated that if the Channel Tunnel had been built it might have prevented the war and in any case would have shortened it by half, and that a year or two later Mr. Winston Churchill came out strongly in its favour. In the light of what happened in France in 1940 some may think it was a very good thing that the proposal never got beyond the blue-print stage. But if the tunnel had been built we might have rendered more effective succour to our ally, and from Dunkirk our men might have brought back their guns and equipment. And it would have been an easy matter to block or blow up the tunnel so as to prevent the Germans using it ; indeed, the plans allowed for a dip in mid-tunnel which could be flooded in wartime. Now the Germans are building the tunnel—so they say. So if you go bathing this summer don't be surprised if you step on a pickelhaube's spike . . .

MUCH has been written of the dramatic arrival in Britain of Alfred Horn, more famous (or infamous) as Rudolf Hess, boon companion of the Fuehrer. The story is told again—and this time I suppose it is really official—in Roof Over Britain: the Official Story of the A.A. Defences 1939-1942, recently published by H.M. Stationery Office at 9d. But this story is only one of many in a book which is primarily concerned with the air battle that was fought so short a time ago. The Great London Barrage, the Blitzes on the Humber, Portsmouth Fights Back, A.A. Women, Balloons in Battle, Balloons at Sea—this selection of chapter-headings will indicate Roof Over Britain's contents.

DRAMATIC END OF A U.S. TRANSPORT. On Dec. 12, 1942 it was announced that the President Coolidge, former American luxury liner but of late a troopship, had been sunk off the Solomons. She struck a mine; and though she was rammed on to a coral reef, she slipped off and turned turtle. Of the 4,000 troops on board only four were drowned, so fine was the rescue effort. Built in 1931 this ship, a turbo-electric vessel, was the tenth U.S. transport to be sunk since America entered the War. Above, troops are seen swarming over the side of the doomed ship. *Photo, New York Times Photos*

Printed in England and published every alternate Friday by the Proprietors, THE AMALGAMATED PRESS, LTD., The Fleetway House, Farringdon Street, London, E.C.4. Registered for transmission by Canadian Magazine Post. Sole Agents for Australia and New Zealand: Messrs. Gordon & Gotch, Ltd.; and for South Africa: Central News Agency, Ltd.—April 16, 1943   S.S.   *Editorial Address:* JOHN CARPENTER HOUSE WHITEFRIARS, LONDON; E.C.4.

Vol 6   *The War Illustrated*   Nº 153

Edited by Sir John Hammerton

SIXPENCE   APRIL 30, 1943

VICTORS OF THE MARETH LINE. This Eighth Army tank crew had a part in the smashing of Rommel's defences and are again ready to advance against the retreating Afrika Korps. They have put ticks against Alamein and Tripoli, and their next objective appears to be Tunis. "Another severe defeat has been inflicted by the Desert Army upon the Axis forces they have so long pursued," declared Mr. Churchill on March 30, 1943.

Photo, British Official: Crown Copyright

NO. 154 WILL BE PUBLISHED FRIDAY, MAY 14

THE BATTLE FRONTS

by Maj.-Gen. Sir Charles Gwynn, K.C.B., D.S.O.

ROMMEL'S eviction from the Mareth Line and from the Wadi Akarit position marks the end of the first phase of the Battle of Tunisia. The intermediate pursuit phase that followed was of short duration; the speed of the Eighth Army's pursuit compelled Rommel to abandon any intention he may have had of fighting rearguard action or of counter-attacking the First Army's columns which threatened his lines of retreat. It is not surprising that he has made good his escape in view of his readiness to cut his losses and sacrifice his Italian allies. Opposed by strong flank-guards holding highly defensible positions, the First Army columns operating from Fonduk, even if they had been more experienced troops, had little real chance of intercepting his retreat unless he had attempted to delay the advance of the Eighth Army.

By April 15 the stage was set for the second main phase of the battle—the attack on the outer ring of the final Axis position with which by that date the Allies were everywhere in contact. There may be a pause in land fighting for re-grouping and preparation before the attack is delivered; but meantime the air offensive continues with a growing intensity which would seem to prohibit any attempt to carry out a "Dunkirk" evacuation. The final phase of the battle will not, however, be completed until Bizerta is captured, and it must be realized that it is defended by an inner ring of fortifications which may prove more capable of prolonged defence than the outer ring, strong as the latter undoubtedly is.

Now that the winter offensive in Russia has been brought to a close, I discuss below the events of the last year, and draw deductions from them as they seem to affect the outlook for the coming summer. Reasonable conclusions may, I think, be drawn.

TUNISIA

The battle of the Wadi Akarit, which was something more than a rearguard action, reduced Rommel's power for mischief. It compelled him to abandon his apparent intention to strike again at the Americans coming from El Guettar, and to withdraw the troops opposing them which he had reinforced with his Panzer reserves. With the Eighth Army in hot pursuit and with the net closing round him, he was left with no alternative but again to save what he could of his army by speed of flight. The Akarit battle that ended on April 6 was therefore not only an outstanding tactical victory but has had major strategical results. It was in many ways perhaps the most remarkable of the 8th Army's achievements under Montgomery's leadership.

The speed with which the attack was prepared, involving among other things the accumulation of reserves of ammunition for a heavy initial bombardment, for the barrage covering the assault and for subsequent pursuit, evidently exceeded Rommel's expectations—or otherwise he would not have dared to detach his Panzers to operate against the Americans. That the delivery of the attack in pitch darkness surprised the enemy is not to be wondered at, for it was practically without precedent. It has been universally accepted that attacks in complete darkness should be limited to small enterprises against well-defined objectives, and that large-scale attacks would court confusion and disaster. Montgomery, confident in the quality and experience of his troops, accepted the risk. The battle has practically brought to a close the operations of the 8th Army in an independent role. It has still heavy tasks ahead, but henceforth it will act as one of a group of armies and its actions in timing, direction and scale must be adapted to the general plan of the group.

RUSSIA

Germany, we know, has carried through a drastic comb-out of her man-power, apparently with the object not only of replacing her heavy casualties, but in order to raise new divisions. Great troop movements towards the Russian front are also reported. Does this mean that she intends to launch another great attempt to deprive Russia of all offensive power, or can it be otherwise interpreted? An analysis of the achievements and failures of her last year's offensive shows little to encourage a new major attempt.

Last year, although the Reichswehr had suffered heavy casualties and had had desperate experiences of the rigours of the Russian winter, yet German man-power had not been seriously affected; and there was no real difficulty, once the effects of winter hardships had worn off, in providing a striking force of formidable size and consisting of well-trained troops. Losses and expenditure of material, though heavy, cannot have been comparable with those of the last six months. The Germans had come very near to disaster, but as a whole their army had escaped. Russia in the preceding summer had had even more disastrous experiences, and her new armies were still neither fully trained nor equipped.

The prospects for an offensive, after a period for recuperation, were therefore on the whole distinctly favourable; and when it was launched it met with immediate success to an encouraging degree. Yet the outstanding fact is that, in spite of great initial success, the momentum of the offensive was lost, and it was brought to a standstill short of almost all its objectives before the Russian counter-offensive turned partial success into disaster. Moreover, it was brought to a standstill by Russian troops that had suffered heavy initial defeats and without excessive employment of reserves earmarked for ultimate offensive employment.

Mr. Stalin has told us that the Germans' original intention was to force the crossing of the Don on the Voronezh front to reach the Volga and then to wheel northwards towards Moscow, cutting its communications with the east and south. This plan, he holds, was only abandoned, in favour of the wheel south between the Don and Donetz, in consequence of the failure at Voronezh. British unofficial opinion, on the other hand, saw in the offensive an attempt to secure the Caucasian oilfields and the use of Caucasia as a base for the development of a great pincer movement against the British in the Middle East.

Either of these interpretations may represent the ultimate directions in which success might have been exploited, but it seems more probable that the primary aim was to defeat decisively the whole left wing of the Russian armies, to reach the Volga in order to reduce Russia's offensive potential by cutting her off from her main source of oil supply, and to secure the oilfields of Northern Caucasia for Germany.

The successful Russian defence at Voronezh had certainly far-reaching results, for it made it more difficult to reach the Volga, and left the Russians with lateral railway communications from the centre to the south—communications which were essential to the defence of Stalingrad and to the development of the ultimate counter-offensive. It is, however, hard to believe that the German

'CONGRATULATIONS, GENERAL!' Striding through the rough stubble of an airfield not far from the Mareth Line, General Eisenhower, Allied C.-in-C. in North Africa, greets General Montgomery, intrepid commander of the Eighth Army. "The record of the Eighth Army is too brilliant to need any praise," said General Eisenhower on March 31.

Photo, British Official: Crown Copyright

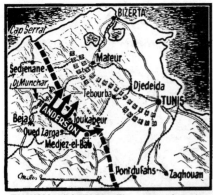

TUNISIAN BATTLES. These maps show the approximate fronts at April 9, 1943. In the north General Anderson's First Army was thrusting hard towards Tebourba and Mateur, while 150 miles to the south General Patton's Americans had joined the Eighth Army.
By courtesy of The News Chronicle

wheel south was an improvised change of plan, and it seems more probable that it was a development of the pursuit of Timoshenko's defeated army and aimed at co-operating with the forces attacking in the Donetz basin towards the Lower Don.

Be that as it may, the wheel was undoubtedly up to a point a successful manoeuvre, though it failed to turn Timoshenko's defeat into a complete disaster. He, in fact, was able to make a determined stand on the Don at Tsimlyansk, and gained much valuable time. He was unable, however, permanently to maintain his position ; with the result that his Army of the Caucasus became isolated from the Army of the Volga at Stalingrad. The failure of the Russians to hold the line of the Lower Don opened the way for almost the only German success brought to fruition in the capture of Novorossisk and Maikop.

From then onwards the German offensive was brought to a standstill before reaching its immediate objectives. It failed to reach the port of Tuapse and the Grozny oilfields ; and though it did succeed temporarily in closing the Volga to through traffic, Stalingrad held out, and attempts to reach the Lower Volga at Astrakhan also failed. After an auspicious beginning the offensive had failed to achieve its main purposes, however moderate we may assume them to have been, and in particular it had failed to rob the Soviet armies of their offensive potentialities. A part only of those armies had been struck by an immense concentration of German land and air power, yet it had survived.

The German failure was certainly not due to a falling-off in the fighting quality of their troops or in the executive skill of their commanders. Nor apparently was failure due to lack of numerical strength, though possibly the available forces were given too many objectives. The main reason for failure was undoubtedly the improved quality of the Soviet armies, due to the experience the troops and their leaders had gained. The result of failure was to leave the offensive armies in a dangerous bulge, and the whole army with an immensely longer front to defend.

We know the consequences. The Germans are almost everywhere back to the line from which the offensive started last summer and, so far as their picked troops are concerned, in seriously reduced strength.

Is there anything in this record to encourage hopes that a renewed large-scale offensive would have greater success even if numerical strength may be recovered or even increased by the arrival of inexperienced and less well-trained formations ? The Germans certainly have again staved off complete disaster, though more through luck of the weather than by a display of genius by the higher command. Strategical genius has been much more apparent on the Russian side ; and the chief credit that can still be given to the Reichswehr is the fighting quality of its troops and the executive skill of its staff and subordinate commanders. But even in that respect is there much difference in the opposing armies ? The one thing which appears to me to favour the Germans is that they retain control of a good and well-organized system of railway communications which would enable them rapidly to concentrate an offensive force ; whereas for a considerable time the Russians must operate in a devastated area which cannot quickly be reorganized. Those conditions certainly offer the Germans opportunities to stage an early offensive with strictly limited objectives, provided they can

muster an adequate striking force—which the relief of experienced divisions on defensive sections of the front by newly-formed divisions might enable them to do. But to undertake a far-reaching sustained offensive would require much longer time for preparation, and thus give the Russians a chance of improving their recovered communications and generally recuperating and reorganizing after their winter exertions.

The conclusion I arrive at, therefore, is that the Germans probably intend a limited offensive as soon as possible after the thaw. The troop movements from Germany seem to indicate the arrival of newly-formed divisions for the relief of experienced formations, required either for offensive purposes or for withdrawal to Germany to form a central reserve in view of possible developments in the West or in the Mediterranean theatre. The divisions which recently appeared on the Dnieper to save the situation which threatened armies in the Donetz were probably drawn from some such central reserve, and if so would certainly require replacement in view of the growing threat in the West.

I cannot believe that in view of their disappointing experiences last year the Germans would entangle themselves in another attempt to secure decisive results in Russia—unless, and until, the general war situation should take a definite turn in their favour.

LENINGRAD TO THE CAUCASUS. After the fierce and bloody riposte which carried the Germans for the second time into Kharkov, most of the Russian front subsided into an uneasy stability. The spring thaws were reported to be hampering movement. This map shows at a glance the territories regained by the Russians between Dec. 6, 1942 and early April of this year.
By courtesy of The Times

Yet Another Battle Honour for the 8th Army

THE MARETH LINE, so strong by nature and made infinitely stronger by the military art of French (and most recently German) engineers, proved no great obstacle to the 8th Army. On March 29, 1943 an announcement from Allied Headquarters in North Africa said that : " The whole of the strong organized defences of the Mareth position are now in our hands." Our lower photograph is of a British Bren-carrier passing a shop wellnigh destroyed by shellfire in the village of Mareth. Top, men of the Durham Light Infantry " dug in " in an anti-tank ditch . a photograph taken in an early phase of the grim battle for Wadi Zigzau. (See p. 718.) *Photos, British Official*

Not *All* Our 20,000 Prisoners were Italians

THOUSANDS OF PRISONERS were captured by Montgomery's men in the battle for the Mareth Line, and the subsequent pursuit to Sfax and Sousse. The majority were Italians; our upper photograph shows a couple surrendering with characteristic demonstrativeness to a Highland officer at the revolver-point. Most of the available transport was used by Rommel to get away his cherished veterans of the Afrika Korps; but, all the same, a number of Germans fell into our bag. Below, quite a considerable batch is being watched over by a Green Howard. *Photos, British Official*

Rommel's Flank Rolled Up by the Americans

TROOPS OF THE U.S. FIFTH ARMY have seen some hard fighting while operating against Rommel's right flank in Central Tunisia. Among the places the Americans captured in their offensive towards the end of March was Maknassy; the railway station is shown in 1, with U.S. soldiers patrolling the deserted track. 2, An American air pilot explores an enemy "fox-hole." 3, Italian prisoners captured by the Americans near El Guettar 4. Bombs bursting near a convoy of American trucks.

Photos, U.S. Official; Associated Press

Gabès Greets the Victors with Smiles and Flowers

WELCOMING THE EIGHTH ARMY INTO GABÈS, these excited inhabitants of the port clambered on to a British armoured car bearing the emblem of the famous Highland Division, as New Zealanders and men of the Black Watch entered the town on March 30, 1943. Gabès was plundered by the Germans before they abandoned the place. Shops and houses were stripped of doors, windows and furniture, and streets were left in a well-nigh ruined condition.

Photo, British Official: Crown Copyright

THE WAR AT SEA

by Francis E. McMurtrie

THE Battle of the Atlantic continues to be the outstanding feature of the situation at sea. Upon its issue depends the whole fate of the War, for without the food, munitions and other supplies which are brought to this country, Russia and Africa the campaign against the Axis Powers could not be waged.

Undoubtedly the Germans are making a supreme effort to intensify the U-boat war against commerce, an effort which has been foreshadowed in these columns. How far their plans have been fulfilled it is impossible to say without fuller knowledge than is likely to be vouchsafed until the end of the struggle. Such information as is available tends to be

swollen by the Berlin propaganda department to any extent deemed expedient.

Against this alarming background may be placed the announcements made on both sides of the Atlantic by those in charge of anti-submarine operations, or responsible for informing the public concerning them.

Mr. Elmer Davis, director of the U.S. War Information office, has admitted that March was worse than either of the two preceding months for the number of U-boat sinkings; but he added that the figure was far lower than the total for the worst month in 1942. Mr. A. V. Alexander's statement that during the past eight months Allied shipping gains have exceeded losses by a good deal more

DRIFTING IN THE NORTH ATLANTIC after their ship had been torpedoed by a German U-boat, these three exhausted survivors were picked up by a Canadian corvette. When found —two in the small boat and one on the raft—they were overcome by shock and exposure, and had fallen asleep.

Photo, Planet News

conflicting; and the public may well be puzzled at times to know whether things are going well or badly.

IT is, of course, beyond doubt that enemy claims are invariably exaggerated, but to what extent is somewhat doubtful. In their latest figures it is alleged that U-boats destroyed 13 vessels of 851,600 tons during the month of March. This statement is almost certainly intended to excite comparison with the month of April 1917, the worst period in the whole of the last war, when 881,000 tons of shipping were lost. It may therefore be regarded as pure propaganda—designed to depress the spirits of the Allies and to raise those of the German and Italian peoples.

Apart from this, it has long been known that U-boat captains are in the habit of claiming as a total loss every merchantman upon which an attack is made, thus providing an inflated basis which can be still further

than 2,000,000 tons threw little further light on the present situation. Next came a gravely-worded warning from Colonel Knox, Secretary of the United States Navy, that during March shipping losses in the Atlantic had taken a serious turn for the worse.

Apart from all these vaguely-worded utterances, there is the known fact that for some time past the enemy have been turning out new U-boats faster than we have been sinking them. Against this it may be urged that the number of escort vessels is also being increased at a more rapid rate than ever before; but it may be doubted whether convoys are yet sufficiently strongly escorted to withstand all the attacks they may meet under present conditions.

It is the settled policy of the Allies not to reveal figures of shipping losses, lest these prove a useful guide to the enemy. Yet it

must be agreed that the absence of such figures is apt to cause disquiet in Allied countries. There is indeed something to be said for the argument advanced recently by the New York Times, that it should at least be possible to devise some means of public information—such as a monthly percentage of cargoes safely delivered in terms of those shipped—which would illuminate the present darkness. Without some such indication of the trend of the battle—which could if thought fit be withheld for a couple of months before publication—vaguely reassuring announcements are apt to fail in their purpose.

ROMMEL'S Predicament and the Dunkirk Precedent

As I write, Rommel is in retreat from his positions north of the Gabès gap and speculation is rife concerning the chances of the Axis armies in Tunisia staging a withdrawal of the Dunkirk type. Circumstances are at first sight very similar, but a good many differences reveal themselves on examination.

To begin with, the enemy must have realized for a long time past that there could be only one end to his resistance, however protracted. With their customary thoroughness, the German General Staff would have made plans to evacuate the maximum number of troops when the time came. At Dunkirk, on the other hand, the crisis developed so rapidly and unexpectedly that much had to be left to improvisation; and but for the prescience of the Admiralty in arranging beforehand for a pool of small craft to be held in readiness for any emergency, it is doubtful if more than a fraction of the force that retreated on Dunkirk could have been saved.

At Dunkirk only the port itself and a few beaches in its immediate vicinity could be used for embarkation, whereas in Tunisia the indented coastline from Bizerta to Sousse is not far short of 200 miles in length, with numerous points suitable for taking off troops in small vessels.

IT may be assumed that generals, with their staffs and some of the picked troops, will be flown off in transport planes, probably under cover of darkness. In fact, as far as possible it is likely that evacuation by sea will also be attempted at night, as being less liable to interruption by air attack.

It is not believed that big liners will be employed by the enemy as transports to take troops from Tunisia. Half-a-dozen such ships have been lost during 1941-42 while in transit from Italy to Libya, proving that they are ideal targets for submarines and aircraft. Ships used will doubtless range from medium-sized merchant ships to quite small craft, such as schooners, barges, etc. It is reported that a number of French vessels have proceeded from Marseilles to Cagliari, the capital of Sardinia. That port lies at the south end of the island, and being only 120 miles from Bizerta is the nearest harbour of importance to which troops could be transported.

It may also be expected that the Luftwaffe will concentrate all the aircraft that it can spare to provide some sort of umbrella for the evacuation—if one is attempted. There is always, of course, the possibility that at the last we shall close in on the enemy forces with such rapidity that only a minority will succeed in embarking.

That the Italian fleet will issue from its harbours of refuge in the north of the peninsula to cover the retreat of the Germans from Tunisia is hard to believe, in view of its past record, to say nothing of the fact that in every recent action the Germans have left their allies in the lurch with a single eye to their own advantage. In any case, the British fleet in the Mediterranean may be trusted to look after the situation and to miss no chance of intercepting enemy ships.

Slowly but Surely Are Our Lost Ships Replaced

BRITAIN'S FAST NEW MERCHANTMEN, replacing those lost by enemy action, are designed to carry the maximum of cargo with the greatest measure of safety. 1, Women painters hard at work. 2, This girl heats rivets which are punched in to secure the top deck of the ship. 3, Hoisting a propeller into position preparatory to fitting. 4, Arriving by rail, these prefabricated parts are to be incorporated in a 10,000-ton cargo ship. Some 60 of these ships were recently built in two well-known British yards, their type being closely related to the many hundreds of U.S. "Liberty" ships.

Photos, Keystone, Daily Mirror, Topical Press

How 'Sparrow Force' Fought the Japs in Timor

Exploits of Australian guerillas who have defied the Japs ever since the enemy occupation of Timor Island (E. Indies) over a year ago, make one of the most thrilling stories of the war. Right, three members of this band, officially known as "Sparrow Force," snipe at the enemy in the jungle.

Using a Morse buzzer, this operator (below) tries to get through to Darwin. When the first messages were received Darwin suspected an enemy trap to lure rescuers into ambush; but the identity of the guerillas was established and medical supplies, letters and food are now reaching them.

Following the dispatch of supplies, Australia sent a photographer by a secret route. He filmed scenes showing the Australians and Dutch raiding enemy posts and pinning down a large Japanese force. The guerillas spread terror among enemy troops by lightning raids, killing over 100 Japs for every one of their own men lost. Above, letters being given out by the commander, Capt. G. Laidlaw.

Some of the Australians and the natives they befriended (left) brandish weapons as they dash through an enemy village which they have set alight. This village was occupied by antagonistic tribes in the pay of the Japs, and a fierce fight developed. The "Sparrow Force" has become adept at hiding from Japanese scouting aircraft in the jungle-covered hills of Timor.

Photos, British Newsreels Association

Life Is Good Again in Russia's Liberated Towns

NOW THE NAZIS HAVE BEEN DRIVEN OUT the people—such of them, that is, who have survived the murders and deportations of the occupation —of the areas freed by the Red Army are making heroic efforts to recapture the life that was theirs before the invasion. 1, Radioed from Moscow, this photograph of a passenger train leaving Rostov's main station is evidence of speedy reconstruction. 2, Gathered in Engels Street, Rostov folk listen to an open-air broadcast of the latest battle news from Moscow. 3, Electricians repairing the installation at a Stalingrad power-station. Peasants returning to their liberated village.

Photos, U.S.S.R. Official; Planet News

Are There Really British Paratroops In Norway?

Three years have passed since British troops helped the Norwegians to defend their country against the Nazi invaders. Now there come reports that British soldiers, paratroops this time, have returned to Norway, and are once again in action against the common foe.

STRANGE things are afoot in Norway's "plateau of a hundred lakes," as the Hardangervidda, great mass of mountain and valley which occupies the southwestern corner of Norway, to the east of Bergen, is called. From Oslo via the Swedish radio came the report on March 30 that the plateau, a matter of about 6,000 sq. miles, was to be closed from April 1 to all civilian traffic, and all hotels, sports establishments, and cabins were being taken over by the German military authorities. Hundreds of troops had been rushed to the district under the direct control of Terboven, the Nazi gauleiter, and the whole area was being subjected to a rigorous combing.

One of the reasons for the closure is stated by a Stockholm newspaper to be the German belief that the Allies will endeavour to establish aerodromes on the mountain plateau from which fighter aircraft could operate to protect invading troops; another is that the Germans are afraid that Hardangervidda may be used as a meeting-place for Norwegian patriots who could gather in the mountains to give support to Allied airborne troops. Apparently they suspect that a British paratroop H.Q. has already been established amid the barren heights—hence the careful search of the countryside; and some of the "invaders" are supposed to have been in action already.

Thus that highly successful act of sabotage which a few weeks ago put out of action the giant Norsk Hydro-Electro chemical plant at Rjukan, about 80 miles west of Oslo—Norway's biggest industrial concern and one which is of vital importance for Germany's war needs—was attributed to "three Norwegian-speaking men in British uniforms." The saboteurs escaped capture. A day or two later, on March 1, Oslo radio reported that twelve "British agents" had boarded a coastal steamer at a small port and forced the captain and crew, at the point of the revolver, to steam westwards, presumably to Great Britain.

Another week went by, and some of the R.A.F.'s Mosquitoes bombed the molybdenum mines at Knaben, near Stavanger, and the plant, Germany's main source of molybdenum, so important for hardening steel, received serious damage so that it will probably be out of action for a year. The German manager was killed. It is reported that as the Mosquitoes flew over Stavanger,

Norwegian patriots, defiantly ignoring the ever-watchful Germans in their midst, stood up and waved enthusiastically.

Shortly after the raid on Knaben a German transport ship in Trondheim harbour was damaged and had to be beached. The saboteurs were not found, but six hostages were seized and 200 other people in Trondheim arrested on a charge of "illegal activity." Following the sabotage at Rjukan about ninety people were arrested, including some of the Norsk Hydro officials, and a curfew between 11 p.m. and 5 a.m. was imposed. Some of the arrested (reported a Swedish newspaper) were shot, and others sent to concentration camps.

To add to German nervousness, light craft of the Norwegian Navy are now operating in their own home waters against enemy shipping. For obvious reasons many of their offensive operations are not made public, but it was recently revealed that two large German transport ships were sunk by Free Norwegian Forces in a daring raid on the port of Floroe, north of Bergen, on March 14. The commander of one of the participating vessels is reported as saying, "We have a really enjoyable job. The best thing about it is that we really get to grips with the Germans on Norwegian soil, or at least in Norwegian waters."

YET another incident was reported by Oslo radio a little later. On the night of March 22 a group of saboteurs were landed on a German island-base off the Norwegian west coast by British motor torpedo-boats. According to the German story, the landing was repulsed "with heavy losses," the party leaving behind them ammunition, food supplies, maps and other material. The German losses were stated to be one man killed and another wounded.

Taken separately, these "incidents" may be regarded as being of no great consequence judged on the scale of world-wide war. But added together they have an altogether different complexion. They serve to keep the Germans in Norway "on the jump," and there are abundant signs that the invaders are getting very jittery indeed. More than eleven hundred miles long, with a coastline—such are the innumerable indentations, the fjords and islands—of some twelve thousand miles, Norway is an exceedingly difficult country to occupy by an invading

S.W. NORWAY, showing the Hardanger Plateau, 75 miles E. of Bergen, which was declared a forbidden zone by the Germans from the beginning of April 1943.

force; and the task is made all the more difficult, even impossible, by the relentless hostility of the vast majority of the Norwegian population. There are some Norwegians who have come to terms with the Germans—the Fascists who form the Nasjonal Samling headed by Major Vidkun Quisling, father of all the quisling tribe; but these traitors are regarded with a contemptuous hatred by the Norwegian folk as a whole. Quisling's party has probably never touched the fifty thousand mark, and his Hirdmen, equivalent of Hitler's Brownshirts, number only some two thousand. Efforts to raise a Norwegian legion to fight against the Russians have failed dismally.

AFTER three years of German occupation Norway's spirit is still unsubdued; and none know better than the Nazis that about 98 per cent of Norwegians are but waiting a favourable opportunity to revolt. That opportunity (the Nazis fear) will be afforded by an Allied invasion. In Norway—and also in Denmark, where there are likewise reports of landings by British paratroops—the Germans are openly discussing the possibility of an Allied landing in Scandinavia, and they have reported that the Allies are massing ships, barges and troops in Scotland and Iceland.

There would seem to be little doubt that the Germans in Norway really do fear an invasion, since they have made apparently such immense preparations to meet it. The civilian population has been evacuated from much of the coastal area, harbours have been mined, islands fortified, the whole coastline is constantly patrolled and coastal shipping subjected to close watch. Villages have been converted into strong points, towns and cities cluttered up with tank obstacles. A West Wall has been built somewhere inland, and to it have been transferred some of the guns from the Maginot Line. The country has been dotted with airfields, wherever the state of the ground has permitted their construction; and Trondheim, Bergen, Stavanger, and Narvik have been converted into naval bases. Then there is the army of occupation; how large we do not know, but 250,000 is a reasonable guess.

For sixty-two days in 1940 there was fighting in Norway. Now after three years the war has returned to Scandinavia.

HARDANGER PLATEAU, a wild and desolate region in S.W. Norway (see accompanying text), might seem to offer ideal conditions for paratroops' activities. On April 9 the Swedish newspaper Dagens Nyheter reported the arrival in this area of large numbers of Austrian Alpine troops to take part in the search for Allied saboteurs. PAGE 716 *Photo, Norwegian Official*

These Women Win Honour for Devotion to Duty

MILLICENT I. RICHARDSON, A.T.S., awarded B.E.M. for displaying courage and devotion to duty on A.A. work during enemy raids in the Midlands. She is 23.

MARGARET JOHNSON, A.T.S., awarded B.E.M. An ambulance driver, she tried to rescue the occupants of a burning plane. Her hands were badly burned in her heroic efforts. Her home is at Altrincham.

DORIS ADAMS, W.L.A., awarded the Silver Medal of Our Dumb Friends' League for fearlessly rescuing two lambs from being gored to death by an infuriated bull. This medal is one that is very rarely presented.

MRS. MARION PATTERSON, awarded the G.M. for rescuing a sailor buried under 15 ft. of debris by a bomb explosion. She also crawled under wreckage and put out a fire.

SERGT. DORIS BLANKS, W.A.A.F., mentioned in dispatches for devotion to duty at R.A.F. Fighter Command. She was the first W.A.A.F. to work as a teleprinter.

CPL. DYSON and A.C.W. P. M. BEESON, W.A.A.F. balloon operators who, despite heavy bombing of their site in a London raid on Jan. 17-18, 1943, sent up their balloon to the required height. They are seen in a bomb crater.

CPL. JULIA SANDFORD, W.A.A.F., a sparking-plug tester, has been mentioned in dispatches for devotion to duty and maintaining a high standard of efficiency.

ACT. MATRON EFFIE TOWNEND, Q.A.I.M.N.S., awarded the R.R.C. for distinguished services in connexion with the evacuation of British wounded from Tobruk in a hospital ship. She has helped to look after hundreds of wounded in the Mediterranean, displaying remarkable devotion to duty.

LADY JUNE HOBSON, lady superintendent of the St. John Ambulance Brigade, Burma, awarded M.B.E. for her splendid services during the Japanese bombing of Rangoon. She is a daughter of the 7th Earl of Carrick.

MARGARET M. CANGLEY, awarded the B.E.M. A stewardess, she was twice a torpedoed victim. She attended wounded in a lifeboat, helped to look after passengers, giving a splendid example of courage when her ship was shelled by a German submarine. Her home is in Victoria, Australia.

Photos, British Official: Crown Copyright; Wright and Logan, Daily Mirror, Planet News, Keystone Hay Wrightson

How Montgomery Captured the Mareth Line

"In the battle that is now to start," said General Montgomery in his message to his troops on the eve of the battle against the Mareth Line, "the Eighth Army will destroy the enemy now facing us in the Mareth positions; will burst through the Gabès gap; will then drive northwards on to Sfax, Sousse, and finally to Tunis. We will not stop or let up until Tunis has been captured and the enemy has either given up the struggle or has been pushed into the sea."

IN a dramatic interpolation towards the end of his soon-to-be-famous broadcast on March 21, 1943, Mr. Churchill said that he had just heard from General Montgomery that "the Eighth Army are on the move and that he is satisfied with their progress."

Like Montgomery's first great attack at El Alamein, this new offensive was a frontal assault on the most vital sector of Rommel's front. As at El Alamein, too, it was preceded and accompanied by tremendous artillery and air bombardments. Launched on the evening of Saturday, March 20, against the Mareth Line between the sea and the road from Medenine to Gabès, in its initial stages it was reported to be highly successful. On Sunday evening it was stated at Allied Headquarters that the Eighth Army had captured all its preliminary objectives in the face of the most bitter resistance from the Afrika Korps. "Fierce fighting ensued," stated the official communiqué; "operations are still continuing satisfactorily."

On the next day the news continued to be good. The Eighth Army was reported to have smashed a gap in Rommel's first main defence line between the villages of Mareth and Zarat, and through the gap into the bridgehead that had been won General Montgomery was pouring tanks, guns and infantry, British, Dominion, and Indian, under cover of a terrific bombardment. Yet on Wednesday morning, March 24, the Prime Minister found it incumbent upon him to utter a word of warning in the House of Commons. "Much very hard fighting still lies before the British and United States' forces," he said. "The latest information from the Mareth Front shows the Germans by counter-attacks have regained the greater part of the bridgehead which had been stormed, and that their main line of defence in that quarter has been largely restored."

ALTHOUGH the communiqué issued later in the day from Allied Headquarters referred only to fierce fighting in the Mareth area and enemy counter-attacks successfully repulsed, Algiers radio and dispatches from the Press correspondents confirmed that Rommel had succeeded in recapturing most of the terrain gained by the 8th Army in its initial leap forward. How had the bridgehead been lost? Let us go back to the opening of the story.

Attacking by moonlight, British infantry of the 50th Northumbrian Division fought their way across the Wadi Zigzau, a formidable, deep ravine, wide and wet and very difficult for tracked or wheeled vehicles to cross. The Northumberland sappers, however, struggled across under terrific fire and put down a causeway of brushwood and boulders, over which a few tanks and more infantry were got into the bridgehead. Then with nightfall the attack was renewed, and several of the pill-boxes—small fortresses, 20 feet or so in diameter and with walls 5 ft. thick—beyond the ravine were entered, although enemy resistance was not entirely overcome.

Torrents of rain falling during the previous nights turned the wadi into a morass, and the causeway, being under point-blank fire from the enemy's artillery, was continually being broken up. Efforts were made to construct a stronger causeway, so as to enable more tanks and anti-tank guns to be rushed into the bridgehead in readiness

for the expected German counter-attack. But before it could be built the 15th Panzers launched an assault on the afternoon of the second day (Monday, March 22). Fighting with magnificent courage and devotion, the men from Northumberland were gradually forced back across the ravine by sheer weight of numbers (*see* page 700). On the southern side were massed a great weight of tanks, guns and men, but these could do nothing to help. That narrow defile, so slippery, so swept by enemy fire, lay in between. So the British withdrew—from the further pill-boxes, then from the other side altogether except for Ksiba Ouest; then that, too, had to be abandoned, such was the absolutely overmastering strength of the enemy. But (as will be seen) the men who died in that bloody ravine had not died in vain.

CONQUERORS' SMILES. Wounded but jubilant are these men of the 8th Army—"the greatest army that has fought in this war anywhere," as American flyers in Tunisia declare. *Photo, British Official: Crown Copyright*

Meanwhile the attackers elsewhere were having better fortune. The Americans at Gafsa pushed on steadily along the road to Maknassy, while a second American force, supported by a French force, made through El Guettar for Gabès. More important still, south of the salt marshes another Allied column, under Lt.-Gen. Freyberg, was developing a threat against Rommel's right flank at El Hamma.

As things turned out it was this column which tipped the scale against Rommel. Shortly before Montgomery opened his main attack he had dispatched Freyberg across the rocky desert in a great turning move. Travelling from Foum Tatahouine by night and lying hid during the day, Freyberg reckoned on March 19 that he had been spotted by Nazi reconnaissance planes, so all the next day he marched and attacked that night, driving a wedge into the German defences north of the Matmata hills. When the bridgehead at Wadi Zigzau had to be abandoned on March 23, General Montgomery decided to switch the main attack from the Mareth Line to the flank where Freyberg was making such good progress. So reinforcements and supplies were rushed to the New Zealand general; for mile after mile the lorries were nose to tail without a break. On Friday, March 26, the newly-arrived forces were put into the line under cover of darkness and the khamsin (hot desert wind) which by good fortune was blowing for once in the enemy's face.

At two in the afternoon the great attack was opened by the R.A.F.'s Kittihawks: a bombing attack was made every thirty seconds for two and a half hours by these heavily-armed fighters, during which over 300 sorties in low-flying bombing and strafing attacks were carried out. At 4 p.m. the artillery opened up and blasted every foot of the enemy's positions. Then the rocky plain became alive with tanks and infantry which had been hidden there. Shermans and Grants were in the van, followed by Crusaders and Valentines. They charged down the road that leads to El Hamma across a saddleback some ten miles wide, crowned by ruins of a two-foot-high wall constructed by the Romans centuries ago. Wrote The Times' Special Correspondent:

"Roaring and lurching over the uneven ground, the mechanized mass moved with awesome slowness in six columns towards the Roman wall across the saddleback. As it neared the gap from the east newly-arrived troops, with tanks and infantry, advanced and wheeled right to face the enemy just out of range.

"As one watched and listened one tried to put oneself in the soul of a German or Italian watching from the other side and imagine the cold horror with which he saw, as shells fell thick round him, and bombs crashed in destruction behind, while the wind blinded and stifled him with its acrid dust, the mighty array of Allied power rolling inexorably against him."

SWEEPING across the Roman wall, Freyberg's infantry carried the enemy's positions at the point of the bayonet. Then they stormed the gun positions two miles back. Passing through the infantry, the armour drove steadily on to the outskirts of El Hamma. All night and well into the next day the battle continued. The Italians surrendered in large droves, but the Germans continued to fight with desperate ferocity like rats in a trap—as indeed they were. For their line of retreat lay towards the Mareth Line, and the Mareth Line was now dissolving. Unable to withstand the tremendous weight of the El Hamma blow—his famous Panzers were far too heavily involved at Wadi Zigzau to be switched to the west—Rommel decided to withdraw while the way to the coast remained open. Montgomery was hard on his heels: on that same Sunday (March 28) the Eighth Army occupied Mareth, Toujane and Matmata, taking several thousands of prisoners. At the same time the Americans and French east of El Guettar developed their threat against Rommel's line of retreat.

Speaking in the House of Commons on March 30, Mr. Churchill announced that "General Montgomery's decision to throw his weight on to the turning movement, instead of persisting with the frontal attack, has been crowned with success. Another severe defeat has been inflicted by the Desert Army upon the Axis forces they have so long pursued." Then after giving the news that El Hamma had been occupied the previous night and that "our vanguards passed through Gabès this morning," the Prime Minister added that "the decisive break-through of General Freyberg's turning troops had been aided to an extraordinary degree by novel forms of intense air attack in which many hundreds of British aircraft had been simultaneously employed." Without any underrating of the task which still lies before the Allies in Tunisia, the Premier concluded with the remark that "we have every reason to be satisfied with the progress already made by our superior forces and superior equipment under their skilful and resolute commanders."

Victor of El Hamma

One of the heroes of the last war—did he not win his V.C. on the Somme in 1916, was he not wounded nine times, six times mentioned in dispatches, awarded the D.S.O. and two bars ?—Major-General Sir Bernard Freyberg, as the Allied C.-in-C. in Crete two years ago and as G.O.C. of the 2nd New Zealand Expeditionary Force since 1939, has won fresh laurels in the present struggle. The most recent of his triumphs was the flank attack by his New Zealanders at El Hamma in Southern Tunisia on March 29, 1943, which compelled Rommel to withdraw from the Mareth Line.

719

Before the Assault on Mareth

When these photographs were taken the Mareth Line was still in enemy hands, but preparations were afoot which would soon send Rommel once again on the run. In 1, men of a famous Home Counties regiment operating in the coastal sector are using a Service rifle to fire H.E. or smoke grenades from a cup fixed to the muzzle. 2, British infantry passing along an anti-tank ditch constructed by enemy engineers. 3, Rommel's lines at Mareth bombarded by Montgomery's guns.

Phot

Yet Another 8th Army Triumph

Now the attack has begun ; the 8th Army is advancing yet again.   In the frontal assault on the Mareth Line particularly bitter fighting developed at Wadi Zigzau, a rocky gully—still with a stream in it—which was crossed at night under fierce fire.   Casualties were heavy : 4, A first-aid post by the side of the Wadi.   The attack was pressed home : 5, British infantry after storming an enemy pill-box. 6, In a peaceful interlude Bonzo is intrigued by the " innards " of a Vicker's machine-gun.

Busy Scenes in Benghazi

In the years of fierce fighting in the Western Desert the little Libyan port of Benghazi was now in enemy hands, now in British. But almost always it was a target for the bombers, so that its quays were shattered or blown into the water. Now the battle has left it far behind, but still the tide of war flows strongly through it as a most important link in the 8th Army's supply line. These recently-taken photographs show war stores being unloaded in Benghazi harbour.

Clerks of the Weather Now Go By Air

Vitally important is the work of the Meteorological Flights of the R.A.F.—of the men whose job it is to secure the data on which the weather forecasts are based. As will be seen from this article by W. J. BENTLEY, they fly in all weathers—to find out about the weather.

"WE fly in weather which compels even the birds to walk!"

There may have been some slight exaggeration about this remark, made by a Coastal Command meteorological pilot in Iceland, but it certainly conveyed a good idea of the difficulties the "weather pilots" encounter in the Arctic.

Fog and cloud, almost down to ground level, do not stop the "Met" flight aircraft taking off to chart the weather, sometimes

W.A.A.F. WEATHER FORECASTERS, after intensive scientific training, draw up reports from meteorological bulletins. This photo shows the Stevenson screen which contains a standard thermometer. *Photo, Sport & General*

on a course stretching hundreds of miles out to sea. During a recent month the weather plane was flying on 28 days of the month.

In the Arctic winter they are dangerous flights—suicidal to any but the most skilful pilots. A water-spout added to the difficulties of one weather pilot recently. He was flying over the sea when the giant column of water suddenly swept up right in front of his machine.

Commanding the Meteorological Flight in Iceland is a young Flight-Lieutenant who was formerly a Ferry Command instructor at Montreal.

WEATHER pilots send in their reports by code and radio to "Central Forecast." This is the nerve-centre of the organization. It is responsible for the collection of the observations which constitute the raw material of the meteorological "factories," and for their distribution throughout the whole organization. It is also responsible for the management of the meteorological stations which make observations and furnish reports from places other than Royal Air Force aerodromes; and, above all, for deriving from the study of the observations and the charts based on them the general deductions about future weather.

These observations are coded in a manner designed to concentrate the information into the shortest possible message. Collection of these messages from a wide network of stations is completed in a few minutes. As soon as it is completed the messages are distributed in one collective message at high speed to all the meteorological stations at the different Commands, Groups, and aerodromes. By this means an instantaneous picture of the meteorological conditions over the whole country is available every hour within a remarkably short time of the observations having been made.

At the Central Station while the observations are being collected and distributed they are also being plotted on blank outline maps, according to a system which enables practically the whole of the information to be shown on a single map. Actually there are several maps, and on some of them only a selection of the information is given in order that a broad picture may be obtained over a wider area. It is from a study of these maps that the forecaster prepares his analysis and his prognosis of the meteorological situation.

THE analysis and forecasts made by the meteorologists at the central station are distributed regularly throughout the day for the information and guidance of the meteorologists at the stations at the various commands.

Our wartime weather charts, the secret information that may be known only to the Services—with the exception of Dover, the Channel weather reports of which are not secret—would be impossible to draw up if weather pilots were not willing to risk their lives in the attempt.

This weather chart is an outline map of the region in which the assistant is working; and shows the coast, certain height contours, and a series of circles which are situated at the positions of stations from which reports are received. Each station is identified by a number which is printed upon the chart and also appears in the message. On this chart the observations from the different stations are plotted. In the British Isles charts of this nature are prepared at intervals of about every three hours seven days a week. The purpose is to produce a weather chart of the area which can be used by the assistant's superior officer for the preparation of aviation forecasts.

Forecasters utilize charts and observations made by assistants to prepare forecasts, and to explain to R.A.F. officers the meteorological situation over the area with which they are concerned, and the changes and developments which will take place in it.

When the observations have been plotted and scrutinized the forecaster must complete the charts, draw the isobars, insert the "fronts" and diagnose the meteorological situation. He must examine the significance of the observations in their relation to each other and of the charts in their relation to the preceding charts, and must arrive at a sound conclusion as to what succeeding charts will be like, because he is concerned not only with the subsequent meteorological conditions at a single place, but with the weather over large areas during substantial periods of time and at different levels.

If the technical work behind the scenes seems dull, remember that a few pilots have to risk their lives so that hundreds of other pilots and air-crews will not be in danger in bad weather.

A YOUNG Flight-Lieutenant told me of some of his adventures over icy seas. "One of the worst flights I ever made took place a few weeks ago," he said. "We flew blind all the way out and back—exactly ten hours of blind flying. When we approached our base we were told that the clouds were right down to 100 ft. over the airfield. I didn't dare to come low because of the mountains, so I climbed and broke out of the top of the clouds at 7,000 ft." He looked for a way down and found it, a few miles away. "It was a hole in the clouds, only about 200 yards across, but it was enough. I spiralled down in tight turns and saw the runways of another airfield below."

Sometimes "weather spotters" are able to prevent other aircraft running into danger. Only a short time ago a "Met" pilot, 200 miles out to sea, found heavy cloud and squalls approaching Iceland at 50 m.p.h. He signalled base, and all the aircraft were immediately recalled. The last returned only a few minutes before the squalls arrived.

WEATHER PILOTS (see accompanying text) climb to 25,000 ft. twice a day over Britain, taking readings of the humidity, temperatures and barometric pressures. The men here shown in the contact office keep in touch with the pilot, and in bad weather inform him how and where to land.

Photo, Keystone

VIEWS & REVIEWS
Of Vital War Books

by Hamilton Fyfe

Two queries disturb the minds of a great many people. Can we win the war against Germany by breaking through its Home Front as we did last time ; and, if so, can that break through be accomplished by means of bombing ?

I say " as we did last time," because I think there is no doubt the Kaiser's armies could have gone on fighting much longer than they did if the mass of the nation had not shown very clearly they had had enough. Military opinion on our side—not British only, but American and French also—was that fighting might go on for the best part of another year. Balfour based on this his public statement that there would have to be a 1919 campaign. Northcliffe built on it his private remark in October 1918 that the war was not near its end. It was the collapse on the " German Home Front " that settled the matter. A book by a well-known German exile just published with that title (Gollancz, 10s. 6d.) is therefore of great interest, although it records events and minds and opinions only up to the middle of last year.

Dr. W. W. Schütz has been able to compile a volume crammed with evidence that numbers of Germans were at that time losing faith in the Nazis ; that those who had always been opposed to them were doing what they could to make their opposition effective ; that certain high Catholic ecclesiastics were worried about Nazi attacks on their Church (though not apparently about the cruelties perpetrated in occupied countries and on Jews) ; that the heavy losses in Russia had caused doubts even as to the wisdom of the Fuehrer ; and that efforts were being made all the time by Goebbels and his gang of propagandists to persuade their dupes to hold on.

Often these efforts throw a comical light on the belief so general not many years ago, that the Germans were the best-educated people in the world. Education is seen to have had in their case the result of making them utterly stupid and sheep-like. Here is an illustration. In order to counteract the depression caused by the success of the Russian offensive during the winter of 1941-42 and the damage to Hitler's popularity which this entailed, a sudden boosting of Frederick the Great was started. Why ? Because " Old Fritz " was often defeated, often seemed to be beaten, but came up on top in the end ! That showed the very low estimate the Nazis had of German intelligence. But this estimate was, according to Dr. Schütz, too low.

The Home Front proved a strangely unwilling audience to the High Priests of the latest Nazi myth. It was rapidly swallowed up by the immense dry sand-dunes of public distrust, a genuine wave of depression and a longing for peace. This wave was bound to reach even Hitler's sacred person. No artistry of Goebbels could shelter Hitler the man, and all those round him, from the questions, doubts, and the silent, still silent, demands of the people.

Goebbels knew what effect the comparison between his chief and the king who is infamous in history as one of the worst of double-crossers was having, but he was "too clever, too cautious, too sly " to take the bull by the horns. The organ of the S.S. (the Black Guard) and the Gestapo jumped in with both feet. It declared that Hitler must not be thought of as a modern version of Siegfried in the Nibelungen Lied. This comparison had been insisted on by Nazi propaganda for years, but it was all wrong. Hitler was not Siegfried, the noble, stainless knight. He was a reincarnation of the villain of the piece — of Hagen, who " defended himself against fate without any consideration for what mankind regards as inviolable and sacred. Hagen in pursuing his aims used all methods, treason if necessary. He showed no mercy to his enemies, nor to himself. Thus he was true to the highest conception of the German heroic ideal."

Will Our Bombs Break Germany?

Here we have the harvest of German education, which warped history and distorted legend to suit the political needs of the hour. It had the effect of making a few crazily ingenious (recollect the theory these few put forward that British people endured bombing because they got some sort of sexual kick out of danger to life!), and of turning the mass into nit-wits liable to be taken in by almost any nonsense their rulers might put over to them, even when that nonsense directly contradicted what they had been told before. But it seems they were at any rate puzzled by the Frederick the Great rubbish, and so even greater rubbish had to be evolved by the Black Guard to counter that puzzlement.

Again, it seems to us incredible that a nation should allow a man like Goering, who has been proved utterly false in his assurances ("German cities can never be bombed") and utterly incompetent in his actions, to retain authority and power. In his new book Is Bombing Decisive ? (Allen and Unwin, 5s.) the clever Czech writer, Capt. F. O. Miksche, gives an example of Goering's ineptitude, Taken in by the predictions of an Italian general (Douhet), he embraced the theory that Britain could be decisively beaten by the German Air Force. This theory he put into practice in 1940. Hitler believed in it, and promised that our cities should be "erased." Yet, when this promise was made to look silly, neither Hitler nor the German people had the sense to sack Goering, though, if Capt. Miksche is right, Hermann has never been really Commander-in-Chief of the Luftwaffe since. He "only functions in the capacity of a party supervisor in the aeroplane industry and the Luftwaffe." But he still keeps the title and presumably draws the pay.

What does Capt. Miksche say about the possibility of breaking the German Home Front by bombing ? He says it cannot be done. The Germans learned from their experience in the Battle of Britain that "the bombing of towns has no decisive effect, and that such operations are only useful in proportion to their high cost if they can be exploited by the surface forces," that is, on the ground and at sea. For the true aim in war is the destruction of the enemy's living force, and, even if the German masses' will to resist could be broken by bombing, they could not, Dr. Schütz and Capt. Miksche tell us, stop the war as they did in 1918.

There are in Germany, Dr. Schütz calculates, over a million well-equipped men in key positions, stationed at strategic points, controlling all means of communication. They make revolution impossible. As for the Army, it is controlled by ten determined Nazis among every hundred privates, these ten having agents of the Gestapo to look after them ! That disposes of any chance to mutiny. In Capt. Miksche's view, the German Home Front means a "police system to keep careful watch on the people and a well-organized propaganda to continuously influence them, also the S.S. divisions to suppress them with armed strength in an emergency." If we relied on bombing to force the Germans to rise against their rulers—which, however, we do not—we should be deluding ourselves.

We delude ourselves equally, however (we are warned by Capt. Miksche), if we believe Air Marshal Sir Arthur Harris when he says that "by bombing we can beat Germany," meaning we can do it by destroying fifty or sixty German industrial towns. For the Nazis have been "feverishly organizing new industries, making use of the occupied parts of the Soviet Union, building new factories in Prague, Pilsen, Maribor, and other places, compelling the Hungarian's to work for their war machine, and all of these prospective targets lie out of the effective range of our aviation."

Capt. Miksche's book is an answer to Alexander Seversky, who maintained that the War could be won in the air ; there is too much Seversky in it. But it is a contribution of real value to the debate on the best and quickest way to force on the Nazis that unconditional surrender which the Casablanca Conference declared to be essential. Close cooperation between the Air Force and the Army, and of both with the Navy, is what Capt. Miksche, and all other reasonable folk, believe in. There is no doubt we should have done better if we had had this close cooperation from the start.

RAID DAMAGE IN BERLIN. Now at long last Berlin is receiving punishment such as the Nazis have inflicted so often on the cherished cities of other peoples. This photograph shows Berlin A.R.P. workers striving to overcome a fire engendered by R.A.F. bombs.

Photo, Keystone

After Two Years the Yugoslavs Still Fight On

IN THE MOUNTAINOUS HEART OF YUGOSLAVIA the Germans and Italians are hard put to it to hold their own against the bands of patriots who refuse to accept the defeat of two years ago as final. 1, German soldiers taking to an unknown destination, and fate, Bosnian women suspected of having carried food and ammunition to their menfolk resisting the invader. 2, German storm-grenadiers, employing local oxen for transport, move through a burning Bosnian village. 3, Nazi soldiers captured by Serbian " chetniks."

Photos Keystone, Associated Press

THE WAR IN THE AIR

by Capt. Norman Macmillan, M.C., A.F.C.

THE United Nations' air forces engaged in the Tunisian war zone are now referred to as though they have been divided into a strategic and a tactical force. Here, at last, is the logical application of air power. Probably it has not before been possible to establish the two divisions of air power in the South Mediterranean, simply because there were not enough aircraft to make it feasible to do so. That it has become possible now is the best evidence that the output of the aircraft factories of Britain and America has put a greatly augmented air power into the hands of the commanders in the Mediterranean theatre of war.

Hitherto, one force has had to do both duties as best it could ; and it cannot always have been easy to apportion to each the strength of aircraft the commander would have liked to use.

Until recently the tactical force has had to come first, and ever since General Auchinleck's withdrawal to El Alamein in June 1942 the main air strength in North Africa has been devoted to the winning of the battles on the ground. It is probable that history will accord to the air its due place in the successes which were achieved. At the moment the fighting is of a nature too cohesive to be dissected. The Eighth Army has shown itself to be a precise-working machine, employing air, sea, and submarine collaboration in a manner so dovetailed into its own operational needs as to make the working of all three Services a combined operation.

The first application of divided tactical and strategic air power was the creation in the autumn of 1917 of the Independent 41st Wing of the Royal Flying Corps which was sent to Ochey in north-eastern France under Lieut.-Colonel Cyril Newall (now Marshal of the R.A.F. and Governor-General of New Zealand). This force was later called the Independent Air Force, and its command was taken by Major-General H. M. Trenchard (now Viscount Trenchard) in June 1918.

The independence of the air force from the other Services was recommended by General Smuts in his Memorandum to the Cabinet in 1917, together with its employment in a strategic capacity in addition to its normal use as a tactical weapon. It is therefore the more fitting that the greatest example of this combined use of air power to a common end should have been displayed in North Africa, the theatre of war within which Field-Marshal Smuts' Parliament sanctioned the earliest employment of South African forces, including the South African Air Force, after the cleaning up of the Italians in north-east Africa.

In North Africa this logical development of the employment of air power has been carried to a nicely-balanced state, firstly, by the collaboration of the United States air forces, and, secondly, by the appointment of an air generalissimo (which Air Chief Marshal Sir Arthur Tedder is) to co-ordinate the air operations of the whole recently created Mediterranean Command.

The organization of this Mediterranean zone, and the part allotted to air power therein, are of more than passing interest. For it would appear that it is from having got things right at the top first, so that the organization was smooth and the allocation of responsibility precise, that all subsequent success has derived.

MOUNTING Power of Allied Air Force in Mediterranean

IT may not be disclosed until after the War ; but do we see again here the guiding mind of Field-Marshal Smuts, who came to London last autumn ? That is quite probable. And the arrangement no doubt was completed and strengthened between President Roosevelt and Mr. Churchill at their Casablanca conference. Today, the combined air power of the United Kingdom, the Dominions, and the United States sweeps over the Mediterranean with irresistible force, and with mounting power. The forces at the command of the Luftwaffe cannot compare with the superb air force which has been created by the United Nations in the Mediterranean. The Italian Regia Aeronautica must have a sense of being overwhelmed by the air power opposed to Italy. Their aircraft are inferior to ours, and they are far fewer.

ROMMEL MEETS KESSELRING somewhere in the Western Desert. This excerpt from a captured German newsreel gives a close-up of the redoubtable commander of the German Afrika Korps (right) and his fellow field-marshal who commands the Luftwaffe in the Mediterranean. *Photo, Ministry of Information*

In Sicily, Field-Marshal Albert Kesselring (smiling Albert of the Luftwaffe), German Air Commander in the South, must feel anxiety mount as the air power opposed to his grows ever greater. He was one of the advocates in Germany of the use of the Luftwaffe to quell all opposition in an enemy, by terror bombing in addition to tactical and strategic bombing. He lost (with Field-Marshal Sperrle) the Battle of Britain when he was matched against Sir Hugh Dowding and the boys of Britain's Fighter Command. Now he is matched against Sir Arthur Tedder. Will he fare better ? I doubt it. And so must he. For now he faces an air arm far stronger than the comparatively tiny fighter force that hurled back the German geschwadern over Britain.

It is said that Kesselring and Rommel are personal enemies. If this be true it will not help either in the storm which is breaking over them.

WHAT are we going to achieve in the air when the Axis forces are driven from Africa ? The cordon will have been drawn about the Axis forces and they will have been contained for the first time since the War began. We shall then have complete air protection for passage of ships through the Mediterranean. With that supply line secure under air cover it will be possible to augment the rate of supply to all Middle East and Eastern theatres of war. We shall be better able to aid Russia at the southern end of her front. We shall be better placed to take the offensive against the Japanese invaders of Burma.

We shall possess air bases along the whole coastline of North Africa (except Spanish Morocco) from which we can attack by air Axis-held Europe at any point at will.

We shall be in a position to attack Europe across the narrow bridge of the Mediterranean between Tunisia and Sicily, if we wish to do so, but we shall also have a range of choice as great as that we can now make in relation to the western coast of Europe.

The Axis forces will have a long-spread-out line to defend, in Russia, along the Mediterranean, and facing the Atlantic and the Arctic Ocean, of about 8,000 miles.

It will then become possible to apply against that great area the lessons we have learned about tactical and strategic air power working to a common end, not in a single theatre of war, as in Tunisia now, but against Axis-held Europe as a whole. It should be possible to co-ordinate the Russian effort, which hitherto has necessarily been fought in isolation, within the grand framework of the master strategy. And for this purpose our air power can be concentrated at the tactically decisive point, or points.

DIRECTORS OF ALLIED AIR POWER in North Africa. Taken on Castel Benito airfield after the 8th Army's triumphant entry into adjacent Tripoli, this photograph shows three of the men who were among the chief architects of the Allied victory. Left to right : Air Vice-Marshal Sir Arthur Coningham, General Carl Spaatz, U.S.A.A.F., and Air Chief Marshal Sir Arthur Tedder. *Photo, British Official : Crown Copyright*

Allied Aircraft Hammer the Japs in Burma

R.A.F. AND U.S. PLANES are playing a vigorous part in the Burmese fighting. 1, R.A.F. armourers ride on a bomb-train carrying its load to a waiting plane at an Indian airfield. 2, Allied aircraft drop a shower of incendiaries on Jap positions in the Taungdaung area. 3, Indian pilot of a Hurricane gives the " thumbs-up " sign on returning from a sortie. The I.A.F.'s 1943 target is 10 squadrons equipped with the latest aircraft. 4, R.A.F. Blenheims swoop over a Jap base in the Myitkyina valley.

Photos, British Official: Crown Copyright

Helicopters Should Be Useful Against U-Boats

IN THE ANTI-SUBMARINE WAR helicopters are seen to possess obvious advantages, chief among them being the small space they require when taking off and landing. By using a revolving rotor the element of "lift" is obtained when most or all of the forward movement has ceased. Normal aircraft need speeds ranging from about 40 m.p.h. to provide sufficient turbulent air over the wing surfaces to keep the craft airborne.

Here in this drawing is shown a composite craft making a vertical take-off from the deck of a warship. The engine (A) drives the three-armed

lifting screw or rotor at about 200-250 revolutions per minute, making a circle 30 ft. in diameter. The gear box (B) takes the drive through the shaft (C) to the rotor-head (D), which contains the pitch-changing mechanism. The pilot, by means of a control column, can change direction even sideways, and, in some cases, backwards, by adjusting the pitch of the rotors and use of rudder and tail planes, etc. At (E) are seen the pneumatic floats suitable for deck or sea landing. A helicopter with rotor arms folded, and stowed in its hangar, is shown at (F).

Specially drawn for THE WAR ILLUSTRATED *by Haworth*

HELICOPTERS can hover over the precise spot where they intend to land. This photograph shows one of these aircraft preparing to descend. The Vought-Sikorsky helicopter is a wingless, two-engined, two-seater machine which can fly forwards, backwards and sideways. It can operate from any type of terrain.

Photo, Associated Press

BRITAIN has placed orders in America for helicopters, announced Capt. H. Balfour, Under-Secretary of State for Air, in the House of Commons on March 11. These aircraft, he went on to state, would be employed to help protect our shipping against U-boat attacks. Capt. Balfour's announcement followed reports from the U.S.A. that the Vought-Sikorsky helicopter was being produced in quantities for service tests for the American Army.

The U.S. Naval authorities have also decided to use this aircraft as an anti-submarine weapon owing to the facility with which it can take off and land vertically from the deck of a ship. The helicopter can carry depth charges or bombs, which it drops with a hundred per cent accuracy.

Designers have long been attracted to rotating-wing aircraft, that is, the type with thin flexible blades rotating on a vertical axis. The helicopter works on different principles from those of the autogyro. It does its flying by means of its rotor, the angle of whose blades can be altered to fly the machine in any direction of the compass, in addition to a rising or descending angle.

The present version of the helicopter is the result of more than 30 years' work on the problem of direct-lift aircraft, begun in Russia in 1910 by Major Sikorsky, and continued in America after the last war. In France also Bréguet carried out numerous experiments in helicopter research. Model experiments confirmed results obtained by the Chinese hundreds of years before.

The Vought-Sikorsky helicopter has extraordinary manoeuvrability, and is able to stop its forward travel in a matter of seconds

Right on the Target—Direct Hit by U.S. Bombers

BULL'S EYE ON A JAP SHIP deprived enemy forces in Burma of badly needed supplies. The vessel was steaming across the Bay of Bengal, south of Rangoon, when she was spotted by U.S.A.A.F. aircraft. Swooping over the 7,000-ton ship, the American planes dived low and dropped their bombs. This remarkable photograph, taken just after a big explosion had occurred, shows boats pulling away and another swung out on the davits waiting to be lowered as the crew take to the water.

Photo, British Official

THE HOME-FRONT

by E. Royston Pike

IN the first three days of September 1939 a million and a quarter schoolchildren and children under school age, mothers and expectant mothers, blind, cripples, mental defectives, hospital patients and "helpers" were evacuated from the most vulnerable areas of our great cities into the countryside. In the reception areas the people as a whole met this summary invasion of their homes with good will and helpfulness; but hardly had the billeting been completed when the country rang with accusations against some of the mothers and children. Letters to newspapers, reports to the Ministry of Health, and speeches in Parliament voiced a disgust which had in it an element of horror. The "submerged tenth," as the slum-dwellers used to be called in the days of General Booth and that other Booth who studied and described the life and labour of the Londoners of the 'nineties, came to the surface, revealing a foul beastliness which had never been suspected or realized save by those, health visitors and the like, whose duties took them into the lowest dens of London's East End, the dock areas of Mersey and Tyne, the teeming tenements of Leeds and Birmingham and Manchester.

AFTER three months 88 per cent of the mothers had returned to their homes, taking with them 86 per cent of their young children; but they left behind them a fearful memory. Against some of the mothers and young children the complaints were extraordinarily intense and bitter. To quote a passage from Our Towns: A Close Up (Oxford University Press, 5s.), a recently-published book which takes the lid off the slums as never before, one written in such plain language that a spade is called a nit-comb:

It was said that they were dirty, verminous, idle and extravagant; that they could not hold a needle and did not know the rudiments of cooking and housecraft, and that they had no control over their young children, who were untrained and animal in their habits. Some of these women were said to be foul-mouthed, bullying and abusive, given to drinking and frequenting public houses, insanitary in their habits and loose in their morals.

WITH such mothers what can one expect of the children? Much was forgiven the unaccompanied schoolchildren, and the sight of them filled many hostesses with a burning zeal to improve their condition.

Dirty and verminous, ill-clad and ill-shod (some had never had a change of underwear or any night-clothes and had been used to sleeping on the floor), suffering from scabies, impetigo, and other skin diseases, refusing to eat wholesome food, but clamouring for fish-and-chips, sweets and biscuits, refusing to go to bed at reasonable hours, destructive and defiant, foul-mouthed, liars and pilferers— these are some of the charges in the indictment against the future parents of our race. Some parents were said to have deliberately sent their children away ill-clad in order to get free clothing, to send them pocket-money, sweets, and "comics" instead of the clothing they needed, and to descend, often accompanied by relatives, for week-end visits which were an imposition and a scourge, expecting their whole party to receive free hospitality. The country rang with such accusations . . .

Back in their old quarters, these appalling dregs of humanity, who in their habits put the animals to shame, have aggravated the enormous difficulties presented by bombing, blackout, and large-scale transference of labour. At their last meeting the Education Committee of the London County Council learned of the uphill struggle encountered in the re-establishment of school facilities.

" . . . For many months children spent nights regularly in public shelters, under conditions which made it difficult, if not impossible, to observe reasonable standards of cleanliness of body and clothing, and of hygiene generally. Moreover, the damage by air attacks to houses, schools and other buildings made it necessary to improvise accommodation which normally would never have been accepted as reasonable for living and for schooling. Rationing of clothes, soap, and towels makes difficulties in the schools where in peacetime very useful work was done in the making and providing

YOUNG FARMERS' EXAMINATION arranged by the Berkeley Hunt Agricultural Society, was successfully revived this year. For the first time there were two women candidates, one of whom is here seen estimating the value and weight of a sheep, under the watchful eye of a judge. *Photo, E. W. Tattersall*

of garments for schoolchildren, work which was both educational and of immense assistance to the families concerned." Then many of the schools are still in the occupation of Civil Defence organizations. Yet while the children who have returned from evacuation show an all-round improvement in well-being and vitality (though they are often behindhand in their book-learning), the children who have remained in London show (it is claimed) no signs of physical or mental deterioration.

In London, as elsewhere, the schools are putting up a tremendous fight against the evils which war has brought in its train, and the evils which, alas, were carried over from peacetime. Few are aware of the difficulties which have to be faced (hence the importance of such books as Our Towns).

One speaker at the L.C.C. meeting revealed that he had just found a school where the mistress was trying to get every child to bring a handkerchief to school, even if it were only a bit of rag. Whereupon Miss Agnes Dawson said that years ago she herself had "made it a point to give every child in my school a handkerchief as a Christmas present, with her name woven into the corner. They didn't last long, it is true, but it was an

experiment worth trying." Another speaker, Mrs. E. M. Lowe, in a plea to cut the cant and face facts, declared that you can inculcate clean living by the age of fourteen, but you can't teach good housekeeping by that age.

THAT many of the young women of England are completely ignorant of housewifery was one of the criticisms made by a W.A.A.F. officer at a meeting of the Women's Adjustment Board Committee in London on March 5.

"I have seen thousands of women coming into the Forces," said Squadron Officer W. Wood, "who have never lit a fire in their lives. It is appalling that our young women of seventeen and eighteen should not know the elementary rules of housewifery and cooking. The extent of their cookery is to open a tin and make a cup of tea." The Services, she went on, are doing good work in teaching girls to mend their underclothes and stockings, and to foster standards of cleanliness. "It is astonishing how many weeks some of these girls can go without washing," she commented . . .

Letters published in the Press, so far from resenting, bore out the allegations.

Thus one printed in The News Chronicle reads: "The washing conditions are frightful: just six grubby-looking baths and two sinks in a hut about a hundred yards from the house for about five hundred W.A.A.F.s; these are only open at certain hours, and we have to get dressed in the morning without washing and also go to bed unwashed. You can imagine how sweet-tempered that makes me."

FOR the most part it is women who are bearing the burden and heat of the day on the home front: it was a band of gallant women who, for instance, obtained the information for Our Towns. It is all the more surprising, therefore, that Mrs. Mavis Tate, M.P., should have had to fight so long and so hard for what must seem to be a stroke of elemental justice—the granting to women who are injured in air raids the same compensation as is paid to men.

Following the division reported in our page 410 the Government set up a House of Commons Select Committee to consider the matter; and having received the Committee's report, Sir Walter Womersley, Minister of Pensions, announced in the House on April 7 that the Government had accepted its recommendations. The rate of injury allowance and disablement pension for women would be raised to the men's rate; and, moreover, non-gainfully occupied persons of both sexes would have their rates increased to those hitherto paid to gainfully-occupied men. Those most benefited by this latter provision are the housewives. Under the old order a housewife hurt by bomb-blast while doing her duty in her home received only 16s. 4d. weekly compensation, whereas if she had been injured while doing duty as a part-time warden she would have received 28s. Under the new order men and women will each receive 35s. (plus 8s. 9d. for a married man). Well might Mrs. Tate be jubilant over the removal of "this great injustice that has been suffered by women."

DOWN the Mile End Road rumbled a tractor-plough, driven by a girl in the uniform of the Women's Land Army. To the People's Palace it went, to a great East End rally—part of the campaign to enlist 60,000 voluntary helpers for holiday-work on the farms in the Home Counties. Camps are being established in the country, each equipped with main water and modern sanitation, a bed for every worker. Men and women and boys and girls over 16 are required; pay is 1s. an hour for men, 10d. for women, and 8d. for the youngsters, and the cost of living at the camps will be 4s. a day. Another food "flash" is that all the King's horses, including the famous greys seen in the Coronation procession at Ascot, are to help this year to bring in the harvest on the Windsor estate.

Plough that We May Reap the Victory Harvest!

TWO out of three of Britain's population are now fed on home-grown food, but Mr. R. L. Hudson, Minister of Agriculture, is urging us to do even better. In March 1943 he demanded that Britain's ploughing acreage of 600,000 be increased to 1,000,000.

The photographs in this page show how men and women are tackling the drive for food on the home front. 1, A drill sowing barley in a 60-acre field in Herts. It was stated recently that no cereal from the next harvest would be allocated to whisky manufacture. 2, Engaged in reclaiming 6,000 acres of Cheshire marshland by ditching, these Land Girls knock-off for lunch. 3, This member of the W.L.A. wears battledress while tilling the soil. 4, Ploughing a Yorkshire field.

Photos, The Times, Daily Mirror, Fox

I WAS THERE! Eye Witness Stories of the War

Our Sub. Destroyed a Nazi Plane in Mid-Air

Enemy-hunting in the Mediterranean, the submarine Umbra (see page 649) achieved a grand " bag "—including 12 Axis ships sunk, totalling about 49,000 tons, 13 prisoners captured, and credit for the destruction of a Nazi plane. Here is part of the great story, told by the Umbra's commanding officer, Lieutenant S. L. C. Maydon, D.S.O., R.N.

MY submarine was commissioned in August 1941, and our first success was, paradoxically, a disappointment to me. We encountered a very small craft on a very dark night. As soon as the alarm was given I went up on the bridge and, when my eyes became accustomed to the darkness, I thought we were on the trail of a U-boat. It was a small black box-shaped thing that I saw. We fired our torpedoes, and I immediately dived. We waited a bit in case there were other enemy naval craft in the vicinity, then surfaced cautiously.

We dived again, and returned to the spot next day, when we found two survivors on rafts. From one of these we learned the identity of our victim. It was not a U-boat, as I had hoped, but an Italian salvage ship, the Rampino, of 301 tons. The one satisfaction we had was that we must have fired a very accurate, or at least very lucky, shot to hit such a small target in the dark.

We encountered larger prey on the night of June 14-15, 1942—the Italian battle fleet ! We saw flares dropped by our aircraft, in line, in the most amazingly accurate manner. On the morning of the 15th I knew the Italian warships were coming in our direction. We stayed on the surface as long as we dared ; then we dived, and we could hear the threshing of ships' propellers. When I came to periscope height I saw two battleships, three cruisers and many destroyers. I moved into position to attack, and was within twenty seconds of firing the torpedoes when there was the devil of a noise.

At first we thought it was depth charges. Then we realized that it came from the bombs of our own aircraft attacking the Italian fleet. They were American Liberators, I believe ; and the sight that I watched through the periscope was an astonishing one. The sky was filled with tracer shells and there were bomb splashes everywhere on the surface of the water. I was so astonished and fascinated by the sight that the idea of danger just did not occur to me, although we were in the same peril from the bombs as were the Italian warships. I figured that the Italians might come round in a big circle, and I moved into a likely position to intercept them. They did come round, going as fast as ever they could. This time we got off our torpedoes, and obtained one hit at least. We learned later that the battleship we hit was under repair in dock at Taranto for a considerable time.

A TRENTO class cruiser had been hit by a bomb and set on fire. She was blazing well, and we started stalking her. She was protected by three destroyers, circling round her continually as she limped towards the Italian coast. A rather ineffective smoke screen was being put down. We got in fairly close, and then two of the destroyers came in right over us. We had to go away a bit. We came in again, and it was remarkable that although the cruiser was on fire aft there were sailors standing on the forecastle leaning on the rail. We fired two torpedoes, then several depth charges were dropped, but we got clear. That, I think, was the most exciting day I have ever spent. The cruiser sank a few minutes after 10 p.m. I did not see her go down, as my idea was to get away quickly. There was someone, however, who saw our torpedoes hit, and he reported that the cruiser broke up and sank in three minutes.

On August 27, 1942—the first birthday of Umbra—we carried out another attack, on two heavily-escorted enemy supply ships. We sighted them with their attendant destroyers, and I fired my torpedoes when the ships were more or less in line. One was definitely hit, and probably sank. We had twenty-nine depth charges dropped around us that time. The following month we again sighted two enemy vessels, and I had never before seen such a heavy air escort for two merchant ships. I fired a complete salvo of torpedoes, and at least one hit was obtained. The target was seen stopped and down by the stern. Then came counter-attacks by the escorting destroyers, and seventeen depth charges were dropped close to us.

Later we saw that three destroyers had been left behind to go round the damaged merchant ship in an endless circle. The moon came up and the light was good. We worked our way in again, and I dived straight through the destroyer screen. Suddenly there was a heavy explosion. We thought at first of a depth charge. Then we saw that the ship had disappeared. The explosion must have been her blowing up.

ON Dec. 2, 1942, off the Tunisian coast, we saw an Italian collier, going quite slowly. I did not attack immediately, as I hoped something better might be following her. I reckoned that if nothing else came along we should still be able to catch up with her and carry out an attack. Nothing did come, so we went after her, surfaced and attacked with gunfire. With our second shot we severed her main steam-pipe. She came to an abrupt halt, and then we sank her. We picked up an Italian and he told us that some Germans had been on board. We found them—a nice capture of ten. All save one were German air force personnel.

Lt. S. L. C. MAYDON, D.S.O., R.N.. commander of H.M.S. Umbra, who describes in this page the splendid achievements of his craft against enemy shipping in the Mediterranean. *Photo, British Official*

One of them, an Austrian, could speak a fair amount of English, so we made him interpreter. Some of the Huns, we gathered, had been in hospital and were going home to Germany on sick leave. Others were in the ordinary course of transfer of duty. They had been waiting in Tripoli for some time for an air passage. They had taken off in a Junkers 52, which had promptly run out of petrol, and they had come down in the sea. They had been picked up by the Italian collier, and then they were picked up again—by us.

A week later we had the good fortune to meet a munitions ship escorted by four aircraft. We fired our torpedoes, obtained a hit, and the ship blew up. When we looked again there were only three escorting planes : and that is how we came to be credited with the destruction of an aircraft. The suggestion is that the fourth was blown up by the force of the explosion of the ammunition ship.

I Rode 'The Weapon That Will Win the War'

This vivid description of aerobatics in one of the world's fastest warplanes—the Mosquito—is condensed from an article by Ronald A. Keith and reprinted here from the February issue of Maclean's, Canada's National Magazine.

THE familiar terrain of Toronto stands on edge and gyrates like a spinning platter. A mighty weight presses on your head and shoulders like an invisible drop hammer. Then your vision clears and a cow barn tilts past the window in a blur of speed.

It could be a horrible dream, but it isn't. It is the exciting reality of flight with Geoffrey de Havilland, Jr., in the Canadian-built Mosquito, one of the swiftest warplanes in the world.

After secret preparations the event had been heralded by a cryptic telegram : "CAN YOU BE AT AIRPORT NEAR TORONTO TO GET INSECT STORY EARLY THURSDAY?" We could. For that "insect" would be one of those deadly "Mosquitoes" which are breeding in this country's war-plants and will be rising in swarms to sting the Nazis into frenzies. This bomber, now being manufactured in Canadian plants, has been described by an R.A.F. Air Marshal as "the weapon that will win the war."

As our Mosquito stood on the tarmac its long legs were like slender stilts propped under the long slim belly of the fuselage. The sun sparkled on the plexiglass dome of the cockpit and slanted through the transparent bomb-sighting snout. The plywood body and wings, sheathed in fabric and slicked with silver dope, gleamed like the surface of a hardwood floor, hinting at one of the secrets of the plane's phenomenal speed. It has been claimed that freedom from the thousands of rivet-heads, which mar the metal plane's surface like a rash, adds up to twenty per cent more speed for the same power.

The Merlins were coughing discreetly as they idled ; we mounted a ladder to find Geoffrey de Havilland seated at the controls, checking his instruments in the compact two-man cabin. In a chocolate-coloured jacket, white shirt and correct tie he looked more like an alert young businessman in his office than a famous test pilot ready for take-off. Buckling on his aerobatic shoulder harness, which would clamp him firmly to the seat in any position, de Havilland smiled.

"You may buckle yours up if you like, but you really won't need it. She is very gentle in aerobatics," he suggested. We were already busy buckling, also taking some care to check the parachute harness. Its two snap hooks in front were ready to grip corresponding rings on the parachute pack which lay in a compact bundle on the floor.

The escape hatch too came in for some attention. A normal exit involves raising a hinged floor section, unfastening a down-swinging hatch, pulling a small tubular ladder from a hidden compartment, and climbing down. To abandon the aircraft while "upstairs," however, it is permissible to forget the ladder, as long as you remember to snap on your parachute pack, otherwise it would be one long step to the ground. For baling out, the belly hatch would seem to be ideal because it eliminates the danger of being struck by the rudder or tailplane. For quick action you simply lift the floor section and step on a pedal which jettisons the outer door and away you go.

The air brakes hissed and sighed, the engines rumbled in slight acceleration and the black tarmac rolled under the transparent nose as we taxied out to the take-off position. The pilot was fanning his glance across the instrument panel in a final cockpit check, his left hand nursing two ivory cubes which crowned the throttle levers. Fuel levels; air, hydraulic and oil pressures; oil, car-burettor and cylinder head temperatures; flying instruments, tachometers, fuel selector switches . . . everything checked. The engines were revved up and we were all set to go.

THE propeller pitch levers went forward into "fine" for take-off, which meant that the blade angles were set to bite thin slices of air while swirling at maximum speed, thus developing full power, like a car in low gear. Then the ivory throttle-handles went forward, the tail lifted, and there was a vivid cata-pulting impression as the plane surged forward. In an incredibly brief moment we were suddenly rocketing along at 130 miles

an hour and the Mosquito leaped into the air. We shot upward in an astonishing mile-a-minute climb which simply snatched the airfield out of sight and left us floating in space 7,000 feet above the flat contours of the city.

Once aloft, operation of the aircraft appeared to be amazingly simple. There was the control column rising between the pilot's knees and surmounted by a semi-wheel, something like vertical handlebars. Turning the wheel banked the plane, while pushing or pulling dived or climbed it. The pilot explained that in such a fast aircraft the rudder pedals were almost unnecessary, even in aerobatics, because when the plane banked it turned of its own accord. De Havilland proceeded to demonstrate.

Toronto Was Upside Down!

WITHOUT even diving for extra speed, as in slower planes, he simply eased back on the wheel . . . The nose came up sharply and the world seemed to be clinging to our tail; then the Mosquito arched over on to its back and, momentarily, there we were in the weirdest of attitudes. We seemed to be quite normal, but there was the city of Toronto fantastically hanging upside down. We could see it by peering *up* through the plexi-glass of the cockpit roof. Then, without the slightest stress or discomfort, we were around the invisible barrel hoop and flying level again.

" The roll is just as simple," the pilot said. And even as he spoke, the nose came up slightly above the horizon and he turned the wheel sharply to the right. Suddenly we were following the contours of an imaginary corkscrew and once again the world was performing weirdly. There it was on edge, pivoting against the right wing tip, then it

careened up over our heads and slid down the other side to flash by the left wing tip. Around it went, once, twice, three times. Then it settled down beneath us and stayed put for a few moments.

As our pilot had promised, there was none of the unpleasant sensation of hanging upside down out of the seat and against the safety belt that would be taken for granted in slower planes. The centrifugal force of those high speed manoeuvres kept us pressed comfortably against the seat cushions regardless of the plane's attitude. Thus the acrobatics were simple. To the passenger it was just a case of sitting there in serene comfort while the world went "haywire."

The only unpleasant gyrations were the tight vertical bank and the pull out from a steep dive. The tight vertical bank was something like the motor-cycle " wall of death" in the midway but infinitely faster. In both instances there seemed to be an irresistible pressure seeking to shove you through the seat, draining the blood from your head and dimming your vision. Eventually this titanic squeeze play knocks you unconscious and you black out; but our manoeuvring was slightly less terrific than that.

We plummeted almost to deck level, skimming the waves along the waterfront. Coming out of that dive, a glance at the airspeed dial showed the needle quivering on 450 miles per hour! There was still no over-powering sensation of great speed until we flashed by docks and warehouses. Then it was not difficult to understand why they claim it takes two men on the ground to watch the Mosquito, one to see it coming, the other to see it going. It is reported that the first English farmer to see the original Mosquito unlimbering had only one word to describe his impression. "Crikey!" he said.

'Those Crazy Airmen!'

NOW we were low over downtown Toronto, looping, rolling, twisting and finally shooting skyward in a spectacular vertical roll. In all the confusion the writer sometimes lost track of the city and didn't know whether to look up, down, sideways or back over the tail to see it. But otherwise it was an altogether comfortable ride.

Thus we sat in relative ease and safety, while throngs of people in the streets below craned their necks, muttered about "those crazy airmen," and narrowly escaped death under the wheels of automobiles whose drivers were also gazing upward. According to subsequent newspaper reports, Geoffrey de Havilland's aerobatics were tying up city traffic in blocks.

Sighting a fast Norwegian attack bomber as it wheeled over Island Airport, de Havilland proceeded to make its pilot feel pretty silly. We literally flew circles around the single-engined bomber, looping up over its nose and down behind the tail, barrel rolling around it and finally twisting almost straight up in front of it.

RETURNING to the airport, we encountered a camouflaged Lockheed Ventura, one of the fastest of twin-engined bombers. It was winging eastward, probably destined for transatlantic ferrying to England. Our pilot calmly shut off one engine, advanced the throttle of the other Rolls, then proceeded to skim past the Ventura in an astounding demon-stration of single-engined speed. To empha-size his point, he then put the Mosquito through several slow rolls, still on the single engine.

In a final flourish our Mosquito, now on both engines, swooped down over the tele-phone wires to flash across the airport at something more than seven miles a minute, then careened gracefully up and over to execute a roll off the top of the loop. The engines blurped, backfired, then purred softly as the throttles came back and we sloped steeply to a "hot" three-point landing.

MOSQUITOES, as told in this and the preceding page, have great powers of attack. A force of these machines bombed railway workshops and installations at Namur, Belgium, on April 3, 1943. This photo was taken during the raid, and shows a Mosquito lit up by a bomb-burst in the foreground.
Photo, British Official: Crown Copyright

In Burma We Explored a City of the Dead

An Indian Army observer who has recently returned across the frontier
to India was one of a British patrol that penetrated enemy-occupied Burma
to what was once a busy town, but is now strewn with human skeletons.
His grim story of this scene of horror and desolation is given below.

"ROUTINE" operation they called the patrol when we left our base on the 'home' side of the border, where for the last few months cloud, mist and rain enveloped the countryside. We struck off the road after a few miles and followed a bridle path which plunged through dense tropical foliage. Soon we were provided with our first typical example of the high degree of improvisation which is a feature of these operations in Burma.

Across a raging stream, a temporary bridge of bamboo and telephone wire had been constructed by an earlier patrol. To supports on either side of the river had been fastened several strands of wire, from which the super-structure of the temporary bridge was suspended. The roadway was formed by inter-laced bamboo, covered with cane matting, and in an emergency would be capable of bearing a light motor vehicle. Across the bridge the ground rose to over 2,000 feet in a distance of just under two miles. The path up which we struggled, during a downpour of rain, was a mountain stream in full flood. Our arrival, drenched and exhausted, at the summit brought us to the end of the first of many days of marching—and to an advanced post situated in a Naga village.

Next day we continued down into a valley. The rain had stopped for a while, but as we descended the temperature increased and our clothing was as wet from perspiration as it had been on the previous day from rain. The going was easier now, and in the early afternoon we contacted our most advanced

position, which is held by Indian troops; in fact it has never been evacuated. So far we had not met opposition. Occasionally a snake would slither across the path in front of us, and deep in the jungle we would hear the screaming and chattering of monkeys disturbed by our approach.

IN BURMA, as told in this page, the horrors of war have been fully experienced. Here is a glimpse of the lighter side—men of the Lancashire Fusiliers at a jungle "cookhouse."
Photo, British Official

From time to time figures, semi-naked but carrying a rifle and ammunition, would leap out in front of us from the jungle and make a mystic sign. They were members of the guerilla force, drawn from Naga and Kuki tribesmen, who operate throughout the hills. Having satisfied themselves as to our bona fides, they would disappear again into the depths of the jungle.

Once we met a party of refugees, numbering about forty, making for India. They told a pitiful tale of Japanese and traitor-Burman cruelty and treachery. Burmans whom we occasionally met towards the end of the outward journey appeared to be friendly and answered freely all the many questions that were asked by the Intelligence Officer who accompanied the patrol.

Late one afternoon we arrived at our destination—formerly a busy centre, now literally a city of the dead. There was no sign of life. Buildings appeared as if they were still occupied. On entering we found sometimes only emptiness, but sometimes human skeletons lying around. Cars were parked along the streets as though the owners had stopped for a moment to do some shopping. I opened the door of one of these cars. Inside was a skeleton.

There was horror in that town, an atmosphere of death and decay. It had been the end of a long, hard journey for many exhausted, diseased and hunger-stricken people who had died rather than give in.

We turned then towards India. We waded through rivers and mud, into which at times we sank knee deep. Day after day swarms of mosquitoes and sand flies tormented us. Here we improvised a bridge; there we hacked a way through dense undergrowth. Always we watched for—hoped for—signs of the enemy, for the memory lingered of the city of the dead in the Burmese jungle.

OUR DIARY OF THE WAR

MARCH 31, 1943, Wednesday 1,306th day
Air.—U.S. Flying Fortresses raided shipyards at Rotterdam in daylight.
Mediterranean.—Nearly 100 Flying Fortresses raided three aerodromes and harbour at Cagliari, Sardinia.
Russian Front.—In the Kuban Soviet troops occupied Anastayevskaya.
Burma.—R.A.F. Blenheims bombed oil installations at Bhamo.

APRIL 1, Thursday 1,307th day
Air.—Mosquitoes raided power station and railway workshops at Trier and Ehrang in W. Germany.
North Africa.—Very heavy Allied air raid on El Maou airfield at Sfax.
Mediterranean.—R.A.F. and U.S. bombers made low-level raid on Messina.
India.—Thirty Jap bombers attacking Feni, S.E. Bengal, were intercepted by Hurricanes.
Australasia.—Air battle off Guadalcanal; 16 Jap fighters shot down for loss of six American aircraft.

APRIL 2, Friday 1,308th day
Air.—R.A.F. made night raid on Lorient and St. Nazaire.
Australasia.—Allied heavy bombers attacked Jap shipping at Kavieng, New Ireland.
U.S.A.—American aircraft made eight raids on Kiska, Aleutians, and also bombed Attu.

APRIL 3, Saturday 1,309th day
Air.—Daylight raids on Abbeville and docks at Brest; another heavy night attack on Essen.
North Africa.—Allied troops occupied Cap Serrat, 40 m. W. of Bizerta.
Australasia.—Allied heavy bombers again attacked Jap warships at Kavieng.

APRIL 4, Sunday 1,310th day
Sea.—Admiralty announced loss of sub-marine Tigris.
Air.—U.S. Flying Fortresses made daylight raid on Renault works near Paris. At night Kiel received its heaviest bombing from the R.A.F.
Mediterranean.—Heavy raid on Naples by Allied bombers; Palermo and Syracuse also attacked.
Russian Front.—On Donetz front Russians repelled German attacks near Izyum; in the Kuban Soviet troops made progress.
India.—Jap aircraft raided airfield near Chittagong on Bay of Bengal.

Australasia.—Jap shipping at Kavieng again attacked by Allied bombers; in all seven warships and five merchant ships were sunk or damaged.

APRIL 5, Monday 1,311th day
Air.—Large force of U.S. bombers raided Erla aero-engine works at Antwerp; Venturas attacked Brest docks.
Mediterranean.—Allied bombers made heavy day and night raids on airfields in Sicily and N. Tunisia.
India.—R.A.F. Hurricanes drove off more than 50 Jap bombers raiding S.E. Bengal.
Burma.—U.S. bombers attacked Mandalay and Prome by day; R.A.F. made night raid on railway station at Rangoon.
U.S.A.—American bombers and fighters made six attacks in the Aleutians.

APRIL 6, Tuesday 1,312th day
Air.—R.A.F. fighter-bombers raided airfield at St. Omer and steel-works near Caen.
North Africa.—Eighth Army launched attack north of Gabès against Wadi Akarit. Heavy air raid on Sfax.

APRIL 7, Wednesday 1,313th day
North Africa.—Eighth Army advancing from Wadi Akarit made contact with Second U.S. Army Corps from El Guettar.
Australasia.—Japanese aircraft sank three Allied ships off Guadalcanal; in air battle U.S. fighters brought down 39 Jap planes.
General.—Hitler and Mussolini began four-day conference at Fuehrer's H.Q. Bolivia at war with Axis nations.

APRIL 8, Thursday 1,314th day
Air.—Announced that in daylight raids on Renault works on April 4 and Erla works at Antwerp on April 5 a total of 70 German aircraft were shot down by Flying Fortresses and Liberators. R.A.F. made heavy night attack on the Ruhr.
North Africa.—Allied aircraft carried

out heavy attacks on enemy transport on coastal road from Mahares to Sfax.

APRIL 9, Friday 1,315th day
Sea.—Admiralty announced that destroyer Harvester had been torpedoed and sunk in Atlantic after battle with U-boats.
Air.—R.A.F. made another night attack on the Ruhr, with Duisburg as main target.
North Africa.—Germans announced evacuation of Pichon, Central Tunisia.

APRIL 10, Saturday 1,316th day
Air.—R.A.F. made night raid on S.W. Germany. Koenigsberg bombed by Soviet aircraft.
North Africa.—Eighth Army occupied port of Sfax.
Mediterranean.—Italian heavy cruiser Trieste sunk and Gorizia damaged by Flying Fortresses in harbour of La Maddalena, Sardinia. Lightning fighters shot down 30 enemy transport planes in Sicilian straits.
Burma.—Japanese infiltration through the jungle led to further withdrawal by our troops in the Mayu peninsula.
Australasia.—Heavy bombers attacked Jap base at Wewak, New Guinea.

APRIL 11, Sunday 1,317th day
North Africa.—First Army troops entered Kairouan; First and Eighth Armies made contact near Fondouk.
Mediterranean.—Lightning fighters shot down 31 enemy transport planes in the Sicilian straits.
U.S.A.—American aircraft made four raids on Jap bases in Kiska, Aleutians.
Australasia.—Jap dive-bombers and fighters attacked Allied shipping in Oro Bay, New Guinea.

APRIL 12, Monday 1,318th day
Air.—Koenigsberg again raided by Soviet aircraft.
North Africa.—Eighth Army occupied port of Sousse.
Mediterranean.—U.S. Liberators raided Naples; R.A.F. made night attacks on Palermo and Messina harbours.
Russian Front.—Soviet troops beat off German attack on Volkhov front, aimed at cutting Leningrad's lifeline with east.
Australasia.—One hundred Jap aircraft made heaviest raid yet on airfields near Port Moresby, New Guinea; 37 destroyed or badly damaged.
General.—Antonescu, Rumanian Prime Minister, received at Hitler's H.Q.

★ ══════ *Flash-backs* ══════ ★

1940

April 8. Allied Governments notified Norway of mine-laying in Norwegian waters.

April 9. Germans invaded Norway and Denmark.

April 10. First Battle of Narvik; destroyer Hunter sunk, Hardy beached.

1941

April 1. Asmara, capital of Eritrea, surrendered to British.

April 3. Benghazi evacuated in face of Rommel's advance.

April 5. In Abyssinia British forces entered Addis Ababa.

April 6. Germans invaded Greece and Yugoslavia.

April 10. British and Imperial

troops made contact with Germans in northern Greece.

1942

April 1. Japanese launched heavy attacks on Bataan peninsula.

April 3. In Burma British withdrew from Prome.

April 5. Japanese air raid on Colombo.

April 6. First Japanese raids on India: Cocanada and Vizagapatam bombed.

April 9. Aircraft-carrier Hermes sunk by Japanese aircraft, loss of cruisers Dorsetshire and Cornwall announced. Trincomalee, Ceylon, raided by Japanese. American resistance ended on Bataan; Corregidor holding out.

NEVER since the War began has London seemed so full as now, when those who, because of their business or habitation, may call themselves Londoners are jostled by crowds of suburban and provincial visitors, when it is thronged by men and women in a rich variety of uniform and speaking all the tongues of the United Nations. Many of these have never seen London before, and all will return to their homes in distant parts without ever seeing it as we who have loved and lived in it for so long would have liked it to be remembered. For there is no denying that the London of today is decidedly shabby and in-parts down-at-heel. Bombs have left monstrous chasms, beautiful churches are burnt-out shells, once-graceful buildings are as gaunt and ugly as a toothless harridan. In one detail, however, lack of material has worked for temporary good. I refer to the horrible disfigurement first introduced by our good American friends by way of cinema publicity. Finely-proportioned façades used to be plastered over with crudely-coloured mammoth pictures so that only scraps of the buildings remained visible. I hope the authorities will take steps after the War to prevent a recrudescence of these abominably inartistic displays, which might be in place on Coney Island or at Blackpool's show grounds, but were eyesores in the Strand, the Haymarket, and many of our best thoroughfares.

"A THOUSAND Germans were killed," "the enemy suffered heavy losses" . . . How often do we find some such statement in the communiqués coming from the Russian front! And the unthinking receive the news with a half-smile of satisfaction. But in a battle the casualties are never all on one side ; if thousands of Germans have been killed, we may be sure that a great host of gallant Russians has fallen too. Our ally has won great victories, but only at a great price—and there's a limit to the price that can be paid. So many people, and among them some who ought to know better, write and talk as if Russia's manpower were inexhaustible—that the Soviet must crush the Axis by sheer weight of numbers. Yet, with practically the whole of Europe under his control, Hitler can call upon a population of over 300 millions, while Soviet Russia with fifty millions of her people in Nazi-occupied territory has a population of about 130 millions. Not numbers but generalship won Stalingrad for Russia. Well may Negley Farson write again and again in The Daily Mail of " the Red Army Millions Myth." He never hears a " Salute to Russia " programme without feeling a bit sick, he says, since, though they spring directly from the heart, " these cheers and pageants must be ashes in Stalin's mouth when *he* (and possibly he alone) is handed the terrible casualty lists showing the death-roll of his people." Farson is absolutely right in his declaration that Russia's death-roll should never be out of our thoughts—should temper our rejoicing over Red Army victories with sadness, even a measure of apprehension.

A FEW days after I had referred in these notes to those unhelpful officials, " swanking around clothed in a little authority," I received a letter from a reader in a township north of the Forth complaining bitterly of the conditions in the munitions factory in which he works. Inches of snow on the floor at times in the winter of a year ago, flooding in time of heavy rain, damp and chilly atmosphere, heating system broken down so that the men had to work with their raincoats on—these are some of the conditions he described ; and he went on to tell of women having to stand twelve hours a day without so much as a cup of tea and forbidden to speak to one another. "No appeal seems possible," he concluded ; " the factory inspector is but a name to workers, and one finds the official mind always suspicious of a worker and his complaints."

QUITE frankly I found these allegations a little hard to swallow ; but I know, too, that there is no smoke without a fire. So I sent a note of the complaints—mentioning the factory, but not my correspondent's name—to the Ministry of Labour, in the

Sqdn.-Ldr. J. A. F. MacLACHLAN, D.S.O., D.F.C., and bar, one of the most successful of R.A.F. " night-intruders." He lost an arm during a fierce fight over Malta, and has destroyed fourteen enemy aircraft.
Drawn by Eric Kennington, Crown Copyright reserved

belief that they would give the matter proper attention. In that I need hardly say I was well justified. The Ministry at once took up the matter with the District Inspector of Factories, and the terms of his report have been communicated to me. The Inspector considers that my correspondent's allegations are not substantiated. True, the factory is in a very exposed position, so that when the weather is very severe the firm have occasionally had trouble with snow coming through the windows and with flooding. But the Inspector has no knowledge of the heating system having broken down ; and though the work on which the women are employed is usually done standing, there are seats for them to use at such times as there is an opportunity for them to sit down. I am afraid my correspondent is still not satisfied, but that is not for me to judge. Even in peacetime it was often said that factory inspectors had an impossible job, and nowadays their duties are infinitely more onerous. Conditions, too, in any particular factory change from day to day. But when Mr. Bevin's officials are receiving so many brickbats it is only fair to put on record this little instance of their courteous efficiency.

ON the face of it, it is a little surprising to find the Army Bureau of Current Affairs co-operating with the University of London Institute of Archaeology and C.E.M.A. (Council for the Encouragement of Music and the Arts) in arranging an exhibition of photographs entitled The Present Discovers the Past. But as one who has had the satisfaction of awakening an interest in archaeology in the minds of a host of readers, I confidently recommend a visit to the London Museum. The exhibition will remain on view until May 30. Its object is to vindicate the relevance of archaeology to modern life, and it is most interesting to study the comparisons between modern and ancient roads, houses, domestic appliances, agricultural implements, etc. Most striking, however, are the aerial photographs of such ancient wonders as Maiden Castle, Silbury Hill, the Uffington White Horse, Woodhenge, and the Cerne Giant. But most fascinating of all, perhaps, are those photographs of ordinary English fields which, when photographed from the air, are seen to be indelibly marked with the outlines of Roman walls, Saxon barrows, and Celtic fields. For a hole or ditch once dug in the chalk can never be obliterated ; the soil tends to be more moist and less compact so that the corn grows taller and ripens later. Over ancient foundations the corn is short and ripens early.

READING the many tributes to Cardinal Hinsley, the Roman Catholic Archbishop of Westminster who died at his country home at Buntingford, Herts, on March 17, one could not but be struck by the universal recognition of his qualities as a churchman, as an English patriot, and as a man of fine and rich personality. Not so long ago Rome was "the scarlet woman," and it is less than a century since the Pope's appointment of Wiseman as first Archbishop of Westminster and Cardinal gave rise to the most bitter and prolonged agitation in religious circles. But today we have the Archbishop of Canterbury declaring that all whose aspirations are set upon a Christian Britain mourn Cardinal Hinsley ; "many of us also mourn a most kindly and warm-hearted friend," and the Moderator of the Free Church Council (Dr. J. S. Whale) paying tribute to the Cardinal's warm humanity, moral directness, and fine Christian simplicity.

VERY much more cheerful is the latest letter I have received from our worthy correspondent in Malta, Mr. G. Fabri. It is dated early in March, when the much-bombed island had just assumed the offensive in real earnest. He speaks most appreciatively of the convoy ships that had entered the harbour and so swelled the island's stocks of food that whereas only a short time since the "hungry eyes of the thousands lining the bastions penetrated into the ships' holds and visualized their contents—flour for bread and milk for the babies," today the Maltese housewife has to make two trips to the grocer to bring in the fortnightly rations. "And as she stores them away in the kitchen cupboard she cannot fail to notice how the United Nations are striving to help Malta in every possible way. Salmon and butter, milk, sweets, and other important items : how closely knit is this small island to the large family of Allied Nations ! " But he goes on to say that though things have changed so much for the better in Malta, that does not mean that there may not be a new flare-up at any time. "The Nazis may one day return—but how different is Malta in April 1943 from April of last year ! "

This Pillbox Did Not Halt the Desert Army

ROMMEL'S DEFENSIVE LINE was brilliantly outflanked and the whole of the Mareth area occupied by Gen. Montgomery's forces by March 30, 1943. The battered Axis transport and armour, incessantly attacked from the air, streamed up the Tunisian coast towards Sfax and Sousse as the 8th Army vanguard swept without pause through the Gabès gap. These cheerful British sergeants have seen some hard fighting and are photographed at the entrance of their pillbox in the Mareth Line.

Photo, British Official: Crown Copyright

Printed in England and published every alternate Friday by the Proprietors, THE AMALGAMATED PRESS, LTD., The Fleetway House, Farringdon Street, London, E.C.4. Registered for transmission by Canadian Magazine Post. Sole Agents for Australia and New Zealand : Messrs. Gordon & Gotch, Ltd. ; and for South Africa : Central News Agency, Ltd.—April 30, 1943   S.S.   *Editorial Address :* JOHN CARPENTER HOUSE, WHITEFRIARS, LONDON E.C.4

Vol 6   *The War Illustrated*   Nº 154

Edited by Sir John Hammerton

SIXPENCE   MAY 14, 1943

THE ELEPHANT RETURNS TO ACTIVE SERVICE.   U.S. troops in India, constructing bases near the Burmese border, have adopted the elephant (no newcomer to battlefields of the East) as a powerful ally : as, before them, the Japanese used elephant transport in their advance into Burma early in 1942.   American soldiers in a jungle outpost in the Naga Hills region are here shown adjusting a load while their patient beast of burden waits to lumber off.
Photo, Sport & General

NO. 155 WILL BE PUBLISHED FRIDAY. MAY 28

THE BATTLE FRONTS

by Maj.-Gen. Sir Charles Gwynn, K.C.B., D.S.O.

AFTER the short lull which followed the battle of Akarit, the final phase of the battle for Tunisia opened on April 19 with the attack by the 8th Army. In the following days it was taken up along the whole front by the other armies of General Alexander's command; while the Allied forces maintained a devastating attack on the enemy's sea and air communications, on his airfields and on every vulnerable target. The Navy was no less active in attacking his sea communications. It would seem, therefore, that the fight this time will be to a finish, for the alternative of evacuating any large part of the Axis forces can hardly exist.

The struggle is, however, likely to be long and costly; for the enemy holds a fortress naturally strong and powerfully fortified. In it he has picked troops of the highest quality and they are certain to fight in a spirit of fanatical desperation. Moreover, the Allies will have to depend chiefly on their infantry and artillery, for the superiority in armour they now possess will avail them little. The terrain gives few opportunities for its employment. Air cooperation will, of course, be of immense assistance, but where so much cover for the defence is available it can only be really efficient if land attacks force the enemy into the open.

Progress during the final ten days of the struggle, though slow, has been highly encouraging. One after another the enemy's most fiercely held strong points have been taken and his main outer position has been weakened. Even when that is taken his citadel at Bizerta will remain to be captured; however confident we may be in the final outcome, initial successes achieved by the 8th Army should not raise premature hopes of rapid victory.

In Russia the lull in major fighting will probably continue till the beginning of May, but both sides are evidently preparing rapidly for a renewed offensive. With their better communications the Germans are likely to secure the initiative, except in the Kuban.

THE MIDDLE EAST

Before the Libyan campaigns are overshadowed by greater events to come, let us review their achievements and note some of the critical decisions taken and opportunities lost by the enemy. The achievements of Montgomery's 8th Army have been so outstanding that its campaign is sure of its place in military history, but we should not forget how much it owed to Wavell's Army of the Nile and to Auchinleck's 8th Army. The experience of desert fighting and the knowledge of the enemy's methods and armament which they acquired were invaluable.

Moreover, the great base organization on which Montgomery's success so largely depended had been steadily built up during the earlier campaigns. Montgomery's army had to break new ground and to adapt itself to many new circumstances, but the foundation had been well laid, even in the matter of close cooperation between land, sea and air forces which was brought to such perfection.

Wavell's campaign, considering the inadequacy of his resources and the fact that he was a pioneer, was in some ways the most brilliant of all, and it should not be underrated because he had a less formidable opponent than Rommel. His decision to take the offensive and his brilliant victory at Sidi Barrani decided the issue of the campaign just as did Alamein. The capture of Bardia and Tobruk were outstanding achievements, but it was the brilliant interception of the retreat of the remnants of Graziani's army by the Armoured Division that fully revealed the potentialities of mechanized troops in desert warfare.

How impossible it was for Wavell, with his small force exhausted and already with a long and inadequately equipped line of communication, to advance to Tripoli is clearly proved by the difficulties Montgomery had later to overcome. Any such premature attempt would have invited disaster; for, dominating as was the position Admiral Cunningham had acquired by his bold offensive attitude, he could not prevent the dispatch of reinforcements to Tripoli. Rommel's appearance was shortly to prove this, and Malta had not yet become an unsinkable aircraft carrier and an offensive base. Wavell had achieved his main object — the elimination of the immediate threat to Egypt; and by securing the airfields of Cyrenaica had rendered a service to the Navy.

Yet Wavell's success was due primarily to the bold decision of the War Cabinet to send him reinforcements of troops and material, ill as they could be spared after Dunkirk; and it was due to Admiral Cunningham's offensive attitude that an important part of them was able to take the Mediterranean route, thereby arriving at the critical moment. The fruits of Wavell's victory were largely sacrificed to the Greek campaign, and the enemy's capture of Crete deprived Admiral Cunningham of the dominating position he had established in the Eastern Mediterranean; but Tobruk, retained by another notable decision, held out, preventing Rommel from fully exploiting his success.

THE degree of success achieved by Rommel on his first appearance draws attention to the great opportunity Germany had lost. If Germany, with masses of troops and armour in excess of what she could possibly employ for the invasion of Britain, had decided to stiffen Graziani's army for the invasion of Egypt, could Wavell have successfully resisted the onslaught? Why did Hitler neglect the opportunity? Was it because he was confident that the war would be won in Britain, or was it because his General Staff, till Wavell showed them the way, did not realize the possibilities of mechanized desert warfare? Opportunities lost seldom recur, and I suggest we have here one of the major mistakes Germany has made.

Auchinleck's campaign, though by hard fighting it inflicted heavy losses on the enemy from which he never fully recovered, failed to come up to expectations at any time, and ended in disaster. I am convinced that Rommel had not foreseen and had not prepared for the invasion of Egypt; and, justifiably exploiting success, he drove his troops to exhaustion till they were brought to a halt by Auchinleck's reserves summoned from Palestine. With an immensely long line of communication he was then obviously in a dangerous position. Elsewhere I wrote at the time that I hoped he would meet the fate I was convinced would

EIGHTH ARMY IN SFAX received an enthusiastic welcome from the inhabitants of the town on April 10, 1943. This photograph shows a British tank passing through one of the main streets which is lined with civilians who delightedly cheer the entry of Gen. Montgomery's forces.
Photo, British Official: Crown Copyright

BREAK-THROUGH AT GABÈS GAP. By March 31, 1943, the vanguard of the 8th Army, New Zealanders and men of the 51st (Highland) Division, were in contact with rearguards of the retreating Afrika Korps near Oudref, 10 miles N. of Gabes. This photograph, which was taken from an advanced observation post immediately after Gen. Montgomery's forces had broken through the narrow gap, shows our tanks and other vehicles moving forward in their northward advance.
Photo, British Official : Crown Copyright

have been Wavell's if he had attempted to reach Tripoli. My hopes were in due course confirmed, but I admit I had to wait longer than I expected.

Rommel no doubt expected that he would receive adequate reinforcements before a counter-offensive could be launched against him ; but the Navy and the Middle East air force, taking full advantage of their offensive base at Malta and of Rommel's desperately long and restricted line of communication, saw to it that he was largely disappointed. Before he was strong enough to strike again, Alexander and Montgomery were in command of a force that had grown proportionally at a greater rate. Control of sea communications, even with enforced detours, had again vindicated its decisive importance.

R ECONSTITUTED, re-equipped and given new commanders, but retaining many of its original constituents with their great records and wealth of experience, the 8th Army was again formidable. But before the processes of reorganization and re-equipment could be completed Rommel again took the initiative in the hopes not only of carrying his ambitious invasion plans to fruition but of anticipating the arrival of British reinforcements, which he must have known were still in passage. His attack, met by skilful and ingenious defensive tactics, was repulsed with heavy loss, and he had no option but to fall back to the naturally strong and heavily fortified position.

There he no doubt confidently expected to defeat attacks and possibly to deliver a decisive counter-blow. The mere fact that, in his withdrawal, after the failure of his attack, no counter-attack on a major scale was

delivered against him may have increased his confidence and caused him to underrate his enemy. But Alexander bided his time till his preparations for the decisive struggle were complete, and in particular he awaited the arrival of Sherman tanks which would make good deficiencies revealed in Auchinleck's campaign. The story of the battle of Alamein needs no retelling.

The courage and determination displayed by the troops and the great skill with which every arm was employed to wear down the enemy's defence and to dissipate his reserves before the delivery of the final thrust, all contributed to make victory decisive. Only by deserting his Italian allies and by the speed of his flight was Rommel able to save the remnants of his army. Pursuit was amazingly rapid, but it could not keep pace with an elusive mechanized force which could travel by an intact road and leave mines on it to delay the pursuer.

Even air pursuit, which at first created havoc, was eventually out-distanced ; for

airfields, required by short-range aircraft, had to be captured and cleared by the land forces. Falling back on his depots and bases in Cyrenaica, Rommel's supply difficulties were less than those of the pursuit with its ever lengthening lines of communication, and he was also able, by picking up reserve equipment and personnel, to make good some of his losses. Pauses in the pursuit were therefore inevitable.

His flight had in fact become an orderly retreat. But by tempering the speed and vigour of pursuit with caution Montgomery gave his opponent no opportunity either for counter-offensive action or to make a protracted stand. The pursuit was certainly one of the major achievements of the 8th Army. The vigour and dash of the fighting troops, the skill and courage of the sappers in their endless mine-clearing task, and the ceaseless toil of the supply and maintenance services, in which the Navy and Air Force took a notable share, all contributed to produce a model display of sustained dynamic energy.

The battle of the Mareth Line and the Wadi Akarit, with which the role of the 8th Army as an independent force ended, served to give its commander a new opportunity to show his versatility and capacity to adapt methods to circumstances, and the troops to display their courage and tactical skill in whatever task was given them. These were actions in which boldness and promptness of decision and tactical initiative were even more essential than in the set piece of Alamein. To have fought two such engagements in quick succession and to have followed them by vigorous pursuit testifies to the thoroughness of the administrative preparations carried out during the pause after the occupation of Tripoli.

Victors and Vanquished in the Tunisian Hills

WITH THE FIRST ARMY IN TUNISIA : 1, Gen. Anderson (left) and his A.D.C., Maj. Clarke (U.S.), confer with a Brigadier during the G.O.C.'s visit to the forward position of a famous county regiment. 2, Men belonging to a squadron of the R.A.F. Regiment ready for action with their 2-pounder anti-tank gun. 3, Some of the prisoners, mostly Austrians, captured during an infantry and tank attack on enemy-held hills N. of the Medjez-el-Bab road on April 7, 1943.

    Photos, British Official: Crown Copyright

Doughboy Joins Tommy on the Road to Gabès

TUNISIAN LINK-UP. On April 7, 1943 news was flashed from Gabès to Gafsa that the U.S. 2nd Corps and the 8th Army had met near the Chemsi Mountains, 16 miles E. of Guettar. Top, American and British patrols welcome each other on the Gafsa-Gabès road, when a junction was effected between the two forces for the first time. Below, 8th Army men leave their trucks, Doughboys clamber from their tanks, and there is hearty hand-shaking and back-slapping. Helmets were temporarily exchanged, and, in the absence of beer, the historic meeting was celebrated with cigarettes and chewing-gum.

PAGE 741   *Photos, British Official: Crown Copyright; British Newsreels*

Montgomery's Masterstroke at Wadi Akarit

After he was flung out of the Mareth Line by the 8th Army Rommel retired some forty miles to the north, where along the Wadi Akarit he made another stand—but not for long. The storming of this position by Montgomery's troops was generally hailed as among the finest achievements in the North African War.

TWENTY miles or so to the north of Gabès lies the Wadi Akarit. There, is little to distinguish it from its fellows. It is just another watercourse : a raging torrent in winter and in summer a dried-up ditch. When a few weeks ago it was a battlefield it was still the springtime ; and down the middle of the wadi ran a sluggish, dwindling stream, fringed on either side by mud, difficult for a man to cross and wellnigh impracticable for a tank. It empties into the Mediterranean, almost at the very middle of the Gulf of Gabès ; from the shore it runs south-eastwards to a belt of salt-marsh lying to the north of El Hamma. Then the ground rises to the quite considerable heights of the Shott el Fejej.

It was on March 23 that Rommel was booted out of the Mareth Line. On Wednesday, March 31, General Montgomery's patrols were in contact with the powerful enemy forces holding the Wadi Akarit line. By the following Sunday Montgomery had brought up sufficient guns and ammunition for a forty-eight hours' bombardment. Then before it was light on Tuesday, April 6, the attack went in.

That an attack could be mounted on so huge a scale in so short a time was amazing ; it reflects the very highest credit on the 8th Army's command and commissariat. But just as amazing was the fact that the attack was launched at night—and not a moonlight night either, but one that was pitch dark. Only troops at the very peak of training and battle experience could tackle successfully such a task ; only a general supremely confident in his plans, and in the men who were his instruments, could venture on such a hazard. But Montgomery *had* the fullest confidence in his men, and in himself. Once again that confidence was to be justified to the full.

FIVE hundred guns opened the battle, splashing the enemy's hills with a hail of metal. Then at 4 a.m. British infantry, the last of whom had been brought up in position an hour before, moved up the foothills towards a gash in the mountain rampart between two hills, the 400-ft. Jebel Roumana, and "Hill 275," the 1,000-ft. Jebel Fatnassa. This gap, about two miles wide, was the 8th Army's main objective. The assault was witnessed by Lloyd Williams, Reuters special correspondent with the 8th Army. This is his picture of the scene :

While the infantry moved forward across the dark valley, artillery of the 8th Army kept up its mighty concentration of shellfire, aiming into the gap in the hills and on to the southern slopes of the mountains. A running line of angry red explosions began to move backwards over the enemy positions as the guns let go. For more than an

hour shells fell steadily and heavily in hundreds and hundreds. For more than an hour the guns continued, and stopped only when the infantry swept into the hills.

From the rising ground in front of Rommel's line I watched this assault. Red and white lines of tracer bullets criss-crossed the valley, and now and again the rapid fire of machine-guns could be heard. Over the enemy lines Very lights rose and fell as our infantry pressed home their attack. German guns feebly answered the might of the 8th Army's barrage.

As darkness faded the battle increased in intensity, and when morning came the whole plain was chocked with grey smoke from shells. In the distance the brown hill of Roumana appeared distorted into fantastic shapes as our shells exploded round it. Hill 275 was wreathed in dust and smoke, and the highest peak—about 1,000 ft. high—seemed to be erupting like a volcano.

By this time British infantry were already nearing the summits of both these hills. High up from them came sharp flashes, while the bitter cold dawn wind carried the sound of machine-guns and mortars over the valley. As the sky lightened our tanks dashed forward to exploit the gap between the hills across the route prepared by our infantry They rumbled over the hill, crossed the valley under shellfire, and as they disappeared from sight I saw them fanning out into an inferno of smoke and explosions.

British transport columns followed them, bouncing over the plain straight for the gap. More and more tank squadrons came along, disappearing into the pall of smoke. Anti-aircraft shells, bursting in the sky behind the enemy front lines, showed that bombers and fighters of the Western Desert Air Force were already on their job, attacking Axis guns and transports.

From the outset the attack went like clock-

work. This was shown by the fact that the infantry who had been ordered to capture Jebel Roumana by 5.22 a.m. actually completed their task by 5.15 a.m. But not without hard fighting. Indeed the assault on these two vital heights by men of the 51st (Highland) Division was described as " one of the greatest heroic achievements of the war."

THEIR precipitous slopes intersected by deep wadis, the heights had been thickly strewn with machine-gun, mortar, and anti-tank gun emplacements, hewn by the defenders out of the solid rock. The Seaforth Highlanders and the Cameron Highlanders had to attack across two miles of meadowland (says Reuters) and were actually in the foothills when our barrage opened. When our last shell dropped they swarmed up the slopes and charged the defences. Within an hour both heights had surrendered and nearly a thousand Italian prisoners were streaming back. Aware that the positions were lightly held, the Germans put in a fierce and courageous counter-attack, and gave the men of the 51st Division an anxious time. At one moment the Seaforths could muster only 40 men. They called on clerks, the Intelligence Staff and orderlies to man Bren guns, to keep the enemy off ; then held on until tanks and the Black Watch came to the rescue.

The extreme left flank was occupied by the 4th Indian Division—that gallant body of Punjabis and Rajputana Rifles, Gurkhas, Mahrattas, Baluchis, Garhwalis and Sikhs, with two or three battalions of British infantry as their tried and trusted comrades, who have been in every battle of the North African campaigns since they first went into action in December 1940. In the black of night they stealthily scaled a high massif, and surprised its garrison, destroying them without a shot being fired.

In the afternoon the Germans counter-attacked time and again, but every assault was repulsed with heavy loss. In fact the enemy had been decisively defeated, and during the night it became clear that they could not maintain their Wadi Akarit positions. Early on April 7 British mobile forces, having passed through the gap the infantry had won, started the pursuit. In the afternoon men of the 8th Army made contact with American forces operating from El Guettar.

ROMMEL was in no position to make a further stand. Closely pursued by the veterans of the 8th Army, attacked on his flank by Americans and French, threatened in the rear by the First Army—he hastened to withdraw from the great plain of Central Tunisia. Sfax was entered by the 8th Army on April 10, and the 1st Army were in Kairouan the same evening. Sousse fell two days later. Not until the attackers had reached Enfidaville did they come up against any really serious opposition. On April 12 it was announced that the 8th Army had taken 20,000 prisoners since the opening of the onslaught on the Mareth Line on March 20.

GABÈS and El Hamma, of vital importance to the enemy, were occupied by the 8th Army on March 29, 1943. Twenty miles to the north lies the Wadi Akarit, the storming of which is here described.

STORMING OF THE WADI ZIGZAOU, foremost defence of the Mareth Line, developed into a savage hand-to-hand fight that began on March 20, 1943, and was not finally concluded until eight days later (see page 718). This photo gives a vivid idea of the difficulties that confronted the attackers : men of the 8th Army show the cameraman how they scaled the steep sides of the Wadi.

Photo. British Official : Crown Copyright

How the Northumbrians Scaled the Wadi Walls

ROMMEL'S MARETH LINE DEFENCES constituted a fortress of tremendous strength, both natural and artificial ; its principal features are shown in the upper drawing. Very noticeable is the deep Wadi Zigzaou, across which the 50th (Northumbrian) Division advanced under very heavy fire to establish a bridgehead deep in the heart of the enemy's lines. The Green Howards led the attack, some scaling the sides of the wadi with the aid of ladders (lower drawing). The main attack was delivered by the Durham Light Infantry, who did all that brave men could do to maintain the bridgehead. The engineers built a causeway of brushwood over the slippery mud of the wadi bottom, but this proved inadequate for the passage of more than a handful of British tanks. Eventually, on March 22 Rommel brought up his armour, and, despite their determined resistance, the Durhams were forced back across the wadi. But only a few days later the Northumbrians swept forward again, this time victorious (see pages 700 and 718).

Drawings by Percy Home and E. Byatt, by courtesy of The Sphere

H.M.S. INDOMITABLE, one of Britain's largest and most powerful aircraft-carriers, was begun in 1937, and belongs to the Illustrious class. She has a displacement of 23,000 tons and a complement of 1,600. According to details published when the Indomitable was laid down, her length is 753 feet and she carries sixteen 4·5-inch guns. The Indomitable played a leading part in the N. Africa landings last November, and achieved a fine record in the Mediterranean. In August 1942 she was one of the carriers protecting the famous convoy to Malta. This powerful vessel also carried fighter-planes to Malaya and Ceylon. She is equipped with Seafire fighters and Albacore torpedo-bombers. Some of the latter are here shown ranged on the flight-deck. Capt. G. Grantham (inset) commands the Indomitable.

Photos, Planet News

THE WAR AT SEA

by Francis E. McMurtrie

It is some time since any heavy sea fighting was reported in the Solomon Islands area. Indeed, the last action which could properly be termed a battle took place on the night of November 30-December 1 last. The official name for this action was the Battle of Lunga Point. It was the outcome of a desperate attempt by the Japanese to run reinforcements through under cover of darkness to their hard-pressed forces in Guadalcanal. Not only were many transports sunk with troops on board, but the enemy lost six destroyers on this occasion. The only American loss was the 9,000-ton cruiser Northampton.

Operations since have been mainly confined to the air, though they have involved naval losses on both sides. Thus the United States Navy had the heavy cruiser Chicago and two destroyers torpedoed by enemy aircraft, while the Japanese have had six cruisers and as many destroyers sunk by air attack.

In spite of their losses the Japanese are believed to be massing forces for a fresh attempt to pierce the Allied defences in New Guinea and the Solomons, with the ultimate object of invading Australia. There is always the possibility that the next serious approach may come from a fresh quarter ; such as Timor, for example. That the Commonwealth Government view the position with considerable concern is apparent from the warning words of Mr. Curtin, Dr. Evatt and other Australian speakers.

It is pointed out that so long as Japan controls the sea lines of communication between her home bases and the conquered territories to the north of Australia, very large forces can always be concentrated at some selected point beyond bomber range, such as Truk, in the Caroline group, and directed to the attack whenever the enemy thinks fit. In short, until the main Japanese fleet has been definitely defeated the danger will remain imminent.

PREPARATIONS for Heavy Blow at Japanese Sea Power

Fortunately the United States Navy is increasing in strength almost daily, and the numbers of ships of all classes available for service in the Pacific must be very much greater than, say, six months ago. That the Japanese can add to their strength in similar measure is beyond belief, for their ship-building resources are definitely limited ; moreover, a great part of those resources must be fully engaged in making good the steady depletion of the Japanese mercantile fleet, which has lost a serious amount of tonnage not only in the Solomons operations but also through the activities of American submarines. There are probably twice as many of the latter in service as there were a year ago, so enemy shipping losses are likely to go up rather than down in future months.

When the time is ripe it may be expected that the U.S. fleet in the Pacific will make a forward move. Whether this move will come from the Solomons or from some other direction it is useless to speculate ; but one of the first requirements for such an undertaking is a strong force of aircraft-carriers. In October last the loss of the Hornet reduced the number available to three—the Enterprise, Ranger and Saratoga. But since that date several new ones are believed to have been completed, including the Essex, Lexington, Bunker Hill, Independence, Princeton and Belleau Wood ; and at least five more have been launched and are nearing completion. It may therefore be inferred that preparations for striking a heavy blow at Japanese sea power are well advanced.

Suggestions continue to be made that the German warships which have been stationed in Norwegian waters for some twelve months past may be preparing for an incursion into the Atlantic, with the object of wiping out a convoy or two. Thus it is argued that the 40,000-ton battleship Tirpitz, the 26,000-ton battleships Scharnhorst and Gneisenau, the heavy cruisers Admiral Hipper and Prinz Eugen, and the aircraft-carriers Graf Zeppelin and Peter Strasser might well be employed in company as a squadron for this purpose.

The prospects of such an enterprise succeeding today are far poorer than they were when the Bismarck and Prinz Eugen made their sortie in May 1941. Not only

U.S. AIRCRAFT-CARRIER SANGAMON, a merchantman converted into an auxiliary aircraft-carrier, is here seen under the protecting guns of a heavy cruiser as she steams ahead with an American Navy task force. Converted merchantmen are playing a vital and increasing part in carrying planes which can be launched for the protection of convoys. *Photo, Associated Press*

should our present resources place us in a much better position to observe the movements of German naval forces than we were then, but our naval strength is decidedly greater. A squadron of seven ships would require much more in the way of supply vessels than the six which the enemy sent out for the benefit of the Bismarck and her consort. Preparations on such a scale could hardly fail to become known.

So far as can be ascertained, neither the Scharnhorst nor the Gneisenau has left the Baltic. Moreover, it is doubtful if the latter ship has completed the big refit rendered imperative by the torpedo damage received when six Swordfish aircraft of the Fleet Air Arm attacked her in the Straits of Dover over a year ago. She has indeed been undergoing what almost amounts to reconstruction in the dockyard at Gdynia, the Polish port seized by the Germans in 1939.

Though the Graf Zeppelin is believed to have been completed, she has never ventured out of the Baltic, and it looks as though she

had proved a failure, or surely some use would have been made of her before now. She was launched as long ago as December 1938. Her sister ship, the Peter Strasser (named after the officer who was in command of the German airship force in the last war), has not yet been put into service, and may not even have been launched, affording additional support for the belief that the Graf Zeppelin is regarded as a white elephant

U-BOAT the Most Promising Weapon Left to Dönitz

My own belief is that, while the Commander-in-Chief, Grossadmiral Dönitz, would have no objection to sacrificing any of these ships if he saw any possibility of using them to advantage, he has come to the conclusion that they are of very little value to Germany, except possibly for attacking convoys bound for North Russia. It is known that the officers and men of the ships in Norwegian waters have been warned that they may be called upon to undergo training for sub-marine service. Dönitz is a fervent believer in the U-boat as the most promising weapon left to him, and he may be expected to subordinate everything else to its use.

Recently Mr. Elmer Davis, who holds a position in the United States Government organization corresponding to that of Mr. Brenden Bracken here, gave a somewhat pessimistic account of the capabilities of the majority of the U-boats now operating in the Atlantic. He stated that they were of the double-hulled type, with considerable capacity for resisting depth-charge explosion, and that they could dive to 100 fathoms, at which depth it was difficult to reach them. These particulars do not altogether accord with those of a U-boat which fell into British hands last year, for she was of saddle-tank (single-hulled) design and would be comparatively vulnerable to depth-charge attack.

In any case the depth which they can reach will not affect the fact that so long as they are kept under the surface they are more or less impotent. It is for this reason that the presence with a convoy of numerous scouting aircraft is so valuable. .

Daring Submarine Raid on Jap-held Makin

RAID BY U.S. MARINES ON MAKIN ISLAND (Gilbert Isles) in the Pacific on Aug. 17, 1942 resulted in a seaplane base being wrecked. Makin Island was occupied by the Japanese on Dec. 10, 1941. Top, Marines lined up on the submarine which took them to their objective. Inset, Lt.-Col. Carlson (left), leader of the raiders, Maj. J. Roosevelt (centre), his second-in-command, and Lt.-Cmdr. Pierce, skipper of one of the submarines. Below, the Marines' first glimpse of Makin through their escorting submarine's periscope.

Bismarck Sea Was a Disaster for the Japanese

HEADING FOR LAE, IN NEW GUINEA, a Japanese convoy consisting of some 22 ships, among them 3 cruisers, 4 destroyers and a large number of transports, was attacked by U.S. and Australian aircraft on March 2 and 3, 1943. The convoy was dispersed, isolated, and then virtually annihilated, not one vessel reaching its destination. The Japs tried to protect their ships with an air umbrella, but lost some 70 planes. 1, Zero fighter destroyed on the ground at Lae. 2, Jap destroyer set on fire by Allied bombs. 3, Medium bombers swoop on one of the transports while another enemy ship burns on the horizon.

Photos, New York Times Photos, Central Press

There's Now a West Point Over Here

Everyone has heard of the United States Military Academy at West Point, New York ; since it opened in 1802 it has trained many thousand highly educated and efficient officers for the U.S. Army. This article by LEIGH M. SCULLY describes another and much younger "West Point"—one which the War has caused to be established "somewhere in England."

SERGEANT NORRIS NEVILS has been selected and is just starting his training as an officer. He is 30, his home-town is at Charleston, South Carolina. He used to be swimming and diving instructor at Miami Beach, Florida, and among his best friends is Johnny Weissmuller. But that's not why Sergeant Nevils and 64 other men with him are the centre of attraction. The reason is that he's among the first members of the United States Forces in Europe to train as an officer at " West Point Somewhere in England." And that's of vital interest to everybody in Britain, because it is positive proof that the expansion of the United States Forces in Europe is so big that now new officers have to be found from the ranks of the men serving here.

West Point, the U.S. officers' training college in America, is famous all over the world, chiefly because of Hollywood interpretations of it. But at this "West Point" of England, young and old soldiers, from the sunny beaches of Miami to the crowded streets of New York City, are going through a three months' course packed into which is the military, tactical and toughening training which America's West Point spreads over four years.

The curriculum is divided into four sections : Weapons, tactics, general subjects and specialized subjects.

IT is not sufficient for candidates to know all about—and how to operate—every pattern of American rifle, light and heavy machine-gun, anti-tank gun, mortar and grenade ; they must also know all about British arms.

On the tactical side the candidates learn to command soldiers, squads and units up to battalions. Under this heading, too, are air-craft identification and combat drill. Daily calisthenics, toughening over a 450-yard obstacle course eight times a week, hand-to-hand combat, forced marches from four to 23 miles, night problems for scouting and

BRIG.-GEN. BENJAMIN O. DAVIS, referred to in this page, is the highest ranking coloured officer in the U.S. Army. He serves with the American Command in Britain.
Photo, Associated Press

patrolling—these are other means of turning out better than the best.

Here is a typical day's work. Reveille at 6.30, parade ; 7.15, breakfast ; 8.0, class-room, when talks on various subjects are given by trainees ; lectures until noon, lunch ; 1 p.m., drill ; 2 p.m., obstacle course, cross-river bridge building ; then weapons class until 6 p.m. ; dinner ; 7 p.m. to 9 p.m., study for the next day's subjects. Bed at 10 o'clock, tired but still enthusiastic.

This goes on for six days of the week. Some of the men have to polish up subjects on Sunday. And there is no leave in the whole three months !

Colonel Walter Layman, Commandant of the training centre, believes in living as his students do. He has no orderly, and relies on an alarm clock to awaken him. The other day he had a guest, and the colonel promised to wake him early.

The guest was roused by a knock on the door. " Five-thirty," called the colonel. The guest looked at his watch and saw it was only 12.10 a.m. Half an hour later there was another knock, and the colonel asked : " Are you ready ? " The guest protested that Colonel Layman had made a mistake, that the time was not 5.30 but 12.40. The colonel called a major and asked the time. The major confirmed that the guest's watch was right. The colonel had bathed, shaved and was fully dressed. He even had his gloves on. He went back to bed, but was up again at 6 a.m.

OF the 65 men now training at "West Point," 14 are coloured soldiers. They were chosen by the only negro General in the U.S. Army, Brig-Gen. Benjamin O. Davis. A list of 84 men was put up to Davis, and the 14 now at "West Point" are the pick —not only fine strapping fellows but also A.1. in mental ability. One was a law student, another a doctor, before the War. They all work with their other colleagues at "West Point" without any consideration of colour.

At the original West Point there is a magnificent chapel with stained glass windows in which are depicted mottoes for each phase of training. At this "West Point" the young officers attend a village church that is similar to the one in the film Mrs. Miniver.

The only motto they have is on a banner fixed with drawing pins to the wall above Colonel Layman's fireplace. It reads *Melior Quam Optimus* (Better than the best). Col. Layman explained this by saying : " We've got to turn out officers who know more, can take more, and are better leaders than Germany can produce. To be as good is not enough."

U.S. FORCES IN BRITAIN are very well catered for. In London a palatial club has been organized in Curzon Street, under the direction of the American Red Cross : Left, troops find the Club's post-office extremely useful. To house the ever-growing U.S. Army in this country the American Corps of Engineers has erected a number of camps throughout Britain : Right, interior of one of the comfortable huts at a camp in the Home Counties.

Photos, Topical Press, L.N.A.

American Troops Learn from British Commandos

U.S. RANGERS IN BRITAIN undergo the most rigorous battle-inoculation. These photographs show men of a Ranger battalion recently in training at a Commando depot of British Combined Operations Command in Scotland. All equipment used in these exercises is American. 1, Mines explode as attacking troops cross a river by means of a toggle rope bridge. 2, Serving as a warning to the foolhardy, the grave of an imaginary victim bears the inscription: "This man took up a position on the skyline." 3, Flame-throwers advance for a final assault on an "enemy" hedgehog position.

Photos. Central Press Photos. Associated Press. New York Times Photos

General Montgomery—The Man as I Know Him

"As a member of my Staff for some years I may claim to know Gen. Montgomery well, both professionally and, as a friend," writes MAJ.-GEN. SIR CHARLES GWYNN, K.C.B., D.S.O., and in this intimate pen-portrait our distinguished contributor throws revealing light on the personal characteristics of the man who inspires and brilliantly leads the triumphant 8th Army.

Mr. Churchill does not often choose the wrong word, but for once I think he made a mistake when he spoke of General Montgomery as " that Cromwellian soldier." The Press not unnaturally followed suit, for it is always ready to stick a label on any sailor, soldier or airman who suddenly steps into the limelight. Should he already have a nickname, that provides easy copy ; and to invent one is not difficult. But thumbnail portraits of the new star are apt to be misleading caricatures.

First impressions produced on the general public, including politicians, are liable to persist, sometimes with unfortunate results. Kitchener was a sufferer in this respect ; he was labelled as a formidable, unapproachable, inhuman person. Formidable he certainly was, but those most closely connected with him have testified that he was remarkably easy to work with and neither inhuman nor unapproachable. He was also labelled as a great organizer, whereas he was essentially a great improviser with remarkable intuition, rather than an organizer in the ordinary sense. As a result many approached him with nervous suspicion and his reputation as an organizer led to many misunderstandings.

Before General Montgomery reaches even higher positions than that he now occupies I should like to try to correct any false conception of his characteristics. As a member of my Staff for some years I may claim to know him well, both professionally and as a friend. Of his professional attainments it would be out of place for me to speak in any but general terms. From the position he held he was bound to be a keen, highly trained officer ; but at the time I am speaking of it was impossible to form any clear conception of what armies of the future would look like, or of the nature of the operations they would be engaged in, or of how officers would adapt themselves to developments. Speculation there was, but there were no data to provide a basis for definite conclusions. Still less was it possible to forecast the careers of even the most brilliant of the rising generation of officers outside the narrow avenue of normal peacetime promotion.

Professionally, the most I can claim is that I valued Montgomery's opinions and felt little doubt that given opportunities he would rise to the occasion. His main interest in life was quite obviously his profession, but his approach to its problems was not heavy-footed. Criticisms, the courses of action he proposed to take, or the views he held were incisively and concisely expressed in short phrases, sometimes epigrammatic and touched with humour. His outlook was, I think, essentially practical, and he was more concerned with the Army as he knew it or as it had reasonable prospect of becoming, than with armies whose composition and armament were still entirely of a speculative character. Like most of us he realized that tanks, aircraft, and other important developments of mechanization held great possibilities, but that did not shake his faith in his own particular arm of the service—the infantry.

He was not a fanatical believer in any particular weapon or theory, but was interested mainly in the co-ordinated development of the Army as a whole, with unprejudiced introduction of such weapons as science placed at its disposal. He was, in fact, no specialist, but a general practitioner who, though he had not lost faith in old-fashioned remedies, was well abreast of the times and always ready to call in the specialist. I was not surprised to hear that he was commanding a Division in France, but I was surprised, though glad, when his appointment to the command of the 8th Army was announced. I had not realized that his qualities had been so fully appreciated. That he has exceeded my own expectations I admit, though I was confident that Mr. Churchill had collected a first-class team.

Alert in Mind and Body, Lighthearted in Spirit

Of Montgomery's personal characteristics I am better qualified to speak. Anyone less like my conception of a Cromwellian soldier I can hardly imagine. That he drank water at dinner I had noticed, but whether on principle or by preference I did not inquire ; and he certainly did not impose his principles on his own guests. I also knew that he attended Church regularly ; but so did many others, and if he had strong religious views he certainly was not censorious of the less devout nor did he seek to convert them. But it was even more in his general characteristics that he did not come up to my conception of a Roundhead.

There was nothing ponderous about him, and the impression he particularly gave was of alertness in mind and body and of lightheartedness. Judging from published photographs and from his recorded sayings and actions, he apparently retains these qualities. Physically active, he was a better than average games player, especially at those which, like tennis and squash racquets, require quickness of foot and a sense of anticipation. Perhaps because the effects of wounds made it inadvisable for him to over-exert himself he took his games lightheartedly, but with his sense of anticipation he was difficult to catch on the wrong foot. Golf he refused to take seriously.

LADY MONTGOMERY, mother of the 8th Army's commander, photographed in the garden of her home at Moville, County Donegal, Eire. Gen. Montgomery's father was Bishop of Tasmania. *Photo, Planet News*

Successful people are always targets for criticism, and the censorious have expressed themselves shocked at the tone and wording of his messages to his Army. They have been termed bombastic and undignified, ignoring their intention or how far they were adapted to fulfil it. That they were bombastic in a personal sense is, I think, a ridiculous suspicion and they clearly made no attempt at dignity—with which I do not think General Montgomery is much concerned ; at any rate they were not pompous—a common failing. Surely their intention was obvious. They were not merely exhortations to fight hard ; they gave to all ranks of the Army a clear picture of the scope of their task. It was not only to defeat the enemy in one battle and thus remove the immediate threat to Egypt, its full object was to destroy or drive Rommel out of Egypt altogether.

Now that, I think, was important, for at the time public opinion in Egypt was gravely and mainly concerned with the vital and pressing problem of local security. It would not have been surprising if that feeling had had its influence on the Army, or if it had resulted in some slackening up after the security of Egypt had been ensured. Montgomery's messages seem to me well calculated to defeat any such tendency, to define clearly in language easily understood what the object was, and to infect all ranks with the drive and energy of their leaders. The message in fact broadcast Mr. Churchill's instructions to General Alexander in terms that would appeal to the troops and perhaps touch their sense of humour.

I should imagine they had less effect on the conduct of the troops in the battle of Alamein than in the sustained and wearisome effort of the pursuit. The troops knew what was required of them and there was no slackening off. In the last war, most notably perhaps at Suvla Bay, the troops very often knew little of the purpose of the operations they were engaged in and their interest seldom extended beyond the limited objectives that were made known to them.

GEN. MONTGOMERY attending a show of the " Balmorals " concert party of the 51st (Highland) Division in Tripoli last January to celebrate the 8th Army's victory. Here we see him enjoying the famous troupe's performance.
Photo, British Official : Crown Copyright

He Rules the Mediterranean Skies

Leader of the new Mediterranean Air Command, Air Chief Marshal Sir A. W. Tedder was seconded from the Army to the Royal Flying Corps in 1916 and, after seeing much service in France and Egypt, transferred to the R.A.F. three years later. In between the Wars he held a number of Air commands, the most recent being that of Air Officer C.-in-C. R.A.F. in the Middle East.

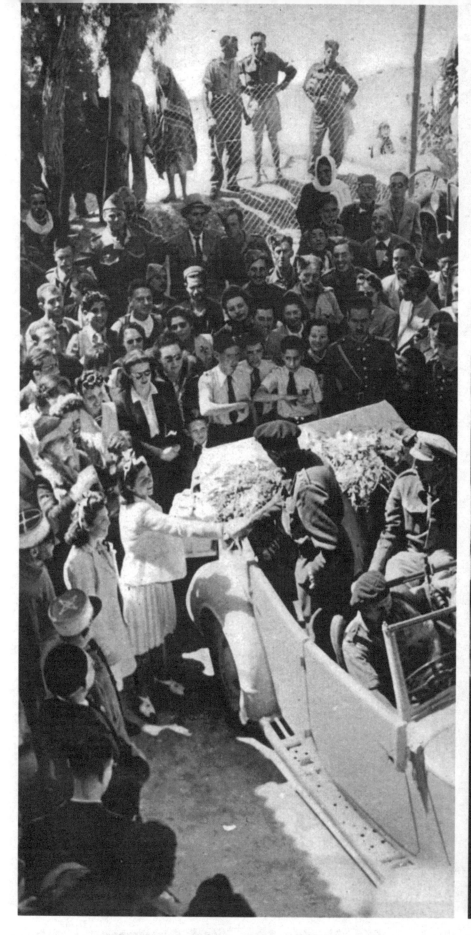

Gabes Greets the Conquering Heroes

Following the storming of Rommel's positions at Mareth and Wadi Akarit, the 8th Army swept across the Tunisian plain with irresistible élan. Everywhere the population gave the victors a great welcome. In Gabès girls wearing the colours of the Fighting French presented General Montgomery with bouquets of flowers, while some strove to shake the hand of the great captain who had delivered them from the ruffianly invaders.

Ovation for Montgomery and His Men

Down the main street of Gabes, the Tunisian township on the Mediterranean shore that fell to the 8th Army on the morrow of their capture of the Mareth Line, marches a Black Watch battalion of the 51st (Highland) Division, their pipers making martial music in the van. Good reason have they to swing past with such forceful pride. Have they not avenged in overrunning measure their brother clansmen who fought to the bitter end in France?

Victory Wings in the Tunisian Air

Air power working in perfect combination with the forces on the ground put the crown on the Desert Army's triumph in the battles for Tunisia. Hurricanes presented to the R.A.F. by the great Indian State of Hyderabad are seen in the upper photograph flying above a North African village. Below, a parachute being retrieved by men of the R.A.F. mobile parachute packing unit now in Tunisia.

VIEWS & REVIEWS Of Vital War Books

by Hamilton Fyfe

BY far the most interesting pages in the history of modern warfare are those which tell of the development of tanks. They were called so by mere chance. When General Swinton was writing in 1915 a report of a conference about what were then known as "landships," he wanted to use some word that would disguise what they really were. He thought of "cistern," and "reservoir," because they looked something like that. Then "tank" occurred to him. It was written down, and it stuck.

That conference was on Christmas Eve. Fifteen months earlier General Swinton had proposed to use caterpillar tractors with enclosed armoured cars carrying guns as a means of destroying machine-gun nests. He was then "Eye-witness," appointed by Headquarters in France to supply the British Press with news of the war. Capt. J. R. W. Murland, who has produced a most instructive little book, The Royal Armoured Corps (Methuen, 7s. 6d.), is not quite accurate in saying that "at the beginning of the last war no newspaper correspondents were allowed in France." I was there from the beginning, in August until October 1914—so long as the mode of fighting was mobile. I was not authorized, it is true. Indeed, Lord Kitchener said if he could catch me he would have me shot. This was just after he had announced in the House of Lords that no war correspondents were in the field, and had read next day in the Daily Mail a page dispatch from me about the arrival of the first trains of wounded at Rouen. He was naturally annoyed.

WHEN trench warfare clamped the armies down, I could no longer operate on my own. I was sent to Russia. Col. Swinton, as he was then, was left for a while to furnish the newspapers with such little bits of information as Headquarters would let him send. He did not send anything about the possibility of overcoming "the almost insuperable obstacle" of the enemy's trenches, wire and machine-guns by building a new weapon that would cross trenches, take no heed of wire, and crush out machine-gunners. But he did forward the suggestion to the War Council and the Committee of Imperial Defence. Lord Kitchener pooh-poohed it. Even when the idea had had time to sink in, and after he had seen these new weapons in actual use some months later, he sneered at them as "pretty mechanical toys."

Very different was the impression they made on Mr. Churchill, then First Lord of the Admiralty. He had seen during his expedition to Antwerp in October 1914 how useful armoured cars were and how vastly more useful they could be if they went across country and made their way over trenches. At once he saw the possibilities of the Swinton suggestion. He told Mr. Asquith, the Prime Minister, when he found that nothing was being done about it, that "it was extraordinary the Army in the field and the War Office should have allowed nearly three months of warfare to progress without addressing their minds to its special problems." He did not stop at that either.

Tragic Story of the Tanks

He formed an Admiralty Landship Committee ; Royal Naval Air Service officers at once began making experiments.

All through the early stages "the attitude of the War Office" was, Capt. Murland says, "painfully clear." It opposed the tank by every means in its power. It had had in its possession since 1912 a plan for a fighting vehicle with caterpillar tracks, but had put it away and forgotten all about it. When the author of this plan turned up in 1919 and claimed from the Royal Commission on Awards to Inventors some recognition of his foresight, the War Office pretended never to have heard of him and only "under pressure" produced his papers. By this time the invention had got far beyond what had been in his mind when he made his blueprints.

But, in spite of good results obtained, the War Office still obstinately obstructed the production of tanks. Sir Albert Stern, who was in charge of certain experiments, gave an order for 700 engines when he was satisfied that the right type had been designed. The War Office "disapproved strongly and had the order cancelled." Colonel Stern fortunately persisted and increased the order to 1,400. Not till eight months later was this officially recognized ; and, as that was in October 1917, it is unlikely that, but for Sir Albert's firm action, any of the tanks would have been ready when they were needed for our advance in 1918. He actually got them into production before the official O.K. came through.

Here is another instance of the military mind's reaction to the new weapon—or ought I to say the cavalryman's mind, for at the War Office the highest posts were nearly all held by cavalrymen ? Of course, they hated the deposition of the horse. They clung to the traditions in which they had grown up. They knew nothing about machines and heartily disliked them. So, when Sir Ernest Swinton submitted in March 1916 a set of rules (elementary enough) for tank fighting, they tucked it away and did not even send a copy to the Tank Corps Staff in France. "It was November 1917 before the use of tanks was governed by these now obvious precepts."

FOR ten years, 1928-1938, the conversion of cavalry regiments into armoured car regiments was held up. Then a fresh lot under Lord Gort and Mr. Hore-Belisha were given control of the Army, and mechanization was wholesale. But "no one can doubt that ten years was too long a delay." If our policy had been more progressive, we should have been able to start the War with a very large number of highly-trained men and more tanks. That might have made all the difference in France in 1940.

The points that had to be considered in designing tanks were chiefly three : thickness and weight of armour, speed, and fire-power. As quickly as the "ironclads" were launched when wooden ships went out, new and more penetrating shells and torpedoes were produced. So at equal pace with the clothing of tanks in steel plates went the improvement of guns to pierce those plates. That sort of thing has happened since the first ages of organized war. Attack and defence have been elaborated side by side. Tanks have therefore been getting heavier. Light tanks are obsolete. "No tank can be sufficiently protected and yet remain in the light category." We may yet come to the landship a hundred feet long, weight 1,000 tons, wheels 40 feet in diameter, three turrets with two quick-firing naval guns in each, and 300 shells to every gun. That was proposed in 1914 by an officer of the Royal Naval Air Service named Heatherington.

Of the much-debated Churchill tank Capt. Murland remarks drily that "its origin cannot be traced to any previous design. Very heavy armour and a powerful armament increased its size and weight above those of any contemporary British machine." But reports from North Africa have been showing that in its very much altered and improved condition it has done well. It must be remembered, too, that it was "put straight into production off the drawing-board" at a time when we needed tanks very urgently indeed. Capt. Murland does not mention this, but after Dunkirk (Mr. Churchill told the miners on Oct. 31st 1942) "we had not 50 tanks, whereas we now have 10,000 or 12,000."

Though many units of the Royal Armoured Corps have seen distinguished action in the North African campaigns, the Great Tank Battle that has been so often predicted has not been fought so far. The author thinks it will be when we invade the Continent. "This will be the armoured battle which future historians will point to as the culmination of tank design and development." We need not fear, when it comes, for either our machines or for the men inside them.

BRITISH MARK VI B TANKS which went to France with the B.E.F. in 1939. Compare these fragile, 5-ton armoured vehicles with their formidable successors operating in Tunisia to-day. "Light Tanks are obsolete" says the author of The Royal Armoured Corps, dealing with tank development, which is reviewed in this page. *Photo, British Official : Crown Copyright*

Military Camouflage Is a Very Fine Art

To keep the enemy from seeing what he would very much like to see is obviously a matter of supreme importance, and calls for the expenditure of immense ingenuity and effort. In this article ALEXANDER DILKE gives some little-known and seldom appreciated details of the work that is performed by our " Deception Corps."

THE Eighth Army fighting in Tunisia is having to learn new disappearing tricks. The camouflage that was so immensely successful in concealing men, guns, and vehicles behind the El Alamein line does not serve when sand gives place to a greener landscape. The principles of deception remain the same, however, and the experts, who, by developing desert camouflage to its highest pitch, completely deceived Rommel about the position of the Eighth Army's reserves, can have no difficulty in adapting their materials and methods to a different landscape.

These men include a famous magician, a noted biologist, who is the author of a standard book on the protective colouring of animals, theatre and film scene painters, and others whose peacetime work is the harmless deception of the public. Farther north Major Godfrey Baxter " stage-manages " the Army soldiers and vehicles as once he stage-managed the chorus and scenery of the famous Glyndebourne Opera.

Tunisia is greener than the Western Desert, but presents problems in camouflage hardly less difficult, for the plains are almost treeless—which means that everything in the open has to be camouflaged. It also means that a great deal of work has to be done at night. It is little use camouflaging a munitions dump, however skilfully, if the enemy's aerial photographs show you at work on it ! Where an important new building is to be camouflaged by merging it with the landscape, it is necessary for the building process itself to be hidden by, for instance, camouflaging the piles of bricks and the lorry tracks leading to the site. Otherwise the enemy's photographs would ensure that his maps showed the village church and scattered cottages to be, in fact, an army depot, a tank repair workshop or whatever it might be, and he would bomb it at the first opportunity.

Camouflage is a science we have learned from animals. Hence the professor of biology. When faced with the apparently impossible task of hiding men, guns, and materials on a completely featureless desert, the scientists studied the animals that inhabit the desert. The tricks and colouring used by the gazelle and the jerboa were used to hide gun-barrels and Bren gun-carriers. " Hide," perhaps, is not the right word. Camouflage aims rather at presenting no feature to attract the enemy airman or camera. The gun emplacement or vehicle is " seen " by the enemy, but he takes it for a normal feature of the landscape. That is why camouflage experts giving instruction always emphasize to their pupils that camouflage is tactical as well as technical.

IT is an excellent idea to make your shell dumps look like half-a-dozen native houses, but if the enemy airman sees half-a-dozen houses in the middle of miles of nothing, without even a road leading to them, he is likely to become more suspicious rather than have his suspicions lulled !

There is no standard method of camouflaging anything in every circumstance. No branch of warfare calls for greater imagination and less reference to textbooks. But there are sound principles, worked out by experts ; and these are learned at a special Army school for camouflage in the Midlands. Here the pupils learn a way of thinking as well as a way of doing. The courses they take last several weeks or about three days according to the work they are going to do. Models of landscapes, not only in Britain but also of present and future zones of battles, are used for teaching.

The pupil learns that it is not colour alone that matters but also texture. It is not sufficient to paint the roof of a building. It must be given a " texture " that will deceive eye and camera. The introduction of the aerial camera has greatly increased the difficulties of camouflage. It is not only that the photographs show up what may deceive the eye, but that they can be studied at leisure under special instruments and recent photographs compared with those taken a month or six months ago. A little patch of a different shade on a photograph may be the first intimation that a new building has been erected. This, in fact, was the case with one important target in Germany, and when

THREADING SCRIM through a camouflage net. This photograph was taken at the Berkeley Square, London, A.R.P. Post, where the personnel make camouflage nets in their spare time. As explained in this page netting plays a very important part in camouflage.
Photo, Keystone

more information came from " other sources," it was promptly and effectively bombed by the R.A.F.

Complete deception of the enemy about the existence of the dump, aerodrome, vehicle park or whatever it may be is, perhaps, the ideal. But this is not always possible, especially in the case of static targets such as aerodromes. The camouflage expert then tries to make the target difficult to find and identify. The enemy, perhaps, knows the exact whereabouts and even the type of camouflage used on many aerodromes. But it is still immensely difficult when flying at 300 m.p.h. to pick out the group of suburban villas, say, which is really a hangar, and get it in the bomb-sight.

One aerodrome is so well camouflaged to look like a peaceful rural scene that experienced pilots coming down to land have suddenly gone up again fearing that they had made a mistake !

For the concealment of guns, vehicles and every sort of mobile weapon, netting " garnished " with scrim is the great standby. Hundreds of thousands of yards of the netting are made and the scrim—green for Britain and similar landscapes, brown and white for the desert—is made from scraps

from textile factories. Wonders of concealment can be performed with this netting : it provides a covering that is opaque from a distance yet does not cast a heavy shadow. Hiding shadows is not the least of the arts of camouflage.

The camouflage expert must keep his eye on the weather. British airmen discovered a German landing-ground that had been cleverly camouflaged by having irrigation ditches in neighbouring fields carried across it in paint. When the temperature fell the water in the real ditches froze to ice. That in the fake ditches remained beautifully liquid—a miracle of Nature in which our air observer refused to believe ! Where faked trees are used, they must shed their leaves in the autumn and assume them again in the spring. This is one of the disadvantages of using natural foliage except for rapid emergency camouflage. The leaves start changing colour very soon after being picked, and the change is shown in photographs in a matter of hours.

SOLDIERS who are " camouflage conscious " will perform wonders of improvisation. Perhaps the most remarkable instance was in Burma when Japanese bombers approached a number of R.A.F. crates just landed, a tempting target. Our airmen jumped on the crates by the dozen and lay flat, " disrupting " the lines of the pile and also giving it a deceptive texture ! The ruse worked, and the bombers passed over without apparently noticing.

Experts can teach camouflage and, in the case of static buildings, work out detailed plans to be carried out by workmen who do not understand the why and wherefore. But for camouflage in the field it is important that every man should know the principles, for he will have to do his bit in carrying earth from trenches to scatter it far away, or whatever it may be, and he will do it more enthusiastically if he understands why. In fact, camouflage experts say that a few bombs in the neighbourhood are the best teachers !

So far I have written only of what might be called negative camouflage. There is another important side : making the enemy believe that there are vehicles or guns when in fact there is nothing. This form of deception is very old, but has been carried to new lengths by aerial warfare. False fires are lit in the neighbourhood of German towns being attacked, to mislead our bombers ; " guns " are made of poles laid across boxes ; imitation tanks are set up. But in this battle of wits the deception has to be carried far : a sort of double double-cross. The dummies must be made to look as if they were camouflaged, and yet not camouflaged so well that they are not noticed ! It calls for a nice estimate of the enemy's psychology. The British have scored some good successes with camouflage, especially against the impressionable Italians.

In Nature, camouflage is not only visual but also, sometimes, aural—an animal making a noise like one which is very much more dangerous. Noise camouflage in warfare is still in its infancy, but it presents enormous possibilities, especially against inexperienced soldiers, as the Germans have demonstrated.

The " Deception Corps " is a small band of élite workers, but their hints and instruction help every soldier. They have grown considerably since war began, and no unit in the future will be complete without its camouflage experts.

Appearances Are Sometimes Very Deceptive!

INGENIOUS METHODS OF CAMOUFLAGE are employed on all the battlefronts. Top left, an effectively concealed fighter at a U.S. air base in China; this airfield is invisible from the sky. Top right, trees form the motif of a camouflage "backcloth" along the façade of a building near Tripoli. Left centre, personal camouflage: a British soldier, wearing specially-designed clothing, assume a prone position by the side of a hummock and becomes part of his surroundings. Below, snow camouflage: this photograph from an enemy source shows a skilfully concealed German gun and crew in the Lake Ilmen sector of the Russian front.

Photos, British Official; Crown Copyright; Pictorial Press, Sport & General, Planet News

THE WAR IN THE AIR

by Capt. Norman Macmillan, M.C., A.F.C.

MODERN conditions of war involve the lifting of enormous tonnages of supplies. Never have armies been so dependent upon transport. The former military method of living upon an invaded country—relatively easy in the days of small armies equipped with horses—has largely vanished. Even if the Japanese troops can subsist more readily in the countries they have overrun than can troops of the United Nations, they still require great quantities of military supplies to be brought to them.

Our current age of mechanized war has created a monster with a ravenous appetite. It devours most of the output of the industrial man-power of the world. It demands the allocation of most of the world's transport systems to carry its supplies.

Germany was one of the first nations to appreciate the importance of air transportation in war. The Luftwaffe generals had the method built up for them by the Deutsche Luft Hansa A.G. (German Air Transport Company) with Junkers aircraft. When it was found that air transport offered the only means of getting heavy mining machinery into the interior of New Guinea to exploit the gold which was known to be there, Junkers aircraft were found to be the only suitable transport aircraft to carry the heavy units involved ; even if other planes could carry the weight, they did not possess hatches through which the large sections of mining machinery could be loaded into their fuselages.

When the Luftwaffe was formed in 1933 the man appointed to organize it was Erhard Milch, for seven years the principal organizer of the Deutsche Luft Hansa. He is now a Field-Marshal in the Luftwaffe. Milch created a transport section of the Luftwaffe. It grew concurrently with the development of the fighter, bomber, army cooperation and naval cooperation branches.

In 1936, when I visited Tempelhof and Staaken aerodromes, considerable numbers of Luftwaffe transport aircraft were parked there. They were camouflaged Junkers 52s. They were ready for war. German officers explained with a smile that they were " postal " aircraft.

The Junkers 52 was chosen because it was easy to make, reliable (as a civil transport aircraft its airframe did 270,000 miles between overhauls), and more commodious than most other German transport aircraft of that time which (like the Junkers 86 and the Heinkel 111) were actually prototypes of bombers. The Junkers 52 was really the only existing German aircraft which could be at once employed for military troop-transport.

IN the early stages of the War the Junkers 52 was a marked success. It could land, or crash-land, almost anywhere, for it possessed a low alighting speed, due partly to its Junkers wing-aileron. It could carry fifteen fully armed men. It was good for the dropping of parachutists. It could transport a load of about 2½ tons. About 300 were used in Norway and they contributed greatly to the rapid fall of that country before the German onslaught.

In spite of the design of other types of troop-transports by other German aircraft constructors, the Junkers 52 is still the principal type of aircraft upon which the Luftwaffe relies for transportation of men, material, petrol, and vehicles (some in parts for quick assembly) to her war zones where speed of supply is important or where other means of supply are doubtful, non-existent, or in need of assistance.

Our 255 m.p.h. Gladiator fighters in Norway found the Junkers 52 easy prey. The Russian Air Force shot down large numbers during the period when the Germany Army was cut off in Stalingrad, and could be supplied only by air.

The Junkers 52s met with their greatest successes in the four days' battle for Holland. They crash-landed on the beaches at Scheveningen and disemplaned troops. They came down in droves on the Dutch aerodrome of Waalhaven-Rotterdam, and the three aerodromes near The Hague. They had again a phenomenal success in the capture of Crete, where there was scarcely any fighter opposition, and but little anti-aircraft gunfire.

Now they have been in large-scale use again, running supplies to the German forces in north-eastern Tunisia. It must be difficult for the German forces there to obtain supplies by sea, for every port on the northern side of the Mediterranean—in Sicily, Sardinia, and Southern Italy—has been under heavy air bombardment for weeks, and the harbours at Bizerta and Tunis have been subjected to rhythmic raids that must have reduced their value very greatly. Loading and unloading facilities for ships are almost as important as the ships themselves, and if the stevedoring cannot be carried out because the machinery has been smashed by bombs, the value of ships for the purpose of transporting stores is largely diminished. Under these conditions the possibility of running in supplies from aerodrome to aerodrome assumes great importance.

HEADACHE for Air-Line Organizer Luftwaffe Chief Milch

When, as has been the case in the central Mediterranean for many weeks, Axis shipping has had to run the gauntlet of submarine and air attack, the difficulty of maintaining supplies to Rommel and von Arnim is augmented and its cost in ships lost may become an almost intolerable strain on Italo-German communications.

Little is heard of the work of the Fleet Air Arm in the Mediterranean, but it is more than probable that their torpedo aircraft have sunk as many tons of enemy shipping as the surface and under-water ships of the Navy. The R.A.F. and Dominion air forces have lent a hand with torpedoes and bombs. The U.S. air forces also have hit many ships.

Now, more than at any time during the whole North African campaign, the use of the opposing air forces, United Nations' versus the Axis, will determine the speed of outcome of the final battles to eject the vassals of Hitler and Mussolini from Tunisia.

AIR Vice Marshal Harry Broadhurst and Air Marshal Sir Arthur Coningham have demonstrated their ability to take the stage in the Tunisian skies. Coningham in command of the Tactical Air Forces, and Broadhurst in command of the Desert Air Force, sent their fighter boys after Milch's Junkers 52s in British Spitfires and American Warhawks (the latest of the long series of Curtiss Hawk fighters, this one is fitted with a Packard-built Rolls-Royce Merlin engine).

A force of about 100 Junkers 52 transports leaving Tunisia for the northern shores of the Mediterranean suffered 68 casualties, shot down into the sea or forced to crash-land on the Tunisian shore. In addition, 16 of their escorting Messerschmitt 109 and 110 fighters were destroyed. We lost eleven aircraft.

It looks as if the day of the Junkers 52 as a war transport is over. Its 190 miles an hour top speed is too slow to escape modern fighters. The Battle of Britain proved that German fighters cannot protect German bomber (or transport) formations. So bigger fighter escorts will not provide the answer. Air-line organizer Luftwaffe chief Milch must get a headache when he thinks of the Junkers 52s that he provided to give the Luftwaffe world supremacy in military air transportation. Antiquated and outnumbered, they are a liability to the Luftwaffe and to the German Army. And, as for Goering, let us remember that Junkers was the firm that Goering seized and turned into a Government factory.

SKODA WORKS, Pilsen, Czechoslovakia, devastated by the R.A.F. on April 16-17, 1943, was one of Europe's largest armament centres. On the same night Mannheim-Ludwigshafen factories in W. Germany were also attacked. This photo shows the vast area of the Skoda works. Inset, map giving distances from London to the target areas.

Sweeping the Luftwaffe from the African Sky

SMASHING ROMMEL'S AIRFIELDS in Tunisia, Allied planes have inflicted crippling blows on vital targets. 1, Her left wing and engine nacelle riddled by flak, this B.26 (Martin Marauder) flies home after a bombing attack. 2, Air Commodore "Bing" Cross, D.S.O., D.F.C., named by Sir A. Coningham on April 14, 1943, as leader of fighter squadrons carrying main weight of Tunisian air attacks. 3, Taken by a U.S. cameraman after a devastating raid by Flying Fortresses on the Axis airport of El Aouina, N.E. of Tunis, this photograph shows smoke-columns rising from bombed enemy transport planes.

Photos, British Official: Crown Copyright; U.S. Official, Associated Press

Stalin's Airmen Smite Hard at Nazi Königsberg

'WINGS FOR VICTORY' campaign among the collective farmers of the Gorky and Chkalov regions of the U.S.S.R. was responsible for the production of this impressive line-up of planes for the Red Air Force, photographed from the air.

KÖNIGSBERG, capital of E. Prussia, suffered heavily three times in one week when Soviet bombers attacked the port on April 10-11, 12, 16-17, 1943. Great fires and explosions occurred on each occasion as port installations and other vital objectives were subjected to intensive bombing. The raid on April 16-17 coincided with the fierce assault by the R.A.F. on the vast armament centre of Mannheim-Ludwigshafen in Western Germany. At Königsberg the Russian aircraft kept up their attack for two hours, when 10 explosions and 20 fires were observed. All but three planes returned safely.

A number of the Soviet pilots, navigators and radio operators who took part in these raids had already distinguished themselves in attacks on the Reich. Major A. Radchuk, who was over Königsberg on the night of April 12, has recorded his impressions: "The Germans, scared by the previous raid, had taken extraordinary precautions. The sky was full of searchlights. In spite of heavy fire from the German ground defences our planes reached the target area dead on time. Our bombs were effective, for we observed a number of terrific explosions down below."

MEN OF THE RED AIR FORCE are seen in the above photograph receiving presents and comforts from admiring delegates representing the people of the Kuibyshev region. The delegates paid a visit to the fighting-line and were very much impressed by the magnificent skill and courage displayed by the Russian airmen in action. Lt. Vassily Dobrovolsky (below) led four fighter planes to cover Soviet troops from the air. Six Messerschmitts attacked the Russian aircraft and three of the German planes were shot down. Dobrovolsky has brought down 13 enemy planes, and has made 254 operational flights.

LONG-RANGE BOMBER RAIDS made recently by Soviet airmen have included attacks on Danzig, Tilsit, and the triple assault on Königsberg described above. Port installations, railway and military objectives suffered heavily. Men of the Long-Range Bomber Regiment of the Guards are here seen loading up bombs before one of their long operational flights.

Photos, U.S.S.R. Official; Planet News'

Allied War Chiefs Meet in India's Capital City

IMPORTANT CONFERENCE IN NEW DELHI following the Casablanca meeting last January was announced on Feb. 11, 1943 to have secured the closest Allied cooperation against the Japanese. Leaving the Imperial Secretariat Building after joint staff talks are (left to right, front): Field-Marshal Sir Archibald Wavell and Lt.-Gen. Joseph W. Stilwell. Immediately behind them (left to right) are Lt.-Gen. Brehon B. Somerville, Field-Marshal Sir John Dill and Lt.-Gen. Henry H. Arnold.

Photo, Sport & General

THE HOME FRONT

by E. Royston Pike

Do you smoke Woodbines? If you are one of the people who smoke ten Woodbines a day and cut that down by one cigarette a day you will be almost square with your pre-Budget expenditure. If you cut down your smoking by two cigarettes a day you will be in pocket. This little calculation, made by the Chancellor of the Exchequer in the course of the Budget debate, was intended to cheer up those who thought that another twopence on ten cigarettes was a pretty stiff imposition. Take a heavy smoker (Sir Kingsley Wood continued)—he had seen them and knew them, and they were not of one sex only—who smoked, say, fifteen cigarettes a day; if he cut that number down to thirteen he would be spending no more than before the Budget was introduced. So, too, with drink. The man who used to drink four to seven pints a week could save the extra tax (1d. per pint on beer of average gravity) if he drank only half-a-pint a week less. Then as for pipe-smokers, a man need only give up every sixth pipe to be all square. " That is the quota suggested by Charles Lamb, who said : 'One pipe is wholesome, two pipes toothsome, three pipes noisome, four pipes foulsome, and five pipes quarrelsome.' " And not one of those five pipes has the pipe-smoker to go without !

As the Chancellor said, when one has regard to the suffering and hardship in so many parts of the world, to go without a few drinks or smokes is a small thing enough. Taken all in all, the Budget—the sixth of the War—was an attack on unessential spending, one aimed at people "who have some money to spare for expenditure on luxuries." Beer, wines and spirits, tobacco and entertainments all have to pay more in tax; and the purchase tax on such things as silk dresses, fur coats, gramophone records, musical instruments, cut glass, jewelry, electric shavers, perfumery and cosmetics is increased from the present 66⅔ to 100 per cent. The tax increases are intended to raise £100 million in the course of a year, bringing the total revenue from taxation to £2,900 million, leaving about £2,250 million to be covered by borrowing, while the sale of overseas investments is expected to yield something over £600 million. The expenditure for the current year has been estimated at the truly tremendous total of £5,756 million.

Speaking in the same debate, Capt. Crookshank, Postmaster-General, quoted some remarkable figures. Since the beginning of the War the number of telegrams sent each year has increased by ten millions to over seventy millions a year. The Greetings service has doubled, from about four millions to over 8,500,000. There has also been an enormous increase in trunk telephone calls ; before the War they numbered 528,000 a week, now they are 952,000—80 per cent of them Government and business calls. So great is the strain on the telephone service, indeed, that the charges for trunk calls are being increased, not so much with a view to more revenue as to permit a reduction in the Post Office's man-power. As statistics these figures are dry enough, but they are warm with life when they are translated into terms

of wartime separations and changes in the location of home and industry.

You and I and all the other people making up Britain's population spent £4,800 million in 1942 on "consumption at market prices," while in 1938 our expenditure was "only" £4,035 million. Some of the chief items are as follows, the 1938 figure being given in brackets, and million pounds in each case understood : food, 1,320 (1,198) ; drink and tobacco, 912 (452) ; rent and rates, etc., 520 (500) ; fuel and light, 242 (194) ; clothing, 462·(441) ; travel (including private motorcars, etc.), 215 (296). These figures are taken from a White Paper (Cmd. 6348, H.M. Stationery Office, 6d.) prepared by the Treasury and published as a kind of postscript

WATCH YOUR STEP, CHILDREN! A thousand children who recently attended a safety-first demonstration at Grocers' Schools, Hackney, London, were urged to become " traffic conscious " by a police inspector who pointed the moral with the statement that, on the average, every day in 1942 saw four children killed in road accidents in this country. *Photo, Topical Press*

to the Budget. Another of its Tables gives the total private incomes for 1942 as £7,836 million as compared with £4,920 in 1938.

Taken at face value, the figures would seem to show that Britain's population are both receiving and spending very much more than in the year before the War. But we must have regard to the very considerable changes in the purchasing power of money. The Treasury statisticians estimate that consumption in 1942 was probably about ·82 per cent of that in 1938, i.e. it had fallen off in actual volume by about a fifth. Then there is the immense increase in taxation. But it is remarkable that out of every £ spent on "consumer goods" by the people of this country 3s. 9d. goes on alcoholic drink and smoking. Compare this with about 6s. 7d. on food, 2s. 2d. on rent, and 2s. on clothing. The amount spent last year on drink and smoking represents about 19 per cent of all

personal expenditure as compared with 11 per cent in 1938. But don't jump to the conclusion that people are drinking nearly twice as many pints and tots and smoking nearly double the number of cigarettes as before the War. What did a bottle of whisky cost in 1938—and a packet of ten ?

Why did we take up our allotments ? If the question were suddenly put to us we should answer, very likely, with the phrase "Digging for Victory." Yet a recent survey of allotment-holders (reports The Economist) has disclosed that only one in twenty took an allotment to help in the war effort. Rather more than half, fifty-five per cent to be exact, gave as their reason to obtain fresh food. Nearly eighteen per cent said that they wanted to save money, and seven per cent wanted to reduce the trouble of shopping. And fourteen per cent said that they wanted to obtain fresh air and (shade of Adam !) health-giving exercise. For one reason or another—and in most people, no doubt, all these and probably other reasons have had their influence—more than half a million people have taken up allotments since the War began. The latest figures available show that in April 1942 there were 1,586,888 allotments, covering 172,861 acres ; figures of production are not available, but the average weekly yield from a hundred well-planned 10-rod allotments in 1940–41 was 19¾ lb. edible weight in the winter, 11¼ in the spring, 12½ in the summer, and 14¾ in autumn. Very likely these yields are a bit on the high side, but there is no reason to doubt that the nearly two million families in this country who have allotments or large gardens are practically self-supporting in vegetables and salads.

How are things going on the Fuel Front? Speaking in London on April 14, Major Lloyd George, Minister of Fuel and Power, announced that, thanks to the splendid effort of consumers and producers alike (and also because of the mild winter), the gap between production and consumption of coal has now been closed. Three days later, however, the outlook seemed nothing like so rosy. " I cannot say I am satisfied with the position since the beginning of 1943," said Major Lloyd George at Bristol ; " I have been watching the production returns in the last few weeks with serious concern. Although there are at the moment over 5,000 more men in the industry than a year ago, the production each week is nearly 100,000 tons less than in the same weeks of last year and absenteeism is higher than it should be."

Carelessness is exacting a heavier toll than valour. In the first two years of the War the casualties of the Armed Forces of the United Kingdom on the Battlefields were 145,012. On the roads last year the casualties were 147,544. The death rate on the roads is not less than before the War, but greater. Three more lives were lost every day in January this year than in the last January of peace. In February, 93 children were killed—more than in any February since the records were first kept. One sixth of the road casualties last year were children under fifteen, and in conjunction with the falling birth-rate the disturbing significance of this loss is underlined. These figures were given in a recent speech at Blackburn by Mr. Hore-Belisha, M.P., who dotted our pavements with Belisha beacons in an altogether commendable attempt to reduce the number of road casualties. Of course, excuses can be made. Road improvements have been stopped. Sign-posting has been discontinued. There is the black-out. But, says Mr. Hore-Belisha, " All these factors enjoin upon us the necessity for greater care, not less."

So That's How They Use the Bombs We Make!

ONE MILLION TRENCH MORTAR BOMBS were recently produced in such record time by a small West Country arms firm that the men and women who made them were invited to visit the practice range, where they saw their work in action. 1, A director reads the Ministry of Supply's telegram congratulating the workers on their millionth bomb. 2, A soldier loads a bomb into one of the mortars preparatory to discharging it. 3, Women operatives riding to the range in Bren-gun-carriers.

Photos, British Official

I WAS THERE!

In Denmark They Wear Britannia Brooches

Mrs. Isobel Coffey, a Scotswoman who recently arrived in Britain after escaping from Denmark—where she had been living since 1939—reveals how this Nazi-occupied country is keeping its end up and presenting a cold shoulder to the hated invader. Her story is reprinted here from Free Denmark, a Danish weekly paper published in London.

BRITANNIA BADGE, cut from an English penny, was brought back by Mrs. Coffey, who tells of her experiences in occupied Denmark in this page. *Photo, Daily Express*

It would be a gift to the enemy if I were to tell you how I managed to escape from Denmark. It is, however, no secret that as late as January last I was living at Damehotellet (Ladies' Hotel) in Gammel Mont in Copenhagen, and that the Germans phoned the hotel several times a week to make sure that I was still there. And, like all other foreigners, I had to report to the Danish police every week.

In August 1939 on my doctor's advice I went to the Vejlefjord Sanatorium for a cure. Then the war came, and after Christmas I decided to return to Britain. I bought the ticket for the plane journey home, which had been arranged for April 17, 1940. But the Nazi invasion put a stop to my plan and I had to stay in the Sanatorium until, in April 1942, I went to Copenhagen. During all this time I was allowed to move freely about the country, except in the restricted area of Jutland where it is necessary to have a special permit.

I examined, of course, all chances of returning to England, where my three sons, aged 17, 13 and 11 years, are at school. One day I went to Gestapo headquarters in Dagmarhus to try to solve my problem. I was shown into an office where an official was seated. He kept me standing before his desk for more than ten minutes before looking up. At last he asked me, in the most brutal manner, what I wanted. I never hated anybody as I hated that man at that moment, and I felt certain that the hate was reciprocated. I need hardly say that the result of my visit was negative.

The streets of Copenhagen are crowded with Germans, especially sailors. Wherever you go you realize how the Danes cold-shoulder the Germans; they make it a rule to leave a tramcar or a railway compartment as soon as a German enters. To avoid this humiliation the Nazis usually prefer to stand outside in the corridor or on the platform. And how the Danes enjoy the obvious nervousness of the Nazis when an air raid alert is sounded! The swastika dangles over many buildings taken over by the Germans. The other day they requisitioned a large school building near Osterport Station

and built deep shelters within the houses, for use, I believe, as safe and commodious Nazi headquarters in Copenhagen.

As a rule, the Nazi troops are allowed to remain only a few months in Denmark; the German authorities don't regard it as desirable that their soldiers should become accustomed to the relatively good conditions there. The occupying troops are terribly afraid of being sent to the Russian front, and many prefer to commit suicide. I have been told that, at the beginning of the occupation, the Germans wanted to buy the equipment of the Danish army, but the offer was declined by the Danish government. Then the Nazis simply asked for it and, as far as I know, half of it had to be surrendered. The Danish Nazis are hated even more intensely than the Germans. Never had I seen the loyal population give vent to this icy contempt so openly as on the occasion of the Danish volunteers returning from the Eastern front and marching through the capital. One day one of my young student friends had a fight with five of Denmark's few Nazi students; he gave me the comforting assurance that the five looked much worse than he did after the encounter.

All the time I was in Denmark I enjoyed many manifestations of sympathy and friendship, simply on account of my being a British subject. I always wore, as a brooch, a British penny with Britannia cut out as a silhouette, this being a popular fashion there. Unfortunately, owing to lack of " raw material," the demand for these emblems cannot be met. The interest taken in Britain is tremendous, and no noise sounds more

welcome in the ears of the Danes than the roaring of British planes on their way to German targets inside or outside Denmark.

In fact, the Danes have felt neglected by the R.A.F. because the Germans in Denmark have not been attacked on the same scale as in other countries. While I was in Vejlefjord Sanatorium a British pilot being chased by German fighters had to jettison his bombs, and as a result thousands of window-panes were broken in the town. But I never heard a word of blame for British airmen. On the contrary, pilots taken prisoner are greeted cordially, and graves of R.A.F. men are kept decorated with flowers.

I always got the underground papers Frit Danmark (Free Denmark) and De Frie Danske (The Free Danes). Those responsible for these print on the envelopes in which they are sent to subscribers the name of a government office, or a well-known business firm or some German headquarters as the sender! In this way the greater part of these clandestine papers get through; only a few fall into the hands of the Gestapo.

Torpedoed by U-boat Twice in Twenty Minutes

This is the story of what happened after the torpedoing by a U-boat of the liner Avila Star (see also p. 216). The author is 19-year-old Maria Elizabeth Ferguson, awarded the British Empire Medal for her great courage and the services she rendered to wounded men during 20 days and nights in an open lifeboat. She has written the story of this tragic ordeal specially for THE WAR ILLUSTRATED.

I HAD been two years in the Argentine with my father, who is a planter, when I decided to return to England and join up. I put my name down as a volunteer and started on the journey home, to join the Boat Section of the W.R.N.S. One night, when we were 300 miles off Portugal and were down below in the lounge chatting, there sounded a metallic thud.

The ship quivered, the engines stopped, the lights went out. A torpedo had struck us. We rushed up and slithered across the sloping deck to the lifeboats. It was pitch dark, but emergency lights were quickly switched on. Unfortunately, we had some difficulty in lowering our boat—the poor old Avila Star was listing at thirty degrees—and twenty minutes elapsed before we were

pushing away from the ship's side. Suddenly, without warning, I found myself splashing about in the water.

A second torpedo had struck the ship, passing just below our lifeboat and blowing us all into the air; although I do not remember either going up or coming down, having had a knock on the head. I do not know how I managed to keep afloat, but when I recovered consciousness I saw a half-submerged lifeboat quite near. I managed to clamber into it and then helped to haul in another struggling figure.

I helped the others in the wallowing lifeboat to push off, and soon after we got away we heard the dull roar of boilers exploding as the Avila Star went to the bottom. I sat in the boat's stern, nursing two injured men, whilst others signalled with torches to try to locate the other boats. And so, tossing about in the darkness, that first dreadful night passed. In the morning, when it grew light, we discovered that our boat had no bottom. It was kept afloat only by the airtight tanks round its sides.

The five other boats, which we could now see, came closer, and the seventeen of us swam across to two of them. The boat into which I scrambled now had 37 men and one other woman aboard, and in that open boat we remained for twenty days and nights. At first the boats all managed to

Mrs. Coffey has many interesting stories to recount of life in Denmark under the Germans. Here she is seen with two of her sons, both of whom were at school in Surrey when she arrived home. *Photo, Daily Express*

MISS M. E. FERGUSON, B.E.M., whose courage and endurance brought her through a severe ordeal after being torpedoed, describes her adventures in this and the preceding page.
Photo, L.N.A.

keep together, but when the weather worsened we became separated and lost touch.

Sleep was almost impossible, icy water splashing over us as we huddled together in effort to keep warm. None of us was equipped for this sort of thing. I was wearing a borrowed playsuit several sizes too large and the second officer's heavy bridge coat. Some were wearing only pyjamas. The only thing to relieve the awful monotony of the daylight hours was the serving out of skimpy rations. When one meal was over we looked forward to the next share-out—ship's biscuits, milk tablets, chocolates; and we had about three mouthfuls of water each three times a day. Water was precious !

Those who were wounded—several were cut or scalded—we tended as well as our equipment allowed. But we had only a small first-aid box, and ten men died before we were picked up. We lowered them over the side. Three more died later. For seventeen days we saw nothing but a bird, some empty bottles, seaweed, and once a piece of meat and a loaf floating by. The sight of the latter raised our hopes, and on the afternoon of the seventeenth day we heard aircraft. Anxiously we lighted flares to attract the attention of the pilots. But I wondered if we had any real cause for hope , for I knew that from no great height a fairly large ship looks no bigger than a small fishing smack, and a lifeboat must seem like a pinhead—almost invisible.

But they sighted us, and dropped tins of biscuits and small kegs of fresh water. We picked these up and drank the water immediately ; but salt water had got into the tins and the biscuits were quite uneatable. They also dropped us a chart, showing our position and with a written message that help would come soon. From the chart we learned that we had sailed about 1,500 miles, and were now about 100 miles from the African coast. If that promised help did not come we might never reach land at all.

For three weary days after the planes had come and gone we saw nothing but sea, and our spirits were at the very lowest ebb when at last we sighted a ship. We soaked a dry rag in petrol, tied it to a boathook, put a lighted match to it, and to our intense joy the vessel altered course in our direction. As it approached we saw that it was a Portuguese sloop, the Pedro Nunes. We were taken aboard, and sent to hospital at Lisbon. Eventually I reached England—at least five weeks later than I had bargained for.

M.G.B. CREW who took part in the successful action against E-boats described by Lt. Bradford in this page, proudly display their flag upon which a " kill " is recorded.
Photo, British Official

of about 50 degrees. It seemed to us as though we had gone straight through her.

Just before we rammed we could see the whole of the E-boat's deck lit by our gunfire. There appeared to be only three men still alive on her deck. Her captain was dancing about on the bridge and waving his arms frantically. After the ramming we circled round to see what remained of the two E-boats. There was nothing but wreckage.

As there were still three boats at large we resumed the chase. But they saw us in time and retreated at full speed. Nevertheless, we managed to score four direct hits on the bridge of the rear E-boat, and then one of our engines gave us a little trouble. It turned out that our engine-room staff had been working under great difficulties,

And That Was the End of an E-boat!

A thrilling engagement between two of our motor gunboats and five enemy E-boats took place in the North Sea on March 29, 1943. How one of the E-boats was blown up and the remainder were dealt with is here described by Lieut. D. G. Bradford, R.N.R., of Over Hulton, Lancs.

WE came upon the E-boats lurking near our convoy route and gave chase at full speed. They were so surprised that they were unable to get a proper start before we were upon them. At about 70 yards we opened fire. The E-boats split up into two groups, three in one and two in the other. I took the larger group, and the other M.G.B., commanded by Lieutenant Philip Stobo, R.N.V.R., of Rickmansworth, gave chase to the other.

We closed to within 25 yards and concentrated our fire on the second of the three E-boats. Our first bursts must have put their guns' crews out of action. Our heavier armament was scoring repeated hits on the engine-room, hull and bridge. Lumps could be seen flying off the E-boat. From the light of our gunfire we could see one of the enemy gun crews completely flaked out at the foot of their gun. There was no sign of life on board.

The third E-boat made a half-hearted attempt to engage and a few bullets went through our superstructure, one shattering our searchlight. But we were determined to destroy one E-boat at a time. We continued to pump shells into the second E-boat in the line when suddenly there was a terrific explosion and a flash from its engine-room. The decks opened up like a tin can. And that was the end of an E-boat !

The leading E-boat, which I believe was commanded by the senior German officer, was our next target. We overtook him and engaged with our for'ard guns. There were several direct hits, and the E-boat tried to take evading action by changing course. This presented us with a wonderful opportunity. We were about 40 yards away and

by a sharp alteration of course came into direct line to ram. We bore down at full speed and struck the E-boat with our bows about 20 feet from her stern. There was a shudder as the E-boat heeled over at an angle

AVILA STAR'S LIFEBOAT, seen almost on the horizon, was sighted by the Pedro Nunes, from which this photograph was taken (see accompanying text). The lifeboat drifted in the ocean for twenty days and nights before the Avila Star's survivors were picked up by the Portuguese ship, whose crew are shown in the foreground.

caused by escaping exhaust fumes. The engine-room ratings had been taking turns at getting a breath of fresh air through the engine-room hatch.

We carried on at reduced speed and managed to keep contact with the fleeing E-boats for half an hour before they finally got out of range. Our guns were firing all the time, but it was not possible to observe the results. The final phase of the battle came shortly afterwards when we found two groups of E-boats, one of eight and another of three boats. We saw them by the light of star-shells fired from a British destroyer which put them to flight. We tried to intercept them, but with a damaged engine we did not have sufficient speed to close in and attack. Our gunners did what damage they could, but again we could not observe the results.

My crew, nearly all of whom are under 21, put up a splendid show. I have got the toughest crew in coastal forces, and they share with me the ambition to board an E-boat and have a hand-to-hand show-down. We thought it might happen this time and we were all prepared for boarding.

I Was a 'Naughty' Prisoner in Italian Camps

Among the first prisoners of war in Italian hands exchanged in the Middle East in March 1943 to reach home, Cmdr. W. L. M. Brown, D.S.C., of Cheltenham, tells (in The Evening News, from which this account is reprinted) how war-weary Italians are now reacting to the depressing news of Axis reverses—and to R.A.F. bombing.

COMMANDER W. L. M. BROWN said on his arrival in London that Italians now said "let's hope the war finishes soon," without any reference to who wins it. The remark was used as a greeting, cut down to one word "speriamo," meaning "let's hope . . ." It was usually accompanied by a shrug of the shoulders.

"The Italians," he said, "definitely hate and fear the German despite the propaganda telling them to treat the German as a brother. On the other hand, also in spite of propaganda, they still respect the British and like them."

He got the impression that the Germans were not running Italy in detail. They might be running it from the top. There were no Germans in control of prison camps, and, though there were German railway transport officers at stations they seemed to be there to keep the two sides separate, rather than to control the Italian side of things.

"The reaction to R.A.F. bombing that I heard most often—though I am not convinced it was a genuine reaction—was 'Get on with your bombing,' 'Finish off this business,' 'Get on with the second front.' The prison officers from whom we got that are not normally allowed to speak to prisoners and, therefore, we had access only to those who were disgruntled. There was no tendency to run Mussolini down, and I don't think the Italians are on the verge of a revolution."

Commander Brown described himself as a "naughty" prisoner. Captured in July 1940, when his reconnaissance aircraft from the Warspite was shot down off Tobruk, he was in five prison camps during his captivity. He reached his final camp at Gavi eight months before the exchange because of incidents that occurred at a previous camp.

"This concerned a tunnelling episode for which I was blamed," he said. "But the Italians never really bawled me out."

CMDR. W. L. M. BROWN, D.S.C., who recently reached England after being a prisoner since 1940, describes in the accompanying text some Italian reactions to the present phase of the war.
Photo, C. Weston

OUR DIARY OF THE WAR

APRIL 13, 1943, Tuesday *1,319th day*
Sea.—Admiralty announced loss of submarine depot-ship Medway, sunk in Mediterranean last year.
Air.—Heavy night raid by R.A.F. on Italian naval base of Spezia.
North Africa.—Forward troops of 8th Army made contact with enemy prepared positions at Enfidaville.
Mediterranean.—Flying Fortresses attacked enemy aircraft on airfields at Milo and Castelvetrano in Sicily.
U.S.A.—American bombers and fighters made ten attacks on Kiska, Aleutians.

APRIL 14, Wednesday *1,320th day*
Air.—R.A.F. made heavy night raid on Stuttgart; 23 bombers missing. Soviet aircraft raided Danzig and Königsberg.
North Africa.—First Army troops captured peak of Jebel Ang N.W. of Mejez-el-Bab.
Mediterranean.—Flying Fortresses attacked enemy airfields at Elmas and Monserrato in Sardinia.
Australasia.—From 75 to 100 Jap aircraft raided Milne Bay, New Guinea; 30 destroyed or damaged.
U.S.A.—American aircraft made eight more attacks on Kiska.

APRIL 15, Thursday *1,321st day*
Sea.—Strong force of E-boats off east coast was routed by light naval forces.
North Africa.—First Army repelled enemy counter-attacks and held Jebel Ang.
Mediterranean.—U.S. Liberators made daylight raids on Catania and Palermo. R.A.F. attacked Naples and Messina by night.

APRIL 16, Friday *1,322nd day*
Air.—Large-scale daylight attacks by R.A.F. and U.S.A.A.F. on Brest, Lorient, Ostend, Havre and Haarlem. In biggest night operation of the year more than 600 R.A.F. bombers raided Skoda works at Pilsen and Mannheim-Ludwigshafen; 55 missing.
Mediterranean.—Flying Fortresses bombed docks and shipping at Palermo.
Russian Front.—Soviet troops repulsed German counter-attacks in the Kuban.
General.—Mussolini decreed that Sicily and Sardinia were operational areas. Adm. Horthy, Regent of Hungary, at Hitler's H.Q.

APRIL 17, Saturday *1,323rd day*
Air.—Daylight raid by U.S. heavy bombers (unescorted) on Focke-Wulf factory at Bremen; 63 enemy aircraft

destroyed; 16 bombers lost. Soviet night raids on Danzig and Königsberg.
North Africa.—Flying Fortresses raided docks at Ferryville (Bizerta) by day; enemy aircraft bombed Algiers area.
Mediterranean. — R. A. F. heavy bombers made night raid on Catania.

APRIL 18, Sunday *1,324th day*
Air.—R.A.F. made another heavy raid on Spezia naval dockyard and barracks.
North Africa.—In aerial engagement near Cape Bon, U.S. and R.A.F. fighters shot down 58 Ju52 transports and 16 of their escorting fighters. Five enemy bombers destroyed over Algiers.
Mediterranean. — Flying Fortresses made heavy attacks on Palermo.
U.S.A.—American aircraft made nine more attacks on Kiska.

APRIL 19, Monday *1,325th day*
North Africa.—During night of 19th-20th Eighth Army attacked enemy positions at Enfidaville.
U.S.A.—Americans made 15 more raids on Kiska.
General.—Norwegian Prime Minister, Quisling, at Hitler's headquarters.

APRIL 20, Tuesday *1,326th day*
Sea.—Admiralty announced loss of trawler Adonis.

Air.—R.A.F. made daylight attacks on Boulogne, Cherbourg and Zeebrugge. By night heavy bombers raided Stettin and Rostock, Mosquitoes attacked Berlin, Soviet Air Force bombed Tilsit.
North Africa.—Enfidaville occupied by Eighth Army.
Australasia.—Allied heavy bombers raided aerodromes and shipping at Wewak, New Guinea.

APRIL 21, Wednesday *1,327th day*
Sea.—Admiralty announced loss of submarine Thunderbolt (formerly Thetis).
North Africa.—Enemy attacked First Army positions near Mejez-el-Bab, but withdrew, losing 33 tanks. Eighth Army troops captured Takrouna, N.W. of Enfidaville.
Australasia.—U.S. bombers made daylight raid on Nauru Island.
General.—President Roosevelt announced execution by Japanese authorities of American airmen captured during raid on Tokyo in April 1942.
British Government renewed warning that use of gas against Russians would be followed by use of gas against military objectives in Germany.

APRIL 22, Thursday *1,328th day*
Air.—Soviet aircraft made mass raid on Insterburg, East Prussia.

North Africa.—First Army launched attack in Goubellat-Bou Arada sector.
Mediterranean.—U.S. and R.A.F. fighters shot down 31 Me323 transports and 11 fighters in Gulf of Tunis.
Australasia.—Japanese bombers raided positions in Ellice Islands occupied by American forces.

APRIL 23, Friday *1,329th day*
North Africa.—Eighth Army captured Jebel Terhouna, N.W. of Enfidaville.
Australasia.—U.S. bombers attacked Jap air base at Tarawa, Gilbert Is.

APRIL 24, Saturday *1,330th day*
Mediterranean.—Ten more enemy supply ships sunk by our submarines.
Australasia.—Allied heavy bombers raided Kendari, air base in Dutch E. Indies.
U.S.A.—American warships bombarded Holtz Bay and Chitagof Harbour in the Aleutians.
General.—Swedish Government sent Germany note of protest following sowing of mines in Swedish waters and firing on Swedish submarine.

APRIL 25, Sunday *1,331st day*
North Africa.—French announced capture of Jebel Mansour, on road to Pont du Fahs.
Burma.—Japanese renewed their attacks on British line in Mayu peninsula.

APRIL 26, Monday *1,332nd day*
Air.—R.A.F. bombers made one of War's heaviest night raids on Duisburg.
North Africa.—On the First Army front, British infantry captured the whole of Longstop Hill.
Mediterranean.—Daylight raid by U.S. heavy bombers on airfield at Bari, Italy, followed by night attack by R.A.F.
U.S.A.—Eleven American attacks on Kiska, and two by Canadian fighter-pilots.
General.—Soviet Government announced suspension of relations with Polish Government in London, following German story of massacre of Polish officers near Smolensk.

APRIL 27, Tuesday *1,333rd day*
North Africa.—In Mejez-el-Bab sector the First Army was engaged in ceaseless attack and counter-attack; French troops made progress towards Pont du Fahs.
Mediterranean.—Flying Fortresses raided airfields at Villacidro, Sardinia.

★ ═══════════ *Flash-backs* ═══════════ ★

1940
April 13. *Second battle of Narvik; seven German destroyers sank.*
April 15. *Announced that British forces had landed in Norway.*
April 25. *Enemy pressure forced withdrawal of Allied forces in southern Norway.*

1941
April 14. *Siege of Tobruk began.*
April 16. *Heavy night raid on London; repeated on the 19th.*
April 17. *Yugoslavia capitulated.*
April 23. *Announced that Greek armies in Macedonia and Epirus*
had capitulated. *Greek Government moved to Crete.*
April 24-25. *Imperial forces began to evacuate Greece.*
April 27. *German troops entered Athens.*

1942
April 18. *U.S. bombers from aircraft carrier Hornet raided Tokyo.*
April 23. *R.A.F. made first of four heavy raids on Rostock.*
April 24. *Germans made "Baedeker" raid on Exeter.*
April 25. *Bath heavily bombed.*
April 27. *Reprisal raid on Norwich.*

IN these days, when women have proved themselves the equal of men in so many occupations once believed to be entirely outside their capacity, both physically and mentally, it is interesting to discover as I did the other day in picking up one of my favourite books, The Life of Colonel Hutchinson, by his Wife, that nearly three hundred years ago the first faint beginnings of the N.F.S. might be traced. Mrs. Hutchinson, in her classic description of her husband's life and his defence of Nottingham Castle against the Cavaliers, puts on record the fact that the women in Nottingham went about during the siege in bands of fifty, "to put out the smouldering fires lighted by the firebrands of the enemy." Her famous book lay in manuscript for many years and was not given to the world until 1806, when the Rev. Julius Hutchinson, one of the Colonel's descendants, edited it and added numerous footnotes. His reflection on these early N.F.S. workers will no doubt raise a smile today among the valiant women who adorn that service: "This is a curious fact," says he, "and points out a useful way of turning to use and profit the timorousness and watchfulness of the sex."

TEN years have passed since Franklin D. Roosevelt assumed the Presidency of the U.S.A. It was a dark hour, the darkest perhaps in modern American history. But from the day of his inauguration he has been in very deed the captain of his people. Some men are great in deeds, some in words; a few, like Winston Churchill and President Roosevelt, are great both in expression and in action. On this side of the Atlantic we have come to recognize in the President's voice the voice of a friend; and so there should be a wide welcome for the book, Addresses and Messages of Franklin D. Roosevelt, which has been recently published in this country by H.M. Stationery Office at 1s. Here is what the President said in 1933, in 1942 and in the years between; here is his Good Neighbour speech, his Fireside Chat in which he called America the Arsenal of Democracy, his Third Inaugural Address, his joint statement with Mr. Churchill on the Atlantic Charter, his addresses to Congress calling for a declaration of a state of war against the countries of the Axis. The book is a reprint of a document printed by order of the United States Senate, and its reprinting by order of our Government is, I believe, an unprecedented recognition of a great man's great words.

ARE you up to date in R.A.F. slang? You know what browned off means, and could possibly define Get cracking, piece of cake, and stooge; but when you hear a young pilot-officer saying that "So and so has been shot down in flames" you will be relieved to find that he is referring not to a battle in the sky but to a set-back on the amatory front—a mere crossing in love. The phrase may also mean that the victim has been severely reprimanded; a close relation is, tear off a strip—meaning, to take down a peg. Perhaps you may guess that a blonde job is a young woman with fair hair; by the exercise of a little imagination you may realize that flinging a woo means meeting a young lady, blonde or brunette. Shagbat officer stands for a somewhat plain W.A.A.F. officer. Tail-end Charlie is, of course, the rear-gunner; the dustbin is his position in the aircraft, and the drink is what he drops into

when he falls out. But you may not recognize an R.A.F. photographer in stickyback, the doctor as quack, the chief engineer as chief plumber, the senior W.A.A.F. officer as Queen Bee, and a W.A.A.F. motor-coach as the passion wagon. Perhaps I may add that I have learnt of these phrases in preparing a new edition of The A B C of the R.A.F., which contains a glossary of R.A.F. slang.

ONE of the most famous of R.A.F. slang terms is Mae West, used to describe the rather rotund and billowy stole or waistcoat which has saved the life of many a gallant airman. That the world-renowned film-star rather welcomes than otherwise this use of her name seems to be evident from a letter which was quoted recently by Hannen Swaffer in The Daily Herald. So pleased was

F/L. E. S. LOCK, D.S.O., D.F.C., whose short stature earned him the nickname of "Sawn-off Lockie." An intrepid and fearless fighter in the air, he was reported missing in 1941 and presumed killed in action the following year. He was 22.
Drawn by Capt. Cuthbert Orde, Crown Copyright reserved

she on discovering in the war film Air Force that its airmen referred to their bulging life-jackets as "Mae Wests" that she wrote to the local training unit of the R.A.F.

"Dear boys, I've just seen that you flyers have a jacket you call a 'Mae West' because it bulges in all the right places. Well, I consider it a swell honour to have such great guys wrapped up in me, know-what I mean? I hear that I may get into the dictionary because of this. I've been in 'Who's Who,' and I know what's what, but this'll be the first time I ever made a dictionary."

NOT long ago I gave a "mention" in these notes to an eye-witness account of the Dieppe raid of last August (Wing-Commander Austin's We Landed at Dawn). Here is another, Rehearsal for Invasion (Harrap, 6s.), written by Wallace Rayburn, the Montreal Standard's war correspondent with the Canadian Forces over here. It goes without saying that it makes interesting reading; how could it be otherwise when a man with a journalist's trained eye saw the things that Rayburn saw? He tells how they left for France, how they struggled ashore

or Pourville beach and fought their way through the little seaside town's streets, how at last those who were left managed to get away and back to England. Among those who didn't come back was 33-year-old Lieut.-Colonel C. C. I. Merritt, O.C. of the South Saskatchewans, who for his courage at Dieppe became Canada's first V.C. of this war. Rayburn, who was himself wounded in the raid, had a last glimpse of the Colonel striding down a street in Dieppe on the way to tackle a very hot spot of a bridge. "He showed no sign of concern at the muck' that was flying round him. His tin hat dangled from his wrist, and he twirled it around as he walked. His men followed him as he advanced into the very face of the white concrete fortress on the hill. Watching this display of bravery and inspired leadership I felt a thrill run through me. A stretcher-bearer standing beside me shook his head incredulously and said: 'My God!'"

WHEN introducing his Budget on April 12 Sir Kingsley Wood, the Chancellor of the Exchequer, said that he had not overlooked the suggestion that had been made to levy income tax on the basis of current earnings. No acceptable plan has been forthcoming so far, but a close examination of the matter is still proceeding. Certainly conditions may arise which may add point and weight to the proposal. As everyone knows, we pay tax based on our incomes during the year up to the previous April 5. As long as we continue in employment, this is satisfactory enough. But as The Economist pointed out recently, this state of affairs can hardly last for ever. After the War many workers will wish to retire from industry; women, especially housewives, will wish to return to their homes. Are they to be saddled with an income-tax liability for which they have not made, and could not have made, provision? Will husbands whose own earnings have declined shoulder their wives' tax liability in addition to their own? Are soldiers who owed something to the tax-collector before they joined up to return to civilian life saddled with debts? Here is the making of a pretty problem.

TWICE in a Lifetime. The title is apt enough for a well-illustrated shilling booklet published for the Belgian Information Office by Evans Brothers Ltd., giving details of the oppression and privations inflicted by the German invaders on the Belgian country and people. Only too exact is the resemblance of 1940 to 1914; only too plain is it that today as in the years of the last war, hunger, imprisonment, deportation and execution have been, and are, the lot of an unknown number of brave Belgian patriots. Perhaps this time it is even worse than the last, since then the Belgians' King captained his army in the battle-line, and a corner of Belgian soil remained unpolluted by the German stain. The text describes and compares the two wars, and the photographs show how only too often what happened in 1914 was all too closely paralleled in 1940 and since. Among them is one of the front page of the old Libre Belgique on which is a picture of Governor von Bissing holding in his hands a copy of the banned publication; facing it is a reproduction of another front page, bearing a photograph of General von Falkenhausen, showing that he "follows the example of his predecessor in seeking the truth in La Libre Belgique of today."

Who Said the Horse Was Obsolete in War?

Photo, British Official: Crown Copyright

MOUNTED PATROL IN TUNISIA uses horses under cover of uneven ground and scrub with marked success. This patrol was the idea of Sgt.-Maj. L. A. Dumais, a Canadian, and it has brought in, besides valuable information, a quantity of enemy equipment left on the battlefield. This photograph shows the colonel of a famous British regiment leading the patrol on a white horse. Some of the riders are men who were connected with racing stables before they joined the Army.

Printed in England and published every alternate Friday by the Proprietors, THE AMALGAMATED PRESS, LTD., The Fleetway House, Farringdon Street, London, E.C.4. Registered for transmission by Canadian Magazine Post. Sole Agents for Australia and New Zealand: Messrs. Gordon & Gotch, Ltd.; and for South Africa: Central News Agency, Ltd.—May 14, 1943. S.S. *Editorial Address:* JOHN CARPENTER HOUSE, WHITEFRIARS, LONDON, E.C.4

Vol 6 · *The War Illustrated* · № 155

Edited by Sir John Hammerton

SIXPENCE

MAY 28, 1943

TUNISIAN ARABS WELCOME A BRITISH SERGEANT at Chaouach, N.W. of Medjez-el-Bab, which Gen. Anderson's men captured on April 10, 1943. This N.C.O. of the Field Security Police, who managed successfully to evade his German captors in Tunis and rejoin his comrades of the 1st Army, describes in fluent Arabic the Axis defeat in this sector. These Arabs were able to return to their homes at Toukabeur, a near-by village.

Photo, British Official : Crown Copyright

NO. 156 WILL BE PUBLISHED FRIDAY, JUNE 11

THE BATTLE FRONTS

by Maj.-Gen. Sir Charles Gwynn, K.C.B., D.S.O.

ON May 6, 1943 the battle of Tunisia was decisively won by a blitzkrieg attack following on a series of desperate encounters in which the enemy's troops were exhausted and his reserves expended. The enemy had been out-fought, out-generalled, and induced to make the mistakes that no doubt General Alexander hoped he would make.

The world stood amazed when it was realized that within two and a half weeks after the 8th Army's initial attack on April 19 at Enfidaville, the boasted, impregnable Axis stronghold had been penetrated, and that nothing remained but to mop up the fragments of its defeated garrison. A blow had been struck at German military prestige almost as heavy as it had received at Stalingrad. The confidence of the German nation and its satellites in the competence of the High Command which had thus twice wilfully exposed its armies to disaster must be approaching vanishing point. Will belief in the effectiveness of the elaborate wall of fortifications which fringes the coastline of Europe survive ? Will the German people now realize that the amateur armies of the democratic nations are as formidable fighters as the professional soldiers of the Reich, and better equipped ?

The storm is still brewing in Russia ; and it may break before this article is published. Meanwhile, there seems every possibility that part at least of the German bridgehead in the Kuban may meet the fate of the bridgehead in Tunisia. The notable superiority which the Russian Air Force is steadily gaining over the Luftwaffe may prove as important a factor as the air superiority established by the Allies in Tunisia.

NORTH AFRICA

No one expected the final phase of the battle of Tunisia to develop with such amazing rapidity. The enemy in his outer defence ring had positions of exceptional natural strength, and these had been artificially improved with the usual German thoroughness. The position did not lack depth, for behind the mountain strongholds there were second lines of defence almost equally strong, in addition to the fortress of Bizerta itself and the inner defences of Tunis and Cape Bon.

WITH fifteen divisions of picked and experienced troops, Von Arnim had a formidable army with which to conduct a protracted defence if he handled it skilfully and economically. Except in the matter of armour and petrol supply there was no immediate prospect that he would run short of munitions or food. Although he could not hope to equal the immense weight of artillery that could be concentrated against him, that is a disadvantage the defence always experiences. On the other hand, in minefields he had a weapon which has proved highly effective in strengthening the power of

defence, and he had ample supplies of mines to enable him to develop its use to the utmost.

The chief disadvantage he suffered from was inferiority in the air, owing to the limited number of airfields available for short-range aircraft and to shortage of petrol. There can be no doubt that the supremacy in the air established by the Allies, if not the main cause of the initial breakdown of the enemy's defence, contributed immensely to its rapid and complete collapse. Valuable as had been air cooperation during the initial attacks on the enemy's defences, it was in exploitation of success and in pursuit that air supremacy became the decisive factor.

Credit for victory must primarily be given to the skill and courage of the attacking infantry, which can seldom have been equalled, and to the support given by artillery. It was their efforts which wore down the enemy's defences and opened the way for the decisive exploitation by aircraft and armour which produced such astoundingly rapid results.

It may be long before the full account of the exploits of the fighting troops can be fully recorded, but it can already be seen with

what consummate generalship their efforts were directed. It is abundantly clear that the enemy was not merely out-fought and crushed by greater weight of armament, but that he was completely out-generalled.

THE sequence of General Alexander's operations is interesting. First came the very quick attack of the 8th Army on the Enfidaville line, which drove the enemy back to his main position. Some surprise was expressed by the critics that the 1st Army did not attack simultaneously. Presumably the reasons were that the 8th Army attack was only a preliminary operation, intended to establish a threat to the enemy's southern flank while the regrouping of Alexander's command was in progress. Faced with a particularly strong position, with its advanced depots probably still insufficiently stocked for a prolonged major effort, the 8th Army had little chance of achieving decisive success. Its main task was to mislead the enemy and to contain a large part of the strength he had available.

The 1st Army with which Alexander meant to make his decisive attack had a considerable distance to advance and a number of enemy strong-points to capture before it had a reasonable chance of effecting a breakthrough. Its initial attacks began two days after the 8th Army attack and in combination with the action of the French towards Pont du Fahs served further to mislead Von Arnim into believing that his southern flank was chiefly threatened. The enemy consequently expended a considerable part of his armour in meeting the 1st Army in the Koursia plain, where the threat to Pont du Fahs was developing.

The 1st Army's drive towards Tebourba was also vigorously opposed, and met with counter-attacks. These preliminary attacks, however, made considerable progress, and the taking of Longstop Hill and Jebel Bou Aoukas, combined with the partial encirclement of Pont du Fahs and the 8th Army's attitude, all tended to convince Von Arnim that Alexander's main effort would be made in the south and that, therefore, he had little to fear in the north.

EVEN when the American 2nd Corps appeared on the northern front, having by a wonderful cross-country march been switched from the extreme right to the extreme left of Alexander's line, it did not excite his suspicions. Possibly underrating the offensive capacity of American troops, he may have thought they had been brought in on what was likely to be a quiet part of the front, and so been all the more convinced that the 1st Army was the immediate danger. Characteristically, and in accordance with German doctrine, he decided to meet that danger by counter-attacking ; and it seems probable that he drew on his northern front reserves to provide the striking force he required. With the 8th Army apparently engaged in preparations for renewed attack, it is unlikely that he weakened his force facing it.

During the last week of April Von Arnim delivered his counter-attacks with the greatest ferocity, but they were met with equally fierce resistance and succeeded only in recovering a little lost ground, though this included the recapture of the important key point of Bou Aoukas. By Sunday, May 2, both sides appeared to have fought themselves to exhaustion ; but whereas Von Arnim had expended his reserves, Alexander had still strong forces in hand, including those of the 8th Army which was still uncommitted to a major attack. That Alexander switched a considerable part of the 8th Army—the 7th Armoured Division and the 4th Indian Division—to take part in the decisive attack on the 1st Army front, has just been reported.

The enemy having expended his reserves and exhausted his troops in the counter-attacks, Alexander was now in a position to

LAST LAP TO TUNIS. Near Bou Arada on the S. Tunisian front, these men of the 1st Army move up through standing corn preparatory to attacking Axis positions in this area. Furious fighting at Bou Arada in mid-April, 1943, developed into one of the decisive battles for Tunis.
Photo, British Official: Crown Copyright

FINAL PHASE IN TUNISIA. With the occupation of Tunis and Bizerta by the Allies on May 7, 1943 the surviving fragments of Von Arnim's once-great army were hounded into the Cap Bon peninsula. All organised resistance ceased on May 12. This map shows (dotted) the line on April 24, and the direction of subsequent Allied thrusts. *By courtesy of The Times*

make his decisive onslaught. He may have postponed it for a day or so in hopes that the weather, which for a week had been restricting air operations, would improve. At any rate before it was delivered came the unexpected collapse of the northern front.

The Americans, far from having been given a defensive role, had been attacking-with great vigour, magnificently assisted on their left by the French Moroccan Corps. They had made considerable progress and captured important key-points with the support of an ever-increasing weight of artillery fire.

LACKING reserves and under the onslaught of troops that had with experience made immense strides in tactical efficiency, the defence wilted. Apparently hoping to escape the grave danger of a sudden collapse, withdrawal to the inner Bizerta defences was ordered. The decision entailed the abandonment of the important road junction of Mateur and the possible complete isolation of the Bizerta fortress. But the decision came too late. At the first signs of retreat, the Americans and Moroccans, without hesitation or delay, started in fierce pursuit ; and the enemy never succeeded in rallying effectively in spite of the strong defences available. Once again it was proved that the strongest works cannot be held by demoralized troops. The capture of Mateur on May 3 also opened a line of approach to the flank of the Axis troops opposing the 1st Army at Tebourba.

Yet this unexpected success was probably not the signal for the decisive 1st Army attack which was by now almost ready for delivery. Preceded on May 5 by a local attack to recover J. Bou Aoukas, the main attack was delivered on the next day. The infantry assault, preceded by a devastating air and artillery bombardment, broke through the weakened crust of the Axis mountain defences and, as at Alamein, opened a gap for the waiting armour to break through into the open

country. Delivered on a narrow front and aimed, not as in previous attacks towards Tebourba or Pont du Fahs, but straight at Tunis through Massicault, it was a blitz-krieg attack which in a matter of a few hours disrupted completely the whole German scheme of defence.

But we may ask ourselves, could our infantry have forced the gap for the armour if German reserves had not previously been exhausted and wrongly used ? The village

of Massicault, which had been prepared for hedgehog defence, fell without resistance. The counter-attacks which Von Arnim had delivered may have caused a few days' delay, but at the sacrifice of ability to offer prolonged resistance. When the crisis came Von Arnim's reserves were either exhausted or in the wrong place.

Perhaps the most astounding feature in the German collapse was the fall of Bizerta, a fortress designed and equipped to stand a long siege. It is evident that it was no part of the German plan to abandon the place in order to concentrate their whole force for a final stand in the Cape Bon peninsula. Every credit must be given to the Americans and French for the speed and vigour with which they pressed home their attack ; but it is inconceivable that they could have reached the fortress but for the breakdown of German morale, due very largely to the mistakes made by Von Arnim.

NOW that the battle has been won so decisively, we may consider whether after all in the long run it was not to our advantage that the first attempt to seize Tunis and Bizerta failed. It induced Hitler to expend a substantial number of his best troops and to incur immense losses of men, aircraft, and shipping in maintaining them in their dangerous position—and that at a time when all his resources were needed in Russia. The defeat he has suffered is immensely damaging to his prestige, and it has still further undermined belief in German invincibility and military capacity.

Still more important perhaps, the campaign has given the Allied army invaluable experience, and welded it into a magnificent striking force. An easy occupation of Tunisia would have left it far from prepared to undertake the more difficult operations that may be believed to lie ahead.

The six months that have passed since the first landing in Algeria do not therefore represent lost time. As a matter of fact, in any case a considerable part of the time would have been needed to disembark the whole force with its stores, to build up its base establishments, and to complete its organization. Those processes, no doubt, have been expedited under the pressure of the immediate needs of the campaign ; and opportunities have been given to correct faults which might not otherwise have been detected. Now the war in Africa is won. A new phase begins.

AXIS PRISONERS IN TUNIS were rounded up and marched away after our men entered the capital. It was estimated that 50,000 were taken in Northern Tunisia in two days, and very shortly the number was more than trebled. This radioed photo—the first to be received from the captured city—shows some of the great host of the vanquished moving off under the guns of a British tank.
PAGE 771
Photo, Planet News

After Six Months Struggle in the Mountains

Gen. G. S. PATTON watches his men advance during a battle for enemy-held hills in Central Tunisia. Commander of the 2nd U.S. Army Corps, he was succeeded (it was announced on May 9, 1943) by Maj.-Gen Bradley.

Sherman tanks (right) advance towards the Goubellat Plain, between Medjez-el-Bab and Pont du Fahs (see panorama in p. 797).

REMOVING AXIS MINES from the path of the advancing American troops in Central Tunisia. These U.S. Army Engineers are shown clearing one of the innumerable death-traps set by the enemy to impede the Allied push towards Tunis and Bizerta. Having located the mines by their detectors, these specially-trained men remove them by hand. The soldier on the right holds a mine which he has just extracted from its hiding-place in the ground.

Photos, British Official: Crown Copyright, Planet News, Keystone

Eisenhower's Armies Enter Upon the Last Lap

MEDJEZ-EL-BAB was the scene of some of the fiercest fighting on the Northern Tunisian front during the second and third weeks of April 1943. Desperate battles were fought by the 1st Army in the hills N. and N.W. of the town where the enemy was strongly entrenched between Sidi Nsir and Jebel Ahmera (Longstop Hill).

Medjez was originally taken by us on Nov. 25, 1942, and was of great strategic importance. 1st Army men had many savage hand-to-hand encounters with Von Arnim's crack troops during the last offensives. Left, a long column of German prisoners marches through the ruined street of the town en route to a prisoners-of-war camp

Below, a "Priest" 105-mm. gun mounted on a Gen. Grant chassis in action with the 8th Army.

8th ARMY IN ENFIDAVILLE, Tunisian town N. of Sousse, taken by them on April 20, 1943. The men shown above are searching a row of houses for enemy stragglers. Enfidaville was the coastal anchor of the Axis line running west through the mountains. It was here that Rommel launched an un-successful counter-attack against Gen. Montgomery's forces as the latter advanced towards the town. When our infantry entered the place they found that the enemy had withdrawn completely.

Photos, British Official: Crown Copyright

Meanwhile, in the northern sector of the Tunisian front the 1st Army were also heavily engaged. On May 3 the capture of Mateur by the U.S. 2nd Corps greatly facilitated further advances. Vital road and railway junction, 20 miles S.W. of Bizerta, Mateur was taken after a 15-mile advance. Above, British troops advance in single file along the Mateur road. Their way lies across a rocky landscape which is characteristic of this region of Northern Tunisia.

The Truth About Britain's Tank-Busters

Recently the phrase "tank-buster" has made frequent appearances in accounts of the fighting in North Africa. This article by HAROLD A. ALBERT explains the term and mentions by name some of the men who have developed the technique of "tank-busting" into a fine art.

TANK-BUSTING — the concentrated and scientific "tin-opening" that punished the Panzers so severely in Tunisia— is not new, although its secret was fully revealed only in the break-through at the Mareth positions. It first hit the enemy between the eyes at Alamein last October. The man behind the punch was a secret ace from India, Wing-Commander Roger Cave Porteous.

Thirty years old, holding a commission for seven years in the R.A.F., he had never been decorated although he had commanded his squadron since its arrival in the Middle East. A brilliant and courageous flyer, he was probably chosen by Air Marshals Tedder and Coningham for his great skill and his distance from the limelight.

Tank-busting as he developed it, in a Hurricane fitted with special heavy-calibre guns for attacking armoured vehicles, was born of dive-bombing and an idea dating from the old R.F.C. days, when planes were fitted with a Heath Robinson device which exploded a charge backwards in order to compensate for the powerful recoil of the guns. The Nazis had come near the idea in the twin-engined Henschel 129, with a 30-mm. cannon slung externally beneath its fuselage. They missed success, perhaps in tactics, perhaps in inferiority of armament. In the hands of Roger Porteous, however, it was clear from the start that we had hit on an innovation of power and supremacy.

The secret lay in the two 40-mm. (about 1·57 in.) Vickers cannon, one beneath each wing. Weighing 320 lb. apiece, too large to go inside the fuselage, they were the biggest weapons ever mounted in single-seater fighters. The shells alone weighed 2½ lb.

each and the guns were capable of automatic or single-shot fire.

In the course of nine sorties during the bitter sky-fighting of the Gazala line, Porteous destroyed 5 enemy tanks, 7 lorries and innumerable other vehicles. Encountering two troop carriers on the way home during one trip, he was tempted to try out the combat strength of his unexpected armament, and the carriers were literally shattered to fragments. Soon he was leading in actual training flights over the enemy lines the sweeps that became known as the Porteous school of tank-busting.

SPECIALIZED knowledge—the need for distinguishing at a glance the silhouette of Allied and Axis tanks and armoured cars— could be taught on the ground. The ice-cold technique of low-level precision attacks into enemy armour could be gained only in the sky. Flying skill exceeding the average, plus iron nerves, was essential. The star "pupil," Wing-Commander Howard Burton—who with Squadron-Leader Weston-Burt was to head the great break-through towards Gabes—had won the Sword of Honour at Cranwell. In addition, he had gained the D.F.C. for "coolness" after 50 or 60 sorties had brought him a bag of six enemy aircraft. Another pioneer, South Africa's Captain Johannes Faure, had been mentioned in dispatches as "an exceptionally good leader" and had destroyed at least five enemy planes.

Ace flyers all, the first "tin-openers" were frankly aware of the risks involved. In taking aim, sighting first on a burst of tracer, they might be below the bursts from the Breda guns, but there could be "no

room to wriggle," no chance to avoid ground fire, indeed no time for evasive action. The vital essential was pre-arranged team-work. Spattering the target, the first tank-buster would be closely followed by a second, swerving in sharply from a different direction and confusing the gunners.

That was the primary, simple, but dangerous trick of the Porteous school. Before the enemy knew what it was all about, tank-busters were operating in Libya. Six Italian tanks were caught, sitting in a straight line —and were smashed to pieces. One pilot crippled as many as twenty tanks in less than a week. On the opening day of the Alamein offensive 19 enemy tanks were hit by a single wing. This success foreshadowed the 32 enemy tanks wrecked at El Hamma in April last and the 50 vehicles destroyed and hundreds damaged on the Sfax road, when the further refinement of fighter cover for the Hurriguns enabled tank-busting as a fine art to be almost doubly effective.

Before long, as the tank-busters swept through to Daba and Fuga, many new men had won their laurels in "double sorties," as they were called. Flying Officer William McRae harvested a D.F.C. for his "fearless determination to achieve success." Sergeant George Chaundy, formerly an Oxford mechanic, Flight Sergeant Kevin Clarke, of Birmingham, and Aberdeen's Sergeant Forbes Fraser—all these flyers of 148 Squadron were conspicuously successful.

IT was never easy. The road to success in this new branch of flying technique was paved with heroism. Thus one of Porteous's right-hand men, Flight-Lieut. Allan Simpson, was wounded in the chest by ground fire as he swept into the armour clusters at Bir Hacheim. Still he continued to attack, scoring one hit after another. Then, weakened by loss of blood and with his right arm useless, he attempted to gain height. His plane was hit by the barrage. Hot oil spraying his face, blinded by smoke, Simpson parachuted at only 500 feet. The citation to his D.F.C. justifiably described this deed of gallantry as "an outstanding devotion to duty."

Then there was Sergeant John Price, formerly a Yorkshire electrician, who was wounded in the head by a shell splinter and, though dazed and suffering from concussion, still carried on. There was Lieutenant Douglas Rogan, who had his right foot virtually shot off during an attack on a tank concentration, but still brought his plane back to base—an amazing effort in face of the pain and shock—and made a good landing. And there was Sergeant John Strain, who had an artery punctured and was nearly blown off his machine by a burst of flak but remained undaunted . . .

These are a few among the many tank-busting founder members. Today they and many newcomers to the business have spread their work from auxiliary attacks on armoured vehicles to dug-in emplacements and ground offensive formations of all kinds.

Rommel undoubtedly planned a surprise with his Mark IVs and Vs at Mareth. They were dug into pits in the sides of the wadis, and only tank-busting tactics could have opened them up. That scores of tanks were destroyed and hundreds damaged without—in some instances—a chance to fire a shot is now a matter of history. In General Montgomery's phrase, such intimate and close support between air and army had never been achieved before. It was an inspiration to all the troops—and a surpassing sign of Hurrigun victories yet to come.

HURRICANE IID FIGHTER'S ARMAMENT includes two 40-mm. guns. Fitted under the wings, each gun fires a 2½-lb. shell and is capable of automatic or single-shot fire. This photograph shows the formidable armament of one of these specialized aircraft which have played so successful a part in attacks on enemy tanks and armoured fighting vehicles in N. Africa. (See also p. 775).

Photo, British Official: Crown Copyright

How the R.A.F. Deals with the Nazi Armour

DUAL ATTACK BY R.A.F. 'TIN OPENERS' IN TUNISIA. This drawing gives a vivid impression of the tactics employed by our Hurricanes when carrying out their paralysing assaults on enemy tanks. By working in pairs and coming in from different directions, they make it impossible for the tank under attack to follow the movements of both aircraft with its turret, and it is thus apt to fall a victim to the 'tank-busters' when unsupported by other fighting vehicles. (See article opposite.)
Drawing by courtesy of The Sphere

'TANK-BUSTERS' IN FLIGHT. Each of the 40 mm. guns carried by these aircraft weighs only 320 lb., and in addition to the cannon the Hurricane is armed with two ·303 Browning machine-guns. These machines first went into action against Rommel's armoured vehicles in Cyrenaica in June 1942. During the following month one squadron alone accounted for 74 tanks, 46 lorries, eight armoured cars, four six-wheeled troop carriers and three bowsers—all for the loss of one pilot.

PAGE 775
Photo, British Official; Crown Copyright

GIANT LANDING BARGE, filled to capacity with troops who are standing shoulder to shoulder, is here shown doing ferry duty in the harbour at Tripoli. Italian apprehensions of an Allied invasion deepened considerably as the Axis suffered defeat after defeat in Tunisia. Landing-craft, such as that seen above, might well be employed one day in taking troops and equipment across the Mediterranean.

Photo, Associated Press

THE WAR AT SEA

by Francis E. McMurtrie

ONE of the direct consequences of the fall of Bizerta will be the facility afforded the British Mediterranean Fleet for making use of that port as a base. Any damage done to the harbour installations can hardly affect this fact.

Since the French occupied Tunisia in 1881, Bizerta has been systematically developed as a naval base, for which it is naturally well adapted. At Bizerta itself is the commercial port and outer harbour ; this is connected by a dredged channel, having a uniform depth of water of 39 feet, with Bizerta Lake. Here are situated the naval dockyard and the town of Ferryville. There are four dry docks, of which the largest, 800 feet in length, could take a battleship or aircraft-carrier. Two others, each 656 feet long, are able to accommodate cruisers. The remaining one, 295 feet in length, is suitable for small destroyers, sloops or corvettes.

In the lake, which is eight miles across and roughly circular, there is room for a whole fleet. Its obvious weakness is that ships sunk in the dredged channel might insert the cork in the bottle, as it were ; but if this were done by the Germans before surrendering, the obstacle should not take long to remove, judging from the rapidity with which Benghazi and Tripoli harbours were cleared.

DRY docks cannot be destroyed, though the pumping plant by which they are either flooded or emptied might be wrecked. Heavy cranes and other mechanism may have been sabotaged ; but it may be assumed that the possibility of such obstacles having been left will have been foreseen, and that every possible arrangement will have been made in advance for putting in hand the necessary repairs as soon as the port is taken over by the Allied naval authorities.

Strategically, Bizerta is admirably situated for launching an attack upon Sicily or Sardinia, distant respectively some 90 and 125 miles. In the lake there is ample space for transports and landing-craft to assemble—though for that matter there are several hundred feet of quayage in the outer port from which troops could be embarked.

Interference by Axis aircraft from the other side of the Sicilian Channel should not be serious so long as we maintain our present superiority in the air. Actually, that advantage should tend to increase as time goes on, so that the passage of supplies through the Mediterranean to Egypt and Syria should soon be possible. This will obviate the long delay hitherto involved by the necessity of employing the route round the Cape of Good Hope. It was estimated some time ago by Admiral of the Fleet Sir Andrew Cunningham that this shortening of our sea supply route would be equivalent to an addition of 2,000,000 tons to Allied shipping resources. This implies a corresponding gain in the unceasing battle against the U-boats.

WHAT Could Italy's Navy Do in the Event of Invasion ?

In some quarters it has been predicted that the Germans will now seek to concentrate the greater part of their submarine strength in the Mediterranean, with the object of obstructing any invasion of Europe from Africa. This rather loses sight of the fact that similar efforts to interfere with seaborne supplies to our armies in North Africa failed to prevent their annihilating Arnim's forces. That being the case, what chance have German submarines of accomplishing anything appreciable, now that the whole of the southern shores of the Mediterranean are under Allied control ?

It is far more likely that the Germans will leave the unenviable task of meeting the menace of invasion from Africa to their wretched dupes, the Italians. In view of the consistent failure of the latter to accomplish anything at sea in the past, it may be questioned whether such opposition need be reckoned formidable.

At the same time, an examination of Italian naval strength may be of interest. It comprises seven battleships, the majority of which were last reported to be at Spezia, in Northern Italy. A report that three of these ships had proceeded to Taranto, in the south, is a little difficult to credit. Not only is it obviously bad strategy to divide forces in this way, but the disaster of November 8, 1940, when the Italian fleet at Taranto was crippled by a torpedo attack from British naval aircraft, proved that port to be no longer a safe one.

How many cruisers Italy has in service is uncertain. Not more than two, and probably only one, of the heavy 10,000-ton type have survived the hazards of war. There may be seven or eight of between 5,000 and 8,000 tons ; and in addition, several of the twelve new fast ships of the Regolo class, of 3,362 tons, are believed to have been completed. One of them was torpedoed and probably destroyed by a British submarine not long ago.

When the War began the Italian Navy possessed a strong force of destroyers and seagoing torpedo-boats, but losses in these classes have been very heavy. In the three weeks preceding the fall of Bizerta and Tunis at least eight were disposed of by the Royal Navy and Allied air forces. It is questionable if more than 60 could be mustered to meet an invasion threat, so many having been uselessly expended in escorting Axis convoys to Africa.

There are, of course, the small craft which we should class as motor torpedo-boats and motor gunboats, but which the Italians refer to as M.A.S.—an abbreviation for *motoscafi anti-sommergibili*, or anti-submarine launches. They were extremely proud of these little craft in pre-War days, boasting that they would accomplish marvels in the way of torpedoing enemy warships. In practice they have proved a sad disappointment, even though the greatest bravery was shown by Italian officers in abortive attacks on the harbours of Alexandria, Malta and Gibraltar. How many of them still remain at the enemy's disposal it is impossible to say, as they can be built very rapidly—possibly a hundred.

ITALIAN submarines numbered over 100 when war began, but losses have probably reduced this figure by at least half. Some of the larger ones are believed still to be operating outside the Mediterranean, in conjunction with the U-boat packs ; but there should remain available a considerable number which would have to be reckoned with when attempting a landing on Italian soil.

For submarine operations, however, the Mediterranean is not an ideal sea, as the water is unusually clear and the weather is often bright. At this time of year, too, the hours of daylight are so many that an additional handicap is imposed. In such circumstances the remarkable achievements of our own submarines are more than ever to be commended ; but up to now the Italians have not shown themselves to be capable of such feats.

It would seem, therefore, that any serious naval resistance to an Allied invasion of Europe from Africa is scarcely to be feared. Should the Italians at last take their courage in their hands and send their entire fleet out to do or die, no one (we may be sure) would welcome the decision more warmly than Sir Andrew Cunningham.

Air Force Girls Lend a Hand with the Sea Balloons

W.A.A.F. PERSONNEL IN BALLOON COMMAND are doing a front-line job. These airwomen help to keep our sea balloons aloft, for among their many important tasks they service the barges and drifters of our water-borne barrage. Daily rations for the men aboard the barges have to be weighed and checked, and then the ration-vessel sets out for the balloon boats. W.A.A.F.s are here seen loading ration-containers on to a drifter of the sea balloon fleet.

Photo, Keystone

Gentlemen, a Toast: The Charwomen of the Sea!

Prepared for the Admiralty by the Ministry of Information and published by H.M. Stationery Office, His Majesty's Minesweepers is a well-illustrated ninepenny booklet describing the work of that great fleet of little ships which clear the seaways of the deadly "fish" strewn with such indiscriminate devilry by enemy planes and ships.

CHARWOMEN of the sea: it is a well-chosen description. In every town and city those hard-working women, the "chars," are "up with the dawn, sweeping and clearing passage and office before their betters are abroad. Most people take their work for granted. Few know how they live; few even see them, save perhaps for a glimpse of one adjusting her bonnet as she departs. They are sturdy, weather-beaten and good-humoured. Rain, hail or snow finds them at their task; and when there is a blitz they take it with a jest." To continue the quotation from the official account of His Majesty's Minesweepers:

Like them, the minesweepers are as undeterred by blizzards as by bombs, and they have a spirit and tradition of their own. They are seen by few outside their own calling, for by the time the big ships are due their sweeping is done, their gear packed, and they are under steam for home.

Over twenty-five thousand men are now engaged in the Minesweeping Service of the Royal Navy, and every month new ships go from the yards to join those which have been sweeping since the War began. Fleet sweepers and trawlers, paddlers, motor-minesweepers, whalers and drifters have been and are engaged in continuous sweeps, making the channels safe for the convoys and the ships of war. Most people seem to think that minesweeping is confined to the English Channel, but in fact these handy men of the Navy have cleared up many a minefield in the Mediterranean, off the coasts of Africa, in the waters of Australasia, in the Indian Ocean and the South China Sea. In Arctic waters, too, they have provided a safe passage for the convoys proceeding to Murmansk. It is impossible to calculate the value of their service; they have caught and detonated thousands of mines, any one of which might have blown a ship to pieces. Every minefield cleared is a battle won.

Headquarters of the Minesweeping Service is H.M.S. Vernon, which came into prominence when (as is fully told in the book under review) Lt.-Cmdr. Ouvry and other members of its staff solved the dangerous puzzle of that "scientist's paradise," the German magnetic mine.

IN this war as in the last trawlers are the mainstay of the Minesweeping Service. At scores of ports round the British coast they may be seen, lying three or four abreast alongside the quay, steaming out to their sweeping grounds, or returning to port after a stiff spell of duty. They are seaworthy little vessels of steel construction with high bows, with a length of about 140 ft. and a displacement of between 200 and 300 tons. At sea they are just numbers, but in harbour they display their names in white letters on a black board. Many of them have their distinctive badges; many have a swastika painted on their funnel, indicating a Nazi plane brought down, while the tally of mines destroyed is kept by chevrons and stars. H.M.T. Rolls Royce holds the record at present of over 150 mines to her credit.

The larger and faster of the minesweepers operate with the Fleet; and their increased armament enables them to undertake escort and anti-submarine duties when they are not actually sweeping. Recently one of them rammed and destroyed a German submarine in Arctic waters, and when H.M.S. Edinburgh was torpedoed in May 1942 three of the Halcyons—a type of Fleet sweeper, having a displacement of some 800 tons, a complement of 80, and a speed of 17 knots—put up a spirited fight which will live in the history of the Service.

The Flag Officer in command had given orders that they should retire at full speed under a smoke screen if attacked by surface-craft. These orders never reached them. When the Edinburgh was hit, instead of turning away they turned towards the enemy destroyers, "going in like three young

FIGHTING AN UNSEEN ENEMY lurking under the surface of the sea, men aboard our minesweepers carry out their hazardous tasks by day and night. These officers maintain a keen vigil from the bridge of their sweeper.
Photo, Planet News

terriers," as the Admiral said, and firing whenever visibility permitted. Then, while one made a smoke screen, the other two went alongside the sinking cruiser and took off the whole ship's company. The Admiral was among the last to leave. As he stepped on to the sweeper's quarter-deck her Commanding Officer saluted.

"Everything correct, sir. Your flag is hoisted."

The Admiral looked upwards. Flying at the masthead was the Cross of St. George, with two red balls in the upper and lower cantons. Its ragged edge suggested that it was a Senior Officer's pendant from which the tails had been cut, and the red balls looked as though they had been hastily daubed on with red paint. But there was no mistaking it for anything but a Rear-Admiral's flag.

It was a gesture which no German could hope to understand: but one that Nelson himself would have appreciated.

These Halcyons, it may be mentioned, are mostly named after minesweepers of 1914; Halcyon herself was built under the 1931 Naval estimates, and 16 further ships of the same class were added in later years. One of them, Seagull, was the first rivetless ship built for the Royal Navy, her construction being entirely welded. Then there is the Bangor class of 20 or more ships, which have a displacement of about 700 tons, and a main armament of a 3-inch gun forward and a pom-pom aft; their complement is about 80.

Yet a third class of Fleet minesweepers is the Albury, consisting of 20 ships built under the emergency programme of the last war, and launched between June 1917 and August 1919. Their displacement is 710 tons, and their speed 16 knots. They have a complement of 73, and are armed with a 4-inch gun apiece. They are the only coal-burners left in the Royal Navy: hence their nickname of "Smoky Joes."

IN the annals of minesweeping "Operation Dynamo" stands out as one of the most amazing achievements of the little ships. "Operation Dynamo" was the evacuation of Dunkirk. The Smoky Joes were there, the paddle-sweepers and the drifters.

The senior ship of the paddle-sweeper flotilla, the Sandown (Commander K. M. Greig, R.N.), was bombed repeatedly on every passage across the Channel, but was never hit; her ratings ascribed her good fortune to their mascot, a dachshund who became known as Bombproof Bella. But two other ships of the flotilla were not so fortunate. The Gracie Fields sank on her second trip, and the Brighton Queen sank after striking a wreck on her first return passage. As she went down the fourth ship of the flotilla, the Medway Queen (Lt. A. T. Cook, R.N.R.), took off all the survivors. The Medway Queen made seven trips to and from Dunkirk, so setting up the sweepers' record.

Of another flotilla of paddle-sweepers that reached Dunkirk from Harwich, the Waverley (Lt. S. F. Harmer-Elliott, R.N.V.R.) had embarked 600 troops when twelve Heinkels bombed her from a height of 8,000 ft. A bomb passed straight through the ship, and within a minute of the order "Abandon ship" the Waverley had gone down. Lt. Harmer-Elliott was rescued after being 45 minutes in the water, but many of his ship's company perished, together with between 300 and 400 of the soldiers. The other ships of the flotilla, Marmion, Duchess of Fife, and Oriole, were more fortunate, doing magnificent work in the evacuation. For four days and nights their men worked without sleep, almost without food, and between them they brought 4,755 troops safely home.

Finally, mention is made of H.M.T. St. Melanté (Skipper F. Hayward).

When the Germans invaded Holland she was sweeping off The Hook, and the skipper and several members of the crew were wounded by bomb splinters. Then she went to Flushing, where with her consort the Arctic Hunter she was bombed and raked by machine-gun fire. After sweeping the harbour entrance at Zeebrugge, St. Melanté went in turn to Dunkirk, Le Havre, and St. Nazaire. From St. Nazaire she took off 670 men and carried them safely to the transports waiting in the harbour. She was there when the Lancastria went down. Then as the troopships were ready to sail Skipper Hayward was told, "Although your crew are off their feet, you must sweep us out."

So at dawn the St. Melanté and the trawler Asama went ahead of the great convoy—twenty merchant-ships packed with troops with ten fishing trawlers and the escort of destroyers. They swept from the lock gates into the open sea; then on either side of the convoy steamed with it to Britain.

Hitler's 'Secret Weapon' Was Met and Mastered

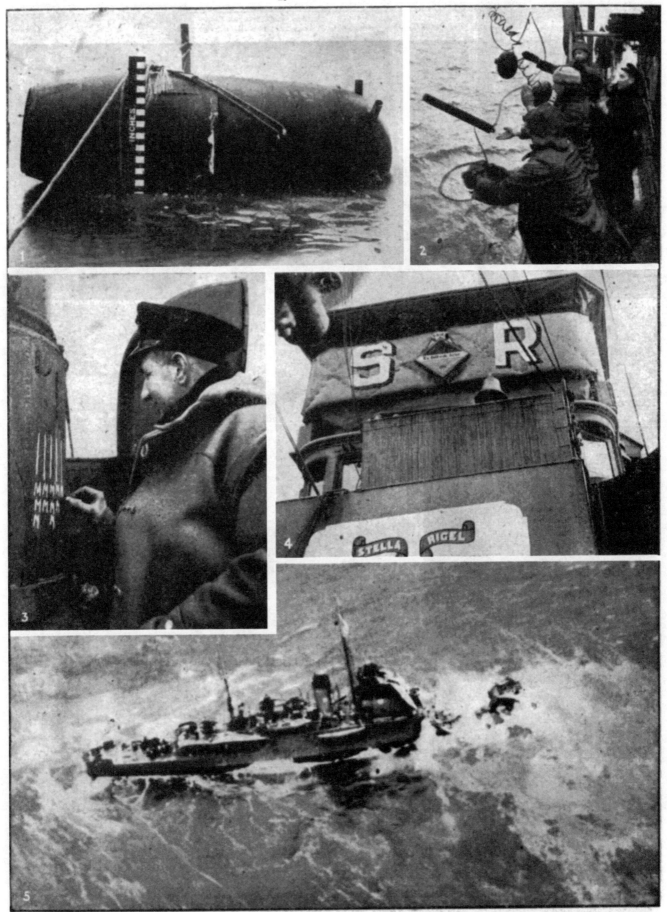

FREEING THE SEA TRAFFIC LANES. 1, This German magnetic mine—Hitler's secret weapon—dropped in the Thames Estuary on Nov. 23, 1939, was the first to be recovered intact. 2, "Bosun's Nightmare," so-called because of its tangles, was the first answer to the magnetic mine. 3, M's denote magnetic mines destroyed, and strokes seapaths cleared. 4, "To hell with Hitler," is Minesweeper Stella Rigel's motto. 5, This sweeper makes for home after being badly damaged by a mine.

Photos from His Majesty's Minesweepers

Heroic Figures in Britain's Submarine Service

MEN AND SHIPS ON OUR UNDERWATER FRONT: 1, Lt. J. S. Stevens, described by Gen. Eisenhower as "the maddest captain in the trade," has been awarded the D.S.O. He served in the Thunderbolt—previously Thetis—when she sank a U-boat on her first patrol, and was later appointed to command to another submarine. On April 21, 1943 the Thunderbolt's loss was announced. 2, H.M. Submarine Ursula has a long and distinguished war record, dating from her daring raid on Nazi warships in the R. Elbe in 1939. Here she flies the Jolly Roger recording her tally of victims. Bars represent supply ships sunk, the oil installations, viaducts and trains denote shore bombardments, while the stars indicate gun actions. 3, Cmdr. J. W. Linton, D.S.O., D.S.C., R.N., who, it was announced on May 3, 1943, was lost with his ship Turbulent. He was estimated to have sunk some 27 enemy vessels. 4, "Torpedo running, sir!" is telephoned to the captain in the control-room. 5, Gun action aboard a British submarine. 6, End of the patrol; a submarine enters port.

This Way for the Air Route Across Africa!

ON THE BRITISH W. AFRICAN COAST is the airfield pictured above, a vital link in the supply of aircraft to the African front and Middle East. Here, crated machines, shipped from Britain, are unpacked, assembled and tested before being flown across Africa by pilots who will later use them for Operations. The creation of an airfield from a tropical forest was a formidable task. 1, Palm tree falls to native workers' axes. 2, In building runways "metalling" was carried in baskets on the heads of labourers. 3, Hurricane fuselages, wings and tail units being taken from crates for assembly. Two native porters on the left are carrying on their heads long-range petrol tanks to be fitted under fighters' wings. 4, Hurricanes ready for flight-testing before being handed over to pilots who will then fly them to their destination. 5, Hawker Hurricane on flight-test after assembly on the tropic aerodrome.

Women Make Good as Aircraft Surgeons

That the duties performed by the women in the Services are many and varied, and often highly responsible, will be clear from what we have said about them in our pages. And here W. J. BENTLEY writes of yet another job which feminine brains and hands have learnt to do —and learnt to do well.

Now it can be revealed that on many R.A.F. stations—where pilots train for daylight sweeps and mass raids, on Master I and III trainers—nearly 80 per cent of the flight mechanics are women. They're the girls who nurse the planes, and Waafs in the servicing parties—a special branch of flight mechanic, which is a Group II trade, the second highest group of skilled tradesmen and tradeswomen to be found in the entire Royal Air Force.

Each aircraft is inspected every 24 hours, and thoroughly overhauled after it has flown a stipulated time. In the 24-hour inspection of the Masters the girls check up on the filling of the oil, fuel and supercharged oil tanks, check over the controls and run the engines on the ground, just as the men do, before signing certificates of airworthiness. At some stations a special mixed team, of men and women, is responsible for the airworthiness of each individual machine ; at Master training centres all take a share and have a joint responsibility for all aircraft.

"Like the men of our group," a girl flight mechanic says, "we are divided into 'flight mechanics A,' who do the routine inspections and maintenance of air-frames and undercarriages, and 'flight mechanics E,' who are responsible for inspection, starting and running of aero-motors." When girls first arrived at one station a few months ago the men did all the work, but the girls have now taken over an equal and independent share under the N.C.O. gang-leaders.

On that station the other day I saw a girl fitting a new filter to a Pratt and Whitney Twin Wasp motor, while another was fitting new plugs—a very different job from changing the plugs of a family car ! Another girl at work on the Kestrel motor of a Master I was fitting new H.T. leads, while two girls together were shortening the jack on an undercarriage leg because the mechanism was not locking properly. Their job had to be done with the utmost care, for a crash-landing would otherwise result.

Official opinion has been against the use of girl flight mechanics on operational stations, as it was felt they would not be able to stand the irregular hours. Few of the girls knew anything about engineering in "civvy street." One I met had been a dressmaker, another a housekeeper ; one a shop assistant, another an armament inspector. As recruits they were given a psychology test before beginning the course of training ; and though they do not have to fly on Operations, they nevertheless do have to fly on occasion.

All R.A.F. flight mechanics, men and women, must expect to fly in aircraft for which they have signed certificates of airworthiness. The flying instructors of the stations take them up and can explain to them anything slightly awry in the performance of the machine better than they could do on the ground.

There's a team of flight mechanic "A" girls fixing on their parachute harness now before going up. They wear flying helmets and seat-type parachutes are attached over their blue overalls.

Air-screws of the planes are swung by girls, others hang on to the tails to keep them down, and girls, too, remove the chocks in professional manner.

The spirit of these ground crews is perfect. They get little glory, but they love the job with a craftsman's pride in it. And at an engineering centre not far away are other girls who make the mass raids and day sorties a success. They are the girls of a Spitfire hospital who "nurse" broken planes. At one of these centres 150 girls—ex-domestic servants, clerks and housewives—have become skilled nurses for damaged fighter aircraft.

When you hear on the radio that "two of our fighters were damaged," or that "the pilot, his machine badly shot-up, returned safely" —these are the girls who bring the aircraft back into commission again, often within a few hours.

TWO W.A.A.F. CORPORALS, E. Chapman (left) and K. Donovan (right), sparking-plug testers of Coastal Command, flew some hundreds of miles recently to complete urgent work in connexion with the servicing of aircraft in the North.
Photos, British Official : Crown Copyright

All the girls working on this scheme are expert aircraft surgeons, though none has been at the factory more than 10 months, working on a scheme suggested to the Ministry of Aircraft Production by Lord Nuffield. They work so swiftly that a "fly-in"—a machine badly shot-up but capable of being flown—is usually in the air again on Operations in a matter of hours.

Sometimes the machines are "ferried" in, but often a Spit or a Hurribox is flown in from its squadron by the pilot himself. "That's why we can feel we really are helping the pilots," one of the girls explained, as she looked up from a riveting job in the cockpit of a Spitfire VB. "When the boys come in here and tell us how they escaped with their lives after getting over the target, and so getting badly shot-up, it's all the incentive we need to get those planes back into action again as quickly as possible."

As each girl finishes her job it is wheeled outside, and an R.A.F. test-pilot takes it up for fault-finding. Cynics might think that he risks his neck by having to fly once-damaged aircraft that have been mended by women.

But there is striking proof how well these girls keep the Spits and Hurriboxes in the air. You see, as the test-pilot taxies in he sees a slim girl standing at the far end of the field. She is easily identifiable in her white linen suit. She is the checker. In her book have to go details of all the defects spotted by the test-pilot, and which must be put right before the machine is flown back to the Operational station. In her book there are barely four pages of complaints in the course of the whole ten months. That's proof.

W.A.A.F. FLIGHT MECHANICS are doing splendid work for the R.A.F. in Flying Training Command. The safety of our pilots depends to a considerable extent upon the skill and care of these airwomen. They check the filling of fuel and oil tanks, etc., and finally they fly with the pilot to test the machine which they have serviced. Here some of them are hard at work on a trainer.
Photo, British Official : Crown Copyright

He Led the Victors of North Africa

Second to America's General Eisenhower in command of the armies of the United Nations in the Mediterranean basin, General the Hon. Sir Harold Alexander served in France for the greater part of the last war, receiving the D.S.O., M.C., and the Legion of Honour. In this War he was in command of the last British forces at Dunkirk, and won deserved renown for his masterly leadership in Burma two years later. Then as C.-in-C. Middle East he launched at El Alamein the great series of victories which was crowned on May 7, 1943 by the Allies' triumphal entry into Tunis and Bizerta.

Nature Aided the Nazis in Tunisia

Through April and into May the great battle of the Tunisian " box " went on, as Von Arnim strove desperately to avoid being thrown into the sea. To the uninitiated the Allies' progress seemed disappointingly slow, but these photographs show a countryside most admirably suited for defence by a determined adversary. 1, American M-10 tank destroyers, a new Ford product representing an improvement on the M-4 medium tank, rolling through an Arab farm ; 2, German 60-ton Tiger tanks, knocked out by gunners of the 1st Army, litter a Tunisian battlefield. Yet they were " invincible " !

Photos,
Crown Cop

Hard Was the Way Up Longstop

Barren mountain slopes, crags and precipitous gorges, forbidding heights towering above the plain—these are the main characteristics of the rocky wilderness whose conquest has demanded such a toll of human life and labour. Desolate appears the landscape seen by this machine-gunner perched above Heidous (3); but on Longstop Hill, the black ridge in the middle distance, the enemy lies ensconced. A craggy crest above Kelbine just captured by our men (4). Churchills approaching Longstop (5). So rough was the country that supplies had to be taken on mules (6); the village is Chaouach.

So This Is Tunis

When on the morrow of victory, Alexander's men go sightseeing in Tunis, what do they find? A city where the crust of modern French culture is pierced by such relics of Roman rule as this aqueduct (1), where the voice from the minaret calling the Moslem faithful to prayer (2) stills the noise of Oriental bazaars (4), a city of palm-lined avenues (3) and of close-packed homes of Arab and Jew in the native quarter, dominated by the great Mosque of the Olive Tree (5).

VIEWS & REVIEWS

Of Vital
War Books

by Hamilton Fyfe

I MUST confess to a prejudice. It is a prejudice against women in uniform. Very few of them seem able to wear it as a matter of course. Far too many have their hair absurdly frizzed or fluffed—I mean it looks absurd under a Service cap. Make-up on the face of a woman in uniform suggests the chorus of a revue. Indeed, I think I agree with a friend of mine who says that with rare exceptions they look like chorus girls or else like schoolmarms. Uniform destroys any distinction or personal charm a woman may possess when she is dressed like a woman; and it appears to bring out and emphasize all her less attractive points—in particular, ugly legs.

But when I read a book like Wings On Her Shoulders (Hutchinson, 8s. 6d.) I feel I have to take all that back. I feel that my prejudice is misplaced. I am moved to admiration and gratitude for the work women in uniform are doing—and, by the way, the photographs of them by Cecil Beaton are first-rate. The book is about the Women's Auxiliary Air Force—I suppose they must be called W.A.A.F.s, though I dislike the term as much as most of them (I believe) dislike it. I have seen lips curl and eyes flash at the query, "Do you prefer the Waafs to the Ats or the Wrens?"

Mrs. Bentley Beauman, the author, was once Woman Editor of The Yorkshire Post; she has put her book together with journalistic skill. It isn't literature, nowhere near it. Yet I can imagine it being a godsend to any historian writing a hundred years hence. For it isn't only about what the Waafs do in uniform; it throws light on the social, intellectual and economic standing of women generally at this present time. Take the matter of pay, for instance. The lowest ranking officer gets 7s. 10d. a day.

This brings her approximately £132 a year when income-tax has been deducted—or £11 a month. In addition she has allowances amounting to about 32s. a month. Her mess bill might be about £5; when she has paid it she has £7 13s. over for all other personal expenditure. As her uniform grant does not cover the cost of an officer's outfit, with tailors' bills rising, part of this has to go to pay the difference in the first months after she is commissioned. If she can provide her own amusement, has private money or friends in the R.A.F., she is well off. Otherwise, with her nose to the war wheel she must argue that all work doesn't necessarily make a dull dog; and if her mind runs in financial channels, there is always the thought that she may some day become a Squadron Officer at 19s..4d. a day and allowances.

ALL Waafs now get a hot, well-cooked dinner in the middle of the day if they are at a big station or in camp. Earlier on, their meals were not well arranged. Landladies at billets were paid 10d. a day for lodging and attendance, 9d. for breakfast, 8d. for high tea or supper. The airwomen got 1s. 2d. a day for their dinner at N.A.A.F.I. canteens, which were supposed to supply meat, two vegetables and a sweet for 11d., "leaving 3d. for a cup of tea and bun. But practice was not so good." Drawing rations and being fed from the station kitchen makes a lot of difference.

The Waafs are, I suppose, the most popular of the women's war Services. Formed by Royal Warrant on June 28, 1939, there were 48 companies in being when, a bare two months later, the outbreak of war necessitated an immediate call for thousands more airwomen. There was a rush to join as soon as a B.B.C. appeal for recruits had been put on the air. The Director at Adastral House, London, was told a policeman wanted to see her. She had him in.

"You can't do this sort of thing, ma'am," he said.

"What sort of thing?" she asked.

"These 'ere women," he said.

"What women?" she asked.

"These women queueing up."

"Oh, that's all right. Don't worry about that. I've got a perfectly good recruiting staff to cope with them."

"But have you seen them, ma'am?"

"No, why?"

"Well, there's thousands of them. There's a queue stretching right down Kingsway to the Strand, goodness knows where it ends! We can't keep them in order!"

So all who were any good were enlisted. They were not always welcomed. "Old-fashioned officers of misogynistic outlook

Wings On Her Shoulders

said rather rudely nothing would induce them to have any sort of women hanging around their station, in uniform or out." Other officers asked if the Waafs couldn't be put in charge of their wives, "but war did not allow of such happy family parties." However, the system was for some time so informal that difficulties often arose. The women "agreed to certain conditions, but it was a gentleman's agreement. If they cared to break it and go off, leaving their uniform behind so that they could not be sued in the civil courts, nothing could be done to them. Nothing but the minor punishments of fatigues and stoppage of privileges could be imposed if they were absent without leave. Desertions in the first 18 months of war were serious."

Now conditions of service for women are like those for men. This is how a persistent offender against discipline is dealt with: Sergeant's evidence is that she came in late after a dance, and when asked what had happened said, "Shut up, it's none of your business," and threw her pass down without waiting to be booked in, and went out of the Guard Room banging the door. The sergeant has her own view of the case. She thinks there is a boy friend in it. The offender has been "very difficult lately. I can't do anything with her." Having been on the charge sheet for the third time in a fortnight, she is given seven days' minor punishment, which means that after work she must report every hour at the Guard Room, not be allowed to leave camp or go to any entertainment, and be given fatigues such as cleaning out boxrooms or scrubbing floors.

On the whole, women officers are probably rather more sympathetic to women in the ranks than men are inclined to be. One Wing Officer, asking for names of any who were suitable for commissions to be sent in, added "And send ones who are kind." Mrs. Beauman remarks drily that "sympathy and efficiency had sometimes been regarded as

awkward bedfellows." Men often do take that view. Women have done very useful work in proving this a mistaken view.

As for the pluck and dogged persistence in sticking to duty when in peril of death that many of the Waafs have displayed, these qualities men gladly and fully recognize. Among the awards for gallantry it is hard to pick out any particular cases. Here are three:

When enemy bombers heavily attacked an R.A.F. Fighter Command Station, Sgt. Turner was the switchboard operator and Cpl. Henderson was in charge of a special telephone line. Bombs were falling around the building, but both airwomen carried on with their jobs, although they knew there was only a light roof over their heads. When the building received a direct hit both continued working till it caught fire and they were ordered to leave.

Cpl. Robins was in a dug-out which received a direct hit during an intense raid. A number of men were killed and two seriously injured. Though dust and fumes filled the shelter, Cpl. Robins immediately went to the assistance of the wounded. She displayed courage and coolness of a very high order in a position of extreme danger.

An aircraft crashed near W.A.A.F. quarters. Cpl. Pearson rushed out and, although the aircraft was burning, and she knew there were bombs aboard, she stood on the wreckage, roused the pilot, who was stunned, and assisted him in getting clear. While he was on the ground, a 120-lb. bomb went off. Cpl. Pearson threw herself on top of the pilot to protect him from blast and splinters. Her prompt and courageous action undoubtedly helped to save the pilot's life.

Yet many who set such magnificent examples of "sticking it" are what would be called "just ordinary girls." One, for instance, turned up on a wet morning with an umbrella. Her explanation was that her raincoat had gone astray, "and I can't get my nice new uniform wet!" Others were heard screaming after a bad raid which they had borne very well. They were afraid not so much of the bombs that were dropping as of the mice in their impromptu quarters! Now, if they had been Nazi mice!

Cpl. PEARSON, E.G.M., whose heroic action is told in Wings On Her Shoulders, reviewed in this page. Her portrait by Dame Laura Knight, R.A., officially commissioned in 1940, is here reproduced.

Crown Copyright Reserved

From Italian Prison to the Free Air of England

HOME FROM ITALY. Some four hundred repatriated British prisoners arrived in the hospital ship Newfoundland at a West Country port on April 23, 1943. 1, Women of the British Colony in Lisbon proffer cigarettes to our men en route for England. 2, First men ashore. 3, Capt. Frame, of Glasgow, captured at Tobruk, enjoys his first impressions after landing. 4, A wounded accordion player leads the singing on the upper deck as the ship comes alongside.

Photos, G.P.U., Keystone, P.N.A.

Training Tank Captains for the Coming Battles

CADETS OF THE ROYAL ARMOURED CORPS are trained at the Royal Military College, Sandhurst, to become the best tank officers in the world. Above are illustrated some of the tests they have to undergo. 1, Negotiating a rope bridge at tree-top level. 2, Jumping test in parachute-landing training : a 12-ft. drop. 3, Scaling a 30-ft. wooden "cliff" by means of small hand-and-foot holes. 4, A stomach traverse on double ropes slung between two trees. 5, Learning to recognize salient features of tanks from true-to-scale models.

Photos, Central Press

THE WAR IN THE AIR

by Capt. Norman Macmillan, M.C., A.F.C.

It seems a far cry back to the days when our air power appeared to be insufficient to stem the tide of Axis domination. Yet only three years have passed since we were fighting odds of 30 to 1 against us in Norway, seven to one against in France, four to one against in the Battle of Britain. Then there were but three machines for the defence of Malta—three Gladiators nick-named Faith, Hope, and Charity. "And the greatest of these is charity." I am not sure that "Charity" was the greatest of the three Gladiators in Malta, but I do know that not Mussolini, nor Hitler, nor Kessel-

What immense courage the British people, all the British people, all over the world have displayed! They have not broken faith during the greatest ordeal in the history of mankind, nor faltered once; although before the War their memory had grown dim, and there were few who chose the unpopular path of trying to revive it.

It is not an easy task to assess how much we owe today to the steady growth of our air power during the past three years, but it is indeed much. The great deliverance of Egypt, the absolute defeat of the Italian and German armies in North Africa, could not

Generals Alexander and Montgomery, and later with General Eisenhower of the American Army. The great victory in Africa was the work of a team. The one-man band of Rommel could not stand up to that team, nor could his ultimate successor Von Arnim.

Our great increase in air power, effected during the course of the actual war, will be regarded by historians as perhaps the greatest feat of industry the world has ever seen. For we have had to build up our strength in the air at the same time as we have had to expend it upon defence and offence. For the successful balancing of aircraft output and aircraft expenditure we have to thank the team of air experts working immediately under the direction of the Prime Minister. It has been rather like the private financial budget of a prudent householder, who, having the wisdom to work and save, has yet been able to spend wisely in order to improve the conditions under which he lived.

Every Plane We Can Turn Out Needed to Win the War

It has not been accomplished without a tremendous effort from the aircraft industry. And it has not been done without complications. We have seen the directors of aircraft companies asked to resign their positions in favour of Government-appointed directors; controllers have been appointed in other cases; in one case, Short Bros. of Rochester, the shares of a company have been taken over entirely by the Government.

Various opinions have been expressed upon the application of the powers which war-time legislation has placed in the hands of the Government. I do not propose to add anything to what has been already said elsewhere upon this subject but this : Now that the war in North Africa has reached its appointed end, we and our Allies face the task of reducing the fortress of Europe which stands embattled in the hands of the two ruthless dictators and their slave-driving minions. However fortunate we may continue to be in action, there can be no doubt that the most difficult task of all lies ahead. If we are to achieve success with the minimum loss in life, and in the shortest possible time, we shall have need of every aeroplane we can turn out to enable us to breach the walls of Fortress Europe and destroy the power of Hitler and Mussolini. And all the time we must maintain, too, the air war against the submarine (our air arm in ever-increasing measure is reducing our losses at sea), and keep up our air pressure against the Japanese, which already has saved the Hawaiian Islands and Australia from invasion.

To achieve so much we must have the greatest possible output of aircraft. Nothing can be permitted to stand in the way of the achievement of our object of producing the biggest obtainable number of aircraft in the ensuing months. Now that we have achieved superiority, it must be kept at all costs. To that end the speeding-up of output is imperative, to make allowance for a possible increase in aircraft losses when our assault upon Fortress Europe commences.

We are fortunate in having the Commonwealth Joint Air Training Plan to give us the opportunity to train air-crews in areas of the world free from enemy interference, where rationing is less onerous, and where changes of climate will improve the physical tone of the air-crews of tomorrow.

Looking back along the years of war, we can marvel at the roughness of the way we have trodden to reach our present happier position in the air. Looking ahead, we have every reason for confidence, for air power has been demonstrated to be the factor essential to military victory; and air power is now almost overwhelmingly in our hands. The power that blasted the enemy out of Africa is seeking fresh fields to conquer.

Air Marshal Sir A. CONINGHAM, A.O.C. N. African Tactical Air Force, photographed recently when giving an address to pilots in his Command in Tunisia. "Thanks to your efforts," he is reported as saying, " the Allies have unchallenged supremacy in the air. We must go on hitting the enemy until he stops from sheer exhaustion."
Photo, British Official : Crown Copyright

ring, the tactical general of the two dictators who was personally responsible for the tremendous air assault upon the Mediterranean island, betrayed charity.

Now the scales have turned. The R.A.F. is a greater air force, measured in the number of our aircraft, than the Luftwaffe. When the relative quality of the aircraft of the two air forces is taken into the account, the power of the R.A.F. is even greater than is indicated by its numerical superiority. But the R.A.F. is not the end of the force that the Axis has to face. There are the United States air forces of the Army and Navy, and there is the Red Air Force of Russia. The present disparity in air power—now so clearly in our favour—will grow and grow until the Axis forces will be overwhelmed by the weight of our blows.

There are two quotations that are particularly applicable to the present change of fortune in the air. One is from Mr. Winston Churchill's broadcast to the world on July 14, 1940. He said : " . . . be the ordeal sharp or long, or both, we shall seek no terms, we shall tolerate no parley. We may show mercy—we shall ask none."

And the other is from that moving poem of Colonel Macrae's, from which I take :

If ye break faith with us who die
We shall not sleep though poppies blow
In Flanders fields.

have been accomplished without first obtaining superiority in the air. The tank-buster Hurricanes with their two 40-millimetre guns played havoc with Rommel's tanks. Never before have such large guns been mounted to the wings of an aircraft. When one remembers that the Hurricane is a low wing monoplane with full cantilever wings, the successful fitting of these guns represents an engineering triumph characteristic of British technical skill. (See illus. p. 774.)

The pattern of tactical bombing and machine-and-cannon-gunning of the battle areas by the tactical air force of the Middle East was a perfected piece of military organization. The shooting of the Italian and German fighters from the skies and the destruction of large numbers of these machines upon the enemy aerodromes displayed the pertinacity of the British fighting spirit. The large-scale operations of the Middle East strategic air force upon the ports, communication lines, and industry of the Mediterranean Axis-held zone was a clever dovetailing of the use of air power to prepare the way for conquests yet to come. Indeed, it is possible to say that the successful outcome of the surface fighting in Egypt, Libya, and Tunisia was pre-determined by the air planning of Air Chief Marshal Tedder, operating in concert with his colleagues of the British Army,

Latest and Fastest of Britain's Fighter Planes

HAWKER TYPHOON, first officially-released photographs of which are seen above, has had many successes against the Luftwaffe. On April 29, 1943 it was stated that these aircraft had destroyed 40 enemy raiders since the beginning of the year. 1, Typhoon in flight and (2) on the ground. It has a span of 41 ft. 7 in., an overall length of 31 ft. 11 in., and a 2,000-h.p. Napier Sabre engine giving a speed of over 400 m.p.h. Armament consists of four 20-mm. Hispano cannon. 3, Black-and-white camouflage distinguishes it from the F.W. 190. *Photos, Barratts. New York Times Photos. Planet News*

Brave Men of the Air: Some Recent Awards

Act. F./Lt. R. RANKIN, R.A.A.F., awarded D.F.C. for displaying skill in many raids, notably in that on El Aouina last November.

L./A.C. J. A. SKINGSLEY, awarded D.F.M. for throwing overboard a blazing oxygen bottle, thus saving his plane from destruction.

F./Sgt. KEEN, D.F.M., awarded C.G.M. for repairing damaged radio when his plane was hit. He was badly injured.

Sgt. Air Gunner D. SMITH, awarded D.F.M. for trying to save a comrade's life by parachute from blazing bomber. He was made prisoner.

Sgt. L. PARISH, posthumously awarded G.C. for attempting to save a passenger's life in a burning plane in the Sudan.

Sgt. D. NABARRO, aged 21, awarded the first "pooled medal," the D.C.M.—formerly a military decoration, but since last Jan. open to all the Services.

Maj.-Gen. J. LE MESURIER, S.A.A.F., awarded D.F.C. for completing a fine record of operational flying and displaying remarkable powers of leadership.

Act. W./Cdr. G. GIBSON, D.S.O., D.F.C., awarded a bar to the latter decoration for his splendid achievement in completing 172 sorties.

F./O. D. GREAVES (right) and 2nd W./O. F. ROBBINS, awarded D.F.C. As pilot and observer they flew together and cooperated in the destruction of 5 enemy planes. They are seen with an improvised gramophone in N. Africa.

F./Lt. J. LE ROUX, awarded a bar to his D.F.C. for courageously destroying 5 enemy planes. He has also successfully attacked shipping and ground targets.

Act. F./Lt. E. H. Glazebrook, R.C.A.F., awarded D.F.C. for displaying outstanding leadership in many sorties over Sicily and in heavy fighting over Malta. He has destroyed three enemy aircraft.

F./O. E. L. MUSGRAVE, R.A.A.F., awarded D.F.C. for successfully bombing an enemy merchant ship in the Channel despite heavy opposition. Although his plane was damaged he managed to fly it to safety.

F./O. D. IBBOTSON, R.A.F.V.R., awarded D.F.C. for destroying seven enemy aircraft during the W. Desert campaign. His keenness and determination have been an inspiration to all with whom he has worked.

Spring's Promise of a Bountiful Fruit Crop

APPLE BLOSSOM IN KENT, appearing a month earlier than had been known in this orchard for 30 years, surrounds these oasthouses in pink and white clouds. So fine a display should portend a record apple harvest. Tests in drying English fruit last season proved that colour and flavour of apples, pears, etc., could be perfectly preserved. Further tests are to be carried out this year. Oasthouses in which for years malt and hops have been dried are suitable for drying the fruit.

Photo, News Chronicle

This Strike Was a Gamble with Men's Lives

"The Russian man in the street," cabled Harold King, Reuter's Special Correspondent in Moscow, on May 4, "is somewhat taken aback at the thought that half a million men could abstain or even threaten to abstain from work in a vital industry in the middle of the War." This reaction to the American coal strike found worldwide expression. What lies behind the strike? This article should help to provide an explanation.

THEY'RE turning out the stuff in America, *yes sir* ! The stuff that wins wars, that in brave and capable hands will win this war, sooner perhaps than some folks expect.

Planes ? If you want to know just how many we are producing, says Mr. Donald Nelson, Chairman of the U.S. Production Board, airplane output in March reached a new high of 6,200 ; and for the first time heavy bomber production passed the 500-a-month mark. Tanks ? Not far short of 3,000 were delivered. Guns ? In the first quarter of 1943 we produced nearly 18,000 artillery pieces, including 7,000 anti-aircraft and more than 8,000 anti-tank guns. Our factories also turned out 235,000 machine-guns and more than a million rifles and sub-machine-guns. Ships ? Well, March was a bumper month there, too. We put the battleship Iowa into commission, not to mention a number of smaller vessels that gave the month a lead of 17 per cent over February. As for merchant vessels—deliveries by the U.S. Maritime Commission climbed in March to five *a day*. Of the 134 major-type ships delivered, 103 were liberty ships. Motor vehicle output was up by 8 per cent over February's total, clothing production was up 10 per cent. And if you are among that dwindling majority who think that money still means something big in wartime, you may like to know that the U.S. Treasury and Government Corporations spent more than seven thousand million dollars in March on war purposes, compared with " only " six thousand millions the month before.

These are just some of Mr. Nelson's figures. They make encouraging reading, particularly when they are taken in conjunction with the figures of Lend-Lease shipments announced at about the same time by Mr. Stettinius, U.S. Lease-Lend administrator. But this is the bright side of a picture which has a not-so-bright reverse. On the last Saturday night in April all but a few thousands of America's 530,000 coal miners answered the strike call of their union, the United Mine Workers—biggest and most powerful of America's trade unions, whose president is Mr. John L. Lewis.

Why was the strike call issued ? Not, we are assured, because the mine workers are against the war or politically disaffected in any way. The miners of America are held to be as patriotic as their fellows in Britain. Not politics, but an economic issue brought out the men with the cap-lamps from the pits of Ohio and Kentucky, Pennsylvania, West Virginia and Illinois ; that, and a complicated tissue of intense antagonisms and rivalries which for years past has been playing the devil with America's industrial set-up.

Briefly put, the economic issue boils down to that race between wages and cost of living about which we know something—too much, indeed—in this country.

America's miners have a hard job—though not so hard seemingly as the men working in our own coalfields, since over there the coal is got at more easily : the layers lie flat, and the miners go down only a thousand feet or so, whereas here in Britain the layers are mostly tilted and we have mines burrowing 4,000 ft. under the ground, even some way under the sea. Then in America, as in Britain, the miner's life is a dangerous one, thousands being killed or injured every year. But it isn't these things that the American miner grumbles about. The real trouble apparently is that, as Don Iddon, The Daily Mail's New York correspondent, put it the other day in a highly-informative dispatch, " the men who dig coal are having a fierce struggle to make ends meet, and that is the simple truth."

The United Mine Workers are seeking an increase in pay of two dollars a day so as to catch up with the cost of living. According to figures presented on May 6 by the coal owners to the War Labour Board (on which public, management, and labour are represented) the cost of living for miners increased by only 24 per cent from 1941 to January 1943, while wages increased 73 per cent from October 1940 to February 1943. These figures would no doubt be challenged by the U.M.W., but their spokesman, J. L. Lewis, was ostentatiously absent from the inquiry. "The latch-string is on the outside of the door," said Mr. Morris Cooke, the chairman ; but John Llewellyn showed no inclination to pull it. He has no time for the War Labour Board apparently. The Board is not a statutory body, but one appointed by Mr. Roosevelt ; and Mr. Lewis is opposed to the President and all his works.

Years ago the situation was very different. In his early days Lewis was a member of the Republican party ; but he supported Mr. Roosevelt's candidature in the election of 1936. But by 1940 the President had incurred Mr. Lewis's ire ; and before the presidential election of 1940 the labour chieftain pledged himself to retire from the presidency of the C.I.O. (Committee of Industrial Organizations) if Mr. Roosevelt were re-elected. Roosevelt beat Willkie, and Lewis was as good as his word. Philip Murray, No. 2 of the U.M.W., took his place as the head of the C.I.O., and Lewis was forced to concentrate on his job as president of the United Mine Workers. But of late he has been able to stage something of a comeback ; and in company with "Big Bill" Henderson, head of the Carpenters' Union (one of the craft unions comprising the American Federation of Labour, for years the deadly rival of the more recently established C.I.O., union of the general or industrial unions), he is said to be forming a Republican faction in the ranks of organized labour.

A dynamic personality, pugnacious and self-assertive, highly gifted in organization and a powerful speaker, Lewis has the enthusiastic, possibly unthinking, support of not only the miners but many thousands more of American workers. He himself thinks he is strong enough to challenge the President. If there is to be a show-down, it will be (he believes) the wealthy squire of the White House and Hyde Park who will take the count...

BUT here he has not made sufficient allowance for the President. He too is a powerful personality, and one, moreover, more calculated to appeal to the great mass of Americans, white-collared and horny-handed, to the betterment of whose lot no American has contributed more. On May 1 Mr. Roosevelt ordered Mr. Harold Ickes, who is Administrator of Solid Fuels as well as Secretary of the Interior, to take immediate possession of all the coalmines affected by the stoppage ; and within a few hours the U.S. military were on guard at the pits, above which flew the Stars and Stripes. In a broadcast to the nation two days later the President revealed himself in fighting mood.

" I want to make it clear," he forcefully declared, " that every American coalminer who has stopped mining coal—no matter how sincere his motives, no matter how legitimate he may believe his grievances to be—every idle miner directly and individually is obstructing our war effort . . . The stopping of the coal supply, even for a short time, would involve a gamble with the lives of American soldiers and sailors and the future security of our whole people. It would involve an unwarranted, unnecessary and terribly dangerous gamble with our chances of victory."

In face of so resolute an attitude it was hardly surprising that the strike was called off ; indeed, twenty minutes before the President's voice was heard on the air Mr. Lewis had given out that he had reached agreement with Mr. Ickes for the members of his union to return to the pits for a 15-day period beginning on May 4. The miners, he said, had now a new employer, the U.S. Government, and negotiations for a settlement would be resumed forthwith.

So for the time being—a fortnight at least—there was a truce. But the problem itself remained—a challenge to those who, on either side, direct America's industrial life ; a menace, only averted for a brief space, to the successful effort of all the United Nations.

E. ROYSTON PIKE

WORKERS OF AMERICA have " taken their coats off " so as to make their country the Arsenal of Democracy in very deed. All the same, that there is grave dissatisfaction in their ranks, particularly over the rising cost of living, is evidenced by the coal dispute which is still far from settled. Above is a typical crowd of U.S. shipyard workers. *Photo, Sport & General*

Into War's Byways Goes Our Roving Camera

VOLUNTEER LAND CORPS CAMPS are being erected in various parts of the country. Above, a number of volunteers waiting to register at a recently completed camp at Staines, Middlesex.

OVER TWO TONS OF KEYS were recently collected by the Gas Light and Coke Co. in a salvage drive. Among the 150,000 brought in were keys of every shape and size. This girl examines a giant specimen from the vast pile.

SIXTY TONS OF A.T.S. CLOTHING are issued every week by one hundred and fifty A.T.S. auxiliaries, storekeepers and clerks. The A.T.S. have taken over a section of a large Midland store which clothes a proportion of the British Army, and are entirely running their own organization. This photograph gives some idea of the vast quantities of clothing required. Civilian workers are busily stacking a pile of battledress to be worn by their military sisters.

PLAQUE TO U.S. AIRMAN. Lt. H. D. Johnson, D.F.C., U.S.A.A.F., sacrificed his life last Nov. when he crash-landed his plane on a football ground to save civilians living in Edward Road, Walthamstow. A piece of the plane's propeller mounted in a glass case was unveiled at the scene of his sacrifice on April 4, 1943.

SCHOOL FOR RIVER FIREMEN at Cheyne House, Chelsea Embankment, teaches men of the National Fire Service how to combat river fires during heavy air bombardments, a task which calls for considerable skill and courage. This fire float is shown passing downstream as it approaches Albert Bridge on one of its practice tests.

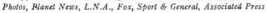

Photos, Planet News, L.N.A., Fox, Sport & General, Associated Press

Even the Italians Flocked to Greet Us at Sfax

" There really isn't much to laugh at in desert warfare," says Clifford Webb, War Correspondent in Tunisia of The Daily Herald (from which this story is reprinted). But he encountered amusing incidents that lightened the grimness of the general scene preceding and during the 8th Army's triumphal entry into Sfax on April 10, 1943.

FOUR or five hours earlier I had crouched in a ditch just off the road between Mahares and Sfax, while the enemy hurled across the last few shells in his rearguard defence before being nosed out of this important harbour town and sent running by our spearhead force.

The delay between the enemy's withdrawal and the actual entry into Sfax was due to the discovery of a minefield. It stretched across the road and effectively barred the way to all traffic until the sappers went forward and cleared it. While the engineers prodded the road and road verges with bayonets, I saw the front wheels of a lorry hurtle into the air as one deadly mine exploded with a shattering roar. Fortunately, all the occupants escaped without a scratch.

An Italian officer, leading a straggling column over the field towards the road, was called on to surrender. He was highly indignant at the request. He explained with much hauteur that he and his men had already surrendered a couple of miles farther forward, and that it was not usual to surrender twice.

British infantrymen and machine-gunners, who had successfully tackled the last German rearguard in a spirited night action, munched bread and bacon and sipped steaming tea as they waited for the mines to be lifted. The sun rose, and soon it was time for the cavalcade of battle to move off. I accompanied the triumphal parade.

About a mile outside the town the infantry debussed, formed up and swung into a march behind the leading tanks. Delighted French people, who had cowered in their battered buildings from the noise of war during the night, came out to greet the conquerors.

The ceremonial parade took the main thoroughfare to the harbour, while platoons of shock troops threaded their way through side streets and made for the aerodrome. Sfax had certainly taken a battering from the air, but there was no doubt about the genuine nature of the French people's welcome.

So hard have Rommel's rearguards been pressed they have scarcely had time to dig in roadside positions before our troops were among them. Moving columns of guns, light tanks and lorried infantry have swung off the road and into action in a matter of minutes, cleaning up enemy pockets relentlessly and pushing forward with all speed.

On Friday (April 9) there were light artillery duels at little more than 2,000 yards range, and on one occasion our gunners, running off the road to shoot, found that they had set up their guns right in an abandoned enemy ammunition dump.

" Any Jerry stuff landing near would have blown up half Tunisia," a gunner officer told me, " but there was no time for finessing. We just shot him out of the way before he had time to reply with any accuracy." Another incident typifying the close nature of the chase was the arrival in our lines of a German ambulance, complete with wounded.

I don't know who was the more astonished, our men or the German driver, who had no idea that that particular part of the country was in our hands. He climbed down from the cabin with a gesture and almost comic look of bewilderment to join the already long line of prisoners, while our medical men took charge of the wounded.

It is difficult to give you in Britain any real idea of what this kind of advance means. On paper or on the radio it is Medenine one day, Gabès a couple of days later, a brief battle at Akarit and then Sfax, and so on.

I travelled 140 miles on Saturday to cover about 70 miles in a straight line. Blown-up roads and bridges and mines were expected, and we were rarely disappointed. Charred and wrecked enemy transport, blasted by the R.A.F., littered the roads. Men who died when the vehicles were hit had been hastily buried in the roadside almond groves, their steel helmets decorating the rough graves and their names scribbled on pieces of wood.

Officers tore up and down the road in Jeeps, returning or going out on reconnaissance patrols, during which they sometimes deliberately offered themselves as targets to enemy gunners to discover the guns' position.

The manner in which the Italians have flocked over to us during the past few days has suggested mass desertion rather than genuine surrender. They amble back towards our rear positions unguarded, but perfectly happy and quite brazenly delighted that their war efforts have finished.

As told in this page, Sfax's inhabitants welcomed the 8th Army on April 10, 1943. This radioed photo shows some of them riding on a British tank. _Photo, British Official_

There isn't much to laugh at in desert warfare. But it is funny to see a head-scratching military policeman puzzling what to do with a mob of gesticulating Italian prisoners, who surround him like a lot of children surrounding the vicar at a Sunday school treat.

How We Flung the Nazis Off Longstop Hill

One of the most strongly fortified Axis positions in Tunisia, Longstop Hill dominating the Medjez-el-Bab-Tunis road, stood in the path of the First Army's westward drive. Bitter fighting cleared the last German from the formidable height on Easter Monday morning, April 26, 1943. War Correspondent Alan Moorehead sent to The Daily Express (from which we reproduce the story) the following front-line dispatch a few hours after the victory.

A BLINDING hot sun blazes down on scrub, and there is a watery heat haze on each succeeding height. As you tramp upward you are half-choked with fine white dust from returning ambulances and tanks, and then sweat makes runnels through the dust on your arms and face as you go higher and get hotter.

Every few yards the ground is pitted with mortar shell blast, and the surrounding grass is dead and withered—as though some disease had blighted the plants. You reach the top of each ridge only to find another ahead, and then you see the front-line infantry. They seem to swarm everywhere. This particular spot where I have been standing almost looks like a stage set. A zigzag trench makes an open suture through the

LONGSTOP, the formidable height on the road to Tebourba, was stormed by the 1st Army on April 26, 1943. Infantry are here moving up in the initial stages of our shattering attack, an account of which commences in this page. In the background is one of " those incredible Churchills " which clawed their way up gradients of 1 in 3. _Photo, British Official_

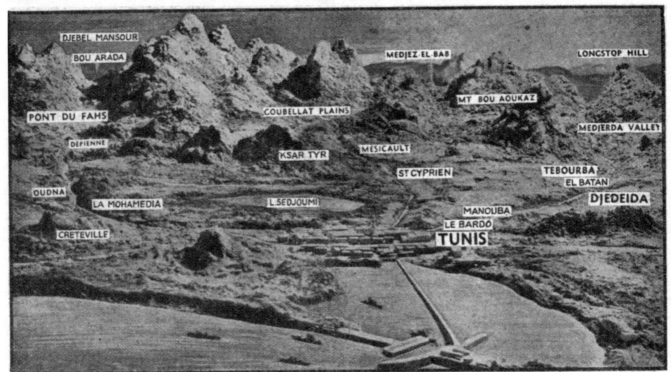

TUNIS AND ITS APPROACHES. The comprehensive relief-map above, in which distances are necessarily foreshortened, depicts the wide battle-field stretching down from the heights to Tunis Harbour and the open sea in the foreground. In the background, extreme right, Longstop Hill (see accompanying text) 25 miles from Tunis, rises above the Medjerda Valley. Below, an impression of twin-peaked Longstop during our storming of this vital objective.   *Top, Courtesy of Sunday Times and Sunday Graphic.   Bottom, Drawing by F. D. Blake; Courtesy of The Daily Express*

camel thorn, and on the freshly-turned yellow earth the men have flung their battledress jackets, their mess tins and empty ammunition boxes.

Men lie about, half in and half out of the trench, not talking much, but smoking, waiting, watching. Each time a shell comes over they cock their heads slightly, listen shrewdly to its whine which gives the direction, and then relax, hardly bothering to look where it falls in billowing smoke—perhaps half a mile away, perhaps 200 yards, but anyway not in the trench. They have been shelled all night, and far heavier than this. They stormed these heights against point-blank fire three days ago, and have been mortared on and off ever since. Perhaps two men in three are left.

Month-old copies of London newspapers lie about, and one big headline is turned up: " *No more wars after this, says Eden.*" They laugh right along the trench until another shell goes over, and then the talk goes round to something else : " *Where is the Eighth Army ? What is happening across the valley ? You can tell Winston Churchill this—we have been in the line since December.*" There is no bitterness about their complaints. They are just practical. The only thing that stirred them was the report made in one paper that front-line troops are getting poached eggs on toast for breakfast, and that does not sound very funny to men who had nothing much but bully and water for four days.

Down the slopes of the hill odd groups of prisoners are still being rooted out of caves. All Germans these. Canvas jackboots, corduroy trousers, gabardine jackets, cloth caps with red, white and black badge. They wear wings over their breast pockets. They are from Rommel's Afrika Korps. Their eyes are red-rimmed from fatigue, but otherwise they march in good order through the dust, unable to comprehend they are prisoners, but dumbly grateful that they are alive.

Each time a shell comes over—ours or German—they break ranks and scatter through the scrub. Only one German captain makes a fuss, demanding to see a British officer. A Scots corporal bleakly motions

him forward. In a farmyard shed the Germans are searched, and they stand and watch while British Tommies go through their packs.

I saw a letter sent to one prisoner from Germany. It is an hysterical account of the damage done to Berlin ; and it concludes, " Be pitiless, for the English have no pity." Mounting to the heights of Longstop you meet other infantry. Beneath several layers of grimy beard you see the face of a major to whom they already gave the D.S.O. before he led this charge straight over each crest of hill, and it is not much good asking him what happened.

He says vaguely : " Oh, I don't know. I shouted, 'Come on,' and the boys jumped up and ran forward yelling at the top of their voices. We found Germans cowering in their trenches—it was probably the noise that made the Jerries give in."

Those incredible Churchills. One of them mounted to the ultimate crest of Longstop, a place where you would think hardly a fly could cling. They outclimb any German tank. I watched a couple of them tilted at an impossible angle climb to the crests of Djebel Ang. As they ground through rocks over the summit they suddenly found themselves confronted with six German tanks, two of them Tigers. These were sheltering in the next valley, and the Germans were apparently so astonished at seeing British tanks among crags that they turned round and scooted in the direction of Tunis.

With a good deal of evidence to back him up a general said to me here today : " Put a Churchill against German infantry and they will surrender at once." And yet here on Longstop they were dug-in as well as troops may be behind mines.

I have been hiding myself in some of their shallower trenches, but I believe there are others that go six feet into the earth and then have a cave cut horizontally at the bottom. The Germans simply hid down there while our barrage was on, then when our infantry charged they fired their machine-guns on fixed lines by remote control. They just squeezed the trigger from below ground.

Standing here on Longstop you see all the battlefield spread out below and all the figures and facts given you back at divisional and brigade headquarters suddenly become alive and have meaning. Straight south across the unbelievably green and flowering Medjerda Valley we saw shells bursting ten miles away. That was the battle for Wadi Ahuror we crossed last night.

A bridge blew up behind our troops there and now they are holding on while reinforcements come up by a detour. Ahead our fighters are plastering lines of trees. That is the Tebourba road where German transport is hastening eastward. I heard the calm, reasonable voice of a brigade major calling for this raid only one hour ago.

Away to the south on Goubellat plain there is a steady grumbling of bombing and artillery. That is where our tanks are advancing on German armour. They got six 88-mm. guns yesterday, and one of these is already in action on our side.

We cannot, of course, see Djebel Mansour, another landmark in this campaign. It dominates the Bou Arada-Pont du Fahs valley, and now today there is news we have that height without resistance. In the far north, too, French Goums are within five miles of Bizerta lakes. All this we can either see or hear about on Longstop, and from here on a clear day you almost look into Tunis itself.

This the administration has done with due regard to humanitarianism and with due avoidance of molly-coddling. One particular thing has impressed the Arabs—deliverance from Italian rule. The second is rain. The Eighth Army have made the Arab a present of both.

I went to a tea party to meet the leaders of the Arabs in Tripolitania, and, sipping green tea with them, I learned that they are grateful and happy for their deliverance. These intelligent leaders refer to the Eighth Army as "the army with wet feet," which is quite a different thing from the army with cold feet.

They regard Montgomery as a kind of miracle man who brought them a prodigious wet season. In rural areas farmers are looking forward to the best crops for 12 years.

The Jews are grateful for their release from Italian rule, and, like the Arabs, they are receiving with delight the news of the success of the Eighth Army in Tunisia. Under the old regime the rule for the 30,000 Tripolitanian Jews was "to us all doors are closed doors."

In Tripoli I Found No 'Little Caesars'

When the 8th Army marched into Tripoli on January 23, 1943, the British military administration found it to be a bankrupt city in a bankrupt country. Peter Duffield, Special Correspondent in Tripoli of The Evening Standard (from which this account is reprinted), describes how this region of Mussolini's much-vaunted African empire is now progressing under the new management.

I HAVE talked today to 46-year-old Brigadier Lush, head of the British Military Administration in Tripolitania, who has already had experience in the "rebirth of nations" in Ethiopia and Madagascar. Under him are men drawn from almost every British, Colonial and Foreign service—from Nigeria, East Africa, Palestine and Egypt.

It is months since the Eighth Army marched into Tripoli, and Mussolini might be interested to hear how this region of his much-vaunted, much-vanished African empire is progressing under new management.

First, it ought to be remembered that the British military administration found Tripoli a bankrupt city in a bankrupt country—a people bankrupt financially, materially, and mentally. Public works had been sabotaged, stores had been looted, food exhausted. The colonists had been left unprotected.

And in Tripoli itself, where the upper crust of civic and political rulers had shamelessly fled, the beaten, stupefied, listless and casually abandoned Italians had been forced to watch the whole fiduciary façade of Fascism crumble in front of them.

Into this town, and facing this bankruptcy, came the British political officers. They sat at the grandiose desks in the grandiose offices. They slept in the hotels. They took over from the hierarchy of little Caesars who had been running the market garden empire. They tried to make a motionless concern into a going concern.

It was, and is, their job to maintain order and to see that the lives, domestic peace, honour and religious convictions of the inhabitants are respected, and generally to weld, as best they can, the civil administration with the demands of the Eighth Army.

One of the most interesting men I talked to was the Italian manager of the Tripoli brewery, now producing beer for the British troops, who is a typical deluded Fascist, and who insists that Britain provoked this war. But he is nevertheless astonished to read each day in the Italian newspaper published by the British the Italian communiqué—verbatim.

I met, too, Italian colonists who wish to be left alone with their acres. They have accepted the British administration, essentially a stop-gap, short-term authority, until the end of the war. Until the peace conference decides the ultimate fate and ownership of Tripolitania, the British can merely care for and maintain the country and the people.

OUR DIARY OF THE WAR

APRIL 28, 1943, Wednesday *1,334th day*
 Sea.—Light naval forces, including destroyers Goathland and Albrighton, attacked heavily-escorted enemy convoy off-Ushant and hit two supply-ships and two escort vessels.
 Air.—Large-scale mining operations by R.A.F. in Baltic caused loss of 23 bombers. Soviet aircraft again raided Königsberg.
 Mediterranean.—Daylight raids on Messina and Naples by U.S. bombers.

APRIL 29, Thursday *1,335th day*
 North Africa.—Enemy counter-attacks in Medjez-el-Bab sector repulsed after bitter fighting.
 Australasia.—Allied bombers raided Jap seaplane base on Amboina.
 General.—Laval received at Hitler's headquarters.

APRIL 30, Friday *1,336th day*
 Air.—Essen heavily bombed by R.A.F.
 North Africa.—Very heavy fighting continued on First Army front.
 Mediterranean.—U.S. aircraft again raided Messina during daylight.
 Australasia. — U.S. aircraft raided Kahili and Vila in Solomons and Munda in New Georgia.
 U.S.A.—American aircraft made 13 more attacks on Kiska and also bombed Attu.
 General.—U.S.A. broke relations with Adm. Robert, Governor of Martinique.

MAY 1, Saturday *1,337th day*
 Air.—U.S. heavy bombers made daylight raid on St. Nazaire.
 Mediterranean.—Announced that 15 Axis ships, including two destroyers, had been sunk by Allied bombers and submarines.

MAY 2, Sunday *1,338th day*
 Sea.—Admiralty announced loss of ex-American destroyer Beverley.
 Air.—Mosquitoes made dusk raid on railway workshops at Thionville.
 North Africa.—U.S. and French troops in N. Tunisia advanced towards Bizerta.
 Russian Front.—Soviet H.Q. announced failure of six-day German offensive in area of Novorossisk.
 Australasia.—Fifty Jap bombers and fighters raiding Darwin were intercepted by Spitfires.
 U.S.A.—Eight more American air raids on Kiska.
 General.—German S.S. leader in Poland, Wilhelm Krueger, killed in Cracow.

MAY 3, Monday *1,339th day*
 Sea.—Admiralty announced loss of submarine Turbulent.

North Africa.—American troops occupied Mateur, S. of Bizerta.
 Mediterranean. — Fighter-bombers from Malta raided Lampedusa aerodrome.
 Russian Front.—Soviet bombers made night attacks on Gomel, Minsk and Briansk.
 U.S.A.—American bombers and fighters made nine more attacks on Kiska.
 General.—Gen. Andrews, U.S. Commander in Europe, killed in air accident over Iceland.

MAY 4, Tuesday *1,340th day*
 Air.—Daylight raids by U.S. heavy bombers on Antwerp and by R.A.F. at The Hague and Abbeville. By night R.A.F. made first major attack on Dortmund ; 30 bombers missing.
 North Africa.—French launched attack S. of Zaghouan, near Pont du Fahs.
 China.—U.S. bombers raided Jap bases in Hainan and Indo-China.
 Australasia.—Announced that U.S. forces had occupied Russell I., N.W. of Guadalcanal.

MAY 5, Wednesday *1,341st day*
 North Africa.—Jebel Bou Aoukas, N.E. of Medjez-el-Bab, captured by First Army troops.
 Russian Front.—Krymskaya, in the Kuban, captured by Soviet troops. Russian

bombers raided Dnepropetrovsk and Briansk by night.

MAY 6, Thursday *1,342nd day*
 Sea.—Admiralty announced loss of submarine Sahib.
 North Africa.—First Army, with strong air support, launched major offensive in Medjez-el-Bab area ; Massicault, 16 m. from Tunis, taken by storm. In northern sector Americans and French launched offensive towards Bizerta.
 Mediterranean.—Liberators made heavy daylight raid on Reggio, in toe of Italy, following night attack by R.A.F.
 Russian Front.—Soviet bombers and fighters destroyed or damaged 350 aircraft in raids on enemy airfields.
 U.S.A.—U.S. Army aircraft made five attacks on Kiska and seven on Attu.

MAY 7, Friday *1,343rd day*
 North Africa.—Tunis captured by First Army and Bizerta by U.S. troops ; French occupied Pont du Fahs.
 Australasia.—Allied heavy bombers raided aerodrome at Madang, New Guinea.
 U.S.A.—Navy Dept. announced that in January U.S. forces had occupied Amchitka, in Rat Island group of Aleutians.

MAY 8, Saturday *1,344th day*
 North Africa.—Tebourba and Djedeida occupied by Allied troops ; French cap-

tured Zaghouan ; naval forces shelled enemy positions on Cape Bon.
 Mediterranean.—Allied aircraft made heavy attack on island of Pantellaria.
 Australasia.—Another heavy Allied raid on Madang ; Japanese troopship sunk in harbour.

MAY 9, Sunday *1,345th day*
 North Africa.—Organized fighting ceased in N.E. Tunisia, where six German generals surrendered to 2nd U.S. Corps ; enemy resistance continued round Zaghouan and in Cape Bon peninsula, which was blockaded by naval forces and heavily attacked from the air.
 Mediterranean.—Over 400 U.S. aircraft made daylight raid on Palermo, Sicily ; Messina also bombed.
 Burma.—Announced that in Arakan British had evacuated Buthidaung in face of Japanese threat of encirclement.
 Australasia.—Catalina flying - boats raided aerodrome at Babo, New Guinea.

MAY 10, Monday *1,346th day*
 Sea.—Admiralty announced loss of destroyer Pakenham.
 North Africa.—Armoured units of First Army drove across neck of Cape Bon, cutting off enemy troops in the peninsula from those holding out round Zaghouan.
 Russian Front.—Soviet Air Force made heavy raids on Kiev, Briansk and Orel.
 Mediterranean.—Flying Fortresses made heavy attacks on airfields in Sicily ; Pantellaria docks and airfield again raided.
 Australasia.—Jap fighters raided airfield on Millingimbi Island, off N. Australia.
 General.—Lt.-Gen. Devers arrived in London as U.S. Commander in Europe.

MAY 11, Tuesday *1,347th day.*
 North Africa.—First Army patrols made complete circuit of Cape Bon peninsula ; First and Eighth Armies closed in on enemy still resisting near Zaghouan.
 Mediterranean.—Heavy U.S. raid on Catania, Sicily ; Marsala and Pantellaria also attacked.
 Russian Front.—Soviet Air Force raided railways at Briansk, Orel, Kharkov, Krasnograd, Poltava, Lozovaya, and Dnepropetrovsk.
 Burma.—In the Arakan peninsula our troops withdrew from Maungdaw.
 U.S.A.—American forces landed on Japanese-occupied island of Attu, in the Aleutians.
 General. — Announced that Mr. Churchill had arrived in Washington. Announced that troops from Barbados had embarked for Dominica in connexion with the "Martinique affair."

★ Flash-backs ★

1940
May 2. Allied troops in Norway S. of Trondheim evacuated from Aandalsnes and Namsos.
May 10. Germans invaded Holland, Belgium and Luxemburg. Mr. Churchill became Premier. British troops landed in Iceland.

1941
May 2. Announced that evacuation of Greece was completed ; 43,000 out of 60,000 men withdrawn.
May 5. Haile Selassie re-entered Addis Ababa in triumph.
May 6. Stalin replaced Molotov as Russian Premier.

May 10. Very heavy night raid on London ; 33 bombers destroyed. Hess landed in Scotland by parachute.

1942
April 28. "Baedeker" raid on York.
May 1. Japanese entered Mandalay.
May 2. Cruiser Edinburgh sunk during passage of Arctic convoy.
May 3. Seven-day Battle of the Coral Sea began.
May 5. British troops landed in Madagascar.
May 6. Corregidor, Philippines, fell after five months' siege.

Editor's Postscript

OF the many books that I should have liked to write were the allotted span anything over a hundred years rather than a mere seventy, was one that would tell the world something of what Britain has done, not merely to save Europe and America, but to save civilization. It is a grand theme, but the ingrained habit of the Briton not to boost in print his own achievements explains no doubt why so little has been written about it. When I managed to interest my colleague, Mr. Hamilton Fyfe, in the idea, I was happy because he, who has given hostages as a journalist to the people's cause, would command a sympathetic audience where I might be regarded as a mere Imperialist. So he has written his book with my title: But For Britain . . . I have read his manuscript with pleasure and approval, although his thesis does not run on the lines mine would have followed; and I am glad to know that it is being published immediately by Macdonald & Co., the enterprising firm of publishers who have issued Mr. Shinwell's The Britain I Want. If you can afford the modest price of 5s. I am sure you will be glad to add it to your bookshelves; and if not, I hope you will ask for it at your library.

WHEN the "amenities" on which people can spend their money nowadays are so few, it is a little surprising to learn that the number of convictions for drunkenness is falling rapidly. In large measure, of course, this happy state of affairs is due to the tremendous increase in taxation on alcoholic drinks of every kind: there is not a Budget which does not put something on the cost of the working-man's pint and the wealthy fellow's bottle of whisky. Then, too, as regards beer it is so very much weaker than it used to be. As Lord Woolton told us some time ago, those who, like himself, were anxious to see some reduction in the amount of excessive drunkenness in the slums of this country twenty-five years ago, "begged and prayed for a light drink which the working people might have which would give them more pleasure and satisfaction without the bestiality that followed from excessive drinking. We have got that beer now (Lord Woolton went on); people are enjoying it, and it is doing them at any rate very little harm." These reasons —and no doubt there are others—account for the fact that, whereas in 1941 in the Metropolitan Police area 10,799 persons were convicted of drunkenness, in 1942 the number had dropped to 7,491. Most of the other great cities, and indeed the majority of our towns and counties, show similar decreases.

ANOTHER vivid sidelight on the nation's drinking habits shows us the women visiting public houses regularly. "In the past the public house has been, in the main, a man's sanctum," says the Chief Constable of Newport, Mon.—his words are quoted in the Fellowship of Freedom and Reform's Bulletin for April; "Now it would appear that women are not only doing men's work, but are gradually acquiring the habits of men. This applies to women in the Services as well as to those in industry." Rightly enough, the Chief Constable thinks that this constitutes an interesting sociological problem which must have its bearing on future licensing legislation. Should women be kept apart from men, and separate rooms be provided for them on licensed premises, he asks; or should there be a revolutionary alteration in the design of public houses— these to be built with open façades, with "nothing to suggest that the customers are being hidden from public view, and encouragement given to make licensed premises the resort of the family as are wine shops and beer gardens in some continental countries?" One may feel a certain wry amusement from the reflection that the frosted windows of the saloon bar may be put there by magistrates' behest so that the people passing along the street shall not be demoralized by the spectacle of men (and women) "knocking back" their mild-and-bitter . . .

SO the Navy knows its Shakespeare . . . During a recent operation in northern waters, in bitter weather, with frequent snowstorms, when the sea was covered with sludge ice, a sudden call to "Action stations" sounded on a British cruiser. Apparently the Yeoman of Signals had sighted an enemy vessel which *might* have been the Luetzow. Steaming "flat out" through the storm, with her guns trained in the direction of the supposed enemy cruiser, the ship at daybreak finally came out "into the clear" to find— nothing at all! After a lengthy consultation on the bridge, the conclusion was reluctantly reached that what had been seen was only a shadow on the snowstorm. Whereupon, says Arthur Oakeshott, Reuters Special Correspondent, who was there at the time, the Admiral caused the following signal to be sent to the other cruisers in company: "Macbeth, Act IV, Scene I, lines 110 and 111." When turned up this was found to be, "Come like shadows, so depart!" Mr. Oakeshott then proffered a gem from Julius Caesar, which the Admiral signalled also: "Ha! Who comes here? I think it is the weakness of mine eyes that shapes this monstrous apparition." Next the Admiral noticed that the guiding cruiser had suddenly turned incorrectly: "Haven't you turned the wrong way?" he signalled. Swift came the reply: . "Sorry, we were so busy looking up our Shakespearean signal books." Another of the cruisers straightway capped this with a further Macbeth quotation: "Turn, Hell-hound turn!" Not surprisingly the erring vessel is now known as H.M.S. Hellhound.

NEVER since the Napoleonic age have pamphlets had such a vogue as now, when limited supplies of paper and limited leisure for reading make it necessary that as much information as possible shall be given in the smallest possible space. Among the host of pamphlets that are appearing a very high place must be accorded to the series on World Affairs, published by the Oxford University Press. Some noteworthy additions of recent appearance are Violet Conolly's Soviet Asia, and J. H. Stembridge's Atlas of the U.S.A. (Mr. Stembridge's Atlas of the U.S.S.R. in the same series appeared last year). Over four million copies of the World Affairs series have been sold. Now the first numbers have appeared of another sixpenny series, the Oxford Pamphlets on Home Affairs. How Britain is Governed, by Mr. R. B. McCallum, is the first; and its companions are Mr. R. F. Harrod's Britain's Future Population, Professor A. G. Pigou's Transition from War to Peace, and The Newspaper, by Mr. Ivor Thomas, M.P. All are first-rate, but perhaps I may be permitted to give an individual pat on the back to a fellow journalist's attempt to convey a mass of information concerning the British Press to that great body of readers who seldom have even the foggiest notion of the immense effort and enterprise involved in the production of their favourite newspaper.

WITH this number we have completed Volume 6 of THE WAR ILLUSTRATED. Those of my readers who are having their loose Parts bound in volume form will find in this page brief instructions how to go about it. As it may be assumed that all who will bind Volume 6 have already had the preceding volumes bound, nothing more than a reminder and instructions here given are needed. But the publishers ask me to emphasize that all loose Parts sent for binding must be free from pencil or ink marks of any kind. That is most important. And once again I would remind those subscribers that the difficulties of labour and material which have vastly increased since the easier days when our first two Volumes were produced, have in no way diminished during the run of Volume 6, and our publishers will greatly appreciate the forbearance of subscribers in allowing much more than the ordinary time for the execution of their binding orders. They can have the assurance that everything possible is done to expedite the work, as well as to provide the best workmanship and material at reasonable prices. Compared with almost all other commodities, the value given in the bound volume of THE WAR ILLUSTRATED is exceptional. I am more than satisfied at the response of my readers to the final change which transformed the publication into a fortnightly, without any advertising wrapper and using every inch of space to the best advantage. The introduction of an extra colour into some of our pages will enrich the bound volumes, which in themselves will not only contain a remarkable record of events throughout the War, but will indicate the changing conditions of production that prevailed during their publication.

Arab Setting for a British Supply Base

Photo, Paul Popper

STREET SCENE IN SOUK-EL-ARBA, a key town in the Northern sector of the Tunisian front. Situated W. of Medjez-el-Bab on the Mejerda River and the main Bizerta line, this road and rail centre became one of our most important supply bases, feeding as it did the First Army's growing offensive in the vital Medjez-el-Bab region—the offensive which on May 7 carried it triumphant into Tunis.

Printed in England and published every alternate Friday by the Proprietors, THE AMALGAMATED PRESS, LTD., The Fleetway House, Farringdon Street, London, E.C.4. Registered for transmission by Canadian Magazine Post. Sole Agents for Australia and New Zealand : Messrs. Gordon & Gotch, Ltd. ; and for South Africa : Central News Agency, Ltd.—May 28, 1943.   S.S   *Editorial Address :* JOHN CARPENTER HOUSE, WHITEFRIARS, LONDON, E.C.4.